Irwin's Legal and Regulatory Environment of Business

Irwin Legal Studies in Business Series

Adamson
Basic Business Law
1995

Barnes/Dworkin/Richards
Law for Business
Fifth Edition, 1994

Bennett-Alexander/Pincus
Employment Law
1995

Blackburn/Klayman/Malin
The Legal Environment of Business
Fifth Edition, 1994

Bowers/Mallor/Barnes/Phillips/Langvardt
Law of Commercial Transactions and Business Associations
1995

Dworkin/Barnes/Richards
Essentials of Business Law and the Regulatory Environment
1995

Dworkin
Contract Law Tutorial Software
1993

Klayman/Bagby/Ellis
Irwin's Business Law
1994

Metzger/Mallor/Barnes/Bowers/Phillips/Langvardt
Business Law and the Regulatory Environment: Concepts and Cases
Ninth Edition, 1995

McAdams
Law, Business and Society
Fourth Edition, 1995

McCarty/Bagby
Irwin's Legal and Regulatory Environment of Business
Third Edition, 1996

Richards
Law for Global Business
1994

Tucker/Henkel
The Legal and Ethical Environment of Business
1992

Irwin's Legal and Regulatory Environment of Business

F. William McCarty
Western Michigan University

John W. Bagby
Pennsylvania State University

Third Edition

IRWIN

Chicago • Bogotá • Boston • Buenos Aires • Caracas • London • Madrid • Mexico City • Sydney • Toronto

Irwin Book Team

Executive editor:	Craig Beytien
Sponsoring editor:	Karen Mellon
Marketing manager:	Brian Kibby
Project editor:	Lynne Basler
Production supervisor:	Pat Frederickson
Assistant manager, graphics	Charlene R. Breeden
Designer:	Keith McPherson
Interior designer:	Stuart Paterson
Cover designer:	Stuart Paterson
Art studio:	Weimer Graphics, Inc.
Compositor:	Weimer Graphics, Inc.
Typeface:	10.5/12 Times Roman
Printer:	R. R. Donnelley & Sons Company

Times Mirror
Higher Education Group

Library of Congress Cataloging-in-Publication Data

McCarty, F. William, date

The legal environment of business / F. William McCarty, John W. Bagby — 3rd ed.

p. cm.

ISBN 0-256-14071-5

1. Industrial laws and legislation—United States. 2. Commercial law—United States. 3. Law—United States. I. Bagby, John W. II. Title

KF1600.M39 1996

346.73′07-dc20

[347.3067] 95–24860

Printed in the United States of America

1 2 3 4 5 6 7 8 9 0 DO 2 1 0 9 8 7 6 5

To:
Alma, Julie, Cari, Chris, David,
Dianne,
and to:
Robin, Julia Marie, and Jack.

PREFACE

The legal and regulatory environment of business continues to be of significant concern for both small firms and large global enterprises. The regulatory environment within the United States is changing as existing federal legislation and regulations are reviewed, revised and sometimes totally eradicated. Globally, new international institutions, such as the World Trade Organization, and changing regional agreements, such as the North American Free Trade Agreement and the Maastricht Treaty of the expanded European Union, have altered the rules affecting many business activities.

The countries of Europe are moving closer together as laws within the European Union are harmonized and those in former Eastern Bloc countries like Bulgaria, the Czech Republic and Poland are altered to enhance their free enterprise developments. In Asia, China is adopting new intellectual property laws and establishing commercial banks to make loans based on business criteria rather than political considerations. The opening up of China, the demise of the Soviet Union, the continued growth of southeast Asia economies, and the integration of North American economies have globalized the business environment.

This third edition integrates international perspectives into topical legal problems. The business manager preparing for the twenty-first century needs to understand the legal environment wherever business is transacted. What are some of the differences in the legal environments in Germany and in Korea? How are contract disputes usually resolved in business relations with Japan? What actions are prohibited by the competition policies in the European Union? How can firms protect their intellectual property in countries without a long history of enforcement of property rights?

As the first chapter of the text notes, ethical and legal analysis of problems are each important of business managers. As business customs, practices, and legal rules often differ from one country to the next, firms transacting global business must carefully establish, review and communicate clear guidelines for ethical behavior to mangers as they move from one culture to another.

Critical thinking skills are essential to legal analysis. By analyzing the issues, reasons and conclusions reached by judges in court cases, one can better determine how particular legal policies are applied. Just as evidence presented in courts is subject to cross-examination, the business manager reading a report, article or memorandum of understanding must question assumptions and challenge illogical assertions based on faulty data. In this edition of the text, we have brought to the fore the need for critical thinking. Each chapter begins with several critical thinking questions, cases and contextual introductions are followed by critical thinking questions, and each chapter concludes with questions and exercises that review legal principles, apply legal reasoning to problems and reinforce critical thinking skills.

We have retained our use of chapter introductions that provides historical, political, economic and social context to the subjects of each chapter. This provides a framework for present legal concerns by noting past, present, and possible future developments. The case extracts which illustrate important chapter principles, include many classic and well-received cases from prior editions as well as newer cases on developing legal issues. Each case is followed by several case questions, usually including at least one calling for a critical thinking analysis. By posing questions at the beginning of each chapter, after each case, at times within the textual material, and at the end of the chapter, this edition continues the proven SQ3R pedagogy: study, question, read, recite and review.

We have designed this text to respond to the accreditation standards of the American Assembly of the Collegiate Schools of Business (AACSB). Those standards state:

> Both undergraduate and MBA curricula should provide an understanding of perspectives that form the context for business. Coverage should include:
>
> - Ethical and global issues
> - The influence of political, social, legal, regulatory, environmental and technological issues, and
> - The impact of demographic diversity on organizations.

In the beginning chapter, we introduce the reader to both ethical as well as legal analysis. Throughout the subsequent chapters, ethical dilemmas are presented within the chapters and the concluding chapter focuses specifically on the social responsibility of business firms. The international environment of business, which was the penultimate chapter in the previous edition, has been moved to the first part of the text so that the understanding of the global legal environment is studies alongside the national legal environment of the United States.

This is a comprehensive text. We have added a new chapter on commercial transactions and new material on intellectual property while condensing, where appropriate, some material from previous chapters into fewer pages and chapters.

Text Organization

The text is organized into eight parts, based on concepts important to an understanding of the social, political, legal and regulatory environment of modern, competitive business firms. Throughout the chapters contained in each part there are discussions of ethical, international, and controversial matters.

Part 1 introduces the legal systems of the United States and contrasts this with systems in other nations. This focuses on topics concerning legal process and institutions, and dispute resolution techniques. Chapter 3 provides comprehensive coverage of the legal environment of international business and creates a framework from which to study the remaining international matters throughout the book. Chapter 4 consolidates ADR and the court systems into one chapter.

Part 2 focuses on governmental powers over business as dictated by constitutional and administrative law. Fundamental constitutional rights are organized numerically by amendment and placed within the framework of a business environment. Regulatory matters such as agency controls, hearing requirements, administrative remedies, etc. are simplified and made more accessible.

Part 3 focuses on the private law concerns of property, torts, contracts and commercial transactions. Property law is fundamental to nations with a tradition of market economics, capitalism, and democracy, like the United States. The discussion of torts addresses the responsibilities between individuals. Contract and commercial law is the basis of all transactions and provides the foundation for international commerce. The separate commercial law chapter in this edition provides comprehensive business law topic coverage.

Part 4 addresses several particular legal problems that business firms face. The United States offers consumers more legal redress than most other nations. However, product liability and consumer financing laws are spreading throughout the world, changing the relationship between consumers and producers of goods and services.

Part 5 discusses the formation, financing, operation, and internal and external problems of operating business organizations. A wide variety of forms are discussed: sole proprietorships, Subchapter S corporations, and corporations. Regulations of the securities markets govern firms' access to the public capital markets.

Part 6 addresses the competition laws known as antitrust in the United States. While antitrust enforcement diminished during the 1980s, there are signs of its resurgence. The European Economic Community (EC), Japan, and other industrial nations are now beginning to adopt and enforce anti-monopoly laws largely based on the U.S. model. These considerations are likely to become more important considerations as the 21st century approaches.

Part 7 addresses the important considerations of employee relations. The expanding direct regulation of employment by the federal, state, and local governments has led to somewhat greater coverage of these areas in this edition. Workplace safety, compensation matters, employment contract conditions, and equal employment laws are discussed in two separate chapters.

Part 8 provides an integrative capstone to the study of the legal environment. This part focuses on environmental law and the social responsibility of business. These matters have received increasing attention during the 1990s but are placed last to highlight how they apply concepts discussed earlier. This also provides an opportunity for students to integrate other concepts learned earlier into a more complex framework.

Case Features

The text combines our analysis of important legal principles with extracts from court cases that apply some of the principles to specific situations. Each chapter includes three to six cases. All cases are introduced by a factual summary in the authors' language so that the reader can understand the situation being discussed by the court. Both recent and later cases are used to portray both a historical context for the development of the law and the current conditions in which legal problems occur. New cases have been added in every chapter so that students can see how contemporary legal problems are being addressed.

Because the law is subject to individual opinions and different interpretations, some dissenting opinions are included. They present contrasting legal views and often pose different approaches to solving particular problems. We continue to include case questions so that vital concepts of each situation are addressed by the reader.

Chapter Pedagogy

Each major topic is introduced with contextual matters covering the historical, social, political, and economic influences that have shaped the legal environment of business. The text employs the SQ3R study method that is introduced more fully in Chapter 1. This method enhances students' critical thinking skills by emphasizing the survey, question, read, recite, and review method of study.

Each chapter begins with several survey techniques to engage student interest:

- **Critical Thinking Questions** open each chapter, identifying important topics and encouraging students to strive for higher levels of learning related to important topics.
- **Introduction . . . Past, Present, and Future** sections present contextual matters that provide integrative perspective for the issues that have been addressed by law and regulation.
- **Thought Questions** at the end of the introductory section draw attention to the core concepts presented.

Within the Chapters, other techniques are used to highlight content and features:

- **Case questions** follow each judge's decision. These questions address important expressed or implied concerns raised by the case.
- **Ethical Dilemma boxes**, identified with the ■ symbol, draw points of law into the context of ethical considerations.
- **International Perspective and Commentary** boxes, identified with the ▼ symbol, focus the student's attention on the global impact of points of law in business.
- **Margin Glossary** terms provide students an immediate definition for key words and phrases presented in the body of the text.
- **Readings** from the business press coverage of key controversies, presented in shaded boxes, enhance students' ability to question important contemporary issues.

At the end of each chapter, there are three elements that review important concepts:

- **Summary** text restates main ideas in a brief, narrative form to provide a quick review for the student.
- **Critical Thinking Review Questions** encourage students to describe, compare and contrast, distinguish between, and make assumptions about issues raised by the authors.
- **Critical Thinking Exercises** probe to deeper levels of learning, urging students to interpret, apply, analyze, and identify differences among issues.

Additional Features

The text includes both a brief and a detailed table of contents to enhance the survey features of the text. The end-of-book glossary, which is more detailed than that in many texts, defines each term that is boldfaced or italicized in the text. This frees the reader from constantly consulting outside references and legal dictionaries. The appendixes present the U.S. Constitution, excerpts from the Uniform Commercial Code, and Spanish-English equivalents for important legal terms.

Supplements

The Instructor's Manual, prepared by the authors, contains answers to case and problem questions, transparency masters, and excerpts from important laws and regulations. Computest 4, a computerized text bank, is also available to enhance the preparation of quizzes or examinations.

Acknowledgments

We wish to acknowledge the collegial support received from faculty, staff, and administrators at Pennsylvania State University and the Haworth College of Business at Western Michigan University. The insights and recommendations of our colleagues have been useful. We also wish to thank the following reviewers for their valuable suggestions as they reviewed our draft manuscripts for the first two editions of this text:

William Burke, *Trinity University*

Sandra Burns, *Arkansas State University*

Larry Clark, *Louisiana State University*

Theodore M. Dinges, *Longview Community College*

Michael Engber, *Ball State University*

Gamewell Gant, *Idaho State University*

James Hill, *Central Michigan University*

Jack Hires, *Valparaiso University*

Susan Jarvis, *Pan American University*

Paul Lansing, *University of Iowa*

Nancy Mansfield, *Georgia State University*

Keith Maxwell, *University of Puget Sound*

John Norwood, *University of Arkansas*

Steve Palmer, *Creighton University*

Sheelwant Pawar, *Idaho State University*

Daniel Reynolds, *Middle Tennessee State University*

Ira Schwartz, *Towson State University*

Burke T. Ward, *Villanova University*

William Wines, *Boise State University*

Larry Zacharias, *University of Massachusetts at Amherst*

We also give our thanks to the reviewers who helped shape this current, third edition:

Jack M. Hires, Valparaiso University

Paul Lansing, University of Illinois

Janice Loutzenhiser, California State University—San Bernardino

John Norwood, University of Arkansas

Lloyd Peake, California State University—San Bernardino

Leo Stevenson, Western Michigan University

Our special thanks and gratitude to our editor, Karen Mellon; and our project editor, Lynne Basler, at Richard D. Irwin. Both of these talented individuals gave wise counsel and extended their efforts to bring this edition to publication.

Finally, we appreciate the patience, support, and encouragement of our spouses, Alma McCarty and Robin Bagby.

F. William McCarty
John W. Bagby

Contents

Part 1

The Legal System and Business, 3

Chapter 1

Introduction to Legal and Ethical Analysis, 4

Law and the Legal Environment, 6
Legal Analysis, 10
The Nature of Law and Legal Theories, 15
Law and Ethics, 18
Ethical Analysis, 19
Textual Treatment of Ethics, 22

Chapter 2

Law and the Legal System, 30

The Legal System, 32
Classification of Law, 38
Tasks of a Legal System, 43
Significant Characteristics of the U.S. Legal System, 45
The Legislative Branch, 54
The Executive Branch, 54
The Judicial Branch, 55

Chapter 3

The Legal Environment of International Business, 66

Overview, 68
Conducting International Business, 69
Sources of Law, 70
International Trade, 81
Laws Affecting Exports, 83
Laws Affecting Imports, 84
Licenses, 86
Ethical Dilemmas and International Business Law, 89
International Investments, 92

Chapter 4

Litigation and Alternative Dispute Resolution, 104

Litigation in the U.S. Legal System, 106
The Civil Litigation Process, 110
Participants in Civil Litigation, 120
Alternative Dispute Resolution, 132
Arbitration, 134
Mediation, 138
The Minitrial, 140
Private Trials, 141
Comparing Litigation and ADR, 142

Part 2

Governmental Powers Over Business, 153

Chapter 5

Constitutional Law, 154

The Basis for Constitutional Powers, 156
Specific Powers of Government, 164
Constitutional Rights of Businesses and Individuals, 173

Chapter 6

Administrative Law, 190

Administrative Agencies: General Concerns, 192
Controls Over Administrative Agencies, 195
General Functions of Administrative Agencies, 198
Administrative Rulemaking, 199
Administrative Adjudication, 202

Informal Administrative Activities, 204
Judicial Review and Administrative Agencies, 206
Business Interaction with an Administrative Agency, 215
Regulation and Deregulation, 217

PART 3

PRIVATE LAW AND BUSINESS, 223

CHAPTER 7

PROPERTY, 224

The Nature of Property, 226
Intellectual Property, 230
Computer Law, 244
Ownership and Transfer of Personal Property, 246
Ownership of Real Property, 247
Sale of Transfer or Real Property, 252
Legal Control of Real Property, 255

CHAPTER 8

TORTS, 264

Business and Vicarious Liability, 266
Classification of Torts and Business Activities, 267
Intentional Torts, 270
Negligence Torts, 277
Strict Liability Torts, 288
Tort Law Reform, 290

CHAPTER 9

CONTRACTS, 294

Importance of Contracts, 297
Classification of Contracts, 297
Mutual Assent: The Agreement, 298
Consideration, 305
Capacity, 310
Reality of Consent and Defenses to Contract Formation, 311
Illegality, 313
Written Contracts, 317
Interpretation of Contracts, 319
Third-Party Rights, 321
Contract Performance and Remedies for Breach, 325

CHAPTER 10

COMMERCIAL LAW, 330

Sales of Goods, 333
Leases of Goods, 346
Commercial Paper, 346
Creditor's Rights, 355
International Sales Transactions, 363

PART 4

CONSUMER LAW AND BUSINESS, 373

CHAPTER 11

PRODUCT AND SERVICE LIABILITY, 374

Introduction, 376
Product Liability Theories, 379
Liability of Parties in Distribution Chain, 393
Affirmative Defenses, 402
Product Liability Reform, 405
Product Liability Risk Management, 408

CHAPTER 12

CONSUMER PROTECTION, 412

Consumer Protection by the Federal Trade Commission, 414
Advertising Regulation, 418
Trade Regulation Rules and Deceptive Trade Practices, 424
Consumer Financing, 427
Consumer Product Safety Regulation(s?), 438

PART 5

BUSINESS ASSOCIATIONS, 445

CHAPTER 13

AGENCY, 446

The Nature of an Agency Relationship, 448
Creation and Termination of an Agency Relationship, 449
Duties Owed by Principal and Agent to Each Other, 457

The Contract Liability of the Principal for Agency Activities, 467
The Tort Liability of the Principal for Agency Activities, 470

CHAPTER 14

BUSINESS ORGANIZATIONS, 480

The Forms of Business Organization, 482
The Proprietorship Form of Business Organization, 482
The Partnership Form of Business Organization, 485
Franchises and Business Organizations, 494
The Corporation Form of Business Organization, 495
Types of Corporations, 500
The Role of Corporate Participants, 503
Comparison of Business Organization Forms, 510

CHAPTER 15

SECURITIES REGULATIONS, 516

The Primary Federal Securities Statutes, 518
Registration of Securities, 520
Insider Trading, 531
Proxy Solicitations and Tender Offers, 541
Miscellaneous Securities Laws, 549

PART 6

ANTITRUST LAW AND BUSINESS, 553

CHAPTER 16

MONOPOLIES AND MERGERS, 554

U.S. Antitrust Laws, 558
Trusts and Monopolies, 561
Enforcement of Antitrust Law, 564
Monopolies, 571
Mergers, 578

CHAPTER 17

RESTRAINTS OF TRADE, PRICE DISCRIMINATION AND UNFAIR TRADE PRACTICES, 592

Horizontal Combinations and Restraints of Trade, 594
Vertical Restraints of Trade, 603
Price Discrimination, 618
Unfair Trade Practices, 626

PART 7

EMPLOYMENT LAW AND BUSINESS, 631

CHAPTER 18

TERMS AND CONDITIONS OF EMPLOYMENT, 632

The Employment-at-Will Doctrine, 634
The Fair Labor Standards Act, 641
Unemployment Compensation, 645
Retirement Income and Pensions, 646
Workers' Compensation, 650
Occupational Safety and Health Act, 655

CHAPTER 19

LABOR–MANAGEMENT RELATIONS, 666

Role of the NLRB, 671
Representation Elections, 672
Employer Interference with Union Organization, 675
The Labor Negotiation Process, 683
Labor Dispute Resolution: Concerted Activities, 689
Internal Union Democracy, 699

CHAPTER 20

EQUAL EMPLOYMENT OPPORTUNITIES, 706

Equal Pay Act, 709
The Civil Rights Act of 1964, 711
Enforcement of the Antidiscrimination Laws, 728

PART 8

SOCIETAL POWERS AFFECTING BUSINESS, 739

CHAPTER 21

ENVIRONMENTAL LAW, 740

The Environment and Legal Regulation, 742
The National Environmental Policy Act, 743
Environmental Compliance Audits, 746
Air Pollution, 746
Water Pollution, 754
Land Pollution, 755
Other Federal Environmental Concerns, 760
State and Local Concerns, 762

CHAPTER 22

THE SOCIAL RESPONSIBILITY OF BUSINESS, 768

White-Collar Crime, 770
Business Crimes, 773
Corporate Social Responsibility, 782
The Divergent Goals of Business and Society, 786

APPENDIX A THE CONSTITUTION OF THE UNITED STATES OF AMERICA, A-1

APPENDIX B UNIFORM COMMERCIAL CODE, B-1

APPENDIX C SPANISH-ENGLISH EQUIVALENTS FOR IMPORTANT LEGAL TERMS, C-1

GLOSSARY, G-1

CASE INDEX, CI-1

INDEX, I-1

List of Cases

Allied Structural Steel Co. v. Spannaus, 170
Amax, Inc. v. Water Quality Control Commission, 209
American Academy of Pediatrics v. Heckler, 200
Anheuser-Busch, Inc. v. Stroh Brewery Co., 237
Atari Games Corp. v. Nintendo of America Inc., 240
Board of Regents of State College v. Roth, 229
Bowsher v. Synar, 51
Brooks v. Brooks, 35
Brown Shoe Co. v. United States, 583
Business Electronics Corp. v. Sharp Electronics Corp., 611
California Retail Liquor Dealers Assn. v. Midcal Aluminum, Inc., 606
Central Hudson Gas & Electric Corp. v. Public Service Commission, 175
Chevron, USA, Inc. v. Natural Resources Defense Council, Inc., 748
Cipollone v. Liggett Group, Inc., 391
Citizens to Preserve Overton Park v. Volpe, 214
Commission on Human Rights and Opportunities, et al., 60
Conklin Development v. Acme Markets, Inc., 250
Cooke v. Lynn Sand & Stone Co., 507
Dirks v. SEC, 536
Dolan v. City of Tigard, 159
Dolan v. City of Tigard, 258
Donovan v. Burger King Corp., 642
Eastern Dist. Co., Inc. v. Flynn, 316
Edmonson v. Leesville Concrete Company, Inc., 123
Escott v. BarChris Construction Corp., 529
Federal Trade Commission v. Procter & Gamble Co., 585
Gallagher & Ascher v. Simon, 203
Harris v. Forklift Systems, Inc., 721
Hensley v. Sherman Car Wash Equipment Co., 403
Hoffman v. Red Owl Stores, Inc., 309
In re Playboy Enterprises, Inc., 780
Intern. Ass'n of Machinists v. OPEC, 79
International B'hd. of Teamsters v. United States, 727
J. Apablasa v. Merritt & Co., 303
Joseph Albanese's Case, 653
Joseph v. Norman's Health Clubs, Inc., 428
Katko v. Briney, 25
Lechmere v. National Labor Relations Board, 677
Macke Co. v. Pizza of Gaithersburg, Inc., 324
MacPherson v. Buick Motor Co., 376
Marshall v. Barlow's, Inc., 205
Martin v. McDonald's Corp., 291
Massey v. Tube Art Display, Inc., 475
Masterson v. Sine, 320
McCabe v. L.K. Liggett Drug Co., 381
McGowan v. St. Regis Paper Co., Inc., 287
McQuade v. Tucson Tiller Apartments, Ltd., 256
Merrill, Lynch, Pierce, Fenner & Smith, Inc. v. Boeck, 458
Metro Edison v. People Against Nuclear Energy, 744
Miller v. City Bank & Trust, 486
Mills Co. v. Crawfish Capitol Seafood, 497
Mitsubishi Motors Corp. v. Soler Chrysler-Plymouth, Inc., 136
Mitsubishi Motors v. Soler Chrysler-Plymouth, 91
N.L.R.B. v. Gissel Packing Co., Inc., 679
O'Leary v. Moyer's Landfill, Inc., 757
Orkin Exterminating Co. v. F.T.C., 426
Pacific Mutual Life Ins. Co. v. Halsip, 184
Palmer v. United States, 116
Perez v. U.S., 166
Price Waterhouse v. Hopkins, 713
Principe v. McDonald's Corp., 614
Quinnipiac Council, Boy Scouts of America, Inc. v. Commission on Human Rights and Opportunities, et al., 60
Rasmussen v. South Florida Blood Service, 272
S.E.C. v. Howey, 525
Schoenberger v. Chicago Transit Authority, 454
Science Accessories v. Summagraphics, 462
Smith v. American Express Travel Services, 472
State v. McGraw, 774
Sztejn v. J. Henry Schroder Banking Co., 365
T.S.C. Industries v. Northway, 544
Texaco, Inc. v. Pennzoil Co., 275
Texaco v. Hasbrouch, 623

Thompson Printing Machinery Co. v. B. F. Goodrich Co., 338
Timberlane Lumber Co. v. Bank of America, 76
Trans World Airlines, Inc. v. Hardison, 717
Twigg v. Hercules Corp., 639
United States v. Nachtigal, 34
United States of America v. Economy Muffler & Tire Center, Inc., 751
United States v. Socony-Vacuum Oil Co., Inc., 597
United States v. Park, 440
United Paperworkers Int'l. Union v. Misco, Inc., 698
United Parcel Service v. Fetterman, 652
United States v. Beusch, 792
United States v. Aluminum Co. of America, 575
United States v. E.I. du Pont de Nemours & Co., 574
United Steelworkers of America v. Weber, 731
Upjohn v. United States, 129
Van Hooser v. Keenon, 490
West Michigan Environmental Action Council, Inc. v. Natural Resources Commission of the State of Michigan, 762
Westinghouse Electric Corp. v. Nutt, 397
Whirlpool Corp. v. Marshall, 661
Williams v. Jackson Co., 278
Williams on Behalf of Williams v. Bowen, 212
Wisconsin Public Intervenor v. Mortier, 47

Irwin's Legal and Regulatory Environment of Business

PART 1

The Legal System and Business

1 Introduction to Legal and Ethical Analysis

2 Law and the Legal System

3 The Legal Environment of International Business

4 Litigation and Alternative Dispute Resolution

CHAPTER

1

Introduction to Legal and Ethical Analysis

Critical Thinking Questions

- What makes society's established standards or guidelines for action or behavior *law?* Does law originate from a higher authority as well as from common practices and customs?
- How does deductive reasoning differ from inductive reasoning as used in *legal analysis?*
- Can you explain how identifying issues, reasons, and conclusions and evaluating evidence as utilized in studying law involves the use of *critical thinking skills?*
- Does the concept of *stare decisis* require that any prior court decision be followed in subsequent cases?
- Compare and contrast how the natural law and legal positivism *theories of law* look differently at the relationship of law to human actions.
- How are moral principles used in *ethical analysis?*
- What are the main distinctions between the *two major ethical theories:* the consequence-oriented, or teleological, utilitarian theory and the duty-based, or deontological, universalism theory?

Introduction... Past, Present, Future

The study of law begins by realizing its importance to both personal and business activities. The importance of law in society is not new. Hundreds and even thousands of years ago, some societies sought to codify local customs and practices so that individuals and businesspeople would know what they were expected to do and not to do. Today, these codes constitute the most important source of law in countries that have *civil law* legal systems. In other societies, customs and practices evolved into legal standards when courts resolved disputes by referring to those practices. Countries in which court decisions predated attempts to codify the law developed *common law* legal systems based on those *precedent* court decisions grounded in common law. In many societies, religion has played an important role in the development of both ethical standards and legal rules. Today, the *Islamic* legal system, based on the *Koran*, predominates in many countries.

Legal analysis requires the use of both deductive and inductive reasoning. General principles of law referred to in the text can be reviewed deductively by using the *SQ3R* (Survey, Question, Read, Recite, and Review) method of study. As *critical thinking* skills require readers to identify issues, reasons, and conclusions and to evaluate the evidence presented by the author, the study of law serves as an ideal context in which to develop those skills. Briefing of case excerpts help the reader to analyze the main components of a court decision and to induce from that case to other situations. The theories of natural law, legal positivism, sociological, legal realism, critical legal study, and the economic school, all help to enhance our understanding of the role of law in our society. Although both law and ethical standards are based on moral norms, only those rules or standards for behavior that are explicitly enforced by the society are considered laws.

Because there is a close relationship between a society's legal rules and its moral values, the relationship between law and ethics is reviewed. Ethical precepts such as the Golden Rule form the basis for the universal ethical theory, which, along with the utilitarian theory, may be used for examining the ethical nature of business decisions and individual actions. *Ethical analysis* involves a process of examining motives and actions from the perspective of moral principles. Both the utilitarian and the universal theories provide a method of analysis that can be used to evaluate the ethical nature of many business decisions. Today, corporations are more aware of the responsibilities they have to customers, suppliers, employees, and local citizens. Therefore, the importance of conducting both legal and ethical analyses of proposed actions is growing.

Increasingly, actions in one part of the world have consequences elsewhere. The transfer of a firm's operations from Canada to the United States may prompt workers to protest the loss of jobs. The destruction of chemical plants in Russia may cause environmental pollution in dozens of neighboring countries. The development of an "abortion pill" in France leads to demands for the drug in some countries and protests against its use in others. As the world becomes smaller, both ethical standards and legal rules begin to harmonize, and international norms gradually develop. For example, the level of protection afforded to copyrights, patents, and trademarks (intellectual property) is becoming more similar across countries. Ethical standards regarding inappropriate contributions and gifts to public and private officials are more comparable. The future is likely to require business managers to increase their knowledge of the global legal environment surrounding their firm and industry and to become more aware of their corporation's ethical behavior.

Thought Questions

1. How might legal analysis differ in a common law country, where case law is an important source of law, from that practiced in a civil law country?
2. Do you think there is a common ethical standard among some countries regarding the use of inside information when selling or purchasing corporate securities (stock)?
3. What is the most significant difference between legal and ethical standards? What is the most significant similarity?

Law and the Legal Environment

This book describes and analyzes the legal environment of business. Laws affect businesses in many ways. Contract, property, and tort laws directly influence business agreements, real estate transactions, and liability concerns. Laws also regulate a wide range of business activities, from the hiring of employees to the warranties that accompany the sale of products. Securities regulations influence business financing decisions. Environmental laws, employee safety regulations, and consumer protection rules attempt to limit the harmful side effects of economic activity by imposing penalties for violations and, therefore, requiring compliance from business firms.

Law in Today's Society

Both national and local news stories focusing on legal matters appear almost every day. For example, constitutional provisions in many states require governments to begin each year with a balanced budget. States and cities are frequently forced to cut services, lay off employees, and seek ways to raise revenue without overtaxing citizens in order to meet this legal obligation. Students at public colleges and universities are directly affected: they often find higher tuition and fees accompanied by fewer professors and services.

Increasing global competition and technological changes are transforming many industries and individual businesses. Managers at all firms must be cognizant of many legal concerns as they prepare for a new environment. If a firm seeks to lay off workers, a state law or labor contract may require specific procedures be followed in determining who can be fired and how they are to be notified. If workers are to transfer to a different location or to begin a business in a different state or country, labor laws, investment regulations, and taxation provisions are among the concerns that must be addressed.

Firms moving into new markets are concerned with the corporation and securities laws that affect how the business may best be organized and financed; the tort laws that establish the basis for liability to customers and other product users; and the employment, environmental, and commercial sales laws that directly affect business operations.

Even on college campuses, the law has made its presence known. Ivy League universities were accused of violating antitrust law by collaborating to set common tuition charges and financial aid packages for students. They settled out of court and agreed to disband their annual meetings. Stanford University's practices for billing federal research projects were questioned when yachts and parties appeared to have been financed by the taxpayers. Students, too, are more aware of the law's intrusion into their lives. As society comes to recognize that many rapes and assaults are committed by acquaintances and dates, young people on campus realize that they may face both criminal and civil liabilities if they don't heed the "no" of their friends. New laws require public institutions of higher education to issue annual statistics regarding specified crimes committed on campus. Fraternities that condone hazing and organizations that sell alcohol to underage purchasers have been found liable for injuries to those affected by their actions.

In addition to the headline stories, hundreds of less visible cases affect the livelihood of many businesspeople each day: An arbitration provision inserted in contracts between stockbrokers and their clients is upheld; a court determines that under certain conditions, accountants can be held liable for negligence in reviewing corporate annual reports; a sexual harassment case is decided in favor of a female attorney with the Securities and Exchange Commission. Furthermore, many legal problems are resolved without going to trial—in part due to the precedent represented by other cases. Cigarette manufacturers routinely settle claims of smoking-induced injury without going through a public trial. Rutgers University settled a suit brought by the parents of a student who died at a fraternity initiation party. Local residents opposing the development of existing green space in Kalamazoo, Michigan, reached an accord with the developer after forcing him to modify his original plan. As the law is clearly part of our environment, we must understand how it may affect our business activities.

What Is Law?

The term *law* has several different meanings, each of which captures a different sense of the source of law, its legitimacy, and its use as a process.

Law: Definition One

> That which is laid down, ordained or established. A rule or method according to which phenomena or actions coexist or follow one another.
>
> *Black's Law Dictionary*

Law: Definition Two

> A binding custom or practice of a community. A rule or mode of conduct or action that is prescribed or formally recognized as binding by a supreme controlling authority or is made obligatory by a sanction made, recognized, or enforced by the controlling authority.
>
> *Webster's Third New International Dictionary*

Each of these definitions emphasizes several different aspects of law. The definition from *Black's Law Dictionary* notes that law refers to a result regardless of the process used to bring it about, that is, whether the result was ordained or established. Therefore, this definition focuses on the behavior that results from the establishment, creation, or recognition of the law. Actions or phenomena, whether involving particles of matter or people in a society, may be expected to act as they do because of law.

According to the *Webster's* definition, law is not generated by an outside source or higher authority; rather, it flows from the customs and practices the people in a society follow. The second segment of this definition emphasizes that sanctions are needed to make law effective. Therefore, only those societal customs or practices that are recognized as binding and are enforced by the authorities can be called laws.

law
Established standards or guidelines for action or behavior in a society, whether they originate from a higher authority or from the common practices and customs of people.

By combining these two definitions, we can conclude that **law** refers to established standards or guidelines for action or behavior in a society, whether they originate from a higher authority or from the common practices and customs of people. To be law, however, the standards must be "binding"; they must be made obligatory by the authorities in a society.

Why Study Law?

As the stories noted above make clear, law reaches pervasively into our personal and professional lives. From arbitration awards and bankruptcy proceedings to securities fraud and waste disposal requirements, the law and the legal environment cannot be ignored by business managers. One of the primary reasons that business students in particular study law is to gain the knowledge necessary to plan the numerous activities that hinge on what the law allows or requires. The legal environment in the 1990s is not the same as in the 1960s or even in the 1980s.

When studying the laws of the United States, it is important to realize that laws are made at various levels and by different branches of government. State courts and state or local regulatory bodies make thousands of decisions that determine where a business locates and, for certain industries (e.g., insurance, public utilities), what services can or must be offered and what rates can be charged for them. Contract, property, and liability laws in the United States originate primarily at the state level; there is little regulation in these fields at the federal level.

In addition, as economic ties between countries have multiplied and strengthened, the world has shrunk. Many companies find that their domestic market has become too small. Even the biggest companies in the biggest countries cannot survive if they compete in global industries but their activities are limited to one or two countries. Thus, international sources of law must be consulted. In the 21st century, business managers must take into consideration regulations and legal decisions made in Tokyo and Brussels as well as those coming from Lincoln, Nebraska; Charleston, South Carolina; and Washington, D.C., when determining tomorrow's legal environment.

The legal institutions and methods commonly used to resolve disputes are changing, both in the United States and in many other countries. For example, Chapter 4 discusses several emerging methods of dispute resolution: the minitrial and rent-a-judge, as well as arbitration and mediation. Arbitration is favored as a method for resolving many international contract disputes, while mediation and conciliation are most accepted in many Asian countries. Thus, it is important that business managers have a general knowledge of the legal system and the most important laws affecting their activities. A society's laws embody and reflect its customs and values. Since the laws of a society change and evolve, the legal environment of business is dynamic. Business managers must be aware of those changes and the forces that cause them. Businesspeople who are aware of important legal rules and emerging legal developments can perform more efficiently and effectively than those who lack such knowledge.

What Is the Legal Environment of Business?

Many studies have attempted to define the legal environment of business. The term suggests something more than merely memorizing rules of law. The **legal environment of business** is generally concerned with the study of the legal, regulatory, and political institutions and processes affecting business activities. In essence, the legal environment of business relates primarily to those laws that affect how business activities are conducted. Although public regulatory laws are central to a study of the legal environment, certain areas of private law, such as contract, tort, and property law, also require attention.

legal environment of business
The study of the legal, regulatory, and political institutions and processes affecting business activities.

Finally, ethical problems should also be discussed as part of the legal environment of business because law and ethics guide behavior in tandem. Several of the legal cases referred to earlier, for example, raise ethical questions. Is it right for a firm that has received special tax incentives for building in one state to move to another state or country without compensating for the benefit it has received? Is insider trading not only illegal, but also ethically improper? Business cases involving pollution, misleading advertising, and unconscionable contracts also clearly raise ethical concerns.

Components of the Legal Environment of Business

- An introduction to the fundamental legal institutions and processes in both domestic and international settings.
- An overview of the primary private law fields of property, tort, contract, and commercial transactions, which directly affect many business activities.
- An examination of specific areas in which there is significant regulation of business endeavors. These include consumer protection laws, securities regulations, antitrust concerns, labor and employment laws, and environment policies.
- An analysis of the relationship between law and ethics, including an examination of ethical problems as they relate to specific fields of law and a discussion of the social responsibility of business firms.

Legal Analysis

legal analysis
The study of court cases that solve specific disputes by applying general legal principles.

Legal analysis involves the study of court cases that solve specific disputes by applying general legal principles. Throughout this text, extracts from court opinions are presented in conjunction with the text material. This mixture permits the study of law and the legal environment to combine both inductive and deductive reasoning.

Inductive Reasoning

inductive reasoning
The process of examining specific situations to determine if they have some common attributes.

Inductive reasoning is the process of examining specific situations to determine if they have some common attributes. A reader who studies several related cases gains an understanding of how the application of legal principles in similar cases leads to the formation of general legal rules. Case summaries reveal the logic used by a court to decide specific legal problems. Generalizations from those specific situations become the basis for solutions to other, similar problems. By reviewing different cases related to the same topic, a reader can see how individual decisions lead to the establishment of general legal principles.

stare decisis
"Let the decision stand."

The common law legal system of the United States relies on decisions in prior cases as an important source of law. At the center of the common law legal system is the doctrine of ***stare decisis,*** which means "let the decision stand" (see page 33 in Chapter 2 for a further discussion of this term). Courts within the same jurisdiction are required to follow the legal principles set forth in earlier cases. Thus, the law applied to one case not only decides the case for the parties involved, but also establishes a legal "precedent" for future similar cases. It is for this reason that legal analysis in the United States involves the study of cases. This text includes end-of-chapter questions and exercises requiring the application of legal concepts based on situations that are similar to the court cases and text examples.

Deductive Reasoning

deductive reasoning
The process of examining general principles derived from induction or legislation and applying them to specific situations.

Deductive reasoning is the process of examining general principles derived from induction or legislation and applying them to specific situations. Many countries of the world use a civil law legal system based on a code of law that contains the society's most important general principles. By examining those general principles, one can deduce how to apply them to other specific problems.

For example, consider the general principle that all real estate contracts must be in writing to be enforced. A specific real estate contract between the ABC firm and the XYZ firm can, therefore, be enforced only if it is written. The same principle should apply equally for a contract between the XYZ firm and John Jones or for one between John Jones and Mary Brown. To fully understand a general legal concept, its application to several different situations or cases must be examined. This text presents numerous legal principles and cases illustrating how judges apply general legal principles to solve specific problems. After reading and understanding the court's opinion in a specific case, generalizations can be made and used to resolve other, similar problems and cases.

Thus, in order to solve the questions and problems you see on examinations and in professional activities, you must go beyond memorizing important legal principles. You must be able to determine if a principle fits the test problem or the business situation in the same way in which it fit the case you studied. Legal analysis requires you to understand how specific case decisions give rise to general principles and how general principles apply in specific case situations.

Reading the Text Material

The study of law calls for a different approach than reading a newspaper, magazine, or book. A widely used study method known as **SQ3R** can be very effective in improving your ability to retain and comprehend the information presented in this text. SQ3R stands for survey, question, read, recite, and review. The organization of this text, and of each of its chapters, has been prepared in a manner intended to facilitate the use of the SQ3R method of study.

SQ3R
A study method whose name stands for survey, question, read, recite, and review.

Your first task should be to *survey* the material assigned. Thus, if you are reading a chapter, look carefully at the content and organization of the material presented. The critical thinking questions and introduction sections at the beginning of each chapter facilitate this process. Take a few minutes to read each section heading and one or two subsequent sentences. Remember that you are surveying what topics are addressed in the chapter. You are not yet seeking to comprehend the details.

The second segment of study focuses on *questions*. Before you begin each section, formulate questions about the subject matter and about the key terms in order to focus your reading. In this way, the relevant points are more readily apparent. The questions following the chapter introduction and those appearing after each case assist in highlighting important aspects of your reading.

After you *read* the material, return to the questions you formulated and *recite* the answers to them. If you asked what was the meaning of a certain term, recite the definition for it. If you asked how to differentiate between two concepts, recite how each concept applies to particular situations.

The last step consists of a *review* of the material studied. A review helps you to retain the information presented. Again, asking questions may be helpful. What were the major points addressed by the cases? Which legal concepts do they illustrate? How do the section headings relate to each other? A summary, critical thinking review questions, and critical thinking exercises are presented at the end of each chapter to assist your review.

Developing Critical Thinking Skills

Critical thinking skills enable students to become independent learners. Because legal rules change frequently, managers who understand the issues and policymaking processes underlying lawmaking, regulation, and litigation are better able to make informed and intelligent business decisions. Critical thinking is fundamental to legal analysis.

Critical thinking requires an evaluation of the reasons, logic, and weight of evidence used in any argument. To perform the required analysis, you must understand the speaker or author's issue, conclusion, and reasons. These elements are also used in reading and briefing a judge's written court opinion. The next section and Appendix A review these elements as they apply to case opinions.

Only after the issue, conclusion, and reasons are identified can the audience evaluate the quality of the evidence and determine if the reasons support the conclusion. There are a variety of steps to critical thinking; the most important components include locating ambiguity, evaluating the evidence, generating rival hypotheses and conclusions, suggesting analogies, discovering reasoning errors and logical fallacies, and questioning value and descriptive assumptions. Figure 1–1 depicts each of the major critical thinking inquiries, describes their function in critical analysis, and notes tips regarding their place in critical thinking.

Identifying Issue, Conclusion, and Reasons *Issues* are the primary subject for review. What is the problem or question being addressed by the author or by a judge's court opinion? The *conclusion* is the writer's judgment about how that issue is to be resolved based on the evidence reviewed. Some conclusions are descriptive; they explain how things are. Other conclusions are prescriptive; they suggest what ought to occur.

What are the *reasons* given in support of the conclusion? Reasons answer why the conclusion should be accepted. Assume the facts show A was driving his car too fast when he injured B as he crashed into B's car. Also assume the law says that negligent or careless drivers should compensate those who are injured by their actions. The conclusion, that A should compensate B, is supported by the reasoning that A's driving too fast was negligent and it was the cause of B's injuries.

Locating Ambiguity Ambiguity may be significant if it creates misunderstanding. It is important that both the author and the reader attach the same meaning to key terms. Some ambiguity is inevitable, as the author and the reader generally have different backgrounds. Some ambiguity in the law is intentional; terms may be left vague so that they can cover a variety of circumstances. The term *security* as it relates to corporate stocks and bonds is vague so that it can apply to a variety of financial instruments, even some that do not yet exist. Sometimes the meaning of an ambiguous term is clarified when you review the context in which it is used. If you find an alternative meaning to a term, that meaning may change the author's conclusion or your evaluation of the reasons being used. Although not every ambiguity is important, ambiguities that link reasons with conclusions create the greatest misunderstanding.

Evaluating the Evidence Authors provide evidence, alleged to be facts, to support their reasons and conclusions. That evidence needs to be evaluated. Factual claims come from examples, empirical research, analogies, metaphors, or acknowledged authorities. There may be a failure in following a scientific method for determining the facts. A survey may not be representative, the conditions studied may not be adequately controlled, or the percentages found in the conclusion might be misleading. A study showing "five out of seven college students surveyed drink beer" does not indicate the size of the sample being surveyed or the relative frequency of their drinking. Conclusions based on the mean or median response to certain questions do not show the variance or spread between the top and bottom values.

FIGURE 1-1

Critical Thinking Inquiry	Definition	Function in Critical Analysis	Critical Thinking Tips
Issue	Subject addressed in author's expression	Essential to understanding points under discussion	May be hidden by unclear or technical language
Conclusion	Author's answer to the issue under controversy	Summary of author's view	Look for indicator words: *therefore, thus, as a result, it follows that*
Reasons	Statements of facts, evidence, analogies, or beliefs used to support a conclusion	Suggests why audience should accept author's conclusion; relationship of reasons to conclusion is focus of critical thinking inquiry	Look for indicator words: *because, the fact is, as a result of, by reason of, due to, in view of, on account of, thanks to*
Ambiguities	Words or phrases susceptible to alternate meanings	Although often inevitable given the imprecision of language good authors prevent much ambiguity	Examine context meaning; request author clarification; substitute alternate meaning to test whether conclusion changes
Statistical Flaws in Evidence	Failure in rigor of scientific method; nonrepresentative or biased sample; uncontrolled conditions; research method not replicable; deceptive but impressive large numbers; misleading percentages	Factual-based claims may be misleading if statistical flaws in empirical evidence; sampling is often a practical necessity	Demand author "show me"; use personal experience or others' studies as benchmark for comparison; examine controlled conditions; search for sample bias
Rival Hypotheses and Conclusion	Alternate hypotheses consistent with author's reasons or conclusion; alternate conclusion consistent with author's reasons or hypothesis	Author's reasoning weakened by rival hypotheses or conclusions	Use personal experience to search for alternate explanations consistent with author's conclusion, then generate alternate conclusions consistent with author's reasons
Analogies	Similarities between different things, suggesting that other similarities exist	Can provide convincing reasons, particularly when scientifically gathered evidence is missing or difficult to collect; law uses analogy significantly; although people accept analogies, weak analogies can be misleading	Carefully examine both the similarities and differences between two things compared; analogy is weak reason if differences predominate; generate competing yet plausible analogies to weaken author's analogies
Reasoning Errors and Logical Fallacies	Analytical flaws that weaken or contradict author's reasoning:	Fallacious argument misleads the reader	Be vigilant; always look for all these fallacies
	• **Diversions** lure reader from critical thinking • **Glittering generalities** divert and evoke emotion	Diversions and glittering generalities obscure reasons, assumptions, and analogies or evoke emotion	
	• **False dilemma** raises conflict between reasoning of author and author's opposition	False dilemma incorrectly forces misbelief that there are only two choices	

FIGURE 1-1 continued

Critical Thinking Inquiry	Definition	Function in Critical Analysis	Critical Thinking Tips
	• **Circular reasoning** simply restates conclusion as evidence	Circular reasoning disguises conclusion as reasons by begging the question	
Value and Descriptive Assumptions	Unstated beliefs implicit in author's reasoning	Assumptions that seem to strengthen conclusions through use of value-laden terms	Look for value-laden phrases and how author moves from incomplete reasons to partially supported conclusions

Generating Rival Hypotheses When the author suggests a cause-effect relationship, the reader should search for alternative connections. Causation is the relationship between the reasons given and the author's conclusion. In the case of the car accident noted above, while A was driving too fast, what do we know about B's conduct? If B stopped his car suddenly prior to A's car hitting his car, there may be an alternate or at least a second cause for the accident. Critical thinkers use alternate hypotheses as a means of evaluating the author's conclusion. Any alternate hypothesis must itself be tested for soundness and consistency. A rival hypothesis that is consistent with the author's evidence casts doubt on the author's conclusion.

Suggesting Analogies Reasoning by analogy compares two things to find their shared characteristics. The author first notes that the two things that are being compared, one familiar and one unfamiliar, have some common characteristics. Then, the author implies there must be other characteristics that they also share. Finally, by asserting some facts about the familiar thing, the author suggests those facts also apply to the unfamiliar thing. For example, an author might be discussing the organizational structure of a U.S. automobile firm while comparing it to that of a Japanese firm. Some common characteristics of Ford (the familiar) and Honda (the unfamiliar) are that they both sell their cars throughout the world, that each has a range of car models from deluxe to basic, and each also manufactures trucks. In evaluating analogies, both the similarities and the differences in items should be evaluated. If there are only a few similarities, the analogy is weak. A reader who suggests alternative analogies may weaken the author's conclusion.

Discovering Reasoning Errors and Logical Fallacies Because the reasoning process involves several steps, critical thinkers should evaluate each step of the process for logical fallacies. An author may use *emotional language* as a diversion from the real issue. An *appeal to an authority* or a *testimonial* implies that the audience should accept the conclusion because some famous person agrees with it. Advertising messages may feature testimonials that suggest you should use the product because the celebrity spokesperson has endorsed it. A *false dilemma* is a conflict created by an author that suggests you have only two choices in reaching a conclusion. Most controversies involve more choices. *Circular reasoning* occurs when a conclusion is restated as evidence. Something is bad because it is undesirable; the conclusion that it is bad is not supported by restating the conclusion and attempting to use that new term as evidence for the conclusion. Critical thinkers remain sensitive to common types of poor-quality evidence; they don't generalize or jump to the suggested conclusion based on biased or incomplete evidence.

Questioning Values and Descriptive Assumptions An author's assumptions affect the reader's movement from the evidence to the conclusion. Values are abstract ideas that form the basis for making decisions. Equal opportunity, justice, fairness, impartiality, excellence, cooperation, competition, and equality are among the values that authors and readers may or may not share. Although authors generally do not express their value assumptions, critical thinkers should identify the author's value assumptions as well as those of the audience to see if there are value conflicts. For example, if an author wants to continue to apply the law as it existed in a prior case to a new case, the author may argue that precedent requires following the prior case. However, if the result of the prior case is not now seen as fair or just, the author opposed to the prior case may argue that fairness, not precedent, is more important.

An author's unstated factual belief may or may not be shared with the audience. Descriptive assumptions are hidden facts that must be true in order for the reasons stated to support the conclusion. Critical thinkers try to identify these assumptions to evaluate the author's perspective. An audience should accept an author's argument and conclusion only if it also shares the author's descriptive assumptions.

Reading Case Opinions

The court opinions found in this text are taken from the decisions of the various state and federal courts. Some are recent cases dealing with problems affecting contemporary business managers. Others are classic cases that represent important developmental changes in the application of law to certain activities. Some cases include both majority and dissenting opinions. Dissenting judges often provide insight into the terms of a conflict or the range of economic, social, or political views on an issue. Furthermore, dissenting opinions sometimes pave the way for later changes in the law.

At first, cases can be difficult to read and understand. It helps to look for certain elements that facilitate the review of a case's important aspects. It is often useful to write a short summary of the case, known as a **brief.** A brief helps to clarify the opinion and helps you to understand the issues addressed by the court. Appendix A contains a sample case, a discussion of items to include in a brief, and a sample brief.

brief
A short summary of a case.

The Nature of Law and Legal Theories

Theories concerning the nature of law attempt to answer questions about the source of law, the extent of an individual's obligation to observe the law, and the adequacy and justice of particular laws. No single set of answers to these questions receives general acceptance. Rather, several theories contribute various perspectives that enhance our understanding of the role of law in society.

Natural Law Theory

Natural law theory holds that nature ordains the law independently from human action. In the U.S. Declaration of Independence, the second and most famous sentence provides a good example of natural law: human beings are "endowed by their Creator with certain inalienable rights," including "Life, Liberty and the pursuit of Happiness." The theory of natural law assumes that people will find rational justice by using their natural reasoning abilities.

The primary concerns of natural law theory are laws that deal with the human condition and with situations relating to fundamental human rights, including laws that guarantee the right to life, laws that guarantee a person's civil rights, laws that promote equal housing opportunities, and laws that protect a person's freedom of speech. According to the theory, natural law establishes fundamental human rights for all people, regardless of their culture or society. Natural law is the same for poor farmers in Afghanistan, steel workers in Germany, and businesswomen in the United States.

People have espoused many variations of the natural law theme. Underlying each is the belief that certain higher principles of justice exist for all people, regardless of their present situation. Thus, the U.S. Constitution's Bill of Rights protects all people, even the criminals and hate mongers in society. Natural law theorists believe these principles can and should be implemented through legal institutions. Natural law theory continues to influence some laws today, particularly right-to-life laws. Because murder is inherently wrong according to natural law, the protection of the life of a fetus overrides non-life threatening concerns of the mother or the circumstances of conception when being considered by legislators or judges seeking to follow natural law precepts. Sometimes natural law is described as normative, prescribing what "ought to be," because it emphasizes a body of higher law that individuals must attempt to understand and obey.

Positivism Theory

In the 18th century, scholars developed a positivism philosophy of law that continues to influence the teaching of law in many universities today. Positivism theorists contend that any accurate explanation of the nature of law should be based on what actually occurs in society, not what ought to be. Legal positivism theory analyzes law and legal institutions as they actually exist. Positivists regard as law only those rules that the state adopts to obligate people to generally do (or to refrain from doing) particular activities. For example, if a society has not adopted laws to prohibit the use of confidential information by the owner of a company's stock, the seller who knows the company's finances are not in good shape would be able to sell his stock to an innocent purchaser without concern about the legality of his actions. This view emphasizes law as being the commands of a sovereign power. In some countries, sovereign power resides with a monarch or dictator; whereas, in other societies it is vested in elected officials, legislators, or even the people at large.

Note that the positivism theory emphasizes both the commands of the sovereign and the analysis of law based on observations of what occurs in the application and enforcement of those commands. This analytical approach presents an important contrast to natural law theory. The focus of positivism is on the here and now (what is), not on a normative objective (what ought to be). Some legal scholars criticize legal positivism for its lack of concern for moral content of laws.

Sociological Theory

Sociological theory, developed during the 20th century, views law as society's response to economic, political, historic, and social pressures. For example, in the late 19th century, the United States and many countries in western Europe reacted to the social turmoil that accompanied the Industrial Revolution by passing laws and using legal institutions to provide remedies for those in need. Antitrust laws restricted certain anticompetitive business practices, and child labor laws limited the use of children as workers in factories and offices. Sociological theorists believe the legal system and laws of a society are closely integrated into its social structure. Because social structures differ from one society to the next, so too do laws and legal systems. They reject both the relationship between law and logic suggested by legal positivists and the universal truths of natural law. Instead, the law is examined and understood by observing how the law operates in society's legal institutions.

Sociological theory inspired several important concepts of 20th century legal thought. For example, the focus on the interaction between law and society recognizes that both society and laws are dynamic. Society changes as the balance of power shifts between various interests. Laws, in turn, change to reflect the changes taking place in society. Conversely, the legal system and the laws also influence society. Law can resolve conflicts between public and private interests or between the interests of groups and individuals. Because law can balance competing interests in a society, it can be used to assert social control. A society's governmental authorities use law to encourage, direct, change, or repress certain behavior. For example, tax law makes retirement earnings contributions exempt from income tax to encourage savings; licensing rules prohibit other behaviors as harmful or unprofessional conduct (selling real estate without a license); and criminal laws impose penalties such as fines and jail sentences to discourage socially undesirable conduct.

Realism Theory

The legal realism theory is a variation of the sociological theory. Both consider law and legal institutions as reflections or implementations of economic, political, and social influences. However, realists are more concerned with how the legal system actually operates than with the more theoretical relationship between laws and the interests of society. Oliver Wendell Holmes's definition of law illustrates the realist point of view: "The prophecies of what the courts will do in fact, and nothing more pretentious, are what I mean by the law." To the realist, the law is determined not just by looking at a written statement, but also by examining the behavior of judges, lawyers, police officers, sheriffs, and administrative enforcement personnel in the legal system. The realist views law not as a mere set of established rules, but as a system of rules that fluctuate as the people in the legal system and the society itself change.

A realist studies the actions of legal officials rather than either existing or normative rules. Therefore, no unified concept of law underlies the realism theory. Instead, the realist is concerned with the operation of an ever-changing legal system. Article 2 of the Uniform Commercial Code (UCC) reflects adherence to this philosophy of law. The UCC was drafted on the basis of observed business practices, and it mandates the most desirable practices of merchants. In many instances, the code requires merchants to follow "commercially reasonable" practices, such as accepting payment made within 30 days as incurring no interest charges. Although such practices are not set in concrete and are subject to change, the UCC reflects the realist view.

The Economic School Theory

The economic school of thought was developed in 1970 by Richard Posner, a former law professor at the University of Chicago Law School and now a judge on the United States Court of Appeals for the Seventh Circuit. This theory holds that most laws may be evaluated according to economic theory since it is assumed that people seek to maximize their own welfare. Law is viewed as means by which efficient economic outcomes are achieved. If you are injured in an accident, you may decide to seek compensation from the party at fault through mediation or litigation. The choice you make may depend on your view as to which forum offers you the best chance of receiving the most money.

Critical Legal Study Theory

Critical legal study theorists believe that law, like literary criticism, is the product of political and moral values. To critical legal theorists, law is not stable and predictable, but rather is subject to interpretations by those involved in the legal system (legislators, judges, lawyers) and by ordinary people who behave according to what they believe the law means. The interpretation of law is based not only on logic and reason, but also on political and moral beliefs.

Historical Theory

Historical theorists look to the past as well as to the present. They see law as more than the current laws that the positivists are most concerned with. Customs and practices change and through time, some evolve into new legal standards. Although laws in the United States now require integrated public schools, that was not always the case. Understanding both past and present conditions and legal standards helps to prepare new laws that will address future problems. Historical theorists look at law as embodying a society's customs. Customs and cultural values influence and become the basis of law. As customs change, a society's laws change. Laws that do not reflect the customs in a society are likely to disappear or not be enforced.

Law and Ethics

Both law and ethics prescribe guidelines for behavior. Some people believe that obeying the law means they are also behaving ethically. Others believe that laws establish minimum standards whereas a system of ethics may actually impose stricter obligations. Thus, some argue that in certain situations, ethical standards may require people to violate the law. As Figure 1–2 notes, legal actions may be unethical, and illegal actions may be ethical. The principle of civil disobedience, as practiced by Mahatma Ghandi and Martin Luther King, Jr., is based on the belief that people should actively oppose unethical laws.

Although law and ethics are closely related, both reflecting moral judgments, they are fundamentally different. Legal rules require all people to follow certain clearly defined standards or face explicit consequences. If we violate criminal rules, we could be prosecuted and imprisoned. If we do not adhere to contract requirements, our agreements may be unenforceable and of little value. Ethical standards, by contrast, are subjectively determined on an individual and institutional basis. Unethical behavior often goes unpunished by society. In some groups, unethical behavior is tolerated or accepted; in others, it is frowned upon and discouraged.

One of the areas in which the relationship between law and ethics arises concerns the imposition of a legal duty to provide information or even assistance. Consider the following ethical dilemmas.

	Legal actions (L)	Illegal actions (I)
Ethical actions (E)	(L) + (E)	(I) + (E)
Unethical actions (U)	(L) + (U)	(I) + (U)

FIGURE 1-2

The Interplay of Laws and Ethics

ETHICAL DILEMMA

Today, some parties on both sides of the pro-life/pro-choice abortion debate believe so strongly in their positions that they are willing to violate the law. Pro-life advocates have chained themselves to the entrance of clinics where legal abortions are performed in order to prevent those abortions from taking place. A pro-life activist recently killed a doctor who was performing abortions. According to some pro-life proponents, it may be ethical to "kill a killer." Pro-choice activists in some jurisdictions are subject to laws that require clinics not to provide abortion information to pregnant clients; the activists nevertheless provide that information because they believe their ethical duty overrides the legal rules they are supposed to follow. Do you think it is acceptable to violate laws if ethical action is promoted in doing so? Are the actions of pro-life and pro-choice activists ethical?

Next, consider a U.S.-owned chemical plant located outside the United States. Some employees are exposed to toxic substances on a daily basis. Does the U.S. firm that is the controlling owner of the foreign plant have a legal duty to warn the foreign employees of the potential danger from the toxic chemicals? Should the firm consider the "duty-to-warn" laws of the United States or the foreign country or both? Is there an ethical obligation to provide a warning even if there is no legal duty?

Finally, assume you are walking along a beach on a small lake when you spot a person in the water about 100 meters from shore. As you look closer, you see that the person in the water appears to be drowning. You look around, see no one else nearby, and knowing that you are a good swimmer and that the water is not too cold or too deep, you consider whether to rescue the drowning person whom you now hear crying for help. Do you have a legal obligation to begin the rescue? If you begin the rescue, whether you have to or not, does the law impose on you a duty of care? Do you think the law would be the same in the United States as it is in another country, such as the Netherlands? Do you have an ethical duty to help the drowning person who is a complete stranger to you?

ETHICAL ANALYSIS

Ethics is a field of philosophy that examines motives and actions from the perspective of moral principles. **Morality** refers to human behavior that is found to be good and just. **Moral reasoning** involves the process of moving from premises to conclusions in determining the right course of action. The moral principles that form the basis for evaluating behavior are generally drawn from several different sources.

ethics
A field of philosophy that examines motives and actions from the perspective of moral principles.

morality
Human behavior that is found to be good and just.

moral reasoning
The process of moving from premises to conclusions in determining the right course of action.

Some ideals come from principles espoused by philosophers. Religious principles, such as the Golden Rule, the Ten Commandments, or similar precepts from the Buddhist or Muslim religions also frequently provide the starting point from which ethical analysis proceeds. The early Greek philosophers—Socrates, Plato and Aristotle—focused on good and doing the right thing. Socrates talked of acquiring knowledge of the "true good," asking each individual to "know thyself." Plato said ethical behavior consists of praiseworthy acts while Aristotle talked about doing "right" and "good."

Religious commands have also been the source of many ethical standards. All major religions emphasize doing good for others, being fair, and treating people in a way that shows respect. In Islamic and Hindu countries, the standard for proper behavior is linked to established precepts based on divine revelations or prophetic teachings. The separation of law and moral standards found in western countries is not present where there is a religious-based legal system.

More recently, the person with self-centered values considers all behavior that is in one's self-interest, or at least that which is acceptable to others or that which produces desired results, as being ethical. By contrast, expectancy ethics and ethical realism looks at ethics on an expectancy basis. If you borrow money from a banker, you expect to be told truthfully the interest and fees you are being charged. You might expect, however, that a salesman would not disclose to you all problems related to the product you contemplate purchasing. The standard for behavior depends on what people realistically expect.

ethical analysis
Studying ehtical concepts and theories and applying them to particular situations.

Like legal analysis, **ethical analysis** involves studying concepts and theories and applying them to particular situations. Ethical analysis cannot be accomplished simply by instinctively trying to determine what is right. Instead, using ethical theories, you must ask questions, examine alternatives, and seek solutions that coincide with ethical goals. Several ethical theories exist, each of which determines what is good or right in a different manner. You determine which approach will be most helpful to guide you in different situations.

Even people who follow the same approach may apply moral standards to specific problems in different ways. Some people argue that because different cultures have varied customs and moral codes, no universal moral truth can be defined. According to this view, a practice that is considered morally wrong in one society may be commonly accepted in another. Critics strongly object to this belief. If, for example, there is discrimination based on race in South Africa, is the practice acceptable because it is permitted and approved by the dominant group in that country? From either viewpoint, ethical truths are conclusions that are backed by reasons and values, not merely subjective opinions of good and bad.

Two important ethical theories influence the formation of our moral concepts today. They are the teleological, or consequence-oriented, utilitarian theory and the deontological, or duty-based, universalism theory.

Utilitarian Theory

utilitarian theory
Defines an action as morally right and ethical if it produces the greatest amount of good for the greatest number of people.

Utilitarian theory examines the consequences of a given action and defines an action as morally right and ethical if it produces the greatest amount of good for the greatest number of people. In order to reach this goal, there must be agreement on what is good and on the number of people affected by different actions. Different philosophers have reached varying conclusions about what is good (individual happiness, the common good, or material wealth) and about the number of people affected (focusing on those most directly affected, on anyone even slightly affected, or on no one being worse off).

The utilitarian does not focus on the inherent correctness of a given action, but rather examines its consequences. In order to maximize the good from a given action or course of conduct, we must measure the costs and benefits from possible alternative activities. Thus, the utilitarian ethical analysis may require the performance of a societal cost-benefit analysis. Consider the decision to close a plant in Ohio and invest in a new one in South Carolina. This action may permit the company to produce at a lower cost, benefiting its customers. If production expands, the company may provide more employment, though at lower wages, and increased profit for the firm, its managers, and its owners. How do you determine if these benefits outweigh the adverse effect on the community in Ohio, the Ohio workers, and the company's suppliers in that region?

Utilitarian theory is the dominant ethical theory used in business today. When used at the micro level of the firm rather than at the macro level of the society, the firm seeks to maximize the benefit to the firm without considering the effects of its actions on society. Theories that focus on the consequences of actions, as does utilitarian theory, are known as teleological theories. There are no basic principles of good or right; good is determined by maximizing the good consequences of an action and minimizing the bad ones.

Kantian or Universal Theory

The second major ethical theory is referred to as the **Kantian** or **universal theory.** Immanuel Kant (1724–1804) is commonly considered the father of modern philosophy. Unlike the utilitarian, Kant did not look at the consequences of actions to determine if they were ethical. Instead, Kant argued that a commitment to universal principles (the categorical imperative) should guide people. He believed that actions are moral only if those actions can be undertaken by everyone in good conscience. Thus, your actions should be guided by determining if your conduct could serve as the standard for universal conduct.

universal theory Defines actions as morally good if those actions can be undertaken by everyone in good conscience.

The Golden Rule exemplifies this duty-based standard: You are to act in the way you expect others to act toward you. Kant also focused on ends rather than means. Other people should be treated as individuals with worth, not as means to an end. This duty-based theory is known as a deontological theory. Conduct should be guided not by looking at its resulting consequences, but by whether it coincides with preexisting duties. Consider a business situation. What is ethical behavior for a person who sells a product knowing of some defect in it? Kant would examine the need for the seller to disclose to a potential buyer what he or she knows about the product by asking universal-based questions.

Using Kantian Ethical Analysis

1. Would I want everyone, regardless of the product being sold, to be able to refrain from disclosing what they know about a defect in the product? Does it matter what product is being sold, whether it is a used car with defective brakes, a ladder with a defective rung or step, or a bookshelf that lacks support on one of its shelves?
2. Would I want the principle of nondisclosure applied if I were the buyer instead of the seller?
3. Am I treating the other people involved (the buyer) as an end, according them respect, not as a means (to achieve a sale and profit for me)?

Business Ethics

business ethics Application of traditional ethical analysis to business decisions.

Business ethics can be viewed as an application of traditional ethical analysis to business decisions. However, although decisions made by individuals in a business organization obviously affect that organization's actions, a business organization often has its own history, tradition, rules, and ethical standards. The actions of a business firm may be influenced by values, interests, and principles that differ from those of its individual managers. Ethical analysis, therefore, can sometimes be difficult to implement in a business context. Problems arise in (1) identifying common values within a firm or industry, (2) deciding how much emphasis to place on collective benefits, (3) projecting side effects, and (4) defining the extent of a firm's responsibilities to outside groups.

Numerous business decisions require managers not only to know the law, but to make ethical decisions as well. For example, a beer manufacturer had planned to target its advertising for selling a beer with a high alcoholic content in predominantly low-income neighborhoods. By using such terms as "bold" and "high-performance," the manufacturer sought to increase sales of the product to consumers who might want a little extra "kick" from the beer. The campaign promised to return additional sales and profit, but were the ethical aspects of the advertising aimed at low-income consumers and distributed only in certain neighborhoods sufficiently analyzed? How would a universalist or a utilitarian analyze this venture? McDonald's offers a lean hamburger that has lower fat content and cholesterol than its other menu items. Did McDonald's respond to the marketplace's demand for such items, or did it determine what it should offer and then have the market respond?

Public opinion regarding the honesty and ethical standards of business executives, politicians, and even religious leaders has become less favorable in recent years. For example, President Clinton, House Speaker Newt Gingrich, Senator Alphonse D'Amato, and several of President Clinton's Cabinet appointees have been targets of ethics probes by Congressional Committees or by the Attorney General's Office. Business executives of several Fortune 500 firms have used corporate funds to purchase works of art, to furnish resort villas, and to pay questionable expenses for their traveling companions. The former chairman of the United Way faced criminal charges based on his billing exorbitant personal expenses to that not-for-profit agency. Some television evangelists who have raised money for "their" church and its operations have used the contributions to pay for lavish lifestyles. The ethics scandals seem to occur in almost all walks of life.

Textual Treatment of Ethics

Law is often based on ethics. The area of business ethics is of growing concern to the public, business leaders, and lawmakers. Therefore, it is important for future business managers to be able to examine the relationship between their actions and ethical standards. This text uses three approaches to study business ethics. First, this chapter provides an overview of the relationship between law and ethics that should guide your reading of cases and text material in later chapters. Second, the text incorporates ethical dilemmas pertaining to particular legal areas into the chapters and includes end-of-chapter ethical exercises. Third, Chapter 22 is devoted to a discussion of corporate social responsibility and business ethics. After reviewing the laws noted throughout the text, the final chapter provides an opportunity to summarize the social and business ethics problems that influence the legal environment of business.

SUMMARY

The study of law involves the study of court cases and textual materials. The law plays an important role in all societies, and its role in the United States is very significant. Law affects both personal and business activities. In the business world, an understanding of the legal environment of business is vital for managers taking part in financing, advertising, product development, and human resource decisions. The legal environment of business concerns not only the rules of law, with particular attention to the areas in which there is significant regulation of business conduct, but also the study of domestic and international legal institutions and legal processes affecting business activities.

Legal analysis combines inductive reasoning, based on individual case study, with deductive reasoning, which focuses on general legal concepts. By looking at numerous similar specific cases, you can inductively formulate general principles; and by examining general concepts and applying them to different situations, you can deduce whether the general principles are indeed valid. This text incorporates a variety of items so that the reader can use the SQ3R method of study. In this method, you survey and formulate questions about the material, read the assigned material, recite questions and answers about your reading, and review what you have read. Because legal rules and the policies they implement change frequently, the person whose critical thinking skills are sharp will better understand the issues, policies, and lawmaking and regulatory processes at work in a legal system. It is for this reason that critical thinking analysis, which requires an evaluation of the reasons, logic, and weight of evidence used in any argument, is included in this beginning chapter of the text. The cases in the text can be studied by preparing a brief that contains the important elements of the court's decisions. Your brief should include the facts, the central issue, the holding, the rationale, and, for some cases, a dissent and commentary.

A number of theories attempt to explain the nature of law. Natural law theory sees law as ordained by nature and separate from the customs of a particular society. The positivism theory emphasizes both the commands of the sovereign power and the analysis of law based on its application and enforcement in particular situations. Sociological theory views law and legal systems as an inherent part of a society, whereas the realism theory views law as emerging from the existing legal institutions of a society. The economic, critical, and historical theories see law in the context of other disciplines.

Both law and ethics prescribe guidelines for behavior. Ethics is concerned with examining motives and actions from the perspective of moral principles. Religious precepts and philosophical theories are common sources of such principles. Among the most influential ethical theories are utilitarian theory, which looks at the consequences of actions to determine their costs and benefits, and the Kantian, or universalist, theory, which examines whether moral standards can be universalized. Business ethics can be viewed as an application of traditional ethical analysis to business decisions. Because business organizations often have their own history, tradition, and values, the actions of a business firm may be influenced by values that differ from those of its managers.

CRITICAL THINKING REVIEW QUESTIONS

1. Give three different definitions of law and furnish an example of how each can be applied.
2. Write a short statement describing four of the legal theories discussed in the text. Provide an example illustrating the views of each theory.
3. What is the purpose of briefing a case? In what way does a case affect parties who are not involved in the case?
4. What is the difference between deductive and inductive reasoning? How is each used in the study of law?

CRITICAL THINKING EXERCISES

1. Three sailors and a cabin boy were adrift in an open lifeboat, 1,000 miles from land. On the 20th day, having been without food for 9 days and without water for 7 days, two of the sailors killed the cabin boy, who was in a very weak condition. He would probably have died had he not been

killed. The three sailors ate his body and drank his blood for three days. Four days later, the sailors were rescued, and the two who killed the cabin boy were subsequently tried for murder. How do you decide this case as the judge? Under what jurisprudential theory? (*Regina v. Dudley & Stephens,* 14 Q.B.D. 273, 1884).

2. Mary, a 16-year-old high school student, had an opportunity to sing with a small band. To enhance her singing abilities, she entered into a contract with Mrs. Thompson for a course of vocal music lessons. The lessons were scheduled to occur for 10 weeks, and Mary agreed to pay Mrs. Thompson $500. She paid $200 at the beginning and was to pay the remaining $300 when the lessons were finished. Mary quit after completing six lessons and notified Mrs. Thompson that she was disaffirming the contract. She asked for the $200 she had paid to be returned, but Mrs. Thompson refused. Mary then sued Mrs. Thompson for the return of the $200. Assume that the law entitled Mary to have the $200 returned. Was it ethical for her to seek it? Do you think Mary had any ethical duty to pay Mrs. Thompson for the lessons she did have? Why?
3. You are the vice president for international sales of A-One AirSeat Corporation, which manufactures seats used in airplanes. Recently you have been discussing your product with an airline representative from Chinan Express, the government-subsidized airplane manufacturer in a heavily populated country in Asia. In order to sell products to this firm, you need a license from the government. In your discussion with the representative from Chinan Express, you learn that if you pay a certain individual $100,000, and have him apply for the license on behalf of your firm, it is very likely that the license will be granted within two months. On the other hand, if you apply directly, it may take up to two years for your firm to obtain the license. You hope to sell over $5 million in seats to Chinan Express. The president asks what you think would be the right thing for the company to do. What would be your recommendation to the president regarding this transaction? Consider both the Kantian and utilitarian ethical theories in formulating your answer.
4. Alpha Construction Company is considering who to promote to the position of regional sales manager for its heavy equipment division, which sells equipment to firms engaged in highway construction activities. In the past, the person promoted has usually been the top salesperson from the various branch offices in the region. You are the vice president of human resources and need to make a recommendation to the company's board of directors concerning this position. Two candidates are being considered. Bob, a 10-year employee, is a good salesman from the company's New York office, is well liked by the customers, and knows many of the salespeople who he would have the responsibility to manage. Susan has been a saleswoman with the firm for six years, and for the last three years has been the top salesperson. Some of the salespeople in the region are not sure how they would like having a woman as their manager. They suggest that customers with whom the regional manager would have to meet, entertain, and negotiate may not want to do business with a woman sales manager. Who will you recommend? Use ethical analysis to explain your decision.
5. Discuss the relationship between law and ethics. Give examples of acts that may be legal but unethical and acts that may be illegal but ethical.
6. Solar Sights, Inc., manufactures solar panels to be used in small office buildings and residences. Although the firm can demonstrate an energy savings if there is a specified amount of sunlight on the panel, many firms are reluctant to purchase the panels because trees on neighboring property may block out the sunlight. There is no law to protect access to the sun for solar panels in any of the states in which the firm does business. Refer to four legal theories noted in the chapter and explain why you think there should or should not be such a law.

APPENDIX

A

Reading a Case and Writing a Brief

The following case is presented to sharpen your skills in case analysis and brief writing. Carefully read the *Katko v. Briney* case and the review questions that follow. Next, read the section on what items to include in a case brief. Prepare your own brief of the *Katko* case based on the format suggested. Finally, compare your brief with the sample brief. Although your brief should be similar to the sample, it need not be identical.

If you take the time to brief many of the cases in this text, both your understanding of the cases and your writing of briefs will improve. Writing a brief also helps to improve your analytical skills. It is almost impossible to write a good brief for a case unless you have first thought about the important facts, determined how the legal principle is applied, and analyzed the court's reasoning and decision.

A Sample Case

Katko v. Briney

183 N.W.2d 657 (1971)
Supreme Court of Iowa

Plaintiff Katko sued for damages resulting from serious injury caused by a shot from a 20-gauge spring shotgun set by defendant Briney in a bedroom of an old uninhabited farmhouse. Briney had set the shotgun because there had been numerous housebreakings in the area. The shots from the gun hit Katko, who had broken into and entered the house to find and steal old bottles and dated fruit jars that were considered valuable antiques. Briney claimed he had a right to protect his property against thieves such as Katko. Katko claimed that Briney's shotgun trap was wrongful and illegal. At the trial, the jury returned a verdict for Katko against Briney for $20,000 actual damages and $10,000 punitive damages. The trial judge approved the jury's verdict, and Briney appealed to the Iowa Supreme Court.

Chief Justice Moore

The primary issue here is whether an owner may protect personal property in an unoccupied boarded-up farmhouse against trespassers and thieves by a spring gun capable of inflicting death or serious injury. We are not here concerned with a man's right to protect his home and the members of his family. Defendant's home was several miles from the scene of the incident to which we refer.

For about 10 years there occurred a series of trespassing and housebreaking events with loss of some household items, the breaking of windows, and messing up of the property in general. Through the years, the defendant boarded up windows and doors in an attempt to stop the intrusions. He also posted a no trespassing sign some 35 feet from the house. On June 11, 1967, defendant set a shotgun trap in the north bedroom. It was rigged with wire from the doorknob to the gun's trigger so it would fire when the door was opened. Briney first pointed the gun so an intruder would be hit in the stomach, but at his wife's suggestion it was lowered to hit the legs. He admitted he did it "because I was mad and tired of being tormented," but he "did not intend to injure anyone." The spring gun could not be seen from the outside, and no warning of its presence was posted.

Plaintiff entered the old house by removing a board from a porch window. . . . [When p]laintiff went to open the north bedroom door, the shotgun went off, striking him in the right leg above the ankle bone. Much of his leg was blown away. He crawled to his vehicle and was then rushed to a doctor and the hospital, where he remained for 40 days.

Plaintiff . . . pled guilty to the criminal charge of larceny in the nighttime of property of less than $20 value from a private building. . . . [H]e was fined $50 and costs and paroled . . . from a 60-day jail sentence.

The main thrust of the defendant's defense is that the law permits the use of a spring gun in a dwelling or warehouse for the purpose of preventing the unlawful entry of a burglar or thief. The trial court instructed the jury that the law allows one to "use reasonable force in the protection of his property, but such right is subject to the qualification that one may not use such means of force as will take human life or inflict great bodily injury. Such is the rule even though the injured party is a trespasser and is in violation of the law himself."

The trial court also stated that "an owner of premises is prohibited from willfully or intentionally injuring a trespasser by means of force that either takes life or inflicts great bodily injury. The fact that the trespasser may be acting in violation of the law does not change the rule. The only time when such conduct of setting a spring gun or like dangerous device is justified would be when the trespasser was committing a felony of violence or when the trespasser was endangering human life by his act."

The overwhelming weight of authority, both textbook and case law, supports the trial court's statement of the applicable principles of law. Prosser on Torts, third edition, pages 116–18, states:

> The law has always placed a higher value upon human safety than upon mere rights in property; it is the accepted rule that there is no privilege to use any force calculated to cause death or serious bodily injury to repel the threat to land or chattels, unless there is also such a threat to the defendant's personal safety as to justify a self defense. . . . Spring guns and other man-killing devices are not justifiable against a mere trespasser, or even a petty thief.

Restatement of Torts, Section 85, page 180, states:

> The value of human life and limbs, not only to the individual concerned but also to the society, so outweighs the interest of a possessor of land in excluding from it those he is not willing to admit thereto that a possessor of land has no privilege to use force intended or likely to cause death or serious harm against another . . . unless the intrusion threatens death or serious bodily harm to the occupiers or users of the premises.

In *Allison v. Fiscus* (1951), the facts were very similar to [this case]. There, plaintiff's right to damages was recognized for injuries received when he broke a door latch and started to enter defendant's warehouse with intent to steal. As he entered, a trap of two sticks of dynamite buried under the doorway by defendant owner was set off and plaintiff seriously injured. The Ohio Supreme Court recognized the plaintiff's right to recover punitive damages in addition to compensatory damages.

The judgment of the trial court is affirmed.

Case Questions

1. Could Briney, as the owner of this unoccupied farmhouse, do anything to protect his property against thieves such as Katko?
2. Would this case be decided differently if Briney had posted a notice outside the house that there was a shotgun rigged to one of the bedroom doors?

3. What would be the decision in a case in which attack dogs are used to protect a jewelry store from burglars?

4. Would the case be decided differently if Briney were living in the house?

Items to Include in a Case Brief

Case Title and Citation In reading cases, look at the first several lines preceding the court's opinion. The first line states the title of the case and identifies the parties to the suit. Most of the cases cited in this text are appellate cases, not trial court cases, so generally the first party named is the **appellant,** the one who is bringing the appeal. The second party, known as the **appellee,** is the party who is satisfied with the trial court's decision. Some courts do not put the name of the appellant first; instead, they continue to place the names in the sequence used by the trial court.

If the court is a trial court, the name of the party bringing the case to trial, the **plaintiff,** appears first, whereas the name of the party against whom the suit was brought, the **defendant,** appears last. These two sets of litigation designations (appellant/appellee and plaintiff/defendant) indicate different characteristics about the parties, but sometimes the terms are used together. A plaintiff-appellee, such as Katko in the preceding case, is the party who originally brought the case to trial and who was satisfied with the trial court's decision. Briney, the defendant-appellant, is the party who was sued and was dissatisfied with the trial court's decision because he lost.

The second line contains the **citation,** which tells the reader and legal researcher where the case may be found. Court opinions are collected and bound together in books known as *reporters.* The numbers and abbreviations in the citation indicate in which book and on what page to find a case. The Katko case begins on page 657 of volume 183 of the second series of *North Western Reporter* books. The date indicates when the case was finally decided by the reviewing or appellate court. Several years may pass between the original trial and the decision by the reviewing court.

The third line gives the name of the court that wrote the opinion. Generally, this is an appellate court, which reviews the decision made by a lower court. In some cases, it may be a trial court, a state's supreme court, a federal court, or even an administrative agency. Chapter 2 discusses the organization of state and federal courts.

Facts Only those facts that provide information needed to resolve the problem confronting the court should be stated in a brief. You should read the entire case before beginning the brief so that you can distinguish salient facts important to deciding the issue from irrelevant or tangential facts. Notice in the sample brief how unimportant facts are omitted and the important facts are summarized.

Issue Court opinions frequently resolve several issues. Cases in this text are generally edited to present only the issue considered most important to the context of a discussion. The issue identifies the legal problem that must be answered to determine which of the disputing parties wins the case. Generally, the issue should be posed in the form of a question permitting a yes–or–no answer.

Holding The holding contains the court's answer to the question posed by the issue. The holding comprises the legal rule and precedent for which that case stands. It may also be useful to note which party won the lawsuit. The holding is the opinion of the majority of the judges of the court. It may not be the holding of all of the judges and you may disagree with it.

Rationale The court's reasoning explains the decision it reached. Be careful not to simply restate the decision as the rationale. In order to extract general rules from the court's decision, you must understand the court's reasoning. Ask yourself, "If the facts in this case were changed slightly, would the case be decided the same way? Why? Which facts or policies would lead a court in a slightly different case to reach the same opinion?" The premises used and the chain of reasoning form the basis for the court's decision.

Dissent Some cases that contain both a majority and dissenting opinion are presented to highlight controversies. A good brief should include a few sentences to summarize the views of the dissenting judges. Your comments should address the reasoning used to reach the dissenting opinion. When no dissent appears but there are obvious criticisms to the holding, you may voice these criticisms independently.

Comment and Rule of Law In your briefs, it may be helpful to include a section expressing your thoughts about the case. In this section, you may comment on the court's reasoning and on the consequences of the decision or the holding when it is later used as precedent. You may also want to summarize the rule of law from the case. The rule of law is generally limited to a one- or two-sentence statement that could be used as precedent in similar cases. Writing such a rule at the end of every case highlights the importance of that particular case to the development of law as well as to the litigating parties.

A Sample Brief

Katko v. Briney

Supreme Court of Iowa (1971)

Facts

Katko entered a boarded-up and uninhabited farmhouse owned by Briney with the intent of stealing some old bottles he believed to be there. Although a No Trespassing sign had been posted in front of the farmhouse, there was no notice that Briney had rigged a shotgun to go off when a bedroom door in the farmhouse was opened. When Katko opened that door, the shotgun went off, blowing away part of his leg. Katko sued Briney for damages caused by the shotgun blast. Briney claimed that he was not liable because he did not intend to seriously injure anyone and he is entitled to protect his property against thieves.

Issue

May an owner protect private property in an unoccupied house against trespassers and thieves by a spring gun capable of inflicting serious injury or death?

Holding

No. An owner cannot use deadly force in protecting personal property; the person using such force is liable for damages for any injury caused.

Rationale

The law places a higher value on human safety than on property rights. Deadly or dangerous force is permitted to protect property only if there is a threat of death or serious injury to those on the premises. Because these premises were unoccupied, deadly force could not be used. Although Briney said he did not intend to injure anyone, he should know that a shotgun can cause serious injury or death, and what he should know, not his stated intent, is the basis for judging his actions.

Comments

Even if there had been notice of the danger to an intruder, such as a sign indicating there was a shotgun trap, the law would hold the person who injures liable for doing so. The case does not deal w force that a person may use to protect both people property because no one inhabited the premises. T law seeks to balance the interests of the property owner against a person's interest in being free from injury by others. Even when committing a trespass or larceny, people have an interest in being free from injury by others. Human life is given a higher priority than property.

CHAPTER

2

Law and the Legal System

Critical Thinking Questions

- Are the functions of law the same for all societies? Is the role of law in a country with an Islamic legal system different from the role of law in countries using either a civil law or common law legal system?
- Compare the legal reasoning process in a common law legal system with a civil law legal system.
- How does substantive law differ from procedural law?
- How are conflicts between state and federal laws resolved in the United States?
- How does each branch of the federal government exercise rule-making powers?
- Why do some states have fewer levels of courts than other states? Compare the organization of the federal judicial branch with the organization of the judicial branch in the state where your university or college is located.

Introduction . . . Past, Present, Future

Law is not simply a set of rules that can be classified, memorized, and written for exams or for solving specific problems. The nature of law, and our understanding of it, has changed through the ages. Codes of law date back to 2000 B.C. when Hammurabi codified the practices and rules of ancient Babylon. In the United States, law is based on the "common" law, derived from England; whereas, the "civil" law in the majority of the world's countries is derived from the codified Roman law. Islamic law is dominant in many countries, particularly in the Middle East; it is also used in conjunction with a civil law legal system in a few countries. Some countries' legal systems, such as those in Japan and Egypt, reflect the influence of both civil and common law.

In the 20th century, many changes have occurred in both the rules and sources of law in the United States. For example, rules that a buyer had to beware of purchasing possibly defective goods were abandoned. Instead, new statutory laws and court decisions now protect consumers by imposing implied warranty obligations on sellers. Administrative agencies that address consumer protection, employee safety, and environmental problems today provide a source of rules and orders that affect many business activities.

Internationally, the legal systems in many countries have changed dramatically in the last few years. The eastern European countries have adopted some of the property and contract concepts from the West. The dissolution of the former Soviet Union has led to the privatization of much of the property formerly owned by the state. Each of the republics that were once a part of the Soviet Union is now in the process of designing its own legal system. In western Europe, the European Union (EU) has expanded to include several new countries while also further integrating the economies of its existing member countries and unifying its laws on product liability, product labeling, intellectual property, and consumer protection. No one could have predicted that all of these changes would occur so rapidly.

In the future, it seems likely that many legal systems will be in a state of change. Some countries will transfer significant lawmaking powers to international regional organizations (as is occurring in European Union countries and is beginning in some South American countries), while other areas (such as the Czech Republic and most of the republics of the former Soviet Union) will shift lawmaking authority from the former national level to the province, state, or republic level. In the United States, some industries may face less regulation (such as the television cable and telecommunication fields), while others (such as the health care and biogenetic firms) are likely to be subject to greater regulation. Similarly, while freedom from significant governmental control is important in the contract and property fields, environmental hazards, speculative financial products, and continuing consumer concerns will likely bring about new regulations and laws. The domestic and international legal environment will continue to be a significant concern for both small and large business firms as we move into the 21st century.

Thought Questions

1. As more countries become a part of regional organizations such as ASEAN and MERCOSUR, is it likely that the legal systems in those countries will become more similar?
2. What areas of law are likely to change the most in a country that is moving from governmental ownership and control to one based on capitalism and free enterprise?
3. Would it be easier for a country that had been under communist control to structure a new legal system on the civil law or the common law legal system model? Why?

The Legal System

A society's legal system is made up of several components. The institutions that create or amend the laws in a society constitute one component. The complexity and method of organizing legal institutions vary greatly from one society to another. The substantive laws regulating conduct constitute a second component. Some societies allow individuals and businesses significant freedom concerning their activities; whereas, others scrutinize even minor aspects of business and personal life. Procedural laws, a third component, also differ greatly among societies. For example, the U.S. legal system has numerous procedural laws aimed at providing fair and impartial civil and criminal trials. The trial procedural laws in some other countries are less comprehensive.

Components of a Legal System

The origin of the institutions that create or apply a society's laws presents important questions for business. Does a society establish many institutions, such as legislative bodies, administrative agencies, governmental bureaus, and judicial entities? Or does the lawmaking power reside in one person (a dictator, premier, or king) or in one small group (the House of Saud or the mullahs of Iran)? The **legal institutions** of a society constitute one component of its legal system.

A second component of a society's legal system is the **substantive law** that regulates the activities of the people in that society. As noted later in this chapter, substantive law answers fundamental questions about the rights and responsibilities of a society's members. What criminal activities are prohibited? How formal must contractual agreements be to be considered valid? What business activities are subject to government control? The scope of the substantive law's regulation of individual conduct differs according to the society's political, economic, and cultural values.

A third component of a society's legal system is the **procedural law** that enforces that society's substantive laws. Procedural law answers questions about the processes used to enforce substantive laws. Does the legal system guarantee that a person charged with a crime has the right to be represented by an attorney at a trial? Will the trial allow the accused to offer testimony? In civil disputes, are the parties required to testify? These questions concern procedural laws that are important in determining the characteristics of a society's legal system.

Common Law Legal System

The legal system of the United States is a **common law legal system.** Because this legal system originated in England, it is sometimes known as the Anglo-American legal system. Over two dozen countries, including the United States, Australia, New Zealand, and most of Canada, use a common law legal system. In common law systems, the courts are recognized not only as interpreters of the law, but also as creators of law.

Origin of the Common Law In England, the courts existed long before the legislative body known as Parliament. Furthermore, since no written constitution existed, the courts first began to create, interpret, and apply laws. These interpretations, found in written court decisions, reflected local customs and practices. After the Norman Conquest in 1066, the King and his successors used the King's courts to unify the country under a common, or uniform, set of customs. The common rules applied by these courts replaced local customs and formed the basis from which the common law evolved.

Stare Decisis* Concept** As court decisions became recognized as a primary source of law, the doctrine of ***stare decisis developed. According to this concept, a judge's decision in a case not only constitutes the interpretation and application of the law to the controversy between the litigating parties, but it also sets a precedent for future cases.

The concept of *stare decisis* brings predictability to the law. By reading a prior case based on essentially the same facts, the decision for later cases can be predicted. However, *stare decisis* is applicable only within a given court system. Thus, a decision by the Michigan Supreme Court has to be followed by lower courts in Michigan but not by lower courts in Pennsylvania. Only the lower courts in the same jurisdiction are bound by the precedents set by a given higher court.

Even within the same court system, applying the concept of *stare decisis* is difficult. Often, several precedent cases exist that bear upon some aspect of the case under

legal institutions
The institutions in a society that create or apply a society's law; these institutions are one of the components of a society's legal system.

substantive law
The law that regulates the activities of people in a society by defining their rights and duties; it constitutes a second component of a society's legal system.

procedural law
The law that enforces a society's substantive law and details the methods by which those duties and rights are enforced; it constitutes a third component of a society's legal system.

common law legal system
The legal system that originated in England and that recognizes courts as creators of law.

stare decisis
The concept that a judge's decision in a common law legal system sets a precedent for future cases because it is recognized as a primary source of law.

consideration. For example, in the *Nachtigal* case that follows, the District Court and the Court of Appeals determined that the facts of the case being considered were controlled by a previous decision the Court of Appeals had made in the *Cranton* case. The United States Supreme Court, however, determined that its decision in the *Banton* case was the correct precedent for the *Nachtigal* case.

United States v. Nachtigal

113 S. Ct. 1072 (1993)
United States Supreme Court

Jerry Nachtigal was charged with operating a motor vehicle in Yosemite National Park while under the influence of alcohol, in violation of a federal regulation governing national parks. The driving under the influence (DUI) offense is a misdemeanor that carries a maximum penalty of six months' imprisonment and a $5,000 fine. As an alternative to a term of imprisonment, the sentencing court may impose a term of probation not to exceed five years, and it also may attach other conditions to the probation term. At the trial before a magistrate, Nachtigal asked for a jury trial. The magistrate, applying our decision in *Blanton v. North Las Vegas* (489 U.S. 538 (1989)), denied the request. He reasoned that because DUI carries a maximum term of imprisonment of six months, it is a "petty" offense, not within the jury guarantee of the Sixth Amendment. At the trial, defendant was convicted of operating a motor vehicle under the influence of alcohol, fined $750, and placed on probation for one year. The District Court reversed the magistrate, commenting that the *Blanton* decision was at variance with the Court of Appeals decision of *United States v. Cranton* and that our *Blanton* decision did not expressly overrule *Cranton*. The Court of Appeals agreed with the District Court and noted that because the Secretary of the Interior, not Congress, had set the maximum prison term at six months, there was no determinative legislation regarding the seriousness of this offense. The Supreme Court granted certiorari.

Per Curiam

In *Blanton,* we held that in order to determine whether the Sixth Amendment right to a jury trial attaches to a particular offense, the court must examine "objective indications of the seriousness with which society regards the offense." The best indication of society's views is the maximum penalty set by the legislature. While the word "penalty" refers both to the term of imprisonment and other statutory penalties, we stated that "[p]rimary emphasis . . . must be placed on the maximum period of incarceration. We therefore hold that offenses for which the maximum period of incarceration is six months or less are presumptively "petty." A defendant can overcome this presumption, and be entitled to a jury trial, only by showing that the additional penalties, viewed together with the maximum prison term, are so severe that the legislature clearly determined that the offense is a "serious" one.

Applying the above rule, we held that DUI was a petty offense under Nevada law. . . . The present case, we think, requires only a relatively routine application of the rule announced in *Banton*. Because the maximum term of imprisonment is six months, DUI is presumptively a petty offense to which no jury trial right attaches. The Court of Appeals refused to apply the *Banton* presumption, reasoning that the Secretary of the Interior, not Congress, ultimately determined the maximum prison term. But there is a controlling legislative determination present within the regulatory scheme. Congress set six months as the maximum penalty the Secretary could impose for a violation of any of his regulations.

The additional penalties imposed under the regulations are not sufficient to overcome this presumption. . . . The discretionary probation conditions do not alter this conclusion; while they obviously entail a greater infringement on liberty than probation without attendant conditions, they do not approximate the severe loss of liberty caused by imprisonment for more than six months. We hold that the Court of Appeals was wrong in refusing to recognize that this case was controlled by our opinion in *Banton* rather than by its previous opinion in *Craner.* An individual convicted of driving under the influence in violation of the regulations [for national parks promulgated by the Secretary of Interior] is not constitutionally entitled to a jury trial.

The judgment of the Court of Appeals is reversed.

Case Questions

1. Is it possible that a person charged with violating a federal statute that carries a penalty of no more than six months' imprisonment and payment of a large sum of money or probation for a number of years would be entitled to a jury trial?
2. What do you think is the primary reason that the *Banon* case, not the *Craner* case, is the controlling precedent for this case?
3. Do you think a state could allow defendants charged with "petty" crimes to be tried by a jury? Why would states probably prefer such cases to be tried without a jury?

***Stare Decisis* and Changing Circumstances** A further, limiting aspect of *stare decisis* is that in some cases, the circumstances surrounding the decision made in the earlier case may have drastically changed. Thus, the same court, when faced with a similar case years later, could decide to make a different decision. In such a case, the court generally expressly notes that it is overruling the prior case, and it explains why. Consider, for example, the historic 1954 *Brown v. Board of Education* case in which the United States Supreme Court clearly rejects the "separate but equal" doctrine it had earlier spelled out in the 1896 *Plessy v. Ferguson* case.

> In approaching this case, we cannot turn the clock back to 1868, when the [14th Amendment to the U.S. Constitution] was adopted, or even to 1896, when *Plessy v. Ferguson* was written. We must consider public education in the light of its full development and its present place in American life throughout the Nation. . . .
>
> We come then to the question presented: Does segregation of children in public schools solely on the basis of race, even though the physical facilities and other "tangible" factors may be equal, deprive the children of the minority group of equal educational opportunities? We believe that it does.
>
> . . . Whatever may have been the extent of psychological knowledge at the time of *Plessy v. Ferguson,* this finding is amply supported by modern authority. Any language in *Plessy v. Ferguson* contrary to this finding is rejected.

Review the *Brooks* case that follows to see why the Supreme Court of Alaska changed the law regarding prenuptial agreement.

Brooks v. Brooks

733 P.2d 1044 (1987)
Supreme Court of Alaska

Leora and Vern Brooks were married on August 5, 1978. It was each party's third marriage. At the time of their divorce, the Brookses had been married approximately 5 years. Leora was 57 and Vern 54. The Brookses had no children together, but each has adult children from prior marriages.

At the time of their divorce, Leora was a resource management officer with the state of Alaska and a licensed real estate agent. Vern was an engineer with the FAA for 22 years and had worked briefly for the Coast Guard in Juneau. He is currently retired on a medical disability and receives disability benefits.

On July 31, 1978, five days before their marriage, the Brookses executed a prenuptial (or premarital) agreement. It provides in pertinent part:

> During their marriage each of them shall be completely independent of the other as to all property owned by either of them before said marriage, and shall be subject to his or her disposition as his or her separate property in the same manner as if said proposed marriage had never been celebrated. Any and all property or monies acquired after said marriage shall be considered the joint property of husband and wife and in the event of termination of said marriage shall be divided equally.

The trial court granted the Brookses a divorce and held that the parties' "[pre]nuptial agreement was validly entered into" and would be "enforced in its entirety." Leora Brooks appealed to the Supreme Court, contending that the trial court improperly valued some of the parties' mutual property. The Supreme Court of Alaska decided it first had to review the validity of the prenuptial agreement. "We have yet to pass upon the validity of prenuptial agreements in this state. Thus, even though neither party challenges the agreement here, we must address this threshold issue."

Burke, Justice

The traditional common law view was that prenuptial agreements in contemplation of divorce (hereinafter prenuptial agreements) were inconsistent with the sanctity of marriage and the state's interest in preserving marriage and maintaining the financial security of divorced persons. Courts uniformly viewed these agreements as inherently conducive to divorce and as allowing a husband to circumvent his legal duty to support his wife. Thus, prior to 1970, prenuptial agreements that stipulated terms regarding alimony and property settlements upon divorce were almost universally considered *void ab initio* [void from inception] as contrary to public policy. The reason prenuptial agreements were thought to promote divorce was stated in *Crouch v. Crouch* (Tenn. App. 1964):

> [S]uch [a] contract is promotive of divorce and void on grounds of public policy. Such contract[s] could induce a mercenary husband to inflict on his wife any wrong he might desire with the knowledge that his pecuniary liability would be limited. In other words, a husband could through abuse and ill treatment of his wife force her to bring an action for divorce and thereby buy a divorce for a sum far less than he would otherwise have to pay.

The policy grounds most frequently cited by the courts were that prenuptial agreements (1) are incompatible with and denigrate the marital relation, (2) tend to facilitate and induce divorce, and (3) burden the state by casting indigent spouses on public charity. Since 1970, however, public policy has changed markedly. With the advent of no-fault divorce laws and the changes in society such laws represent, the traditional rule has rapidly given way to the more realistic view that prenuptial agreements are not *void ab initio* but are valid and enforceable if certain standards of "fairness" are met. Although the standards vary from state to state, the following three criteria are typically considered:

1. Was the agreement obtained through fraud, duress or mistake, or misrepresentation or nondisclosure of material fact?

2. Was the agreement unconscionable when executed?

3. Have the facts and circumstances changed since the agreement was executed, so as to make its enforcement unfair and unreasonable?

If none of the above factors are present, prenuptial agreements have generally been accorded judicial recognition. As the West Virginia Supreme Court recently noted:

> The older rule was grounded in yesteryear's sound public policy: in general, thirty years ago women did not work in the market economy; society enjoyed a consensus that favored lifetime marriage and disfavored divorce; and prenuptial agreements that lim-

ited the support obligation in favor of former wives encouraged divorce and made divorced women potential charges of the state.

Circumstances have changed dramatically in the last three decades, however. . . . [T]oday 58.7 percent of all married women are gainfully employed. [W]e no longer have a society-wide consensus on the sanctity of marriage: . . . Currently divorces are being granted at the rate of approximately 1,200,000 per year.

Today, divorce is a "commonplace fact of life." As a result there is a concurrent increase in second and third marriages, often of mature people with substantial means and separate families from earlier marriages. The conflicts that naturally inhere in such relationships make the litigation that follows even more uncertain, unpleasant, and costly. Consequently, people with previous "bad luck" with domestic life may not be willing to risk marriage again without the ability to safeguard their financial interests. In other words, without the ability to order their own affairs as they wish, they may simply forgo marriage for more "informal" relationships. "This society's staggering divorce rate can only place any reasonable person on notice that divorce is as likely an outcome of any marriage as a permanent relationship."

Prenuptial agreements, on the other hand, provide such people with the opportunity to ensure predictability, plan their future with more security, and, most importantly, decide their own destiny. Moreover, allowing couples to think through the financial aspects of their marriage beforehand can only foster strength and permanency in that relationship. In this day and age, judicial recognition of prenuptial agreements most likely "encourages rather than discourages marriage." . . .

In sum, both the realities of our society and the policy reasons favor judicial recognition of prenuptial agreements. . . . Therefore, we join those courts that have recognized that prenuptial agreements legally procured and ostensibly fair in result are valid and can be enforced. "The reasoning that once found them contrary to public policy has no place in today's matrimonial law."

The trial court's decision is affirmed in part, reversed in part, and remanded for reconsideration not inconsistent with the instructions set forth in the body of this opinion.

Case Questions

1. Why did prior case law hold that prenuptial agreements were contrary to public policy and thus illegal?
2. What data is presented to document the conclusion that changes have occurred since the earlier cases were decided?
3. How would people benefit if the court declared that prenuptial agreements would be generally valid and enforceable?

ETHICAL DILEMMA

Are judges who are faced with prior cases that seem to dictate the settlement for the dispute under consideration free to ignore those decisions if they believe the precedent cases are not well-reasoned? Under what circumstances should judges who disagree with prior court decisions ignore them or seek to distinguish them in any possible manner rather than follow their holdings? Would you give different answers if the judges were on trial courts rather than on a state supreme court? Why? Suppose judges believe that the laws are "behind the times" and not current with the wishes and needs of society? Is that a reason for prior court precedents to be ignored? What about cases in which the judge believes the majority of the citizens want to follow the prior law, but the judge believes that a change should be made in that law? Is it appropriate to make changes in the law even if neither the opinions in prior cases nor the wishes of the society indicate any desire for a change? What factors should be considered by judges in reviewing the applicability of precedent cases to the case under review? Do you think either the universalist or utilitarian ethical theories help in answering these questions? Why?

Civil Law Legal System

civil law legal system The legal system that has a code of law as the primary source of law in the society; the customs that became recognized as legal rules in the society were organized and codified into one source or code of law.

A **civil law legal system** is based on a code of laws that organizes and codifies the legal rules of a society into one source or code. Civil law legal systems can trace their origin back to around 1750 B.C., when Hammurabi codified the laws of Babylon. From that time on, Babylonian laws were derived from the codes rather than from the society's common past practices. Thus, the codification of law represents a compilation of the existing laws. The code also represents a reformation of the legal system, as after the code becomes effective, past societal practices not in the code are no longer used as a basis for the law.

Most of the civil law legal systems in the world today are based on Roman law. Although Roman law existed as early as A.D. 100, its influence was minimal for centuries. By the 18th century, however, the codified Roman law had become the basis of the legal system in over 60 countries in western Europe, Asia, South America, and Africa.

Today, many countries have a hybrid system of civil and common law. For example, in Egypt, the modern legal system has been influenced by both French civil law and English common law. In addition, Islamic law, discussed later, plays an important role in Egypt's legal system. The Japanese legal system, which was first greatly influenced by Chinese legal institutions and administrative processes, borrowed from the French Code Civil in the late 19th century. Later, Japan transformed its system into a German type civil law system. Finally, at the end of World War II, the Allies imposed on Japan a constitution and regulatory reforms modeled on the U.S. common law legal system.

Differences in Civil and Common Law Legal Systems

There are several major differences between the common law and civil law legal systems. First, the civil law legal system places greater importance on the governmental or administrative interpretation of law than does the common law legal system. In a common law system, while courts often defer to a governmental explanation of what the law means, the courts clearly have the authority to interpret the law.

Second, the trial procedures of the two systems are also different. Litigation in the civil law legal system is like an investigation conducted by all parties. The judge whose powers are inquisitorial heads the investigative team, but both attorneys have duties to assist the judge and the court in determining the facts in dispute. In contrast, the common law legal system uses an adversarial trial process. Each party looks after its own interests, and the judge acts somewhat like a neutral umpire or a referee. Neither party must divulge information that harms its own case if the opposing party does not request that information.

Finally, unlike a common law legal system, civil law legal systems rarely have jury trials. Each of these characteristics, depicted in Figure 2–1, is discussed in more detail in subsequent sections of this chapter.

Classification of Law

Law can be classified in a variety of ways. Some laws fit into more than one classification. For example, contract laws are generally private, substantive civil laws.

FIGURE 2-1

Comparing Features of a Common Law and a Civil Law Legal System

Common Law Legal System

1. The development of law by a system of judicial precedent (*stare decisis*).
2. The use of an adversarial trial process.
3. The use of a jury to decide issues of fact in many court cases.

Civil Law Legal System

1. The development of law through applying general principles from a code of law; administrative or governmental interpretations of the code may be very important.
2. The use of an inquisitorial trial process.
3. The use of a judge to decide facts and law in most court cases.

Substantive Law and Procedural Law

Substantive laws define rights and impose on members of society the duty to respect those rights. Laws that detail the means or methods by which those rights or duties will be enforced are known as *procedural law.* For example, substantive law defines the elements necessary to create an enforceable contract. By examining those elements, we can determine if a person has to be a certain age to make a valid contract. We also would know whether if one contracting party does not make any commitment to the other party their agreement would be a contract. On the other hand, procedural law determines how that substantive law will be enforced. Will the person who seeks to enforce another person's contractual commitment be entitled to a trial? Should a jury be used at the trial? These questions can be answered by examining procedural laws.

Criminal Law and Civil Law

Another method of categorizing laws focuses on the rights that the law seeks to protect. If the purpose of a law is to protect the society as a whole rather than one of its members, the law is a **criminal law.** If a law concerns the rights of individuals (often including a corporation as a "person") or the duties owed to people in the society, the law is a **civil law.** Essentially, civil law focuses on wrongs against individuals, whereas criminal law focuses on wrongs against the whole society.

criminal law
Laws that seek to protect society as a whole; their aim is to protect society and to punish the wrongdoer.

civil law
Laws that concern the rights and duties of people in a society; civil laws seek to have a wrongdoer compensate the injured party for his or her loss.

As an action may involve both a criminal wrong and a civil wrong, a person accused of committing improper acts may face both a criminal case and a civil case. The two cases would involve different parties and distinct and separate problems. Furthermore, both the substantive and procedural laws involved in the civil case would differ from those involved in the criminal case. For example, if an official of a company is believed to have spent corporate funds for unauthorized private purposes, that person may face both criminal prosecution and civil suits. If his or her actions constitute criminal fraud, the state or federal government, or both, can prosecute and seek to have the official jailed and/or fined. In addition, the official could also face civil suits brought by shareholders of the bankrupt firm. A shareholder could sue for damages to compensate for his or her loss, claiming the negligence of the officer caused the loss of value to the firm's stock owned by the shareholder.

Who Initiates the Case? In a criminal case, the society initiates the legal action. The most serious criminal case is a homicide, where someone has been killed. Homicides range from first degree murder cases, where someone is charged with intentionally and with premeditation, taking another person's life to involuntary manslaughter, where neither the intent nor the premeditation is present but some degree of negligence on the part of the defendant is alleged to have caused a person's death. Larceny, rape, robbery, and criminal assault are other types of criminal cases frequently litigated in the nation's courts. The society starts a criminal case because the society, rather than the individual victim, is the primary victim of the wrong. The commission of a crime makes all people, not just the victim of the crime, feel less safe and secure. Thus, the society acts on behalf of all of its members (including, of course, the victim). Generally, the attorney representing the society may hold the office of district attorney, prosecuting attorney, state's attorney, or U.S. attorney. In a civil case, the lawsuit is brought by an individual person who claims that his or her rights have been infringed. The individual plaintiff selects and pays an attorney to represent him or her. The society is not a party to such lawsuits between two or more of its members.

Frequently, you can tell by the title of a case whether it involves a criminal or civil action. A criminal case, brought by the society, will be titled *People v. Smith,* or *United States v. Smith,* or *Michigan v. Smith.* Of course, since the United States or Michigan could be either a plaintiff or a defendant in a civil case, a case with the society named as one of the parties is not always a criminal case. However, most of the cases in which the society is the plaintiff are criminal cases. A civil case, on the other hand, would be titled *Jones v. Smith* or *ABC Corporation v. Smith,* because individuals or organizations are parties on both sides. Review the title of the two cases excerpted earlier in this chapter. Are they civil or criminal cases?

Purpose The purpose of a criminal case is to determine whether the defendant committed a criminal act and whether the court must therefore impose some punishment. A person convicted of a crime might face a fine or be sent to jail or prison. The penalty should punish the wrongdoer as well as deter would-be criminals from committing similar acts. The punishment may even rehabilitate the criminal, so that he or she will be less likely to commit future wrongs against the society.

A civil lawsuit seeks to compensate the person who has been wronged instead of endeavoring to punish the wrongdoer. If Laura breaks a contractual agreement she made with David, he may bring a civil lawsuit against her. Generally, David would seek an award of damages as a remedy. He would want the court to order Laura to pay him a sum equal to the money he lost when she did not perform as agreed in their contract. Suppose that Laura had agreed to sell David 50 desks for his furniture store, each priced at $100, or a total of $5,000, and that at the last minute she told David she would need $7,500 to sell the desks as promised. If instead of paying the higher amount, David finds he can purchase similar desks for $125 each, or a total of $6,250, David could sue Laura for damages to compensate for what he has lost by not being able to buy the desks for $5,000. Thus, he would ask that Laura be ordered to pay his damages of $1,250.

Differences in Substantive Laws Substantively, the law specifying what acts constitute robbery differs from the law specifying what acts must occur in order to have an enforceable contractual agreement. In criminal cases, most actions considered criminal are defined by legislative enactments, such as federal or state statutes, administrative regulations, and municipal ordinances. In civil actions, a person's rights or duties toward other persons can be based either on statutory laws or on the common law of court decisions. What substantive law was the defendant in the *Nachtigal* case charged with violating? Was that a legislative enactment? What law was of concern to the court in the *Brooks* case? What was the source of that law?

Differences in Procedural Laws The procedures followed in the two types of lawsuits also differ. Legal standards, known as the **burden of proof,** indicate which party has the obligation to submit proof to the court and the quantity and quality of the evidence that is needed to prevail. In the *criminal lawsuit,* the accused defendant is presumed innocent until proven guilty. The individual defendant will win unless the society can prove *beyond a reasonable doubt* that he or she committed the criminal act. That is the amount or standard of proof that must be met to prove a person guilty in a criminal case. In the *civil lawsuit,* the burden of proof is not the same. It is only necessary for the plaintiff to prove the case against the defendant *by a preponderance of the evidence.*

burden of proof The standard as to the amount of proof needed to find the defendant guilty or liable; in a civil case, the standard is by the preponderance of the evidence; while in a criminal case, the standard is beyond a reasonable doubt.

For example, suppose that in a given civil case both the amount and quality of the evidence is a little more in the plaintiff's favor than in the defendant's favor. Because a preponderance of the evidence is in the plaintiff's favor, the plaintiff would win the case. However, the same amount and quality of evidence in the plaintiff's (prosecutor's) favor in a criminal case would not be sufficient to convince a jury or a judge of the defendant's guilt beyond a reasonable doubt. Thus, the defendant, not the plaintiff, would win the criminal case. The amount and quality of evidence required of the plaintiff to win a criminal case exceeds what is required to win a civil case. The differences in these burdens of proof highlight the controversy surrounding some laws with both civil and criminal provisions. For example, the racketeering laws (RICO), discussed in Chapter 22, provide for both criminal and civil suits. Because the plaintiff who brings a civil case will not have to meet the same burden of proof he or she would need if seeking to apply the criminal provisions, civil suits are encouraged.

Common Law and Statutory Law

The terms *common law,* law found in court decisions, and *statutory law,* law based on legislative enactments, are used to indicate the general sources of law within a society with a common law legal system. Although the common law of the United States originated in the customs and practices of the people in England, today in the United States the term **common law** generally refers to the case law that results from court decisions.

common law The law based on court decisions in a common law legal system.

Where does one find the common law? Consider the following excerpt, known as the Erie Doctrine, from a famous U.S. Supreme Court case, *Erie R. Co. v. Tompkins,* 304 U.S. 64 (1938):

> Except in matters governed by the Federal Constitution or by acts of Congress, the law to be applied in any case is the law of the state. And whether the law of the state shall be declared by its Legislature or by its highest court in a decision is not a matter of federal concern. There is no federal general common law. Congress has no power to declare substantive rules of common law applicable in a state whether they be local in their nature or "general," be they commercial law or a part of the law of torts. And no clause in the Constitution purports to confer such a power upon the federal courts.

Of course, there is federal common law applicable to federal questions, interpretations of constitutional provisions, federal statutes, and regulations. The concern of the

Erie Doctrine is the laws that states have the authority to make. It is the state courts, not the federal courts, that determine the common law of each state.

statutory law
The law based on legislative enactments.

The term **statutory law** generally refers to the laws that have been formally adopted by legislative bodies. In the United States, legislative bodies include the U.S. Congress, the state legislatures, and local city councils or commissions. Administrative rules and regulations, which are discussed more fully in Chapter 6, are also generally classified as statutory laws. Finally, while the laws and regulations of municipal bodies are sometimes referred to more specifically as *ordinances,* they are also a type of statutory law.

Law and Equity

courts of law
Courts originally organized to give a remedy to a specific problem, one mentioned in a writ.

equity courts
Courts established to hear cases that could not be adequately addressed by the law courts; the chancellor decided by referring both to law and equity.

Historically, England first organized the courts solely as **courts of law** under a writ system. Those courts of law could grant specific remedies to redress various legal problems. There was a specific writ and a specific remedy for each specified problem. If you had unusual problems or wanted a unique remedy, the law courts would not help you. As English society evolved, it found the rigid legal system for addressing grievances and resolving disputes unresponsive to many legitimate claims.

In response, the king of England appointed his spiritual adviser as the chancellor, and eventually separate courts known as courts of chancery or **equity courts** were established to hear such cases. In these courts, the judges or chancellors could decide disputes with greater discretion than that exercised by the law courts. They could base their decisions on concepts of justice and equity, not just the provisions of the law. Further, the equity courts could grant remedies not available to the law courts. Today, *equitable remedies,* such as specific performance or an injunction, are used when the traditional legal remedies are not adequate to serve justice.

These two systems of courts, each with their own procedures, existed for hundreds of years in England before being brought to the United States. Law and equity courts continued to exist separately for years after the United States first formed its legal system, but eventually these two types of courts were merged.

Today, except for the lowest level of courts, judges in federal and state courts hear both legal and equity cases. The distinction between law and equity cases, however, still has some importance in our legal system. For example, juries hear and decide factual issues in law cases but not in equity cases. The plaintiff seeking an equitable remedy must first prove that the normal legal remedies are inadequate to properly remedy the injury in question.

Public and Private Law

public law
Law that concerns the relationship between people and their government, such as constitutional or administrative law.

private law
Law that concerns relations between individuals or firms in a society such as contract, property, and tort law.

Public law concerns the relationships between people and their governments. Thus, criminal law is classified as public law because it involves a wrong against the society. Both constitutional law and administrative law, discussed in Chapters 5 and 6, are also types of public law. Constitutional law concerns the power of government to perform certain activities, whereas administrative law concerns the lawmaking powers of administrative agencies.

Private law concerns the relationships between individuals and firms within the society. The private law topics of property, torts, contracts, and commercial transactions are discussed in Chapters 7–10. While private law may seem more relevant to business firms than public law, public law has become increasingly important to many businesses because it regulates and often restricts business activities.

Tasks of a Legal System

Each society organizes its legal system to perform several different tasks. The institutions and functions of the legal system vary greatly from one society to the next. In both China and Japan, for example, business institutions often provide the means for resolving disputes, whereas in the United States that function is performed primarily by the legal system. Despite the differences among the legal systems in various societies, these systems generally perform certain similar functions. Maintaining order and providing a forum for resolving disputes are functions common to most legal systems. Other common functions, such as protecting expectations and maintaining a political authority while accommodating change, are briefly noted below.

Maintaining Order The most important function of a legal system is maintaining order within the society. For example, although societies as diverse as those in Poland, South Africa, China, and the United States have different laws concerning the activities of their people, each of these societies uses the legal system to maintain order. In a society without order, people cannot function efficiently because they must spend more time and energy protecting themselves and their property than in productive pursuits. Thus, the purpose of legal rules is to promote conforming conduct or to discourage nonconforming conduct. A liberal society may be one where there are fewer legal rules that seek to maintain order; instead, customary rules are used. Thus, spitting or littering on public property is generally nonconforming conduct in most societies. Some societies, like Japan, rely more on custom, while in other societies, as with Singapore, legal rules are used to deter the nonconforming conduct. The most important rules in a liberal society are the rules against rules—the rules that restrict the government's power so that the liberal order itself can exist.

Providing a Forum for the Resolution of Disputes A society's legal system usually provides methods and places for individuals and organizations to resolve disputes. It should be noted, however, that in societies that have borrowed heavily from the Chinese legal system, private disputes historically were not to be settled in the courts. Harmonious settling of the quarrel, rather than a settlement that conforms to established norms, was the primary concern. In some Asian societies today, the emphasis on the duty to maintain peace and order (and thus amicably settle any dispute) outweighs an emphasis on the rights of the complaining party to have a public forum determine the dispute in accord with established rules. In the West, however, the greater emphasis on the rights of individuals and on achieving a settlement that conforms to established rules, applied by a neutral decision maker, has generally led to the legal system playing an important role in resolving disputes. For this reason, one finds in the United States a legal system that provides numerous local, state, and federal courts that assist parties in resolving their disputes. Of course, courts are not the only forums for settling disputes. Numerous alternatives exist, and many of them are increasing in popularity, as is noted in Chapter 4.

Other Tasks

While maintaining order and providing a forum for disputes are generally recognized as the more important tasks for a legal system, there are other tasks as well. A legal system protects people's expectations while both maintaining the political authority and promoting social change.

Protecting Expectations The legal system protects expectations by providing a framework of rules on which people in the society can rely. When a consumer buys a ladder, the legal system reinforces the consumer's expectation that he or she will not suffer injury because the ladder is defective. The legal system cannot guarantee that the consumer will not be injured. Instead, it requires the maker of a defective ladder to compensate the consumer who has been injured as a result of the defect. The legal system thus encourages the use of reasonable care by the ladder manufacturer while assuring the consumer that it will protect his or her expectations for the use of a nondefective ladder. The legal system may also set minimum design or performance standards for products that are to be sold in the society. If you want to sell an automobile, it must be equipped to meet established safety standards (seat belt, bumpers, shatterproof windshield, etc.) and environmental requirements (use of lead-free gasoline, refrigerants that do not deplete the ozone).

Maintaining the Political Authority In almost all societies, the legal system maintains a dominant political authority. That authority generally punishes or expels people who turn over secret governmental documents to its opponents. It may even permanently imprison or execute its opponents. In the 1980s, for example, the then established political authority in Poland and in China used the legal system to protect themselves against those who sought to challenge their power. Some legal systems permit a wider range of conduct and criticism against the existing political authority than do others. The United States tolerates significantly more political discussion and dissent than do most other countries.

Promoting Social Change Decisions of a legal institution such as a court, a state agency, or a legislative body may bring about social change because people generally support such decisions. Of course, not everyone in society agrees with each new court decision, administrative regulation, or statute. However, once a decision is made, most people generally conform their behavior to its requirements. For example, the Occupational Safety and Health Administration (OSHA) imposed new safety standards on many factories and firms. Generally, court interpretations requiring the use of safer equipment have been adhered to, even when some of the rules and interpretations do not seem to make sense in certain situations.

Similarly, in recent years, state legislatures have adopted antiabortion laws that vary rather significantly from state to state. Obviously, in each state some people believe their state law is appropriate while others think they are very wrong. Nevertheless, with few exceptions, most people within the state will follow the decision of their legislature.

International Perspective and Commentary

The most significant event affecting the world's legal systems during the last decade has been the disintegration of the socialist legal system in Poland, the former East Germany, the former Czechoslovakia, Hungary, Bulgaria, Romania and even in the former Soviet Union. Monumental economic and political changes have reshaped these countries' boundaries and both new and old countries are seeking to install vastly different legal systems.

While each country is attempting to establish its own legal system, their former socialist legal systems are most likely to be replaced with civil law and in some instances Islamic law legal systems. Some countries are patterning their legal systems after those of countries in the European Union so that their eventual application for entry into that regional association will be approved.

The most dramatic legal changes occurring in these countries is in the creation of property law. State-owned lands and businesses are being privatized and various methods are being used to sell off the businesses to citizens and in many cases to foreign investors. For many citizens, this is their first experience as owners of land or shares of stock in a business. Other changes include establishing private financial institutions and gradually making the currency in the country convertible. New investment laws are being written to attract private investments and existing contract, commercial transaction, and corporation laws are being updated.

Significant Characteristics of the U.S. Legal System

The U.S. Constitution provides the framework for the organization of the U.S. legal system. Two significant characteristics determine which governmental authority has lawmaking powers in a given situation. **Federalism** is the division of powers among federal, state, and local governments. The **separation of powers** is the splitting of lawmaking authority among the three branches of government: legislative, judicial, and executive. Each branch has separate powers to perform its specific functions, and each provides checks and balances on the other branches. Together, these characteristics shape the sources of law in the U.S. legal system. In addition to the Constitution, the legislative, executive, and judicial branches, along with administrative agencies, constitute the sources of law in the U.S. legal system.

federalism The concept of shared lawmaking powers between the federal and state or local governments.

separation of powers The splitting of lawmaking authority at one level of government among the executive, legislative, and judicial branches.

The U.S. Constitution determines whether the state or federal legal system has the lawmaking powers to handle particular problems. Each state also has a constitution that describes the organization of its government and legal system. Although state constitutions differ in many ways, each separates the powers of governmental branches and preserves federalism by dividing power between the central state authority and local units of government, such as cities and counties.

Federalism

The term *federalism* describes a dual form of government, in which powers are divided between the states and the federal government. Before the Constitution was signed, state governments had shared lawmaking powers under a confederative form of government. Soon after the Revolutionary War, however, the states began to experience problems in building a common defense, conducting foreign affairs, and maintaining economic stability. Nevertheless, the states did not want to return to a strong central government like the one that had ruled over the colonies. Their compromise solution created a federalist government dividing lawmaking powers between the states and the central federal government.

Businesses and individuals often find this sharing of lawmaking authority confusing. What if there are different laws at the state and federal level or at the state and local level? Sometimes rules from different sources impose conflicting requirements. For example, the federal Environmental Protection Agency monitors air pollution emitted by new plants. However, state or local laws generally impose conditions on the construction of new plants and factories. These sources of law may impose inconsistent requirements regarding the construction of new plants. Another example concerns corporate directors. While state law governs their actions, a federal law regulates some

FIGURE 2-2 Sharing of Federal and State Lawmaking Powers

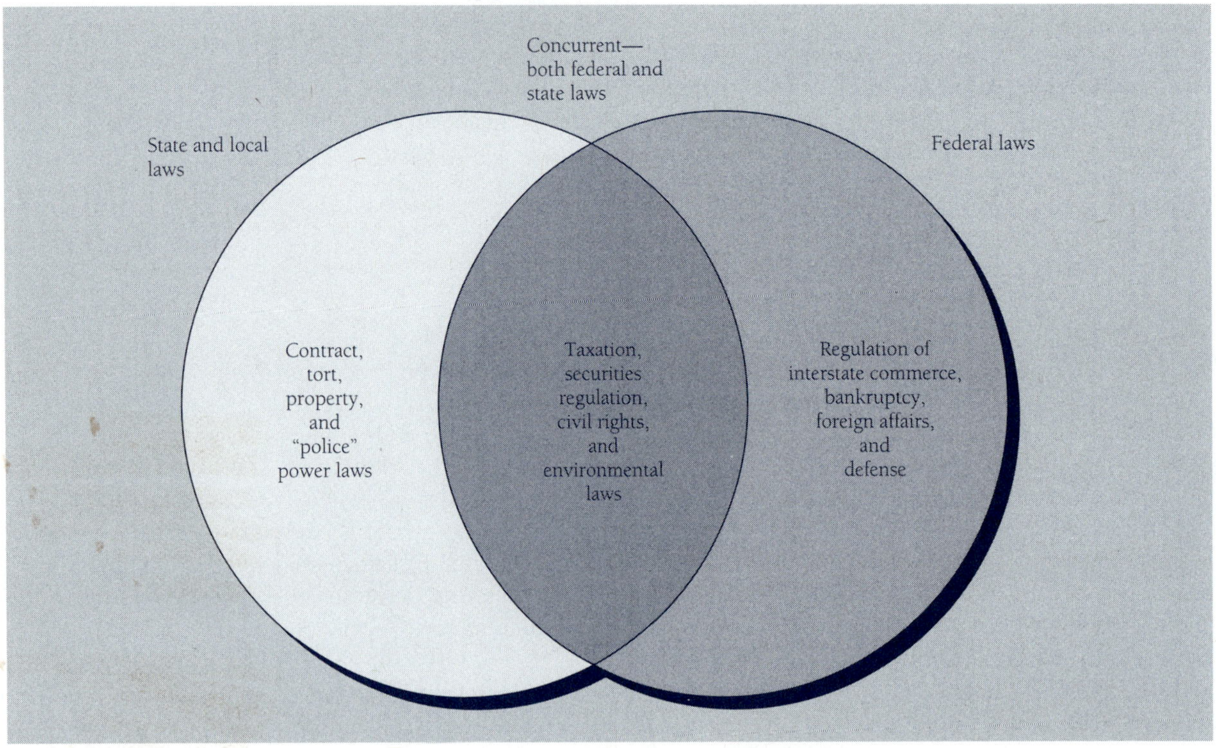

of the activities of investment advisers, even if those advisers are also directors of a corporation.

Some business representatives are in favor of greater federal regulation so that they will face uniform federal rules rather than differing state laws. Peter Hutt, a Washington, D.C., lawyer who represents trade groups in the medical-device and food industries says that "one national rule is better than 50 inconsistent rules of any kind" (*The Wall Street Journal*, May 10, 1993, page B3). Furthermore, as so many products and services are sold nationally, uniform laws may better suit our more homogeneous population.

Despite the problems that result from the existence of two major legal systems, federalism has substantial benefits. First, because state lawmakers are closer to a problem and can often act more quickly than lawmakers from the federal Congress, state legal systems can deal with many problems within the states more effectively than can a distant federal government. Second, the division of power between the state and federal legal systems reduces the authority of each system. Consequently, special interest groups are less likely to dominate at all levels of those legal systems. Finally, the states do not all face similar problems; some states are densely populated, while others are not. Coastal states have different concerns than many of the farming states in the Midwest. Federalism allows states to use diverse solutions for their own problems. Figure 2–2 illustrates the sharing of lawmaking powers between the federal and state legal systems.

Federal Supremacy

Sometimes a state law conflicts with a federal law. As a result, the state law may be preempted or nullified by the federal law. However, since the purposes for state and local laws may be different from that of the federal laws or regulations, sometimes both sources of law may be enforced. In such cases, the fact that a business has complied with federal law generally does not exempt it from meeting the separate requirements imposed by state and local law.

Where Congress is clearly establishing a federal policy, by enacting a statute, ratifying a treaty, or regulating a specific activity by federal regulation, the supremacy clause of the U.S. Constitution prohibits state law from contradicting federal law. That clause of the U.S. Constitution provides:

> This Constitution, and the Laws of the United States, which shall be made in Pursuance thereof; and all Treaties made, or which shall be made, under the Authority of the United States, shall be the supreme Law of the Land.

The existence of a conflict between a state law and a federal law is not always obvious. Courts analyze such conflicts by examining the intent of Congress in passing a statute or in authorizing an administrative agency's regulation. A federal law *preempts* a state law if a court determines there was legislative intent to supersede state law. The intent may be based on explicit language found in the federal law, or it may be implicitly contained in the structure and purpose of the federal regulation. In the following case, Mortier, a resident of Casey, Wisconsin, claims the town's ordinance, which required that anyone using a pesticide had to obtain a permit before applying it, was preempted by the federal insecticide law.

Wisconsin Public Intervenor v. Mortier

111 Supreme Court 2476 (1991)
United States Supreme Court

The Federal Insecticide, Fungicide, and Rodenticide Act (FIFRA) was enacted in 1947 to replace the federal government's first effort at pesticide regulation, the Insecticide Act of 1910. Like its predecessor, FIFRA was primarily a licensing and labeling statute. In 1972, growing environmental and safety concerns led Congress to undertake a major revision of FIFRA through the Federal Environmental Pesticide Control Act. It granted additional authority to the Environmental Protection Agency (EPA) to enforce the law and transformed it into a comprehensive regulatory statute.

FIFRA specifies several roles for state and local authorities, including allowing the states to regulate the sale or use of pesticide so long as the state regulation does not permit a sale or use prohibited by the Act. In 1985, the town of Casey, a small rural community in Wisconsin, adopted an ordinance requiring a permit for the use of pesticides on any public land, on private land used for a public purpose, or for the aerial application of pesticides to private land. Towns and villages in Wisconsin had been granted the authority to regulate the use of pesticides by the Wisconsin legislature. The applicant had to provide information about the pesticide use at least 60 days prior to the desired use. The town had the authority to deny the permit or attach conditions to the use of pesticides for "any reason related to the protection of the health, safety and welfare of town residents."

Mortier applied for a permit for aerial spraying on a portion of his land. The town granted the permit but restricted the land on which it would allow the aerial spraying. Mortier sued, claiming the town's law was preempted by state and federal law. The trial court and the Wisconsin Supreme Court agreed with Mortier. The state Supreme Court found that FIFRA clearly prohibited any regulation of pesticides by local governments. On appeal, the United States Supreme Court granted certorari.

Justice White

Under the Supremacy Clause, U.S. Constitution Article VI, clause 2, state laws that "interfere with or are contrary to the laws of Congress, made in pursuance of the Constitution, are invalid." The ways in which federal law may pre-empt state laws are well established and in the first instance turn on congressional intent.

Congress' intent to supplant state authority in a particular field may be expressed in the terms of the statute. Absent explicit pre-emptive language, Congress' intent to supercede state law in a given area may nonetheless be implicit if a scheme of federal regulation is "so pervasive as to make reasonable inference that Congress left no room for the States to supplement it," if "the Act of Congress . . . touch(es) a field in which the federal interest is so dominant that the federal system will be assumed to preclude enforcement of state laws on the same subject," or if the goals "sought to be obtained" and the "obligations imposed" reveal a purpose to preclude state authority. When considering preemption, "we start with the assumption that the historic police powers of the States were not to be superseded by the Federal Act unless that was the clear and manifest purpose of Congress."

Even when Congress has not chosen to occupy a particular field, pre-emption may occur to the extent that state and federal law actually conflict. Such a conflict arises when "compliance with both federal and state regulations is a physical impossibility or when a state law stands as an obstacle to the accomplishment and execution of the full purposes and objectives of Congress." It is, finally, axiomatic that "for the purposes of the Supremacy Clause, the constitutionality of local ordinances is analyzed in the same way as that of statewide laws."

As the Wisconsin Supreme Court recognized, FIFRA nowhere expressly supersedes local regulation of pesticide use. [The statute includes the following language: "A State may regulate the sale or use of any federally registered pesticide or device in the State, but only if and to the extent the regulation does not permit any sale or use prohibited by this subchapter." The State Supreme Court reasoned that while the statutory language alone did not evidence the intent to pre-empt local regulations, it was possible to infer from the language and the legislative history that Congress had occupied the field to the exclusion of the States.] But it is our view that even when considered together, the language and legislative materials relied on below are insufficient to demonstrate the necessary intent to pre-empt. As for the statutory language, section 136 v plainly authorizes the "States" to regulate pesticides and just as plainly is silent with reference to local governments. Mere silence, in this context, cannot suffice to establish a "clear and manifest purpose" to pre-empt local authority. Properly read, the statutory language tilts in favor of local regulation. The exclusion of political subdivisions cannot be inferred from the express authorization to the State(s) because political subdivisions are components of the very entity the statute empowers.

The evidence from the legislative history, which centers on the meaning of what would become section 136 v, is at best ambiguous. The House Agricultural Committee Report stated that it had "rejected a proposal that would have permitted political subdivisions to further regulate pesticides." But . . . the Senate Commerce Committee observed that while the Senate Agricultural Committee bill does not specifically prohibit local governments from regulating pesticides, the report of the Committee states explicitly that local governments cannot regulate pesticides. None of the Committees . . . asserted that FIFRA preempted the field of pesticide regulation. Like FIFRA's text, the legislative history thus falls far short of establishing that preemption of local pesticide regulation was the "clear and manifest" purpose of Congress.

Likewise, FIFRA fails to provide any clear and manifest indication that Congress sought to supplant local authority over pesticide regulation. . . . While the 1972 amendments turned FIFRA into a "comprehensive regulatory statute," the resulting scheme was not "so pervasive as to make reasonable the inference that Congress left no room for the State to supplement it." . . . FIFRA nowhere seeks to establish an affirmative permit scheme for the actual use of pesticides. It certainly does not equate registration and labeling requirements with a general approval to apply pesticides throughout the nation without regard to regional and local factors like climate, population, geography, and water supply. Whatever else FIFRA may supplant, it does not occupy the field of pesticide regulation in general or the area of local use permitting in particular. . . . The specific grant of authority in [the statute section referred to earlier] . . . acts to ensure that the States could continue to regulate use and sales even where, such as with regard to the banning of mislabeled products, a narrow pre-emptive overlap might occur.

Finally, like the EPA, we discern no actual conflict either between FIFRA and the ordinance before us or between FIFRA and local regulation generally. As we have also made plain, local use permit regulations—unlike labeling or certification—do not fall within an area that FIFRA's "program" pre-empts or even plainly addresses. We hold that FIFRA does not pre-empt the town of Casey's ordinance regulating the use of pesticides.

The judgment of the Wisconsin Supreme Court is reversed.

Case Questions

1. In this case, the statutory language is not clear, and the legislative history is ambiguous; thus the presumption the court states at the beginning is very important to the reasoning. What is that presumption, and why do you think it exists?

2. What are some of the specific reasons why Congress might have wanted local instead of federal regulation regarding the use of pesticides?

3. Assume you are a member of Congress who wants the federal statute to pre-empt local regulations; how would you modify or add to the current section of the law as quoted at the beginning of the case?

Shared Lawmaking Authority

Even though there may be both federal and state laws affecting a particular activity, on some occasions, courts find the federal law does not intend to crowd out or preempt the state law. In these areas of concurrent jurisdiction, both state and federal laws may exist together. For example, there are federal and state laws regulating taxation, antitrust, environmental, work safety, and securities matters. The federal legislation in these areas permits the states to also make and enforce laws. Thus, a person who violates an antitrust law or an environmental requirement could, in some cases, be found liable in both federal and state courts.

In other cases, the enforcement of shared laws is the responsibility of either the federal or the state regulators. For example, in the *Mortier* case, the Supreme Court of the United States determined that a local law regulating the use of pesticides was not pre-empted by the federal law regulating various aspects of pesticide labeling, sale, and use. The Court in that case found that as Congress had not clearly expressed an intention to pre-empt all state and local laws related to pesticide use, both the federal and state/local law could exist together.

Separation of Powers

The government's powers, at both the federal and state levels, are separated into the executive, legislative, and judicial branches. Each branch is authorized to exercise only the powers that it possesses. Generally, the legislative branch makes the law, the judicial branch interprets the law, and the executive branch executes and enforces the law. The separation of powers is designed to provide checks and balances among the three branches of government. The framers of the Constitution included this principle because there was little accountability by the English crown to the American colonies. Although checks and balances are cumbersome and inefficient at times, they prevent any one branch of government from becoming too powerful.

No one branch has enough power to dominate the entire government. Each branch exercises some authority over the other branches, so that a checking mechanism exists. For example, as Figure 2–3 portrays, as chief of the executive branch, the president can veto the laws passed by the legislative branch. The legislative branch has a variety of powers. It confirms many federal officials and through its "power of the purse," can even refuse to appropriate money for a program that the executive branch wants to encourage. The judicial branch has the authority to interpret and even declare void unconstitutional laws enacted by the legislative branch.

FIGURE 2-3 Separation of Powers in the Federal Legal System

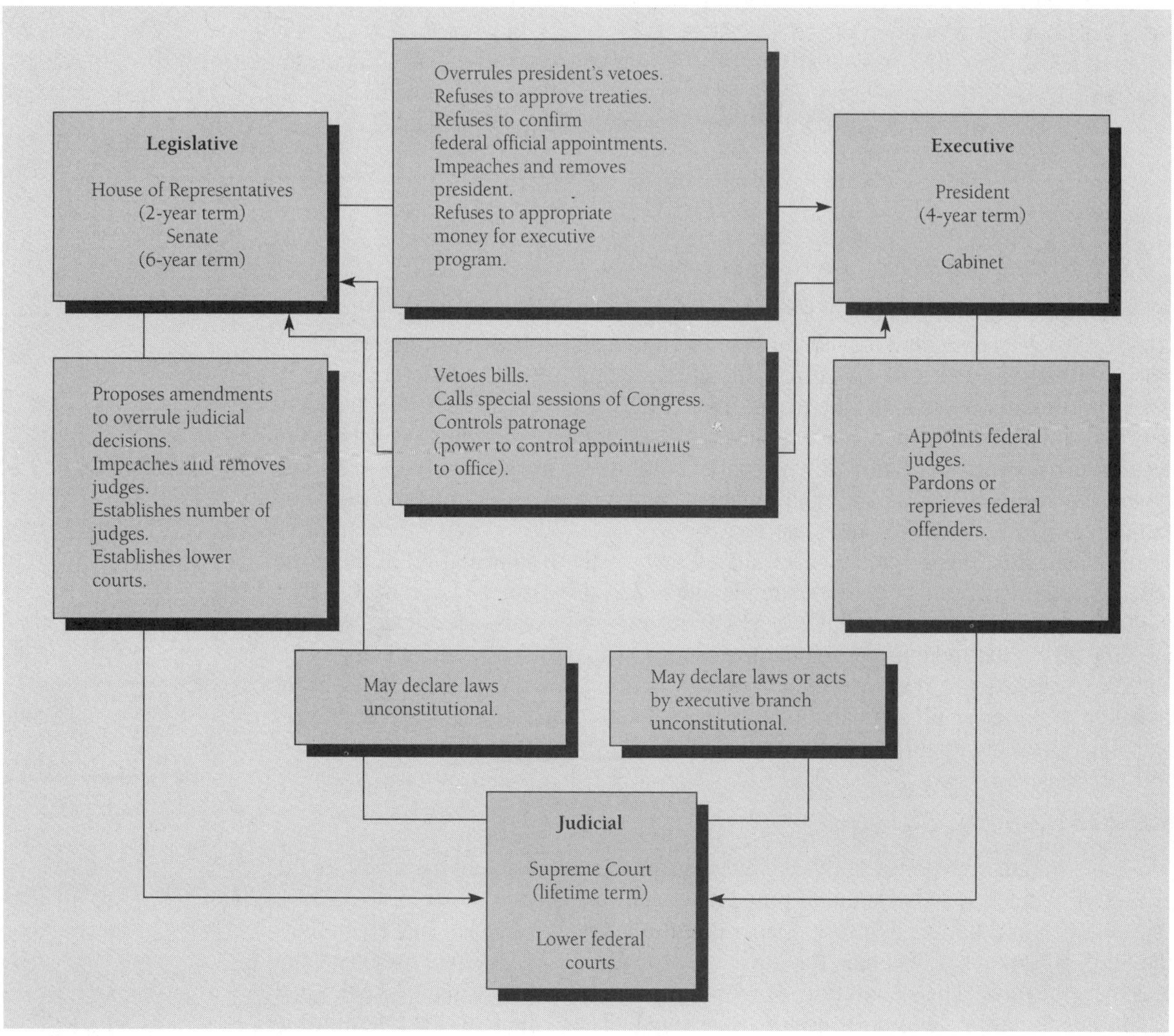

The principle of the separation of powers has been used to restrict the actions of both the legislative and executive branches of the federal government. In the case that follows, the Supreme Court examined a federal statute that granted significant budget-cutting authority to the comptroller general. Several congressmen claimed that since the comptroller is under congressional control, he could not perform executive branch functions without violating the separation of powers.

Bowsher v. Synar

478 U.S. 714 (1986)
United States Supreme Court

This case arose when Congress passed the Balanced Budget and Emergency Deficit Control Act of 1985 in an attempt to balance the federal budget. That law requires the comptroller general (Bowsher) to prepare a report projecting the federal budget deficit so that the spending reductions necessary to reach annual budget targets could be made. The law gave the comptroller general the ultimate authority to determine the budget cuts to be made if Congress could not agree on them. Congressman Synar asserted that the law violated the separation of powers because the comptroller general, who was under the control of Congress, could not be authorized to perform executive branch functions, such as determining how much spending to cut from the federal budget. The trial court held for Synar, and Bowsher appealed.

Burger, Chief Justice

. . . We noted recently that "[t]he Constitution sought to divide the delegated powers of the new Federal Government into three defined categories, Legislative, Executive, and Judicial." The declared purpose of separating and dividing the powers of government, of course, was to "diffus[e] power, the better to secure liberty." Justice Jackson's words echo the famous warning of Montesquieu, quoted by James Madison in The Federalist No. 47, that "'there can be no liberty where the legislative and executive powers are united in the same person, or body of magistrates'. . . . "

Even a cursory examination of the Constitution reveals the influence of Montesquieu's thesis that checks and balances were the foundation of a structure of government that would protect liberty. The Framers provided a vigorous legislative branch and a separate and wholly independent executive branch, with each branch responsible ultimately to the people. The Framers also provided for a judicial branch equally independent with "[t]he judicial Power . . . extend[ing] to all Cases, in Law and Equity, arising under this Constitution, and the Laws of the United States." Art. III, sec. 2.

Other, more subtle, examples of separated powers are evident as well. Unlike . . . parliamentary systems, the President, under Article II, is responsible not to the Congress but to the people, subject only to impeachment proceedings which are exercised by the two Houses as representatives of the people. Art. II, sec. 4. And even in the impeachment of a President, the presiding officer of the ultimate tribunal is not a member of the legislative branch, but the Chief Justice of the United States. Art. I, sec. 3.

That this system of division and separation of powers produces conflicts, confusion, and discordance at times is inherent, but it was deliberately so structured to assure full, vigorous, and open debate on the great issues affecting the people and to provide avenues for the operation of checks on the exercise of governmental power.

The Constitution does not contemplate an active role for Congress in the supervision of officers charged with the execution of the laws it enacts. The President appoints "Officers of the United States" with the

"Advice and Consent of the Senate. . . . " Article II, sec. 2. Once the appointment has been made and confirmed, however, the Constitution explicitly provides for removal of Officers of the United States by Congress only upon impeachment by the House of Representatives and conviction by the Senate. An impeachment by the House and trial by the Senate can rest only on "Treason, Bribery or other high Crimes and Misdemeanors." Article II, sec. 4. A direct congressional role in the removal of officers charged with the execution of the laws beyond this limited one is inconsistent with separation of powers.

This was made clear in debate in the First Congress in 1789. . . . This Court first directly addressed this issue in Myers v. United States. At issue in *Myers* was a statute providing that certain postmasters could be removed only "by and with the advice and consent of the Senate." The President removed one such postmaster without Senate approval, and a lawsuit ensued. Chief Justice Taft, writing for the Court, declared the statute unconstitutional on the ground that for Congress to "draw to itself, or to either branch of it, the power to remove or the right to participate in the exercise of that power . . . would be . . . to infringe the constitutional principle of the separation of governmental powers."

. . . [I]n Humphrey's Executor v. United States, . . . Justice Sutherland's opinion for the Court also underscored the crucial role of separated powers in our system:

> "The fundamental necessity of maintaining each of the three general departments of government entirely free from the control or coercive influence, direct or indirect, of either of the others, has often been stressed and is hardly open to serious question." . . . In light of these precedents, we conclude that Congress cannot reserve for itself the power of removal of an officer charged with the execution of the laws except by impeachment. To permit the execution of the laws to be vested in an officer answerable only to Congress would, in practical terms, reserve in Congress control over the execution of the laws. The structure of the Constitution does not permit Congress to execute the laws; it follows that Congress cannot grant to an officer under its control what it does not possess. . . .

Appellants suggest that the duties assigned to the Comptroller General in the Act are essentially ministerial and mechanical so that their performance does not constitute "execution of the law" in a meaningful sense. On the contrary, we view these functions as plainly entailing execution of the law in constitutional terms. Interpreting a law enacted by Congress to implement the legislative mandate is the very essence of "execution" of the law. Under sec. 251, the Comptroller General must exercise judgment concerning facts that affect the application of the Act. He must also interpret the provisions of the Act to determine precisely what budgetary calculations are required. Decisions of that kind are typically made by officers charged with executing a statute . . . .

. . . By placing the responsibility for execution of the Balanced Budget and Emergency Deficit Control Act in the hands of an officer who is subject to removal only by itself, Congress in effect has retained control over the execution of the Act and has intruded into the executive function. The Constitution does not permit such intrusion . . . .

No one can doubt that Congress and the President are confronted with fiscal and economic problems of unprecedented magnitude, but "the fact that a given law or procedure is efficient, convenient, and useful in facilitating functions of government, standing alone, will not save it if it is contrary to the Constitution. Convenience and efficiency are not the primary objectives—or the hallmarks—of democratic government. . . . "

We conclude the District Court correctly held that the powers vested in the Comptroller General under sec. 251 violate the command of the Constitution that the Congress play no direct role in the execution of the laws. Accordingly, the judgment and order of the District Court are affirmed.

Case Questions

1. Is there a way to rewrite the duties of the comptroller general that would make the Act constitutionally valid?
2. If the portion of the Act that allows Congress to appoint and remove the comptroller general were deleted, would the law then be constitutional?
3. In designing the Constitution, why did the Founders want to separate the powers of the legislative and executive branches?

FIGURE 2-4

Arguments Advanced When Debating the Role of the Jury

Advantages of Using a Jury

- Deliberations by a jury tend to expose the biases of any one individual; the result is less biased than if only one judge were used.
- The public has become accustomed to the jury and acepts it as an integral part of the U.S. legal system.
- The law is written in general terms—reasonable doubt in criminal cases and reasonable conduct in negligence cases—and it is a jury, drawn from a cross section of the community, that can best apply those standards.
- Juries offer a sense of involvement in the legal system.
- The role of the jury balances the power of the judge.

Disadvantages of Using a Jury

- The jury selection process and trying cases to juries greatly increases the length of trials.
- A jury is no more capable of applying community standards for a particular case and party than is a judge.
- Juries have not been shown to have less bias than judges.
- Juries may be less qualified in complex and technical cases than a judge; if one or more jurors does not understand the problem, the jury's verdict may not make sense.

Role of the Jury

Another characteristic of the common law legal system is in its use of the jury. The jury is used to determine facts; the questions of law in a case are determined by a judge. Although the jury is not unique to common law legal systems, it is more prominent in common law countries than in civil law legal systems. In the United States, the jury's role in both civil and criminal cases is constitutionally protected under Amendments 6 and 7. Therefore, the right to trial by jury is a fundamental right. Historically, the jury has had an important place in the American legal system since the union's inception. The colonists brought the jury with them as a measure to prevent royal abuses in the judicial systems. The Stamp Act of 1765 stated that the trial by jury was an inherent and invaluable right of every British colonist. Then, in 1774, the First Continental Congress declared that the colonies were adopting the common law of England, including the right to be tried by a jury of one's peers.

While the right to trial by jury in the United States thus sprang from the existence of the jury in 18th-century England, the first popular use of the jury dates back to 590 B.C. in Athens, Greece. Modern critics of the jury system note the ancient origin of the jury and assert that its use as a trier of fact in today's society is outdated. They note that in modern English civil cases, the jury is used only on rare occasions. The debate over the advantages and disadvantages of a jury trial usually rests on several arguments, such as those listed in Figure 2–4.

Sources of Law

The three branches of government in the United States are granted express lawmaking powers by the Constitution. In addition to those sources of law, administrative agencies at both the federal and state levels that have been created by the legislative branch possess significant lawmaking authority. A review of the sources of law thus should include not only the three branches of government, but also the rules and decisions coming from agencies, bureaus, and commissions at the federal, state, and local levels.

The Legislative Branch

legislature
An officially selected body of persons responsible for making laws for a political unit such as a state or nation.

A **legislature** is an officially selected body of persons vested with the responsibility to make laws for a political unit, such as a nation or a state. The federal legislature in the United States is the Congress. Most state legislatures consist of two houses, which together have the authority to make laws known as statutes, enactments, or legislation.

The legislative process at the federal level is similar to that used in most states. Potential legislation begins when a bill is introduced in either the House of Representatives or the Senate. After a bill is introduced, it is referred to a specialized committee with responsibility for reviewing legislation regarding certain subjects. Most bills die when a committee refuses to take action. The committee can act on a bill by holding hearings, by submitting it to staff members for research and review, and by "marking it up," reviewing it line by line and rewriting its terms. Once a committee recommends a bill, it is forwarded to the floor of the house of Congress in which it was introduced. The committee attaches its report, which focuses on the policy for the proposal and its intended effect. A minority report may be included if some members of the committee disagree with the majority's recommendations. If the bill in that house of Congress is approved, it will be sent to the other house of Congress.

The other house pursues the same process: committee consideration study, review, and eventual vote by that full house. If the bills approved by each house of Congress differ, a conference committee consisting of members of both houses will seek to find a compromise that satisfies both houses. The compromise version must then be approved by votes of each house. Once both houses of Congress approve a bill, it is sent to the president for review. This is one of the checks that the executive branch has on the actions of the legislative branch.

The president may approve the bill or veto it. If the president vetoes the bill, it is returned to the house from which it originated and may be voted on again. If Congress seeks to override the president's veto, a two-thirds vote from each house of Congress is needed. Former President Bush vetoed over two dozen bills sent to him by Congress, but none of the bills were subsequently approved by two-thirds of the Congress.

One other option is open to the president; he or she can take no action for a period of 10 days after receiving the bill. In that case, the bill becomes law unless Congress adjourns and thus prevents the president from returning the bill. If Congress adjourns, inaction by the president will be considered a *pocket veto,* preventing the bill from becoming law.

The Executive Branch

The **executive branch** consists of the chief executive (the president or state governor), the cabinet, and those administrative agencies that derive their authority from the executive. Section 1 of Article II of the Constitution states that "The executive Power shall be vested in a President of the United States of America." Other provisions of the

Constitution give the president the power to make treaties (with the advice and consent of two-thirds of the Senate) and the authority to act as Commander in Chief of the Armed Forces.

executive branch The chief executive (president or governor), cabinet, and administrative agencies that derive their authority from the executive.

The *executive order* is the most common method by which the executive branch makes law. Executive orders may be based on powers expressly granted to the president, powers implied from the Constitution, or powers delegated to the president from the Congress. For example, the president's authority to negotiate trade agreements with other countries is based on powers granted to the president by Congress in the Tariff and Trade Act; while the authority to send military personnel within the country, and perhaps on a limited basis outside the country, to provide assistance in times of emergency, or to defend the country is based on constitutional powers. One executive order that has had significant impact on business is the executive order requiring federal contractors to take affirmative action to ensure that their employment practices are not discriminatory. This executive order is discussed in Chapter 20.

Administrative Agencies

Administrative agencies generally are created by the legislative branch to deal with specific governmental problems. The agencies usually are housed in the executive branch of government. Agencies frequently possess extensive lawmaking powers, which may include executive functions such as conducting investigations and administering governmental programs. An agency may also be granted legislative functions such as rule making and judicial functions such as adjudicating individual cases or claims. Administrative agencies at the state level include the Worker's Compensation Bureau, the Secretary of State, and the Department of Commerce; while the Social Security Administration, the Customs Bureau, and the Internal Revenue Service are federal agencies with a variety of lawmaking powers.

Administrative agencies must use certain uniform procedures, which are generally specified by the legislature in an Administrative Procedures Act (APA). If the required procedures are followed, the rules and regulations of the administrative agencies have the force of law. While courts may review administrative agency actions, agency decisions are often deferred to by a court exercising its judicial review. Chapter 6 discusses administrative agencies and their functions in greater detail.

The Judicial Branch

The courts, which have the power to interpret laws, constitute the **judicial branch** of government. Article III, Section 1 of the U.S. Constitution provides:

judicial branch The courts, which have the power both to interpret laws made by other branches and to make laws when deciding cases.

> The judicial Power of the United States shall be vested in one supreme Court, and in such inferior Courts as the Congress may from time to time ordain and establish.

In addition to interpreting laws from the other branches of government, statutes from the legislature, or executive orders and agency regulations, courts are also a source of law. However, laws emerging from the judicial branch are different from legislative acts. Whereas statutory law is usually general and prospective, the common law of court decisions is particular and retrospective. Thus, legislative bodies usually make laws affecting future norms of society, while courts make decisions affecting past events. Of course, important judicial decisions, through precedent cases, can affect many people who are not parties to an actual case.

State Judicial Systems

jurisdiction
A court's power to hear and decide cases.

A court's power to hear and decide cases is referred to as its **jurisdiction.** The term also refers to the political entity (e.g., state) that exercises the power to hear cases. The jurisdiction of various courts, both at the state and federal levels, is established by statute. Since cases are originally heard by trial courts, these courts are courts of *original jurisdiction.* Appellate courts do not hear trials; instead, they review trial court decisions. These courts are said to have *appellate jurisdiction.* Figure 2–5 depicts a multilevel state court system. Courts at level 1 are courts with original jurisdiction, while courts at levels 2 and 3 are courts with appellate jurisdiction. Some states have fewer than 3 levels of courts, and the names of courts in each level differ among the states. A trial court's jurisdiction to hear a case involves both *jurisdiction of the person* (jurisdiction over both participants) and *jurisdiction of the subject matter* (jurisdiction over the problem that a case concerns).

A general trial court has the power to hear almost any type of dispute. Thus, it has subject matter jurisdiction over almost all cases, except for minor or special disputes heard by inferior courts. Personal jurisdiction requires that the parties to the dispute be properly before the court. The plaintiff who files a complaint with a court thereby agrees to have that court resolve the dispute and grants it personal jurisdiction over the plaintiff. Personal jurisdiction over the defendant is acquired by using a document known as a *summons* to serve notice of the lawsuit on the defendant.

Most state laws allow for other methods of obtaining personal jurisdiction over the defendant. Occasionally, publication in a local newspaper provides sufficient notice to the defendant. When a potential defendant is outside the state where the court is located, a *long arm statute* is used. For example, if a citizen of California is involved in an accident in Oregon that injures an Oregon citizen, the Oregon long arm statute grants personal jurisdiction over the California defendant to an Oregon

FIGURE 2–5

A Multilevel State Court System

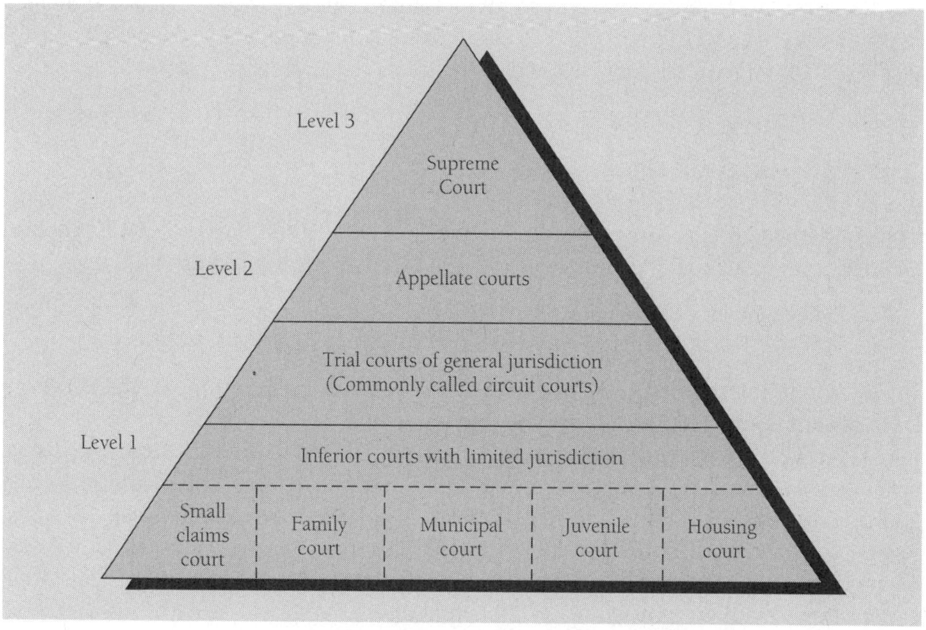

court even if summons is served on the defendant in California. As long as some minimum contact exists between the out-of-state defendant and the state with the long arm statute, the notification to the defendant need not take place inside the state where the court is located. Without some minimum contact, it would offend traditional notions of fairness and justice to pull an out-of-state defendant into court.

An *inferior trial court* is generally limited to hearing certain kinds of cases or minor disputes that might otherwise have to be brought into the general trial courts. For example, the district court in the Michigan judicial system hears minor criminal cases and civil disputes involving less than $10,000. This court is much like a municipal court, its jurisdiction and power being limited to a given geographic area, such as a city. Pennsylvania has a comparable court, known as the court of common pleas.

Probate courts sometimes hear juvenile cases as well as estate cases involving a deceased person's will. Some states have family courts that hear divorce and child custody cases. Traffic courts and housing courts are also inferior courts that decide only certain types of cases.

Many states have special courts for minor disputes that can be settled quickly. For example, a small claims court generally hears civil cases involving less than a certain dollar amount, such as $3,000. Parties usually appear in such courts without an attorney, and the decisions of these courts generally cannot be appealed. "The People's Court" television program is based on actual disputes that qualify for presentation in a California small claims court.

Federal Judicial System

As Figure 2–6 depicts, the basic three-tier system is used by the federal judiciary, with trial courts at the bottom, appellate courts in the middle, and the U.S. Supreme Court at the top. In addition to the regular three-tier courts, the federal judicial system has several special courts, including the Claims Court (determines monetary claims against the United States), the Tax Court, Bankruptcy Courts, and the Court of International Trade. As these courts hear only certain types of cases, their jurisdiction is called *limited subject matter* jurisdiction.

As noted, the *Supreme Court of the United States* is expressly referred to in Article III of the U.S. Constitution. It hears appeals from the federal appellate courts and from the highest state courts. The Constitution also provides that a few cases, such as disputes between two states, may originate in the Supreme Court. The federal appellate courts, known as the *circuit courts of appeal,* are organized into 13 circuits, spread geographically across the nation. There is one circuit for the District of Columbia, one for appeals from the court of international trade and the court of claims, and the remainder for appeals from federal trial courts within each of 11 circuits or regions across the country.

At the trial level of the federal judicial system is the *federal district court.* There is at least one district court, often with numerous judges, in each state, and many states have several district courts. While state courts at the trial level can generally hear any type of dispute, the jurisdiction of a federal trial court is limited to two basic types of cases: those involving federal questions and those involving diversity of citizenship. *Federal question cases* focus on the source of law that governs the case. Such cases are resolved by reference to federal statutes, the U.S. Constitution, a U.S. treaty, a federal administrative regulation, or an executive order of the president.

FIGURE 2-6 The Federal Judicial System

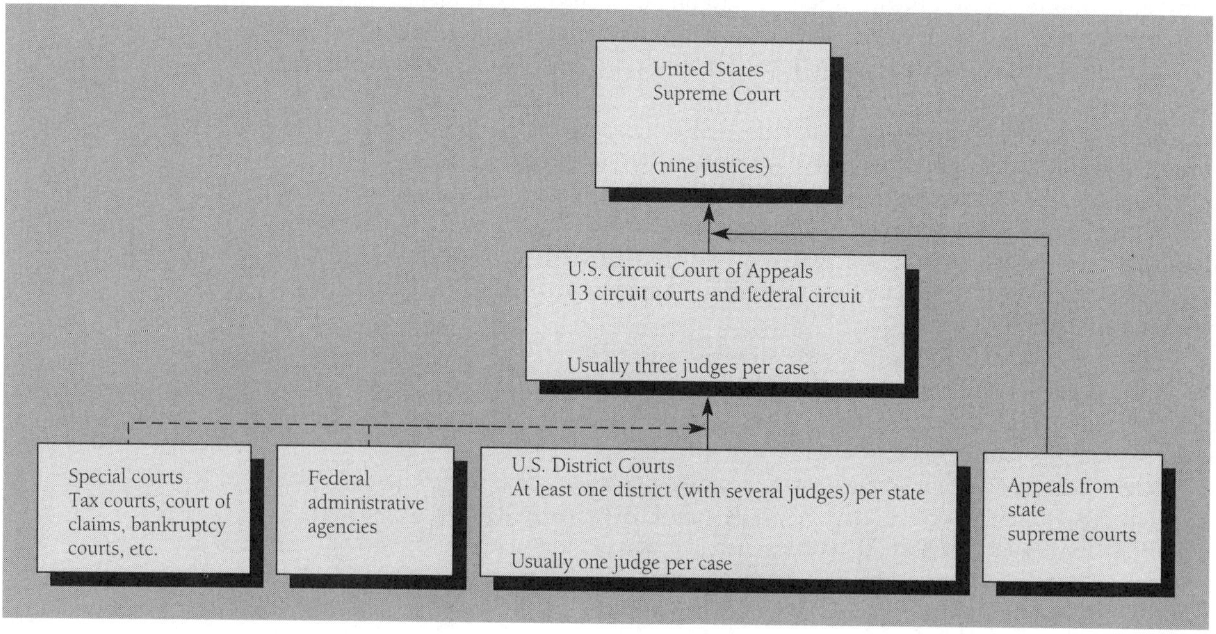

On the other hand, *diversity of citizenship cases* focus on the parties' citizenship, regardless of the nature of their problem. Such cases require all plaintiffs to have state citizenships diverse or different from those of all defendants. Diversity of citizenship cases also require that the damages being sought exceed $50,000. Recently, there have been proposals to eliminate the diversity of citizenship of the litigants as a basis for bringing a case to a federal court.

In determining an institution's citizenship, a corporation is considered a citizen of either the state where it was incorporated or where it has its principal place of business. Thus, the General Motors Corporation, incorporated in Delaware, could be a citizen of either Delaware or Michigan. For this reason, if General Motors sues a citizen of Georgia, the dispute, regardless of its subject matter, may be brought in a federal district court. However, if it sues a citizen of Delaware or Michigan, it cannot use the federal court system unless the case concerns a federal question.

Certain special aspects of the federal district court's diversity of citizenship jurisdiction should be noted. First, the federal district court's jurisdiction is not exclusive; it is concurrent or shared with that of the state courts. A plaintiff who wishes to sue defendants from other states may do so in either a state court that has jurisdiction or in a federal district court. If the suit is started in the state's judicial system, the defendants may be able to remove the case to a federal district court for trial. In most cases, however, the plaintiff controls the court system used. Second, if a case is brought in a federal district court solely because of diversity of citizenship, that court must apply substantive state law (such as the contract law of Georgia) to resolve the parties' dispute. However, the district court will apply federal, not state, procedural rules.

Finally, some cases must be filed in either the federal or state court system. For example, bankruptcy or patent cases must be heard in special courts in the federal court system. These subjects are covered only by federal laws. Conversely, a contract dispute between two California residents with no federal questions must be heard in the California state courts. In such a dispute, there would be no subject matter jurisdiction for a federal court and probably no personal jurisdiction for the courts of other states. Thus, you should distinguish between concerns focused on bringing a case in the federal or state legal system and concerns regarding the rules that determine the proper substantive law. Just as the federal courts apply state laws in most diversity of citizenship cases, the state courts sometimes apply federal law in resolving disputes brought to them. Determining where a case is heard and decided is not the same as determining which substantive laws apply. The latter determination is governed by **conflict of law rules,** which establish criteria to aid the judge in applying the most appropriate law.

conflict of law rules Rules that establish criteria to determine what law governs transactions involving different states or countries.

How Courts Make Law

Laws emerging from the judicial branch are different from legislative acts. Legislative bodies can usually respond to political, social, and economic change more quickly than the judiciary. Because judges act only when a case or controversy is presented, they cannot react directly to such change. Further, whereas statutory law is general and prospective, the common law of judicial decisions is particular and retrospective.

Of course, exceptions exist. Some statutes are intended to affect only a few companies or individuals, and important judicial decisions, through precedent, affect many people who are not parties to an actual case. Courts make law by deciding cases and controversies. The law controlling a particular case may originate from prior court decisions, from statutory laws, from administrative regulations, or occasionally from the court itself if a law is made for that case. When a court uses a prior decision as a source of law for a later case, it is adhering to the concept of *stare decisis.* A court may also decide a case by interpreting statutory law. In so doing, it attempts to determine the legislature's intent in passing the statute so that the statute can be properly applied to the case. In interpreting administrative regulations, courts generally follow the interpretation principles they use for statutory laws. Sometimes a court confronts a new problem, one not addressed by prior cases, administrative regulations, or existing legislation. When that happens the court's determination decides the case for the litigating parties and also establishes a precedent for later cases.

Applying Law from Prior Cases One purpose of applying law from prior cases is to promote stability and predictability in the law. If a court changed the rule of law or applied it differently when confronted with facts similar to those at issue in a prior case, the law would be unpredictable. Frequent changes in the law would make it impossible for people to base their future conduct on existing interpretations. More litigants might appeal court decisions in the hope that appellate judges would use a different interpretation. Consistent application of the same law to different people facing similar problems promotes uniformity in the law.

The concept of *stare decisis* requires a court to follow the decision made in an earlier similar case. However, in some situations, a court finds that the overall circumstances of a case are not the same as those in earlier situations. Although adherence to precedent is needed to promote stability and predictability in the law, the law must also be flexible enough to change as society encounters changes in technology, science, morals, economics, or politics. The *Brooks* case discussed earlier provides an example of the Supreme Court of Alaska's determination that a change was needed regarding the law governing the enforceability of prenuptial agreements.

Interpreting Statutory Laws Many cases require courts to interpret the meaning of language in a statute. One aspect of that activity focuses on determining what an informed reader would understand from the text. A second aspect focuses on determining the legislature's intent; what did the drafters of the statute have in mind when they selected certain words or phrases? In general, courts use a combination of these methods in interpreting statutes.

Courts have established several rules to aid them in interpreting statutes. Generally, they begin by looking at the *plain meaning* of a statute. If the plain meaning of a word or phrase used in a statute is obvious, no further analysis is required. However, the legislature may use the same word in different contexts to mean different things. For example, does the term *person* include a corporation? Corporations are not commonly thought of as persons. Yet some statutes, such as the Uniform Partnership Act, intentionally include a corporation as a person. Thus, the plain meaning of the term *person* in one statute may differ from its plain meaning in another statute.

If the plain meaning of statutory words or phrases is unclear, courts frequently turn to the *legislative history* to determine the legislature's intent in selecting those words or phrases. The Supreme Court in the *Mortier* case examined the legislative history of the FIFRA legislation when it considered whether Congress intended to preempt all state and local regulation regarding the use of pesticides. A court usually asks several questions when examining a law's legislative history. What were the words in the original draft of the bill? How were those words changed in the version of the bill that became law? Is there any record from a legislative committee regarding why certain changes were made? Did the sponsors of the statute make any comments concerning the inclusion of particular words or phrases? Inquiries of this kind assist a court in determining the legislative intent of an unclear or ambiguous statute.

Another method of determining the meaning of words or phrases in a statute is to analyze the policy or *purpose* behind the statute. Why was this particular statute passed? The questionable words or phrases should be interpreted in a manner that furthers the purpose of the statute. Courts also examine the context of such words or phrases.

Which of the methods of statutory interpretation referred to above are used in the following case? Note that the court focused on several specific phrases in the statute, such as "place of public accommodation" and "deny access."

Quinnipiac Council, Boy Scouts of America, Inc. v. Commission on Human Rights and Opportunities, et al.

528 A.2d 352 (1987)
Supreme Court of Connecticut

Catherine Pollard requested that she be appointed scoutmaster of Boy Scout Troop 13 in Milford. Pollard had a long history of active involvement in scouting as a merit badge counselor, a Cub Scout den mother, and a Troop 13 committee member. In this latter capacity, she had acted as de facto scoutmaster for Troop 13 when it lacked a functioning scoutmaster and as an assistant scoutmaster during the years 1972 to 1976. Nonetheless, Pollard's application to be scoutmaster was turned down because of the policy of the Boy Scouts of America that scoutmasters be men at least 21 years of age.

Although the official policy statement of the Boy Scouts of America imposes no gender qualification for employment, and encourages women to undertake volunteer leadership roles, the national organization does not permit women to serve in certain positions: scoutmaster, assistant scoutmaster, Webelos den leader, assistant Webelos den leader, and lone scout friend and counselor. The plaintiff rejected Pollard's application solely because of this national policy, without making any judgment whatsoever about her individual qualifications to perform the duties required of a scoutmaster.

Pollard filed a complaint with the Commission on Human Rights. After a hearing, it determined that the Quinnipiac Council, a Boy Scouts of America Council serving central Connecticut, was statutorily obligated to offer Pollard a position as scoutmaster. The Quinnipiac Council appealed that decision to the superior trial court, which reversed the Commission's decision. Pollard and the Commission on Human Rights appealed that decision to the state supreme court.

Peters, Chief Justice

The dispositive issue in this case is whether the refusal to permit a woman to serve as a scoutmaster for a Boy Scout troop is a violation of our public accommodation statute. . . .

In our determination of the merits of the defendants' appeals, it is important to identify, at the outset, what is and what is not at issue. The central question before us is whether the defendants can sustain their *statutory* claim that sec. 53-35(a), our public accommodation statute, forbids the plaintiff from denying to Pollard, because of her gender, the opportunity to serve the plaintiff as a scoutmaster. . . .

It is a discriminatory accommodation practice, under section 53-35(a), to deny any person within the jurisdiction of this state "full and equal accommodations in every place of public accommodation, resort or amusement . . . by reason of . . . sex. . . . " The phrase "place of public accommodation, resort or amusement" is itself defined "within the meaning of this section [as] any establishment which caters or offers its services or facilities or goods to the general public. . . . "

In deciding whether section 53-35(a) makes a gender based refusal to consider an application for scoutmaster a discriminatory public accommodation practice, we operate under well established principles of statutory construction designed to assist us in ascertaining and giving effect to the apparent intent of the legislature. "If the language of a statute is plain and unambiguous, we need not look beyond the statute because we assume that the language expresses the intention of the legislature." When we are faced with ambiguity in a statute, however, we turn for interpretive guidance to its legislative history, the circumstances surrounding its enactment, and the purpose the statute is to serve. . . .

We first address the question whether section 53-35(a) . . . entirely excludes the Boy Scouts of America. The plaintiff urges us to hold that the concept of "*place* of public accommodation" necessarily involves a specific physical site and hence automatically excludes its organization from the coverage of the statute. . . .

The statute defines a "place of public accommodation" as "any establishment, which . . . offers its services. . . . " The legislature has itself linked its definition of "place" not with a site, but rather with "any establishment." The meaning of this linkage is sufficiently ambiguous on its face to require us to look further to determine what the legislature intended to encompass within its prohibition of discriminatory accommodation practices.

Inquiry into the statute's legislative history makes it exceedingly doubtful that linkage to a physical site is a necessary element of the present definition of a "place of public accommodation." Public accommodation statutes in general have their origins in the common law duties of innkeepers and common carriers to offer their services to the general public without discrimination. In Connecticut, as the trial court correctly observed, our public accommodation statutes have repeatedly been amended to expand the categories of enterprises that are covered and the conduct that is deemed discriminatory. . . . In 1953 . . . the definition came to be, as it remains today, "any establishment which caters or offers its services or facilities or goods to the general public."

In order to draw appropriate implications from this legislative history we must consider the remedial purpose that the public accommodation statute was designed to implement. . . . [T]he unconditional language of the statute, the history of its steadily expanded coverage, and the compelling interest in eliminating discriminatory public accommodation practices persuade us that physical situs is not today an essential element of our public accommodation law. [O]ur statute now regulates the discriminatory conduct and not the discriminatory situs of an enterprise which offers its services to the general public.

Our conclusion that our public accommodation statute does not automatically exclude the plaintiff from coverage because it does not have a fixed physical situs does not, however, end our inquiry. The next question . . . is whether its conduct in denying Pollard an opportunity to become a scoutmaster was a discriminatory public accommodation practice. We hold that it was not.

In the decision of whether a discriminatory public accommodation practice has occurred, the determinative issue is whether an "establishment" that serves "the general public" has denied access to its goods and services to a member of a protected class. . . . Unlike the statutes in some other jurisdictions, our statute does not expressly limit its coverage to "business enterprises" nor does it expressly exclude private clubs or organizations.

We can discern no reason to interpolate a "business" limitation into the legislature's unadorned reference to "any establishment." Like the question of situs, the question of coverage must reflect the legislative purpose of eliminating discriminatory conduct by those who serve the general public. From that vantage point, the organizational status of the enterprise that is the service provider cannot be the determinant of statutory coverage. . . . Although no private organization is duty-bound to offer its services and facilities to all comers, once such an organization has determined to eschew selectivity, under our statute it may not discriminate among the general public. This construction accords with that of other courts in our sister states construing similar legislation. . . .

. . . All of our antidiscrimination law is essentially fact-bound. As the Supreme Court of the United States has frequently reminded us, and as we have repeatedly stated in our own opinions, the *individual* is the focal point of the legislation that defines and prohibits discriminatory practices. The purpose of antidiscrimination legislation is to afford access to opportunity on the basis of individual abilities rather than on the basis of stereotypical generalizations.

In considering the opportunity of which an individual claims to have been deprived, the focus is equally on the particular opportunity, the particular position, rather than on access to an organization or an industry as a whole. The corollary to these well established principles is that a person seeking recovery for discriminatory practices must demonstrate that he or she has personally been deprived of access to goods or services or positions in a manner forbidden by the statute governing access to public accommodations.

The issue in this case therefore is whether the record sustains Pollard's claim that she has personally been deprived of a public accommodation when she was denied the opportunity to become a scoutmaster. . . . It is important to note the precise claim that the defendants advance. They maintain that Pollard was denied access to an "accommodation" because the plaintiff denied her the opportunity *to be of service* to the plaintiff. This claim raises an issue of first impression not only in this state but apparently in the country as a whole.

We observe first that a statute that addresses a discriminatory denial of *access to goods and services* does not, on its face, incorporate an allegedly discriminatory refusal by an enterprise to avail itself of a claimant's desire to *offer services*. . . .

Our public accommodation statute gives no indication that it was intended to encompass the proffer of services within its definition of discriminatory accommodation practices. . . . We therefore conclude that, in denying Catherine Pollard the opportunity to serve as scoutmaster of Boy Scout Troop 13, the plaintiff did not deprive her of an "accommodation" as that term is used in our public accommodation statute.

The trial court's decision in favor of the Quinnipiac Council is affirmed.

Case Questions

1. Do you think the legislature intentionally chose the terms "place of public accommodation" and "establishment" instead of using words like "location" or "business firm"?

2. What does the Court conclude regarding the need for an establishment to have a "physical site" after reviewing the legislative history? Which party does that conclusion favor?

3. What is the difference between what the statute protects regarding discriminatory action and the activity Pollard complained of?

SUMMARY

Although a society's laws may be viewed as determining the nature of the society's legal system, the institutions in a society that create or apply laws are also an important part of its legal system. The role of the courts in making or applying law differs significantly between the common law and civil law legal systems. Other differences in these legal systems lead judges and lawyers to use different reasoning processes to determine the law that should apply to resolve a specific problem.

Despite their differences, all legal systems perform similar functions. Probably the most important of these functions is the maintenance of order within the society. They also provide a forum for the resolution of disputes and provide some certainty and stability while accommodating changes in society.

Laws can be classified in various ways. Substantive law generally defines both rights and duties; procedural law details the methods by which those rights and duties are enforced. Significant differences in the parties, procedures, rules, and purposes distinguish criminal law cases from civil law cases. Both common law and statutory law are sources of law. Laws can also be classified by the extent to which the problems with which they deal affect the public rather than private parties.

Two distinctive features of the U.S. legal system are the division of lawmaking authority vertically between the states and the federal government and horizontally among the legislative, judicial, and executive branches of government. The twin bases of federalism and separation of powers shape the structure of the U.S. legal system. The *Mortier* case concerns the federalism principle, while the *Synar* case illustrates the application of the separation of lawmaking powers among the branches of government. The supremacy clause, which resolves most of the conflicts between state and federal laws in favor of the federal laws, also shapes the legal environment in the United States.

Each of the three branches of government performs distinct roles in the federal and state legal systems. The legislature, generally consisting of two houses, is the primary lawmaking branch of government. Although both the federal and state legislatures make law through a process that begins with the proposal of a bill, much of the work is done through committees.

The executive branch consists of the chief executive, his or her staff advisers, and the departments of government that administer and enforce the laws. The chief executive, who has express and implied lawmaking authority, uses executive orders to implement certain executive policies. Administrative agencies are sometimes also considered a part of the executive branch.

The federal and state judicial branches are usually organized into trial courts, appellate courts, and a supreme court. Both federal and state courts can hear some similar types of cases. For example, diversity of citizenship cases that do not involve special federal laws can generally be filed in either federal or state courts. The federal and state court systems each also have exclusive powers to resolve certain legal questions. Patent, bankruptcy, and federal tax cases must be brought to the federal courts. Property matters or contract disputes involving citizens of the same state generally must be brought to the state courts.

Courts make law by applying laws from prior cases, by interpreting constitutional and legislative provisions, and by deciding cases that raise novel questions. Although the precedent of prior cases is usually followed, in some situations a court declines to follow prior case law. When this happens, as in the *Brooks* case, the court's decision sets a new precedent for future case decisions.

Courts follow several principles when seeking to interpret statutes. The plain meaning of words or phrases, the legislative history of statutes, and analysis of the context surrounding questionable words or phrases are used by courts to determine statutory intent. Even when deciding a question that has not been answered by prior cases or existing legislation, a court makes law. In such instances, an appellate or supreme court's decision and statements of law will be followed by other courts in the same jurisdiction in future years.

Critical Thinking Review Questions

1. How would you describe the components of the U.S. legal system to a student from Poland who is enrolled in your school?
2. Compare and contrast the common law and civil law legal systems.
3. Distinguish between *(a)* procedural and substantive law, *(b)* criminal and civil law, and *(c)* common law and statutory law.
4. Federalism and the separation of powers are fundamental concepts in the U.S. legal system. The term *separation of powers* refers to the notion that lawmaking power in our government is divided among the executive, judicial, and legislative branches. Each branch acts as a check on the others, thus preventing one branch from exercising too much power. What assumption supports the concept of *federalism?* What similarities are there between the concepts of federalism and the separation of powers?

Critical Thinking Exercises

1. If your manufacturing company sells its product in 20 states, would you prefer regulation by state law or by federal law? In what courts can your company be sued? Will the substantive law of that state be applied in your court case?
2. What is the major advantage of *stare decisis* in a precedent-oriented system?
3. The basic characteristic of common law is that the courts will follow a case that establishes a precedent when similar issues arise in later cases. However, the courts do not always follow precedent. Why?
4. Mrs. Plaintiff sues the defendant church to recover damages for injuries sustained when she tripped on a loose stair tread at the church. For many years prior to this suit, the courts of the state have followed the rule that nonprofit organizations, such as churches, are not to be liable in such situations even where the injury is a result of their own carelessness. You are a judge of the court deciding whether or not the defendant church should be held liable. In deciding the issue of charitable immunity, should you apply the rule of *stare decisis,* overrule the old precedent, or let the legislature resolve the issue through the legislative process?
5. Give an example of rule making through the legislative process. How is this process different from the making of rules by a court?
6. A state statute prohibits the "carrying on one's person of any gun, knife, or other concealed weapon or implement of violence." Several women who were suspected of prostitution were arrested outside a large hotel in a major city. After a search of their handbags, several small canisters of mace were found. Have these women violated the statute's terms? What principles would be used to interpret the statute?

CHAPTER

3

The Legal Environment of International Business

Critical Thinking Questions

- As nations want to regulate and restrict activities that can adversely affect their economies, can the laws of one country regulate activities taking place in other countries if those activities affect it, or does the law of the country where the activity occurs always displace all other national laws?
- How are laws used to encourage exports?
- As international trade involves the payment of money for the delivery of goods, can laws regulating the exchange of a local currency for a foreign currency as well as laws regulating which goods can be traded through imports or exports be used to seek to manage international trade?
- Compare and contrast the role of the courts and the role of administrative agencies in interpreting laws in a civil law legal system and in a common law legal system.
- What are some of the issues that should be addressed in an agreement between a licensor of a trademarked, copyrighted, or patented product and a foreign licensee who will make or sell that product?
- Why might a firm that wants to invest directly in another country find it desirable to enter into a joint venture with a partner firm from the country where the investment is made rather than investing on its own?

Introduction... Past, Present, Future

International trade, and attempts to regulate it, has existed for thousands of years. While in the past national laws and regulations have dominated international commerce, by the 17th century the international "law merchant" was applied in many different countries to resolve disputes between international traders. Today, a combination of national, regional, and international laws affect international business activities. Laws in the country of source regulate the import of goods, determine the acceptability of provisions in licensing agreements, and affect the organization and operation of joint-venture or direct-investment facilities. Laws in the country of origin may be given extraterritorial application so as to affect foreign business activities that have an impact on commerce in that country.

Organizations such as the recently expanded European Union (EU), the Association of Southeast Asian Nations (ASEAN), the Gulf Cooperation Council (GCC), the Southern Common Market (MERCOSUR), the Andean Pact (ANPAC), and the Organization of Petroleum Exporting Countries (OPEC) have emerged in recent decades as regional sources of law. Some regional organizations are concerned with particular problems (OPEC's concern with the world price for petroleum products) or with encouraging trade within the region (ASEAN nations currently focus primarily on regional trade issues), whereas at least one organization now has a variety of institutions that make laws in numerous fields (the EU).

Global business has become so important to nations and business firms that national laws and regulations increasingly must be designed and harmonized with those of other countries. New regional organizations are encouraging business firms and national lawmakers to enlarge their "borders" and to give equal treatment to firms and products crossing old boundaries. The legal environment is changing most dramatically in the republics of the former Soviet Union and in many eastern European countries. China, the world's most populous country, is attracting thousands of international business firms by revising portions of its legal structure and clarifying some of its administrative practices.

In the United States, a firm's investment decisions once focused on comparing the legal environment in Ohio and South Carolina. It is the investment and regulatory environment in Mexico and China that is being studied for the future. U.S. firms in Pennsylvania that once faced competitors from Illinois or Georgia now find French, Dutch, Japanese, and even Chinese-owned firms transacting business in the United States. The 21st century is certain to require an increased appreciation and understanding of the legal environment for international business.

Thought Questions

1. How do the rules and regulations of international organizations and regional associations affect private international business transactions?
2. If future global business transactions are more likely to involve high-tech products and services rather than standard commodity items, which laws and regulations in the global legal environment will increase in importance?
3. How are lawmakers in one country affected by the legal environment in other countries and by the increasing globalization of business?

Overview

Although this chapter concerns "international" business, that term is often used as a synonym or substitute for the term "global" business. While the terms *international* and *global* are often used interchangeably, sometimes the two terms have distinct meanings. For example, an international investment fund differs from a global investment fund; the international investment fund makes investments outside the country where the fund is listed, whereas a global fund invests both inside and outside that country. From a legal perspective, **international law** concerns the law among nations (*inter* national), while the newer term **global legal environment** is used primarily to consider the laws, institutions, and legal processes that affect private business firms. Although the focus of this chapter is on the "global legal environment," we use the term **legal environment of international business** to examine the international, regional, and national laws affecting global business transactions.

international law
Laws governing conduct among nations.

global legal environment
Laws, institutions, and legal processes that affect private business firms.

legal environment of international business
The international, regional, and national laws that affect global business transactions.

The first section of this chapter discusses the current status of international trade and investment. Conflicts between global business firms and the nations that seek to regulate their conduct are noted. International business activities may be regulated by national, regional, and international laws. The second section focuses on the sources of laws and on the special problems that arise when one nation attempts to apply its laws to events occurring outside its borders. The third section examines the laws that most directly affect international trade. Trade may involve the export or import of products or services, or it may involve the licensing of patents, trademarks, copyrights, or know-how to foreign manufacturers or distributors that make or sell products or services globally. The final section discusses laws that affect foreign investments through joint ventures and direct investments by single firms.

Conducting International Business

International Trade

Although the United States has not been as dependent on world trade as are other nations with fewer resources or less-developed markets, it has long played an important role in world trade development. The most recent development in world trade is the formation of a new organization, the World Trade Organization (WTO). At the beginning of 1995, the World Trade Organization replaced the General Agreement on Tariffs and Trade (GATT), which came into existence at the end of World War II. While the GATT regulated much of the world's trade for several decades, both developing and developed nations sought to develop a new institution. Developing nations felt the GATT's "most-favored nation" standard, which emphasized equal treatment of imported goods from all member countries, did not adequately address their special needs. Developed countries, which over time reduced tariff barriers through GATT negotiations, wanted to add provisions for addressing nontariff barriers, which too often arose in place of the tariffs that had been removed.

In recent decades, countries on the Pacific Rim have intensified their involvement in world trade. Japan has been in the forefront of world trade for many years. Taiwan, South Korea, Singapore, and Hong Kong have become world trade centers, and China is dramatically increasing its role in international trade. The volume of world trade in goods in 1993 was almost five times the volume in 1975. Figure 3–1 depicts both the growth of world trade from 1975 through 1993 and the dominance of trade among the industrialized countries.

International Investment

Although international trade is generally more visible, international investment has been increasing and has reached significant levels in many countries. Foreign investment occurs when individuals or firms purchase securities (typically stocks or bonds) of foreign firms. If the amount of the investment by the purchaser from one country gives that person or firm at least 10 percent ownership of a foreign firm, the investment is known as a **foreign direct investment.** A purchase of foreign securities that results in the purchaser owning less than 10 percent of that firm is known as a **foreign portfolio investment.**

foreign direct investment
The purchase by a person or firm from one country of at least 10 percent of the ownership of a firm in another country.

foreign portfolio investment
The purchase by a person or firm from one country of less than 10 percent of the ownership of a firm in another country.

In recent years, foreign firms have made significant direct investment in EU countries, the United States, Mexico, and several countries in eastern Europe. For the United States, the amount of investment by foreign firms, known as foreign direct investment in the United States (FDIUS) has recently surpassed the level of direct investment abroad (DIA) by U.S. firms. Figure 3–2 illustrates the origin of foreign investment in the United States, while Figure 3–3 depicts the major countries in which U.S. firms invest.

Nations and International Business Firms

Different nations have different policies and laws regarding the conduct of business by foreign-based firms. As early as the 1950s, some governments began to realize that their goals could conflict with the goals of the local business subsidiaries of foreign corporations. Consequently, some nations imposed a variety of laws, administrative rules, and investment codes on foreign investors. By contrast, other nations welcomed foreign investors because those investments provided many people with jobs and

FIGURE 3-1 Trends in World Trade

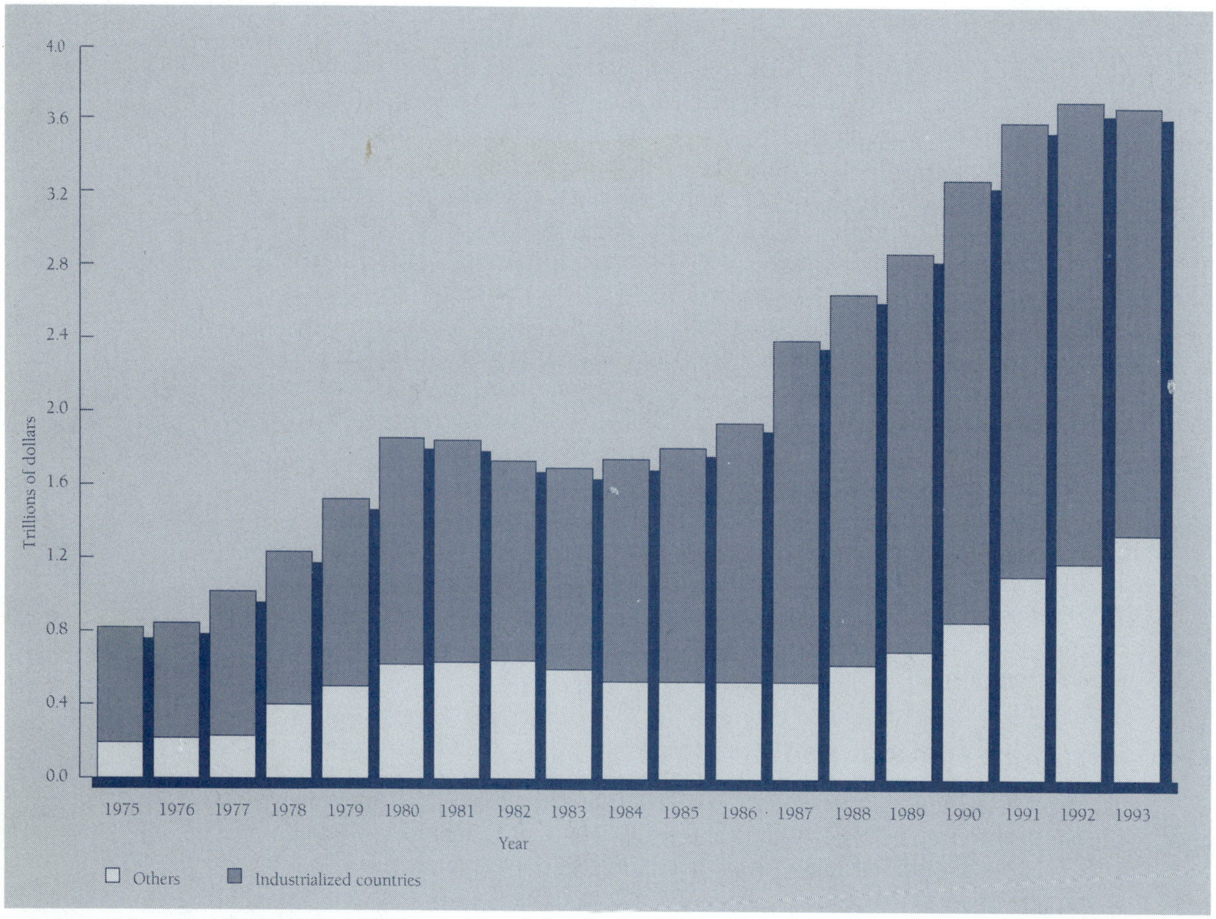

Source: *Direction of Trade Statistics: 1980–1989 Yearbooks*, Washington, D.C.: International Monetary Fund 1989; and International Financial Statistics: 1994, Washington, D.C.: International Monetary Fund 1994.

helped to improve the country's economic conditions. These nations modified their tax laws, currency exchange regulations, and administrative policies to attract global business enterprises.

Countries also vary in the manner in which they regulate how their own firms conduct international business activities. For example, although exports are generally encouraged, they are sometimes restricted. Moreover, within any one country, some national laws may promote international business, whereas others seek to restrict its influence.

Sources of Law

A domestic or national legal problem is approached by attempting to relate the facts to a known legal framework. When doing business in the United States, a business manager assumes the existence of written legal rules established by legislatures or administrative agencies and interpreted by the courts. However, the national or

FIGURE 3-2 Foreign Investments in the United States: 1980 and 1992

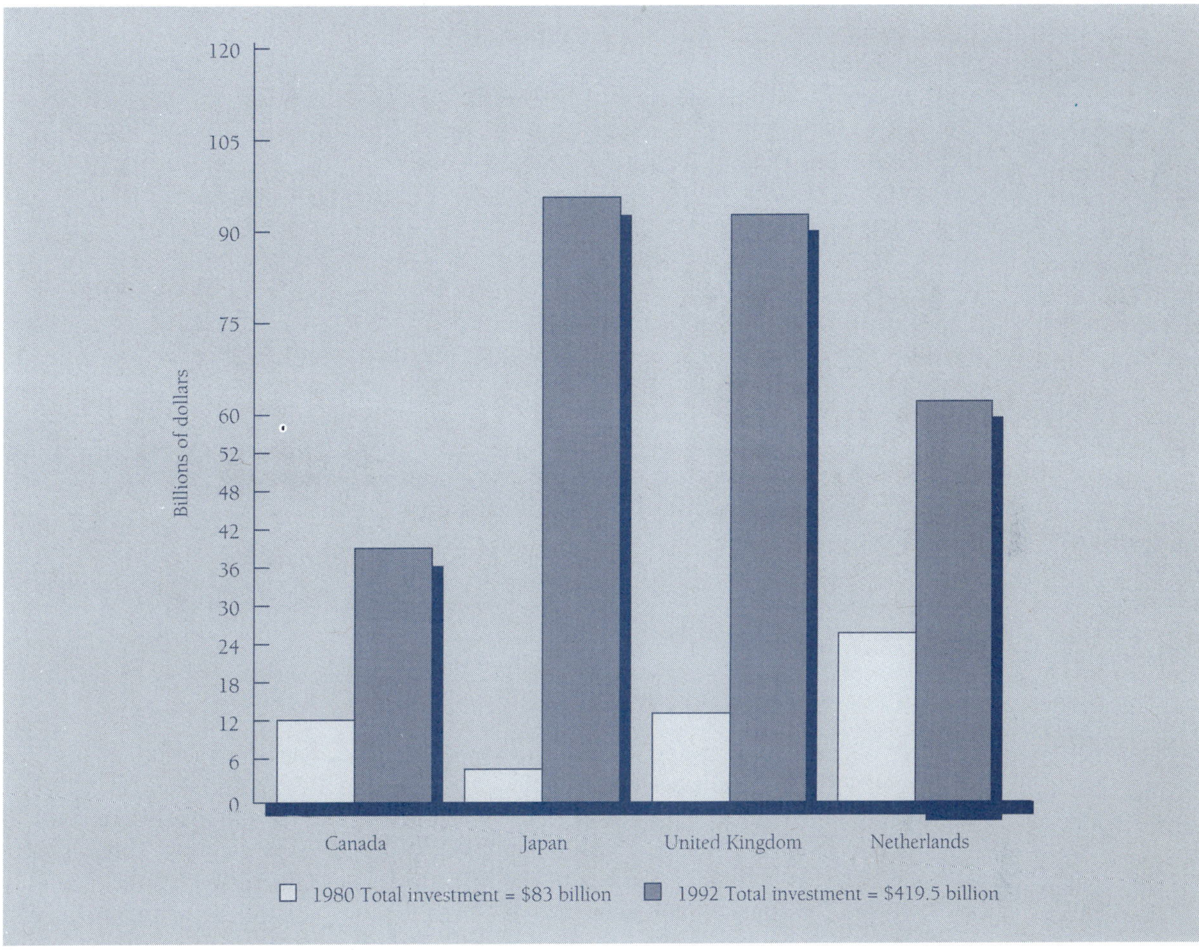

Source: *Statistical Abstract of the United States, 1994* (Washington, D.C.: U.S. Government Printing Office, 1994), U.S. Department of Commerce, Bureau of the Census, p. 777.

regional laws governing foreign transactions may be based on social, political, and economic values different from those of the United States. Moreover, the role of law and even the type of legal system in other countries are often quite different from the U.S. legal environment.

Thus, in the 15 countries that are a part of the European Union (see Figure 3–4, page 73 for a map of the countries in the European Union), some laws originate at the national or local level, while directives and regulations come from the Commission and Council of the Community. The legal systems in Poland, Hungary, and the Czech Republic, and the republics in the Commonwealth of Independent States (CIS) are changing rapidly. In some places, a new legal order has not yet replaced the old system. For example, the new republics of Estonia, Latvia, and Lithuania are each seeking to attract foreign investment by offering tax incentives to firms willing to build facilities there. Only a few years ago, the legal environment in those republics was not attractive or even stable for foreign business firms.

FIGURE 3-3 U.S. Investments Abroad: 1980 and 1992

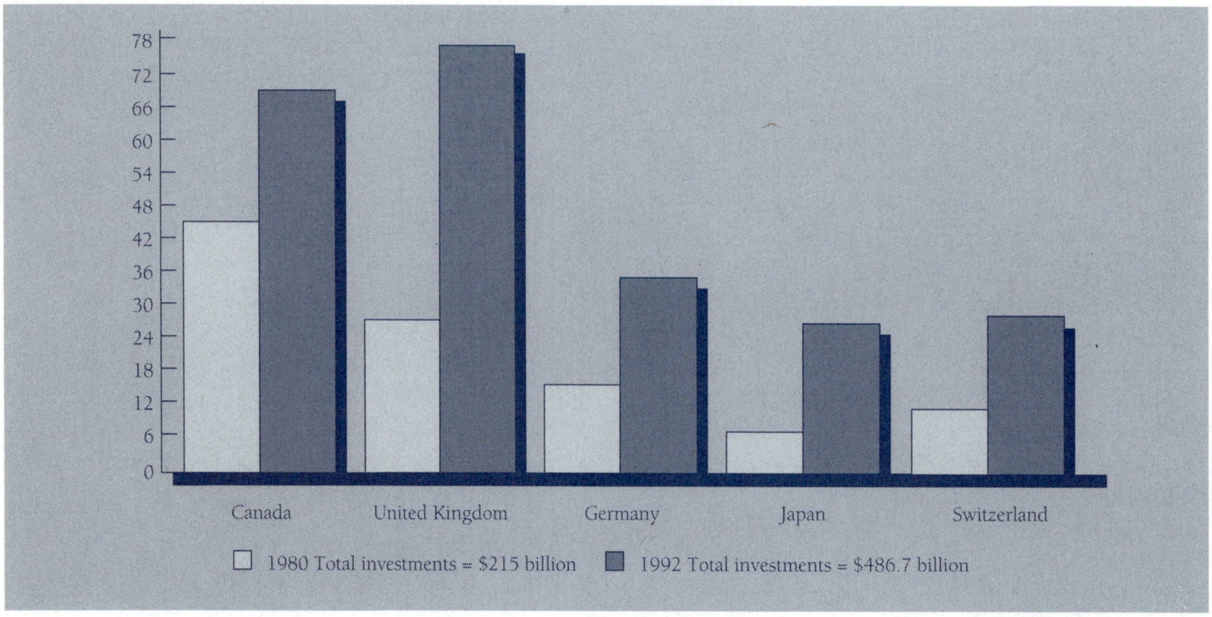

Source: *Statistical Abstract of the United States, 1994* (Washington, D.C.: U.S. Government Printing Office, 1994), U.S. Department of Commerce, Bureau of the Census, p. 797.

In the Middle East and in countries such as Malaysia and Indonesia, one must be cognizant of the influences of the Islamic religion on the legal system. The Islamic sources of law affect both the substantive and procedural laws in many countries. To complicate matters, many rules are unpublished customs. For example, foreign firms sometimes have difficulty in competing in Japan because the rules on how to comply with governmental requirements may not be in writing, or they are written in general terms and their interpretation by officials is known only to local firms. Just as the foreign investor in the United States is faced with a new and complex legal environment when doing business here, the legal environment in other countries will differ from that to which U.S. businesses are accustomed.

National, Regional, and International Laws

When a firm engages in international business, its activities are regulated by national, regional, and international laws. The dominant source of the laws that affect international business is national law.

bilateral treaty
An agreement between two nations that is generally given national and international effect.

National Laws The laws of different countries often have conflicting aims. Countries frequently regulate overlapping aspects of business transactions. Some countries seek to resolve conflicting rules by entering into **bilateral treaties**, agreements between two countries that generally have both national and international effect. Typically, bilateral treaties govern the conditions under which firms from other countries are permitted to do business in the host country and the taxation of income derived in one country and remitted to an affiliate firm in the other country. These and

FIGURE 3-4 European Union Members

other relevant treaties are an important source of law that should be consulted before transacting international business.

Absent treaty provisions resolving conflicts between different national laws, a business should assume that a transaction could be subject to the law of more than one nation. In some situations, the laws of a nation can regulate activities or transactions occurring outside its geographic boundaries. (These extraterritorial laws are discussed in a subsequent section of the chapter.) In such situations, a business must seek to comply both with the law of the nation where the transaction occurs and with the national law that is given extraterritorial effect.

Regional Laws The regional coordination of policies by different nations is a fairly recent development affecting the conduct of international business. Regional organizations provide a larger framework for the regulation of business activities than do individual nations. They are more cohesive, though smaller, groups of nations than the groups found in international organizations. Regional organizations take a variety of forms.

Some nations cooperate for rather limited and specific purposes. For example, the member nations of the Organization of Petroleum Exporting Countries (OPEC) cooperate in seeking to stabilize the price at which oil is sold. Many of those nations have very limited activities with one another in other international business matters. The members of the ASEAN nations seek to promote trade among their countries even though substantial differences exist as to how best to accomplish that goal.

Other regional groupings seek to harmonize parts of their national legal system. While the North American Free Trade Agreement (NAFTA) aims at removing all tariffs among the countries of Canada, Mexico, and the United States, it also includes important legal guarantees for investment in the area by any of the region's firms. NAFTA also establishes a variety of panels to be used to resolve disputes among members. There are panels for disputes regarding financial services and for special labor and environmental problems. These dispute resolution techniques use panels of experts from the member countries rather than existing legal institutions of any of the countries. For example (subject to several minor exceptions), if a business firm from Canada has a dispute with the government of Mexico regarding its investment in Mexico, the Canadian firm has the right to submit the dispute to a three-person arbitration panel whose decision will be binding on both the investor and on the Mexican government.

The European Union (EU) is the most important of the world's regional organizations. Its role as a lawmaker affecting international activities is discussed later in the chapter.

International Law In some cases, the nations of the world have given law-making powers to international organizations. For example, such organizations as the International Monetary Fund, the World Trade Organization, and the World Bank sometimes have significant effects on the international legal environment. Recent international conferences about the law of the sea, environmental problems, trade barriers, and monetary matters provide examples of the continuing development of new international laws that affect business activities.

National Law and Legal Systems

The national law of the country in which a firm is doing business usually has a greater impact on the firm's activities than do any other types of law. The laws of most countries, despite much variation, can be classified as belonging to one of three major legal systems. The socialistic legal system is no longer considered significant for international business activities because it has been discarded in recent years by many of the countries that once followed it.

Major Legal Systems

1. Civil law or code law system, as in France.
2. Common law legal system, as in the United States.
3. Islamic legal system, as in Pakistan.

Despite the variety of legal systems found among the countries of the world, the recognized legal sources within most countries are customs, judicial practices, and legislation. Significant differences, however, lie in how each legal system uses these sources of law. For example, judicial decisions are recognized as a primary source of law in a nation with a common law legal system. In such countries, courts may interpret legislative acts and declare them void if they conflict with the nation's constitution. By contrast, civil law or code law legal systems give a more limited role to courts. For example, because in France only laws derived directly from the *Code Civil* are considered primary sources of law, French court decisions have a lower status than legislative enactments as a source of law. Conversely, the administrative or governmental interpretation of the Code has greater importance.

There are also important differences in the application of substantive laws. For example, even though contract laws occupy an important role for individuals and business firms in many countries, the details of a particular contract may differ significantly. In the United States, a contract is apt to include language for every contingency. The approach of businesspeople and their lawyers is to use the contract as the written expression of everything the parties have agreed to do. If the parties did not include something in the contract, the law assumes they intentionally omitted possible terms.

By contrast, in Germany, contracts do not need to include all the terms on which the parties agree. If there are standard practices and ways of conducting business in a certain industry, the parties are expected to know and abide by those practices; reference to them is not found in a contract. Still further, in Japan, the parties undertaking the same type of business activity might not even make a written contract. If a contract is prepared, it likely will be less extensive than its counterpart in either the United States or in Germany. In Japan, if conditions assumed by the contract do change, the parties will expect to renegotiate the contract, regardless of what the contract provides. The contract terms are regarded as less important than is the relationship between the parties. Consequently, each party expects that the other will accommodate needed changes so as to allow the other party to profit from and to continue the relationship.

Legal institutions also have varying degrees of independence and authority in different countries. Even where the letter of the law seems to be similar, its interpretations, application, and enforceability can differ greatly. For example, the dozens of countries that have a legal system based at least in part on Islamic law differ in their interpretations of the Shari'a and Koran. Similarly, while Japan's legal system is modeled on Germany's and France's civil law legal system, cultural factors influencing legal processes differ significantly. In Japan, the role of the state and legal institutions to officially intervene and enforce practices and policies is remarkably weak. As a consequence, there is greater dependence on rather pervasive and powerful extralegal and informal means of enforcing social control, and less on legal institutions and officials, than is true in either Germany or France.

Extraterritoriality of National Laws

extraterritorial law The law of one nation that seeks to regulate activities or conduct outside its geographic border because of the consequences occurring within its territory.

A conflict may occur between national laws if attempts are made to extend the effects of one country's law beyond that country's boundaries, thereby creating **extraterritorial law.** For example, both the U.S. income tax and antitrust laws have extraterritorial application. If a U.S. corporation derives income from export sales to Germany, license royalties from Brazil, or dividends from a Japanese subsidiary, all of these sources of income are subject to the U.S. income tax. There may be double taxation of such income because the country where the income is earned, the country of source, generally seeks to tax income earned within its boundaries. However, credit provisions in the U.S. tax laws and bilateral treaty agreements between the United States and many other countries often reduce or even eliminate this potential double taxation.

Another example of an extraterritorial law is the Sherman Act, the keystone of U.S. antitrust law, discussed in Chapter 15.

Extraterritorial Language of the Sherman Antitrust Act

> Every contract, combination or conspiracy in restraint of trade or commerce . . . with foreign nations is declared to be illegal.

In 1945, Judge Learned Hand made it clear that the Sherman Act applied to restrictive practices of non-U.S. firms acting abroad if their practices were intended to affect and did affect imports into the United States:

> It is settled law . . . that any state may impose liabilities, even upon persons not within its allegiance for conduct outside its borders which the state reprehends.

How does a U.S. court determine whether U.S. antitrust laws should apply to a restrictive agreement occurring outside the borders of the United States that could affect U.S. commerce? The following case discusses the possible extraterritorial application of a U.S. law.

Timberlane Lumber Co. v. Bank of America

749 F.2d 1378 (1984)
Court of Appeals, Second Circuit

Timberlane Lumber Company, a U.S. firm that purchased and distributed lumber in the United States, formed a partnership with two Honduran corporations to develop alternative sources of lumber for delivery to the United States from Honduras. Timberlane eventually purchased an interest in an existing but financially unstable Honduras lumber mill owned by the Lima family. Before the Timberlane purchase, a part of the ownership of the mill had been transferred to Bank of America. Bank of America refused to sell its interest in the mill to Timberlane.

Timberlane asserted that Bank of America refused to sell its share in the Lima mill because it wanted to protect its interests in competing lumber mills by driving Timberlane out of the Honduran lumber market. As such action by the Bank of America could restrict competition in the United States lumber business in violation of U.S. antitrust laws, Timberlane sued Bank of America in federal court.

The district court dismissed the action, but on appeal, in the case referred to as Timberlane I, the court of appeals set aside the district court's holding and announced a three-part test for determining whether the United States would assert federal jurisdiction over claims alleging illegal antitrust behavior outside the United States. On remand, the district court again dismissed the antitrust claim of Timberlane, which again appealed.

Sneed, Judge

Timberlane I's test undertakes three separate inquiries: (1) the effect or intended effect on the foreign commerce of the United States; (2) the type or magnitude of the alleged illegal behavior; and (3) the appropriateness of exercising extraterritorial jurisdiction in light of considerations of international comity and fairness.

The district court applied Timberlane's analysis and concluded that jurisdiction should not be exercised in this case. Although we agree with the district court's conclusion, we do not expressly approve all of its analysis. Therefore, we discuss each part of the inquiry as set forth in Timberlane I.

1. "Does the alleged restraint affect, or was it intended to affect, the foreign commerce of the United States?"

The first part of Timberlane I's analysis requires "that there be some effect—actual or intended—on American foreign commerce before the federal courts may legitimately exercise subject matter jurisdiction under [the antitrust] statutes." On appeal, Bank of America does not deny that Timberlane has met this requirement. "[B]y alleging the ability and willingness to supply cognizable markets with lumber that they allege would have been competitive with that already in the marketplace, they have satisfied this prong of the circuit's test."

2. "Is it of such a type and magnitude so as to be cognizable as a violation of the Sherman Act?"

The only issue under the second part of the inquiry is whether the magnitude of the effect identified in the first part of the test rises to the level of a civil antitrust violation, i.e., conduct that has a direct and substantial anticompetitive effect. In this case Timberlane alleges that Bank of America conspired with its Honduran subsidiaries to prevent Timberlane from milling lumber in Honduras and exporting it to the United States. Our review of the complaint reveals that Timberlane has alleged an injury that would state a claim under the antitrust laws against Bank of America. Thus, it satisfies the second part of the analysis.

3. "As a matter of international comity and fairness, should the extraterritorial jurisdiction of the United States be asserted to cover it?"

Under the third part of Timberlane I's analysis, the district court must determine "whether the interests of, and links to, the United States—including the magnitude of the effect on American foreign commerce—are sufficiently strong, vis-à-vis those of other nations, to justify an assertion of extraterritorial authority." This determination requires that a district court consider seven factors. This district court here found that the undisputed facts required that jurisdiction not be exercised in this case. We agree. To support our conclusion each factor will be examined.

a. "The degree of conflict with foreign law or policy."

We must determine whether the extraterritorial enforcement of United States antitrust laws creates an actual or potential conflict with the laws and policies of other nations.

Although Honduras does not have antitrust laws as such, it does have definite policies concerning the character of its commercial climate. To promote economic development and efficiency within its relatively undeveloped economy, the Honduran Constitution and Commercial Code guarantee freedom of action. The Code specifically condemns any laws prohibiting agreements (even among competitors) to restrict or divide commercial activity. On balance, we believe that the enforcement of United States antitrust laws in this case would lead to a significant conflict with Honduran law and policy. This conflict, unless outweighed by other factors in the comity analysis, is itself a sufficient reason to decline the exercise of jurisdiction over this dispute.

b. "The nationality or allegiance of the parties and the locations of principal places of business of corporations."

Next we should consider the citizenship of the parties and witnesses involved in the alleged illegal conduct. In this case, with only one exception, all of the named parties are United States citizens or nationals. But it is also true that "[a]ll of the crucial witnesses to the incidents were either Honduran citizens or residents." We believe, therefore, that the citizenship of the parties weighs slightly in favor of the exercise of jurisdiction.

c. "The extent to which enforcement by either state can be expected to achieve compliance."

The weighing of this factor yields no clear answer. Of course, any judgment against Bank of America could easily be enforced in a United States court. Whether such a judgment could be enforced as easily in Honduras is less certain. We believe that the enforcement factor tips slightly in favor of the assertion of jurisdiction.

d. "The relative significance of effects on the United States as compared with those elsewhere."

A more definitive answer emerges when we compare the effect of the alleged illegal conduct on the foreign commerce of the United States with its effect abroad. The insignificance of the effect on the foreign commerce of the United States when compared with the substantial effect on Honduras suggests federal jurisdiction should not be exercised. . . . (T)he relative significance of effects in this case weighs strongly against the exercise of jurisdiction.

e. "The extent to which there is explicit purpose to harm or affect American commerce."

Timberlane has not demonstrated that Bank of America had any particular interest in affecting United States commerce.

f. "The foreseeability of such effect."

Aside from the fact that American commerce has not been substantially affected, Timberlane has not shown that Bank of America should have foreseen the consequences of its actions. We do not believe that a reasonable investor would have foreseen the minimal effect that has occurred here. This weighs against the exercise of jurisdiction.

g. "The relative importance to the violations charged of conduct within the United States as compared with conduct abroad."

Finally, a court should consider the location of the alleged illegal conduct in order to assess the appropriateness of the exercise of extraterritorial jurisdiction. In this case both parties agree that virtually all of the illegal activity occurred in Honduras. This factor clearly weighs against the exercise of jurisdiction.

h. Resolving the Seven Factor Test.

It follows that all but two of the factors in Timberlane I's comity analysis indicate that we should refuse to exercise jurisdiction over this antitrust case. The potential for conflict with Honduran economic policy and commercial law is great. The effect on the foreign commerce of the United States is minimal. The evidence of intent to harm American commerce is altogether lacking. The foreseeability of the anticompetitive consequences of the allegedly illegal sections is slight. Most of the conduct that must be examined occurred abroad. The factors that favor jurisdiction are the citizenship of the parties and, to a slight extent, the enforcement effectiveness of United States law. We do not believe that this is enough to justify the exercise of federal jurisdiction over this case.

Affirmed.

Case Questions

1. What is the assumption behind the court's use of the three-part test in determining whether to exercise jurisdiction? Why doesn't it hear every case in which it has jurisdiction instead of deciding by the use of these factors not to hear a case even though it could do so?

2. How many of the seven factors reviewed by the court do you think would have to favor exercising jurisdiction for it to agree to review Timberlane's claim?

sovereign immunity doctrine International law principle. Courts of one state do not have jurisdiction to determine cases against another sovereign state; there is a recognized exception for

National Laws and Foreign Governments

In the United States, international business activities are conducted primarily by private corporations. In some other countries, international business activities are conducted primarily by governments or by corporations that governments own and manage. If contracts between private business firms and governmental organizations arise, two legal concepts may affect the resolution of subsequent disputes. One of the concepts, the **sovereign immunity doctrine,** which holds that the courts of one country have no jurisdiction to resolve suits brought against another state, is based in international law and is accepted, in one form or another, by practically all countries. The other concept is **the act of state doctrine.** This concept originated in the Supreme Court of the United States and serves as a guide to the determination of whether the judiciary, rather than the executive or legislative branch of government, should seek to resolve certain legal problems.

In the following case, both the sovereign immunity and the act of state doctrines are considered in a suit against sovereign foreign countries, even though their actions may be contrary to U.S. interests.

commercial activities of a sovereign state.

the act of state doctrine Established by the U.S. Supreme Court. U.S. courts will not judge legality of a politically sensitive act of a foreign court; will defer to other branches of the U.S. government.

Intern. Ass'n of Machinists v. OPEC

649 F.2d 1354 (1981)
Court of Appeals, Ninth Circuit

The members of the International Association of Machinists and Aerospace Workers (IAM) were disturbed by the high price of petroleum and petroleum-derived products in the United States. They believed that price-fixing by the Organization of Petroleum Exporting Countries (OPEC) caused this burden on the American public. Accordingly, IAM sued OPEC and its member nations in December 1978, alleging that their price-setting activities violated U.S. antitrust laws. The district court ruled in favor of the defendants, holding that it lacked jurisdiction and that IAM had no valid antitrust claim; the IAM appealed to the court of appeals.

Choy, Circuit Judge

IAM is a nonprofit labor association. Its members work in petroleum-using industries, and like most Americans, they are consumers of gasoline and other petroleum-derived products. They object to the high and rising cost of such products.

OPEC is an organization of the petroleum-producing and exporting nations. . . . The OPEC nations have organized to obtain the greatest possible economic returns for a special resource which they hope will remove them from the ranks of the underdeveloped and the poverty-plagued. OPEC was formed in 1960 by the defendants Iran, Kuwait, Saudi Arabia, and Venezuela. The other defendants, Algeria, Ecuador, Gabon, Indonesia, Libya, Nigeria, Qatar, and the United Arab Emirates, joined thereafter.

OPEC achieves its goals by a system of production limits and royalties which its members unanimously adopt. After formation of OPEC, it is alleged, the price of crude oil increased tenfold and more. Whether or not a causal relation exists, there is no doubt that the price of oil has risen dramatically in recent years, and that this has become of international concern.

Supporters of OPEC argue that its actions result in fair world prices for oil and allow OPEC members to achieve a measure of economic and political independence. Without OPEC, they say, in the rush to the marketplace these nations would rapidly deplete their only valuable resource for ridiculously low prices. Detractors accuse OPEC of price-fixing and worse in its deliberate manipulation of the world market and withholding of a resource which many world citizens have not learned to do without.

In the international sphere each state is viewed as an independent sovereign, equal in sovereignty to all other states. It is said that an equal holds no power of sovereignty over an equal. Thus the doctrine of sovereign immunity; the courts of one state generally have no jurisdiction to entertain suits against another state. This rule of international law developed by custom among nations. Also by custom, an exception developed for the commercial activities of a state. The former concept of absolute sovereign immunity gave way to a restrictive view. Under the restrictive theory, immunity did not exist for commercial activities since they were seen as non-sovereign.

In 1976, Congress enacted the FSIA [Foreign Sovereignty Immunity Act] and declared that the federal courts will apply an objective nature-of-the-act test in determining whether activity is commercial and thus not immune: "The commercial character of an activity shall be determined by reference to the nature of the course of conduct or particular transaction or act rather than by reference to its purposes." The trial judge reasoned that, according to international law, the development and control of natural resources is a prime governmental function. The opinion cites several resolutions of the United Nations' General Assembly, which the United States supported, and the United States Constitution, which treat the control of natural resources as governmental acts. While we do not apply the doctrine of sovereign immunity, its elements remain relevant to our discussion of the act of state doctrine.

The act of state doctrine declares that a United States court will not adjudicate a politically sensitive dispute which would require the court to judge the legality of the sovereign act of a foreign state. This doctrine was expressed by the Supreme Court in *Underhill v. Hernandez* (1897):

> Every sovereign State is bound to respect the independence of every other sovereign State, and the courts of one country will not sit in judgment on the acts of the government of another done within its own territory.

The doctrine recognizes the institutional limitations of the courts and the peculiar requirements of successful foreign relations. To participate adeptly in the global community, the United States must speak with one voice and pursue a careful and deliberate foreign policy. The political branches of our government are able to consider the competing economic and political considerations and respond to the public will in order to carry on foreign relations in accordance with the best interests of the country as a whole. The courts, in contrast, focus on single disputes and make decisions on the basis of legal principles.

When the courts engage in piecemeal adjudication of the legality of the sovereign acts of states, they risk disruptions of our country's international diplomacy. The principle of separation of powers is central to our form of democratic government. Just as the courts have carefully guarded their primary role as interpreters of the Constitution and the laws of the United States, so have they recognized the primary role of the President and Congress in resolution of political conflict and the adoption of foreign policy.

The doctrine of sovereign immunity is similar to the act of state doctrine in that it also represents the need to respect the sovereignty of foreign states. The two doctrines differ, however, in significant respects. The law of sovereign immunity goes to the jurisdiction of the court. The act of state doctrine is not jurisdictional. Rather, it is a prudential doctrine designed to avoid judicial action in sensitive areas. Sovereign immunity is a principle of international law, recognized in the United States by statute. It is the states themselves, as defendants, who may claim sovereign immunity.

The act of state doctrine is a domestic legal principle, arising from the peculiar role of American courts. It recognizes not only the sovereignty of foreign states, but also the spheres of power of the co-equal branches of our government. Thus a private litigant may raise the act of state doctrine, even when no sovereign state is a party to the action. The act of state doctrine is not diluted by the commercial activity exception which limits the doctrine of sovereign immunity. While purely commercial activity may not rise to the level of an act of state, certain seemingly commercial activity will trigger act of state considerations.

The decision to deny access to judicial relief is not one we make lightly. There is no question that the availability of oil has become a significant factor in international relations. It is clear that OPEC and its activities are carefully considered in the formulation of American foreign policy. The remedy IAM seeks is an injunction against the OPEC nations. The possibility of insult of the OPEC states and of interference with the efforts of the political branches to seek favorable relations with them is apparent from the very nature of this action and the remedy sought.

A further consideration is the availability of internationally accepted legal principles which would render the issues appropriate for judicial disposition. While conspiracies in restraint of trade are clearly illegal under domestic law, the record reveals no international consensus condemning cartels, royalties, and production agreements. We are reluctant to allow judicial interference in an area so void of international consensus. The act of state doctrine is applicable in this case. The courts should not enter at the will of litigants into a delicate area of foreign policy which the executive and legislative branches have chosen to approach with restraint. The decision of the district court dismissing this action is affirmed.

Case Questions

1. Did the court find that OPEC's sovereign immunity prevented it from deciding this case?

2. Would the court reach the same conclusion if the OPEC governments had conducted their oil sales through private corporations that they owned instead of through governmental agencies?

3. Compare and contrast the sovereign immunity doctrine with the act of state doctrine.

International Trade

International organizations such as the International Monetary Fund (IMF), the World Trade Organization (WTO), and the World Bank (WB) make rules that affect both investment and trade. Bilateral treaties, such as agreements aimed at eliminating double taxation on firms in one country that do business in the other country, and multilateral treaties, such as the Law of the Sea Convention, are both national and international sources of law.

Since multilateral negotiations under the former GATT organization removed many of the tariff barriers to trade, future international trade negotiations are likely to emphasize the removal of nontariff barriers affecting both goods and services. It is likely that China, and other countries in Asia as well as some of the republics in the Commonwealth of Independent States, and several eastern European countries will be among the areas where the greatest increase in trade is experienced. As countries continue to associate in regional organizations and develop free-trade linkages through multilateral treaties, foreign investment will increasingly be subject to regional developments and legal changes, rather than national laws.

The Sale of Goods

Export—the selling of a domestically manufactured product or a service to a foreign purchaser—is the most common and least complex method of conducting international business. The manufacturer or seller is the exporter; the purchaser is the importer.

All commerce and trade requires a stable legal environment. Special laws and customs known as **law merchant** govern the sale and movement of goods. These laws spread through England and other countries centuries ago, and they remain in effect today. In recent years, the international community has agreed on a common body of international sales laws, the United Nations Convention on the International Sale of Goods (UNCISG). This convention, discussed in detail in the treatment of Commercial Law in Chapter 10, was drafted by representatives from countries with common law, civil law, and socialist legal systems, and embodies principles from each. This treaty has been adopted by over two dozen countries, including the United States, and is being reviewed in many others. The UNCISG applies to contracts for the commercial sale of goods between parties whose places of business are in different nations that have agreed to the terms of the convention.

export
The selling of a domestically produced good or service to a foreign purchaser.

law merchant
The law governing the sale of goods for international traders that was first used in the 17th century and that today forms the foundation for today's international convention on the sale of goods.

Documents Used in International Sales Transactions

The sale of export goods between countries entails risks that differ greatly from those encountered when the sale occurs within national boundaries. The documentary sale has developed to accommodate the needs of both the buyer and the seller in an international sale. The seller doesn't want to release the goods until payment is received from the buyer, and the buyer doesn't want to pay until the goods have arrived and been inspected.

Standardized documents and terms are used to ensure that three objectives are met: (1) each party knows who pays the costs of transporting and insuring the goods while en route to their destination, (2) the buyer will obtain good title to the goods when they are received, and (3) the seller is sure that payment will be made when the title for the contracted goods is transferred.

Transportation Terms The terms under which goods will be transported must be agreed to by the parties. Transportation terms are a part of most sales contracts, whether the sales occur domestically or internationally. In international transactions, the costs, insurance, and freight expenses for sending goods **(CIF)** are generally quoted as one price to the buyer. For example, if a Chicago seller agrees to deliver chairs to a buyer in Paris, the seller will determine the costs of the goods, the insurance needed while they are in transit, and the shipping or freight charges and give the total price to the buyer for the goods CIF to Paris.

In some cases, the contract will call for the seller to ship the goods to a certain spot, beyond which the buyer must pay for their transport to the ultimate destination. For example, if the contract prices the chairs free on board **(FOB)** to Chicago, the seller will deliver the goods free to a common carrier who will then load the goods (onto a truck, railroad, airplane, etc.) in Chicago, and the French buyer must then pay for the freight and insurance costs to transport them from there to Paris.

There are other alternatives for shipping goods from one country to another. The **C & F** contract requires the seller to prepay the freight expenses, but the buyer pays the costs of insurance while goods are in transit. Under an **FAS** contract, the seller places the goods free alongside ships, or a specific ship, in a port, and the buyer assumes the risk of loss and pays all freight charges for loading them onto the ship and transporting them from that point to their ultimate destination.

The Bill of Lading A second objective is to ensure that the buyer obtains good title to the goods. A **bill of lading** is a contract between a common carrier (shipper, airline, etc.) and the firm or person shipping the goods. It describes the terms agreed to regarding the transport and delivery of the goods and acts as a receipt for the goods by the carrier. The bill of lading is also document of title that permits the owner of the goods to transfer them even though the goods are not in the owner's possession.

The bill of lading document has two forms. Under a straight bill of lading, the carrier must deliver the goods only to the person named in the bill of lading. The straight bill of lading does not represent a transferable title to the goods. However, if a negotiable bill of lading is used, title to the goods may be transferred by the owner if he or she endorses it to another party such as a bank or the buyer of the goods. The goods themselves do not have to be delivered to transfer ownership; a negotiation of the bill of lading document transfers title to the goods. Thus, if goods are in transit on a ship or in a truck covering long distances, the title to the goods may be transferred numerous times. For example, the ownership of oil in tankers leaving the Persian Gulf may be transferred more than a dozen times before the oil reaches its ultimate destination.

CIF
The term standing for costs, insurance, and freight, which are totaled together in determining the price of goods for foreign buyers; the CIF term is the most common transportation term used in international sales.

FOB
The term stands for free on board, which describes an international seller's obligation to deliver the goods for a stated cost on board a common carrier (ship, truck, etc.) at a named destination; thereafter, any further transportation or insurance is to be paid by the buyer. The destination may be at the buyer's end (destination) or at the seller's end (shipper).

C & F
The term stands for costs and freight and is a transportation term expressing the seller's obligation to pay these expenses, while the buyer pays any insurance needed to protect the goods.

FAS
The term stands for free alongside and expresses the buyer's obligation to deliver the goods to or alongside a ship, but not to pay to have them loaded onto the ship.

The Letter of Credit A third objective is to make sure the seller is paid when the title to the goods is transferred. A **letter of credit** is used to reduce the risk of nonpayment. The bank guarantees payment when it issues a confirming letter of credit while it only reviews sales and transportation documents when it issues an advising letter of credit. Most common is a transaction in which the buyer contracts with a bank to pay for the goods being sent by the seller. The seller, who may not be ready to offer credit terms to an unknown buyer in a foreign country, will insist on a letter of credit. Thus, a bank's credit is substituted for that of the buyer. For example, the buyer's bank issues a letter of credit and agrees with the buyer to pay the seller, provided that the seller gives it certain documents, primarily the bill of lading, within a specified time. The use of letters of credit is discussed in greater detail in Chapter 10.

bill of lading
The document that represents both a receipt for goods being transported and a title to the goods; if it is negotiable, the goods can be delivered to whomever has the document.

letter of credit
A bank document indicating the bank will pay for goods if the seller submits the prescribed documents to the bank; if the bank issues an advising rather than a confirming letter of credit, the bank will review the documents but will not guarantee payment.

Laws Affecting Exports

Laws may encourage or discourage exports. Laws may discourage the export of products that are scarce in the exporting country. For example, U.S. export quotas have been imposed on wheat and soybeans during crop shortages. Laws may also discourage exports out of concern over their possible misuse by the importer. For example, the United States restricts the export of military equipment and technologically advanced computer hardware because these may have adverse military uses.

Despite these concerns, laws usually encourage exports because the penetration of foreign markets by domestic producers helps a country's balance of trade. Governmental assistance and tax benefits are among the most common methods used to encourage exports.

License Regulations for Exports

Businesses should investigate the domestic laws of their home country to be certain that the goods in question may be freely exported. Laws may require prior approval before particular goods are allowed to leave the country. Such laws generally prohibit the export of these goods to any country. However, certain export controls target specific countries. For example, U.S. computer parts may be freely exportable to many countries but not to Iraq.

Governmental Assistance for Exports

Numerous governmental programs assist exporters. In addition to providing exporters with tax assistance, discussed more fully in the following section, governments frequently provide them with a great deal of valuable information. Publications of the U.S. Department of Commerce, for example, assist potential exporters in identifying countries and firms that seek certain products. The Department of Commerce also assists U.S. exporters in contacting foreign representatives. In addition, the department sponsors exhibits and trade shows in U.S.-owned trade centers throughout the world. Many U.S. firms participate in these events to facilitate meetings with foreign businesspeople who are interested in U.S. products.

The Export Trading Company Act of 1982 also assists exporters. This act assures U.S. firms that their export activities are not illegal under U.S. antitrust laws. A firm must first file information regarding its export activities. If the firm meets certain conditions, it will be immune from antitrust prosecution by the U.S. government. The Export Trading Company Act also permits U.S. banks to invest capital and make loans to trading companies that seek to export U.S. goods and services. The intent of the law is to encourage the formation of such companies that provide information on export opportunities and provide trading services to small firms that may find it expensive and difficult to do on their own. Trading companies are common in Japan and in several other Asian countries.

Several U.S. governmental organizations make financial assistance available to exporters. The Export-Import Bank (EX-IM) offers medium- and long-term loans and credit guarantees. Loans are made directly to exporters as well as to commercial banks that relend them to exporters.

Tax Assistance for Exporters

Exports are generally encouraged because they provide jobs and revenue for the economy. Special programs often give tax assistance to exporters. For example, the turnover or value-added tax (VAT) levied in many European countries is often refunded to the seller if the goods are sold for export. Thus, the cost of goods purchased in these countries will be less for the foreign buyer than for the local buyer (as long as the rebate of the tax is passed along to the ultimate purchaser). In the United States, the Foreign Sales Corporation Act of 1984 exempts from U.S. tax approximately 5 percent of the income of foreign sales corporations. Thus, a corporation that has $100,000 of income from its foreign sales will pay income tax on approximately $95,000 instead of $100,000. A foreign sales corporation (FSC) must be located outside the United States in a country with a tax information exchange agreement. Most of the income of the FSC must be derived from qualified export transactions.

Laws Affecting Imports

Legal controls are often imposed on products by both the importing country and the exporting country. Importing countries may want to protect domestic products from competition with foreign products. Some importing countries may simply lack the capital necessary to pay for imports.

Legal restrictions against imports range from prohibitions declaring that certain products cannot be imported, to quotas limiting the number of products imported, to tariffs taxing imported products, to various forms of discrimination against foreign goods or in favor of domestic goods. Although each nation may adopt its own import policy, a nation's commitment to international trade agreements, such as the World Trade Organization (WTO), limits the restrictions it may impose.

Prohibitions on Imports

prohibition
A prohibition totally restricts imports into a country.

A **prohibition** totally restricts the import of a product. For example, in the United States, the Trading with the Enemy Act grants the president the power to restrict all imports from countries considered enemies of the United States. Thus, there may be a prohibition on all or some products from Libya or Cuba into the United States. Other U.S. laws restrict the import of products, such as certain firearms, narcotics, and certain perishable commodities, regardless of their country of origin. Brazil prohibits the import of small computers and light passenger airplanes, and Taiwan keeps out chemicals used in making drugs if those chemicals can be produced domestically.

Quotas on Imports

A **quota** limits the quantity of a product that may be imported. Thus, it is less restrictive than an outright prohibition but more restrictive than merely taxing the product. While the rules of the WTO prohibit certain quotas, some significant exceptions to the ban on quotas exist. Quotas, which are widely regarded as an effective form of restricting imports, are frequently disguised as "voluntary" agreements between trading partners. The EU has pressured Japan to limit its shipments of quartz watches, stereo equipment, and computer-controlled machine tools. The United States has obtained similar promises from Japan to limit its auto exports and from European and South American countries to limit their exports of steel.

quota
A quota limits the number of specified goods that may enter a country.

Tariffs

A **tariff** is a tax on an imported product. Tariffs are invariably discriminatory because domestic products are not subject to the same taxes. Usually, tariffs are levied to protect infant industries from the better-developed industries of foreign countries. An *ad valorem tariff* is levied on a value basis (the tariff represents a percentage of the value or price of the item imported), while a *flat rate tariff* is levied on each unit imported (such as a barrel of oil, a foot or meter of pipe, or a kilogram of nails).

tariff
A tax on imported goods; the tax may be based on the value of the goods (ad valorem) or simply be levied on goods of a certain type (flat rate).

Other Duties

In addition to tariffs, two other duties may be imposed on imports that are regarded as unfairly traded goods. **Antidumping duties** are used when goods are *dumped* or sold in the importing country at a price lower than that in their home market. Rules of the WTO permit an importing nation to impose an antidumping duty that is equal to the difference between the sales price of the imported product and the price of a comparable product in the home market.

antidumping duties
Antidumping duties are levied when imported goods are sold in a foreign market at a price lower than in their principle market.

In the United States, the International Trade Administration first determines that foreign merchandise is being sold in the United States at less than fair value (LTFV). Then, the International Trade Commission determines whether a domestic industry is materially injured or is threatened with a material injury. The International Trade Commission's determinations may be appealed to the federal Court of International Trade, which in turn can be reviewed by a federal court of appeals.

Countervailing duties are assessed to counteract foreign subsidies of imported products that materially injure competing domestic products. The foreign subsidy may be in the form of tax rebates, favorable financing terms, or other special governmental assistance. Under international agreement, where it can be proved that a subsidy causes or threatens to cause material injury to a domestic industry, countervailing duties may be levied as long as they do not exceed the amount of the subsidy. In the United States, if the subsidy is granted by a country with which the United States does not have an international trade agreement, countervailing duties can be imposed whether or not a U.S. firm is injured by the subsidy.

countervailing duties
A countervailing duty is imposed by an importing country to counteract a subsidy for certain goods from the exporting country.

Nontariff Barriers

nontariff barrier
Any governmental restriction that discriminates against imports or favors exports is a nontariff barrier.

Any governmental regulation that discriminates against imports or in favor of exports is a **nontariff barrier.** It is difficult to list all of the major types of nontariff barriers, but they include prohibitions, quotas, import licensing controls, foreign exchange controls, import fees, financial deposit requirements for imported producers, and duplicative or unnecessary product testing and certification requirements.

Nontariff barriers can be classified into nontariff barriers effective upon entry (barriers that affect goods as they come into a country) and nontariff barriers effective subsequent to entry (programs, practices, and policies of an importing country that discriminate against imported goods already in the country).

Nontariff Barriers Effective upon Entry Import licensing controls require importers to obtain a governmental license to import products. The license may require payment of a fee, completion of extensive documentation regarding the products and their manufacturing firms, or approval by regulatory agencies. An import license may be available only if a business has certain export "credits" with which to purchase the imported products. In some Central American countries, import licenses often take months to process, and chosen officials are given complete discretion to approve such licenses. Standards, procedures, and guidelines for determining an official verdict may be unknown or nonexistent; and given the absence of such criteria, court appeals may be pointless.

Nontariff Barriers Effective Subsequent to Entry Nontariff barriers effective subsequent to entry include governmental procurement policies, internal tax policies, subsidy programs, and other practices giving domestic industries an advantage. For example, the "Buy America" Act prohibits the purchase of foreign goods by federal agencies if domestic equivalents are available at comparable prices or if national security interests are involved.

The United States requires all imported items to carry a marking that identifies their *country of origin.* This requirement is intended to ensure that the American consumer knows that such items were produced in foreign countries. No import that lacks a marking of this kind is permitted, so this nontariff barrier is effective upon entry. Since marking all imports with he country of origin gives American consumers the choice of selecting American-made alternatives, the marking requirement is also a nontariff barrier effective subsequent to entry.

LICENSES

license
A license is a certificate or document that permits a licensee to make use of the licensor's property.

In addition to exporting, another method of conducting international trade uses licensing agreements. A **license** is a certificate or document that gives the licensee permission to produce or distribute the licensor's product under the licensor's name. For example, a patent license is a written authorization to make or use the patented article for a limited time in a designated territory.

Terms of a Licensing Agreement

A license agreement generally contains the grant of a license from the licensor, details the conditions of its uses, establishes other assistance that the licensor may provide to the licensee, fixes the compensation payable to the licensor, determines the governing law, and establishes methods for resolving disputes.

Scope of the License The grant of the licensee usually states the nature of the license being granted and expresses limitations on its use by the licensee. For example, confidentiality requirements are usually imposed on the licensee, particularly where trade secrets, rather than patents, are being licensed. The licensor will try to require confidentiality over a long period of time, whereas the licensee will seek a shorter period. In addition, both parties will be concerned about how to treat new technologies that are developed under the agreement. The licensor will seek the right to use any new related "know-how" that the licensee develops. The licensee will want to ensure that updated information and improvements developed by the licensor are transferred so that the licensee can maintain its competitive position.

Manufacturing and marketing limitations may also be imposed on a licensee. For example, a licensee may be allowed to manufacture or sell products only in certain locations. Permitted use limitations may restrict the applications for which licensed technology may be used. For example, licensed plastics manufacturing technology might be allowed to be used for cups, boxes, and other containers, but not for automotive products.

Assistance Provided In addition to granting the license, the licensor may also agree to provide training assistance, marketing programs, or manufacturing guidance. Training of personnel may be more necessary at the beginning of the licensing period, but in some cases periodic review of updated and emerging uses for the technology is also included. Marketing assistance may consist of advertising prepared by the licensor or perhaps a financial contribution to advertising prepared or purchased by the licensee. Manufacturing guidance in laying out the manufacturing or assembly processes may be necessary for some licensed products.

Compensation Terms As compensation for the use of the license, the licensee generally pays a royalty to the licensor. The royalty must be at a rate that allows both the licensee and the licensor to make a fair return on their investment in developing and using the licensed technology. The parties to any license agreement also must determine the frequency of the royalty period and whether royalties are determined on net or gross income, and designate the currency of payment. Some countries restrict the methods used to determine royalties. For example, in India, the government, which must approve all licensing agreements, will not allow the licensor to require a minimum guaranteed royalty to be paid. Instead, royalties must be tied to income earned: if no income is earned, no royalty is due.

Governing Law The determination of the governing law may be difficult. In some situations, the country where the licensee is located will not approve contracts where the law of the licensor's country is selected. In most countries, however, the parties are free to select the governing law, and the courts of each nation will enforce the law selected by the parties. Although each party often prefers its law, the critical question concerning applicable law is whether the governing law effectively recognizes and protects intellectual property. Some countries fail to adequately protect all forms of intellectual property, and others take no steps to discourage piracy of transferred technology. In those situations, a gray market of goods may develop from unlicensed competitors or from third country licensees for goods produced by the appropriate licensee.

Taxation of Licenses

The tax treatment of licensing agreements concerns both the licensor and the licensee. Both the licensor's country and the country in which the licensee manufacturers, uses, or sells the licensed product will probably seek to tax a share of the royalties stipulated in the licensing agreement. In the absence of tax treaties, royalties are usually subject to income tax in the licensee's country, which is the *country of source* for the activity giving rise to royalties. The tax authorities in the country of source generally withhold the tax due from royalty payments that the licensee makes to the licensor. Royalty income is generally taxed a second time in the licensor's country, the *country of origin.*

Tax treaties may either exempt royalty income from taxation in one of the countries or give the licensor credit for income tax paid in the country of source. Generally, if the licensor has a permanent establishment (branch, office, factory, or warehouse) in the country of source, royalty income is taxed only there.

License and the Gray Market

gray-market goods Gray-market goods are goods that are imported into a country without the consent of the trademark holder.

Gray-market goods are products that are imported into a country without the consent of the authorized trademark owner. There are several types of gray-market goods. *Parallel imports* are products imported into one country through an authorized trademark licensee in a second country. For example, if a U.S. manufacturer makes computers and obtains trademark protection for them with an IBM trademark, the manufacturer may license one firm in South Korea and another firm in Japan to sell the IBM computers in their respective countries. However, if a Japanese firm purchases IBM trademarked computers from the Korean licensee, rather from the Japanese licensee, and sells them in Japan, those computers are parallel imports.

A second type of gray-market good is the *reverse import.* Reverse imports are products produced in a second country by a firm that also produces goods in the country where the products from abroad are imported. For example, the Honda automobile firm has its headquarters and primary manufacturing facilities in Japan. However, it also produces Honda automobiles in the United States. When Honda imports cars it makes in the United States into Japan and sells those imports, in competition with its own domestically produced automobiles, the imports are regarded as reverse imports. They are the reverse of the automobiles manufactured in Japan and then exported to the United States.

Finally, there are *illegally trademarked goods.* Even though a manufacturer has no permission from the trademark owner or any authorized licensee, manufacturers do sell goods with what appear to be valid trademarks. Generally, goods that have high brand recognition will face competition from illegally trademarked goods. Watches, perfumes, pharmaceuticals, sporting goods, luggage, and handbags are common gray-market goods. Although sometimes these goods are distributed through normal channels, frequently flea markets or temporary vendors on urban street corners throughout the world seek to pass off their products, at significantly lower prices, as authentic and thus produced according to the trademark owner's specifications.

Gray-market goods present a problem to both the trademark owner and its licensee when the illegal goods, produced outside the country where the trademarked goods are produced, make their way back into that country and compete with the licensor's or licensee's goods. The prices of the gray-market goods undercut the prices of the validly trademarked products, which are made comparatively higher by either the high quality associated with the product or the fluctuation of international currency values. In addition, the producer of gray-market goods does not have to pay the royalties that the licensor uses to recoup its research, developmental, and marketing expenses.

Despite the concerns of the trademark holder, the law regarding gray-market goods is not all one-sided. Consumers and some retailers argue that the gray market allows goods of quality comparable with well-known brands to be purchased at significantly lower prices. U.S. courts have not been decisive in answering gray-market problems. Most foreign jurisdictions allow the entry of gray-market goods. In the EU, the use of intellectual property law provisions and licensing agreements to block trade in gray-market goods has been repeatedly denied by the European Court of Justice.

Ethical Dilemmas and International Business Law

Many ethical questions are raised when a firm does business internationally. Is it ethical for the manufacturer of gray-market goods to knowingly sell them, misleading consumers to believe that the goods are genuine? Is it ethical for a firm to import gray-market goods or for consumers to knowingly buy them?

Should a product that is banned in one country be sold in other countries? This question poses ethical dilemmas when manufacturers are faced with substantial inventories of products that the legal institutions, regulators, or consumers in one country have determined are too dangerous to sell. Should managers take advantage of people in less developed countries who may lack information and awareness of possible hazards associated with products?

Such ethical dilemmas arise for food producers when products do not meet governmental standards in one country; should those products then be sold instead to other countries that have less stringent regulations? Similarly, when products designed for use by parents of infants or by elderly people require careful preparation or mixing of ingredients, will the producers ensure that people in countries wherever the products are sold are properly advised about how to prepare those products?

Environmental concerns also affect the disposal of waste. Is it ethical to contract with governments in poor countries to dispose of trash or toxic waste in those countries? What if the disposing firm has reason to believe that money paid to foreign officials will not be used to protect people from the hazards associated with the product?

Another area that poses ethical dilemmas for firms doing international business concerns the payment of money to foreign officials. Although most countries have laws against bribery, sometimes significant differences exist regarding customary and acceptable practices affecting payments made to officials. A payment made for services performed by a government official may be ethically and legally proper in one country but not in another. Firms engaging in international business must be aware of the legal and ethical standards in the country where the business activity is performed. In the United States, the Foreign Corrupt Practices Act (FCPA), which amends the securities laws, outlaws foreign bribery by all domestic concerns. The FCPA is discussed in greater detail in Chapter 22.

Licenses and International Dispute Resolution

The careful drafting of licensing agreements and other international contracts may eliminate many disputes, but some cannot be avoided. For example, disputes may arise over the method of transferring new production techniques or over the licensee's adherence to required quality standards. To resolve such disputes, the parties could submit their disagreements to national courts or use mediation. In international transactions, however, many disputes are often resolved by arbitration.

In the next chapter, Chapter 4, the various methods of dispute resolution are reviewed in detail. As is noted there, whereas mediation is a voluntary, nonbinding dispute resolution method, arbitration is a binding procedure. Firms that frequently engage in international business transactions often select arbitration at the time they enter into contracts because it is quicker and less complicated than litigation and because the decisions are binding on the parties involved.

Significant international consensus exists regarding the enforceability of both the agreement to arbitrate and the arbitrator's award. Over 70 countries have signed the United Nations Convention on the Recognition and Enforcement of Foreign Arbitral Awards. A variety of bodies are used to determine the rules and processes for international arbitration. These include the American Arbitration Association, the International Chamber of Commerce in Paris, the Euro-Arab Chamber of Commerce, and the United Nations Commission for International Trade Law (UNICTRAL).

The UNICTRAL rules were developed in 1985 by the United Nations, which attempted to take into account concerns from all legal systems in all parts of the world. The model law developed by UNICTRAL can be applied to all international commercial arbitration, whether administered on an individual case basis or by an established institution (such as the AAA or the International Chamber of Commerce).

Courts have limited roles regarding arbitration under the UNICTRAL rules. They can select a neutral arbitrator if the parties do not, refer the parties to arbitration, review challenges to the arbitrators, and set aside arbitration awards for a few specific reasons. According to the model law, an arbitration is international in nature if it meets the requirements noted below.

Requirements for an Arbitration to be International Pursuant to UNICTRAL Provisions

1. Parties have their place of business in different countries at the time the arbitration agreement is concluded.

2. Parties agree that the subject matter of the arbitration relates to more than one country.

3. The place of arbitration as determined by the arbitration agreement is outside the countries in which the parties have their place of business; or the place where a substantial part of the commercial relationship is performed, or the place with which the subject matter of dispute is most closely connected, is outside the countries in which the parties have their place of business.

While U.S. legislative enactments, judicial opinions, and treaty provisions clearly noted that arbitration agreements entered into by U.S. firms would be enforceable, Soler, an automobile dealer in Puerto Rico, thought than an exception might be made for the U.S. antitrust law. Essentially, he argues that the public policy behind the U.S. antitrust law is unique and that therefore only U.S. judges, not internationally selected arbitrators, are qualified to determine whether or not that law is violated by a party to an international contract. The U.S. Supreme Court responds to this argument in the following case.

Mitsubishi Motors v. Soler Chrysler-Plymouth

473 U.S. 614 (1985)
United States Supreme Court

Mitsubishi Motors (MM) is a Japanese corporation that manufactures automobiles and has its principal place of business in Tokyo, Japan. It is the product of a joint venture between Chrysler International S.A. (CISA), a Swiss corporation wholly owned by Chrysler Corporation, and Mitsubishi Heavy Industries Inc., a Japanese corporation. The aim of the joint venture was the distribution through Chrysler dealers outside the continental U.S. of vehicles manufactured by MM and bearing Mitsubishi or Chrysler trademarks. Soler is a Puerto Rican corporation with its prime place of business in Puerto Rico.

Soler made an agreement with CISA and MM to sell cars in Puerto Rico, including an agreement to arbitrate all disputes "which arise between Mitsubishi and Soler of or in relation to . . . this Agreement or for the breach thereof." The disputes were to be "finally settled by arbitration in Japan in accordance with the rules and regulations of the Japan Commercial Arbitration Association."

Initially, Soler did a good business, but in 1981 it ran into difficulty selling the required number of cars provided by the agreement. Attempts to work out the difficulties failed, and Mitsubishi sued Soler in the U.S. District Court for Puerto Rico and asked the Court to refer the dispute to the Japan Commercial Arbitration Association. Soler claimed Mitsubishi and CISA had conspired to divide the market in restraint of trade in violation of the U.S. antitrust laws. It argued its antitrust claim could not be resolved by arbitration.

Justice Blackmun delivered the opinion of the Court.

We granted *certiorari* primarily to consider whether an American court could enforce an agreement to resolve antitrust claims by arbitration when that agreement arises from an international transaction. . . . The "liberal federal policy favoring arbitration agreements" manifested in by the [Arbitration] Act as a whole, is at bottom a policy guaranteeing the enforcement of private contractual arrangements: the Act simply "creates a body of federal substantive law establishing and regulating the duty to honor an agreement to arbitrate." By agreeing to arbitrate a statutory claim, a party does not forgo the substantive rights afforded by the [antitrust] statute; it only submits to their resolution in an arbitral, rather than in a judicial forum. It trades the procedures and opportunity for review of the courtroom for the simplicity, informality, and expedition of arbitration. . . .

There is no reason to assume at the outset of the dispute that international arbitration will not provide an adequate mechanism. To be sure, the international arbitral tribunal owes no particular allegiance to the legal norms of particular states; hence, it has no direct obligation to vindicate their statutory dictates. The tribunal, however, is bound to effectuate the intentions of the parties. Where the parties have agreed that the arbitral body is to decide a defined set of claims which includes, as in these cases, those arising from the application of American antitrust law, the tribunal therefore should be bound to decide the dispute in accord with the national law giving rise to the claim. . . .

As international trade has expanded in recent decades, so too has the use of international arbitration to resolve disputes arising in the course of trade. The controversies that international arbitral institutions are called upon to resolve have increased in diversity as well as in complexity. . . . If they are to take a central place in the international legal order, national courts will need to "shake off the old judicial hostility to arbitration," and also their customary and understandable unwillingness to cede jurisdiction of a claim arising under domestic law to a foreign or transnational tribunal. To this extent, at least, it will be necessary for national courts to subordinate domestic notions of arbitrability to the international policy favoring commercial arbitration.

Accordingly, we "require this representative of the American business community to honor its bargain" . . . by holding this agreement to arbitrate "enforce[able] in accord with the explicit provisions of the Arbitration Act."

Case Questions

1. Does the United States have a federal policy regarding arbitration agreements? What is that policy and where is it found?

2. What assumption does Soler make about an arbitration panel's ability to review a legal dispute based on the U.S. antitrust law? Why doesn't the Court agree with that assumption?

3. Why do you think the Court believes it is likely that arbitration will continue to be used as a method to resolve international contract disputes?

International Investments

Legal constraints on exporting and licensing often make international investment a more desirable method of engaging in international business. If significant barriers to international trade exist, investment may be the only means of selling products in a foreign market. Local laws may erect discriminatory barriers against foreign products that only the establishment of plants in those countries can overcome. For example, many Japanese firms have made investments in European countries to bypass the tariff barriers imposed by the EU.

Crucial business factors may also make investment preferable to exporting or licensing. The on-site locations obtained through investment enable foreign firms to market goods and to provide after-sales service on them more effectively. For large items, the transportation expenses incurred in exporting often make trade arrangements so costly that investment may be the only profitable means of selling internationally. These factors help explain why many companies that export goods to the United States from Japan, Korea, and other Asian countries have begun to produce these goods in the United States and why most firms seeking to do business in China are already investing there.

direct investment
An international direct investment is one in which the investing firm purchases or owns all (or almost all) of the stock of a foreign firm.

Both direct investments and joint ventures are methods of investing internationally. An international **direct investment** is an investment in a firm in another country that is totally or almost totally owned by the investing firm. If a firm in the United States organizes and owns the stock of a German firm that it uses for all of its business activities in Germany, the German firm, owned by the U.S. firm, constitutes a direct investment by the U.S. firm. Because it is the German firm that is located in the country where the German business is transacted, the German firm would generally be regarded as the local firm and the U.S. firm as its foreign owner.

Similarly, as the U.S. firm created the German firm and owns it, the U.S. firm could be called the parent firm and the German firm its subsidiary. Today, the term "affiliate" firm is often used in place of the term *parent* or *subsidiary* firm. The *affiliate* term better describes and recognizes the contributions of various firms which are related to one another rather than suggesting that one firm is more dominant than the other.

An international **joint venture** always has two or more active participants and usually involves the establishment of a separate corporation. Frequently that new corporation, owned partially by a foreign firm and partially by a local firm, is organized in the host or local country. In a joint venture, each party shares in contributions and ownership. For example, a foreign firm may contribute capital and management experience, while a local firm may contribute raw material resources and local marketing expertise. A comparison of a direct investment with a joint venture is shown in Figure 3–5.

joint venture
An international joint venture is formed when two or more participating firms agree to share in a common project with limited scope and duration; usually, a separate firm is created and is jointly owned by the two parties.

The laws of the countries in which the operations are conducted must be closely examined to determine the benefits of international investment, whether through direct investments or joint ventures. However, as Table 3–1 illustrates, international investment is also affected by certain rules of international law, extraterritorial aspects of the laws of the country of origin, treaty obligations between the country of origin and the country of source, and relevant rules of international institutions.

FIGURE 3-5 Comparison of Foreign Affiliate and Branch Organizations

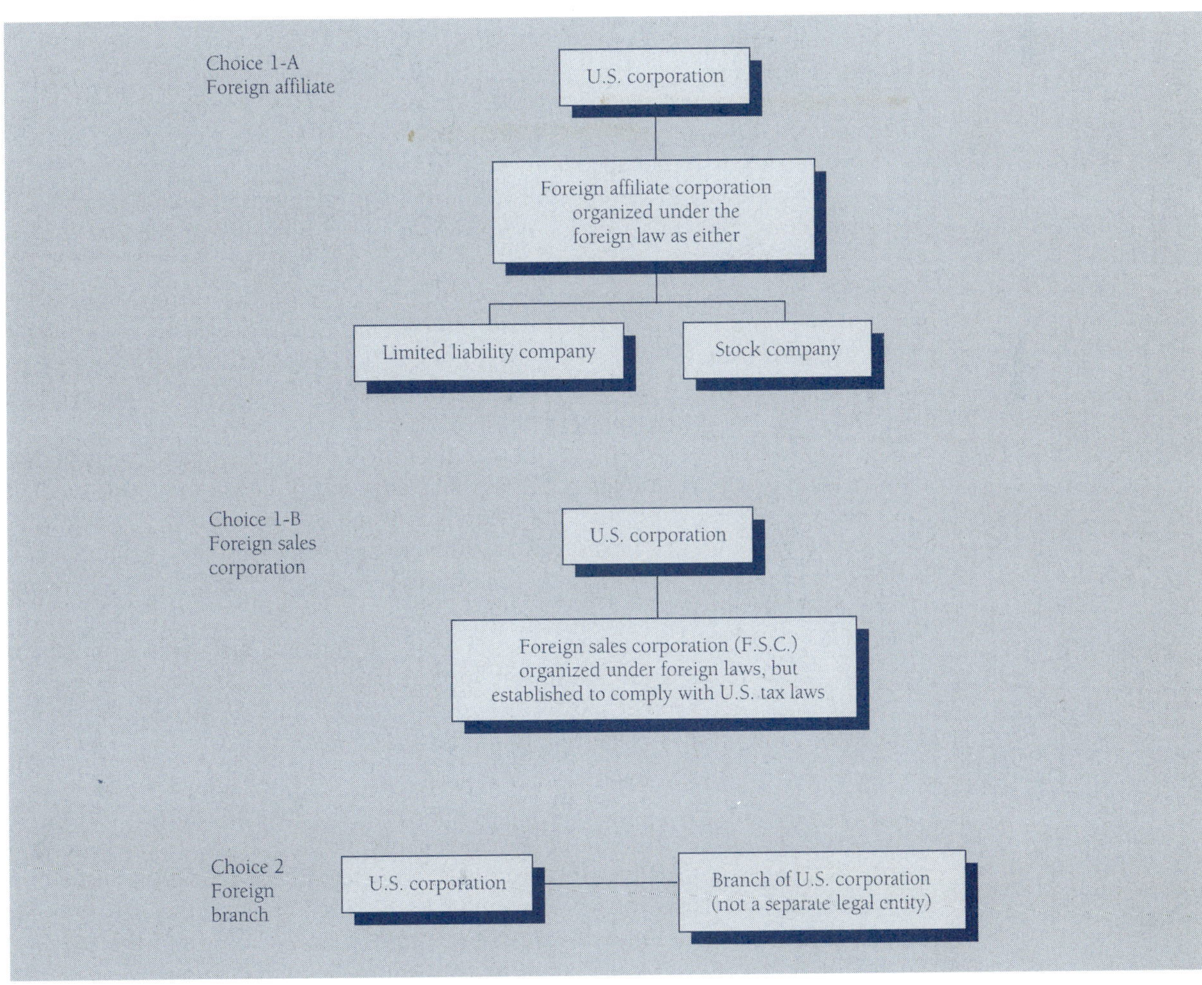

TABLE 3-1

Sources of Law Affecting International Business Investment in Germany by a U.S. Firm

Type of Law	Specific Legal Source
Laws of country in which investment is made (country of source)	German laws
Laws of regional organization	EU laws
Extraterritorial laws of country of origin	U.S. tax or antitrust laws
Treaty agreements between countries	U.S.–German treaty on double taxation
Relevant rules of international institutions	Rules of World Trade Organization (WTO)

Investing in Joint Ventures

Joint ventures are commonly used by companies engaged in international business. In the Mitsubishi Motors case, for example, the facts indicated that Mitsubishi Motors, a Japanese firm, is a joint venture between Chrysler International (CISA) and Mitsubishi Heavy Industries, Inc. A joint venture is a form of partnership that is limited in scope. The parties to a joint venture do not agree to merge all of their activities, but instead agree to cooperate in some areas while perhaps continuing to compete in others.

Joint venture arrangements have recently replaced direct investments in wholly owned subsidiaries as the most prevalent method for establishing foreign manufacturing facilities. In many countries, investment codes prohibit many types of direct investments and require that a specific percentage of a joint venture be owned by local individuals, firms, or government units. In such countries, the joint venture may be the only means of foreign investment.

Absent legal restraints requiring the use of joint ventures, this method of international investment may be preferable where direct investment is too expensive. Political and business risks may be so great that it may be best to share them. There may be critical ingredients of business success, such as access to local capital, political contacts, personnel, and local suppliers, that only a local partner can provide.

In some countries, laws require that the government itself be a part owner of any joint venture. Such an arrangement has both advantages and disadvantages. If a government is a part owner, the joint venture is generally assured that governmental agencies will grant needed licenses and regulatory approval. However, governmental participants may lack business experience or may be subject to removal if they fall out of favor with the ruling party.

The unique legal problems associated with the international joint venture are primarily those that affect its organization and its relations with the firms that created it. A number of legal sources must be consulted to determine the profitability of the venture. These are discussed further in the next section.

Direct Investments

Direct investment is the most involved method of conducting international business. Most nations have mixed views about granting foreign firms the right to participate directly in economic activities within their borders, and the policies adopted on this score vary according to political and economic considerations. A country's historical experiences with foreign investors, its level of economic development, its need for foreign capital and technology, and its political ideology are important factors. Numerous legal questions must be answered before a foreign investment is made.

Legal Questions Affecting Foreign Direct Investments

1. What are the country's investment laws or policies?
2. Which form of business organization is most appropriate for an investment?
3. Are there exchange controls affecting movement of money into or out of the country?
4. What is the taxation policy of the source country?
5. Do labor laws require worker representation on a company's board of directors or the hiring of a certain percentage of the labor force from the source country?
6. Is expropriation or nationalization a possibility?
7. What are the antitrust policies, and how have they been developing?
8. Is intellectual property (patents, trademarks, and copyrights) protected?

Highlights from several legal areas illustrate the primary importance of the laws of the source country. These considerations influence decisions regarding both direct investments and international joint ventures.

Investment Laws and Policy The impact of foreign investment laws is probably the first area that should be investigated. Many countries attempt to attract foreign investors by creating a favorable legal environment, including incentives to invest in particular industries, in stipulated depressed localities, or in special programs. Such incentives are often implemented by means of tax holidays, increased depreciation, or other benefits aimed at making the country's tax rate favorable for foreign investors. Ireland and Scotland have recently attracted numerous manufacturing operations largely though tax incentives.

Many countries try to stimulate some foreign investments while restricting and controlling others. Analysis of the overall objectives of a country's investment code—as well as detailed analysis of its provisions—is required to determine whether the country's policy of promoting and encouraging foreign investments is counteracted by the restrictions and regulations found in more specific laws.

Forms of Business Organization The choice of a particular form of business organization for international investment often has critical tax consequences. For a U.S. firm, the U.S. tax laws, the tax laws of the country of source, and tax treaties between the United States and the country of source may influence which form is chosen.

When regarded from the viewpoint of a firm in the United States, a business organization formed under the laws of another country is regarded as a foreign corporation. Thus, when a U.S. firm establishes a German corporation, to the U.S. firm and to the U.S. government that corporation is foreign. Of course, it is regarded under German law as a local corporation and it appears that way in Figure 3–6. There are several options available to a firm seeking to do business in another country.

The Affiliate The first option is to organize a corporation in the country where business is to occur or in a country with favorable corporation and taxation laws. Typically, an affiliate known as a **foreign affiliate** firm (foreign to the firm organizing the new entity) is incorporated under the laws of the country where its business activity is to take place, thereby increasing the likelihood that it will be treated by that country as a local company. Generally, such firms are separate legal entities and are not usually considered part of the parent corporation. In some cases, however, such as the chemical disaster in Bhopal, India, involving the Union Carbide Company and its Indian affiliate, Union Carbide, Ltd., the "parent" firm, because it has the right to and sometimes does seek to control activities of its affiliate, may be held liable for activities of that affiliate.

foreign affiliate
A foreign affiliate is a firm that is located in a country other than the firm that owns it; usually it is organized in the country where it transacts business.

The U.S. Foreign Sales Corporation (FSC) The Internal Revenue Code permits U.S. corporations with international sales to establish a U.S. firm know as a **foreign sales corporation.** This firm is incorporated under U.S. law, not the laws of the country where the firm does business. It is referred to as a foreign sales corporation because its sales and income must come from outside the United States. The U.S. parent firm that establishes an FSC subsidiary owns all the shares of the subsidiary's stock. Although there are several specific requirements such firms must meet, an FSC is essentially a "shell" or "paper" corporation. The parent firm sells its export products to the FSC, which then resells them to foreign buyers. For this reason, the FSC, not the parent firm, derives income from export sales. Approximately 5 percent of the income from an FSC may be exempt from U.S. income tax. For example, if a U.S. firm has sales of $1,000,000 and would normally make income of $100,000 on those sales, it would be taxed on the $100,000. However, if the U.S. firm instead establishes an FSC and sells its products to it so that the FSC then sells to customers and it, not the parent firm, derives $100,000 of income, only $95,000 would be taxed as approximately 5 percent of the $100,000 of income is exempt from tax.

foreign sales corporation
A foreign sales corporation is a corporation that is organized under U.S. laws and that derives almost all of its income from foreign sales; often, it is practically a paper corporation established primarily for tax reasons.

The Branch Another option is to establish a foreign branch of a firm's existing corporation. **Branches** of any corporation are not independent entities but a part of the parent corporation. Thus, legally, for a U.S. firm with its headquarters in New York and branches in Chicago, Frankfort, Germany, and Mexico City, each branch is regarded as a part of the firm in the United States. The choice between the branch and subsidiary firms is often based on the activities to be conducted. If an initial loss is anticipated for a foreign venture, a branch may be preferable since the firm with U.S. and foreign branches may use the loss from the foreign branch to offset income from domestic branches. A firm with several branches, whether local or domestic, reports and is taxed on its net or combined income, not on the amount of income or loss of each branch. On the other hand, special tax benefits may be available in the country where business occurs if a separate foreign affiliate (regarded as local in the country where the business activity occurs) exists.

branch (foreign branch)
A branch is not a separate firm, but a part of another firm; a foreign branch is not in the same country as the main office of the firm, but it is a part of that firm.

While the tax consequences of using different forms of business organization are very important, liability concerns or market-oriented issues may also affect the choice of organizational form. In these matters, a firm incorporated where the business is being transacted will usually be more favorable than other business organization forms. Figure 3–7 (p. 98) illustrates the differences between the foreign affiliate, the U.S. foreign sales corporation, and the branch form of business organizations.

FIGURE 3-6

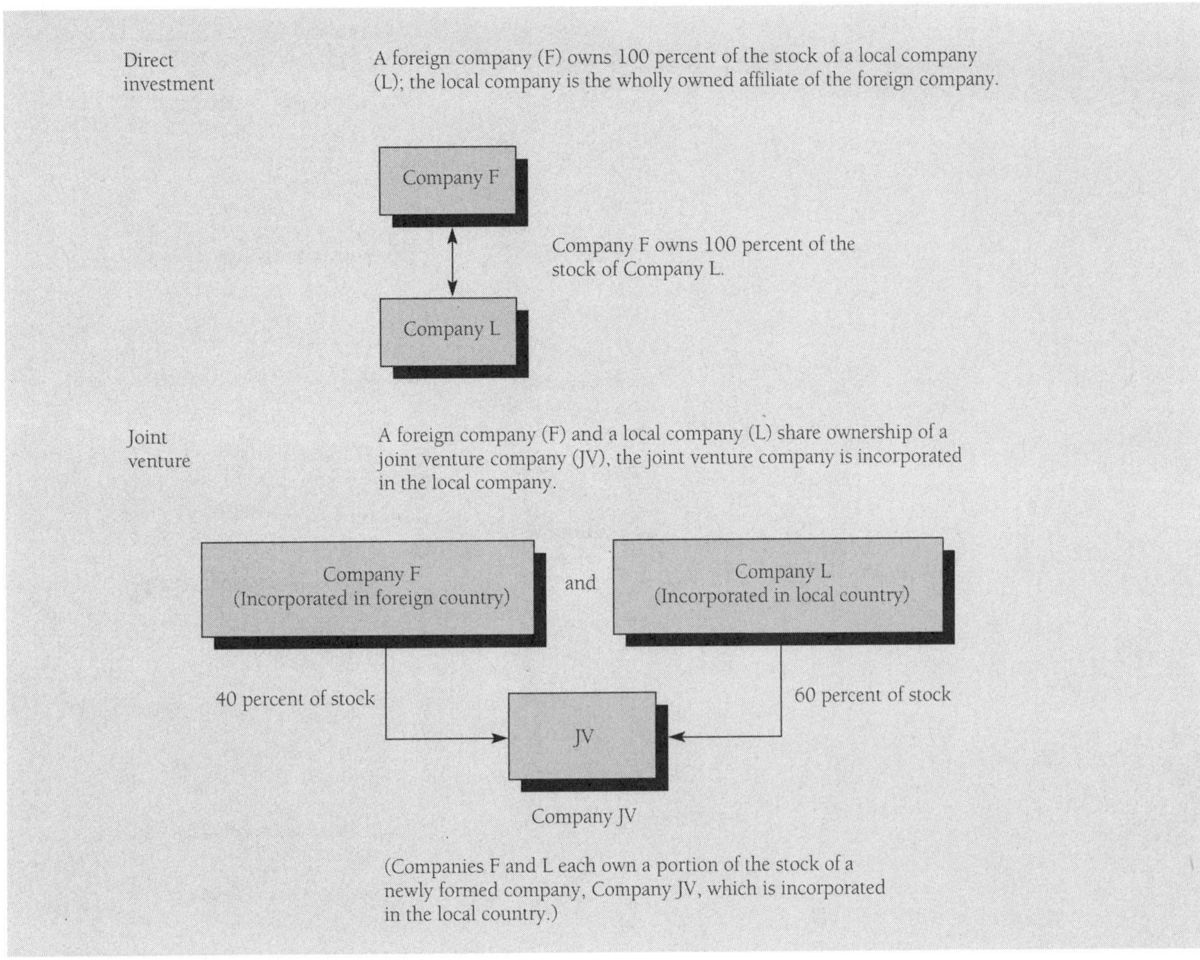

Exchange Controls Foreign direct investment decisions may be affected by currency exchange controls designed to limit the investing firm's right to withdraw profits, interest, dividends, or portions of the invested capital. Some protection against the most severe restrictions is available to U.S. corporations pursuant to treaty provisions. Firms may also secure insurance protection against the risk of inability to convert investment receipts from the local currency into dollars.

Tax Considerations Foreign direct investors must examine both direct and indirect taxes. Many countries derive most of their income from indirect taxes, such as sales taxes, turnover taxes, or excise taxes. Indirect taxes are easier to collect than direct taxes and are less dependent on a high level of taxpayer income. Thus, for example, almost 50 percent of France's taxes are indirect taxes.

Municipal or state taxes, as well as national taxes, must be reviewed to determine the total tax burden. In Switzerland, for example, the municipal or canton taxes on corporate income are far more significant than the Swiss federal tax.

FIGURE 3-7

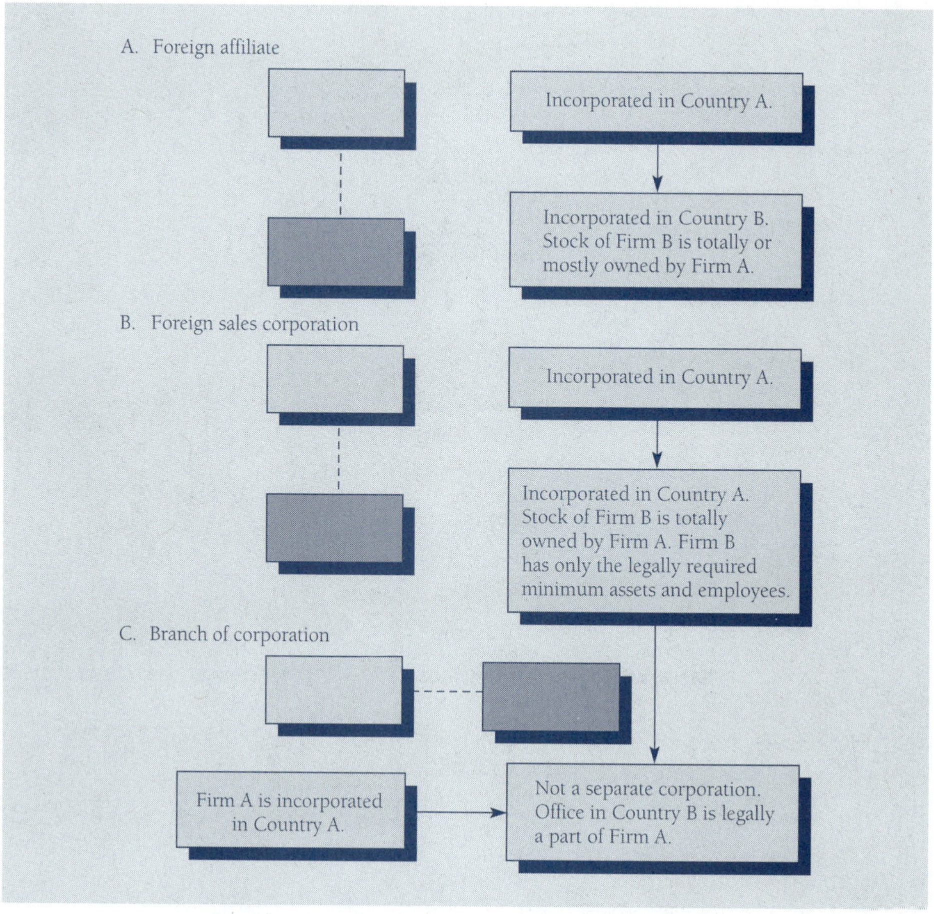

Tax treaties play an important role in determining the tax burden of some transactions. As previously stated, tax treaties may alleviate the double taxation imposed by conflicting or overlapping tax laws of the country of source and the country of origin.

Labor Laws Labor costs are generally a significant part of the cost of doing business and therefore influence most foreign investments. International investments are affected not only by minimum or prevailing wage laws, but also by legal provisions regarding hours of work, workers' compensation, retirement benefits, and vacation bonuses. In most European countries, for example, bonuses of one month's pay generally are required by legislation or practice for salaried and hourly workers. In Japan, bonuses of at least one month's pay or more are awarded to most workers in July and December; often each semiannual bonus may be as high as four months' pay. Severance payments equal to at least six months' salary must accompany any notice of termination for many workers in numerous countries.

In some countries, workers have a vested right to their jobs; Mexican and Colombian laws restrict an employer's right to discharge workers except under specifically prescribed conditions. Local laws often require foreign workers to obtain work permits, such as work visas or green cards in the United States. Further, laws may require that local nationals comprise a minimum percentage of the labor force. All foreigners working in Saudi Arabia must obtain work permits, and all companies in Saudi Arabia that employ foreigners must employ 75 percent Saudi nationals and pay at least 51 percent of their total payroll to Saudi nationals. Indian law required Union Carbide to have Indian managers at its Bhopal facility.

Safety of Investment from Expropriation or Nationalization Expropriation or nationalization occurs when a government takes over the ownership and management of private firms. Although the terms are often used interchangeably, the government pays compensation to the former owner when **nationalization** takes place; no compensation is paid when **expropriation** occurs. In 1982, France nationalized many of the banks operating in France, both foreign and domestically owned; in the 1960s and 1970s, Cuba expropriated many of the foreign banks operating there.

If sizable investments are contemplated, legal protection against the risk of expropriation should be considered. Such protection may be available from a variety of sources. The local investment code may have express nonexpropriation guarantees. Treaties signed by some foreign countries with the United States indicate agreement as to the standard for "reasonable compensation." Certainly, the insurance protection offered through such U.S. agencies as the Export-Import Bank, the Foreign Credit Insurance Association, and the Office of Private Investment Controls should be examined if there is any danger regarding the safety of expropriation or nationalization. In any event, firms should analyze the risk of expropriation before investing in politically unstable foreign countries.

nationalization
Nationalization is the taking of private property and making it public or governmental property; when property is nationalized, the former owner of the property receives compensation.

expropriation
Expropriation occurs when private property is taken by a government and no, or clearly inadequate compensation is paid to its former owner.

Antitrust Laws Firms operating in the United States, whether of domestic or foreign origin, have long been aware of the possible effects of the antitrust laws on their operations. The U.S. antitrust laws, discussed in Chapters 15 and 16, are intended to preserve a relatively free system of competition by controlling anticompetitive practices and by regulating the growth and use of economic power.

Countries other than the United States have also enacted antitrust laws, though U.S. antitrust law has had more influence on international business transactions than the antitrust law of any other country. Antitrust laws were enacted in most of the major European countries after World War II. Those national laws were subsequently supplemented and to some extent replaced by Article 85-90 of the Treaty of Rome, which created the European Community (now the European Union). Article 85-90 of that treaty prohibits practices and agreements that restrict or distort competition within the EU or among its member states. Furthermore, the EU has clearly indicated that Article 85-90 also applies to extraterritorial activities that affect trade or commerce in the member states even if one of the parties to such activities is a nonmember of the EU.

Patents, Trademarks, and Copyrights Intimately connected with antitrust law is the legal protection afforded trademarks and patents. Whereas antitrust law is antimonopolistic, patent law gives a limited monopoly to certain processes, products, or designs, and trademark law gives a limited monopoly to symbols or words. Trademarks designate the source of origin of a product, while patents give their owner a monopoly over a product's manufacture, sale, or use.

A country cannot give extraterritorial effect to its patent laws; therefore, a patent confers rights that are protected only within the boundaries of the country in which the patent is issued. Thus, a U.S. patent and a Canadian patent, even when granted for the same invention, create separate and distinct rights that may differ in scope and effect in each of the issuing countries. For example, until 1995, patents in Japan were valid for 15 years from the date of publication, in the United States for 17 years from the date a patent is issued, and in many other countries for 20 years. Now, both the U.S. and Japan have changed their laws to conform to the laws in most other countries—patents are valid for 20 years from the date the application is filed. A proposal to establish 20 years as the length of time for protecting patents seems to be gathering significant agreement among the leading patent issuing countries.

U.S. courts have held that a foreign patent confers no rights on its owner with respect to acts done in the United States. Under U.S. patent laws, inventors are not required to use their patents or to permit others to use them; no taxes are due to maintain their patents. In some other nations, however, these obligations must be performed to maintain a patent's validity. While the United States and Japan currently will issue a patent to the first person who files as opposed to the first inventor, most countries give preference to the first person to invent even if another person files first.

The principal international agreement relating to patents and trademarks is the International Convention for the Protection of Industrial Property (Paris Union), of which the United States and over 80 other countries are members. This agreement creates uniformity by allowing applicants in one member country to apply subsequently for protection in other member countries. A person in one member country who files an application in another member country within six months of the original filing date is entitled to priority based on the original filing date.

The oldest multilateral treaty for the protection of copyrights is the Berne Convention. Over 70 countries are members. A literary, artistic, or musical work whose publication first occurs in a member country qualifies for protection in other member countries. The Universal Copyright Convention is another major multilateral copyright treaty. It provides for national treatment of copyright holders of member countries if the copyrighted work was written by a citizen or resident of a country that is a party to the treaty or was first published in a member country. The United States is a member of the Uniform Copyright Convention and recently has signed the Berne Convention.

Summary

International business is conducted through international trade or investment. International trade has increased dramatically over the last several decades. In recent years, many Pacific Rim countries have accounted for an increasingly larger portion of international trade. International investment occurs when businesses from one country open offices, plants, and factories in other countries. Foreign investment by firms from a variety of countries is increasingly rapidly. The greatest growth in the situs for foreign investment in this decade has been in China and in other Asian countries.

A variety of laws affect firms engaged in international business. The organization and operation of international business is subject to national, regional, and international laws, but national laws have the greatest effect. If the country of source has a legal system with which the businessperson is unfamiliar, its laws should be closely reviewed. Common law, civil law, and Islamic law are the main categories of legal systems.

Some laws of the country of origin may have extraterritorial effect. The antitrust and income tax laws of the United States have effect outside its territory. Regional laws may be superimposed on national laws. Thus, business operations are affected, for example, by the regional laws of the European Union and the North American Free Trade Agreement. International organizations such as the International Monetary Fund and the World Trade

Organization create and implement rules that become part of the international legal environment.

International trade is affected by laws that encourage or restrict exports and by laws that restrict imports. Laws restricting exports are intended to preserve scarce resources or regulate access to vital national products and information. Laws encouraging exports often take the form of subsidies or tax incentives. Laws affecting imports include prohibitions, quotas, tariff barriers, and nontariff barriers. Although the tariff barriers of many developed countries have been reduced, a variety of nontariff barriers remain in place in many countries. International trade occurs not only through the export of products but also through the licensing of patents, trademarks, and know-how. Licensing agreements usually require the licensee to pay the licensor a royalty in exchange for information on or use of a product developed by the licensor. The parties to any international licensing agreement need to consult the laws of the country of origin, where the licensor is located, and the laws of the country of source, where the licensee is located. International contract disputes are generally submitted to arbitration rather than court litigation.

International investments usually occur either through joint ventures by two or more firms or through one firm's direct investment in a foreign country. In either case, the laws of the country in which the investment is made have the greatest weight. Frequently, national legal requirements force firms to do business through joint ventures; however, even where joint ventures are not required, they are often a preferred method of entering a new business environment. Many countries have an investment code that details the treatment given to the investments of foreign firms. Laws that affect the appropriateness of specific forms of business organization should be consulted. The tax laws of the country in which an investment is contemplated should be carefully examined.

Clearly, the safety of any international investment must be determined before the investment is made. Labor laws, antitrust laws, and patent and trademark laws vary significantly among countries. The international legal environment for business investment is affected by the laws of the country of source, extraterritorial laws of the country of origin, and applicable regional and international laws.

Critical Thinking Review Questions

1. Some writers suggest that regional organizations that create free trade associations for their members, but not for other countries, are interfering with world trade patterns and are merely diverting trade between member and nonmember countries to trade between member countries. What alternative explanation might indicate that regional trading associations are beneficial to world trade?
2. Assume that a firm is doing business in three countries: one with a common law legal system, one with a civil law legal system, and one with a system based primarily on Islamic law. Which particular aspects of the laws affecting the firm are likely to vary significantly among these countries?
3. What are the biases behind laws that permit the entry of all types of gray-market goods into a country? Who benefits from these laws, and who is hurt? Which countries would you expect to be most permissive about gray-market goods?
4. Why are letters of credit needed? Why are documents like the bill of lading used to transfer title to goods instead of having the title to the goods transferred when the possession of the goods are transferred?
5. Assume you read that of all the firms investing in country X last year, 75 percent formed joint ventures while only 25 percent invested through direct investing, and that the author of the article concluded that "joint ventures are obviously the preferred method of doing business in country X." Explain why that conclusion might be fallacious.

Critical Thinking Exercises

1. A U.S. firm is thinking of opening a new manufacturing facility in Poland. Before it makes a direct investment in that country, it seeks your advice as to which types of laws it should review

to determine if it should make the investment. Assume that Poland welcomes foreign investment of the type planned by this firm. What advice would you give?

2. The United Kingdom imposes quality standards on domestic producers of milk and dairy products. It has also passed a regulation prohibiting the import of pasteurized milk and unfrozen dairy products as a measure to protect its people from milk that may not meet its standards. Other European Union member countries protest that the regulation does not provide a method whereby their milk and dairy products can pass the health and safety standards the U.K. imposes on its producers. Does the U.K. regulation violate the "free movement of goods" provisions of the Treaty of Rome governing the EU countries or the directives of its Commission prohibiting national laws interfering with that free movement?
3. Assume that the United States, France, and Germany have signed the UNCISG Treaty, but Portugal and Mexico have not done so. Baachus Wines, a U.S. importer of wine and beer, contracts with a French winery to buy French wines. A dispute arises regarding the quality of the wines sent to Baachus. Does the UNCISG apply? What if the contract is for German beer? What if Portuguese wine is being purchased? Would your answer to these questions be different if Baachus wanted the products delivered to its Mexican office?
4. A U.S. firm sells caustic soda to a firm in India under a CIF contract. The soda was loaded on the ship, but a labor strike made it impossible for the ship to leave the U.S. port where it was docked. As a result, the soda arrived in India six months late, and the Indian buyer sued. Who should prevail? Would your answer be different if the seller knew that a labor strike was imminent? Why?
5. Union Carbide Corporation owned 50.9 percent of Union Carbide India, where a leak of toxic methyl isocyanate killed more than 2,000 people in 1984. A lawsuit on behalf of the victims was filed in the United States against Union Carbide Corporation, the parent corporation, claiming that it had effective control over Union Carbide India. What factors do you think a court should consider in determining whether a parent corporation has control over its subsidiary/affiliate corporation? If the law in India required a majority of the officers and directors of the Union Carbide India firm to be Indian citizens, would that affect your answer?
6. Griffin is the holder of both a U.S. and an Italian patent for a composting machine. Griffin granted an exclusive license to Longwood to make and sell the machine in the United States and an exclusive license to Carminati for Italy and other countries in the European Community. Keystone purchased three machines from Carminati; he used one in his business in the United States and sold the other two to U.S. purchasers. Griffin claims Keystone violated its and Longwood's patent rights. Keystone said that as he bought the machine from one who had a license to sell it, he could do whatever he wanted with the machines. If you decide for Keystone, what policy would your decision be promoting? What policy is promoted if you decide for Griffin?

CHAPTER

4

Litigation and Alternative Dispute Resolution

Critical Thinking Questions

- While some writers point to the relatively high number of lawyers as the major reason for litigation, alternative explanations often focus on cultural factors and on characteristics of the U.S. legal system. What alternative explanations do you think explain the use of litigation in the United States?
- Compare and contrast the role of the jury with the role of the judge in a civil trial.
- Although the attorney is perhaps best recognized as a litigator, most attorneys spend the greatest portion of their time performing other functions. Describe those functions and explain why they are less recognized.
- Why is arbitration a preferred method of dispute resolution for most international contract matters?
- Explain why litigation may be preferable in some cases to alternative dispute resolution methods. Give reasons why alternative dispute resolution may be preferable to litigation.

Introduction... Past, Present, Future

Litigation is a dispute resolution process in which parties present evidence through their attorneys to a jury and judge. Through court determinations of disputes, laws are interpreted, applied, and created. Most court cases that are filed are not concluded in the courts; usually, they are resolved through negotiations. In some cases, parties turn to authorities outside the courts for assistance in resolving their disputes. A variety of methods are used. While litigation is the most visible and formal method of dispute resolution, mediation, arbitration, and other alternative methods are often used.

litigation
A process for solving disputes involving presentation of evidence by parties through attorneys before a jury and judge.

Litigation is important not only for the parties to a controversy, but also to the development of law. In the United States, almost all judicial decisions beyond the trial level generally must be explained in written opinions that become public information. It is through such opinions, exemplified by the cases in this text, that laws are applied to specific facts and legal principles are established.

In the past, the U.S. civil litigation system handled far fewer cases than it does today. Some of the cases and controversies litigated today were practically unknown until recently. Controversies regarding biogenetic products, class-action suits regarding asbestos exposure, the role of cigarette usage in causing cancer, the ownership and protection of computer programs, and sexual harassment cases are among today's disputes that have added to the caseload before the nation's courts.

In almost all fields of business litigation, the number of disputes brought to the courts has increased dramatically over the past several decades. Not only are there new controversies that must be resolved, even in the traditional areas there are more people and more products and more business and consumer transactions than ever before. Another reason for this increase may be that as a result of advertising by law firms, televised court proceedings, and increasing educational exposure, people are more familiar with and less afraid to access the legal system to resolve their disputes. As a result of the increased caseload, the legal system has become overburdened.

Both state and federal courts generally face a backlog of cases. Civil cases throughout the country face delayed resolution as criminal cases take priority on court dockets due to the requirement that defendants accused of crimes be given a prompt trial. The increasing costs and delays associated with litigation have led many firms to use alternative methods of resolving disputes and to find new ways to better manage their legal costs.

In the future, it is likely there will be more attempts to manage and control the cost of litigation. Legal restrictions of access to litigation or of compensation awarded to an injured party may be imposed in the next few years. The increasing use of alternative dispute methods by individuals, small business owners, and global business firms alike may halt the trend of increasing litigation. While litigation will continue to draw significant public attention, mediation, arbitration, and other methods of dispute resolution are prone to greater usage.

Thought Questions

1. Think about the role of litigation in the United States and in Japan. Compare and contrast the characteristics that make the United States more likely to foster litigation as a method of dispute resolution than Japan.
2. If you were a manager of a firm that was facing mounting legal costs, what steps would you consider taking to reduce those costs?
3. Give reasons for using each of the following methods of dispute resolution: litigation, arbitration, mediation, negotiation.

Litigation in the U.S. Legal System

The United States is a litigious society—that is, a society in which people often prefer to sue rather than settle disputes by other methods. Although more publicity is given to criminal litigation than to civil litigation, civil litigation is of greater concern to both the average citizen and the business manager. Sometimes business managers use litigation as a part of their management strategy. For example, in 1990 Johnson and Johnson, the manufacturer of Extra Strength Tylenol, sued Bristol Myers-Squibb, manufacturer of Aspirin Free Excedrin, for falsely claiming in its advertisements that Excedrin is a better pain reliever than Extra Strength Tylenol. Johnson and Johnson accused Bristol Myers-Squibb of incorrectly analyzing three studies in which patients were asked about the effect of Extra Strength Tylenol and Aspirin Free Excedrin. Johnson and Johnson's claim also stated that Bristol Myers-Squibb "has a history of habitual false advertising."

There are several reasons why litigation in the United States may be more common than in most other countries. In the United States there is little stigma to litigation, and perhaps more willingness to use it to solve problems that are not satisfactorily resolved

FIGURE 4-1 Civil Suits Filed in Federal Courts

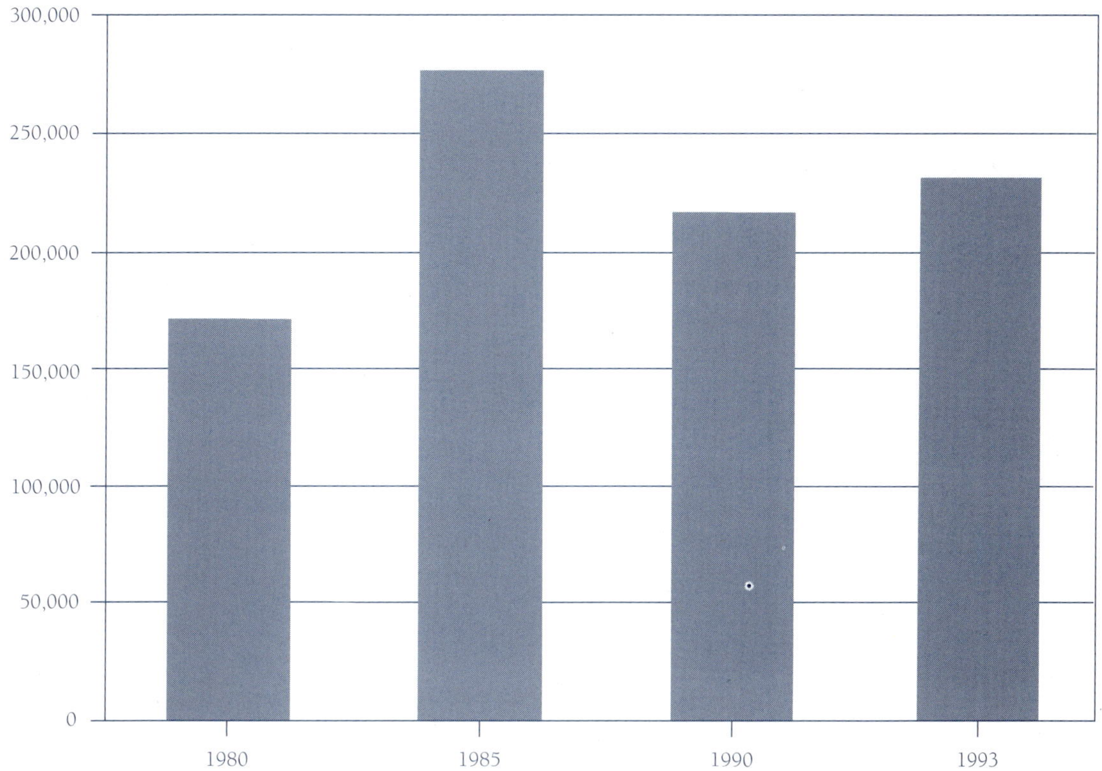

Source: U.S. Department of Commerce, Bureau of the Census, *Statistical Abstract of the United States, 1994.* (Washington, D.C.: 1994) Figure 211.

through negotiation than there is in countries where confrontation is discouraged. For example, consensus practices aimed at harmonizing conflicting goals are such a part of the Japanese business environment that litigation between business firms is viewed as disruptive to long-term trust building. A survey of Japanese manufacturing firms found that only 24 had ever faced a product liability suit in Japan, and only 7 of those firms had ever been held liable.[1]

Another reason why litigation is used more frequently in the United States may be that there is greater trust in the legal system. People who do file lawsuits generally anticipate that their claim will be listened to, that there is a realistic chance that they may prevail, and that the court decision is enforceable. Where the legal process makes it difficult to file claims, to prove a wrong committed by the defendant, and to enforce a court judgment, there is little incentive to litigate.

As Figure 4–1 shows, over 225,000 civil suits were filed in federal courts in 1993; fewer than 4 percent of these suits reached trial. The majority of federal cases involve claims based on specific statutes. While contract and tort cases each account for approximately 15 percent of the number of federal civil cases filed, the greatest

[1] "Survey: The Legal Profession," *The Economist*, July 18, 1992, p. 14.

FIGURE 4-2 Filings in State Courts in 1989*

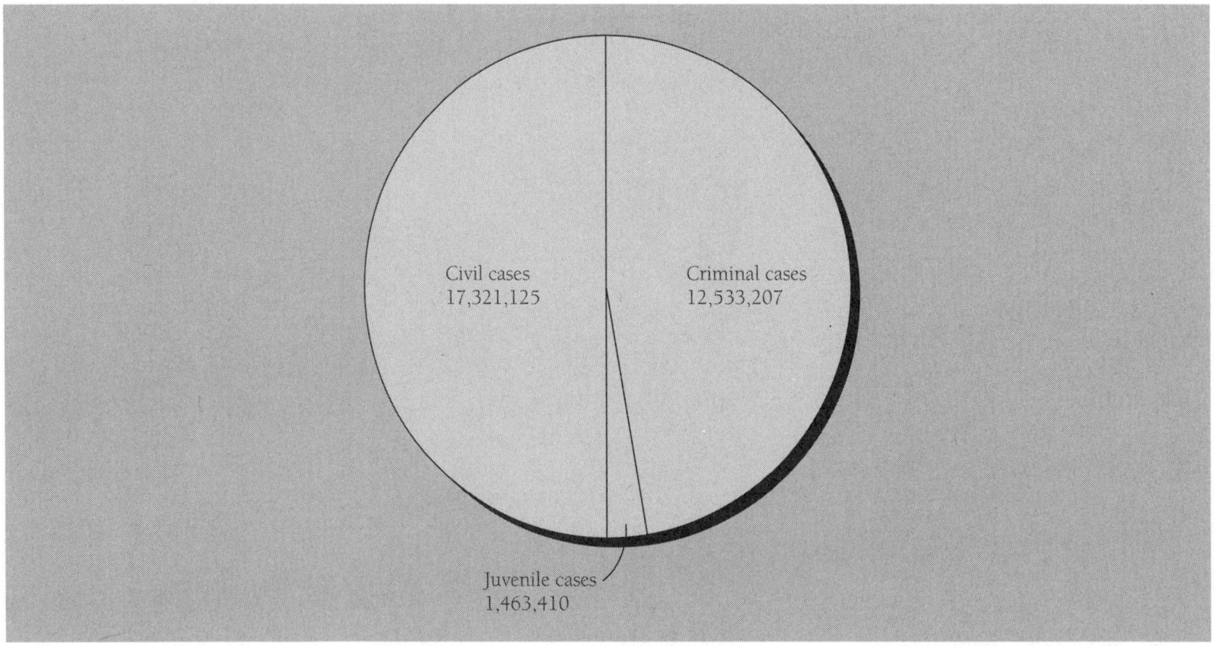

*Does not include traffic cases.

Source: *Guidebook to the Use of State Court Caseload Statistics*, National Center for State Courts (Williamsburg, VA., 1991) Table 1, p. 9.

caseload increase during the 1990s has been in civil rights cases. However, because most civil cases involve questions of state law, such as contract, real estate, and personal injury law, they are generally litigated in state courts rather than federal courts. In 1989, the year for which the most recent data was accessible, over 17 million civil cases were filed in our state courts (see Figure 4–2).

The causes and effects of the increase in litigation are varied. Some suggest that one cause may be the weakening of such social units as the family, church, and neighborhood. In earlier times, these social units often helped people resolve their disputes without court intervention. Others argue that greater numbers of more severe injuries have resulted from technological changes in our complex society. Finally, some writers note that the increase in the number of civil lawsuits parallels the increase in the number of lawyers. Figure 4–3 shows the increase in the number of attorneys employed in the United States since 1970. Of the over two million lawyers in the world, nearly 40 percent are in the United States. Only Pakistan and Singapore have more lawyers per 100,000 people than does the United States (Pakistan has over 500, Singapore approximately 400, and the United States slightly over 300 lawyers per 100,000).[2]

A noticeable effect of the increase in civil litigation is the increase in the cost of liability insurance. Less noticeable are the effects of civil litigation on entrepreneurial

[2] Ibid., p. 4.

FIGURE 4-3 Attorneys Employed in the United States

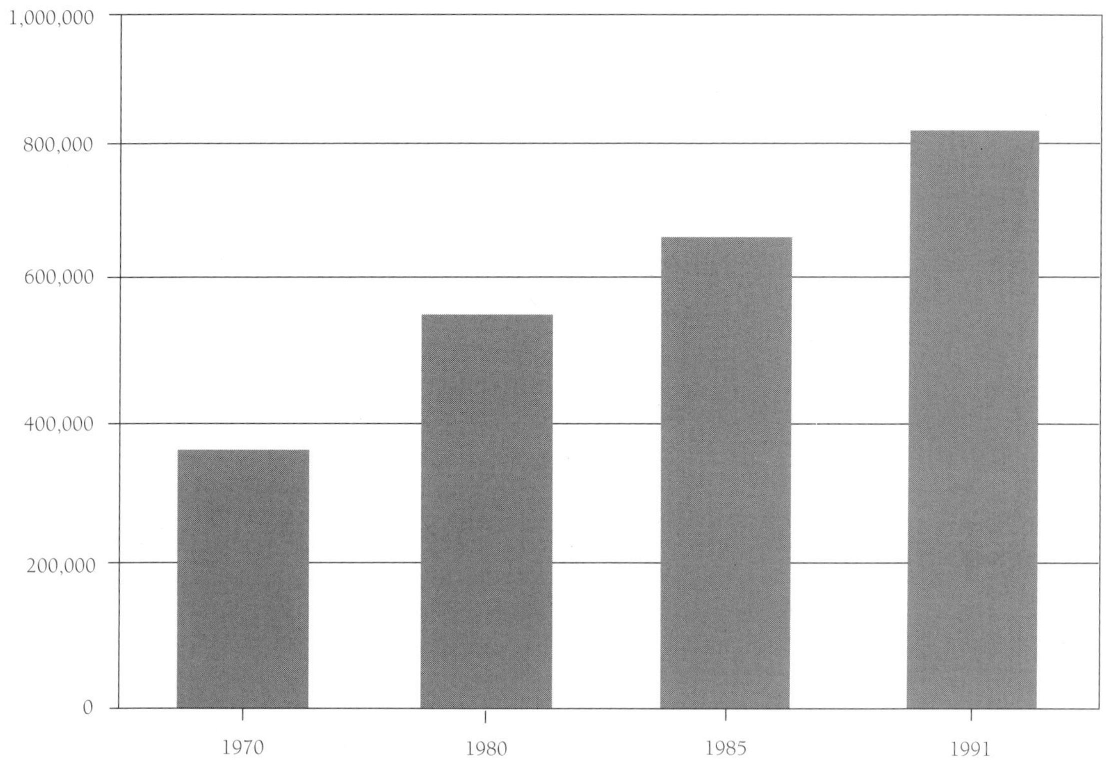

Source: U.S. Department of Commerce, Bureau of the Census, *Statistical Abstract of the United States, 1994* (Washington, D.C., 1994) Figure 210.

risk taking. Is fear of product liability lawsuits making companies more conservative in developing new products? Are the expense and aggravation of malpractice claims causing doctors to shy away from emergency or surgical fields? Is the prospect of litigation increasing the time it takes to open new chemical plants or to place innovative drugs in the marketplace?

Criminal and Civil Litigation

Criminal cases are brought by a public official representing the society at large. Civil cases are brought by individuals and business enterprises. As noted in Chapter 2, criminal litigation and civil litigation differ significantly in their use of a jury and in their parties, purpose, and processes. Thus, in examining any court opinion, legal process, or principle of law, it is important to bear in mind the differences between criminal and civil litigation.

adversarial process A process in which the parties have the responsibility for developing evidence that will prove their claims; parties also determine which witnesses to call and when to object to opposing evidence.

Adversarial Process

In the legal system of the United States, all litigation is modeled on the adversarial principle that charges the parties with responsibility for the development and proof of their claims. In an **adversarial process,** the parties, not the judges, must decide what evidence to present, which witnesses to use, and when to object to something that the opposing party seeks to do. Because most people are not familiar with the complexities of litigation, the parties to litigation generally hire attorneys to represent them and present their case.

The rationale for the use of the adversarial process is that truth and justice are more likely to emerge if each litigant is responsible for preparing, presenting, and defending his or her case. A neutral judge brings impartiality to the process, and the biased parties are expected to bring greater concern and dedication to their case than would parties who are merely assisting in an investigation. Critics of the adversarial system argue that winning or losing a case too often depends on the skill of the attorneys rather than the merits of the case. It is also argued that the adversarial process leads parties to hide or distort facts in order to strengthen their positions. Accordingly, legal reforms adopted in recent decades have sought to lessen the impact of the adversarial principle in litigation. In addition, use of the adversarial process may decrease as a consequence of an increased use of administrative tribunals (discussed in Chapter 6), and alternative methods of dispute resolutions (discussed later in this chapter).

International Perspective and Commentary

When one compares litigation from one country to the next, differences are likely to emerge both in the matters that are subject to litigation and in the litigation process being used. There are also some notable differences among legal systems in determining which disputes are to be resolved by courts and which by other means. Most civil law systems do not litigate family law cases such as divorce or adoptions; removing those cases from courts significantly reduces the volume of litigation. Similarly, a registration system is often used for all transfers of real property. Thus, routine changes in the title to land do not require judicial action in most civil law countries, whereas some of those changes do require court action in many common law legal systems.

inquisitorial process A process in which the judge, with the assistance of the parties, investigates the facts and determines the evidence to be presented in a trial.

Most nations do not employ the adversarial process in conducting litigation. Instead, the **inquisitorial process,** which requires all parties to assist the judge in investigating the facts of the controversy before the court, is generally used in countries with either a civil law legal system or an Islamic legal system. In cases litigated according to the inquisitorial process, the judge, somewhat like an orchestra leader, takes an active part in determining the facts. By contrast, the judge in a trial using the adversarial process is more like a referee in a sports event, essentially reacting to objections posed by the attorneys. The weight given to oral testimony, subject to cross-examination, and to documentary evidence also varies. All legal systems protect certain records of individuals and business entities while precluding some oral testimony. There is, however, significant variation in the records protected and the testimony prohibited from nation to nation.

The Civil Litigation Process

As many of the civil cases that are filed never reach trial, it is necessary to look at the entire civil litigation process, not just the trial itself, to understand the nature of civil litigation. The civil litigation process can be divided into stages that begin before a case has been filed and end after a trial has been decided.

Stages of the Litigation Process

- Prelitigation concerns
- Pleadings stage
- Pretrial activities
- Trial procedures
- Post-judgment concerns
- Appellate process

Prelitigation Concerns

Before any litigation begins, the disputing parties should consider a number of matters. Several important questions relate to the attorney's role. Should the party consult an attorney as soon as there is the possibility of litigation? Can the disputing parties investigate the facts and settle the dispute without seeking the assistance of attorneys? Would turning the dispute over to attorneys at an early stage take too much control away from the parties themselves? If the parties try to work things out themselves, will their discussions, notes, and documents hurt their cases if the dispute later appears in civil litigation? Answering such questions helps determine when an attorney should be consulted.

Even after a decision to consult and retain an attorney has been made, several matters must be addressed before any litigation begins. These matters are the who, what, when, and where of the dispute.

Questions to Ask Before Litigation

Who are the parties that could be sued? Often there are multiple defendants, and the plaintiff has to decide whether to sue some or all of the parties that might be liable.

What is the basis of the suit? A party who may be able to sue on the basis of a contract, breach of warranty, or tort may need to determine the advantages to pursuing one theory rather than another.

When will the litigation begin? Should the party seek to file suit as soon as possible, or should the onset of litigation be delayed in the hope of achieving a settlement?

Where could the litigation take place? If a party has a choice of several courts, the place of suit may affect the applicable law or who can be sued.

Pleadings Stage

A civil lawsuit is begun by filing a complaint with a court that has jurisdiction. Typically, the plaintiff's attorney files the complaint with the court and has a copy of the complaint and a summons delivered to the defendants.

The **complaint** is a document that gives the plaintiff's version of the *historical facts*—allegations about the circumstances that led to the claimed wrongful acts by the defendant. It also generally includes *jurisdictional facts*—statements showing why the case is being brought before this particular court. Finally, the complaint concludes with a *prayer or request for relief.* This specifies the remedy that the plaintiff wants the court to impose. If the plaintiff is seeking to be compensated for loss, the prayer for relief will request damages. A copy of a complaint appears in Figure 4–4.

The **summons** is a court order that gives the defendant notice of the lawsuit and requires the defendant to respond within a prescribed period of time (frequently 20 days). If no response is filed within that time period, a *default judgment* will be entered. This judgment is entered as a result of the defendant's nonappearance.

complaint
The document a plaintiff files to begin a civil lawsuit. It gives the plaintiff's version of the facts, shows the court's jurisdiction, and requests a remedy by its prayer for relief.

summons
A court order giving the defendant notice of a lawsuit and a certain time period in which to respond or face a judgment by default.

FIGURE 4-4

State of Michigan
Kalamazoo County Circuit Court

Ace Electronics
Plaintiff(s)

v.

Jane Smith
Defendant(s)

Judge Joyce Sanchez
(Assigned Judge)

Civil Action No.
95-987654-MI
(Year-File-Code)

Jones & Robinson (23232)
Attorney(s) for the Plaintiff

3825 N. Crosstown Parkway ,
Address

616-432-5678
Phone Number

There is no civil action between these parties arising out of the same transaction of occurrence as alleged in this complaint pending in this court, nor has any such action been assigned to a judge.

COMPLAINT

Plaintiff. Ace Electronics, by its attorneys, Jones & Robinson states:

1. Between the dates of July 1, 1994 and October 10, 1994 Plaintiff sold and delivered certain goods, wares, and merchandise to the Defendant, upon open account, upon the promise of Defendant to pay for these goods.

2. There is now unpaid upon this account the sum of $12,250.00.

3. The account has become stated between the parties.

4. As a consequence, Defendant is justly indebted to Plaintiff in the amount of $12,250.00 plus interest from and after October 10, 1994 plus costs of suit.

5. A copy of the account and an affidavit verifying the account are attached as Plaintiff's Exhibits A and B.

PLAINTIFF REQUESTS judgment in its favor and against Defendant in the amount of $12,250.00 plus interest, cost, and attorney's fees.

Jones & Robinson
(Firm Name)

By Robert Robinson
(Typed Name of Attorney)

3825 N. Crosstown Parkway
(Address)

(616)-432-5678
(Phone Number)

---

answer
A document filed by the defendant that responds point by point to the allegations in the plaintiff's complaint.

The response to the plaintiff's complaint is generally found in the defendant's answer. The **answer** is a document that responds point by point to the allegations and statements of the plaintiff's complaint. If the defendant agrees with a statement, the defendant may admit that the statement is true. If the defendant disagrees with an allegation, the answer will show that the defendant denies the allegations. In this way, the defendant addresses each essential segment of the plaintiff's claim.

The answer may also include an affirmative defense. An *affirmative defense* provides a legal justification for the defendant's conduct. It states a legal reason why the defendant would be found not liable even if the plaintiff's claims were found to be true. A *counterclaim,* which is essentially a suit by the defendant against the plaintiff, may also be a part of the defendant's answer.

In addition to the answer, the defendant's response to the plaintiff's complaint, the defendant may also make a variety of other responses by motions. A *motion* is a request to the court for some type of court order. Motions may be made throughout the pleading, pretrial, trial, and post-trial stages of litigation. During the pleadings stage, most motions are made in writing. Before the court acts on a motion, notice is provided to the opposing party, and oral arguments on the motion are presented to the judge. The judge either grants or overrules motions before litigation continues.

If the defendant's answer raises facts not addressed in the plaintiff's complaint, the plaintiff files a reply document. A *reply* either admits or denies the new facts raised by the defendant's answer. Once all of the pleadings have been filed, the framework or outline of the litigation emerges. Matters that the defendant has admitted in the answer are not at issue and need not be proved at trial. The disputed facts and allegations form the basis for further investigation during the pretrial stage and at the trial.

Pretrial Activities

Discovery Procedures After the pleadings have been filed, but before the trial begins, each party seeks to discover as many important facts as possible about the dispute. The U.S. legal system has a very open approach to litigation in general and to discovery procedures in particular. Because both of the parties to a lawsuit have access to the same information, documents, and potential witnesses, any surprise at the time of trial is usually eliminated.

Discovery procedures are the methods used by each of the parties in a lawsuit to uncover facts or documents that are in the exclusive knowledge or possession of the opposing party or that party's witnesses and may be used as evidence. Discovery is less significant in criminal litigation than in civil cases because in criminal litigation some of the defendant's information does not have to be made available to the prosecution. A variety of discovery procedures are used in civil suits.

discovery procedures The methods used by litigants to uncover facts or documents in the exclusive knowledge of the opposing party or that party's witnesses.

Depositions A **deposition** is transcribed testimony that a witness gives under oath and outside court. The witness is examined by the attorney for one party and then cross-examined by the attorney for the other party; all of the questions and answers are recorded by a court reporter. Depositions enable the parties to find out prior to a trial, when the witness's recall is fresh, what that person might say when called on to testify at the trial. If a witness is unable to appear at the trial, his or her deposition may be used and the testimony preserved. Because both deposition and trial testimony are given under oath, conflicts between a deposition statement and trial testimony can be used to discredit a trial witness. Clearly, before testifying at a trial, a well-prepared witness will carefully review his or her deposition statement.

deposition Testimony that a witness gives under oath and outside the courtroom; depositions are used to find out prior to trial the testimony of opposing witnesses and to preserve that testimony for use at trial if the witness is unavailable.

Examinations An examination may be a physical or mental examination of a litigant or an examination of personal or real property. Thus, a doctor hired by the opposing party may conduct physical examinations of a party to determine the extent of a claimed injury. A psychiatrist may conduct mental examinations to assist in determining a party's mental state. Examinations of buildings by contractors, engineers, and architects may reveal hidden defects in design or construction.

Inspections and Production of Records and Documents A unique feature of the U.S. legal system is that the records and documents of each litigant relating to the matters in dispute must be made accessible to the other litigant. Bookkeeping records, correspondence, medical files, and financial documents in the possession of either party may be requested and must be made available for inspection and review by the opposing party. Only privileged or totally irrelevant information is exempt from such a request.

interrogatories Written questions submitted to the opposing party that must be answered under oath.

Interrogatories **Interrogatories** are written questions submitted to the opposing party that must be answered under oath. Although the opposing party need not provide answers that go beyond the questions asked, this discovery device sometimes uncovers information that only the opposing party has. A question might ask, for example, if the opposing party has or knows of any correspondence relating to defects in products sold to the plaintiff.

INTERNATIONAL PERSPECTIVE AND COMMENTARY

DISCOVERY OR DISCLOSURE

Two different systems exist in the United States and in most European countries for obtaining information needed for trial. In the United States, a civil suit may be filed even though the plaintiff has very little information regarding potential witnesses and what their testimony may indicate about the issues in the trial. The filing of the case generally occurs first, and then the parties seek to *discover* information from the other party that will enhance their case. The discovery entails interrogatories to the opposing parties, numerous depositions from the parties and their witnesses, and frequent requests for files and documents that might have any possible bearing on the case. The objective of the discovery process is laudable—it seeks to produce all relevant evidence—but it often becomes too extensive, repetitive, and expensive for the parties.

In European countries (including England, a common law country), a case is investigated before it is filed. The potential litigants *disclose* documents and possible witness information before the case is filed. Once suit is filed, preliminary pleadings are filed to see if the case has legal merit. If it does, a trial date is set, and the parties exchange their witness lists and a short statement of what the witnesses will say. Exhibits to be used are exchanged, and the trial proceeds. Depositions may not be used at trials unless a witness is outside the court's jurisdiction.

In contrast to both the U.S. and the European systems, Japanese discovery procedures are very limited. A plaintiff who might bring a personal injury or product liability case against a manufacturer of a product that may have caused injury to the plaintiff cannot require the manufacturer to disclose reports it has regarding any problems encountered in the manufacturing process or complaints from other consumers of similar products. As a consequence, plaintiffs in Japan, who usually have little knowledge about the manufacturing process or the safety record of a manufacturer's product, generally find it very difficult to prove the defendant's negligence or the product's defective nature. Thus, potential plaintiffs in Japan do not perceive that there is much to gain from litigation. Civil cases in Japan often take a very long time to resolve, the likelihood of success is low, and the society encourages settlement through negotiation or mediation rather than litigation. As a result, legal costs associated with product liability concerns obviously differ significantly for Japanese and U.S. manufacturers.

Although each system has merit, there is a growing belief that the discovery procedure currently used in most U.S. courts is too cumbersome, expensive, and time-consuming. How it may be modified is unclear; the disclosure system is being carefully reviewed to see how it might apply in the U.S. legal environment.

Pretrial Conference A **pretrial conference** is a meeting of several persons, such as the attorneys and the judge, held prior to trial to enhance the interchange of opinions and eliminate differences or disputes. Pretrial conferences seek to narrow the issues in dispute and to move the controversy toward either trial or settlement. Some pretrial conferences are quite formal: The judge, attorneys, and perhaps the parties meet in court and review outstanding issues. Other pretrial conferences are informal: The attorneys and judge discuss the case in the judge's office, and no formal record of their conversation is kept.

pretrial conference A meeting of attorneys and the judge prior to trial held to narrow the issues in dispute and to move the controversy toward trial or settlement.

A judge may ask the parties to submit documents, such as briefs, showing the sources of law that back up their claims. If a trial is to be conducted, the use of expert witnesses may be discussed and the possible date and length of the trial determined. Settlement options that could resolve the controversy without a trial are also reviewed. For example, if an injured party is seeking compensation, the parties may agree that the plaintiff's medical expenses incurred since the injury amount to $100,000. The defendant may not admit liability, and the plaintiff may be seeking additional compensation, but the question of what medical expenses have been incurred will not need to be proven at the trial.

Trial Procedures

Most civil cases do not result in a trial; instead, they are settled by the parties outside the courtroom. Approximately 5 percent of the civil cases filed in federal courts are tried. Usually, when a trial does occur, it is because the parties are unable to agree about what actually happened. Thus, this is the primary purpose of most civil trials. In the American legal system, questions of fact are usually determined by a jury.

However, in some civil cases, the parties do not have a right to a jury trial. The Seventh Amendment to the United States Constitution provides: "In suits at common law, where the value in controversy shall exceed twenty dollars, the right to trial by jury shall be preserved . . . " Thus, suits that were tried in the chancery or equity courts (without benefit of a jury) instead of "at common law" are not covered by the Seventh Amendment's jury trial guarantee. Equity cases include cases in which the plaintiff asks the court to grant an unusual remedy, such as an injunction or a specific performance order. Those remedies are equitable remedies that historically were not available in common law suits; suits asking for such relief are not tried before a jury.

In some cases, the parties agree to waive their rights to a jury trial. In non-jury trials, the judge not only determines the legal questions, but also decides the facts. In the *Palmer* case that follows, a third-party defendant in the case (a third-party defendant is a party whom the original defendant brings into the case) claims he is entitled to a jury trial; whereas, the government claims a case like his is not guaranteed a jury trial by the Seventh Amendment. The court also considers whether that party has waived the right to a jury trial.

Palmer v. United States

652 F.2d 893 (9th Cir. 1981)
United States Court of Appeals

Palmer was injured after being struck by an automobile driven by an employee of the United States. At the time of the accident, Palmer was standing in a public highway directing traffic around Fisher's automobile, which had been disabled after colliding with another vehicle. Fisher, who later admitted having drunk an alcoholic beverage prior to his collision, had left the scene of the accident before Palmer was struck by the government vehicle.

Palmer sued the government under the Federal Tort Claims Act, seeking damages for negligence. The government then sued Fisher as a third party defendant, demanding he reimburse the government if it was held liable to Palmer. Although both Palmer and Fisher asked for a jury trial, no jury was impaneled. During the trial, neither Palmer nor Fisher objected to the court's apparent failure to rule on the jury demands.

The trial court found that the negligence of both the government and Fisher had contributed to the injuries sustained by Palmer. Under California's doctrine of comparative negligence, the court held the government responsible for 30 percent and Fisher responsible for 70 percent of the negligence causing Palmer's injuries. Damages were determined to be $88,600. Because the government was the only named defendant in the plaintiff's actions, the court ordered it to pay the entire amount to Palmer. It then held that the government was entitled to a judgment against Fisher for 70 percent of the damages it paid. Fisher appealed, contending the trial court erred in denying him a jury trial. Fisher argued that because the government's claim against him was a tort claim under the common law, a jury trial was needed. The government argued that its claim for compensation due from Fisher derived from the doctrine of contribution, an equitable doctrine, and therefore did not warrant a jury trial under the Seventh Amendment.

Ferris, Circuit Judge

Whether the Seventh Amendment authorizes a jury trial in a particular case does not depend on the character of the overall action, but instead is determined by "the nature of the issue to be tried." An issue is considered "legal" when its resolution involves the ascertainment and determination of legal rights or justifies a remedy traditionally granted by common law courts.

Here, the government's claim against Fisher requires a determination of the extent to which Fisher's negligence contributed to Palmer's injuries, the relative fault between Fisher and the government, and whether the government has in fact satisfied the judgment rendered against it in Palmer's original negligence suit. Each of these issues involves determinations of rights and liabilities traditionally arising in common law suits for negligence. Moreover, the government seeks to recover from Fisher a portion of the damages which it was required to pay to Palmer. Recovery of damages is a remedy traditionally granted by common law courts. Accordingly, we hold that Fisher, as a third-party defendant who was not joined as a defendant in Palmer's original action, had a right to a jury trial on the government's claim for partial comparative indemnity.

There is no dispute here that Fisher filed a timely demand for a jury trial. Federal Rule of Civil Procedure 38(d) specifically provides that, once a timely demand is filed as required by Federal Rule of Civil Procedure 5(d), the demand can only be withdrawn by consent of the parties. Hence, the precise issue here is whether Fisher waived his right to jury trial by withdrawing his demand. Under Federal Rule of Civil Procedure 39(a), a consensual withdrawal of a jury demand can be effected by the parties through either (1) written stipulation filed with the court or (2) oral stipulation made in open court and entered in the record. The record before us reveals neither an oral nor a written stipulation by the parties to withdraw Fisher's jury demand. Under the terms of the procedural rules applicable here, then, Fisher's jury demand was never properly withdrawn.

The government argues, however, that Fisher withdrew his jury demand by failing to object and by otherwise acquiescing to the bench trial format of the district court proceedings. We decline to create an exception to the precise terms of Federal Rules of Civil Procedure 38(d) and 39(a), although we recognize that other courts have done so. Because the constitutional right to a jury trial is fundamental, we must indulge every reasonable presumption against its waiver. A party's acquiescence to the district court's maintenance of a bench trial, without more, is insufficient to establish a withdrawal of a jury demand.

We hold, therefore, that there was no withdrawal of Fisher's demand for a jury trial.

Reversed and remanded.

Case Questions

1. What criterion is used to determine whether a party in a civil case is entitled to a jury trial? When is an issue a legal issue?
2. What are the two reasons the court gives for Fisher being entitled to a jury trial?
3. If a party in a federal case wants to waive the right to a jury trial, how can he or she make that waiver?

Selection of a Jury Usually, the first step in any trial is the selection of the jury. In most states, the number of jurors varies with the type of case. Approximately three-fourths of the states have civil case juries consisting of from six to eight people. In many states, the jury's decision or verdict need not be reached by unanimous vote. In Michigan, for example, all civil case juries consist of six people, and a decision on which five of the six agree constitutes the jury's verdict. A *hung jury* occurs if fewer than the minimum required to make a valid decision agree.

Prospective jurors are chosen from various sources in the community. The selection process is meant to obtain a cross-section of the community. Of course, some of the people who are called to serve may not be impartial with regard to the issues in specific cases. If it can be shown that a person's biases might influence his or her decision in a particular case, the judge will grant a challenge to exclude that person from serving as a juror on that case. Challenges to potential jurors and other aspects of the jury's role are discussed in a subsequent section of this chapter.

Presentation of Evidence Once the jury is selected, the presentation of evidence begins. First, each party is given a chance to make an *opening statement,* an overview of the case to be presented. This statement indicates to the judge and jury what testimony, documents, and exhibits the party intends to present as evidence. Opening statements are not considered evidence.

The plaintiff, who begins the presentation, has the burden of proving the complaint's allegations by the preponderance of evidence. Most of the evidence presented is the oral testimony of witnesses who are questioned by the attorneys. Documents, charts, or other exhibits are also submitted. After a witness has answered the questions of the plaintiff's attorney on direct examination, the defendant's attorney asks the witness questions through cross-examination.

Direct examination is the questioning of a witness by the party on whose behalf the witness has been called, while *cross-examination* is the questioning of a witness called by the opposing party. The questioning of a witness can continue through redirect and re-cross-examination if new issues are brought out in the witness's answers.

Once the plaintiff has called all of the witnesses who are to testify and has introduced the exhibits to be considered by the jury, the plaintiff's primary case is complete. If the testimony presented is not sufficient to allow a jury to decide for the plaintiff, the defendant can present a motion to the judge to direct the verdict and dismiss the case. If the judge agrees with the request, the judge will grant the *motion to direct the verdict* in favor of the defendant. When this occurs, the jury has nothing to do; the case is over and has been decided in the defendant's favor. If the judge does not grant the motion, the trial continues and the defendant presents evidence.

Oral testimony of witnesses called by the defendant and cross-examined by the plaintiff is then presented to the jury and the judge. If either litigant believes that the rules of evidence prohibit the introduction of certain evidence, that party may object to the evidence. The judge then makes a legal decision to allow the evidence (*overruling* the objection) or to prohibit its use (*sustaining* the objection). Each major decision that the judge makes concerning the admissibility of evidence can later be reviewed by an appellate court.

Rules of Evidence The rules of evidence assure that information presented during a trial is relevant, unbiased, and reliable. Testimony that has been determined to be unreliable or irrelevant should not be presented. For example, the fact that a witness committed several traffic offenses in the past five years would be irrelevant in a civil trial involving a contract dispute. If one of the parties seeks to ask the witness a question concerning those offenses, the other party can object to such evidence as irrelevant to the trial. The judge would then rule on the objection and should exclude the evidence by sustaining the objection.

Similarly, information contrary to a rule of evidence may be offered at a trial. One such rule concerns *hearsay* testimony. This rule of evidence, which has many exceptions, excludes as unreliable any testimony based on what a person has heard other people say. Testimony is restricted to statements based on the witness's knowledge and observation. For example, if Chris witnesses a fight between Dave and Jim, Chris may testify as to what he saw. However, if Chris tells Dianne about that fight, Dianne may not testify as to what she heard Chris say. Hearsay testimony is excluded because the opposing party cannot probe Chris's perceptions if only Dianne is available to report the hearsay.

Concluding the Trial After both the plaintiff and defendant have finished presenting evidence, each is usually given a chance to offer rebuttal evidence contradicting the evidence that was presented by the opposing party. The parties are then usually allowed to make *closing statements,* or summations, that organize the evidence to assist the jury in arriving at that party's desired conclusion. Like the opening statements, these statements are not evidence, and the jury cannot consider them facts in reaching its decision.

After the closing statements have been presented, the judge gives the jury *instructions* as to the law it should apply to the dispute and as to the evidence presented by the parties. The judge's instructions summarize the law, and the jury reviews the evidence and determines the facts. The **verdict** is the jury's determination based on the application of the law, as provided in instructions from the judge, to the facts, as determined from the evidence by the jury.

verdict
The jury's decision at the end of a case based on instructions regarding the law from the judge and the jury's determination of the facts.

Although people often think of the jury's verdict as the end of a trial, the trial judge may legally set aside or change a verdict. Most judges are hesitant to alter a jury's verdict, but if a judge believes that a jury's verdict is not based on the evidence presented or does not follow the instructions of law, the judge may reverse the verdict by granting a *judgment notwithstanding the verdict (JNOV).* Of course, a judge's reversal of a verdict may be appealed.

Post-Judgment Concerns

It is the court's **judgment,** or decision, that ends the trial court proceedings. If either party considers the judgment wrong, that party can appeal the judge's legal errors. Such errors may arise if the judge admits or denies the use of certain testimony or exhibits as evidence or makes mistakes in instructing the jury as to the law. If the judgment is not appealed within a specified period, it becomes final.

judgment
The judge's determination or decision at the end of a trial; it may be different from the jury's verdict. If the judgment is not appealed within a certain time, it becomes final.

A plaintiff may obtain a judgment against a defendant for $100,000, yet fail to receive that amount. The judgment is a legal determination of the amount of money owed. If the defendant does not pay the determined amount voluntarily, the plaintiff may use legal means to enforce the judgment.

One method used to enforce a judgment is garnishment. *Garnishments* of wages or bank accounts are court orders to other persons, such as the defendant's employer or bank, to pay the plaintiff some of the defendant's money.

Another method is to attach assets of the defendant, such as a car or other personal property. An *attachment* is an order allowing one person, such as the plaintiff, to sell personal property of the defendant, such as equipment, inventory, or furnishings, so that the proceeds may be used to pay off a judgment. The judgment also gives the plaintiff a *lien,* an interest in real estate owned by the defendant. If that real estate is sold, some of the proceeds will be paid to the plaintiff.

The judgment of a court usually remains in effect for several years and may be renewed. Any time during that period, property acquired by the defendant can be garnished, attached, or subjected to a lien so that it can be used to satisfy the judgment. Only after the judgment has been fully paid or satisfied, does the defendant's legal obligation to the plaintiff terminate.

Appellate Process

An appellate court reviews the legal rulings that one or both of the parties think were incorrectly made by the trial court judge. The trial court is charged primarily with deciding factual discrepancies between the parties. In an appeal, therefore, a determination of the facts is unnecessary because all of the factual issues were decided prior to or at the trial. Because trial courts perform different functions than do appellate courts, the appellate process varies substantially from the trial process.

The *trial court record* consists of the transcript of the testimony of all the witnesses, the exhibits used as evidence, the judge's rulings on all objections to the introduction of evidence, the judge's instructions to the jury, the jury's verdict, and the judgment of the court. The comments of the parties generally consist of oral arguments, supported by written presentations called briefs. A *brief* used in an appeal highlights the claims made by a party at the trial. It usually provides references to other cases that support those claims.

Appellate court judges make decisions based on the trial court record, the oral arguments, written briefs of the parties, and research and discussion conducted by the appellate court itself. An appellate court generally consists of three judges who act by a majority vote. If the appellate court agrees with the trial court's judgment, it affirms that court's determination. If the appellate court determines that the trial court's judgment was incorrect, it reverses the judgment. Finally, the appellate court can either modify the legal remedy provided by the trial court or remand (return) the case to the trial court for some redetermination.

Suppose an appeal is made because the plaintiff that lost the case wanted to use certain testimony at the trial that the judge excluded. If the appellate court determines that the judge's interpretation was wrong and that the plaintiff's testimony should have been allowed as evidence, the appellate court would probably remand (return) the case to the trial court. If the excluded testimony was critical to the plaintiff's case, the verdict of the jury (which was against the plaintiff) might have been different. Because there is no way to tell whether the jury's decision would have been different, the case is sent back to the trial court, which must now allow the plaintiff to use the excluded testimony.

Participants in Civil Litigation

Each of the participants in civil litigation have distinct and important roles. Because litigation in the United States uses an adversarial process, attorneys, as representatives of the parties, are given significant responsibilities for investigating facts and presenting evidence. The parties and their legal representatives, not the judge, control this part of the litigation process. The judge determines the applicable law and rules on the evidence that can be used. The jury analyzes the evidence presented and determines a verdict after receiving instructions from the judge. The roles of the judge, jury, attorney, and parties involved in civil litigation each balance and check the power granted the others.

The Trial Judge

Judges are selected in several ways. Federal judges are appointed by the president, with the advice and consent of the Senate. Usually, the senior senator who is from the same political party as the president approves the selection, and the entire Senate consents. If there is no senator from the president's political party, the president then selects a person who still must be approved by the Senate as a whole. Justices of the Supreme Court are closely scrutinized by the Senate as a whole after being nominated by the Senate.

The states use a mixture of appointive and elective processes to choose judges. Most states use some form of an election with judges being nominated by political parties. The judges are then elected either through identification with a political party or after running on a nonpartisan ballot. In the Missouri plan, the governor of a state appoints judges by selecting from a list of people nominated by a nonpartisan board. At the next election, voters then determine whether to retain the judge for a full term, which is usually six or eight years.

A judge in the American legal system must perform several functions. The parties in a case have a right to a judge who is able to act as an impartial decision maker at the trial by deciding legal issues based on existing laws, not on the basis of individual beliefs or because of bias toward one of the parties. The judge must also instruct the jury regarding the law that it is to use in arriving at its verdict. After the trial, other judges, who act as an appellate court, provide a check on the trial court judge by reviewing the judgment.

The Jury

The jury's primary role in the American legal system is to determine the disputed facts. Either of the parties involved in a civil trial can request a jury. Nevertheless, waiving of the right to a jury trial is quite frequent in civil cases. In many of the world's legal systems, no jury is available for most civil lawsuits. Thus, the role of the jury is most often discussed as a part of the criminal trial process rather than the civil trial process. The following commentary presents an unusual situation: The prosecutor desires a jury trial that the defendants want to waive.

Judge or Jury? Federal Prosecutor Wants Lay People to Hear Insider-Trading Case

By Stephen J. Adler

NEW YORK—In a surprise move, the U.S. attorney's office has refused to allow defendants in the Marcus Schloss & Co. insider-trading case to have a judge, rather than a jury, decide their case.

While defendants in criminal cases have a constitutional right to trial by jury, ordinarily they can waive that right and allow a judge to hear the case in a so-called bench trial. But under federal procedural rules, both the judge and the prosecutor have to consent to the waiver. And in this case, the prosecutor refused.

In his letter Friday opposing the bench trial, Manhattan U.S. Attorney Benito Romano said, "Jury trials occupy a special place in the framework of our government and therefore, absent extraordinary circumstances not present here, it is the general policy of this office not to consent to a defendant's waiver of a jury."

Defense lawyers said . . . that juries are likely to be unsympathetic to well-to-do defendants, particularly in cases involving alleged abuses on Wall Street.

Stanley S. Arkin, attorney for defendant D. Ronald Yagoda, said, . . . "A jury is not going to understand the professional's advantage in trading stocks as opposed to the advantage that a crook gets."

In the case, Mr. Yagoda, the former head of trading at Marcus Schloss, was charged with conspiring with members of the "Yuppie Five" ring, allegedly to trade on inside information. He was also charged with perjury and obstruction of justice in connection with his testimony before the Securities and Exchange Commission. Marcus Schloss was charged with insider trading in connection with its arbitrage activities. Both defendants pleaded innocent.

. . . Mr. Romano extolled trial by jury in general and added that there was a particularly important reason for such a trial in this case. "It is not secret that certain recent indictments charging securities law violations and related offenses have engendered a great deal of public debate and controversy," he wrote. "The public interest in the prosecution of these 'white-collar' criminal cases suggests to us that primary responsibility for deciding such cases should be placed in the hands of a jury drawn from the lay community."

Defense lawyers in the case agree that they have no legal appeal available because the federal rules and court cases clearly give the prosecution the right to veto their request for a bench trial.

Source: Reprinted by permission of *The Wall Street Journal*, February 27, 1989.

Two major types of juries are a part of the American legal system. The *grand jury* (discussed in Chapter 22) generally has from 17 to 23 members and investigates possible criminal activity. It plays no role in the civil litigation process. The more common type of trial jury, which has 12 or fewer members, is known as the *petit jury* because it is smaller than the grand jury.

Selection of Potential Jurors Potential jurors are generally selected from the adult population of the community in which the court hearing the case is located. The pool of available people is usually drawn from voter registration or drivers' license lists. Although state laws differ, most eligible adults called are required to serve if selected. If a segment of the community is excluded from jury service, such as women over sixty or day-laborers, the jury does not adequately reflect the community.

The Impartiality of the Jury Several special concerns have been expressed regarding the use of a jury in the American legal system. In some cases, there is such pretrial publicity surrounding a case that it may be difficult or impossible to find an impartial jury. Is an impartial jury obtainable if a case being tried is the subject of intense pretrial publicity? Can potential jurors who read the papers, watch television, or listen to the radio be impartial? The murder case against O.J. Simpson certainly raised these questions. Consider the answers suggested to these questions in the following extract from *United States v. Haldeman,* a criminal case involving several advisers to former President Nixon.[3]

> It is fundamental that "the right to jury trial guarantees to the criminally accused a fair trial by a panel of impartial 'indifferent' jurors." To be indifferent a juror need not be ignorant. In these days of swift, widespread and diverse methods of communication, an important case can be expected to arouse the interest of the public in the vicinity, and scarcely any of those best qualified to serve as jurors will not have formed some impression or opinion as to the merits of the case. To hold that the mere existence of any preconceived notion as to the guilt or innocence of an accused, without more, is sufficient to rebut the presumption of a prospective juror's impartiality would be to establish an impossible standard; *it is sufficient if the juror can lay aside his impression or opinion and render a verdict based on the evidence presented.*
>
> We find the pretrial publicity in this case, although massive, was neither inherently prejudicial nor unforgettable. We therefore turn to an examination of the voir dire itself. . . . After determining the venireman's [a venireman is a potential juror, a preson called to court for possible jury service] degree of interest in and exposure to the case, the court inquired whether he had formed or expressed an opinion of the guilt or innocence of any defendant. If the venireman had formed an opinion, the judge attempted to determine whether that opinion was firmly held or could be set aside. In closing he was asked whether he could return a fair and impartial verdict based solely on the evidence presented at trial and the court's instructions on the law. . . . Mere familiarity with the facts and issues involved in the case would not have rendered a venireman unqualified to sit.

The Representative Nature of the Jury Another concern regarding the jury focuses on its representative nature. Is a jury that does not reflect the community's racial, economic, social, or educational makeup still qualified? Potential jurors who have been brought into a court to determine whether they can serve on a specific case go through a process called *voir dire,* which means "to speak the truth." The judge and

[3] 559 F.2d 31 (D.C. Cir., 1976).

each of the parties have a right to question the potential jurors to determine whether they have any bias that would prevent them from rendering an impartial verdict.

A party that considers a juror biased will challenge that person by using either a challenge for cause or a peremptory challenge. A *challenge for cause* cites a legal reason for not selecting the person, such as the person's being related to one of the parties, having a financial interest in the case, or holding a firm opinion about the case. If the judge agrees with the party's reason, the challenge for cause is granted and the person is dismissed. An unlimited number of challenges for cause can be granted. A *peremptory challenge* does not cite any reason for dismissing a potential juror. A limited number of potential jurors may be dismissed through the use of such challenges.

In 1986, the U.S. Supreme Court decided the *Batson* case.[4] The court determined that Batson, a black defendant, was denied equal protection of the law when the prosecutor used peremptory challenges to strike all black veniremen from the panel. The court found the State's privilege to strike individual jurors through peremptory challenges was subject to the equal protection clause and that when those challenges were used in a discriminatory manner, they violated the rights of the defendant. Following the *Batson* case, attorneys and litigants in civil cases wondered about the right of a private party in a civil case to use peremptory challenges to exclude jurors on account of their race. The answer to that question came five years later, in the *Edmonson* case.

Edmonson v. Leesville Concrete Company, Inc.

III. S. Ct. 2077 (1991)
United States Supreme Court

Edmonson, a black construction worker, was injured in a job site accident at Fort Polk, Louisiana, a federal enclave. Edmonson sued Leesville Concrete Co. for negligence in the federal district court, claiming it had permitted one of the company's trucks to roll back and pin him against some construction equipment. Edmonson invoked his Seventh Amendment right to a trial by jury. During *voir dire,* Leesville used two of its three peremptory challenges authorized by statute to remove black persons from the perspective jury. Referring to the *Batson* decision, Edmonson asked the court to require Leesville to provide a race-neutral explanation for the peremptory challenges. The trial court judge denied the request on the grounds that *Batson* does not apply to civil cases.

The jury found for Edmonson in the amount of $90,000, but as it determined he was 80 percent at fault, it reduced his award to $18,000. Edmonson appealed, and the court of appeals reversed, holding that *Batson's* decision that peremptory challenges could not be used to exclude jurors on the basis of race also applies to civil cases. On an en banc (full panel) rehearing, the court of appeals upheld the district court. Edmonson then appealed to the Supreme Court.

[4] *Batson v. Kentucky*, 476 U.S. 80 (1986).

Justice Kennedy delivered the opinion of the Court.

We must decide in the case before us whether a private litigant in a civil case may use peremptory challenges to exclude jurors on account of their race. Recognizing the impropriety of racial bias in the courtroom, we hold the race-based exclusion violates the equal protection rights of the challenged jurors.

In *Powers v. Ohio,* we held that a criminal defendant, regardless of his or her race, may object to a prosecutor's race-based exclusion of persons from the petit jury. Our conclusion rested on a two-part analysis. First, following our opinions in *Batson* and in *Carter v. Jury Commission of Greene County,* we made clear that a prosecutor's race-based peremptory challenge violates the equal protection rights of those excluded from jury service. Second, we relied on well-established rules of third-party standing to hold that a defendant may raise the excluded jurors' equal protection rights.

Powers relied upon over a century of jurisprudence dedicated to the elimination of race prejudice within the jury selection process. Indeed, discrimination on the basis of race in selecting a jury in a civil proceeding harms the excluded juror no less than discrimination in a criminal trial. In either case, race is the sole reason for denying the excluded venireperson the honor and privilege of participating in our system of justice.

That an act violates the Constitution when committed by a government official, however, does not answer the question whether the same act offends constitutional guarantees if committed by a private litigant or his attorney. The Constitution's protection of individual liberty and equal protection apply in general only to action by the government. Racial discrimination, though invidious in all contexts, violates the Constitution only when it may be attributed to state action. Thus, the legality of the exclusion at issue here turns on the extent to which a litigant in a civil case may be subject to the Constitution's restrictions.

. . . This fundamental limitation on the scope of constitutional guarantees "preserves an area of individual freedom by limiting the reach of federal law" and "avoids imposing on the State, its agencies or officials, responsibility for conduct for which they cannot fairly be blamed." One great object of the Constitution is to permit citizens to structure their private relations as they choose subject only to the constraints of statutory or decisional law.

To implement these principles, courts must consider from time to time where the governmental sphere ends and the private sphere begins. We begin our discussion within the framework for the state action analysis set forth in *Lugar.* There we . . . asked first whether the claimed constitutional deprivation resulted from the exercise of a right or privilege having its source in state authority, and second, whether the private party charged with the deprivation could be described in all fairness as a state actor. There can be no question that the first part of the *Lugar* inquiry is satisfied here. By their very nature, peremptory challenges have no significance outside a court of law. Their sole purpose is to permit litigants to assist the government in the selection of an impartial trier of fact. . . . Peremptory challenges are permitted only when the government, by statute or decisional law, deems it appropriate to allow parties to exclude a given number of persons who otherwise would satisfy the requirements for service on the petit jury.

. . . In the case before us, the challenges were exercised under a federal statute that provides, "In civil cases, each party shall be entitled to three peremptory challenges." Without this authorization, granted by an Act of Congress itself, Leesville would not have been able to engage in the alleged discriminatory acts. Given that the statutory authorization for the challenges exercised in this case is clear, the remainder of our state action analysis centers around the second part of the *Lugar* test, whether a private litigant in all fairness must be deemed a government actor in the use of peremptory challenges. Although we have recognized that this aspect of the analysis is often a fact bound inquiry, our cases disclose certain principles of general application. Our precedents establish that, in determining whether a particular action or course of conduct is governmental in character, it is relevant to examine the following: the extent to which the actor relies on governmental assistance and benefits, whether the actor is performing a traditional governmental function, and whether the injury caused is aggravated in a unique way by the incidents of governmental authority. Based on our application of these three principles to the circumstances here, we hold that the exercise of peremptory challenges by the defendant in the District Court was pursuant to a course of state action.

. . . As discussed above, peremptory challenges have no utility outside the jury system, a system which the government alone administers. In the federal system, Congress has established the qualifications for jury service, and has outlined the procedures by which jurors are selected. To this end, each district court in the federal system must adopt a plan for locating and summoning to the court eligible prospective jurors. This plan . . . must implement statutory policies of random juror selection from a fair cross section of the community, and nonexclusion on account of race, color, religion, sex, national origin, or economic status.

At the outset of the selection process, prospective jurors must complete jury qualification forms as prescribed by the Administrative Office of the United States Courts. . . . In a typical case, counsel receive these forms and rely on them when exercising their peremptory strikes. The Clerk of the United States District Court, a federal official, summons potential jurors from their employment or other pursuits. . . . Whether or not they are selected for a jury panel, summoned jurors receive a per diem fixed by statute for their service.

The trial judge exercises substantial control over *voir dire* in the federal system. In some cases, judges may even conduct the entire *voir dire* by themselves, a common practice in the District Court where the instant case was tried. When a lawyer exercises a peremptory challenge, the judge advises the juror he or she has been excused.

As we have outlined here, a private party could not exercise its peremptory challenges absent the overt, significant assistance of the court. The government summons jurors, constrains their freedom of movement, and subjects them to public scrutiny and examination. . . . Without the direct and indispensable participation of the judge, who beyond all question is a state actor, the peremptory challenge system would serve no purpose. By enforcing a discriminatory peremptory challenge, the court "has not only made itself a party to the [biased act], but has elected to place its power, property and prestige behind the [alleged] discrimination." In so doing, the government has "create[d] the legal framework governing the [challenged] conduct," and in a significant way has involved itself with invidious discrimination.

In determining Leesville's state-actor status, we next consider whether the action in question involves the performance of a traditional function of the government. A traditional function of government is evident here.

In the federal system, the Constitution itself commits the trial of facts in a civil cause to the jury. Should either party to a cause invoke its Seventh Amendment right, the jury becomes the principal factfinder, charged with weighing the evidence, judging the credibility of witnesses, and reaching a verdict. The jury's factual determinations as a general rule are final. These are traditional functions of government, not of a select, private group beyond the reach of the Constitution. . . . Though the motive of a peremptory challenge may be to protect a private interest, the objective of jury selection proceedings is to determine representation on a governmental body. Were it not for peremptory challenges, there would be no question that the entire process of determining who will serve on the jury constitutes state action. The fact that the government delegates some portion of this power to private litigants does not change the governmental character of the power exercised.

Race discrimination within the courtroom raises serious questions as to the fairness of the proceedings conducted there. Racial bias mars the integrity of the judicial system and prevents the idea of democratic government from becoming a reality. To permit racial exclusion in this official forum compounds the racial insult inherent in judging a citizen by the color of his or her skin.

A civil proceeding often implicates significant rights and interests. Civil juries, no less than their criminal counterparts, must follow the law and act as impartial factfinders. And, as we have observed, their verdicts, no less than those of their criminal counterparts, become binding judgments of the court. Racial discrimination has no place in the courtroom, whether the proceeding is civil or criminal. The Constitution demands nothing less. We conclude that the courts must entertain a challenge to a private litigant's racially discriminatory use of peremptory challenges in a civil trial.

It may be true that the role of litigants in determining the jury's composition provides one reason for wide acceptance of the jury system and of its verdicts. But if race stereotypes are the price for acceptance of a jury panel as fair, the price is too high to meet the standard of the Constitution. The quiet rationality of the courtroom makes it an appropriate place to confront race-based fears or hostility by means other than the use of offensive stereotypes. Whether the race generality employed by litigants to challenge a potential juror derives from open hostility or from some hidden and unarticulated fear, neither motive entitles the litigant to cause injury to the excused juror.

The judgment is reversed, and the case is remanded for further proceedings consistent with our opinion.

Case Questions

1. Do the constitutional guarantees of individual liberty and equal protection usually apply to private parties? Why?

2. What are the reasons the Court gives for finding that the use of peremptory challenges to jurors in a civil case constitute "state action"?

3. What sequence of steps in the selection of a jury are outlined in the case?

The Attorney

attorney-at-law
A person who acts for someone else in legal matters; attorneys are licensed by state law.

An **attorney-at-law** is a person who acts for someone else in legal matters that may concern real estate, tax, contract, or civil litigation problems. In the United States, the license to practice law is granted by the states, not by the federal government. The requirements differ somewhat among the states, but graduation from an approved law school and the successful completion of a state-approved bar examination are generally prerequisites to obtaining a license to practice law.

Attorney's Office Environment Some attorneys have their own law offices. Others are members of firms with as few as two or three partners or as many as 500 or more attorneys. Still others are salaried employees of corporations. Many attorneys are employed by federal, state, and local governmental agencies. A significant number of attorneys do not even practice law: They work as bankers, business managers, or educators.

Businesses that regularly use attorneys to perform a variety of functions have developed several organizational means for working with them. Many businesses hire attorneys as employees and either disperse them among operational units or centralize them into a separate legal department. A staff of lawyers who work as attorneys for a business is generally referred to as *corporate counsel* or *inside counsel.* This is the role played by Mr. Thomas in the *Upjohn* case, which appears on page 129.

A different type of business-attorney relationship exists when a business retains a lawyer or a law firm. This relationship is usually based on a contract specifying the fee that the business will pay in exchange for the services provided for the business by the lawyer or law firm. A business may not want to hire a lawyer each time it has a legal problem. Instead, it may agree to pay a set sum to retain a law firm and thus ensure that when it needs that firm's services, it can consult with the firm's lawyers. The attorney-client relationship is formed once the retainer agreement has been made, and it remains in effect whenever the law firm performs work for the business.

Many businesses work both with attorneys who are employees and with attorneys in law firms. The inside counsel usually perform functions while some legal specialized services are provided by the attorneys in law firms. In many cases, an outside law firm is hired to act as a litigator if the legal problems of a business involve court proceedings. Some companies bargain with law firms to reduce their fees for the services they provide. Figure 4–5 depicts some of the methods being used by business to reduce legal fees.

Firms incurring rising legal costs are also likely to more carefully scrutinize legal costs in general and litigation expenses in particular. Attorneys who are employees of corporate firms may be given more of the legal work of the firm to perform and may act as managing supervisors on projects requiring the use of outside law firms.

FIGURE 4-5

Methods Used by Business Firms to Reduce Legal Fees

- **Bidding on proposals** Clients send proposals to several law firms; the law firms detail their plans, specify attorneys who will be used, and state the fee to be charged.
- **Blended rates** Clients pay an hourly rate that blends the rates normally charged by senior level partners and junior level associates; the law firm then determines who to assign to the client.
- **Flat fees** Law firms agree to handle a project for a flat fee, no matter how many attorney hours are needed.
- **Mix of hourly and contingent fees** Some portion of the firm's hourly fees is dependent upon success in the case.
- **Volume discount** A business agrees to send a law firm all of a specific kind of work (e.g., environmental litigation), and the law firm agrees to discount its normal fees.

INTERNATIONAL PERSPECTIVE AND COMMENTARY

LAWYERS AND GLOBAL BUSINESS

Business firms engaged in international business rely on the advice of those attorneys who know the rules of international trade and investment. These attorneys may be employees of the business firm itself or may be practicing in a law firm. Many U.S. law firms have followed their clients overseas and are now located in cities such as Beijing, Moscow, Tokyo, and Mexico City.

Some nations, such as Japan, admit very few foreign attorneys, while others, such as France, allow foreign attorneys in their country to do only those activities their lawyers could do in the foreigner's home country. The restrictions on attorneys most often affect the attorney's representation of a client in court; few nations allow foreign attorneys to represent a client without assistance from a local attorney. Some restrictions are also imposed on foreign attorneys who seek to negotiate with government or business representatives.

In the European Community, attorneys from one member nation are allowed to move freely among the other member nations to establish law firms and to provide legal services. It may be that this freedom will expand beyond the Community's borders. However, even in the Community, the restrictions on court appearances and formal representation of a client are enforced.

The growth of international business activities has led to an expansion of multinational legal departments and international law firms. The mixture of lawyers from different nations who work side by side on international business matters is leading to the development of an international legal practice.

Functions Performed by Attorneys Most of the time practicing attorneys spend on legal matters does not relate to the conduct of trials. The attorney acting as litigator performs the most visible type of legal work, but counseling, negotiating, and drafting functions are the predominant and most time-consuming activities of many attorneys.

An attorney acting as a *counselor* for a firm gives the firm advice regarding its activities. How do tax laws affect the firm's decision to purchase or lease a building? What should the contract forms say when the firm sells products to consumers? Should the firm organize a separate corporate entity to sell its products internationally? Although the officers and directors of a firm are responsible for such decisions, they generally seek the counsel of both inside and outside attorneys concerning the laws that affect the firm's activities.

Attorneys also work as *negotiators.* If a business is purchasing a sizable real estate parcel, developing a mall, or contracting to install computers in a university, specialized attorneys may be called on to negotiate contract terms. Businesses having contractual relations with labor unions frequently hire attorneys to negotiate collective bargaining agreements. Attorneys often negotiate with governmental representatives. For example, an attorney for a business may negotiate with a local government about a variance in the zoning code or a reduction in the local property taxes. Negotiations at the state level may focus on agency investigations, licenses, permits, or compliance reports. At the national or international level, attorneys may negotiate a joint venture or license agreement for a business firm.

Attorneys are also *drafters* of documents. They often write wills for clients, prepare contracts regarding the purchase and sale of businesses, or draft partnership agreements. An attorney who drafts documents seeks to ensure that their language addresses and resolves as many legal problems as possible. Given this objective, it is not surprising that the contract terms for what appears to be a simple transaction are often detailed and complex. The parties expect attorneys to draft documents that cover all of the essential concerns and foreseeable problems, including concerns the parties may be unaware of.

The attorney who works as a *litigator* in a trial is engaged in the most visible of legal tasks. Because of the publicity given to certain types of lawsuits (product liability, environmental protection, and securities regulation), many people assume that a business is almost invariably the defendant when it is in court. In fact, the bulk of business litigation involves corporations as plaintiffs. Generally, lawsuits in the fields of contract and commercial law involve two businesses. Because the American legal system is an adversary system, the attorney's role in a civil trial is clearly that of an advocate for the client's interests from the prepleadings stage through the trial or appeal.

FUNCTIONS PERFORMED BY ATTORNEYS

Attorncy Function	Examples
Counsellor	Advises business on whether to incorporate. Counsels on whether tax laws favor a lease rather than a purchase of property.
Negotiator	Negotiates labor contract for business with employees' representative. Negotiates a contract for a major purchase—such as a new computer system.
Drafter	Prepares contracts for sale of business. Drafts will and trust agreement.
Litigator	Represents individual or business acting as plaintiff in lawsuit. Defends business or individual being sued by other parties.

Attorney–Client Privilege A business firm wants to select an attorney who can be trusted, whether as an employee or by means of a retainer agreement. The attorney-client relationship is based on trust. Frequently, the attorney requires confidential information in order to perform his or her function. To counsel, negotiate, draft, or litigate, the attorney must be informed about business activities relating to that function. The **attorney–client privilege** provides that an attorney cannot be forced to divulge such confidential information regarding his or her client. In the *Upjohn* case, which follows, the U.S. Supreme Court reviews the role of Upjohn's attorney. Is a corporate attorney permitted to keep confidential information obtained from employees about questionable payments made to foreign officials, or must the attorney reveal that information to the Internal Revenue Service (IRS)?

attorney–client privilege Provides that an attorney cannot be forced to divulge confidential information regarding his or her client.

Upjohn v. United States

449 U.S. 383 (1981)
United States Supreme Court

After Thomas, the general counsel for Upjohn, was informed that one of its foreign subsidiaries had made questionable payments to foreign government officials in order to secure business, he began an internal investigation. He sent all of Upjohn's foreign managers a questionnaire and also interviewed them and other company officials and employees. Subsequently, based on a voluntarily submitted report, the IRS began an investigation to determine the tax consequences of the questionable payments. It demanded that Upjohn furnish it with the replies to the questionnaire, notes of the interviews, and the memoranda regarding the payments. Upjohn refused on the ground that these documents were protected from disclosure by the attorney–client privilege. The United States then sued to obtain them. The trial court concluded that the summons should be enforced. Upjohn appealed to the court of appeals, which affirmed the trial court's decision. Upjohn then filed for review by the Supreme Court.

Justice Rehnquist delivered the opinion of the Court.

The attorney–client privilege is the oldest of the privileges for confidential communications known to the common law. Its purpose is to encourage full and frank communications between attorneys and their clients and thereby promote broader public interests in the observance of law and the administration of justice. The privilege recognizes that sound legal advice or advocacy depends upon the lawyer's being fully informed by the client. Admittedly complications in the application of the privilege arise when the client is a corporation, but this Court has assumed that the privilege applies when the client is a corporation, and the Government does not contest the general proposition.

In the case of the individual client, the provider of the information and the person who acts on the lawyer's advice are one and the same. In the corporate context, however, it will frequently be employees beyond the control group (officers and agents responsible for directing the company's action in response to legal advice) who will possess the information needed by the corporation's lawyers. Middle-level and indeed lower-level employees can embroil the corporation in serious legal difficulties, and it is only natural that these employees would have relevant information needed by corporate counsel if he is adequately to advise the client.

The communications at issue were made by Upjohn employees to counsel for Upjohn acting as such, at the direction of corporate superiors, in order to secure legal advice from counsel. . . . Information, not available from upper-echelon management, was needed to supply a basis for legal advice concerning compliance with securities and tax laws, foreign laws, currency regulations, duties to shareholders, and potential litigation in each of these areas. The communications concerned matters within the scope of the employees' corporate duties. The questionnaire identified Thomas as "the company's General Counsel" and referred in its opening sentence to the possible illegality of payments such as the ones on which information was being sought.

Consistent with the underlying purpose of the attorney–client privilege, these communications must be protected against compelled disclosure.

Application of the attorney–client privilege to communications such as those involved here puts the adversary in no worse position than if the communication had never taken place. The privilege only protects disclosure of communications; it does not protect disclosure of the underlying facts by those who communicated with the attorney.

"A fact is one thing and a communication concerning that fact is an entirely different thing. The client cannot be compelled to answer the question, 'What did you say or write to the attorney?' but may not refuse to disclose any relevant fact within his knowledge merely because he incorporated a statement of such fact into his communication to his attorney." . . .

Our decision that the communications by Upjohn employees to counsel are covered by the attorney–client privilege disposes of the case so far as the responses to the questionnaires and any notes reflecting responses to interview questions are concerned. The summons reaches further, however, and Thomas has testified that his notes and memoranda of interviews go beyond responses to his questions. To the extent that the material subject to the summons is not protected by the attorney–client privilege as disclosing communication between an employee and counsel, we must reach the ruling by the Court of Appeals that the work-product doctrine does not apply to the summonses issued. While conceding the applicability of the work-product doctrine, the Government asserts that it has made a sufficient showing of necessity to overcome its protection.

We think a stronger showing of necessity and unavailability by other means than was made by the Government in this case would be necessary to compel disclosure. Accordingly, the judgment of the Court of Appeals is reversed, and the case remanded for further proceedings.

Case Questions

1. What is the difference between the attorney–client privilege and the work product rule?
2. What is the purpose of the attorney–client privilege?

The Litigating Parties

A person who may become a party in a civil lawsuit should know what action to take to avoid litigation, what action to take when there is the potential for litigation, and what action to take as a party involved in litigation.

How to Avoid Litigation One midwestern law firm suggests to its clients that the following steps may help to avoid litigation.[5] First, important transactions should be reduced to a signed writing. The writing should be prepared before any performance is required. Where possible, written promises should be secured (i.e., payment assured), either by property or by an indemnification clause, one that makes the promising party liable for actual expenses and damages incurred by the other party if the first party breaches the agreement.

Second, the person who is about to sign a written agreement should make sure that he or she understands it before signing. Although this may seem elementary, many people are more prone to simply sign an agreement, particularly one that uses rather specific legal terms, than to ask questions about it. The more complex the transaction, the more important it is to review and question the meaning of terms used in the written agreement.

Finally, it is important to be alert to situations with high litigation potential. Transactions that have a substantial value or especially difficult consequences to one of the

[5] *Understanding Litigation*, a booklet by Howard & Howard Attorneys, P.C., September 7, 1983.

parties (such as with an employee discharge) require planning before action. In these situations, consideration of the legal consequences regarding words spoken, letters written, or actions taken need to be carefully reviewed before any such action occurs.

Actions Anticipating the Potential for Litigation People who are owners or managers of business firms may want to have a formal program of procedures to follow when their employees become aware of circumstances that might lead to litigation. In order to document a claim or properly defend one, there are several steps that should be followed in most cases.[6] Figure 4–6 highlights some of those steps.

Actions to Take after Becoming a Party to Civil Litigation A party in a civil lawsuit must be aware of how his or her role relates to the roles of the judge, jury, and attorney. During the trial, the judge's role is to be an impartial decision maker. Thus, neither party should try to discuss a pending case with the judge. During the trial, the judge must allow only legally proper evidence to be presented for the jury's consideration. Accordingly, a party should not volunteer information while testifying during a trial.

Each of the parties in a civil lawsuit aids in selecting the jury. Acting in cooperation with his or her attorney during the *voir dire* (voir dire, meaning to speak the truth, is the process for questioning potential jurors to determine if they are free from bias), a party may seek information from potential jurors that may help ensure the selection of a sympathetic jury. Although impartial juries are an objective of our legal system, the parties each seek a jury that is more sympathetic to their position than to that of the

[6] Ibid.

FIGURE 4-6

Documenting or Defending a Potential Claim

1. Preserve relevant evidence	Identify and preserve the item causing the injury (defective part, exploding coke bottle) and document who can identify it as having been involved in the case and having been in the same condition as when it was received by your firm.
2. Prepare photos and diagrams	Take photos of the accident scene, damaged parts, and other items that are not large enough to preserve. Identify who took the photos and diagrams and when they were prepared.
3. Obtain eyewitness statements	As soon as possible after the event, each witness should write what he or she saw or heard about the accident in as much detail as possible (just the facts, no conclusions or opinions). Have the person sign the written statement. Consider using tape recorded interviews in which you ask detailed questions about the accident and clearly identify the witness, date, and interviewer.
4. Consult your attorney	This is necessary for two reasons. First, the attorney can provide guidance as to what facts are important regarding liability and the evidence to be preserved. Second, early involvement of your attorney may protect against adverse information being obtained by others due to the attorney–client privilege.

other party. If a party is testifying in a case, he or she must try to answer questions persuasively. Most experienced observers believe that jurors are adept at telling when a witness is lying. Thus, truth is not merely the best policy; it is the only policy.

ETHICAL DILEMMA

ETHICAL DILEMMAS IN LITIGATION

Although the alternative dispute resolution methods discussed later in this chapter sometimes offer meaningful cost and time savings when compared to litigation, parties still often choose to pursue litigation. Is it ethical for a party to seek to litigate a questionable case or to harass the opponent into settlement by threatening or conducting costly pretrial procedures? If a large firm has significant resources and easy access to legal counsel, is it ethical for that firm to pursue litigation if it suspects its small firm opponent will be unable to bear the time and cost such litigation will require? Similarly, if the cost of litigation for a defendant is significantly more than the cost of settlement of a minor claim, is it ethical to file a nuisance claim against that party?

Before bringing a suit, a client should have a reasonable belief that wrongful conduct has occurred, that damages have resulted, and that genuine issues exist. Litigation can be an ethical method of settling disputes, but unfounded or vindictive litigation wastes scarce societal resources and brings about disrespect for the law. The law provides remedies for victims of unfounded litigation. Thus, the fraudulent use of legal processes is both unethical and illegal.

ALTERNATIVE DISPUTE RESOLUTION

Alternatives to court litigation have been studied and supported since early in the 20th century. Congress passed the Federal Arbitration Act in 1925, and the American Arbitration Association was founded a year later. However, it was not until the 1970s that the emphasis on alternative dispute resolution (ADR) increased as the delay and expense associated with litigation drove both businesses and individuals to opt for other methods of solving disputes.

alternative dispute resolution
Various methods for resolving disputes that are alternatives to litigation; the term usually refers to arbitration, mediation, minitrials, and private trials.

The term **alternative dispute resolution** (ADR) covers a broad range of options to the adversarial system of litigating disputes. These options generally include arbitration, mediation, the minitrial and summary trial, and the private trial or rent-a-judge methods. The term *alternative* not only contrasts these methods with litigation, but it also conveys a sense of choice and selection as to the method by which parties will seek to resolve their disputes. Contracts requiring the use of arbitration, commonly used in international business transactions, are becoming more common for health care providers, landlords, and securities brokers.

Large corporations use ADR as a means to solve complicated disputes while cutting burgeoning legal costs. In some jurisdictions, civil cases of less than a specified dollar amount and divorce property matters must be submitted to mediation before being litigated. Some states require the use of mediation, minitrials, and arbitration within the judicial system. Thus, ADR has become mandatory in some situations. By the beginning of the 1990s, alternatives to litigation for both individuals and firms had become a significant part of the legal environment. Neighborhood mediation centers, mandatory contract arbitration, and increased use of minitrials are today well-accepted dispute resolution methods.

ADR in the Corporate Arena

In 1977, the first minitrial was used by Telecredit TRW to settle a patent dispute.[7] The parties had spent two years and over $1 million in their pretrial activities. Telecredit claimed TRW had infringed its patents, and TRW wanted a showing of how the patents had been infringed. Telecredit asked TRW who it would believe, and TRW said it wanted the opinion of a neutral outside expert. A former court of claims judge was picked by the parties to be an adviser but not to act as a judge or arbitrator. Gradually, they agreed to procedural rules, and the minitrial method of dispute resolution was born. The parties settled their dispute less than three months after the minitrial agreement, no doubt saving another $1 million in legal fees for the disputing firms.

In 1985, IBM demanded arbitration in a long-standing dispute with Fujitsu. Two arbitrators were chosen, and they soon became mediators and negotiated new agreements between the parties. The parties followed the lead of the arbitrators/mediators and resolved their existing problems without litigation. Further, the two firms also agreed to use the ADR method for resolving any future problems. These firms used alternate dispute resolution techniques to solve problems when they realized they had not moved toward resolution in their prelitigation maneuvers.

In 1987, the U.S. Supreme Court pointed to the Federal Arbitration Act as its basis for determining that customers of a brokerage house, Shearson/American Express were required to arbitrate claims charging violation of several federal securities laws. The broker had a compulsory arbitration agreement provision in the contract with the customer:

> The Federal Arbitration Act provides that arbitration agreements "shall be valid, irrevocable, and enforceable, save upon such grounds as exist at law or in equity for the revocation of any contract. . . . The Act thus establishes a 'federal policy favoring arbitration.' "[8]

ADR in the Neighborhood

In the last several years, a network of diverse dispute resolution programs have evolved to mediate, arbitrate, and facilitate conflicts into agreement with a minimum of stress on the disputing parties and the courts. Today, these programs may be found in state, city, or county agencies. Trade associations have consumer action panels. University systems often use student volunteers and employ ombudsmen to serve as mediators. Some cities have independent organizations that provide mediation service for the community as a whole. Several common questions about neighborhood dispute resolution centers are answered below.

1. **Who are the mediators?** Mediators are community volunteers who receive at least 25 hours of specialized training in conflict resolution techniques and communication skills. They are laborers, counselors, attorneys, senior citizens, and employees at various community organizations.

2. **What kind of matters are appropriate for mediation?** Each center has guidelines that generally include neighborhood disputes (fences/driveways), consumer/merchant disputes, business and contract disputes, landlord/tenant problems, family disputes, and small claims. Disputes involving controlled substances and serious violence are not appropriate for mediation.

---

[7] *Business Week*, October 13, 1980, p. 170.

[8] [The case is *not* excerpted in 3d ed.]

3. Why do people use mediation? Mediation is quick, usually occurring within 10 days from the time both parties have agreed to mediate. The mediation usually lasts less than two hours. It is inexpensive, since the centers provide free mediation to indigent people and low costs to others. It is successful because the goal is to have all parties satisfied. Mediation aims at a win-win situation. It offers privacy, since all discussions related to the subject of mediation remain confidential and cannot be used in a lawsuit. Its effectiveness rate is high, with approximately 80 percent of all mediations ending in agreement.

Arbitration

arbitration
A process for resolving disputes that uses an individual or panel, often selected for their expertise, authorized by the parties to make a binding decision after hearing evidence presented through established procedures similar to those used in litigation.

Arbitration is probably the best known of the alternative dispute resolution methods. In **arbitration,** an arbitrator, or arbitration panel, generally has authority to make a binding decision of the dispute. One person or a panel of people gather evidence from the contending parties under generally less complicated procedures than those followed in court. Courts generally recognize and enforce the disputing parties' choice of arbitration and the arbitrator's decision.

Arbitration is commonly used in international commercial transactions, in health care provider contracts with patients, in settling disputes between professional athletes and their team owners, and in contracts between securities brokers and their clients. Parties select arbitration by inserting clauses in a contract to govern future disputes or by agreeing to use arbitration after a dispute arises. A sample arbitration offer found in a patient information booklet given to health care patients is shown in Figure 4–7.[9]

[9] This provision appears in a booklet approved by the Michigan Commissioner of Insurance. It was written by the Michigan Arbitration Advisory Committee, a group of consumers, doctors, hospital administrators, nurses, and lawyers.

FIGURE 4–7

Arbitration Offer Found in Patient Information Booklet

Michigan Medical Arbitration Program Standard Offer

Arbitration is a method of deciding disputes without going to court. The offer of this agreement is authorized under Michigan law to provide the patient with a choice between arbitration or going to court to resolve any health care complaint which may arise.

In arbitration, a 3-person panel made up of a doctor or other health care professional, a lawyer, and a member of the public will hear and decide your case. In most cases a decision made by the arbitration panel is final and cannot be appealed to court.

Please take a moment to review the agreement. Signing the agreement is your choice. You will receive the same quality of health care whether or not you sign. If you do sign, you have 60 days after you are discharged to change your mind.

The patient information booklet you receive should answer any questions you may have. Questions can also be answered by calling the American Arbitration Association's toll-free number in the booklet.

The arbitrator is usually a specialist familiar with the type of problem underlying the dispute. Because the arbitrator handles fewer cases than a judge does, the dispute can be resolved more quickly than if it went through the courts. Further, arbitrators are often familiar with the nature of the dispute and the commercial practices of firms in the same or similar industries. By contrast, judges who are randomly assigned to the controversy may not have the expertise permitting appropriate decisions.

Voluntary Agreements to Arbitrate

The most important first step in initiating arbitration is the agreement to arbitrate. That agreement may be one of two kinds: (1) a future dispute arbitration clause in a contract, or (2) in cases where the parties did not agree in advance, a submission of an existing dispute to arbitration. If the parties agreed in advance to arbitrate a dispute, the party initiating the action serves a demand for arbitration on the other party and also files it with an arbitration association, such as the American Arbitration Association (AAA). The *Mitsubishi* case that follows exemplifies a situation in which the parties at the time of contracting agree to arbitrate any future disputes. The AAA rules of arbitration generally require that the other party be given a certain time period in which to respond to the claim before any documents are submitted or a hearing occurs.

Parties who have not agreed in a contract to arbitrate may nevertheless use arbitration. They both sign a submission to arbitration agreement, which constitutes a contractual obligation of the parties that will be enforced by the courts as long as it is not contrary to public policy or illegal. Both a future dispute arbitration clause and a submission agreement, which needs to be signed by both parties, are depicted below.

> *For the Arbitration of Future Disputes:* Any controversy or claim arising out of or relating to this contract, or the breach thereof, shall be settled by arbitration in accordance with the Commercial Arbitration Rules of the American Arbitration Association, and judgment upon the award rendered by the arbitrator(s) may be entered in any court having jurisdiction thereof.

> *For the Submission of Existing Disputes:* We, the undersigned parties, hereby agree to submit to arbitration under the Commercial Arbitration Rules of the American Arbitration Association the following controversy: (cite briefly). We further agree that the above controversy be submitted to (one)/(three) arbitrator(s) selected from the panels of arbitrators of the American Arbitration Association. We further agree that we will faithfully observe this agreement and the rules, that we will abide by and perform any award rendered by the arbitrator(s), and that a judgment of the court having jurisdiction may be entered upon the award.

INTERNATIONAL PERSPECTIVE AND COMMENTARY

Although courts in the United States were at one time hesitant to allow arbitrators to oust the jurisdiction of courts in resolving international disputes, there are now a number of sources that ensure the recognition and enforcement of arbitration agreements. First, statutes in every state of the United States recognize arbitration. Second, several recent decisions of the U.S. Supreme Court have eliminated all obstacles to U.S. enforcement of agreements to arbitrate made by parties in international contracts. The *Mitsubishi* case is one of these cases.[10] Finally, the United Nations Convention on the Recognition and Enforcement of Foreign

[10]This case is also excerpted in slightly different form on page 91 in Chapter 3 in the discussion of international dispute resolution.

Arbitral Awards, ratified by most of the world's leading commercial nations, is a multilateral treaty that provides for the recognition of arbitral awards and prevents courts from litigating disputes the parties agreed to arbitrate. Arbitration is common in international business situations for several reasons. Each party fears bringing its dispute to hostile foreign courts with unfamiliar and perhaps bewildering procedures. Each party believes the judges or jurors in a foreign court will be partial toward the party from that country. Finally, each party generally perceives that prior disputes resolved through arbitration were more favorable than those resolved through litigation.

Mitsubishi Motors Corp. v. Soler Chrysler-Plymouth, Inc.

473 U.S. 614 (1985)
United States Supreme Court

Mitsubishi Industries, a Japanese corporation, and Chrysler International, a Swiss corporation, formed a joint venture company, Mitsubishi Motors, to distribute through Chrysler dealers outside of the United States vehicles manufactured by Mitsubishi and bearing Chrysler and Mitsubishi trademarks. Soler Chrysler-Plymouth, an automobile dealer incorporated in Puerto Rico, and Chrysler entered into a distributor agreement that provided for the sale by Soler of Mitsubishi-manufactured vehicles within Puerto Rico. Paragraph VI of the Agreement, labeled "Arbitration of Certain Matters," provided that:

> All disputes, controversies, or differences which may arise between Mitsubishi and Soler out of or in relation to . . . this Agreement or for the breach thereof, shall be finally settled by arbitration in Japan in accordance with the rules and regulations of the Japan Commercial Arbitration Association.

Initially, Soler maintained brisk sales, but following a slump in the new car market in 1981, Soler requested Mitsubishi delay or cancel shipment of several orders. A year later, Soler disclaimed any responsibility for failing to sell cars under its contract. Mitsubishi brought suit in the United States in Puerto Rico, seeking an order to compel arbitration in accord with Paragraph VI of the Agreement. The district court ordered Soler to arbitrate, even as to its antitrust claims. The Court of Appeals reversed because it felt Soler's antitrust claim should not be subject to arbitration because of public policy concerns. Mitsubishi appealed to the Supreme Court.

Justice Blackmun delivered the opinion of the Court.

We granted certiorari primarily to consider whether an American court could enforce an agreement to resolve antitrust claims by arbitration when that agreement arises from an international transaction. Soler reasons that, because it falls within a class of whose benefit the federal and local antitrust laws were passed, the clause cannot be read to contemplate arbitration of these statutory claims.

We do not agree, for we find no warrant in the Arbitration Act for implying in every contract a presumption against arbitration of statutory claims. The "liberal federal policy favoring arbitration agreements," manifested by the Act as a whole, is at bottom a policy guaranteeing the enforcement of private contractual arrangements: the Act simply "creates a body of federal substantive law establishing and regulating the duty to honor an agreement to arbitrate."

There is no reason to depart from these guidelines where a party bound by an arbitration agreement raises claims founded on statutory rights. Of course, courts should remain attuned to well-supported claims that the agreement to arbitrate resulted from the sort of fraud or overwhelming economic power that would provide grounds "for the revocation of any contract." But, absent such compelling considerations, the Act itself provides no basis for disfavoring agreements to arbitrate statutory claims.

By agreeing to arbitrate a statutory claim, a party does not forgo the substantive rights afforded by the statute; it only submits to their resolution in an arbitral, rather than a judicial, forum. It trades the procedures and opportunity for review of the courtroom for the simplicity, informality, and expedition of arbitration.

We now turn to consider whether Soler's antitrust claims are nonarbitrable even though it agreed to arbitrate them. We conclude that concerns of international comity, respect for the capacities of foreign and transnational tribunals, and sensitivity to the need of the international commercial system for predictability in the resolution of disputes require that we enforce the parties' agreement, even assuming that a contrary result would be forthcoming in a domestic context.

There is no reason to assume at the outset of the dispute that international arbitration will not provide an adequate mechanism. To be sure, the international arbitral tribunal owes no prior allegiance to the legal norms of particular states; hence, it has no direct obligation to vindicate their statutory dictates. The tribunal, however, is bound to effectuate the intentions of the parties. Where the parties have agreed that the arbitral body is to decide a defined set of claims that includes, as in these cases, those arising from the application of American antitrust law, the tribunal therefore should be bound to decide that dispute in accord with the national law giving rise to the claim.

As international trade has expanded in recent decades, so too has the use of international arbitration to resolve disputes arising in the course of that trade. The controversies that international arbitral institutions are called upon to resolve have increased in diversity as well as in complexity. Yet the potential of these tribunals for efficient disposition of legal disagreements arising from commercial relations has not yet been tested. If they are to take a central place in the international legal order, national courts will need to "shake off the old judicial hostility to arbitration," and also their customary and understandable unwillingness to cede jurisdiction of a claim arising under domestic law to a foreign or transnational tribunal. To this extent, at least, it will be necessary for national courts to subordinate domestic notions of arbitrability to the international policy favoring commercial arbitration.

Accordingly, we "require this representative of the American business community to honor its bargain" . . . by holding this agreement to arbitrate "enforce[able] in accord with the explicit provisions of the Arbitration Act." The judgment of the Court of Appeals is affirmed in part and reversed in part, and the cases are remanded for further proceedings consistent with this opinion.

Case Questions

1. Does U.S. policy favor or disfavor arbitration agreements?
2. What is the difference between arbitration panels and courts regarding an "allegiance" to the norms of particular states?
3. Compare the benefits of litigation that are "traded off" to those that arise as a result of an agreement to arbitrate.

Court-Mandated Arbitration

In some cases, courts require litigating parties to submit their cases to arbitration. California is one of the leading states requiring the use of court-mandated arbitration. For example, cases seeking damages of less than $50,000 may be ordered to arbitration. In these cases, the parties are still involved in selecting the arbitrators, and the hearing is similar to that used in voluntary arbitrations, but there is no judge or jury, and no written decision with reasons is provided. Instead, the arbitrator issues an award that is binding if it is not appealed. There are several procedural differences, involving the use of subpoenas and the discovery methods, between the court-mandated arbitration and the voluntary arbitration. Nevertheless, even court-mandated arbitration is generally quicker and less expensive than a trial.

Enforcement of Arbitration Agreements

In recent years, the U.S. Supreme Court has upheld arbitration provisions in a number of different circumstances. In the 1987 *Shearson/American Express* case referred to earlier, arbitration of a claim brought under the 1934 Securities and Exchange Act (Exchange Act) and the Racketeer Influenced and Corrupt Organizations Act (RICO) was found not to be too complicated for arbitration. Later that same year, the Court found that a federal court could not refuse to enforce an arbitration agreement rendered under a collective bargaining agreement.[11]

Recently, several large U.S. banks recently told holders of deposit and credit card accounts that any complaints they have would be subject to arbitration. BankAmerica and Wells Fargo Bank sent notices to their customers in early 1993 that the banks were adopting the new policies. According to an article in *The Wall Street Journal,* bank representatives stated that the move is an attempt to get a handle on legal fees.

However, Ken McEldowney, executive director of the nonprofit San Francisco–based Consumer Action group, says that "arbitration robs bank customers of important legal protection." He notes the class-action lawsuit, which has been used to challenge business practices that don't amount to much individually, but that cause large financial harm collectively. McEldowney also says the lack of discovery, the lack of legal precedent in arbitration, and the concern over impartiality of arbitrators called on frequently by banks are all problems with arbitration.

The Consumer Action association and several bank customers have filed suit seeking to halt the banks' use of arbitration in consumer disputes. We don't know whether the courts will enforce the agreement to arbitrate, when the bank but not all of their customers agree with that choice. However, based on the case decisions we have noted, the likelihood is that such agreements to arbitrate will be enforced.

Over 60 countries have signed the New York Convention on the Recognition and Enforcement of Arbitral Awards. In these countries, arbitral agreements are recognized, and courts will not adjudicate disputes that the parties have agreed to submit to arbitration.

Mediation

mediation
A dispute resolution process whereby a third party seeks to persuade the disputing parties to settle their differences; unlike arbitration, the recommendation or decision of the mediator is not binding on the parties.

Mediation is a process of dispute resolution whereby a third party seeks to persuade the disputing parties to settle their differences. Mediators are used for a variety of reasons. A mediator can defuse emotions between parties who may be angry or upset with each other. Mediators may suggest alternative strategies to the parties and encourage the use of unforeseen compromise positions. Mediators may point out weaknesses to each party in their respective positions, thereby encouraging more realistic settlement discussions.

[11] *United Paperworkers Intern. Union v. Misco, Inc.*, 108 S. Ct. 364 (1987).

Mediation is used in international conflicts, labor-management disagreements, and in numerous contract disputes. Former President Carter has assisted in seeking to resolve several international conflicts through his role as mediator. The Federal Mediation and Conciliation Service has experienced mediators who serve in labor–management disputes. In the winter of 1995, President Clinton asked the head of the Federal Mediation and Conciliation Service to discuss with baseball owners and the major league players association their differences so that the baseball strike might end. That particular effort was not successful. Mediation has worked well in the insurance industry. Its Dispute Resolution Procedures for Insurance Claims is used to settle thousands of claims annually. Sometimes the law requires the use of mediation. For example, the Magnuson-Moss Product Warranty Act authorizes mediation in disputes regarding malfunctioning consumer products.

Mediation and Arbitration

While mediation, like arbitration, is used to resolve disputes, the most important difference between them is that arbitration is usually binding, while mediation is not. The mediator usually acts as a go-between who encourages the parties to modify their positions. Usually in mediation, the mediator derives authority from the parties; he or she is invited to assist the parties. The mediator's role is not to judge, but to persuade and seek compromise and reconciliation. The mediator's recommendations are not binding and usually do not have to be accepted by the contending parties. In most cases, those recommendations are not directly enforceable through the legal system.

While an arbitrator renders a decision and thus acts as a substitute for the judge, the mediator merely emphasizes the reasonableness of the parties' demands. With arbitration, the parties must accept the arbitrator's findings and, except in unusual cases, there is no right to appeal that decision. Generally, if the contract or agreement between the parties provides for arbitration, the arbitrator's decision is final.

Court-Annexed Mediation

In many state trial courts, mediation is used as a part of the pretrial litigation procedure. For example, in Michigan, rules of procedure dictate that all eligible actions will be considered for mediation if not resolved by a certain point, normally at the close of discovery. An action may be selected for mediation by the court, by agreement of the parties, or by motion of one of the parties and an order of the court. In a few states, for example, Maine and California, mediation is required for all divorce cases. Consequently, most divorce cases never get to trial; they are resolved through mediation.

When mediation is used in a pretrial setting, a panel is usually used. Typically, a mediation panel consists of three persons. In Michigan, there is an attorney associated primarily with plaintiffs' cases, an attorney normally associated with defendants' cases, and an attorney not normally associated with either. Only 28 days' notice is required before a mediation hearing can occur. At the hearing, each side generally has 15 minutes to orally argue its position to the panel. The statements made at the mediation hearing are not admissible evidence in any court. The panel has 14 days to evaluate the case and inform the attorneys of its evaluation. Each party then has 28 days to accept or reject the mediation award; the failure to file a written acceptance or rejection is treated as an acceptance.

If all parties accept the award, a judgment is entered in accordance with the panel's recommendation. If all or a part of the award is rejected, the trial may proceed. The mediation award and the acceptance or rejection of the parties is sealed and may not be opened until after the judge enters a judgment. If a party has rejected a mediation award and the case proceeds to trial, that party must pay the opposing party's actual costs, including attorneys' fees, unless the verdict is more favorable to the rejecting party than the mediation award.

THE MINITRIAL

minitrial
A dispute resolution process involving informal presentation of the evidence regarding a dispute to the senior executives of the firms that are parties to a dispute; occasionally, an independent adviser observing the minitrial may make settlement recommendations to the executives of the disputing parties.

Informal presentations of disputes before senior executives of the disputing parties are known as **minitrials.** Occasionally, an independent adviser is also a part of this process. Once the senior executives have heard the presentations, settlement of the dispute becomes more likely because the strengths and weaknesses of the parties' cases become evident.

A neutral party is often present as a moderator or an independent adviser. In some situations, the adviser is asked for his or her opinion, while in others the senior executives of the disputing firms meet to discuss settlement as soon as the presentation has been completed. Once the senior executives have heard both sides of the dispute and become aware of the relative strengths and weaknesses of their positions, settlement may be more likely to occur.

The minitrial requires all of the parties to agree to its use. It allows the parties to resolve questions of law and fact in complex disputes through the use of an abbreviated discovery process. The abbreviated discovery procedure, requiring exchange of documents and names of witnesses, gives the parties fuller knowledge of the facts involved in the dispute and makes them more ready to reach a settlement. After the discovery stage, the adviser meets with the parties and seeks to resolve procedural issues. The actual trial generally lasts only a day or two and occurs months, not years, after the case begins.

The adviser at the hearing does not take the role of the judge, but instead derives his or her authority from the parties. In some cases, the minitrial will be presented to the respective parties, and the adviser will merely conduct the hearing. In other cases, the adviser may be given authority to render an advisory opinion as to the outcome of the case if in fact it goes to trial.

Minitrials have been used in patent disputes, product liability cases, unfair competition controversies, and antitrust claims. The advantages of the minitrial include:

1. The parties can design the processes and rules to be used.
2. The process may allow for influence of mediation and creative problem solving.
3. The use of some discovery techniques allows each party to learn the facts and pertinent issues about its opponent; this promotes an informed settlement.
4. The adviser can be selected for her or his expertise and can be granted varying degrees of authority.
5. Both the preparation for the trial and the trial itself are relatively brief.
6. The case is generally presented to the executives of the parties themselves, the people with authority to settle the dispute.
7. The hearings are confidential; the parties and the adviser agree not to disclose information regarding the proceedings to others.

PRIVATE TRIALS

A **private trial** uses retired judges or attorneys to resolve disputes. Parties using a private trial can avoid crowded court calendars and select judges with specialized expertise rather than randomly be assigned judges in the courts. The parties generally agree to share all expenses incurred in proceeding with a private trial. They also usually concur that the decision will be binding. While decisions at private trials generally are not recognized and enforced, some states, such as California, do recognize these rent-a-judge decisions as valid trial judgments. Appeals to higher courts are permitted in states recognizing private trial decisions.

private trial A dispute resolution process using a retired judge or senior attorney selected by the parties to resolve a dispute. While the parties generally agree that the decision will be binding, private trial judgments usually are not enforced by public officials unless state law recognizes such judgments.

A California statute originating in the early 1900s permits the parties to bypass the formal court system and use paid judges or referees. This statute allows the decision of the rent-a-judge to have the finality of trial court judgments. Although some of the problems with civil litigation are overcome by using these private trials, some people believe private trials also pose problems. The commentary that follows discusses some of the common questions about private courts.

PRIVATE COURT ALTERNATIVES TO THE PUBLIC COURT LOGJAM

Surely more than a few Americans serving on civil juries have asked themselves why private disputes are litigated at public expense. What public interest is served, for example, when lawyers bid for big settlements, and big fees, in class-action suits they themselves organized? What entitles such entrepreneurs to a taxpayer subsidy and a claim on the valuable time of jurors? Or why should public facilities be used to resolve big-money disputes between corporate giants over a contract they willingly signed?

Those questions, interesting as they are, are not threatening to bring down civil justice. But that edifice is tottering a bit from overload, without any clear enthusiasm among taxpayers for expanding it to meet a seemingly insatiable demand. As a result, some litigants, to save time and legal costs, are turning to private justice, and it seems to serve quite well.

If "Alternative Dispute Resolution," or ADR, continues to expand, it might well stimulate serious debate over privatization of some civil litigation as a means of freeing up the public courts for faster administration of criminal justice. The broad public clearly has a direct and significant interest in that, what with bailed-out criminals awaiting trial, roaming the streets to commit new crimes. . . .

The American Arbitration Association . . . has provided ADR services for many years, as have similar groups. But while arbitrators often have special expertise, some lawyers complain of an absence of legal precedents and procedures and the tendency of some arbitrators to merely split differences.

A newer and more fascinating development is the private court. One of the most ambitious private-court enterprises is Judicate, Inc., set up in Philadelphia in 1985 to offer services nationwide. . . . Judicate courtrooms are miniature public courtrooms, with a bench for the judge, a chair for the witness and chairs on either side for the litigants. Many of the judges are retirees from the public bench. Unlike a public court, Judicate allows litigants to choose the judge they want from a panel. Trials use public-court processes, but the rules are simpler and things move faster. Most cases, however, are dispatched with a simple settlement hearing, which can be held almost anywhere and may cost disputants as little as $75 each.

Private courts have sometimes been tabbed as "justice for the rich," but Mr. Seid, President of Judicate, says that is not the real life experience. "Many of our clients are low-income people. For an insurance company to get a dollar to a plaintiff in a normal case, it's going to cost them two dollars out of pocket because of delays, litigation costs and court fees. If this system works right, you can get more money to the plaintiff with less cost to the defendant and everybody benefits."

A more serious charge is that private justice contributes nothing to the total body of law. "The criticism is that we are not helping the court system and the system of justice, because some cases should be in a public forum," says Mr. Seid. "The fact is that not every case should go to us. We're not here for the cutting edge, for the case that's breaking new ground, for novel, complex legal arguments. Those cases should be tried in public courts. What we're trying to do is free the public courts of routine existing law cases or cases where liability isn't really in question but you're just trying to figure out how much the case is worth."

Public courts are so seldom challenged as institutions because of their long and honorable English common-law tradition. There is widespread agreement that anyone, however humble, deserves a day in court if wronged. This assurance contributes to a sense of fairness that prevents private resentments from becoming widespread public discontents that might threaten the social and political order. . . .

While the beauties of English common law are well accepted, the U.S. court systems—federal, state and local—are faced with new practical realities. Judges must try to cope with new conflicts arising out of scientific advances—whether a computer microcode can be copyrighted—that might best be settled by someone with technical expertise. Corporate lawyers sometimes practice "strategic litigation," just to tie up competitors in court. Tort litigation has exploded.

Given the old saying, "Justice delayed is justice denied," there clearly is room for new thinking about dispute resolution.

Source: Reprinted by permission of *The Wall Street Journal,* February 7, 1989, p. A21.

Comparing Litigation and ADR

Both litigation and ADR constitute important segments of the U.S. legal system. The Constitution establishes the courts as a forum for resolving disputes. The courts are open to all people (although they are difficult for poor people to access), and they involve citizens in dispute resolution through juries. Although litigation is costly and inefficient, the courts play an important role as a check on the other branches of our government. Through the application of the Bill of Rights and due process guarantees (discussed in the next chapter), the courts enforce the rights of the minority. Most people support a strong and independent court system because it forces the government and other people in society to act according to rule of law.

Although litigation is sometimes used as part of a business strategy, in many situations ADR techniques usually offer a more effective means of resolving disputes. ADR techniques are generally fairly quick, not too expensive, and private. None of those attributes are common to litigation. ADR involves the parties in a nonadversarial environment, encouraging each party to participate in seeking a solution that both

FIGURE 4–8

Comparison of Dispute Resolution Methods

Method of Dispute Resolution	Binding/ Reviewable	Selection of Decision Maker	Nature of Decision	Public/ Private
Civil trial	Yes—can appeal	Judge not selected by parties	Written decision with reasons	Public
Arbitration	Yes—limited review	Selected by parties; generally has expertise on subject in dispute	Sometimes a written decision with reasons	Private except when court reviews
Mediation	No, but can be enforced if in contract	Selected by parties	Based on agreement by parties; written decision is sometimes required	Private
Minitrial	No, but can be enforced if in contract	Selected by parties; sometimes has expertise on subject in dispute	Based on agreement by parties	Private
Private trial/rent-a-judge	Sometimes—then subject to appeal	Selected by parties	Written decision; sometimes with reasons	Private unless enforcement needed

parties can live with in both the short- and long-term. Business managers need to be cognizant of different ADR techniques so that an optimal method is selected for any dispute the business confronts. Effective dispute resolution management is too important to be ignored either by individuals or by firm managers.

Factors to Consider

A comparison of the different methods of dispute resolution should consider a number of factors. Among those depicted in Figure 4–8 are:

1. Is the decision reached through each method binding? Can the decision be reviewed?
2. How is the decision maker selected? Does that person generally have expertise in the particular type of dispute?
3. Is the decision written? Are reasons given? Do the parties have to agree with the decision?
4. Is the process by which the dispute is resolved public or private?

ADR essentially refers to less adversarial methods of dispute resolution, whether used as a part of a court process or as an alternative to it. There are several basic differences between the adversarial method of dispute resolution followed in civil litigation and the ADR processes. First, in the adversarial process, the neutral party (judge) makes a decision after hearing from the disputing parties, whereas in ADR the hearing officer may help formulate the result during the process. Second, in adversarial litigation, one party wins and the other loses. By contrast, ADR methods allow for each party to benefit from the resolution. Third, whereas ADR requires communication and trust between the parties, the adversarial system nurtures distrust and animosity. Finally, the parties in litigation expect their case will be governed by a general legal principle found in a statute, administrative regulation, or court decision. In an ADR matter, the outcome of the dispute need not be based on general legal principles. Although legal rules are followed in most arbitration hearings, most ADR methods do not require the decision or result to be based on recognized legal rules.

Compare the following excerpts from *The Wall Street Journal;* the first article, "Some Disputes Still Deserve Their Day in Court," compares litigation to ADR and notes that litigation is still preferable in some situations. The second article, "Built-In Protection Against the Litigation Blues," notes how ADR is being used to cut legal expenses in several large firms.

Some Disputes Still Deserve Their Day in Court

By Campbell Killefer

Most non-lawyers say "Amen" to criticism that litigation afflicts American business and everyday life. But one highly touted cure has many attributes of snake oil—it is believed to be cheap, foolproof and easily stomached. The trend to use alternative dispute resolution—commonly known as ADR—in business disputes is healthy, but its promoters often indulge in considerable hype.

. . . One of the principal strengths of ADR is that it allows, even encourages, the parties to design the format, rules and schedule to fit the particular dispute. Unlike traditional litigation, ADR attempts to show each side its own weaknesses, the other side's strengths, and the virtues of compromising so that the parties' relationship can move forward.

[The author then discusses a successful ADR and notes] That sums up a successful ADR—a fair settlement that inflicts some pain on all parties but allows them to maintain their commercial relationship in the future.

The case of a failed ADR may illustrate even better the critical ingredients necessary for out-of-court settlements. A utility tried to settle a big dollar dispute with one of its equipment vendors. The equipment vendor proposed a form of ADR: a mini-trial before the parties' senior executives. The parties' lawyers made summary presentations to the executives, who became even more entrenched in their battle lines. The ADR failed and led to fierce and extremely costly litigation for years now with no trial date set.

There were several problems with this ADR. First, the equipment vendor appeared to start the ADR without truly wanting to resolve the dispute through compromise; the ADR was just a detour from the parties' fight. Additionally, there was no neutral mediator [independent adviser] present to provide a reality-check. Thus, the companies continued deluding themselves about the impregnable strength of their cases. Finally, because the companies trusted each other so little, neither side presented its "real" case. Instead, both pulled their punches and hid parts of their cases. The executives were never shown the whole picture, which probably doomed the ADR from the outset.

Here are several points to consider when you or your company are deciding between ADR and litigation:

Is a jury important to your case?

Some types of claims, such as fraud or malicious harm to a victim, have greater appeal to a jury of average citizens than to a well-educated, neutral mediator. Many people want their "day in court" before a jury of their peers.

Is the dispute so complicated or technical that an expert decision maker would be best?

Highly technical cases in such areas as computer engineering, accounting rules, or other non-intuitive disciplines can fly over the heads of juries, whereas an expert in your particular industry may readily grasp the facts and issues in an ADR.

Do you need discovery to develop the facts of your case?

If you know your basic claim but need the formal court discovery process to unearth facts and documents from the other side . . . , ADR may not be right for you. Conversely, can you bear the costs and distraction of massive discovery by your adversary?

Is a confidential proceeding and decision important?

Most court proceedings are open to the public and [some] are covered by the press. The flexible procedures of ADR allow you to ensure confidentiality.

Is a speedy decision more important that a perfectly just result?

A fast ADR may produce a compromise that is no thing of beauty but gets the dispute behind you and your company. . . .

Do you need a decision, or must you establish a broader principle?

An ADR produces a compromise; a court judgment often announces a principle. . . . If you only need your dispute resolved, forget about establishing principles.

Do you need a neutral person cracking heads to get results?

Judges have little free time and are understandably reluctant to get their hands dirty in forcing rough compromises. A distinguished industry expert, a retired judge, or an eminent senior lawyer may be quite effective in pulling both sides to the middle ground. Special masters appointed in Agent Orange cases, asbestos cases and other mass torts have streamlined settlements that could have reached gridlock in the federal courts.

ADR is a healthy trend that is here to stay. But you should evaluate ADR vs. litigation for your business dispute in light of the above issues as you would any other tough commercial decision. Let the buyer beware.

Source: Reprinted by permission of *The Wall Street Journal*, October 12, 1992, p. B10.

Built-In Protection Against the Litigation Blues

By James F. Henry

If you want to do business with General Mills, then you'd better be willing to forgo formal litigation of any future dispute. Why? Because this Fortune 500 company will not sign a contract unless you agree that conflicts will be resolved through the use of a minitrial, mediation or another alternative dispute resolution (ADR) procedure.

ADR is not brand-new. Lawyers have deployed it in countless disputes, often with great success. Some creative managers and lawyers are institutionalizing the use of ADR. They are making these techniques a permanent element of corporate strategy—in relations with customers, with suppliers and with employees. Some examples:

Deere & Co., the heavy equipment maker, routinely mediates its product liability cases through a company that provides ADR services. In 1990, Deere lawyers directed 36 cases to mediation; by early this year [1991], 20 had settled.

Grappling with the banking crisis, the FDIC has trained 100 "dispute coordinators" in its offices nationwide. Directed by FDIC lawyers, these staffers negotiate and mediate certain bank loan disputes. In 1990, they saved the FDIC $3 million in legal costs.

General Motors has devised a two-step ADR system for resolving disputes with its many dealers, encompassing such common issues as termination, service obligations and product allocation.

When work-related disputes arise in the ranks of its 42,000 nonunion employees, Northrop uses four different ADR methods to resolve them.

The main mission of IBM's industry relations department, which consists of 16 staffers with sales and marketing backgrounds, is to prevent and resolve disputes between IBM and other companies in the computer industry.

Despite the diversity of processes and disputes, there are common themes to these varied programs. One, a feature of IBM and FDIC initiatives and many others, is the central role assigned to the business manager. No longer does a manager simply tell his lawyers to sue, and then wait for the call to a deposition. It is a main tenet of ADR that the talents and skills of executives are invaluable in dispute resolution. In minitrials, mediations and other ADR procedures, senior business executives participate as fully as their lawyers in resolving disputes.

The flip side of this development is that lawyers are viewing disputes in a more businesslike, managerial fashion. According to Motorola general counsel Richard H. Weise, "Our product is the resolution of disputes, and with ADR we think we can deliver a higher-quality product with less cost and in a shorter time."

But despite the compelling rationale underlying the use of ADR, the task of instituting it within a corporation is difficult. Clearly, rooting out the litigation habit is arduous, piecemeal and prone to setbacks. Many lawyers and top managers, inured to litigation, look with distaste on the so-called ADR "wimp" factor. Old habits die hard, especially when substantial effort is needed to learn the new ones. Lawyer Marguerite Millhauser, who counsels companies about ADR, compares it to another revolution: computers. In winning over a person wedded to his typewriter or pencil, the computer advocate must confront the former's " fear of the unknown, fear of making a mistake, fear of failure and fear of being judged," Ms. Millhauser says.

But the effort is worth it. . . . The promise of ADR—in saving time and money, in preserving business relationships, in better "win-win" results—far exceeds the cost of institutionalizing it.

Source: This Reprinted by permission of *The Wall Street Journal,* July 22, 1991, p. A8.

ADR: Pros and Cons

ADR has grown because each of the methods possesses some advantage when compared to litigation. The text has referred to the generally lower cost and quicker resolution of the dispute as significant advantages usually attributed to ADR methods.

Comparisons among ADR methods and between those methods and litigation are depicted in Figure 4–8. The authors of *The Wall Street Journal* articles also present their views regarding ADR and litigation. Figure 4–9 summarizes many of the pros and cons of ADR. Business managers and individuals alike must be aware of the attributes of each method of dispute resolution. Sometimes, one also faces an ethical dilemma in selecting the most appropriate method to use. Consider the following commentary.

ETHICAL DILEMMAS AND ADR

ETHICAL DILEMMA

The goal of dispute resolution is equity. Whether they choose a civil trial, arbitration, mediation, minitrial, or rent-a-judge, most people want what is rightfully theirs. The cost of alternative dispute resolution methods may vary from one type to the next. Mediation through community dispute resolution centers generally is the least expensive method. Arbitrators are a bit more expensive, and rent-a-judges are generally the most expensive. If you pay for a more expensive method of dispute resolution, are you going to receive a better result?

FIGURE 4-9

Pros and Cons of ADR

Pros: Advantages of ADR over litigation

1. Less time from beginning of controversy to resolution of dispute.
2. Less cost because of lower attorneys' fees, less time away from work by corporate employees, and lower "court" costs for the prevailing party.
3. Parties can select a more experienced decision maker or facilitator rather than being randomly assigned to a judge.
4. Parties are able to select where the dispute will be heard; they are not bound to use the court system where each party does business.
5. The nonadversarial nature of ADR makes it easier to do business in the future with an opponent. The parties are actively involved in solving a problem and are not passive participants.
6. The informality of ADR methods is less formidable than are the evidentiary rules governing court procedures.
7. ADR is more confidential than litigation, which becomes a matter of public record.

Cons: Disadvantages of ADR as compared to litigation

1. The longer time frame for litigation may be advantageous to one of the parties if it will have to make a payment to the other party once the dispute is resolved. Passage of time naturally decreases both the cost to the defendant and the value of the plaintiff's recovery.
2. The use of discovery in litigation allows each party to obtain valuable information from the other party.
3. The rule of law generally governs the dispute; if the law is on one party's side, the case is more likely to be decided in that party's favor.
4. Only the courts can establish precedent. If a party has concern about future cases as well as the present controversy, litigation may establish the needed precedent.
5. Litigation is generally preferred if the case involves new or complex legal theories.
6. Litigation is more public and thus may be used to let other parties know that disputes will not be settled for their nuisance value.

If the job of deciding cases is taken out of the hands of judges, what standards will be imposed on the parties who instead perform that task? What types of checks and balances will guarantee that they are doing an equitable job? Will poorer people get an inferior quality of justice merely because they cannot afford to use certain methods of dispute resolution? Would the universalist and the utilitarian both find private trials ethical?

SUMMARY

The American legal system provides a variety of ways in which parties to a dispute can seek to resolve it. Litigation in the United States is based on the adversarial principle, which makes the parties and their attorneys responsible for presenting needed information and arguments about the law. The parties, pretrial procedures, and trial practices of criminal and civil litigation are quite dissimilar.

The civil litigation process consists of several stages. As most cases are not resolved through trial, many of the concerns of civil litigation must be addressed early. The pleadings and pretrial stages are often crucial to the outcome of civil litigation since most cases are settled during these preliminary stages.

Civil cases that do go to trial may be tried before a judge alone or with both a judge, who determines the legal questions and instructs the jury on the law, and a jury, which determines the facts. Each party in a civil case has a role in selecting prospective jurors through the use of challenges. The plaintiff begins the presentation of evidence, and then the defendant follows. Witnesses testify through direct and cross-examination conducted by the attorneys. Rules of evidence determine the type of information presented at a trial; the rules are intended to prohibit use of irrelevant, biased, or unreliable evidence. The jury verdict occurs after closing statements are made but before the judgment is rendered. Post-judgment collection methods include garnishment or attachment. If legal errors in a trial are made, a trial court's judgment may be appealed.

The judge, jury, attorneys, and parties each perform specific roles in the civil litigation process. To some degree, each acts as a check on the others. The attorney–client privilege protects the information that clients give to attorneys in confidence. The privilege exists so as to encourage full and frank communications between attorneys and their clients and thereby promote broader interest in the observance of law and the administration of justice.

Alternative dispute resolution (ADR) refers to nonadversarial methods of dispute resolution that are used instead of civil litigation. Arbitration, mediation, minitrial, and private trials are among the more common ADR methods. Firms engaged in international business, such as those involved in the *Mitsubishi* case, have used arbitration to resolve disputes for many years, and arbitration is widely used in many commercial cases. Arbitrators can usually make final and binding decisions. Voluntary arbitration occurs as a result of a contract clause governing future disputes or a submission agreement signed by both parties concerning an existing dispute. Some courts also require the use of arbitration. Agreements to arbitrate and arbitration awards are recognized and enforced in over 60 countries. Because arbitrators usually handle fewer cases than judges and work primarily with certain types of business transactions, arbitration can be a quicker and more efficient method of dispute resolution than civil litigation.

Mediation is used by parties seeking an informal and nonbinding method of resolving disputes. It is also used both with the civil litigation process and as an alternative to it. When used with civil litigation, mediation is often required before a party proceeds to trial. The trial takes place only if the mediation decision is not accepted. However, if a party proceeds to trial after rejecting the mediation award, that party must pay the opposing party's costs unless the trial verdict was more favorable than the mediation award. The mediator's role is not to judge but to persuade and seek to reconcile differences. Court-mandated arbitration and mediation procedures vary among the states.

The minitrial features a presentation to the executives of the parties and the use of a neutral adviser. After the presentation, the parties seek a settlement. Sometimes, the adviser gives an opinion as to how a court would likely resolve the dispute. The minitrial process usually allows the parties limited discovery before the trial and only a one- or two-day presentation at the trial. Generally, it is the executives of the parties, not the adviser, who have the authority to settle the dispute. Thus, the minitrial, like mediation, is nonbinding in nature. In the private trial, a retired judge or attorney is hired to hear and decide a case. The parties can select the judge and will have their case heard more quickly than if they had used litigation. While the private trial is generally nonbinding, statutes in some states, such as California, do allow the decision of this rent-a-judge to be as final as trial judgments.

ADR may not always be preferable to litigation; instead, there are pros and cons to each. The informed business manager will be aware of the variety of methods for resolving disputes and select the method that is most likely to accomplish his or her objectives.

Critical Thinking Review Questions

1. Compare and contrast the common law adversarial system with the civil law inquisitorial system of litigation.
2. An attorney for a plaintiff argues that as preemptory challenges are to be used at the sole discretion of the parties, he should be able to use the preemptory challenges granted him in a civil suit by state law to exclude potential jurors regardless of their sex or race. What reasons would you give to counter his argument?
3. Identify each of the following terms and place them in the proper sequence in civil litigation: motion to direct the verdict, counterclaim, answer, deposition, motion to dismiss for lack of jurisdiction, verdict, complaint, direct examination of plaintiff's witnesses.
4. Very few legal systems make as extensive use of the jury as does the United States. Evaluate the role of the jury in the U.S. legal system. Do you think its role should be changed? Why?
5. Describe three situations in which a manager might prefer to use litigation rather than an ADR method to solve a dispute.
6. Compare and contrast the role of the parties toward each other, the role of the parties in determining the process and rules to be used, and the role of the decision maker in litigation with his or her role in the ADR methods.
7. Under what circumstances would it be best to use each of the various methods of alternative dispute resolution?

Critical Thinking Exercises

1. Thiel sued Southern Pacific Company for injuries he received from a moving train. The jury in the case returned a verdict for Southern Pacific, but Thiel appealed, claiming the jury had not been properly selected. The jury selection process deliberately excluded from the jury list anyone who worked for a daily or hourly wage. Should the judgment and jury verdict at the trial level be upheld? *Thiel v. Southern Pacific Co.*, 328 U.S. 217 (1946).
2. Assume that several employees of your company inform you, your firm's in-house counsel, of their concern about your company's safety violations. Should those communications be protected by the attorney–client privilege? How does their contract with you differ from the attorney–client contact in the *Upjohn* case?
3. Nancy sues Martha in Kentucky and recovers a judgment for $25,000. The decision of the trial court was not appealed. Martha has not paid Nancy any of the money. What can Nancy do to collect from Martha?
4. Guzman was charged with violating the federal selective service laws because he refused to report for a physical examination and for induction into the armed services. Before trial, Guzman claimed the jury selection system used by the court violated his right to a jury represented by a

cross section of the community because it excluded persons under the age of 21 from serving on the jury. At the time of the indictment, Guzman was 20. Guzman also claimed that because the state uses the voter registration list as the sole source of names, there would be a substantial underrepresentation of young persons on the jury because these persons have a significantly lower registration rate. How should the court decide? See *United States v. Guzman*, 337 F. Supp. 140 (S.D.N.Y., 1972), aff'd. 468 F.2d 1245, cert. denied 410 U.S. 937.

5. USF, a real estate development firm, expanded and grew from a small accounts receivable financing firm to an international conglomerate. It then began having financial problems and numerous criminal, administrative, and civil cases were filed against it. Because there were common legal issues based on contract, tort, and securities laws in most of the civil cases, they were consolidated and scheduled to be tried together. The trial court judge ruled that the legal and factual issues were so complex as to be beyond the abilities of a jury; thus, he denied all demands for a jury trial. Should the complexity of a case be a basis for denying a party's right to a jury trial in a civil case? *In re U.S. Financial Securities Litigation*, 609 F.2d 411 (9th Cir., 1979).
6. Some scholars have suggested that attorneys have both ethical and legal duties to inform their clients who are considering litigation about alternative dispute resolution methods. These scholars believe attorneys have an obligation to fully inform their clients of all available options before pursuing litigation. How could the teleological and deontological ethical theories guide an attorney who is discussing litigation, and alternatives to it, with a client?
7. The firm where you work is a large firm that is involved in a multimillion dollar antitrust and breach of contract suit with another large firm. The two firms are competitors in the same industry, but each also has license agreements and a joint venture with the other. Each firm expects to spend several hundred thousand dollars in attorneys' fees and other costs to prepare for the suit. The case is scheduled to come before the court in about a year. The executives of your firm are upset with the slow pace of litigation and the long time period it will take to get the case into and out of court. If appeals occur, several years could come and go before the case is resolved. You are invited to a brainstorming session called by one of the executives who is in charge of managing the litigation. He has asked a group of people to gather together to pose suggestions for ways in which this dispute could be solved without going to court. Which of the alternative resolution techniques would you recommend, and why?
8. AMF Inc. and Brunswick Corp. each manufacture automatic scoring devices for use in bowling. Brunswick advertised that its automatic scoring device was more reliable than any others in use, and AMF brought suit claiming the advertisement was false and deceptive. AMF sued Brunswick, and the litigation was resolved by an agreement whereby each party would submit any future disputes regarding advertising claims to an arbitration panel for nonbinding arbitration. Later, Brunswick ran several advertisements that claimed its laminated lanes were more durable than the wood lanes manufactured by AMF. AMF sued to have Brunswick submit its information to the arbitration panel, but Brunswick refused. Should the court force Brunswick to provide the arbitration panel with information on its laminated lanes?
9. Rodriguez de Quijas signed a standard arbitration agreement with his stockbroker when when he opened an account with it. The contract obligates the parties to settle any controversies through binding arbitration. De Quijas sued the stockbroker firm alleging that the broker made false and fraudulent transactions in his account and violated the 1933 Securities Act. The Securities Act authorizes a person who is injured by a breach of that act to sue for damages, and de Quijas asserts that language allows him to bypass the arbitration. Do you agree?
10. All-Right Electric Company contracted with Careful Construction Company to do electric work on several commercial office buildings Careful had contracted to build. Their contract provided that any dispute between them was to be submitted to a private court. A dispute arose as to whether All-Right's work conformed to the standards it had agreed to in the contract. All-Right wanted to bring the dispute to trial, but it

made a token appearance before a private judge. It presented no evidence, called no witnesses, but simply read statements indicating that its work conformed to the contract. The private judge decided in favor of Careful, but All-Right refuses to abide by that decision. Would a court enforce the private judge's decision and decline to hear a case if All-Right sues?

PART 2

Governmental Powers over Business

5 Constitutional Law

6 Administrative Law

CHAPTER

5

Constitutional Law

Critical Thinking Questions

- How does the U.S. Constitution establish the structure of the federal government and clarify the relationship between the federal government and the separate states or local governments? Why does the Constitution limit governmental encroachment on the personal lives of individuals and their business affairs?
- Why is the judicial branch given significant law-making powers to interpret legislative, constitutional, and common laws at both the state and federal government levels?
- What federal government power forms the basis for most federal laws affecting business activities? How do the powers to tax and spend facilitate this regulation?
- What interests are protected by the First Amendment freedom of speech guarantee for individuals and business?
- Why do the Fifth and Fourteenth Amendments provide for due process in state and federal governmental processes and in substantive laws? Who does the equal protection clause prohibit from committing discrimination?

Introduction...Past, Present, Future

Nearly every major provision of the U.S. Constitution reflects a reaction to the tyrannical rule the English crown exercised over the American colonies. The Constitution restricts the potential misuse of governmental powers by the central government, which the colonies experienced. The federal system created by the Constitution spreads governmental powers among separate branches at each level of government and separates powers between the federal and local governments. The colonies first organized into a confederation to confine the central government's powers. However, the confederation could not coordinate the states' activities, resulting in protectionism and conflicting policies that were harmful to the whole country's strength. The Constitution was then developed as a compromise between the Federalists, who desired a strong central government, and the Anti-Federalists, who supported stronger states' rights. The resulting U.S. Constitution forms the basis for all American law and represents the foundation for power at all levels of government. As the supreme law of the land, the Constitution establishes the basic structure of the federal government, provides for the states' self-government, and limits government encroachment on business and personal activities.

The Constitution consists of two major parts and several subparts. The first part contains the Preamble and seven substantive articles that establish and empower Congress, the executive branch, and the judiciary, then regulate relations among the states and authorize Constitutional amendments. The second part contains the Constitutional amendments. The first 10 amendments, called the Bill of Rights, were ratified in 1791 to protect fundamental freedoms and liberties. Since then, over 5,000 amendments have been proposed, but only 18 have passed; they deal with liquor prohibition, taxation, the abolition of slavery and its effects, congressional pay, and election matters. Amendment proposals in recent years have sought to require equal rights for women, balance the federal government budget, outlaw desecration of the American flag, and establish the right to life for the unborn.

The courts have reinforced the federal government's pervasive power to regulate business and interstate commerce. Nevertheless, there are still disputes over the relative roles of the states in our federal system. Many cases hold that the federal powers to regulate business activities are so pervasive that they preempt any state interference with interstate commerce. By contrast, other cases have carved out pockets of states' rights to regulate the local incidents of local business activity. However, state laws that interfere excessively with the federal government's enumerated lawmaking powers are held unconstitutional under the supremacy clause.

In the future, constitutional law will probably focus more on relations between individuals and government. Conflicts may arise between the rights of individuals as stated in the Bill of Rights and reinforced by numerous antidiscrimination and privacy statutes and other laws intended to cure social problems. The new federalism movement of the 1980s may continue to put greater financial and regulatory responsibilities on the states. The renewed regulatory activism of the states' legislatures, administrative agencies, and attorneys general are challenging the present concept of resolving conflicts in federalism.

Thought Questions

1. What role has the conflict over centralized or local government played in the development of American constitutional law?
2. How does the U.S. Constitution remain relevant given changes in technological, social, and economic developments?

The Basis for Constitutional Powers

The Historical Perspective

Conflict over the separation of powers has dominated the history of American constitutional law since the Revolutionary War. Our government represents a compromise between opposing views of where the most legitimate, efficient, and responsible places for governmental power are to be. America has continually struggled between two political forces in the search for the best model for government. The *Federalists* advocated the unitary form of central or national government. The *Anti-Federalists* represented regional interests that advocated stronger local governments. A general theory of government, known as **federalism** or *dual federalism,* recognizes that it is legitimate for power to reside at both the central and local levels. Much of American history and the contemporary legal issues affecting business turn on federalism and the separation of powers among and within both state and federal governments.

federalism
Debate over best place for government power: centrally or locally.

Constitutional Development during the Revolutionary War England's pervasive and tyrannical rule over the American colonies led to the Revolutionary War. The

English crown was dictatorial and abused the colonists, having little respect for their opinions. Therefore, the Constitutional framers included provisions to restrict any similar misuse of power by separating the central government's powers into distinct branches. The separation of powers into many governmental units may not seem like the most economically efficient form. However, it more effectively prevents tyranny.

The original 13 colonies derived their political powers from colonial charters granted by the English crown. These documents eventually developed into separate state constitutions and were ultimately modeled after the U.S. Constitution with similar separation of powers structures. Because the colonies had divergent social and economic interests, they considered themselves separate, distinct, and sovereign political entities. While the colonies united during the Revolutionary War to oppose English tyranny, their main motivation was to oppose their common enemy and provide for their collective defense.

The Articles of Confederation The colonies' first attempt to unify was an overreaction to the stong English central government. Soon after the Declaration of Independence, the states used a confederation form of government. This was no more than a loose aggregation of the states, similar to early Swiss, Germanic, and Papal state experiments. A **confederation** is a loose alliance of independent entities that seek to retain separate autonomy and self-determination. Confederating states join together for limited common goals, such as defense. They reject stronger forms of central government.

confederation Loose aggregation of autonomous states for limited mutual benefits.

The **Articles of Confederation** created the first American confederation. It provided a benchmark for the strongest form of states' rights in American federalism. Ever since the Articles were ratified, between 1777 and 1781, the trend has generally been toward increased central government powers and away from state powers. However, there have been intermittent periods of states' rights sentiment, most notably, the Civil War.

Articles of Confederation First form of U.S. constitution used between 1781 and 1789.

The Articles gave the new American Congress very limited power to conduct foreign affairs, raise armed forces, or levy taxes. It created no branches of government with executive or judicial power. The early Congress had no power to raise money and could only request that the states contribute money for their collective efforts. Indeed, the states had different currencies, creating havoc in interstate commerce and runaway inflation. The central government had great difficulty maintaining domestic peace and preventing violence. This strife reflected deep political, social, and economic problems. Domestic unrest caused a general loss of prestige for the U.S. government under the Articles. In response, the states attempted to revise the Articles, but instead they wrote an entirely new document, the U.S. Constitution.

Development of the U.S. Constitution The Constitution is a compromise between the two dominant political groups of that time. The Federalist party initially succeeded in securing a strong national government in international affairs, interstate commerce, and taxation. The **Federalists** were largely well-to-do northeastern merchants who stood to gain most from unlimited interstate commerce. The **Anti-Federalists** represented the states' rights interests fighting for the states to retain some governmental powers. The Anti-Federalists were largely populists representing the agrarian interests of the South. They distrusted both the Federalists and central governments. This power struggle resulted in a compromise reserving the police power to the states and providing regional strength through state representation in the U.S. Congress.

Federalists Early advocates of strong central or national government in the United States.

Anti-Federalists Early states' rights advocates in the United States.

INTERNATIONAL PERSPECTIVE AND COMMENTARY

OTHER NATIONS' CONSTITUTIONS

The U.S. Constitution is a unique document in world history. No other existing constitution has survived longer. This success is probably due to the Constitution's promise of freedom, the vastness of U.S. natural resources, the rugged individualism and motivation of immigrants from all over the world, and their rejection of the rigid feudal class systems of most other nations. The U.S. Constitution provides a blueprint for minimum government intervention while permitting fundamental democratic principles. It balances efficiency with freedom and rewards individual achievement while protecting individual rights. It accommodates the powers of numerous competing economic, social, and political interests, unlike the ethnically dominated governments of the privileged few in most other nations.

The U.S. Constitution was influenced by other nations. Principles of democracy were drawn from the Greeks and Romans. The common law tradition was drawn from England. The lack of a written English constitution inspired the American founders to rely on more than just the unwritten English customs and conventions. The Magna Carta, reluctantly issued by England's King John in 1215, provided a model for due process by guaranteeing fundamental personal liberties such as the enjoyment of life, liberty, and property except after judgment by one's peers. The French also exerted considerable influence. Montesquieu's writings on the shortcomings of monarchy and despotism inspired the design of the U.S. republic.

Today, Europeans stand to benefit from the experience of the United States under the Constitution. The nations of the European Union (EU, formerly the EC) are moving through confederation by lowering their mutual borders. The EU nations face many of the collective problems of balancing central governance with culturally diverse sovereignties. The EU is following in many of the footsteps of the United States: economic harmonization, a common currency, encouraging intra-EU commerce, integrating varying laws and traditions, and a unified interaction with outside nations.

The United States' post-World War II occupation of Japan led to that nation's adoption of its constitution. Most of Japan's laws are based on U.S. law. Eastern European nations are now using the U.S. Constitution in designing their forms of democracy. These Europeans are discovering a preference for free markets and private property. The U.S. Constitution provides a workable pattern for encouraging economic activity throughout the world.

The Powers of Government

Most governmental powers are provided in the U.S. Constitution. *Enumerated powers* are expressly delegated to the federal government by the states. Implicit powers permit Congress to legislate where it is "necessary and proper" to implement particular enumerated powers. The *reserved powers* of the states include the police power to look after the general health, safety, welfare, and morals of their people.

Not all powers are given exclusively to either the federal or state government. Both governments share or have *concurrent powers* to make laws in several areas (e.g., taxation). Certain potential powers are *prohibited* to both the state and federal governments. For example, neither government may make laws that establish a religion. The supremacy clause denies to the states the power to legislate in areas where the powers of the federal government are exclusive.

Enumerated, Delegated, or Exclusively Federal Powers The federal government has several exclusive powers; the most important to business is the power to regulate interstate commerce. The states are prohibited from making laws that would unduly burden interstate commerce. Other exclusive powers give only the federal government the power to act in matters of foreign affairs. The states have no power to make war, sign treaties, naturalize citizens, or regulate aliens. The federal government has power over the post office and the construction of post roads, which has given rise to the federal road system.

Reserved and Concurrent Powers The Tenth Amendment reserves to the states any powers not specifically delegated to the federal government.

The Tenth Amendment

> The powers not delegated to the United States by the Constitution, nor prohibited by it to the States, are reserved to the States respectively, or to the people.

Despite this reservation by the Tenth Amendment to the states of remaining governmental powers, the states share most of their powers with the federal government. Examples include the power to tax and the powers of eminent domain.

The **police power** is the primary source of states' power permiting each state to protect its citizens' "health, safety, welfare, and morals." It enables the states to legislate in the areas of criminal law, tort law, contract law, commercial law, divorce law, regulatory law, and property rights. However, the state police power is not unlimited, so legislation is often invalidated when it imposes an undue burden on interstate commerce or constitutes an uncompensated taking of private property, as discussed below.

police power
State reserved legislative power to protect the health, safety, welfare, and morals of the people.

Takings States have the power of eminent domain, permiting the **taking** of private property for public purposes, such as taking farmland to build a highway or a city lot to construct a government building, or flooding farmland to create a lake bed. The Constitution requires the government to pay "just compensation." This clause was included as a response to England's practice of confiscating colonists' property for use by the English crown. What constitutes a taking, and what rights does a property owner have if the government wants to use the power of eminent domain to take that owner's property? Several recent takings cases illustrate the balancing of individual property rights with society's various interests.

taking
Government appropriation of private property for which just compensation is usually due.

Dolan v. City of Tigard

114 S. Ct. 2309 (1994)
United States Supreme Court

Dolan applied for a permit to expand her plumbing supply store and pave the parking lot. The City Planning Commission of Tigard, Oregon, conditioned approval of the permit upon her dedication of land (1) for a public greenway along the adjoining Fanno Creek to minimize flooding and (2) for a pedestrian/bicycle pathway to relieve traffic congestion in the Central Business District. Dolan appealed the Commission's denial of variances from these standards alleging that the land dedication requirements were unrelated to her development proposal and therefore constituted an uncompensated taking of her property under the Fifth Amendment. The appeals board, the state court of appeals, and the state supreme court all affirmed, and Dolan appealed to the United States Supreme Court.

Chief Justice Rehnquist delivered the opinion of the Court.

[In response to Oregon law] Tigard, a community of some 30,000 residents on the southwest edge of Portland, developed a comprehensive [land use management] plan [that] requires property owners in the area zoned Central Business District to comply with a 15% open space and landscaping requirement, which limits total site coverage, including all structures and paved parking, to 85% of the parcel. New developments [must] facilitate this plan by dedicating land for pedestrian pathways where provided for in the pedestrian/bicycle pathway plan. The city also adopted a Master Drainage Plan. Flooding occurred in several areas along Fanno Creek, including areas near petitioner's property. Increase in impervious surfaces associated with continued urbanization would exacerbate these flooding problems. Other recommendations included ensuring that the floodplain remains free of structures and that it be preserved as greenways. Cost of these improvements should be shared based on both direct and indirect benefits, with property owners along the waterways paying more due to the direct benefit that they would receive. Variances are granted only where it can be shown that, owing to special circumstances related to a specific piece of the land, the literal interpretation of the applicable zoning provisions would cause "an undue or unnecessary hardship."

One of the principal purposes of the Takings Clause is "to bar Government from forcing some people alone to bear public burdens which, in all fairness and justice, should be borne by the public as a whole." The authority of state and local governments to engage in land use planning has been sustained against constitutional challenge. "Government hardly could go on if to some extent values incident to property could not be diminished without paying for every such change in the general law." A land use regulation does not effect a taking if it "substantially advance[s] legitimate state interests" and does not "den[y] an owner economically viable use of his land." Undoubtedly, the prevention of flooding along Fanno Creek and the reduction of traffic congestion in the Central Business District qualify as the type of legitimate public purposes we have upheld. A nexus exists between preventing flooding along Fanno Creek and limiting development within the creek's 100-year floodplain.

In some States, very generalized statements as to the necessary connection between the required dedication and the proposed development seem to suffice. Other state courts require a very exacting correspondence, described as the "specifi[c] and uniquely attributable" test. We think the "reasonable relationship" test adopted by a majority of the state courts is closer to the federal constitutional norm than either of those previously discussed. But we do not adopt it as such, partly because the term "reasonable relationship" seems confusingly similar to the term "rational basis" which describes the minimal level of scrutiny under the Equal Protection Clause of the Fourteenth Amendment. We think a term such as "rough proportionality" best encapsulates what we hold to be the requirement of the Fifth Amendment. No precise mathematical calculation is required, but the city must make some sort of individualized determination that the required dedication is related both in nature and extent to the impact of the proposed development. We see no reason why the Takings Clause of the Fifth Amendment, as much a part of the Bill of Rights as the First Amendment or Fourth Amendment, should be relegated to the status of a poor relation in these comparable circumstances. It is axiomatic that increasing the amount of impervious surface will increase the quantity and rate of storm-water flow from petitioner's property. Therefore, keeping the floodplain open and free from development would likely confine the pressures on Fanno Creek created by petitioner's development. The Community Development Code already required that petitioner leave 15% of it as open space, and the undeveloped floodplain would have nearly satisfied that requirement. But the city demanded more—it also wanted petitioner's property along Fanno Creek for its Greenway system. The city has never said why a public greenway, as opposed to a private one, was required in the interest of flood control.

The difference to petitioner, of course, is the loss of her ability to exclude others. As we have noted, this right to exclude others is "one of the most essential sticks in the bundle of rights that are commonly characterized as property." It is difficult to see why recreational visitors trampling along petitioner's floodplain easement are sufficiently related to the city's legitimate interest in reducing flooding problems along Fanno Creek, and the city has not attempted to make any individualized determination to support this part of its request. Petitioner would lose all rights to regulate the time in which the public entered onto the Greenway, her right to exclude would not be regulated, it would be eviscerated. We conclude that the findings upon which the city relies do not show the required reasonable relationship between the floodplain easement and the petitioner's proposed new building.

Dedications for streets, sidewalks, and other public ways are generally reasonable exactions to avoid excessive congestion from a proposed property use. But on the record before us, the city has not met its burden of demonstrating that the additional number of vehicle and bicycle trips generated by the petitioner's development reasonably relate to the city's requirement for a dedication of the pedestrian/bicycle pathway easement. The city simply found that the creation of the pathway "could offset some of the traffic demand and lessen the increase in traffic congestion." No precise mathematical calculation is required, but the city must make some effort to quantify its findings in support of the dedication for the pedestrian/bicycle pathway beyond the conclusory statement that it could offset some of the traffic demand generated.

Cities have long engaged in the commendable task of land use planning, made necessary by increasing urbanization particularly in metropolitan areas such as Portland. The city's goals of reducing flooding hazards and traffic congestion, and providing for public greenways, are laudable, but there are outer limits to how this may be done. "A strong public desire to improve the public condition [will not] warrant achieving the desire by a shorter cut than the constitutional way of paying for the change."

The judgment of the Supreme Court of Oregon is reversed, and the case is remanded for further proceedings consistent with this opinion. It is so ordered.

Case Questions

1. What is a taking? For what reasons does the Constitution prohibit the taking of private property? What reasons might justify a governmental taking of private property?
2. What are examples of government takings of private real property?
3. What evidence must government gather to justify a taking, such as in the case above?

The *Dolan* case illustrates how a partial taking is of particular interest to business. For example, a *partial taking* may be arise where: (1) a landowner is prevented from exploiting the property's greatest economic value, (2) a landowner must let others use the property, or (3) a landowner does not receive just compensation, usually appraised at fair market value, for the taking. Government regulations generally involve no compensable taking where the property is simply restricted from some uses. To do otherwise would severely restrict government's ability to regulate. However, the Supreme Court considers some partial takings as compensable. For example, partial compensation was required when a government body took an easement for public beach access[1] and when the use of property in a flood plain was temporarily restricted.[2] A more expansive taking occurred when a regulatory agency sought to prevent coastal beach erosion by denying a building permit to a resedential beach lot.[3] The Supreme Court balances the economic impact of a regulation against its anticipated public benefits in determining the extent of compensation for such regulatory takings.

---

[1] *First English Evangelical Lutheran Church of Glendale v. Los Angeles County,* 482 U.S. 304 (1987).

[2] *Nollan v. California Coastal Comm'n,* 483 U.S. 825 (1987).

[3] *Lucas v. South Carolina Coastal Council,* —S. Ct. — (1992).

Judicial Review

The common law legal heritage in English-speaking nations such as the United States has evolved into a hybrid of the common law and civil law legal systems. Both types of law periodically require interpretation, a function historically provided by the courts.

Constitutional Interpretation Many constitutional provisions are precise enough that interpretation is unnecessary. For example, most of the numerical limitations are clear. Thirty-five is the minimum age for the president, 30 for senators, and 25 for house members. Similarly, the requirement of a simple majority vote to pass legislation, two-thirds to override presidential vetoes, or three-fourths of state legislatures needed to amend the Constitution are all quite precise. However, much of the remainder of the Constitution contains vague terms. The founders deliberately placed vague terms in the Constitution to permit flexibility as society changed. They realized they could not find precise and timeless language that would effectively anticipate the whole range of potential human behaviors. The courts' flexibility and discretion in interpretation helps to encourage compliance with the "spirit" and not just the "letter" of the law.

Judicial Restraint The Supreme Court's power to interpret the Constitution is important because the formal constitutional amendment process is so cumbersome. Only 27 constitutional amendments are currently in effect and the proposed balanced budget amendment seems to be sidetracked for now. By contrast, the Supreme Court constantly interprets the Constitution, thereby effectively changing it.

case or controversy Constitutional requirement for genuine adversariness in litigation.

strict constructionism Ideology limiting judicial interpretation.

A court's power to make laws is limited in several important ways. First, most courts may adjudicate and interpret only after a real **case or controversy** arises. Advisory opinions are not generally permitted except in a few states. Second, most judges exercise judicial restraint by trying not to make sweeping changes in the law. Judicial decisions are generally made in conformance with established precedents. The common law rule of precedent ensures consistency, provides some notice, and restricts judges from constantly imposing their personal economic or social beliefs. **Strict constructionism** is a view contrary to judicial activism. It presumes the legislature is better suited to solve societal or economic problems because this is precisely the legislature's purpose and because it is more immediately responsible to the electorate.

Although courts have significant law-making powers, they are generally powerless to enforce their decisions. The legislature must appropriate funds for enforcement by the executive. Legal precedents are also subject to later legislation. In 1944, for example, the Supreme Court held that insurance was within interstate commerce, which would have exposed the insurance industry to antitrust law.[4] However, Congress quickly passed the McCarran-Ferguson Act, reversing the decision and providing antitrust exemption to the insurance industry. There are contemporary pressures to abolish this exemption.

judicial review Power of courts to review legislation or the acts of administrative agencies.

Supreme Court Review of Legislation Before 1803, the judicial review of legislation was generally unknown. However, today any conflicts between the Constitution and a statute subject the legislation to **judicial review.** The power of judicial review flows naturally from both the common law of precedent and from the supremacy

[4] *United States v. South-Eastern Underwriters Ass'n,* 322 U.S. 533 (1944).

clause. Although no specific constitutional provision empowers the Supreme Court to hold legislation unconstitutional, the Supreme Court conferred this power on itself in the landmark 1803 case, *Marbury v. Madison*.[5]

In the last few days of his administration, President John Adams made several special appointments to federal office before the new president, Thomas Jefferson, was inaugurated. After Senate confirmation, President Jefferson directed James Madison, the new secretary of state, to withhold several of Adams's appointments, including Marbury's commission as justice of the peace for the District of Columbia. Marbury sought a *writ of mandamus* in the Supreme Court, an order to force Madison to deliver Marbury's commission. Chief Justice John Marshall declined to grant Marbury's request because no statute gave the Supreme Court trial court jurisdiction over mandamus cases. In so ruling, Marshall effectively made it a judge's duty to interpret statutes in light of constitutional provisions. When a controversy involves the constitutionality of legislation, Marshall's decision empowered the courts to invalidate legislation in conflict with the Constitution.

COMMENTARY

THE SUPREME COURT— IDEOLOGY AND POLITICS

From time to time, throughout American Constitutional history, the Supreme Court's political independence has been questioned. Supreme Court judges are appointed by the president with the "advice and consent" of the U.S. Senate. This provides a check on the power of the executive branch, balancing the executive and judiciary's powers. However, critics often charge the nomination process is too political, thereby assuring the appointment of political ideologues. For example, when the president and a Senate majority are from the same political party, the president can appoint and the Senate will probably confirm cabinet members or federal judges who are clearly sympathetic to their own party's ideology. Observers charge that President Franklin D. Roosevelt, a Democrat, used the politically sympathetic Senate majority to appoint liberal Supreme Court Justices supportive of FDR's New Deal and more aggressive government regulation.

Supreme Court justices' political and ideological leanings become important in close questions. A single swing vote on Constitutional questions is decisive, possibly changing established Constitutional interpretations. For example, *Roe v. Wade* inferred the abortion rights rule from a constitutional right to privacy. However, the right to privacy is not expressly stated in the U.S. Constitution. A conservative court majority may overturn the abortion right, leaving the matter to be settled by the states.

When the presidency is held by a member of one party and the Senate is controlled by the other party, new Supreme Court justices probably reflect ideological balance. Senate hearings usually reveal a nominee's extremist views, which can pressure the president to nominate more moderate candidates. This conflict emerged in President Reagan's failed 1989 nomination of Robert Bork to the Supreme Court. Judge Bork's conservative free market ideology was well documented in his law review writings and speeches. His testimony before the Senate Judiciary Committee clearly reinforced this perception. Judge Bork was not

[5] *Marbury v. Madison*, 1 Cranch 137 (1803).

confirmed allegedly because he was successfully portrayed by liberal interest groups as a strict constructionist and hostile to privacy, civil rights, and antitrust enforcement. Critics charge that subsequent Supreme Court nominations have been chosen because their ideological views were not well known. Consequently, they avoided being "Borked," that is, defeated by lobbying pressure on Senate members. Political grandstanding on nationwide television by several senators from both parties contributed to public discontent over the advice and consent process during Judge Clarence Thomas's 1991 confirmation.

The advice and consent process was designed to permit open debate of a nominee's ideology and qualifications. The president should be given some free reign to select ideologically compatible individuals for the cabinet. These people must regularly work with the president's team and harmonize with the administration. However, judges and other independent government officials, like SEC or FTC Commissioners, are independent of the administration. Their experience and job qualifications are more important than ideological conformity. The nomination and confirmation process has permitted a shift of emphasis from ideological compatibility to qualifications necessary for the position. The president and Senate should return to the true spirit of the U.S. Constitution's "advice" provision, which appears to require the president first seek counsel from the whole Senate. This could help avoid the divisiveness of nominating an ideologically unacceptable candidate. Future replays of the destructive treatment of Judges Bork and Thomas may weaken public faith in the nomination process applicable to all federal judges, cabinet members, and other important federal officials.

Specific Powers of Government

Commerce Clause

The power over commerce, an enumerated power of the federal government, forms the basis for nearly all economic regulation. The commerce clause is the most important constitutional provision affecting business.

The Commerce Clause

> The Congress shall have the Power . . . To regulate Commerce with foreign Nations, and among the several States, and with the Indian Tribes.

intrastate commerce Commercial activities conducted wholly within one state and having negligible impact on other states.

The commerce clause affect business in two major ways. First, it gives Congress power to regulate interstate commerce. Second, by implication, it denies the states the power to regulate or impede interstate commerce. This leaves states control over **intrastate commerce,** that is, local incidents of commerce. States may validly use their police power to protect the health, safety, welfare, and morals of their citizens. In practice, both federal and state laws may regulate certain aspects of commerce, providing the state law's purposes are proper.

Regulation of Foreign Commerce The states made inconsistent compacts with foreign nations under the Articles of Confederation. Under the Constitution, regulation of trade with foreign nations is an exclusively federal power. This provision presumes that decisions to make treaties, conduct foreign relations, and regulate foreign commerce are best made by a single, unified entity representing the will and needs of the whole nation.

The definition of foreign commerce is unclear because foreign commerce with the United States necessarily begins or ends within a state. State regulation of imports or exports with foreign nations is invalid if it restricts trade or requires any special treatment of foreign goods. The states may exercise limited regulation over foreign goods once these goods are in the hands of a retailer and the bulk of a wholesale lot has been broken down into smaller commercial units. This happens, for example, if the international bulk unit, a large container or pallet, has been broken down into cases. State regulation is invalid if it discriminates between domestic and foreign commerce, even if the regulation is arguably based on public welfare concerns. Some other nations permit their political subdivisions to affect foreign commerce. For example, the Canadian provinces regulate Canada's securities markets. Provincial regulators can make international agreements with other nations' regulators, as they have done on enforcement matters with the U.S. Securities and Exchange Commission (SEC).

Federal Regulation of Commerce The framers intended the commerce clause to grant Congress sufficient power to govern in all areas of economic activity. In 1824, however, the Supreme Court in *Gibbons v. Ogden*,[6] restricted Congress from regulating *intrastate,* matters wholly within only one state, by narrowly interpreting the word *interstate*.

INTERSTATE COMMERCE

> Commerce, undoubtedly, is traffic, but it is something more: it is . . . commercial intercourse between nations, and parts of nations, in all its branches, and is regulated by prescribing rules for carrying on that intercourse.

By the early 20th century, the Supreme Court restricted Congress's interstate commerce powers to include only those matters involving some transportation of goods across state lines. Therefore, almost all manufacturing was considered intrastate and not subject to federal regulation.

Commerce Power and the New Deal New Deal economics influenced the Supreme Court's interpretation of the commerce clause. During the Great Depression, public pressure mounted for federal solutions to the economic devastation. The legislative efforts of F.D.R. and Congress pitted them against the Supreme Court's laissez-faire predisposition. After F.D.R.'s 1937 power struggle with the Supreme Court, it validated nearly all of Congress's remedial legislation regulating commerce, including such major laws as the National Labor Relations Act, the securities laws, and the Fair Labor Standards Act. Since 1937, the commerce clause has become the most significant source of congressional power to regulate business. Today, federal legislation is upheld even when it develops a federal police power to preserve health, safety, and welfare. The *affectation doctrine* invalidates regulation over interstate commerce

[6] *Gibbons v. Ogden,* 6 L.Ed. 23 (1824).

unless some reasonable link exists between that activity and an aspect of interstate commerce. The determination by Congress that such a link exists is usually sufficient to satisfy the courts, even though the link may be tenuous. How strong must the link be between interstate commerce and the activity to validate the regulation? The next case illustrates this link in instances that might first appear as wholly intrastate.

Perez v. U.S.

402 U.S. 146 (1971)
United States Supreme Court

Perez was alleged to be a "loan shark," a profession that Congress found to be largely controlled by organized crime. Loan sharks enter into extortionate credit transactions characterized by the use of threat or violence to enforce repayment. Perez, a local loan shark, lent Miranda $1,000 to be repaid in $105 installments for 14 weeks, which was increased to $130 after 6 weeks. An additional $2,000 loan was to be repaid in $205 installments, which Perez increased to $330 after threatening Miranda. Perez increased the payment until Miranda sold his butcher shop, unable to make further payments. Perez continued to threaten violence to Miranda and his family, suggesting that collections would soon be made by Perez's more violent associates. Perez was charged with the federal crime of loan-sharking.

Justice Douglas delivered the opinion of the Court.

Chief Justice Marshall in *Gibbons v. Ogden* said: "government . . . action is to be applied to all the external concerns of the nation, and to those internal concerns which affect the States generally; but not to those which are completely within a particular State. The completely internal commerce of a State, then, may be considered as reserved for the State itself."

Chief Justice Stone wrote for a unanimous Court in 1942 that Congress could provide for the regulation of the price of intrastate milk, the sale of which, in competition with interstate milk, affects the price structure and federal regulation of the latter. The commerce power, he said, "extends to those activities intrastate which so affect interstate commerce, or the exertion of the power of Congress over it, as to make regulation of them appropriate means to the attainment of a legitimate end, the effective execution of the granted power to regulate interstate commerce." *Wickard v. Filburn* soon followed in which a unanimous Court held that wheat grown wholly for home consumption was constitutionally within the scope of federal regulation of wheat production because, though never marketed interstate, it supplied the need of the grower which otherwise would be satisfied by his purchases in the open market. In *United States v. Darby*, the decision sustaining an Act of Congress which prohibited the employment of workers in the production of goods "for interstate commerce" at other than prescribed wages and hours, *a class of activities* was held properly regulated by Congress without proof that the particular intrastate activity against which a sanction was laid had an effect on commerce. That case is particularly relevant here because it involved a criminal prosecution, a unanimous Court holding that the Act was "sufficiently definite to meet constitutional demands." Petitioner is clearly *a member of the class* which engages in "extortionate credit transactions" as defined by Congress and the description of that class has the required definiteness.

It was the "class of activities" test which we employed in *Heart of Atlanta Motel, Inc. v. United States* to sustain an Act of Congress requiring hotel or motel accommodations for Negro guests. The Act declared that "any inn, hotel, motel, or other establishment which provides lodging to transient guests affects commerce *per se.*" That exercise of power under the Commerce Clause was sustained. In a companion case, *Katzenbach v. McClung,* we ruled on the constitutionality of the restaurant provision of the same Civil Rights Act which regulated the restaurant "if . . . it serves or offers to serve interstate travelers or a substantial portion of the food which it serves . . . has moved in commerce." Apart from the effect on the flow of food in commerce to restaurants, we spoke of the restrictive effect of the exclusion of Negroes from restaurants on interstate travel by Negroes.

Extortionate credit transactions, though purely intrastate, may in the judgment of Congress affect interstate commerce. In an analogous situation, Mr. Justice Holmes, speaking for a unanimous Court, said, "[W]hen it is necessary in order to prevent an evil to make the law embrace more than the precise thing to be prevented it may do so." It appears, instead, that loan-sharking in its national setting is one way organized interstate crime holds its guns to the heads of the poor and the rich alike and syphons funds from numerous localities to finance its national operations.

Case Questions

1. What is the logical link between loan-sharking and interstate commerce?
2. If local activities may affect interstate commerce, what might be left as wholly intrastate activities beyond federal control?

Some scholars believe the *United States v. Lopez* case signals a reversal in the expansion of federal powers over interstate commerce.[7] In 1995, the Supreme Court held that Congress exceeded its commerce clause powers in banning possession of guns within 1000 feet of schools. However, upon reflection *Lopez* probably just restrains growth in the federal police power. The school gun ban was invalidated because it had little if any real connection to the federal commerce power.

The broad commerce power to regulate business can be further implemented through the *necessary and proper clause*, a catchall phrase in Article I, Section 8, following the list of delegated powers. This permits regulation even beyond an enumerated power such as regulating commerce. Legislation covering such additional matters is valid when it makes regulation of an enumerated power more effective. For example, a limit on tort remedies against nuclear power generators was based on the necessary and proper clause as a way to encourage development of the nuclear power industry.

The Necessary and Proper Clause

> The Congress shall have Power . . . To make all Laws which shall be necessary and proper for carrying into Execution the foregoing Powers.

State Regulation of Commerce While the Constitution does not specifically deny the states power to regulate interstate commerce, case law has limited state power. The dual-federalism concept permits the states to regulate intrastate activities so long as they impose only minor burdens on interstate commerce under a "balancing test." First, the state regulation must bear a rational relationship to a valid state goal. Second, the effect of the state regulation on interstate commerce must be slight. Third, the extent to which the state regulation discriminates against interstate commerce must be small. Fourth, the necessity for the state regulation must be great. These four factors balance the state's interests in regulating against the need for federal uniformity. If a state law regulating commerce is reasonably related to a strong and necessary state goal and the burdens and discrimination that it places on interstate commerce are small, the law should be valid. A long line of cases on the states' powers to regulate

[7] *United States v. Lopez*, 93-1260 (U.S. 1995).

interstate commerce is discernable in three basic groups: (1) state regulation of interstate transportation, (2) state regulation of production and trade, and (3) state taxation of multistate and multinational businesses.

State Regulation of Transportation In the 1925 case of *Buck v. Kuykendall,*[8] a Washington State statute for licensing common carriers was an invalid burden on interstate commerce. Buck was refused permission to use the Washington State highways to operate an "auto stage line" because the territory was "already being adequately served." The Supreme Court found that the state was attempting to unconstitutionally regulate interstate commerce, not simply the safety of its highways. In the 1938 case of *South Carolina State Highway Dept. v. Barnwell Bros.*,[9] the state's restriction on truck width and weight was upheld as a legitimate safety concern, despite the incidental burden the restrictions placed on interstate commerce. Long trucks presented similar safety concerns to Iowa, which validly restricted double trailers over 60 feet long.[10]

State safety concerns must be actual, not conjectural, a problem addressed by the arbitrary train-length restrictions in the 1945 case of *Southern Pac. Co. v. Arizona.*[11] Arizona attempted to collect penalties from Southern Pacific Railway for violating the 14-car passenger-train maximum limit and the 70-car freight-train limit. This case introduced the "balancing test," which the Supreme Court then used to invalidate the Arizona statute as arbitrary. *Bibb v. Navajo Freight Lines, Inc.*[12] presented a similar problem in 1959. Illinois attempted to require all trucks to use a particular type of curved mudguard for their wheels. The statute was found unconstitutional because the mudguards, manufactured by an Illinois company, were expensive and offered little additional protection compared with the equipment already in use by most trucking companies. This illustrates that there must be a compelling local interest before local regulations imposing burdens on interstate commerce are upheld as constitutional.

Discriminatory State Regulation of Production Most state restrictions on out-of-state products are discriminatory and impose an undue burden on interstate commerce. However, there is an exception for state quarantine restrictions. For example, laws prohibiting transportation of diseased cattle into Iowa and New York were upheld. To protect their fruit trees from disease, Arizona and California legitimately restrict the fruit brought into those states. However, local efforts to prevent local disposal of imported solid wastes (e.g., trash, garbage) are generally unsuccessful.[13] While state regulations may ostensibly try to prevent the spread of disease, unwholesome foods, or undesirable materials, their economic effect is to favor in-state producers. A state or local economic interest in maintaining access to domestic products, in conserving local resources or favorable local prices, or in restricting exports outside the state seldom justify burdening interstate commerce.

The celebrated milk import cases have been particularly troublesome. Although states may use their police power to assure food safety, several milk regulations have been invalidated. States have attempted to control the price, place of production, or distance that milk travels to market on the pretext of maintaining the milk's wholesomeness. The New York State Milk Control Act of 1933 established minimum prices

---

[8] *Buck v. Kuykendall,* 267 U.S. 307 (1925).

[9] *South Carolina State Highway Dept. v. Barnwell Bros.,* 303 U.S. 177 (1938).

[10] *Kassel v. Consolidated Freightways Corp. of Delaware,* 450 U.S. 662 (1981).

[11] *Southern Pac. Co. v. Arizona,* 325 U.S. 761 (1945).

[12] *Bibb v. Navajo Freight Lines, Inc.,* 359 U.S. 520 (1959).

[13] *Fort Gratiot Sanitary Landfill, Inc. v. Michigan Dept. of Natural Resources,* 112 S. Ct. 2019 (1992).

for milk in order to ensure sanitary conditions. The city of Madison, Wisconsin, restricted milk sales in the city to milk produced within 25 miles of the city.[14] A Mississippi regulation allowed the sale of milk produced out of state only if the state of origin permitted the import of Mississippi's milk. The Supreme Court found all these state laws to be excessive regulations for their limited objective because other means already existed to control milk purity.

State Taxation of Interstate Business States may impose burdens on interstate commerce by taxing out-of-state businesses. Taxation is justifiable if the out-of-state business has some connection, local operations, or *nexus* with the taxing state. The nexus is a valid basis for taxation because all residents and non-residents should pay for their use of governmental benefits. These benefits include the protection of the state's laws, police, fire department, and courts, as well as the use of its public facilities, such as the direct use of roads or the indirect use of parks or schools by employees. Several types of tax are valid, although each must apply fairly to both in-state and out-of-state businesses. For example, *property taxes* are legitimate if they are levied on real estate or personal property residing within the state on "tax day." *Use taxes* can be legitimately levied on an out-of-state mail order retailer that is exempt from paying sales tax if the purchaser resides within the taxing state and the retailer actively solicits orders by mail or phone order.[15]

There have been difficulties with the "unitary" income taxes levied by some states on multistate and multinational businesses. States may validly tax only the portion of a business's income that is derived from property or activities within the state. For example, an auto assembly plant might be located in the taxing state, but all of the component parts are produced in other states. The taxing state may tax only the assembly operations, not the manufacture of the components. However, it is difficult to accurately compute the portion of income derived from a particular state if companies do a substantial amount of out-of-state business. Income taxes on multistate or multinational businesses, both foreign and domestic, are valid if they meet the following criteria. First, a reasonable formula must apportion the tax. Second, a nexus or minimum contact must be established between the state and the business being taxed. Third, the tax may not discriminate against or unconstitutionally burden interstate or foreign commerce. Fourth, the tax must be fairly related to the benefits the state provides to the taxpayer.

Contract Clause

The contract clause prohibits the states from impairing private contracts. This limitation restricts the states, but not the federal government, from passing statutes or administrative regulations that modify the duties owed under existing contracts. Nineteenth century Supreme Court decisions interpreted the contract clause to prohibit the states from imposing economic regulations.

THE CONTRACT CLAUSE

No State shall . . . pass any . . . Law impairing the Obligation of Contracts.

---

[14] *Dean Milk Co. v. Madison,* 340 U.S. 349 (1951).

[15] *Quill Corp. v. North Dakota,* 112 S. Ct. 1904 (1992).

The framers included the contract clause in response to the economic chaos that existed under the Articles of Confederation and to prevent political pressure to pass *debtor relief laws*. Because more people were debtors than creditors, the framers feared the debtors might elect legislators who promised to pass laws modifying debt contracts.

Some early interpretations of the contract clause restricted public grants by the states to individuals and institutions (e.g., colleges). Modern interpretations of the contract clause permit the states to modify existing contracts only in emergency situations, for example, where this is necessary to protect the public health, safety, welfare, or morals.

Should the contract clause be interpreted literally to prohibit all state regulation of business? The following case illustrates how the Supreme Court may be beginning to reevaluate the growing intervention of state governments into business affairs, signaling some limited return to more laissez-faire attitudes.

Allied Structural Steel Co. v. Spannaus

438 U.S. 234 (1978)
United States Supreme Court

A Minnesota statute required most employers to pay a "pension funding charge" if its pension plan were terminated or if the firm permanently closed its Minnesota offices. The charge applied if pension funds were insufficient to cover liabilities for employees who had worked for the company for at least 10 years. Allied notified the state of its intention to close its Minnesota office. It discharged nine employees who had no pension plan but qualified as pension obligees under the statute. Minnesota assessed Allied a $185,000 pension-funding charge. The statute created a contract liability for pensions that had not previously existed.

Justice Stewart delivered the opinion of the Court.

First of all, it is to be accepted as a commonplace that the Contract Clause does not operate to obliterate the police power of the States. "It is the settled law of this court that the interdiction of statutes impairing the obligation of contracts does not prevent the State from exercising such powers as are vested in it for the promotion of the common weal, or are necessary for the general good of the public." The first inquiry must be whether the state law has, in fact, operated as a substantial impairment of a contractual relationship. The severity of the impairment measures the height of the hurdle the state legislation must clear. Minimal alteration of contractual obligations may end the inquiry at its first stage. Severe impairment, on the other hand, will push the inquiry to a careful examination of the nature and purpose of the state legislation.

The severity of an impairment of contractual obligations can be measured by the factors that reflect the high value the Framers placed on the protection of private contracts. Contracts enable individuals to order their personal and business affairs according to their particular needs and interests. Once arranged, those rights and obligations are binding under the law, and the parties are entitled to rely on them.

Here, the company's contracts of employment with its employees included as a fringe benefit or additional form of compensation, the pension plan. The company's maximum obligation was to set aside each year an amount based on the plan's requirements for vesting. The plan satisfied the current federal income tax code and was subject to no other legislative requirements. And, of course, the company was free to amend or terminate the pension plan at any time. The company thus had no reason to anticipate that its employees' pension rights could become vested except in accordance with the terms of the plan. It relied heavily, and reasonably, on this legitimate contractual expectation in calculating its annual contributions to the pension fund.

The effect of Minnesota's Private Pension Benefits Protection Act on this contractual obligation was severe. The company was required in 1974 to have made its contributions throughout the pre-1974 life of its plan as if employees' pension rights had vested after 10 years, instead of vesting in accord with the terms of the plan. Thus a base term of the pension contract—one on which the company had relied for 10 years—was substantially modified. The result was that, although the company's past contributions were adequate when made, they were not adequate when computed under the 10-year statutory vesting requirement. The Act thus forced a current recalculation of the past 10 years' contributions based on the new, unanticipated 10-year vesting requirement.

Not only did the state law thus retroactively modify the compensation that the company had agreed to pay its employees from 1963 to 1974, but also it did so by changing the company's obligations in an area where the element of reliance was vital—the funding of a pension plan.

Entering a field it had never before sought to regulate, the Minnesota Legislature grossly distorted the company's existing contractual relationships with its employees by superimposing retroactive obligations upon the company substantially beyond the terms of its employment contracts.

The statute in question here nullifies express terms of the company's contractual obligations and imposes a completely unexpected liability in potentially disabling amounts. There is not even any provision for gradual applicability or grace periods. Yet there is no showing in the record before us that this severe disruption of contractual expectations was necessary to meet an important general social problem. It did not operate in an area already subject to state regulation at the time the company's contractual obligations were originally undertaken, but invaded an area never before subject to regulation by the State. It did not effect simply a temporary alteration of the contractual relationships of those within its coverage, but worked a severe, permanent, and immediate change in those relationships—irrevocably and retroactively. And its narrow aim was leveled, not at every Minnesota employer, not even at every Minnesota employer who left the State, but only at those who had in the past been sufficiently enlightened as voluntarily to agree to establish pension plans for their employees. [The statute's impact on Allied's pension liabilities was nullified.]

Case Questions

1. Is the contract clause given literal meaning in this case?
2. What is the most important initial factor that must be determined in a contract clause case? How is this factor determined?
3. What reasons might justify a state's impairment of contract?

Today, the Employee Retirement Income Security Act of 1975 (ERISA) generally protects pensioners from pension plan termination. It probably preempts state laws such as the one discussed in the *Allied* case above. ERISA is discussed further in Chapter 18.

Full Faith and Credit Clause

An important element of federalism is that each state must recognize the laws and legal processes of the other states. Without this recognition, some of the states could become a refuge for persons seeking to evade their legal obligations elsewhere. To prevent such misuse of the states' borders, the framers of the Constitution formulated the *full faith and credit clause.*

Full Faith and Credit Clause

Full Faith and Credit shall be given in each State to the public Acts, Records, and judicial Proceedings of every other State.

Full faith and credit is distinguished from *stare decisis,* the rule of precedent. Precedents are previous cases that establish rules of law applicable to other similar disputes arising later in that jurisdiction. Full faith and credit does not require states to adopt other states' precedents, only to enforce other states' laws when applicable or their judgments between particular disputing parties when suit is brought in another state. The full faith and credit clause requires application of the doctrines of *res judicata* and *collateral estoppel.* These doctrines require that when a competent court with jurisdiction over the subject matter renders a final decision, there can be no further litigation, except for appeals. The doctrines are similar to the criminal law doctrine of *double jeopardy,* which prohibits the prosecution of an individual twice for the same crime. All of these doctrines require a halt to litigation so that a defendant cannot be subjected to repeated suits on the same issues. The courts of other states must recognize and enforce the final decisions of all sister states. For example, if a creditor wins a judgment against a debtor in one state and the debtor flees to another state, the creditor may enforce that decree in the second state. This is true even if the second state does not have the same law as the state rendering the decree. Thus, Indiana need not require the payment of alimony in divorce actions between its citizens. However, it must enforce the alimony awards decreed in other states. Otherwise, Indiana could become a haven for alimony defaulters from other states.

Another important effect of the full faith and credit clause is that the courts of each state must apply the law of the state having the closest relationship to the events at issue in a suit. For example, parties may form a contract in one state, but one of the parties might bring suit for breach of the contract in another state. The *forum state* in which the suit is brought must apply the law of that state with the closest connection to the contract. The Supreme Court has approved several definitions of this "closeness." This may require a complex *conflicts of law* analysis to predict the proper choice of law if the forum state's substantive law differs from that of the other states involved. Similar problems exist in tort, domestic relations, and corporation law. For example, the law of the state of incorporation applies to questions of corporate governance. Conflicts of law rules often make it difficult to *forum shop,* that is, to look around for a court in a state with more favorable law.

Privileges and Immunities

The *privileges and immunities clause* is another aspect of federalism that prohibits the states from erecting barriers at their borders.

Privileges and Immunities Clause

The Citizens of each State shall be entitled to all Privileges and Immunities of Citizens in the several States.

No state may discriminate against the citizens of other states by prohibiting travel or denying access to its courts. Corporations do not have all the same rights as natural persons under the privileges and immunities clause. Thus, out-of-state corporations may be charged higher taxes than domestic corporations as long as the taxes are not confiscatory. Foreign corporations, those chartered out-of-state, must register when doing business in other states to have the privileges and immunities of domestic corporations chartered in that state. Since state taxes support state educational institutions financially, nonresident students may be required to pay higher college tuition at state universities than resident students. The commerce, full faith and credit, and privileges and immunities clauses work together to unify the nation while preserving states' rights.

Taxing and Spending Power

The federal government has the power to tax in order to raise revenue or discourage certain activities. Even if Congress does not have a specific power to directly regulate a particular activity, the taxing and spending power may be used for that purpose. Earlier cases invalidated taxes intended only as indirect regulation rather than for revenue raising. However, today the Supreme Court focuses less on Congress's motives in levying the tax and more on whether or not the tax is valid as a regulatory measure. For example, taxes have been validated to discourage gambling and the sale of marijuana and firearms. In reality, these taxes are indirect regulations of these activities.

Congress also has the constitutional power to spend tax receipts on matters both related to and not directly related to an enumerated power. Funds raised by taxes may be spent on nearly any policy Congress chooses, so long as it does not violate another constitutional provision. Both the taxing and spending powers of the federal government are used to expand its powers to regulate in many areas not originally enumerated in the U.S. Constitution. Today, political constraints are more influential than are constitutional constraints on Congress's taxing and spending habits.

Constitutional Rights of Businesses and Individuals

The adoption of several fundamental rights known as the *Bill of Rights* amended the Constitution during its initial ratification process. The Fourteenth Amendment reinforces these rights. The *First Amendment* contains several rights, most notably freedom of speech, freedom of the press, freedom of assembly, and freedom of religion. The *Fourth Amendment* ensures the right to be secure from searches and seizures except on the issuance of a warrant. The *Fifth Amendment* includes several provisions ensuring fair judicial process, such as protection against self-incrimination, the right to a grand jury indictment, protection against double jeopardy, and the right to due process. The *Sixth Amendment* guarantees a speedy trial, an impartial jury, the confrontation of witnesses, subpoena powers, process to obtain witness testimony, and the right to legal counsel. The *Seventh Amendment* preserves the right to a trial by jury in actions at common law. The *Eighth Amendment* prohibits excessive fines.

These constitutional rights are not absolute; they have been interpreted and refined over the last 200 years. Courts balance the need for constitutional protection against other important policies. The Bill of Rights protections specifically apply to natural persons, but they frequently extend to other entities, such as corporations, that are considered artificial persons. Corporations have protection of many constitutional rights, particularly during criminal investigations and proceedings, as discussed in the remainder of this chapter.

The First Amendment

The First Amendment includes fundamental rights of free speech, press, assembly, and religion. People are specifically protected from federal and state action under the absorption doctrine. The Fourteenth Amendment applies the bill of rights and other constitutional protections to governmental action at all levels and branches of government. Freedom of religion in the business context is discussed further in Chapter 20.

The First Amendment

> Congress shall make no law respecting an establishment of religion, or prohibiting the free exercise thereof; or abridging the freedom of speech, or of the press; or the right of the people peaceably to assemble, and to petition the Government for a redress of grievances.

Freedom of Speech The freedom of speech guaranteed by the First Amendment provides society with open access to the general marketplace of ideas. It protects speakers by affording expressive access to the public, which improves the quality and quantity of available ideas. Speech includes both verbal and nonverbal methods of expression. For example, the courts uphold union picketing for lawful purposes as nonverbal speech. However, laws may regulate some of the incidents of speech to preserve safety and public order. For example, the number of pickets and the manner of picketing may be controlled.

Not all types of speech are protected because society's need for some types of expression does not outweigh the social costs of allowing them. Obscenity, defamatory statements, incitement to riot, fraudulent statements, and subversive speeches receive little protection under the First Amendment. However, prior restraint laws that prohibit certain classes of speech are suspect. *Prior restraint* arises, for example, if a city denies a permit to assemble or a court prohibits a public meeting even though the potential for violence is quite low. It is also impermissible prior restraint when government restricts speech opposing politicians in power.

Commercial Speech Initially, the courts were not sympathetic to the protection of commercial speech. Legislation regulating advertising was approved by assuming commercial speech was less justifiable than other forms of speech because it primarily resulted only in personal gain for the advertiser. Commercial speech was not presumed to have as legitimate a social purpose as political speech. More recent cases recognize that commercial speech disseminates important information. By making adequate information available to all market participants, the free exercise of commercial speech helps ensure more efficient operation of the market.[16]

Commercial speech may be restricted as to time, place, and manner, but only where society's need for regulation outweighs the speaker's interest. The criteria below apply

---

[16] *Virginia Pharmacy Board v. Virginia Citizens Consumer Council*, 425 U.S. 746 (1976).

to the regulation of commercial speech. How do they apply to restrictions on the advertising of tobacco or alcohol?

Criteria to Regulate Commercial Speech

The commercial speech must concern lawful activity and not be misleading.

The degree of restriction must directly relate to the degree of governmental interest.

The restriction must reach no further than necessary to protect the governmental interest, and no other practical method exists to protect this interest.

The time, place, and manner of the speech may be regulated, provided that no change is made in the substance of the speech.

This commercial speech analysis affects both federal and state law. In a recent case, the federal ban on advertising the alcoholic content of beer was invalidated.[17] Some groups had argued that ads touting the percentage of alcohol in beer would encourage alcohol abuse. However, the societal interest in banning such ads was too tenuous to be sustained as a restriction on commercial speech. Should problems such as the energy crisis outweigh an electric utility's right to advertise? The following case established the analysis that is used to evaluate restrictions on commercial speech.

Central Hudson Gas & Electric Corp. v. Public Service Commission

447 U.S. 557 (1980)
United States Supreme Court

Responding to the energy crisis, the New York Public Service Commission prohibited electric utilities from advertising to promote electricity use. It permitted only informational advertising that encouraged shifts of consumption from peak to off-peak times. Central Hudson Gas and Electric opposed the ban on First Amendment grounds.

Justice Powell delivered the opinion of the Court.

The Commission's order restricts only commercial speech, that is, expression related solely to the economic interests of the speaker and its audience. The First Amendment, as applied to the States through the Fourteenth Amendment, protects commercial speech from unwarranted governmental regulation. Commercial expression not only serves the economic interest of the speaker, but also assists consumers and furthers the societal interest in the fullest possible dissemination of information. In applying the First Amendment to this area, we have rejected the "highly paternalistic" view that government has complete power to suppress or regulate commercial speech. "[P]eople will perceive their own best interests if only they are well enough informed, and . . . the best means to that end is to open the channels of communication, rather than to close them." Even when advertising communicates only an incomplete version of the relevant facts, the First Amendment presumes that some accurate information is better than no information at all.

---

[17] *Rubin v. Coors*, 93-1631 (U.S. 1995).

If the communication is neither misleading nor related to unlawful activity, the government's power is more circumscribed. The State must assert a substantial interest to be achieved by restrictions on commercial speech. Moreover, the regulatory technique must be in proportion to that interest. The limitation on expression must be designed carefully to achieve the State's goal. . . . First, the restriction must directly advance the state interest involved; the regulation may not be sustained if it provides only ineffective or remote support for the government's purpose. Second, if the governmental interest could be served as well by a more limited restriction on commercial speech, the excessive restrictions cannot survive.

In commercial speech cases, then, a four-part analysis has developed. At the outset, we must determine whether the expression is protected by the First Amendment. For commercial speech to come within that provision, it at least must concern lawful activity and not be misleading. Next, we ask whether the asserted governmental interest is substantial. If both inquiries yield positive answers, we must determine whether the regulation directly advances the governmental interest asserted, and whether it is not more extensive than is necessary to serve that interest.

The Commission offers two state interests as justifications for the ban on promotional advertising. The first concerns energy conservation. Any increase in demand for electricity—during peak or off-peak periods—means greater consumption of energy. The Commission argues, and the New York court agreed, that the State's interest in conserving energy is sufficient to support suppression of advertising designed to increase consumption of electricity. In view of our country's dependence on energy resources beyond our control, no one can doubt the importance of energy conservation. Plainly, therefore, the state interest asserted is substantial.

The State's interest in energy conservation is directly advanced by the Commission's order at issue here. There is an immediate connection between advertising and demand for electricity. Central Hudson would not contest the advertising ban unless it believed that promotion would increase its sales. Thus, we find a direct link between the state interest in conservation and the Commission's order.

We come finally to the critical inquiry in this case: whether the Commission's complete suppression of speech ordinarily protected by the First Amendment is no more extensive than necessary to further the State's interest in energy conservation. The Commission's order reaches all promotional advertising, regardless of the impact of the touted service on overall energy use. But the energy conservation rationale, as important as it is, cannot justify suppressing information about electric devices or services that would cause no net increase in total energy use. In addition, no showing has been made that a more limited restriction on the content of promotional advertising would not serve adequately the State's interest.

The Commission's order prevents appellant from promoting electric services that would reduce energy use by diverting demand from less efficient sources, or that would consume roughly the same amount of energy as do alternative sources. In neither situation would the utility's advertising endanger conservation or mislead the public. To the extent that the Commission's order suppresses speech that in no way impairs the State's interest in energy conservation, the Commission's order violates the First and Fourteenth Amendments and must be invalidated.

Case Questions

1. What reasons justify bans on commercial speech?
2. What types of commercial speech are presumed to be unjustified?

Political Speech First Amendment protection also extends to the political speech of commercial entities. Corporations may validly disseminate ideas and influence political thought as long as they do not violate the campaign finance laws, discussed more fully in Chapter 22. However, the subject of the political speech should be general and may not receive protection if it identifies specific political parties or candidates.

In *First National Bank of Boston v. Bellotti*,[18] a Massachusetts statute prohibited a corporation from making expenditures or contributions for the purpose of influencing

[18] *First National Bank of Boston v. Bellotti*, 435 U.S. 765 (1978).

the vote on questions submitted to voters unless the questions materially affected the corporation. The statute also prohibited corporate advocacy on legislation involving taxation. Corporate violators could be fined up to $50,000, and the corporate officer who authorized the expenditures could be fined and imprisoned for up to one year. First National Bank of Boston and others desired to publicize their views that a ballot question on a graduated individual income tax was unconstitutional. The Court held:

> [The First] Amendment protects the free discussion of governmental affairs. . . . The inherent worth of the speech in terms of its capacity for informing the public does not depend upon the identity of its source, whether corporation, association, union, or individual. . . . The press does not have a monopoly on either the First Amendment or the ability to enlighten. . . . The First Amendment goes beyond protection of the press and the self-expression of individuals to prohibit government from limiting the stock of information from which members of the public may draw.

If a legislature may direct business corporations to "stick to business," it also may limit other corporations—religious, charitable, or civic—to their respective "business" when addressing the public. Such power in government to channel the expression of views is unacceptable under the First Amendment. The First Amendment is plainly offended when a statute suppresses speech and thereby gives one side an advantage in the debate.

Litigation Threat Chills Freedom of Speech

Ethical Dilemma

The Bill of Rights includes constitutional freedoms most Americans consider sacred, fundamental rights. These rights are the product of political struggles over several millennia, which track the evolution of civilization. However, the First Amendment freedom of speech may appear to conflict with other civil and property rights. This problem has arisen in recent years with public participation by individuals and interest groups. They may write editorials, give speeches, organize boycotts, complain to regulators, testify before public bodies, or otherwise become involved in political participation that arguably harasses particular businesses. For example, some interest groups have made public attacks on real estate developers alleging environmental or aesthetic destruction. In other cases, citizens have complained to regulators about a manufacturer's allegedly unsafe products. As a result of these attacks, the targeted business can suffer declining sales or a loss of reputation, or face toughened new regulations.

Some of these targeted businesses have responded by suing for damages or to enjoin the speech. Such responses are termed *SLAPP* suits, *Strategic Litigation Against Public Participation*. Such suits by either side may involve an ethical dilemma of constitutional proportions. Either an unfair pressure is brought on the targeted business, or costly litigation is brought by affluent firms, chilling the free speech or government participation by individuals and thereby frustrating these fundamental constitutional rights.

Some targeted businesses bring SLAPP suits alleging the public participants of one or more torts: defamation (libel, slander), trade disparagement, trademark infringement, misrepresentation or fraud, tortious interference with contract relations, interference with prospective advantage, and/or privacy violations. In many cases, the target's mere initiation of suit intimidates the public participant, effectively silencing any public participation. However, some public participants challenge SLAPP suits and are usually successful in blunting the SLAPP to vindicate their participation rights. Indeed, in some SLAPP-back suits the public participants have won damages for abuse of process or malicious prosecution against the originally targeted business.

Targeted businesses should never be denied judicial access to redress malicious damage by a public participant acting in bad faith. However, public participants should not be intimidated from exercising legitimate First Amendment rights of free speech and petitioning the government for redress of grievances. Vindicating constitutional rights and abusing the political and legal systems pose ethical dilemmas for all involved.

The Fourth Amendment

Of all the constitutional provisions discussed, the Fourth Amendment provides business with the greatest protection from unfair governmental investigations. Typically, the Fourth Amendment protection arises before a criminal defendant is indicted or before a civil administrative case is filed. The Fourth Amendment protects both natural persons and corporations from unreasonable searches and seizures.

Fourth Amendment: Unreasonable Searches and Seizures

> The right of the people to be secure in their persons, papers, and effects, against unreasonable searches and seizures, shall not be violated, and no Warrants shall issue, but on probable cause, supported by Oath or affirmation, and particularly describing the place to be searched and the persons or things to be seized.

The administrative regulation of business often involves several methods of investigation. After suit has been filed, an administrative agency may use discovery to obtain information for its case. Discovery devices include interrogatories and depositions to question opposing parties and witnesses. A production of document request permits the examination of private files. Before suit is filed, investigators may get information from required reports, on-site inspections, and subpoenas. After assessing this information, the agency may decide whether there is sufficient evidence to prosecute or sue.

Statutes require the keeping of many records for the public's benefit, so they are considered *public* records with no right to privacy. Accordingly, no Fifth Amendment privilege protects them from disclosure. Administrative agencies may share with other agencies the nonprivileged evidence they gather. Federal agencies may generally refer investigative files to the Justice Department for criminal prosecution. For example, the Securities and Exchange Commission may inform the Justice Department about the information it has on inside trading, which may lead to criminal charges.

subpoena Government order requiring a witness to testify.

Subpoenas The statute creating administrative agencies usually gives them the power to subpoena documents. **Subpoenas** require pretrial and trial testimony from witnesses. A *subpoena duces tecum* requires the production of documents. Agencies may not abuse the subpoena power for ulterior motives. For example, agencies may not harass a business by issuing excessive subpoenas, and they may not publicly disclose trade secrets and other private matters examined under subpoena. To ensure that agencies do not exceed their subpoena powers, administrative subpoenas are not *self-executing.* This means the recipient of an administrative subpoena may validly refuse to either testify or to produce the documents requested until ordered to do so by a court.

An agency must justify a subpoena before a court will order enforcement. Four fairness standards, established in *United States v. Powell,*[19] require the agency to prove that its investigation is legitimate and that the information it seeks is relevant. The subpoena recipient must comply if the agency satisfies the *Powell* criteria. The extent to which law enforcement officials may search private business premises for evidence of wrongdoing is also limited by the Fourth Amendment as discussed in Chapter 6.

United States v. Powell Subpoena Enforcement Standards

1. Agency has a legitimate purpose to investigate.
2. Inquiry must be relevant to that legitimate purpose.
3. Agency may not already have the requested information in its possession.
4. Agency must follow all its own administrative procedures in issuing the subpoena.

The Fifth and Fourteenth Amendments

The Fifth and Fourteenth Amendments contain two major provisions to maintain fundamental fairness: the due process and equal protection clauses. The Fifth Amendment applies these protections to actions taken by the federal government.

Fifth Amendment Due Process Clause

No person shall be . . . deprived of life, liberty, or property, without due process of law.

The Fourteenth Amendment applies the Fifth Amendment to the states under the *absorption* or *incorporation* doctrine. This doctrine assures that the fundamental protections of most constitutional rights also apply to the actions of state government.

Fourteenth Amendment: Due Process and Equal Protection Clauses

. . . nor shall any State deprive any person of life, liberty, or property, without due process of law; nor deny to any person within its jurisdiction the equal protection of the laws.

Equal Protection of the Laws The need for equality under the law after the abolition of slavery demanded a definitive constitutional statement. The equal protec-

[19] *United States v. Powell,* 379 U.S. 48 (1964).

tion clause of the Fourteenth Amendment provided blacks with protection from arbitrary legislative distinctions. Today, that clause applies to all types of arbitrary and unreasonable classifications in legislation. By its very nature, legislation necessarily selects which persons or entities are subject to the law, based on such classifications as conduct, size of business, or level of income. However, establishing fair classifications of this kind is difficult, requiring careful statutory design. For example, only murderers, not lesser criminals, should receive punishment under criminal statutes prohibiting murder. Similarly, the Uniform Commercial Code imposes special obligations on merchants; it requires a higher level of conduct in commercial transactions from merchants than from nonmerchants. These classifications are fair only when they adequately discriminate.

Legislative classifications with no reasonable purpose are unconstitutional under the equal protection clause. Under the rational basis test, laws should have general applicability unless there is sufficient reason to discriminate against certain people. This test applies in many situations, but it seldom invalidates legislation. Another test, the strict scrutiny test, applies in situations involving discrimination against protected classes of persons or discrimination in matters of fundamental rights. When strict scrutiny applies, many statutes are held unconstitutional. Quasi-strict scrutiny is an intermediate test that is important in some business contexts.

rational basis
Equal protection test of legislation validity requiring a rational connection between a permissible governmental purpose and the statute in question.

Rational Basis The equal protection clause does not disturb the constitutionality of a statute if there is a rational connection between the statute's classification scheme and a permissible governmental purpose. Under this **rational basis** test, the statute is first presumed constitutional. Government may regulate in areas that are normally and legitimately the role of government. For example, Congress may pass laws pursuant to an enumerated power, such as the regulation of interstate commerce. State legislatures may pass criminal laws implementing the police power. Any classifications used in statutes enacted for such purposes must have a reasonable basis and not be arbitrary.

In *Minnesota v. Clover Leaf Creamery Co.*[20] the Supreme Court found that a Minnesota statute provided adequate equal protection even though it prohibited disposable plastic packaging only for milk. The statute sought to diminish the solid-waste problem and save energy by banning nonreturnable plastic milk containers, yet it permitted the use of nonreturnable plastic containers for other products. The rational basis test, which was used here, invalidates only the most outrageously arbitrary classification schemes. This case permits states to implement a regulatory program in steps, eliminating evils only partially at first and deferring complete elimination to future regulations.

strict scrutiny
Equal protection test of legislation validity requiring the legislation be necessary to and the only means to achieve a compelling governmental interest.

Strict Scrutiny In more recent years, courts have used the **strict scrutiny** test to invalidate legislation that violates certain fundamental rights or discriminates against suspect classes. When the rigorous criteria of the strict scrutiny test are applied, legislation is seldom acceptable if any conceivable alternative could achieve the same legitimate regulatory end. Under strict scrutiny, the suspect legislation must be necessary and the only means to achieve a compelling governmental interest. To survive a strict scrutiny attack, a statute must relate to the governmental interest more closely than is required under the rational basis test, and the governmental purpose must be more important. There must be clear legislative intent to reach the legitimate governmental goal.

[20] *Minnesota v. Clover Leaf Creamery Co.*, 449 U.S. 456 (1981).

Strict scrutiny applies only to fundamental rights and to discrimination against suspect or protected classes. *Fundamental rights* include voting rights, interstate travel, immunity from mandatory sterility, and criminal procedural protections. *Suspect classes* are demographic classifications of people who deserve greater protection because they have been subjected to intentional discrimination and because they are nearly powerless to overcome the discrimination. Suspect classes include classifications based on race, national origin, and alien status. Employment discrimination is governed by the antidiscrimination laws discussed in Chapter 20.

Quasi-Strict Scrutiny A third classification, *quasi-strict scrutiny,* has arisen in recent years. It falls between the rational basis and the strict scrutiny tests. This standard applies where the rights involved are clearly important but are not quite considered fundamental rights, or where the classifications in the statute are only partially suspect. For example, classifications based on sex, gender, or legitimacy must be substantially related to an important government objective under this middle ground test. The quasi-strict scrutiny test validates some classifications while invalidating others. Clearly every equal protection inquiry must be quite fact specific.

Equal protection issues arise most often in cases of racial segregation. Equal protection has required reapportionment of state legislatures under the principle of "one man, one vote," as when two nearby congressional districts in a state have grossly unequal numbers of citizens. The courts have ruled military regulations as unconstitutional that afford spouses of servicewomen lesser benefits than the spouses of servicemen. The denial of voting rights in school district elections to nonparents or nonowners of property was found unconstitutional under strict scrutiny.

Due Process of Law The due process clause is intended to prevent unfair and predetermined outcomes at criminal trials like those in colonial times held before English judges. Due process requires that government observe at least a minimum level of fairness in trial procedures. This fairness doctrine prohibits arbitrary, biased, and unreasonable outcomes in trials and administrative hearings. The due process clause applies to a wide variety of criminal, civil, and administrative hearings. Certain private determinations by nongovernmental entities are also subject to some form of due process. However, due process rights are not identical in all cases. Criminal defendants usually receive more specific and extensive protections than do civil or administrative litigants.

Due process prohibits government from depriving any person of life, liberty, or property without due process of law. A *person* in this context is broadly construed to include both natural persons and artificial persons, such as corporations or unincorporated associations. A *deprivation of life* usually denotes capital punishment and arises in right to die or euthanasia cases. A *deprivation of liberty* occurs when one is denied the ability to move freely in public areas, that is, while not trespassing on private property. A *deprivation of property* occurs when a person must pay a fine or money damages or when property is taken by government. Due process permits government to deprive one of life, liberty, or property, but only if due process is followed.

Due process has developed into two separate limits on unreasonable governmental action. *Procedural due process* incorporates the traditional issues regarding the processes of investigation, arrest, detainment, trial, and appeal. *Substantive due process* involves issues concerning the fairness of legislation in the way it defines rights and duties. These due process issues arise whenever government attempts to vindicate rights, whether those attempts are prosecuted by government attorneys, initiated in court or administrative agencies, or conducted by private entities affected with a public character (e.g., private universities). To successfully claim a due process right, some form of state action or governmental process must be involved because constitutional rights provide protection only from oppressive governmental actions, not oppressive private acts. There is no constitutional protection from an individual's actions unless the individual is acting under the color of government. For example, a basketball coach suffered no due process violation when the NCAA required the university to punish its coach for alleged NCAA rule violations. The NCAA is a private organization, so there was no state action involved even though the state university implemented the NCAA's order.[21]

Procedural Due Process Two basic rights in litigation involve due process protections. The first right is intended to assure defendants a fair opportunity to offer a defense and the use of fair trial procedures. This is why in some cases a notice of suit, a *service of summons*, must be personally delivered to the defendant. *Substituted service* of process is a valid alternative if it is impossible to deliver the notice directly.

The second basic due process right in litigation concerns the conduct of the trial. The precise fair trial procedures vary according to the rights adjudicated, the type of trial, and the severity of the penalties. The trial procedures should afford the utmost protection to a criminal defendant charged with a capital crime. At the other extreme, a college disciplinary proceeding can provide sufficient due process even without many of the procedural technicalities of a criminal trial. The Fifth, Sixth, and Seventh Amendments also require several fair trial procedures.

Defendant's Due Process Rights

1. Confront witnesses with cross-examination.
2. Present evidence.
3. Subpoena witnesses.
4. Have an impartial decision maker.
5. Appeal the trial decision.

Is a full trial by jury necessary to review a university's dismissal of a student for poor scholarship? Informal administrative processes need not include the full spectrum of evidentiary rules yet must still provide minimum due process. In *Board of Curators of the University of Missouri v. Horowitz,*[22] Horowitz was dismissed from the university's medical school for failure to meet academic standards. She had been fully informed of the faculty's dissatisfaction with her progress and the adverse impact on her timely graduation. The ultimate dismissal decision was deliberate and careful. Horowitz sued the university, claiming a lack of due process in the dismissal process. The Supreme Court compared academic dismissal to disciplinary proceedings, reserving the broader due process procedural steps such as notice and opportunity to present evidence only for disciplinary proceedings. Justice Rehnquist said that:

[21] *National Collegiate Athletic Ass'n v. Tarkanian,* 488 U.S. 179 (1988).

[22] *Board of Curators of the University of Missouri v. Horowitz,* 435 U.S. 78 (1978).

> The decision to dismiss respondent rested on the academic judgment of school officials that she did not have the necessary clinical ability to perform adequately as a medical doctor and was making insufficient progress toward that goal. Such a judgment is by its nature more subjective and evaluative than the typical factual questions presented in the average disciplinary decision. Like the decision of an individual professor as to the proper grade for a student in his course, the determination whether to dismiss a student for academic reasons requires an expert evaluation of cumulative information and is not readily adapted to the procedural tools of judicial or administrative decision making.

Substantive Due Process The substantive due process doctrine allows a court to declare a statute unconstitutional if the statute fails to provide due process. In the late 19th and early 20th centuries, the *economic due process* doctrine was applied to invalidate early regulatory statutes that required minimum wages or maximum working hours, or allowed union membership. Many such statutes were unconstitutional because they unjustifiably restricted the freedom of business to contract or they deprived business of its property without due process. Today, economic substantive due process is inapplicable.

In the area of personal liberty and rights, the substantive due process doctrine retains some validity. It requires that legislation meet two tests. The first test is an ends-means test similar to that found in equal protection cases. This test requires that legislation be directed toward a legitimate governmental purpose and that the means used be closely connected to that purpose. Second, the test prohibits vague legislation. A statute is unconstitutional if it does not provide ascertainable criteria for the identification of unlawful conduct. For example, a law enforcement officer cannot arrest someone based on the officer's interpretation of what constitutes wrongdoing. Laws permitting this level of discretion are vague. For example, in *Coates v. City of Cincinnati*,[23] the city passed a criminal ordinance prohibiting "three or more persons to assemble . . . on any of the sidewalks . . . and there conduct themselves in a manner *annoying* to persons passing by . . ." (emphasis added). On the basis of this ordinance, the Cincinnati authorities prosecuted Coates for participating in a student demonstration. The ordinance violated due process because it subjected Coates's constitutional right of assembly to an imprecise standard, the term *annoying conduct*. Conduct that some people find "annoying" does not annoy others, so people of common intelligence must necessarily guess at the word's meaning. Substantive due process also protects business from prosecution under vague laws.

Punitive Damages There is a widespread perception that juries are awarding increasingly larger punitive damage awards. *Punitive damages* are an additional component of damages above and beyond compensatory damages. Compensatory damages reimburses the plaintiff for losses actually suffered. Advocates of punitive damages argue they deter the adverse side effects of business activities on society. The argument is that without the threat of severe penalties, business managers have little incentive to avoid endangering the public with harmful products, manufacturing processes, or business practices. Additionally, managers are too well insulated personally from lawsuit pressures; that is, they seldom bear the financial effects of their decisions directly because the firm pays. Highly visible punitive awards signal managers to more carefully consider the impact their decisions have on others.

---

[23] *Coates v. City of Cincinnati*, 402 U.S. 611 (1971).

Punitive damages can have an adverse impact on companies. Critics charge that punitives are unpredictable and counterproductive for the economy. For example, a multimillon-dollar punitive award could wipe out a company's profitability for years, force it to drop products, slow its innovation, force the closing of facilities, require layoffs, or even drive the company into bankruptcy. Recent challenges to punitive damages have alleged they violate two fundamental constitutional rights: (1) punitives allegedly constitute excessive fines prohibited by the Eighth Amendment, and (2) unrestrained jury discretion to assess punitives violates the defendant's due process under the Fourteenth Amendment.

In *Browing-Ferris Indus. v. Kelco Disposal*,[24] the Supreme Court rejected the Eighth Amendment argument. A regional BFI executive instructed the local BFI office to cut prices and drive Kelco, a competing waste collector, out of business. The Supreme Court reaffirmed the jury's award to Kelco of $51,146 in compensatory damages and $6 million in punitives in Kelco's monopolization suit. The Eighth Amendment was intended to protect convicted defendants from excessive punishment by government, not from civil actions between private parties. Should the due process clause apply to restrict punitive damages? The following case reexamines the constitutionality of punitives.

Pacific Mutual Life Ins. Co. v. Halsip

499 U.S. 1 (1991)
United States Supreme Court

The health insurance for Halsip and other employees of Roosevelt City, Alabama, lapsed after Ruffin misappropriated health and life insurance premiums. Ruffin was agent for both Union Fidelity Life Insurance Co. and Pacific Mutual Life Insurance Co. Premiums for this coverage were deducted from city employee paychecks and remitted by the city clerk to Ruffin for payment to the insurers. Ruffin misappropriated the premiums and never forwarded the insurer's notice warning the insureds that their health insurance coverage would lapse. After hospitalization, Halsip was forced to pay her hospital bill. Her physician placed her unpaid account with a collection agency that obtained a judgment against her, adversely affecting her credit. Halsip sued Ruffin for fraud. The jury held Pacific Mutual vicariously liable for Ruffin's wrongful acts. Halsip was awarded $1,040,000 of which nearly $840,000 was punitive damages.

Justice Blackmun delivered the opinion of the Court.

Alabama's common-law rule is that a corporation is liable for both compensatory and punitive damages for fraud of its employee effected within the scope of his employment. We cannot say that this does not rationally advance the State's interest in minimizing fraud. Alabama long has applied this rule in the insurance context, for it has determined that an insurer is more likely to prevent an agent's fraud if given sufficient financial incentive to do so. Imposing exemplary damages on the corporation when its agent commits intentional fraud creates a strong incentive for vigilance by those in a position "to guard substantially against the evil."

[24] *Browing-Ferris Indus. v. Kelco Disposal,* 492 U.S. 257 (1989).

Under the traditional common-law approach, the amount of the punitive award is initially determined by a jury instructed to consider the gravity of the wrong and the need to deter similar wrongful conduct. The jury's determination is then reviewed by trial and appellate courts to ensure that it is reasonable. So far as we have been able to determine, every state and federal court that has considered the question has ruled that the common-law method for assessing punitive damages does not in itself violate due process. In view of this consistent history, we cannot say that the common-law method for assessing punitive damages is so inherently unfair as to deny due process and be *per se* unconstitutional. One must concede that unlimited jury discretion—or unlimited judicial discretion for that matter—in the fixing of punitive damages may invite extreme results that jar one's constitutional sensibilities.

We need not, and indeed we cannot, draw a mathematical bright line between the constitutionally acceptable and the constitutionally unacceptable that would fit every case. We can say, however, that general concerns of reasonableness and adequate guidance from the court when the case is tried to a jury properly enter into the constitutional calculus.

To be sure, the instructions gave the jury significant discretion in its determination of punitive damages. But that discretion was not unlimited. It was confined to deterrence and retribution, the state policy concerns sought to be advanced. And if punitive damages were to be awarded, the jury "must take into consideration the character and the degree of the wrong as shown by the evidence and necessity of preventing similar wrong." The instructions thus enlightened the jury as to the punitive damages' nature and purpose [and] identified the damages as punishment for civil wrongdoing of the kind involved.

Before the trial in this case took place, the Supreme Court of Alabama had established post-trial procedures for scrutinizing punitive awards. In *Hammond v. City of Gadsden*, it stated that trial courts are "to reflect in the record the reasons for interfering with a jury verdict, or refusing to do so, on grounds of excessiveness of the damages." Among the factors deemed "appropriate for the trial court's consideration" are the "culpability of the defendant's conduct," the "desirability of discouraging others from similar conduct," the "impact upon the parties," and "other factors, such as the impact on innocent third parties." The *Hammond* test ensures meaningful and adequate review by the trial court whenever a jury has fixed the punitive damages.

Also before its ruling in the present case, the Supreme Court of Alabama had elaborated and refined the *Hammond* criteria for determining whether a punitive award is reasonably related to the goals of deterrence and retribution. It was announced that the following could be taken into consideration in determining whether the award was excessive or inadequate: (a) whether there is a reasonable relationship between the punitive damages award and the harm likely to result from the defendant's conduct as well as the harm that actually has occurred; (b) the degree of responsibility of the defendant's conduct, the duration of that conduct, the defendant's awareness, any concealment, and the existence and frequency of similar past conduct; (c) the profitability to the defendant of the wrongful conduct and the desirability of removing that profit and of having the defendant also sustain a loss; (d) the "financial position" of the defendant; (e) all the costs of litigation; (f) the imposition of criminal sanctions on the defendant for its conduct, these to be taken in mitigation; and (g) the existence of other civil awards against the defendant for the same conduct, these also to be taken in mitigation.

The application of these standards, we conclude, imposes a sufficiently definite and meaningful constraint on the discretion of Alabama fact finders in awarding punitive damages. The Alabama Supreme Court's post-verdict review ensures that punitive damages awards are not grossly out of proportion to the severity of the offense and have some understandable relationship to compensatory damages. Pacific Mutual thus had the benefit of the full panoply of Alabama's procedural protections. Pacific Mutual's due process challenge must be, and is, rejected.

The judgment of the Supreme Court of Alabama is affirmed. It is so ordered.

Justice O'Connor, dissenting

Punitive damages are a powerful weapon. Imposed wisely and with restraint they have the potential to advance legitimate state interests. Imposed indiscriminately, however, they have a devastating potential for harm. Regrettably, common-law procedures for awarding punitive damages fall into the latter category. States routinely authorize civil juries to impose punitive damages without providing them any meaningful instructions on how to do so. Rarely is a jury told anything more specific than "do what you think best."

In my view, such instructions are so fraught with uncertainty that they defy rational implementation. Instead, they encourage inconsistent and unpredictable results by inviting juries to rely on private beliefs and personal predilections. Juries are permitted to target unpopular defendants, penalize unorthodox or controversial views, and redistribute wealth. Multimillion-dollar losses are inflicted on a whim.

Due process requires that a State provide meaningful standards to guide the application of its laws. A state law that lacks such standards is void for vagueness. The void-for-vagueness doctrine applies not only to laws that proscribe conduct, but also to laws that vest standardless discretion in the jury to fix a penalty. I have no trouble concluding that Alabama's common-law scheme for imposing punitive damages is void for vagueness.

Case Questions

1. What procedures does Alabama provide to assure due process in the assessment of punitive damages?
2. In what situations does the Supreme Court suggest that punitives could violate the defendant's due process rights?
3. For what reasons does Justice O'Connor's dissent suggest there is a potential for due process violations remaining under Alabama's punitive damage process?

Several states now limit punitives by statute; Alabama "caps" punitive damages at $250,000 per case. Tort reform discussed further in Chapter 8 and product liability reform discussed in Chapter 11 are part of this. The courts since *Halsip* are in conflict; some have narrowed punitives, some have invalidated limits on damage awards, and others continue awarding punitives without any arbitrary dollar limitation. Critics of the tort reform movement charge that stories about punitive damages are distorted to advocate statutory limitation. Most large punitive awards are newsworthy but are eventually reduced after settlement or appeal through *remittitur*. Many huge awards are never paid at all, and most tort reformers fail to acknowledge these facts.

There have been several comprehensive empirical studies of damage awards that contest the false claims of some tort reformers. Researchers find that most large damage awards: (1) were made in asbestos cases, (2) have declined since 1986, (3) are made by state courts, (4) predominate in the South, (5) are usually based on the failure to warn consumers of known defects, and (6) involve plaintiffs who are victims of catastrophic injuries.[25] Other studies confirm that few of the huge damage awards publicized are ever paid out.

Self-Incrimination The protection of witnesses from compelled self-incrimination constitutes one of the best-known aspects of the Fifth Amendment. By "pleading the Fifth," witnesses may refrain from giving evidence that might tend to show their own guilt. The Fifth Amendment constrains the investigatory activities of administrative agencies, prosecutors, police, and congressional committees.

An important limitation on the protection against self-incrimination has developed. That protection is a personal right, so it protects only a natural person from whom testimony is sought. Therefore, corporations and other business entities do not receive protection against incriminating evidence taken from an employee's testimony in matters involving the corporation. Employees may assert the privilege of protection

[25] Michael Rustad, *Demystifying Punitive Damages in Product Liability Cases: A Survey of a Quarter Century of Trial Verdicts,* Research Monograph Paper of the Roscoe Pound Foundation, Washington, D.C., 1991.

TABLE 5–1

U.S. Constitution's Bill of Rights

Amendment Number	Rights Established
First Amendment	Freedom of religion, speech, press, assembly, petition government for redress of grievances
Second Amendment	Right to bear arms
Third Amendment	Limits on quartering soldiers in private homes
Fourth Amendment	No unreasonable searches and seizures without warrant issued on probable cause
Fifth Amendment	Indictment required for serious crimes; no double jeopardy for crimes; no compelled self-incrimination; no deprivation of life, liberty, or property without due process; no takings without just compensation.
Sixth Amendment	Criminal trial rights: speedy and public trial, trial by impartial jury, notice of trial, confront adverse witnesses, subpoena witnesses, representation by counsel
Seventh Amendment	Civil trial rights: jury trial, limited appeal of jury verdict
Eighth Amendment	No excessive bail or fines, no cruel and unusual punishment
Ninth Amendment	Enumerating these rights does not make an exclusive list; other rights are retained by the people
Tenth Amendment	Powers not delegated to federal government are retained by states or the people

against self-incrimination to protect their own interest. However, the privilege does not protect the employer from incrimination.

In many instances, evidence that incriminates one party is in the hands of someone else. For example, accountants or attorneys often hold tax documents for their clients, and when government officials seek these documents, the clients may try to claim that the Fifth Amendment privilege against self-incrimination applies to the documents. This argument usually fails on the grounds that the privilege is testimonial, so it protects only verbal, not documentary, evidence. There are other types of evidentiary privileges. These privileges usually protect the accused from the release of confidential information by close associates. Such associates include spouses, attorneys, priests or ministers, and, in some states, accountants. Table 5–1 summarizes the Bill of Rights.

SUMMARY

The U.S. Constitution is the basic and supreme law that establishes the structure and limits of American government. It is a compromise on the optimal "residence of power" that is effected through a system of checks and balances (separation of powers) and the sharing of power between the federal and state governments (federalism). Through adoption of the U.S. Constitution, the federal government gained broad enumerated powers over foreign affairs, interstate commerce, and taxation. Federal law prevails when in conflict with state laws. However, states may exercise the reserved police power to protect the health, safety, welfare, and morals of its citizens, when done for legitimate objectives.

There are several specific governmental powers that affect business. The commerce clause permits the federal government to regulate trade and commerce with foreign countries and among the states. The states cannot erect protectionist trade barriers. Since most commercial activities have some impact on interstate commerce, state regulation may impose only minor burdens as determined by the "balancing test."

Although the contract clause once restricted the states from regulating business activity, today most courts use the due process clause to invalidate unreasonable state economic regulations. The full faith and credit clause requires each state to respect and give effect to the laws and court decisions of other states. The privileges and immunities clause prohibits a state from discriminating against the citizens of other states. The states do not consider undomesticated out-of-state corporations citizens under this clause.

The Bill of Rights are the first 10 amendments to the U.S. Constitution, which were originally passed to assure fundamental rights for individuals. Most also apply to business. The First Amendment guarantees freedom of the press, speech, religion, and assembly. However, the First Amendment does not prevent reasonable governmental restraints on obscenity, defamation, incitement, fraud, subversion, and commercial speech as necessary to protect society. The Fourth Amendment protects both individuals and corporations from unreasonable searches and seizures that usually arise before a suit is filed. An administrative agency may seek testimony or the production of personal or corporate records if the inquiry is legitimate and the agency has carefully followed its own procedures. A court will enforce administrative subpoenas requiring testimony or the production of documents, but only where the information sought is relevant and not already in the agency's possession.

The equal protection clause of the Fifth and Fourteenth Amendments requires that all individuals receive equal protection of the law without arbitrary legislative distinctions or discrimination. No equal protection problem exists if there is a rational connection between a statute's classification scheme and a permissible governmental purpose. In discrimination cases, however, legislation must survive a strict scrutiny of its purpose and effect if an unequal protection claim arises. The due process clauses of the Fifth and Fourteenth Amendments protect both individuals and corporations from deprivation of life, liberty, or property without due process. Procedurally, due process requires notice of litigation, fair trial procedures, and an impartial tribunal. Substantively, it requires that legislation have a legitimate objective and use only reasonable means to achieve it. The Fifth Amendment also prohibits government from requiring self-incriminating testimony from an accused individual. However, this self-incrimination protection cannot be invoked by corporations because they are not natural persons.

Critical Thinking Review Questions

1. What is meant by judicial review? Does this give the Supreme Court the final word on what the law and the Constitution mean?
2. Explain the constitutional foundation for state and federal government regulatory power.
3. Compare the balancing critieria used in takings cases with the analysis used in equal protection cases.

Critical Thinking Exercises

1. Is there any limit to the ability of Congress to regulate intrastate activity under the commerce clause? Consider the case of an Ohio farmer, Filburn, who was fined $117.11 for exceeding his 1941 acreage allotment for wheat under the Agricultural Adjustment Act of 1938. Filburn was allotted 11.1 acres for this purpose, but he sowed and harvested 23 acres. He sold some of his wheat but used most of it as food for his family and as feed for his cattle. Filburn sued for an injunction against the enforcement of the fine. He argued that his activity had been completely intrastate and

that Congress could not regulate it under the commerce clause. How should the Supreme Court decide the case? Why? *Wickard v. Filburn,* 317 U.S. 111 (1942).

2. An Arkansas statute requires that all motor vehicles sold in the state be equipped with radial tires. A federal statute requires that all automobiles sold in interstate commerce be equipped with a new mechanism that substantially improves wheel alignment. Both statutes have been passed for the purpose of safety and obtaining better gas mileage. Are both statutes enforceable? Why or why not?
3. The Georgia legislature passes a law that requires interstate truckers and moving vans to stay off Georgia highways from 7 A.M. to 10 A.M. and from 4 P.M. to 6 P.M. so that local traffic will move better during rush hour. What constitutional issues are raised?
4. Harry Homeowner resides in Lake City, which the state recently granted a huge sum to erect a civic center. To build this civic center as planned, Lake City condemned the property and residence owned by Harry Homeowner, mailed Harry a check for an amount equal to 25 percent of the appraised value, and ordered Harry and his family to leave the premises with all of their belongings within two weeks. Lake City conducted no hearing concerning this matter. What constitutional issues are raised?
5. Pennsylvania passes a statute requiring all unemployed non-Pennsylvanians present in the state to leave Pennsylvania. What is the problem with this statute?
6. The city of Atlanta passes an ordinance banning the sale of all toys with toxic paint and sharp edges. The effect of this ordinance is to ban the sale of foreign toys, which amount to 70 percent of the toys sold in the Atlanta area. The Atlanta ordinance is much stricter than the federal statutes governing toy safety. Answer the following questions:
   a. Where does the city of Atlanta get the power to ban hazardous toys?
   b. Is a problem presented by the fact that the Atlanta ordinance is more stringent than the federal statutes?
   c. Does the city of Atlanta have the power to regulate the sale of foreign toys?
7. New Hampshire enacted a commuters' income tax that taxed the New Hampshire-derived income of nonresidents. New Hampshire did not tax the income of New Hampshire residents. Residents of Maine and part of New Hampshire challenged the validity of the tax. The case was transferred directly to the New Hampshire Supreme Court, which upheld the statute. The case was then heard by the U.S. Supreme Court on appeal. What was the result, and why?
8. Under an Alabama state law regarding divorce, a wife may recover alimony from her husband if cause is shown. When Mr. and Mrs. Orr filed for a divorce, Mr. Orr claimed alimony from his wife and was denied it under the state statute. He appealed, claiming that the statute denying alimony to husbands was unconstitutional. On what grounds is his claim based? What was the result, and why? *Orr v. Orr,* 440 U.S. 268 (1980).
9. The plaintiffs, consumers of prescription drugs, claimed they would benefit from the advertising of prescription drugs. They brought a suit against the Virginia State Board of Pharmacy in which they challenged the constitutionality of a Virginia statute declaring it unprofessional conduct for a licensed pharmacist to advertise the price of prescription drugs. The board had the power to revoke a license or to impose a fine for violation of the statute. As a result of the statute, all advertising of the price of prescription drugs was effectively forbidden. The Citizens Consumer Council sued the Virginia State Board of Pharmacy. On what grounds would its lawsuit be brought? With what result, and why? *Virginia State Board of Pharmacy v. Virginia Citizens Consumer Council,* 425 U.S. 748 (1976).

CHAPTER

6

Administrative Law

Critical Thinking Questions

- Compare and contrast administrative rulemaking with adjudication in terms of the people generally affected, the processes used to reach decisions, and the scope of judicial review.
- Why does Congress dictate the process by which agencies must make adjudicatory or rulemaking decisions instead of leaving it to the agency to determine?
- Why are informal agency activities such as granting permits, determining eligibility for governmental benefits, or analyzing data subject to only infrequent judicial review?
- Explain several factors that limit the number of administrative actions actually reviewed by the courts.
- How does judicial review of administrative agency actions differ for rulemaking, adjudicatory, and informal activities?

Introduction... PAST, PRESENT, FUTURE

Administrative law concerns the organization and operation of what is known as the fourth branch of government—the administrative agencies. An **administrative agency** is a governmental body that is not included in the Constitution as part of the legislative, executive, or judicial branches. Congress established the first administrative agencies in 1789 to deal with foreign imports and to provide pension fees to disabled soldiers. These agencies, and their modern successors, are known as **executive agencies** because they are subject to control by the executive branch of the government. The first independent administrative agency, the Interstate Commerce Commission, was created in 1889.

administrative agency In the United States, a governmental body that is not defined by the Constitution as being part of the executive, legislative, or judicial branch.

executive agency An agency of the government that is subject to control by the executive branch.

The federal agencies, and their state and local counterparts, were created to meet the changing needs of the country. In the early years of the United States, there was little regulation of business by government. However, as the United States grew and prospered, the Industrial Revolution changed the country from an agrarian to an industrial society. A few businesses began to dominate in certain industries, and their use of power and certain monopoly practices led to the establishment of independent federal regulatory agencies.

In the 1960s and 1970s, laws were passed creating agencies to deal with social problems in such fields as civil rights, consumer protection, the environment, and employee safety. Subsequently, the social regulation of the 1960s and 1970s gave way to policies of deregulation and regulatory reform. In the 1980s, the downsizing and restructuring of firms in the airline, trucking, communication, and financial services industries led to dramatic changes in the regulatory environment. It is likely that political changes occurring worldwide and the demands of global competition will force even more regulatory changes during the remaining years of the 20th century. In the future, a shift to regulation by private groups and by regional or international bodies may replace some of the state and federal regulation of business.

Administrative Agencies: General Concerns

administrative process The methods used by administrative agencies to perform a wide variety of activities.

administrative law The law that governs the grant of powers to administrative agencies, specifies the procedures they are to use in carrying out their operations, and determines the extent to which courts review their actions.

Today, businesses are regulated in many ways by a variety of administrative agencies at the federal, state, and local levels of government. This government regulation occurs through the **administrative process,** the methods used by administrative agencies to perform a wide variety of activities. **Administrative law** is at the heart of that process; it governs the granting of powers to agencies, specifies the procedures that agencies must use in carrying out their operations, and determines the extent to which agency activity is reviewed by the courts.

Administrative agencies deal with many distinct problems and operate in different ways. This chapter examines the creation of administrative agencies and the legislative delegation of their powers. Then, it reviews the functions performed by these agencies as they make rules, adjudicate cases, and perform numerous informal activities. The role that courts play in reviewing agency functions is also noted. After briefly reviewing the interaction between administrative agencies and the businesses they regulate, the chapter concludes with an evaluation of the future of government regulation by administrative agencies.

Creation of Administrative Agencies

Congress created the Interstate Commerce Commission as the first independent federal regulatory agency for reasons similar to those that later led to the establishment of thousands of other federal, state, and local administrative agencies. Most administrative agencies are created to deal with specific problems. Each of the three branches of government has some control over the actions of administrative agencies.

In the late 19th century, while Congress wanted to institute a fair system for establishing rates charged by railroads, it lacked the expertise needed to establish such rates. Should the rates throughout the country be equal on a per mile basis? Should the rates differ with the amount of freight or passenger traffic or with the distance traveled? How could Congress draft one law that would apply to many different situations?

In addition, if Congress did somehow establish fair rates, what would happen if conditions changed? If railroad costs went up and traffic decreased, should the rates decrease? What if some railroads made a profit and others did not? Congress realized that it would be unable to constantly monitor the railroad industry and that an organization capable of examining the industry's problems over a period of years was needed.

Finally, if general railroad rates were established, the courts would have to determine how the rates should apply to specific situations. But the courts were already very busy, and they had little expertise regarding the specific problems of the railroad industry. Thus, the Interstate Commerce Commission was created and granted both the power to determine general rates—a rulemaking or legislative type of power—and the power to resolve disputes regarding the application of those rates—an adjudicative type of power.

As the years passed, Congress created other administrative agencies to deal with other specialized problems. In 1914, the Federal Trade Commission was created to help curb monopolistic practices that the 1890 Sherman Act had failed to address. As radio transmission became common, the need to allocate the available bandwidths led to the creation of the Federal Communications Commission. The airplane brought us the Federal Aviation Agency, now the Federal Aviation Administration (FAA), and the

Food and Drug Administration (FDA) was established to deal with impure foods and quack medicines. The stock market crash of 1929 led to the creation of the Securities and Exchange Commission (SEC), and the development of atomic energy led first to the creation of the Atomic Energy Commission (AEC) and then to its conversion into the Nuclear Regulatory Commission (NRC). Some of the functions performed by selected federal agencies are listed in Figure 6–1.

In recent years, new agencies have been created as additional problems emerged that appeared too complicated for Congress to address and monitor. In 1970, for example, the Environmental Protection Agency (EPA) and the Occupational and Safety Health Administration (OSHA) were created. The Consumer Product Safety Commission (CPSC) emerged in 1972 to protect consumers against unreasonable risks associated with consumer products. This chapter is concerned with the laws and regulatory powers of these and other administrative agencies.

Role of Administrative Law

Administrative agencies, created to deal with specific societal problems, clearly illustrate the connection between law and the changing society. However, administrative law is not concerned with the substance of regulatory laws or with the specific regulations promulgated by these agencies. The substantive rules of the agencies are dealt with in other chapters. Thus, regulatory concerns of the Federal Trade Commission are discussed in Chapters 16 and 17; concerns of the Securities and Exchange Commission, in Chapter 15; and concerns of the Environmental Protection Agency, in Chapter 21.

FIGURE 6–1

Functions of Selected Administrative Agencies

Agency	Function
Consumer Product Safety Commission (CPSC)	Protects the public against risk of injury from consumer products
Environmental Protection Agency (EPA)	Administers laws related to water and air pollution, solid wastes, and other environmental concerns
Equal Employment Opportunity Commission (EEOC)	Enforces civil rights and equal opportunity laws regarding discrimination in employment
Federal Trade Commission (FTC)	Protects the public from anticompetitive behavior and unfair and deceptive business practices
Food and Drug Administration (FDA)	Administers laws that prohibit distribution of adulterated, misbranded, or unsafe foods, and cosmetics
Interstate Commerce Commission (ICC)	Regulates interstate surface transportation
National Labor Relations Board (NLRB)	Conducts union certification elections and holds hearings on alleged unfair labor practices
Occupational Safety and Health Administration (OSHA)	Enforces laws seeking to provide all workers with a safe and healthy work environment
Securities and Exchange Commission (SEC)	Enforces federal securities laws regulating the sale of securities to the investing public

Instead, administrative law is concerned with the procedures that the agencies use to perform the tasks delegated to them by legislative bodies. This chapter examines the processes that administrative agencies generally use to make rules and regulations and to apply laws and those rules and regulations in the cases that they adjudicate and in their informal activities.

Delegation of Authority to Administrative Agencies

As administrative agencies are not mentioned in the U.S. Constitution, their powers must originate from one of the three branches of government expressly granted powers by the Constitution. Legislative provisions that grant powers to agencies enabling them to perform a variety of activities are known as **enabling acts.**

enabling act
Legislative provisions that grant powers to agencies, enabling them to perform a wide variety of functions.

As noted in Chapter 2, the Constitution grants Congress legislative powers while assigning other powers to the executive and judicial branches. These powers are intentionally separated to prevent the concentration of power. However, because administrative agencies may have all three types of governmental powers, several constitutional questions were raised when Congress first created them. If an agency had the power to make general rules and regulations, was Congress giving away its legislative power? Could legislative power, granted to Congress by the Constitution, be exercised by other governmental organizations? Was the separation of powers violated if agencies possessed not only legislative but also judicial and investigative authority?

Some of the early cases dealing with such questions determined that the delegation of authority from Congress to administrative agencies did violate the separation of powers. However, since early in the 20th century, the courts have generally upheld the legislature's delegation of authority to administrative agencies. **Delegation** is the transfer of power by one governmental body (such as the legislature) to another (such as an administrative agency). Although it is unconstitutional for the legislature to transfer *all* of its legislative powers to an administrative agency, it is permissible for the legislature to delegate part of its authority to make rules and regulations to an agency.

delegation
The transfer of powers by one governmental branch to another or to an administrative agency.

Enabling legislation grants some authority to an agency and specifies the activities that the agency may perform. In the Federal Trade Commission Act, for example, the Federal Trade Commission was created and was given authority to protect the public from uncompetitive behavior and unfair and deceptive acts or practices. Similarly, the Securities and Exchange Act of 1934 granted the Securities and Exchange Commission authority to regulate the securities markets.

The legislative provisions that specify which concerns are to be addressed by an agency in performing its functions are commonly referred to as **standards.** If the legislature does not adequately define the standards by which agency actions are guided, the courts may find that the grant of authority to the agency is unconstitutional. A congressional delegation of legislative powers to administrative agencies was held unconstitutional in *Schechter Poultry Corp. v. United States.*[1] In that case, Congress delegated to industry associations the authority to make "codes of fair competition" that the president could approve. That delegation of authority did not

standards
A legislative provision that establishes the specific concerns an agency is to address in performing its functions.

---

[1] 295 U.S. 495 (1935).

supply the industry associations or the executive branch with the necessary standards:

> Section 3 of the Recovery Act is without precedent. It supplies no standards for any trade, industry, or activity. It does not undertake to prescribe rules of conduct to be applied to particular states of fact determined by appropriate administrative procedures. Instead of prescribing rules, it authorizes the making of codes to prescribe them. For the legislative undertaking, section 3 sets up no standards, aside from the statement of the general aim of rehabilitation, correction, and expansion described in section 1. In view of the scope of that broad declaration, and of the nature of the few restrictions that are imposed, . . . [w]e think that the code-making authority thus conferred is an unconstitutional delegation of legislative power.

In the years since the *Schechter* decision, the U.S. Supreme Court and most of the state supreme courts have allowed very broad and general standards to be used in delegating authority to administrative agencies. For example, the Occupational Safety and Health Administration (OSHA) was given the authority to make rules to assure, so far as possible, every worker in the nation "safe and healthful" working conditions. That authority gives OSHA the power to establish safety and health standards for furniture, computer, and automobile manufacturing plants. Obviously, such a broad delegation of power to the agency gives it great discretion. However, each of the three branches of government does exercise some control over administrative agency activities.

Controls Over Administrative Agencies

Administrative agencies are not directly accountable to the people. Administrators, unlike legislators, judges, and the president, are not elected. Thus, controls over administrative agencies are needed to ensure that the agencies are responsive to the country's needs. The legislature that delegates power to an administrative agency maintains some control over the agency's activities. Similarly, the executive that appoints a person to head an agency and the courts that review its activities also exercise some control. Finally, some controls over agencies are exercised by the public through access to agency information.

Legislative Controls

Modification of Agency Authority The legislature has significant controls over the administrative agencies it creates. It may modify the powers granted to the agency in the enabling act or alter the procedures by which agencies are to perform their function. An agency may even be completely disbanded; Congress abolished the Civil Aeronautics Board in the 1980s. In the enabling legislation, Congress generally specifies which activities an agency may perform. If the agency acts beyond that authority, the judicial branch may find the agency action illegal. Congress also establishes the procedures an agency must follow in making rules and adjudicating cases. The **Administrative Procedure Act (APA)** is the statute that specifies these procedures for most federal agencies. Most of the states have a similar act. Figure 6–2 depicts the most recent amendments to the Administrative Procedure Act. The Freedom of Information Act is discussed later in this chapter.

Administrative Procedure Act (APA) The legislative statute that establishes the methods or procedures by which administrative agencies are to perform their adjudicatory or rulemaking function as well as determining the extent of judicial review of those actions.

FIGURE 6-2

Amendments to the Administrative Procedure Act (1946)

Date	Act	Purpose
1966	Freedom of Information Act	Provides public access to agency records
1976	Sunshine Act	Allows public access to public meetings—requires meetings to be open unless reason for closing is explained
1980	Regulatory Flexibility Act	Directs agencies to take into account the size of businesses when preparing rules and seeking information
1990	Negotiated Rulemaking Act	Requires agencies to consider and employ alternative dispute resolution methods in rulemaking and enforcement

sunset laws
Laws that provide for an automatic periodic review of agency activities.

legislative oversight committee
A committee that reviews and scrutinizes agency activities, particularly when the agency is requesting legislative funding.

legislative veto
The exercise by Congress of its disapproval of administrative rules; by law, the veto belongs to the legislature as a whole, not to only one segment of the legislature.

Periodic Review of Agency Activities In many states, an automatic periodic review of agencies is provided by **sunset laws.** Under such laws, the legislature reexamines the records of agencies and determines whether to continue their authority. In addition to a review provided by sunset laws, Congress also has other opportunities to influence the activities of administrative agencies. When agencies request funding, a special **legislative oversight committee** often carefully scrutinizes their activities.

Congress has also attempted to preserve some direct legislative control over the rulemaking powers of administrative agencies. For example, a **legislative veto** gives Congress the chance to veto administrative rules that it finds objectionable. Although Congress as a whole has the power to revoke rules of administrative agencies by amending an agency's enabling act, courts have found the separation of powers principle is violated if only a part of Congress seeks to exercise the legislature's power and there is no presentment to the president for signature. In the *Chada* case, an administrator in the Immigration and Naturalization Service (INS), an agency that acted on behalf of the attorney general, ordered Chada to be deported. On review, an administrative law judge in the INS suspended Chada's deportation. The House of Representatives passed a resolution vetoing the administrative law judge's suspension of the deportation order, but the U.S. Supreme Court found that veto to be unconstitutional.

> The Framers were acutely conscious that the bicameral requirement and the Presentment Clauses would serve essential constitutional functions. The division of the Congress into two distinct bodies assures that the legislative power would be exercised only after the opportunity for full study and debate in separate settings.
>
> Examination of the action taken here . . . reveals that it was essentially legislative in purpose and effect. The one-House veto operated in this case to overrule the Attorney General and mandate Chada's deportation. Disagreement with the Attorney General's decision on Chada's deportation—that is, Congress's decision to deport Chada—no less than Congress's original choice to delegate to the Attorney General the authority to make that decision, involves determination of policy that Congress can implement in only one way: bicameral passage followed by presentment to the President.
>
> The legislative veto doubtless has been in many respects a convenient shortcut: the sharing with the Executive by Congress of its authority over aliens in this manner is, on its face, an appealing compromise. In purely practical terms, it is obviously easier for action to be taken by one House without submission to the President. . . . The choice we discern as having been made in the Constitutional Convention imposes burdens on governmental

processes that often seem clumsy, inefficient, even unworkable, but those hard choices were consciously made by men who had lived under a form of government that permitted arbitrary governmental acts to go unchecked.[2]

Budgetary Control The legislature also has significant control over administrative agencies through its control of the budget. The budget for an agency whose mission or recent action is not popular with the legislature may be cut back. At both the federal and state levels, legislatures are willing to exercise their "power of the purse" to signal their concerns to administrative agencies. This fiscal power is shared with the executive branch because the president proposes the annual budget.

Executive Controls

The executive branch has the clearest line of authority over administrative agencies. Most federal agency heads are appointed to their positions by the president, who retains the authority to hire and fire them. Subject to the civil service system and Senate approval, the president can control the policies of many agency administrators. State governors have similar powers over many state administrative agencies. Candidates for both federal and state executive offices frequently promise to alter, reduce, or eliminate the regulatory activities of administrators in their "bureaucracy."

The administrators of independent agencies do have some independence from the executive; they have fixed terms of office, and they can generally be removed only *for cause.* The Securities and Exchange Commission, Federal Trade Commission, and Federal Reserve Board are among the independent agencies. Agencies may also be reorganized by the president with the consent of Congress. Thus, functions and powers of one agency can be transferred to other agencies.

Judicial Controls

The courts have the authority to review the rules, informal actions, and adjudications of administrative agencies. Judicial review of agency actions by the judicial branch is discussed in a subsequent section of this chapter. Today, it is these controls, not the constitutional challenge to the legislative delegation of authority, that are most important in ensuring that administrative agencies do not act in an arbitrary manner.

Public Controls

Concern over secret agency activities and the misuse of information led to passage of the **Freedom of Information Act (FOIA)** in 1966. Congress sought to increase the accountability of agencies to the public by mandating that agency files be open to public interest groups, scholars, journalists, and other interested parties. Businesses sometimes use the FOIA to review agency information about competing firms.

Freedom of Information Act (FOIA) The law that provides access to information held by administrative agencies for private citizens and firms.

The FOIA has even been useful for people in other countries. A Japanese attorney recounted to one of the authors that while discovery rules in Japan limited the access to information about a Japanese company's testing of its products, that attorney knew that firm had been required to provide such information to an administrative agency in the United States. Using the Freedom of Information Act, the Japanese lawyer obtained

[2] *I.N.S. v. Chada,* 462 U.S. 919 (1983).

from the agency files information not available in Japan about that company's product testing. The information was then used to obtain a settlement of a lawsuit in Japan brought on behalf of a consumer of that firm's product.

Cases have sought to limit this use of agency files, but the courts have held that the FOIA requires all agencies, departments, and independent commissions to make all agency documents publicly available unless the documents qualify for one of the statute's nine exemptions.

Freedom of Information Act Exemptions

1. Documents classified by the president as in the national interest.
2. Documents related to agencies' internal personnel practices.
3. Documents whose disclosure is prohibited by other statutes.
4. Documents containing trade secrets or financial data.
5. Documents reflecting the deliberative process of agency policy formulation or containing advisory opinions.
6. Personnel, medical, and similar files whose disclosure would be an unwarranted invasion of privacy.
7. Selected law enforcement records.
8. Documents regarding the operation of financial institutions.
9. Geological and geophysical maps and data.

General Functions of Administrative Agencies

Administrative agencies perform activities at all levels of government in the United States. Local government agencies coordinate transportation facilities and schedules and establish zoning regulations for business and residential land use. State agencies often include mental and public health boards, departments of commerce and labor, and commissions for employment, construction, natural resources, insurance, and liquor control.

rulemaking The process by which an administrative agency exercises a legislative-type function in making rules of general applicability.

adjudicatory function The performance of a judicial-type function of an administrative agency that holds hearings to determine facts and the application of laws and regulations to those facts.

Of the more than 100 agencies at the federal level, the two that affect the most people are the Internal Revenue Service and the Social Security Administration. The Internal Revenue Service interprets the tax statutes, collects taxes, and makes rules and regulations that specify how taxpayers are to compute the taxes they owe to the federal government. The Social Security Administration determines eligibility for social security benefits and issues millions of checks to eligible recipients.

Administrative agency activities can be classified into three general functions; each is discussed in a subsequent section of the chapter. The first of these functions is **rulemaking.** Many administrative agencies are authorized to make rules and regulations of general applicability that have the effect of law.

The second general function of administrative agencies is adjudicatory in character. An agency performs an **adjudicatory function** when it conducts adjudicatory hearings to determine whether a particular individual or business has violated a legislative statute or an administrative regulation. In a hearing, an agency finds facts and applies laws or rules to those facts. Generally, the procedures of administrative hearings are similar to but less formal than those used in the courts. The federal courts process several hundred thousand cases each year, whereas several million claims are processed annually by federal agencies, and even more are processed by state and local agencies.

The activities comprised by the third general function of administrative agencies are referred to as **informal actions.** Agencies administer grants and assistance programs, undertake investigations, gather and analyze data, and issue reports. Some agencies grant patents, and others regulate immigration, classify grain, or review waste disposal plans.

informal actions
The performance by administrative agencies of activities, such as determining eligibility for government benefits or grants, that are neither adjudicatory nor rulemaking functions.

ETHICAL DILEMMA FOR ADMINISTRATORS

ETHICAL DILEMMA

Regulators, administrative law judges, and caseworkers in administrative agencies hold powerful positions due to their role in making, interpreting, and enforcing the law. An administrator engaged in rulemaking may assign greater importance to the public comments made by parties in favor of a proposed rule than to those made by parties opposed to the ruling. Administrators may decide to proceed to a hearing in some cases while declining to initiate cases based on individual complaints in other situations.

Administrative law judges may consider individual circumstances in one situation where a rule or statute is not followed but refuse to overlook violations in other cases. Some caseworkers may apply one administrative policy in certain cases and another in different cases even though the facts of the problems appear to be similar. It is important for administrators to be fair and impartial, even when doing so may be contrary to the interests of other administrators in their agency, legislators who seek to influence them, or those who have supported the programs and policies of the agency. When there is a lack of impartiality or fairness, or when policies are not applied evenly, the actions of administrators are unethical.

ADMINISTRATIVE RULEMAKING

The line between rulemaking and adjudication is occasionally blurred because both involve hearings. However, an agency action that affects a large number of people and does not depend on facts about individual circumstances is generally regarded as rulemaking rather than adjudication.

Rulemaking Power

The power to make rules originates with the legislature, which then delegates some of its rulemaking power to an administrative agency. Of course, the legislature also can later limit or revoke the agency's rulemaking power. In the early 1980s, for example, the Federal Trade Commission (FTC) began to make rules requiring used car dealers to disclose certain information regarding the defects of the cars they sold. After the dealers lobbied Congress, it specifically revoked the FTC's authority to make such rules.

Imposing Procedural Requirements

The legislature specifies an agency's rulemaking procedures. Sometimes the legislature tailors those procedures to a specific agency in the enabling legislation. More frequently, the legislature refers to another statute that governs rulemaking as well as a variety of other administrative activities. Both Congress and state legislatures have passed special laws detailing the procedural requirements that agencies must follow in making rules and in performing adjudicative functions. The **Administrative Procedure Act (APA)** is the statute that establishes such procedures for federal agencies.

Providing Notice An agency engaged in rulemaking must provide public notice that it will hold a hearing to receive comments about a particular problem or a specific rule proposal. Such notice is usually inserted in the *Federal Register* and mailed to persons who are either known to be affected by a proposed rule or who have requested they be provided with notices from particular agencies. The public notice must generally be provided at least 30 days before the hearing date. Similar notice provisions are usually included in the state Administrative Procedure laws governing rules proposed by state agencies.

Holding a Hearing to Receive Comments Unlike a court trial or an administrative adjudicatory hearing, at a rulemaking hearing there is usually no trial or adversarial proceeding. Instead, people interested in or affected by the proposed rule offer oral or written comments on the proposals. The agency is represented by people who listen to those comments, but they themselves usually do not present testimony at the hearing.

Preparing the Final Rule After the hearing, the administrative agency reviews the comments offered by interested parties and affected businesses. It is required to provide a general and concise summary of the comments. It may revise or withdraw the proposed rule to reflect those comments, but it has no legal obligation to do so. It may be that only a few people attend the hearing or submit their written comments. If only a few people with similar views offered their comments, the hearing would not reflect the diversity of views that may exist regarding a particular proposal. Thus, an agency is usually free to prepare its final rule in a form that it determines to be most appropriate; it need not mirror the comments received at the hearing. Once the agency prepares its final rule, it must then publish the rule. All federal rules appear in the ***Federal Register*** and are later compiled into the *Code of Federal Regulations (CFR).* Rules adopted by state administrative agencies may sometimes be found in sources such as the *Michigan Register.*

Federal Register
The source where proposed rules, final rules, and certain policies of federal administrative agencies are published; the *Federal Registers* when bound together become the *Code of Federal Regulations (CFR).*

In the following case, the agency concerned did not follow the rulemaking procedures established by the Administrative Procedure Act. Heckler, secretary of health and human services, sought to establish a policy that would impose additional duties on hospitals. The court discussed the agency's duty to consider "relevant factors to prevent arbitrary and capricious decision making and to assure rational consideration of the impact of the contemplated regulatory action." What concerns did the court have regarding the establishment of agency policy?

American Academy of Pediatrics v. Heckler

561 F. Supp. 395 (D.C.D.C. 1983)
United States District Court

This case involved the validity of an administrative rule published without benefit of public comment by Heckler, secretary of the Department of Health and Human Services. The rule concerned the care and treatment of newborn infants in hospitals receiving federal funds.

The rule was sparked by a case involving an infant born with Down's syndrome and a surgically correctable blockage of his digestive tract that precluded normal feeding. After the infant's parents refused to consent to surgery, the hospital turned to the state for guidance. Despite the appointment of a special guardian, no judicial intervention occurred. Because the infant needed immediate surgery, he died within six days of birth.

The rule published by Heckler required hospitals and other medical institutions receiving federal aid to post a sign warning that failure to feed and care for handicapped infants violated federal law. It authorized an immediate investigation by officials from the Health and Human Services office to protect the health of such an infant, and it required institutions receiving federal aid to give 24-hour access to hospital records and facilities during the investigation. Physicians, hospital staff members, and families would be questioned.

The American Academy of Pediatrics sued Heckler, contending that the rule was arbitrary and capricious and that no justification existed for dispensing with public comment in the rulemaking process as required by the Administrative Procedure Act.

Gesell, Judge

The Administrative Procedure Act was designed to curb bureaucratic actions taken without consultation and notice to persons affected. Broad delegations of rulemaking authority from the Congress were intended to be tempered by assuring a degree of due process for those to be governed by the rule. The greater the impact of the regulation upon established practices or the greater the number of people directly affected, the more the courts have insisted that the right of comment by those affected be preserved.

Thus the Act has been generally construed to curtail rulemaking without comment. Moreover, the Act requires that all regulations shall issue only after the rulemaker has considered relevant factors to prevent arbitrary and capricious decision making and to assure rational consideration of the impact of the contemplated regulatory action. The instant regulation offends these established precepts to a remarkable extent.

The Court is well aware that the agency rulemaking must be considered deferentially and that this Court is prohibited from substituting its own judgment for that of the agency's decision. Nevertheless, this Court may not, on the other hand, "rubber-stamp" challenged agency decisions and must inquire whether the agency's action was based on a consideration of the relevant factors. Lacking such consideration, the regulation fails to satisfy the test of rationality and cannot be sustained because it is arbitrary and capricious.

The record tendered in support of the Secretary's action here clearly establishes that many highly relevant factors central to any application of section 504 to medical care of newborn infants were not considered prior to promulgation of the challenged rule.

[The] record reflects no consideration whatsoever of the disruptive effects of a 24-hour, toll-free "hotline" upon ongoing treatment of newborns. As indicated, any anonymous tipster, for whatever personal motive, can trigger an investigation involving immediate inspection of hospital records and facilities and interviewing of involved families and medical personnel. In a desperate situation where medical decisions must be made on short notice by physicians, hospital personnel and often distraught parents, the sudden descent of "Baby Doe" squads on the scene, monopolizing physician and nurse time and making hospital charts and records unavailable during treatment, can hardly be presumed to produce higher quality care for the infant.

It is clear that a primary purpose of the regulation is to require physicians treating newborns to take into account only wholly medical risk-benefit considerations to prevent parents from having any influence upon decisions as to whether further medical treatment is desirable. The Secretary did not appear to give the slightest consideration to the advantages and disadvantages of relying on the wishes of the parents who, knowing the setting in which the child may be raised, in many ways are in the best position to evaluate the infant's best interests.

None of these sensitive considerations touching so intimately on the quality of the infant's expected life were even tentatively noted. No attempt was made to address the issue of whether termination of painful, intrusive medical treatment might be appropriate where an infant's clear prognosis is death within days or months or to specify the level of appropriate care in futile cases.

. . . Even if the regulation could withstand the requirements of [the APA], it must be declared invalid due to the Secretary's failure to follow procedural requirements in its promulgation. It is undisputed that the rule was not issued in accordance with either the public notice or 30-day delay-of-effective date requirements of the APA. The Secretary argues that the rule is either a "procedural" or "interpretative" rule not subject to the requirements of these provisions, or that waiver of these requirements is appropriate given the need "to protect life from imminent harm." Neither of these arguments has merit.

This regulation cannot be sustained. It is arbitrary and capricious. . . . At the minimum, wide public comment prior to rulemaking is essential. Only by preserving this democratic process can good intentions be tempered by wisdom and experience.

Case Questions

1. What two requirements does the Administrative Procedure Act impose on agencies contemplating rulemaking actions?
2. What are the appropriate factors that the agency should have weighed but did not consider prior to issuing its rule in this case?
3. If the agency had considered the appropriate factors, would its regulation have been legal? Why?

Administrative Adjudication

In many instances, administrative agencies are authorized to perform adjudicative functions. They may determine facts, apply rules or laws to those facts, and reach a decision. In performing adjudicative functions, both federal and state agencies generally follow court-type procedures. However, there are several important differences between agency adjudicative procedures and those used in traditional court trials. A jury trial is not possible in administrative hearings, and most hearings do not observe all of the traditional rules of evidence. Many of the procedures governing administrative adjudications are specified in applicable administrative procedures law.

Most administrative adjudications follow the traditional sequence of (1) investigation, (2) complaint, (3) hearing, and (4) decision or order. Of course, many of the matters that are investigated never reach the complaint stage. And even after a complaint has been filed, most controversies are settled without a full hearing. For those matters that do reach the hearing stage, the procedures used in a hearing generally are similar to the procedures used in court trials. These procedures include providing adequate notice of the hearing and allowing each party to present evidence by the testimony of witnesses, introduce documentary evidence, cross-examine opposing witnesses, present rebuttal testimony, and offer concluding arguments to the administrative law judge or hearing examiner. At the end of a hearing, the administrative law judge issues an order based on the application of relevant law to the facts presented at the hearing. Frequently, that order may be appealed to some other person or group of persons within the agency. For example, the order of an administrative law judge in the Federal Trade Commission can be appealed to the commissioners themselves. In rendering its decision, the commission has broad powers to modify the order. If a party wishes to appeal the Commission's final decision, the case proceeds to the federal Court of Appeals.

Thus, the courts have the power to review the decisions of administrative agencies. Administrative agencies and the businesses they regulate frequently have different views regarding what procedures the agencies should follow in carrying out their activities. If an agency plans to revoke a license held by a business, does it first have to hold a trial-type hearing? This issue is addressed in the following case.

Gallagher & Ascher v. Simon

678 F.2d 1007 (1982)
Seventh Circuit Court of Appeals

The Customs Service, a division in the Department of the Treasury, determined that Gallagher, an importing business, should lose its license as a customs broker because it had violated a "timely entry" Treasury Department regulation. Gallagher argued that before suspending its license, the Treasury Department should have held an adjudicatory hearing and granted it all the rights and procedures generally available in a trial. Since the Customs Service was a division of the Department of the Treasury, Gallagher sued Simon, the Secretary of the Treasury. After the federal district court decided in Simon's favor, Gallagher appealed to the court of appeals.

Cudahy, Circuit Judge

At the time this case began, Gallagher was a licensed customs broker in Chicago. It had been issued a special permit by the Treasury Department which allowed it to secure the immediate release of imported goods by submitting invoices to customs inspectors for examination at the point of entry. Gallagher was allowed to complete the entry documents and pay the duty at a later time, referred to as making a "timely entry." Regulations defined timely entry as being within 10 days after the day on which the imported merchandise was first released under a special permit.

If a broker fails to make timely entry, the District Director generally sends warning letters. Notice of the suspension of the special permit follows if a broker continues not to make timely entries.

On July 23, 1976, District Director Hertz issued a warning letter to Gallagher, accusing it of making 9 late entries in the preceding month. The warning letter stated the number of violations was unacceptably large and advised that if Gallagher's performance did not improve, its special term permit would be suspended in September. Gallagher took no action. . . . When Gallagher made 21 untimely entries in August, District Director Hertz, in a September 12 letter, issued an order suspending Gallagher's special term permit for a period of 30 days commencing . . . September 17, 1976. . . . Gallagher then filed suit in district court.

The APA provides that the formal adjudicatory procedures described in sections 556 and 557 must be followed "in every case of adjudication required by statute to be determined on the record after opportunity for an agency hearing. . . ." The APA, as many courts have recognized, does not itself mandate that a trial-type hearing be held where none is required under the administrative agency's own governing statute; the APA simply dictates the procedures to be followed when another statute provides for a hearing. Thus, if the governing statute does not require that a hearing be conducted in connection with a particular agency action, [the adjudicatory provisions] "do not come into play." In the instant case, the regulation authorizing the District Director to suspend a broker's special term permit does not provide an opportunity for an agency hearing. Consequently, . . . the APA does not require that a permit suspension comply with the procedures to be used in an adjudicatory hearing.

The plaintiffs argue that all license suspension and revocation cases [include] an independent right to an adjudicatory hearing. Section 558(c) of the APA provides in pertinent part:

> When application is made for a license required by law, the agency . . . shall set and complete proceedings required to be conducted in accordance with sections 556 and 557 of this title or other proceedings required by law and shall make its decision. Except in cases of willfulness or those in which public health, interest, or safety requires otherwise, the withdrawal, suspension, revocation, or annulment of a license is lawful only if, before the institution of agency proceedings therefore, the licensee has been given—(1) notice by the agency in writing of the facts or conduct which may warrant the action; and (2) opportunity to demonstrate or achieve compliance with all lawful requirements.

The instant case involves an agency decision to suspend a license and thus is governed by the second sentence in section 558(c). Read literally, all that this sentence requires of an agency proposing the suspension of a license is that the licensee receive prior written notice of the facts warranting the suspension and an "opportunity to demonstrate or achieve compliance" with all legal requirements. It does not mandate any sort of hearing, let alone a trial-type hearing described in sections 556 and 557. The legislative history . . . indicates that the special treatment accorded licensees was not intended to trigger a right to an adjudicatory hearing meeting the requirements of sections 556 and 557. The district court concluded that the District Director had met his obligations under this section, and we agree. The notice requirement was satisfied in the instant case by the warning letters sent by the District Director to Gallagher.

The second requirement—an opportunity to demonstrate or achieve compliance—was also met in the instant case. An opportunity to achieve compliance was, indeed, the very purpose of the warning letters, which threatened suspension of the term special permits only if the broker's conduct did not improve. Such a notice of violations and a request to comply in the future meet the requirements of section 558(c). We conclude that the impact of the two suspensions, relatively short in duration and affecting only a portion of the customs broker's business, was not so great as to require more formal procedures than were afforded. We conclude that these government interests outweigh the factors supporting additional procedural safeguards, the costs of which would be unduly great. Affirmed.

Case Questions

1. Under what circumstances should an administrative agency consult the Administrative Procedure Act to determine whether a trial-type hearing is required?
2. Which provision of the APA controlled the need for a trial-type hearing in this case?
3. What procedures does the APA require an administrative agency to follow if it is suspending or revoking a license? How were those procedures followed here?

Informal Administrative Activities

General Activities

Most agency actions are informal rather than adjudicative or legislative. Administrative agencies engage in a wide variety of informal actions, many of which are not subject to court review. In some instances, however, such decisions are reviewed informally within the agency. Frequently, the action taken by the initial decision maker is reviewable by an immediate supervisor and again by a person at the agency's highest level. Critics suggest that such reviews are merely perfunctory and perhaps not impartial. It is important, however, that all of the expert agency personnel consider decisions affecting regulated business so as to assure consistency in matters affecting similar firms.

Information-Gathering Activities

Administrative agencies gather information through three different types of activities. First, many agencies gather and analyze information as they engage in rulemaking or adjudication. Many legislative statutes and administrative regulations require regulated companies to submit reports, financial records, and other documents. As such records are usually considered public documents, the Fifth Amendment privilege against self-incrimination does not protect them from disclosure. Further, an agency may share documents in the public record with other agencies. Since various agencies require many different reports, the cost of complying with agency requests for information can be a significant burden for businesses, particularly small firms. This has led to the Paperwork Reduction Act and to the regulatory cost-benefit analysis discussed later in this chapter.

Second, administrative agencies hold informal hearings in order to gather information. Many agencies use their subpoena power to compel the testimony of witnesses or the production of needed documents at such hearings. The secretary of the Department of Health and Human Services could have held informal hearings with hospital administrators, doctors, and parents to determine whether the department should respond to the situation mentioned in the *Pediatrics* case.

Third, agencies often have the power to inspect the books and records or the premises of regulated businesses. For example, the Securities and Exchange Commission (SEC) investigates complaints against securities brokers. If some basis for such a complaint exists, the SEC may want to inspect a broker's books and records. In recent years, the SEC has conducted several investigations about possible violations of insider trading laws and stock manipulations. Its investigations have led to both criminal and civil charges and subsequent convictions and civil judgments against individuals and securities firms.

OSHA inspectors visit factories and plants to determine whether conditions are unsafe or whether OSHA's safety rules are being violated. Because regulatory inspections serve the public interest, should courts give special interpretations to the Fourth Amendment with regard to administrative inspections? Should the probable cause requirement usually followed in criminal cases be relaxed in dealing with administrative warrant procedures? The following case illustrates the dilemma posed by on-site searches in administrative investigations.

Marshall v. Barlow's, Inc.

436 U.S. 307 (1978)
United States Supreme Court

An OSHA inspector sought to inspect and search Barlow's plumbing business in Idaho. The inspector said that OSHA was simply conducting a routine inspection of the premises. Barlow's refused to permit the inspection, claiming the Fourth Amendment protected it against unreasonable searches, and required that OSHA obtain a warrant before conducting an inspection. The trial court granted Barlow's an injunction to prevent OSHA from conducting a warrantless search, and Secretary of Labor Marshall, who oversaw OSHA, appealed to the Supreme Court.

Justice White delivered the opinion of the Court.

The Occupational Safety and Health Act of 1970 (OSHA) empowers agents of the Secretary of Labor (Secretary) to search the work area of any employment facility within the Act's jurisdiction. The purpose of the search is to inspect for safety hazards and violations of OSHA regulations. No search warrant or other process is expressly required under the Act.

The Secretary urges that warrantless inspections to enforce OSHA are reasonable within the meaning of the Fourth Amendment. . . . The Warrant Clause of the Fourth Amendment protects commercial buildings as well as private homes. To hold otherwise would belie the origin of that Amendment, and the American colonial experience. The Fourth Amendment's commands grew in large measure out of the colonists' experience with the writs of assistance [that] granted sweeping power to customs officials and other agents of the King to search for smuggled goods.

Against this background, it is untenable that the ban on warrantless searches was not intended to shield places of business as well as of residence. This Court has already held that warrantless searches are generally unreasonable, and that this rule applies to commercial premises as well as to homes.

> As we explained in *Camara,* a search of private houses is presumptively unreasonable if conducted without a warrant. The businessman, like the occupant of a residence, has a constitutional right to go about his business free from unreasonable official entries upon his private commercial property. The businessman, too, has that right placed in jeopardy if the decision to enter and inspect for violation of regulatory laws can be made and enforced by the inspector in the field without official authority evidenced by a warrant.

The Secretary submits that warrantless inspections are essential to the proper enforcement of OSHA because they afford the opportunity to inspect without prior notice and hence to preserve the advantages of surprise. While the dangerous conditions outlawed by the Act include structural defects that cannot be quickly hidden or remedied, the Act also regulates a myriad of safety details that may be amenable to speedy alteration or disguise. The risk is that during the interval between an inspector's initial request to search a plant and his procuring a warrant following the owner's refusal of permission, violations of this latter type could be corrected and thus escape the inspector's notice.

We are unconvinced, however, that requiring warrants to inspect will impose serious burdens on the inspection system or the courts, will prevent inspections necessary to enforce the statute, or will make them less effective. In the first place, the great majority of businessmen can be expected in normal course to consent to inspection without warrant; the Secretary has not brought to this Court's attention any widespread pattern of refusal.

Whether the Secretary proceeds to secure a warrant or other process, with or without prior notice, his entitlement to inspect will not depend on his demonstrating probable cause to believe that conditions in violation of OSHA exist on the premises. Probable cause in the criminal law sense is not required. For purposes of an administrative search such as this, probable cause justifying the issuance of a warrant may be based not only on specific evidence of an existing violation but also on showing that "reasonable legislative or administrative standards for conducting an . . . inspection are satisfied with respect to a particular [business]."

A warrant showing that a specific business has been chosen for an OSHA search on the basis of a general administrative plan for the enforcement of the Act derived from neutral sources such as, for example, dispersion of employees in various types of industries across a given area, and the desired frequency of searches in any of the lesser divisions of the area, would protect an employer's Fourth Amendment rights. We doubt that the consumption of enforcement energies in the obtaining of such warrants will exceed manageable proportions.

We hold that Barlow's was entitled to a declaratory judgment that the Act is unconstitutional insofar as it purports to authorize inspections without warrant or its equivalent and to an injunction enjoining the Act's enforcement to that extent. The judgment of the District Court is therefore affirmed.

Case Questions

1. What procedures would OSHA have to follow if it still wants to search Barlow's premises?
2. How does the need for a warrant protect the businessperson if a government official determines that a search by police officers is in fact necessary?
3. Analyze the scope of this decision. Will it affect any activities of other federal agencies or state agencies? How?

JUDICIAL REVIEW AND ADMINISTRATIVE AGENCIES

The scope of judicial review of administrative decisions is limited because administrative agencies are considered experts in the activities assigned to them. Since courts, unlike agencies, hear a wide diversity of cases, they seldom have the specialized knowledge possessed by agencies.

Determining Whether an Agency Activity Is Reviewable

Before a court reviews an activity of an administrative agency, it must answer three questions about the propriety of its review:

Judicial Review Questions

1. Is the agency activity subject to judicial review?
2. If yes, are there reasons not to review this particular problem or decision?
3. What standards or criteria should be used to determine the legality or propriety of the agency's activity?

Agency Activities That Are Not Reviewable Before undertaking a judicial review of an administrative agency's activity, a court must decide whether the activity is, in fact, subject to review. Some agency activities are not subject to judicial review; in such instances, the agency's decision is considered final. For example, the Food and Drug Administration was asked to investigate a state's use of drugs in administering capital punishment. The agency declined to do so, and the court refused to review this agency action. Thus, an agency's decision not to act, not to investigate, or not to file a complaint against a firm is often considered an unreviewable decision. This stance is justified because the agency has discretion to make decisions about how to use its resources to carry out the policies set by the legislature. These *discretionary activities* of agencies are not reviewable by the courts and are immune from private tort liability.

A second category of agency activities is also exempt from judicial review. If the legislature clearly specifies that the agency has the final authority over a matter, the courts will follow the *statutory preclusion* of judicial review. For example, the administrator of Veterans Affairs has the final authority to determine the benefits due to veterans:

standing
The requirement that a person or organization has a sufficient stake in the outcome of an agency activity before challenging it in an administrative proceeding or in court.

Example of Statutory Preclusion of Judicial Review

> [T]he decisions of the administrator on any question of law or fact under any law administered by the Veterans Administration providing benefits for any veterans and their dependents or survivors shall be final and no other official or any court of the United States shall have the power or jurisdiction to review any decision.[3]

ripeness
The requirement that an issue that relates to a challenge to an action taken by an administrative agency is sufficiently final and ready for court determination.

Reasons Not to Review The second judicial review question focuses on whether there are reasons why a court should not review an administrative agency action, even though it could do so. Answering these questions depends on (1) the person seeking review (a matter of **standing**), (2) the finality of the agency's decision (a matter of **ripeness**), (3) the extent to which the agency has reviewed the activities (a matter of

[3] 338 U.S.C.A. Section 211(a).

exhaustion of administrative remedy The requirement that before seeking review by a court, a person challenging an administrative action first must use any and all available administrative methods to review that action.

primary jurisdiction When both a court and an administrative agency are authorized to review some administrative action, the concept that the court will defer to the agency because it should have the first chance to review such matters.

exhaustion of administrative remedies), and (4) whether the agency should review before a court does so (a matter of **primary jurisdiction**). The questions that address the propriety of court intervention in agency activities are summarized in Figure 6–3.

Standards for Review The third question that a court must answer is: What standards should it use to judge or measure the administrative agency's activity? In general, courts examine whether an agency has clearly explained why and how it reached a decision. However, courts do not second-guess agency decisions.

Review of Agency Legislative Activities

While courts are authorized to review administrative rule-making activities, they are not to substitute their judgment for that of the agency. The scope of a court's review varies with the type of activity being reviewed. When an agency performs a legislative function, such as rulemaking, the reviewing court seeks to answer several specific questions.

Questions Affecting Review of Agency Legislative Actions

1. Is the delegation of legislative authority to the agency sufficiently limited?
2. Did the agency's action fall within the powers granted to the agency by the legislature?
3. Did the agency's action violate any constitutional or statutory requirements imposed on the agency?
4. Did the agency follow proper procedures (usually specified by statute)?
5. Is the action of the agency "arbitrary or capricious"?

In reviewing an administrative agency's rulemaking procedures, a court examines the determinations an agency makes to see if its actions are reasonable. In the Colorado case excerpted below, the state legislature passed a Water Quality Control Act and delegated extensive rulemaking powers to the Colorado Water Quality Control Commission. That Commission classified the waters of the state according to their use and then promulgated water quality standards that would protect that use.

FIGURE 6–3

Reasons Why a Court Might Not Review Agency Activities

Concern of Courts	Topic	Reasons for a Court Not to Review
Who seeks review?	Standing	If the person is not an aggrieved party, injured in some way, there may not be a disputed case.
When will problem be ready for review?	Ripeness	If the agency's activity is not yet final, the court should not act.
When is the party seeking review?	Exhaustion of remedies	If the person affected has remedies available in agency, the court should not review.
Where is review to take place?	Primary jurisdiction	If both court review and administrative review are possible, maybe the court should defer to agency.

The plaintiffs in that case, several corporations and a municipality, objected to the standards adopted by the Commission in performing the rulemaking function delegated to it by the legislature. It sought review by the Colorado courts. The Colorado Court of Appeals decision that follows explains the role of the court in reviewing the rulemaking of agencies such as the State Water Quality Control Commission.

Amax, Inc. v. Water Quality Control Commission

790 P.2d 879 (1989)
Colorado Court of Appeals

The Colorado Water Quality Control Act seeks to "conserve state waters, to protect, maintain and improve where necessary and reasonable, the quality thereof for public water supplies. . . . " It authorizes the Water Quality Control Commission (Commission) to develop a program for water quality protection throughout the state by classifying state waters by their use and by then promulgating water quality standards that would protect their use.

The Commission promulgated basic standards and, following an extensive rulemaking proceeding, adopted use classifications and water quality standards for the South Platte River Basin. The plaintiffs, Amax, Inc., Adolph Coors Co., and the City of Golden challenged the use classifications and the water quality standards adopted by the Commission. The Commission's decision was affirmed by the Denver District Court and plaintiffs then appealed to the Colorado Court of Appeals.

Opinion by Judge Metzger

I Standard of Review

Initially, plaintiffs contend that the trial court erred in concluding that the Regulation reflects essentially policy choices, rather than factual determinations, and consequentially, applying a less stringent standard of review. They assert that the record contains insufficient factual support for the Regulation's use classifications and water quality standards and that, therefore, the trial court's order upholding the Regulation must be reversed and the cause remanded to the Commission for further proceedings. We disagree.

In *Citizens for Free Enterprise v. Department of Revenue,* our supreme court articulated the reasoning underlying judicial review of administrative rulemaking procedures. Explaining the "based on the record" requirement of the state Administrative Procedure Act provision governing administrative rulemaking proceedings, the court held that the standard of review in the consideration of agency rulemaking is reasonableness.

A reviewing court should display sensitivity to the range and nature of determinations that must be made by an administrative agency. Postulating the types of rules promulgated by an agency as lying along a continuum, rules may be based primarily upon policy considerations, with factual determinations playing a tangential role. For such rules, specific factual support should not be required, although the reasoning process that led to the adoption of the rule must be defensible.

At the opposite end of the continuum, the court noted, the necessity for the rule may turn upon discrete facts capable of demonstrative proof. In that situation, the reasonableness of the agency action depends upon the presence of factual support for its determination.

Between these two extremes are the numerous agency actions which involve a combination of factual determinations and policy choices. In these instances, the nature and scope of judicial review must be appropriately tailored depending upon which is predominant.

Rules adopted pursuant to a statutory rulemaking proceeding are presumed valid. Accordingly, the burden is upon the challenging party to establish their invalidity by demonstrating that the rulemaking body acted in an unconstitutional manner, exceeded its statutory authority, or otherwise acted in a manner contrary to statutory requirements. A reviewing court may not substitute its judgment for that of the administrative agency. An agency's construction of its own regulation is entitled to great weight.

A

Plaintiffs' argument concerning the predominance of factual determinations in the Regulation rests on two main assertions. First, they contend that, in promulgating the Regulation, the Commission was bound to set use classifications and water quality standards based solely upon existing water uses. Consequently, they argue, to the extent the Regulation is based upon the Commission's assessment of future uses, it is deficient as a matter of law. . . .

The General Assembly, in expressing a forward-looking statement of purpose, and in creating a Commission having broad and extensive powers and duties, determined that an aggressive and sustained effort is required to protect this vital resource. Thus, we conclude, that, here, since the Commission's consideration of future uses was consistent with its statutory mandate, the Regulation is not deficient for that reason.

Second, we are not persuaded that the Commission was restricted to a mere description of existing water uses in the South Platte River Basin when it stated in the purpose clause of the Regulation that "The classifications identify the actual beneficial uses of the water.". . .

In the Basic Standards Regulation, the Commission is directed to employ several considerations in assigning water classifications. In general, these classifications must be directed towards the realization of the water quality goals set forth in the Clean Water Act and the Water Quality Control Act. In both instances, the goals of preservation and enhancement of water quality are specifically set out. . . . Consequently, since the Commission's considerations of future uses was consistent with its overall regulatory scheme, it did not err by considering such uses.

B

Plaintiffs' second argument concerning the predominance of factual determinations in the Regulation is based in the following provision in the Basic Standard Regulation:

"(1) Considerations in Assigning Classifications. The following will serve to guide the Commission in assigning classifications:

(e) Classifications should be for the highest water quality attainable. Attainability is to be judged by whether or not the use classification can be attained in approximately twenty (20) years by any recognized control techniques that are environmentally, economically, and socially acceptable as determined by the Commission after public hearings."

Plaintiffs contend that this language obligates the Commission to set classifications and standards based upon future uses or quality of water if and only if the evidence establishes that these future uses or quality of water can be attained in 20 years. Since, they argue, the record contains no evidence or findings concerning attainability, the Regulation is deficient and the trial court erred in ruling otherwise. We do not agree.

The 20-year attainability provision is couched in discretionary rather than mandatory language. And, its placement in the Basic Standards Regulation as the fifth of six "considerations in assigning classifications" obviates any assertion that it is compulsory in nature. . . .

Inasmuch as the Regulation addresses predominantly policy determinations, judicial review is limited to considerations of reasonableness. The Regulation reflects the Commission's adherence to its statutory mandates and its own regulatory framework. Upon examining the record ourselves and deferring to the Commission's expertise, we conclude that the Regulation is reasonable because of the factual support in the record, together with the Commission's clearly articulated defensible reasoning.

II Scientific Reasoning

Plaintiffs contend that several decisions of the Commission in adopting the water quality standards were based upon either insufficient data or an improper application of scientific methodology to existing data. Upon reviewing the record, we conclude that the standards, both generally and specifically, have an appropriate basis. [The Court's discussion of the Plaintiffs' attack on the scientific reasoning used by the Commission is omitted from this excerpt.]

In summary, we uphold the Commission's action in promulgating the South Platte Regulation. Our analysis of the record in light of the applicable law and the argument by counsel, convinces us that this Regulation constitutes a series of delicate and difficult policy decisions by the Commission. Accordingly, when reviewing the specific contentions of plaintiffs, we have considered whether the record supports the Commission's action by providing an ample factual base, and conclude that it has. In those instances in which the factual base could be arguably less than ample, we are persuaded that the Commission's reasoning for its decision is cogent and defensible under the criteria set out in the *Citizens for Free Enterprise v. Department of Revenue, supra.*

The judgment is affirmed.

Case Questions

1. How would you classify this agency's rulemaking when considering whether the rules are based upon policy considerations, discrete facts, or some combination of both?
2. What are the three types of challenges that the court states can be made to a statutory rulemaking proceeeding? Which of these are used in the portion of the case excerpted here?

Review of Agency Adjudicatory Activities

When an agency performs a review of a judicial function, such as the holding of an adjudicatory hearing, the court's review process is somewhat different from its review of rulemaking. The following questions are generally examined when a court reviews an agency adjudicatory action.

Questions Affecting Review of Agency Adjudicatory Actions

1. Did the agency violate any constitutional or statutory provisions imposed on it?
2. Does the agency have proper jurisdiction to decide the case?
3. Did the agency follow proper procedures (usually established by statute)?
4. Is the agency's decision supported by "substantial evidence" in its record?

When reviewing an agency adjudicatory action, a court is looking to see if there is substantial evidence in the record that supports the agency's determination. The case that follows concerns a denial of disability benefits that the claimant argues she is entitled to under the Social Security Act. The court notes a series of steps involved in a review of this case: initial determination within the agency, request for reconsideration, submission of case to an administrative law judge for hearing, determination by the administrative law judge, appeal to district court, referral by judge to magistrate who reviewed the case and submitted a recommendation to the district judge, decision by district court, and finally appeal to the federal court of appeals. This case is somewhat unusual as it does result in a reversal of the decision of the administrative agency.

Williams on Behalf of Williams v. Bowen

859 F.2d 255 (2d Cir. 1988)
Court of Appeals

On behalf of her then ten-year-old daughter Loretta, Joyce Williams filed a claim for Supplemental Security Income Benefits on November 5, 1984. Born on December 28, 1973, Loretta was diagnosed at birth with having a bilateral congenital hip disease. Loretta first had surgery when she was only a few months old and then twice more before she was two years old. Loretta continued to have a congenital persistent dislocation of her hip when she was eight years old and had an operation in 1984 to arrest bone growth in her right leg. Shortly thereafter, her mother filed this claim on her behalf. The initial application for benefits was rejected and requests for reconsideration were denied. After a hearing, the Administrative Law Judge upheld the denial of benefits. Williams then filed in District Court seeking judicial review; that Court referred the case to a Magistrate who recommended reversing the determination of the Administrative Law Judge, However, the District Court judge instead affirmed the denial of benefits and this appeal followed.

Cardomone, Circuit Judge

This appeal from a denial of disability benefits is somewhat uncommon because it requires us to reverse an administrative determination for lack of substantial evidence. Such a determination must demonstrate a rational connection between the agency's legal connection and the medical and lay testimony presented. Only then can a reviewing court be assured that the evidence on which the administrative determination rests is "substantial." The constituents of this required foundation are wanting in this appeal brought by Joyce E. Williams on behalf of her daughter Loretta Williams. . . .

. . . (T)he district court ruled that substantial evidence supported the Secretary's determination that the claimant had not proven her entitlement to disability benefits. . . .

We set forth an appellate court's power of review in this sort of case. A determination by the Secretary that a person is not disabled is conclusive when that decision is supported by substantial evidence. Substantial evidence has been defined as "such relevant evidence as a reasonable mind might accept as adequate to support a conclusion." It is more than a mere scintilla or a touch of proof here and there in the record.

Within that limitation on its scope, appellate review of an administrative record is plenary, and not merely a rubber-stamping of the administrative conclusion. To determine on appeal whether an ALJ's [administrative law judge's] findings are supported by substantial evidence, a reviewing court considers the whole record, examining the evidence from both sides, because an analysis of the substantiality of the evidence must also include that which detracts from its weight. The entire thrust of judicial review under the disability law is to ensure a just and rational result between the government and a claimant, without substituting a court's judgment for that of the Secretary, and to reverse an administrative determination only when it does not rest on adequate findings sustained by evidence having "rational probative force."

We begin by reviewing the statute under which the instant claim is made. To prove entitlement of disability benefits under Title XVI of the Social Security Act, an adult claimant must establish that she suffers from a medically determinable physical impairment that prevents her from engaging in any substantial gainful activity. In the case of a child under the age of 18, a disability will be recognized, and benefits awarded, if the child suffers from an impairment of "comparable severity." Pursuant to his authority under the Social Security Act, the Secretary has promulgated regulations setting forth specific criteria for determining child disabilities. According to those disabilities, a child will be found disabled if he or she (a) is not doing any substantial gainful activity; and (b) has a medically determinable physical or mental impairment which compares in severity to any impairment that would make an adult disabled. This requirement will be met when the impairment meets the duration requirement and is listed in Appendix I of . . . this Chapter [of the Code of Federal Regulations]. . . . In the instant case, claimant asserts that as a result of lifelong musculoskeletal abnormalities, she suffers a marked reduction in walking speed and distance (as noted in the Chapter's definition) and is, therefore, entitled to disability benefits. The Secretary correctly argues that it is not sufficient that there be a diagnosis of a listed impairment. . . . Rather, the evidence must also establish that the medical findings demonstrate the existence of a specific impairment listed in Appendix I. Accordingly, we review the entire record presented to the Secretary, particularly as it bears upon the requirement that a claimant demonstrate a marked reduction in walking speed or distance.

Unrefuted evidence in the record indicates that Loretta could not perform tasks that involve walking, standing, or bending. The word "gait"—employed by each examining physician—means or describes a manner of walking or locomotion by foot. Each physician has, in turn, noted the abnormality *and* shortness of Loretta's gait. Objective medical evidence and the professional opinions—taken together with common sense—logically connect therefore the evidence presented and the requirements set forth in the agency's Listing of Impairments. . . .

Standing alone, the medical evidence strongly suggests, but does not necessarily prove, that claimant is disabled under sec. 101.03 (A). Beyond that, as earlier mentioned, the ALJ failed to make any finding regarding the credibility of Joyce and Loretta Williams' testimony, which was uncontradicted and generally consistent with the medical diagnosis. Nor did the ALJ give a reason for rejecting the testimony that Loretta could not walk as far as her mother, her brother or her friends. In fact, the ALJ's findings contain no mention of the Williams' testimony.

As a fact-finder, an ALJ is free to accept or reject testimony like that given by Joyce and Loretta Williams. A finding that the witness is not credible must nevertheless be set forth with sufficient specificity to permit intelligible plenary review of the record. The failure to make credibility findings regarding the Williams' critical testimony fatally undermines the Secretary's argument that there is substantial evidence adequate to support his conclusion that claimant is not under a disability.

Further, whatever findings the ALJ makes must be consistent with the medical and other evidence. Put another way, an ALJ must assess subjective evidence in light of objective medical facts and diagnoses. Here, the subjective testimony of pain and disability given by the claimant and her mother is consistent with the objective medical facts and the experts opinions. Consequently, we hold that the record in this case lacks adequate evidence to support the Secretary's determination.

Case Questions

1. What relationship must exist between the evidence presented at the agency's adjudicatory hearing and the conclusions reached by the administrative law judge (ALJ) in order for the reviewing court to find substantial evidence in the record?
2. Does the ALJ have to accept the testimony given by the Williamses? If the ALJ determines some testimony is not credible, what should he or she do? How should the subjective testimony be related to medical facts and diagnoses?

Review of Agency Informal Activities

Courts sometimes review an agency's informal activities. Many of those activities are discretionary, not subject to review by the courts. In the *Overton Park* case that follows, the court first examines the question of reviewability. Once a court determines that an agency's action is subject to review, what other factors influence that review? Read the case and see how the court determines the answers to other questions affecting the judicial review of informal agency activities.

Questions Affecting Review of Agency Informal Actions

1. Is the action in question subject to judicial review?
2. Did the agency act within the scope of its authority?
3. Did the agency follow the procedural requirements?
4. Was the agency's action "arbitrary and capricious"?

Citizens to Preserve Overton Park v. Volpe

401 U.S. 402 (1981)
United States Supreme Court

Volpe, secretary of the Department of Transportation, determined that a federal highway (Interstate 40) could be built through a park in Memphis, Tennessee. Several federal laws prohibited him from authorizing the use of park property to construct a highway if feasible and prudent alternative locations were available. A citizens' group—Citizens to Preserve Overton Park—sued in federal district court, claiming that the secretary's decision was invalid because he did not make formal findings of fact in support of the decision. This group also claimed that the secretary's decision was unsound and argued that it should be reviewed and considered by the courts.

Both the district court and the appellate court rejected the group's claim because they found the secretary's decision to be unreviewable by the courts. The group then appealed to the Supreme Court, asking whether the secretary's decision was reviewable and, if so, what standard of review should determine whether his decision was lawful.

Justice Marshall delivered the opinion of the Court.

A threshold question—whether petitioners are entitled to any judicial review—is easily answered. . . . The Administrative Procedure Act provides that the action of "each authority of the Government of the United States," which includes the Department of Transportation, is subject to judicial review except where there is a statutory prohibition on review or where "agency action is committed to agency discretion by law." In this case, there is no indication that Congress sought to prohibit judicial review and there is most certainly no "showing of clear and convincing evidence of a legislative intent" to restrict access to judicial review.

Similarly, the Secretary's decision here does not fall within the exception for action "committed to agency discretion." This is a very narrow exception.

The very existence of the statutes indicates that protection of parkland was to be given paramount importance. The few green havens that are public parks were not to be lost unless there were truly unusual factors present in a particular case or the cost or community disruption resulting from alternative routes reached extraordinary magnitudes. If the statutes are to have any meaning, the Secretary cannot approve the destruction of parkland unless he finds that alternative routes present unique problems.

Plainly, there is "law to apply" and thus the exemption for action "committed to agency discretion" is inapplicable. But the existence of judicial review is only the start: the standard for review must also be determined. For that we must look [again] to . . . the Administrative Procedure Act, which provides that a "reviewing court shall hold unlawful and set aside agency action, findings, and conclusions found" not to meet six separate standards. In all cases agency action must be set aside if the action was "arbitrary, capricious, an abuse of discretion, or otherwise not in accordance with law" or if the action failed to meet statutory, procedural, or constitutional requirements.

The generally applicable standards . . . require the reviewing court to engage in a substantial inquiry. Certainly, the Secretary's decision is entitled to a presumption of regularity. But that presumption is not to shield his action from a thorough, probing, in-depth review.

The court is first required to decide whether the Secretary acted within the scope of his authority. . . . The reviewing court must consider whether the Secretary properly construed his authority to approve the use of parkland as limited to situations where there are not feasible alternative routes or where feasible alternative routes involve uniquely difficult problems. And the reviewing court must be able to find that the Secretary could have reasonably believed that in this case there are no feasible alternatives or that alternatives do involve unique problems.

Scrutiny of the facts does not end, however, with the determination that the Secretary has acted within the scope of his statutory authority. [The APA also] requires a finding that the actual choice made was not "arbitrary, capricious, an abuse of discretion, or otherwise not in accordance with law.". . . To make this finding the court must consider whether the decision was based on consideration of the relevant factors and whether there has been a clear error of judgment.

Although this inquiry into the facts is to be searching and careful, the ultimate standard of review is a narrow one. The court is not empowered to substitute its judgment for that of the agency.

The final inquiry is whether the Secretary's action followed the necessary procedural requirements. Here the only procedural error alleged is the failure of the Secretary to make formal findings and state his reason for allowing the highway to be built through the park. Here, there is an administrative record that allows the full, prompt review of the Secretary's action that is sought without additional delay which would result from having a remand to the Secretary. That administrative record is not, however, before us.

Thus it is necessary to remand this case to the District Court for review of the Secretary's decision. That review is to be based on the full administrative record that was before the Secretary at the time he made his decision.

Case Questions

1. How does the Court counter the argument that this administrative action is not subject to judicial review?
2. What are the steps a court should use to determine whether an agency's actions were arbitrary and capricious?
3. What will the record have to show in order for the administrator to prevail in his determination that the highway should be built through Overton Park?

Business Interaction with an Administrative Agency

Information and Influence through Trade Associations

Since administrative agencies perform a variety of functions, businesses interact with them in different ways. Almost all businesses seek to keep informed about relevant agency rulings and regulations. Small businesses frequently rely on trade associations to alert them to agency proposals. Trade associations also offer conventions, training courses, and programs that keep members abreast of current political developments. Today, over 2,500 trade associations are based in Washington, D.C., and hundreds more are found in each of the state capitals and in major cities. Trade associations generally seek the adoption of administrative rules and legislation favorable to their members.

Cost–Benefit Analysis

Every business must comply with administrative requirements, orders, and regulations, whether or not it is able to keep informed about and comment on their development. What is the cost of such compliance? Several executive orders issued in the 1980s require executive agencies to make a cost-benefit analysis on all new rules. In addition, some of the independent agencies perform cost-benefit analyses.

Executive Order 12,291, which provides for the evaluation of major regulations on a cost-benefit basis, requires agencies to comply with the following principles:

1. Obtain adequate information in formulating rules.
2. Perform an initial cost–benefit analysis on all rule proposals to determine whether a major rule is present.
3. Maximize the net benefits to society by adopting a regulation only when the social benefits of regulation outweigh the costs of regulation.
4. Consider alternative proposals.
5. Correlate all regulatory proposals to reduce conflicts.

Although the direct cost of compliance with agency regulations can be estimated, it is more difficult to assess the benefit gained from administrative agency activities. If EPA regulations mandating the cleanup of air, water, and land pollution improve the health of individuals, what is the value of this benefit? If the FDA prevents drugs with significant side effects from being marketed, how should we value the many deformities, injuries, or even deaths that may be prevented? If the FAA requires increased maintenance on commercial airplanes, how many crashes are prevented? What is the value to society of less pollution, fewer dangerous drugs, safer air travel, and even reduced injuries and deaths?

Another complication is that while the costs of regulations are often paid for by some people, the benefits often accrue to others or to the public at large. Finally, it is impossible to assign objective values to benefits derived by the society as a whole. Thus, cost–benefit analyses are but imperfect attempts to assess the efficiency of government regulation.

International Perspective and Commentary

The institutions of the European Union (EU) include an administrative Commission. The Commission consists of approximately 20 members who represent the European Community. National interests are represented in the European Union by the Council of Ministers. The Assembly or Parliament and the European Court of Justice are the other major EU institutions. Each commissioner supervises and directs a directorate encompassing a functional area such as transportation, energy, or agriculture. The Commission proposes regulations and directives to the Council and seeks to ensure that Community laws are followed. Regulations are directly applicable in EU countries. Directives, however, leave to the member country the method of achieving the aims noted in the directive.

The administrators or bureaucrats of the European Community are referred to as *Eurocrats.* Brussels is home to over 12,000 Eurocrats who draft rules, bring enforcement actions, and recommend changes in the legislation of member countries. Rule writers are divided into 22 administrative directorates-general. They, and the staff of the 17 commissioners, are at the center of the Brussels bureaucracy.

Rules affecting mergers, worker participation on corporate boards of directors, and telecommunication standards are drafted, discussed, redrafted, voted on, and implemented. In addition, rules on local content requirements and exemptions from antitrust laws are currently being rewritten in response to changing trade problems and court decisions.

Accounting firms, management consultants, law firms, trade associations, and state officials from the United States have active Brussels offices from which they lobby the administrators. Those who are successful say their aim is not to try to have the American rules and practices transferred to Europe. Instead, they demonstrate that the interests of their U.S. clients are compatible and consistent with the European interests.

Regulation and Deregulation

Criticism of Regulation by Administrative Agencies

Criticism One criticism directed at administrative agencies concerns the relationship between their structure and the performance of their functions. In some agencies, rulemaking and adjudication are not completely separated—the personnel who make the rules may also decide whether those rules have been violated in certain cases. In other instances, agency personnel not only establish rules and serve as judges, they also perform the prosecutorial function of deciding when to charge someone with violating the rules. When an agency acts as rulemaker, judge, and prosecutor, the separation of powers within the agency is difficult to envision. Those adversely affected by agency adjudicatory actions claim administrative law judges lack the impartiality to preside over cases involving rules promulgated by the agency and brought after agency investigations.

Another criticism of administrative agencies relates to their role as "regulators." While regulators are charged with imposing legal requirements on businesses and individuals, there are numerous examples of overzealous and unrealistic agency actions. It seems overzealous when an agency determines that all tomatoes sold in the United States must be a minimum size, consequently barring almost half of Mexico's tomato crop and forcing the consumer to pay a much higher price in the grocery store. In pursuit of providing information to the borrower, truth-in-lending regulations have imposed numerous requirements on financial institutions. When considered separately, each regulation may be reasonable, but the cumulative effect of meeting all regulations may be unrealistic. Meeting each new regulation often requires preparing separate documents for the borrower to read and sign. As a consequence, when borrowing money, the borrower, who is faced with pages of detailed information, seldom reads all of it.

A third criticism of administrative agencies concerns the lack of coordination among different agencies. Hospitals and other health care providers complain of expensive, contradictory, and confusing regulations. The government requires the hospital to continually assess and audit its medical care, but the Federal Peer Review Act also requires that an independent agency under contract to the Health Care Finance Administration also conduct a peer review. When Medicare funds are involved, a third audit is performed by the Joint Commission on Health Care Organizations.

Responses to Criticisms

A response can be given to each of the criticisms. The criticism that the separation of functions within administrative agencies still leaves a judge who is not impartial regarding agency actions doesn't mention that today most administrative law judges have quasi-independent roles. They are separated from the head of the agency in which they serve and have no responsibility or influence with regard to rulemaking or prosecutorial decisions of the agency. On the other hand, there is an advantage to having a judge who works primarily with one agency. Administrative law judges generally offer a degree of specialization and knowledge of important details and administrative procedures not found in most courts.

While there are examples of overzealous regulation, they are generally the exception rather than the norm. When there are exceptions, there are procedures within the agency and through judicial review to counter the arbitrary or unreasonable action. Similarly, reforms are underway at both the state and federal level to deal with contradictory or confusing regulations. Many states now have an ombudsman who acts to cut through contradictory or unclear administrative actions on behalf of those affected by interagency conflicts. The health care field is ripe for reform, but at both the national and state level, obtaining the political agreement to implement the reforms will take years of dedicated effort.

The Future for Administrative Regulation

As we move through the last decade of the 20th century, the concern with the role of government has increased. The 1994 Congressional election brought the "Contract with America" from republican Congressional representatives. It promises a smaller government with less administrative intrusion by the federal government into business and personal activities. It is too early to tell whether the main provisions of the Contract will become law and, if so, whether people will be happy with the results.

Deregulation The benefits of deregulation are based in the virtues of a free market. Throughout the world, there has been a move away from government regulation to a free market economy. In Japan, interest rates on bank deposits were deregulated in 1994, allowing banks, not the Ministry of Finance, to determine the rates they would pay to attract deposits from Japanese savers. Within a month, some banks began to pay slightly higher rates. In Hungary and the Czech Republic, citizens were only recently allowed to own shares in private enterprises. Each citizen was given vouchers to use for investing in enterprises and investment funds. As former state-owned enterprises were privatized, they offered projects in which potential investors could use their vouchers. As most of the vouchers were invested in investment funds, controlled by banks, the banks have so far ended up as the effective owners of the enterprises.

According to a Brookings Institute study, airfares in the United States fell almost 30 percent as a result of airline deregulation.[4] With the breakup of AT&T, long-distance rates fell about 25 percent, and new entrants increased competition and offered new services at attractive prices. On the other hand, local telephone rates increased by approximately 30 percent during the same time period.[5]

---

[4] Associated Press, "Deregulation of American Business Had a Price," *Des Moines Register,* December 20, 1989, p. 55.

[5] See "Phone Frenzy," *Business Week,* February 20, 1995, pp. 92–97.

Reregulation Congress deregulated cable television rates in 1984. In the next few years, investment in cable television increased, and many more channels became available. However, consumers complained because the cable companies, free of regulation, dramatically increased the rates. Consequently, by 1991, the FCC authorized local communities to regulate the rates charged for basic service by cable companies. Both less regulation and more comprehensive regulation is being considered by Congress.

As in the past, specific problems may lead to calls for the government to "do something." Concerns with the bailout of the savings and loan industry, the extensive downsizing of corporate hirings, the safety of flying on small airplanes, and the use of derivative financial instruments in many mutual funds and pension funds create cries for "reregulation." As new areas of our economy develop and problems occur within unregulated industries or activities, the need for reregulation will deserve serious attention.

Comment The United States is already one of the least regulated of the industrial nations. Administrative agencies in the United States were not created for ideological purposes; they were born to deal with specific problems in a society that lacked regulation. Congress wanted to build a national railroad system and to consider the needs of other carriers of interstate commerce. Dangerous foods and unsafe drugs that should never have reached the marketplace were freely available. Increasing pollution and the fraudulent sale of speculative securities to the public at large were among the problems that provided the impetus for the creation of administrative agencies.

Most agency administrators perform valuable functions that relieve the courts and legislatures from monumental burdens. Without their expertise and efficiency, activity in the traditional three branches of government would have come to a standstill long ago.

Federal, state, and local agencies appear to be effective organizations for administering the complex laws necessary to regulate numerous societal activities. As some form of governmental regulation is desired by most people, administrative agencies appear to be inevitable. They have developed in almost all independent nations and are likely to increase in importance as technology expands and society becomes more complex. Given the constant tension between the demand for regulation and business criticism of regulatory burdens, the cycle of alternating regulation and deregulation is apt to continue.

SUMMARY

Administrative agencies perform many functions in all legal systems. Agencies at the federal, state, and local levels derive their powers from the legislature. Both federal and state legislatures grant agencies the power to make rules, to hear and adjudicate certain types of controversies, and to perform a variety of informal investigative and administrative tasks.

In making rules, administrative agencies are required to follow procedures usually specified in a federal or state administrative procedure act. Generally, an agency must first provide public notice that it intends to engage in rulemaking and then hold a hearing to receive public comment. A rulemaking hearing is not a trial; it is a forum at which the agency presents its views and receives, in oral or written form, the comments of the public. After a hearing, the agency usually provides a summary of the comments offered at the hearing, and its reaction to them, before adopting a rule. That rule need not, however, be based on those comments. Still, the *Pediatrics* case indicates that a rule is likely to be held invalid if it is adopted without input from the public through comment at a hearing. Furthermore, an administrative agency's adoption of a rule contrary to the public's views may be found arbitrary and capricious when reviewed by a court.

Administrative agencies also make individual determinations concerning possible violations of agency rules or statutory laws. In performing this adjudicatory function, an agency is required to conduct a hearing using procedures similar to those used in a court trial. If the courts do not find substantial evidence in the record that supports an agency decision, the decision can be overturned.

Many informal activities, such as investigating compliance with statutes or agency rules by regulated businesses, are performed by administrative agencies. Administrative agencies may also grant permits, determine client eligibility for benefits, or approve the expenditure of governmental funds for selected projects. Such informal activities are less subject to review by the courts than the rulemaking or adjudicatory activities of administrative agencies. The *Overton Park* case illustrates the limited nature of judicial review of these activities.

Businesses interact with administrative agencies in numerous ways. Many businesses and trade associations become involved in agency rulemaking activities. Numerous industries and individual businesses find that the activities of some administrative agencies are vital to them. The United States has gone through several cycles of regulation followed by deregulation. Currently, there is a much greater regard for deregulation than for reregulation. Many politicians and commentators suggest the economy would improve if our legal system would leave to the marketplace many of the functions now performed by administrative agencies. While significant changes in some administrative activities may occur, in areas such as safety and protection of investors and of the environment, administrative regulations are likely to remain a vital part of the legal and regulatory environment of the United States.

Critical Thinking Questions

1. Define and give examples of the rulemaking and adjudicatory functions performed by an administrative agency in your local and state or provincial government.
2. Compare and contrast administrative rules and administrative orders on the basis of the procedures used to create them and their effect once they become final.
3. Evaluate the sources of controls on administrative agency action. Can you suggest alternative methods to control actions of administrative agencies?
4. Describe each of the steps that generally occur in an agency adjudicatory proceeding. How does an agency proceeding differ from a civil court trial?

Critical Thinking Exercises

1. The federal Mine, Safety, and Health Act of 1977 requires federal mine inspectors to inspect underground mines at least twice a year. The inspection is intended to ensure compliance with health and safety standards. The act also grants inspectors the right to enter any mine without advance notice of an inspection. If a mine operator refuses to allow a warrantless inspection, the secretary of labor is authorized to bring a civil action for an injunction. When a federal mine inspector attempted a follow-up inspection of one company's stone quarries, an officer of the company refused to allow the inspection. The company relied on the *Marshall v. Barlow's* case as authority for denying the inspector admission to the quarries without a search warrant. Do you think the reasoning of that case should apply to this situation? Why?
2. A Florida administrative rule permits a warrantless search of child day care facilities, including private homes used as day care centers, at any time of day. The Florida legislature's concern is to protect the health and safety of children at these centers by eliminating such hazards as inadequate capacity, accessibility to poisonous materials, open pools,

and sexual abuse. Is the Florida warrantless search scheme constitutional as applied to private homes?

3. The state of Georgia has regulations granting compensation to employees for work-related injuries. The Workers' Compensation Board awards compensation after conducting hearings. The findings of the Workers' Compensation Board are subject to judicial review and reversal only if the board acts outside its powers or if the award is not supported by substantial evidence on the record taken as a whole. Does the Workers' Compensation Board exercise legislative or adjudicatory powers in making awards? Explain.
4. The Interstate Commerce Commission (ICC) published a general notice in the *Federal Register* outlining proposed legislation to be submitted to Congress. The notice asked for comments from the general public. Following a period allowed for written comments, instead of submitting legislation to Congress, the ICC issued final rules that affected tour brokers. These regulations put new, expensive "tour broker surety bond" requirements on tour brokers. The National Tour Brokers' Association sued the ICC, claiming the notice provided was inadequate under the APA. Did the ICC comply with the procedural requirements under the Administrative Procedure Act?
5. The National Traffic and Motor Vehicle Safety Act requires the Secretary of Transportation to consider "relevant motor vehicle safety data" in making regulations. In 1977, the secretary promulgated a safety regulation that required new motor vehicles produced after September 1982 to have passive restraints (either continuous pull automatic seat belts or air bags). The regulation left the choice of passive restraints to the manufacturer. In February 1981, the secretary of transportation reopened the rulemaking process because of changes in the economy and problems in the auto industry. Two months later, the secretary proposed rescinding the regulation. The public then submitted comments on this proposal. State Farm Mutual Automobile Insurance sought review of the rescission, claiming the rescission of the safety standard was arbitrary and capricious. Do you agree? Why?
6. The government obtains people with expert knowledge for its regulatory agencies from the very industries they are supposed to regulate. This often gives rise to conflicts of interest. This revolving-door problem is a concern of almost every government agency. The best place to get experts for the Food and Drug Administration is from either the food or the pharmaceutical industries. If an executive from ABC Drug Company is appointed director of the Food and Drug Administration, how should he or she treat a product that ABC is trying to convince the FDA to approve? The reverse of that situation is equally perplexing. If a top-ranking official of the Food and Drug Administration quits and is hired by ABC Drug Company, how should that person's prior affiliation with the FDA influence its approval of ABC's drugs? How could government regulations limit the potential conflicts of interest from the revolving door?

PART 3

Private Law and Business

7 Property

8 Torts

9 Contracts

10 Commercial Law

CHAPTER

7

Property

Critical Thinking Questions

- Why is the protection of property rights so important to the legal systems being adopted in Eastern Europe and in the republics of the former Soviet Union?
- If you were a Chinese government official negotiating with representatives of the United States concerning intellectual property rights, what would you say regarding the importance of legal protection for intellectual property? What arguments would you expect the U.S. representative to make?
- Compare and contrast the different ways in which both real and personal property may be shared by two or more co-owners.
- What are the reasons why a recording system is used for the transfer of interests in real property?
- Compare and contrast the different types of intellectual property, namely copyrights, patents, trademarks, and trade secrets.
- What assumptions lie behind granting government control over real property through eminent domain, public and private nuisance laws, and zoning and land use regulations?

Introduction... Past, Present, Future

Property rights form the foundation of our free enterprise system. The U.S. Constitution (Fifth Amendment) recognizes the importance of property by protecting people from being deprived of property without due process of law and by requiring compensation if private property is taken for a public purpose. Property rights are not the same in every society; the recognition of such rights often evolves within a society. In developing countries, technology must usually be imported to make local businesses competitive on a global scale. The imported patented, copyrighted, and trademarked products drain the scarce resources of these countries. Thus, regulations often encourage the transfer of property rights and their liberal use rather than enforcing restrictions on behalf of the foreign property owner. As developing countries industrialize, their concern for the protection of intellectual property rights generally increases.

For many years, property in the United States consisted primarily of land and tangible items of personal property. The owner of land had nearly absolute rights regarding its use. In fact, some people even had a recognized and enforced property interest in other persons—their slaves. The abolition of slavery not only changed the nation, it also changed the relative importance of land and the property rights of landowners.

In the 20th century, property rights began to conflict with individual rights. Could a restaurant owner prohibit some individuals from using a restaurant open to the public? If pollutants from an owner's use of land fouled the air or water, did neighbors or society have remedies against the landowner? Such questions entail conflicts between enforcement of an owner's property rights and recognition of the rights of other individuals and of society.

On the one hand, the conflict between property rights and individual rights has resulted in a limitation of the law's recognition of the absolute rights of real property owners, thus diminishing the relative role of such property as a source of wealth and status. On the other hand, even though the interests of society in regulating the use of real property has increased, individual property owners have sought successfully to impose limits on the government's interference with or regulation of their use of property.

During the last several decades, many new forms of personal property have been recognized. In the world of investments, warrants and options give investors the right to purchase stock and a wide variety of specialized assets based on or derived from other stocks at some future date. A newly recognized real property right, time-sharing, allows a number of persons to have rights to use one piece of real estate, each at a specified time. Resorts throughout the world sell interested purchasers the right to use homes, condominiums, and luxury yachts. Further, owners of time-sharing rights in different properties subscribe to networks that permit them to exchange their rights with each other.

Finally, the law now recognizes property interests in previously unprotected intangible items. A person may have a property interest in obtaining future employment with a firm or in receiving governmental benefits. A license to practice a profession or to sell such products as securities or liquor is being recognized as property. The recognition of a property interest in computer chips and in specific computer operating systems or programs is vital to create the incentive to innovate. Biogenetic engineering has allowed firms to develop new drugs, plants and products that are changing the very environment in which we live.

The concept of property has undergone significant change in our nation. Land and real estate no longer constitute the most important part of a person's property. Property rights based on such intangibles as status, reputation, and intellectual acquisitions have moved to the fore. It is likely that these newly recognized property rights will become a significant part of our legal environment in the 21st century.

The Nature of Property

When property is discussed, most people think of physical things, such as a book, a boat, or a home. From the legal viewpoint, property consists not of the physical things themselves, but rather the relationship between the individual and those things. **Property** is defined as a bundle of rights that people have in things. The law creates these rights to prevent others from interfering with the owner's use and enjoyment of property.

property
The bundle of rights that people have in things.

Ownership interests are recognized by enforcing the right of a person or a business to use property. For example, the owner of a boat may use the boat, let others use it, or prevent others from using it. If someone takes the boat without the owner's permission, the law may punish this as theft. The courts enforce the owner's right to the boat by ordering the thief to return it or pay damages to the owner. The owner has the right to remodel the boat or even destroy it. The owner can use the boat as collateral for a loan. If the owner sells the boat or leases it to other people, the rights of ownership or possession of the boat will be transferred and recognized by law.

The key concept of property is the law's recognition and enforcement of the rights of people with regard to items considered to be property. Without the law's protection of these rights, property has meaning only to the extent that the possessor can exclude others by force. **Property law** describes a legally enforceable relationship between people or businesses and certain things as a property interest.

property law
The law that describes the legally enforceable relationship between people or businesses and things in which they have a property interest.

Classification of Property

The ways in which the law classifies property are reflected in the laws and procedures that affect ownership rights. For example, the classification of property as real or personal affects how that property is transferred. The transfer of real property, such as a house, requires a formal document such as a deed. To inform other parties of the buyer's interest in the property, the deed must be recorded in a government office. By contrast, the buyer of personal property does not need to use a formal document or to record it in a government office. Instead, delivery of personal property, such as a book, is sufficient to transfer title to the buyer. Despite the different methods used to transfer property, the new owner of real or personal property obtains all the rights that belonged to the former owner.

Real Property **Real property** (also known as realty) is land and everything attached to it, including the air above it and the minerals below the surface. Historically, the owner of land has received extensive legal protection. A person wrongfully thrown off his or her land may sue to recover it. A person who contracts to buy land may sue the seller to require specific performance of the contract and to force transfer of the title to the land.

real property
Land and everything attached to it, including the air above and the minerals below.

In contrast, a person who contracts to purchase personal property may generally sue only for damages. Thus, if a buyer contracts to purchase a vacant lot, and the seller decides not to sell it, the buyer may sue and force transfer of the title upon payment of the contract price. But if a buyer contracts to purchase an item of personal property, such as a boat, the buyer is able to sue only for damages unless the boat is a unique item. All real property is unique, but most personal property is not unique.

Fixtures Items attached to land are considered real property, even if they were once classified as personal property. **Fixtures** are personal property that have become real property through attachment to land or buildings. To determine whether an item of personal property has become a fixture, the courts will examine the intent of the party who attaches the item, the manner in which the item is attached, and the use of the item with that or other real property.

fixtures
Personal property that has become real property through attachment to land or buildings.

These questions arise when someone sells a home. Which items are personal property that generally will not be transferred to the purchaser, and which are fixtures that will be transferred to the purchaser? Would the following items be classified as personal property or as fixtures?

A refrigerator plugged into the wall with an electric cord but otherwise unattached to the walls of the house.

A dishwasher built into a cabinet under a kitchen counter.

An area rug on the floor just inside the front door.

Wall-to-wall carpeting that completely covers the floor of the main bedrooms and is attached to the floor with large staples.

A decorative light fixture in the hallway that the seller informs the buyer will be replaced with a standard light fixture.

Keys to the house door.

personal property Moveable property that has a physical existence and property without a physical existence.

tangible property Personal property that has a physical existence.

intangible property Personal property that does not have a physical existence.

Personal Property **Personal property** (also known as *personalty*) that has a physical existence, such as this textbook, a shirt, a boat, or a pair of shoes, is called **tangible property** because it can be seen, touched, and felt. Unless converted to fixtures, as just discussed, most movable property is considered tangible personal property. Goods are tangible personal property items that are movable at the time they are identified in a sales contract. Items attached to the land, such as crops or minerals, become personal property once they have been detached or extracted.

Personal property that has no physical existence is referred to as **intangible property.** As with tangible property, the law recognizes the owner's right to sell, pledge, use, or give away such property. A stock share, copyright, trademark, account receivable, or bank account is intangible property. Thus, intangible property includes both economic interests in property, as with a bank account or a share of stock, and intellectual property, such as copyrights, patents, and trademarks. However, as the owner of intellectual property has special statutory rights that determine who can copy the author's book, use a patented computer chip, or sell goods affixed with the owner's trademark or symbol, intellectual property is discussed in a subsequent section. Figure 7–1 depicts the different types of property interests.

The federal Constitution and most of the state constitutions prohibit government from taking "property" without due process of law. This makes the determination of what constitutes property an important issue in numerous court cases. Generally, cases of this kind concern items of intangible personal property, such as the right to continued employment. Does the expanded determination of intangible property apply to a college professor's interest in having his employment continued beyond an established term?

FIGURE 7–1

Different Types of Property

Real property—interest in land	One acre of land along with the house, garage, and fixtures in the house
Real property—fixture	The furnace and built-in dishwasher in a house
Personal property—tangible	A chair and sofa in a house
Personal property—intangible	Fifty shares of Exxon stock
Personal property—intellectual	Copyright of a book or magazine article

Board of Regents of State College v. Roth

408 U.S. 562 (1972)
United States Supreme Court

Roth was hired by the Board of Regents to teach political science at Wisconsin State University on the Oshkosh campus. His appointment specified employment for one year. After completing that term, Roth was notified that he would not be rehired. Because he had been hired for a one-year term and had not been granted tenure, the university claimed it had no obligation to give him notice of cause for the decision not to rehire him. Roth claimed that due process of law required that he be notified of the reason for not rehiring him.

Justice Stewart delivered the opinion of the Court

The only question presented to us at this stage in the case is whether the respondent had a constitutional right to a statement of reasons and a hearing on the University's decision not to rehire him for another year. We hold that he did not.

The requirements of procedural due process apply only to the deprivation of interests encompassed by the Fourteenth Amendment's protection of liberty and property. When protected interests are implicated, the right to some kind of prior hearing is paramount. But the range of interests protected by procedural due process is not infinite. To determine whether due process requirements apply in the first place, we must look not to the "weight" but to the *nature* of the interest at stake. We must look to see if the interest is within the Fourteenth Amendment's protection of liberty and property.

"Liberty" and "property" are broad and majestic terms. They are among the "[g]reat [constitutional] concepts . . . purposely left to gather meaning from experience. . . . [T]hey relate to the whole domain of social and economic fact, and the statesmen who founded this Nation knew too well that only a stagnant society remains unchanged."

The Court has also made clear that the property interests protected by procedural due process extend well beyond actual ownership of real estate, chattels, or money. By the same token, the Court has required due protection for deprivations of liberty beyond the sort of formal constraints imposed by the criminal process.

The Fourteenth Amendment's procedural protection of property is a safeguard of the security of interests that a person has already acquired in specific benefits. These interests—property interests—may take many forms.

Thus, the Court has held that a person receiving welfare benefits under statutory and administrative standards defining eligibility for them has an interest in continued receipt of those benefits that is safeguarded by procedural due process.

Similarly, in the area of public employment, the Court has held that a public college professor dismissed from an office held under tenure provisions, and college professors and staff members dismissed during the terms of their contracts, have interests in continued employment that are safeguarded by due process.

Certain attributes of "property" interests protected by procedural due process emerge from these decisions. To have a property interest in a benefit, a person clearly must have more than an abstract need or desire for it. He must have more than a unilateral expectation of it. He must, instead, have a legitimate claim of entitlement to it.

Property interests, of course, are not created by the Constitution. Rather they are created and their dimensions are defined by existing rules or understandings that stem from an independent source such as state law—rules or understandings that secure certain benefits and that support claims of entitlement to those benefits.

Just as the welfare recipient's "property" interest in welfare payments was treated and defined by statutory terms, so the respondent's "property" interest in employment at Wisconsin State University-Oshkosh was created and defined by the terms of his appointment. Those terms secured his interest in employment up to June 30, 1969. But the important fact in this case is that they specifically provided that the respondent's employment was to terminate on June 30. They did not provide for contract renewal absent "sufficient cause." Indeed, they made no provision for renewal whatsoever.

Thus, the terms of the respondent's appointment secured absolutely no interest in re-employment for the next year. They supported absolutely no possible claim of entitlement to re-employment. Nor, significantly, was there any state statute or University rule or policy that secured his interest in re-employment or that created any legitimate claim to it. In these circumstances, the respondent surely had an abstract concern in being rehired, but he did not have a *property* interest sufficient to require the University authorities to give him a hearing when they declined to renew his contract of employment.

Reversed and remanded.

Case Questions

1. Could a person have a property interest in employment that would be entitled to due process protection?
2. What determines whether a person has a property interest in something? Where does that interest come from?
3. What sources would you consult to determine whether you have a property right in your continued employment?

Intellectual Property

intellectual property Intangible property that is created by mental rather than physical effort.

Intellectual property is intangible property created primarily by mental rather than physical efforts. The most common types of intellectual property are patents, trade secrets, trademarks, and copyrights. Figure 7–2 summarizes the protection for the different types of intellectual property. Several types of intellectual property are protected under the common law; however, for all of these except trade secrets, compliance with special federal statutory registration requirements ensures the fullest property rights.

Licensing of Intellectual Property

license Can be either the permit to sell, assemble, manufacture, or use property belonging to someone else or the permit to enter upon or make use of another person's real property.

A **license** is a permit to sell, assemble, manufacture, or use property belonging to another firm. (a license also has a slightly different definition when used in discussing real property; that definition is discussed later in this chapter). Franchisors such as McDonald's and Holiday Inn license to franchisees the right to use their trademarks on the hamburgers and hotel rooms that the franchisees sell. Sometimes, a pharmaceutical firm may license a competing firm to sell one or more of its products in certain parts of the world. *Cross-licensing* occurs where one firm grants a license to a second firm in exchange for a license from the second firm to the first firm. Cross-licensing that adversely affects competition has been determined to be illegal in the United States, but in Japan cross-licensing between a firm that is the original inventor and a firm that makes an improvement on the invention while a patent application is pending has been quite common.

The evolution of the protection offered for intellectual property laws is exemplified by changes in Japanese laws. In the 1960s, each licensing agreement required government

FIGURE 7-2 Chart of Relationships Among Patents, Copyrights, Trademarks, and Trade Secrets

Type of Protection	Functional Patent	Design Patent	Copyright	Trademark or Service Mark	Trade Secrets
What Is Protected?	Functional features of process, machine, manufactured item, or composition of matter	Ornamental designs for article of manufacture	Works fixed in tangible medium of expression, e.g., literary, musical, pictorial, and motion picture works	Words, names, symbols, or devices	Valuable formula, process, or compilation of information known only to its developer
Criteria for Protection	New and "nonobvious"	New and "nonobvious"	Originality	Used to identify and distinguish goods or services	Valuable information that owner intends to keep secret
How Obtain Rights?	Granted only by federal gov't. (U.S. Patent and Trademark Office)	Granted only by federal gov't. (U.S. Patent and Trademark Office)	Federal rights automatic upon creation To preserve rights: Publication with notice and registration of claim with register of copyrights	Common Law: Adoption and use (sometimes secondary meaning required) Federal or state registration: Application and compliance with statutes	Protected by common law
Life Time?	20 years from date of patent application	14 years from date of patent application	Life of author plus 50 years	Common law: As long as properly used as a mark Federal regulation: 20 years (if formalities complied with) renewable for 20-year periods	No time limit—as long as it is valuable and kept secret
Test of Infringement?	Making, using, or selling in U.S. devices embodying the claimed invention	Designs look alike to eye of ordinary observer	Substantial portion copied? Similarity?	Likelihood of confusion, mistake, or deception	Unlawful discovery of information

approval; this allowed the Japanese government to involve itself in all negotiations for firms who were importing technology. By the 1970s, the parties to a licensing agreement did not need prior governmental approval; the only requirement was that the government had to be notified of the licensing. Today, as the government in Japan is more concerned with the export of technology than with its import, the guidelines affecting licensing agreements are intended primarily to make unfair business practices illegal.

FIGURE 7-3

Major International Treaties Affecting Intellectual Property

Name of Treaty	Type of Property	Protection	Parties
Paris Convention	Patents, Trademarks	National treatment, one-year priority period, use of form of country of origin	U.S. + 90 countries
Patent Cooperation Treaty	Patents	File first in local office and eight months later in other countries	U.S. + 40 countries
Madrid Agreement	Trademarks	National registration gives applicant filing in International Bureau Office protection in all member countries if there is no objection by members within one year	30 + countries (not U.S.)
Pan-American	Trademarks	Right to enforce in other countries under terms similar to Paris Union	U.S. + 20 countries
Berne Convention	Copyrights	Works published in one country are automatically eligible for protection in other countries without registration there. If a nation is a member of both the Berne Convention and the Universal Copyright Convention, the Berne Convention is controlling	U.S. + 80 countries
Universal Copyright Convention	Copyrights	National treatment if the applicant complies with its own national law; a copyright notice is required on all works	U.S. + 90 countries

International Protection of Intellectual Property

In some countries, laws that protect certain property, particularly intellectual property such as copyrights, patents, and trademarks, either do not exist or are often not enforced. For example, a country might not grant or recognize patents on certain products. In India, patents for any invention intended for use as a food, medicine, or drug are prohibited. Many U.S. drugs are widely reproduced in India and other developing countries because patent protection is not available. Often, intellectual property is not protected in developing countries because it is easy to misappropriate and difficult to protect, because the property is often in great demand, and because the lack of physical substance to the property weakens its exclusivity.

Similarly, some countries have laws that recognize property rights, but the laws are not commonly enforceed. In Brazil, copyright laws are similar to those in other countries, but piracy of videocassettes and computer software and unauthorized translation of literary works is widespread. In Singapore, "Lotus 1-2-3" copies sell for approximately $5, and fake Rolex watches can be found for $25. The United States and China settled a trade dispute in early 1995 when China agreed to destroy some government-owned factories that were producing millions of uncopyrighted compact discs.

In other countries, the legal processes that affect property rights are slow and cumbersome. Whereas trademark applications in the United States are processed in a little over a year, in Japan the processing period is almost four years. During the time the application is pending, there is no penalty for trademark infringement.

Firms competing internationally need to be aware of the steps required to protect international property. As the case stories in the accompanying International Perspective indicate, failure to consider the legal consequences of actions that may seem innocent can be disastrous. Intellectual property is often the subject of a licensing agreement in international business transactions. This topic was discussed in greater detail in Chapter 3, which focused on the international legal environment.

A variety of international treaties affect intellectual property. The protection of intellectual property is becoming a greater concern for many Western firms, and there is increased negotiation regarding this topic in both bilateral and multilateral treaties. Several of the more important multilateral treaties to which the United States is a party are depicted in Figure 7–3.

INTERNATIONAL PERSPECTIVE AND COMMENTARY

Case Stories on Protecting Intellectual Property

According to a recent article prepared by officials at the Patent and Trademark Office of the U.S. Department of Commerce, U.S. firms competing internationally need to protect their intellectual property. The difference between an advantageous competitive arrangement and commercial disaster may depend on forethought and planning regarding intellectual property. The following are recent examples of successes and failures drawn from composite experiences of U.S. firms.

Company A sent product literature to a potential foreign business partner. Soon, the would-be partner cornered the market for the product in its region. Although company A had a U.S. patent, its public disclosure made its product unpatentable in most foreign countries.

Company B knew pirated copies of its computer programs were being sold in some foreign countries. It blocked commercial importation of its product in those countries, enforced its copyright country by country, and was successful in stopping infringements in its major markets.

Company C did business on a handshake. Its closely guarded technology was very useful to its competitors.

Company D believed its exclusive rights to inventions and writings were very valuable, and it sought the best protection in each country in which it did business. If adequate protection was not available, it avoided investing there.

Source: U.S. Department of Commerce, "An Introductory Guide for U.S. Businesses on Protecting Intellectual Property Abroad," *Business America,* July 1, 1991.

Patents

A **patent** is issued for products and processes that are original, novel, useful, and nonobvious. For example, patents have been issued for the ballpoint pen, new drugs, and photographic equipment. The owner of a patent has a legal monopoly to make, sell, and use the patented product or process throughout the United States and its territories and possessions. After the United States signed the recent GATT (now administered by the World Trade Organization), it changed the time period for which a patent is valid. As in most other countries, U.S. patents are now valid for 20 years from

patent
A new and nonobvious process, machine, manufactured item, or composition of matter that is protected by national law.

the time a patent application is filed. Under the old law, the time period was 17 years from the date a patent was issued. Design patents, which protect ornamental designs rather than a product's function, grant an owner the right to exclude others from making, using, or selling any product embodying a protected design for a period of 14 years.

Obtaining a patent is often consuming and expensive, usually requiring a patent search by a patent attorney. The search must prove that the product is new and significantly different from any previously patented products. The owner of a patented product may assign this property interest in a license to others. This is frequently done in exchange for royalty payments. Typically, the patent is assigned to a firm that agrees to manufacture and market the patented product. Research scientists and engineers at corporations are often requested, as part of their employment contract, to transfer to the corporation the rights to any products that they develop. The patents for these products are then issued to the corporation.

A patent gives its owner a monopoly; its unauthorized use is a patent *infringement.* The patent owner may sue the infringer for damages and seek an injunction prohibiting future infringements by the wrongdoer. For example, Polaroid won a patent infringement case that it brought against Kodak, thus forcing Kodak out of the instant photography market.[1] After the patent on a product expires, the product is considered to be in the public domain. Thereafter, any firm or individual may freely use the patented information. For example, the drug Motrin, used to treat arthritis, was a product patented by the Upjohn Company. After the patent expired, other pharmaceutical firms were free to manufacture similar products, such as Advil, based on the Ibuprofen ingredient originally described in the Motrin patent.

Trade Secrets

trade secret
A valuable formula, process, or compilation of information that is known only to its developers.

A **trade secret** is a valuable formula, process, or compilation of information known only to its developer. To obtain legal protection for a trade secret, two elements must be present. First, there must be some valuable information, such as a special recipe, a customer list, or a manufacturing process. For example, "the Colonel's secret ingredients" used in preparing Kentucky Fried Chicken and the secret formula for Coca-Cola are considered valuable information.

Second, the owner must attempt to keep the information secret. Information that becomes widely known to competitors or the general public cannot remain a trade secret. For example, a competitor of Du Pont obtained aerial photographs of the layout of a newly built Du Pont manufacturing facility, and the competitor's photographer claimed that Du Pont had not kept secret its manufacturing process for producing methanol. However, the court ruled that even though Du Pont's process was discoverable through aerial photography, Du Pont had made considerable effort to maintain confidentiality. Thus, the information was not freely available to the public and was therefore protected by trade secret law.[2]

No time limit is placed on trade secrets. As long as information is valuable and kept secret, it is protected. The absence of a time limit on trade secret protection sometimes makes a trade secret more valuable than a patent. However, reliance on trade secret protection is much riskier than reliance on patent protection because lawful discovery of the secret information terminates the protection; whereas, patent protection now

[1] *Eastman Kodak Company v. Polaroid Corporation,* 479 U.S. 850 (1986).
[2] *E.I. Dupont de Neumours & Co. v. Christopher,* 431 F.2d 1012 (1970).

exists for 20 years. Trade secrets are protected by state tort laws, discussed further in Chapter 8. By contrast, as a Supreme Court case notes, federal laws protect patents.

A Comparison of Patents and Trade Secrets

Trade secret law and patent law have coexisted in this country for over one hundred years. Each has its particular role to play, and the operation of one does not take away from the need for the other. Trade secret law encourages the development and exploitation of those items of lesser or different invention than might be accorded protection under the patent laws, but which items still have an important part to play in the technological and scientific advancement of the nation. Trade secret law promotes the sharing of knowledge and the efficient operation of industry; it permits the individual inventor to reap the rewards of his labor by contracting with a company large enough to develop and exploit it. Congress, by its silence over these many years, has seen the wisdom of allowing the States to enforce trade secret protection.[3]

ETHICAL DILEMMA

MISAPPROPRIATING INTELLECTUAL PROPERTY

Industrial espionage has received increasing attention in recent years. In high-technology industries, numerous attempts have been made to steal trade secrets. Although the federal patent and copyright laws provide some protection for trade secrets, these laws have several limitations. The formal procedure for patenting a machine, process, or design is expensive. Moreover, there are often long delays in securing a patent, and some designs may be useful for only a short time. Sometimes, the cost of patent infringement litigation outweigh the benefits of the patent. Patents valid in only one country provide insufficient protection because foreign firms may ignore U.S. patent laws.

Some new processes are very complex, requiring many separate patents and many years for development into commercial viability. During this time, the public and competitors of the patent holder may have access to the disclosed information on which the patents are based. To avoid the costs and the loss of privacy that patenting entails, many of the fruits of research and development are not patented.

It is not improper to use "reverse engineering." This is a method of discovering trade secrets (but not copyrights or patents) hidden in a finished product that is already being marketed. For example, in the early 1980s, GM bought 10 Volvos to disassemble and learn how to make safer cars. GM could validly use any trade secret information learned from this reverse engineering. However, any patented technology discovered in such a process must be licensed to be legitimately used.

When the owner is taking reasonable precautions to preserve secrecy, others are prohibited from using devious methods to misappropriate trade secrets if no reasonable defense is available. In *Du Pont v. Christopher,* the court said: "Our devotion to freewheeling industrial competition must not force us into accepting the law of the jungle as the standard of morality expected in our commercial relations. Our tolerance of the espionage game must cease when the protection required to prevent another's spying costs so much that the spirit of inventiveness is dampened."

[3] *Kewanee Oil Co. v. Bicron Co.,* 416 U.S. 470, 493 (1974).

Trademarks

trademark
A distinctive mark on goods that designates their origin and distinguishes them from those of competitors.

A **trademark** is a distinctive mark on goods that distinguishes them from those of competitors. The mark may be a picture, a design, words, or a combination thereof. The golden arches design used by McDonald's and the words *Coca-Cola* and *Xerox* are trademarks. They are used on storefronts and packages and in advertisements to show consumers that products originate from a particular firm.

Like patents, trademarks are usually registered under a special federal statute—in this case, the Lanham Act. The trademark owner first applies to the Patent and Trademark Office for registration and then conducts a search of existing trademarks to determine whether the intended use of the trademark conflicts with the use of existing trademarks. Owners of existing trademarks may challenge an application for a new trademark if they consider it too similar to their trademarks or confusing to the public. Federal registration upon the Principal Register gives constructive notice to all later users that its owner intends to enforce the trademark nationwide, even where the mark is not in current use.

While trademark rights are acquired through use, a trademark can be "reserved" for a period of up to 20 years based upon an intent to use. The term *trademark* is often used to describe four different types of marks protected by federal law.

Types of Marks Protected under the Lanham Act

1. Trademarks—identify goods originating from particular companies, such as IBM or Pepsi.
2. Service marks—identify services provided by particular companies, such as Holiday Inn or Hilton.
3. Certification marks—certify that certain standards have been met by the manufacturer of the products on which a seal is displayed, such as the Good Housekeeping Seal of Approval, the seal of the American Meteorological Service, the designation of approval from Underwriters Laboratories (UL approved).
4. Collective marks—used by associations such as the Boy Scouts of America to identify products that they manufacture, approve, or endorse.

Registered marks of all four types are generally valid for 20 years and may be renewed for a second 20 years. To qualify for registration, a trademark must be associated by the public with the firm or source from which it originates. For example, if the public associates Coke, a registered trademark, with any cola drink, the trademark may eventually become generic, able to be used by anyone.

The term *LITE* was first used by the Meister Brau company in 1967 to designate a low-calorie, low-carbohydrate beer. The company registered the trademark and later sold the name and trademark to the Miller Brewing Company. Later, other brewers began to manufacture low-calorie beers, and Miller sued to protect its trademark. In 1977, the Court of Appeals determined that the term *light beer* had become associated in the minds of the public with generic products rather than the products of a particular producer. Accordingly, trademark protection became unavailable to the manufacturer of any light beer.[4] A somewhat similar problem is discussed in the following case.

---

[4] *Miller Brewing Co. v. Heileman Brewing Co.*, 561 F.2d 75 (1977).

Should trademark protection be granted for a product whose trade name represents the initials for a generic term?

Anheuser-Busch, Inc. v. Stroh Brewery Co.

750 F.2d 631 (1984)
8th Circuit Court of Appeals

In January 1984, Anheuser-Busch applied for registration of the trademark "LA" for a low-alcohol beer that it had developed. It began marketing the beer in March 1984. That month, Stroh Brewery announced its plans to market two beers using the "LA" label, one for Schaeffer beer and the other for Old Milwaukee. In April 1984, Anheuser-Busch sued Stroh for trademark infringement, trademark dilution, and unfair competition. Stroh argued that the mark "LA" was generic and descriptive of products, so that trademark laws could not protect it. The trial court found for Anheuser-Busch; accordingly, it issued an injunction, an order stopping Stroh from using the "LA" label on its beer. Stroh appealed that decision.

Gibson, Circuit Judge

Stroh first argues that the initials of a generic term such as "low alcohol" cannot assume trademark status.

Rather, the question in the instant case is whether, when a party seeks to protect initials alone which are also the initials of a generic or descriptive phrase, the initials are to be equated with that phrase. The key issue, as the case demonstrates, is the nature of the relationship or tie between the initials and the generic or descriptive phrase and the relationship or tie between the initials and the product. As the district court properly held, if some operation of the imagination is required to connect the initials with the product, the initials cannot be equated with the generic phrase but are suggestive in nature, thereby rendering them protectible. Stroh also refers us to some thirteen cases in support of their contention. We have examined these cases carefully and find that in none is it stated as a matter of law that initials of generic or descriptive phrases are unprotectible. We conclude that the district court did not err as a matter of law in engaging in a factual determination of the proper classification to be accorded the initials LA.

Stroh next argues that the district court erred as a matter of law in relying primarily on consumer perceptions in its classification of LA. It asserts that consumer perceptions should not be used as the principal test for "terms that have started out as generic category descriptors." Stroh's assertion assumes that LA is a "generic category descriptor." As discussed above, the district court specifically found LA to be neither generic or descriptive. Thus *Miller Brewing Co. v. Jos. Schlitz Brewing Co.,* the case Stroh cites as authority, is not on point: that case deals with the irrelevance of a survey of the responses of 988 beer drinkers to "the meaning of a familiar word of Anglo-Saxon heritage" (i.e., "light"). The mark LA in a beer-drinking context obviously is not so familiar. As the *Miller* case itself points out, when "a coined word for a commercial product" is involved, the proper test becomes "what 'buyers understand by the word.' "

In *WSM, Inc.* we specifically stated that "[t]he test for deciding whether a word has become a generic title of a product or service is one of buyer understanding: 'What do the buyers understand by the word for whose use the parties are contending.' " The same test applies when deciding whether a word is descriptive.

Stroh argues that since the term LA was merely generic or descriptive, the district court improperly relied on the consumer survey offered into evidence. Stroh further attacks the methodology of the survey. . . .

In determining the viewpoint of the prospective purchasers in trademark and unfair competition cases, substantial weight may be accorded the result of a properly conducted survey. Courts have frequently relied upon properly conducted surveys in determining whether marks are generic or descriptive. Indeed, survey evidence may be the most practical manner of approaching the evaluation of public reaction in such cases.

Stroh also argues that the consumer survey was improperly designed. The survey was designed by Dr. Yoram Wind, Professor of Marketing and Management, Wharton School, University of Pennsylvania. The district court found that the consumer survey was fairly and scientifically conducted by qualified experts and impartial interviewers, that the study drew responses from a sample of a relevant portion of potential consumers, that the questions upon which the results relied did not appear to be misleading or biased, and that the recordation of responses was handled in a completely unbiased manner. Stroh . . . argues the survey was defective because respondents who were familiar with low alcohol beer were not asked what LA meant.

Dr. Wind also stated that if a student of his had included such a question in "a research design he would have gotten an F in the course." We believe the district court did not err in finding Dr. Wind's defense of his research design persuasive. The district court therefore properly looked to the consumer survey in reaching its conclusion that "LA . . . stands for an idea which requires some operation of the imagination to connect it with the product."

As we observed before, the district court grounded its analysis of the protectibility of LA on four mutually exclusive categories: the generic, descriptive, suggestive, and arbitrary or fanciful. The district court found the term LA to be suggestive in nature.

Stroh argues that the term is generic. We have addressed above and found wanting Stroh's contention that initials of generic phrases must similarly be so classified.

We affirm the issuance of the injunction by the district court.

Bright, Circuit Judge, dissenting

In this case, a major beer brewer, Anheuser-Busch, invokes federal jurisdiction seeking trademark protection for its brand name "LA." I would deny protection because its claim to the mark "LA" reflects a preemptive and anticompetitive intent to capture the emerging market for low alcoholic content beer by converting the initials of "low alcohol" (l.a.) into a trademark.

The objectives of the trademark law are: (1) to prevent confusion among the consuming public as to the source of goods or services and (2) to indicate ownership and permit the trademark owner to control the product's reputation. To realize these objectives, a trademark must distinguish a product from similar products and identify its owner or producer. Consequently, only those marks characterized as distinctive may receive trademark protection. Thus, to gain trademark protection for the mark "LA," Anheuser-Busch must demonstrate by clear and convincing evidence that LA primarily serves to designate its source (from Anheuser-Busch) rather than to describe or indicate a characteristic that it shares with other beers of low alcoholic content produced by other brewers.

The majority relies heavily on the district court's determination that the initials "LA" do not describe but merely suggest the beer's low alcoholic content. This finding rested upon a market survey, conducted at the behest of Anheuser-Busch in contemplation of this litigation. The survey concluded that consumers perceived LA as the brand name of the product and not as a description for low alcohol beer.

. . . However, the market survey introduced by Anheuser-Busch in the district court suffers several fatal defects. . . . The perceptions of a group of wholly uninformed consumers are, however, simply legally irrelevant. Dr. Wind's approach essentially measures consumer perception in an abstract, hypothetical context: What does a mark convey immediately to a consumer who has never before seen the product and who might not even know that such a product category exists.

Thus, a legally relevant test of consumer perceptions must reflect the real world and a real market. In this case, then, the appropriate group of consumers to survey would have been an informed group of consumers, familiar with low alcohol beer.

Examination of the market survey reveals serious defects—namely, that the conclusion that LA does not connote low alcohol beer was drawn from the legally irrelevant sample group of uninformed consumers asked to draw meaning from an isolated product label, and that the survey was otherwise insufficient because of the questionable structure and make-up of the questions asked. Thus, upon analysis, this survey does not, in my view, support the district court's finding that LA is suggestive.

Case Questions

1. If *low alcohol* is a generic term that cannot be trademarked, what is the reasoning used by the court for granting trademark protection to "LA" beer?
2. What test did the court use to determine whether a word was generic?
3. What alternative explanations does the dissenting judge give for his denial of protection to the LA trademark?
4. What criticisms does the dissenting judge make regarding the empirical method used in the market survey in question?

Copyrights

copyright
The protection granted to protect the original work of authors, musicians, and painters that makes it illegal to copy their work without permission.

Copyrights protect the original work of authors, musicians, and painters who produce works of artistic or intellectual merit. This book has been copyrighted, making it illegal to take the authors' words without permission. Like corporate researchers who invent patentable products, authors who contract to write a book generally transfer their copyright to the publishing firm that seeks to sell it.

Copyright protection exists under the common law once a work has been created. However, it is also possible to register copyrights. The registration process for copyrights is much simpler than those for patents or trademarks. With copyrights, unlike patents or trademarks, no one conducts a search to determine originality or the absence of conflict. This means that a copyright holder may be subject to an infringement suit by another copyright holder.

While a copyright notice is not required to obtain copyright protection, such notice may be helpful in a case involving an infringement from a person who might otherwise claim to be innocent because he or she had not noticed that a work might be protected. When a notice is used, it may take the form of the word *copyright,* the abbreviation *copr,* or the symbol © followed by the year and the name of the copyright holder. The copyright for this book is located on the page following the title page. Copyright protection under the Copyright Act of 1976 lasts for the life of the creator plus 50 years. If there is more than one creator, as with this book, the copyright lasts for 50 years beyond the life of the longest surviving creator.

Copyrights protect the words, music, or composition of the author, composer, or painter, but not the ideas expressed in the copyrighted material. Thus, you have the right to read a portion of a book, take some of the author's ideas, and use them to create new, noninfringing text. However, as the term *copyright* suggests, you do not have the right to copy the particular words, the "form of expression," that the author used or to photocopy material in the book without permission unless the purpose is exempt. Does the developer of a computer operating system have a right to copyright that system, or does the system represent an idea not subject to copyright protection? The case presented at the end of this section indicates how the copyright law applies to computer programs.

Some use of copyrighted material is permitted. The *fair use doctrine* allows the quotation of several paragraphs in a book for use in a report or in a published review or commentary. This doctrine also permits taping for personal use songs played on the radio. Similarly, a 1984 Supreme Court case determined that television shows could be copied onto a VCR for later personal enjoyment without violating the rights of the copyright owners.[5] However, as the broadcasters of professional sports events remind us, further use is prohibited.

---

[5] *Sony Corp. v. Universal City Studios,* 464 U.S. 417 (1984).

A Typical Copyright Notice Announcement

No rebroadcast or other use of this copyrighted game and the play-by-play announcement of it is permissible without the consent of major league baseball and the competing teams.

The case that follows, *Atari v. Nintendo,* illustrates the interrelationship among the various aspects of intellectual property. Issues of patent infringement, copyright infringement, and trade secret violations are raised, some by both parties. Read carefully the judge's explanation of the different protection offered by the copyright and patent laws.

Atari Games Corp. v. Nintendo of America Inc.

975 F.2d 832 (1992)
United States Court of Appeals, Federal Circuit

Nintendo brought action against Atari for unfair competition, patent infringement, copyright infringement, and trade secret violations. Atari then sued Nintendo, claiming unfair competition, Sherman Act violations, and patent infringement. After the cases were consolidated for trial, the District Court judge issued a preliminary injunction barring Atari from exploiting Nintendo's copyrighted computer programs. Atari appealed to the Court of Appeals.

Rader, Circuit Judge

Nintendo's home video game system, the Nintendo Entertainment System (NES), includes a monitor, console, and controls. The console is a base unit into which a user inserts game cartridges. These cartridges contain the various game programs for the NES. As dictated by the program on the cartridge, the console controls an image on the video monitor, often a television set. In response to this video display, the user interacts with the system by manipulating controls. Thus, by operating the controls in response to the video image, an individual plays the game on the cartridge in the NES console.

For instance, the game program may control a maze or a set of obstacles on the video display. The user then manipulates the controls to guide an object through the maze or set of obstacles. The game program then awards the user points for proficiently passing through the maze or obstacle.

Nintendo designed a program—the 10 NES—to prevent the NES from accepting unauthorized game cartridges. Both the NES console and authorized game cartridges contain microprocessors or chips programmed with the 10 NES. The console contains a "master chip" or "lock." Authorized game cartridges contain a "slave chip" or "key." When a user inserts an authorized cartridge into a console, the console detects a coded message and accepts the game cartridge. When a user inserts an unauthorized cartridge, the console detects no unlocking message and refuses to operate the cartridge. Nintendo's 10 NES program thus controls access to the NES.

Atari first attempted to analyze and replicate the NES security system in 1986. It could not break the 10 NES program code by monitoring the communication between the master and slave chip . . . or by analyzing the chips themselves. In December, 1987, Atari became a Nintendo licensee. The license terms, however, strictly controlled Atari's access to Nintendo's technology, including the 10 NES program. . . .

In early 1988, Atari's attorney applied to a Copyright Office for a reproduction of the 10 NES program. The application stated that Atari was a defendant in an infringement action and needed a copy of the program for that litigation. Atari falsely alleged it was a present defendant in a lawsuit. . . . In fact, no suit existed between the parties until December 1988 when Atari sued Nintendo for antitrust and unfair competition. Nintendo filed its suit against Atari in November 1989.

After it deciphered the 10 NES program, Atari developed its own program—the Rabbit program—to unlock the NES. . . . Because Atari chose a different microprocessor and programming language, the line-by-line instructions of the 10 NES and Rabbit programs vary. Nonetheless, as the district court found, the Rabbit program generates signals functionally indistinguishable from the 10 NES program. The Rabbit gave Atari access to NES owners without Nintendo's strict licensing requirements. The district court issued an injunction against Atari's infringement of Nintendo's 10 NES.

Because this action involves patent infringement claims, this court has jurisdiction over his appeal. To resolve issues of copyright law, the court applies the law as interpreted by the regional circuits, in this case the United States Court of Appeals for the Ninth Circuit.

The Ninth Circuit sustains preliminary injunctions if the movant shows either a likelihood of success on the merits and the possibility of irreparable injury, or that serious questions going to the merits were raised and the balance of hardships tips sharply in its favor. In a claim for copyright infringement, a showing of reasonable likelihood of success on the merits raises a presumption of irreparable harm. . . . Thus, following Ninth Circuit case law, this court must determine whether Nintendo has shown a likelihood of success on its prima facie case of copyright infringement and a likelihood that it will overcome Atari's copyright misuse defense.

To prevail on its copyright infringement claim, Nintendo must show ownership of the 10 NES program copyright and copying by Atari of protectable expression from the 10 NES program. The parties do not dispute that Nintendo owns the 10 NES copyright. Therefore, Nintendo must only prove that Atari copied protectable expression from the 10 NES program. Nintendo can show copying by proving that Atari made literal copies of the 10 NES program. To show nonliteral copyright infringement, Nintendo must ultimately prove substantial similarity between the 10 NES and the Rabbit in protectable expression. To determine whether Nintendo is likely to so prove, this court must first distinguish protectable expression from the unprotectable elements of the 10 NES program.

Article I, sec. 8, cl. 8 of the Constitution gives Congress power to "promote the Progress of Science and useful Arts, by securing for limited Times to Authors and Inventors the exclusive Right to their respective Writings and Discoveries." The Copyright Act of 1976, in general protects "original works of authorship fixed in any tangible medium of expression." The statutory definition of "works of authorship" embraces computer programs. . . . The 1976 Act, however, sets limits on the scope of the copyright protection. In the words of the Supreme Court, "the mere fact that a work is copyrighted does not mean that every element of the work is protected. In no case does copyright protection for an original work of authorship extend to any idea, procedure, process, system, method of operation, concept, principle, or discovery, regardless of the form in which it is described." . . .

Judge Learned Hand devised an abstraction test to separate the ideas from expression in written or dramatic works:

> Upon any work . . . a great number of patterns of increasing generality will fit equally well, as more and more of the incidents is left out . . . There is a point in this series of abstractions where they are no longer protected, since otherwise the playwright could prevent the use of his ideas to which, apart from their expression, his property is never extended.

Our sister circuit recently applied his test in a computer program copyright. Judge Hand's abstraction analysis forces differentiation of the unprotectable idea and protectable expression. The abstraction method also properly recognizes that a computer program contains many distinct ideas.

After separating the program into manageable components, the court must next filter the unprotectable components from the protectable expression. The court must filter out as unprotectable the ideas, expressions incident to the idea, expressions already in the public domain, expressions dictated by external factors (like the computer's mechanical specifications) and expressions not original to the programmer or author.

In addition copyright protection does not extend to any procedure, process, system or method of operation. In conformance with the standards of patent law, title 35 provides protection for the process or method performed by a computer in accordance with a program. Thus, patent and copyright laws protect distinct aspects of a computer program. Title 35 protects the process or method performed by a computer program; title 17 protects the expression of that process or method. While title 35 protects any novel, nonobvious and useful process, title 17 protects a multitude of expressions that implement that process. If the patentable process is embodied inextricably in the line-by-line instruction of the computer program, however, then the process merges with the expression and precludes copyright protection.

Nintendo's 10 NES program contains more than an idea or expression necessarily incident to an idea. Nintendo chose arbitrary programming instructions and arranged them in a unique sequence to create a purely arbitrary data stream. This data serves as the key to unlock the NES. Nintendo may protect this creative element of NES under copyright. Nintendo seeks to protect the creative element of its program beyond the literal expression used to effect the unlocking process. The district court defined the unprotectable idea or process as the generation of a data stream to unlock a console. Nintendo has shown that there are a multitude of ways to generate a data stream that unlocks the 10 NES. The district court properly discerned that the 10 NES program contains protectable expression. At a minimum, Nintendo may protect under copyright the unique and creative arrangement of instructions in the 10 NES program.

Atari acquired a copy of the 10 NES program from the Copyright Office and used it to replicate the 10 NES source code. [Copyright regulations permit accessing material from the Copyright Office by parties who are in litigation with a copyright holder; it was under this regulation that Atari accessed Nintendo's 10 NES source code.] The Copyright Act states that copies obtained from the Copyright Office in violation of the regulations are unauthorized reproductions. Atari had no reason to fear a copyright infringement suit from Nintendo. Thus, no controversy at all existed when Atari acquired the 10 NES program from the Copyright Office. Without an actual controversy, Atari's acquisition of the 10 NES source code violated Copyright Office rules.

The Copyright Act permits an individual in rightful possession of a copy of a work to undertake necessary efforts to understand the work's ideas, processes and methods of operation. This permission appears in the fair use exception to copyright exclusivity. . . . When the nature of a work requires intermediate copying to understand the ideas and processes in a copyrighted work, that nature supports a fair use for intermediate copying. Thus, reverse engineering object codes to discern unprotectable ideas in a computer program is a fair use. Fair use to discern a work's ideas does not justify extensive efforts to profit from replicated protected expression. The fair use reproductions of a computer program must not exceed what is necessary to understand the unprotected elements of the work.

To invoke the fair use exception, an individual must possess an authorized copy of a literary work. Because Atari was not in authorized possession of the Copyright Office copy of 10 NES, any copying or derivative copying of 10 NES source code from the Copyright Office does not qualify as fair use.

Reverse engineering, untainted by the purloined copy of the 10 NES program and necessary to understand 10 NES, is fair use. An individual cannot even observe, let alone understand, the object code on Nintendo's chip without reverse engineering. . . .

Even in the absence of verbatim copying, a copyright owner may show infringement by showing that the infringer had access to work and that the two works are substantially similar. This doctrine prevents a plagiarist from escaping infringement by making immaterial changes in the protected work. The Ninth Circuit uses a two-step analysis to evaluate substantial similarity:

> First an extrinsic test is used to determine whether two ideas are substantially similar. This is an objective test which rests upon specific criteria that can be listed and analyzed. Second, an intrinsic test is used to compare forms of expression. This is a subjective test which depends on the response of the ordinary reasonable person.

In the context of computer programs, the ordinary reasonable person with the ability to intelligently respond to computer expression is a computer programmer.

The district court noted that the Rabbit program incorporates elements of the 10 NES program unnecessary for the chip's performance. The Rabbit program contains instructions from the original 10 NES program that have since been deleted by Nintendo. These unnecessary instructions strongly suggest that the Rabbit program is substantially similar to the 10 NES program.

In sum, Nintendo is likely to show that its 10 NES program contains protectable expressions. As Nintendo is likely to show misappropriation and copying of the unauthorized Copyright Office copy, it is likely to succeed on its infringement claim. Alternatively, Nintendo is likely to prove substantial similarity between the Rabbit and 10 NES programs sufficient to support its infringement claims. This record justifies the trial court's granting of a preliminary injunction.

As a defense to copyright infringement, Atari asserts Nintendo has misused its copyright of the lockout program because it has conditioned the license of its copyright program on the acceptance of contract provisions that give it control over the games developed by independent, third-party software developers. In the absence of any statutory entitlement to a copyright misuse defense, however, the defense is solely an equitable doctrine. Any party seeking equitable relief must come into court with "clean hands." The Ninth Circuit has noted that the doctrine of unclean hands can preclude the defense of copyright misuse. The district court states, "Atari lied to the Copyright Office in order to obtain the copyrighted 10 NES program." This record supports the district court's conclusion and suggests that Atari's unclean hands prevent it from invoking equity.

Affirmed.

Case Questions

1. Apply the court's unprotectable idea versus protectable expression differentiation to a book (such as this textbook) or a play or movie you have seen. Which are the unprotectable ideas and which are the protectable expressions?
2. Why does the law permit patented products to be "reverse engineered"?
3. Atari sought to counter its copying from the unauthorized Copyright Office program by claiming Nintendo misused its copyright. Assume that Nintendo did in fact improperly use its copyright to seek to restrict competition from others. What reason does the court give for dismissing Atari's claim?

MISAPPROPRIATION OF INTELLECTUAL PROPERTY

ETHICAL DILEMMA

The law of intellectual property rights—patents, copyrights, trademarks, and trade secrets—is designed to encourage innovation in areas that could eventually affect society. These property rights are based on an implied contract between the innovator and the government. To encourage the development of new products, the innovator is given a monopoly for a limited time. In exchange, the innovator must share the innovation's benefits with society.

The major ethical problem with intellectual property arises from its intangible nature. It is easy to understand that stealing tangible property is unethical and illegal. The owner immediately knows of the loss, and society generally condemns the misappropriation. By contrast, intangible property (e.g., information, ideas, inventions, designs) appears to be inexhaustible. When one person misappropriates a copy of intangible property, the owner still has the original property. However, this misappropriation diminishes the owner's opportunity to fully exploit the intangible property right. There is a common misunderstanding that nothing has been misappropriated because the owner still has the original.

However, an ethical problem clearly arises because the misappropriator has gained value without expending development efforts to earn it or pay the owner for it. Misappropriation or infringement of intellectual property is a tempting act because it is often easy to do and may go undetected. Unauthorized photocopying and software duplication exemplify this unethical misappropriation.

Computer Law

Computers are used by millions of business firms to accomplish a wide variety of tasks. From word processing to data storage to product scanning, the computer has become ubiquitous in both the back rooms and executive offices of most business organizations. Of course, some people who use computers may do so for unauthorized and illegal purposes. Such crimes as fraud, embezzlement, and sabotage are easy to commit for knowledgeable computer users. Businesses therefore need to be vigilant and informed about actions they may take to prevent computer crimes or to prosecute if necessary.

Laws Applicable to Computer Hardware and Software

computer law
Laws related to the protection of computer hardware or software or to the illegal use of computers or computer technology.

Computer laws are those laws that are related to the protection of computer hardware or software or to the illegal use of computers or computer technology. The unique aspect of computer law deals more with software than with hardware. *Software* concerns the programming involved with a computer; it is often divided into operational and application programs. Computer hardware is regarded as equipment. In most cases, the hardware is movable, and so it is tangible personal property. Contract law is applicable when it is purchased, leased, or sold. The relationship between contract and personal property laws is discussed in Chapter 9.

Even if software is sold with the hardware, courts have held that a sale of goods takes place. However, if only software is sold, such as to a business that already has its computer hardware, many courts have held that no goods are involved. Thus, contract law, not sales law, applies to that transaction. Other courts, referring to the existence of a tangible disk or tape and manuals, have applied sales law to the lease or sale of computer software. Over a decade ago, the courts determined that computer programs are property that could be copyrighted. Another problem the law has resolved is that the theft, unauthorized use, or destruction of the data in a computer's memory constitutes a violation of criminal laws. A variety of different computer crimes may be committed. Someone may enter false data into a computer's memory (indicating a fictitious person has a bank account or insurance policy), alter or destroy files (erase records of loans owed or of telephone calls made), make unauthorized use of a computer system (access a competitor's data or classified military information), or commit theft by computer (have bank funds transferred to an account in a thief's name and then withdraw the funds from the bank).

Computer Crime

computer crime
Any illegal act that requires knowledge of computer technology or the use of a computer.

A **computer crime** is any illegal act requiring knowledge of computer technology or involving the use of a computer. As both the ethical and criminal aspects of computer crime are discussed in Chapter 22, this chapter provides only a brief review of computer crime. There are two categories of computer crime. First, a computer may be used as a tool in committing a crime. In one case involving insurance fraud, employees of an insurance company entered fictitious names of new policyholders into their company's computer system. The company then used the computer's list of its policyholder names to obtain financing. When the fraudulent scheme was uncovered, the value of the company's stock declined, and several company officials were convicted for their criminal actions.

A second category of computer crime occurs when information stored on a computer is stolen or damaged. As computer microchips allow thousands of pages of data to be stored in a computer's memory, many businesses store customer account information, financial data, and product inventory records in computer files. Like other valuable property, the records and data may be damaged or stolen. Damage may occur when someone introduces a computer virus program into the computer records. The virus may alter or destroy existing records. A theft occurs when there is any unauthorized entry into a computer system. As the *McGraw* case in Chapter 22 notes, the theft of computer time may be regarded as a criminal act. Access to a computer system by illegal means may allow the thief to find out financial, personnel, or trade secret information about a company.

Laws Affecting Computer Crimes Computer crimes are addressed several ways by the law. The definitions of some general criminal acts, such as the unauthorized taking of property, have been interpreted to apply to computer crimes as well as to other crimes. Thus, the definition of property in a theft statute also applies to software, business information, and customer lists.

Similarly, many states have enacted specific laws addressing specific computer-related crimes. Computer trespass, computer tampering, the unauthorized use of computer files, and the unauthorized use of computerized data are among the acts considered criminal.

There is also some protection against computer crimes in the federal laws. The Fair Credit Reporting Act (discussed in Chapter 11) makes illegal the unauthorized access to credit reporting information. The Semiconductor Chip Protection Act provides a special system of legal protection for mask works (the layout design) used in the production of semiconductor chips. It confers the exclusive right to reproduce and distribute mask works for 10 years, subject to registration by the Copyright Office. In addition, we have noted that copyright law applies to computer programs and that the unauthorized use or reproduction of copyrighted material is both a tort and a crime.

Finally, the Counterfeit Access Device and Computer Fraud and Abuse Act of 1984 makes it a crime to use or access federal or private computers without authorization in several situations. Accessing a computer to get classified military or foreign policy information is a felony if done with the intent to harm the United States or to benefit another country. Unauthorized access to financial records of federal financial institutions (banks, savings and loans, credit unions, and registered securities brokers) is also prohibited by this law.

Entertainment and Computer Software

Ethical Dilemma

Ethical dilemmas have been emerging in other areas of intangible property. For example, should television or movie actors, or recording artists have the right to control when and where their movies are viewed or their records are heard? The question seemed to be settled before videocassette recorders (VCRs) began selling widely. Music broadcast over the radio may be recorded legally by listeners for replay later, so long as they do not attempt to pirate the music by reselling it for profit.

Now that stereo manufacturers are selling digital audiotape (DAT), this question is again becoming clouded. The video- and audiotaping techniques of the past produced imperfect copies of the original. Static and distortion introduced in the broadcasting and recording processes made copies less desirable than the original. However, DAT and recordable CDs permit an exact copy to be produced. This may give pirates an incentive to reproduce a copyrighted work, which, in turn, would prevent the copyright holder from receiving "just" compensation. An ethical dilemma arises because the property rights of the copyright holder are outside the copyright holder's exclusive physical control. This motivates pirates to misappropriate the copyrighted work. Music companies have made arrangements requiring DAT recorder manufacturers to include a device making such recordings impossible.

A similar problem arises with computer software. The ability of personal computers to precisely duplicate software has led many software companies to include devices that make unauthorized copying difficult (copy protection). An ethical dilemma confronts software owners whose private access to the computer source code enables them to duplicate the software. If they make duplicate copies for their backup purposes, the copyright owner suffers no loss. However, if the copies are used by others who might have purchased the software, the copyright owner may be deprived of revenue. A tougher ethical question arises when the software duplicator simply seeks to test a software program before actually purchasing it. If the duplicator is favorably impressed with the software and purchases it, this may actually benefit the software owner. Despite this potentially favorable impact on software owners, software piracy is illegal unless the license permits duplication, or the software is in the public domain. Both civil and criminal penalties can be imposed on those who violate the software copyright law. Many corporations are strictly enforcing rules prohibiting software pirating by their employees.

Ownership and Transfer of Personal Property

It is possible to transfer the right to use or have custody of items of personal property without transferring the ownership of those items. When only the right to use or maintain custody of personal property is involved, a bailment is created. Bailments are widely used in personal and business transactions and selected personal property laws deal with bailments. The ownership of personal property is to be transferred either during a person's life or at death. Transfers during a person's lifetime may be made either by sale or by gift. At death, personal property may be transferred by making a valid will. In the absence of a will, state intestacy laws determine the recipients of a decedent's personal property.

Bailments

bailment
The transfer of possession and custody of property without a transfer of ownership.

A **bailment** arises if one person transfers or loans personal property to another person for a specific purpose. For example, if John gives a watch to a jeweler for repair, a bailment occurs. The jeweler is the *bailee* (custodian of the property transferred) who must exercise reasonable care over the *bailor's* property (John's watch) while it is in the bailee's custody. By contrast, transfer of the possession of personal property that is also intended to transfer its title (the right to ownership of the property or evidence thereof) is either a sale or a gift. A valid will may postpone the transfer of personal property until after death.

Transfer of Title

Sale The most common method of transferring the title to personal property is a *sale.* State contract laws generally regulate the methods for effecting sales of goods. Article 2 of the Uniform Commercial Code, enacted into law in 49 states, is the primary source of such regulation. Most of the states also have special statutory provisions for the sale of motor vehicles, such as cars, trucks, or motor homes. Such contracts are discussed further in Chapters 9 and 10.

Gift Personal property may also be transferred by a gift. A gift made by a living person is referred to as an **intervivos gift**. A gift of personal property is valid if the donor intends to make the gift and delivers possession of the item. Actual delivery of the item is not necessary if something is done to evidence the transfer of ownership. For example, transferring the keys and title certificate of a car is sufficient to transfer the title to the car, and putting the donee's name on a savings account book is sufficient to transfer the money in the account.

inter vivos gift
A gift of personal property made by a living person.

Transfer at Death An owner of personal property may transfer it at death by making a valid will. The will may specify who is to take specific personal property owned by the decedent: "I give my automobile to my sister Susan." The will may also make a general statement such as, "I give all the furniture in my home to my wife Sally." Even a statement such as, "All the remainder of the property I own I give to my daughter Julie" will transfer the title to personal property at a person's death.

If a person dies without a valid will, state laws, known as **intestacy laws,** provide a method for distributing the decedent's property to the surviving heirs. The spouse and children and then the parents and siblings of the decedent are usually the recipients of property that is transferred by a state's intestacy laws. The law of the state where the decedent was domiciled (had a primary residence) is applied to the disposition of personal property. The laws governing the transfer of personal property differ from those that govern the descent of real property. The law of the state where the real property is located controls that transfer.

intestacy laws
The state laws that provide for the distribution of property of a decedent who died without a valid will.

State laws also define the process for determining whether a will of a decedent is valid and what property is transferred at death. Thus, **probate laws** specify the number of witnesses who must have seen the testator make her or his will and the proof that is needed to show the required competency to transfer property at death. Probate laws also provide for the appointment of a personal representative to administer a decedent's property until it can be transferred to those heirs who are to receive it. Probate laws do not affect the property that a person has transferred to others prior to death. Thus, property that is owned by two people as joint tenants with each having survivorship rights, life insurance benefits, and property already transferred to a trust is not subject to the probate process.

probate laws
The laws defining the process for determining if a decedent had a valid will and what property is transferred and who inherits it at the decedent's death.

Ownership of Real Property

The law recognizes different interests in real property; for example, the ownership of things under, on, or above land may be separated. Several interests in the same piece of land may exist at the same time. Those interests can be grouped into three categories: possessory interests, nonpossessory interests, and undivided interests.

Types of Possessory Interests

estate
The nature, quantity, and quality of a person's interest in real property.

Estates in land and leasehold interests concern rights that relate to the possession of land. The term ***estate*** is used in real property law to indicate the nature, quantity, and quality of an ownership interest. The extent of an estate is determined by its duration and by when the rights to possess and enjoy it begin. These rights may include life estate, leasehold estate, and dower rights.

life estate
An interest in real property that gives a person the right to use it for as long as some designated person is alive.

Life Estate A **life estate** gives a person the right to use property during his or her life (the life could also be that of another person). After that time, the owner loses any interest in the property, and another person receives the remainder of the ownership interest. For example, if an elderly parent transfers a residence to a child while retaining a life estate, the parent has the use of the residence for life, but the child will receive the ownership when the parent dies.

leasehold estate
A possessory interest in property that allows a person to possess real property for a designated term.

Leasehold Estate A **leasehold estate** is a possesory interest in property that allows a person (the lessee or tenant) to possess real property owned by another party (lessor) for a designated term. The lessee has the right to possess and control the property during the term of the lease. Leases are commonly used in business for both personal and real property. Where law prevents a person or a company from owning property, long-term leases (such as 99-year leases) are quite common. One of the most famous leases is the lease granted to Great Britain by China in 1897; it granted Great Britain the right to rule the territory known as Hong Kong for a period of 100 years, or until 1997. As the reversionary owner of the property, Hong Kong comes under Chinese rule as of July 1, 1997.

dower interest
The interest in land owned by a decedent granted to his or her surviving spouse.

Dower Interest A **dower interest** is an interest in land granting a surviving spouse either a life interest in or full ownership of some portion of the deceased spouse's real property. While originally the dower interest was available only to the surviving wife, most state laws now grant a dower interest to either a male or female surviving spouse.

The Leasehold Estate

The leasehold estate or lease is the most common possessory interest in real property. The tenant's interest in the property is called a *leasehold,* and the landlord's interest is called a *reversionary interest.* Both the landlord and the tenant may transfer their interests to other people unless their lease agreement restricts this right. Residential leases commonly require the landlord's written approval of any transfer by the tenant.

assignment
The transfer by a tenant of all his or her rights in a leasehold estate to another person.

Assignment of Lease If the lease does not prohibit assignment, a tenant may assign a leasehold interest in property by transferring that interest to an assignee. However, the assignee does not replace the tenant on the lease agreement. A lease **assignment** grants the assignee all the rights the tenant had, such as the right to live in an apartment. An assignment also imposes the tenant's duties on the assignee, such as the duty to pay the rent. However, the tenant must pay the rent if the assignee does not.

Suppose that Cari, who leases and manages a frozen yogurt store on Main Street, decides to leave that location for a better location on North Rose Street, and that Jim contracts with her to take over her lease on the Main Street store in an assignment. Jim is the *assignee,* the person to whom the assignment is made, and Cari is the *assignor,* the person who makes the assignment. Jim becomes a party to the original lease agreement with the owner. He must pay the rent on the Main Street store, but Cari remains secondarily liable if he fails to do so.

Sublease In a **sublease,** the subtenant has a contract only with the tenant, not with the owner, and the subtenant does not receive all of the tenant's rights. Subleases are for a shorter period than that of the original lease. For example, assume that Cari, who has a two-year lease on a yogurt shop, decides to vacation in Hawaii for 10 months and therefore subleases the shop to Jim for one year. After that year, Cari will still have one year left on her lease. In this sublease, Jim is not a party to the lease made with the owner. Cari still owes the rent for the entire two years of her lease, but the sublease entitles her to receive from Jim the rent due under the sublease agreement. Jim's rights are based only on the sublease terms, not on the lease between Cari and the owner. Figure 7–4 illustrates the differences between an assignment and a sublease.

sublease The transfer by a tenant of some but not all of his or her rights in a leasehold estate to another person.

FIGURE 7–4 Comparison of Assignment and Sublease of Real Property

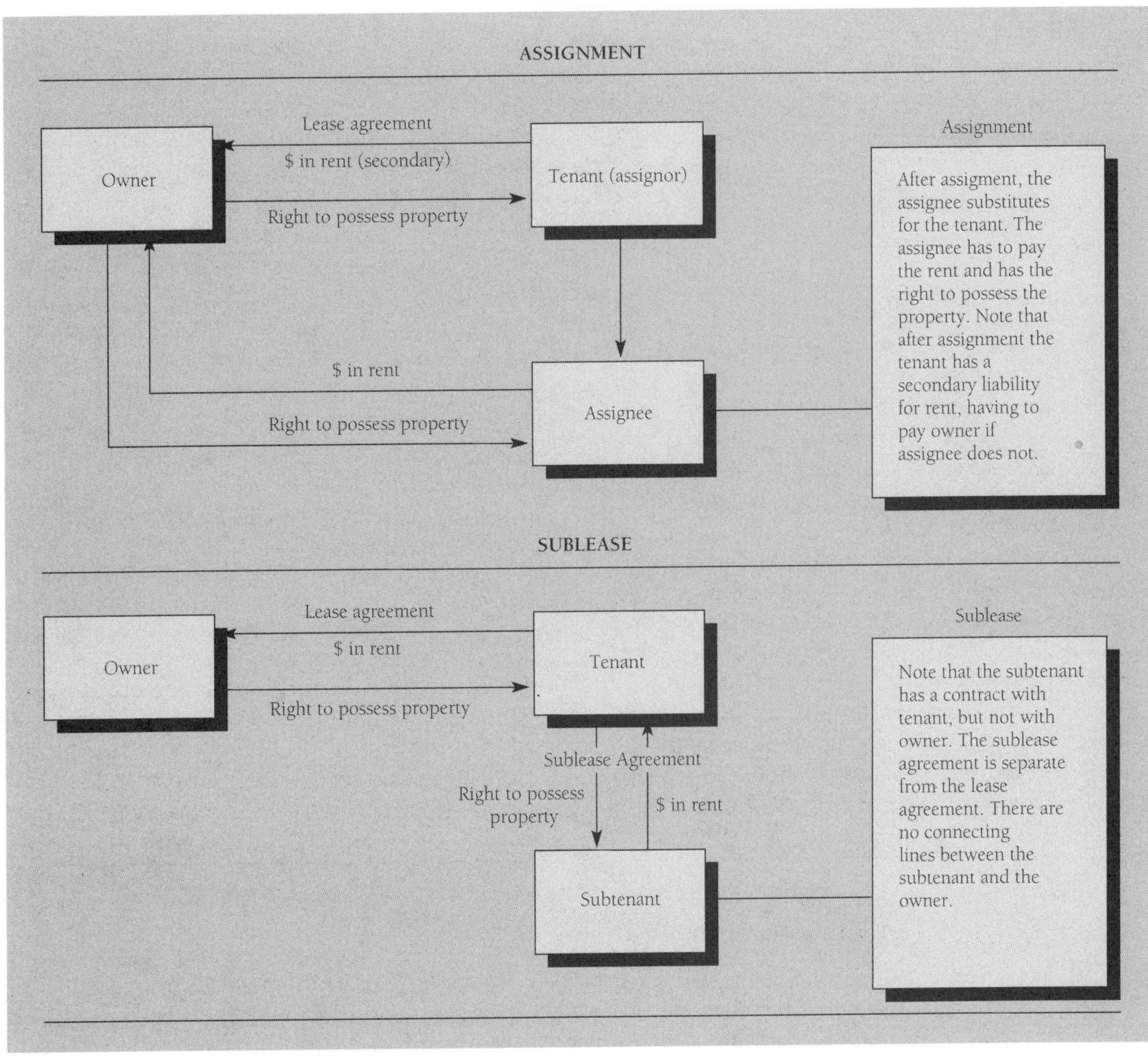

An assignee receives the rights granted in the original lease between the landlord and the tenant, while a subtenant receives none of those rights. The subtenant's rights and duties arise solely from the sublease agreement. In the following case, a clause in the lease between Conklin and Acme prohibited Acme from assigning its lease without obtaining written permission from Conklin. However, the lease agreement did not expressly prohibit a sublease. What factors did the court examine to determine whether Acme's transfer was a permissible sublease or a prohibited assignment?

Conklin Development v. Acme Markets, Inc.

453 N.Y.S.2d 930 (1982)
Supreme Court, Appellate Division

The Plaintiff, Conklin Development, signed a contract leasing space in a shopping mall to the defendant, Acme Markets. The lease agreement prohibited assignment of the lease by Acme but allowed Acme to sublease the space. Conklin claimed that Acme had violated the lease by assigning its lease interest to P & C Markets (P & C). Acme asserted that its agreement with P & C was a permitted sublease because Acme's lease term expired on May 31, 1983, whereas P & C's term expired on May 1, 1983.

Memorandum Decision

There is no question that the agreement between Acme and P & C was a sublease, not an assignment. In order to constitute an assignment, the transfer from the original lessee must convey the entire interest of the lessee. If he retains a reversionary interest in the real property transferred, privity of estate does not arise between the landlord and the transferee. [*Privity of estate* is the mutual or successive relationship to the same rights in property.] . . . The transfer under such circumstances constitutes a sublease, and the relation of landlord and tenant does not exist between the original lessor and the transferee.

The instrument between Acme and P & C specifically reserves unto Acme the right to exercise the renewal options in the prime lease, distinctly and explicitly subordinates any renewals of the sublease to Acme's right to exercise renewal options of the prime lease and recites that Acme remains liable to plaintiff for the performance of the obligations of the prime lease. Based on these provisions, Special Term correctly found the instrument to be a sublease.

Having found that the Acme-P & C agreement was a sublease and not an assignment, no privity of contract or estate between plaintiff and . . . P & C could exist.

Affirmed.

Case Questions

1. What issue determines the outcome of this case?
2. What is meant by the term *privity of estate* as it applies to this case?
3. If the agreement between Acme and P & C was a sublease, what rights did Conklin have in the sublease?

Nonpossessory Interests

A second category of real property interests grants a limited use or enjoyment of property that does not involve exclusive possession. Easements, licenses, and liens exemplify nonpossessory property interests.

Easements An **easement** is a nonpossessory interest permitting its owner to make limited use of some portion of another's property. An easement might allow a gas or electric utility company to install and service underground cable. It might also grant an adjoining landowner access to a landlocked parcel. For example, if Anna owns land that backs onto a lakefront, and Brad's land is across the street from Anna's front yard, Brad might have an easement over a portion of Anna's land, permitting him to cross her land to get to the lakefront.

easement
A nonpossessory interest in land allowing its owner to make limited use of some portion of another's property.

Licenses Insofar as real property is concerned, a **license,** like an easement, is a nonpossessory interest which allows one party (the licensee) to use another party's (the licensor) land for a limited purpose. However unlike an easement, a license is generally personal in nature and revocable by the property owner. A license is granted, not to the owner of a specific lot (say, the owner of the property across the street), but to a specific person. When land is sold, an easement is generally transferred to the new owner, but a license is not. Thus, a license might permit a neighbor to cut wood on the owner's property or to use the lakefront at the back of the owner's lot. However, it does not grant that privilege to the purchaser of the licensee's property, and it can be disregarded by the purchaser of the licensor's property.

license
A nonpossessory interest in land, personal in nature and revocable by its grantor, which allows the owner of the license the right to use the land of another (the grantor) for a limited purpose.

Liens A **lien** gives one person a nonpossessory, collateral-like interest in another person's property. Typically, a lien is granted to a lender who accepts it as security against a borrower's promise to repay a debt. A *mortgage* is a common type of lien on real property. Liens also exist on personal property. For example, when a mechanic does repair work on a car, a *mechanic's lien* is generally created by statute. If you do not pay the repair cost, the mechanic can sell the car and use the proceeds to pay the repair bill. In most types of personal property, security interests such as liens are governed by Article 9 of the UCC, which is discussed in Chapter 11.

lien
An interest in property, real or personal, that gives one person a collateral-like interest in another person's property.

Undivided Interests

The third category of real property interests is comprised of those held by several parties jointly. Some methods may be selected by the parties; others are imposed by law.

Co-ownership Property may be co-owned by taking title to it either as joint tenants or as tenants in common. If joint tenancy is selected, each of the joint tenants has an equal right to possess the entire property, and no joint tenant can exclude the others from possession. If there are only two tenants and either dies, the survivor becomes the sole owner of the property. Such joint tenancy, referred to as **joint tenancy with rights of survivorship,** generally must be intentionally created.

A **tenancy in common** also allows each co-owner an undivided right to possess the entire property. It does not, however, include a right of survivorship. If one tenant dies, the court generally partitions the property, giving a portion of it to each cotenant and also to the deceased co-owner's heirs. For example, assume two people own an apartment building, a boat, or a store as tenants in common. If one of the co-owners dies, the decedent's heirs, not the surviving cotenant, usually inherit his or her share.

joint tenancy with right of survivorship
The ownership of property by at least two people that automatically transfers the interest of one party to the other upon that party's death.

tenancy in common
An interest in property owned by two or more people that gives each an undivided right to possess the property and gives the property to a party's heirs upon death.

Community property ownership The laws of several states, mostly in the Southwest, consider a husband and wife co-owners of all property acquired during their marriage, regardless of who purchased or paid for it. For example, if cars, furniture, or jewelry are purchased by one spouse, and title is placed in only that spouse's name, community property law nevertheless treats the property as belonging equally to both spouses. Gifts, individually inherited property, and separate property owned prior to or after the marriage are generally not considered community property: Such items may be kept separately by each spouse.

Condominium and cooperative ownership Many people desire to share ownership in real property yet maintain their own living space. This may be done through condominium or cooperative ownership. For example, individual control over a specific area (an apartment) may be given to each owner of an apartment building, while the common areas (the pool, lobby, hallways, and outside lawn area) may be co-owned by all the owners. Each owner of a *condominium* owns an individual apartment unit and agrees to share the upkeep expenses of the common areas. Owners may sell individual units at will.

By contrast, a corporation usually owns *cooperative* buildings or developments. Occupants of individual units buy shares in the corporation and then lease a unit from it. In many cooperatives, each shareholder-owner must obtain the approval of the other shareholder-owners before selling or subleasing an individual unit.

Sale or Transfer of Real Property

Transfer by sale is the most common and the most important method of obtaining title to real estate. Contract law, discussed in Chapter 9, plays an important role in most real estate transactions because purchase and sale of real estate is based on the contract made by the parties.

Most people participate in several real estate transactions during their lives. Lease provisions and landlord–tenant laws are most relevant to apartment tenants. The purchase of a home may occur several times during a person's life. Small firms often buy buildings for office space, and larger firms often build and develop numerous parcels of real estate in locations across the country and perhaps throughout the world. Because numerous legal documents must be prepared and reviewed in any real estate transaction, the advice of an attorney and the assistance of real estate agents should be sought before any of the steps discussed below are taken.

The Sales Agreement

A seller of real estate usually contacts a real estate agent to establish the terms of sale. The seller and agent must agree on how long the agent will have the right to list the property for sale. The seller may give the agent the exclusive right to list the property. Such listing contracts usually require the payment of a commission to the agent after he or she produces a person who is "ready, willing, and able" to purchase the property. Even if the seller later decides not to sell to that person, the real estate agent may usually collect the commission because he or she has successfully performed the obligations of the listing contract.

A contract to sell real property is generally prepared in one of two ways. For many residential real estate transactions, the seller or the seller's agent prepares a document known as the *purchase agreement* or *offer to purchase.* Standardized form contracts that have blanks for the insertion of variable information are often used. This document becomes the contract after being signed by the purchaser and accepted and signed by the seller.

The contract must be in writing to be enforceable. It details the purchase price to be paid, the type of deed to be provided by the seller, the seller's obligations regarding the title to the property, and the financing terms. As the purchaser generally must obtain mortgage financing, the purchase agreement is usually contingent on obtaining the mortgage on specified terms. Any personal property that is to be included in the sale, such as drapes, major appliances, or furniture, also is listed in this agreement.

For most commercial real estate transactions, the parties do not begin with a formal contract or a document prepared by one of them. Instead, they first negotiate the terms, and then one of them prepares a contract reflecting the negotiated terms. The terms of their agreement are usually found in the contract they sign at the end of negotiations.

The Legal Documents

After the contract has been signed by the parties, both the seller and the purchaser must perform certain actions to consummate their transaction. The seller must provide satisfactory proof of title to the property being sold. Depending on local custom, either title insurance (an insurance company's policy that the seller has title to the property) or an abstract of title (a history of the transactions transferring title to property), with an attorney's opinion of its appropriateness, generally satisfies this requirement. A survey of the property or a termite inspection may be required. A certificate showing that the local property taxes have been paid is usually needed. The seller's mortgage lender must be notified so that its loan balance is paid and its security interest in the property is discharged.

Generally, after the contract is signed, the purchaser will try to obtain a lender's commitment to finance some portion of the purchase price to be paid to the seller. A lender that commits to lend the money needed for the purchase price will require the purchaser-borrower to sign a promissory note and mortgage agreement.

The Mortgage A **mortgage** gives the lender an ownership interest in the property being purchased. It creates a security interest or lien to provide collateral for the *promissory note* that evidences the purchaser's debt. The purchaser-borrower is known as the *mortgagor,* and the lender is known as the *mortgagee.* If the proof of title and other documents furnished by the seller are acceptable to the mortgagor and the mortgagee, a closing date for the sale is set.

mortgage
The lien interest in property retained by an individual or firm providing financing to the purchaser of the property.

The Deed The *closing* of the real property sale is an event at which the parties sign and exchange several documents. The seller provides the purchaser with a deed to the property. Generally, the deed is a **warranty deed,** one that warrants or guarantees that the title is good and free of any liens or encumbrances by others who might have an interest in the property. A warranty deed must include certain words to effectively transfer the property. A typical warranty deed appears in Figure 7–5.

warranty deed
The deed a seller of property usually transfers to a purchaser; it warrants that the title is good and free of claims by others.

If the purchaser agrees, the seller may instead promise to transfer only whatever interest the seller has in the property by using a *quitclaim deed.* Such deeds are not used in most sales because if it turns out that the seller does not own the property, a quitclaim deed transfers nothing to the purchaser. Quitclaim deeds are used in transactions between spouses, partners, or joint tenants. A quitclaim deed is sufficient to transfer the legal interest in property owned by the seller to the purchaser, where the parties know each other and the purchaser knows the interest owned by the seller.

FIGURE 7-5 Warranty Deed

The Grantor(s) ROBERT A. BROWN AND MARILYN B. BROWN, HUSBAND AND WIFE AS JOINT TENANTS, whose address is 4488 S. 15th ST., GRAND RAPIDS, MI convey(s) and warrant(s) to THOMAS A. STEVENSON AND MARY R. STEVENSON, HUSBAND AND WIFE AS JOINT TENANTS, whose address is 1803 W. PARK ST., LANSING, MI the following described premises situated in the CITY of GRAND RAPIDS, County of KENT and state of Michigan:

LOT 47 OF THE WEST PORT PLAT IN THE CITY OF GRAND JUNCTION, MASON COUNTY, MICHIGAN, EXCEPT THE WEST 20 FEET THEREOF, ACCORDING TO THE PLAT THEREOF AS RECORDED IN LIBER 1 OF PLATS ON PAGE 69, KENT COUNTY RECORDS

for the sum of ONE HUNDRED THOUSAND AND NO/100 DOLLARS ($100,000.00) subject to easements and building and use restrictions of record and further subject to

NO OTHER ENCUMBRANCES.

Dated this 8TH day of JANUARY, 1995

Signed in the presence of:	Signed by:
* MARTHA BLACK	* ROBERT A. BROWN
* JAMES GREEN	* MARILYN B. BROWN
	*
	*

STATE OF MICHIGAN } SS
COUNTY OF KENT }

The foregoing instrument was acknowledged before me this 8TH day of JANUARY, 1995 by

ROBERT A. BROWN AND MARILYN B. BROWN

* PATRICIA SAEL
Notary Public, KENT County,
Michigan
My commission expires: DECEMBER 13, 1995

County Treasurer's Certificate	City Treasurer's Certificate	
When recorded Return To: JOHN ALLEN ALLEN & BOOTH P.C. (name) 433 W. STATE STREET (street address) GRAND RAPIDS, MI (city and state)	Send Subsequent Tax Bills To: THOMAS A. STEVENSON 4488 S. 15TH ST. GRAND RAPIDS, MI	Drafted by JOHN ALLEN Business Address ALLEN & BOOTH P. C. 433 W. STATE ST. GRAND RAPIDS, MI

Tax Parcel * ____________ Recording Fee ____________ Transfer Fee ____________

*TYPE OR PRINT NAMES UNDER SIGNATURES.

Other Documents Along with the warranty deed, the seller and the mortgage lender provide a closing statement that itemizes what amounts the purchaser is to pay. After reviewing the deed, the proof of title documents, and the closing statement, the purchaser and the mortgagee-lender pay the purchase price, less any credits for money paid.

Recording Then, the lender or the purchaser records the deed. All important documents affecting the title to real property must be recorded—entered into the public record. Deeds, mortgages, long-term leases, easements, liens, and assignments are generally recorded to provide notice to other parties of the various interests in specific parcels of real property. Although an unrecorded deed is effective between the purchaser and the seller, it has no effect on the rights of any third parties to their transaction. Recording a document such as a deed or a mortgage gives notice to the world that a certain person has an interest in particular real estate. Thus, persons interested in purchasing must consult the record to determine who claims an interest in the property to be purchased.

Legal Control of Real Property

The most stringent control on real property regulates who can own it. Such control is uncommon in the United States, but some governments restrict the right of aliens to own real property. In Saudi Arabia, for example, foreign businesses or individuals are usually not allowed to own real property. They must lease it from local owners, or have a trust hold title for their benefit. In the United States, state laws generally prohibit minors from owning real property while permitting them to own personal property. Some of the states limit the ownership of certain real estate by foreigners.

The most common controls over real property are found in federal environmental restrictions, state nuisance laws, and local land use regulations. For example, federal environmental laws and regulations restrict the development of property in coastal areas and where wildlife habitats exist. This topic is discussed more extensively in Chapter 21. State nuisance laws grant relief to persons adversely affected by another person's use of property. Zoning ordinances and development regulations restrict the types of buildings that property owners may erect or the activities that they may engage in on their property.

These laws, regulations, and ordinances are imposed primarily to benefit the general public. Private restrictions, though not favored by the law, are enforced if they are reasonable and if they benefit other property owners. Finally, property may be taken by the government through its power of **eminent domain** if the property is needed for a public purpose and the owner is adequately compensated.

eminent domain The power of the government to take private land for public purposes if adequate compensation is paid.

Nuisance Laws

State **nuisance laws,** which are a part of tort law, provides that an owner of real property cannot use it in a way that injures others. A *private nuisance* exists if an owner's use of real property deprives others of their right to use and enjoy their own property. The playing of a loud stereo through the night might be a private nuisance to a neighbor. A *public nuisance* involves conduct that affects a broad group of people. A back-to-school block party attracting thousands of students and other individuals to several residences might constitute both a private nuisance and a public nuisance. A private nuisance might occur because neighbors are unable to use and enjoy their

nuisance laws Laws that provide that an owner of real property cannot use it in a way that injures others.

property. A public nuisance might occur because members of the public are unable to use streets and walkways for travel. Public nuisance cases are usually brought by the government; whereas, private nuisance cases are brought by individuals.

How should a court resolve a dispute when residents in an apartment complex complain that the periodic rock music concerts in the neighboring shopping center interfere with their right to peace and quiet?

McQuade v. Tucson Tiller Apartments, Ltd.

543 P.2d 150 (1975)
Arizona Court of Appeals

Tucson Tiller Apartments (Tiller) is located next to the McQuade shopping center, Plaza Antigua. The trial court found that in the past two years McQuade has held 5 to 10 rock music events that attracted between 3,000 and 7,000 people. The court found that the noise from these events was so loud as to interfere with the reasonable use of Tiller's property and that the McQuade premises could not accommodate such large crowds without interfering with the reasonable use of Tiller's property. The trial court enjoined McQuade from holding concerts with loud music and from holding mass attendance events larger than its property could handle. McQuade, referred to in the opinion as the appellant and defendant, sought review by the court of appeals.

Hathaway, Judge

It is undisputed that appellants intend to continue holding mass music events. The purpose of these concerts is to promote the businesses in Plaza Antigua. As this is a continuing business practice, we will treat this case as one involving a continuing nuisance rather than an anticipated nuisance. The fact that the injury is only occasional does not prevent an injunction.

Music does not constitute a nuisance per se, but it may become a nuisance because of loud noise or the attraction of large crowds. Noise, to be enjoined, must produce substantial injury and annoy the normal person.

In determining whether the acts constitute a nuisance, the court should consider all the circumstances, including the locality and character of the surroundings, the nature of the defendant's business and the manner in which it is conducted, the value to the community of the defendant's activities, the defendant's ability to reduce the harm, and the extent to which the defendant would be damaged by an injunction and the plaintiff damaged by the failure to enjoin. The court can also consider priority of use.

In sum, the court looks at the reasonableness of the defendant's activities in the locality. This involves a balancing test.

Here the area is neither residential nor industrial. Appellants' mass musical events are not of great utility to the community. Although appellants can take steps to reduce the harm, any improvements will be minor so long as the loud music and large crowds continue. Appellants are not greatly harmed by this injunction. The mass events are not necessary to running the shopping center, and appellants are free to engage in other activities which advertise their shopping center.

On the other hand, if the injunction is not upheld, appellee's tenants will continue to suffer from the long days of loud noise, parking problems, trespass, and other annoyances.

Applying a balance test, we have no hesitancy in holding appellee's right to use and enjoyment outweighs appellants' interest in continuing to hold loud, mass attendance events.

It is conceded that appellants held events at their shopping center before appellee's apartments were built. However, coming to the nuisance is not a complete defense, but only one factor to consider along with the others. That portion of the injunction prohibiting loud noise and crowds greater than appellants' property can accommodate is upheld.

The injunction is affirmed as modified.

Case Questions

1. What test was used by the court to determine whether the rock music events at the plaza constituted a nuisance?
2. If the shopping center was there before the apartments were built, would the shopping center have the right to continue using the property as it did previously?

Zoning and Development Restrictions

Local governments have **police power,** the power to impose reasonable regulations that promote the public health, safety, morals, and general welfare of their community. **Zoning ordinances** are laws that restrict the use of real property in furtherance of these objectives. Such ordinances generally regulate the structure, size, and design of buildings, the density of population, the size of lots, the setback requirements for the placing of buildings, aesthetics, and the use of property for commercial, residential, or industrial purposes.

police power
Laws that allow state or local governments to impose reasonable regulations that promote the public health, safety, morals, and general welfare of a community.

Many local governments also have ordinances that impose regulations on the development of vacant real property within their jurisdiction. For example, sewer and water requirements must be met, and street or road plans must be approved before any development can begin. In some cases, open spaces must be set aside by real estate developers for use as parks and public facilities. Some large planned developments have been allowed to combine various uses of the entire property, such as residential and commercial uses, in one area despite the limitations that zoning ordinances impose in other areas. Such developments are known as *planned unit developments (puds).* As people have become more aware of the limitations of land use controls at the local level, there has been a trend to move some of these legal controls to the regional or state level. Local land use control laws are sometimes ineffective because developers may move to adjacent communities or nearby unregulated areas. In other cases, conflicting local regulations leave regions with patchwork designs rather than systematic patterns that emerge from coordinated activities.

zoning ordinances
A local law that restricts the use of real property in furtherance of benefiting the general public.

Enforcement of Private Restrictions

A private agreement limiting the use of real property is called a **restrictive covenant.** Such covenants are usually written directly into the deeds to properties when these are sold by the real estate developer so that purchasers of properties in a development are bound to the consistent use of the properties. Thus, purchasers of any parcel of property will receive a deed requiring them to abide by the restrictions imposed for the benefit of the owners of the remaining properties in the development. For example, a deed may require that all garages be attached to houses or that all buildings on lots be set back a stipulated distance from lot lines.

restrictive convenant
Private agreement restricting the use of real property.

Restrictive covenants generally *run with the land.* This means that the restrictions are imposed on whoever buys the land and are not canceled by its sale. Restrictive covenants commonly require that houses built on property be at least a certain size and limit the use of property to residential purposes. Thus, restrictive covenants are often similar to zoning regulations in the limits they impose on the owners of property.

However, because restrictions originate from an owner of private property and limit the use of property by other owners, they are not favored by the law. Nevertheless, they are generally enforced if they benefit the other property owners whom they were intended to benefit. At one time, some deeds contained restrictions prohibiting persons of certain races from owning the deeded property. A 1947 U.S. Supreme Court decision made such restrictions unenforceable.

The Power of Eminent Domain

Eminent domain is the power of the government to take private property without the owner's consent. There is clear constitutional authority for acquisitions of private property by the government—including federal, state, and local units and even private corporations that have been delegated this power by the appropriate government. However, several limitations are imposed on the exercise of eminent domain.

First, the property must be taken for a public purpose. Clearly, this requirement is met if the property is needed for the building of a school, a new road, or a prison facility. Second, the property owner must be adequately compensated. This requirement is a firm component of the concept of eminent domain in the United States, though not in some other countries. Third, the property owner is entitled to due process of law before the property is taken. Thus, a hearing regarding the need for the property and the adequacy of the compensation must be held prior to its taking. Finally, the government may be considered to have "taken" privately owned property if it imposes significant limitations on the uses of that property. In such a case, the owner will be entitled to compensation for that taking.

That was the decision in a recent Supreme Court case, which in a 5–4 decision reversed the decision of the local city authorities, the Court of Appeals, and the Oregon Supreme Court.

Dolan v. City of Tigard

114 S. Ct. 2309 (1994)
United States Supreme Court

Florence Dolan owns a plumbing and electrical supply shop on Main Street in Tigard, Oregon. She applied to the city for a permit to nearly double the size of her 9,700 square feet store. The City Planning Commission granted her permit application subject to two conditions. First, she was to dedicate the portion of her property that was within the 100-year floodplain for improvement of a storm drainage system along Fanno Creek, which flowed along the western boundary of her property. Second, she was to dedicate an additional 15-foot strip of land adjacent to the floodplain as a pedestrian/bicycle pathway. Ms. Dolan requested a variance from those conditions from the City Planning Commission. They denied her request as they found a relationship between the dedicated conditions and the projected impact of her project. She then appealed to the Land Use Board of Appeals, but they also found reasonable relationships between her project and the conditions imposed on her expansion. The Oregon Court of Appeals and the Supreme Court of Oregon affirmed those local decisions.

Rhenquist, C.J, delivered the opinion of the Court.

The Takings Clause of the Fifth Amendment of the United States Constitution, made applicable to the States through the Fourteenth Amendment, provides: "(N)or shall private property be taken for public use, without just compensation." One of the principal purposes of the Takings Clause is to bar government from forcing some people alone to bear public burdens which, in all fairness, should be borne by the public as a whole. Without question, had a city simply required petitioner to dedicate a strip of land along Fanno Creek for public use, rather than conditioning the grant of her permit to redevelop her property on such dedication, a taking would have occurred. Such public access would deprive petitioner of the right to exclude others, one of the most essential sticks in the bundle of rights that are commonly characterized as property.

On the other side of the ledger, the authority of the state and local government to engage in land use planning has been untainted against constitutional challenges long ago as our decision in *Euclid v. Ambler Realty Co. (1926).* Government hardly could go on if to some extent values incident to property could not be diminished without paying for every such change in the general law. A land use regulation does not effect a taking if it substantially advances legitimate state interests and does not deny an owner economically viable use of his land.

The sort of land regulations discussed in the cases just cited, however, differs in two respects from the present case. First, they involve essentially legislative determinations classifying entire areas of the city, whereas here the city made an adjudicative decision to condition petitioner's application for a building permit on an individual parcel. Second, the conditions imposed were not simply a limitation on the use petitioner might make of her own parcel, but a requirement that she deed portions of the property to the city. . . . Under the well-settled doctrine of constitutional conditions, the government may not require a person to give up a constitutional right—here the right to receive just compensation when property is taken for a public use—in exchange for a discretionary benefit conferred by the government where the property sought has little or no relationship to the benefit.

In evaluating petitioner's claim, we must first examine whether the essential nexus exists between the legitimate state interest and the permit condition exacted by the city. If we find a nexus exists, we must then decide the required degree of connection between the exactions and the projected impact of the proposed development. . . . Undoubtedly the prevention of flooding along Fanno Creek and the reduction of traffic congestion in the Central Business District qualify as the type of legitimate public purposes we have upheld.

The second part of our analysis requires us to determine whether the degree of the exactions demanded by the city's permit conditions bear the required relationship to the projected impact of the petitioner's proposed development. A use restriction may constitute a taking if not reasonably necessary to the effectuation of a substantial government purpose.

The city required that petitioner deed to the city as greenway all portions of the site that fall within the existing 100-year floodplain and all property 15 feet above the floodplain boundary. In addition, the city demanded that the store be designed so as not to intrude upon the greenway area. The city relies upon the Commission's rather tentative findings that increased stormwater flow from petitioner's property can only add to the public need to manage the floodplain for drainage.

The city made the following specific findings relevant to the bicycle/pedestrian pathway. In addition, the proposed expanded use of this site is anticipated to generate additional vehicular traffic thereby increasing congestion on nearby collector and artery streets. Creation of a convenient, pedestrian/bicycle pathway system as an alternative means of transportation could offset some of the traffic demand on the nearby streets and lessen the incremental traffic congestion.

The question for us is whether these findings are constitutionally sufficient to justify the conditions imposed by the city on the petitioner's building permit. Since state courts have been dealing with this question a great deal longer than we have, we turn to representative decisions made by them. Some form of reasonable relationship test has been adopted in many jurisdictions. Despite any semantical differences, general agreement exists among the [state] courts that the dedication should have reasonable relationship to the needs created by the development.

We think a term such as "rough proportionality" best encapsulates what we hold to be the requirement of the Fifth Amendment. No precise mathematical calculation is required, but the city must make some sort of individualized determination that the required dedication is related both in nature and extent to the proposed development. Because petitioner's property was in the Central Business District, the Community Development Code already required that petitioner leave 15% of it as open space and the undeveloped flood plain area has nearly satisfied that requirement. But the city demanded more—it not only wanted petitioner not to build in the floodplain, but it also wanted petitioner's property along Fanno Creek for its greenway system. The city has never said why a public greenway as opposed to a private one, was required in the interest of flood control.

The difference to petitioner, of course, is in the loss of her ability to exclude others. As we have noted, this right to exclude others is one of the most essential sticks in the bundle of rights that are commonly characterized as property.

The city seeks to impose a permanent recreational easement upon petitioner's property that borders Fanno Creek. Petitioner would lose the right to regulate the time in which the public entered the greenway, regardless of any interference it might pose with her retail store. Her right to exclude would not be regulated, it would be eviscerated. We conclude that the findings on which the city relies do not show the required reasonable relationship between the floodplain easement and the petitioner's proposed new building.

With respect to the pedestrian/bicycle pathway, we have no doubt that the city was correct in finding that the larger retail facility proposed by petitioner will increase traffic on the streets of the Central Business District. The city estimates roughly 435 additional trips per day. But, on the record before us, the city has not met the burden of demonstrating that the additional number of trips generated by the petitioner's development reasonably related to the city's requirement for a dedication of the pedestrian/bicycle pathway easement. As Justice Peterson of the Supreme Court of Oregon explained in his dissenting opinion, "The findings of fact that the bicycle pathway system could offset some of the traffic demand is a far cry from a finding that the bicycle pathway system will or is likely to offset some of the traffic demand. The city must make some effort to quantify its findings in support of the dedication for the pedestrian/bicycle pathway beyond the conclusory statement that it could offset some of the traffic generated.

The judgment of the Supreme Court of Oregon is reversed and the case is remanded for further proceedings consistent with this opinion.

Case Questions

1. As this was a 5–4 decision by the Supreme Court, what arguments do you think the dissenting opinions would make to support the city?
2. Suggest several alternative findings or studies that could have been made by the city to strengthen its case.
3. Justice Rhenquist mentions that the right to exclude others is one of the biggest sticks in the bundle of property rights; what are some of the other sticks?

Summary

The law defines property as a bundle of rights. These rights are recognized and enforced by law when other people interfere with the owner's use or enjoyment of property. For example, the due process clauses of the U.S. Constitution's 5th and 14th Amendments protect people from governmental action that would deprive them of property without due process.

Property can be classified as real or personal, usually based on whether it is attached to land or movable. Although fixtures may have originally been personal property, permanently attaching them to real property transforms them into real property. Both tangible objects and intangible rights are recognized as property. Copyrights, trademarks, patents, and trade secrets are types of intellectual property. The first three are generally protected by federal registration, and some treaties provide means for intellectual protection. The common law offers some protection for copyrights, trademarks, and trade secrets.

Because law sometimes grants special protection to property, the courts must determine what constitutes an interest in property. In some situations, rights to governmental benefits or job security may be recognized as intangible property.

The transfer of personal property may create a bailment or constitute a delivery of title. A bailment transfers only possession and custody to the bailee; whereas, a delivery of title transfers ownership. Title to personal property may be transferred by sale or gift; a gift may be made during life or after death. If a decedent did not make a valid will for transferring property at death, state intestacy laws determine who will inherit a decedent's property. Probate laws determine whether a will is valid and provide for the administration of a decedent's property until it is distributed to the rightful heirs.

Both possessory and nonpossessory interests in real estate are recognized. A lease agreement creates a possessory interest in real property. Frequently, the lessee or tenant is prohibited from transferring all of his or her possessory rights through an assignment. A sublease differs from an assignment because in a sublease the transferor keeps some rights. A subtenant's rights are based on the sublease agreement, not on the rights of the lease.

Easements, licenses, and liens are nonpossessory interests in real property. An easement usually runs with the land and gives its owner the right to perform specific activities on someone else's real property. A license permits someone to perform an activity on another's real property; unlike easements, licenses are personal in nature and are not automatically transferred to other parties. A lien provides a security interest in real property for a mortgage lender; liens such as the mechanic's lien can also exist in personal property.

Co-ownership of personal property may take several forms. The joint tenancy, tenancy in common, and community property methods of sharing real property provide different rights to co-owners. Condominium and cooperative ownership of real property provide methods for individually owning or possessing specific space while sharing ownership of common areas.

The sales contract is the basic document governing the sale of real estate. A deed, usually a warranty deed, actually transfers title to property, while a mortgage protects the interest of the lender of some or all of the property's purchase price. All documents transferring interests in real estate must be recorded to indicate to third parties the owner's interests in the property.

Real property is subject to control from both common law and regulatory statutes or ordinances. Nuisance laws and zoning restrictions regulate the use of real property so that it is consistent with the uses of other property. Although private restrictions on real property are not favored by the law, reasonable restrictive covenants are enforceable. Upon payment of adequate compensation, government may exercise its power of eminent domain and take private property for a public purpose.

Critical Thinking Questions

1. Apply the chapter's information on intellectual property to the software industry. Compare and contrast copyright protection and patent protection for software. What arguments could you make supporting the position that, for protecting the software industry and the public, trade secret protection may have greater advantages than copyright or patent protection?
2. George agrees to sell his home to you and to give you a warranty deed to the property. If the delivery of that deed to you effectively transfers George's ownership to you, why should you also record the deed in the county where the real estate is located?
3. Five years after graduation, you decide to purchase your first home. What legal documents will you be asked to review and sign as part of the purchase of real estate?
4. Allen, Bob, and Charles own a piece of real estate as joint tenants with right of survivorship. Who would own the property if Charles transferred his interest to Doris?
5. Private property owners argue that local, state, and federal zoning ordinances, land use regulations, and federal environmental laws restricting what they can do with their property constitute an unconstitutional taking of their property. Lawmakers and environmentalists assert that such regulation of property is in the public interest and that the community and public interest takes precedence over the interests of the private property owner. What tests would you use to resolve these differences in numerous individual disputes?

CRITICAL THINKING EXERCISES

1. Jane and Joe were business partners who owned real estate as joint tenants and not as tenants in common. At the time of Jane's death, a dispute arose between Jane's children, who were her heirs, and Joe as to who now owned her half interest in the property. Who is entitled to the property interest that she had? Why?
2. A residential developer owned property that fronted a small pond and property just across the street. All of the property was developed except for one front lot on the pond that was used as a means of access to the pond for property owners across the street. What is the best way for the property owners across the street to gain access to the pond if the remaining front lot is sold?
3. John signed a contract to purchase a home from Bill. When John took possession of the home, he noticed that Bill had removed several antique lighting fixtures, a built-in double self-cleaning oven, a furnace, and planter boxes that had been on the deck. The contract between John and Bill said nothing as to who was entitled to these items. Who would win if John sued Bill for their return? Why?
4. Beard owned an apartment building and leased an apartment to Frances. Subsequently, Frances sublet the apartment to Jane and went on a long vacation. Beard then began eviction proceedings because the lease agreement prohibited assigning the apartment. Is there a difference between a sublease and an assignment? May a landlord prohibit both a sublease and an assignment?
5. The California Portland Cement Company manufactures cement in a plant built on land it has owned for 20 years. When the company bought the land and built the plant, the surrounding land was vacant and unimproved. Colbert, who owns land near the plant on which he lives and raises citrus crops, files suit to have the plant enjoined as a nuisance because of the dust and smoke it produces. Is he entitled to an injunction?
6. Carl purchased two adjoining lots. A restrictive covenant accompanying the sale of the lots stated that "no lot shall be used for a nonresidential purpose." On one of the lots, Carl constructed a large garage in which he refurbished expensive classic cars. Did construction of the garage violate the restrictive covenant? Who can enforce the covenant?
7. Most computer software packages are protected by a copyright and may also have a "write-protected" lock on the program to prevent its duplication. Usually, however, someone, or some company, finds a way to unlock the program shortly after it hits the market. There are legitimate companies that design software that helps duplicate copyrighted packages. Such duplication may be illegal as a violation of copyright laws and counterproductive as it reduces the profitability of designing new programs.

   People rationalize purchasing duplicated software because of the high prices charged for the software itself. Software companies claim that this practice forces them to artificially inflate the price charged to the legitimate buyer to make a profit on the sale of fewer products. What arguments would you make to encourage consumers to refrain from purchasing software that is duplicated from copyright protected packages? Is the software company that circumvents copyright protection of other companies acting ethically?

CHAPTER

8

Torts

Critical Thinking Questions

- Compare torts with contract violations and criminal laws by describing the purpose of each action and what a plaintiff must prove in each different type of case. Describe a fact situation that could involve a tort, breach of contract, and criminal act.
- Why are employers sometimes held liable for the torts committed by their employees? What determines the employer's liability? Is the employee who commits a tort also liable?
- Describe the elements of three different types of intentional torts.
- Explain how each of the elements in a negligence case—duty, nonperformance of duty, proximate cause, and injury—relate to each other.
- Punitive damages may be awarded in a case where an intentional tort is committed. Recently, the U.S. House of Representatives voted to restrict punitive damages in all civil litigation cases. Victims of intentional torts and their attorneys argue that punitive damages serve as both a punishment on the wrongdoer and a message to firms not to engage in such conduct. Tort reform advocates argue that punitive damages bear little relationship to compensatory damages and are rendered with little basis. What are two additional arguments that each side is likely to present if Congress as a whole considers whether to restrict the amount of punitive damages?
- Explain what is meant by comparative negligence, contributory negligence, and an assumption of risk; give an example of how each might be used.

Introduction... Past, Present, Future

In the past, the primary concern of tort law was to protect people from wrongful acts causing personal injury or damage to property. Victims sought compensation for torts such as assault, battery, and trespass. Over the years, tort law has expanded significantly. People sought to protect their reputation, right to privacy, and freedom from tortious actions causing mental distress. Today, interference with personal rights (sexual harassment) and economic relations (interference with contracts) is of greater concern to many people than are actions that interfere with property rights (trespass).

In the negligence area, most states have switched from the "all-or-nothing" contributory negligence defense to a comparative negligence standard. This standard ensures that minor negligence on the plaintiff's part will not completely bar recovery for injuries caused by the defendant's negligence. Although the negligence requirements have not changed through the years, several recent cases have sought to impose on governments, business firms, and individuals new duties, which if not properly performed could leave them liable for injuries to plaintiffs.

The future is difficult to predict. Some reform in tort law appears to be very likely. U.S. manufacturers argue that the current system makes their products more expensive as compared to those manufactured in countries with less stringent liability laws and that the state laws are too disparate for firms manufacturing in the national and global economy. Among the areas most ripe for reform are restricting damages recovered in some tort cases, particularly in the medical liability area, imposing some restriction on punitive damages and perhaps modifying the joint and several liability concept. Possible reforms also are likely in product liability laws; those reforms are discussed in Chapter 11.

Business and Vicarious Liability

tort law
Imposes duties on people to act in a reasonable manner toward others and to refrain from intentionally causing others to be injured.

Tort law imposes duties on people to act in a reasonable manner toward others and to refrain from intentionally causing others to be injured. Tort law is an important legal concern of businesses because they may be held liable for the actions of their employees if those actions cause injury to others. Most businesses act through other people: officers, employees, and independent agents. Corporations, partnerships, and most sole proprietorships (discussed in Chapter 14) employ people and other firms to implement their activities. The law holds a business responsible for the actions of people the business has a right to control.

Vicarious Liability: The Agent and the Independent Contractor

vicarious liability
The liability of the business for the actions of its agents.

If an agent commits torts while working on behalf of a business, the injured person can sue the business and/or the agent. The liability of the business for the actions of its agents is known as **vicarious liability.** The business is called a *master* or *principal,* and its agents are also known as *servants.* Vicarious liability arises when an agent causes injury to a third party, an individual, or another business while acting on behalf of a principal.

independent contractor
A person employed by a business solely to do a particular job without the business having any control over how the job is to be done.

A business is not held vicariously liable for the act of an agent if the business has no right to control that agent's means of conducting the act. For example, if a person is employed as a plumber or an electrician by a business solely to do a particular job, such as installing a kitchen sink or new electrical outlets, without the business having any control over how the job is to be done, only that person, known as an **independent contractor,** is responsible for his or her acts. The business is not generally liable for the torts committed by an independent contractor. The vicarious liability of businesses for the acts of agents or contractors is discussed in greater detail in Chapter 13.

Vicarious Liability and Individual Direct Liability

Although a business is held vicariously liable for an employee's torts, this fact does not alter the direct liability of the employee. All persons are directly liable for their tortious acts. The vicarious liability imposed on a business for employee torts is in addition to this direct liability. For example, if ABC Trucking Company employs John to drive a delivery truck and John's negligent driving causes injury to pedestrians, John will be directly liable and ABC vicariously liable to the pedestrians for their injuries.

There are several reasons why the vicarious liability of a business is generally so significant. First, because both the business and the employee may be held liable, the injured party usually sues both of them. The injured person may be unsure whether the employee is solely responsible as an independent contractor or whether the business is also liable because the employee is a servant. By suing both, the injured plaintiff forces the business and the employee to determine the extent of the control that the business can exercise over the employee. Second, the business usually has greater financial resources than the employee; this basis for suing the business is known as the *deep*

FIGURE 8–1 Relationship of Tort Law to Criminal Law and to Other Branches of Civil Law

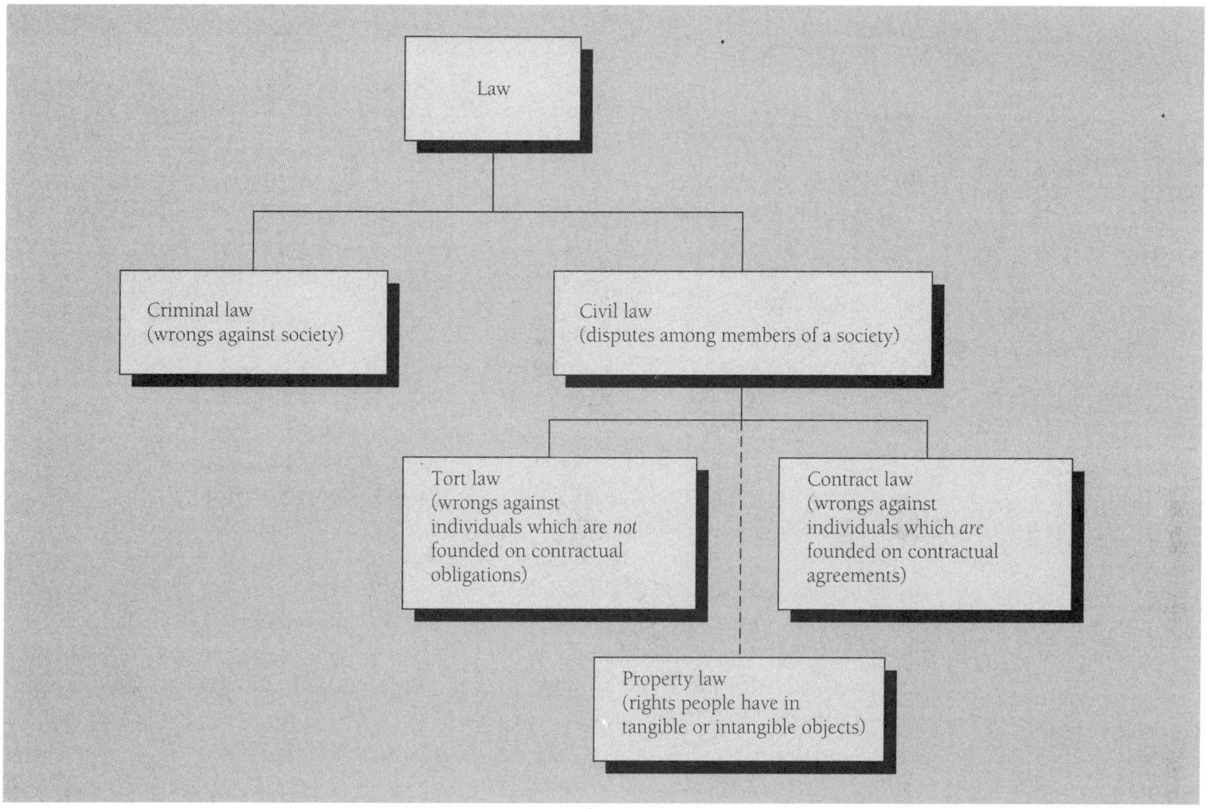

pocket theory. Whereas the business usually secures insurance to cover its potential liability to injured parties, the wages or other financial resources of the employee are frequently insufficient to satisfy large damage awards. Given this disparity in resources, the business, with its deep pocket, is generally the primary target in litigation brought by the injured person.

Classification of Torts and Business Activities

Both criminal acts and tortious acts are wrongs. Torts are civil wrongs that may be redressed by the victim of the wrong, while criminal acts are wrongs against society that are redressed when society initiates criminal charges. Tort law is a part of the civil segment of our legal system. While criminal law is regarded as public law, property, tort, and contract law are each regarded as essential elements of our private law. As Figure 8–1 illustrates, it may also be contrasted with the civil law of contracts discussed in the next chapter.

Tort Law and Criminal Law

An action that results in personal injury may also constitute a criminal action. Torts are wrongs committed against individuals or businesses, whereas crimes are wrongs committed against society. The tort case is primarily concerned with compensating the victim of a legal wrong, whereas the criminal case is primarily concerned with punishing the person who commits a wrong against society. Although criminal law originally depended on common law precedents, it is now based primarily on statutory laws passed by the federal and state legislatures. By contrast, tort law principles emerge primarily from common law precedents, though some statutes affect tort law liability.

There is no double jeopardy if a person is tried for a civil tort and a criminal act, even if both arise out of the same wrongful act. *Double jeopardy* occurs only when a person is tried twice for the same crime. The substantive law, trial procedures, and burdens of proof are different for tort cases than for criminal cases. Thus, although a tortious action could be a crime, it need not be; it is a wrong for which the injured party can be compensated.

Suppose that a tenant in an apartment causes damage to the apartment owner's property. If the tenant intentionally causes the damage, say by writing on the walls, the tenant would be committing both a tort and a crime. The tenant could be guilty of the crime of malicious destruction of property and also liable to compensate the owner for the damage. A prosecutor could sue the tenant for the criminal act, and the owner could sue the tenant for the tort that damaged the property. However, if the damage caused by the tenant was unintentional and resulted from negligence or carelessness, such as allowing water to spill over from the bathtub onto the floor, the tenant would be held liable only for the tortious action. The owner could bring a civil damage suit against the tenant, but the prosecutor could not bring a criminal action.

Tort Law and Contract Law

If a business or an individual breaches a contractual obligation while also committing a tort, the injured party may bring both a breach of contract case and a tort case. Since both cases involve civil (noncriminal) actions arising from the same events and involving the same parties, the two actions must usually be brought together in one legal proceeding. For example, suppose a consumer purchases a thermos bottle and later notices that the inside is chipped, so that pieces of the bottle are floating in the liquid. The contract of purchase was that the bottle was fit for the ordinary purpose; since the bottle did not meet that standard, the seller breached the contract. However, the purchaser could also sue the manufacturer of the thermos bottle in tort because the manufacturer breached its responsibility for being reasonably careful in the manufacture of its product. Both the manufacturer and the seller could be sued in one suit alleging a negligent tort against the manufacturer and a breach of contract by the seller.

A plaintiff may recover damages if either the nonperformance of a contract or the commission of a tortious act is proved against the defendant. Whether the plaintiff proves that one or both wrongs have occurred, the compensation to the plaintiff is generally based on the seriousness of the injury. Because the injury is the same, the compensation due, whether from both or either of the defendants, is also generally the same. In tort cases involving intentional torts, however, the law permits the plaintiff to collect punitive damages in addition to compensatory damages. Punitive damages are not available in a breach of contract action.

INTERNATIONAL PERSPECTIVE AND COMMENTARY

Where to Hear a Tort Case and What Law to Apply

The general legal principle governing a tortious act is that the law of the place where the tort occurs is usually applied. Of course, it is not always easy to determine where a tort action occurs. In the *Union Carbide* case, a U.S. court was asked to hear a tort case against Union Carbide Ltd. (an Indian corporation) and Union Carbide, Inc. (a U.S. corporation), which owned a majority of the Indian corporation.[1] The plaintiffs alleged that the lack of supervision by the U.S. firm made it responsible for the deaths and damage caused by an explosion at the Indian manufacturing facility. It asked the U.S. court to hear the case and to apply U.S. tort law in determining liability.

The U.S. court refused to hear the case because the parties, witnesses, and documentary evidence were primarily in India. The court applied the concept of *forum non conveniens,* determining that the U.S. court was not a convenient forum in which to hear and decide the case. Likewise, the court looked at the *conflict of law* rules and determined that the substantive law to apply in determining liability for the explosion should be the law of the place where the wrong occurred: India.

Types of Torts

There are three different types of torts: intentional torts, negligence, and strict liability. Each type imposes liability on individuals or businesses that injure others. Yet, as Figure 8–2 illustrates, each type of tort has distinctive requirements for proof. In some situations, however, there may not be a clear line differentiating the requirements of one type of tort from another.

FIGURE 8-2

Requirements for Proof in Different Types of Torts

Type of Tort	Requirements	Examples
Intentional tort	Intent to commit act Causal connection of act to injury	Battery—hitting a person in the face Trespass—stepping on the property of another person without permission
Negligent tort	Duty to act in a reasonable manner Breach of duty Proximate causation connecting act to injury Injury to plaintiff	Driving a car carelessly and causing injury Improperly cleaning a floor in a store, causing a customer to slip and fall
Strict liability in tort	Ultrahazardous activity or inherently defective product The activity or defect causes plaintiff's injury The defect exists when the product is under the defendant's control	A company dynamiting an old building causes injury to a person across the street A person is injured while drinking from a defective and chipped coffee thermos

[1] *In Re Union Carbide Corp. Gas Plant Disaster,* 809 F.2d 195 (2d Cir., 1987).

Intentional Torts

intentional tort
An intentional, wrongful act causing injury to another person.

An **intentional tort** is an intentional, wrongful act causing injury to another person. The plaintiff must prove that the defendant *tortfeasor,* the person committing the tort, intended to perform the act that caused the injury. Tortious actions that interfere with personal rights may pertain to physical or mental injury, interference with private property (such as trespassing), and interference in economic relations.

General Requirements

Intentional torts require the plaintiff to prove only that the defendant intended to perform the *act* that caused the injury; it is not necessary to prove that the defendant intended to cause the injury. If, however, the plaintiff can prove evil motive or desire to harm, he or she may collect punitive damages in addition to compensatory damages. *Compensatory damages,* such as damages for medical expenses, lost income, and pain and suffering, compensate the injured person for the loss actually suffered. *Punitive damages* punish the wrongdoer for his or her actions and are intended to deter others from committing similar actions. Punitive damages are usually available only in intentional tort cases where there is proof of malice or a clear disregard of the rights of others.

Required Elements of Intentional Torts

1. The defendant *intended* to do the act.
2. The act committed, not something else, *caused* the plaintiff's injury.
3. The plaintiff suffered *injury,* such as personal injury, property damage, or the deprivation of a right.

The clearest cases of intentional torts generally occur in situations in which one person causes physical injury to another person. For example, a punch in the nose can be the basis for an intentional tort if it causes injury. The law requires that people refrain from intentional actions that injure others. It allows recovery of damages for an injury caused by someone's intentional interference with the right not to be injured. The compensation depends on the amount needed to restore the injured person to the state in which he or she would have been if no tort had been committed.

Several kinds of intentional acts interfere with personal rights and are therefore torts. Torts may arise from physical or mental injury, from interference with property rights, and from interference with economic relations. Inducing a supplier to breach a contract with a business is an example of tortious interference with economic relations.

Intentional Torts That Interfere with Personal Rights

Assault Assault is the intentional act of putting someone in apprehension of immediate, offensive, harmful touching. The victim need not be frightened; as used here, *apprehension* means expectation. Words alone typically do not constitute an assault because they are not sufficient to make an ordinarily reasonable person apprehensive of immediate harm. Words coupled with a menacing gesture, however, can constitute an assault. The relevant intent in assault is that of the actor. The apprehension is based on the victim's state of mind, judged by a reasonable standard. Note that actual physical contact need not take place for an assault to occur. A person who points a gun or a knife at another person in a threatening manner commits an assault, even though the victim is not actually touched.

Battery Battery is the intentional offensive touching of another person without justification or consent. Battery also includes the unprivileged touching of another with some instrumentality put in motion by the aggressor. For example, shooting with a bullet that hits someone constitutes a battery. "Reasonable justification" is usually the key to determining whether a battery occurs. Minimal, social, or unavoidable touching, such as occurs on a crowded bus or at a sporting event, is usually not considered battery because it is expected, justified, and not offensive to a reasonable person.

A person imminently threatened or battered by another may respond in self-defense with similar force without incurring liability. However, if the threat is to either a third party or to the threatened person's property, it is less likely that the retaliator's "defensive battery" will be justified.

False Imprisonment False imprisonment is the intentional confinement of a nonconsenting individual within a bounded area for an appreciable time. False imprisonment may be charged against a business that attempts to deal with suspected shoplifters or with employees suspected of dishonest behavior. Under common law, a storekeeper could be held liable for detaining a suspected shoplifter if that person was later found to be innocent. Now, state statutes limit the liability of storekeepers for false imprisonment to unreasonable actions or bad faith detentions. If storekeepers have probable cause or act in good faith in detaining a suspected shoplifter, they will not be liable. The privilege is a qualified one; if it is abused, the storekeeper could be held liable for detention without reasonable cause.

Defamation A defamation is the publication of an untrue statement about another person that injures the person's reputation or character. *Slander* is oral defamation, and *libel* is written defamation. The reason for the publication requirement is that a person's good name exists only in terms of evaluations by others. If the audience does not consider the statement derogatory or if no one hears or reads the statement, there is no injury to the person's reputation or character and thus no defamation. Truth constitutes an absolute defense; true statements are considered legally justified. Certain statements are defamatory per se (automatically)—for example, accusing a person of murder or alleging that a person has a loathsome communicable disease such as syphilis.

Another defense to defamation exists if the person who makes the statement has a qualified or absolute privilege to do so. During litigation, judges, attorneys, and witnesses have an absolute privilege. A qualified privilege exists for private matters if the statement is made by someone who has a duty to make statements and if the statement is communicated only to those with an immediate interest in the information. For example, if a prospective employer asks a former employer about a former employee's character, the former employer's statement is privileged. Thus, if the former employer acts in good faith and not in malice, there is no defamation even if the statement is untrue.

Another exception occurs with public figures. No defamation of a person who is a public figure exists unless the statement is both untrue and made with malice. Malice is often difficult to prove. However if, for example, a reporter writes an untrue story about a public figure, the defamation may be regarded as malicious if the reporter did not take reasonable steps to substantiate the statements of his or her sources.

Infliction of Mental Distress The courts are beginning to recognize that the intentional infliction of emotional harm is a separate tort. Liability is usually limited to outrageous acts that cause detectable emotional injury. For example, if a person is bullied or made to view gory or gruesome photographs or watch a relative confront, but escape from, a dangerous situation, the resulting mental distress may lead to a damage award. Although courts frequently hold that there has to be some physical injury to allow recovery for mental distress, some courts allow recovery even in the absence of physical injury.

Invasion of Privacy The right of privacy protects a person from unwarranted interference with the right to be left alone. Recent cases have involved the unauthorized revelation of private facts about a person's intimate life. For example, a television portrayal of a person's life, even if disguised as fiction, is wrongful if the viewers are likely to know whose life has been portrayed. The use of a person's commercial endorsement without consent is an unlawful appropriation. Unlike defamation, truth is not a defense to an invasion of privacy.

An important issue regarding the right of privacy arises with regards to persons with AIDS (acquired immunodeficiency syndrome). How should the right of privacy be balanced against public protection when a person with AIDS seeks the names and addresses of blood donors whom he or she suspects transmitted the disease? The case that follows discusses the right of privacy and the competing public interest in maintaining a volunteer-based blood supply.

Rasmussen v. South Florida Blood Service

500 So. 2d 533 (1987)
Supreme Court of Florida

In 1982, Donald Rasmussen suffered injuries when struck by an automobile while sitting on a park bench. While hospitalized as a result of those injuries, he received over 50 units of blood by transfusion. In July 1983, he was diagnosed as having AIDS; he died a year later. In his suit for negligence against the driver who caused his original injuries, he attempted to prove the source of his aggravated AIDS injury. He served South Florida Blood Service (Blood Service) with a subpoena that requested its records and documents indicating the names and addresses of blood donors. There was no allegation of negligence against Blood Service, and it was not a defendant in Rasmussen's negligence suit.

Blood Service asked the trial court to bar it from disclosing the requested information, but the trial court ordered it to comply with Rasmussen's subpoena. The Court of Appeals reversed, concluding that the requested material should not be discovered. Rasmussen's heirs appealed to the Florida Supreme Court.

Barkett, Justice

The Supreme Court first recognized a right of privacy based on the United States Constitution in *Griswold v. Connecticut* (1965). This right of privacy has been described as "the most comprehensive of rights and the right most valued by civilized man." In recent cases, the Court has discussed the privacy right as one of those fundamental rights that are "implicit in the concept of ordered liberty such that neither liberty nor justice would exist if they were sacrificed."

In *Whalen v. Roe* (1977), the Supreme Court specifically recognized that the right to privacy encompasses at least two different kinds of interest, "the individual interest in avoiding disclosure of personal matters, and . . . the interest in independence in making certain kinds of important decisions." In *Nixon v. Administrator of General Services* (1977), the Supreme Court reaffirmed the confidentiality strand of privacy.

Moreover, in Florida, a citizen's right to privacy is independently protected by our state constitution. In 1980, the voters of Florida amended our state constitution to include an express right of privacy. In approving the amendment, Florida became the fourth state to adopt a strong, freestanding right of privacy as a separate section of its state constitution, thus providing an explicit textual foundation for those privacy interests inherent in the concept of liberty which may not otherwise be protected by specific constitutional provisions.

A principal aim of the constitutional provision is to afford individuals some protection against the increasing collection, retention, and use of information relating to all facets of an individual's life.

It is now known that AIDS is a major health problem with calamitous potential. At present, there is no known cure and the mortality rate is high. As noted by the court below, medical researchers have identified a number of groups that have a high incidence of the disease and are labeled "high-risk" groups. Seventy-two percent of all AIDS victims are homosexual or bisexual males with multiple sex partners and seventeen percent are intravenous drug users. [Note: These are 1987 statistics.]

As the district court recognized, petitioner needs more than just the names and addresses of the donors. His interest is in establishing that one or more of the donors has AIDS or is in a high-risk group. Petitioner argues that his inquiry *may* never go beyond comparing the donors' names against a list of known AIDS victims, or against other public records (e.g., conviction records in order to determine whether any of the donors is a known drug user). He contends that because a limited inquiry *may* reveal the information he seeks, with no invasion of privacy, the donors' privacy rights are not yet at issue.

However, the subpoena in question gives petitioner access to the names and addresses of the blood donors with no restrictions on their use. There is nothing to prohibit petitioner from conducting an investigation without the knowledge of the persons in question. We cannot ignore, therefore, the consequences of disclosure to nonparties, including the possibility that a donor's coworkers, friends, employers, and others may be queried as to the donor's sexual preferences, drug use, or general life-style.

The threat posed by the disclosure of the donors' identities goes far beyond the immediate discomfort occasioned by third party probing into sensitive areas of the donors' lives. Disclosure of donor identities in any context involving AIDS could be extremely disruptive and even devastating to the individual donor. If the requested information is released, and petitioner queries the donors' friends and fellow employees, it will be functionally impossible to prevent occasional references to AIDS. As the district court recognized, AIDS is the modern day equivalent of leprosy. AIDS, or a suspicion of AIDS, can lead to discrimination in employment, education, housing and even medical treatment.

By the very nature of this case, disclosure of donor identities is "disclosure in a damaging context." We conclude, therefore, that the disclosure sought here implicates constitutionally protected privacy interests.

. . . Society has a vital interest in maintaining a strong volunteer blood supply, a task that has become more difficult with the emergence of AIDS. The donor population has been reduced by the necessary exclusion of potential blood donors through AIDS screening and testing procedures as well as by the unnecessary reduction in the donor population as a result of the widespread fear that donation itself can transmit the disease. In light of this, it is clearly "in the public interest to discourage any disincentive to volunteer blood donation." Because there is little doubt that the prospect of inquiry into one's private life and the potential association with AIDS will deter blood donation, we conclude that society's interest in a strong and healthy blood supply will be furthered by the denial of discovery in this case.

In balancing the competing interests involved, the probative value of the discovery sought by Rasmussen is dubious at best. The potential of significant harm to most, if not all, of the fifty-one unsuspecting donors in permitting such a fishing expedition is great and far outweighs the plaintiff's need under these circumstances.

Accordingly, we approve the decision of the Third District.

Case Questions

1. State the competing interests that were involved in the search for information in this case.
2. Why did the court determine that the disclosure of the requested information would do greater harm than its nondisclosure?

Intentional Torts That Interfere with Property Rights

Interference with property rights concerns one person's unauthorized appropriation or use of another person's property. The person owning or possessing the property may be injured even if the property is not damaged. Trespass and conversion are torts that interfere with property rights. The right to possess real property is violated by trespass; the right to possess personal property is violated by a conversion, destruction, or taking of that property.

Trespass A person who enters someone else's real property without consent is committing a trespass. The intentional act of entering the possessor's property causes the injury. Even if the property is not damaged, the possessor is harmed by the unpermitted entry. A person who owns real property, such as land and the trees attached to it, has the right to have that property remain free from interference. Of course, if the property is also damaged, there is need for greater compensation.

Conversion Conversion occurs when one person appropriates property that is rightfully in another person's possession. The theft of goods from someone's house represents not only a crime, but also the tort of conversion. Thus, the defendant may be held responsible both for the criminal act of larceny and for the tort of conversion. Conversion also occurs when a person fails to return borrowed property or property placed in a bailment for a specific purpose. For example, if Joe lends Sue his computer for one month, but she keeps it for three months, Sue commits conversion. Sue has wrongfully denied Joe the use and enjoyment of his computer for two months. Generally, a successful conversion suit requires proof of the owner's demand for the return of property, followed by an intentional refusal to return it.

The victim of conversion may sue for damages measured by the rental value of the converted property. Thus, in the above example, Joe could sue for damages based on two months' rental value of a similar computer. If the defendant destroys or permanently deprives the owner of property, the damages would equal the market value of the property.

Intentional Torts That Interfere with Economic Relations

Both individuals and businesses are protected from unreasonable interference with their economic relations. The intentional torts of disparagement, interference with contract rights, and interference with prospective business relations all pertain to the area of economic relations.

Disparagement The tort of disparagement comprises disparaging statements regarding the business activities of a person or a business. This tort arises if the plaintiff can prove that specific business losses occurred as a result of the statements. For example, if the advertising of a business states that the products of another business are not of normal quality, that another business buys stolen goods, or that another business does not pay minimum wages to covered employees, the disparaged business could sue in tort.

Disparagement is sometimes referred to as *trade libel.* Unlike traditional libel, disparagement concerns only an individual's business or trade; it does not concern an individual's personal activities. Further, the plaintiff in a disparagement suit must prove that the disparagement is false. In a libel case, however, the defendant must prove that the libelous statements are true.

Interference with Contract Rights The tort of interference with contract relations involves intentional tampering with the contract of a person or a business. The contract may be between an employer and an employee, a business and a supplier, or a business and a customer. Intentionally causing the breach of a valid contract constitutes wrongful interference with contractual relations. The tort occurs if the defendant, knowing of a contract between the plaintiff and another party, intentionally induces that other party to breach the contract, thus causing injury to the plaintiff.

Interference with Prospective Business Relations The tort of interference with the prospective economic advantage of an individual or a business is similar to the tort of interference with contract relations. Individuals and firms have a legal duty not to tamper with the business relations of others. This is true whether those business relations involve currently enforceable contracts or merely the expectancy of contracts. The following case discusses the Pennzoil–Texaco fight over Getty Oil Company. Pennzoil sued Texaco for its wrongful interference with an agreement between Pennzoil and Getty Oil. Texaco claimed it did not knowingly interfere with their agreement.

Texaco, Inc. v. Pennzoil Co.

729 S.W.2d 768 (1987), certiorari denied 108 S. Ct. 1305 (1988)
Texas Court of Appeals

In December 1983, Pennzoil announced an unsolicited offer for 16 million shares of Getty Oil at $100 per share. Subsequent to that offer, discussions progressed between Gordon Getty, who as trustee owned over 40 percent of Getty Oil's stock, and Pennzoil, and a Memorandum of Agreement was signed by Pennzoil and Getty, who, with others, owned a majority of the Getty Oil stock.

However, the Getty Oil board of directors voted to reject the Pennzoil offer, requesting instead a revised offer of slightly more than $110 per share. At the same time, Gordon Getty began to seek offers from other firms. Meanwhile, Pennzoil agreed to the Getty Oil request, and on January 4, 1984, Getty Oil's lawyers and public relations staff began to draft a press release describing the terms of the agreement with Pennzoil. Pennzoil's lawyers also began to draft a more detailed transaction agreement.

On January 5, Texaco's board of directors authorized its officers to make an offer for 100 percent of Getty Oil. Gordon Getty that day agreed to sell his shares of stock to Texaco for $125 per share. The next day, Getty Oil's board of directors voted to withdraw its counterproposal to Pennzoil and to accept Texaco's offer. After Texaco announced that it would merge with Getty Oil, Pennzoil sued Texaco for wrongful interference with its merger contract with Getty Oil. Texaco claimed that no binding contract existed between Pennzoil and Getty Oil and that if such a contract did exist, it had not knowingly interfered with the contract.

The trial court found for Pennzoil. It awarded Pennzoil $7.53 billion in damages as a result of Texaco's interference. It also found that Pennzoil should receive $3 billion in punitive damages. Texaco appealed to the Texas Court of Appeals.

Warren, Justice

First, Texaco asserts that Pennzoil failed to prove that Texaco had actual knowledge that a contract existed. New York law requires knowledge by a defendant of the existence of contractual rights as an element of the tort inducing a breach of that contract. However, the defendant need not have full knowledge of all the detailed terms of the contract.

There is even some indication that a defendant need not have an accurate understanding of the exact legal significance of the facts giving rise to a contractual duty, but rather may be liable if he knows those facts, but is mistaken about whether they constitute a contract. . . . Since there was no direct evidence of Texaco's knowledge of a contract in this case, the question is whether there was legally and factually sufficient circumstantial evidence from which the trier of fact reasonably could have inferred knowledge.

Texaco argues that the writings known to Texaco and the verbal assurances it was given are matters of undisputed fact that do not add up to actual knowledge of a binding contract. It states that the only written evidence known to Texaco was the Memorandum of Agreement, the January 4 press release, and the January 2 "Dear Hugh" letter from Gordon Getty to Hugh Liedtke, Pennzoil's CEO. Texaco contends that these writings confirm the absence of a binding agreement.

Based on the other evidence at trial, different inferences could have been drawn from the fact that the press release did not state exactly the same information contained in the Memorandum of Agreement. It was for the jury to decide what weight to give to the evidence, and where conflicting inferences were possible from the evidence, it was the jury's task to choose between them.

Texaco's next contention is that the unambiguous wording of the press release, i.e., the "subject to" and agreement "in principle" language, demonstrated that there was no contract. We disagree that the press release is unambiguous, and our discussion above of the press release's use of the terms: agreement "in principle," and "subject to" a definitive agreement applies equally here. That language did not in itself preclude the existence of a contract, nor a jury finding of Texaco's knowledge of one.

We find that an inference could arise that Texaco had some knowledge of Pennzoil's agreement with the Getty entities, given the evidence of Texaco's detailed studies of the Pennzoil plan, its knowledge that some members of the Getty board were not happy with Pennzoil's price, and its subsequent formulation of strategy to "stop the [Pennzoil] train" and "take care of Liedtke."

Pennzoil contends that the jury could also draw an inference of Texaco's knowledge of its agreement from the evidence relating to a *Wall Street Journal* article dated January 5. That article reported on the terms of the Pennzoil/Getty merger and referred to an "agreement" 17 times.

Finally, Pennzoil points out that certain demands made by the [Getty] Museum and the [Getty] Trust also gave Texaco knowledge of their contractual obligations to Pennzoil. The jury could reasonably infer that Texaco was given knowledge of the Pennzoil agreement from this evidence. . . .

The jury was not required to accept Texaco's version of events in this case, and this Court may not substitute its own interpretation of the evidence for the decision of the trier of fact. There was legally and factually sufficient evidence to support an inference by the jury that Texaco had the required knowledge of an agreement.

From the evidence, the jury could have concluded that Texaco deliberately seized upon an opportunity to wrest an immensely valuable contract from a less affluent competitor, by using its vast wealth to induce the Museum, Gordon Getty, and Getty Oil to breach an existing contract. The evidence shows that the wrongful conduct came not from . . . mid-level employees but from top-level management. Apparently the jury believed that the conduct of Texaco's top-level management was less than the public was entitled to expect from persons of such stature. There is no evidence that Texaco interfered with the contract to injure Pennzoil, but the jury could reasonably conclude from the evidence at trial that Texaco cared little if such injury resulted from its interference.

Considering the type of action, the conduct involved, and the need for deterrence, we are of the opinion that the punitive damages are excessive and that the trial court abused its discretion in not suggesting a remittitur.

If within thirty days from the date of this judgment, Pennzoil files in this Court a remittitur of two billion dollars, as suggested above, the judgment will be reformed and affirmed as to the award of $7.53 billion in compensatory damages and $1 billion in exemplary damages; otherwise the judgment will be reversed and remanded.

Case Questions

1. What "knowledge" of the Pennzoil–Getty Oil contract by Texaco was required to prove that Texaco committed the tort of inducing a breach of contract?
2. The court states that "apparently the jury believed that the conduct of Texaco's top-level management was less than the public was entitled to expect from persons of such stature." Explain what you think this statement means regarding public expectations regarding conduct of top business managers.

Negligence Torts

Under the law of negligence, a person or a business must act responsibly and will be held liable for breach of the duty of care when others are injured because of such a breach. A **negligence tort** occurs when a person breaches a duty to use reasonable care toward others, and the breach of duty causes injury. Whereas an intentional tort is actionable only if there is intent to do the act causing injury, a negligence tort occurs if a careless act causes injury to others. Thus, negligence is based on fault. People have an obligation to act reasonably. When the carelessness of an individual or a business causes injury to others, tort law holds that individual or business liable to compensation for the injury.

negligence tort Occurs when a person breaches a duty to use reasonable care toward others, and the breach of duty causes injury.

General Requirements

Four requirements must be proved by a plaintiff in a negligence case:

1. The defendant owes a *duty of care* to the plaintiff.
2. The defendant *breached* or did not perform that duty.
3. The nonperformance or breach of the duty was the *proximate cause* of the plaintiff's injury.
4. The plaintiff suffered *injury,* and damages can be determined to compensate the plaintiff for the injury.

Cases often focus on particular elements of negligence. However, the *Williams* case, which follows, reviews each of the four major elements. Note, however, that it combines into one the last two elements listed above—proximate cause and injury. Which of the four required elements was found to be lacking in the *Williams* case?

Williams v. Jackson Co.

359 So. 2d 798 (1978)
Court of Civil Appeals of Alabama

The Williamses purchased a house and later found that serious defects in the subflooring had led to termite infestation. The Williamses then sued both the real estate company (the Jackson Company) that had prepared the deed transferring ownership of the house to them and the firm (Pest-Ex) that had inspected the house for termites. Both firms claimed they were not liable because they owed no duty to the Williamses. The trial court agreed with the firms and the Williamses appealed.

Wright, Presiding Judge

In every action in tort three elements must be present: (1) a duty of defendant to protect plaintiff from the injury of which he complains; (2) a failure to fulfill that duty; and (3) an injury to the plaintiff proximately caused by the failure of defendant. Plaintiff contends that when defendant [Jackson Company] drew the deed for the transfer of title in the purchase of the house and lot, it undertook the practice of law. By such undertaking it assumed the duty of not only properly drawing a legal instrument but also the duty of giving full legal advice to plaintiffs concerning the purchase, including informing them that the doctrine of caveat emptor applied. We are unable to accept this contention for recovery.

There is no contention that Jackson Company represented to plaintiffs that they were skilled or qualified to give legal advice, or assumed any contractual obligation to provide such advice. Assuming that the preparation and furnishing of the deed by Jackson Company constituted the unauthorized practice of law in violation of statute and was negligence as a matter of law, the duty arising thereby was only to provide a proper and legal deed resulting in transfer of title. Jackson Company could not thereby be said to have assumed the duty of providing full legal advice. . . . We further consider that plaintiff's theory breaks down as to the third element necessary, that of proximate cause. The negligent act charged is the drawing of the deed. The injury complained of is the purchase of a defective house. There is no conceivable chain of causation between the breach of a duty to draw a valid deed and the purchase of a house with holes in the floor. The decision to purchase has been made before a deed is drawn. In fact, it is stated in the claim that the contract to purchase was executed before Jackson Company was ever contacted. Even if that were not so, it is not reasonably foreseeable that the preparation of a deed would result in the purchase of a defective house. The test of reasonable foreseeability is not met.

The claim of plaintiffs against Pest-Ex alleged that on July 15, 1976, plaintiffs signed a contract with a real estate agent for the purchase of a house and that after signing the contract of purchase, they applied for a commitment from the Federal Housing Administration to guarantee a loan for the purchase. A commitment letter was subsequently issued by F.H.A. but was subject to inspection for termites by an approved termite control company and a report thereof on a form furnished by F.H.A. Defendant Pest-Ex did perform the inspection and submitted the report, a copy of which was required by F.H.A. to be furnished the buyer and seller. The claim is that Pest-Ex negligently failed to inspect and state in the report that there was damage to the subflooring and that as a proximate sequence of the failure to report the presence of damage, plaintiffs suffered injury. The issue on appeal is whether the court was correct in finding that Pest-Ex owed no duty to plaintiffs because they were not a party to the contract for inspection.

In dismissing the claim through a finding that Pest-Ex owed no duty to plaintiffs because they were not parties to the contract Pest-Ex made with F.H.A., the court erred. Privity of contract is not a required basis of duty in such cases. It has now been expressly stated by our supreme court that duty may arise from a social relationship as well as from a contractual relationship; that a duty to use care may arise from the reasonable man test of foreseeability of injury. Thus one who undertakes to perform a contract may be determined to owe a duty to others not privy to the contract to perform his obligations under the contract without negligent injury to such others. Such duty may arise from the foreseeability that such others may be injured by negligent performance, or duty may arise from the knowledge that others are relying upon a proper performance. This latter source of duty could surely be shown by evidence in support of the claim against Pest-Ex in this case. The trial court was incorrect in its holding that plaintiffs could not recover from Pest-Ex because there was no privity of contract.

Case Questions

1. Which of the four elements that must be proved in a negligent tort case were found to be lacking in the Williamses' case against Jackson Company?
2. How does the court's analysis of the case that the Williamses brought against Pest-Ex differ from the case against Jackson Company?

Duty of Care The law imposes a duty on all individuals and businesses to act carefully toward others when it is foreseeable that a lack of reasonable care could cause injury. That **duty of care** is based on the premise that many actions involve a predictable danger of injury. It is not necessary to foresee the precise harm that could occur if reasonable care is not exercised, but only that the failure to exercise reasonable care poses an unreasonable risk of some harm. However, if no risk of harm is foreseen, there is no duty to use reasonable care. In such situations, causing an injury to someone would not constitute a negligent tort.

duty of care The duty imposed on all individuals and businesses to act carefully toward others when it is foreseeable that a lack of reasonable care could cause injury.

Certainly, it is reasonable to foresee that driving a car too fast risks harm to other drivers and pedestrians. Therefore, a duty to use reasonable care requires the driver to guard against such harm. A driver who fails to perform the duty of driving carefully may be committing a negligent tort. Some of the states apply no-fault laws to motor vehicle accidents. In those states, in most cases the injured party need not prove the driver's negligence to be entitled to compensation.

Breach or Nonperformance of Duty The plaintiff must prove either that the defendant did not perform the duty of care or that the defendant is responsible for the nonperformance of that duty. For example, if you have a party in your home, the law imposes on you a duty to use reasonable care in maintaining the property and in conducting the party so as to protect guests from foreseeable risks. Does a room have loose rugs on which a guest could slip and fall or loose ceiling tiles that could fall on someone? If the homeowner or apartment tenant does not take precautions with regard to such items of foreseeable danger, the duty of care is not performed (and thus is breached). Thus, nonperformance of the duty of care occurs if a person acts in a careless, reckless, or unreasonable manner.

For example, in a case filed against Los Angeles International Airport, no liability was placed on the airport for the death of a person who was killed when a bomb that had been placed in a public coin-operated locker exploded. The court found the airport itself was not in dangerous condition and that the city that operated the airport had taken reasonable steps to guard against terrorism: "The complaint here sets forth no facts which give rise to the duty on the part of the City to expand its policing of the airport terminal."[2]

The law does not require that a person or a business be an insurer or a guarantor of the absolute safety of others. Negligence is based on a comparison of a person's actions with the standard for the actions expected from the mythical, ordinary, reasonable person. Sometimes a person or a business acts reasonably yet still causes injury to others. For example, a company that manufactures room heaters uses a process to ensure that they do not overheat, risking fire. If the company has acted reasonably, as compared to the standard expected of manufacturers of similar products, there would be no negligence even if the heater became defective and caused injury to its user. In such a case, the company could not be held liable for negligence, though it might be held liable on some other basis, such as an implied warranty or strict liability.

proximate cause The standard used in negligence cases to establish the required causal relationship between the defendant's nonperformance or breach of duty and the plaintiff's injury.

Proximate Cause Once the plaintiff has shown that the defendant breached the duty of care, the defendant's act must also be shown to be the proximate cause of the plaintiff's injury. **Proximate cause** is the standard used in negligence cases to establish the required causal relationship between the defendant's nonperformance or breach of duty and the plaintiff's injury. Only injuries with a close (proximate) causal connection to the actions of the defendant or injuries caused by actions whose consequences can be reasonably foreseen can trigger the defendant's liability. The law does not impose unlimited liability on the defendant whose actions are only weakly linked to the plaintiff's injury.

For example, suppose that a person standing on a curb and seeking to board a bus takes a big stride to reach the bus step and then falls and is injured. The proximate cause of the person's injury would probably not be the distance of the bus from the curb. Instead, the person's act of striding too far to reach the bus instead of walking off the curb and then climbing onto the bus would be the proximate cause of the injury. If the causal connection between the actions of the bus driver and the injuries suffered by the plaintiff is not close, there is no liability on the bus company.

There is no negligence in situations in which happenstance or intervening events lead to unforeseen consequences. For example, suppose that Adam, who is camping in the woods, fails to carefully extinguish a campfire. If the fire spreads from the campground to a nearby building, Adam would probably be liable because there would be a close causal connection between his breach of duty and the damage to the building. However, if soon after the building begins to burn, an unusually strong wind causes the fire to spread for miles and miles, the rule of proximate cause would excuse Adam from liability for damage caused to more distant property.

Even if a duty of care is not performed, there must be a close connection between the plaintiff's injury and the nonperformance. In the *Moncur* case against Los Angeles International Airport, the court examined whether the explosion was sufficiently connected to the alleged lack of reasonable care by the Airport Commission. Courts traditionally look to the defendant's actions to see whether *but for* those actions the injury to the plaintiff would still have occurred. This "but for" test is generally used to determine proximate cause. "But for" the actions of the defendant, would the injury to plaintiff have occurred?

---

[2] *Moncur v. City of Los Angeles Dept. of Air,* 137 Cal. Rptr. 239 (1977).

Injury The final element of a negligence case requires proof that the plaintiff's injury is compensable by some amount of damages. The injury need not be physical. Legal injury occurs whether the plaintiff sustains pain, suffers embarrassment, or loses money. The trier of fact—this is normally the jury in a negligence case—determines the amount of damages necessary to compensate the plaintiff.

The plaintiff generally has the burden of proving the injury and the extent of damages necessary to compensate for it. In a negligence trial, both the plaintiff and the defendant frequently use expert witnesses to aid them in presenting evidence related to the damage issue. For example, the plaintiff may have a doctor testify regarding the extent of the injuries suffered and the likelihood of permanent disability. The defendant usually has a doctor testify that the plaintiff's injuries are less severe than claimed.

The plaintiff also has an economic or financial expert testify that based on his or her calculations and projections, and taking the doctor's testimony into account, the plaintiff will have a diminished earning capacity in the future. This expert usually concludes that the jury should award the plaintiff a sum of money computed as the present value of the plaintiff's future earnings loss. The defendant can, of course, cross-examine the plaintiff's financial expert and can produce an expert witness who testifies that a smaller amount of damages would compensate for the plaintiff's earnings loss, and the plaintiff's attorney can, of course, cross-examine the defendant's expert witness. It is for the jury to determine the believability of these conflicting economic projections.

Each of the elements in a negligent action must be proven. Generally, the duty to act is imposed on firms; they do not "voluntarily" assume the obligation to act. In determining whether a firm has a duty to act, recall that the law imposes a duty to act in a reasonable manner when it is foreseeable that a lack of reasonable care could cause injury. Is it foreseeable that if McDonald's does not take precautions to make its premises safe that its employees or customers might be injured or even killed by people committing criminal acts?

While firms are not guarantors for the safety of those who may be in danger, once a firm assumes a duty to act in a reasonable manner, it can be held liable for negligence if its nonperformance of that duty causes injury to customers. Each of the elements in a negligent tort is discussed in the following case.

Martin v. McDonald's Corp.

572 N.E.2d 1073 (1991)
Appellate Court of Illinois

McDonald's Corporation is the world's best known franchisor of fast-food restaurants. It authorizes franchisees to operate fast-food restaurants using the McDonald's trademark, service marks, and know-how. One of its franchises is located in Oak Forest, Illinois. As McDonald's restaurants were often open late in the night and as the daily cash transactions at any given franchise location could be significant, McDonald's realized there was a threat of armed robbery for its franchisees. Accordingly, McDonald's established an entire corporate division to deal with security problems at its franchises. It prepared a manual for restaurant security operations and required its franchisees to adhere to those procedures.

Regional security managers periodically inspected McDonald's franchises to examine how the procedures were being implemented.

Jim Carlson, a regional security manager for the area in which the Oak Forest franchise was located, visited the Oak Forest franchise on October 31, 1979. At that time, he informed the manager of security procedures and specifically noted that no one should take garbage out the back door after dark and that trash and grease were to be taken out the side door at least one hour prior to closing. Carlson also noted that the locks had to be changed and that an alarm system should be installed for the back door.

On November 29, 1979, a six-woman crew, all teenagers, was working to clean up and close the Oak Forest restaurant. A gunman, later identified as Peter Logan, appeared at the back of the restaurant with a gun and ordered the crew to open the safe, get him the money, and then get into the refrigerator. In moving the crew into the refrigerator, one person, Laura Martin, was killed and two were assaulted. The parents of Laura Martin and the injured crew members sued McDonald's to recover damages for its negligence. The trial court ordered McDonald's to pay the Martins over $1 million and also ordered it to pay $125,000 to the injured workers. McDonald's appealed.

Justice McNulty delivered the opinion of the Court

In order for plaintiffs to recover on a theory of negligence, they must establish that there was a duty owed to them by the defendant, that the defendant breached its duty, that they were injured, and that the defendant's breach of duty, or negligence was the proximate cause of their injuries. The question of duty, the legal obligation imposed upon one for the benefit of another, is a question of law to be determined by the court.

Defendant McDonald's Corporation, contends that it had no duty to protect Laura Martin, Maureen Kincaid or Therese Dudek (the injured crew members) since it was merely the licensor of the business that was operated by McDonald's Restaurants of Illinois, and plaintiffs were employees of the licensee. McDonald's asserts that it had no duty to plaintiffs as it had no "special relationship" (such as common carrier/passenger, innkeeper/guest, possessor of land/member of the public) with them as required by the Restatement (second) of Torts.

Plaintiffs . . . insist that McDonald's owed them a duty of care because it had voluntarily assumed such a duty. Case law supports the proposition that liability can arise from the negligent performance of a voluntary undertaking. . . . Plaintiffs argue that McDonald's, like the insurance company in *Nelson* and the Chicago Housing Authority in *Phillips* and *Cross,* had assumed an increased responsibility for their care and protection, and as such, was liable for the negligent performance of this voluntary undertaking.

Even though McDonald's had no duty imposed by law to protect plaintiffs against the criminal acts of third parties, it had voluntarily recognized the threat of armed robbery and the importance of security in the restaurants, especially in the time period immediately after closing. It had created a branch of its corporation assigned to deal with security problems, and had prepared a bible for store security operations. McDonald's, through its regional security manager, Jim Carlson, undertook not only the obligation to check for security problems, but also to communicate to store management what the security policies were and to "follow up" to be certain that the problems had been corrected and the "recommended" security procedures "followed." . . .

Defendant urges the court to consider the separate and distinct nature of McDonald's Corporation and McDonald's Restaurants of Illinois . . . No matter what legal relationships existed, it was McDonald's Corporation which undertook to provide security and protection to plaintiffs. It was McDonald's Corporation's regional security manager, Jim Carlson, who acted directly as security supervisor for the newly-acquired Oak Forest McDonald's, even though this restaurant was directly owned by McDonald's Restaurants of Illinois, Inc.

On October 31, 1979 . . . Carlson . . . visited the Oak Forest store. Carlson met with the store manager, Karl Ferret, and although he did not provide Ferret with a copy of the McDonald's bible of security procedures which Carlson had written, he did inform Ferret about McDonald's proper closing procedures, specifically stating that no one should throw garbage out the back door after dark. . . . During this visit to the store, Carlson also did a security check, and suggested certain security changes be made such as changing the locks and ordering a new security window and Detex alarm system for the back door.

The trial court correctly determined that McDonald's Corporation had a duty to protect plaintiffs . . . from harm. [T]here is ample support in case law and in the facts of this case to support a determination that McDonald's Corporation voluntarily assumed a duty to provide security to plaintiffs and to protect them from harm.

Once McDonald's Corporation assumed the duty to provide security and protection to plaintiffs, it had the obligation to perform the duty with due care and competence, and any failure to do so would lead to a finding of breach of duty. . . . McDonald's clearly established a security policy which unquestionably included a follow-up. McDonald's argument that the employees were already familiar with security procedures and did not need to be instructed is belied by the facts of the actual operation of the restaurant. Trial testimony proved that the work crew used the back door exclusively, both before and after dark, and emptied garbage and grease through this door all day and all night. . . . In view of this established operating procedure, it is meaningless for McDonald's to argue that its employees were familiar with back door security, and that a follow-up was unnecessary. Therefore, the duty which McDonald's defined for itself included a follow-up which was doubly necessary because of the operating conditions of the restaurant. Accordingly there was ample evidence for the jury to determine that McDonald's had breached its assumed duty to plaintiffs.

McDonald's argues that even if it had breached a duty to plaintiffs, that there is no evidence to support the contention that anything McDonald's Corporation did or failed to do was the proximate cause of the entry of Logan on the premises and the subsequent injury to the plaintiffs. . . . While it is true that there is no direct evidence that Peter Logan entered the store through the rear door, there is more than ample circumstantial evidence on which the jury could conclude that Logan did indeed gain entry to the McDonald's through the rear door and that the failure of McDonald's security procedures facilitated that entry and were thus the proximate cause of injury to plaintiffs.

Defendant McDonald's Corporation also contends that even if it had breached a duty to plaintiffs which proximately caused their damage, that such damages consists of emotional injuries only and as such are not compensable under the law. As support for this proposition, McDonald's relies on the zone of danger rule and the physical injury requirement established by the Illinois Supreme Court in *Rickey v. Chicago Transit Authority (1983).*

We find the *Rickey* analysis inappropriate to the instant case. Plaintiffs Kincaid and Dudek (the injured crew members) were not bystanders in a zone of danger who suffered emotional distress as a result of observing the murder of their co-worker. Rather, they were direct victims of an assault and battery perpetrated by Peter Logan and proximately caused by McDonald's negligence. . . . (Based on the facts of this case, we find that plaintiffs Kincaid and Dudek have stated a valid claim for the negligent infliction of emotional distress and are entitled to damages recognizable under the law.

We affirm the trial court's determination of defendant McDonald's negligence and its award of damages to the parents of Laura Martin for their daughter's wrongful death and to Maureen Kincaid and Therese Dudek for negligent infliction of emotional distress.

Case Questions

1. Why do you think McDonald's assumed the duty to monitor the security at its restaurants, even those owned by its franchisees? If it had not assumed that duty, what argument would you make on behalf of the plaintiffs?

2. Review each of the elements of negligence as discussed in this case. What was the basis of McDonald"s duty to plaintiffs? What actions show nonperformance of that duty? Explain the causal connection between McDonald's actions and the death or injury of the plaintiffs.

3. Assume you are a security official or corporate manager for McDonald's. After reviewing this case, what actions could McDonald's take to limit its future liability for injuries caused by the criminal actions of others?

COMMENTARY

Will the Proximate Cause Requirement Be Changed?

By Amy Stevens and Junda Woo

The California Supreme Court has made it easier for victims to win personal-injury and product-liability lawsuits, in a technical decision with wide implications.

The ruling will affect virtually all jury trials statewide in which it has been alleged that there were multiple causes for a person's injuries. The 6–1 ruling struck down the state's traditional jury instruction on negligence liability, substituting one that would permit juries to find that there can be more than one cause of harm.

The court's decision requires an instruction that asks the jury to determine instead whether the defendant's conduct was a "substantial factor" in bringing about harm, and would allow a jury to hold defendants liable even if their behavior was only a contributing factor in the injury.

The rejected jury instruction required a jury to find that harm wouldn't have occurred "but for" the defendant's actions. "Proximate cause," the rejected standard, has been criticized by legal scholars and disapproved by many state courts nationwide, because it tended to mislead juries into thinking that the defendant had to be physically near the injured party, or that the defendant's actions had to have occurred close in time to the harm. The decision by the influential California high court could encourage even more states to move away from the "but for" test.

The "substantial factor" test developed as an alternative, discretional instruction about 25 years ago. The effect of the new ruling is to make that instruction mandatory.

Source: Reprinted by permission of *The Wall Street Journal,* Amy Stevens and Junda Woo, "California Eases Standards on Negligence," December 12, 1991, p. B5.

Negligence Per Se and *Res Ipsa Loquitur* In two circumstances—negligence per se and *res ipsa loquitur*—the burden of proof on the plaintiff is less than it is in most negligence cases. **Negligence per se** applies when the plaintiff uses the defendant's violation of a criminal statute as proof of the defendant's negligence. For example, if a statute requires a moving firm to have certain safety equipment on its trucks and the defendant moving firm did not have such equipment, the statute creates a conclusive presumption that the defendant was negligent. In some of the states, the presumption is not conclusive, but can be rebutted by other evidence.

negligence per se Applies when the plaintiff uses the defendant's violation of a criminal statute as a presumption of defendant's negligence.

res ipsa loquitur Means "the thing speaks for itself"; in some situations, circumstantial evidence is used to establish a first-impression case of negligence.

Res ipsa loquitur means "the thing speaks for itself." In some situations, circumstantial evidence is used to establish a prima facie (first impression) case of negligence. Unless the defendant counters this evidence, the doctrine of *res ipsa loquitur* is sufficient to prove negligence. This doctrine is used in situations in which the plaintiff cannot know the exact cause of negligence, as in cases involving product liability or negligent building construction. A building will not usually crumble or collapse unless there was some negligence in its design or construction; thus, even though the exact cause of the failure is not known, circumstantial evidence suggests there was negligence.

Intentional and Negligent Torts

Ethical Dilemma

The intentional and negligent state of mind accompanying a tortious act can be exposed to ethical analysis. Clearly, when a tortfeasor knows that an act will injure others, performing that act is unethical. Intentional aggression on another person illustrates an ethical conflict between the actor's self-interest and the victim's rights. Fraud is a classic form of ethical dilemma, in which the perpetrator breaches the victim's trust. For example, a salesperson who has gained the trust of a potential customer knows that the customer is likely to rely on the salesperson's statements. This salesperson commits fraud by intentionally making a statement contradictory to fact.

Negligent actions can also be analyzed with ethical principles. To the extent that wrongdoers have had sufficient experience with harmful or damaging instrumentalities, they should know when extra precautions are necessary to avoid injury. Evidence of carelessness, recklessness, or a wanton disregard of the consequences of an act indicates that the actor is making an unethical decision to ignore the dangers. This is not to say that all negligent acts are unethical. However, when the actor should know that an outcome could cause injury and fails to adequately guard against it, the actor's reckless disregard of consequences approximates intentional misconduct, an unethical act. For example, society increasingly believes that driving under the influence of alcohol is both an unethical act and an illegal criminal act. The person who knows, or should know, that his or her conduct can cause injury to others, but, disregarding the possible consequences, operates a motor vehicle while under the influence of alcohol is acting unethically.

Defenses to Negligent Torts

There are three basic defenses to negligence claims: contributory negligence, comparative negligence, and assumption of risk.

Contributory Negligence The **contributory negligence** defense, which must generally be raised by the defendant, alleges that even though the defendant may have been negligent, the plaintiff was also somewhat negligent. In the past, the law prohibited any recovery by the plaintiff from the defendant if the defendant proved any contributory negligence by the plaintiff. This is commonly known as the *all-or-nothing rule* because the plaintiff wins all if contributory negligence is not proved and nothing if contributory negligence is proved.

contributory negligence The negligence defense that even though the defendant may have been negligent, as plaintiff was also somewhat negligent, plaintiff cannot recover.

Comparative Negligence Because of the harsh effect of contributory negligence on plaintiffs who were only slightly at fault, most states now use comparative negligence as the most common defense in negligence cases. **Comparative negligence** weighs the relative negligence on the plaintiff and the defendant. In some states, it does not matter how much negligence is attributable to the plaintiff. Even if the plaintiff can prove that the defendant is only 15 percent negligent in causing the plaintiff's injuries, the plaintiff (who would be 85 percent negligent) can still recover damages equal to 15 percent of the money needed to totally compensate for those injuries. For example, suppose that a two-car accident occurs in a state using this type of comparative negligence defense. Assume that the plaintiff (the driver of one of the cars) is found to be 85 percent at fault for his own injuries. If $100,000 is needed to totally compensate the plaintiff for his injuries, the plaintiff would be able to recover $15,000 from the defendant (the driver of the other car), who was 15 percent at fault.

comparative negligence The negligence defense that weighs the relative negligence of the plaintiff and the defendant and holds defendant liable only for a portion of plaintiff's damages.

FIGURE 8-3

Comparative Negligence: Recovery Under Different State Standards

	State A	State B
Recovery for plaintiff who is 85% at fault and whose injuries amount to $100,000	$15,000	0 (Plaintiff cannot recover if more than 50% at fault.)
Recovery for defendant who is 15% at fault and whose injuries amount to $50,000	$42,500	$42,500

In State A, the court would actually award the plaintiff nothing, and the defendant would receive the net amount of $27,500, the difference between the amount due the plaintiff and the amount due the defendant.

Other states permit the plaintiff to recover damages from the defendant only if the defendant is responsible for at least 50 percent of the plaintiff's injuries. In the states that follow this interpretation of comparative negligence, the plaintiff in our example would recover nothing from the defendant.

However, suppose that the defendant was also injured in this accident, in the amount of $50,000. Figure 8–3 compares the amount that each party would recover under both systems of comparative negligence if the plaintiff was 85 percent at fault and suffered $100,000 in injuries and the defendant was 15 percent at fault and suffered $50,000 in injuries.

assumption of risk The defense to negligence or strict liability that prevents plaintiff's recovery if he or she knew or should have known of the risk inherent in a particular situation and voluntarily assumed that risk.

Assumption of Risk Like comparative negligence, the assumption of risk defense is based on the concept of fault. **Assumption of risk** applies if a plaintiff knew, or should have known, of the risk inherent in a particular situation and voluntarily assumes that risk. The defendant in such a case is not responsible for the plaintiff's injury even if the defendant was negligent. A classic example of this defense occurs when a plaintiff is injured while riding in a car with an intoxicated driver. Although the defendant driver is negligent in driving while intoxicated, the plaintiff, who knows the risk of riding with an intoxicated driver yet voluntarily does so, may be denied recovery due to his or her assumption of that risk.

Some of the states that accept the defense of comparative negligence do not also accept the defense of assumption of risk. In their view, the plaintiff's assumption of risk is a form of negligence comparable to the defendant's negligence. In these states, the assumption of risk and comparative negligence defenses are viewed as one defense. As is indicated in the case that follows, there is significant overlap between the two concepts. However, even if a state dropped the use of contributory negligence in favor of comparative negligence, a distinction generally exists between comparative negligence and assumption of risk.

Assumption of risk occurs when a person who knows of a risk nevertheless proceeds in the face of that risk. Contributory or comparative negligence compares the action of the one person to the action of a reasonable person (to determine whether there is any negligence) and of the defendant (to determine the relative negligence of the parties). A person's actions can contribute to causing an injury even if he or she does not know of the risk involved. In the following case, what was the basis for the distinction between these two defenses in Mississippi?

McGowan v. St. Regis Paper Co., Inc.

419 F. Supp. 742 (S.D. Miss. 1976)
United States District Court

McGowan was injured while unloading wood chips for his employer, Columbia, at the St. Regis paper mill. He had performed similar work at the paper mill before, so he knew that oil or grease often built up on the ramp he used. In fact, he admitted he had seen the oil and grease that caused him to fall. When McGowan sued St. Regis for negligence, St. Regis claimed McGowan had assumed the risk when he continued to use the ramp after knowing it to be in a dangerous condition. The trial court's decision follows.

Nixon, District Judge

The owner or occupier of business premises owes invitees, such as plaintiff, the duty to exercise reasonable or ordinary care to keep its premises in a reasonably safe condition and to warn them of any dangers which are known or should be known to the owner through the exercise of reasonable care. However, in the interest of his own safety, an invitee is required to use that degree of care and prudence which a person of ordinary intelligence would exercise under the same or similar circumstances, and in the usual case, there is no obligation to protect him against dangers which are known to him or which are obvious and apparent. Against such conditions it may normally be expected that the visitor will protect himself, and for this reason it is frequently held that reasonable care requires nothing more than a warning of danger.

In this case, although the defendant did not post any warning signs or give any other type of warning to plaintiff or other truck drivers unloading the wood chips on the defendant's ramp, they nevertheless knew, or in the exercise of reasonable care, should have known, of the probable existence of oil or grease being present on the ramp, which lifted many trucks while unloading chips therefrom; in fact, the plaintiff testified that he actually saw the oil or grease which subsequently caused him to slip and fall and realized that it constituted a dangerous condition. Therefore, the defendant was under no duty to warn him of that obvious and known danger.

There is no proof that the defendant caused the oil or grease to be present on the ramp, that they had knowledge thereof, or that it had existed for such a period of time that they were charged with such knowledge. As a matter of fact, ten trucks had unloaded on this ramp on the morning in question prior to the time that the plaintiff was injured, and one had just left the ramp after unloading. Thus, the plaintiff has failed to prove by a preponderance of the evidence that the defendant was guilty of any negligence which proximately contributed to cause the plaintiff's injuries.

. . . The Mississippi Supreme Court has held that where assumption of the risk overlaps and coincides with contributory negligence, the contributory negligence or comparative negligence rule of Mississippi is applicable. However, the Court refused to abolish the doctrine of assumption of the risk as a bar to recovery and recognized that the application of the rule of comparative negligence, which is not a complete defense, where it overlaps and coincides with contributory negligence, "does not prevent a defense on the ground that the plaintiff's injury was caused by his negligence, if his negligence was the sole proximate cause of the injury."

The defense of assumption of the risk is in fact quite narrowly confined and restricted by two requirements: first, that the plaintiff must know and understand the risk he is incurring, and second, that his choice to incur it must be entirely free and voluntary. As the Mississippi Supreme Court pointed out in the case of *Daves v. Reed,* the significant difference between assumption of the risk and contributory negligence is between risks which were in fact known to the plaintiff and risks which he merely might have discovered by the exercise of ordinary care. The former defense is governed by the subjective standard of the plaintiff himself, whereas the latter is measured by the objective standard of the reasonable man. Assumption of the risk is a jury question in all but the clearest cases.

The undisputed facts of the instant case constitute one of the rare instances where the doctrine of assumption of the risk as a complete bar to recovery is applicable, inasmuch as the plaintiff subjectively knew, as admitted in his sworn testimony, that the oily or greasy substance was present on the unloading ramp, that it constituted a dangerous condition, and that he voluntarily and freely was walking through the substance with a chain in his hand in an attempt to "tie down" his truck prior to tilting the ramp and unloading wood chips from the truck. He did not notify the employee of the defendant who was on duty in the control house a short distance away of this condition or ask that anything be done in connection therewith, but freely and voluntarily subjected himself to the danger which he recognized. Thus, he is barred from recovery by the doctrine of assumption of risk as it has been enunciated by the Mississippi Supreme Court.

Case Questions

1. Why wasn't St. Regis obligated to warn McGowan of the danger presented by the oil and grease on the ramp?
2. Did the court find that St. Regis was negligent in maintaining the ramp?
3. Compare and contrast the court's analysis of assumption of risk with its discussion of contributory or comparative negligence.

International Perspective and Commentary

Tort Law and the European Community

In the European Union (E.U.), Article 215 of the Treaty of Rome provides that the noncontractual liability of the community is governed by the "general principles common to the laws of the member states." Much of the work of the European Court of Justice is now handled by the European Court of First Instance. This court was authorized by the 1987 Single European Act, and its jurisdiction is limited to actions or proceedings by individuals or legal persons (firms).

When damages are sought in litigation involving community law, the European Court of Justice and the Court of First Instance must determine what principles of noncontractual liability (tort law) are common to the laws of member states. This is not easy, as there are now 15 member nations. Two members are common law jurisdictions, whereas the others are civil or code law countries. The European Community tort liability principles are not based on those national laws that impose the highest duty. Instead, it is common law national principles, such as fault being required for finding of negligence, that create community liability principles. Although the laws of many EU member states base liability for defective products on negligence, today the EU uses a no-fault liability standard for damages caused by defective products. Product liability laws in both the United States and in Europe are discussed in Chapter 11.

Strict Liability Torts

The traditional view of strict liability is that a person engaging in inherently dangerous or ultrahazardous activities is liable to any injured party, regardless of the actor's intent or fault. Therefore, strict liability is different from intentional torts and negligence because strict liability requires neither a finding of intentional wrongdoing nor a finding of fault.

General Requirements

Strict liability recovery is relatively easy to establish compared to either the negligence or intentional tort standards. A **strict liability tort** occurs if one person does something dangerous that injures another person who is within the scope of risk. The determination of whether an activity is extrahazardous is the important question in strict liability cases. By reading past cases, we can make a list, though not an exhaustive one, of activities that courts find to be extrahazardous. The dusting of crops, the keeping of wild and vicious animals, and the use of explosives and certain chemicals are activities that have been found to be ultrahazardous. On the other hand, such activities as mining coal, driving automobiles, and keeping gasoline in service station tanks have been found not to be ultrahazardous.

strict liability tort Occurs if one person does something dangerous that injures another person who is within the scope of risk; some product liability cases now are based on this standard.

In the last several decades, an increasing number of suits involving defective products have been decided on the basis of strict liability. There is strict liability for a product found to be defective if the product is unreasonably dangerous and the danger is not readily apparent to the buyer. Typical strict liability cases have involved such products as foods and drinks, playground equipment, defective consumer appliances, and automobiles. In these cases, the plaintiff must meet the following three requirements, which are discussed further in Chapter 11.

Required Elements of a Strict Liability Defective Products Case

1. There was a *defect* in the product.
2. The defect *caused* the plaintiff's *injury*.
3. The defect existed when the product left the defendant's *control*.

Defenses

Because proof of negligence is not required in strict liability cases, the contributory or comparative negligence defenses are not available. However, most states do recognize as defenses the assumption of risk and *misuse,* which is a form of assumption of risk based on improper product use. If a cigarette manufacturer warns the purchaser or user of cigarettes of a specific risk associated with their use, the manufacturer is generally not liable for compensation for injuries resulting from that risk to a person who knowingly assumed it. A recent Supreme Court case discussing this issue is found in Chapter 11. If a product that is intended to be used to kill ants or insects outside the house is used to kill household insects, despite a clear warning on the product, and the product injures the plaintiff, the defense of misuse could be used against the injured plaintiff.

Policies

Several policies underlie the allowance of recovery on the basis of strict liability. First, such liability tolerates an extrahazardous activity if it has some social value. Second, compensation for a victim is more likely in strict liability cases than in negligence cases. Allowing the defendant to spread the costs of the injury among many users enables society to receive the benefits of the extrahazardous activity while sharing the cost of compensating the injured party. For example, society benefits from allowing miners and road or bridge builders to have explosives available for their work. Society also shares in the cost of compensating a party injured by the use of such explosives because blasting insurance obtained by the miners and the road or bridge builders is expensive, due to strict liability laws, and that affects the cost of our minerals, roads, and bridges.

On the other hand, there are some policy reasons against the concept of strict liability. The most obvious is that the defendant can escape liability only by forgoing the extrahazardous activity. Thus, the law does not distinguish between a good and bad business that performs an extrahazardous activity except to the extent that good users undertake extra precautions.

Tort Law Reform

Because so many cases involving strict liability have applied to sales of products that cause injuries, many manufacturers have sought federal and state legislative changes in the area of product liability law. This area involves not only the strict liability and negligence tort concepts but also warranty and misrepresentation laws. Because product liability laws are important to consumers of products as well as their manufacturers and sellers, Chapter 11 is devoted to this subject. However, this section discusses some possible areas of tort reform.

The Future of Tort Law

The 1980s were a period of dramatic growth in litigation. Tort law expanded as more extensive duties were recognized by the courts. Juries became more sympathetic to victims of accidents, product failures, and unsafe conditions, applying the deep-pocket theory to hold accountable corporate defendants that were perceived to have extensive financial resources. Eventually, insurers of these firms claimed that they were unable to accurately predict the outcome of tort litigation. As a result, insurance premiums skyrocketed, some types of insurance became unavailable, and both insurers and potential corporate defendants called for tort reform in the media, through various legislatures, and in the courts.

Proponents of tort reform claim that it would create a fair, predictable, and equitable fault system while reducing the costs of litigation. They assert that the tort crisis had increased the cost of goods and services, stifled innovation in new products, delayed the introduction of new drugs, and postponed the sharing of benefits in many research breakthroughs. The tort reforms that have been sought include changes in the allocation of liability among several defendants, limits on certain types of damages, restriction of double recoveries by plaintiffs, reduction of the contingency fee incentives of plaintiff attorneys, sanctions against frivolous suits, and periodic payments of damages over a number of years. The first two areas of potential reform are noted in subsequent sections. In the years ahead, astute managers will closely monitor both legislative and judicial endeavors to address this important segment of the legal environment.

Joint and Several Liability

Joint and several liability requires the complete satisfaction of a plaintiff's damage award from any or all of the responsible defendants, regardless of the degree of fault of any single defendant. A defendant may be required to pay more than its share of the damage award if the other defendants are *judgment-proof* (uninsured or unable to pay). This provides an incentive to plaintiffs to sue a deep-pocket defendant that may be only slightly at fault because the whole compensatory and punitive amount must be paid by any defendant with sufficient financial resources. For example, drivers injured in traffic accidents often sue the state as well as the other driver because the state is responsible for road conditions. If the other driver is at fault but has insufficient insurance to satisfy the plaintiff's damages, the state's deep pocket is liable for the remainder.

Since 1985, almost half of the states have reformed the laws of joint and several liability. Six states—Alaska, Arizona, Kansas, Utah, Vermont, and Wyoming—have totally abolished it. Many states have kept joint and several liability but have limited its applicability. California and Ohio use it only for economic damages such as lost wages and medical expenses. Parties who are less than 50 percent or 25 percent at fault will not be jointly liable in New York and Illinois, respectively. A change from joint and several liability to proportionate liability is the goal of many proponents of tort reform. With proportionate liability, a defendant 15 percent at fault would be liable for only 15 percent of the plaintiff's damages.

Damage Caps

Tort reform efforts usually attempt to significantly limit or eliminate such *noneconomic damages* as (1) pain and suffering, (2) lost of consortium with a spouse, (3) emotional distress, (4) embarrassment, and (5) punitive damages. For example, some states have imposed specific dollar amount ceilings for noneconomic damages in all negligence cases. Other states have such ceilings only for specific types of suits, most notably medical malpractice or product liability cases. Still other states require "clear and convincing evidence" before allowing noneconomic damages to exceed the ceilings. The House of Representatives has passed a bill limiting noneconomic damages in medical malpractice cases to $250,000. That proposal is based on California's Medical Injury Compensation Reform Act, which includes the $250,000 limit.

Punitive Damages

Twenty-nine states have made changes in the law of punitive damages. In five states, Louisiana, Massachusetts, Nebraska, New Hampshire, and Washington, punitive damages are generally unavailable. As Chapter 5 notes, the United States Supreme Court has indicated that the due process clause of the Constitution limits a jury's discretion in awarding punitive damages (because it is depriving the defendant of property). Many states have adopted laws that specify more clearly the limited circumstances that would support awarding punitive damages.

Summary

Tort law is an important area of legal concern to businesses. Liability is imposed on a business for the actions of its employees, agents, and even its contractors if they are acting within the scope of their authority and are subject to control by the business. Since a business usually has greater insurance coverage and financial resources, the deep-pocket approach generally leads tort victims to make more and larger claims on businesses than on individual wrongdoers.

Three classes of torts can form the basis for the liability of a business to an injured party. Intentional torts are based on actions that have been committed intentionally. Negligence torts result from the wrongdoer's carelessness or lack of reasonable care. Strict liability torts require no proof of fault or of intent to act in a wrongful manner; instead, they are based on dangerous or ultrahazardous activities. Since many strict liability torts involve product liabilityconcerns, this area is treated in greater detail in Chapter 11.

Intentional torts require not proof of intent to harm, but proof of intent to commit the act that causes harm. Among the intentional torts are actions that interfere with personal rights, such as battery or false imprisonment, and actions that impair a person's reputation or state of mind, such as defamation, the infliction of mental distress, and invasion of privacy. Other intentional torts are those that interfere with property rights, such as trespass and conversion, and those that interfere with economic relations, such as interference with contract rights.

Negligent torts occur when a person or a business having a duty to act reasonably toward others does not perform that duty, and that nonperformance is a proximate cause of the injuries of others. In negligence cases, the presence of each of the four elements of negligence—duty, nonperformance, proximate cause, and injury—must be proved. Several defenses may be asserted by a business sued in a negligence case. The defenses of contributory and comparative negligence examine whether the plaintiff contributed to causing the injuries suffered. In contributory negligence, any negligence on the plaintiff's part prevents recovery, whereas in comparative negligence, which is a defense in most of the states, the negligence of the injured plaintiff reduces, but does not totally bar, the compensation that the defendant must pay to the plaintiff. The assumption of risk defense is used in a negligence case if the plaintiff performed some activity closely associated with a specific risk of which he or she was, or should have been, aware.

In strict liability cases, no proof of the defendant's fault is required. A defendant that makes dangerous products, such as firearms or caustic chemicals, is liable for any injuries resulting from the use of those products. Strict liability cases were originally concerned only with wild animals or inherently dangerous products, but today almost any defective product can be the basis for such a case. The only defenses to a product liability case are the plaintiff's assumption of risk or misuse of the product.

The chapter also notes some of the proposals for reforming tort law that have been advanced so as to alert the reader to potential changes in this legal area.

Critical Thinking Questions

1. Susan left work after dark one evening. She was assaulted and battered in the parking lot. The security guard detained the assailant. Both Susan and the local district attorney brought separate cases against the defendant. Did their cases cause double jeopardy for the defendant? Compare and contrast the causes of action Susan brought on the basis of tort assault and battery with the causes of action the district attorney brought on the basis of criminal assault and battery.
2. Give examples of four negligence cases where the issue in each focuses on a different element that is required to prove negligence.
3. John, a relatively inexperienced skier, brought a negligence action against Big Bear Ski Resort for injuries that allegedly occurred when he became entangled in underbrush concealed by loose snow. John was skiing on the resort's intermediate trail. No warning signs regarding the underbrush were posted. What would be the basis for holding Big Bear Ski Resort liable?
4. Black sued a retail store for injuries. He slipped on rainwater as he stepped on a mat just inside the door to the store. Prior to the fall, a store employee placed a "Caution: Wet Floor" sign approximately five feet in front of the door. In accordance with store procedure, the employee mopped the entrance area periodically on rainy days. What defense will the retail store assert? Is this defense different from contributory negligence?
5. Explain the concept of joint and several liability, how it is applied, and the grounds on which it is criticized.

Critical Thinking Exercises

1. Mrs. Davis was in debt to a finance company. She informed the company that she was no longer employed, that she was on public aid, and that she was unable to make payments on her loan. Over an eight-month period, in attempting to collect the debt, employees of the finance company called her several times a week, sometimes more than once a day, using obscene and threatening

language. Employees of the finance company visited her home weekly to demand payments on the debt. On one occasion, an agent from the finance company even telephoned her at a hospital where she was visiting her sick daughter. Mrs. Davis sued the finance company for damages, alleging severe emotional distress. Was the finance company's conduct toward her tortious? What kind of tort is she alleging has occurred?

2. The plaintiff, who was injured in an automobile accident caused entirely by the defendant driver, was not wearing his seat belt. He was thrown from the car and sustained a head injury when he landed on the pavement. The defendant offered evidence that had the plaintiff been wearing his seat belt, he would not have been thrown from the car. If the doctrine of comparative negligence is followed, should the plaintiff's nonuse of the seatbelt reduce the damages awarded to plaintiff? Why?
3. The defendant company has been a bicycle manufacturer for 50 years. It has always used reputable raw material suppliers. During the manufacturing process, it always follows quality control standards, making safety checks on every tenth bicycle that comes off the assembly line. Jane purchased a new bicycle from the company. While riding under normal conditions, she jumped a low curb. Because three spokes of the front wheel were defective, the wheel collapsed, and Jane was injured. As a result of the accident, she is now paralyzed from the waist down. Discuss the liability of the company on the grounds of both negligence and strict liability.
4. A man ran to catch a commuter train in Grand Central Station. An employee of the Long Island Railroad negligently tried to assist the man as he jumped for the train, causing the man to drop a package he was carrying. The package, which contained legal fireworks, exploded. The explosion shook the train platform, causing a weighing scale to fall over and injure Mrs. Palsgraf and her daughter, who were standing some distance away from the explosion. Mrs. Palsgraf sued the Long Island Railroad. What was the result, and why? *Palsgraf v. Long Island Railroad Co.,* 248 N.Y. 339, 1928.
5. The plaintiff (a salesman) sought damages for statements that were alleged to have been made by his former employer. He alleged that following the termination of his employment, the sales manager of his former employer made statements to his friends, business associates, and customers accusing him of theft of company property and that the sales manager knew these statements to be false. The plaintiff's wife testified that the sales manager's statements caused her husband to become depressed and to have more sleepless nights than he had had before he learned of the statements. The plaintiff testified that the accusations caused him anxiety, depression, humiliation, and many sleepless nights. Has the plaintiff made out a cause of action for slander? Is the truth a defense to a cause of action based on defamation? Is the truth a defense to a cause of action based on invasion of privacy? *Hennis v. O'Connor,* 388 N.N. 2d 470, 1986.
6. Consider the following cases related to drug testing by employers. On May 26, 1986, the city of Plainfield, New Jersey, ordered all its firefighters to submit to a surprise urinalysis while under the surveillance and supervision of bonded testing agents employed by the city. A similar process was repeated on two separate occasions until over 100 employees were tested. There was no notice of the intent to conduct the mass urinalysis. Later, 16 firefighters were informed they had tested positive for the presence of controlled dangerous substances; they were immediately terminated without pay. The plaintiff firefighters claimed their right to privacy and their freedom from unreasonable searches and seizures were violated. Do you agree? What torts would you argue have been committed? See *Capua v. City of Plainfield,* 643 F. Supp. 1507 (1986).

   Recall that while government employees are protected by the federal Constitution against unreasonable searches and seizures, employees in the private sector have no such protection. Would your answer be different if the employees worked for Disney World? What if the employees worked for a nonprofit agency such as the Boy Scouts or the Red Cross? Should it matter if the private firms receive substantial federal funds? Analyze these cases from an ethical perspective. See C. Stone, "Corporate Vices and Corporate Virtues: Do Public/Private Distinctions Matter?" 130 *University of Pennsylvania Law Review* 1441 (1982).

CHAPTER

9

Contracts

Critical Thinking Questions

- Contracts are the basis for most business relationships. Why do valid and enforceable agreements require: (1) genuine mutual assent, (2) legal contractual capacity, (3) consideration supporting the parties' promises, and (4) a legal contractual purpose?
- Mutual assent of the parties exists when a valid, definite, and intentional offer is communicated by the offeror and accepted by the offeree. What is the purpose for requiring that the acceptance terms mirror the offered terms?
- Contracts must be supported by consideration or have a legal substitute, such as promissory estoppel. How does consideration separate idle, unimportant, or social promises from the more serious ones that deserve legal enforcement?
- Some contracts may be voidable by one party because the law protects minors and drunken, drugged, and insane persons. How do victims of coercive negotiations rescind their contracts due to mistake, misrepresentation, fraud, duress, undue influence, or unknown illegality?
- Generally, contracts need not be in writing unless they involve the sale of land, guarantee other's debts, last more than one year, or involve the sale of $500 or more of goods. What additional evidence is admissible to vary a written contract?
- Outside third parties may have rights in the contracts of others if these parties are intended to benefit by the contracts or receive their rights by way of assignment. What alternate circumstances would make the assignment of contract rights or delegation of contract duties impermissible?

Introduction... Past, Present, Future

Modern contract law evolved from common law court decisions. Contract-like devices were recognized by the ancient Egyptians. However, early English law failed to enforce promises, holding persons liable only for defective performances. Modern contract law developed to support laissez-faire capitalism and the Industrial Revolution. There was a growing number of transactions, and contracting parties became more physically remote, necessitating more certainty in commercial transactions. The U.S. Constitution has libertarian ideals emphasizing individual free will and limiting the states from interfering with existing contracts. When these ideals are applied to commercial contracts, the law creates freedom of contract. Although parties are not completely free to contract for anything, particularly illegal objectives, freedom of contract encourages free enterprise by satisfying the reasonable expectations of contracting parties, permitting better planning.

The common law of contracts has been collected and rephrased by legal scholars into a compilation known as the *Restatement (Second) of Contracts.* Although the *Restatement* is not the definitive law, many courts nevertheless make the *Restatement* authoritative by citing it to resolve disputes as if it were legislation. In the United States, contract law is a combination of common law precedents, the *Restatement,* and statutory contract law. The most important statutory law of contracts is the *Uniform Commercial Code (UCC).* The UCC governs many types of contracts and now applies in varying forms in all U.S. states. The UCC is based on the *law merchant,* which evolved from the trading practices and conventions adopted by European merchants during the Middle Ages. The UCC is divided into several parts, and Article 2 governs contracts for the sale of goods. These are discussed further in Chapter 10.

In the future, contract law is likely to evolve from the somewhat inflexible historical requirements to reflect real-world business practices. The UCC is a good example of this trend. The law will need to respond to the mechanization of commercial contracting through computer communications, a process known as electronic data interchange (EDI). For example, parties will adopt common contract terms embodied in an umbrella contract for their numerous future dealings, permitting them to use electronic communications to make their offers and acceptances. The rule of consideration may be further weakened as the courts recognize that the parties to contracts are in the best position to know the seriousness of their expectations. The rights of incapacitants may be further eroded because minors are becoming quite sophisticated. This chapter examines the formation and performance of contracts through the events and conditions affecting their legal validity.

In the future, many more contract disputes will be resolved by alternative dispute resolution, particularly arbitration, now commonly used in international contracts. This is consistent with the need for greater trust and good faith by commercial parties, perhaps reducing contract formalities. Market discipline will replace aspects of legal enforcement.

Thought Questions

1. What assumptions does the U.S. Constitution make concerning the role of contracts in the economy and ultimately for public prosperity?
2. How will contracting evolve as technical developments occur in the future?

INTERNATIONAL PERSPECTIVE AND COMMENTARY

VARYING CONCEPTIONS OF CONTRACT

Contract law varies, often quite widely, between nations and even within a nation's political subdivisions, states, or provinces. International custom has clearly influenced national contracting laws toward uniformity, particularly among nations successful in international trade. Nevertheless, there are often some fundamental differences in each nation's historical and cultural view of commercial transactions. International commercial law reflects concern over the heightened risk affecting cross-border transactions, the arbitrary and protectionist intervention of some governments, foreign currency fluctuations, and the greater physical distances involved. Details of international commercial transactions and dispute resolution are discussed further in Chapters 3 and 10.

Certainty in international transactions is complicated because there are varying approaches to contracting that reflect different legal systems: (1) the common law system applicable in the United States, Canada, and other nations of the former British empire; (2) the civil law system applicable in nations with a European continental heritage; (3) Islamic law; (4) socialist law; and (5) law in developing countries. Each system has unique cultural, political, and historical differences that impact contract duties, formation, performance, and expectations. For example, uncertainties will probably increase in dealings with Eastern bloc nations as they evolve away from the socialist system probably to civil law. Socialist theory was antagonistic to profit; economic decisions were made through central planning; contracts were negotiated exclusively with highly bureaucratic foreign government agencies; written contracts were required; and terms were exhaustively specified, particularly the price term. Socialist governments were inflexible about supplementing vague contracts with trade customs or "market prices." These practices are nearly extinct as the former socialist nations embrace democracy and capitalism. Civil law nations fill in contract gaps with statutory terms common to all contracts, as is the case under the UCC in the United States.

Trade between developing countries and industrialized nations reflects an imbalance in bargaining power and legal system development. The United Nations' Vienna Convention for the International Sale of Goods (CISG), discussed further in Chapter 10, reflects concerns over these problems. Dealings between firms in developing and developed nations raise ethical concerns because contracts are negotiated with foreign government officials. In some cases, foreign officials demand special favors before granting business to foreigners. Concern over these practices led the United States to adopt the Foreign Corrupt Practices Act (FCPA) discussed in Chapter 22, to prohibit U.S. firms from making bribes or corrupt payments to gain business.

Importance of Contracts

Contracts are the most basic of all business relationships. All sales of personal property, goods, real estate, services, and employment result from contracts. The interactions of businesses with suppliers, customers, and employees are all based on various contract for services, sales of land, and sales of goods. Even less formal relations that many college students encounter are contracts. For example, the following involve enforceable contracts whether or not they are in writing: dormitory and food service agreements, apartment leases, textbook purchases and sales, social commitments such as hiring a band or DJ for a party, charitable fund-raisers, student organization sponsored events such as plant tours or office visits, and arrangements for an outside speaker. Contracts are intangible relationships among parties that provide for enforceable duties that the parties voluntarily assume. Many contracts are put into written documents to evidence the relationship. There is no tangible "contract," only the legally enforceable rights resulting from the parties' agreement. A **contract** may be defined as an enforceable set of mutual obligations for which the law provides a remedy, recognizes a duty, or provides for court enforcement.

contract
An enforceable set of mutual obligations for which the law provides a remedy, recognizes a duty, or provides for court enforcement.

Contracts are enforced so that commerce may proceed in an orderly fashion. If businesses could not rely on their reasonable expectations that contracts will be performed, commerce might be reduced and would become less stable. In such an uncertain world, only face-to-face agreements could be made with reasonable certainty, and many agreements would be breached. Because contracts create legally enforceable obligations, businesses may plan for future purchases, production, and sales. Contracts assure business a reasonable remedy when an obligation is breached. Such commercial disputes comprise a rising proportion of the current boom in litigation.

Classification of Contracts

Contracts are classified in several ways. *Express contracts* arise from the parties' outward expressions of mutual assent such as their oral or written statements or gestures. *Implied in fact contracts* are inferred from the parties' actions. For example, a written employment agreement is an express contract, whereas the contract between a taxi driver and a passenger is implied. Quasi-contracts are implied in law and discussed later in this section.

Bilateral contracts exist where there are two promises, one from each party. A *unilateral contract* arises where one of the parties does not expect a return promise but instead asks the other party to actually perform. For example, a reward poster is an offer to enter into a unilateral contract: The offeror promises to pay the reward if some other party provides the information sought. The other party does not accept the reward contract by promising to provide the needed information, but instead accepts the reward offer by performance in providing the information. While both bilateral and unilateral contracts are possible under the UCC, most contracts are bilateral.

A *valid contract* is completely enforceable by either party if it meets all of the necessary legal requirements. A *void contract* is invalid and unenforceable and arises when a contract has an illegal objective or when one party is adjudged to have been insane or incompetent during negotiations. A *voidable contract* allows one or both of the parties to rescind or cancel if there is a problem with incapacity, fraud, misrepresentation, duress, undue influence, or mistake. *Executed contracts* have been fully performed by both parties, and *executory contracts* have at least some duties that are not yet performed.

Contracts are created when one party's proposal, called the offer, is agreed to by the other party making an acceptance. The original author of an offer is the *offeror.* The person to whom the offer is made is the *offeree.* Only the offeree may create a binding contract, and that is when the acceptance is communicated. In a bilateral contract, each party makes at least one promise, making each party a *promisor.* As a result of making contractual promises, the contract makes each party an *obligor,* obligating their performance. This also makes each party the recipient of the other party's promise, so each promisor is also a *promisee.* Usually, each party is also an *obligee* to whom the duty of performance is owed unless the rights of third parties are involved.

Contracts Implied in Law

quasi-contract
Contract-like duty imposed to prevent unjust enrichment after a benefit is conferred.

A **quasi-contract,** though not a real contract, is treated like a contract for many purposes. Quasi-contractual agreements do not arise from agreements between the parties. Instead, certain obligations are *implied in law* under special circumstances. If one of the parties is *unjustly enriched* because a *benefit is conferred* by the other party, then quasi-contractual liability may arise. A quasi-contract frequently occurs where a benefit is conferred accidentally and the recipient could have prevented the mistake. Quasi-contractual liability can also arise in an emergency, such as when a doctor supplies lifesaving services to an unconscious victim. Even though there is no actual agreement and no actual contractual liability arises, the courts often require payment because it is unjust to receive benefits without paying for them. For example, suppose that an adult knowingly permits a neighborhood child to cut the adult's lawn by mistake. Although there is no contract for the child's services, it would be unjust for the adult to keep the benefits without paying if the adult could have prevented the work.

Mutual Assent: the Agreement

Before a bilateral contract arises, the parties must agree to the contract's terms, a step known as *mutual assent.* In most cases, the parties begin preliminary negotiations of the contract by communicating their expectations about the terms. For example, an advertisement or the initial sales pitch of a salesperson may start the negotiations. The contract terms usually identify the parties, adequately describe the subject matter, state the price (i.e., the cash, property, or services), indicate the quantity of the property or services, fix the time for the parties' performance, and include any other key terms (e.g., credit, warranties). These early communications may be in the form of offers and counteroffers, or they may be merely informational. A fine line distinguishes informational communications from one of the 5 operative contracting communications of offer, acceptance, counteroffer revocation, or rejection. This distinction is based on the *objective theory of contracts,* discussed below.

NEGOTIATING CONTRACT TERMS

INTERNATIONAL PERSPECTIVE AND COMMENTARY

Dealings between U.S. and Japanese companies contrast with contracts between Western developed nations. The Japanese prize long-term relations slowly nurtured on trust, long-term commitment, and superior performance. They do not rush into contracts with foreign firms. Instead, Japanese firms rely on a drawn-out negotiation of relationships, focusing on the prospects for harmony and the evolution of their relationship and less on the favorability of particular terms (price). Extensive socializing is used in Japan to probe the intentions of another firm's representatives before a deal is finalized. Negotiators in Mexico follow a similar negotiations model. While this practice appears extremely time-consuming to historically impatient American negotiators, it is fundamental to making sound relationships of trust with the Japanese and many other Asians and Latin Americans.

Today, most international commercial contracts seek to foresee and address all possible contingencies by resolving disputes in advance. Most contracts use choice of law provisions and binding international arbitration. By contrast, the Japanese prefer to solidify relationships between firms first, resolving any disputes through consensus, compromise, and accommodation. They do not welcome the intrusion of an outside arbitrator or the embarrassing visibility of public adversariness with a trial.

Offer

An **offer** is a proposal to contract that contains all the necessary contract terms. The proposal must be intended by the offeror to confer a power of acceptance on the offeree. An offer becomes effective only after it is communicated to the offeree. The offer is usually made in an oral or written manner, but occasionally it can be communicated by gestures, such as bids made at some auctions.

offer
Proposal to contract, containing all the necessary contract terms communicated to the offeree.

Objective Theory of Contracts All expressions of the contracting parties are judged by how a reasonable person would respond. The objective theory of contracts applies to all communications between parties, including offers, counteroffers, acceptances, revocations, rejections, preliminary negotiations, and inquiries regarding terms. An offeror's statement is a legal offer if a reasonable person would conclude that the offeror's communication was clearly intended to confer a power of acceptance on the offeree and that the offeree need only accept to create a contract. The offeror's hidden intent or secret hesitation is irrelevant if the average reasonable person would believe the offeror intended to make an offer. For example, an emotional person may make a proposal, but only in jest. Such a proposal might be an offer irrespective of the emotional person's intent if a reasonable person believes the offeror intended to make an offer.

FIGURE 9–1

Offer and Acceptance

After preliminary negotiations, A's offer passes a power of acceptance to B, who exercises that power and a contract results when B dispatches an acceptance to A. For example, if A offers to purchase B's house and B mails an acceptance to A, an enforceable contract exists.

Usually, a reasonable person will express *definite terms* by including all or nearly all of the proposed contract's essential terms in the offer. However, this is not always necessary because the parties may presume they are using reasonable or customary terms. For example, the UCC permits terms to be left open for future determination or inference, as discussed in Chapter 10.

Preliminary Negotiations Problems may arise in interpreting whether business communications are really offers. Generally, advertisements for goods or services are merely intended to be invitations to deal; they are seldom actual offers. This is so because most reasonable persons would presume that advertisements, solicitation letters, catalogs, and price lists are intended merely to arouse the buyer's interest. These communications seldom confer a power of acceptance because most people expect to negotiate after receiving such information.

Many problems could arise if advertisements were routinely considered offers. A contract might be created if the prospective purchaser merely accepted an advertisement. For example, many sellers would not be prepared with sufficient inventory if too many of these "offerees" responded to a particular advertisement. It is reasonable to assume that advertisers do not want this "stockout" problem, so their advertisements are not offers, only preliminary negotiations. However, an advertisement can be worded to clearly indicate that it is an offer. An advertiser could invite immediate acceptance. For example, language such as "while they last" in an advertisement can create an offer.

Acceptance

acceptance
Conduct reasonably indicating approval and commitment to a proposed contract.

For a contract to be formed, the offeree must *make an* **acceptance** of the offer, as illustrated in Figure 9–1. A contract comes into existence when the offeree accepts the exact terms proposed. This results in an exact agreement, a *meeting of the minds.* In one form of negotiating, informal communications between the parties take place before either actually makes an offer. Later, a formal offer, containing all of the terms already acceptable to both parties, is made by one party and formally accepted by the other. Businesses often use this form in more complex contracting such as with a supplier or commercial customer.

In another form of negotiating, the parties exchange several offers, most of which are not accepted. Instead, each response to the previous offer is a *counteroffer.*

FIGURE 9-2

Counteroffer

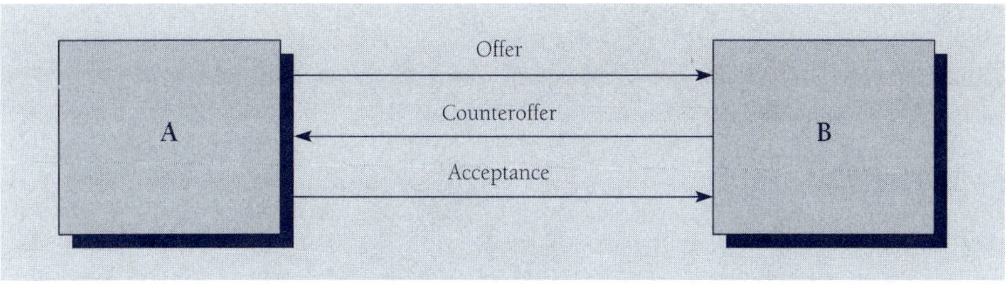

A's offer is terminated by B's counteroffer or conditional acceptance, but B extends a new offer to A. The contract results when A dispatches an acceptance in response to B's counteroffer. For example, if A offers to purchase B's house but B counteroffers at a higher price, then no contract exists unless A accepts B's counteroffer.

Eventually, when one of the counteroffers is finally accepted, a contract results. This second form is often used in sales of residential real estate and is illustrated in Figure 9–2. In either form of negotiating, a binding contract is formed when the last offer made is unconditionally accepted by the offeree.

Termination of Offers

As long as an offer remains open, the offeree is free to accept and create a contract. However, offers may be terminated, ending the offeree's ability to exercise the contracting power. Offers are terminated by the passage of time, revocation, rejection, acceptance, the death of either party, or the destruction of the contract's subject matter.

Lapse of Time Offers do not confer a permanent power of acceptance. Offers are terminated by the passage of a reasonable time, a period that varies depending on the circumstances. Offers terminate quickly in volatile markets, such as the stock, currency, or commodities exchanges. By contrast, in more stable markets, such as some real estate markets, offers live longer, perhaps for days, weeks, or even months. An offeror who wants the offer to terminate at a specific time may limit its duration by specifying the offer lapses under its own terms after the time passes. For example, prospective home buyers often specify when their offers lapse, such as in a few hours or days. This tactic creates an imminence that may induce a reluctant seller to accept a particular price.

Revocation Usually, the offeror may withdraw an offer by the act of **revocation.** A revocation is effective when expressed directly by the offeror to the offeree. A revocation may also be implied, as when the offeree receives reliable knowledge that the offered property was sold to another person. Revocation is illustrated in Figure 9–3.

revocation Offeror's withdrawal of an offer terminating the offeree's power of acceptance.

Option Contracts In some instances, an offeror may promise not to revoke an offer. Such *irrevocable offers* are useful, for example, when the offeree must expend significant sums to survey or research the subject matter before agreeing. If the offer is held open, the offeree has more time to study it without fear of losing the deal. There are two ways to make an offer irrevocable: option contracts and firm offers.

FIGURE 9–3

Revoked Offer

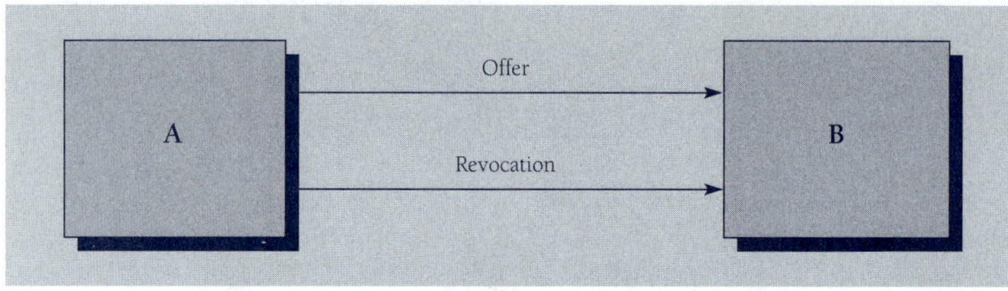

A's offer is terminated by A's revocation of the offer, and if made before B responds, no contract results. For example, if A offers to purchase B's house but has a change of heart before B responds, A may withdraw the offer by revocation and no contract results.

FIGURE 9–4

Rejected Offer

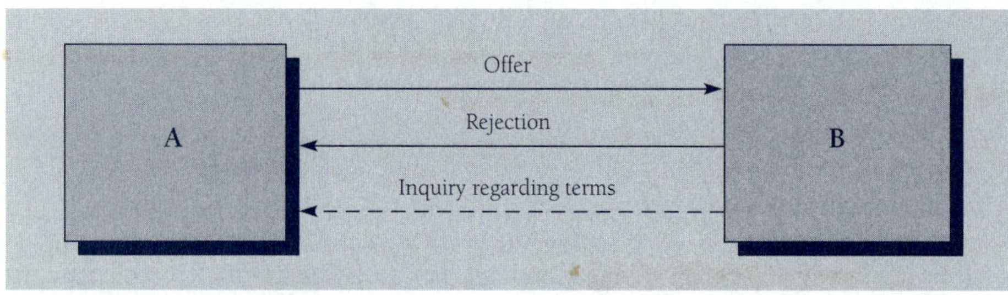

A's offer is terminated by B's rejection of the offer so no contract results. For example, if A offers to purchase B's house and B immediately rejects the offer, no contract results. However, a mere inquiry regarding terms does not terminate the offer.

option
A contract making an offer irrevocable, gives the offeree a specified time to further consider the offer.

An **option** contract is formed when the offeree pays a price (consideration) for irrevocability. The option becomes a separate contractual commitment in which the offeror gives up the right to revoke. A *firm offer* is also irrevocable even without payment of consideration under UCC requirements, as discussed in Chapter 10. If the offeror revokes an option, the offeror is liable for damages for breach of the option contract. For example, a homeowner who sells optioned property to another buyer is liable to the offeree holding the option.

rejection
Offeree's refusal to contract on the offered terms.

Rejection An offeree may refuse an offer by communicating a **rejection** that terminates the offeree's power of acceptance. Rejection is illustrated in Figure 9–4. However, an offeree's response to an offer may not be an unequivocal rejection. For example, an offeree might appear to accept an offer but also attach additional or different conditions to the acceptance. This type of response is often called a *conditional acceptance*. When an offeree revises the offered terms in any way, it is considered a *counteroffer*. Both conditional acceptances and counteroffers are considered rejections because they lack exact agreement with the offered terms. Where deviations are found between the offered terms and the accepted terms, no contract results because the parties have failed to agree and have not arrived at a mirror-image meeting of their minds. However, it is not a rejection for an offeree to merely request the offeror provide additional information or to ask the offeror to consider changing the terms. This is an *inquiry regarding terms*.

Mirror-Image Rule The common law requires that the acceptance mirror the offered terms under the *mirror-image rule.* This rule applies to contracts for land sales, services, or employment. The UCC is more liberal, permitting some deviations between the offered and accepted terms, as discussed in Chapter 10. When parties correspond about a possible contract, how do they know when a binding contract arises? The following case illustrates the problem of obtaining an exact mirror image between offer and acceptance.

J. Apablasa v. Merritt & Co.

1 Cal. Rept. 500 (1959)
California Court of Appeals

The plaintiff and the defendants wrote three letters to each other concerning the marketing of the plaintiff's invention. On August 24, 1955, the defendants wrote the first letter to the plaintiff. The plaintiff responded to that letter with a response dated August 27, 1955. The defendants did not reply to the plaintiff's August 27 letter, so the plaintiff wrote to the defendants on September 20, 1955. Plaintiff alleges the first and last letter constituted a contract. Defendants deny a contract was formed by these communications. Defendants' August 24 letter:

> I think you have a very fine invention. Undoubtedly with the right design worked out for the various models, proper sales brochures, and a concentrated direct-sales effort, the returns should be most gratifying. I feel confident that 50,000 units at $50.00 each could be sold within the first year.
>
> For us to work out the proper sales program and devote ourselves one hundred percent to the adaptability and perfection of various designs is, in itself, going to involve a great deal of time and money. I feel if the enterprise is going to be a success we should use all the money we have to develop and market the product, and pay you your fee out of the operating profits.
>
> Should you decide to give us a try in merchandising and marketing the item, instead of the $50,000 cash you mentioned as your selling price, I should suggest $100,000 as a bonus payment to be paid from a fixed percentage of the earnings and when this has been paid, that you should receive a continuing graduated percentage of the profits thereafter.
>
> Trusting something like this would be acceptable to you, and looking forward to hearing from you quite soon, I am
>
> Sincerely yours,

Plaintiff's August 27 letter:

> After due consideration, and in view of my age and other circumstances, I would like to sell the invention outright as I have already expressed to you, possibly taking less down payment—$5,000 instead of $10,000 and the balance on or before five years to make up the $50,000, which I have no doubt would be fair to assume would be available from the profits.
>
> I hope that within the different views we have expressed, something of mutual interest may be worked out.

Plaintiff's September 20 letter:

> After careful consideration I have decided to accept your proposition as outlined in your letter to me of August 24th, 1955, with this proviso: that you agree to put this product in production within a definite period of time from the date of the signing of any agreement between us.

An analysis of the writing fails to disclose the definite terms necessary to constitute it an offer to manufacture or have manufactured, merchandise and market plaintiff's invention—for an offer must be certain and definite.

It is well settled that if the offer is so indefinite as to make it impossible for a court to decide just what it means, and to fix exactly the legal liability of the parties, its acceptance cannot result in an enforceable agreement. The letter, a definite rejection by defendants of the idea of an outright sale of the device and an invitation to consider their services in merchandising and marketing the same, omits any reference to manufacturing; indeed, nothing therein relates to how or by whom the article is to be produced; production cost and who shall bear the same; how raw materials, patterns, designs and samples will be supplied; in what manner plaintiff's invention and patent if one exists, shall be transferred and to whom; and when production is to begin. Likewise, as to the marketing of the item, absent is any reference to territory, whether distribution is to be exclusive, who is to set the price, and the minimum amount to be sold in what period of time. Relative to the $50 figure mentioned, it appears to be only a suggested possible sales price used as a basis for speculation as to within what time, how many, and at what amount the items could be sold; and far from fixing the selling price, the figure constitutes no more than an expression of opinion of what possible returns "could" be expected and what "could" be done if sufficient time and money are expended on a proper program. Nor is there mention of how much out of any established sales price defendants are to receive on each item for their services, and how much is to be paid plaintiff. The "suggested percentage" is exactly what it purports to be—a suggestion of what "could" be worked out in the future "should (plaintiff) decide to give (them) a try to merchandising and marketing the item." That this letter was by no means intended to constitute an offer is found in the last paragraph wherein defendants expressed their hopes that "something like this" would be acceptable to plaintiff. (Emphasis added.)

Herein plaintiff rejected consideration of any arrangement to market and merchandise his invention and professed interest only in its outright sale. Appellant does not dispute that defendants' August 24 letter relates only to marketing and merchandising; and it is obvious his reply actually proposes a plan altogether different than that suggested by defendants, revealing an absence of any meeting of the minds and complete lack of interest in any program excluding outright sale. At most his letter of August 27 amounted to no more than a counter-proposal by him rejecting any plan heretofore proposed by defendants.

Where a person offers to do a definite thing and another introduces a new term into the acceptance, his answer is a mere expression of willingness to treat or it is a counter-proposal, and in neither case is there a contract; if it is a new proposal and it is not accepted it amounts to nothing.

Case Questions

1. What shows the defendants' intent to confer a power of contracting on the plaintiff in the August 24 letter? What language in the August 24 letter indicates that the defendants had mental reservations?

2. What could have been the practical effects of the plaintiff's August 27 and September 20 letters?

The Parties' Communications

For one party's communications to confer, exercise, or terminate the power of acceptance, the communications must be intended to affect the power of contracting. Most of the communications between contracting parties are effective only when actually received. There is one exception, the *mailbox rule,* which makes an acceptance effective when it is dispatched. Unless the offer states otherwise, a *dispatch* occurs when the offeree has done everything that can be done to send off the acceptance. For example, a contract immediately comes into existence when the offeree drops a properly addressed, stamped letter of acceptance into a Postal Service mailbox. The acceptance is effective even if a rejection or revocation arrives before the acceptance arrives. However, if the offeree uses an unreasonable means of communication, the offeree's acceptance does not become effective until it is received. Alternatively, the offer could specifically state the offeror must actually receive the offeree's

FIGURE 9-5

Mutual Promises

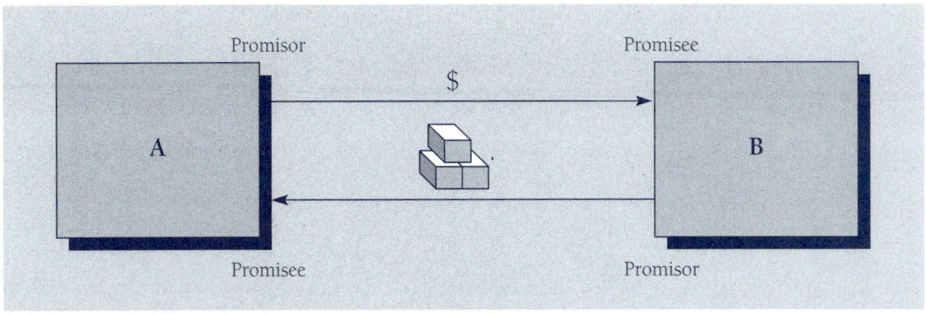

In the contract resulting from mutual assent between A and B (offer and acceptance), A promises to pay for goods that B promises to deliver. Each of them is a promisor and each is a promisee on the two respective promises.

acceptance before a contract becomes binding. Acceptances are generally effective only upon receipt in civil law nations. The UCC permits acceptance by any method reasonable under the circumstances.

CONSIDERATION

The law does not enforce all agreements. Mutual promises must go beyond a certain minimum threshold to create a contract for two reasons. First, many promises are made idly or lightly, with no intention of creating binding obligations. For example, promises to make a gift, to do a favor for another, or to participate in a social arrangement are considered less serious than business promises. Second, only sufficiently important cases should burden the judicial system. Although it might be socially desirable to rely on all promises, there must be some limit on the enforceability of promises, a limit corresponding to the seriousness and motivation of the promisor and the reasonableness of the promisee's expectations. These reasons justify the **consideration** requirement. Consideration distinguishes serious, enforceable promises from less serious and unenforceable promises. The rule of consideration requires that the parties mutually give value or make obligations. It is the principal measure of the importance of promises, but its significance is declining. The mutual promises necessary for adequate consideration are illustrated in Figure 9–5.

consideration Test for contract enforceability that judges the seriousness of the promises made.

Tests for the Presence of Consideration

There are several tests of consideration that are cast in terms of value, benefits, detriments, mutuality of obligation, and the exchange of promises. A common misconception about consideration is that value must pass physically between the parties. Another misconception is that there must be a real detriment to the promisor and a real benefit to the promisee. While the consideration requirement is usually satisfied if property or labor is exchanged, it can be satisfied with less, such as the parties' new promises. Only *legal detriments* or *legal benefits* need be present in the new promises such as when the parties make promises that obligate themselves in the future. A promise to do something new, something the promisor was not previously

FIGURE 9-6

Consideration: Detriments and Benefits

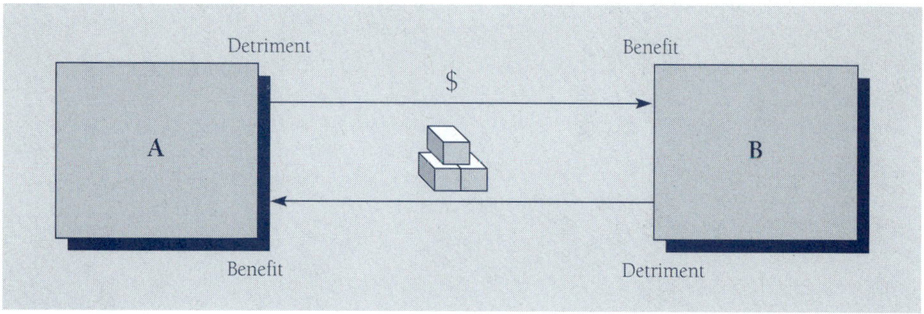

Consideration exists for a contract when the two parties exchange new promises. Above, A promises to pay money to B because B promises to deliver goods to A, and B promises to deliver goods to A because A promises to pay money to B. A's promise to pay B for the goods that B delivers is a benefit to B and a detriment to A. B's promise to deliver goods to A is a benefit to A and a detriment to B.

obligated to do, is sufficient consideration to support a counterpromise. A promise is quite different from an actual transfer of property or services pledged in a promise. All that is necessary is that the promise create a legally binding obligation. Promises alone have sufficient legal value to show seriousness. Actual performance is not required to satisfy the consideration element.

A *forbearance* is a promise not to do something or to refrain from doing something; it can also constitute sufficient consideration. In the settlement of a dispute over an automobile accident, for example, the party at fault usually promises to pay money in exchange for the victim's promise to refrain from suing for damages. This explains why contracts to release a negligent driver are enforceable to prevent suit after the victim accepts an insurance company settlement. The proper test of consideration is whether the parties make mutually binding new promises. Enforceable promises may be either promises to do something new or promises to refrain from doing something previously permissible. The promises that both parties make must change their legal obligations in order to satisfy the consideration test, as illustrated in Figure 9–6.

Mutuality of Obligation

The exchange element of consideration is an important concept. Parties that exchange promises are more likely to intend to be legally bound. Each party makes a promise "on the condition" that the other party make an acceptable return promise. With few exceptions, the mutual or bilateral nature of the promises clearly indicates their seriousness and the parties' intent to be bound. Each party makes a promise "in consideration" of the other party's promise, so the promises are mutually given in exchange for each other. Each party is induced or motivated to promise something new because the other party has made a new promise in return. Stated another way, each party's promise must be supported by the consideration found in the other party's counterpromise.

The classic formulation of consideration holds that there must be a legal *detriment to the promisee* or a legal *benefit to the promisor* when the promises of the parties are analyzed. Detriment to the promisee is illustrated in Figure 9–7, and benefit to the promisor is illustrated in Figure 9–8, on page 308. Each of these is an efficient test because each demonstrates that two promises are made and that each party gives and

FIGURE 9-7

Consideration: Detriment to the Promisee

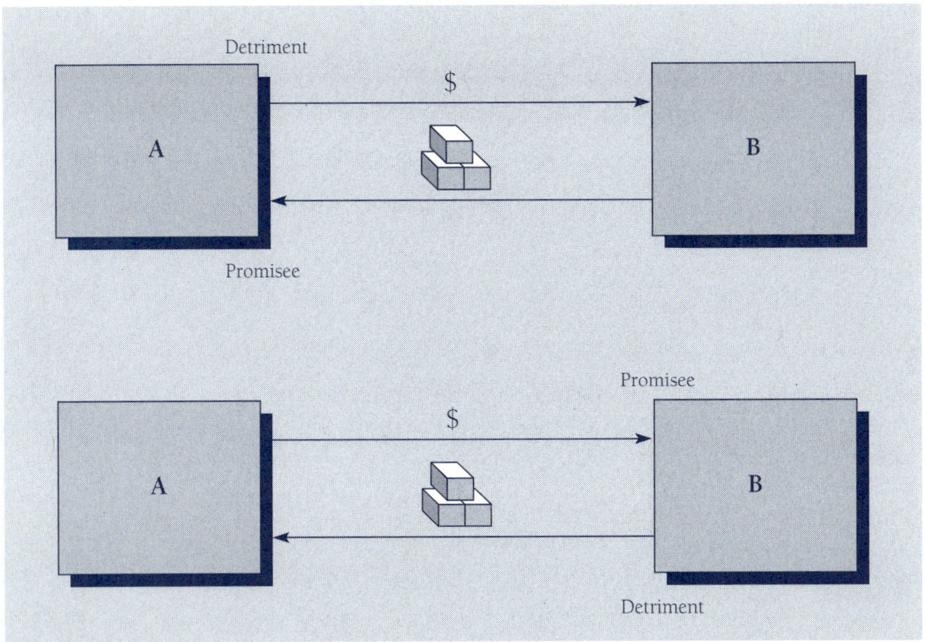

Consideration exists for the whole contract because, from A's perspective, there is a "detriment to the promisee." A's detriment is the promise to pay money to B, made in exchange for B's promise to deliver goods to A. (top)
Consideration exists for the whole contract because, from B's perspective, there is a "detriment to the promisee." B's detriment is the promise to deliver goods to A, made in exchange for A's promise to pay money to B. (bottom)

received legal value. Another formulation holds that each party must consciously give legal value in an outgoing promise in return for the incoming promise. Still another formulation holds that consideration will exist whenever the offer and acceptance result in two new promises made in exchange for each other. Each formulation includes elements of legal value given for and legal value received from the conscious mutual exchange of interdependent promises. While the theoretical nature of consideration may seem obtuse, it need not pose interpretation problems because the following situations usually indicate when consideration is lacking.

Unenforceable Promises: Consideration Is Lacking

In several common situations, consideration is found lacking and the agreement becomes unenforceable. If either party's promise is subject to that party's wish, will, or desire, then the promise is *illusory.* For example, an unlimited right to cancel the contract gives the promisor a way to "back out" at any time. A promise that is never binding is an illusion, so these contracts lack consideration. If the cancellation right is limited, such as with 30 days' notice, then the promise provides good consideration.

preexisting legal duty Repromising an old duty is insufficient consideration for a new contract.

When one party is already legally bound to perform an obligation and later simply repromises it, that second promise is a mere stale repetition. Nothing new is given in exchange for the promisee's return new promise. When there is a **preexisting legal duty,** the promisor is already legally obligated to do or refrain from doing the activity

FIGURE 9-8

Consideration: Benefit to the Promisor

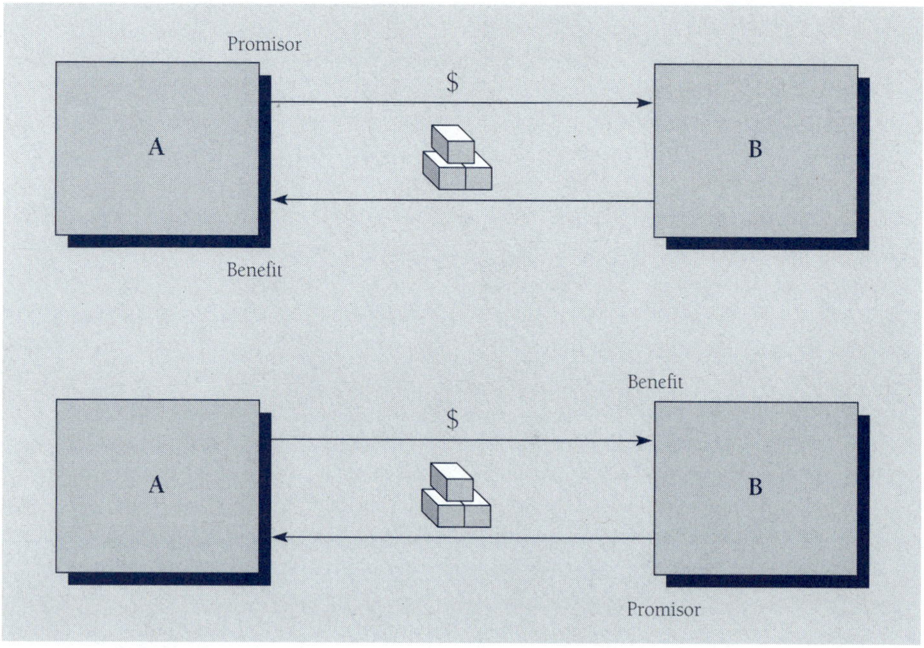

Consideration exists for the whole contract because, from A's perspective, there is a "benefit to the promisor." A's benefit is the expectation of receiving goods from B, made in exchange for A's promise to pay money to B. (top)
Consideration exists for the whole contract because, from B's perspective, there is a "benefit to the promisor." B's benefit is the expectation of receiving payment from A, made in exchange for B's promise to deliver goods to A. (bottom)

repromised. There is no new consideration making the contract unenforceable when based on a restated promise. Thus, if a jockey under contract to ride a horse in the Kentucky Derby pressures the horse's owner for more pay when the odds become more favorable for the horse to win, the owner's promise to pay more is not supported by any new consideration. The jockey has a preexisting legal duty to ride that race under the original contract terms.

accord and satisfaction An agreement and its performance that discharges a previous obligation.

There is sufficient consideration in an **accord and satisfaction** when a debtor agrees to settle a disputed or unliquidated debt. For example, a client may not have agreed to a consultant's fee before the services are rendered, so the bill may be in dispute. By contrast, agreements to settle undisputed debts with the debtor promising to pay less are usually not supported by consideration because the debt amount is the debtor's preexisting legal duty. However, if the debtor promises to pay the amount sooner or in a different medium, then the creditor receives something different than originally promised, and consideration is present.

Promises Enforceable without Consideration

Enforceable obligations do not always require consideration. There are a few unusual cases in which single, one-way, or gratuitous promises, though unsupported by consideration, become enforceable to preserve fairness and equity. The doctrines of *promissory estoppel* and *charitable subscriptions* permit enforcement when the promisee suffers damage by relying on a promisor's promise and the unfairness is balanced.

Elements of Promissory Estoppel

1. Under the circumstances, should the promisor reasonably expect that the promisee will rely on the promise and then act in some definite and substantial way? This is known as a *detrimental reliance*.
2. Has the promisee *in fact relied* on the promise to his or her own detriment?
3. In *balancing the equities* of enforcing or not enforcing the promise, would substantial unfairness be avoided if the promise is enforced?

The doctrine of charitable subscriptions applies when a charity relies on a donor's promise to contribute. Typically, the promisor pledges to donate something, and the charity relies on that pledge to its detriment by changing its position. For example, if a church member's promise to make a big contribution induces the church to remodel its building, the one-way charitable subscription becomes enforceable as soon as the church contracts with a builder. Should private businesspersons be given a similar protection? The following case illustrates the protections of promissory estoppel even when no remedy exists under traditional contract law.

Hoffman v. Red Owl Stores, Inc.

133 N.W. 2d 267 (Wis. 1965)
Wisconsin Supreme Court

During 1960, Hoffman had numerous negotiations with representatives of Red Owl Stores urging him to establish a Red Owl food store in Wautoma, Wisconsin. Hoffman bought a small independent store to gain experience in grocery retailing. After three months, his store was operating profitably and Red Owl representatives then convinced him to sell the store to his manager. Hoffman was assured that if he sold his bakery business, Red Owl would set him up in a new Red Owl store, so he leased a building site for the Red Owl store. Hoffman was advised on each successive occasion that he needed more investment capital than previously stated by Red Owl representatives. Hoffman's negotiations with Red Owl finally broke down when Red Owl insisted that his father-in-law make him a $13,000 gift for use as investment capital.

Currie, Chief Justice

Sec. 90 of Restatement, 1 Contracts provides:

> A promise which the promisor should reasonably expect to induce action or forbearance of a definite and substantial character on the part of the promisee and which does induce such action or forbearance is binding if injustice can be avoided only by enforcement of the promise.

Because we deem the doctrine of promissory estoppel is a needed tool we endorse and adopt it.

The record here discloses a number of promises and assurances given to Hoffman by Lukowitz on behalf of Red Owl upon which plaintiffs relied and acted upon to their detriment.

Foremost were the promises that for the sum of $18,000 Red Owl would establish Hoffman in a store. After Hoffman had sold his grocery store and paid the $1,000 on the Chilton lot, the $18,000 figure was changed to $24,100. Then in November 1961, Hoffman was assured that if the $24,100 figure were increased by $2,000, the deal would go through.

Hoffman was induced to sell his grocery store fixtures and inventory in June 1961, on the promise that he would be in his new store by fall. In November, plaintiffs sold their bakery building on the urging of defendants and on the assurance that this was the last step necessary to have the deal with Red Owl go through.

We conclude that injustice would result here if plaintiffs were not granted some relief because of the failure of defendants to keep their promises which induced plaintiffs to act to their detriment.

Case Questions

1. What explanation might be given for the behavior of Red Owl?
2. How could Red Owl have avoided liability in this case?
3. What consideration would have been given by Hoffman if Red Owl's actions were construed as an offer for a unilateral contract?

The consideration requirement is waived in several other, but limited, situations. For example, a debt barred by either the statute of limitations or the debtor's discharge in bankruptcy may be revived if the debtor reaffirms the original promise to pay the debt or makes partial payment without new consideration. Debts barred by bankruptcy must be approved by the bankruptcy court judge. *Composition* agreements entered into by several creditors and a debtor are enforceable without new consideration because the parties have a mutual interreliance similar to actual consideration. The UCC permits contract modifications without consideration, as discussed in Chapter 10. However, a common law modification contract lacks consideration unless both parties' obligations are changed.

Capacity

Not all persons are legally capable of entering into contracts. Some persons lack the mature judgment, experience, cognitive development, or ability needed to understand the effects of their promises. Minors and drunken, drugged, or insane persons lack contractual capacity, so they are protected from harsh dealings of another party. However, the mental and negotiating capabilities of incapacitated persons are not evaluated in every case. Rather than invalidating outright all the contracts of incompetents, the law gives each incompetent the right to avoid unfair contracts. An incompetent may usually withdraw or *disaffirm* a contract. This protection lasts until the minor reaches the age of majority, usually 18, or the drunken, drugged, or insane person becomes lucid.

In most of the states, both deserving and shrewd minors are protected by the right to disaffirm a contract. For example, a minor can disaffirm a reasonable contract even if the adult party is damaged by the disaffirmance. Adults can protect themselves by assuring they deal only with adults or by insisting an adult parent or guardian join in or cosign the contract. Adults cannot disaffirm contracts they have made with minors.

Voidability of an Incompetent's Contracts

Before majority, minors may disaffirm their contracts at any time but must generally return the contractual benefits still in their possession. It is usually irrelevant that some of these benefits are missing or are depreciated. Many states now limit the minor's absolute right of disaffirmance when the minor misrepresents their age by making the minor liable for the adult's losses. After a minor attains majority or after an incompetent becomes lucid, disaffirmance can only be done within a reasonable time. During this grace period, the minor can assess the fairness of contracts made during minority and decide to either disaffirm or ratify them. Once the minor who reaches majority ratifies the contract, there is no longer any right to disaffirm.

The contracts of minors and other incompetents are not automatically considered void. As voidable contracts, only the minor's intentional act of disaffirmance releases liability. A voidable contract may be ratified only after the incapacity is removed. Therefore, a minor cannot make a legally binding contract during minority, so it is impossible to ratify a contract during minority. Ratification can occur when a minor reaches majority or when a drunken, drugged, or insane person becomes lucid. The law may imply ratification if the incompetent either refrains from disaffirming beyond a reasonable time after the incapacity is removed or acts in a manner inconsistent with disaffirmance. For example, if after reaching 18, a person continues to use property bought during minority, the courts will usually infer that ratification should be implied from the person's conduct.

Necessaries

In some instances, an incompetent's right to disaffirm is further limited, making them responsible to pay for **necessaries,** the necessities of life: food, clothing, and shelter. Necessaries may also include contracts for services and property that aid in sustaining life, such as tools of the trade, employment placement services, vocational education, and medical services or supplies. The possibility of an unfair bargain may still exist in a contract for necessaries that is overpriced. The law implies quasi-contractual duties on the incompetent to pay the reasonable value of the necessary items. This amount may be less than the price originally agreed to. However, these items are not necessary if the incompetent's parent or guardian could provide them, so the contract is still voidable.

necessaries
Necessities of life for which quasi-contractual liability exists even if an incompetent disaffirms that contract.

Reality of Consent and Defenses to Contract Formation

In some cases, the parties' mutual assent is not genuine, such as when either party is unwillingly coerced. The law generally favors stability to satisfy the reasonable expectations of contractors, so it is difficult to cancel an agreement. However, if the misunderstanding or coercion is so great that enforcement would be unfair, an agreement can be canceled. Such situations usually arise when one party misrepresents material facts to the other, when certain mistakes are made, or when one party is coerced.

Misrepresentation and Fraud

It is unjust for either party to provide incorrect information to the other about the contract's subject matter. From an economic perspective, the allocation of resources is not optimal if contractors have inaccurate information. The law prohibits a wrongful party from enforcing a contract based on misrepresentation. The innocent victim may rescind a contract premised on misrepresentation of a material fact on which the victim has justifiably relied and suffered damages. The UCC implies a good faith requirement of "honesty in fact in the conduct or transaction concerned" in every contract or duty.

The initial focus in a misrepresentation case is on the person making the statements and on the statements themselves. However, not all representations are facts that can be misrepresented. *Facts* are matters susceptible to exact knowledge, such as past events or current conditions. Usually, predictions of future events are merely opinions. Unless the representer is a recognized expert or appraiser, statements of opinion or prediction cannot be misrepresented. For example, a salesperson's use of generalized statements concerning the value of goods is known as *puffing*. Most reasonable people realize that puffing statements are usually too vague to be misrepresented as facts. If the person making representations of facts knows, or should know, the statements are false, then action is fraudulent and more serious. *Fraud* is not only a reason to rescind or cancel a contract; it may also provide the basis for monetary damages under the tort of *deceit,* and fraud is criminal under various state and federal laws.

The second focus in a misrepresentation case is on the victim. In negotiating a contract, the victim's *reliance* on the other party's representations must be reasonable. Sometimes the victim should not believe a particular representation. If the victim has superior experience with the contract subject matter, the victim should make an independent investigation. If there is no actual reliance by the victim, there is no causal link between the misrepresentation and the victim's alleged damage. A lack of reliance releases the misrepresenter from liability, because contract law aids only victims damaged as a direct result of another's wrongdoing. However, if the victim of fraud honestly and reasonably believed the misrepresenter's statements, the contract may be canceled. For example, if a landowner promises there were never any toxins dumped on the land, the buyer may rescind if there is proof the landowner contaminated the land.

Mistake

In most instances, the law refuses to aid those who blunder in contract negotiations by making mistakes of judgment in assessing either the contract's value or their own capabilities. However, some mistakes concern such key terms as the identity, existence, or character of the contract's subject matter. When both parties are mistaken about the subject matter, a *bilateral* or *mutual mistake* occurs, permitting either party to rescind. If only one party is mistaken, there is a *unilateral mistake*. A contract is voidable for a unilateral mistake only if the nonmistaken party knowingly takes advantage of the victim's mistake.

Duress

The terms of most contracts are dictated by market forces or by one party's business needs. Laissez-faire freedom of contract prevents the law from changing the terms of freely negotiated contracts. However, if one party unduly pressures the other party, the resulting contract may be voidable. The threat or actual use of force is an obvious type of coercion that might force a person to agree to unfavorable terms. This constitutes *duress,* and the victim may rescind the contract. The threat of criminal prosecution is duress, but the threat of civil suit is not duress unless the claim is unfounded and malicious. *Economic duress* arises if one party threatens to breach an existing contract unless the victim agrees to another, usually unfavorable, contract. However, economic duress is not a justifiable basis for cancellation if the economic circumstances are imposed by the market or if the victim makes mistakes of judgment. Unfair commercial contracts may be modified under the UCC concept of *unconscionability* discussed further in Chapter 10.

There is a subtle form of coercion where *undue influence* is exerted by someone owing a fiduciary or family relationship to the victim. A victim of undue influence may rescind a contract if a position of trust is used to divert property from its normal course. For example, a young boy's grandmother became his guardian after his parents died leaving him heir to their corporate stock. However, the grandmother induced the boy to sign over the stock to her. Her undue influence deprived him of the stock, so he later disaffirmed the stock transfer to the grandmother, and the corporation was required to replace his shares.

Economic Duress

Ethical Dilemma

The use of threats or intimidation to coerce someone to agree to an unfavorable contract is unethical. If the coercion amounts to duress or undue influence, the contract may also be unenforceable under contract law. However, many contracting activities are not illegal, but still pose ethical dilemmas. The decision maker should analyze the type of coercion used in negotiating a contract. If the pressures employed are typical of market forces, they are legal and probably also ethical. For example, supply and demand pressures that relate to price, quantity, or other standard contract terms would seldom pose an ethical issue unless one party had the power to corner a market or single-handedly change supply or demand. Tactics may be unethical if they are clearly coercive; are not tied directly to contract terms; or threaten, coerce, or intimidate.

It is considered commercially reprehensible to threaten a breach of contract to pressure the other party into an undesirable agreement. Market outcomes are optimal only if participants have reasonable expectations their contracts will be performed. Consider the case of *Totem Marine Tug & Barge, Inc. v. Alyeska Pipeline Service Co.*[1] Alyeska became dissatisfied with Totem's slow progress in moving construction materials up to the trans-Alaska pipeline, so Alyeska commandeered the vessels while en route. This voided Totem's insurance, and Alyeska terminated Totem's contract. Totem billed Alyeska for expenses of over $500,000. Alyeska knew that without cash to pay other creditors soon, Totem would go bankrupt. Alyeska delayed making payment and eventually coerced Totem to settle for less than 20 percent of the billings. Alyeska's nonpayment illustrates how unethical conduct is distinguished from simply taking advantage of market conditions. An act is both illegal and unethical if the stronger party creates a business compulsion in bad faith to exact more favorable terms than possible without the coercion.

Illegality

The common law doctrine of *illegality* holds that the law should not aid lawbreakers; therefore, the courts usually do not aid either party to an illegal contract. Illegality arises if the principal contract objective calls for the commission of a crime or tort. Illegal contracts are void and unenforceable. However, illegality doctrine is not straightforward if the contract calls for acts that may not appear illegal, but an illegal

[1]*Totem Marine Tug & Barge, Inc. v. Alyeska Pipeline Service Co.*, 584 P.2d 15 (Ala. 1978).

performance is likely. When the most likely method of performing the legal acts is illegal, the contract itself may be illegal. By contrast, an otherwise legal contract is not made illegal simply because it is possible that one party may perform an illegal act during performance. The court must determine the legality of the subject matter and assess how the principal duties are likely to be performed.

Because the courts refuse to enforce the duties of either party to an illegal contract, it is often said that the parties must be left as the court finds them. For example, if one party has already paid for an executory illegal act, the other party will not be required to perform that act. Neither will the courts help the party that paid for the unperformed illegal act get the money returned. Illegal contracts cannot be rescinded or enforced, despite the unfairness when both parties likely know of the illegality, they are called *in pari delicto.*

Types of Illegality

The courts generalize about four common illegality areas in which they modify the rule prohibiting enforcement of illegal contracts. These areas are licensing, gambling, public policy, and restraints of trade.

Licensing Many states and municipalities require certain professionals and most businesses to obtain licenses before engaging in the licensed activity. Before a court refuses enforcement of contracts with unlicensed persons, the type of license must be determined. Some licensing statutes, such as municipal business licenses, have only a *revenue-raising* objective. Such statutes and ordinances do not usually test the expertise or qualifications of licensed individuals. Instead, the objective of the license is revenue raising, so contracts made by unlicensed persons or businesses are generally enforceable even if they have neglected to obtain the required license. However, there may be a penalty.

On the other hand, all states and most nations require the licensing of certain professionals. The primary objective of these statutes is to protect the public from unscrupulous and unskilled practitioners. These *regulatory licensing statutes* require satisfaction of certain professional qualifications before professional practice by lawyers, doctors, engineers, teachers, real estate brokers, and barbers. Professionals must demonstrate their good character and professional skills. Contracts of an unlicensed person to provide regulated services are unenforceable and illegal. Because licensing statutes are designed to protect the public from unskilled and unscrupulous persons, customers or clients are usually permitted to rescind their contracts with unlicensed professionals and regain funds paid. The client is within the class of persons to be protected.

Gambling In all of the states, the free exercise of gambling is illegal except in licensed casinos, at licensed pari-mutuel racetracks, at licensed offtrack betting parlors, at sales locations for state lotteries, or at limited charitable functions (e.g., bingo games). Contracts to pay illegal gambling debts are unenforceable.

One of the most perplexing problems with gambling is determining what activities constitute illegal gambling. *Gambling* is the creation of a risk primarily for the purpose of shifting the risk to expose the parties to gain or loss. If two parties bet on the price level that a particular stock will reach on a particular day, an unenforceable gambling contract arises. Although a similar economic event seems to occur if one party sells a stock and another party buys it, there is a fundamental difference between betting and a legitimate securities transaction. Stock carries the risk of uncertain price movements with its ownership. Betting on the price of a stock creates a brand-new risk that is not associated with stock ownership, but is created in the gambling contract.

Insurance contracts are also susceptible to gambling. If the beneficiary or loss payee (the person designated to receive the policy proceeds) has a close connection with the insured person or property, the insurance contract is legal because the beneficiary's risk existed before purchasing the insurance. This close connection or nexus, called an *insurable interest,* indicates that the insurance policy is not illegal gambling.

An insurable interest in a person's life exists where there is a close family relationship (i.e., spouse, child, parent) or where the insured is a key employee of a business. An insurable interest in property exists where the beneficiary owns, leases, or holds a lien on the property (collateral) or where a seller identifies specific goods as destined for shipment to a particular buyer under the UCC. If the purchaser of insurance has no insurable interest, the insurance contract is like illegal gambling. In the case of a loss, no benefits are paid, and only the premiums are returned to the purchaser.

Public Policy As a matter of public policy, the courts usually do not enforce agreements that violate society's ethical and moral norms as found in statutes and court decisions. Public policy prohibits contracts that seek to bribe or unduly influence public officials, fiduciaries, agents, or law enforcement officials in the performance of their duties. Such contracts are illegal and unenforceable. For example, public policy prohibits certain terms in the contracts of parking lot operators, pawn shops, or checkrooms. These parties are *bailees* because they hold custody of other persons' property. Bailees often use *exculpatory clauses* to escape liability for losses of the owner's property while the bailee has custody. Such clauses are generally unenforceable if the bailee seeks to be free of liability for willful misconduct. Exculpatory clauses are valid only to relieve the bailee of liability for negligence, and the terms must be communicated to the property owner. For example, a coat room's "not responsible for loss" language on the receipt is enforceable only if the customer reads this exculpatory clause.

Restraints of Trade Many contracts that attempt to restrain trade are illegal because they violate public policy. For example, contracts that prohibit the transfer of property and contracts among competitors to fix prices, divide markets, allocate customers, or create monopolies are illegal under both contract law and federal antitrust law. However, some trade restraints are economically useful, justifying their enforcement when *ancillary*, or closely related, to another agreement and protecting interests in that other agreement.

Employment Contracts Employers often may have legitimate interests in restricting their employees from quitting and going to work for a direct competitor. Employers often give their sales staff confidential customer lists, teach them innovative sales tactics, or provide them with secret new product information that could damage the employer if the employee quit to join a competitor. Designers, engineers, and persons in upper management often learn trade secrets, so disclosure would damage the employer's competitive position. To protect these legitimate confidential interests, an employer may contract to restrain an employee from immediately working for a direct competitor by insisting the employee sign a *covenant not to compete*. The restraints imposed by the covenant must be limited to a reasonable geographic region and may last for only a reasonable time after the employee leaves the employer, usually for two or three years.

Employment contract covenants not to compete are not favored by the law, particularly if they deprive the employee of a reasonable livelihood. There has been a trend toward refusing enforcement if the covenant is too broad or vague or if it damages the employee. Overbroad covenants not to compete are limited to reasonable periods of time and to reasonable geographic regions in which the employee formerly had a direct impact. Some overbroad covenants are completely unenforceable, suggesting that employers should draft them carefully or risk losing all protection. Alternatively, employers use confidentiality agreements to protect valuable trade secrets and use patent assignments clauses to clarify ownership of innovations. What does an employer risk if a salesperson quits to join a competitor? The following case illustrates such legitimate protectable interests.

Eastern Dist. Co., Inc. v. Flynn

567 P.2d 1371 (Kan. 1977)
Kansas Supreme Court

Flynn became dissatisfied with his job at Eastern Distributing Company, a wholesale liquor distributor in Kansas City, and joined a competitor. He immediately began to service the same customers he had previously served as Eastern's route salesman. Flynn's written contract of employment with Eastern restricted him from disclosing Eastern's list of customers to a competitor or from soliciting those customers if he ceased to be associated with Eastern for any reason. The contract also restricted him from any connection with a competitor of Eastern's within a 50-mile radius of his former sales territory for one year following his termination from Eastern. Eastern sought an injunction ordering Flynn to cease from competing with Eastern.

Kaul, Justice

It has become well established that a noncompetition clause is valid if it is ancillary to any lawful contract, but it is subject to the test of reasonableness of the covenant and whether it is inimical to the public welfare.

Professor Blake points out that if contacts are infrequent and irregular there may be no sufficient risk to the employer to support any degree of restraint and further that frequency of contact may also affect the permissible period of restraint; the important consideration being that the employer should be given a reasonable period of time in which to overcome the former employee's personal hold over the customers. With respect to locale of the contact the important factor is whether the contact is made at the employer's place of business, which involves less risk to the employer, or at the customer's home or business establishment, which is more likely to direct the customer's loyalty primarily to the employee and support some degree of restraint.

It is also generally recognized that the "customer contacts" theory gains added weight where the business is one in which the employee is the sole or primary contact with the customers and in which a close personal relationship with them is fostered, enabling the employee to control such business as a personal asset.

It is well-settled law that the mere desire to prevent ordinary competition does not qualify as a legitimate interest of an employer and a restrictive covenant is unreasonable if the real object is merely to avoid such ordinary competition.

However, it is also a well-recognized principle that "customer contacts" is a legitimate interest to be protected by an employer. It is clear from the import of the language of the instant contract that "customer contacts" was the principal incident which Eastern intended to protect.

While the names of customers and their places of business are matters of public record, Baird testified that the hours a licensee is available, the names and ordering habits of their clerks are not. The evidence disclosed that a salesman's calls on customers were frequent and regular; that they were made at the customer's place of business rather than at Eastern's; and that the salesman was Eastern's principal, if not its sole, contact with customers. Defendant was hired away from Eastern to continue to serve the same customers he knew while employed by Eastern. There is ample evidence to support the trial court's findings which viewed in the light of the foregoing authorities establishes a legitimate interest subject to protection by a court of equity.

We think the trial court in the exercise of its equitable powers fairly and reasonably reduced the area restriction to only that which was necessary to protect plaintiff's interest. We find no public policy or public interest involved under the facts and circumstances of this case sufficient to avoid or render unenforceable a reasonable restraint.

Case Questions

1. What factors make a noncompetition clause ancillary to an employment contract?
2. What interests can be protected by a reasonable covenant not to compete?
3. What alternate treatment other than invalidating a covenant not to compete might a court use to enforce the covenant if it were worded too broadly as to include an unreasonable geographic area or last for an unreasonable duration?

Sale of a Business In the sale of a business or a professional practice, a similar need arises to protect the intangible property rights transferred. The purchaser of a business often pays a premium price for its "going concern" value, an amount that often exceeds the fair market value of its tangible assets. This premium paid for the goodwill of a business may need the protection of a covenant not to compete.

Most buyers are willing to purchase a seller's business only if the seller promises not to compete with the buyer. This helps assure that the seller's customers, clients, or patients will not simply follow the seller to a new location. Covenants not to compete that are intended to protect either goodwill or business trade secrets are considered *ancillary* (closely connected) to the sale of business contract and are enforceable if drafted reasonably. Such covenants must cover only a limited geographic region, but unlike employment restrictions, a sale of business restriction may last indefinitely.

Written Contracts

Contrary to a popular misconception, most oral contracts are fully enforceable and legally binding. Generally, contracts do not have to be in writing. Of course, it may be difficult to prove the precise terms without a written document. To reduce the possibility of inaccurate fact-findings in court, the law requires that some contracts be in writing. For contracts that fall into several special classes, the **statute of frauds** requires a written contract signed by the *party to be charged.* This is this party who usually denies the existence of a contract and is allegedly in breach. Written contracts need only be signed by the party against whom the plaintiff seeks enforcement.

statute of frauds Requirement for written contracts in the sale of interests in land, guarantee contracts, contracts not to be performed within one year, and sales of goods of $500 or more.

memorandum
Written contract minimally sufficient to satisfy the statute of frauds.

To be effective, a written contract must appear in a certain form, known as a **memorandum.** A memorandum may be an informal document or even a collection of several documents referring to the same transaction. It may be pieced together from separate documents, receipts, telegrams, letters, order forms, confirmations, addressed envelopes, and the like. The signature may be any tangible sign that is used to authenticate a writing. A cursive signature is usually sufficient, but so is a stamp, seal, initial, printing, typing, or even the letter *X* if it is intended by the party for authentication. Written contracts are necessary in four major business-related activities: (1) sales of land, (2) guarantees to pay the debts of others, (3) contracts incapable of performance within one year, and (4) sales of goods of $500 or more (discussed in Chapter 10).

Sales of Land

A contract that calls for the transfer of any *interest in land* must be in writing to be enforceable. This requirement applies to contracts that transfer a variety of real estate interests, including full ownership, called a fee simple; an easement; covenant; mortgage; condominium ownership; mineral rights; growing vegetation; and leases lasting more than one year in most states (three years in some other states, such as Pennsylvania).

An exception permits enforcement of a *part performance* of an oral land sale contract if the buyer has (1) paid part or all of the purchase price, (2) taken possession of the property with the seller's knowledge, and (3) made valuable improvements on the land. Enforcement of an oral land sale is justified because it would be unfair to let the seller use the technicalities of the statute of frauds to back out of an unattractive oral deal if the buyer has taken possession. In such instances, most courts grant a *specific performance,* ordering the seller to deed the property over to the buyer even without a written contract.

Guarantee Contracts

If an outsider promises a creditor that the outsider will pay the original debtor's debt, the promise must be in writing. These promises are known as collateral contracts of *guarantee.* While the original debtor's contract of debt need not be in writing, the guarantor's promise to pay if the debtor defaults *must* be in writing. A true collateral contract of guarantee is enforceable only after the debtor defaults. For example, assume that C, a creditor, is willing to extend credit to D, the debtor, only if G, the outside guarantor, provides additional assurance that the debt will be repaid. G's promise to pay D's debt if D defaults is a collateral contract of guarantee, and it must be in writing.

An exception to this requirement exists when the guarantor's *main purpose* or *leading object* is merely to protect the guarantor's own interests. An oral guarantee is enforceable in this situation because fraud is less likely to be present. For example, a corporation in financial difficulty may be able to borrow money only if its president agrees to guarantee the loan. Because the president's main purpose in guaranteeing the loan is to protect the presidency, the guarantee need not be in writing.

The guarantee contract should be carefully distinguished from collateral and security arrangements that need no writing to be enforceable. Since loan cosigners or comakers are both primarily liable on the debt, their promises are not collateral guarantees, so they need not be in writing.

Contracts Incapable of Performance within One Year

Long-term and complex contracts are the most susceptible to problems of proof after time passes. If a breach of contract suit is brought long after contracting, witnesses may forget the facts. Therefore, a contract that is incapable of being performed within one year must be in writing. This requirement is less onerous than it may seem. In many instances, the parties choose to take longer than a year to perform contracts that were capable of full performance within a year. But the fact that a contract *might* take longer than a year to perform is immaterial, so this does not require a writing. Instead, contracts that set a specific starting and ending date that lasts over one year must be written. The time begins to run when the contract is made and ends with the last required performance. Similarly, contracts that require a number of years for full performance must be in writing.

Interpretation of Contracts

Disagreements over the meaning of contract terms are resolved under the objective rule of contracts. Terms are interpreted by how a reasonable person would understand the words used. Common words are given their general meaning unless the particular line of business applies a unique *usage of trade* to the words in question. For example, the word *gross* commonly means large, shameful, or out of proportion, but among wholesalers and retailers it refers to 12 dozen, or 144. UCC usages are discussed in Chapter 10.

Parol Evidence Rule

Before a contract is finalized, the parties frequently negotiate or "dicker" about its terms. The negotiation process often involves proposals and counterproposals of alternative terms that replace previously withdrawn terms. As the proposed terms change, advantages are granted to one side, and burdens are imposed on the other. The final agreement usually represents a compromise in which both parties give up some of their original demands and find agreement in a middle ground. This process of give-and-take through negotiation has led to the parol evidence rule.

The **parol evidence rule** prohibits either party from proving any different terms than those stated in the written document. The parol evidence rule excludes from the jury's consideration oral or written evidence that would alter or vary the terms in the written contract. Thereby, neither party may seek the jury's sympathy by introducing evidence of a contract term that may have only been considered during preliminary negotiations but was later omitted when the parties reached a final agreement.

parol evidence rule Evidence rule prohibiting admission of contradictions to an integrated written contract intended to be the whole and complete agreement.

If the parties intend the written contract to embody all the terms of their agreement, the law presumes that they expect it to "tell the whole story." Such an intentionally complete document is known as an *integration,* which is distinguished from the memorandum required to "satisfy" the statute of frauds. Conceivably, a memorandum might be neither intended nor complete enough to be considered an integration.

The parol evidence rule is also distinguished from the statute of frauds because it is "triggered" by an integration. The parol evidence rule tends to protect the integrity of written contracts and the parties' expectations of performance as specified in the writing. As a practical matter, the rule requires the party that did not prepare the writing to read it carefully before signing. This extra care assures that all of the finally agreed-upon terms actually appear in the written contract.

The parol evidence rule does not exclude evidence to clarify ambiguities or show fraud, duress, mistake, illegality, incapacity, or later modifications. What policies are furthered by the parol evidence rule? The following case illustrates the admissibility of parol evidence that might alter the written contract.

Masterson v. Sine

436 P.2d 561 (Cal. 1968)
California Supreme Court

Dallas Masterson and his wife, Rebecca, transferred their ranch to Dallas's sister Medora and her husband, Lu Sine, with a grant deed. The deed reserved to the Mastersons an option right to repurchase the ranch within the next two years for the sale price plus the depreciated value of improvements added by the Sines. After the sale, Dallas was adjudged bankrupt. Both the trustee in bankruptcy and Rebecca brought suit to establish their right to enforce the option.

Traynor, Chief Justice

The parol evidence rule precluded admission of extrinsic evidence offered by defendants to show that the parties wanted the property kept in the Masterson family and that the option was therefore personal to the grantors and could not be exercised by the trustee in bankruptcy.

When the parties to a written contract have agreed to it as an "integration"—a complete and final embodiment of the terms of an agreement—parol evidence cannot be used to add to or vary its terms. When only part of the agreement is integrated, the same rule applies to that part, but parol evidence may be used to prove elements of the agreement not reduced to writing.

The crucial issue in determining whether there has been an integration is whether the parties intended their writing to serve as the exclusive embodiment of their agreement. The instrument itself may help to resolve that issue. It may state, for example, that "there are no previous understandings or agreements not contained in the writing," and thus express the parties' "intention to nullify antecedent understandings or agreements." . . . Circumstances at the time of the writing may also aid in the determination of such integration.

In formulating the rule governing parol evidence, several policies must be accommodated. One policy is based on the assumption that written evidence is more accurate than human memory. This policy, however, can be adequately served by excluding parol evidence of agreements that directly contradict the writing. Another policy is based on the fear that fraud or unintentional invention by witnesses interested in the outcome of the litigation will mislead the finder of facts.

McCormick has suggested that the party urging the spoken as against the written word is most often the economic underdog, threatened by severe hardship if the writing is enforced. In his view the parol evidence rule arose to allow the court to control the tendency of the jury to find through sympathy and without a dispassionate assessment of the probability of fraud or faulty memory that the parties made an oral agreement collateral to the written contract, or that preliminary tentative agreements were not abandoned when omitted from the writing.

Evidence of oral collateral agreements should be excluded only when the fact finder is likely to be misled. The rule must therefore be based on the credibility of the evidence. [T]he Restatement of Contracts permits proof of a collateral agreement if it "is such an agreement as might *naturally* be made as a separate agreement by parties situated as were the parties to the written contract."

The draftsmen of the Uniform Commercial Code would exclude the evidence in still fewer instances: "If the additional terms are such that, if agreed upon, they would certainly have been included in the document in the view of the court, then evidence of their alleged making must be kept from the trier of fact."

The option clause in the deed in the present case does not explicitly provide that it contains the complete agreement, and the deed is silent on the question of assignability. Moreover, the difficulty of accommodating the formalized structure of a deed to the insertion of collateral agreements makes it less likely that all the terms of such an agreement were included. In the present case, defendants offered evidence that the parties agreed that the option was not assignable in order to keep the property in the Masterson family. The trial court erred in excluding that evidence. The judgment is reversed.

Case Questions

1. Compare and contrast an integration agreement with a memorandum.
2. What kinds of evidence are still admissible despite the parol evidence rule?
3. Why is there a parol evidence rule?

Third-Party Rights

It seems logical that only contracting parties may seek judicial enforcement of their contracts. In four distinct situations, however, outsiders have legally enforceable rights or responsibilities in the contracts made by others. The first two situations involve contracts specifically identifying an outside third party who is intended to receive the contract benefits. Such third parties are either creditor beneficiaries or donee beneficiaries. The third and fourth situations arise when either contracting party transfers contractual rights or obligations under an existing contract to an outsider. In such situations, the outsider may enforce the contract or be required to perform a contractual duty if transferred from one of the original contracting parties.

Third-Party Beneficiaries

An outsider intentionally identified as a beneficiary or obligee in the original contract is known as a *third-party beneficiary*, illustrated in Figure 9–9, on the following page. A third-party beneficiary may enforce the contract against the original obligor. If the person to whom a performance is promised intends for the contract to confer a gift on another, then the third party has no right to sue this promisee. For example, if one person purchases flowers from a florist for a spouse, the recipient, as a *donee* third-party beneficiary, can enforce the contract against the florist (the obligor) but cannot sue the spouse who purchased the flowers. The spouse conferring the gift simply used the florist's services to make the gift.

There are greater rights for a third party who was previously owed a duty by the promisee, and the promisee uses the obligor to discharge this duty. Such an outsider is a *creditor* third-party beneficiary and may enforce the obligation against either of the original contracting parties. The promisee is liable to the third party because that duty existed prior to and independently of the third-party beneficiary contract. For example, a home sale contract may identify the lending bank as a creditor third-party beneficiary. The buyer assumes the seller's mortgage, thereby promising to repay the original mortgage loan. Unless the bank releases the seller from making the payments, the bank may sue either the seller or the buyer for loan default because the seller originally borrowed the money.

FIGURE 9–9

Third-Party Beneficiary

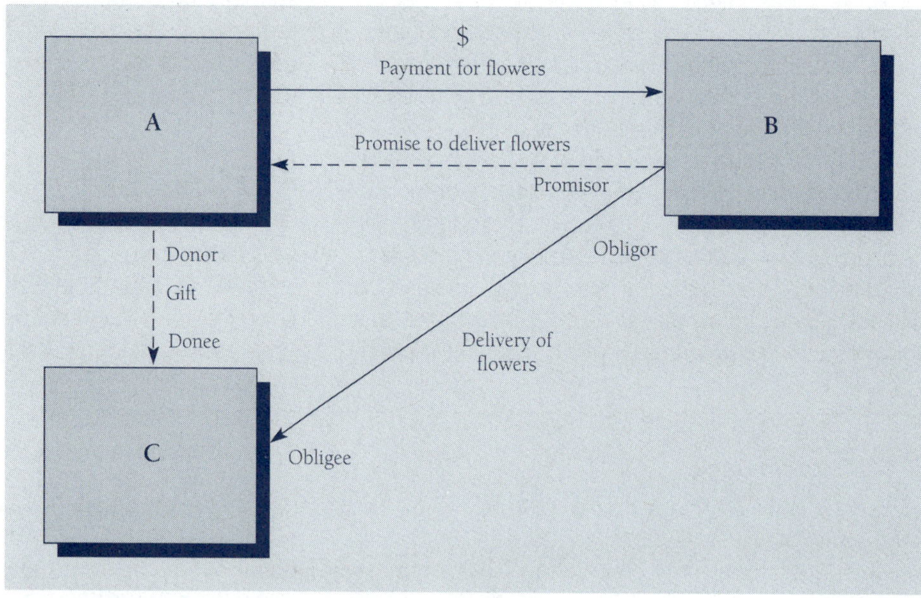

A buys flowers from B to be delivered to C, and the contract between A and B identifies C as the recipient of B's performance. Thus, C is a donee third-party beneficiary of the contract between A and B. C may require B, but not A, to perform the contract.

Incidental Beneficiaries

Some outsiders, *incidental beneficiaries,* benefit only by coincidence from the contracts of others. They have no rights to enforce a contract because they are neither identified in the contract nor intended to benefit from it. For example, contracts for the construction of a new factory often generate significant economic benefits or positive externalities, for the surrounding community. However, community members cannot enforce the construction contracts because they are merely unintended and incidental beneficiaries.

Assignment and Delegation

Contract rights and duties are sometimes transferred to an outsider in a separate contract. Such transfer contracts can be made either before or after the original contract. The law distinguishes between the *assignment* of a right to enforce the original contract, illustrated in Figure 9–10, and the *delegation* of a duty to perform under the original contract, illustrated in Figure 9–11. In the sale of an ongoing business, for example, assignments of rights to enforce contracts with others (e.g., accounts receivables) are often combined with delegations of duties previously undertaken with others (e.g., accounts payables). The purchaser of the business may collect previously outstanding accounts receivables and must perform contract duties the seller formerly owed to its customers.

The transfer of rights or duties is sometimes accomplished without the permission of the other party to the original contract. Such transfers are effective only when they do not materially change the obligations or rights of the nonconsenting party. For example, a wholesaler may assign past-due accounts receivables to a collection agency

FIGURE 9–10

Assignment of Rights

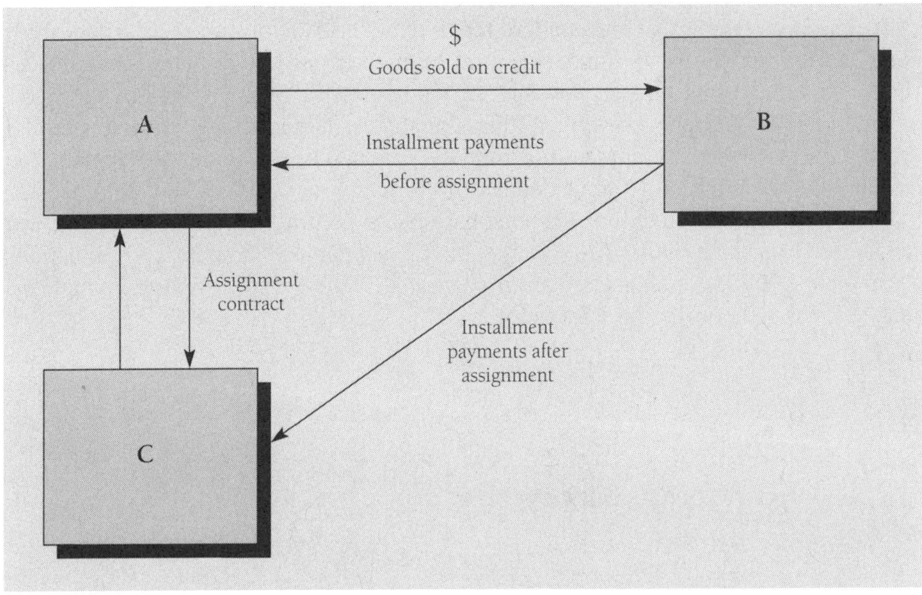

A's account receivable is factored to C, an assignment of rights. C is the factor that obtains the right to receive the installment payments that B originally promised to A. B's consent is necessary only for the assignment of personal services, not this payment duty.

FIGURE 9–11

Delegation of Duty

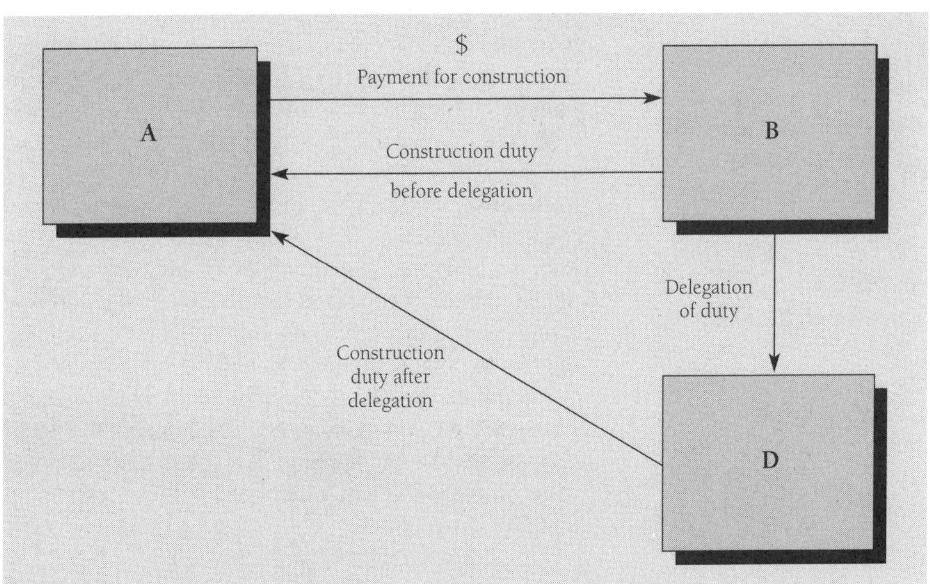

B's obligation to perform construction services is delegated to D. In this delegation of a duty, D is the delegate that becomes obligated to perform the construction services to A. A's consent is necessary to delegate personal services and also to release B's original duty to perform.

or factor. The debtors cannot complain when notified because they can simply redirect their payments to the assignee. Rights and duties are freely transferable if they involve obligations to pay money or are standard repair and construction contracts. The test for transferability focuses on the nonconsenting contracting party. A transfer is unenforceable if the nonconsenting party would suffer a material change in duty or right. Personal service contracts are typical unassignable or nondelegable contracts unless the original contractor consents to substitute the new party as assignee or delegate. The original contract can validly limit delegation.

What is the distinction between a personal service contract that involves a material change and a contract that is fully assignable or delegable? The next case illustrates how to identify duties or rights that are freely transferable without imposing a material change on the nonconsenting contractor.

Macke Co. v. Pizza of Gaithersburg, Inc.

270 A.2d 645 (Md. 1970)
Maryland Court of Appeals

Virginia Coffee Service, Inc., contracted with Pizza of Gaithersburg, Inc., to provide cold-drink vending machines for each Pizza location. The Macke Company later purchased all of Virginia's assets and received its contracts by assignment, including the contract with Pizza. Pizza attempted to terminate these contracts, and Macke brought suit to determine its rights under the combined assignment and delegation.

Singley, Judge

In the absence of a contrary provision—and there was none here—rights and duties under an executory bilateral contract may be assigned and delegated, subject to the exception that duties under a contract to provide personal services may never be delegated nor rights be assigned.

[This court has] held that the right of an individual to purchase ice under a contract reflected a knowledge of the individual's needs and reliance on his credit and responsibility and could not be assigned to the corporation which purchased his business. In *Eastern Advertising Co. v. McGaw & Co.,* our predecessors held that an advertising agency could not delegate its duties under a contract which had been entered into by an advertiser who had relied on the agency's skill, judgment, and taste.

We cannot regard the agreements as contracts for personal services. . . . The appellees earnestly argue that they had dealt with Macke before and had chosen Virginia because they preferred the way it conducted its business. Specifically, they say that service was more personalized, since the president of Virginia kept the machines in working order, that commissions were paid in cash, and that Virginia permitted them to keep keys to the machines so that minor adjustments could be made when needed. Even if we assume all this to be true, the agreements with Virginia were silent as to the details of the working arrangements and contained only a provision requiring Virginia to "install . . . the above listed equipment and . . . maintain the equipment in good operating order and stocked with merchandise." We think the Supreme Court of California put the problem of personal service in proper focus a century ago when it upheld the assignment of a contract to grade a San Francisco street:

> All painters do not paint portraits like Sir Joshua Reynolds, nor landscapes like Claude Lorraine, nor do all writers write dramas like Shakespeare or fiction like Dickens. Rare genius and extraordinary skill

> are not indispensable to the workmanlike digging down of a sand hill or the filling up of a depression to a given level, or the construction of brick sewers with manholes and covers, and contracts for such work are not personal, and may be assigned.

Moreover, the difference between the service the Pizza Shops happened to be getting from Virginia and what they expected to get from Macke did not mount up to such a material change in the performance of obligations under the agreements as would justify the appellee's refusal to recognize the assignment.

Restatement, Contracts §160(3) (1932) reads, in part:

> Performance or offer of performance by a person delegated has the same legal effect as performance or offer of performance by the person named in the contract, unless, (a) performance by the person delegated varies or would vary materially from performance by the person named in the contract as the one to perform, and there has been no . . . assent to the delegation. . . .

Uniform Commercial Code §2–210(5) permits a promisee to demand assurances from the party to whom duties have been delegated.

As we see it, the delegation of duty by Virginia to Macke was entirely permissible under the terms of the agreements.

Case Questions

1. What is a personal service?
2. Why would it be unjust or inefficient to require an obligee to accept a personal service performance from someone other than the original obligor?
3. What alternative arrangement would have avoided this outcome?

Contract Performance and Remedies for Breach

Sometimes one party to a valid contract finds performance is no longer advantageous, either because of their personal incapability or because the contract's value has disappeared. The law usually enforces such contracts. There are several degrees of performance quality. An executory contractual duty can be discharged if it becomes impossible to perform. However, in most cases if one party breaches, the other party may be entitled to a legal remedy such as damages or specific performance.

Conditions

Certain events or **conditions** are often necessary before a parties' rights are enforceable. Some contracts contain *conditions precedent,* events which must happen *before* a duty is owed. For example, a home buyer is usually not required to purchase the house until sufficient financing is obtained. Financing is a condition precedent to the buyer's obligation to purchase. *Concurrent conditions* arise when each party's performance is conditioned on the other party's near simultaneous tender of counterperformance. For example, in most retail sales the buyer's payment is concurrently conditioned on the seller's delivery, and the seller's delivery is concurrently conditioned on the buyer's payment. Occasionally, *conditions subsequent* arise to provide service until a condition subsequent occurs. For example, the expiration of the warranty period or consumer abuse in failing to make necessary oil changes is a condition subsequent to a car manufacturer's warranty liability. Contract remedies may be granted after a condition occurs.

conditions Express or implied contract terms that trigger a party's performance duty.

Discharge by Performance

material breach
Failure of contract obligee to perform as promised, triggers the obligee's remedies.

substantial performance
Slightly defective but still acceptable contract performance which entitles obligor to an adjusted payment.

Each party's performance is judged by the degree of perfection that a reasonable obligee can objectively expect to receive. To fully discharge contractual duties in most situations, each party must perform exactly as promised or be guilty of a **material breach.** In the event of a material breach, the innocent party may suspend counterperformance and sue for a remedy. However, when a complex performance is required, something less than perfect, *full performance* may suffice. In construction contracts, for example, a contractor acting in good faith may deviate slightly from the plans and specifications if deviations are minor and unintentional. The required materials may be unavailable, so a reasonable substitute may be used, but the contractor should still be paid. Sometimes it may be necessary to adjust the purchase price to reflect the lesser quality of this **substantial performance.**

Late deliveries, payments, or performances of services are also judged in this way. If the performance delay is so serious that it constitutes a material breach, the innocent party is relieved from performance and may sue for breach. Slight delays must be tolerated, perhaps with a price adjustment made. However, at the time of contracting either party may insist that *time is of the essence,* mandating timely performance.

Either party may notify the other party of inability to perform in the future; this is an *anticipatory breach,* called an *anticipatory repudiation* under the UCC. Such a preannounced breach permits the innocent party to immediately sue for breach or pursue other remedies without waiting for the time originally set for performance.

Impossibility of Performance

The doctrines of delegation and impossibility are fundamentally interrelated. Sometimes an obligor becomes ill and cannot perform services or cannot deliver goods that were destroyed, or the factory halted production. A strike or a boxcar shortage may also prevent performance. In such situations, the contract becomes *subjectively impossible* to perform. That is, the obligor cannot perform as promised, but perhaps others must be substituted as delegates to perform.

Consider the contrast between a contract for the services of a famous portrait painter and a painting contractor. If the artist becomes ill, there is no substitute for the quality of the expected performance. Because no one else can paint the portrait as specified, the painter's duty is either justifiably delayed or excused altogether by impossibility. By contrast, if the painting contractor suffers a strike, there is no objective legal impossibility because house painting is not a unique service. Another house painter could paint the building. In such cases, the obligor must delegate the duty or risk paying damages. The doctrine of impossibility excuses performance only when unique services are justifiably excused or unique subject matter is destroyed after mutual assent but before performance. Other variations of this defense are the *frustration of purpose* and *commercial impracticality* doctrines. Some courts release an obligor if, after the contract has been made, events occur that render the other party's performance worthless.

Force Majeure Clauses The parties may agree to define some of the particular events that trigger an impossibility of performance. *Force majeure* clauses are often used when one or both parties could be exposed to uncertain and debilitating events. Force majeure clauses are enforceable as privately bargained for impossibilities. Oil and gas contracts typically contain force majeure clauses. These excuse performance if, through no fault of either party, performance becomes impossible due to labor troubles, war, transportation failures, acts of God, or any other event the parties agree to include.

Damages

Contract law is intended to satisfy the parties' reasonable expectations of performance. In most cases, money damages are efficient and satisfactory remedies. *Compensatory damages* are the most typical damage awards because they represent the losses actually suffered in obtaining a replacement, realizing the promisee's original expectations, or securing a substitute performance. For example, the party breaching a contract must usually pay any of the innocent party's out-of-pocket expenses. Of course, the promisee has a *duty to mitigate damages* by avoiding and minimizing such damages when possible. *Punitive damages* are rarely awarded in breach of contract cases unless the promisor is also guilty of tortious and willful misconduct.

Damages for breach can be made more certain if the parties agree to a *liquidated damage* provision in which the parties specify a damage sum payable if one party breaches. Liquidated damage provisions are enforceable only if they are a legitimate estimate of uncertain future damages. Any attempt to use liquidated damages as a penalty to discourage breach is generally unenforceable. For example, if a wholesaler presold a quantity of goods to be acquired from a manufacturer, an unreasonably large liquidated damage provision in the manufacturer's supply contract would be unenforceable as a penalty because the wholesaler's potential loss is limited to the difference between actual and resale price. However, if the wholesaler had not presold the goods and the market for the goods was uncertain, a liquidated damage provision might still be reasonable.

Specific Performance

Although damages are the most typical remedy, a specific performance of the contract may be ordered in cases involving unique property (e.g., land, collectibles, or particular goods previously identified for purchase). *Specific performance* is a court order requiring the parties to perform as originally promised. When money damages are inadequate to satisfy the promisee's expectations, the extraordinary remedy of specific performance may be ordered. However, no specific performance will be ordered for personal services.

Summary

Contracts are the most basic and important business relationship. They are made up of legally enforceable obligations arising from mutual promises. Contracts are enforced to permit orderly business, satisfying the parties' reasonable expectations. Contracts for service and land sales are governed by the common law of each state, and the UCC governs sales of goods. Valid and enforceable contracts arise when the parties (1) have legal capacity and (2) mutually assent to a single agreement that is (3) supported by consideration and (4) the contract has a legal objective.

Mutual assent is based on the parties' communications. The offer confers the power to contract and must include key terms: parties' identity, subject matter, description, quantity of goods, price, and time for performance. A contract results when the offeree unconditionally accepts the offeror's precise proposal. Slight differences between the written form used by buyers and sellers of goods are often permissible. Except for acceptances, which are usually effective when dispatched, all communications are effective when received.

Contracts may be unenforceable, particularly those that are unimportant or not serious. Contracts become enforceable if consideration exists as where two parties make promises in reliance on each other's counterpromise. Promises to do something or to refrain from doing something are sufficient. However, a repromise of a previously made promise is unenforceable under the preexisting legal duty rule. Some promises made without consideration are enforceable under promissory estoppel.

Minors and drunken, drugged, or insane persons are protected from unwise contracts. Minors can usually disaffirm a contract until a reasonable time after reaching majority. Then the law implies a ratification of the contract, eliminating the right to disaffirm. Minors must usually pay the reasonable value of necessaries.

A contract obligation may be avoided if either party's assent is obtained by coercion, including duress, or under the threat or actual use of force. If one party to a contract misrepresents material facts to the other, the victim may cancel the contract. Mistakes concerning the identity, existence, or subject matter of a contract permit rescission. Where both parties to a contract are mistaken or where one party knowingly takes advantage of the other's mistake, the contract is voidable.

A contract is unenforceable if its primary objective violates a criminal or tort law. A contract is also unenforceable if its objective appears legal but will probably involve an illegal act. Contracts made by unlicensed professionals are illegal if the licensing statute is regulatory but not if it is revenue raising. Most gambling contracts are illegal and unenforceable. Public policy disfavors exculpatory clauses in which one party attempts to avoid all responsibility. Restraints of trade are illegal unless they are reasonably worded to protect valid interests arising in an employment contract or the sale of a business.

Not all contracts must be in writing to be enforceable. The statute of frauds requires a simple written memorandum, signed only by the party denying the contract, and only if the contract involves (1) land sales, (2) guarantees, (3) contracts incapable of performance within one year, and (4) sales of goods of $500 or more. The following exceptions may permit enforcement of oral contracts: part performance of land sales or contracts whose main purpose protects the loan guarantor.

If the parties put their agreement into a complete and formal writing (integration), neither party can alter that agreement with testimony of different terms. Evidence of misrepresentation, fraud, duress, undue influence, illegality, incapacity, or later modifications or clarifications is still admissible.

Third parties may have enforceable rights or duties in the contracts of others, but only if one or both of the contracting parties specifically intend it. Incidental and unintended beneficiaries have no rights in contracts. A contracting party may transfer contract rights or duties by assignment or delegation. The transferee may enforce the transfer if the other contracting party suffers no material change in duty or right.

A contract obligor that is unable to perform as promised should find a substitute to perform. Parties may be relieved of their duty to perform contract obligations if performance of those obligations becomes impossible or too burdensome. Innocent parties may sue for a remedy such as damages or specific performance.

Critical Thinking Review Questions

1. For what reason has the concept of consideration remained in the law of contracts? When is consideration required? When is consideration not required?
2. How does the objective theory of contracts clarify ambiguities in the communications of contracting parties during negotiations?
3. How does the parol evidence rule resolve ambiguities in a written integration contract that the parties envision to be the whole and complete embodiment of their agreement?

Critical Thinking Exercises

1. The plaintiff, a real estate developer, requested that the defendant utility company extend power lines to a new subdivision but never signed a contract promising to pay for the installation. After the utility company completed the installation of the new lines, the plaintiff sought a declaratory judgment that it was not liable for the cost of extending the lines. Under what theory would the real estate developer be liable?
2. Larry and Bo were playing a friendly game of golf at Callaway Gardens. As Larry was about to drive from the tee, Bo said, "If you make a hole in one, I'll give you $500." Larry made a hole in one. Does Bo have to pay?
3. Nancy had a contract to work for Ace Construction for two years when financial difficulties developed at the company. In oral conversation with the owner of Ace Construction, Nancy offered to resign. The owner did not accept that oral offer. Later, the owner wrote Nancy a letter accepting her oral offer to resign. Has the offer lapsed?
4. The plaintiff purchased an option to buy the defendant's hunting lodge. The written option agreement stated that the option to purchase was to expire on May 1. On April 15, the plaintiff refused to exercise the option in a notification to the defendant. Subsequently, on April 29, the plaintiff attempted to exercise the option. Where an offeree (the plaintiff in this case) refuses to exercise an option and subsequently decides to exercise it, does the first refusal extinguish the offer? Does it make a difference if the offeror (the defendant/seller in this case) has not changed his position after the refusal?
5. SupplyCo's sales representative, Jack Jenkins, has made numerous sales calls on ABC Manufacturing, usually negotiating with Henry Smith, ABC's purchasing manager. SupplyCo sells industrial solvents that could be used in ABC's manufacturing processes. ABC's solvent needs currently amount to several hundred thousand dollars annually and are fulfilled by IndusSolvCo, under a long-term supply contract. Henry suggested to Jack that if SupplyCo would permit Henry's family to use the SupplyCo corporate beach house for Henry's family vacation, he would terminate the IndusSolvCo contract prematurely to make future purchases from SupplyCo. None of this is put in writing, and Henry's family used the beach house for their two-week summer vacation. Thereafter, Henry did not terminate the IndusSolvCo supply contract and never makes any orders from SupplyCo, although he is apologetic when Jack again visits ABC. What ethical issues are apparent for both men and their companies? Comment on the role of the statute of frauds in controlling the unethical behavior of these parties.
6. Jane contracted for the purchase of a house. Before the closing, she discovered that the house had a leaky roof. At the closing, she would not pay until the seller promised to repair the roof. The seller promised to repair, and she paid the purchase price. Is the seller's promise enforceable? Why or why not?
7. The plaintiff/purchaser bought a sporting goods store located near the athletic field of a major university. As part of the contract, the defendant/seller agreed that he would not open a competing business in the university town for the next three years. The following summer, the seller opened a competing sporting goods store on the other side of town. The plaintiff/purchaser claimed he was entitled to money damages for breach of contract. Can the seller of the sporting goods store open a competing store and solicit business from his former customers?
8. John was employed by Acme Development Company as a commercial real estate salesman. His employment contract provided that if he left Acme's employment, he could not engage in the real estate business for five years within 10 miles of its offices. He brought an action for declaratory judgment to determine his rights under the contract. Acme counterclaimed and sought an injunction to prevent him from working for a competitor. Can an employer automatically enforce a restrictive covenant in an employment contract?
9. Jane purchased a life-cycle exercise machine at Body Works. The written installment sales contract disclaimed any warranty obligations to the seller. Jane experienced several problems with the exercise machine that Body Works refused to repair. Jane sued the Body Works on its oral promise that if problems arose, it would "take care of them." Is this oral promise admissible in court?
10. Jones had an oral agreement to purchase 1.3 acres of land in a 10-acre tract owned by seller. Seller refused to close on the contract. If the buyer sues for specific performance, will the statute of frauds be a valid defense?

CHAPTER

10

Commercial Law

Critical Thinking Questions

- Compare and contrast the common law strict rules of offer and acceptance with the UCC's more realistic mutual assent rules.
- For what reasons does the UCC place special duties on merchants?
- How do the title and risk of loss rules address the ambiguity in a contract of sale and the method chosen for transporting goods from seller to buyer?
- What is presumed by intermediaries in the banking system about the reliability of their transactions in taking and giving value for commercial documents?
- Why would anyone take a negotiable instrument rather than cash for payment of goods or services?
- What interests are subjugated when an insolvent debtor is subjected to creditors' rights and the bankruptcy process?

Introduction... Past, Present, Future

The amount of commerce has reliably expanded only as mechanisms developed to satisfy the uncertainties of trading partners. Since medieval times, the risks of travel on the high seas, war, pirates, and the unreliability of distant trading partners could have confined trade to just local barter and exchange. However, the emerging merchants of that era developed customs and practices that eventually evolved into the **law merchant** to better satisfy their needs and fulfill their expectations. These customs have evolved into the modern Uniform Commercial Code (UCC), the Vienna Convention for the International Sales of Goods (CISG), and other commercial customs and practices discussed in this chapter.

law merchant
Evolution of merchants' customs and practices from the middle ages into modern commercial law.

The common law of contracts discussed in Chapter 9 largely applies to transactions in land and services. A significant portion of the economy involves the sales of goods and the underlying payment and credit transactions involved with the manufacturing sector. This chapter explores the additional laws applicable to these commercial transactions. Most of this law is derived from the Uniform Commercial Code (UCC), a consistent set of laws now adopted in all of the U.S. states. Commercial transactions are a combination of sales contracts governed by UCC Article 2, payments made by negotiable instrument for goods and services governed by UCC Article 3, relations between banks and their customers governed by UCC Article 4 and 4A, the need for collateral to secure commercial loans governed by UCC Article 9, and provisions for the orderly satisfaction of creditors' rights against insolvent persons and entities governed by federal bankruptcy and various

FIGURE 10–1

Uniform Commercial Code (UCC)

Article Number	Title	Coverage
1	General Provisions	Definitions common to the whole UCC
2	Sales	Contract rules for sales of goods
2A	Leases	Contract rules for leases of goods
3	Commercial Paper	Negotiations and transfer of checks, notes, drafts, and certificates of deposit
4	Bank Deposits & Collections	Relationships between banks and depositors; collection process for commercial paper
4A	Funds Transfers	Relationships among commercial entities and banks in processing funds transfers by wire (electronic funds transfers for consumers is governed by federal law)
5	Letters of Credit	Parties' obligations and process for using letters of credit to finance international sales of goods
6	Bulk Transfers	Notice and protection of creditors from merchant selling all inventory and absconding with sale proceeds
7	Warehouse Receipts Bills of Lading, Documents of Title	Negotiation and transfer process for evidence of title to goods in transit or storage
8	Investment Securities	Negotiation and transfer of investment securities (e.g., stock, bonds)
9	Secured Transactions	Creation and enforcement of liens on goods; priorities among secured creditors

state creditor–debtor laws. This uniformity encourages interstate commerce and reduces transaction costs by providing an efficient form of commercial contract terms on which businesses from all parts of the United States have developed expectations. As first suggested in Chapter 2, international commercial law is more challenging given the difficulties of enforcing contracts across borders. However, workable international commercial practices have developed into codes to make a somewhat uniform global pattern similar to that in the United States. Figure 10–1 summarizes the various parts of the UCC and their applicability.

In the future, commercial transactions will become even more mechanized, with the majority of transactions being processed electronically. The initial negotiating of contracts will increasingly take place via computer and phone links. Videoconferencing or teleconferencing may become standard practice. The final establishment of the definitive contract terms will be conducted by *Electronic Data Interchange (EDI)* over telecommunication systems, satellite links, and other communication devices. This may follow international standardization under the United Nations/ Electronic Data Interchange for Administration, Commerce and Transport (UN/ EDIFACT). Payment for goods and services will increasingly bypass the physical document-processing system of banks instead using electronic funds and wire transfers that simply credit and debit the parties' accounts. Transfer of important certification documents showing inspection, proving ownership, or satisfying customs will also take place electronically. Standard forms and umbrella agreements will be utilized to reduce transactions costs and lessen surprise. Such systems will necessitate additional recognition of the importance of evolving uniform laws from prevailing customs and practices. This chapter discusses the UCC, the major source of commercial law in the United States, as well as several international laws and practices useful in international trade.

Thought Questions

1. What reasons support the evolution of law from the actual practices of commercial parties and how does this reflect changes in international relations and technology?
2. What is ambiguous about trade among political entities when the parties are from different states or nations?

Sales of Goods

The common law of contracts in the United States is supplemented by the UCC, which is applicable in all 50 states and the District of Columbia. The UCC governs only the sale of goods, so the threshold choice of law question in commercial problems is always: What is the predominant subject matter of the contract? *Goods* are all things movable at the time of contracting. The common law of contracts applies where land or services predominates and any accompanying sale of goods is only minor. By contrast, where the sale of goods predominates and land or services is only an insignificant part of the contract, Article 2 of the UCC applies. For example, the common law applies to a beautician's largely service contract to provide hair coloring despite the incidental use of the hair coloring product. By contrast, the UCC applies to the sale of an automobile despite the incidental promise to provide maintenance services under the accompanying warranty. Article 2 does not apply to other transactions in goods such as those classified as a gift, a sale of investment securities, or a bailment.

The UCC encourages freedom of contract while reflecting business practice. Therefore, the UCC reinforces commercial expectations about how parties should act but still gives them great leeway to design optimal agreements. Nevertheless, all parties must act in *good faith,* defined in UCC §1-201 as honesty in fact in that transaction. Merchants are sometimes held to even higher standards of conduct. **Merchants** are persons who deal in goods of the kind, or profess to be experts in that trade or business, or use expert agents. In general, merchants must read their mail and become familiar with commercial practices in their chosen trade or business.

merchants Persons who deal in goods of kind, profess to be experts, or hire expert agents to conduct their business; the UCC implies special duties on merchants.

The United Nations Commission on International Trade Law (UNCITRAL) developed the Vienna Convention for the International Sale of Goods (CISG) as international sales law similar in many respects to UCC Article 2. However, there are some significant differences discussed in this chapter. Many deal with the formation of international sales contracts. The CISG applies to contracts for the international sales of goods where the parties' places of business are in different "states," which is the international term for nations. The CISG applies only to commercial contracts because the variety of consumer protection laws worldwide might too easily conflict with the CISG. The CISG applies only if both parties' nations have ratified the CISG, although parties from non–CISG nations could agree to apply the CISG. The United States

FIGURE 10-2

Nations Adopting the CISG (by 1995)

Argentina	France	Romania
Australia	Georgia	Russian Federation
Austria	Germany	Singapore
Belarus	Ghana	Slovakia
Bosnia/Herzegovina	Guinea	Spain
Bulgaria	Hungary	Sweden
Canada	Iraq	Switzerland
Chile	Italy	Syrian Arab Republic
China	Lesotho	Uganda
Cuba	Lithuania	Ukraine
Czech Republic	Mexico	United States of America
Denmark	Netherlands	Venezuela
Equador	New Zealand	Yugoslavia
Egypt	Norway	Zambia
Estonia	Poland	
Finland	Republic of Moldova	

ratified the CISG in 1986. Figure 10–2 lists the other nations that have adopted the CISG as of this writing, either by ratification, acceptance, approval, accession, or succession. The CISG would not apply to an international sales contract between a U.S. and Japanese firm because Japan has not yet signed the CISG. In such cases, the complex international conflicts of law rules noted in Chapter 2 apply in determining whether U.S. or Japanese law applies or whether the parties have chosen some other dispute resolution method such as arbitration. Parties may also specifically opt out of the CISG by stating so in their sales contract. This may be advisable for large firms experienced in international trade. However, the CISG is useful in reducing transaction costs and in reducing the uncertainties of potential application of obscure foreign law, particularly if foreign law might plague the contract's performance or one party is new to international sales transactions.

Formation of a Sales Contract

The UCC generally requires the same elements of a valid contract as the common law: mutual assent, consideration, no defenses to formation, and legality. The UCC adopts most common law offer and acceptance doctrines but simplifies the formation of a sales contract consistent with commercial practice. UCC §2-206 permits both bilateral and unilateral contracts. The UCC rejects the rigid common law acceptance rules by permitting acceptance in any commercially reasonable manner. An acceptance of an order (offer) is possible with either a prompt promise to ship or with a prompt shipment of goods that conform to the order's specifications. The shipment of nonconforming goods is the simultaneous acceptance and breach of contract unless the seller indicates the shipment is made as an accommodation.

Open Terms Usually, a reasonable person will definitely express all or nearly all of the proposed contract's essential terms when making an offer. In some circumstances, however, the parties may assume that reasonable or customary terms should be included even if they are not expressed. Under UCC §2-204, for example, terms of a contract may be left as *open terms* for future determination and later inferred from the circumstances. The contract will be enforced as long as a "reasonably certain basis" exists "for giving an appropriate remedy." For example, the price of goods may be determined later if the parties leave the price term open, if they say nothing about price, or if they intend to use the market price at the time of delivery. The UCC provides additional *gap-filling* terms to supplement vague sales contracts. For example, UCC §2-304 infers a reasonable price that is set as of the time the parties intended delivery of the goods. An open delivery term is interpreted as requiring delivery at the seller's place of business and at a reasonable time after contracting. A payment term left open obligates the buyer to pay when the goods are received. Even the quantity term can be left vague until determined by the sellers' actual *outputs* or the buyers' actual *requirements*. Terms can also be supplied by trade custom, which will be discussed later. The CISG does not clearly encourage the use of open terms, except in setting the price according to some outside force, such as index, formula, or third party. The CISG imposes no good faith duty on the parties like the UCC does.

Firm Offers To make a commercial offer irrevocable, the option contract or firm offer can be used. Options require consideration such as when the offeree pays a price for the privilege of irrevocability. However, a **firm offer** made by a merchant in a signed writing creates an irrevocable offer even without payment of consideration. A firm offer is irrevocable for up to three months as stated in the offer. An offeror who revokes a firm offer or sells optioned property to another person will be liable for damages for breach of contract. For example, assume that in a signed writing a goods merchant makes an offer to sell 500 widgets to a buyer at $30 each. If the merchant promises to keep the offer open for two weeks but then withdraws it the next day, the buyer may enforce the contract. In some civil law nations, offers must stay open for a minimum length of time, such as three days. The CISG makes firm offers enforceable even if they were not made in writing.

firm offer
UCC (§2-205) option that makes an offer irrevocable, enforceable without consideration, if made by a merchant in a signed writing.

FIRM OFFER (UCC §2-205)

An offer made by "a merchant to buy or sell goods in a signed writing which by its terms gives assurance that it will be held open is not revocable . . . [even without consideration] during the time stated or . . . for a reasonable time, but in no event . . . [for longer than three months]."

Battle of the Forms Commercial organizations often fail to adhere strictly to the common law mirror-image rule. Goods sales often involve a **battle of the forms** in which buyers and sellers, with the aid of their attorneys, construct invoices, order forms, and confirmation forms containing terms very favorable to themselves. Inevitably, there are differences between terms found in the offer and acceptance forms. Minor differences usually go unnoticed unless a dispute arises. UCC §2-207 provides a more practical solution to this problem than the common law mirror-image rule.

battle of the forms
Nonconformity of contract terms between buyer and seller's forms, often resolved in goods sales by UCC §2-207.

Additional Terms in Acceptance or Confirmation (UCC §2-207)

1. A definite and seasonable expression of acceptance or a written confirmation which is sent within a reasonable time operates as an acceptance even though it states terms additional to or different from those offered or agreed upon, unless acceptance is expressly made conditional on assent to the additional or different terms.
2. The additional terms are to be construed as proposals for addition to the contract. Between merchants such terms become part of the contract unless:
   (a) the offer expressly limits acceptance to the terms of the offer;
   (b) they materially alter it; or
   (c) notification of objection to them has already been given or is given within a reasonable time after notice of them is received.
3. Conduct by both parties which recognizes the existence of a contract is sufficient to establish a contract for sale although the writings of the parties do not otherwise establish a contract. In such case the terms of the particular contract consist of those terms on which the writings of the parties agree, together with any supplementary terms incorporated under any other provisions of this Act.

UCC §2-207 applies to forming a contract when there are only minor deviations between the parties' written documents in sales of goods. Unlike under the common law mirror-image rule, slight differences between the offer and the acceptance do not always cause a contract to fail. A contract is formed if there are no material differences on key terms in the parties' communications. However, either party may reimpose the mirror-image rule. Counteroffers are possible only if highly material terms are in dispute between the writings. *Highly material terms* include essential terms such as the parties' identity, price, quantity, or subject matter. For example, differences in the size, color, or grade of goods would be highly material, so the return communication containing these differences would be a counteroffer.

Material additions, deletions, or changes found in the acceptance or confirmation form do not destroy the contract, so the parties have a binding agreement. If different terms appear in the second communication, they are considered mere proposals to modify, but the contract still exists on the originally offered terms. Such proposals may be accepted or rejected by the offeror. *Material terms* are those that would cause surprise to either party, such as changes in standard warranty protection or customary credit terms.

When both of the parties are merchants, immaterial differences in the second communication generally become part of the contract, as long as the offeror does not object. If the parties' conduct implicitly recognizes their contract exists, it is enforceable. In that case, the contract's terms are those on which the writings agree, together with other terms automatically supplied by the UCC. For example, if the buyer pays for the goods or the seller delivers them, a contract exists even if the parties' forms do not agree. The CISG rejects UCC §2-207 by following the mirror-image rule. As EDI becomes better established, battles of the forms problems may disappear.

Auctions Auction sales present a problem of identifying which party is the offeror and which is the offeree. Under the common law of auction sales, the identities of the offeror and offeree are defined by the apparent intent of the parties. Sellers at most auctions want to retain the right to withdraw goods from the auction block if there are only inadequate bids. In that case, the bids are considered offers and the auctioneer's final act of knocking down the goods to the highest bidder is the acceptance. Many auctions concern goods, so the UCC rules often apply. Under UCC §2-328, an auction of this kind is called an *auction with reserve* because the seller reserves the right to withdraw goods from the auction block before final sale.

Of course, it is possible to switch the offeror–offeree designations in an auction so that a bid is an acceptance of the auctioneer's offer. As each next bid comes in higher, it replaces the previous bid as the acceptance, until bidding stops and a contract is formed when the goods are "knocked down" to the last and highest bidder. An auction of this kind is called an *auction without reserve* because the auctioneer does not reserve the right to withdraw the goods after bidding starts. Auctions are usually with reserve unless the auction notice explicitly indicates otherwise. Auctions without reserve often draw bargain hunters expecting sales even if only low bids are made.

Mailbox Rule UCC §2-206 is more lenient than the common law mailbox rule in which a contract is formed when the acceptance is dispatched. Absent an agreement to the contrary, an acceptance is effective if it is communicated by any means reasonable under the circumstances, if it is in common use, and if it is as fast as or faster than the means used by the offeror. The CISG rejects the mailbox rule altogether, making acceptances effective only upon receipt.

Consideration Consideration is generally required for sales of goods contracts. However, there are several important exceptions that eliminate the consideration requirement and facilitate flexibility. To modify an existing goods sale contract, there is no need for consideration if both parties agree, even if only one party's obligation is changed given the UCC good-faith obligation. No consideration is required for written merchants' firm offers.

UCC §2-302 permits the court hearing a contract dispute to modify an adhesion contract, one with unfair provisions, under the **unconscionability** doctrine. The parties may present evidence of the purpose and commercial setting of any clause brought into question. A consumer contract may be designated unconscionable if it is one-sided and oppressive, causes unfair surprise, and unfairly allocates risks because one side clearly has superior bargaining power. Courts are increasingly applying unconscionability beyond the UCC context to achieve fairness in common law contracts. However, unconscionability seldom applies to commercial parties; it is reserved for the uniquely vulnerable position of consumers. Commercial parties generally are more experienced and better informed, have better access to legal counsel, possess stronger bargaining power, and negotiate contracts more carefully than do consumers.

unconscionability Unfair adhesion contract with inadequate consideration; can be canceled by a court under the UCC.

UCC Statute of Frauds The common law statute of frauds has been amended by the UCC for contracts involving the sale of goods for $500 or more. The UCC statute of frauds is less restrictive than under the common law. The memorandum required by the UCC need not state all the terms of the contract accurately, but is enforceable only up to the quantity stated in the writing. The UCC's "gap fillers" infer any needed terms, such as permitting oral testimony or other proof to supply terms of price, delivery, quality, or industry customs. There are four major exceptions to the UCC statute of frauds.

First, if both parties to an oral contract are merchants and one party sends a written confirmation of an oral agreement to the other party, then no writing is necessary if the receiver fails to object within 10 days. This *receiver-bound* exception provides an incentive for merchants to carefully read and quickly respond to their mail. A second UCC exception exists for *specially manufactured* goods, defined as goods unsuitable for sale in the seller's ordinary course of business. An oral telephone order for $1,000 of unique manufactured goods becomes enforceable as soon as the seller makes a substantial beginning in procuring or making the goods. Goods requiring special printing, embossing, unusual colors, trademarks, or emblems are usually specially manufactured.

A third UCC exception permits enforcement of an oral contract if the party seeking to deny the contract nevertheless confirms the agreement by making an *admission*. The admission may appear in testimony, in pleadings, or otherwise in a court proceeding. The statute of frauds will not aid a party to renege on a contract actually entered into orally. The fourth UCC exception permits enforcement of oral contracts if there has been either a *partial payment* for goods by the buyer or an acceptance of a *partial delivery* by the seller. Contracts are enforced under this part-performance doctrine only for the quantity paid for or accepted. The next case illustrates the receiver-bound exception for merchants.

Thompson Printing Machinery Co. v. B.F. Goodrich Co.

714 F.2d 744 (7th Cir. 1983)
U.S. Court of Appeals, Seventh Circuit

James Thompson made an oral contract with Ingram Myers, a Goodrich agent, to purchase approximately $9,000 worth of used equipment displayed at the B.F. Goodrich surplus machinery department. Thompson confirmed the oral purchase with a written purchase order sent to Goodrich four days later, which included Thompson's name, address, phone, and information about the purchase. Copies of the document were not received by Myers but distributed within Goodrich to determine who made the sale. The machinery was sold to another purchaser. Thompson claimed that Goodrich received the confirmation letter and was bound by it. Goodrich claimed the statute of frauds was not satisfied because it had not signed any memorandum.

Cudahy, Justice

Uniform Commercial Code section 2–201(2) provides:

> Between merchants if within a reasonable time a writing in confirmation of the contract and sufficient against the sender is received and the party receiving it has reason to know its contents, it satisfies [the statute of frauds] against the [receiver] unless written notice of objection to its contents is given within 10 days after it is received.

We must emphasize that the only effect of this exception is to take away from a merchant who receives a writing in confirmation of a contract the statute of frauds defense if the merchant does not object. The sender must still persuade the trier of fact that a contract was in fact made.

Goodrich argues Thompson's confirmation cannot qualify for the exception. Thompson erred in not specifically designating on the envelope, check, or purchase order that the items were intended for Myers or the surplus equipment department. Goodrich was unable to "find a home" for the check and purchase order in accordance with its regular procedures of sending copies of the documents to several of its departments.

The literal requirements are met that a writing is received and that Goodrich has reason to know its contents. There is no specific or express requirement that the "receipt" be by any Goodrich agent in particular. Section 1-201 provides that notice received by an organization is effective for a particular transaction from the time when it would have been brought to [the proper individual's attention] if the organization had executed due diligence.

The question comes down to whether Goodrich's mailroom, given the information it had, should have notified the surplus equipment manager of Thompson's confirmatory writing. If Goodrich had exercised due diligence in handling Thompson Printing's purchase order and check, these items would have reasonably promptly come to Myers' attention. The purchase order on its face should have alerted the mailroom that the documents referred to a purchase of used printing equipment. Since Goodrich had only one surplus machinery department, the document's home should not have been difficult to find. Even [with difficulty in identifying the transaction] the purchase order had Thompson Printing's phone number printed on it. Thus, we think Goodrich's mailroom mishandled the confirmatory writings. This failure should not permit Goodrich to escape liability by pleading nonreceipt [of the confirmatory note].

Case Questions

1. What two important duties does the receiver-bound rule place on merchants about their incoming mail? Considering the size and geographic dispersion of many corporations, is 10 days a reasonable time?
2. What could a merchant like Goodrich do in its contracts to avoid the problem encountered in this case? What other procedures should be adopted?

Title and Risk of Loss

Before the UCC, the concept of *title* or ownership of property triggered numerous concerns: the right to insure the property, the risk of financial loss if the property was damaged or destroyed in transit, and legal remedies against the seller or a wrongdoer. The UCC has changed this by separating the incidents of ownership from insurable interest and risk of loss. Title to goods affects ownership, the owner's creditors' rights, and taxation.

Title Title cannot pass from the seller to the buyer until after the goods are identified. *Identification* occurs when particular goods are designated as being for the buyer. This can occur explicitly in the contract or occurs when the seller ships goods or designates them as for the buyer. Title passes when the agreement dictates. If the contract does not mention title transfer, the title to goods passes when the seller completes the obligation to deliver, either (1) when they are delivered to the carrier in a contract requiring the seller to "ship," (2) when they are delivered to the buyer in a contract requiring the seller to "deliver," or (3) at the time of contracting if delivery is not mentioned or will occur without moving the goods, for example, goods held in an independent warehouse. If the buyer rejects the goods, title immediately reverts to the seller. The CISG makes no provision for title and most international title transfers are determined by documents of title.

Documents of Title Many commercial transactions use written documents that accompany the goods in transit, facilitate the buyer's payment between the parties' banks, and verify inspections or government clearances. UCC Article 7 governs the use of *documents of title,* which include bills of lading, dock warrants, dock receipts, and warehouse receipts. These are instruments entitling the holder to possess, receive, or dispose of specified goods, which are usually in the possession of a bailee. As discussed in Chapter 7, *bailees* are temporary custodians of goods who usually act for the true owner's benefit, such as a when carrier or warehouse acts for the parties by moving or holding goods. A **bill of lading,** illustrated in Figure 10–3, is a document

bill of lading
Document of title entitling holder to delivery of goods in transit.

FIGURE 10-3 Bill of Lading

Bill of Lading

Shipper	
Consignee: (Complete name and address)	Forwarding agent
	Point and country of origin / Place of receipt
Notify party	Domestic routing instructions
Pier	Place of delivery
Ocean vessel / Port of landing	
Point of discharge	

CARRIER'S RECEIPT — PARTICULARS FURNISHED BY SHIPPER

Marks and numbers	Number of packages	Description of goods	Gross weight	Measurement

- Received in apparent good order and condition except as otherwise noted hereon the goods, containers, or other packages for transportation from the place of receipt or port of loading subject to exceptions, limitations, and conditions and to be delivered to the consignee or assigns.

(TERMS OF THIS BILL OF LADING CONTINUED ON REVERSE.)

TOTAL FREIGHT $ ________

DATE ________ BY ________ (Agent)

of title used by carriers or freight forwarders that often doubles as the contract of carriage. A **warehouse receipt,** illustrated in Figure 10–4, is a title document issued by a warehouse that often doubles as the contract of storage.

warehouse receipt Document of title entitling holder to possession of goods held in a warehouse.

Documents of title can be made negotiable so they will physically accompany the flow documents through the banking system. An endorsement is required to transfer rights from transferor to transferee of a negotiable document of title. There

FIGURE 10-4 Warehouse Receipt—Not Negotiable

Warehouse Receipt-Not Negotiable

Receipt and lot number ______________ Vault no. ____ ____ ____ ____ ____

____ ____ ____ ____ ____

Date of issue ______________ 19 __________

Received for the account of and deliverable to ______________________________

of (address) ____

the goods enumerated on attached schedule and stored in Company warehouse, located at

______________________________________ . These goods are accepted upon the following conditions.

That the value of all goods stored is not over $ ______________________ per pound unless a higher value is noted on the schedule, for which an additional monthly storage charge of

$ ______________ on each $ ______________ will be made.

Ownership. The Customer, Shipper Depositor, or Agent represents and warrants that he is lawfully possessed of goods to be stored and/or has the authority to store or ship said goods. (If the goods are mortgaged, notify the Company of the name and address of the mortgagee.)
Payment of Charges. Storage bills are payable monthly in advance for each month's storage or fraction thereof. The Depositor will pay reasonable attorney's fee incurred by the Company in collecting delinquent accounts.
Liability of Company. The Company shall be liable for any loss or injury to the goods caused by its failure to exercise such care as a resasonably careful person would exercise under like circumstances. The Company will not be liable for loss or damage to fragile articles not packed, or articles packed or unpacked by other than employees of this Company.
Change of Address. Notice of change of address must be given the Company in writing, and acknowledged in writing by the Company.
Transfer or Withdrawal of Goods. The warehouse receipt is not negotiable and shall be produced and all charges must be paid before delivery to the Depositor, or transfer of goods to another person; however, a written direction to the Company to transfer the goods to another person or deliver the goods may be accepted by the Company at its option without requiring tender of the warehouse receipt.
Access to Storage, Partial Withdrawal. A signed order from the person in whose name the receipt is issued is required to enable others to remove or have access to goods. A charge is made for stacking and unstacking, and for access to stored goods.
Building-Fire-Watchmen. The Company does not represent or warrant that its building cannot be destroyed by fire. The Company shall not be required to maintain a watchman or sprinkler system and its failure to do so shall not constitute negligence.
Claims or Errors. All claims for non delivery of any article or articles and for damage, breakage, etc, must be made in writing within ninety (90) days from delivery of goods stored or they are waived. Failure to return the warehouse receipt for correction within ______ ( ) days after receipt thereof by the depositior will be conclusive that it is correct and delivery will be made only in accordance therewith.
Warehouseman's Lien. The Company reserves the right to sell the goods stored, in accordance with the provisions of the Uniform Commercial Code (Business and Commerce Code if stored in Texas), for all lawful charges in arrears.
Termination of Storage. The Company reserves the right to terminate the storage of the goods at any time by giving to the Depositor thirty (30) days' written notice of its intention so to do, and, unless the Depositor removes such goods within that period, the Company is hereby empowered to have the same removed at the cost and expense of the Depositor, or the Company may sell them at auction in accordance with state law.

THIS DOCUMENT CONTAINS THE WHOLE CONTRACT BETWEEN THE PARTIES AND THERE ARE NO OTHER TERMS, WARRANTIES, REPRESENTATIONS, OR AGREEMENTS OF EITHER DEPOSITOR OR COMPANY NOT HEREIN CONTAINED.

Storage per month or fraction thereof $ __________ Wrapping and preparing for storage $ __________
Warehouse labor $ __________ Charges advanced $ __________
Cartage $ __________ __________ $ __________
Packing at residence $ __________ __________ $ __________

By ______________________________

is a special status for bona fide purchasers of negotiable documents of title similar to the holder in due course status, discussed later in the commercial paper section. Some documents of title are nonnegotiable. Carriers must take reasonable care of the goods in their possession and deliver them to the person designated in the document of title, the *consignee*. A warehouse operator must take care of goods in his or her possession, deliver them to the consignee, and accurately prepare the warehouse receipt. Other negotiable documents used in international sales transactions are discussed later.

Warranty of Title The UCC implies in every contract for sale that the seller has the right to sell the goods, that there are no outstanding liens on the goods, and that the seller can pass good title to the buyer. This is known as the *warranty of title.* It differs from express and implied warranties of fitness and merchantability discussed in Chapter 11 because the latter are warranties covering the product's quality. For example, a seller is liable under the warranty of title if the true owner of stolen goods reclaims them after a sale to the buyer. The warranty of title can be specifically disclaimed or does not arise if the circumstances, a sheriff's sale, for example, suggest the goods are of questionable origin. However, a general statement disclaiming "all warranties" does not disclaim the warranty of title.

Risk of Loss Risk of loss is still important because goods can be damaged or lost in shipment, sometimes as a result of natural catastrophes. After risk of loss passes to the buyer, the purchase price must be paid even if the goods are damaged or lost. By contrast, the seller is liable for breach if a loss occurs before risk of loss passes to the buyer. Therefore, the parties have conflicting incentives to alter the risk of loss by the use of favorable contract language and both should consider insuring the goods during transit. The buyer has an *insurable interest* as soon as the goods are identified, and the seller retains an insurable interest for as long as the seller has either title or a security interest (lien) in the goods.

Passage of risk of loss is made according to numerous technical determinations. First, the parties may designate in the contract when risk passes. If they do not agree and no carrier is used, risk passes when a nonmerchant seller tenders delivery to the buyer or a merchant seller makes actual delivery to the buyer. In sales using a carrier, risk generally passes at either the point of the shipment's origin or at the point of arrival at the destination when *mercantile terms* are used: FOB, FAS, CIF, C&F, or Ex-Ship. Consider the example of goods shipped from a Philadelphia manufacturer to a Detroit wholesaler. In an "FOB Philadelphia" contract, risk and title pass when the seller tenders the goods to the carrier in Philadelphia. In an "FOB Detroit" contract, risk and title pass when the carrier delivers the goods to the buyer in Detroit. The risk remains on the seller in a *sale on approval* until the buyer confirms the purchase after the trial period. By contrast, risk remains with the buyer in a *sale or return* until the goods are returned to the seller. Risk reverts to the seller if the goods are rightfully rejected or there is a rightful revocation of acceptance by the buyer. Common mercantile terms are summarized in Figure 10–5.

Performance and Remedies

The UCC imposes a four-year statute of limitations for bringing suits for breach of contract. However, much of the focus in the UCC is to provide reasonable self-help mechanisms to avoid confrontation or litigation. The UCC gap-filling terms provide certainty to those commercial contracts originally made without specifically resolving unforeseen matters. There are special rules for the performance of sales contracts that trigger some special remedies unlike those in the common law. For example, disagreements over the meaning of commercial contract terms are resolved by *usages*, unique meanings given in a particular trade or line of business. A **usage of trade** is a common method or expectation in the contracts of a trade or business derived from custom or

usage of trade Customary business practices unique to an industry giving special meanings to terms.

FIGURE 10-5

Mercantile Abbreviation	Mercantile Term	Mercantile Term Meaning
FOB	Free on board	Requires payment of fright charges: (1) by buyer if FOB (named place of seller's shipment), (2) by seller if FOB (named place of buyer's destination), (3) by seller if FOB (named carrier vessel, car, or vehicle). Title and risk of loss pass from seller to buyer at the named place.
FAS	Free alongside	Requires seller to deliver goods alongside vessel designated by buyer. Title and risk of loss pass from seller to buyer alongside the vessel.
CIF (CF)	Cost, insurance, freight	Seller's price includes cost of goods, loading, transit insurance, and freight charges for transport to the named destination. Seller must contract for the transportation. Title and risk of loss pass from seller to buyer when the goods are delivered to the carrier.
C&F	Cost and freight	Seller's price includes cost of goods, loading, and freight charges for transport to the named destination. Seller must contract for the transportation. Title and risk of loss pass from seller to buyer when the goods are delivered to the carrier.
Ex-Ship	Ex-Ship	Requires unloading of goods from ship at named port; title and risk of loss pass from seller to buyer when unloaded.

precedent. Clarifications may also come from a recognized **course of dealing** from previous conduct between the parties in previous contracts or through a **course of performance** of a single contract between the parties with repeated performances—installment payments or deliveries. For example, a buyer who fails to object to consistently late deliveries may not claim breach of contract for another late delivery until after notifying the seller that late deliveries will no longer be tolerated. As is the case under the common law, ambiguities are resolved against the drafter of a written contract. This is a particularly important rule for businesses using their own form contracts because the ambiguities in such contracts cannot burden consumers. The CISG encourages reliance on international usages but does not encourage domestic usages.

course of dealing Precedents in performing prior contracts between parties giving special meanings to terms.

course of performance Precedents in performing prior installments in a contract between parties giving special meanings to terms.

The UCC permits a contract to be reinstated after *anticipatory repudiation* if the innocent party has not yet sought a remedy. This concept is similar to anticipatory breach under the common law. If either party repudiates the contract by threatening breach before the time set for performance, the innocent party may treat the repudiation as a breach and sue for damages, cancel the contract, or ignore the repudiation and await performance. The wrongful party may withdraw the repudiation so long as the other party has not acted on it, such as by contracting with another or bringing suit. At any time, either party may demand *adequate assurances of performance* from the other party. For example, a seller uncertain about the buyer's solvency or a buyer disturbed with the seller's erratic deliveries may lose trust. If the other party fails to give assurances after a request and within a reasonable time, the innocent party may pursue remedies for breach even if the time for performance has not yet arrived. The UCC releases parties from performing if an unforeseen event makes the obligor's performance highly impractical. For example, if a seller's cost of goods increases by 10 times or more, the contract might be discharged for *commercial impracticality*.

Both buyer and seller have particular rights, duties, and remedies during the contract's performance. Both parties must stand ready to perform until the other party fails to *tender* performance as required, that is, indicate a willingness and immediate ability to perform. The UCC generally permits either buyer or seller to recover *consequential damages,* those additional damages that flow naturally from the breach, including lost income or profits. However, the UCC requires any aggrieved party to *mitigate* damages by trying to minimize them whenever practical. Either party can *cancel* the contract if the other party is in breach of contract.

Buyer's Remedies In addition to the extensive UCC express and implied warranties of quality discussed in Chapter 11, the buyer has several other remedies. The buyer has the right to receive goods *conforming* to the contract description. The seller must tender delivery at a reasonable time and place, give the buyer notice, and hold the goods for a reasonable time to give the buyer the opportunity to take delivery. The buyer has the right of *inspection* to assure the goods are conforming, unless the delivery is COD or is a "shipment against documents," for example, document of title, draft, or letter of credit. This inspection right creates a duty on the buyer, possibly limiting the buyer's warranty protection, as discussed in Chapter 11. That is, to the extent the buyer fails to discover a defect on reasonable inspection, the buyer's warranty is excluded, and there is no remedy.

If the seller delivers *nonconforming goods,* goods that do not meet the contract specifications, the buyer has three choices: (1) *accept* the nonconforming goods, (2) *reject* nonconforming goods and sue for damages, or (3) accept whatever commercial units (e.g., case, crate, pallet) are reasonable under the circumstances and sue for damages. An *acceptance* of goods occurs when the buyer indicates willingness to keep them, fails to reject within a reasonable time, or treats the goods as belonging to the buyer (e.g., uses or resells them). Even after acceptance, the buyer retains a limited right of *revocation of acceptance.* Defects that are difficult to discover in a normal inspection or defects the buyer reasonably believes the seller will cure permit the buyer to revoke the acceptance. If the buyer rejects or revokes acceptance, the goods must be held for the seller to pick up, or the buyer must reship them to the seller. The 1994 bankruptcy amendments permit an insolvent debtor to return goods to the seller if a hearing determines this is in the best interest of the bankruptcy estate.

The buyer's rights after rejecting nonconforming goods are limited by the seller's right to *cure.* The seller may correct the breach by notifying the buyer that substitute conforming goods will be provided before the time originally set for performance expires. If the seller fails to deliver conforming goods by the time set for performance, the buyer may *cover* by purchasing substitute goods from another seller. Alternatively, the buyer may sue for *specific performance* to force the seller to deliver unique goods, that is, *replevy* goods already identified to the contract. The buyer has the right to collect damages when the seller fails to perform. *Damages* are computed as the difference between the contract price and the higher market price on the day of the breach or are computed as the increased price paid for cover, including incidental and consequential damages.

Consider how these remedies would affect a retailer who was promised a widget shipment on Thursday just before the retailer's well-advertised Saturday tent sale. If the wrong goods arrive on Tuesday, the seller still has until Thursday to cure this by delivering conforming goods. If nothing shows up by Thursday, the buyer may cover by purchasing widgets from another supplier on Friday. However, if no goods arrive for the Saturday tent sale, the buyer can sue the seller for consequential damages from the lost profits that would have been made.

Seller's Remedies The seller's basic right is to receive the price paid on or before the time set for payment. The seller has four basic monetary remedies if the buyer refuses to accept delivery of conforming goods: (1) collect damages equal to the difference between the contract price and a lower market price prevailing at breach, (2) collect damages on the difference between the contract price and a lower resale price to another buyer, (3) recover lost profits if the buyer's breach causes the sale of fewer units by the seller, or (4) sue for the price if the goods are unsuitable for sale to anyone else. When the buyer's solvency is in question, the seller has some additional remedies: (1) stop the shipment of goods already in transit with a common carrier, (2) refrain from delivering goods the seller still holds, or (3) demand return of goods for the 20 days following delivery to an insolvent buyer. The 20-day period was extended in the 1994 Bankruptcy Reform Act, as discussed below. The period is also extended if the buyer has made a written misrepresentation of solvency within the prior three months. However, the seller must deliver as promised if an insolvent buyer tenders cash. The CISG closely mirrors the UCC remedies for both buyer and seller. The differences between the UCC and common law are summarized in Figure 10–6.

Leases of Goods

Increasingly, the tax law and the incentive to reduce debt has made leasing an attractive alternative to purchasing goods for both consumers and businesses. The UCC is amended, with Article 2A filling a gap in the law with a more reliable and uniform treatment of leases. As of this writing, UCC Article 2A has been adopted by 45 states and the District of Columbia and is proposed to the legislatures in two other states. Each lease contract is known as a *lease agreement,* in which the *lessor* grants to a *lessee* the right to possess and use goods for a period of time in return for a consideration. UCC Article 2A treats leases of goods more like sales of goods than leases of real property (e.g., apartment, storefront). UCC Article 2A provisions generally parallel UCC Article 2 in issues such as firm offers, contract formation, statute of frauds, the parol evidence rule, performance, assignment and delegation, remedies, warranties, cure, and cover.

Commercial Paper

By the Industrial Revolution, commerce had evolved beyond the limits that payment by barter imposed on contracting parties. Fundamental to the growth in trade has been the development of alternatives to payment for goods, services, and land by barter or currency. Mercantilists in Medieval Europe developed important alternative payment mechanisms by permitting the transfer of rights to receive payment that buyers and borrowers originally exchanged for goods and services. These customs and practices became the *law merchant,* which facilitated trade using negotiable instruments as a reliable substitute for currency. Today, the U.S. Federal Reserve System processes nearly 50 billion negotiable instrument payments annually; most are the familiar personal and corporate checks.

FIGURE 10-6

Comparison of Common Law with UCC Article 2 Sales

Provision or Characteristic	Common Law	UCC Article 2 "Sales"
Application	Land sales, employment, services	Sales of goods (e.g., personal property)
Source of law	State case law precedent; *Restatement*	Uniform state adopted code
Acceptance of unilateral offer	Perform act requested	Prompt shipment of conforming goods
Terms left open in offer? Essential terms	All essential terms must be present in offer	Enforceable contract possible even with certain terms left open for future determination or inference; quantity term is essential
Option contracts	Consideration required	No consideration required if firm offer made in merchant's signed writing (valid up to three months)
Mirror-image rule	Offered terms must exactly match acceptance terms	Mirror image unnecessary unless highly material terms differ (price, quantity, subject matter, parties' identity)
Mailbox rule	Contract formed when acceptance dispatched using offeror's means of communication	Contract formed when acceptance dispatched using any reasonable means under the circumstances
No consideration required	Barred debts, promissory estoppel, charitable subscription, composition	Modification of existing contract, merchant's firm offer (option)
Adhesion contract	Freedom of contract and consideration requirement usually not helpful to victim	Unconscionability prohibited mainly in consumer contracts
Statute of frauds, written contract requirement	Sales of land, contracts incapable of performance within one year, guarantees of other's debts (see exceptions below)	Sales of goods for $500 or more (see exceptions below)
Statute of frauds exceptions	Land sale part performance, main purpose (leading object) in guarantees	Merchant receiver bound, specially manufactured goods, admissions, partial payment/delivery
Memorandum	All terms must be stated somewhere in the assembled documents	UCC gap filing terms may provide any term except quantity; UCC memo enforceable only up to quantity stated
Remedies	Anticipatory breach, damages, impossibility, frustration of purpose, rescission	Anticipatory repudiation, demand adequate assurance of performance, cancellation, damages, cure, cover, specific performance

Modern commercial paper law has evolved from the customs of medieval merchants because of the willingness of lawmakers to encourage payment with instruments and by legislative recognition that uniformity among the states and between nations is needed to facilitate commerce. UCC Article 3 on Commercial Paper, Article 4 on Bank Deposits, and Article 4A covering Electronic Funds Transfers define the rights and liabilities of parties involved in negotiable instrument transactions. Several of the UCC Articles have been revised in recent years, reflecting the evolution of commercial practice. As of this writing, revised UCC Article 3 on Commercial Paper has been adopted by 37 states and the District of Columbia. The remaining states still have the older version, but may soon adopt the revision. Revised UCC Article 4A on Funds Transfers has been adopted by 49 states and the District of Columbia.

Essential to the usefulness of commercial paper is that after it is given by the buyer to the seller, usually as payment by check or note, the seller finds it useful to assign the paper by transferring it through the banking system for eventual payment by the buyer or the buyer's bank. This is the concept of negotiability, making commercial paper a substitute for money. Negotiable paper are formal contracts meeting strict requirements for form. They are transferred by the negotiation process. The law gives a special status to intermediaries who willingly transfer the paper in exchange for the value it represents. Most of these intermediaries become *holders in due course* and are given greater rights than the assignees in a simple contract. This encourages them to handle commercial paper.

Definitions

UCC Article 3 covers two types of commercial paper: notes and drafts. A **note** (promissory note, installment note, collateral note, mortgage note) is a two-party instrument in which the **maker** *promises to pay* the **payee** a specified amount in the future. A bank's *certificate of deposit* is also a form of note in which the bank acknowledges the receipt of customer funds and promises to repay them with interest. A **draft** is a three-party instrument in which a **drawer** issues a draft that *orders* a **drawee**, often the drawer's bank, *to pay* money to the third-party payee. *Checks* are the most common form of draft. When a drawer writes the check, this directs his or her drawee bank to pay the specified amount of money to the payee or to someone else to whom the payee endorsed the check. Other forms of drafts are widely used in commerce. A *time draft* is payable on a specified date in the future, possibly days, months, or even years away. A *sight draft* is payable on sight, that is, when presented and a demand is made for payment. A *trade acceptance* is a commercial draft used to pay for goods. Also known as *sales drafts,* they can be drawn by payee, such as when the seller of goods draws the purchase price on the buyer's bank and payment is conditioned on the buyer's approval.

note
Two-party instrument in which one party promises to pay a specified amount in the future.

maker
Party promising to pay amount stated in note.

payee
Party named to receive payment in note or draft.

draft
Three-party instrument in which the drawer issues a draft ordering drawee (bank) to pay money to a payee.

Negotiability

Negotiable commercial paper must meet strict rules of form to facilitate easy and quick verification of the terms and enforceability. This regularity encourages participants in the banking system to willingly take the paper by assignment in exchange for value, usually by paying money for the paper or crediting a customer's bank account. Commercial paper must meet the negotiability requirements of UCC §3-104 by strictly (1) being in writing, (2) being signed by the maker or drawer, (3) containing unconditional promise or order to pay, (4) indicating a fixed amount of money, (5) containing no

drawer
Party directing drawee to make payment on a draft.

drawee
Party directed to make payment on a draft.

other promise than the promise or order to pay. (6) being payable on demand or at a definite time, and (7) being payable to order or to bearer.

The *writing* requirement permits the use of handwritten, typed, preprinted, or mixed inscriptions that are made in a tangible form. While the use of paper is traditional, it is unnecessary. Computer and telecommunication transfers are covered by UCC Article 4A on electronic funds transfers. The *signature* may be handwritten, either cursive or printed; supplied by stamp, computer, or check-cutting device; or provided by some other mechanized form or symbol so long as it intended to authenticate a writing. However, forgeries do not obligate the maker or drawer who is named on the forged instrument.

There must be an *unconditional promise or order to pay* setting the terms of payment. A *promise* makes a commitment to pay. This is more than a simple acknowledgment of a debt, so a simple IOU is not a promise to pay. Alternatively, an *order* directs some agent to make the payment; typically, it directs payment by the customer's bank or lender. The payment cannot be made conditional on some event or on other agreement. Otherwise, no one would freely accept the paper in commerce. For example, a promissory note would be nonnegotiable if written by a buyer who included an express condition that payment should not be made until the payee delivered specified goods. Similarly, paper is nonnegotiable if made expressly subject to or governed by some other writing or contract. Banks and other intermediaries would have no way to easily confirm whether the goods were delivered, nor could they easily verify the contents of some other writing. However, it is permissible to merely reference or mention some other obligation or writing without destroying negotiability. For example, check writers often use the memo line to reference a particular billing or the underlying contract or agreement. It is also permissible to state that a note is secured with a lien on specified collateral. Payment can be limited to a particular fund, such as when a customer's check is drawn only against one of several accounts at a particular bank.

Instruments are negotiable only if the extent of the obligation is easily ascertained by looking only at the paper. This means a *fixed amount* must be stated. Nevertheless, some adjustments are permissible. For example, interest may be specified at a rate or in a formula if stated on the paper or determined by an index referred to if generally available as published rates, for example, three points over prime rate. Variable rate paper is now negotiable under the 1990 revision to UCC Article 3. Paper remains negotiable even if the fixed amount can be adjusted by a stated discount for early payment or a premium for late payments. There can be adjustments for additional costs of collection, for example, attorneys' fees. Payment must be promised or ordered only *in money,* that is, domestic or foreign currency sanctioned by a government. Payment promised in foreign currency can also be paid in domestic currency, determined at the spot exchange rate quoted by banks as prevailing on the date of payment. However, payment cannot be promised or ordered in goods or services. A check to pay in gold leaf, cigarettes, or bus tokens is nonnegotiable even if these have become an acceptable medium of exchange in some communities.

Negotiable paper must make it clear when payment is promised or authorized. Because there is a time value to money, intermediaries are willing to handle paper only if their obligations and rights are easily determined. A *demand instrument* is payable "on demand," when presented "at sight" or if no time is stated, as with most checks. Many notes and time drafts are often made payable at a definite, future time. Sellers and lenders take these instruments as a form of credit, effectively giving the buyer some time to settle up. The *definite time* that payment will be made must be readily ascertainable when the paper is originally made. Negotiable time paper includes those made payable a fixed period after a stated date (30 days after June 1, 1996), on or before a particular date (payable October 30, 1997), on stated alternate dates, or on some other readily ascertainable date. However, paper is nonnegotiable if made payable only after some uncertain event. For example, a note made payable "after I sell my house" is nonnegotiable. Notes remain negotiable even if they contain *acceleration clauses* giving the holder a right to demand early payment for some stated reason. For example, it is common in real estate loan notes to include an acceleration clause requiring early payment if the owner sells the house. Borrowers are also often given the right to prepay their loan early without destroying their note's negotiability. A note remains negotiable even if the holder is given the right to extend payment to some later date if stated on the note. However, it is nonnegotiable if the maker alone can extend payment.

Commercial paper must contain the magic words of negotiability "payable to order or bearer," indicating to intermediaries that they should willingly take the paper because it will flow freely to others and the maker or drawee will honor the payment. *Bearer* paper is negotiable by anyone who rightfully possesses it. For example, "pay to bearer," "pay to Joan Doe or bearer," or "pay to cash" all contain sufficient magic words of negotiability. *Order* paper is somewhat more restrictive than bearer paper because only a stated person can rightfully demand payment. Order paper requires negotiation; usually, an endorsement must be supplied by the person named in the order or by some other rightful transferee. For example, order paper is negotiable if there are magic words such as "pay to the order of Joan Doe" or "payable to the assigns of John Doe." However, paper is nonnegotiable if it says only "pay to Joan Doe" because this does not encourage intermediaries to handle the paper. The person must be clearly identified by name, account number, or office. Some preprinted forms use both order and bearer language, such as "pay to the order of ________ or bearer," where a specific name will be supplied in the blank when issued. Paper with both order and bearer language are treated as bearer paper. Checks commonly indicate "pay to the order of ________" but remain negotiable even if the maker crosses out the wording "~~to the order~~."

Negotiable paper may be antedated, postdated, or undated without affecting its validity. Written words are given preference over contradictory numeric writing; the written amount on a personal check must be honored even if the numerals do not match. Handwritten terms are given preference over typed or pre-printed terms, and typewritten terms are given preference over pre-printed terms. An incomplete instrument may be completed by some authorized person. For example, a blank check that the maker authorizes to be filled in for the purchase price is enforceable. However, a blank check that has been completed for a higher amount is considered a *material alteration*. The negotiability of instruments must be readily determinable by looking only at the instrument itself for the elements discussed above. These must all appear on the face of the paper, with the few exceptions noted. Figure 10–7 illustrates the formal negotiable instrument requirements appearing directly on a check.

Negotiation and Transfer

The transfer of commercial paper is really the assignment of a contract right to receive the payment as stated. Intermediaries (e.g., merchants, banks) seek a special status conferred by the UCC. These are rights superior to what an assignee under a simple contract normally receives, that is, only the assignor's rights. This special status encourages the participation of intermediaries in the payment system. It is not enough that the instrument be in the negotiable form defined above. The instrument must be transferred and assigned by the *negotiation* process, giving most intermediaries the special status of a

FIGURE 10-7

Negotiability Determined on the Face of a Draft

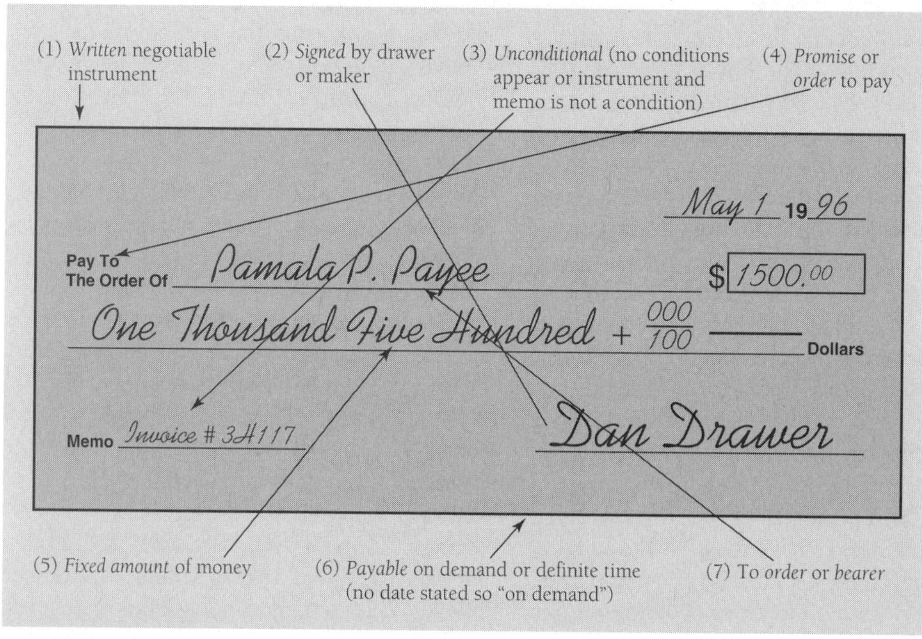

holder in due course. This gives reasonable assurance of payment free from any defenses the original maker might assert against a normal contract assignee.

When a maker or drawer initially writes the paper and makes the first delivery to another person, this is known as *issue*. Most paper is delivered many times in subsequent *transfers* from *transferors* to *transferees*. For example, many personal checks are issued by the drawer to a merchant in exchange for goods or services. The merchant is a transferee who further transfers the check to his or her own bank. The check is quite possibly further transferred through other correspondent banks and is ultimately presented for payment to the drawee, which is the buyer's own bank. *Negotiation* is a special type of transfer to a *holder* who rightfully possesses (actual physical control) and has good title to the instrument. Anyone in possession of bearer paper (including a thief) is a holder with power to transfer title to a holder in due course. For this reason, it is best to make paper to order, to endorse with restrictions and to safeguard paper as if it were cash. Order paper is negotiated when the previous holder physically transfers it after making an endorsement. Endorsement shows the transferor knowingly grants the transferee rights in the paper. If paper is made payable to multiple transferees in the conjunctive (e.g., "Jack *and* Julia") then both must endorse. If the paper is made payable in the disjunctive (e.g., "Jack *or* Julia") then either of their endorsements alone will suffice.

Endorsements An *endorsement* (or indorsement) is the signature of a payee or subsequent party and is usually made on the back of the instrument. It is valid even if it corrects a misspelling or changes the name to the holder. It is preferable to sign the name both ways if misspelled. An endorsement can broaden or limit further negotiation. In a *blank endorsement,* the payee simply supplies her or his signature, converting the paper from order to bearer paper. In a *special endorsement,* the payee

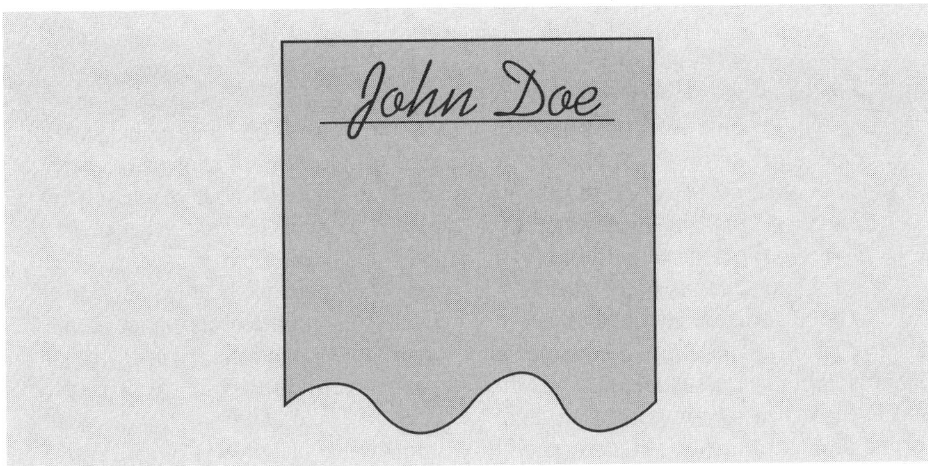

FIGURE 10–8

Blank Endorsement

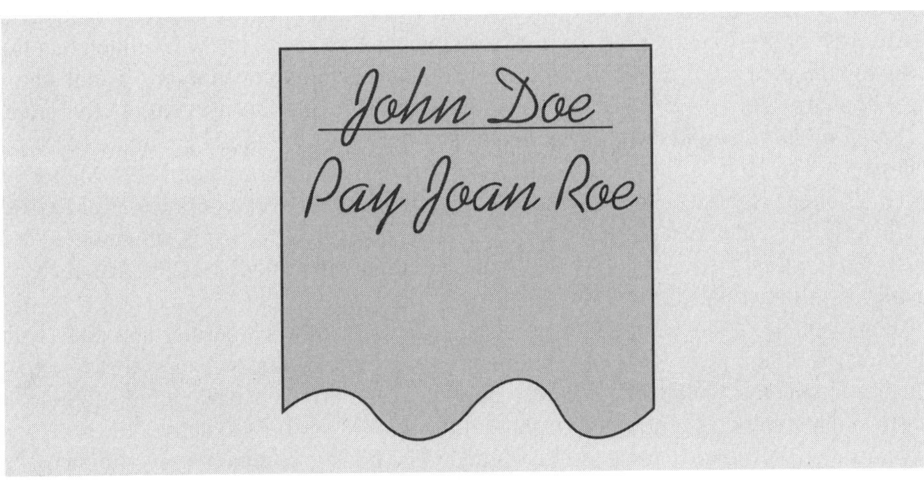

FIGURE 10–9

Special Endorsement

supplies his or her signature but restricts further negotiation to a person named in the special endorsement. This implicitly makes the paper to the order of the newly named person. For example, Figures 10–8 and 10–9 show the backs of two checks made payable to John Doe. John's blank endorsement in Figure 10–8 makes the check into bearer paper. However, in Figure 10–9, John alternatively made a special endorsement over to "pay Joan Roe." This preserves the check's character as order paper and serves as a security measure. It must be signed by the *special endorsee* Joan Roe for any further negotiation. Bearer paper can be given a special endorsement, and this converts it into order paper.

A *restrictive endorsement* that adds some condition generally does not destroy negotiability. For example, an endorsement by the payee John Doe that adds the words "pay only if the maker performs the contract" would be disregarded. However, it is possible to restrict further negotiation somewhat such as to its transfer only through the banking system. "Pay any bank" or "for deposit only" are common and enforceable restrictive endorsements that do not destroy negotiability. For example, anyone paying on a stolen check that had a restrictive endorsement "for deposit only" may be required to pay a second time to the rightful owner of the check.

All endorsers are presumed to make *unqualified endorsements*, that is, they impliedly promise to pay on any instrument they endorse if it is not paid when due. This explains why all intermediaries usually must repurchase a bounced check after the drawee bank dishonors it for insufficient funds. However, any endorser may make a *qualified endorsement* by signing their name and writing "without recourse" on the back. Of course, qualified endorsements reduce the transferability to further intermediaries who may become unwilling to give value for qualified paper.

Forged endorsements on bearer paper are irrelevant because bearer paper does not have to be negotiated. However, a forgery needed to negotiate order paper is ineffective to pass title. Therefore, it becomes important to understand the *chain of title* on the paper if forgeries are suspected. This often requires determining who is each transferor and each successive transferee, noting the order and dates where possible. While a forged drawer or maker's signature will not obligate the true drawer or maker, it does not effect the holder's status with respect to others in the chain of title. Therefore, the ultimate dishonor still gives holders the right collect from their immediate transferors.

Holders in Due Course Intermediaries in the banking system have incentive to participate in transferring payment rights so long as they need not worry much that the commercial paper will be dishonored. Holders can obtain an even more special status as a *holder in due course* (*HDC*) if they take a transfer of an instrument (1) for *value*, (2) *in good faith*, and (3) *without notice* of any defenses or another's claim to owning the paper. The HDC's special status is much better than that of a contract assignee or even a holder. Assignees take subject to any defense the maker or drawer could assert in the original and underlying contract. The HDC takes free of (that is, unburdened by) such *personal defenses*. It is this fact that encourages intermediaries to participate in handling commercial paper.

For example, assume a retailer purchases goods from a wholesaler and pays with a nonnegotiable promissory note. The wholesaler then assigns (factors) the note to a finance company, which immediately pays the wholesaler a discounted amount in cash. What effect on negotiability is there if the wholesaler fails to deliver the goods as promised or if the goods are not as warranted? The finance company is an assignee of a simple contract right to receive the buyer's payment. The finance company could not force the buyer to pay because the seller breached the contract. Commercial practice has developed the HDC as a special status to encourage intermediaries like banks and finance companies to willingly handle notes and drafts. The HDC takes free of personal defenses to the underlying contract. That is, the HDC will not be denied payment even if the maker or drawer has the personal defense of breach of contract against the seller who was the original payee. Additional personal defenses are discussed below.

The HDC must *give value* for the instrument or there are no out-of-pocket losses for the law to protect. Generally, value is given if the HDC pays money for the transfer of the paper. There is also value given when the HDC acquires the paper as collateral, takes the paper as payment for another separate previous debt (antecedent claim), gives another negotiable instrument in exchange (pays for a note with a check), or makes an irrevocable obligation to a third party (issues a letter of credit). Banks usually give value when they give cash for a check or when a customer's account is given unrestricted credit for the amount of a deposited check. HDC status is only given to a holder who takes the paper *in good faith*, that is, honesty in fact, a subjective standard of whether the person actually knew of any wrongdoing. The UCC also imposes an objective standard of sincerity by prohibiting HDC status to a holder with any *notice* of several specified problems: the paper is overdue, went unpaid after demand, or was accelerated; the paper was obviously altered or forged; the paper was dishonored; or anyone has defenses or claims to payment on the underlying transaction. Checks are presumed overdue 90 days after the stated date; intermediaries after that date are not HDCs. The bank may still pay if there are sufficient funds available.

Subsequent transferees from an HDC inherit the HDC's special status under the *shelter rule*. Unless a transferee from a HDC was a party to the fraud, the transferee also shares the HDC's special rights to ignore personal defenses in the underlying transaction. For example, assume the buyer of goods issued a note to a seller who in turn negotiated the note to a HDC. If the HDC made a gift of the note to his or her spouse, the spouse would have HDC protections even though the spouse gave no value to the HDC in return.

The HDC takes free of personal defenses, which means the HDC can demand payment even if the original maker or drawer can assert a defense against the original payee. *Personal defenses* include the usual contract law defenses: breach of contract, fraud in the inducement, misrepresentation, mistake, failure of consideration, failure of a condition precedent, impossibility, and so on. However, a HDC takes subject to real defenses, meaning the HDC may be prevented from receiving payment for any of the following *real defenses:* incapacity (incompetence, infancy), fraud in the execution (tricked into signing the wrong instrument, such as a note rather than an autograph as pretended), instrument discharged in bankruptcy, forgery, material alteration, and illegality.

The Federal Trade Commission (FTC) has abolished the HDC rule when the maker of a note is a consumer purchasing goods or services. This means that consumers who purchase on credit can still assert personal defenses such as breach of the goods sale contract. The FTC rule constrains the transfer of consumer financing notes and effectively pressures the sellers of goods to refrain from breaching the underlying sale contract or risk angering finance companies forcing the seller to hold all consumer financing contracts as their own accounts receivables.

Liabilities of the Parties

Holders, HDCs, and other intermediaries in the commercial banking system willingly participate because their rights and liabilities are predictable on a dishonored negotiable instrument. UCC Article 3 provides for both contract liability and warranty liability. On these bases, most transferees are assured of recourse against either an immediate or remote transferor, such as when a check bounces or a note is not paid. Many parties, such as corporations, are not natural persons, so their negotiable instruments are signed by their authorized agents. Only an authorized agent can obligate an entity to liability on an instrument. The agent is not personally liable on the instrument if the principal is identified and the agent clearly signs in a representative capacity. This is the disclosed principal rule, which will be discussed in Chapter 13.

There are different forms of liability implied for nearly everyone signing a negotiable instrument. Nearly absolute and unconditional *primary liability* exists for makers, drawers, and for drawees after an instrument is accepted. Endorsers generally have only *secondary liability*, typically conditional on certain events or rights. A maker is primarily liable to pay a note according to its terms. The drawer on a check or draft has secondary liability, but this does not arise unless the drawee dishonors the draft. A drawee is not primarily liable until *acceptance* of the draft by the drawee, which usually occurs after the bank verifies the drawer's signature and concludes that a sufficient balance is available. However, if a check presented is not dishonored by midnight on the next business day, it is then accepted. Acceptance makes the drawee into an *acceptor*.

An endorser becomes secondarily liable after payment is refused. This happens if after the holder made *presentment* of the instrument demanding payment from the drawee or maker, there was *dishonor* by inaction or refusing payment and a *notice of dishonor* was given to the endorser, either orally, in writing, or electronically. A *protest* is a notarized certificate of dishonor sometimes used in international banking. An endorser can avoid liability by endorsing "without recourse." Presentment of checks must usually be made within 30 days from the date of endorsement. Endorsers are also liable to all subsequent transferees under five implied warranties: (1) the transferor had *good title* to the instrument, (2) *all signatures are authentic*, (3) the instrument has *no material alterations*, (4) there are *no claims or defenses* against the transferor, and (5) the endorsor has *no knowledge of insolvency* by the maker, drawer, or acceptor. If one of the warranties is breached, an endorser may be liable to any subsequent transferee who gave value for the instrument. Warranty liability is an inducement additional to the protections provided by primary and secondary liability to encourage a holder's participation in handling paper. Warranty liability may be disclaimed.

Bank Relations with Customers UCC Article 4 governs bank relationships with its customers. The drawee bank is a debtor holding its customer funds, and the customers are creditors, depositors, and drawers. A bank's basic obligation runs only to its customers, not to third parties who present checks for payment. The bank must *honor* drafts or other *items* by making payment upon presentment. Wrongful dishonor makes the bank liable to the bank's customer for compensatory damages that may arise if, for example, the drawer is arrested for bouncing checks. However, the bank need not pay an item for which there are insufficient funds available on deposit.

Forgeries The bank may charge the customer's account with properly paid items. However, the bank may not charge a customer's account, or if the bank mistakenly pays the account must be recredited, for items with the following problems: (1) forged signatures of the drawer or an endorser, (2) altered items, (3) payments made before the date stated on the draft, or (4) payments made in violation of a valid stop order. Bank customers must use reasonable care by promptly examining each periodic bank statement for forgeries or bookkeeping errors. A customer who delays may lose the right to contest forgeries or material alterations. Banks can recover from anyone forging a necessary endorsement. The bank, not the customer is liable for payment on an item with a forged drawer's signature. However, if the bank dishonors a check with a forged signature of a drawer or endorser or if the item has a material alteration (i.e., zeros added to raise dollar value), the first transferee who took the check from the forger bears the loss.

Electronic Funds Transfer Considerable transfers of funds are occurring outside the bank handling system for physical documents, as discussed above. The Electronic Funds Transfer Act of 1978 (EFTA) governs consumer transfers with financial institutions. Newly revised UCC Article 4A governs the wholesale transfer of funds between businesses and financial institutions. There are electronic systems operated by the Federal Reserve banks and private clearing houses processing direct deposits, ATM transactions, ATM point-of-sale transfers, telephone transfers, and interbank transfers. These laws provide for certain consumer protections and disclosures, require documentation, require records retention and availability, require error resolution, and allocate liability for risk of loss or inaccurate transmissions. EFT consumer matters are also discussed in Chapter 12.

Creditor's Rights

As it is clear now, a critical underpinning of the commercial law system is the protection given parties when contracts are breached. Much of commerce depends on seller-financed transactions or on financing provided by third-party financial institutions such as banks. Long experience has shown the need for legal and contractual safeguards for lenders when debtors' insolvency leads to default on their loans. These insolvency protections include the orderly and fair administration of the insolvent debtor's remaining holdings to avoid the debtor's disappearance with assets or the inevitable favoritism some creditors receive over others. This section examines the de-financing end of commercial practice as provided by contract, state creditor's rights laws, and the federal bankruptcy law.

Secured Financing

The creditor's willingness to extend credit often depends on how adequately the debtor assures repayment. The debtor's promissory note provides a legal right to sue for the unpaid debt, but this becomes inadequate if the debtor is insolvent. There are other repayment assurances: investigation of the debtor's creditworthiness beforehand, credit insurance, surety and guarantee contracts made by others, and the creditor's rights in collateral. Many loans are made on the condition that the debtor grants legal rights in some property, permitting the creditor to foreclose on the collateral to satisfy defaulted debts. The land mortgages discussed in Chapter 7, new car liens, and a corporate bondholder's security interest in machinery are common examples of *security interests*.

UCC Article 9 provides the legal machinery for securing loans with rights in collateral other than real estate. The debtor creates a **secured transaction** in personal property, goods, or intangibles. The *secured party*, usually the lender, is given special rights to keep or sell the collateral if the debtor defaults by missing payments. It is common for the loan proceeds to be used to purchase the collateral, creating a *purchase money security interest (PMSI)*. Some UCC Article 9 rules depend on the type of property the collateral represents: inventory, consumer goods, farm products, or equipment. Enforceable secured transactions are generally made with two basic steps: (1) attachment creating the security interest and (2) perfection determining the secured party's place in the order of priorities.

secured transaction Contract granting lien on collateral as security for a loan.

Attachment The creditor is responsible for making the security interest effective by assuring attachment with a *security agreement,* which is a writing, signed by the debtor, describing the collateral. This makes the security interest effective between the debtor and the creditor. The security interest is created by **attachment** when three things occur. First, the borrower must sign a security agreement, or the creditor must take possession of the collateral. Second, the secured party must give value, a form of

attachment Creation of a security interest through written agreement or the secured party's possession of the collateral.

consideration, to become entitled to a security interest. Usually a lender advances the loan principal to purchase some property, perhaps the collateral. Third, the borrower must have some rights in the collateral, although full ownership is not necessary. After a security interest attaches, a careful secured party must assure that no other secured party acquires superior rights in the collateral. This is the perfection process.

perfection Public notification of a security interest establishing priority for the secured party.

Perfection Debtors are usually free to grant numerous security interests in the same collateral to several secured parties. This may cause disputes among the various secured parties, particularly if the collateral becomes worth less than the total of all outstanding debts. Therefore, secured parties should take the additional step of **perfection** to put the world on notice of their preferred position. Perfection usually occurs when the secured party files a *financing statement* describing the collateral and the security interest, at an appropriate local government office required by state law. This is a non-possessory security interest. Alternatively, a possessory security interest arises when the secured party perfects by taking possession of the collateral. This seems certain to alert third parties of a potential security interest. Most vehicles have title certificates so that notice of the security interest is written directly on the title certificate, a document necessary to transfer ownership. Perfection of a PMSI is automatic with consumer goods; PMSI perfection is given a 10-day grace period for equipment; and PMSI perfection is given a preference in inventory cases if the secured party gives notice to other secured parties.

Priorities If the debtor becomes insolvent and defaults on making secured loan payments then disputes can arise among competing secured parties. If the sale of the collateral brings less than the claims of all the secured parties, questions will arise about *priority.* Generally, the secured party that perfected first will be first to have the debt completely satisfied out of the foreclosure sale proceeds. Among unperfected parties, the first party to attach a security interest will win. Article 9 provides for many complex additional priority rules that depend on a number of factors about the types of secured parties, the types of collateral, whether the loan created a PMSI, whether the debtor is in bankruptcy, and whether the collateral was purchased by a good-faith purchaser for value.

Default After the priority problems are resolved, the secured party may often choose between selling the collateral in a public or private sale or simply keeping the collateral in complete satisfaction of the debt. If the sale brings more than the secured party's debt, the surplus first pays the expenses of the repossession and sale, then other debts secured by the collateral, and finally the remainder is returned to the debtor. The debtor is still responsible for the deficiency if the sale proceeds are insufficient to satisfy these claims. Many secured transaction foreclosures are settled in the context of the debtor's bankruptcy.

Bankruptcy

The Constitution empowers Congress to pass uniform bankruptcy laws. The Bankruptcy Act of 1898, which governs bankruptcy in the United States, has been revised several times. Substantial amendments were made in the Bankruptcy Reform Acts of 1978, 1984, 1986, and 1994. After a bankruptcy filing, the debtor may lose control and ownership of many assets so they can be liquidated (sold), the proceeds eventually being distributed to creditors. Usually, most of the unpaid portion of the bankrupt's debts are *discharged*, or eliminated altogether, resulting in a "clean slate." Thus, bankruptcy law provides the overextended debtor with a "fresh start" and assures fair and equal treatment of all creditors within each of several creditor classes irrespective of their home state. There are several forms of bankruptcy that may be used by individuals, businesses, and certain government units.

Straight Bankruptcy The best-known form of bankruptcy is found in Chapter 7 of the bankruptcy law; it is known as *straight bankruptcy*. It provides for a complete liquidation of the debtor's assets and partial satisfaction of most debts. The bankruptcy courts administer the process of (1) collection and sale of the debtor's assets, (2) verification of creditor claims, (3) distribution of the liquidation proceeds, and (4) granting the debtor a discharge of most debts.

Insolvent individuals, partnerships, and corporations may be liquidated in straight bankruptcy. However, several highly regulated industries such as banks, savings and loan associations, railroads, most governmental units, and insurance companies in financial distress do not receive this traditional liquidation treatment in bankruptcy. Instead, they may be merged with financially healthy entities or assisted through their financial crisis by regulators. Insolvency is determined on either the cash flow basis or the balance sheet basis. A debtor unable to pay debts as they become due is insolvent on the cash flow basis. A debtor with liabilities in excess of assets is insolvent on the balance sheet basis.

The Bankruptcy Stay From the time the bankruptcy petition is filed until the final disposition of the case by the bankruptcy court, an automtic stay or suspension order is in effect. The *bankruptcy stay* prevents creditors from collecting debts or foreclosing on collateral. During the bankruptcy proceedings, the bankrupt, its creditors, the bankruptcy court, and the bankruptcy trustee each play particular roles.

Voluntary and Involuntary Petitions A debtor may file a *voluntary petition* with the bankruptcy court, or creditors may "throw" a debtor into bankruptcy by filing an *involuntary petition.* A minimum number of creditors is required to file an involuntary petition. If the debtor has more than 12 creditors, at least 3 must join in the involuntary petition. If there are 12 or fewer creditors, only 1 creditor needs to file the involuntary petition. The creditors that file an involuntary petition must also have *unsecured claims* (debts without collateral) amounting to at least $10,000. These requirements are intended to prevent creditor misuse of bankruptcy to retaliate or intimidate.

Duties of the Debtor In order to qualify for a discharge from debts, the debtor must perform several duties and cooperate in good faith during bankruptcy proceedings. Within a reasonable time after the petition is filed, the debtor must file documents with the bankruptcy court, including (1) a list of creditors, (2) a schedule or list of assets and liabilities, and (3) other financial statements. The debtor must give up all nonexempt property to the bankruptcy trustee, who becomes the legal owner until liquidation. All tangible and intangible property, such as goods, real estate, intellectual property rights, and accounts receivable, are surrendered. The debtor must appear at creditor meetings and at the final hearing.

Bankruptcy Trustee Soon after the petition is filed, the bankruptcy court appoints an interim trustee to call the first meeting of the creditors, at which a permanent trustee is elected by majority vote. The debtor is examined (questioned) at this first meeting to determine such things as the whereabouts of the debtor's property. The permanent trustee carefully collects and disposes of the property to accumulate a fund to pay off creditor claims. The trustee determines whether each creditor's claim is genuine and may challenge any fraudulent claims against the debtor. The trustee may also sue outsiders for property and debts owed to the debtor.

The trustee has the power to set aside (invalidate) both preferential and fraudulent transfers. *Preferential transfers* are payments or property transfers the debtor made to outsiders in the 90 days prior to the filing of the petition if the transfer gives that particular creditor a greater percentage of the assets than would have been distributed in normal bankruptcy proceedings. For example, if the debtor paid off an old debt in the month before filing bankruptcy, the trustee may recover the payment, thus requiring equal treatment among creditors. *Fraudulent transfers* are sales or gifts for unfair value that the debtor made to closely related third parties, such as relatives, partners, or corporate officers, at any time within the year before the petition is filed.

The trustee must keep adequate accounting records and must file detailed statements of the disposition of assets with the bankruptcy court. Professionals, such as accountants, appraisers, attorneys, and auctioneers, are hired as necessary to assist the trustee. The proceeds from liquidation of the bankrupt's property, called the bankrupt's estate, are used to pay these and other costs of bankruptcy.

Exemptions Individual bankrupts may keep certain property necessary to continue life after liquidation of the bankrupt's estate.

Property Exempt from Bankruptcy Liquidation (Federal)

1. Not more than $7,500 equity in the homestead.
2. Not more than $1,200 equity in one automobile.
3. Not more than $200 per item in all household items.
4. Not more than $500 in jewelry.
5. Not more than $400 worth of other property not listed above, including any unused portion of the $7,500 homestead equity.
6. Not more than $750 in tools of the debtor's trade.
7. Life insurance interests (i.e., whole life cash value and dividends).
8. Prescribed health aids.
9. Government benefits (e.g., social security, veteran's benefits, alimony).

When a husband and wife go bankrupt as joint petitioners, they may add their individual exemptions together. Unless a state prohibits it, the bankrupt may choose either the federal exemptions listed above or any other exemptions applicable under the state's creditor rights law, whichever is preferable for the bankrupt. State exemptions and amounts vary greatly. Some states provide more generous exemptions.

Distribution There are three basic types of creditors in bankruptcy proceedings. *Secured creditors* have security interests, such as mortgages or liens on specific property. Security interests give these creditors a preference on the sale proceeds after the secured items are sold in liquidation, but only up to their contractual security and up to the liquidation value of the collateral. To the extent that the collateral is insufficient to satisfy secured creditor claims, a secured creditor becomes equivalent to an unsecured creditor. Secured creditors may demand assurances from the trustee that their security will not be diminished during bankruptcy or reorganization. The excess of an asset's liquidation value over the secured party's claim goes to satisfy unsecured creditor's claims.

Unsecured or *general creditors* have no security interests to protect their debts. They must take their shares of the distribution proceeds equally as a group on a pro rata basis. For example, trade creditors that supply inventory or equipment to the debtor without retaining a lien are unsecured. Credit card issuers are generally unsecured.

Priority creditors gain priority over unsecured creditors, but not over secured creditors, as to their specially defined claims. Each of the classes of priority creditors may have its claims totally paid before the next class receives any payment. If there are insufficient funds to pay all the claims of a particular class of priority creditors, they share pro rata, and all lower-priority creditors receive nothing.

Priority Creditor Classes

1. Administration expenses of bankruptcy; accountant and attorney's fees, court costs, trustee's fees, costs of preserving bankrupt's property.
2. Debts incurred after the filing of an involuntary petition and before appointment of a trustee.
3. Wages up to $4,000 per employee of the bankrupt in the 90 days preceding the petition or cessation of business, whichever is first.
4. Unpaid employer contributions to employee benefit plans within the 180 days preceding the petition or business cessation, to the extent that the $4,000 in wages per employee is unused.
5. Consumer claims up to $1,800 in deposits or prepayments for undelivered goods or unperformed services.
6. Taxes of local, state, and federal governments with various limitations.
7. Alimony and child support

Discharge of Debts After liquidation, a discharge in bankruptcy is usually ordered, giving the bankrupt a clean slate for preexisting debts. However, a discharge can be denied if the bankrupt has concealed assets, made fraudulent transfers, destroyed books or records, disobeyed a bankruptcy court order, failed to explain the loss of assets, declared bankruptcy within the six prior years, or made fraudulent statements in the bankruptcy proceeding. If no discharge is granted, the bankrupt will lose its assets in the liquidation but will still owe the unpaid portion of all debts. Some debts, such as alimony, child support, federal taxes, and federally insured student loans, are never discharged.

Alternatives to Liquidation It is not necessary for all debtor-bankrupts to submit to a complete liquidation. If the debtor is in a moderate state of financial health and suitable arrangements can be worked out with creditors, there are alternative procedures to continue without liquidation.

Wage Earners Under Chapter 13, individuals with regular income from salary, wages, or commissions as employees may have their debts readjusted but not discharged. The Chapter 13 adjustment procedure is available if the income earner has aggregate unsecured debts of less than $250,000 and aggregate secured debts of less than $750,000. The debtor remains in possession of his or her assets during the proceedings and after the approval of an adjustment plan. The *plan* provides a cash flow and payment schedule to repay all debts. If the readjustment is ultimately approved, creditors may not involuntarily force the debtor into liquidation during or after the initiation of the Chapter 13 process. Debtors unable to adhere to the plan may later switch to straight bankruptcy.

In most Chapter 13 proceedings, the individual debtor, sometimes with counseling, devises and files the debt repayment plan with the bankruptcy court. Under the plan, the debtor has flexibility to combine or extend existing debts so as to facilitate repayment. The terms of the debts are usually readjusted by the bankruptcy court to enable the debtor to budget payments without going into liquidation. *Composition* arrangements allow for the payment of a lesser principal and/or interest rate. *Extension* terms permit the debtor to make smaller payments by extending the maturity date and/or the number of debt payments. Most such plans must be completed within three years unless the bankruptcy court approves a longer period. Any new debts taken on after the plan has been implemented and before all debts are repaid must be approved by the bankruptcy court.

The plan must be approved by the bankruptcy court but not necessarily by the creditors. The approval of unsecured creditors is unnecessary as long as the plan gives them as much as they would receive under a liquidation. Secured creditors need not approve the plan if the debtor surrenders the secured property to them or they retain a lien of their debt principal. Priority claimants must receive full payment or agree to accept a lesser sum.

The debtor's employer or the debtor pays a certain sum periodically (usually monthly) to the bankruptcy trustee. The trustee apportions that sum among the creditors pro rata in accordance with the plan. If the debtor complies with the plan, there is a discharge even if some creditors have received less than the original amount of their debts plus interest and penalties.

reorganization Continuation of business in bankruptcy without liquidation.

Corporate Reorganizations Corporations may take advantage of Chapter 11, a **reorganization** process similar to the Chapter 13 arrangement. This process permits businesses with going-concern value to continue operation during financial difficulties. The purpose is to balance the negative impact of business failures among creditors, customers, suppliers, employees, the community, and the economy. In a Chapter 11 proceeding, a debtor corporation is reorganized pursuant to a voluntary or involuntary petition. Individuals who do not qualify for Chapter 13 may use Chapter 11.

The reorganization process is usually more complex and time-consuming than a Chapter 13 proceeding. Each *class* or group of similar creditors and shareholders forms a separate committee to propose, modify, and approve a master *reorganization plan*. After a thorough investigation into the debtor corporation's business prospects, financial condition, and activities, these committees meet and attempt to negotiate an acceptable plan. The plan may include elements of composition, extension, and/or reduction or *cram down,* which means that the debtor corporation's shareholders, bondholders, and creditors will receive less than the stated value of their claims. For example, some creditors may be converted into shareholders, preferred shareholders may be converted into common shareholders, and common shareholders may lose shares of stock. All claimants of a Chapter 11 debtor generally receive smaller amounts than their original claims.

If the debtor corporation's management is unable to continue the business, the committees may require that a special trustee be appointed. This trustee will operate the business without interference from the debtor's former management. Alternatively, if the debtor's management is considered capable of successfully continuing the business, no trustee is appointed, and the debtor's management is given the first opportunity to propose the reorganization plan.

The reorganization plan must be presented within the first 120 days after the bankruptcy court orders relief. In more complex reorganizations, the creditor committees consider the merits of various proposed plans. Approval occurs when a majority of the creditors in a committee, holding at least two-thirds of the aggregate debt in that class, vote for it. Stockholder committees must also approve plans with a two-thirds vote of the members of each class (common or preferred stock). Some Chapter 11 proceedings are referred to as "pre-packs" in which the various claimants negotiate the plan before filing the petition. This allows for the plan to be worked out amicably and reduces the bankruptcy court's involvement to approval of a plan that is fair to all parties. A pre-pack can be more efficient and avoid goodwill losses because the proceeding occurs quickly and with less publicity.

If the bankruptcy court finds that a particular plan is fair and equitable to all the classes of creditors, the whole plan may be approved even if some committees have not approved it. The final court approval of the plan discharges the corporation from its former debts and equity interests and substitutes the new claims as defined in the plan. A corporate reorganization can be converted into a liquidation if this appears to be in the best interest of all involved.

Chapter 11 has been used recently to reduce the impact of labor union contracts, product liability claims, and court judgments. For example, Texaco declared bankruptcy to avoid paying Pennzoil $11 billion because of Texaco's alleged interference with Pennzoil's takeover of Getty Oil Company. Eventually, the two companies agreed to a $3 billion settlement, which was later approved as a reorganization plan by Texaco's creditors, stockholders, and the bankruptcy court. The asbestos product liability claims against Johns-Manville were delayed and probably reduced by its Chapter 11 filing. In these cases, Chapter 11 bankruptcy is not used by insolvent corporations; it has been used by solvent corporations to avoid possible future insolvency if huge claims are won.

Insolvency Administration

International Perspective and Commentary

The U.S. constitutional founders envisioned a uniform administration of debtor insolvency because of the fragmented handling by the various states under the Articles of Confederation. The uniformity of the single federal bankruptcy scheme promotes predictability that encourages lending activities for multistate businesses. However, there is no such reliable and uniform treatment of insolvencies between nations. Even regional trading blocs like the EU and NAFTA have yet to provide for orderly creditors' rights for bankrupt multinational corporations with assets and operations in several nations. This problem is compounded as the newly independent former socialist nations discover the boom and bust of their embryonic capitalism.

The problem with varying insolvency standards is becoming evident with several of the recent high-visibility multinational bankruptcies. For example, the BCCI scandal and resulting insolvency tested the interoperability of several nations' bankruptcy laws. Most nations protect their immediate local interests by quickly asserting jurisdiction over an insolvent debtor's local assets. This effectively fragments a multinational's bankruptcy administration into numerous concurrent insolvency proceedings. It also generally fails to treat banks and trade creditors equally between nations. The resulting unpredictability and appearance of unfairness may deter unsecured creditors from participating in the foreign investment that many nations need to attract.

The solutions to this problem could follow two courses. First, nations can work to harmonize their insolvency rules. Most nations give similar treatment to secured creditors as well as giving some priority to employees and suppliers to the firm during bankruptcy. However, many nations disagree with the U.S. Chapter 11 reorganization practice of permitting the insolvent's management to continue its operations. Many nations refuse to continue making creditors' interests subservient to the very managers who were responsible for the bankrupt firm's financial crisis. Full harmonization may be impossible as the differences in various nations' culture and history dictate different debtor treatment. Second, cooperation among different nations' bankruptcy courts could reduce unfairness. Unfortunately, there has been little progress among affiliated trading groups or among any nations in adopting the Model International Insolvency Cooperation Act. The Model Act is inspired by U.S. law. Until progress is made on uniformity, varying treatment of nondomestic creditors will persist in international bankruptcies.

The Bankruptcy Reform Act of 1994 The most recent 1994 amendments have overruled some troublesome court decisions and streamlined the bankruptcy process. There are numerous technical changes mentioned here. Participation on Chapter 11 committees is expanded. Compensation for the bankruptcy trustee is raised. Chapter 13 is opened to higher-income debtors. Bankruptcy judges are empowered to hold jury trials on civil claims related to the bankruptcy. Bankruptcy law is conformed to state law for PMSI priorities. Protection is provided to lessors leasing real estate from the bankrupt debtor. Partner's liability conforms to new state laws creating limited liability partnerships and limited liability companies. A fast track is created for small business Chapter 11 proceedings. A new federal crime of bankruptcy fraud is created, and bankruptcy fraud becomes a predicate offense under RICO. The dollar limitations are generally raised as mentioned above and will be indexed for inflation to the CPI every three years. The law also clarifies numerous other matters: late claim filings, statutes of limitation, equipment lease obligations, borrowings to pay taxes, the return of goods by the debtor to a seller, money orders, redemption on defaulted home mortgages, tools of the trade, nondischargeability of fines, avoidance of liens on exempt property, protection of child support and alimony, nondischargeability of luxury goods debts, and liability for nonlawyer bankruptcy petition preparers. Finally, a bankruptcy review commission is established to study bankruptcy problems and recommend reforms.

ETHICAL DILEMMA

ETHICAL DILEMMAS IN BANKRUPTCY AND INSOLVENCY

Bankruptcy presents ethical dilemmas to both creditors and debtors. The framers of the Constitution intended the bankruptcy laws to eliminate the English practice of imprisoning defaulting debtors. Although such imprisonment was a strong disincentive to avoid default, it prevented debtors from earning money to repay their debts. Society believes that fairness demands that debtors who have borrowed more than they can repay should be given another chance through bankruptcy. On the other hand, debtors who misuse bankruptcy increase the cost of credit and limit the availability of credit to others. Both creditors and debtors face ethical dilemmas in relation to bankruptcy.

Some people argue that protection under the bankruptcy reorganization provisions is too readily available to solvent corporations. The bankruptcy stay is imposed after a corporation voluntarily files for reorganization under Chapter 11, preventing creditors from collecting their debts. The stay forces negotiation for a reduction of their collective claims, it is a costly process, and it raises fairness issues for creditors with legitimate claims. Creditors of bankrupts most certainly receive less than they originally expected. Should the threat of bankruptcy filings be used as a bargaining point in negotiations with liability claimants, labor unions, or judgment claimants? Is it ethical for profitable business corporations to avoid their debt responsibilities under government protection? Can claimants actually receive more in reorganization than in straight bankruptcy?

In the 1980s, the managers of some publicly traded corporations purchased all the outstanding corporate stock in a transaction called a *leveraged buyout (LBO)* or *management buyout (MBO)*. Most companies had unused borrowing capacity that was used to finance the purchase of shares from public shareholders. Some LBO companies were restructured by selling off profitable divisions to pay down this new debt. As a result of this leveraging, many LBO companies became excessively debt-laden at a time when their best assets were being sold off. When the business cycle turned down and the recession hit in the early 1990s, many LBO corporations were forced into bankruptcy. Some creditors argue that MBO managers sold off the only profitable divisions, leaving the company insolvent. Is such activity unethical and an unlawful fraudulent conveyance under the bankruptcy laws? Some observers argue that managers of solvent MBO companies acted unethically because they kept secret their plans for expansion or new products when shares were purchased from the former shareholders. Is it unethical for corporate managers with fiduciary duties to shareholders to hide promising plans so they can purchase the stock more cheaply? ■

International Sales Transactions

U.S. domestic commercial law evolved from international practice and from the law merchant. It balances the risks of parties' nonperformance within a rather certain legal system of enforceable obligations in the United States. However, international sales transactions are far less certain. The physical distance between parties grows, language and cultural barriers arise, currency fluctuations too quickly eliminate profitability, and the cross-border enforceability of contracts is uncertain in many legal systems that are hostile to foreigners. Commerce could be significantly reduced without reliable legal machinery to raise expectations. Therefore, much of international law is designed to improve the reliability of commercial performances. The following section extends the introduction of international law of commercial transactions from Chapter 2. This chapter applies the coverage of the CISG and the negotiability of documents to international sales.

International Documentary Sales

Absent long-standing relations of trust between international buyers and sellers, both buyer and seller risk nonperformance by the other party. The buyer is uncertain whether the goods will arrive as described and when promised. The seller is uncertain whether payment will be made in a timely manner. Both parties risk that the goods may be lost in transit. International commercial practice uses several documents to reduce these risks. A document of title is used to condition delivery and title transfer on the buyer's payment. The buyer can condition payment on documentary proof of inspection, physical delivery, and title transfer. These documents are commonly processed as concurrent performances when the documents are verified and exchanged simultaneously. The parties rely on each carrier, warehouse, dock operator, and intermediary along the route to check the authenticity of documents.

The bill of lading is often transferred between the seller's bank and the buyer's bank. Payment is conditioned on title transfer, while simultaneously delivery and title transfer is conditioned on payment by draft or letter of credit. There are four major methods by which the international buyer makes payment. First, many sellers trust buyers sufficiently who have reliably paid their past bills. Sellers may ship based on the buyer's *open account* and expect timely payment in the near future. Second, some sellers insist on *prepayment* if the buyer is unfamiliar or has uncertain credit risk. However, these buyers risk the seller's default in such situations. Third, payment can be made by *draft* (e.g., bill of exchange, check, sight draft), payable out of the buyer's bank account or credit line. If authorized in the contract of sale the seller rather than the buyer may actually prepare the draft and send it to the buyer's bank for payment along with the bill of lading. Such a *sight draft* is due immediately upon arrival at the buyer's bank. A *time draft* is not payable until some future date, so the seller essentially provides credit. The fourth method uses letters of credit.

letter of credit (L/C) Document promising a bank will make a payment to a third party for the bank's customer.

Letters of Credit The buyer's method of payment in much of international commerce is effected through **letters of credit (L/C).** The L/C is a bank's documentary assurance to the seller that the buyer will pay. The L/C is based on the buyer's bank's creditworthiness and on its international reputation. L/Cs are often made negotiable to facilitate processing through the international banking system. The L/C often accompanies the transaction documents although some L/Cs are nonnegotiable. L/Cs are also used for nonpayment purposes such as performance bonds, guarantees, or other collateral.

L/Cs in the United States are governed by UCC Article 5. However, most international L/C transactions specifically incorporate the *Uniform Customs and Practices for Documentary Credits (UCP)* issued by the International Chamber of Commerce. A new revision of the UCP became effective on January 1, 1994, as *UCP 500.* The UCP governs when invoked by the L/C. When there is any conflict between the UCP and the UCC, the UCC governs only where there is no UCP provision. A sample L/C form appears in Figure 10–10.

The typical international sales transaction using the L/C as payment involves four parties: (1) the buyer is the *account party* who applies to (2) its bank, the *issuing bank,* to establish a line of credit and issue the L/C in favor of (3) the seller, the *L/C beneficiary,* and documents are forwarded and payments transmitted through (4) the seller's bank, known as either a *confirming* or *advising bank.* The whole process involves two other primary documents: the underlying contract for sale of goods and the bill of lading. Many international sales transactions also include one or more of the following supplementary documents and relationships: contract(s) of carriage with one or more common carriers, storage contracts with dock and warehouse facilities, customs clearances, inspection documents, the buyer's application for credit, insurance polic(ies), export licenses, certificates of origin, packing slips, and the relationship of trust built up between the two banks. The 1994 UCP revision creates greater flexibility for L/C parties to use EDI and other electronic documents in international

FIGURE 10-10

Letter of Credit

ORIGINAL
Date: April 6, 1992

Call 828-8327 concerning inquiries on Documents submitted under this letter of Credit

DOCUMENTARY CREDIT — IRREVOCABLE	CREDIT NUMBER Of Issuing Bank 0/00/000 Our No. 0000000
FOR ACCOUNT OF Taiwan Steel Products Co., Ltd. Taipei Taiwan	CORRESPONDENT First Bank Taipei Taiwan
BENEFICIARY John Doe Exporters, Inc. Chicago, Illinois U.S.A.	AMOUNT Six Thousand and 00/100 U.S. Dollars U.S. $6,000.00 EXPIRY June 15, 1992

IN ALL COMMUNICATIONS WITH US, PLEASE MENTION OUR REFERENCE NUMBER

Gentlemen:
We have received from the above named bank a cable dated April 5, 1976 requesting us to inform you that they have opened in your favor their irrevocable Credit particulars of which are as follows:
Available by your drafts at sight ON US.
Accompanied by the following documents (full sets required unless otherwise specified):

Signed commercial invoice in triplicate, describing the merchandise as mentioned below, stating that goods shipped conform with purchase order No. 0/00/0 dated March 5, 1992.

Packing list in triplicate.

Insurance policy or certificate in duplicate covering all risks including war risks.

Full set of clean on board ocean bills of lading issued to shipper's order and blank endorsed, marked "Freight Prepaid" and notify International Forwarders, Keelung.

Evidencing shipment from U.S. Port to Keelung, Taiwan not later than May 25, 1992 of the following merchandise: 200 sets of cookware at the price of $30.00 per one set CIF Keelung, Taiwan.

Partial shipments permitted.

Transshipments prohibited.

Drawings under this letter of credit must be presented for negotiation not later than ten days after the date of issuance of the bills of lading.

☐ This credit is not confirmed by us and therefore carries no engagement on our part, but is simply for your guidance in preparing and presenting drafts and documents.
☒ This credit is confirmed by us and we undertake that all drafts drawn and presented in accordance with the terms of the credit will be honored by us.
The above mentioned correspondent engages with you that all drafts under and in compliance with the terms of this Credit will be duly honored on delivery of documents as specified.
If the Credit has been opened by cable, this advice is subject to correction upon receipt of the mail confirmation. Drafts must be marked "Drawn under First Bank, Taipei, Taiwan, Letter of Credit No. 0/00/0" and presented at our office on or before the above indicated expiry date.
The credit is subject to the Uniform Customs and Practice for Documentary Credits [1974 revision the International Chamber of Commerce Publication No. 290
Should the terms of the above mentioned Credit be unsatisfactory to you, please communicate with your customers and request that they have the issuing bank send us amended instructions. Original Credit must be returned with documents for negotiations.

Yours very truly

J. Smith — FOR CASHIER   *G. Black* — FOR CASHIER

sales transactions. Carefully review the order and flow of documents in the typical L/C process as depicted in Figure 10–11, on the following page.

The seller often prepares the primary documents after negotiating the sales contract with the buyer. All matters called for in the sale contract must be included exactly as

FIGURE 10-11 Document Movements in International Sales Transactions

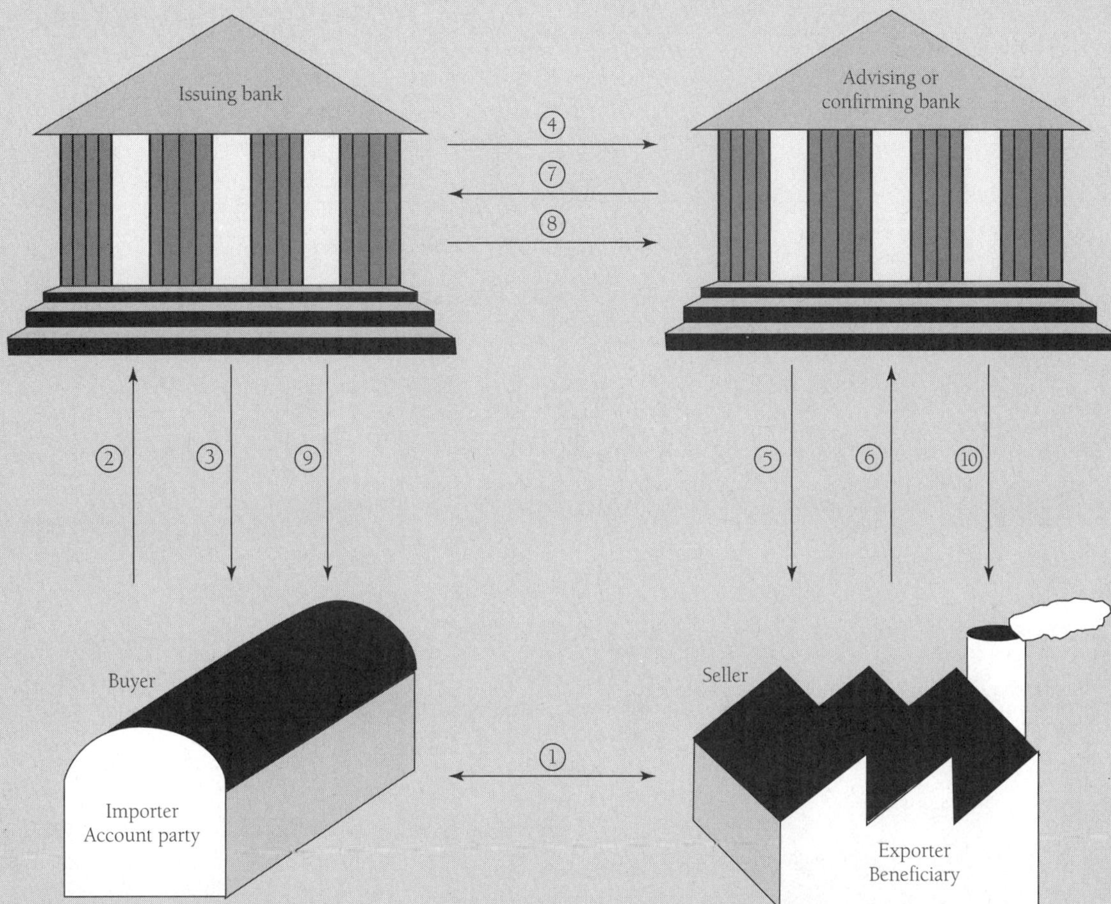

Typical Order of Events:

1. Contract for the international sale of goods.
2. Buyer (account party) applies to the issuing bank for an L/C designating the seller as beneficiary.
3. Issuing bank makes commitment to buyer to issue L/C specifying buyer's terms of full performance.
4. L/C is forwarded from issuing bank to the seller's advising or confirming bank.
5. Advising or confirming bank forwards buyer's L/C to seller for seller's preparation of documents in conformance with L/C.
6. Seller forwards completed documents (e.g., bill of lading, inspection certificates, export license, customs clearance) to advising or confirming bank.
7. Advising or confirming bank carefully checks documents, advises seller to make any necessary revisions, and forwards documents to issuing bank.
8. Issuing bank carefully checks documents for discrepancies and either (a) honors L/C by paying seller or confirming bank; or (b) bank dishonors L/C if there are discrepancies or bank revokes a revocable L/C.
9. Issuing bank forwards bill of lading and any other documents to buyer as necessary to claim goods from carrier.
10. Advising bank pays seller, credits seller's account, or pays transferee if beneficiary negotiated L/C.

they are stated in *all* the other documents. This is a strict form of the mirror image or perfect tender rule from contract law. It prohibits the issuing bank from paying on the L/C if there are any *discrepancies*, that is, major or even minor differences in the terms stated among the documents. For example, discrepancies include any variance between the documents in the description of the goods (e.g., size, quantity, quality, color, specifications), misspellings, missing documents (inspection certificate), late delivery, different named shipping vessel or carrier, expired L/C, or any other error. This *strict compliance rule* is so exacting because time and cost pressures make banks generally unsuitable and unable to investigate or resolve the discrepancy. Banks must examine L/C documents quickly or they are presumed to accept them and thereby become obligated to pay on the L/C. UCC Article 5 gives domestic banks just three banking days to do their document examination. The UCP requires banks to use a "reasonable time," which cannot be more than seven banking days. The general rule is that banks need not "look behind the documents" to determine negotiability and performance of an international sales transaction. Therefore, the parties must draft the documents very carefully and provide for others to verify matters such as inspect the shipment to assure it complies with the sales contract description. The 1994 UCP revision directs banks to ignore any L/C conditions not contained in the documents. Should an issuing bank pay on an L/C if it knows the seller committed fraud? The next case illustrates the *fraud exception* to the strict compliance rule. The UCP has no fraud exception, so this subject is left to national law.

Sztejn v. J. Henry Schroder Banking Co.

31 N.Y.S.2d 631
N.Y. App. Div. 1941

Sztejn negotiated a purchase of hog bristles from Transea Traders, Ltd., an Indian corporation. The price was paid with an irrevocable L/C issued by J. Henry Schroder to Transea. The actual shipment from Transea included 50 cases of cowhair and other refuse under a bill of lading erroneously mirroring the L/C description showing hog bristles. Sztejn sought to enjoin Schroder from honoring a draft sent by Transea's advising bank, the Chartered Bank of India. Sztejn claimed payment should be withheld because of the fraud in the transaction.

Shientag, Justice

It is well established that a letter of credit is independent of the primary contract of sale between the buyer and the seller. The issuing bank agrees to pay upon presentation of documents, not goods. This rule is necessary to preserve the efficiency of the letter of credit as an instrument for the financing of trade. One of the chief purposes of the letter of credit is to furnish the seller with a ready means of obtaining prompt payment for his merchandise. It would be a most unfortunate interference with business transactions if a bank before honoring drafts drawn upon it was obliged or even allowed to go behind the documents, at the request of the buyer and enter into controversies between the buyer and the seller regarding the quality of the merchandise shipped. If the buyer and the seller intended the bank to do this they could have so provided in the letter of credit itself, and in the absence of such a provision, the court will not demand or even permit the bank to delay paying drafts which are proper in form. Of course, the application of this doctrine presupposes that the documents accompanying the draft are genuine and conform in terms to the requirements of the letter of credit.

This is not a controversy between the buyer and seller concerning a mere breach of warranty regarding the quality of the merchandise. It must be assumed that the seller has intentionally failed to ship any goods ordered by the buyer. In such a situation, where the seller's fraud has been called to the bank's attention before the drafts and documents have been presented for payment, the principle of the independence of the bank's obligation under the letter of credit should not be extended to protect the unscrupulous seller. It is true that even though the documents are forged or fraudulent, if the issuing bank has already paid the draft before receiving notice of the seller's fraud, it will be protected if it exercised reasonable diligence before making such payment. However, in the instant action Schroder has received notice of Transea's active fraud before it accepted or paid the draft.

Although our courts have used broad language to the effect that a letter of credit is independent of the primary contract between the buyer and seller, that language was used in cases concerning alleged breaches of warranty; no case has been brought to my attention on this point involving an intentional fraud on the part of the seller which was brought to the bank's notice with the request that it withhold payment of the draft on this account. The distinction between a breach of warranty and active fraud on the part of the seller is supported by authority and reason. As one court has stated: "Obviously, when the issuer of a letter of credit knows that a document, although correct in form, is, in point of fact, false or illegal, he cannot be called upon to recognize such a document as complying with the terms of a letter of credit."

While the primary factor in the issuance of the letter of credit is the credit standing of the buyer, the security afforded by the merchandise is also taken into account. In fact, the letter of credit requires a bill of lading made out to the order of the bank and not the buyer. Although the bank is not interested in the exact detailed performance of the sales contract, it is vitally interested in assuring itself that there are some goods represented by the documents. Accordingly, the defendant's motion to dismiss the supplemental complaint is denied.

Case Questions

1. What is the primary issue in cases like this that seek to invalidate a L/C?
2. Why do courts attempt to enforce L/Cs whenever possible? How could the buyer have better protected itself in this type of situation?
3. What is assumed about the continuation of international commerce if the obligations to honor L/Cs are too easily disregarded?

The bank issuing the L/C has a duty to "pay against the documents" by first checking for discrepancies, endorsing documents as necessary to process the transaction, and either notifying the seller of discrepancies causing dishonor of payment or honoring the payment by paying the seller or crediting the seller's bank. The UCP presumes L/Cs are *irrevocable* although the buyer's bank can make them *revocable,* but this substantially reduces their usefulness. The L/C is often *confirmed,* obligating the seller's bank to credit the seller's account as soon as the issuing bank honors payment. If the L/C is *unconfirmed,* the seller's bank only provides advising functions as a correspondent of the issuing bank by processing paperwork but does not credit the seller's account. The seller's bank must assist in preparing the documents and review them for discrepancies, forward the documents to the issuing bank, and redraft any noncomplying documents returned by the issuing bank if there is still time remaining.

A *standby L/C* is not used for payment, but instead as a performance guarantee or collateral. Payment is due if the account party breaches some duty. For example, Manufacturers Bank was required to pay on a standby L/C that guaranteed the performance of AT&T's contract to install a telephone system in Iran. AT&T stopped performance after AT&T's bills were not paid by the Islamic regime that ousted the Shah. Despite Iran's breach of the installation contract, Manufacturers was still required to pay the standby L/C because AT&T's performance bond was not conditioned on Iran's payments.[1]

---

[1] *American Bell International v. Islamic Republic of Iran,* 474 F. Supp. 420 (S.D.N.Y. 1979).

Alternatives to Traditional Documentary Sales International commercial contracting retains some ancient contracting methods while at the same time it evolves with technology. These alternatives to the traditional documentary sales process described above are widely used today. *Countertrade* is a complex reciprocal barter-like exchange in which international brokers match buyers and sellers who trade goods and services without transferring cash. Many developing countries and former Soviet bloc nations have negative trade balances, their currencies do not convert well into hard currency, they have large debt burdens, or their government restricts currency outflows. These problems restrict the very foreign trade so badly needed to invigorate their economies. There are several general types of countertrade. *Barter* is the direct exchange of different types of goods or services between the two parties. In a *swap,* two sellers of the same goods exchange delivery obligations to reduce transportation costs. *Counterpurchase,* the most common form of countertrade, usually involves a seller from an industrial nation who accepts goods from the buyer, the government, or another firm in a developing nation in exchange for the seller's goods or services. *Buybacks* pay for industrial machinery from the seller with goods eventually produced with the machines sold.

Countertrade raises many legal, ethical, trade policy, and economic policy questions. Legal questions include product safety compliance, complex contracting, and antitrust laws. Ethical issues include foreign bribery and the unfair advantage that rich industrial nations allegedly take of developing nations. Trade policy issues include trade restrictions and dumping laws. Economic problems include circumventing foreign currency translation and the inefficiency that countertrade creates in international markets.

Electronic contracting, document transfer, and endorsement are becoming a much more cost-effective way to process international commercial transactions. These can reduce many uncertainties of performance and even assist developing nations with their hard currency shortages. Eventually, buyers, sellers, their banks, carriers, warehouses, customs officials, and trade brokers will all be linked by computer through telephone lines and satellite connections. This will enable them to enter into contracts, transfer and endorse documents, and make payments electronically. This system of interconnected computers is generally known as **electronic data interchange (EDI).** Already today, many major importers, exporters, and international banks use parts of this technological system. The American Bar Association has issued a model EDI agreement specifying how electronic communications create a contract because electronic contracting poses some novel problems. General terms should be contained in an umbrella contract or *master purchase agreement* providing a documentary source for negotiated terms other than price, quantity, and specifications. Eventually, EDI may replace all documents and payment systems unless computer crime and other security matters impede full implementation.

electronic data interchange (EDI) Computerized commercial contracting through telecommunications.

Summary

Commercial law developed from medieval merchants' practices as they evolved from feudalism. The law merchant was the model for the UCC and for international laws and practices. The UCC governs the sale of goods, payment, and financing by negotiable instruments and the securing of financing with commercial liens on collateral. Federal bankruptcy law, the international CISG, and other customs and practices are also applicable to commercial transactions.

UCC Article 2 differs somewhat from the common law of contracts in the formation, performance, and remedies available. The UCC relaxes the mirror image rule and the requirement for definite terms by permitting open terms and firm offers without consideration, it resolves battles of the forms, and it makes several exceptions to the statute of frauds. The special rules defining when title and risk of loss pass are derived from the use of mercantile terms. Buyers have several remedies: inspect before taking delivery, reject or revoke acceptance of nonconforming goods, cover nondelivery by purchasing substitute goods elsewhere, seek specific performance of unique goods or a replevy identified goods, or sue for consequential and incidental damages. Sellers may cure nonconforming deliveries if time remains, stop or withhold shipment to insolvent buyers, and seek consequential and incidental damages. All parties must act in good faith. Duties can be ignored that become commercially impractical. UCC Article 2A has similar provisions for leases of goods.

UCC Articles 3, 3A, and 4 govern banking and the use of commercial paper and electronic funds transfers to pay for or finance transactions. Negotiable instruments are formal contracts, expected to be assigned to intermediaries. A draft is a three-party instrument in which the drawer orders the drawee to pay the payee. A note is a two-party instrument in which the maker promises to pay the payee. Instruments are negotiable if they are made in writing, are signed by the maker or drawer, and make an unconditional promise or order to pay to order or bearer a fixed amount of money at a definite time and contain no other promise. Banks and payees are encouraged to handle commercial paper if they can become an HDC, giving them special status to avoid personal defenses between the original parties that could hold up payment. Commercial paper is transferred by negotiation and endorsement. The HDC must give value for the instrument, be in good faith, and take without notice of defenses or dishonor. The parties have primary, secondary, or warranty liability that explains how a check bounces because most intermediaries must repurchase a dishonored instrument.

Creditors rights come from UCC Article 9, which creates rights in collateral and by bankruptcy law. A security interest attaches when a security agreement is made. The secured party gets priority over others when the security interest is perfected. There are complex priority rules, specific foreclosure duties, and ways the proceeds must be applied after collateral is sold. Bankruptcy law creates a fair, orderly system to administer insolvent debtor's estates. There are many complex duties, priorities, and exemptions to satisfy before the debtor is granted a discharge, although some debts survive bankruptcy.

International sales are generally more complex and risky than domestic commercial transactions. Several conventions reduce these risks, including the use of bills of lading to transfer title, L/Cs for financing, and banking system intermediaries to assure performance and payment. In the future, EDI may replace much of this document handling.

Critical Thinking Review Questions

1. Explain the major differences between the common law of contracts and the statutory law for sales of goods under the UCC. What is the difference between the subject matter covered by both? For what reasons have the UCC changed the specific rules?
2. Commercial transactions have historically depended more on customs and practices than on enforcement under national laws. For what reasons have the UCC and UCP developed the mechanisms that encourage parties to accept, endorse, and give value for instruments such as checks, notes, drafts, letters of credit, and documents of title?
3. It can be argued the creditor's rights system of collateral, foreclosure, bankruptcy protection, and balanced treatment of creditors is more costly than if debtors and creditors were simply left to their own devices. Criticize this statement from the perspective of the intent behind our creditors' rights laws and practices.
4. Compare and contrast the function of title and risk of loss in the past and how it operates today under UCC Article 2 in sales transactions.

Critical Thinking Exercises

1. The seller and buyer are merchants in the carpet business. The buyer is a carpet retailer in Tennessee who purchases carpets from a wholesaler in Dalton, Georgia. The parties have been involved in a series of transactions over the last six years. Typically, their arrangements involve the following steps: The retailer makes an oral phone offer to buy from the supplier, who then sends back a written acknowledgment, whereupon the retailer sends a written purchase order. In one instance the supplier's acknowledgment form contained the following language: "The acceptance of your order is subject to all of the terms and conditions on the face and reverse side hereof, including *arbitration,* all of which are accepted by the buyer; it supersedes contrary terms on the buyer's order form, if any."

   The retailer's purchase order did not object to any of the terms in the supplier's acknowledgment form. Later, the retailer refused to pay for a shipment of carpet, claiming that the shipment did not meet its specification since some of the carpets in the shipment were not manufactured from a 100 percent Kodel polyester but from a cheaper, inferior fiber. The supplier sued to compel the retailer to arbitrate. Was there an agreement to arbitrate, or was the arbitration provision a "material alteration" of the contract within UCC §2-207? *Dorton v. Collins, Aikman Corp.,* 453 F.2d 1161 (1972).
2. MMI contracted to supply software for Gregory and be compensated at an hourly rate. When the software failed to perform to Gregory's satisfaction, he denied payment and refused to permit MMI to cure the defects. MMI sued for the price, and Gregory counterclaimed breach of warranty of fitness under the UCC. Does the UCC or common law apply to this contract? Explain your reasoning. *Micro-Managers, Inc., v. Gregory*, 434 N.W.2d 91 (Wisc. 1988).
3. Fekkos purchased a tractor from Lykins Oil that was later found to have numerous defects. Lykins agreed to pick up the tractor and Fekkos could leave the tractor in his front yard. When the tractor was stolen, Lykins sued to recover the price. On whom was risk of loss and why? *Lykins Oil Co. v. Fekkos*, 507 N.E.2d 795 (Oh. Ct. Cmn. Pleas 1986).
4. A commercial buyer pays for goods with a signed note promising to pay the agreed sales price in 30 days to the order of the seller. Consider the alternative decisions of the buyer to either (a) make a notation on the bottom of the note showing the invoice number of the goods sale or (b) write the invoice number followed by this statement: "Payment on this note is conditioned on the goods delivered meeting the description in the invoice." What is the issue raised by these notations? What is the impact of each?
5. Assume a supplier sells a shipment of goods to a retailer and that the sale of goods contract calls for the buyer to make three installment payments each month for the next three months. The seller wants to assure repayment by using the secured transaction method available under UCC Article 9. Describe the type of transaction and indicate what two basic steps are important to the supplier's objectives.
6. The buyer of goods from a foreign seller applies to its bank for an L/C to finance the purchase. The buyer's bank issues the L/C, which the L/C "will remain in force for a period of six months." What issue will arise if the bank seeks to revoke the L/C in three months? What interpretation should be given the L/C language and why? See *Conoco, Inc. v. Norwest Bank Mason City*, 767 F.2d 470 (8th Cir. 1985).

PART 4

Consumer Law and Business

11 Product and Service Liability

12 Consumer Protection

CHAPTER

11

Product and Service Liability

Critical Thinking Questions

- Compare and contrast the four primary theories of product liability.
- What key factors distinguish express warranties from implied warranties imposed by the UCC?
- Why are product liability actions based on the seller's alleged negligence usually directed toward the failure to properly design, inspect, or package the goods or the failure to warn users of known dangers?
- Why is the burden of proving that a product's defects render it unreasonably dangerous under a strict liability theory generally easier than proving negligence?
- What is ambiguous about the responsibilities that nearly any seller in the distribution chain has for product safety?
- Why are these affirmative defenses to product liability suits: contributory or comparative negligence, assumption of risk, or misuse?

Introduction . . . PAST, PRESENT, FUTURE

Historically, product liability suits were brought infrequently and were usually unsuccessful. Two basic legal principles limited liability for unsafe products. First, **caveat emptor**, or "let the buyer beware," protected sellers from buyers' suits, requiring buyers to inspect each product for defects prior to purchase. Before the 20th century, products were simple, and buyers had a basic understanding of most materials and mechanisms. Caveat emptor was also the result of the prevailing rugged individualism that demanded self-reliance during the development of the American frontier. It also protected the growth of the new American industrial base in the late 19th century by shielding manufacturers from product liability suits. However, the Industrial Revolution also changed the basic underlying assumptions. First, products became more complex, utilizing electronics, and a flood of new materials were developed with unknown characteristics: plastics, composites, metal alloys, dangerous chemicals, and synthetics. These new materials often have new and unknown mechanisms, with capabilities outside most buyers' general experience. Most people largely understood products made of wood, leather, natural fabrics, and simple metals. Second, after the West was settled, the work skills of most people became increasingly specialized. The capabilities and rugged individualism of the jack-of-all-trades became unsuitable for the increasingly specialized factory work. Third, complex new products were mass-produced in distant factories, breaking the traditionally close contact buyers had with the local craftspeople who made the goods. As a result of these structural changes, buyers had greater difficulties comparing the safety and quality of new products to the experience they had with similar products.

caveat emptor
"Let the buyer beware."

privity of contract Direct relationship between parties, usually by contract, suggesting mutual responsibilities.

The second legal principle limiting liability for defective products was the doctrine of **privity of contract.** Privity presumes legal responsibility only between two parties who deal directly together, such as by contract. When applied to products liability, privity denies the victim the right to sue the seller of an unsafe product unless the victim had a purchase contract directly with that seller. Typically, suits against manufacturers were barred because the victim purchased from a retailer. The assembler/manufacturer, wholesaler, or component part manufacturer lacked privity with the victim and was thus shielded from liability. Privity was also absent if the victim was a bystander, such as a pedestrian in an auto accident or a member of the purchaser's family. The trend today—one of the most significant legal trends of this century—is to relax privity somewhat in product liability cases based on tort theories. However, there is a resurgence of privity in service liability cases. Other vestiges of privity also remain in products liability, particularly under the breach of warranty theory. The relaxation of privity has contributed to a change from caveat emptor to **caveat venditor**, under which the seller must increasingly beware of defective products that harm consumers or bystanders even if there is no direct privity.

caveat venditor "Let the seller beware."

This chapter discusses the theories, remedies, and litigation problems of product liability. The first section examines the historical development of product liability. Next, the various theories of product liability are explored: breach of warranty, negligence, strict tort liability, misrepresentation, and criminal liability. The risk exposure of business is directly related to several procedural concerns: who may sue, who may be liable, the burden of proof required, and affirmative defenses. Tort concepts developed in Chapter 8 and in the following sections are also applicable to service and malpractice liability.

Thought Questions

1. Why has there been a shift from caveat emptor to caveat venditor?
2. Explain the reasoning underlying the privity of contract limitation on product liability suits.

Introduction

Does the fact that an automobile was purchased from a retailer prevent the manufacturer's liability for personal injuries caused by defects in the automobile? The next case was instrumental in dismantling the privity doctrine.

MacPherson v. Buick Motor Co.

217 N.Y. 382, 111 N.E. 1050 (1916)
New York Court of Appeals

MacPherson bought a new Buick from a retail dealer that had originally purchased the car from the manufacturer, Buick Motor Company. The spokes of the car's wooden wheel crumbled, causing the car to collapse and injure MacPherson.

Cardoso, Judge

For a neglect of ordinary care or skill whereby injury happens, the appropriate remedy is an action for negligence. The right to enforce this liability is not to be confined to the immediate buyer. The right extends to the persons or class of persons for whose use the thing is supplied. It is enough that the goods "would in all probability be used at once . . . before a reasonable opportunity for discovering any defect which might exist," and that the thing supplied is of such a nature "that a neglect of ordinary care or skill as to its condition or the manner of supplying it would probably cause danger to the person or property of the person for whose use it was supplied."

We hold that the principle of *Thomas v. Winchester* is not limited to poisons, explosives, and things of like nature, to things which in their normal operation are implements of destruction. If the nature of a thing is such that it is reasonably certain to place life and limb in peril when negligently made, it is then a thing of danger. Its nature gives warning of the consequences to be expected. If to the element of danger there is added knowledge that the thing will be used by persons other than the purchaser, and used without new tests, then, irrespective of contract, the manufacturer of this thing of danger is under a duty to make it carefully.

We have put aside the notion that the duty to safeguard life and limb, when the consequences of negligence may be foreseen, grows out of contract and nothing else. We have put the source of the obligation where it ought to be. We have put its source in the law.

From this survey of the decisions, there thus emerges a definition of the duty of a manufacturer which enables us to measure this defendant's liability. Beyond all question, the nature of an automobile gives warning of probable danger if its construction is defective. This automobile was designed to go 50 miles an hour. Unless its wheels were sound and strong, injury was almost certain. It was as much a thing of danger as a defective engine for a railroad. The defendant knew the danger. It knew also that the car would be used by persons other than the buyer. This was apparent from its size; there were seats for three persons. It was apparent also from the fact that the buyer was a dealer in cars, who bought to resell. The maker of this car supplied it for the use of purchasers from the dealer. The dealer was indeed the one person of whom it might be said with some approach to certainty that by him the car would not be used. Yet the defendant would have us say that he was the one person whom it was under a legal duty to protect. The law does not lead us to so inconsequent a conclusion. Precedents drawn from the days of travel by stagecoach do not set the conditions of travel today. The principle that the danger must be imminent does not change, but the things subject to the principle do change. They are whatever the needs of life in a developing civilization require them to be.

In this view of the defendant's liability there is nothing inconsistent with the theory of liability on which the case was tried. It is true that the court told the jury that "an automobile is not an inherently dangerous vehicle." The meaning, however, is made plain by the context. The meaning is that danger is not to be expected when the vehicle is well constructed.

There is nothing anomalous in a rule which imposes upon A., who has contracted with B., a duty to C. and D. and others according as he knows or does not know that the subject-matter of the contract is intended for their use.

We think the defendant was not absolved from a duty of inspection because it bought the wheels from a reputable manufacturer. It was not merely a dealer to automobiles. It was a manufacturer of automobiles. It was responsible for the finished product. It was not at liberty to put the finished product on the market without subjecting the component parts to ordinary and simple tests.

Case Questions

1. Why does the doctrine of privity no longer apply to product liability suits?
2. What is the duty of care for a manufacturer of goods? To whom is the duty owed?
3. What must a manufacturer do if component parts are purchased from others?

Limitations on Product Liability Suits

The manufacturing industry has been plagued by expansive new product liability theories. One such area of changing law concerns how to deal with *delayed manifestation* of injuries, a very complex issue. In some cases, a product may have *unknown hazards* when made. The victim's injury cannot be detected until several years after exposure to the defective product. Often these injuries are adverse health effects of drugs, medical devices, or environmental exposure to toxic substances. Meanwhile, the statute of limitations may run out, and the victim will be barred from suit. In other cases, the delayed manifestations of injuries make it difficult to later identify the precise manufacturer, among several, of the defective product.

Recent decisions have addressed both of these concerns. In many states, the statute of limitations period begins to run when the injury occurs rather than when the product was purchased. This exposes the seller to potential liability for a longer time after the sale. A few states have reacted to this greater exposure by enacting **statutes of repose**. These limit the time that products must remain defect free.

statute of repose
Time limitation on the period during which products should be defect free.

Some drug cases, such as *Sindell v. Abbott Laboratories*[1] have introduced a new theory of causation when there is difficulty in identifying the manufacturer of the particular product causing the victim's damage. To prevent miscarriage, Sindell's mother took a prescription drug, DES, while pregnant with Sindell. Many years later, Sindell developed cervical cancer due to her mother's use of DES. Sindell could not identify which among the several manufacturers of DES had actually made the dosage in the prescription her mother used. The court developed the concept of **market share liability** to permit victims to bring suit against any or all producers of DES. This concept makes it unnecessary to precisely identify the brand of drug in the actual prescription used. Instead, the extent of a manufacturer's liability may be based on the defendant's actual market share in the drug sales at the time the drug was used. Not all the states have followed this decision, and some recent cases prohibit third-generation plaintiffs (granddaughters) from any recovery.

market share liability
Relieves product liability plaintiff of strict proof of causation against manufacturer(s) of defective product when precise manufacturer cannot be determined.

A limitation on victims' product liability suits has arisen in the asbestos, breast implant, and IUD product liability litigation. Manville, the predominant asbestos producer and a profitable company, filed for bankruptcy reorganization under Chapter 11. Manville continued operations and delayed suits by creditors and liability claimants until it emerged from reorganization. Eventually, the product liability claimants approved a plan to settle their claims without forcing Manville into liquidation. Some observers argue that asbestos claimants generally received less money damages than they could have if not for bankruptcy protection.

Many innovative new products may be withheld from the market in anxiety over the prospects for product liability suits. This possibility is particularly troublesome for national public policy as the need increases for new drugs to treat dangerous and debilitating diseases such as AIDS and cancer. Excessive apprehension over potential product liability may chill America's technological competitiveness in world markets. Legislatures and the courts have been both broadening and restricting product liability duties, making it difficult to accurately estimate product liability insurance premiums. Product liability litigation has increased significantly, which has had a profound impact on manufacturers, wholesalers, and retailers. The cost of product liability planning, insurance, and defense has skyrocketed, creating a cost containment crisis affecting both the manufacturing and insurance industries. Reactions to the product liability crisis by courts, juries, government, insurers, and manufacturers assure that product liability concerns will continue to influence business decision making. This uncertainty may have contributed to the liability insurance crisis and efforts in several states to "roll back" the trend toward higher and unpredictable product liability awards. These and other product liability reforms are discussed at the end of the chapter.

[1] *Sindell v. Abbott Laboratories,* 163 Cal. Rptr. 132, 607 P.2d 924 (1980).

Product Liability Theories

There are several theories of product liability under state law. Managers with an awareness of the range of legal theories available to plaintiffs can better reduce their litigation risk. Contract theories of express and implied warranty usually apply if the goods are purchased. Negligence and strict liability generally expose sellers to even broader potential liability. Each theory, as applied in different states, may have different substantive and procedural requirements.

Warranty Liability

A **warranty** is an affirmation of fact or a promise of performance made in any product sale governed by the Uniform Commercial Code (UCC). In both warranty and strict liability cases, it is unnecessary to determine who is "at fault." Warranties are often stated in contract terms that impose additional duties on the seller. There are three types of product quality warranties: (1) the express warranty, (2) an implied warranty of merchantability, and (3) an implied warranty of fitness for a particular purpose. The UCC also implies a warranty of title, requiring sellers to have rights to pass full ownership to buyers unless the possibility of adverse claims is evident to the buyer.

warranty
Affirmation of fact or a promise of performance made in any product sale under the UCC.

Express Warranties Express warranties are contractual promises relating to the future performance of goods. Goods are defective if they fail to meet the express warranty standards. Warranty liability arises if the seller agrees to provide a remedy to the purchaser. The buyer need not prove any seller misrepresentation or fault. An express warranty arises under UCC 2–313 if the seller's promise forms a *basis of the bargain.* This means that the parties must consider the warranty a part of the description of the goods although no specific reliance needs to be proved for the warranty to be enforceable. The promises that form the terms of the express warranty may come from (1) an affirmation of fact or any promise relating to the goods, (2) a description, (3) a sample, (4) technical specifications, or (5) a model used by the seller to influence the buyer.

Express warranties are formed by the seller's promises or by other conduct. For example, an express warranty is formed if the seller presents technical specifications or a blueprint to the buyer. An express warranty may also be inferred from past deliveries that lead the buyer to presume that future deliveries will involve similar goods. A sample of the goods, such as grain or chemicals drawn from a larger bulk, may represent the expected average quality. A model may be used when the actual goods to be delivered are not available. The creation of an express warranty is illustrated in Figure 11–1.

Generalized statements of value are usually too vague to be warranty promises; such expressions are a seller's *puffing*. For example, when an auto dealer claims that an automobile is "great" or "a bargain," no warranty arises. However, proposed revisions to UCC Article 2 may change the puffing rule. If the revision is adopted by the separate states, the seller will have to prove that the buyer acted unreasonably in believing the puffing created a warranty, for the seller to be relieved of warranty liability. Developments in this area must be closely monitored in the next few years.

For a warranty to be valid, however, warranty statements need not be in any special format, nor labeled as a *warranty* or *guarantee,* nor must the seller intend to create warranty obligations. Express warranties are enforceable to the extent that the seller promises satisfaction. The precise timing of the seller's promise or the seller's display of a sample is not important; even promises made after the sale can create or modify the warranty. What is important is that the statement becomes part of the contract description.

An express warranty may be made in written or oral form as long as the parol evidence rule does not require that it be in writing. As explained in Chapter 9, the parol evidence

FIGURE 11-1 Express Warranty

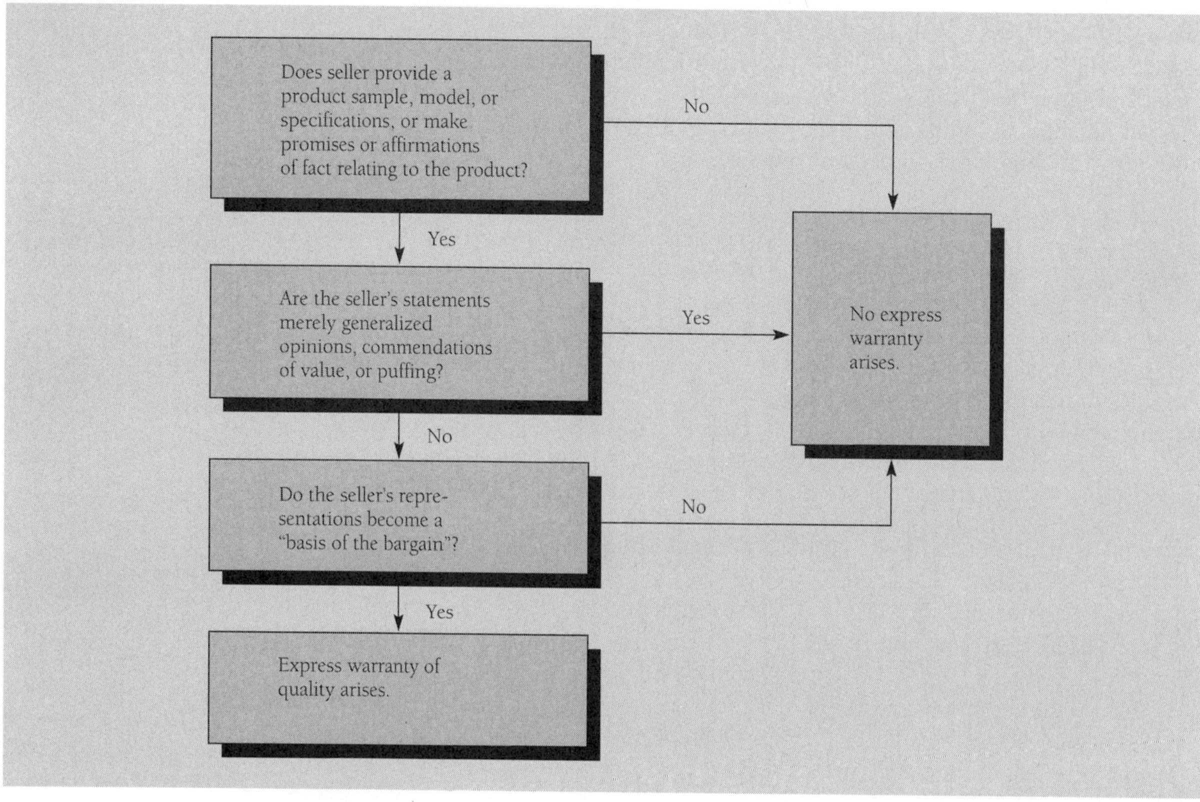

rule applies when a written contract of sale is intended to be the complete contract between buyer and seller. If the written contract is considered an integration and it contains no written warranty, no oral evidence of an express warranty is admissible. However, because promises create a warranty, a car dealer's statements made while showing a car are considered a warranty, even if there is no formal written contract.

merchant
Seller or buyer who deals in goods like those involved in the contract; also someone who professes expertise in the trade.

Implied Warranty of Merchantability A warranty of merchantability is implied under UCC 2–314 whenever goods are sold by a merchant. A **merchant** is a seller or buyer who deals in goods of the kind involved in the contract or who professes to be an expert in the particular trade. Sellers are considered merchants when they employ agents who are merchants. Even secondhand goods must conform to the merchantability standard when sold by a merchant. In isolated sales, those occurring out of the ordinary course of business, no merchantability warranty applies. For example, if a person sells his or her personal car to a neighbor, there is no implied warranty of merchantability. Creation of the merchantability warranty is illustrated in Figure 11–2.

An implied warranty may be inferred from trade customs such as either a *usage of trade,* which is a common practice among most of the firms in a particular business, or a *course of dealing,* which refers to a common practice followed by two contracting partners from their previous dealings. For example, an obligation to provide pedigree papers to substantiate the lineage of a show dog or a bull may arise from a usage of trade. The trade might consider an animal merchantable only where adequate pedigree is demonstrated. Merchantable goods must at least conform to the characteristics of merchantability stated in UCC 2–314(2).

FIGURE 11-2 Implied Warranty of Merchantability

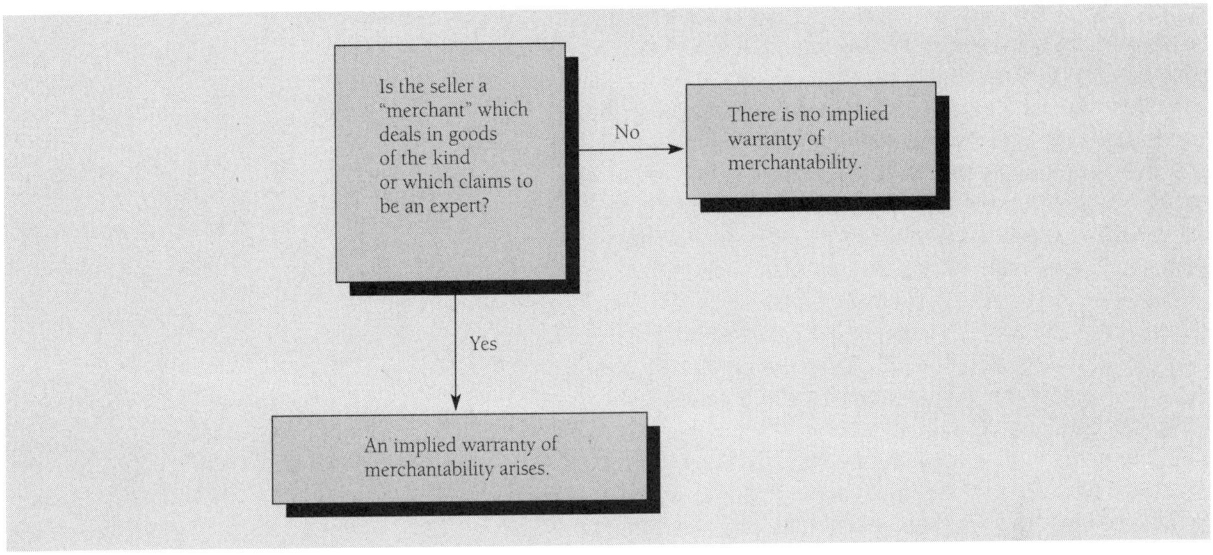

Characteristics of Merchantability [UCC 2-314(2)]

Pass without objection in the trade under the contract description. Are of fair average quality if *fungible* (i.e., all units are equivalent or interchangeable, as with grains or chemicals, and lose their identity when mixed together). Are fit for the ordinary purposes for which they are used. Are of even kind, quality, and quantity within the variations permitted. Are adequately contained, packaged, and labeled as required by the agreement. Conform to the label or container description.

The various definitions for merchantable goods may also provide guidance for the interpretation of an unclear express warranty. Should products be fit for the ordinary uses expected by consumers? The following case illustrates how the implied warranty of merchantability establishes minimum consumer expectations for performance in a coffeemaker that operated similar to an expresso coffeemaker.

McCabe v. L. K. Liggett Drug Co.

330 Mass. 177, 112 N.E.2d 254 (1953)
Massachusetts Supreme Court

The plaintiff purchased a coffeemaker from L. K. Liggett Drug Company. After a few uses, the plaintiff noticed that the water failed to boil up fully from the lower chamber to the upper chamber. The coffeemaker injured the plaintiff when it exploded in her face as she was examining it more closely.

Williams, Justice

Merchantable quality means that goods are reasonably suitable for the ordinary uses for which goods of that description are sold. Whether this coffee maker was of such quality depended on its capability, when properly used, to make coffee. This presented a question of fact for the jury. The evidence consisted of the coffee maker and the testimony of the plaintiff concerning the so-called explosion. The jury could find that she assembled the parts [and used it to make coffee] in accordance with instructions and in the manner that an ordinary person would be expected. The evidence, we think, was sufficient to warrant them in finding why the coffee maker blew up when so used. The appliance had a circular metal filter which fitted over the upper end of the tube in the upper bowl and obviously was intended to hold the coffee grounds in the upper bowl while permitting the water to come up from the lower bowl. This filter was similar in shape to an ordinary metal bottle cap. It had thirty-six small notches in its lower edge which rested on the bottom of the bowl and encircled the opening of the tube. The filter was held in position over the tube by a plunger equipped with springs which reached down into the tube. The plaintiff offered in evidence the opinion of an expert that the area of the notches of the filter was inadequate to provide for the release of the pressure which developed from the boiling water; that this area could be further decreased by the "congealing" of the coffee grounds; and that the pressure in the bottom section, having inadequate release, would build up to a point where it would have an explosive effect.

The fact that the apparatus violently burst apart in the manner described showed that the accumulating pressure was not being released and in the absence of explanation was itself evidence of a defective condition.

If the coffee maker was so imperfect in design that it could not be used without the likelihood of an explosion it could be found that the appliance was not reasonably fit for making coffee and therefore not merchantable.

The plaintiff was not deprived of her right to rely upon the implied warranty either by a failure to inspect or by an inspection before use, as it could have been found that the defect in design would not be obvious to an ordinary person on inspection.

Case Questions

1. When does an implied warranty of merchantability arise?
2. What factors define the minimum performance that consumers may expect from merchantable goods?

Implied Warranty of Fitness for a Particular Purpose The *implied warranty of fitness for a particular purpose* may be made by any seller, whether or not the seller is a merchant. This "fitness" warranty arises under UCC 2–315 whenever the buyer relies on the seller's expertise to select goods suitable for the buyer's intended use. For example, if a paint dealer is asked to select nontoxic paint for use in a child's room, this implies a warranty that the paint contains no lead. The fitness warranty may arise even if the buyer does not directly communicate the particular purpose to the seller. When the seller has reason to know the buyer's purpose and helps select the goods, the fitness warranty arises. However, the buyer must actually rely on the seller's expertise and selection decision before there is a fitness warranty (see Figure 11–3).

The particular purpose at issue in a fitness warranty is distinguished from an ordinary purpose under the merchantability warranty. Particular purposes are specific and planned uses peculiar to the buyer's household or business. Ordinary purposes are the uses customarily made by most buyers. For example, shoes are merchantable when made for walking on normal ground. However, a special pair of shoes might be necessary for mountain climbing so the seller's selection guidance would trigger a fitness warranty because of this special and particular purpose. However, no fitness warranty arises if the buyer ignores the seller's suggestions and insists on a particular brand or model of goods, because in that case there is no buyer reliance on the seller's expertise.

FIGURE 11-3 Implied Warranty of Fitness for a Particular Purpose

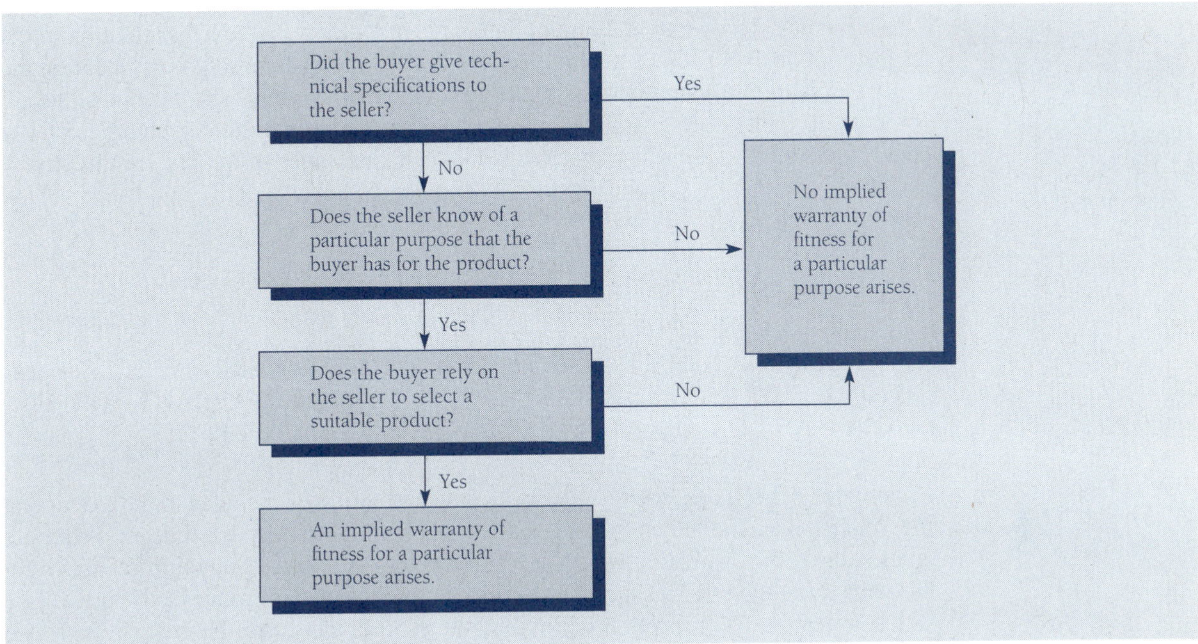

What circumstances might surround a seller's understanding of the buyer's business, permitting an inference that the buyer is relying on the seller's selection expertise? In *Northern Plumbing Supply, Inc. v. Gates*,[2] Gates sought to purchase pipe from Northern Plumbing Supply for use in making a farm implement. Northern's president, Luxem, knew of Gates' purpose because he had visited Gates' farm. Gates showed Luxem a section of pipe with a wall thickness of 0.133 inch as a model for the pipe he desired but simply requested "standard" pipe. Northern supplied Gates with "standard" pipe with a wall thickness 0.116 of an inch, much thinner than the one Gates had shown. This thinner pipe was too weak for the farm implement attachments Gates made with it, causing their failure. Even though Luxem conceded at trial that the thinner wall pipe would not hold up to the stress of Gates' use, he insisted it was not his responsibility to second-guess Gates' request for "standard" pipe. The court held that Gates was a farmer with no way of knowing "standard" pipe had an insufficient wall thickness for his purposes. As a seller, Luxem should know all about pipes and apply this knowledge to Gates' intended use. This case illustrates that the elements of an implied warranty of fitness were present.

Warranty Exclusions Although it would seem advisable for sellers to exclude warranties whenever possible, the seller may need to offer a warranty to be competitive. Some sellers may orally claim warranty coverage, but then exclude the oral warranty in a fine-print provision in the sales contract. UCC 2–316 is intended to prevent such misunderstandings by requiring the seller act in good faith. A warranty

[2] *Northern Plumbing Supply, Inc. v. Gates*, 196 N.W.2d 70 (N. Dak. 1972).

remains in force if a seller engages in any unconscionable conduct in excluding a warranty.

All implied warranty exclusions must be conspicuous in the sale contract. An exclusion must be written in common language that draws the buyer's attention to the exclusion. The exclusion of the implied warranty of merchantability must mention the word *merchantability* or otherwise clearly exclude the warranty. The wordings "as is" or "with all faults" are examples of language that in common understanding call the buyer's attention to the warranty exclusion so all warranties of quality are effectively excluded.

Typical Warranty Exclusion

THE SELLER HEREBY DISCLAIMS ALL OTHER WARRANTIES, EITHER EXPRESS OR IMPLIED, INCLUDING ANY IMPLIED WARRANTY OF MERCHANTABILITY OR FITNESS FOR A PARTICULAR PURPOSE.

Buyer's Inspection of Goods A warranty is automatically excluded to the extent that the seller gives the buyer a reasonable opportunity to inspect the goods before contracting if the inspection would reveal the defect. The seller can reinforce this right by demanding the buyer inspect. For example, if a sales clerk requests the buyer of a stereo to test its FM reception while the unit is on display, but the buyer refuses, no warranty on FM reception will arise. The scope of the examination necessary is based on the buyer's opportunity to inspect and on the buyer's expertise in discovering a particular type of defect. A usage of trade, a course of dealing, or a course of performance may also exclude a warranty.

Inconsistent Warranties and Exclusions Where the terms of an express warranty are inconsistent with an exclusion or a disclaimer, the inconsistency is resolved in favor of the buyer. For example, a two-year express warranty in bold type is inconsistent with an exclusion in fine print. In that case, the buyer will have the benefit of the express warranty. However, it is completely consistent to provide a warranty on some aspect of the goods while disclaiming warranty on other aspects. For example, automobile manufacturers often provide warranties limited to the car's drivetrain (engine and transmission) and expressly exclude any warranty on the tires and battery. The excluded parts are usually covered by warranties from their separate manufacturers, so the buyer can make warranty claims only against the separate manufacturers. The warranty exclusion process is illustrated in Figure 11–4.

Magnuson-Moss Warranty Act Some sellers make outlandish claims about the performance or characteristics of consumer goods. Some sellers have promoted warranties as a major inducement to purchase, calling them "full" warranties when they are not. This led Congress in 1975 to pass the Magnuson-Moss Warranty Act to increase consumer information, prevent deception, and improve consumer product competition. The Federal Trade Commission (FTC) is responsible for implementing this Act.

FTC warranty regulations apply to consumer product sales of $15 or more. While the FTC does not require any express warranty, if any warranty is given it must be (1) conspicuous, (2) found in a single document, and (3) written in readily under-

FIGURE 11-4 Exclusion of Warranties

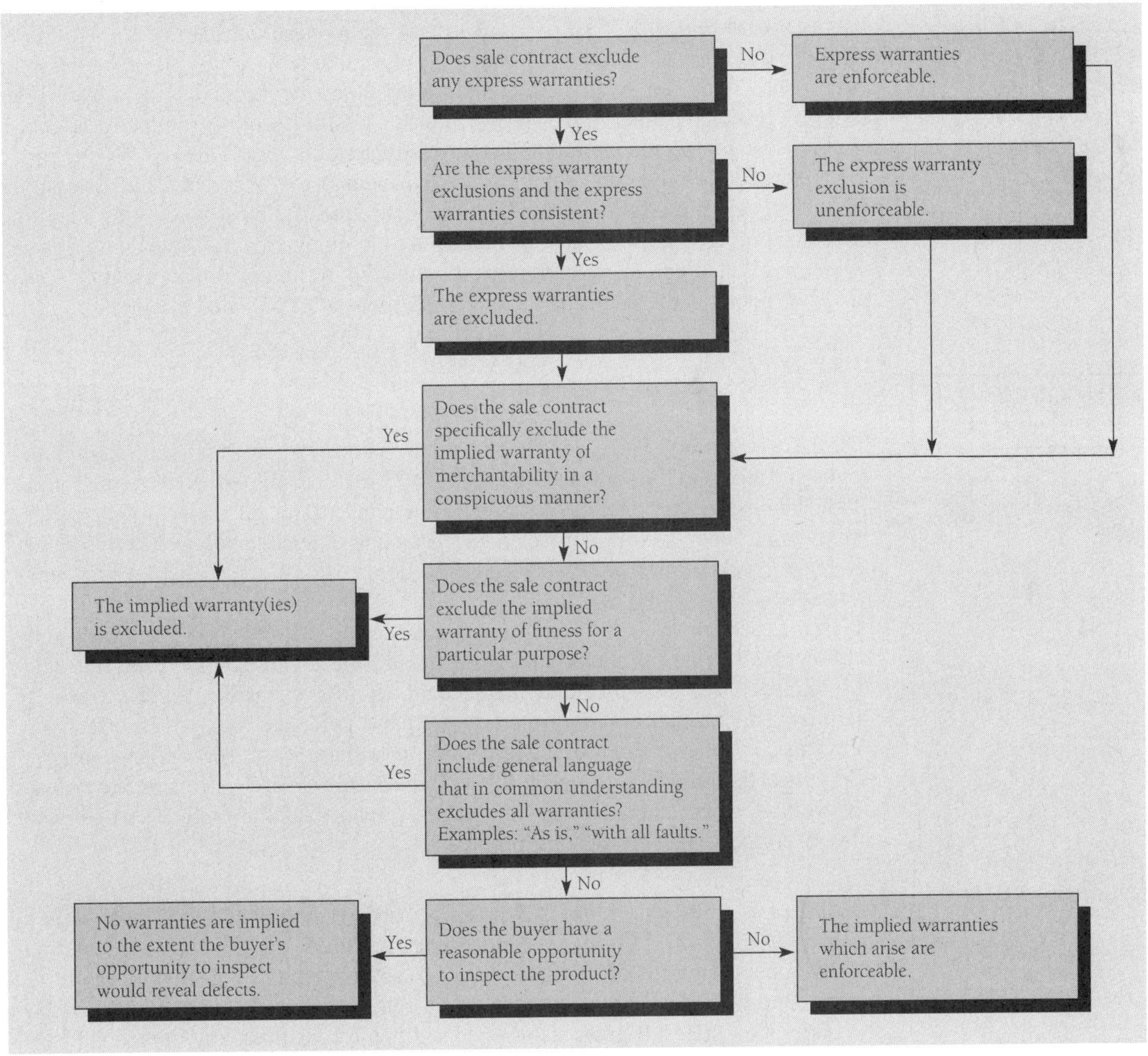

stood language. A warranty must also identify the parties it covers and clearly describe the parts or characteristics excluded from coverage. If a warranty claim is made, the warrantor must state precisely the services provided. The dates of the warranty's commencement and cessation, along with step-by-step procedures for warranty claims, must be stated. If informal dispute settlement procedures such as arbitration are used, the procedures must be described. Usually, the consumer must attempt to resolve the claim through these procedures before taking further action. If the seller provides an express warranty, limitations on implied warranties are invalid, with the exception that implied warranties can be limited to the duration of the express warranty.

full warranty
Magnuson-Moss Act requires that a full warranty provide reasonable repair, refund, or replacement rights and not limit implied warranties.

If consumer merchandise costing over $10 is sold and a warranty is given, the warranty must be conspicuously classified as "full" or "limited." A **full warranty** must provide the consumer with reasonable replacement or repair rights without other charges or conditions. Return of the warranty registration card is not a condition to honor the warranty. *Consequential damages,* those that replace lost profits or earnings if the user is injured by a defective product, may be limited with conspicuous language. If the consumer makes repeated unsuccessful attempts to remedy defects, a refund or free replacement option must be available. This avoids the seller's attempt to "wear down" the buyer and sets minimum standards for "lemons." Full warranties are so costly that few sellers provide them. Consequently, most warranties are either limited or provided as extra-cost insurance-style options. Several states have enacted *lemon laws* that supplement warranties by requiring refund or replacement of certain consumer goods if the dealer is unable to fix them after repeated attempts.

ETHICAL DILEMMA

CONSUMER CONFUSION ABOUT WARRANTIES

The UCC warranty exclusion/disclaimer provisions are an important example of legislated ethics in the warranty area. The UCC requires all parties to exercise good faith and observe fair dealings to meet consumers' reasonable expectations. Sellers have strong incentives to win sales by promising extensive warranties. However, the rising cost of defect claims gives sellers a conflicting incentive to limit warranties.

In the past, some unethical sellers promised warranties in sales literature, in the salesperson's representations, and even in the sale contract. Fine-print warranty disclaimers were also included in the contract to prevent the seller's warranty liability. This problem is reinforced by the parol evidence rule, which effectively prevents consumers from proving that a warranty claim was made. Sellers can avoid this ethical dilemma by (1) complying with the UCC warranty exclusion provisions, (2) prohibiting sales personnel from making outlandish claims, and (3) providing an effective repair and replacement process.

Warranties and Privity Many states apply warranty liability to any business in the chain of distribution. However, some privity requirements still exist for warranty actions in nearly a third of the states. UCC §2–318 permits states to adopt a form of privity or to permit a warranty suit by even remote parties. Alternative A has been chosen by most states. It gives standing to sue to the consumer, any immediate family member, and any guest in the consumer's home who suffers personal injury if their use of the product was reasonably foreseeable. Alternative B expands this beyond the family to cover any natural person's personal injury if their use of the product is reasonably expected (e.g., bystander). Alternative C expands warranty coverage to any person or corporation expected to use the goods; it includes property damage, and it prohibits the seller from disclaiming liability for personal injuries.

Warranties in International Commerce International commercial contracts commonly include no implied warranties. The Vienna Convention on Contracts for the International Sale of Goods (CISG), introduced in Chapter 10, provides for some similar rights, although it does not specifically use the term *warranty.* Sellers must deliver goods fit for the ordinary use for which such goods are intended. Because the CISG applies only to commercial contracts, there is no limitation of this obligation to merchants. Sellers must also deliver goods fit for any particular purpose known if the buyer reasonably relies on the seller's skill or judgment. Goods must conform to any sample or model the seller uses. There is no liability if the buyer knew of the defect when the contract was formed. Goods must be adequately packaged or contained. The use of warranty disclaimers may vary according to local law. The problem of where to bring suit for international product liability is complex, often depending on the substance of treaties between the two nations and on any special choice-of-law, choice-of-forum (e.g., arbitration) clauses in the sales contract.

Negligence

Negligence was the first tort theory used in product liability cases. The plaintiff must prove the damage sustained was the "fault" of the defendant's negligent conduct by establishing a prima facie case of negligence, as discussed in Chapter 8.

The plaintiff must prove that the defendant had a duty to exercise due care and to foresee any unreasonable risk of harm posed by the goods sold. The seller must minimize risks of injury by adequately designing, manufacturing, and inspecting the goods. Primary responsibility to minimize product defects rests with the product manufacturer or assembler. However, in some situations wholesalers and retailers should inspect, assemble, or prepare the goods before delivery. For example, auto dealers have the duty to inspect new cars before delivery to consumers. Manufacturers must warn consumers and give instructions for safe use. **Failure to warn** is now a prevalent negligence product liability theory. The *Cipollone* tobacco liability case discussed later in the chapter exemplifies the duty to warn consumers once dangers of a product become known. Breach of these duties may result in liability to any person who might reasonably be expected to use or be affected by a defective product. For example, it is negligent not to inspect empty beverage bottles before filling them because it is reasonable to expect they could contain a foreign substance that might injure a consumer. By contrast, it is natural to find fish bones in fish chowder, so it would not be negligent for such a product to contain them.

failure to warn Liability theory against seller who fails to warn consumers of known product hazards.

A wide range of injured victims may sue under negligence, including the purchaser, members of the purchaser's family, the purchaser's guests, and even bystanders if they fall within the zone of foreseeability. Foreseeable bystanders are persons reasonably expected to be affected by defective products. For example, it is foreseeable to expect a defective automobile to injure a pedestrian.

Defenses to Negligence Affirmative defenses ordinarily available to a negligence defendant may also be asserted in product liability suits. If the plaintiff contributed to the negligence by not using due care to guard against dangers, the defendant may be partially or completely relieved of liability by comparative or contributory negligence. If the plaintiff misused the product or voluntarily assumed a known risk in using the product or if the risk of injury was unknown or unknowable, the defendant will be relieved of negligence liability. The statute of limitations for negligence torts, often a two-year period, is usually applied to product-liability actions based on negligence.

Strict Liability

The most common theory of product liability used today is based neither on fault nor on the sales contract. Under the strict liability in tort theory, a manufacturer, wholesaler, or retailer that is in the business of selling products may be liable for injuries resulting from defects that make the product unreasonably dangerous. Many states have judicially adopted strict liability, as found in Section 402A of the *Restatement (Second) of Torts.*

Restatement (Second) of Torts, §402A

1. One who sells a product in a defective condition unreasonably dangerous to the user or consumer or to his property is subject to liability for physical harm thereby caused to the ultimate user or consumer, or to his property, if
   (a) the seller is engaged in the business of selling such a product, and
   (b) it is expected to and does reach the user or consumer without substantial change in the condition in which it is sold.
2. The rule stated in Subsection (1) applies although
   (a) the seller has exercised all possible care in the preparation and sale of his product, and
   (b) the user or consumer has not bought the product from or entered into any contractual relation with the seller.

Unreasonably Dangerous and Defective The strict liability claimant must prove the product was (1) defective and (2) in an unreasonably dangerous condition. These standards are purposely vague to cover a wide variety of products and situations.

Defectiveness generally depends on the customer's expectations for product performance. First, the merchantability standards provide some guidance for defectiveness. Products with inadequate safety warnings, that are unfit for ordinary purposes, that have inadequate packaging or labeling, or that would not pass without objection in the trade are probably defective for strict liability purposes. Second, a product dangerous beyond what an ordinary consumer would expect is unreasonably dangerous. Therefore, products with weak parts or mechanical limitations are usually considered defective. By contrast, consider alcohol, caffeine, tobacco, and other common substances with dangerous side effects when used improperly or excessively. Most consumers know these risks, so the products are not unreasonably dangerous unless adulterated with foreign substances.

The strict liability theory exposes business to the broadest potential liability of all product liability theories because of its lesser burden of proof. The privity doctrine and the defenses of contributory and comparative negligence are inapplicable. Some states recognize defenses such as product misuse, assumption of risk, and the plaintiff's failure to discover a defect that should have discovered. Comment (k) to §402A of the *Restatement* exempts products that are unavoidably unsafe, such as prescription drugs. This means plaintiffs in product liability suits for defective drugs must prove negligence because drugs are exempt from strict liability. A few courts have expanded this to exempt defective medical devices from strict liability (e.g., prostheses, IUDs, implants, pacemakers). Commonly, plaintiffs allege all three aforementioned product liability theories when bringing suit, naming all sellers in the chain of distribution. Many European nations are beginning to adopt forms of strict product liability, but most other nations still have procedural rules that make plaintiff suits more difficult than in the United States.

Misrepresentation

Merchants and others engaged in the business of selling goods to the public may be liable for misrepresenting the quality or characteristics of products. Such misrepresentations may result from either negligence or conscious and knowing misstatements. Section 402B of the *Restatement (Second) of Torts* is a common basis for this misrepresentation theory of product liability.

Restatement (Second) of Torts, §402B

> One engaged in the business of selling chattels who, by advertising, labels, or otherwise, makes to the public a misrepresentation of a material fact concerning the character or quality of a chattel sold by him is subject to liability for physical harm to a consumer of the chattel caused by justifiable reliance upon the misrepresentation, even though
> (a) it is not made fraudulently or negligently, and
> (b) the consumer has not bought the chattel from or entered into any contractual relation with the seller.

Although the misrepresentation theory is similar to a breach of express warranty, the two differ in several important respects. Misrepresentation is a tort; it is not based on the UCC or other contract principles. The tort statute of limitations applies, and contractual limitations of remedy, exclusions of warranty, or exclusions of consequential damages are ordinarily inapplicable. There is no privity requirement making the manufacturer, wholesaler, retailer, or other distributor potentially liable. *Consumers* entitled to sue are broadly defined to include employees who use the goods on the job and family members with permission to use the goods.

The misrepresentation must be material and must concern the goods' characteristics. In one case, a windshield misrepresented as "shatterproof" shattered when hit by a stone. The matter misrepresented must be factual and susceptible to exact knowledge. Mere statements of opinion and dealer puffing are not misrepresentations. However, if the consumer is unaware of the misrepresentation, it is not actionable. Only publicly made misrepresentations or advertisements are actionable; individual misrepresentations made only to a particular consumer are not covered by Section 402B.

In one case, a mace weapon was represented in a brochure as capable of "instantaneous incapacitation . . . [of] entire groups." The manufacturer was held liable for injuries suffered by a motel's night auditor who was attacked when the mace weapon failed to repel attackers. In another case, a wire rope failed, permitting a hoisted weight to fall on a consumer. The manufacturer's manual was distributed to dealers for review by buyers. It misrepresented the rope's strength, and formed the basis for liability.

Misrepresentations may be inferred from the way goods are merchandised, even if the marketing efforts are only directed toward a segment of the population. A policeman purchased a riot helmet from his department, relying on a package illustration showing a motorcyclist wearing the helmet. The policeman wore the helmet while riding his motorcycle. The helmet was designed to release quickly on impact and came off his head in a motorcycle accident. The manufacturer was held liable based on the misrepresentation because the helmet was unsuitable for motorcycling. Many plaintiffs allege one or more of the four major product liability theories compared in Figure 11–5.

FIGURE 11-5 Comparison of Product Liability Theories

Theory	Eligible Defendants	Eligible Plaintiffs	Damages Recoverable	Prima Facie Elements Required	Defenses
Negligence	Manufacturer primarily liable; some jurisdictions hold retailers to a duty to discover and disclose defects that are discoverable upon an inspection Franchisors of negligent designs	Any person within the traditional negligence risk perimeter as determined by the concepts of duty and proximate cause, i.e., those within the zone of foreseeability	General and special damages that result directly from the breach Punitive if negligence is "willful"; trend to limit Trend to limit noneconomic damages (pain and suffering)	Duty Breach of Duty Actual cause Proximate cause Damages *Res ipsa loquitur* may establish duty and breach	Contributory negligence Comparative negligence Assumption of risk Misuse of product Statute of limitations State-of-the-art
Strict liability (*Restatement (Second) of Torts,* §402A)	Sellers, manufacturers, retailers, suppliers, or lessors if in the business Franchisors if control retained over defective manufacture or misrepresentations in advertising	Users and consumers; bystanders included increasingly	General and special damages for personal injury, physical harm, or property destruction No punitives Trend to limit noneconomic damages (pain and suffering)	Defect Unreasonably dangerous Consumer expectations Causation Damages	Assumption of risk Misuse of product Should have discovered unreasonable danger (similar to contributory negligence) Statute of limitations Unavoidably unsafe
Breach of warranty (UCC)	Merchants as to implied warranties of merchantability; any seller as to fitness or express warranties	All natural persons who might reasonably be expected to use, consume, or be affected by defective product; most states; only family, guests, or those in household; some states have wider coverage	Trend to limit to purely commercial economic losses, but strongly resisted in some states No punitives	Contract of sale Warranty Breach of warranty Warranty was excluded Damages	Most contract defenses: Failure to notify of breach Lack of privity Misrepresentation Fraud Duress Undue influence Statute of limitations
Misrepresentation (*Restatement (Second) of Torts,* §402B)	Sellers, manufacturers, retailers, suppliers, or lessors if in the business	User, consumer, or bystander if relying on misrepresentation	General and special damages for physical harm	Merchant seller Misrepresentation to public Justifiable reliance Causation Damages	Misrepresentation not made publicly Dealer puffing No reliance Statute of limitations

Should smokers be entitled to allege any of these theories against the tobacco industry? The following landmark case reversed the tremendous successes of the tobacco industry product liability defense efforts.

Cipollone v. Liggett Group, Inc.

112 S. Ct. 2608 (1992)
United States Supreme Court

Mrs. Rose Cipollone smoked cigarettes from 1942 until she died shortly after removal of a cancerous lung in 1984. Thereafter, Antonio Cipollone, her husband, continued her product liability suit against three cigarette manufacturers. Cipollone presented extensive evidence that she was addicted to smoking and that the cigarette manufacturers made misleading advertisements assuring smokers of safety and made advertisements favorably depicting smokers. The cigarette manufacturers alleged that the Federal Cigarette Labeling and Advertising Act of 1965 as amended by the Public Health Cigarette Smoking Act of 1969 preempted state law, thus displacing the product liability laws on which Rose's claims were based. A jury awarded Antonio $400,000 for breach of warranty for advertising before the 1965 warning label requirement, but found that Rose was 80 percent comparatively negligent, denying her any damages. After Antonio's death, the couple's son Thomas appealed a U.S. Circuit Court of Appeals decision overturning the jury's damage award.

Justice Stevens delivered the opinion of the Court.

"WARNING: THE SURGEON GENERAL HAS DETERMINED THAT CIGARETTE SMOKING IS DANGEROUS TO YOUR HEALTH." A federal statute enacted in 1969 requires that warning (or a variation) to appear in a conspicuous place on every package of cigarettes sold in the United States.

Article VI of the Constitution provides that the laws of the United States "shall be the supreme Law of the Land . . . any Thing in the Constitution or Laws of any state to the Contrary notwithstanding." State law that conflicts with federal law is "without effect." Consideration "start[s] with the assumption that the historic police powers of the States [are] not to be superseded by . . . Federal Act unless that [is] the clear and manifest purpose of Congress." In the 1965 preemption provision regarding advertising (§5(b)), Congress spoke precisely and narrowly: "No statement relating to smoking and health shall be required in the advertising of [properly labeled] cigarettes." A warning requirement promulgated by the FTC and other requirements under consideration by the States were the catalyst for passage of this act, which reflected Congress' efforts to prevent "multiplicity of State and local regulations pertaining to labeling of cigarette packages."

The plain language of the preemption provision in the 1969 Act is much broader than that of its predecessor. First, the later act bars not simply "statements," but rather "requirement[s] or prohibition[s] . . . imposed under State law." Second, the 1969 Act reaches beyond statements "in the advertising" to obligations "with respect to the advertising or promotion" of cigarettes. The 1969 Act worked substantial changes in the law: rewriting the label warning, banning broadcast advertising, and allowing the FTC to regulate print advertising. The phrase "[n]o requirement or prohibition" sweeps broadly and suggests no distinction between positive enactments and common law. We must look to each of petitioner's common law claims to determine whether it is in fact preempted. The central inquiry in each case is straightforward: We ask whether the legal duty that is the predicate of the common law damages action constitutes a "requirement or prohibition based on smoking and health . . . imposed under State law with respect to . . . advertising or promotion."

Failure to Warn

Petitioner offered two closely related theories: first, that respondents "were negligent in the manner [that] they tested, researched, sold, promoted, and advertised" their cigarettes; and second, that respondents failed to provide "adequate warnings of the health consequences of cigarette smoking." Petitioner's claims are preempted to the extent that they rely on a state law "requirement or prohibition . . . with respect to . . . advertising or promotion." [Petitioner's] claims that respondents' post-1969 advertising or promotions should have included additional, or more clearly stated, warnings, are preempted. The Act does not, however, preempt petitioner's claims that rely solely on respondents' testing or research practices or other actions unrelated to advertising or promotion.

Breach of Express Warranty

A manufacturer's liability for breach of an express warranty derives from, and is measured by, the terms of that warranty. The "requirements" imposed by an express warranty claim are not "imposed under State law," but rather imposed by the warrantor. While the general duty not to breach warranties arises under state law, the particular "requirement . . . based on smoking and health . . . with respect to the advertising or promotion [of] cigarettes" in an express warranty claim arises from the manufacturer's statements in its advertisements. In short, a common law remedy for a contractual commitment voluntarily undertaken should not be regarded as a "requirement . . . imposed under State law" within the meaning of §5(b). To the extent that petitioner has a viable claim for breach of express warranties made by respondents, that claim is not preempted by the 1969 Act.

Fraudulent Misrepresentation

Petitioner alleges two theories of fraudulent misrepresentation. First, respondents, through their advertising, neutralized the effect of federally mandated warning labels based on a state law prohibition of advertising that tends to minimize health hazards of smoking. Such a prohibition, however, is merely the converse of a state law requirement that warnings be included in advertising and promotional materials. Section 5(b) of the 1969 Act preempts both requirements and prohibitions; it therefore supersedes petitioner's first fraudulent misrepresentation theory.

Petitioner's second theory alleges intentional fraud and misrepresentation both by "false representation of a material fact [and by] conceal[ment of] a material fact." Petitioner's claims that respondents concealed material facts are not preempted insofar as those claims rely on a state law duty to disclose such facts through channels of communication other than advertising or promotion. Thus, for example, if state law obliged respondents to disclose material facts about smoking and health to an administrative agency, §(b) would not preempt a state law claim based on a failure to fulfill that obligation.

Petitioner's fraudulent misrepresentation claims that do arise with respect to advertising and promotions are not preempted by §5(b). Such claims are not predicated on a duty "based on smoking and health" but rather on a more general obligation—the duty not to deceive. Congress offered no sign that it wished to insulate cigarette manufacturers from longstanding rules governing fraud. To the contrary, both Acts explicitly reserved the FTC's authority to identify and punish deceptive advertising practices—an authority that the FTC had long exercised and continues to exercise. This indicates that Congress intended the phrase "relating to smoking and health" to be construed narrowly, so as not to proscribe the regulation of deceptive advertising.

State law prohibitions on false statements of material fact do not create "diverse, nonuniform and confusing" standards. Unlike state law obligations concerning the warning necessary to render a product "reasonably safe," state law proscriptions on intentional fraud rely only on a single, uniform standard: falsity. The phrase "based on smoking and health" fairly but narrowly construed does not encompass the more general duty not to make fraudulent statements. Petitioner's claim based on allegedly fraudulent statements made in respondents' advertisements are not preempted by §(b) of the 1969 Act.

Conspiracy to Misrepresent or Conceal Material Facts

Petitioner's final claim alleges a conspiracy among respondents to misrepresent or conceal material facts concerning the health hazards of smoking. This duty is not preempted by §(b) for it is not a prohibition "based on smoking and health."

The judgment of the Court of Appeals is accordingly reversed in part and affirmed in part, and the case remanded. [Plaintiffs suit may proceed on several theories but not failure to warn after the Surgeon General's warning was implemented.]

Case Questions

1. What product liability theories are preempted by the federal warning requirement?
2. Discuss the immunity a manufacturer receives for compliance with all regulations.

Criminal Product Liability

In recent years, attention has focused on criminal product liability. Several states give prosecutors authority to bring criminal actions against certain product sellers. An Indiana statute outlaws negligent homicide. While most homicide statutes require proof of intent to cause death, the Indiana statute predicates guilt on unintentional death resulting from a negligent failure to exercise due care. In one celebrated Indiana case, Ford Motor Company was charged with negligent design of the Pinto gas tank. Three young women died when their Pinto burst into flames after being rear-ended. Although Ford was acquitted in this case, the case broke new ground in potential punishment for criminal product liability. This area has become increasingly important because the fines, punishment, and adverse publicity resulting from criminal prosecutions or regulatory investigations are harmful to corporate goodwill. However, because criminal punishment penalizes the business and its employees, the full extent of criminal product liability sanctions remains unclear.

Liability of Parties in Distribution Chain

Selection of the proper parties as plaintiffs and defendants is an important part of product liability cases. Substantive laws applicable in the state where the wrong occurs and procedural laws from the forum state may restrict or expand the number of potential plaintiffs or defendants. The clear trend has been to expand the classes of persons entitled to sue for injuries caused by defective products, which exposes business to increasing risks. Possible plaintiffs include both the purchaser and others who are affected by the use of such products. Mass torts and class action suits brought by one person representing all injured plaintiffs has also raised the risk of business and its insurers.

After final distribution of products to the ultimate consumers, there are three classes of persons who may be affected by a defective product. The first group consists of the purchaser and the purchaser's family. The second group consists of the employees of a commercial consumer who use or may be affected by the product. The third group consists of bystanders who may be affected by the product if it fails. Recall that UCC §2–318 permits the states to choose among three privity rules for liability to bystanders.

Product liability law has also expanded the number of defendants potentially liable for defective products. Most entities in the chain of distribution, illustrated in Figure 11–6, are potential defendants, including component part manufacturers, assemblers, wholesalers, and retailers. Most products begin with the refinement of raw materials or the manufacture of component parts. The manufacturer or assembler combines components into finished products. A wholesaler may then purchase the products for resale to retailers, and retailers purchase with a view to resell to ultimate consumers.

FIGURE 11-6 Privity and the Chain of Distribution in the Marketing Channel

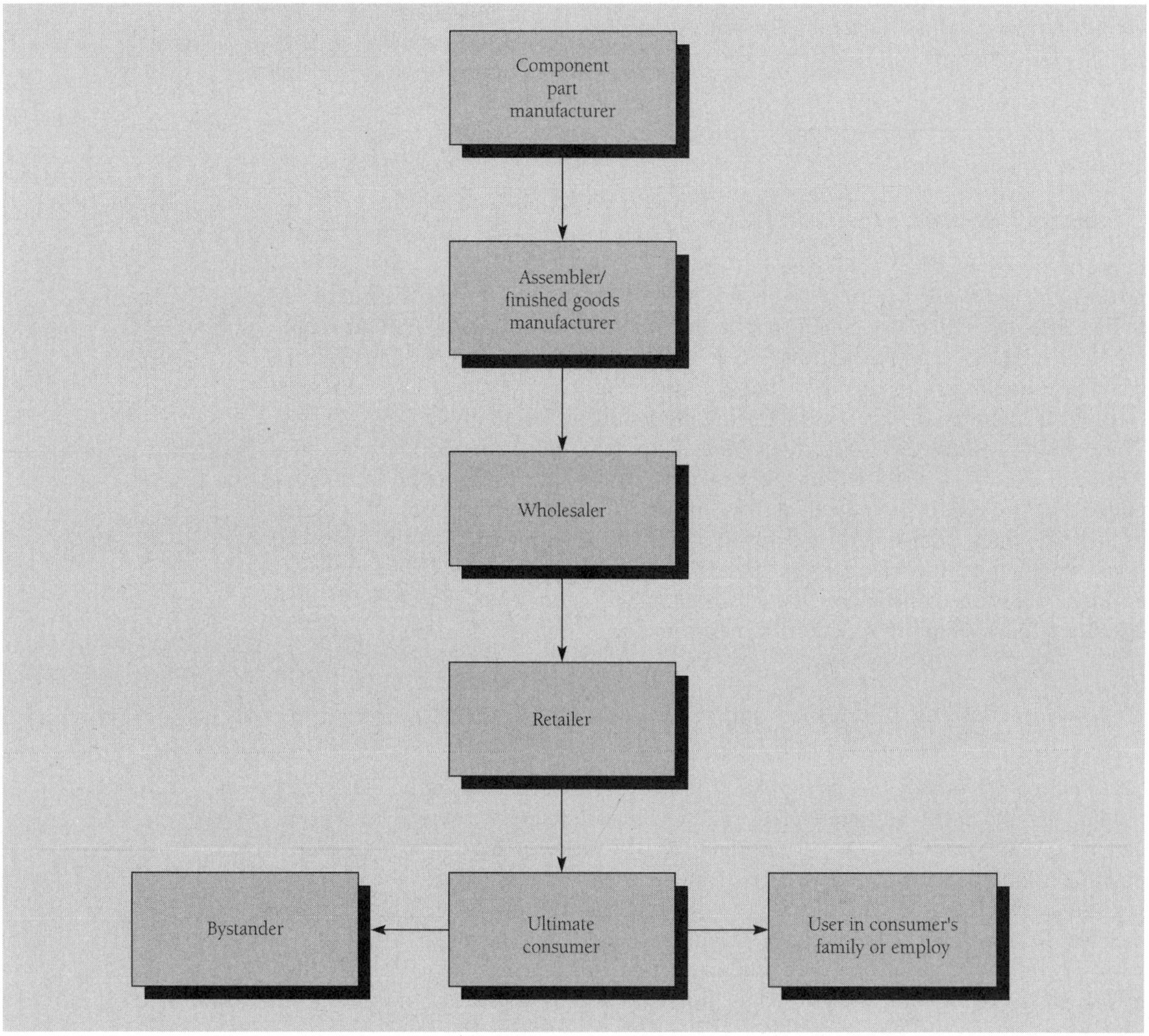

Privity of contract for the sale of products exists only between each level in the chain of distribution. No privity exists between bystanders or users and any seller. No privity exists between the ultimate consumer and any seller other than the retailer.

Manufacturers

Component part manufacturers and assemblers of finished products can be held liable under all product liability theories. However, component part manufacturers may be shielded from liability if (1) the finished product assembler converted the component to an unexpected use, or (2) the component reached the consumer after the assembler, dealer, or buyer made substantial changes in it. For example, a punch press manufacturer sold a machine without safety devices, expecting the industrial customer to add them. The punch press manufacturer was not held liable when an employee was injured after the customer's safety device failed.

Wholesalers

Wholesalers are not usually named as defendants in product liability actions. However, they may be held liable under any of the product liability theories. Such suits are most often brought against the domestic distributors of foreign-made goods. For example, the domestic subsidiaries of foreign automakers can be held liable for automobile defects.

Retailers

Retailers are likely to be sued because they have privity with the buyer. Retailers are held liable under all product liability theories. However, some vestiges remain of a defense known as the *sealed container doctrine.* Under this theory, the retailer has no duty to discover concealed or latent defects. For example, some states relieve retail food stores from liability if a sealed container (e.g., bottled liquids or soft drinks) explodes or leaks out, causing injury or slippery conditions. Certainly, it would be impractical for a retailer to conduct scientific tests or regularly dismantle all goods for inspection. However, a retailer's inspection duty arises when the sealed container is opened, when the retailer suspects poor quality, or when the retailer provides some assembly or installation service thereby introducing a defect. Manufacturers may also be liable for defects introduced by a dealer if final production steps are delegated to the dealer, a common practice in the sale of vehicles. The liability of sellers of used products is still uncertain but is expanding, particularly if the seller has made an express or implied warranty.

Franchisors

Increasingly, patented product designs are either licensed by franchise owners to franchisees for manufacturing, or they carry the licensed trademark of the licensor. Because the franchisee or licensee actually manufactures the product, the franchisor is usually shielded from warranty or strict liability suits. However, if the design is defective, the franchisor may be held liable for negligent design. Additionally, many license or franchise agreements reserve to the franchisor control over the franchisee's quality control, approval of product modifications or adaptations, and oversight of product advertising. The licensor or franchisor may be held liable with such increased control over the franchisee manufacturer.

Allocating Product Liability Among Sellers

Several additional legal doctrines affect the liability of participants in the distribution chain, including joint and several liability, subrogation, indemnification, successor liability, and the market share liability problem discussed previously. Employees who are injured while using industrial machinery for their employers' operations may have a product liability claim against the machinery manufacturers as well as a workers' compensation claim, as discussed in Chapter 18. When the employer or a workers' compensation insurer is required to pay these claims, they are given the right of *subrogation* to sue the defective equipment manufacturer. For example, if the injured employee's claim is paid by workers' compensation, the insurer is substituted as the claimant in the product liability suit against the defective equipment manufacturer. Thereby, subrogation is a form of reimbursement from the equipment manufacturer for the workers' compensation claim payment. Any party ordered to pay a product liability judgment may have the right of *indemnification* from some other responsible party. For example, if a wholesaler were held liable for a defectively manufactured product, it could seek indemnification from the manufacturer if the wholesaler could prove the manufacturer was ultimately responsible for the defect in design, manufacture, handling, or warnings.

The trend in the 1980s to restructure businesses has led to mergers, acquisitions, and corporate breakups involving the sale of various product lines. This raises the question of *successor liability:* Are the purchasers of these businesses liable for defective products previously manufactured or designed by the selling corporation? Generally, business purchasers are liable only for debts they consciously assume, so defective product claims remain the selling corporation's liability. However, if a corporation files for bankruptcy or the seller of a product line is liquidated, product liability claimants could be left with nothing. Some states hold the purchasing corporation liable for these product liability risks, requiring it to inherit these liabilities irrespective of the acquisition contract terms. For example, the purchaser may be liable if the transaction is designed as a sham to avoid liability, the transaction in substance amounts to a merger, or the purchasing corporation inherits the same management and owners of the selling corporation.

Service Liability

Providers of services can be liable if injuries result from their activities. As the service provider is held to a duty of due care, most service liability cases are based on negligence. To avoid liability for negligence or other *malpractice,* professionals who are doctors, lawyers, accountants, and engineers must perform services that are at least equal to the reasonably prudent professional standard. Suits alleging medical malpractice, audit failures, and attorney malpractice have increased at alarming rates in recent years.

The service provider could also be liable for failing to meet a contractual warranty of satisfaction or success. For example, few doctors would promise perfect success in a medical operation, and few lawyers would promise success in litigation. Such promises would obligate them to provide that success and thereby give the patient or client an enforceable contract right. Strict liability is generally inapplicable to sales of services unless they are closely tied to sales of goods. For example, strict service liability is generally limited to such things as a restaurant's defective service of adulterated food or a hairdresser's misuse of hair chemicals that physically injure a client. *Commercial lessors* of goods are sometimes held liable for injuries caused by defective goods they rent to customers. For example, an automobile leasing firm may be liable for a defective rental car, particularly if poor maintenance contributed to an injury. This trend extends the traditional requirement that a sale of goods precede product liability but is consistent with contractual privity found in the lease.

DEFECTIVENESS

The central issue in most product liability suits is whether the product is defective. In a negligence case, the seller must have failed to exercise due care in the product design, manufacturing, handling, inspection, packaging, instructions, or installation or committed a *failure to warn*. Under strict liability, there must be proof the product was rendered unreasonably dangerous by its defect. Warranty theory requires the plaintiff to prove the goods failed to conform to the warranty. The plaintiff must still prove the defect caused the injury.

Defective Designs

Products must be designed to eliminate defects that could lead to injury. Under warranty or strict liability, a defective design is considered a condition of the product. By contrast, negligently designed products result from a lack of due care by the designer or manufacturer. The practical difference is that in negligence suits the design process is examined closely for considerations of the foreseeability of danger. The inquiry is simpler in strict liability suits because forseeability and fault are irrelevant; only the presence of a defect must be proved. A reasonable-acting designer may escape negligence liability if the design appeared reasonable at the time it was designed. However, reasonable design activities are still subject to strict liability if the products are still unreasonably dangerous.

Interaction between the warranty and negligence theories also creates some apparent conflicts. If a buyer specifies a particular need to the seller, the warranty of fitness arises. In such a situation, the manufacturer may nevertheless be negligent because during the manufacturing process the manufacturer is in the best position to assure that a design is not faulty. By contrast, a useful design that is inherently dangerous and thereby unavoidably unsafe may nevertheless be free from defects. For example, although knives are inherently dangerous, they are not defective simply because they can cut things effectively. The manufacturer may limit its liability for such obvious dangers by providing safety devices or warnings. For example, chainsaws are inherently dangerous because of a tendency to "kick back," so chainsaw manufacturers must issue warnings or install chain-stop safety devices to limit their liability. How much misuse must the manufacturer foresee and guard against to avoid a defective design? The following case limits the defective design concept.

Westinghouse Electric Corp. v. Nutt

407 A.2d 606 (1979)
District of Columbia Court of Appeals

Dirickson Nutt, an 11-year-old child, was injured after falling down an elevator shaft built and maintained by Westinghouse. The elevator had stopped between floors, and one rider pulled the doors open to let occupants jump down to the fifth floor below. Nutt slipped through the open doorway, between the floor and the underside of the elevator, injuring his arm, which was eventually amputated. His suit claimed Westinghouse was negligent in designing the elevators so the doors could be opened in this manner.

Gallagher, Judge

Without question Westinghouse, as manufacturer, was under a duty to design a reasonably safe elevator. This duty did not require Westinghouse "to adopt every possible new device which might possibly have been conceived or invented." In a design case, as in other areas of tort law, liability is imposed only for the creation of an unreasonable danger. Thus, Westinghouse's duty was one of reasonableness in designing the elevator "so as to make it not accident-proof, but safe for the use for which it was intended." This duty of care includes the adoption of reasonable safety devices. What constitutes "reasonable care" will vary with the circumstances, and involves "a balancing of the likelihood of harm, and the gravity of harm if it happens, against the burden of precaution which would be effective to avoid the harm."

Westinghouse points to its compliance with existing industry-wide standards as dispositive of the question of due care. Two professional engineers, experts in elevator design, testified at trial that the elevator complied with all applicable safety codes and regulations. An elevator inspector for the District of Columbia government established conformance with the local elevator code. However, compliance with legislative or industry standards "does not prevent a finding of negligence where a reasonable man would take additional precautions."

Similarly, industry-wide custom influences, but does not conclusively determine, the applicable standard of care. As Justice Holmes put it, "What usually is done may be evidence of what ought to be done, but what ought to be done is fixed by a standard of reasonable prudence, whether it is usually complied with or not." Evidence of industry custom, however, may be conclusive when a plaintiff fails to introduce *any* evidence that the product was not reasonably safe for its intended use. Thus, the elevator's conformity to industry and legal standards established Westinghouse's due care unless the Nutts proffered contrary evidence that the product, as designed, created an unreasonable danger.

The sole evidence produced by the Nutts to establish a departure from the standard of care was the testimony of Mr. Foote. In effect, Mr. Foote gave his opinion that a longer toe guard or a different latch placement would have prevented the accident. However, evidence of a design alternative, by itself, is not sufficient to impose liability on the manufacturer.

A finding of unreasonable danger most often turns on the absence of a safety device that was available at the time of manufacture. Adoption of the suggested design alternative by other manufacturers for use in the same or similar equipment would be persuasive evidence. Customary use of another safer design is also relevant to establish the standard of care, and that the defendant's design is unreasonably dangerous. Evidence of available safety mechanisms illustrates what is feasible, and suggests a body of knowledge of which the defendant should be aware. As the court stated in *Moren v. Samuel M. Langston Co.:*

> A manufacturer is held to the degree of knowledge and skill of experts. This standard imposes upon the manufacturer the duty of an expert to keep abreast and informed of the developments in his field, including safety devices and equipment used in his industry with the type of products he manufacturers.

Here, testimony of customary safety features was not introduced. In addition, appellee's evidence failed to establish that an elongated toe guard is known to be feasible, even though not utilized by other manufacturers. This would seem to be the furthest courts have gone in imposing a duty on the manufacturer to keep abreast of recent scientific developments. Mr. Foote admitted on cross-examination that he had no knowledge of the factors involved in design of a toe guard, nor of the feasibility of his suggestions.

Against Westinghouse's evidence that the equipment was reasonably safe as designed, the Nutts mustered little contrary evidence. Mr. Foote's safety suggestions were not competent evidence that Westinghouse, the manufacturer, created an unreasonable danger. Thus, appellees failed to prove Westinghouse's deviation from the applicable standard of care in designing the elevator.

Case Questions

1. For what reason should the court seek out evidence of the function of safety regulations and industry-wide standards in determining the negligence duty of care?
2. What evidence must the plaintiff show to rebut the defendant's proof of compliance with industry standards and safety regulations?

Balancing Risks Against Benefits

Ethical Dilemma

The ethical problems of product safety can be evaluated with a risk-benefit/analysis similar to cost-benefit/analysis. Some recent cases have used this technique to project risks and benefits by assessing the feasibility and economic impact of safer designs. On one side of this analysis are the projected costs of additional safety features, societal decline if fewer useful products are brought to market, the loss of utility if existing and unmodified products are withdrawn, and the loss of useful but unavoidably unsafe products. These costs of product liability and safety regulation are then compared with the benefits of reducing injuries and reduction of the attendant burdens placed on society. Such benefits arise from the lowered risk of injuries, reduced medical and insurance costs, and the worker hours saved with less dangerous designs. The risk-benefit/analysis always involves trade-offs between the product's utility and the societal costs of compensating injuries and avoiding accidents. Society increasingly views it as unethical when manufacturers fail to conduct risk-benefit/analyses in good faith.

Several manufacturers have suffered costs by carelessly considering a product's risk-benefit/analysis. For example, evidence showed that Ford Motor Company management knowingly permitted use of a faultily designed fuel tank filler neck for the Ford Pinto, making the car dangerously vulnerable to explosion in a rear-end collision.[3] Ford executives knowingly postponed costly correction in the design to save $100 million in corporate profits. Confronted with such evidence, at least one jury assessed punitive damages of $125 million, although the award was later reduced on appeal. Ford suffered goodwill and reputational losses in the 1970s and 1980s from adverse publicity about the Pinto, Ford's managerial approach to safety and profits, and its malfunctioning automatic transmissions. Management has an ethical responsibility to consider the social impact of its decisions. The cost of product liability litigation is not the only negative factor for manufacturers.

Sellers can particularly improve safety when the cost to the seller is low, such as by providing warnings to users about known dangers. Adequate product designs and high quality control is always necessary. From time to time, society reevaluates the utility and social costs of certain products. For example, the manufacturers of three-wheel, all-terrain vehicles (ATVs) could not prevent them from flipping over when maneuvered abruptly. Some consumers used their ATVs irresponsibly by refusing to heed warnings; others were too unskilled to appreciate the dangers. After widespread negative publicity, and under pressure from the Consumer Product Safety Commission, manufacturers halted production of the more dangerous three-wheeled ATVs and all children's ATVs. Although ATV use was popular, society refused to accept the level of ethical judgments by both manufacturers and consumers' misuse. This risk-benefit/analysis resulted in complete elimination of the more dangerous models.

The most effective defense to product liability litigation is also the moral high ground: selling safer products. Short-sighted decisions to "cut corners" for profitability, justified as the only survival technique, ignore the adverse impact of selling defective products: product liability financial exposure, reputational losses, and increased regulation. Increasingly, responsible corporations are instituting some quality control program such as "Total Quality Management" or "Continuous Quality Improvement." These firms create a fundamental corporate culture conducive to

[3] *Grimshaw v. Ford Motor Co.*, 119 Cal. App. 3d 757, 174 Cal. Rptr. 348 (Cal. Ct. App. 1981).

quality and the production of safe products. Such firms are more likely to remain competitive in the long run. Attention to quality has the added advantage of improving the firm's reputation in the market as well as enhancing employee morale.

Duty to Warn

Sellers are shielded from liability where adequate directions and warnings of known dangers are provided. However, warnings alone do not replace the manufacturer's duty to provide obvious safeguards. For example, a conspicuous warning about the dangers of a punch press would be insufficient if a simple guard device would protect the operator from serious injury.

To be effective, warnings must be understandable and conspicuous. Sellers are often reluctant to place too many warnings on products because this might alarm purchasers or be ignored. This is not an adequate justification for a failure to warn of known dangers or known allergic reactions. If serious danger would arise when directions are disregarded, the warning must be made more conspicuous. A warning must be calculated to reach the likely users of the product. In one case, employees used machinery purchased by their employer, but a separate warning to users was required in addition to the warnings given only to the employer. In the case of a machine tool used in a factory, the warnings must be conspicuously noted on the machine tool and be made understandable to the average worker. Warnings placed in a bulky user's manual may be insufficient if users are unlikely to ever consult the manual.

Hazardous processing machinery is often covered with many warnings. Manufacturers should foresee and warn against dangers attendant to all uses and even to the service procedures. In *Nelson v. Hydraulic Press Mfg. Co.*,[4] a maintenance worker was injured while attempting to repair an injection molding machine. Melted plastic was placed through a feed tube and forced into molds to manufacture various plastic parts. Nelson climbed a ladder to observe a hardened plastic plug when molten plastic suddenly erupted, causing him severe injury. No warnings appeared on the machine. The court said:

> The jury, as reasonable persons, could have concluded that the defendant manufacturer knew or should have known of the danger to maintenance men from exposure to hot plastic material erupting through the feed hole during maintenance operations to purge the machine of hardened plastic, and that as a result of the failure to warn or instruct concerning said danger the machine in question was unreasonably dangerous and in a defective condition when it left the control of the defendant and that the defective condition was a proximate cause of plaintiff's injuries and damages.

Some product safety laws require warnings and are discussed further in Chapter 12.

Establishing Defectiveness

Proof of a product's defects may come from several sources. Conflicting expert testimony is often heard from engineers, scientists, designers, and production experts concerning the product's performance and design characteristics. Many documents from the seller's files are produced during discovery showing whether a particular design or warning was considered and rejected as too costly during design or production. Defect

[4] 404 N.E.2d 1013 (Ill. Ct. App. 1980).

databases are kept by some federal and state regulators like the Consumer Product Safety Commission and the National Highway Traffic Safety Commission, discussed further in Chapter 12. Their regulations may impact the standard of defectiveness used in the courts. Many other groups accumulate defect, injury, and incident data. For example, consumer groups often track litigation and organize efforts for recalls or class action suits. The Insurance Institute for Auto Safety and various industrial and insurance trade associations also collect extensive defect and claims settlement data. Some plaintiffs lawyers assemble "litigation kits," witch include incriminating documents that suggest strategies for trial or settlement. These are often sold to other plaintiffs and their counsel. Some critics argue this is *champerty*, an illegal contract to promote litigation. A number of defendants have been successful convincing trial judges to issue a *protective order* to withdraw from the public record all court papers filed in a product liability suit. This effectively raises other plaintiffs' costs in accumulating similar evidence, identifying witnesses, and duplicating strategies used in previous successful product liability trials. Confidentiality agreements are often a required part of product liability settlements and like protective orders probably reduce defendants' risk exposure considerably. Clearly, some groups seek to restrain the flow of such information while others try to distribute it widely for personal gain or as part of a crusade.

Regulatory Noncompliance and Damage Suits Plaintiffs in traditional product liability recovery actions can lessen their burden of proof simply by proving that the product fails to meet regulatory standards. In a case involving a poisonous chemical, for example, the manufacturer's failure to include the skull and crossbones or other warning symbol required by regulations triggered liability even though a textual warning was provided. The package failed to adequately warn two migrant workers who could not read English.

Negligence liability may also be established under the doctrine of negligence per se. Whenever a statute or regulation is violated, the product liability plaintiff may have a lighter burden of proof if the plaintiff is the type of person the statute is intended to protect. Some courts hold that negligence per se provides only a rebuttable presumption of the manufacturer's negligence. A violation may be justified if some other protective measure, safety device, or warning is sufficient. Negligence per se only establishes negligence, and the plaintiff must still prove causation.

Several state and some federal statutes provide for private damage suits. For example, the CPSA has an additional private right of action independent of common law product liability theories. In the 1970s Congress passed the Swine Flu Act which relieved the manufacturers of the swine flu vaccine from liability for mass inoculations. The U.S. government was substituted as the defendant in place of the drug manufacturers.

Regulatory Compliance as Due Care Product liability defendants often show their compliance with safety regulations as evidence of their due care. Many courts reject this contention because government regulations are only minimum standards above which there may still be negligence, breach of warranty, or unreasonably dangerous defects. However, compliance with regulations may be evidence of reasonable care, and some product liability reform laws discussed below are moving in this direction.

Res Ipsa Loquitur The legal doctrine *res ipsa loquitur,* which stands for "the facts speak for themselves," permits an injured plaintiff to prove that the defects caused the injury even if there is no proof of causation. An injured plaintiff may sometimes prove a defect this way even if the failure destroys the product. In *Escola v. Coca-Cola*

Bottling of Fresno,[5] a waitress was injured when a bottle of Coca-Cola exploded in her hand either because of carbonation pressure or due to a weakness of the bottle. The injured plaintiff's burden of proof under res ipsa loquitur was established for product liability actions:

> Defendant is not charged with the duty of showing affirmatively that something happened to the bottle after it left its control or management . . . to get to the jury the plaintiff must show that there was due care during that period. Plaintiff must also prove that she handled the bottle carefully. The reason for this prerequisite is . . . to eliminate the possibility that it was the plaintiff who was responsible. . . . It is not necessary, of course, that plaintiff eliminate every remote possibility of injury to the bottle after defendant lost control, and the requirement is satisfied if there is evidence permitting a reasonable inference that it was not accessible to extraneous harmful forces and that it was carefully handled by plaintiff or any third person who may have moved or touched it. Upon an examination of the record, the evidence appears sufficient to support a reasonable inference that the bottle here involved was not damaged by any extraneous force after delivery to the restaurant by defendant. It follows, therefore, that the bottle was in some manner defective at the time defendant relinquished control.
>
> An explosion such as took place here might have been caused by an excessive internal pressure in a sound bottle, by a defect in the glass of a bottle containing a safe pressure, or by a combination of these two possible causes. The question is whether under the evidence there was a probability that defendant was negligent in any of these respects. If so, the doctrine of res ipsa loquitur applies.
>
> The bottle was admittedly charged with gas under pressure, and the charging of the bottle was within the exclusive control of defendant. As it is a matter of common knowledge that an overcharge would not ordinarily result without negligence, it follows under the doctrine of res ipsa loquitur that if the bottle was in fact excessively charged, an inference of defendant's negligence would arise. If the explosion resulted from a defective bottle containing a safe pressure, the defendant would be liable if it negligently failed to discover such flaw. . . .
>
> A pressure test is made by the bottle manufacturer by taking a sample from each mold every three hours—approximately one out of every 600 bottles—and subjecting the sample to an internal pressure of 450 pounds per square inch, which is sustained for one minute. (The normal pressure in Coca-Cola bottles is less than 50 pounds per square inch.) The sample bottles are also subject to the standard thermal shock test. The witness stated that these tests are "pretty near" infallible.
>
> It thus appears that there is available to the industry a commonly used method of testing bottles for defects not apparent to the eye, which is almost infallible. Since Coca-Cola bottles are subjected to these tests by the manufacturer, it is not likely that they contain defects when delivered to the bottler which are not discoverable by visual inspection. Both new and used bottles are filled and distributed by defendant. The used bottles are not again subjected to the tests referred to above, and it may be inferred that defects not discoverable by visual inspection do not develop in bottles after they are manufactured. Obviously, if such defects do occur in used bottles there is a duty upon the bottler to make appropriate tests before they are refilled, and if such tests are not commercially practicable the bottles should not be re-used. [Bottler was liable under res ipsa loquitur.]

Affirmative Defenses

Sellers may assert several defenses to prevent or lessen their liability. Many are typical of the contract or tort defenses previously discussed in those chapters. Disclaimers of warranties and lack of privity are defenses to a breach of warranty suit. Situations in

[5] 150 P.2d 436 (Cal. 1944).

which plaintiffs place themselves in peril are the most widely recognized defenses under tort law. These defenses include contributory and comparative negligence, assumption of risk, and misuse of the product. If the plaintiff failed to exercise due care in using the product, contributory or comparative negligence may completely or partially bar recovery in a negligence or warranty case.

Since strict liability and breach of warranty are not based on fault, the courts are hesitant to apply the negligence doctrines of contributory or comparative fault. However, assumption of risk and product misuse are generally recognized defenses to both strict liability and warranty actions. In many cases involving latent (hidden) defects or the delayed manifestation of injuries, the plaintiff may have trouble proving causation. Successful defendants challenge the plaintiff's weak evidence that the defect led directly to the injury. This is particularly true in novel areas where scientific research is inconclusive to link the use of some drug or substance to an injury like that of the plaintiff's.

Should sellers of products be held liable for injuries sustained by people who have knowingly exposed themselves to danger? The following case illustrates the assumption of risk doctrine in a warranty case.

Hensley v. Sherman Car Wash Equipment Co.

520 P.2d 146 (Colo. 1974)
Colorado Supreme Court

The plaintiff, an employee at a car wash, was injured when she fell into a hole in the floor used for a hookless conveyor. The conveyor moved the cars through the wash area. Although a pivoting safety hood swung down over the hole to permit the cars' tires to pass over it, it reopened after each car passed. She had observed the safety hood's operation, concluding it operated properly.

Pierce, Judge

To establish the express warranty, plaintiff relies on the following language contained in an information sheet provided by defendant:

> 3. SAFE WORKING CONDITIONS. Car wash personnel are assured safe working conditions on all areas of the vehicle by the pivoted safety hood at exit end, over drive box which swings down as tire rides over, and then swings back up to cover the opening after tire has passed over; eliminates all possibility of persons stepping into an open pit.

Defendant contends that plaintiff's inattentiveness amounted to contributory negligence and barred recovery, and that plaintiff "assumed the risk" as she was aware that the safety hood had not been operating properly since the installation of the equipment approximately one month earlier. However, plaintiff testified that on the morning of the accident, a representative of Sherman had worked on the equipment and, specifically, had adjusted the safety hood, assuring her and the manager of the car wash that the device was working properly. Furthermore, she testified that she had observed the hood through the morning; that it operated properly each time a car came through the process; and that, therefore, she assumed that it had been properly repaired.

Other jurisdictions have held that the concept of contributory negligence, as it is known in negligence case law and as distinct from the doctrine of assumption of risk, has no place in actions premised on breach of warranty. In the absence of established Colorado law, we adopt that view.

This case presents a clear example of the distinctions between warranty and negligence theories. While the conduct of plaintiff in looking backwards as she stepped into the opening at the end of the conveyor might well constitute negligence on her part, this part was within the scope of the risk warranted against by defendant. It is uncontested that the purpose of the safety hood was to prevent a person from stepping into the opening at the end of the conveyor unit. As the language relied on by the plaintiff makes clear, the safety hood was designed to assure safe working conditions for employees and to "eliminate all possibility" of persons stepping into the opening. The very risk which defendant warranted not to exist was encountered by plaintiff, and her negligence or lack of due care is irrelevant. Contributory negligence is not a defense where plaintiff's conduct only puts the warranty to the test.

The most common accepted affirmative defense to a warranty claim is unreasonable use of the product by the plaintiff with knowledge of the defective condition and the risk it creates. Defendant was entitled to an instruction to the effect that plaintiff could not recover if she unreasonably exposed herself to a known defective condition. Such activity on her part would be disregard of a known danger, and she would not be proceeding in reliance upon defendant's warranty.

It is uncontested that plaintiff was aware of the fact that the safety hood had not been operating properly at all times. However, if her testimony is to be believed, the fact of her knowledge is attenuated by her apparent reliance on the assurances from the defendant's representative that the safety hood had been repaired and her own observation of the hood just prior to the accident. The issue is her awareness of a defect in the mechanism *at the time of the accident.* Whether or not her reliance on the statements of the repairman and her own observations was justifiable would be a question for the jury to determine.

Case Questions

1. What representations created the warranty in question?
2. Compare and contrast the contributory negligence, assumption of risk, and product misuse defenses.

---

misuse
Product liability defense for an unreasonable and unintended product use.

Abnormal use or misuse of the product by the plaintiff is similar to the assumption of risk defense. A **misuse** is an unreasonable use of the product in a manner that was not intended by the seller or designer. A misuse is sometimes foreseeable by the seller, so warnings or design changes may be necessary. The courts are not consistent in their application of the misuse defense. Some courts recognize this defense in strict liability cases, whereas others refuse to apply it. In one case, the manufacturer of a chair claimed it was misuse for the buyer to stand on the chair and use it as a step-stool. The court found this use to be foreseeable and required that the chair be designed to remain stable even under the pressures of a person standing on it.

state-of-the-art defense
Product liability defense that manufacturer used all known safety improvements at the time the product was designed.

statute of repose
Limitation period for the technological useful life of products.

The **state-of-the-art defense** has been successfully asserted by manufacturers where all known safety improvements have been included in products and further refinements were unknown at the time of manufacture. The state-of-the-art defense might relieve a seller from liability based on negligence. However, it usually has no applicability to strict liability because §402A of the *Restatement (Second)* clearly provides for liability whenever a defect exists, irrespective of the manufacturer's fault. This means products manufactured many years ago may be judged by the technology developed later. This added liability exposure suggests why states are experimenting with **statutes of repose** that limit the time during which there can be products liability. It effectively creates a technological useful life that enables manufacturers to innovate without fear that any improvements must be later installed into all products previously sold before the technology was developed.

Consumers' Personal Responsibility for Product Safety

Ethical Dilemma

Consumers also face ethical dilemmas when they misuse products. Sellers are increasingly considered principally responsible for safety. Consumers may be lulled into complacency and fail to use products responsibly. Safety is a concern for all parties: the manufacturer, the dealer, and the user. Consumers have commonsense duties to avoid exposing themselves, their families, and bystanders to potential dangers. Some states are applying concepts of comparative fault, reducing recoveries paid to plaintiffs whose injuries in auto accidents are increased by not wearing seatbelts.[6]

Product Liability Reform

The product liability crisis is closely related to the general tort reform movement discussed in Chapter 8. Reformers argue that the United States has an excessive product liability system that raises the costs and uncertainties of defending suits, deters new product innovations, adds to consumers' costs for goods, and diminishes the competitiveness of U.S. businesses. Juries allegedly give huge compensatory damage awards, and some large punitive damage awards receive high visibility. These trends allegedly increase the cost of defending product liability cases. Many manufacturers pass the additional insurance and redesign costs on to consumers through higher prices. It is argued that most other nations impose significant barriers to product liability suits such as limiting pretrial discovery, a major source for proof of liability. Additionally, many nations avoid U.S. style attorney–client relations by forcing the loser to pay the winner's litigation costs (the so-called English rule). The English rule requiring the loser to pay the winners' litigation expenses would clearly deter many suits. However, even in the United Kingdom, the English rule applies in less than half the cases. England has an extensive welfare bureaucracy to manage public funds for financing litigation by poor and lower-middle-income plaintiffs. The "loser-pays" rule largely applies only to well-to-do individuals and to business litigants. If the English rule were instituted in the United States, it is likely that a similar publicly financed, legal aid system would arise to soften the harshness of any abrupt shift to a loser-pays system. Other nations restrict the use of a plaintiff's lawyer's contingency fee arrangement. In the United States, the plaintiff's lawyer is permitted to take on a case even if the client cannot commit to paying representation fees in exchange for a percentage of the victim's recovery or settlement. These *contingency fees* arguably encourage frivolous lawsuits, deprive the victim of a significant portion of the recovery, and trigger excessive litigation. However, no one proposes limiting fees paid to defense lawyers.

Many of the same forces are at work in products liability reform as in tort reform. Both reform movements have been triggered by the expansion of theories of liability and the growth in damage awards. U.S. manufacturers and insurers have argued that the tort system is out of control and now requires uniformity. Consumer groups and trial lawyers argue that the liability system is needed as an incentive to design and manufacture safe products. They also assert the so-called crisis is fictitious. Some opponents even speculate that reform will backfire, triggering a huge product safety

[6] *Waterson v. General Motors Corp.*, 544 A.2d 357 (N.J. 1988).

regulatory bureaucracy that could be even more costly and stifling. There is also evidence that the insurance availability crisis of the 1980s was not the result of tort or product liability litigation, but was caused by cutting premiums and destructive competition among insurers, poor underwriting, and collusion among insurers. Indeed, the bulk of civil litigation is commercial suits among businesses; for example, breach of contract. Also, property and casualty insurers' main business is to accept a shift of risk from persons with personal responsibility for their wrongdoing. Without the Western tradition of personal responsibility, there would be little need for this sector of the insurance industry.

Product Liability Reform Proposals

This crisis has led several state legislatures to change the product liability system in an attempt to make it more predictable. Specific product liability reforms have emerged in over half of the states and involve various procedural and substantive law changes. Many successful reforms impose damage caps on punitive damages and on noneconomic damages (pain and suffering). Some reforms would permit juries to be told about collateral source information such as when a victim has already received an insurance settlement, workers' compensation, or medical payments from other sources. Many states and the federal courts are imposing sanctions on plaintiffs and their counsel for frivolous suits.

Some states restrict product liability theories to defective design, failure to warn, or the manufacturer's deviation from the prescribed design so that new theories will not develop in the courts. Other states have reduced the limitations period by redefining when the statute of limitations accrues (begins to run) or by establishing statutes of repose. States have enacted damage caps. Some states permit only one punitive damage award per product defect, effectively encouraging plaintiffs to rush their cases. Another alternative is to bifurcate product liability trials so that punitive damages are determined in a less impassioned proceeding, separate from the main trial. Some states exempt prescription drugs, medical devices, human blood, and tissue products from the strict liability theory. A few states recognize the unavoidably unsafe conditions of products with inherently risky characteristics (e.g., knives) by recognizing that their dangers are not design defects.

Most of the product liability reforms have expanded or confirmed the affirmative defenses: contributory negligence, comparative negligence, and assumption of risk. Some states have adopted the misuse defense or expanded assumption of risk to include situations in which the plaintiff failed to use reasonable caution in using the product or should have appreciated an open and obvious risk or danger in failure-to-warn cases. The state-of-the-art defense is also spreading to some states. Other proposals include modifying the joint and several liability rule by replacing it with proportionate liability that limits each defendant's potential liability to their proportion of fault. Many states encourage settlement of suits with periodic payment schemes often paid from annuities. A few states have modified the privity concept by exempting retailers and other sellers from liability unless the manufacturer was beyond the state's jurisdictional powers, or the reseller modified the product. Some states limit drug liability suits if Food and Drug Administration regulations are met. A few states prohibit evidence of product design changes that eliminated the defective condition for the products produced later.

The state legislatures will probably continue to experiment with limitations on product liability suits. However, federal product liability reform is moving through

Congress again. If it is successful, it may deprive the states from developing local law responsive to their own needs and will prevent states from experimenting with alternative substantive and procedural laws. In recent years, the number and size of tort and product liability awards has continued to decrease by most measures; it has not increased as some tort reformers argue. Recent studies by various groups such as the prestigious and conservative Rand Institute, the National Center for State Courts, the General Accounting Office, and the Insurance Services Office show that the impact of litigation is declining. For example, only 10 percent of personal injury claims use the tort system. Only 7 percent of accident victims receive tort compensation. Only 3.5 percent of claims go all the way to verdict, and fewer than a quarter of defendants are found liable. Most punitive damage awards are reduced, set aside, or otherwise never paid. Juries are becoming less victim oriented and are reducing the lottery jackpot mentality that probably once existed. This is particularly true in courts where the jury is drawn from middle class or affluent suburbs. However, there is also evidence that juries drawn from lower-income neighborhoods allegedly indulge in income redistribution by assessing larger awards. However, comprehensive litigation data is still unavailable. To minimize the adverse impact of product liability, businesses should remain aware of these developments and advance and adhere to industry's standards.

Maintaining U.S. Competitiveness

International Perspective and Commentary

Critics charge that the United States is becoming uncompetitive in world markets because the product liability system imposes excessive costs on U.S. industry. However, many foreign nations impose safety, packaging, labeling, and warranty regulations on all imported products. Some civil law nations have more extensive statutory liability provisions, similar to implied warranties, than do common law nations. The EU has product safety regulations that parallel those in the United States. However, the liability systems of many other nations are currently less financially favorable to injured plaintiffs than the U.S. system is. For example, New Zealand prohibits common law tort actions against the sellers of goods. Instead, New Zealand's government has instituted a regulatory system of no-fault compensation for most types of defective product injuries.

The argument that U.S. firms are becoming noncompetitive relative to foreign based firms is generally false. Probably as a result of restructuring in the 1980s and other economic pressures, many credible studies show that U.S. firms are now significantly more productive and competitive than most other nations, including Japan. Because most major foreign firms sell in the U.S. markets, they are subject to the same product liability laws for U.S. sales. While stringent U.S. laws may deter some foreign firms from competing in U.S. markets, it does not deter the largest, strongest, and most innovative of the world's firms. They can hardly avoid the lucrative U.S. market. Critics might argue that foreign companies design safer but more expensive products for the U.S. market, selling their less safe products at higher profit margins in other nations. Or perhaps innovative products become available first in foreign markets long before they appear in the United States. There is little evidence to support either of these suppositions except in the case of prescription drugs. However, the slow introduction of new drugs in the United States is dictated by regulations of the U.S. Food and Drug regulations, not by fears over product liability under the various state laws. Therefore, the argument that U.S. product liability laws make U.S. firms noncompetitive is at most only a small possibility. Indeed, the contrary proposition is at least as credible: U.S. product liability laws encourage careful design and manufacturing that actually enhance the international competitiveness of U.S. firms.

The burden of differences in product liability safety and testing standards can impose greater costs on those selling in any foreign nation. Many foreign nations impose more stringent standards on imported goods than they do on goods produced domestically. For example, the U.S. automobile industry has long argued that U.S.-built vehicles are priced 40 percent higher in Japan than in the United States because of discriminatory and specious Japanese requirements for imported automobile safety inspections.

Ethical issues arise in product liability when a domestic manufacturer withdraws a defective product from the home market and turns to foreign markets to dispose of existing inventories. For example, critics charge that after U.S. manufacturers stopped selling IUD birth control devices in the United States, they cut their losses by unloading excess inventories in developing countries. As information spreads about business's global social responsibility, the impact of their defective product policies will become a dilemma for public affairs with both international and ethical dimensions for manufacturers and for the public policy debate over product liability.

Product Liability Risk Management

Perhaps in the current political climate, the product liability and tort reform efforts discussed above would appear to be the most effective means to reduce costs. However, such special interest legislation is often viewed as greedy, self-interested, sweetheart deals given to influential groups who lobby hard with political contributions. Such efforts are likely to trigger a severe backlash and an eventual loss of consumer confidence as these facts become public. A better strategy for long-range benefits to companies and their industries is to establish effective product liability risk-management programs. Such programs should provide managers with authority to set policies and procedures to provide oversight of a company's various functions that can impact product safety. Early on in the life of a new product, this effort should involve representatives from design, engineering, manufacturing, marketing, legal, and risk management. If these efforts are relegated to only one of these groups, the group may subjugate sound risk management to that group's individual goals. For example, marketers might delete prominent safety warnings to simplify packaging and avoid alarming consumers, but to the whole firm's disadvantage.

Depending on the circumstances, an effective product liability risk-management program involves most or all of the following elements. First, new products or improvements should be tested for safety under normal consumer use. While in-house testing is usually cheaper, independent testing may be more objective and reliable. Second, design changes intended to reduce cost or simplify manufacturing may degrade the original design specifications. A close and careful risk-management review is clearly necessary for design changes. Third, quality control during production is essential and should be supplemented with safety audits and periodic reviews of quality standards. Fourth, customer feedback systems should be implemented to refine, redesign, and modify production techniques. This should facilitate the collection of customer complaints, sales feedback, repair histories, and product-failure information. Fifth, at frequent intervals and after significant events (e.g., model change or new model introduction, recalls, major litigation, industrial accidents, changes of suppliers), this information should be analyzed with a view to improving quality and safety. Such procedures are an inherent part of the continuous quality improvement used by the world's most successful competitors. Product safety information can also be obtained from trade associations, insurers, and legal counsel. While product liability risk management can be viewed as a sound strategy of bottom-line liability risk prevention, it is also a defensible strategy of high business ethics. Consumers and investors are increasingly demanding such morality in the marketplace.

SUMMARY

As a result of the inroads made on the privity doctrine, businesses are increasingly liable to victims when product failures cause injury. This has caused extensive product liability litigation. Product liability suits have been altered by changes in substantive and procedural legal doctrines such as statutes of limitations, the identification of the precise defendant, and tort reform.

Product liability suits are based on one or more of several theories. The contract theory of express warranties triggers liability when models, specifications, oral promises, or other contractual promises are made. Merchants who regularly sell or act as agents make an implied warranty of merchantability. The implied warranty of fitness for a particular purpose arises when a seller selects goods for the buyer's special purpose. Sellers may exclude express and implied warranties with conspicuous and consistent language. The federal Magnuson-Moss Warranty Act prohibits labeling a warranty as a "full" warranty unless the warranty permits repair, refund, or replacement of defective goods at the buyer's option. All other warranties must be labeled as "limited."

There is even greater expense for torts of negligence and strict liability. The negligence theory holds a manufacturer, wholesaler, or retailer of a defective product liable if the injury should have been foreseen. Sellers must design, manufacture, assemble, and handle products with reasonable care and warn users of reasonably foreseeable and known dangers. Sellers are strictly liable for defective and unreasonably dangerous products. Lack of privity or proof of fault is not a barrier to strict liability suits. Product liability may also be based on the seller's misrepresentation of the product's quality or characteristics in advertising, sales representations, or an owner's manual. Some states permit criminal prosecution of sellers of defective goods. Many victims allege liability under one or more of these product liability theories. The extent to which the perceived impact from product liability litigation has triggered a "crisis" is a contemporary political question that legislators and politicians are rapidly addressing.

CRITICAL THINKING REVIEW QUESTIONS

1. For the most part, privity of contract is invalid as a defense in product liability cases, except under the Uniform Commercial Code. Why? How does the *McPherson v. Buick Motor Co.* case provide insight into this question? *MacPherson v. Buick Motor Co.,* 217 N.Y. 382, 111 N.E. 1050 (1916).
2. In many product liability lawsuits, the plaintiff is suing because the goods purchased had some inherent defect and did not work at all. For other product liability theories discussed in this chapter, goods that may be satisfactory for normal purposes may still be the subject of a product liability lawsuit. Illustrate these two types of lawsuits.
3. Compare and contrast the strict liability theory with liability based on a contractual promise or warranty liability. Explain how it differs from liability based on fault.

Critical Thinking Exercises

1. Read the following three examples. Identify which type of warranty applies to each.
   a. The seller of new boats shows a sample sailboat, claiming that boxed-up sailboats on the back lot are just like the sample. The boxed sailboat purchased is not like the sample at all. There is no written contract of sale.
   b. If a "full warranty" is given, a malfunctioning product must be replaced without charge.
   c. A new sports utility vehicle that has been sold leaks water, and the four-wheel drive is inoperable.
2. A customer requested assistance in selecting a pair of hiking boots suitable for mountain climbing above the timberline in the Rockies. The customer said she would be carrying packs weighing over 75 pounds. The salesperson recommended a pair of traditional hiking boots with waffle soles which lacked adequate support. As a result of wearing the boots, the customer suffered injuries while on the climb and had to be rescued by helicopter out of the wilderness. What is the victim's best warranty theory and why?
3. A man was severely injured when an automobile, left unattended on a hill, struck him as he was playing golf. The car had been left with the gearshift in the "park" position, but the gears became disengaged. The plaintiff brought an action against both the manufacturer and the owner of the car. On what grounds can a "bystander" who receives personal injuries bring action against the manufacturer?
4. Harry Handyman, an accountant, prides himself on doing all the work on his home himself. When the floor in his kitchen needed replacing, he went to the local hardware store and purchased a roll of linoleum and, after a lengthy discussion with the owner, a can of Super-Bind linoleum glue. Harry followed all of the warnings and instructions on the can. He left all the windows in the kitchen open, and he positioned a fan to blow the toxic fumes out of the room. Nevertheless, while he was spreading the glue, an explosion ripped through the kitchen, severely burning him and damaging his home. Later investigation revealed that the cause of the fire was the ignition of the fumes from the glue by the pilot light of a hot-water heater in the utility room outside the kitchen. What cause of action does Harry have, and against whom? Explain.
5. Jones purchased a steel-belted radial tire. The tire had a design defect that caused it to separate, causing an injurious crash. However, Jones was not warned of this defect even though the manufacturer had received several complaints. The tire blew out when she was driving the car on rough terrain. Is Jones entitled to recover for injuries from the manufacturer?
6. Dr. Petri fitted Palmer with a Dalkon Shield intrauterine contraceptive device (IUD). The doctor and patient relied on the manufacturer's promotional materials, which claimed the IUD was a safe and effective birth control alternative. However, Palmer became pregnant anyway, then violently ill, suffered a spontaneous miscarriage, went into septic shock, and developed a blood clotting disorder. Palmer was given an emergency hysterectomy to save her life. If Palmer can prove the IUD was the sole cause of her injuries, what warranty theories would be most effective in claims against the manufacturer? *Palmer v. A.H. Robins Co., Inc.*, 684 P.2d 187 (Colo. 1984).
7. Tetracycline was prescribed for Feldman several times over three years. Eventually her teeth became discolored. Scientific literature existed at the time showing the relationship between tetracycline and tooth discoloration. After FDA review, the manufacturer of the tetracycline Feldman had ingested included warning inserts in its packaging. Did the drug include sufficient warnings when sold to Feldman? Who is responsible for proving the adequacy of the prevailing scientific evidence that triggers a duty to warn? *Feldman v. Lederle Laboratories*, 479 A.2d 374 (N.J. 1984).

CHAPTER

12

Consumer Protection

Critical Thinking Questions

- For what reasons was the Federal Trade Commission given power to regulate unfair and deceptive trade practices in advertising, direct marketing, retail sales and consumer financing?
- What was the historical evidence about creditors' practices in setting and communicating credit terms, their credit billing practices, the bases for selecting borrowers, and the reasonability of their credit collection activities?
- How have the presumptions about credit practices led to laws to protect consumers?
- What market failure is addressed by credit disclosure and advertising regulations?

Introduction... Past, Present, Future

Before the 1930s, common law contract and tort principles of misrepresentation, warranty, and interference with economic relations provided the primary legal protections for consumers. Since 1938, Congress has addressed consumer desires by expanding the authority of the Federal Trade Commission (FTC) to regulate consumer affairs. The FTC's regulatory fervor has varied with the political climate. The Consumer Credit Protection Act expands FTC powers to regulate consumer sales, financing, and credit practices. Over the years, additional consumer protection programs have added powers to the FTC and other agencies.

Consumer product marketing has a checkered past because some sellers took advantage of unsophisticated buyers, failed to admit their products' shortcomings and took advantage of the laissez-faire environment and the caveat emptor (let the buyer beware) attitude. However, as some industries became known for their abusive practices, there were pressures in legislatures to curb these abuses. The protections of the common law of contracts were seen as insufficient, signaling a sea of change in consumer protection by the FTC and the states.

By today's standards, some creditors' past actions seem arbitrary, oppressive, and unrelated to the borrowers' ability to repay. Creditors used unsuitable information and criteria to withhold credit from otherwise creditworthy individuals. Decisions not to grant credit often reflected views held by some niche of society about credit risks or were made to achieve social engineering. Many loan decisions were based on (1) the lender's personal biases, (2) distorted information about borrowers' businesses, lifestyle, associates or family, and (3) credit reports containing unsubstantiated, defamatory and often false allegations of impropriety (gossip). Many creditors ignored the income stability of working women and people of color, believing they had only a limited work ethic or were unable to "hold down a job." There have been major regulations of the credit process as these attitudes spread.

This chapter first examines the FTC's regulatory powers over unfair and deceptive trade practices, deceptive advertising, and consumer protection. The consumer financing relationship is then analyzed with emphasis on the lender's obligations in disclosing credit terms, granting credit, reporting on the credit history of borrowers, and debt collection practices. Finally, the administrative regulation of product safety is addressed.

Thought Questions

1. What changes have occurred in consumer relations to justify consumer protection regulations?
2. What assumptions are sometimes made about borrowers that form no direct or empirical basis for granting credit? Do these assumptions justify credit regulation?

Consumer Protection by the Federal Trade Commission

The FTC is an independent regulatory agency with five commissioners appointed by the president and confirmed by the Senate. There must be political balance on the FTC, with not more than three members from any one political party. The FTC is entrusted by Congress to promote a competitive business environment. Originally created in 1914 under the Federal Trade Commission Act to enforce the antitrust laws, the FTC obtained consumer protection authority in the Wheeler-Lea Act of 1938. The FTC has additional consumer protection powers under the Consumer Credit Protection Act. There is considerable overlap between the FTC's consumer protection function and its powers to promote competition. The FTC fosters competition by monitoring business practices and setting consumer protection policies, such as prohibiting deceptive practices that might divert sales from honest competitors. Deceptive advertisements distort consumers' information, making their purchase decisions inferior, and thus undermine the goals of perfect competition. The FTC's interpretation of this mission changes with its political makeup. For example, the FTC's vigorous industrywide enforcement in the 1960s and 1970s gave way to a restrained case-by-case approach in the 1980s but stricter enforcement is returning in the mid-1990s. The FTC's structure is depicted in Figure 12–1.

The FTC also has the power to prosecute violations of §5 of the FTC Act, which prohibits unfair methods of competition and unfair or deceptive trade practices. The courts have interpreted trade practices to be "unfair" if they offend established public policy and if they are immoral, unethical, oppressive, unscrupulous, or will substantially injure consumers. FTC interpretations may be different from those of the courts, reflecting the prevailing ideology of the FTC and the judiciary. Trade practices are usually found "deceptive" if they tend to deceive the consumer, even if no actual deception is proved. Figure 12–2 summarizes the FTC's powers under various consumer protection laws.

FIGURE 12–1 Federal Trade Commission

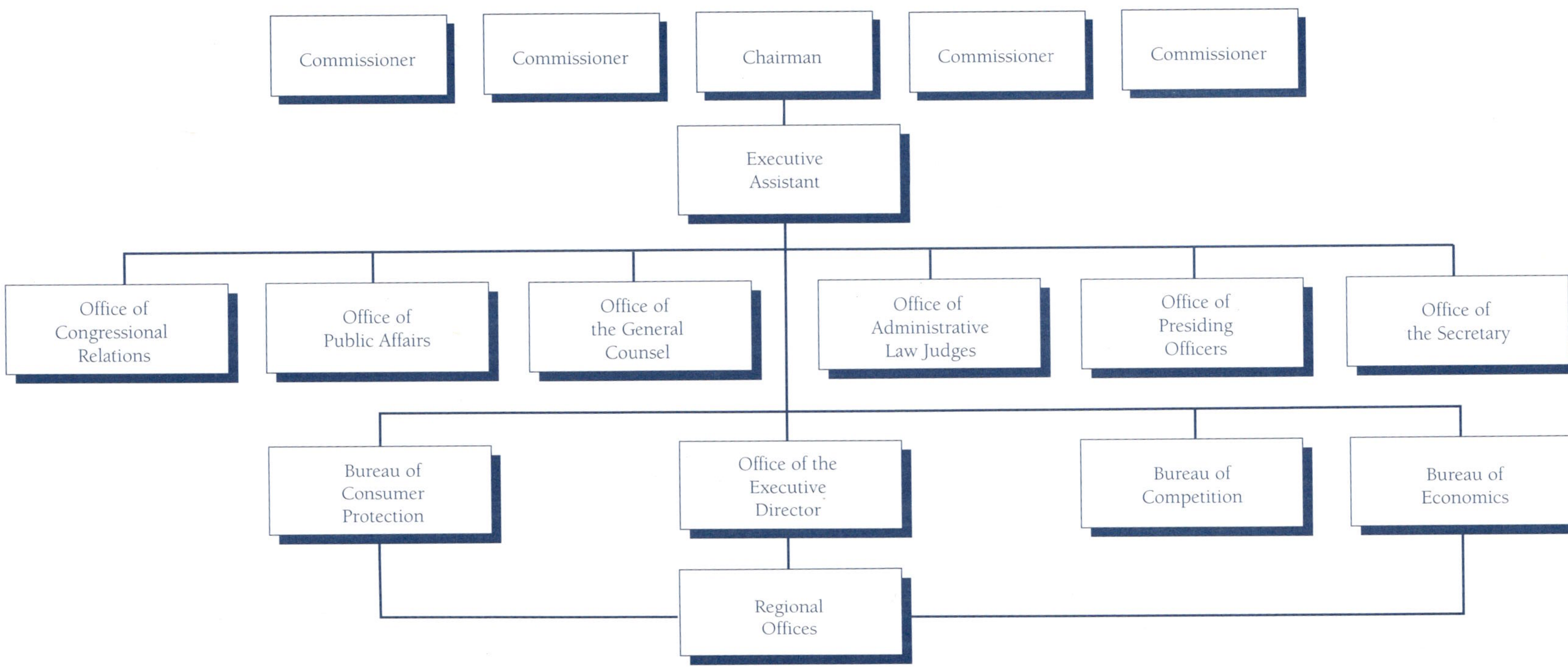

FIGURE 12-2

FTC's Powers under Consumer Protection Laws

Act	Purpose
Federal Trade Commission Act, 1914	Prohibits unfair or deceptive trade practices
Wheeler-Lea Act, 1938	Prohibits deceptive advertising
Truth-in-Lending Act, 1968	Regulates creditor advertising and the disclosure of credit terms
Fair Credit Reporting Act, 1970	Regulates contents and provisions of credit history reports
Equal Credit Opportunity Act, 1975	Prohibits discrimination in the extension of consumer credit
Fair Credit Billing Act, 1975	Prescribes procedures for billing debtors
Magnuson-Moss Warranty Act, 1975	Regulates warranties on consumer goods
Fair Debt Collection Practices Act, 1978	Prohibits deceptive and abusive debt collection practices
Electronic Funds Transfer Act, 1978	Requires disclosure of EFT transactions and processes; provides for detection and correction of errors
Fair Credit and Charge Card Disclosure Act, 1988	Requires disclosure of credit card account terms
Home Equity Loan Consumer Protection Act, 1988	Requires disclosure of home equity loan terms

FTC Powers

The FTC exercises several powers that facilitate the enforcement of the consumer protections laws. The FTC defines unfair and deceptive trade practices by issuing *trade regulation rules,* which have the force of law. These rules prohibit deceptive activity in one or more industries. For example, there are trade regulation rules that address abuses in door-to-door sales, bait and switch sales tactics, direct marketing schemes, and used car sales. The FTC also may issue *advisory opinions* to individual firms seeking to avoid charges of unfair or deceptive trade practices in their proposed activities. More comprehensive advice is sometimes available through *industry guides* addressing the trade practices of an entire industry. Although FTC advisory opinions and industry guides do not bind the courts, there is often deference given to the FTC's expertise. Of course, these policy statements may be amended later by the FTC itself.

Some industries, such as public utilities and the securities industries, are exempt from FTC regulation because they are regulated by another federal, state, or local agency. A few industries, such as food and consumer credit, are regulated by both the FTC and another agency. For example, the FTC and the Food and Drug Administration (FDA) have overlapping jurisdiction over food labeling and ads. The two agencies are beginning to cooperate to avoid costly and conflicting regulations. The FTC can share its investigatory files with other agencies such as to alert the Justice Department (DOJ) to prosecute a criminal violation.

FTC investigations and enforcement actions are initiated after complaints are made from consumers, business competitors, administrative agencies, or Congress. The FTC also initiates its own investigations. The FTC's Bureau of Consumer Protection monitors consumer sales practices to obtain evidence of potential violations. The FTC may then conduct an investigation and gather sufficient evidence to bring an enforcement action. The FTC may issue *cease and desist orders* or settle charges with *consent decrees,* without going to trial. In a consent decree the defendant usually agrees to eliminate the deception.

The FTC may also issue an *affirmative disclosure order,* requiring an offender to provide information in future advertisements. A *corrective advertising order* may be issued to require new advertisements to correct past misleading advertisements. A *multiple product order* prohibits future deceptive advertising by a firm with a history of false advertising in selling any of its numerous products. The FTC has also successfully sought rescission of contracts, returns of property, refunds of the consumer's purchase price, and damage payments to consumers. In one case, the FTC settled charges of false ad claims by requiring a health product retailer to fund health research.

If the business under investigation disputes the charges, an administrative hearing may be held before an administrative law judge (ALJ). Appeals from the ALJ's decision go to the commission and then to the U.S. Circuit Courts of Appeals for judicial review. Violators of FTC regulations or cease and desist orders may be fined up to $10,000 per violation per day. Although the FTC's powers are generally intended to be preventative, the power to fine can add up. For example, *Reader's Digest* was fined $7.75 million for violating an FTC order.[1] However, a 1994 report indicates that since 1980 the FTC has collected only about one-third of the nearly $363,000,000 in fines for advertising or marketing fraud it has levied on 187 companies.

ETHICAL DILEMMAS IN CONSUMER PROTECTION

ETHICAL DILEMMA

Consumer activist groups view product marketing as involving excessive sales pressure and some unfair practices. When goods are oversold, there may be evidence of unethical conduct. The ethical dilemma presented is whether the selling organization, individual salesperson, or advertising consultant has made a conscious decision to mislead prospective purchasers. Unethical conduct arises when a sales presentation or an advertisement makes untrue, fraudulent, or exaggerated claims. Misrepresentations or intentional fraud may appear in documents, sales literature, catalogs, price lists, allegedly "certified" test results, testimonials, advertising, or verbal sales talk provided by the seller or made in response to the buyer's inquiry.

Even where there is no misrepresentation during contracting, a transaction may be viewed as unethical during its performance. The conscious delivery of poor quality goods or goods unsuitable for the buyer is unethical unless the seller notifies the buyer that the substandard delivery is an accommodation. Unfair advantage taken of uneducated consumers is also unethical. Telemarketing fraud is practiced increasingly on the elderly, who are often considered vulnerable to exaggerated claims. As of this writing, the FTC is drafting new telemarketing regulations mandated by a new telemarketing fraud law passed by Congress in 1994. Nevertheless, too few people consciously follow the old adage: If it's too good to be true, it probably is.

[1] *United States v. Reader's Digest Ass'n, Inc.,* 662 F.2d 995 (3d Cir. 1981).

Advertising Regulation

The advertising of consumer products has contributed to the tremendous industrial expansion of the 20th century. A legitimate function of advertising is to inform consumers and eliminate information asymmetries. The legitimacy of advertising and promotional activities declines when it becomes deceptive, when false statements are made, or when misleading practices are used. As introduced in Chapter 5, the U.S. Constitution protects free speech against government censorship. However, there are some limited, permissible restraints on speech that is defamatory, fraudulent, subversive, or that incites riots. Restraint is also permissible when it is essentially related to a compelling governmental purpose. Although political speech is given the greatest protection, *commercial speech* is well protected because information is essential to the efficient operation of markets. Advertising is commercial speech that is regulated under the common law of contracts and under the FTC's consumer protection regulatory scheme.

Common Law Remedies

Although the common law provides remedies for victims of deceptive advertising, they are generally ineffective. Chapter 9 and 10 noted that since the buyer is usually considered an offeror under contract law, the seller's advertisement is seldom treated as an offer. If the product's actual specifications or its price at the store is different from the advertised specifications or price, there is no breach of contract because no enforceable contract yet exists. The warranty liability discussed in Chapter 11 may arise from advertising and other language in the sales materials or contract. Such warranties may form the basis for a consumer's complaint about deception.

The tort of deceit or fraud may exist if an advertiser knowingly makes material misrepresentations of fact on which an injured purchaser justifiably relies. Protection of trademarks and trade names exist under both common law and federal statutes. If an advertiser makes untrue statements in comparing its goods with the goods of a competitor, the defamed competitor may sue for trade libel, slander, or disparagement.

Deceptive Advertising

deceptive advertising Illegal advertising under the Wheeler-Lea Act if capable of deceiving the typical ordinary consumer.

Congress found these common law remedies were ineffective to protect consumers, so it passed the Wheeler-Lea Act in 1938 to deal with **deceptive advertising.** The FTC is authorized to prosecute unfair or deceptive trade practices in advertising. To measure deception, the FTC uses a deception policy that requires assessment of ads by the total impression created in the consumer's mind. To be deceptive, an ad must make a *misrepresentation or omission* in communications with consumers. The misleading statement need only have a capacity to mislead consumers about some *material* aspect of the product. This test is interpreted in a reasonable manner by a hypothetical "*typical ordinary consumer* . . . who is *acting reasonably under the circumstances*." It is not necessary to prove either that the advertiser intended to deceive or that actual deception occurred. However, the deceptiveness must be so strong that a reasonable person, not a gullible one, would be deceived. Courts have admitted survey evidence to show how a reasonable consumer might interpret an ad. All states have false advertising statutes largely patterned on the FTC's powers. With over $100 billion spent annually on advertising, the FTC and states face a big challenge in regulating deception.

Ethical Dilemmas in Advertising

Ethical Dilemma

If advertising creates demand and additional use of some dangerous products or exposure to them increases accidents, safety may be enhanced by restricting the advertising. This type of ethical dilemma has been reduced somewhat for sellers of guns, cigarettes, and alcohol because their advertising is restricted. Some groups believe promoting dangerous products is unethical, such as ads for three-wheel, all-terrain vehicles or ads showing the glamour of smoking or drinking.

Children are a particularly vulnerable audience for certain types of advertising. The use of hero advertising and the merging of children's programming into advertising also pose ethical dilemmas. The private regulation television code encourages broadcasters to use clear transitions between children's shows and ads to weaken the influence of hero advertising. Advertisers must carefully consider how the audience will receive the advertising claims or the lifestyle and activities presented. An ethical dilemma is presented by advertisements that overreach the consumer's ability to appreciate the risks, costs, or utility of a product.

False or Unsubstantiated Claims Ads are deceptive if patently false or if the claims are not supported by a reasonable basis in scientific evidence. Demonstrations must accurately depict the performance of the product advertised and must illustrate some relevant or meaningful attribute. Test results that create the impression of the product's superiority must be based on studies or surveys with a scientific basis. This means clinical tests must be well controlled and use reasonable statistical inference. This *prior substantiation* rule requires that the evidence used in an ad must be gathered before the ads are run. FTC enforcement can require advertisers to submit substantiation at any time.

Product performance claims about composition, durability, capacity, or endurance under adverse conditions must be true. For example, a dishwasher retailer was ordered to cease and desist from claiming that no prewashing was necessary.[2] Numerous sellers of nutritional and health products have been ordered to stop advertising false or unsubstantiated health improvement claims. Kraft was ordered to discontinue ads falsely suggesting its cheese slices had the same calcium content as five ounces of milk. Haagen-Dazs agreed to refrain from advertising its frozen yogurt bars were 98 percent fat free because several flavors allegedly contained over 2 percent fat, some averaging 8 to 12 grams of fat per serving.[3] The FTC prohibited Stouffer Foods from falsely advertising that Lean Cuisine was low in sodium.[4] The FTC order required Stouffer to compare its sodium content to established public guidelines for "low sodium" and the FDA's "recommended daily allowances (RDA)." Now these are called "daily values."

The so-called green ads targeting environmentally conscious consumers are susceptible to abuse. The FTC issued voluntary environmental advertising guidelines in 1992 urging that claims be true and that meaningless claims not be made. In one FTC case, the manufacturer of a spray product containing an ozone-depleting propellant was ordered to stop claiming it was environmentally safe. The manufacturer of a gasoline additive was ordered to stop claiming fuel economy improvements of "up to 15 percent" without significant evidence that consumers could regularly achieve such performance.

---

[2] *Sears, Roebuck & Co., v. FTC,* 676 F.2d 385 (9th Cir. 1982).

[3] *In re Haagen-Dazs Co., Inc.,* FTC File 942-3028 (Nov. 7, 1994).

[4] *Stouffer Foods Corp.,* FTC Docket 9250 (Aug. 6, 1993).

Consumers in many nations have nationalistic pride that encourages the purchase of domestic products. For example, the South Koreans are actively discouraged from buying "luxury goods" produced abroad. Many U.S. manufacturers and retailers encourage consumers to "Buy American" or claim their goods are made in the United States. This has raised questions about the "domestic content" of goods. Wal-Mart's Made in the USA advertising program was subjected to a national TV news magazine probe after the discovery that much of Wal-Mart's apparel was foreign made. Other products touted as made in America are often just assembled in the United States from foreign-made components. This could become a problem for manufacturers of sneakers and computers. Most automobiles made by the big-three U.S. manufacturers have at least some foreign content, and many are assembled in Canada or Mexico. The increasing globalization of the market may eventually curtail such strong claims of domestic source. Some laws have passed that arbitrarily set minimum measures for the "domestic value added" of goods with foreign content. This would then permit ads claiming "Made in the USA."

Puffing A seller's opinion or generalized commendation of value is not a misrepresentation under contract law (Chapter 8), nor does it form the basis for an express warranty (Chapter 10) under the current UCC Article 2. Puffing in ads is not generally considered deceptive by the FTC unless accompanied by more concrete but false statements about the product's characteristics or performance. Obviously false and exaggerated ad claims may not be illegal as puffing if reasonable consumers could easily see the statement is hyperbole—for example, "faster than lightening."

Mock-Ups A *mock-up* is a false demonstration to improve an ad's appearance or effect. The mock-up is deceptive if the viewer believes it represents the real thing. A mock-up that fails to disclose important facts or clearly acknowledge that the demonstration is not genuine is an unfair or deceptive practice. For example, Volvo's ad agency chose to tout the structural integrity and crashworthiness of Volvo cars in a mock-up of a car crushing event. The ad showed a Volvo surviving uncrushed as it was driven over by a "big-wheel" four-wheel drive vehicle, while other brands were crushed. Volvo's ad agency could have cited extensive valid scientific evidence of the Volvo's safety. However, the agency decided the repeated trials necessary to adequately catch the event on film would eventually crush even the Volvo. Volvo fired the ad agency when it was discovered that the Volvo in the film had been extensively reinforced to survive the many film "takes" necessary to shoot a successful commercial. This ad was a mock-up because viewers were led to believe the Volvo in the ad was standard.

Colgate-Palmolive used a series of one-minute commercials allegedly showing Rapid Shave enabling a razor to "cut right through this tough, dry sandpaper." Actually, a mock-up was used in which loose sand was applied to Plexiglas. Real sandpaper would require 80 minutes of soaking with shaving cream to soften enough to be shaved as shown. The U.S. Supreme Court acknowledged the FTC's expertise in determining the deceptiveness of ads and held: "We think it inconceivable that the ingenious advertising world would be unable to conform to the FTC's insistence that the public be not misinformed."[5]

Omissions and Half-Truths Advertisers must also refrain from deception masked with some truth that omits facts necessary for clarification. An *omission* or *half-truth* is

---

[5] *FTC v. Colgate-Palmolive Co.,* 380 U.S. 374 (1965).

deceptive if more information is necessary to keep the ad from being misleading. For example, the selective use of data, comments, or conclusions from scientific studies may be deceptive half-truths. The FTC ordered P. Lorillard to stop advertising that Old Gold cigarettes were lower in tar and nicotine than the six leading brands because the differences were statistically negligible. The ads cited selective data from a *Reader's Digest* article concluding that Old Gold's lower tar and nicotine content was not meaningful for smokers' health. Only the article's most favorable portion was extracted, whereas the more negative conclusion was omitted, creating an "entirely false and misleading impression" in the ad about the article's content and Old Gold's health impact.[6]

In some ads, a false impression is created about the seller's credentials, which is also a misleading omission.[7] For example, persons falsely appearing in ads as scientists or medical doctors are misleading half-truths. Misleading health claims can emerge from literal truths that withhold other important information. For example, the ad for a water purification device claimed to remove several contaminants but failed to mention it added another potentially hazardous chemical. Food ads claiming health benefits such as reduced heart disease from a product's low-fat or low-cholesterol content are misleading if the product contains high sodium content, which is directly connected to heart disease.

Endorsements The FTC has issued several guidelines for endorsements. Endorsements by sports figures, celebrities, or experts, such as those found in shaving, beer, and medical insurance commercials, should reflect the actual opinions of these persons. An advertiser may use such an endorsement only if the celebrity actually uses the product. Ads appearing to be the endorsements of actual consumers must use consumers, not actors. By contrast, fictional dramatizations without endorsements may use unknown actors, so their heartfelt opinion or actual use is unnecessary. Many responsible advertisers use disclaimers indicating the commercial is a fictional dramatization. False endorsements may trigger liability for fraud for the advertiser and for the celebrity.

Corrective Advertisements When an advertiser makes misstatements in advertisements, the FTC assumes that the misconception will remain in the consumer's mind. Only further advertising of a similar magnitude, duration, and creativity can correct such "durable" false impressions from prior false ads. In some cases, a court-approved consent decree requires the advertiser to conduct **corrective advertising** that rebuts the misleading claims of prior ads. The FTC has used corrective advertising orders since the well-known Listerine case in which Warner-Lambert was ordered to conduct $10 million of new ads correcting its former claims that Listerine killed millions of "germs." The germs Listerine eliminated did not cause colds even though reasonable consumers might interpret this from the ads. The U.S. Circuit Court of Appeals dismissed Warner-Lambert's challenge to the FTC's power to order a corrective ad stating: "Contrary to our prior advertising, Listerine will not help prevent colds or sore throats or lessen their severity."[8] Another manufacturer was ordered to run corrective ads for a year admitting its products were not superior insulation to regular glass storm windows.

corrective advertising FTC remedy requiring ads to undo misimpression from former ads.

[6] *P. Lorillard v. FTC,* 186 F.2d 52 (4th Cir. 1950).
[7] *Erickson v. FTC,* 272 F.2d 385 (7th Cir. 1959).
[8] *Warner-Lambert Co. v. FTC,* 562 F.2d 749 (D.C. Cir. 1977).

FTC Corrective Advertising Standard

> [I]f a deceptive advertisement has played a substantial role in creating or reinforcing in the public's mind a false and material belief that lives on after the false advertising ceases, there is clear and continuing injury to competition and to the consuming public as consumers continue to make purchasing decisions based on the false belief. Since this belief cannot be averted by merely requiring respondent to cease disseminating the advertisement, we may appropriately order respondent to take affirmative action designed to terminate the otherwise ill effects of the advertisement.

Comparative Ads and the Lanham Act The FTC favors the recent trend toward scientifically verifiable comparative advertising because it encourages competition. The "Pepsi Challenge" blind taste tests use large random samples performed nationwide by independent testing agents, so these comparisons showing consumer preference are scientifically valid. However, invalid comparisons may be false and deceptive, exposing the advertiser to damages under the common law tort of trade disparagement and for lost profits under §43(a) of the Lanham Act, the federal trademark registration statute. The disparaged competitor may sue if the comparison makes false or misleading statements of fact or misrepresentations about the nature, characteristics, geographic origin, or quality of a competitor's products, services, or commercial activities. The false statement must have a tendency to deceive a substantial segment of the intended audience, it must influence purchasing decisions, and it must be likely to injure the disparaged trademarked product.

Lanham Act comparative ad cases illustrate a false advertiser is subject to suit even if the competitor's precise product is not directly identified in the ad. It is enough that the advertiser misleads consumers about important features, such as a computer monitor's compatibility with a new video standard.[9] Comparison advertising was long condemned by most U.S. businesses as ultimately harmful to their industries. However, comparative ads are appearing with greater frequency, particularly as consumer surveys proliferate from independent research firms. Japanese businesses still avoid active comparison ads because they are believed to disturb the traditional appearance of industrial harmony so important in Japanese culture.

International Perspective and Commentary

International Perspective on Ad Regulation

The regulation of advertising varies considerably among nations. The United States is generally among the most strict. The huge size of the U.S. market, the broad diversity of products available, and the much larger marketing budgets bring about generally more marketing experimentation in the United States than in most other nations. Many deceptive marketing practices are devised in the United States long before the same products, marketing channels, or promotional devices are known in most other nations. However, several northern European nations also have strict ad regulations. The standard in the United Kingdom is somewhat less stringent, holding ads illegal if a product is misrepresented. Government nonintervention in

[9] *Princeton Graphics v. NEC Home Electronics,* 732 F. Supp. 1258 (S.D.N.Y. 1990).

many developing nations may actually indulge misleading advertisers. As advertising becomes even more important in other nations, their ad regulations can be expected to follow the U.S. lead, at least to some extent.

Packaging and Labeling

Congress has passed numerous consumer protection laws directly regulating product packaging and labeling. The Fair Packaging and Labeling Act of 1966 provides for general labeling requirements. As increased packaging obscures the consumer's actual view of the product, accurate label descriptions become increasingly important for product evaluation. Labels must (1) identify the product, (2) identify the name and address of the manufacturer, packer, or distributor, and (3) list the quantity and, if a food product, serving size in a specific manner. FTC rules require particular labeling of numerous diverse products. For example, accurate octane numbers must appear on gasoline pumps. There are numerous additional federal and state labeling laws regulating wool products, cigarettes, flammable fabrics, textiles, poisons, food, drugs, and cosmetics. Some are discussed later in this chapter. Many of these laws empower various agencies to regulate labeling or deceptive practices.

Ethical Dilemmas in Product Labeling

Ethical Dilemma

Recent trends toward better nutrition have generated a flurry of new and repackaged foods and nutritional products. Unfortunately, some food producers began pandering to the public's newfound obsession with healthy eating by taking advantage of consumers' limited nutrition knowledge. Many undertook large-scale advertising that made exaggerated claims of product performance and confused consumers. Such activities pose ethical dilemmas when advertisers misinform consumers by preying on their fears of ill health, their prejudices about body image, and their ignorance about nutrition. The FDA, which monitors unfair and deceptive trade practices in marketing food, drugs, and nutritional products, suddenly became more active regulators in the early 1990s. The FDA now more closely scrutinizes product claims about food content, product descriptors such as *diet, light, fresh, natural,* and *low-fat,* and fad diets.

The promotion of some products as having no cholesterol or low cholesterol falsely suggest that similar products from other manufacturers do contain cholesterol. For example, no major national brand of peanut butter contains cholesterol. There is no cholesterol in peanuts, and no domestic producers add cholesterol-laden lard to peanut butter as they did in the past. Even when factual, a producer's claim of low cholesterol may be an unethical half-truth. High blood cholesterol levels are more closely linked to eating foods high in saturated fat than simply in eating foods high in cholesterol. Similar ethical abuses occur with the use of terms such as *biodegradable* and *recyclable,* which have unclear meanings. Products may decompose very slowly or be difficult to reprocess. For example, composite materials, such as the aluminum foil and plastic used in some juice boxes, are difficult to separate for recycling.

Health claims that products contain lower amounts of suspected unhealthy substances can also be misleading because the comparative descriptors *diet, lower,* or *light* have no meaning except when compared with similar foods that regularly contain more of that substance. For example, the term *light beer* is meaningless unless it contains significantly fewer calories than some average beer. *Light* can also be understood as suggesting lighter flavor, smell, or color.

The FDA has responded to this perceived unethical behavior by requiring more accurate and meaningful nutritional labeling. These rules permit the use of such terms only if accurate comparisons are made or when the descriptor has a legal definition. For example, "low-cal" foods must contain less than 40 calories per serving; "sodium-free" products must contain less than 5 milligrams per serving; "sugar-free" foods must contain less than .5 gram per serving; "reduced-fat" foods may contain no more than half the fat of an identified comparison item. Foods advertised as "high" in some substance must contain 20 percent more per serving of the substance than the recommended daily intake.

Trade Regulation Rules and Deceptive Trade Practices

The FTC may use the notice and comment rulemaking procedure to issue consumer protection regulations. As discussed in Chapter 6, proposed regulations are first published in the *Federal Register.* Affected parties may comment, and the final rule has the force of law. The next sections discuss some of the more significant FTC trade regulation rules issued under §18 of the FTC Act and deceptive practices challenged under §5.

Holder-in-Due-Course Rule

Recall the discussion of UCC Article 3 in Chapter 10. It creates a special rule for persons taking a negotiable check or a promissory note by negotiation, delivery, and/or endorsement, from another. Even if defective goods are purchased by the buyer-debtor who wrote the check or note, the buyer cannot withhold payment if the seller negotiated the paper to a transferee. For example, after a consumer purchases a refrigerator, paying with proceeds from an installment loan, the seller will probably assign (sell) the loan contract (promissory note) to a finance company. If the refrigerator is defective, UCC Article 3 prohibits the consumer from stopping payments as pressure on the seller to fix or replace it. When the finance company purchases the note, it acquires a special legal status as a *holder in due course (HDC)* and may demand payment from the consumer. The HDC rule makes negotiable instrument and commercial paper use more reliable by encouraging financial institutions to regard checks and notes as the "equivalent of cash." Purchasers of checks and notes more readily accept negotiable instruments knowing the seller's breach or defective goods does not affect the right to collect.

The FTC issued a regulation in 1976 suspending the HDC rule for individual consumer purchases or leases of goods and services. This rule requires that any consumer credit contract must contain a boldface clause permitting the consumer to stop paying on debts if the seller committed fraud or breached the contract, or if the goods are defective.

FTC Holder-in-Due-Course Rule Disclosure

NOTICE: ANY HOLDER OF THIS CONSUMER CREDIT CONTRACT IS SUBJECT TO ALL CLAIMS AND DEFENSES WHICH THE DEBTOR COULD ASSERT AGAINST THE SELLER OF THE GOODS OR SERVICES OBTAINED PURSUANT HERETO OR WITH THE PROCEEDS HEREOF.

Purchases made on credit cards are still subject to the special protections given endorsees under the HDC rule. If consumer goods are purchased on a credit card, the loan balance must still be paid off. The consumer must settle any disputes over the defective goods directly with the seller without stopping payment unless the purchase is made within 50 miles of the consumer's home.

Bait and Switch

Some sellers stock a limited supply of inexpensive "loss leader" merchandise as "bait" to lure potential buyers into the store, intending that sales personnel can "switch" them into purchasing more expensive products. This **bait and switch** tactic violates FTC guidelines if a salesperson refuses to show the cheaper merchandise, represents that the bait will be out of stock for a long time, holds an inadequate supply of the bait, or is following instructions to actively switch customers to alternative goods. For example, it is illegal to advertise an inexpensive color TV when insufficient inventory is available and salespeople are instructed to encourage buyers to switch to more expensive models. Ads for cheap eyeglass frames often result in purchases of more expensive, "designer" frames.

bait and switch Deceptive trade practice by seller of placing ads for inexpensive "bait" while intending to "switch" consumers to higher-profit merchandise.

Direct Marketing/Mail Order

The FTC has a *30-day rule* for mail orders, prohibiting sellers from soliciting orders unless the goods can be shipped within 30 days after receiving a prepaid order. Sellers cannot sit on orders, must clearly state expected shipping dates, and must ship promptly. If there are unanticipated delays, the seller may (1) cancel orders and refund payments or (2) notify consumers of the delay and provide an option of shipment or cancellation. High-quality mail-order retailers wait until shipment to charge customers' credit cards, notify customers of their order's status, and remind customers of their alternatives. Many states impose similar mail-order rules.

Door-to-Door Sales

The FTC imposes a *cooling-off period* for door-to-door sales, giving consumers an opportunity to reassess purchases for three days following sales over $25. The rule counteracts the high-pressure tactics often used to sell such merchandise as vacuum cleaners or encyclopedias. Door-to-door sales contracts must tell the buyer that the cancellation right exists and provide a cancellation form. Several types of sales are exempt: real estate, insurance, securities or commodities from a registered broker, and most sales solicited by the buyer. Some state antideception laws apply to door-to-door sales, including some of those exempt under the FTC rule.

Other Trade Regulations

There are several other FTC trade regulations. A used car rule requires a window sticker or buyer's guide on used cars that clearly states the warranties; whether the car is being sold "as is"; estimated repair costs after the sale; suggests an independent mechanical inspection; and reminds consumers that the dealer's oral promises are difficult to prove. The insulation rule requires standardized testing and disclosure of home insulation "R-value" to facilitate comparison shopping. The funeral rule recognizes that consumers are seldom careful comparison shoppers when confronting a funeral. The FTC Funeral Guide requires itemized price lists and the publication of consumer information about various funeral services. Other rules have addressed unfair and deceptive trade practices in the following industries: correspondence schools, hearing aid sales, automobile repairs and estimates, entertainment clubs, health spas, dance studios, insurance, and home improvement. Medical services are under investigation at this writing. For example, there is evidence that excessive and often unnecessary hysterectomies are performed. The FTC is investigating the possibly excessive marketing by ophthalmologists of radial keratotomies, a correction of nearsightedness in which tiny slits are made to flatten the cornea. The procedure has risks many doctors apparently do not disclose and is considered cosmetic because eyeglasses and contacts also correct nearsightedness. Most patients personally pay for radial keratotomies because they are not covered by most insurance plans.

The FTC's early cases focused mostly on "deceptive" trade practices. Increasingly, it also focuses on unfairness (defined as immoral, unethical, oppressive, or unscrupulous activity violating fairness and causing substantial consumer injury). Later refinements to *unfairness* include conduct causing substantial and unavoidable consumer injury not outweighed by consumer benefits or the competition. Is it unfair to raise a fixed fee originally stated in a consumer contract? Unfairness is illustrated in the following case.

Orkin Exterminating Co. v. F.T.C.

849 F. 2d 1354 (11th Cir. 1988)
United States Court of Appeals

Orkin offered lifetime continuous protection guarantees on termite extermination services it provided to over 200,000 customers. For a fixed annual fee, these customers could have their homes re-treated if the home was ever reinfestated. Orkin discovered it was losing money on retreatments, so it raised the annual fees by approximately 40 percent. Orkin's sales personnel pretended there was a billing error if any surprised customers complained that the price was already fixed in their contracts. The FTC issued a cease and desist order to Orkin, and Orkin appealed, claiming the FTC exceeded its §5 authority. FTC precedents had applied only the deception standard, not the unfairness standard it now applied to Orkin.

Clark, Judge

We must decide whether the Commission exceeded its authority in deciding that one company's unilateral breach of over 207,000 consumer contracts could meet the Commission's definition of unfairness. The policy statement's consumer injury standard was the focus of its analysis. The unfairness standard requires a finding of substantial injury to consumers. "The harm resulting from Orkin's conduct consists of increased costs for services previously bargained for and includes the intangible loss of the certainty of the fixed price term in the contract." The Commission's finding of "substantial" injury is supported by undisputed fact that Orkin's breach generated more than $7,000,000 in revenues from renewal fees to which the Company was not entitled. Although the actual injury to individual customers may be small on an annual basis, this does not mean such injury is not "substantial." Because the "increase in the fee was not accompanied by an increase in the level of service provided or enhancement of its quality," no consumer benefit had resulted from

Orkin's conduct. Customers could not have reasonably avoided the harm caused by Orkin's conduct. The Commission generally relies on free and informed consumer choice as the best regulator of the market.

Nothing indicates that the Commission did anything other than that which it purported to do: apply the unfairness standard contained in its Policy Statement. The Commission's conclusion was simply that it was an "unfair" practice to breach over 200,000 contracts. We think that this was a reasonable application of the Commission's unfairness standard. Section 5 by its very terms makes deceptive and unfair practices distinct lines of inquiry. While a practice may be both deceptive and unfair, it may be unfair without being deceptive. The Commission's policy statement assumes the unfairness doctrine differs from, and supplements, the prohibition against deception. For the foregoing reasons, we affirm the Commission's cease and desist order.

Case Questions

1. What is the issue in "unfairness" in FTC enforcement actions under §5?
2. What is the future impact of an agency's prior enforcement interpretations?
3. Is breach of contract a sufficient alternative basis for a finding of "unfairness"? What additional evidence might be necessary?

State Laws Prohibiting Unfair Competition

States have legislation paralleling the FTC Act, the so-called *Mini-FTC Acts.* These laws typically empower the state attorney general or a special administrative agency to enforce prohibitions against unfair and deceptive trade practices and unfair methods of competition. Several states permit private rights of action by consumers for damages, treble damages, punitive damages, attorney's fees, injunctions, rescission of contracts, and class action suits. Attorneys general may seek injunctions, restitution, civil penalties, criminal punishment, and other remedies. One of the most notable developments in the 1980s was the coordination of enforcement efforts by various states' attorneys general through their National Association of Attorneys General organization. Various other state statutes regulate particular aspects of consumer fraud such as lemon laws, door-to-door sales, and use of plain English in insurance contracts. Business must remain aware of this expanding area of federal and state consumer protection.

Consumer Financing

There is such a widespread use of consumer credit in the United States that it can be difficult to rent a car or hotel room without using a credit card. An increase in loan defaults has accompanied the 1980s debt binge and the 1990s restructuring layoffs. This makes it important to discusses the laws administered by the FTC which amended the Consumer Credit Protection Act. These laws are intended to curb abuses in extending consumer credit and reporting and collecting loans.

Consumer Credit Protection

The 1968 Truth-in-Lending Act (TILA) is the basic component of the Consumer Credit Protection Act. It was designed to facilitate the consumer's comparison of creditors' loan terms and thereby encourage competition among lenders. The Fair Credit Reporting Act, requiring consumer credit reports to contain accurate information, was added in 1970. The Fair Credit Billing Act, added in 1975, requires accuracy in consumer credit billings. The Equal Credit Opportunity Act of 1975 prohibits making discriminatory credit decisions. The Fair Debt Collection Practices Act passed in 1978 prohibited creditors from using unreasonable debt collection tactics. The 1988 Fair Credit and Charge Card Disclosure Act and the Home Equity Loan Consumer Protection Act require additional disclosures. These acts are summarized in Figure 12–2 on page 416.

Truth-in-Lending Act TILA is implemented by the Federal Reserve Board under *Regulation Z,* which requires a uniform presentation of credit terms to assist borrowers in comparing the costs of credit. Creditors must use a uniform method to compute and explain credit terms.

Creditors A *creditor* is someone who regularly extends or arranges credit for consumers. Creditors include sellers of consumer goods that hold their own accounts or who arrange the consumer's credit through creditors not regularly engaged in the consumer credit business. Thus, a Ford dealer arranging the buyer's credit through Ford Motor Company Credit Corporation is relieved from making the TILA disclosures, but Ford Motor Company Credit Corporation must make the disclosures.

Most consumer financial institutions (banks or credit unions), consumer retailers, and credit card issuers must comply. Service businesses must also make the disclosures if they regularly grant or arrange credit. For example, contractors, plumbers, lawyers, doctors, dentists, clinics, and hospitals must make disclosures as creditors under TILA.

Consumer Credit TILA requires disclosure from creditors whenever a loan is made for personal, family, or household purposes, not commercial loans. Specifically exempt are loans made to government units, businesses, corporations and broker-dealer loans to investors buying securities or commodities. The Act covers loans of less than $25,000 that are repayable in four or more installments, but no dollar limit applies to real estate loans, so disclosure is required for all consumer real estate mortgages.

annual percentage rate of interest (APR) Standardized computation of the interest cost of credit required by TILA.

Credit Term Disclosures The creditor must conspicuously disclose all the key loan terms including sale price, total of deferred payments, finance charges, and the **annual percentage rate of interest (APR).** *Finance charges* include interest, loan application fees, points, finder's fees, time/price differential, credit life insurance premiums if required by the lender, credit investigation report fees, and miscellaneous service fees. What other fees are part of finance charges? The next case shows that credit transactions not labeled as such must still comply with TILA requirements.

Joseph v. Norman's Health Clubs, Inc.

532 F. 2d 86 (8th Cir. 1976)
United States Court of Appeals, Eighth Circuit

Norman's Health Clubs sold most of its memberships on installment terms. The lifetime memberships cost $360, payable in 24 equal monthly installments, though a few were sold for cash at a discount of between 24 and 46 percent. The customers choosing installments signed a note that Norman's resold at a discount to finance companies, which sent members coupon books for making payments directly to them. This posed the question whether these contracts were actually consumer credit.

Lay, Circuit Judge

The fundamental purpose of the Truth-in-Lending Act is to require creditors to disclose the "true" cost of consumer credit, so that consumers can make informed choices among available methods of payment.

The Act was intended to change the practices of the consumer credit industry, and the statute reflects Congress' view that this should be done by imposing disclosure requirements on those who "regularly" extend or offer to extend consumer credit. In interpreting the Act, the Federal Reserve Board and the majority of courts have focused on the substance, rather than the form, of credit transactions, and have looked to the practices of the trade, the course of dealing of the parties, and the intention of the parties in addition to specific contractual obligations. "Some creditors would attempt to characterize their transactions so as to fall one step outside whatever boundary Congress attempted to establish."

The finance companies operated under a definite working arrangement with the Club. The evidence discloses that (1) the finance companies were alerted almost simultaneously with the customer's execution of a note; (2) an immediate credit check was then made by the finance companies; (3) if the customer's note was accepted, the finance companies paid the Club the amount of the note less the discount; (4) the finance companies accepted assignments without recourse to the Club, thus relying solely on the customer for payment; (5) the finance companies often contacted the customer the same day and upon approving him, the companies would send out their payment book describing the manner of payment and notice of late charges (not mentioned in the note assigned); (6) the finance companies carried the note on their books as a "loan" and listed a "finance charge"; and (7) thereafter, the finance companies treated the club member in the same manner as they did their direct consumer loan customers. The situation was no different than if the finance companies had gone to the Club with the prospective member, paid the Club for the membership and then taken the customer's note just as they did take it. The Act defines "finance charge" as:

> the sum of *all* charges, payable directly or *indirectly by the person to whom the credit is extended,* and imposed directly or *indirectly* by the creditor as an incident to the extension of credit, including . . . any amount payable under a . . . discount . . . system.

"Finance charge" under TILA was intended to include not only "interest" but many other charges for credit.

All of the discount originally agreed upon by the Club and the finance companies was passed along to the customers as a charge for use of credit. It may be, however, that some portion of the subsequent increases in the discount was not passed along to the customers and was rather absorbed by the Club as a reduction in its profit. On the other hand, adding more members may have permitted the seller to so reduce cost per member that it could provide the same services without increasing the face amount of the note. [TILA disclosure must be made by finance companies.]

Case Questions

1. What is the reasoning in applying TILA to finance companies?
2. How would disclosure of the credit terms indicate remove ambiguity in the real cost of the installment contracts here?

Advertised loan terms must be typical of the credit transactions that the lender makes regularly. For example, most 48-month loans have a higher interest rate than 12-month loans. If most borrowers use 48-month loans, then the 12-month loan is not "typical" and should not be the one advertised. All loan terms must be conspicuously indicated if any one loan term is advertised (e.g., interest rate) This itemized information, illustrated in Figure 12–3, permits easier credit comparison shopping.

The Home Equity Loan Consumer Protection Act passed in 1988 because of expansion in the market for home equity loans (second mortgages). Disclosures required are more extensive than for most other loans. For example, more detail is needed about the APR (fixed- or variable-rate terms), additional fees and repayment options must be clearly stated, and advertising standards must be observed. The Act

FIGURE 12-3 Sample Truth-in-Lending Disclosure

Big Wheel Auto Alice Green

ANNUAL PERCENTAGE RATE The cost of your credit as a yearly rate.	FINANCE CHARGE The dollar amount the credit will cost you.	Amount Financed The amount of credit provided to you or on your behalf.	Total of Payments The amount you will have paid after you have made all payments as scheduled.	Total Sale Price The total cost of your purchase on credit, including your downpayment of $ 1500–
14.84 %	$ 1496.80	$ 6187.50	$ 7604.30	$ 9124.30

You have the right to receive at this time an itemization of the Amount Financed.
☐ I want an itemization. ☒ I do not want an itemization.

Your payment schedule will be:

Number of payments	Amount of Payments	When Payments Are Due
36	$211.23	Monthly beginning 6-1-81

Insurance
Credit life insurance and credit disability insurance are not required to obtain credit, and will not be provided unless you sign and agree to pay the additional cost.

Type	Premium	Signature
Credit Life	$120	I want credit life insurance. Signature Alice Green
Credit Disability		I want credit disability insurance. Signature
Credit Life and Disability		I want credit life and disability insurance. Signature

Security: You are giving a security interest in:
☒ the goods being purchased.
☐ __________

Filing fees $ 12.50 Non-filing insurance $ ______

Late Charge: If a payment is late, you will be charged $10.

Prepayment: If you pay off early, you
☐ may ☐ will not have to pay a penalty.
☒ may ☐ will not be entitled to a refund of part of the finance charge.

See your contract documents for any additional information about nonpayment, default, any required repayment in full before the scheduled date, and prepayment refunds and penalties.

I have received a copy of this statement.

Alice Green 5-1-81
Signature Date

*means an estimate

prohibits (1) the use of obscure indexes in setting variable rates and (2) the lender's unilateral termination of the loan or acceleration of principal repayment unless the borrower is guilty of fraud, acts adversely affecting the collateral, or is in payment default.

Credit Cards Credit cards are a form of *open-ended credit* or *revolving charge account* covered by the Truth-in-Lending Act. Credit cards may be issued only on request or on application by the cardholder, though many credit card issuers actively solicit applications and "pre-approve" some applications. A cardholder is liable for the card's use upon accepting the card, usually by signing, using, or authorizing the card's use. TILA limits the cardholder's liability to $50 for unauthorized charges. There is no cardholder liability for unauthorized use after the card issuer is notified of the card's loss or theft. Private credit card protection services are available to insure cardholders against the potential $50 losses and promise to notify card issuers.

The Fair Credit and Charge Card Disclosure Act of 1988 added several disclosure requirements for charge card issuers. These requirements vary, depending on whether the consumer is solicited by telephone, by mail, or by a "take one" application form. When accounts are solicited by mail and variable interest rates apply, this fact, as well as how the rates are determined, must be disclosed. Membership fees, account maintenance fees, minimum finance charges, cash advance fees, late payment fees, and grace periods during which the customer may pay without additional fees must be disclosed.

The terms of open-credit accounts must be disclosed when the account is opened and periodically thereafter, usually with billing inserts. Notice must include the conditions triggering the finance charge, the balance on which charges are computed, the computation method, and the interest rate. A statement of customer rights must be provided, including the amount of the minimum payment required and a description of how additional charges or liens are incurred. Monthly or other periodic statements must disclose the amounts of balances due, finance charges, unpaid balances on which finance charges are computed, APR, and periodic (monthly) rates applied to unpaid balances. Billings must include an address for billing inquiries and state the customer's rights.

Penalties, Remedies, and Enforcement Both criminal and civil liabilities may be imposed for violations of TILA. Willful violators can be imprisoned for up to one year and fined up to $5,000. The civil liability to consumers is set at double the amount of the damage sustained ($100 minimum and $1,000 maximum) plus costs and reasonable attorney's fees. The FTC can issue cease and desist orders. Consumers are entitled to actual damages and up to twice the finance charge.

Ethical Dilemmas in Debtor–Creditor Relations

ETHICAL DILEMMA

The creditor–debtor relationship has evolved significantly over the years. Both the creditor and the debtor face ethical dilemmas in negotiating the terms of their contract, performing the debt payment, and dealing with default and collection. The costs of defaulting debtors are borne by all debtors because higher interest rates and more stringent qualification, security, and collection terms must cover default costs. Debtors act irresponsibly if they have no reasonable intention of repaying credit or if they misrepresent assets or sources of income. Is it ethical for debtors with good credit histories to pay for the expenses of defaulters through higher interest rates?

Some people view the social cost of a creditor's strict collection procedures as intrusive and unfair. If a debt is used to pay for necessities of life, it seems unfair for the creditor to repossess these necessities (home, automobile) after the debtor defaults. How should society balance the unfairness of passing the costs of default risk on to responsible debtors against society's other considerations of fairness? Creditors should continue to refine their methods of screening debtors before granting credit so that they make loans only to creditworthy debtors. A seller that grants credit to uncreditworthy individuals only to increase sales also burdens society.

Fair Credit Billing The Fair Credit Billing Act provides mechanisms to resolve billing disputes with creditors. Creditors must comply with the Act if the credit is payable in more than four installments or if a financing charge is imposed. Creditors are required to inform consumers of their rights and provide an address for billing inquiries.

The consumer may make inquiries regarding billing errors, such as incorrect amounts of improperly billed purchases. Such inquiries must be made in writing within 60 days after receipt of a disputed bill. The creditor must acknowledge an inquiry within 30 days and must explain an error within the next two billing cycles (usually two months). The error must be investigated and corrected if the consumer is correct. The debtor must be informed of the creditor's position and receive copies of documents requested.

While the parties attempt to resolve the disputed debt, the creditor may not attempt to collect the debt, threaten the debtor, make adverse credit reports about the disputed debt, or restrict or close the debtor's account. The creditor may continue to issue bills reflecting the disputed debt and may reduce the debtor's credit line by the disputed amount. The notice and delay provisions of the Act are designed to enable the debtor to respond to the creditor's actions and to encourage investigation and informal settlement. A creditor violating the Act loses the right to collect both the disputed debt and the finance charges and can be fined $50 for each disputed billing item.

Fair Credit Reporting Act Key to assuring fair credit is protecting a debtor's "good credit rating." Of course, ultimate responsibility for good credit lies with the debtor. However, many other people can affect a credit rating. There are approximately 1,900 credit reporting agencies (credit bureaus) throughout the nation which investigate, archive, and report on many personal aspects of debtors. The private services of these agencies enable creditors to evaluate the creditworthiness of loan applicants. Credit standing is also used to indicate character and general reputation in employment, bonding, and insurance decisions. The 1970 Fair Credit Reporting Act is intended to assure fairness in credit reports without unduly burdening the credit reporting system.

Credit Histories Credit reporting agencies collect information on debtors' credit history from the promptness and fullness of installment repayments on loans and credit cards. Credit reporting agencies also collect information about the reputation and character of debtors. The Act permits debtors to correct mistakes in these reports and requires the removal of obsolete information. For example, bankruptcies over 14 years old and bad debt information over 7 years old may not be reported.

Credit Reporting Agency Duties Any entity in interstate commerce that is regularly engaged in the collection or evaluation of consumer credit information provided to third parties must comply with the Act. Reports used only by the reporting agency are exempt.

Reports concerning transactions between the consumer and the reporter are not covered. Credit reporting agencies must verify accuracy of the information. If a consumer disputes information in agency files, whether or not that information has yet been reported, the agency must reinvestigate unless the consumer's dispute is frivolous. If the objectionable information is not deleted, the consumer may include a brief statement of his or her version of the dispute. For example, if two consumers have the same name, but with different spellings (e.g., Johnson vs. Johnsen), an inaccurate report might be made. Each of these consumers is permitted to include a statement in the files concerning this confusion. If adverse information on a consumer is not deleted from an agency's files, all reports on that consumer sent out from the agency must include the consumer's statement or an accurate abstract of it. The consumer may insist that the statement be given to anyone who received the adverse information within the prior two years for employment purposes or within the prior six months for other purposes.

Users Entitled to Credit Reports The customers of credit reporting agencies are usually potential creditors, insurers, or employers. Users must have legitimate purposes to request a report. Reports may be legitimately supplied pursuant to a court order, upon written request of the consumer or to any entity reasonably expected to use the reports in making decisions on such matters as (1) the granting of consumer credit, (2) the issuance of insurance policies, (3) employment, (4) the granting of governmental licenses, or (5) other legitimate purposes.

Remedies The Act and state common law provide remedies for unconscionable conduct in credit investigations. The FTC may designate particular activities of violators as unfair and deceptive trade practices or issue cease and desist orders. Users who obtain information from credit reporting agencies under false pretenses may be criminally liable. For example, falsification of the prospective debtor's authorization for request of credit information is a federal crime. Credit reporting agencies that knowingly provide information for illegitimate purposes may also be held criminally liable, with fines of up to $5,000 and/or imprisonment up to one year. Agencies that willfully or negligently violate the Act may have civil liability for actual damages, reasonable attorney's fees, and court costs. Punitive damages may be assessed for willful violations.

Credit reporting agencies may be held liable for negligence if they do not install and maintain reasonable procedures to ensure the accuracy of reports and supply the reports only for legitimate purposes. The common law torts of defamation and invasion of privacy may also be used by a damaged consumer. Users, credit reporting agencies, and those who supply inaccurate information to credit reporting agencies may be held liable for damages if the information is false or violates the right of privacy.

COMMENTARY

COMMENTARY: INTEGRITY OF PERSONAL FINANCIAL PRIVACY

Personal financial and other data about most individuals is increasingly available from confidential credit records and from publicly available court filings, mortgages, personal property liens, and other sources. Personal profiles or dossiers are regularly compiled from mailing lists, financial surveys, buying patterns, and interviews with neighbors and friends. For example, banks regularly examine the notes customers write on their checks, ask for additional numbers such as credit card, social security, driver's license, or telephone and examine customer deposits to determine income. This information is compiled to determine buying patterns and sold to information services which resell this data to marketers, lenders, employers, and others. The originating phone numbers of calls made to 800 and 900 numbers are captured and matched with reverse phone directories. Clearly this information could be used for other undisclosed purposes.

Many privacy experts believe the information explosion unduly threatens individual privacy and is not adequately addressed by consumer credit law. There is no scientific evidence linking debt repayment problems with poor job performance, yet credit reports are used increasingly in place of prohibited lie detector tests as a job screening technique. Credit reports are the number-one area of consumer complaints to the FTC. In the early 1990s, evidence surfaced that sloppy procedures at credit reporting agencies resulted in individual's records being full of inaccuracies, causing damage to their prospects for credit, insurance, licenses, and employment. The FTC and 19 states' attorneys general settled charges with TRW, the giant credit reporting agency, based on allegations it sold sensitive data to junk mailers, permitted errors to recur, and inadequately investigated customer complaints. The TRW settlement pressured the other two major credit reporting agencies, TransUnion and Equifax, to adopt similar protections or risk further federal regulation.

Proposed legislation could (1) penalize creditors who supply errors, (2) establish tougher penalties, (3) require distribution of corrected reports if employers or creditors were supplied errors, (4) require a free annual credit report to all consumers, (5) require consumer authorization for reports not used for credit, insurance, licenses, or employment, and (6) ban selling data to junk mailers. Such consumer privacy protections are unlikely to pass Congress just now. Additionally, privacy concerns will probably multiply soon, given two developments. First, the information superhighway is fast making personal information much more widely available. Unauthorized computer hackers are increasingly penetrating database security to peer into confidential personal records and even corrupt banking and financial records. Second, smart cars and smart highways are developing as part of the national *intelligent transportation system (ITS)* being promoted by state and federal transportation agencies for several purposes. ITS promises more efficient and less congested transportation. ITS may eventually eliminate road construction and maintenance costs from public budgets as users pay only for their own highway use. ITS also promises a significant increase in highway safety. Private sector participants are encouraged to invest in this infrastructure if profit opportunities arise such as to supply equipment and services to travel services. However, the ITS system will eventually permit the recording of all persons' movements and many of their activities. The potential for privacy loss from surveillance and selling dossiers that show any individual's activities loom large as both governmental and private sector "big brothers" intrude on privacy.

Equal Credit Opportunity Act The Equal Credit Opportunity Act is intended to assure that the creditor's decision to extend or deny credit is not based on the consumer's membership in one of the suspect classes that have historically experienced discrimination. Credit cannot be denied on the basis of race, color, sex, religion, national origin, age, or marital status or on the basis of the fact that public assistance is the source of a person's income. Credit cannot be denied in retaliation against a consumer for exercising rights under TILA. These regulations concern only unlawful discrimination in granting credit; employment discrimination is discussed in Chapter 20.

Generally, the creditor is prohibited from inquiring whether income is derived from separate maintenance, child support, or alimony and from inquiring as to the race, color, religion, or national origin of the applicant. For example, *redlining,* a practice of refusing home mortgage loans in declining neighborhoods, is prohibited. There are a few exceptions to these prohibitions. A creditor may inquire into marital status to determine whether a spouse might assert a state dower right or a community property interest that gives priority over collateral. If public assistance is the source of income, the creditor may make inquiries regarding the stability of that income. For example, a creditor considering an applicant's ability to repay a long-term loan may validly inquire whether unemployment compensation or welfare benefits will soon expire. The Act makes creditors civilly liable for actual and punitive damages if credit is denied on the basis of suspect class membership. Injunctions against future violations are also possible.

Electronic Funds Transfer

Debt and other payments are being made increasingly by paperless **electronic fund transfers (EFT)** using automated teller machines (ATM), electronic or direct deposits, telephone or computer terminal transfers, point-of-sale machines, and automatic payments. To assure that payments are made accurately, that personal privacy is maintained, and that computer hackers do not tamper with electronic payments, Congress passed the Electronic Funds Transfer Act in 1978. This act amends TILA, requiring financial institutions to make disclosures to customers, resolve errors, and provide customer remedies.

electronic fund transfers (EFT)
Paperless electronic money transfer often through ATM machines and telephone transfer.

Financial institutions must notify EFT customers of their rights and send them monthly statements. These statements must show the date and amount of each transfer, the retailer's name, and the particular terminal used. Receipts must be provided for transactions using terminals but not for phone transfers. Allegations of errors must be investigated by the financial institution, and the institution must give the customer notice in writing within ten days. Treble damages may be assessed against the financial institution if it does not resolve errors quickly and accurately. There are criminal penalties for knowingly providing false information.

Financial institutions are liable for damages if a customer's account has sufficient funds but the EFT transaction is not made. Customers may recover damages between \$100 and \$1,000, and there are criminal penalties. Consumers are liable for unauthorized use of their ATM cards up to \$50 if the bank is notified within two days after the consumer learns the card is lost and up to \$500 if notice is given within 60 days. Consumers can be liable up to their available balance and credit line limit if withdrawals are made by someone else who knows that consumer's personal identification number (PIN). There are criminal penalties for using counterfeit, fictitious, altered, forged, lost, or fraudulently obtained debit cards.

Debt Collection

The debt relationship is a consensual one between creditors and debtors. In return for the advancement of cash or goods, the debtor voluntarily promises to repay the debt principal and the interest in fixed or variable installments. As long as payments are made in a timely fashion, the relationship is usually amicable. If the debtor defaults, however, the creditor usually take steps to collect. Many promissory notes contain an acceleration clause permitting the creditor, after the debtor has defaulted on a single payment, to declare the entire principal balance due immediately. This facilitates the collection of the whole debt in a single suit or foreclosure against the collateral without the need to bring a new collection suit for each periodic payment. As long as the creditor or debt collector fairly but tenaciously pursues the debtor, the debtor has little basis to complain. Creditors have several methods to assure loan repayment. Loans are often secured by (1) the cosignature of another debtor, (2) credit insurance, (3) bonding, or (4) forfeiture of rights in the collateral (foreclosure). Debt backed by collateral grants the creditor a legal right to repossess and sell the collateral upon default. The creditor must first attempt to satisfy the debt out of the collateral sale proceeds. Real estate mortgages and automobile security arrangements create security interests of this type.

Debt Collection Practices If unfair debt collection practices are followed, the debtor has several remedies under the common law. Defamation (libel and slander) may be used if a debt collector publishes untrue statements about the debtor. The right of privacy makes it unlawful to use unreasonable collection tactics that intrude on the debtor's solitude or that place the debtor in a false light in the public eye. In some states, laws against the intentional infliction of emotional distress also protects debtors from outrageous actions by creditors.

If a creditor is forced to bring suit on a defaulted loan, the *execution process* is used. This process is somewhat similar to a foreclosure sale. It permits the forced sale of the debtor's noncollateral assets. Execution is available only after a court order, and it typically requires the assistance of the sheriff. Creditors may also use the statutory right of **garnishment.** This is a court order requiring a third party, which holds the debtor's property, to turn it over to the creditor, the sheriff, or the court. The creditor serves a *writ of garnishment* on the debtor's employer or bank, which must deduct a sum of money from wages or a bank account to pay the creditor directly. Because of numerous abuses, Congress amended the Consumer Credit Protection Act to restrict garnishment. With some exceptions, the amount garnished may not exceed 25 percent of the debtor's after-tax income. Employers may not fire garnished employees under the assumption they are irresponsible merely because their wages are garnished.

garnishment
Statutory debt collection procedure from debtor's wages.

Fair Debt Collection Practices Act In an effort to end invasion of privacy, harassment, and other abuses in the debt collection process, Congress twice amended the Consumer Credit Protection Act with the Fair Debt Collection Practices Act in 1978 and 1986. Consumer debts for personal, family, or household purposes may not be collected except as provided in the Act. The Act applies to all parties in the business of collecting debts for others; it does not apply to attorneys or to creditors collecting their own debts.

Debtors may be contacted by a debt collector only between the hours of 8 A.M. and 9 P.M. or at other convenient times. The acceptable methods of contact include telephone, mail, telegram, or visits in person. The debtor may send the debt collector a written request to cease contact within 30 days after the first contact, and the debt collector must stop all contacts except for simple notices to indicate further legal action. A written notice must be sent within 5 days of the debt collector's first contact with the debtor. The notice must include the debt amount, the original creditor's identity, a copy of the debt or judgment, and a statement of the debtor's rights if the debt is not genuine.

A debt collector that violates the Act by using any prohibited collection method may be held civilly liable for actual damages, pain and suffering, emotional distress, invasion of privacy, court costs, and reasonable attorney's fees. Several collection practices are specifically prohibited: threats of violence to person, property, or reputation; obscenities; repeated and annoying telephone calls; false statements about the debtor to anyone; the use of documents falsely appearing to be official statements (e.g., court orders); and contacts at the debtor's work site if the employer prohibits them. Debt collectors may not contact anyone other than the debtor, except that the debtor's attorney must be contacted if the collector knows the attorney's identity. Debt collectors may investigate a missing debtor's whereabouts by contacting third parties. The FTC can enforce the Act with penalties and debtors may seek monetary damages.

Usury Laws

States have passed and revised *usury laws* regulating the highest interest rates that can be charged to consumer debtors. These laws are in direct conflict with the free market theory, which suggests that the market for credit should set interest rates by forces of supply and demand. However, history reveals that usury laws address some abuses: (1) they serve a consumer protection function limiting the cost of credit and (2) they can counteract criminal activity that excessive interest rates induce through *loan sharking*.

Usury law is best known for the credit-like transactions that it does not cover. Usury applies only to consumer loans, not commercial loans. Businesses are expected to adequately protect themselves. Credit card interest rates are governed by separate interest rate ceilings. *Time/price differentials,* in which cash prices are listed separately from deferred payment prices for the purchase of merchandise, are also exempt. These differentials arise when an outright cash price is listed at a lower level than if the price is paid in installments. The penalty for charging usurious interest rates varies among the states, ranging from a small penalty, through forfeiture of some or all of the interest, to complete forfeiture of the loan principal. Some states, notably Arkansas, impose such low usury ceilings that credit can become scarce. However, as a result of the high inflation of the early 1980s, most states' usury ceilings are above 20 percent.

Uniform Consumer Credit Code

The Uniform Consumer Credit Code (UCCC) is a single, uniform, and comprehensive state law governing consumer credit transactions. The controversial UCCC is adopted by only a few states. It is largely superseded by other laws, such as the Consumer Credit Protection Act, in regulating credit contract terms, credit disclosures, retail installment sales, usury, door-to-door sales, garnishment, and creditor remedies.

Consumer Leasing

Leasing has fast become a viable alternative to consumer credit purchases because lease payments are usually lower than loan payments, and the 1986 Tax Act eliminated the deduction for loan interest except on home mortgages and home equity loans. In recognition of the fact that consumer leases of goods are often a substitute for credit transactions, the Consumer Leasing Act has provisions similar to the Truth-in-Lending Act. The Act empowers the Federal Reserve Board to issue Regulation M and provides liability for violations. It applies to all consumer leases of personal property with a total contract obligation of under $25,000. Auto rentals, business leases, and land leases are not covered.

The Act requires disclosures similar to TILA concerning the number, amount, and period of payments; warranties; maintenance responsibilities; purchase options, if any; and premature termination obligations. For example, people who now lease autos rather than finance their purchase must be given a disclosure form indicating typical terms: lease payments, purchase option price (residual value), warranty limitation to the manufacturer's express warranty, that the lessee must service the auto and keep it insured, and that early termination will cost the lessee the present value of all remaining lease payments.

Consumer Product Safety Regulation

There are consumer protection laws that supplement the product liability recovery system discussed in Chapter 11. This section discusses the product safety regulations requiring certain products to maintain minimal safety levels. Food products, drugs, consumer products, and motor vehicles must meet safety specifications. Regulators have both protective and curative remedies. The product liability system compensates victims after an injury, whereas product safety regulations prevent injuries from unsafe products.

Food and Drug Safety and Purity

One of the first areas of consumer product safety to develop was in consumable foods and drinks. Early state statutes concerned the wholesomeness of milk. Today, state and local governments exercise police power to regulate the impact of food and drugs on the health, safety, and welfare of citizens. Regulated foods include bread, milk, milk products, imitations of milk products, soft drinks, intoxicating liquors, fruits, fruit products, grains, grain products, and eggs. Regulatory oversight often covers the production, manufacture, processing, sale, marketing, and transportation of food, often through licensing.

The Food and Drug Administration The Food and Drug Administration (FDA) and the U.S. Department of Agriculture (USDA) also regulate the purity of foods and drinks. Federal statutes dating back to 1906 authorize the regulation of filled milk, meat, poultry, bottled drinking water, vitamins, infant formulas, eggs, food additives, and tea. Agencies control adulterated and misbranded foods, food-level tolerances for poisonous ingredients, and the use of pesticides and additives in foods or raw agricultural commodities. Labeling standards require disclosure of food contents and nutritional profiles.

Drug Safety The Federal Food, Drug, and Cosmetic Act of 1938 empowers the FDA to regulate drugs and devices and any article or component intended to diagnose, cure, mitigate, treat, or prevent disease or to affect the bodily structure of humans or animals. *Devices* include most medical instruments and apparatus such as an IUD, pacemaker, or prosthesis. The states also regulate drugs, including drugs sold over the counter and prescription drugs sold by state-licensed pharmacists. Municipal boards of health have similar regulatory power over drugs as the FDA. Misbranding and adulteration are common classifications of defects.

The FDA and the states may prohibit some types of drug advertising. In one case, for example, claims that a tranquilizer could cure "the anxiety that comes from not fitting in" were found to be misleading. In another case, a manufacturer was held to have overpromoted an antibiotic drug by effectively concealing its warning, leading to liability. State regulatory schemes usually provide remedies to consumers and enforcement powers to local boards of health, including the power to ban, seize, or condemn offending articles and substances.

Consumer Product Safety

The most pervasive federal statute covering defective consumer products is the Consumer Product Safety Act of 1972 (CPSA). The CPSA created the Consumer Product Safety Commission (CPSC) to administer the Act. The Injury Information Clearinghouse compiles product failure statistics, collects research on defects, and funds research to discover defects. Public disclosure of the defects discovered is controlled to minimize undue adverse publicity about particular manufacturers. The CPSC has power to establish minimum product standards and to enforce regulations for noncomplying products. The CPSC also administers the Federal Hazardous Substances Act and the Poison Prevention Packaging Act, which cover the labeling and misbranding of poisons and hazardous substances, and the Flammable Fabrics Act, which sets minimum standards for the fire-retardant qualities of fabrics.

Motor Vehicle Safety

The federalization of automobile safety regulations began with the National Traffic and Motor Vehicle Safety Act of 1966. Congress sought to reduce traffic accidents, deaths, and injuries by establishing vehicle safety standards, supporting related research, and providing mechanisms to remedy defective vehicles. Two major systems were designed to prevent injuries. The first system empowers the U.S. Department of Transportation (DOT) to promulgate practical safety standards for motor vehicles. All newly manufactured domestic and foreign vehicles sold in the United States must be certified as complying with these standards. Extensive civil fines may be imposed for noncompliance. The second system requires remedies for defects arising after sale, such as nonfunctioning or malfunctioning auto parts. These defects are often discovered by customers, testing agencies, manufacturers, or DOT. The manufacturer may be required to (1) recall and repair defective vehicles, (2) replace defective vehicles, or (3) refund the purchase price.

Other state and federal statutes and agencies regulate the safety of particular products. The Federal Aviation Administration (FAA) sets private and commercial aircraft safety standards. The Occupational Safety and Health Administration, discussed in Chapter 18, indirectly sets minimum safety standards for tools.

The Administrative Remedies

Safety regulations establish standards and minimum specifications for the structural integrity and performance of products. Sample products are tested to evaluate their "breaking point." This can facilitate their redesign. A product's resistance to typical operating stresses and patterns must hold within a range reasonably expected under normal use. A hammer, for example, might be required to withstand a minimum pounding pressure before fracturing. Its claw might be required to withstand normal prying pressure.

Agencies are often empowered to "rule in" as legal all safe products and thereby to "rule out" unsafe products. Drugs and food additives may not be sold or used unless they appear on the "legal list." The FDA has established several lists of approved food additives. For example, the *generally recognized as safe (GRAS)* list includes foods and/or food additives that were considered safe for consumption when the list was first published in 1958. The artificial sweetener NutraSweet was separately approved for use in certain foods. The FDA also lists drugs acceptable for prescription and over-the-counter sales. Experimental drugs, such as several AIDS drugs, may not be prescribed or sold until certified after extensive testing.

Certain products and food additives are excluded from distribution. The FDA, USDA, CPSC, and Congress may ban sales of certain products. A product ban may be implemented with a new regulation or after authority to manufacture or sell an existing product is withdrawn. For example, cyclamates were banned as an artificial sweetener in the 1969 Delaney Amendment after evidence mounted about the health hazards.

Warning Labels and Advertising Nearly all safety regulators require that products be branded and that they include instructions for use. Warnings may be necessary to prevent product misuse consistent with the duty to warn. Foods, drugs, cosmetics, and toys are typical of products required to carry conspicuous warnings of known dangers and directions for safe use. Warning labels may help prevent misuse. Mandatory warning labels may also help manufacturers establish misuse by consumers who disregard a conspicuous and known warning. The *Cipollone* case discussed in Chapter 11 illustrates this point.

Several advertising issues arise under product safety regulations. For example, electronic media advertising of cigarettes is banned, relegating tobacco ads only to the print and billboard media. The surgeon general has required that warnings about the dangers of cigarettes be placed on cigarette packages. Even consumer groups oppose the Camel cigarette character because it appeals too much to children.

Searches, Seizures, Forfeitures, and Condemnations Speedy action is often critical in food and drug cases. To avert widespread disaster, the various food and drug regulators have powers to search for adulterated foods and drugs. The Tylenol and other tampering cases justify such immediate and summary action. If an administrative agency's investigation discovers violations of the law, how is the criminal intent of a whole corporation determined? Which individuals in a large business organization should be held responsible if a business fails to adhere to critical safety or health regulations? The next case illustrates an extreme form of administrative product safety enforcement.

United States v. Park

421 U.S. 720 (1975)
United States Supreme Court

Park was the chief executive officer of Acme Markets, Inc., a national retail grocery chain headquartered in Philadelphia. Acme employed approximately 36,000 employees at 874 retail outlets and 12 warehouses. Acme pleaded guilty to numerous charges of violating the FDA Act by failing to maintain sanitary conditions at some food warehouses. During 1971, for example, a food safety inspector found rodent infestation in the Baltimore warehouse. After Acme received FDA citations, the FDA inspector commented that "there was still evidence of rodent activity in the building and in the warehouses, and we found some rodent-contaminated lots of food items." Park testified that although all Acme employees were theoretically under his control, the company had an "organizational structure for responsibilities for certain functions" and assignments "to individuals who, in turn, have staff and departments under them." When Park received notice of the FDA inspections, he conferred with the Acme department responsible for sanitation, which was investigating and attempting to correct the unsanitary conditions. Although Park believed that there was nothing more he could have done to remedy the problem, he conceded that sanitation was ultimately his responsibility, despite delegation of that responsibility to other managers. Park was found guilty of a criminal violation of the FDA Act.

Chief Justice Burger delivered the opinion of the Court.

The rule that corporate employees who have "a responsible share in the furtherance of the transaction which the statute outlaws" are subject to the criminal provisions of the Act was not formulated in a vacuum. Cases under the Federal Food and Drugs Act of 1906 reflected the view both that knowledge or intent were not required to be provided in prosecutions under its criminal provisions, and that responsible corporate agents could be subjected to the liability thereby imposed. Moreover, the principle had been recognized that a corporate agent, through whose act, default, or omission the corporation committed a crime, was himself guilty individually of that crime. The principle had been applied whether or not the crime required "consciousness of wrongdoing," and it had been applied not only to those corporate agents who themselves committed the criminal act, but also to those who by virtue of their managerial positions or other similar relation to the actor could be deemed responsible for its commission. It was enough in such cases that, by virtue of the relationship he bore to the corporation, the agent had the power to prevent the act complained of.

Courts of Appeals have recognized that those corporate agents vested with the responsibility, and power commensurate with the responsibility, to devise whatever measures are necessary to ensure compliance with the Act bear a "responsible relationship" to, or have a "responsible share" in, violations. This is by no means necessarily confined to a single corporate agent or employee—the Act imposes not only a positive duty to seek out and remedy violations when they occur but also, and primarily, a duty to implement measures that will insure that violations will not occur. The Act, in its criminal aspect, does not require that which is objectively impossible. The theory upon which responsible corporate agents are held criminally accountable for "causing" violations of the Act permits a claim that the defendant was "powerless" to prevent or correct the violation to "be raised defensively at a trial on the merits."

Congress has seen fit to enforce the accountability of responsible corporate agents dealing with products which may affect the health of consumers by penal sanctions cast in rigorous terms, and the obligation of the courts is to give them effect so long as they do not violate the Constitution.

The Government established a prima facie case when it introduced evidence sufficient to warrant a finding by the trier of the facts that the defendant had, by reason of his position in the corporation, responsibility and authority either to prevent in the first instance, or promptly to correct, the violation complained of, and that he failed to do so. The failure thus to fulfill the duty imposed by the interaction of the corporate agent's authority and the statute furnishes a sufficient causal link. We conclude that, viewed as a whole and in the context of the trial, the charge was not misleading and contained an adequate statement of the law to guide the jury's determination.

Case Questions

1. Is criminal intent required in corporate crime prosecutions?
2. For what reason should managers be responsible for criminal violations?
3. Does this decision unfairly expose all employees to potential criminal liability?

Repair, Refund, or Replacement Both the CPSA and the National Traffic and Motor Vehicle Safety Act require manufacturers and sellers to remedy defects, commonly with a repair following public announcement of recall. Although recalls are intended to cure defects, the repairs also prevent injuries. Recalls often follow consumer complaints or failure reports. Because recalls enable manufacturers to repair defective products, they probably decrease product liability suits based on product failure. Further interactions between the product liability and product safety regulation schemes are discussed in Chapter 11.

SUMMARY

Numerous state and federal consumer protection regulations apply to businesses that advertise products or services or that grant credit. The FTC regulates this field through informal settlements, corrective advertisements, and litigation. Advertising claims must have a reasonable basis in scientific evidence, must demonstrate relevant product features, must be accurate, and may not omit important facts. Endorsements by celebrities must be based on actual product use, though fictional dramatizations by unknown actors are permissible. Comparison tests should be conducted scientifically.

The FTC holder-in-due course rule permits consumers to stop making installment loan payments if the seller breaches the contract. Sellers are prohibited from luring consumers into showrooms with bait-and-switch tactics. Mail-order marketers must inform the buyer of a stockout or shipment delay and must refund the purchase price or ship the goods within 30 days after an order has been received. Many door-to-door sales may be rescinded within a three-day cooling-off period.

Consumer credit transactions are regulated by the Consumer Credit Protection Act. The Truth-in-Lending Act requires standardized disclosure of loan terms. The APR, sales price, total deferred payments, and finance charges must be disclosed in a uniform format. Charges for unauthorized credit card use are limited to $50 per card account. Cardholders must be notified of the credit terms for card use, and periodic billings must disclose the balance due, the finance charges, the APR, and the monthly interest rates applied to unpaid balances. Violators are subject to criminal fines or imprisonment and civil liability.

The Fair Credit Billing Act provides consumers with notice of billing disputes and with mechanisms for resolving them. Creditors must respond quickly to debtors' inquiries and investigate disputes. The Electronic Funds Transfer Act regulates paperless payments. The Fair Credit Reporting Act requires that reported credit information be accurate or be revised. Credit reporting agencies must reinvestigate information the consumer claims is inaccurate. Only bona fide users of credit history may access credit files and only for legitimate purposes. It is illegal to discriminate against a credit applicant on the basis of race, color, sex, religion, national origin, age, marital status, or welfare status. The Fair Debt Collection Practices Act prohibits harassing debt collection methods.

Federal government and state regulations supplement consumer protection and the product liability system with product safety regulations. Fresh and packaged foods must be handled in specified ways, and certain food producers must be licensed. Administrative agencies may recall adulterated or misbranded foods and may seize, condemn, or impound tainted foods or foods and drugs that have been tampered with. Dangerous food additives may be banned. Similar regulations exist for prescription and over-the-counter drugs. There are similar protections for consumer products and automobiles. The Consumer Product Safety Act and the NHTSC regulate the safety characteristics of these products by setting minimum safety standards and banning unsafe products.

Critical Thinking Review Questions

1. The economy in the southwestern United States is closely tied to the oil industry. A drop in the price of oil during the 1980s played havoc with the economy of the Southwest and caused massive layoffs and lost income for many families. The overall housing market plunged, lowering home prices below what many people still owed on their home mortgages. Some homeowners, confronted with little income and the inability to sell their homes, simply moved out and left the mortgage lenders with large unpaid debts and insufficient collateral value in the homes. Foreclosures locked the lenders into big losses on these loans, leading several lenders to become bankrupt. This created a domino effect, contributing to the Savings and Loan failure problem. What are the ethical issues for (1) home buyers/borrowers, (2) loan officers, and (3) real estate speculators who purchased these homes cheaply at foreclosure sales? Analyze these issues.
2. Identify the following laws, and state the reasons for their enactment:
   a. The Truth-in-Lending Act
   b. The Fair Credit Reporting Act
   c. The Equal Credit Opportunity Act
   d. The Fair Debt Collection Practices Act
3. Explain the reasons why the Truth-in-Lending Act defines the term *finance charge* as broadly as it does. What charges are included as finance charges?

Critical Thinking Exercises

1. The Smell Fresh Company claims that its new aerosol spray will "eliminate all noxious fumes within a one-mile radius of paper mill plants in the area." The Federal Trade Commission doubts that this claim is correct. What will the FTC probably demand that the company do?
2. A department store advertises an inexpensive compact disc player when an insufficient inventory is available. In response to the advertisement, hundreds of customers come into the store to purchase the compact disc player. The salespeople in the store encourage these customers to purchase more expensive models of the compact disc player, which are available. Does this present a legal problem?
3. A door-to-door salesman sells Mary $450 worth of gardening equipment. Mary pays $100 down and signs an installment contract for the balance. Two days later, she decides that she really doesn't need all of the equipment. Does she have a remedy, or is she bound by the installment contract?
4. The Plaintiff Furniture Company sold a television set and a stereo to a customer and retained a security interest in these items to secure the payment of the purchase price. The furniture company did not file a financing statement. The customer pledged the television set and stereo to a pawnbroker as security for a loan. The customer defaulted on the debt to the furniture company after making four payments. There was a contest between the pawnbroker and the furniture company as to who had a prior security interest in the items. Why is it important for the creditor to file a financing statement? Is the furniture company protected in this case?
5. Some of Dan's creditors want to petition him into involuntary bankruptcy. What proof do the creditors need to obtain an order or a release? Are there any alternatives for debtor Dan other than to submit to the bankruptcy court?
6. Eastern Airlines has lost millions of dollars in recent years. One cause of the loss is that Eastern competitors have had lower labor costs and have been able to charge lower fares. Eastern is entitled by law to file a bankruptcy petition requesting a reorganization. In such a petition, Eastern can seek to have the court reject its collective bargaining agreements and other employee contracts. If the request is granted, Eastern would no longer be bound by its collective bargaining agreements. Under such a bankruptcy reorganization, Eastern can continue to do business while arrangements are being made by the court to adjust Eastern's contractual obligations. Would Eastern be morally justified in filing for protection under the bankruptcy laws in an effort to avoid its costly labor contracts?

PART 5

Business Associations

13 Agency

14 Business Organizations

15 Securities Regulations

CHAPTER

13

Agency

Critical Thinking Questions

- Compare and contrast the different methods, actual authority, apparent authority, or ratification of an originally unauthorized act by which a principal can create authority for its agent. Why does the law impose a duty of loyalty on the agent but not on the principal?
- What distinguishes the relationship between the principal and its agents and the relationship between the principal and an independent contractor?
- What issue must be resolved before the law imposes liability on the principal for torts committed by its agents?
- Why does a third party contracting with an agent who represents an undisclosed or partially disclosed principal have the option of holding either the agent or the principal liable on the contract?

Introduction . . . Past, Present, Future

The agency relationship is more important today than it has been in the past century. At the beginning of the 20th century, most business transactions were based on personal relationships. Buyers and sellers usually knew each other and dealt with one another face-to-face. Today, a significant percentage of the world's business is transacted by large corporate organizations that act only through agents, employees, and contractors.

In many instances, an employer today exercises less direct supervision over its employees than it did in the past. Today, fewer people are working in large manufacturing plants in which their actions are overseen by supervisors representing the principal. Instead, current workers are sales representatives, computer operators, customer service agents, production team members, financial analysts, and specialized secretaries who perform highly skilled activities on behalf of their principals or employers. Similarly, separate firms often provide technical service representatives, cleaning assistants, part-time word processors, data entry clerks, nurses, and office assistants for other firms.

In the future, as firms contract for more services instead of hiring additional employees, agency law is more likely to concern the employer-independent contractor relationship than the employer-employee relationship. Accordingly, the law may reexamine the duties of the various parties toward one another. The imposition of liability on the principal for the torts of "its" agents may be extended to some of its contract personnel. This possible liability probably will be viewed as a rather routine cost of doing business.

The Nature of an Agency Relationship

agent
A person who acts on behalf of another person or firm and who has duties to further that person or firm's interests; unlike a distributor, an agent sells the principal's products, not products owned by the agent.

principal
A person or firm that has other people, agents, acting on its behalf and representing its interest.

No one person is able to perform all of the activities required to operate a business. Therefore, businesses select agents to represent them in their activities with suppliers, employees, and customers. In this context, the term **agent** refers to any person who acts on behalf of or represents another person or firm, while the term **principal** refers to the person or firm being represented by someone else.

The Agency Relationship and the Liability of the Principal

The nature of the relationship between an employer or principal and its employees, agents, and independent contractors affects its liability for the tortious acts of those representatives. The greater control the principal has, the more likely the principal will be held liable for torts of its agents. A principal's liability for contracts that its agent agrees to with third parties depends on whether the agent's action was authorized by the principal and whether the third party knew of the principal's existence and identity.

Types of Agency Relationships

The agency relationship is a consensual relationship because it is based on the consent of both agent and principal. Neither can force the other to accept an agency relationship. An agency relationship between a principal and an agent arises once the relationship is created. The duties and rights of the parties as principal and agent are separate from those created by an agreement or employment contract between them.

There are three types of agency relationships, each of which involves different controls and responsibilities for both principal and agent; the three types are depicted in Figure 13–1. As a result of differences in the right of the principal to control the activities of the agent, the principal's contract and tort liability, discussed near the end of the chapter, differs with the type of relationship the principal has with the agent.

master-servant or employer-employee relationship
The relationship between an employer and an employee whose physical conduct is subject to the employer's control and direct supervision.

The **master-servant relationship,** generally referred to today as the **employer-employee relationship,** occurs between an employer and an employee whose physical conduct is subject to the employer's control and direct supervision. The factory worker, household employee, store or office clerk, and farmhand typify the employee in this type of relationship.

FIGURE 13–1

Types of Agency Relationships

Type of Relationship	Degree of Control	Example
Master-servant	Direct control over servant's physical activities	Foreman/factory worker, farmer/farmhand
Principal-agent	Control over general scope of activities but not over details	Owner/manager, department head/sales clerk
Employer-independent contractor	Control of results but not of how tasks are performed	Home owner/plumber, client/attorney

The **principal-agent relationship** involves an agent who is authorized by a principal to carry out a broad range of activities on the principal's behalf. A store manager, a sales agent, and a corporate officer are examples of agents who act in a variety of ways on behalf of their principal-employer.

In the **employer-independent contractor relationship,** the independent contractor is not subject to the control of the employee-principal. The employer who contracts with an independent contractor, such as a plumber, accountant, or attorney, to perform certain activities has no right to control the method of performance used by the contractor.

The principal-agent relationship is separate from the employer-employee relationship. Although all employees are agents, not all agents are employees. For example, although an employer and an independent contractor have a type of agency relationship, the independent contractor is not an employee. Similarly, a person may allow someone to act on his or her behalf without creating an employment relationship. One roommate does errands for another, or one friend consents to help another in a building, repairing, or cleaning project. The roommate and friend acting for others are agents but not employees.

principal-agent relationship
The relationship between a person or firm (principal) who authorizes another (agent) to carry out a broad range of activities subject to the general control of the first person.

employer-independent contractor relationship
A relationship between a person or firm that hires another to perform specific tasks but whose activities are not subject to control by the hiring party.

Creation and Termination of an Agency Relationship

Creation of an Agency Relationship

An agency relationship may be created by conduct less formal than the conduct necessary for a contract relationship. For example, express statements or actions of the principal are sufficient to indicate that an agency relationship has been created. If a purchasing firm tells an IBM salesperson that "the computer will be picked up by a Ms. Jones from our firm," the purchasing firm creates an agency relationship permitting Ms. Jones as its agent to take delivery of the computer.

Similarly, a manager asks an office messenger to deliver documents to another firm, and that request creates an agency relationship even though the manager did not talk directly with anyone from the firm receiving the documents. The messenger is the sending firm's agent while performing the errand. Whenever two people agree that one of them, the agent, may act on behalf of the other, the principal, an **agency relationship** is created.

The burden of proving an agency relationship is on the person who claims it exists. This may be a third party that dealt with an agent and seeks to hold the principal liable on a transaction of the agent. To prove that the principal is liable for the acts of the agent, the third party must show that the agent was authorized to act for the principal. That authority may arise in several ways: actual authority, which is either express or implied; apparent authority; or ratification. These methods of creating the agent's authority are illustrated in Figure 13–2.

agency relationship
The relationship that arises whenever two people agree that one of them, the agent, may act on behalf of the other, the principal.

actual authority
The authority granted to an agent from a principal, based either on express statements or implied from those statements or actions of the principal.

Actual Authority The principal gives the agent **actual authority** through express statements such as "Sell my IBM stock" or by implication from circumstances. For example, a person who has been given the express authority to manage a store has the additional implied authority to do whatever else is

FIGURE 13-2 Creation of Agent's Authority

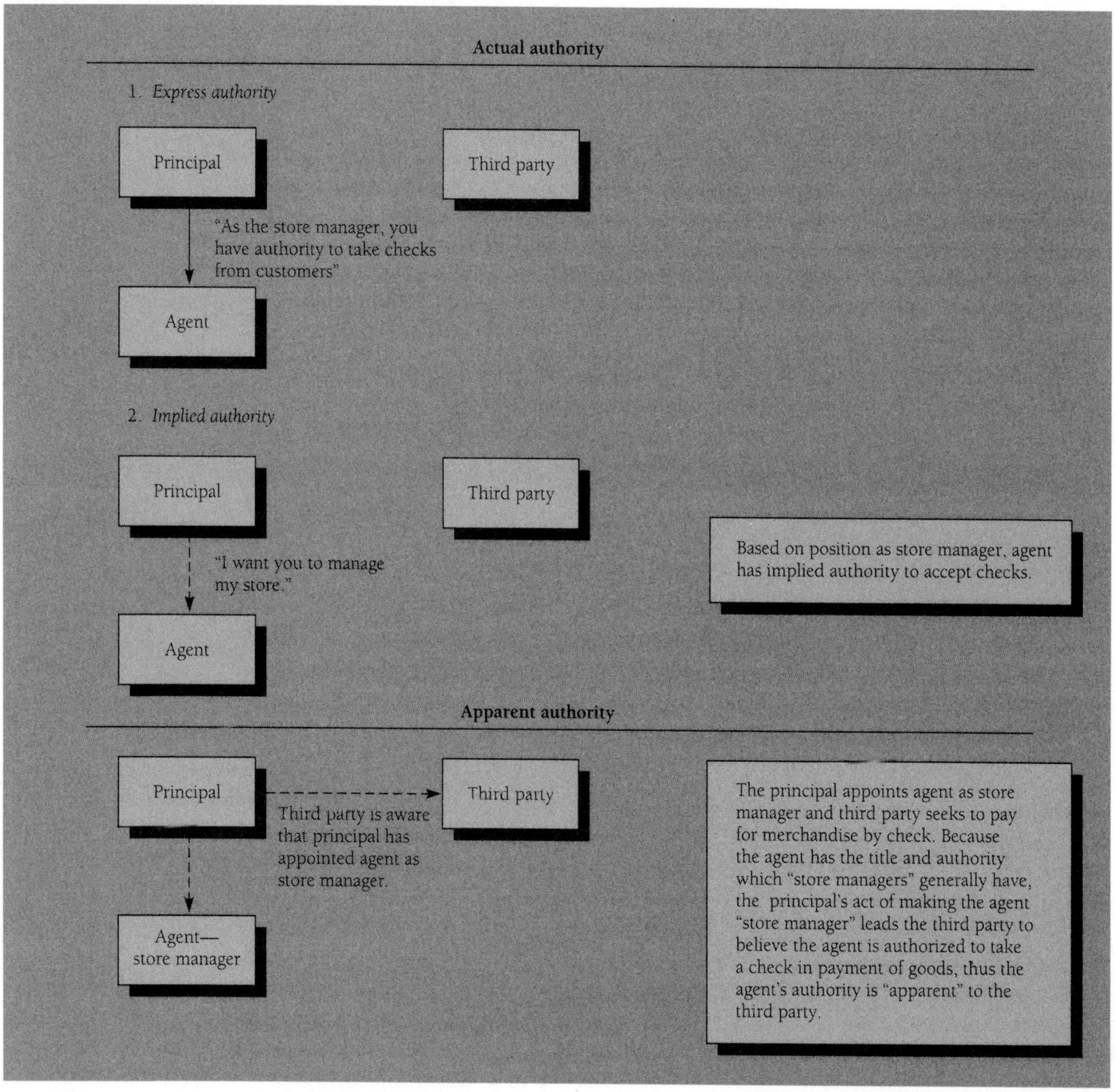

necessary to accomplish that task. If one of the clerks quits, the store manager has the implied authority to hire a replacement. The manager can also accept deliveries made to the store or send someone to pick up needed supplies, even if the owner of the store did not expressly grant such authority. Actual implied authority adds details to a vague or general grant of actual express authority. Such authority enables the agent to perform activities which are normal for a person in that position.

FIGURE 13-2 (concluded)

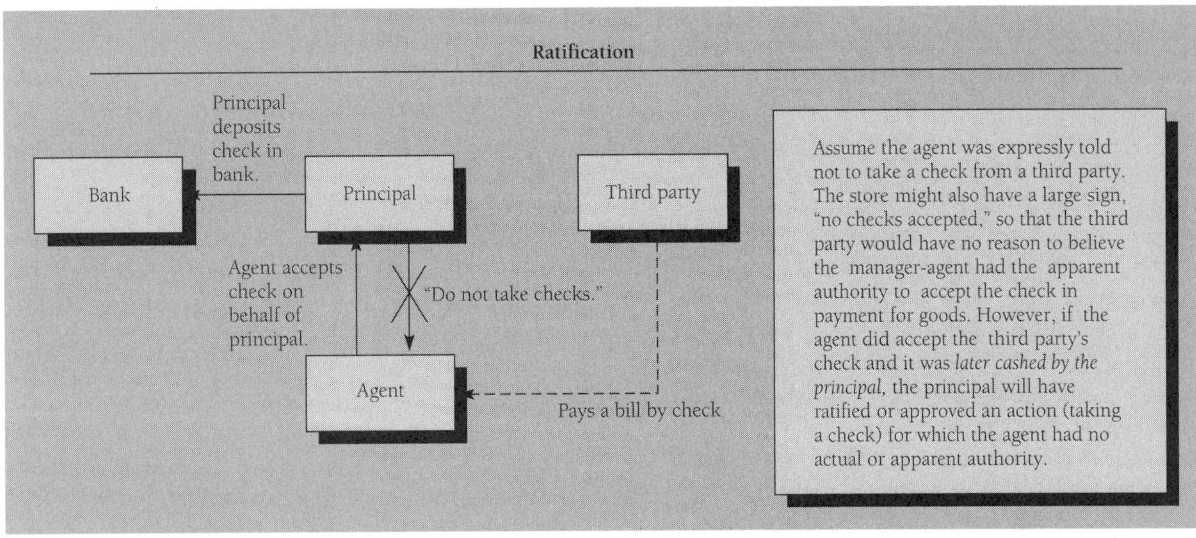

Apparent Authority **Apparent authority** exists when the principal creates the appearance of authority in an agent, even though it does not grant the agent actual authority. If the principal does something that leads a third party to reasonably believe that an agent has authority, the principal is liable for the agent's actions. For example, if you go to a store and the person who is acting as the manager of the store approves the cashing of your check, it is reasonable for you to assume that the owner has authorized the store manager to give such approval on its behalf. Even if the owner did not expressly give the manager that authority, the manager has the apparent authority to act in that manner on the owner's behalf.

apparent authority The authority of an agent that exists when the principal creates a reasonable appearance of authority in an agent, even though it does not grant the agent actual authority.

Of course, if the check is unusually large or is drawn on an out-of-town bank, it may not be reasonable for you to assume that a manager has the authority to approve the check. The question is whether the principal has put the agent in a position that would lead a reasonable person to believe that the agent is authorized to perform certain acts for the principal. The principal is the source of the agent's apparent authority. If the principal does not make it apparent to the third party that the agent can act for the principal, the agent lacks apparent authority.

In the case that follows, Thomas, the chief executive officer of the Commerce Bank of Plano, Texas, signed a letter of credit on behalf of Grant Curtis, one of its customers, to the Bank of Garland. The letter of credit committed the Bank of Plano to pay $100,000 to the Texas Bank of Garland when it presented the letter of credit (LOC) to the Bank of Plano for payment. (A letter of credit, discussed in Chapter 10 and Chapter 3, is a document issued by a bank that indicates it will make payments to the letter's beneficiary under specified circumstances.)

However, the Bank of Plano did not pay and, after it was taken over by the Federal Deposit Insurance Corporation (FDIC), the Bank of Garland sued. The FDIC claims Thomas did not have the actual authority to issue the letter of credit. What is the basis for the court's finding regarding Thomas's apparent authority to issue the letter of credit?

Federal Deposit Insurance Corporation v. Texas Bank of Garland

783 S.W.2d 604 (1989)
Court of Appeals of Texas

On July 28, 1987, Grant Curtis personally delivered the letter of credit (LOC) signed by Sam Thomas to Texas Bank of Garland (TBG), naming TBG as the third-party beneficiary. The LOC, together with a pledged $200,000 certificate of deposit, was collateral for the renewal of a $300,000 note, payable to TBG by Curtis. The LOC reads:

Sam Thomas, III
Chairman of the Board
Chief Executive Officer
Commerce Bank Plano
P.O. Box 865499 Plano, Texas 75086

IRREVOCABLE LETTER OF CREDIT NUMBER 0056

DATE: JULY 28, 1987

FOR THE ACCOUNT OF: GRANT CURTIS
3008 Milton Avenue
Dallas, Texas 75205

TO BENEFICIARY:
TEXAS BANK GARLAND
1919 S. Shiloh
Garland, Texas 75042

AMOUNT
$100,000.00

EXPIRATION:
NOVEMBER 28, 1987

Gentlemen:

We hereby establish our irrevocable Letter of Credit in your favor, available by your draft at sight, on us, accompanied by this Letter of Credit. All drafts must be marked: "DRAWN UNDER LETTER OF CREDIT."

This Letter of Credit is transferable without limitations as to the number of transfers or the number of transferee. Except as expressly stated herein, this Letter of Credit is governed by the Uniform Customs and Practices for Documentary Credits (1984 revision), International Chamber of Commerce Publication.

We hereby engage with you, your transferee, endorsers, and assigns, that all drafts drawn under and in compliance with the terms of this Credit will be duly honored if drawn and presented for payment at our office at 901 W. Parker Road, Plano, Collin County, Texas, on or before 1:00 o'clock P.M., Plano, Texas time, not prior to October 28, 1987, and not subsequent to November 28, 1987. This Letter of Credit can be renewed for an additional period of time if mutually agreed by both Texas Bank Garland and Commerce Bank Plano prior to maturity.

Sincerely,

/s/ Sam Thomas

Sam Thomas
Chairman of the Board
Chief Executive Officer

Curtis defaulted on the note, and on November 23, 1987, TBG presented the LOC, a letter of instruction, and a $100,000 draft drawn against the LOC to Commerce Bank of Plano (CBP). On the same day as presentment, CBP notified TBG that it would dishonor the LOC. CBP provided TBG with a written notice of dishonor on November 24, 1987. On or about November 25, 1987, TBG sued CBP to recover under the LOC. In January 1988, the FDIC was appointed receiver of CBP, and it filed a plea in intervention. The trial court rendered a summary judgment for TBG, and the FDIC appealed.

Ovard, Justice

1. Thomas's Authority

The FDIC contends that the trial court erred in granting summary judgment in favor of TBG because Thomas had no actual or apparent authority to sign the LOC. The FDIC argues that the LOC was not issued by CBP but by Thomas personally.

A corporation can act only through its agents. It is elementary that a bank is bound by the acts of its officers while acting in the scope of their authority, either actual or apparent.

a. Actual Authority

Actual authority can be either express or implied. The record shows that Thomas was denied actual authority to issue the LOC. However, even so, we sustain the trial court's judgment because the record conclusively establishes Thomas's apparent authority.

b. Apparent Authority

The FDIC argues that Thomas did not have the apparent authority needed to issue the LOC, and that even if Thomas possessed the necessary apparent authority, TBG did not exercise reasonable due diligence to ascertain such authority. The doctrine of apparent authority to act as an agent is based on the law of estoppel. The doctrine does not apply unless the person dealing with the agent was misled by the representation or conduct of the principal. The person dealing with the agent must have been induced to act to his prejudice by reason of the principal's conduct, after exercising due diligence to ascertain the truth.

Apparent authority may arise by a principal's action which lacks such ordinary care as to clothe an agent with the indicia of authority, thus leading a reasonably prudent person to believe that the agent has the authority he purports to exercise.

Thomas was CBP's chief executive officer and chairman of the board. Appointing a person to such a position may, in itself, create apparent authority in an employee. Appointing a person as an executive officer impliedly grants in him the authority to issue letters of credit. . . . As TBG's senior vice president for loans testified, "Someone who is chairman of the board and chief executive officer would certainly have the power to issue a letter of credit."

We hold that issuing a letter of credit is within the scope of apparent authority ordinarily entrusted to the chief executive officer of a bank. Thomas had the apparent authority necessary to act as an agent for his bank in issuing the LOC to Curtis.

We will now turn to the question of whether TBG exercised due diligence in ascertaining whether Thomas possessed the necessary apparent authority to issue the LOC. Due diligence is sufficient when it is shown that persons are dealing with bank officers in good faith, without notice of want of authority, and when the officer appears to be acting within the apparent scope of his authority. In a prior transaction, a TBG officer ascertained that Thomas was the chief executive officer and chairman of the board for CBP. Thomas continued in this position on the date that the LOC was issued to Curtis. In addition, an officer of TBG examined the Texas Banking Red Book, a reference manual for the banking industry, and verified Thomas's position with CBP. We hold that TBG exercised due diligence under these facts and that Thomas had the apparent authority to issue the LOC.

c. Thomas as Agent

The FDIC further argues that CBP's operating policy prohibited Thomas from issuing the LOC and that Thomas did not follow CBP's policy requirements. An agent's authority is presumed to be coextensive with the business entrusted to his care. That authority is not diminished at the expense of a third party by private instructions or limitations imposed by the principals, which are not communicated to third parties dealing with the agent.

There is no evidence that CBP communicated its letter of credit policy, or any of the limitations placed on Thomas, to its customers or the banking community. We hold that, before FDIC is entitled to rely upon those policies to diminish an agent's apparent authority, it was CBP's responsibility to communicate its operating policies to the banking public. TBG, as a third-party beneficiary, had no notice of these policies or limitations and was allowed to rely on the validity of Thomas's signature. The chief executive officer and chairman of the board of CBP had the apparent authority to sign and to issue the LOC.

In conclusion, we hold that after considering all of the evidence and the motions, the LOC was a letter of credit; Thomas had the apparent authority to sign and issue the LOC; and federal common law does not bar TBG's recovery because TBG strictly complied with the terms of the LOC.

Consequently, we affirm the judgment of the trial court.

Case Questions

1. Can apparent authority to act as an agent arise because of actions or words from the agent to a third party?
2. What action of the Bank of Plano (FDIC) led the Bank of Garland to reasonably believe that Thomas had the authority to issue a letter of credit for the Bank of Plano? Would your answer be different if Thomas were the vice president of the bank, not its chairman of the board?
3. What changes in the facts of this case might make the Bank of Plano successful in its claim that Thomas lacked apparent authority?

---

ratification
The act by a principal of approving an unauthorized action of an agent; ratification may occur by express action or be implied from the principal's retention of benefits.

Ratification When a principal approves an act performed by an agent who acted without authority, **ratification** occurs. The ratification may be expressed or implied. If a principal agrees to be bound by a contract negotiated by an agent who acted without authority or who exceeded the bounds of his or her authority, an express ratification occurs. If the principal accepts the benefits of the contract and does nothing more, an implied ratification occurs.

What source of authority gives a business manager the power to offer a certain salary to a prospective employee? The following case considers the concepts of actual, apparent, and ratification authority in an employment situation.

Schoenberger v. Chicago Transit Authority

405 N.E.2d 1076 (1980)
Appellate Court of Illinois

Schoenberger sued the Chicago Transit Authority (CTA) to recover contract damages. At issue was whether the CTA might be held liable under agency principles for a promise, allegedly made by its employee ZuChristian when Schoenberger was hired, that he would receive an automatic $500 increase in salary within a year after beginning work. Schoenberger stated that he never inquired into ZuChristian's authority to discuss salary with him but believed that ZuChristian's authority overrode the authority of the placement department, which he thought had only a "perfunctory" role in hiring.

ZuChristian testified that his supervisor had told him to make informal offers to prospective employees. However, ZuChristian stated that when he told Schoenberger of his desire to hire him, he intended for Schoenberger to regard this as an offer. He also stated that he lied to Schoenberger when he told him that the $19,300 salary offer was merely a clerical error, which would later automatically be raised to $19,800. This story, he said, was agreed upon by his superior, John Hogan. Both ZuChristian and Hogan thought their story would lead to Schoenberger's acceptance of the lower salary approved by the employee relations department.

When the increase was not given at the promised time, Schoenberger resigned and filed this suit. The trial court ruled in favor of the CTA, and Schoenberger appealed.

Campbell, Justice

The main question before us is whether ZuChristian, acting as an agent of the C.T.A., orally contracted with Schoenberger for $500 in compensation in addition to his $19,300 salary. The authority of an agent may only come from the principal and it is therefore necessary to trace the source of an agent's authority to some word or act of the alleged principal. Authority may be actual or apparent, actual being either express or implied. The authority to bind a principal will not be presumed, but rather, the person alleging authority must prove its source unless the act of the agent has been ratified.

Both Hogan and Bonner, ZuChristian's superiors, testified that ZuChristian had no actual authority to either make an offer of a specific salary to Schoenberger or to make any promise of additional compensation. Furthermore, ZuChristian's testimony corroborated the testimony that he lacked the authority to make formal offers. From this evidence, it is clear that ZuChristian lacked the actual authority to bind the C.T.A. for the additional $500 in compensation to Schoenberger.

Nor can it be said that the C.T.A. clothed ZuChristian with the apparent authority to make Schoenberger a promise of compensation over and above that formally offered by the Placement Department. Here Schoenberger's initial contact with the C.T.A. was with the Placement Department where he filled out an application and had his first interview. There is no evidence that the C.T.A. did anything to permit ZuChristian to assume authority, nor did they do anything to hold him out as having the authority to hire and set salaries. ZuChristian was not at a management level in the C.T.A., nor did his job title of Principal Communications Analyst suggest otherwise. The mere fact that he was allowed to interview prospective employees does not establish that the C.T.A. held him out as possessing the authority to hire employees or set salaries. Moreover, ZuChristian did inform Schoenberger that the formal offer of employment would be made by the Placement Department.

Our final inquiry concerns the plaintiff's contention that irrespective of ZuChristian's actual or apparent authority, the C.T.A. is bound by ZuChristian's promise because it ratified his acts. Ratification may be expressed or inferred and occurs where the principal, with knowledge of the material facts of the unauthorized transaction, takes a position inconsistent with nonaffirmation of the transaction. Ratification is the equivalent to an original authorization and confirms that which was originally unauthorized. Ratification occurs where a principal attempts to seek or retain the benefits of the transaction.

Upon review of the evidence, we are not convinced that the C.T.A. acted to ratify ZuChristian's promise. According to Bonner's testimony, when he took over the supervision of ZuChristian's group in the fall of 1976 and was told of the promise, he immediately informed ZuChristian that the promise was unauthorized and consequently would not be honored. Subsequently, he informed Schoenberger of this same fact. Mere delay in telling Schoenberger does not, as the plaintiff contends, establish the C.T.A.'s intent to ratify.

For the reasons we have indicated, the judgment in favor of the defendant, C.T.A., is affirmed.

Case Questions

1. Explain why the court found that the CTA did not authorize ZuChristian to offer Schoenberger a salary increase.

2. What did Schoenberger have to prove to show that ZuChristian was acting as the CTA's agent when he discussed Schoenberger's employment at $19,800 instead of $19,300?

3. Who had the authority to commit the CTA to a definite salary for a prospective employee?

Termination of an Agency Relationship

The principal-agent relationship and the agent's authority to bind the principal may be terminated either by the parties or by operation of law.

Termination by the Parties The parties themselves may provide when the relationship ends—for example, "This agency terminates six months after the date of this agreement." Even if nothing about termination is expressed, the agency terminates once the agent has completed the activities spelled out in the agreement creating the agency.

At any time, the parties may mutually agree they will terminate the agency relationship. In most cases, either party may terminate the relationship. However, if the agent has a property interest in the business, the agency may not be terminated without mutual consent. This is because an agent whose reimbursement depends on the continuation of his authority to act as an agent has an **agency coupled with an interest.** Agents who represent media personalities or well-known speakers often have a property interest in the money paid to the principals. The agent's commission comes from the money paid to the principal that the agent collects from third parties.

agency coupled with an interest
The interest of an agent whose reimbursement depends on the continuation of his or her authority to act as an agent.

Termination by Operation of Law The agency relationship may also be terminated by the destruction of its subject matter. For example, if a home owner's agreement with a real estate agent authorizes the agent to list a home for sale for six months, the agency relationship automatically terminates if a flood or fire destroys the home three months later. Death of either the agent or the principal also terminates the agency relationship. Finally, if the law makes illegal the performance of the agent's acts, the agency relationship terminates when the change in the law occurs.

Termination and Notice to Third Parties Even though an agency relationship has been terminated, the principal may still be bound by the agent's subsequent acts if appropriate notice is not given to the third parties with which the agent has dealt. For example, if a company terminates an employee's authority to charge purchases on its behalf at a store where it regularly purchases supplies, the company must inform the store of that termination. Although an agent's actual authority ends when an agency has been terminated, third parties with which the agent has dealt must be informed of the termination for the agent's apparent authority to end.

INTERNATIONAL PERSPECTIVE AND COMMENTARY

Local distributors and agents are often used by firms seeking to sell their products throughout the global marketplace. They can provide knowledge of local markets, governmental regulations, and distribution channels that is difficult to obtain from outside the country where goods are being sold. The terms *agent* and *distributor* have well-defined meanings in the countries of the European Union and in many other civil law countries.

A **distributor** is an individual or firm who assumes the economic and legal risk of selling his or her own goods. The distributor purchases products from the seller and determines the price at which those products will be resold. The distributor deals with the principal-seller at arm's length and does not owe the seller fiduciary duties, as does the agent. However, the distributor usually has a contract obligation to use its best efforts to promote the seller's products. The distributor assumes the risk of ownership of the goods. If the goods are lost or damaged while owned by the distributor, it is the distributor's loss, not the seller's. The distributor, who is more like an independent contractor than an agent, is regarded as an independent businessperson, even if the seller provides technical or financial assistance to the distributor.

distributor An individual or firm who purchases products from the seller and who assumes the economic and legal risk of selling them.

By contrast, an agent acts on behalf of the supplier to obtain business in return for a percentage commission. The agent does not purchase the goods from the seller and thus has no economic or legal risk associated with them. The agent has a fiduciary obligation to the firm it represents and generally also a contract obligation to use its best efforts to try to sell the goods. In many countries, agents may represent several different manufacturers, although generally they agree not to sell goods of one seller that compete directly with goods of other sellers they represent. As the agent generally has no risk with regard to the goods, if they are damaged while in the agent's possession, through no fault of the agent, the seller, not the agent, must assume the loss. The seller of the goods, not the agent, determines the price at which the goods are to be sold.

While both the agent and the distributor are recognized as independent firms, the agency relationship is subject to greater regulation than is the distributor relationship. Some countries require that any agent be a citizen, while others require that all agents be officially registered. The most significant legal concern regarding selecting an agent outside the United States concerns termination. While laws in the United States generally allow agency relationships to be "at will" and freely terminated by either party, in most civil law countries legislation protects agents from unfair terminations. While the content of each country's law varies, most require termination to be based on good cause, to be preceded by adequate notice, and to provide compensation to the agent for the termination. The compensation usually varies with the duration of the agency relationship and the level of commissions paid to the agent.

Duties Owed by Principal and Agent to Each Other

Once an agency relationship exists, the parties owe certain duties to each other. An agent and principal have a special **fiduciary relationship,** one based on trust and confidence. This relationship, which constitutes the basis for many of the legal and ethical problems in business relations, imposes duties on the agent. These fiduciary duties arise in every transaction that an agent undertakes.

fiduciary relationship A relationship based on trust and confidence that gives rise to duties being imposed on the person who acts on behalf of another.

Duties of the Agent to the Principal

Fiduciary Duties Fiduciary duties are duties above and beyond those assumed by the parties in their contract. Fiduciary duties are imposed on the agent (the fiduciary) because the fiduciary is given power and authority over the property and interests of another party (the principal) that places its trust in him or her. As a fiduciary, the agent must act on behalf of the principal, not out of self-interest.

The fiduciary duty is a special form of trust that requires the employee-agent to act in good faith, based on the utmost loyalty and due care for the principal's interest. The agent may not allow conflicts of interest to modify a decision regarding the principal's business. For example, the purchasing agent of a firm cannot allow a conflict of interest to affect his or her selection of automobiles purchased for the firm. The agent's brother may own a car dealership, or a car dealer may promise the agent the use of a personal car in exchange for purchases on the firm's behalf, but the agent's purchasing decisions must be based on the best interests of the firm and not on family loyalty or on self-interest.

The following passage describes the fiduciary duty:

Classic Characterization of the Fiduciary Duty

> Joint adventurers, like copartners, owe to one another, while the enterprise continues, the duty of the finest loyalty. Many forms of conduct permissible in a workaday world for those acting at arm's length are forbidden to those bound by fiduciary ties. A trustee is held to something stricter than the morals of the marketplace. Not honesty alone, but the punctilio of an honor the most sensitive is then the standard of behavior. As for this there has developed a tradition that is unbending and inveterate. . . . Only thus has the level of conduct for fiduciaries been kept at a level higher than that trodden by the crowd.
>
> Source: Justice Benjamin Cardozo, in *Meinhard v. Salmon,* 164 N.E. 545, 546 (N.Y. 1928).

It is sometimes difficult to determine whether there is a fiduciary relationship between parties. In the Boeck case, which follows, Boeck claims that Merrill Lynch had a fiduciary duty toward him in his role as a customer who was buying soybean futures. Merrill Lynch claims that Boeck traded on his own account and that as his broker it merely executed the purchases and sales of commodities he wished to trade. This case has both a majority and dissenting opinion for your review. Which do you agree with? Why?

Merrill, Lynch, Pierce, Fenner & Smith, Inc. v. Boeck

377 N.W. 2D 605 (1985)
Supreme Court of Wisconsin

Merrill Lynch sued to recover $21,712 that Boeck owed on his investment account for soybean futures transactions made during May 1978. Boeck denied liability and counterclaimed for the losses he sustained on the transactions.

Boeck was an experienced commodities investor who had dealt with two other brokerage houses before opening a commodities account with Merrill Lynch in February 1977. Before he began trading with Merrill Lynch, Boeck subscribed to several publications and services concerned with commodities investments. Boeck signed a commodities account agreement that set forth the risky and speculative nature of investing in commodities futures contracts and that warned of the possibility of significant losses. Merrill Lynch had no authority to decide what trades to make in Boeck's account.

Boeck stated that he opened the account at Merrill Lynch because the company had a good reputation for financial services and a strong research program in the commodities field. Douglas Terrill, Boeck's broker at Merrill Lynch, testified that during March, April, and May of 1978, Boeck regularly asked what information Merrill Lynch's research department had about particular commodities. Boeck claims that he based his commodities investment decisions on the information and advice given to him by Merrill Lynch.

The critical time period in the relationship between Boeck and Merrill Lynch was May 15, 1978, through June 1, 1978. On May 15, Boeck claims Terrill told him that Merrill Lynch's soybean expert, David Bartholomew, had just returned from a trip to Brazil and that he had sharply reduced his estimate of the size of the Brazilian soybean crop. Bartholomew was reputed to be a world-renowned expert in the soybean industry, and Terrill advised Boeck of that fact. Terrill allegedly told Boeck that news of Bartholomew's trip and Bartholomew's estimate of Brazil's crop had not been made public and that based on this news, Merrill Lynch's research department soon would make a very strong recommendation to buy, among other things, bull spreads in soybeans and soybean meal.

Terrill denied telling Boeck about Bartholomew's visit to Brazil or that Bartholomew had sharply reduced his estimate of the Brazilian soybean crop. Bartholomew also testified that he never lowered his estimate and that the crop, in fact, was higher than the April estimate. He denied traveling to Brazil during 1978. However, Merrill Lynch never denied telling Boeck the crop estimate was going down.

Boeck claims that on May 17, 1978, Terrill learned that the Brazilian government had increased, not decreased, its soybean crop estimate. Terrill never gave Boeck this information even though Terrill handled numerous soybean and soybean meal trades for Boeck between May 17 and 30. Over 98 percent of Boeck's losses were sustained as a result of investments he made after May 17. Terrill, however, argues that the May 17 information did not indicate a change in Merrill Lynch's estimate, and, in fact, the reports were not consistent or conclusive.

The trial court found Merrill Lynch owed no fiduciary duty to Boeck, and the Court of Appeals affirmed.

Steinmetz, Judge

Both parties rely on *Schweiger v. Loew & Co., Incorporated,* to support their respective claims concerning a broker's fiduciary duty. In that case, this court held that a broker who is "handling" a customer's financial investments owes that customer a fiduciary duty. Boeck argues that this holding imposes a fiduciary duty in broker-customer relationships, such as the one in the present case. Merrill Lynch contends that Schweiger only imposes a fiduciary duty in the case of discretionary accounts. We agree that a broker does not have a fiduciary duty to a customer with a nondiscretionary account absent an express contract placing a greater obligation on the broker or other special circumstances.

We are persuaded by the decisions from other jurisdictions refusing to impose a fiduciary duty in the case of nondiscretionary accounts. In *Robinson v. Merrill Lynch, Pierce, Fenner & Smith, Inc.,* (1971), that court held that a fiduciary duty did not arise to require the transmission of all extrinsic facts or opinions related to the market in question unless there was an express contract or special circumstances which required defendant to transmit to plaintiff such information.

> "To make this defendant or any other broker the guardian of a customer such as the plaintiff would destroy an important part of the marketplace. In every case a trader could recover damages from his broker merely by proving non-transmission of some fact which, he could testify with the wisdom of hindsight, would have affected his judgment had he learned of it." In the instant case, there is no indication of any express agreement or special circumstances between Merrill Lynch and Boeck for the provision of investment decision services. . . .

The record in this case reveals that Boeck had a nondiscretionary account and that he made all the investment transaction decisions on his Merrill Lynch account. Terrill merely placed the orders at Boeck's request. Boeck was an experienced commodities trader who was aware of the risks and uncertainties of that type of investing. There is no express agreement on special circumstances to provide investment advice other than as an incident to brokerage activities. Upon these facts, we hold that a broker does not owe a fiduciary duty to an investor-customer who makes all of the investment decisions, unless there is an express agreement placing a greater obligation on the broker or other special circumstances. We are unpersuaded by the decisions of the Commodities Futures Trading Commission which Boeck construes as reaching a contrary result.

We are also unpersuaded by the concurrence's argument that a broker may become a fiduciary for a person with a nondiscretionary account by gaining the person's trust and confidence and purporting to advise that person with the other's interest in mind. A fiduciary relationship does not arise merely because a broker offers advice and counsel upon which a customer has a right to place trust and confidence. The right to place trust and confidence in the reliability of representations involving commercial transactions already is protected by the law of misrepresentation. A fiduciary relationship arises from a formal commitment to act for the benefit of another (for example, a trustee) or from special circumstances from which the law will assume an obligation to act for another's benefit. The mere fact of reliance on representations, therefore, does not necessarily create a relationship of trust and confidence leading to a fiduciary duty. Thus, we do not hold that a fiduciary duty may arise out of every circumstance where there is a relationship of trust and confidence between the parties.

Here, Merrill Lynch did not formally agree to make investment decisions for Boeck. In fact, Boeck always remained ultimately responsible for making investment decisions, as required by his nondiscretionary account. Also, no special circumstances exist from which we could find that Merrill Lynch should be responsible as a fiduciary for Boeck's investment decisions. Moreover, if we held that a broker is a fiduciary in these circumstances, then an investor could allege that the broker exercised poor judgment when advising the investor. This is because the duty of a fiduciary is greater than simply the duty not to misrepresent. A professional fiduciary, like a broker, also would be held to a higher degree of skill and care than a man of ordinary prudence. Recognizing the full implications of treating a broker as a fiduciary, we refuse to hold that a broker is liable as a fiduciary for representations to an investor with a nondiscretionary account. We would make a broker a guarantor of a customer's investments if we held otherwise. . . . Although the trial court and the court of appeals correctly ruled that Merrill Lynch did not owe Boeck a fiduciary duty and that strict responsibility is not an issue in this case, we conclude that Boeck is entitled to a new trial on the negligent misrepresentation theory of liability. We base this conclusion on the fact that the real controversy was not fully and fairly tried.

Louis, Judge and Cecil, Judge (dissenting)

Although no express contract existed between Merrill Lynch and Boeck regarding investment advisory services, there is no doubt that Merrill Lynch undertook to provide such advice and market information to Boeck as an incident to the commodities account agreement.

It is undisputed . . . that Merrill Lynch never denied telling Boeck that the crop estimate was going down. Nor is it questioned that Merrill Lynch failed to inform Boeck that the Brazilian government had increased its estimate to the country's soybean crop. And no one, not even the majority, disputes that "the size of the Brazilian soybean crop was a significant, material factor affecting the price of soybean futures."

Boeck established that he sustained over ninety-eight percent of his losses in soybean futures as a result of investments made after the critical date of May 17, 1978, the date when Boeck asserts that Terrill first learned that the Brazilian government's soybean estimate directly varied with the Merrill Lynch estimate. Merrill Lynch, through Terrill, never relayed this critical information to Boeck. In other words, the jury found, and nowhere does the majority disagree, that Merrill Lynch undertook to provide its client Boeck with material investment advice and failed to provide Boeck with critical information in its possession which varied with its earlier information. This constitutes a breach of Merrill Lynch's fiduciary duty owed to Boeck. The breach caused Boeck to sustain substantial losses in the soybean market.

The extent of a broker's fiduciary duty in this situation would require that it disclose to the client all significant, material information in its possession regarding the transactions involved. Here, Merrill Lynch would be required to disclose to Boeck all significant, material information regarding the status of the Brazilian soybean crop. Merrill Lynch's fiduciary duty subsumes, at the very least, a responsibility to disclose information it possesses which is contrary to the significant, material information it originally gave to the client. A finding that Merrill Lynch breached its fiduciary duty owed to Boeck would not make Merrill Lynch "a guarantor of [Boeck's] investments." Rather, such a finding would merely make a broker liable for its fiduciary breaches. . . .

The trust and confidence which Boeck placed in Merrill Lynch became legally significant when Merrill Lynch undertook to inform Boeck of the status of the soybean commodities market and of its own decreased projections for the Brazilian soybean crop. Merrill Lynch breached its fiduciary duty when it failed to inform Boeck of the significant, material information of the Brazilian government's promising forecasts for the crop. The jury was correct in its verdict determination regarding breach of fiduciary duty; I disagree with the majority's contrary conclusion.

Case Questions

1. According to the majority opinion, does a broker generally have a fiduciary obligation to customers who use the broker to purchase and sell securities? Is that also true if the customer is buying and selling commodities, futures, or options?
2. If Merrill Lynch had a fiduciary relationship with Boeck, would the broker be able to prove he performed the fiduciary duty if he proved he did not misrepresent any information to Boeck?
3. According to the dissenting opinion, what is the reason for imposing a fiduciary duty on Merrill Lynch and how did it breach that duty?

Note that the fiduciary duty may also be imposed by regulation. For example, the New York Stock Exchange has recently indicated that "discount" stockbrokers who simply execute customer directed trades without providing investment advice may nevertheless be held to the "suitability" duty. This is a derivative of the fiduciary duty requiring brokers to "know their customers' " financial condition and risk preferences and make only "suitable" trades, for example, no risky commodity futures for widows and conservative investors.

Legal and Ethical Lapses for Japanese Firms

International Perspective and Commentary

Ten Japanese securities firms provided over one billion dollars in investment losses to favored clients. Between October 1987 and March 1990, the Big Four Japanese firms—Nomura Securities, Nikko Securities, Daiwa Securities, and Yamaichi Securities—admitted spending over $900 million on behalf of 229 customers. Six more firms provided $260 million to favored clients.

The securities firms sought to make up losses suffered by the clients as the Japanese stock market declined sharply in 1990. The firms also reported they had recorded the compensation to clients as losses for tax purposes. The Japanese Ministry of Finance asked the firms to revise their financial accounts to accurately reflect the compensation paid to the clients.

The securities firms of course not only represented the favored clients, but regular clients as well. How could the firms, as an agent working for all clients, compensate some clients for losses they suffered while not compensating others? Do the securities firms owe ethical and legal obligations to potential clients to disclose their payments to favored clients? Who is injured by these practices?

The Duty of Loyalty Loyalty is the most important fiduciary duty imposed by law on the agent. The agent must honestly represent the principal's interests. Any conflicts between the principal's interests and the agent's interests must be disclosed to the principal or avoided by the agent. For example, the law requires a stockbroker to disclose the brokerage firm's role in underwriting a new issue of a company's stock to its clients.

A stock underwriter receives compensation for selling stock, so it cannot also receive compensation from a client-buyer unless it discloses its dual role to the client-buyer.

The agent's duty of loyalty also prohibits representation of two principals that are contracting together unless these principals know of the agent's dual role and agree to it. Some professions prohibit any *dual agencies.* For example, an attorney cannot represent opposing parties in a case. One of the parties can go unrepresented while the attorney represents the other party, but it must be made clear that the attorney is working on behalf of only one party. However, if an agent is merely a broker seeking to bring two parties together and neither party relies on the broker for advice and assistance in negotiation, the courts will allow the agent-broker to perform this limited *middleman* or *finder* function.

corporate opportunity doctrine
Prohibits the diversion of business opportunities by corporate directors, officers, or key employees if the corporation has an expectancy in the opportunities.

The Corporate Opportunity Doctrine The **corporate opportunity doctrine** prohibits the diversion of business opportunities by corporate directors, officers, or key employees if the corporation has an expectancy in the opportunities. The doctrine is based on applying fiduciary duties, such as the duty of loyalty, to corporate agents. The doctrine prohibits the agents from using their positions in the corporation to identify promising business opportunities for themselves if the corporation might have an interest in those opportunities. The misuse of such opportunities for personal benefit constitutes a breach of fiduciary duty.

In one case, Guth, president of the Loft retail store chain, borrowed the company's money and used its office personnel and credit to purchase Pepsi-Cola stock for himself. Loft's board of directors claimed that the corporate opportunity to purchase the stock should have been offered to the company first. Guth had been alerted to the availability of the stock because he was the president of Loft. Since cola products were sold in the Loft stores, Loft would probably have been interested in the purchase. The Supreme Court of Delaware found that the purchase of the Pepsi-Cola shares was a corporate opportunity belonging to Loft that Guth had wrongfully misappropriated for his own benefit.[1]

Of course, corporate fiduciaries may undertake personal business activities without breaching their fiduciary duties. The key determination is whether the corporation has an interest or expectancy sufficient to establish a "beachhead" in the type of opportunity involved. If the opportunity is in the same "line of business" as existing corporate activities, then the agent's duty is to present it to the corporation. Must a corporate fiduciary present business opportunities to the corporation if the fiduciary learns of them outside his or her business capacity? The following case explores the uncertainties of the opportunities in which the corporation has an expectancy.

Science Accessories v. Summagraphics

425 A.2d 957 (1980)
Supreme Court of Delaware

Three employees of Science Accessories (SAC) quit to develop and market a new product with Summagraphics Corporation. Although the product that Summagraphics sold was conceived by a Dr. Brenner, who had not been associated with SAC, SAC claimed that

[1] *Guth v. Loft, Inc.*, 5 A.2d 503 (1939).

these employees acquired secret information from it that they later used to develop Brenner's product on behalf of Summagraphics. Each of the employees had signed a contract with SAC stipulating that inventions or discoveries made while they were employees of SAC belonged to it. SAC claimed that the employees could not use that secret information without breaching their contractual and fiduciary duties to SAC and without taking a corporate opportunity from SAC. The trial court found for the employees, and SAC appealed to the Supreme Court of Delaware.

Horsey, Justice

The basis of defendants' alleged breach of contractual duties to SAC was a technology disclosure agreement which each of them had signed as an employee of SAC and which, in pertinent part, provided:

> Any invention or discovery which I may make or conceive, either alone or jointly with others, while employed by the Company, for any improvement in process, machine, manufacture or composition of matter, which relates to the Company's business . . . shall be the property of the Company, whether patentable or not and whether made or conceived during regular business hours or otherwise. I will fully and promptly disclose to the Company . . . all information known to me concerning such improvement. . . .

SAC claims that defendants' conduct was in breach of fiduciary duties defendants owed SAC under agency law principles. It is true, of course, that under elemental principles of agency law, an agent owes his principal a duty of good faith, loyalty, and fair dealing. Encompassed within such general duties of an agent is a duty to disclose information that is relevant to the affairs of the agency entrusted to him. There is also a corollary duty of an agent not to put himself in a position antagonistic to his principal concerning the subject matter of his agency.

However, agency law is not without its limitations as to both duty to disclose and duty not to act adversely to a principal's business. Thus, an agent is not under a duty to disclose to his principal information obtained in confidence, the disclosure of which would be a breach of duty to a third person. Similarly, an agent is not prevented from acting in good faith outside his employment even though it may adversely affect his principal's business. Further, an agent can make arrangements or plans to go into competition with his principal before terminating his agency, provided no unfair acts are committed or injury done his principal.

These principles and limitations of agency law carry over into the field of corporate employment so as to apply not only to officers and directors, but also to key managerial personnel. They reflect competing policy interests in the law as to employer-employee relationships. On the one hand, there is ". . . concern for the integrity of the employment relationship [which] has led courts to establish a rule that demands of a corporate officer or employee an undivided and unselfish loyalty to the corporation."

However, there is an offsetting policy "recognized by the courts . . . of safeguarding society's interest in fostering free and vigorous competition in the economic sphere . . . This policy in favor of free competition has prompted the recognition of a privilege in favor of employees which enables them to prepare or make arrangements to compete with their employers prior to leaving the employ of their prospective rivals without fear of incurring liability for breach of their fiduciary duty of loyalty."

The doctrine of corporate opportunity represents one aspect of the law's effort to reconcile these competing policy interests. The doctrine of corporate opportunity is a species of the duty of a fiduciary to act with undivided loyalty. Thus, the law of corporate opportunity is clearly pertinent, if not decisive, to the issue of whether defendants breached any fiduciary duty owed SAC.

Briefly summarized, the law is that if a business opportunity is presented to a corporate executive, the officer cannot seize the opportunity for himself if: (a) the corporation is financially able to undertake it; (b) it is within the corporation's line of business; (c) the corporation is interested in the opportunity. *Guth v. Loft, Inc.* A corollary of the Guth rule is that when a business opportunity comes to a corporate officer which . . . is not one which is essential or desirable for his corporation to embrace, the officer is entitled to treat the business opportunity as his own and the corporation has no interest in it.

Whether the Guth rule or its corollary applies depends, of course, on the facts and the reasonable inferences to be drawn therefrom. Here, the uncontradicted findings of the Court below were that SAC was "neither inclined nor able to develop new products" in the digitizer field by reason of its poor financial condition and its evident unwillingness during the period in question "to develop products suggested by Whetstone." Those findings are clearly sufficient to support the trial court's conclusion that Brenner's concept was not an opportunity available to SAC but one that defendants could legally embrace as their own; and SAC does not claim otherwise.

Since Brenner's concept was found to be an outside opportunity not available to SAC, defendants' failure to disclose the concept to SAC, and their taking it to themselves for purposes of competing with SAC, cannot be found to be in breach of any agency fiduciary duty.

Affirmed.

Case Questions

1. Explain the "competing policy interests" which concern judges in resolving cases claiming that agents who take information with them to competitors are violating their agency obligation.
2. Explain the relationship between the corporate opportunity doctrine and an agent's duty of loyalty to the corporation.
3. What is the primary reason the court in this case found that the agent employees had not violated the corporate opportunity doctrine?

Duty to Communicate Information One of the essential aspects of the principal-agent relationship is that a third party can provide information to an agent and assume that the agent will provide the information to the principal. For example, if an insurance policyholder informs an insurance agent about changes in the insured property, the policyholder assumes that the agent will pass the information on to the insurer. The agent has the duty to pass along information concerning the insured property and can be liable for losses to the principal (insurer) resulting from his or her failure to do so. This duty is sometimes seen as an extension of the duty of loyalty that the agent owes to the principal.

The duty to disclose information was at issue when a savings and loan association, which ordered a termite inspection conducted on a home that it was mortgaging for a potential buyer, was informed by the inspector that the home was infested with termites. Although the savings and loan association argued that the termite inspection had been conducted for its benefit, not for that of the home purchaser-principal, the Supreme Court of Ohio found that it had violated its duty to disclose the information obtained from the inspection to its principal:

> One who acts as an agent for another becomes a fiduciary with respect to matters within the scope of the agency relation. . . . An agent owes his principal a duty to disclose all material information which the agent learns concerning the subject matter of the agency relation and about which the principal is not apprised. Furthermore, where a principal suffers loss through his agent's failure to function in accordance with his duty, the agent becomes liable to the principal for the resulting damages.
>
> From that [agency] relationship arose a duty to inform them of the results of the inspection, and the breach of that duty resulted in the damages found by the jury to have been sustained by appellees. In reliance that the inspection would be conducted and the results made available to them, no separate inspection was initiated by appellees. Appellant was duty-bound to disclose the material facts relating to the termite infestation before recording the deed.[2]

[2] *Miles v. Perpetual Savings & Loan,* 380 N.E.2d 1364 (1979).

Duty of Obedience The principal has the right to direct the agent to perform certain activities, and the agent must obey all reasonable instructions regarding the agency. For example, a firm may direct its employees not to accept personal checks in payment for merchandise that they sell for it. Then, if an employee accepts an uncollectible check on the firm's behalf, the employee can be held liable to the firm. Of course, the agent does not have to follow the principal's instructions to commit illegal acts. And there are even instances in which the agent may act contrary to the principal's instructions.

In an emergency, the agent is allowed to disregard the principal's instructions if doing so is in the principal's best interest. Suppose that a truck driver hauling perishable foodstuffs for a firm was instructed to use the firm's credit card only for gas and oil purchases. If as a result of an emergency situation, such as a flooded roadway or a freak ice storm, the driver has to do something to keep the foodstuffs from spoiling, despite the instructions the driver could use the credit card to pay for their storage during the emergency.

Duty to Use Reasonable Care The agent has the duty to use reasonable care in the performance of his or her duties. The extent of an agent's duty of care is determined by the type of work the agent performs. An accountant performing an audit must use the care that reasonable accountants would use in performing similar work. The agent must use reasonable care in looking after the principal's property. If goods are damaged, lost, or destroyed while in an agent's possession, the agent could be held liable if he or she did not exercise reasonable care. However, the agent is not an insurer of the goods or a guarantor of their safety; only reasonable care is required.

Duty to Account If the agent receives money or property for the principal's business, the agent must provide an accounting to the principal regarding the items received. If the agent is authorized to use the funds for certain expenditures, the agent must keep receipts and record expenditures. One aspect of the duty to account is the agent's duty to give the principal anything of value that the agent receives from third parties in connection with the principal's business. If the agent receives special gifts or money from parties dealing with the principal, the agent must turn over those items to the principal.

Companies usually have policies regarding the amount of personal gifts that key employees, such as purchasing agents, may keep. For example, a company might allow the agent to retain items valued at less than $100. Absent such a policy, the agent must account for all items received while he or she is acting on the principal's behalf.

Duties Owed by the Principal to the Agent

The principal's duties to the agent are based on the contract between them and on agency law, but not on the fiduciary relationship. This is because the agent, acting for the principal, is the fiduciary, but not vice versa. Even if a contract is silent, a principal is usually obligated by agency law to compensate the agent. Further, if the agent spends money on the principal's behalf, the principal must reimburse the agent for those outlays. Finally, the agent who suffers losses due to legal action by a third party is entitled to be indemnified for those losses by the principal.

Duty to Compensate Although usually the principal must compensate the agent, it is possible for the principal and the agent to agree that the agent will not be

gratuitous agency
A relationship in which one person acts on behalf of another without any expectation of being compensated.

compensated for activities performed on the principal's behalf. This creates a relationship known as **gratuitous agency.** One friend may assist another in moving, or several people may volunteer to perform work on behalf of a charitable organization. While these people are agents working on behalf of others, they do not expect to be compensated for their services. On the other hand, a salesperson, truck driver, or stockbroker who acts as an agent on behalf of someone else usually has the right to receive compensation for services performed. Generally, the details of the terms of compensation are expressed in a contract.

The employment contract generally indicates how the compensation is to be paid: by a salary, commission, or bonus arrangement or by some combination thereof. Although it is not uncommon for people to begin an agency relationship without a written contract, using such an agreement can eliminate many future problems. For example, settling the form of compensation ahead of time can prevent disputes; likewise, a clarification of the expenses that will be reimbursed should be included in any agent's contract.

Sometimes an agent's compensation depends on the occurrence of a special event. If the event does not occur, the agent has no right to compensation. For example, attorneys representing personal injury plaintiffs frequently agree to be paid a *contingency fee;* the fee is due only if compensation is awarded to the plaintiff by the court or through settlement. Stockbrokers and salespeople are frequently paid on a commission basis. Brokers are paid a commission for selling stock to customers or obtaining orders from them. Otherwise, they have a right to reimbursement from their employers for expenses, but no right to compensation.

If there is no contract between the principal and the agent detailing the terms and conditions affecting the agent's right to compensation, the law implies that reasonable compensation will be paid for services that the agent renders.

Duty to Reimburse Expenses The agent who advances his or her funds in conducting business for the principal is entitled to be reimbursed by the principal if the principal has authorized the agent's activities. A salesperson instructed to attend a meeting on the principal's behalf would be entitled to reimbursement for registration fees, and travel and lodging expenses incurred while attending the meeting. On the other hand, if a salesperson attended a meeting without first notifying the principal, the principal would not be legally obligated to reimburse the agent for these expenses.

Duty to Indemnify The principal's duty to reimburse the agent for expenses extends to indemnifying the agent for losses that the agent incurs while conducting the principal's business. For example, if the agent loses money while performing a contract, the principal must compensate the agent for the loss. The duty to indemnify also applies to expenses that the agent incurs in defending claims brought against the agent while performing authorized acts for the principal. For example, if a third party claims that a pizza delivery driver damaged that party's property, expenses incurred by the driver-agent in defending the litigation are reimbursable.

Duty to Provide Safe Working Conditions The law requires the principal to provide safe premises and equipment for its agents and employees. The principal has to inspect the workplace and warn the agent of any unsafe conditions. Chapters 18 and 21 discuss specific obligations of employers with regard to employee safety and environmental hazards.

Ethical Dilemma: Your Agent's Obligation—To You?

Ethical Dilemma

"Let's call our travel agent to see where she can find the best price for our trip."

"We've looked at a number of office sites with our real estate agent; do you think she can help us determine which one we can get for the best price?"

"Ted, our insurance agent, says the life insurance policy offered by the Rock Solid Insurance Firm is the best one for us; should we go ahead and get that policy, or do you want to look around some more?"

Each of these statements assumes that a person looking to purchase travel services, real estate, or insurance products can call on an agent to look after their interest. In each case, the agent that the potential purchaser is planning to deal with represents the provider of the services, not the purchaser. The travel agent is paid by hotels and by airlines when they sell a room or a ticket to you. As agents, they have legal duties to their principal, not to you, the third party. The real estate agent represents the seller and is paid a commission by the seller if the agent gets the purchaser to contract to buy the seller's property. The insurance agent does not have an obligation to search for the best policy to fit your needs. Instead, the agent's obligation is to the insurance company(s) he or she represents.

As a possible purchaser of these services, you need to understand that the agent is not working on your behalf. An agent has an ethical obligation to inform third parties that he or she does not represent them. Of course, in promoting the interest of its principal, the agent can and should be helpful to potential customers. Firms that use agents to deal with third parties should take responsibility for the acts of the agent. If travel agents, realtors, or insurance representatives make mistakes or cause problems, it is the firm they represent, not the customer, who has the obligation to rectify the problems.

The Contract Liability of the Principal for Agency Activities

The liability of the principal for both the contractual and tortious activities of its representatives depends on the nature of the relationship between the principal and the representative and on the knowledge and perceptions of third parties regarding their relationship. The knowledge and perception of the third party regarding the relationship determines the principal's liability for contracts agreed to between an agent and a third party. This section examines the three basic agency relationships and the attendant liability of the principal or employer for contracts negotiated by the principal's representative.

Contracts and a Master–Servant Relationship

Where a master-servant relationship exists, the master has the right to control the physical acts of the servant-employee. The servant generally has no authority to make contracts for the master or to act on the master's behalf. No third party should expect a factory employee at General Motors to be able to contract for that corporation. A third party who does contract with such a person would not be able to hold the principal (General Motors) liable because the third party should know that the agent has no authority to act on behalf of the firm.

Contracts and an Employer-Independent Contractor Relationship

Similarly, with an employer-independent contractor relationship, the independent contractor usually has no authority to contract on behalf of the employer. If one person contracts to hire another person as a plumber, dentist, or accountant, the employer does not thereby authorize that person to make contracts for the employer. Further, the hiring of such a person does not give any third party reason to believe that the person has authority to make contracts for the employer. Since the independent contractor does not receive actual or apparent authority from the principal-employer, the principal-employer will not be liable for contracts that the independent contractor makes with third parties.

Contracts and a Principal-Agent Relationship

Difficulties regarding the liability for contracts negotiated by an agent with third parties occur when there is a principal-agent relationship. The principal's liability for contracts that an agent makes with third parties depends on the third party's knowledge of that agency relationship. Principals may be classified as disclosed, partially disclosed, or undisclosed.

disclosed principal
One whose existence and identity is known by the third party when it contracts with the agent.

Disclosed Principal A **disclosed principal** is one whose existence and identity is known by the third party when it contracts with the agent. If the agent discloses the existence and identity of the principal to the third party and the agent acts within the scope of his or her authority, the principal is liable for the contract the agent makes with the third party. Only the principal is liable to the third party; the agent has no contractual liability. For example, when IBM sells computers to a university, a representative of IBM negotiates with a representative of the university. These employees are agents who have disclosed the identity and existence of their principals. Thus, the university as a third party cannot hold the IBM employee personally liable for the performance of the contract. Likewise, IBM cannot hold the employee of the university personally liable for the university's performance of the contract.

If the agent acts beyond his or her authority and the third party has no reason to know that the agent is exceeding that authority, the agent is liable to the third party. The agent's liability is based on a breach of the implied warranty of authority the agent makes to the third party, not on the contract itself. The principal would not be liable for the unauthorized acts of the agent unless there is either apparent authority or ratification.

partially disclosed principal
One whose existence is known by the third party, but whose identity is unknown; the third party knows the agent is acting for someone else but does not know the identity of the principal.

Partially Disclosed Principal A **partially disclosed principal** is one whose existence is known by the third party, but whose identity is unknown; the third party knows the agent is acting for someone else but does not know the identity of the principal. If an agent discloses the existence of a principal but not the principal's identity, the contracting third party may hold either the principal or the agent liable if the contract is not performed.

For example, if a real estate development firm is seeking to build a new shopping mall or an amusement park in an area, it may seek to purchase the needed property by acting through agents. If the developer discloses its intention to buy many different parcels of property, after it has purchased some property the price of the remaining property it hopes to buy will increase significantly in price. Thus, a developer might ask 5 or 10 different agents to seek to buy the desired property, instructing each not to disclose the developer's identity to the sellers. If the owners who are approached by agents interested in buying their property know the agents are representing someone, they know an agency relationship exists between the agent and the undisclosed principal. However, they would not know the identity of the principal.

If a contract between a third party and an agent obligates the agent to pay money over a period of several years, the third party can hold either the agent or the principal liable if the money is not paid as promised. The agent is liable because that is the person with whom the third party negotiated and with whom that party thought he or she was contracting. The principal is liable because the agent was acting within the scope of his or her authority in contracting to purchase the property. The third party's *election* (seeking to hold either the principal or the agent liable on the performance of the contract) usually occurs once he or she discovers the identity of the principal. This may take place even after litigation against the agent has begun. The principal, although undisclosed at the time of the contract, can also enforce the contract against the third party.

Undisclosed Principal An **undisclosed principal** is one whose existence and identity is unknown to the third party. The third party thinks the contract is being made by the agent on his or her own behalf, not as an agent for an unknown principal. If the agent is acting for a totally undisclosed principal, the third party is not aware of an agency relationship. In this case, the third party holds the agent liable on the contract. It is the agent who has to perform the contract because the third party reasonably believed that the agent, not some unknown person whom the agent in fact represented, made the contract. As in the case of the partially disclosed principal, if the third party learns of the existence and identity of the principal, the third party may elect to hold the principal liable instead of the agent. The third party cannot, however, hold both agent and principal liable on the same contract.

undisclosed principal One whose existence and identity is unknown to the third party when it contracts with the principal's agent.

Liability of the Agent

Most agents do not want to be held personally liable on contracts they make on their principal's behalf. The agent who does not want to be held liable for such contracts can clearly indicate the principal party that is to be held liable. If a person signs a contract as "Mike Sleaford," there is no reason to think that he is acting as an agent. He has signed his own name and will be held liable. If he signs the contract as "Mike Sleaford, agent for First Southern Bank," it may not be clear whether Mike or the bank will be held liable. If Mike wants to make it obvious that he is not to be held liable, he can sign as follows: "First Southern Bank, by Mike Sleaford, its agent." Here, Mike has indicated that First Southern Bank is the principal to be held liable and that he signed for it as an agent, not as the principal contracting party.

In some cases, the agent will be liable either as a cosigner or a guarantor. For example, when a small company seeks a loan from a financial institution, the financial status of the company is often too precarious for the lender to make the loan unless the owner agrees to be liable. Thus, if George Smith, president of Smith's Auto Body Repair, Inc., wants to borrow money from First of America Bank, the bank will loan to Smith's Auto Body Repair, Inc., only if George Smith also personally agrees to pay back the loan. The loan is to the corporation as principal, and George as its president is its agent. Because George also signs to repay the loan, he is also a coprincipal. Here, George's liability is based on his being a principal, not on his being the corporation's agent.

FIGURE 13–3

Contract Liability When Agent Makes Contracts with Third Parties

Type of Agent's Authority	Disclosed Principal	Partially Disclosed Principal	Undisclosed Principal
Actual Authority	Principal is liable; agent is not liable.	Third party may elect to hold either principal or agent liable.	Third party may elect to hold either principal or agent liable.
Apparent Authority	Principal is liable; agent is not liable.	Third party may elect to hold either principal or agent liable.	There cannot be both apparent authority (from principal) and an undisclosed principal.
Ratification	Only agent is liable until ratification; only principal is liable after ratification.	Only agent is liable until ratification; after ratification either principal or agent is liable at third party's election.	[Same as for partially disclosed principal.]
Unauthorized Act by Agent	Agent is liable for third party's damages; principal is not liable.	[Same as for disclosed principal.]	[Same as for disclosed principal.]

George would be regarded as a guarantor if he agreed to repay the loan if the corporation were unable to do so. In this situation, while both George and the corporation are liable, the lender must first seek repayment from the corporation before asking George to pay the loan. It is important for agents to understand that when they become comakers or guarantors of loans made to their principals, they become personally liable. Figure 13–3 depicts the contract liability of the principal when its agent makes contracts with third parties.

The Tort Liability of the Principal for Agency Activities

The tort liability of the principal for wrongs committed by its representatives depends both on the nature of the relationship between the principal and representative and on how the action in question relates to the representatives' work for the principal. While the principal is usually liable for the torts committed by its servant-employees, it is usually not liable for torts committed by its independent contractors. As for liability of the principal for torts of its agent, determining whether an agent acts within the scope of his or her authority is critical in assessing the principal's liability. Figure 13–4 portrays the tort liability of the principal for each of the three major types of agency relations: the master-servant, the principal-agent, and the employer-independent contractor.

FIGURE 13-4 Tort Liability of Principal

Type of Relation	General Characteristics	Examples	Principal's Liability for Agent's Torts
Master-servant referred to as employer-employee	Employee is under direct control of employer. Master or employer gives detailed directions to servant or employee.	Restaurant manager supervises dishwashers. Foreman supervises assembly line worker.	Master usually liable for servant's torts.
Principal-agent	Principal has right to control actions of agent but does not exercise detailed control over all of the agent's physical activities.	Sales manager tells sales agent what route to cover and what policies to use. Vice president of bank manages bank activities.	Principal liable if act of agent is within agent's scope of authority.
Employer-independent contractor	Independent contractor is *not* subject to employer's control. Contractor agrees to results but determines how to achieve those results.	Roofing contractor determines how to roof, and home owner agrees to end result. Business firm employs messenger service to deliver messages in town, and messenger service determines how deliveries are to be made.	Employee is usually not liable; exception for nondelegable duties.

Liability of Master-Employer for Torts of Servant-Employee

Since the employer has the right to control the activities of the servant-employee, the employer will be liable to third parties who are injured by the employee's actions. This vicarious liability of the employer is in addition to the liability of the employee-servant who commits the tort. A person is not excused from liability for a tort merely because the tort occurs while the person is working for an employer.

As a practical matter, the injured third party will usually turn to the employee-principal firm, rather than to the employee, for compensation. If the employee is acting to further the employer's business, rather than acting solely on his or her own behalf, the employer will be liable.

Principal's Liability for Torts Committed by Its Agents The firm as principal is liable for the tortious acts of its agent if the activities of the agent are within his or her scope of authority. This rule of **respondeat superior,** "let the superior respond," holds the principal liable regardless of the principal's fault or lack of fault. The principal's liability is based on the agent's tort; it is the agent's tort, not that of the principal, that is the basis for the vicarious liability imposed on the principal.

respondeat superior The term, meaning let the superior respond, is used to describe the liability of the principal for the torts of its agent when the agent is acting in the scope of its authority to further the principal's interests.

For example, if a negligent driver for Pizza Hut causes injury to a pedestrian, the driver is liable, but the injured party can sue both the driver and Pizza Hut. However, the injured party can collect only once, either totally from one party or partially from each of the parties. The fact that Pizza Hut is liable does not displace the liability of the driver. Liability is imposed on the principal because the principal directed or authorized the agent to act in its place. Essentially, in exchange for enabling the principal to do business through the agent, the law imposes liability on the principal when its agent, while acting within the scope of his or her employment, commits torts.

Because "the scope of authority" limits the principal's liability for the agent's torts, it is important to determine what acts are outside the agent's authority. When the agent acts on his or her own and not in furtherance of the principal's business, the principal is not held liable. The acts of the agent are then beyond the scope of the agent's authority. While the law often leans toward compensation for the injured party, the principal will not be liable for acts of its agent that are clearly beyond that agent's scope of authority. Consider one court's discussion of this issue regarding one of the fastest growing torts in the workplace of the 1990s.

Smith v. American Express Travel Services

876 P.2d 1166 (1994)
Arizona Court of Appeals

Smith, a 22-year employee of American Express Travel Related Services (TRS) was employed in Phoenix, Arizona, as a fraud coordinator in the Fraud Operations Department from January 1984 until August 1990. Nally was also a 20-year employee of TRS and was the manager of TRS Fraud Operations for the United States. Nally was not Smith's direct supervisor.

From 1984 until the end of 1987, Nally and Smith had a friendly relationship. Nally occasionally touched her on the arm and shoulders or put an arm around her waist, but Smith was not offended by Nally's conduct. Beginning in December 1987, Nally began to engage in what Smith believes was sexual harassment. In addition to teasing her at her desk, he grabbed or touched Smith's breasts, rubbed up against her, touched her leg under her dress and tossed candy down the front of her blouse, all in the view of other employees. On at least four occasions, he forced her to have sex with him at various locations in the TRS building. Smith submitted to those advances because she felt physically threatened by him and she was afraid she might lose her job even though Nally never threatened her if she refused.

During this time, TRS had a written policy prohibiting sexual harassment. Copies of the policy were posted throughout the building, and TRS distributed a memo to its employees approximately once a year. Smith was familiar with TRS's sexual harassment policies and grievance procedures under which employees could submit written or oral complaints, even anonymously, to TRS's Human Resources Department for investigation.

Between December 1987 and July 1989, Smith complained about Nally's conduct to several nonmanagerial co-workers. Although they suggested she report Nally to the Human Resources Department, Smith declined, requesting that the matter be kept confidential.

In 1989, Smith told a manager in the fraud operations group about the sexual harassment. Another supervisor also learned of the alleged harassment and passed on the information to the human resources department. TRS immediately began an investigation, and it initially placed Nally on an indefinite suspension. Two weeks later, TRS gave Nally the option of resigning or being fired; he resigned.

Smith continued to work with TRS for another year and then left to take a similar position with a bank. Just before she left TRS, Smith filed suit against Nally and TRS. At the trial court, the judge ruled that Nally's conduct was outside the scope of employment, and it determined TRS could not be held vicariously liable for Nally's assault and battery and intentional infliction of emotional distress. The trial court entered judgment for TRS and ordered Smith to pay its attorneys' fees of $57,000 and costs of $4,300. Smith appealed.

Toci, Presiding Judge

We conclude that the trial court correctly ruled that Nally's conduct in sexually assaulting and harassing Smith was outside the scope of his employment. Nally's sexual misbehavior and assaultive conduct was neither the kind of activity for which he was hired nor was it actuated, even in part, by a desire to serve TRS. Thus, we follow the majority of cases that have held that, under common law principles, an employee's sexual harassment of another employee is not within the scope of employment.

We first observe that this appeal involves common law tort and contract claims rather than sexual harassment under either Title VII of the Civil Rights Act of 1964 or Arizona's Civil Rights Act. Title VII liability is much broader than common law tort liability. One reason is that in Title VII actions, employer liability is based on a statutory scheme that broadly defines employer to include agents of the employer. In common law tort actions, however, the acts of the employer's agents generally do not subject the employer to liability unless the elements of the doctrine of *respondeat superior* are met. Consequently, here we look to the common law doctrine rather than to the federal and state antidiscrimination statutes and cases interpreting such statutes.

According to the doctrine of *respondeat superior,* "an employer is vicariously liable only for the behavior of an employee who was acting within the course and scope of his employment." In Arizona, the conduct of a servant is within the scope of employment if it is of the kind the employee is employed to perform, it occurs substantially within the authorized time and space limit, and it is actuated at least in part by a purpose to serve the master.

Under Arizona law, an employee is acting within the scope of his employment while he is doing any reasonable thing which his employment expressly or impliedly authorizes him to do or which may reasonably be said to have been contemplated by that employment as necessarily or probably incidental to that employment. In other words, an employer is liable for the conduct of its employee if at the time the injury occurred the employee was performing a service in furtherance of the employer's business.

Whether an employee's tort is within the scope of employment is generally a question of fact. It is a question of law, however, if the undisputed facts indicate that the conduct was clearly outside the scope of employment.

Here, the trial court properly granted summary judgment finding that Nally's conduct was outside the scope of his employment. Nally's actions were not expressly or impliedly authorized as part of his job duties. Nor could his conduct have been reasonably necessary or probably incidental to his employment. Clearly, Nally did not perform a service in furtherance of TRS's business when he harassed and assaulted Smith. His alleged tortious actions were committed solely to further his own personal interests.

Our conclusion is supported by reported cases in other jurisdictions. Most courts that have considered the question have held that as a matter of law, an employee's sexual harassment of another employee is not within the scope of employment.

Smith claims, however, that the real issue is whether Nally's misconduct was foreseeable as within the range of responsibilities TRS entrusted to him. She argues that because TRS put Nally in a supervisory position where he could assault and harass women he supervised and because he was responsible for administering sexual harassment policies within the department, TRS is liable for his conduct. We disagree.

We conclude that no evidence exists from which a reasonable jury could conclude that TRS knew about Nally's sexual harassment and ratified it. Smith did not report the harassment or assaults to her own immediate supervisor, to Nally's supervisors, or to the TRS Human Resources Department. In fact, she attempted to keep TRS management from learning of Nally's conduct by telling those with whom she had discussed the matter to keep the information a secret. Finally, no evidence exists in this record from which a reasonable jury could conclude that TRS knew or should have known that Nally had created a sexually offensive working environment and thus was capable of sexual harassment.

In an effort to establish TRS's knowledge of Nally's conduct, Smith asserts that Bickel was aware of the sexual harassment when he was functioning as "acting supervisor" in the Fraud Department. This argument has no merit. No evidence exists in the record that Bickel acquired any knowledge of Nally's sexual misconduct while acting within the scope of his authority as an occasional supervisor. Second, although Bickel did act as Nally's temporary replacement, this naturally occurred while Nally was absent from work. On these occasions, since Nally was not on the job, Bickel could not have observed any misconduct by Nally.

Finally, the evidence is undisputed that during the time Bickel substituted for Nally, no person, including Smith, complained to Bickel about Nally's sexual harassment of Smith. Bickel's knowledge of Nally's conduct was necessarily obtained when he was not acting as a supervisor. Such knowledge is not imputed to TRS.

Nally's knowledge of the sexual harassment is not imputed as a matter of law to his employer. . . . [A]n agent's tortious conduct is imputed to the principal only if the agent acquired the information in the scope and course of his employment with the principal. Nally's duties did not include sexual assault or harassment. Thus, his knowledge of these activities cannot be imputed to TRS.

Smith presented no evidence from which a reasonable jury could find that TRS knew that Nally had created a sexually offensive work environment. Smith did not complain about Nally to any corporate employees with authority over Nally or any management employee who was responsible for dealing with such matters. Furthermore, Smith was unable to come forward with any evidence that any prior sexual harassment claim had ever been brought against Nally. . . . In absence of such evidence, a reasonable jury could not conclude that TRS could reasonably have foreseen that Nally would assault Smith.

Affirmed.

Case Questions

1. Explain how each of the three requirements which must be met in order to make an employer vicariously liable for the behavior of an employee acting within the scope of his or her employment are met (or not met) in this case.
2. What is the critical element that is missing in order for Smith to prove that TRS ratified Nally's conduct as its agent?
3. The court discusses several ways in which Smith, or someone who suffers sexual harassment as she did, could prove that the principal should be held liable for the acts of its agent. List two different ways in which she could show that the principal should be held liable for its agent's tortious acts.

Employer's Liability for Contracts Negotiated by an Independent Contractor In the employer-independent contractor relationship, the employer generally does not have the right to tell the independent contractor how to perform the work. Because the employer does not have the right to control the independent contractor's performance of the contract, the employer is generally not in a good position to ensure that the independent contractor performs with due care.

Therefore, an employer generally is not liable for torts committed by its independent contractor. If a roofing contractor repairs the roof on a person's home and some shingles blow off the roof and injure a neighbor, the roofing contractor is liable for the damage caused, but the home owner is not. The roofing contractor determines how to repair the roof, and the home owner does not control, or have the right to control, how the roofing contractor goes about doing so.

There are some exceptions to this general principle. An employer may by law be prohibited from delegating certain tasks to independent contractors. Employers who use independent contractors to perform such tasks will be held liable if the actions of the independent contractors are tortious toward third parties. The last paragraph of the case that follows discusses the circumstances under which an employer can be held liable for the torts of the independent contractor.

Similarly, because it is the absence of the employer's right to control that makes the employer-independent contractor relationship different from the other relationships between the employer and its representatives, courts closely examine the possible control of the employer. If the employer could have exercised some control but did not do so, the employer may be held liable for the torts of the independent contractor. How much control must an employer be able to exercise over an agent-contractor before being liable for the torts of that agent-contractor? The next case illustrates how the employer's right to control determines the nature of the relationship between the employer and its representative.

Massey v. Tube Art Display, Inc.

551 P.2d 1387 (1976)
Court of Appeals of Washington

Tube Art was to move a sign it provided for its client, McPherson Realty, to a new location. It hired Redford, a backhoe operator, to dig a hole at a spot that it marked. While digging the hole, Redford struck a gas pipeline. Finding no leak, he left the site. The next morning, an explosion in the building served by the pipeline killed several people and injured others. Massey, a tenant in the building, sued Tube Art for injuries caused to his property, claiming that it was liable for Redford's negligence as its employee-agent. The trial court agreed with Massey, and Tube Art appealed to the court of appeals, which affirmed the trial court's determination.

Swanson, Judge

Traditionally, servants and nonservant agents have been looked upon as persons employed to perform services in the affairs of others under an express or implied agreement, and who, with respect to physical conduct in the performance of those services, is subject to the other's control or right of control. An independent contractor, on the other hand, is generally defined as one who contracts to perform services for another, but who is not controlled by the other nor subject to the other's right to control with respect to his physical conduct in performing the services.

In determining whether one acting for another is a servant or independent contractor, several factors must be taken into consideration [as] listed in Restatement (Second) of Agency:

a. the extent of control which, by the agreement, the master may exercise over the work details;

b. whether or not the one employed is engaged in a distinct occupation or business;

c. the kind of occupation, with reference to whether, in the locality, the work is usually done under the direction of the employer or by a specialist without supervision;

d. the skill required in the particular occupation;

e. whether the employer or the workman supplies the instrumentalities, tools, and the place of work for the person doing the work;

f. the length of time for which the person is employed;

g. the method of payment, whether by the time or by the job;

h. whether or not the work is a part of the regular business of the employer;

i. whether or not the parties believe they are creating the relation of master and servant; and

j. whether the principal is or is not in business.

All of these factors are of varying importance in determining the type of relationship involved and, with the exception of the element of control, not all the elements need be present. It is the right to control another's physical conduct that is the essential and oftentimes decisive factor in establishing vicarious liability, whether the person controlled is a servant or a nonservant agent.

Our review of the evidence supports the trial court's evaluation of both the right and exercise of control even though Redford had been essentially self-employed for about 5 years at the time of trial, was free to work for other contractors, selected the time of day to perform the work assigned, paid his own income and business taxes and did not participate in any of Tube Art's employee programs. The testimony advanced at trial, which we find determinative, established that during the previous three years Redford had worked exclusively for sign companies and 90 percent of his time for Tube Art. He had no employees, was not registered as a contractor or subcontractor, was not bonded, did not himself obtain permits or licenses for his jobs, and dug the holes at locations and in dimensions in exact accordance with the instructions of his employer. In fact, Redford was left no discretion with regard to the placement of the excavations that he dug. Rather, it was his skill in digging holes pursuant to the exact dimensions prescribed that caused him to be preferred over other backhoe operators. We therefore find no disputed evidence of the essential factor—the right to control—nor is there any dispute that control was exercised over the most significant decisions—the size and location of the hole.

Assuming for the sake of argument that Redford acted as an independent contractor, this court does not accept Tube Art's argument that its liability is, therefore, negated. In the present case, Tube Art exercised control over where the hole was to be dug, the day it was to be dug and how deep the hole was to be. Moreover, it was not unreasonable to expect Tube Art to know that gas pipes might very well be lurking in the vicinity of the proposed excavation. In such a case it was incumbent upon Tube Art to ascertain where other service pipes might be. Failing this, Tube Art cannot now disclaim liability. Rather, where the danger to others is great, a duty is imposed upon an employer to make such provision against negligence as may be commensurate with the obvious danger. It is a duty which cannot be delegated to another so as to avoid liability for its neglect.

Affirmed.

Case Questions

1. Which of the factors suggested in the *Restatement (Second) of Agency* are most important in determining an employee's status as a servant or independent contractor?
2. Would the court have decided for Tube Art if Redford were considered an independent contractor?
3. In what way was Redford negligent? Could Massey have held him liable for that negligence? In what way was Tube Art negligent? Could Tube Art be held liable for its negligence as well as for the negligence of Redford?

SUMMARY

There are three different types of agency relationships: master-servant relationships, principal-agent relationships, and employer-independent contractor relationships. Agency relationships are generally created by contract. Even in the absence of a contract, however, an agency relationship may arise if the parties consent to it. The burden of proving an agency relationship rests with the person who claims it exists. For the agent's acts to be binding on the principal, there must be actual authority, apparent authority, or ratification from the principal. An agency relationship can be terminated by agreement of the parties or by operation of law.

Once an agency relationship exists, each of the parties owes certain duties to the others. The duties of the parties are usually specified in a contract. Even in the absence of an express agreement, however, the agent owes the principal several fiduciary duties: the duty of loyalty, the duty to communicate information, the duty to use reasonable care, and the duty to account. The principal also owes the agent several duties: generally, the principal must compensate the agent, reimburse the agent's expenses, indemnify the agent for losses, and provide the agent with a safe workplace.

Most agency problems spring from the agent's activities with third parties. Usually, the concern focuses on whether a principal can be held liable for the torts committed or the contracts negotiated by its agent. The liability of the principal depends on the type of agency relationship that exists and on the knowledge and perception of third parties regarding that relationship.

In the master-servant or employer-employee relationship, the employer has the right to control the employee's physical activities. Usually, the employee is under the direct control of the employer, which supervises and directs the employee's work. The employer is liable for torts of these employees that cause injury to third parties, but since any servant/employee has very limited authority to negotiate contracts for the employer, the employer is not liable for the employee's contracts.

The principal-agent relationship arises when a principal, such as a business firm, hires an agent to represent it and to work according to guidelines and procedures established by the principal. While the principal may not always be in direct control of the agent's physical activities, it usually retains the right to direct how the agent is to perform assigned tasks. The principal is liable for tortious acts of the agent that are within the agent's scope of authority and for contracts made by agents who disclose (fully or partially) the principal to third parties.

In the employer-independent contractor relationship, the employer contracts with another party, the independent contractor, to have that party perform certain tasks. The independent contractor, not the employer, determines how those tasks are performed. As the employer has no right to control the independent contractor's performance, the employer is usually not liable for tortious acts of the independent contractor. Unless otherwise agreed, the independent contractor has no authority to commit the employer to contracts.

Critical Thinking Review Questions

1. Describe the circumstances under which an agent may be held personally liable on a contract he or she signs on behalf of a principal with third parties.
2. Assume that an insurance company has fired a life insurance salesman who worked for the company for 15 years in a rural community. It does not notify the community at large or any of its former customers that this agent no longer works for it. The agent keeps his rate book, life insurance policies, and other documentation that he received from the insurance company. Three weeks after being fired, he sells a $100,000 term life insurance policy to a former customer. Would the insurance company be bound by the agent's actions? Why?
3. Which party, the master or the servant, is ultimately liable for torts that are the servant's rather than the master's fault? Would your answer change if the servant's torts were caused by the master's improper instructions?
4. Roberts, who lives in Boston, owns 10 acres of land in Florida. He writes Johns to inquire whether Johns would act as his agent in attempting to find a buyer for the land. After some correspondence, Johns agreed to act as Roberts's agent. Roberts relies on Johns's judgment with respect to the value of the land. After Johns wrote Roberts that $1,000 per acre was a reasonable price for it, Roberts agrees to a sale to a firm that purchased the land for $10,000. A short time later, Roberts learned that Johns was one of three partners in the purchasing firm and that the land was reasonably worth $30,000. Assume that the other partners knew these facts. What are Roberts's rights against Johns and the purchasing firm?
5. Chris, a general contractor, entered into a contract to build a house for Melanie. Chris subcontracted all of the carpentry work to Joe. Joe failed to enclose a stairwell, and Andrea, who was examining the house to install windows in it, fell through the stairwell and suffered injuries. Explain whether Melanie, Chris, and Joe would be held liable to compensate Andrea for her injuries.

CRITICAL THINKING EXERCISES

1. A principal employed an agent as a commercial real estate salesman on a commission basis. The principal allowed the agent to draw $1,500 a month as base pay. The salesman/agent worked for the principal for six months, but his commissions averaged less than $500 a month. The principal then terminated the agent's employment and sought to recover from the agent the amount by which the draw payments exceeded the earned commissions ($1,000 a month). Will the principal recover?
2. Jeff Reynolds is a project administrator of a high-tech corporation. His wife Maria, a former computer programmer, develops software in an office at home. Jeff and Maria dream of having their own company someday. Meanwhile, Jeff likes his job and his boss and works hard at the corporation. One day, Bill Fences, a software developer, demonstrates a terrific new software package that he wants Jeff's company to use and promote. Jeff is impressed. He indicates to Bill that the program is not exactly in line with his company's business, but that the company might be interested if the package were seen by the right people. However, Jeff does not offer the software package to his company. Instead, he and his wife plan to strike a deal with Bill and his company to market the package on a freelance basis on their own. Jeff confides in you, telling you what he and Maria are planning to do. He says, "Don't you think this is a great opportunity?" After your study of agency law, how would you reply?
3. Stokely-Van Camp, Inc., hires Lennen & Newell as its advertising agent. Lennen & Newell contracts with CBS for the purchase of advertising time. The contract Lennen & Newell makes with CBS is not signed by Stokely-Van Camp. If CBS is not paid for the advertising time, can it hold Stokely-Van Camp liable? *CBS v. Stokely-Van Camp, Inc.* 456 F.Supp. 539 (1977).
4. Davis was a salaried traveling salesman for Playtex. He had no set hours and worked only when necessary, including evenings and weekends. On a Sunday, he was planning to go to a friend's house to have dinner and do some paperwork. On the way, he was involved in an auto accident with Barnum. Barnum died, and Rappaport, his executor, brought suit against Playtex. Is Playtex liable for Davis' action? *Rappaport v. Playtex Corp.,* 352 N.Y. S.2d 241 (1974).
5. Haven had minor surgery but was paralyzed due to what he claims was negligence on the part of his surgeon. Haven wants to sue both the surgeon and the hospital where the surgery was performed. Dr. Randolph, the surgeon, was not employed by the hospital, and the hospital did not control the way in which Dr. Randolph performed the surgery on Haven. Is there a principal-agency relationship between Dr. Randolph and the hospital such that Haven can hold the hospital liable for Randolph's negligence? *Haven v. Randolph* 342 F. Supp. 538 (1972).
6. A personnel or human resources director at a firm may be given the responsibility for setting the salary level for new employees. Frequently, that person has a salary ceiling or range and, based on the qualifications of the candidate, has the authority to make an offer within those guidelines. Suppose you were the person with such authority and were interviewing a candidate for a position that normally pays $25,000 annually. After discussing the terms of employment with a candidate you'd like to hire, you ask the candidate, "What salary would you expect for this position?" If the candidate replies, "I'd like to be paid at least $20,000," what salary would you offer? Would it make a difference if you know that your performance will be more highly regarded if you hire for the lowest possible salary?

   Do you have legal or ethical obligations to your firm and to the candidate for employment, or to just one of them? If you knew that the candidate likely would later find out that he or she could have asked for $5,000 more in salary, would this change your answer? Does it matter whether the candidate is the sole support of a family and needs the higher salary?

CHAPTER 14

Business Organizations

Critical Thinking Questions

- How does the principle that a fiduciary has obligations to those it represents affect partners in a partnership and officers in a corporation?
- Why does the business judgment rule absolve members of a corporation's board of directors from liability stemming from their negligent acts? Is the rule applied equally to all directors? Why?
- What are the advantages a corporation enjoys by separating managerial control over corporate activities from ownership of the corporation?
- What arguments would you make for disregarding the separate legal status of a corporation if you wanted to hold the shareholders of the corporation personally liable for corporate debts?
- Explain how the limited liability company differs from the corporation and how a limited partnership differs from a general partnership. Why were these organizations created, and what purpose do they serve?

Introduction . . . Past, Present, Future

The sole proprietorship is the oldest and most common form of business organization. No special legal formalities are needed to establish a sole proprietorship; and no special legal rules, since it has a single owner, regulate relations among its participants.

Like the sole proprietorship, the partnership form of business organization has existed for thousands of years. Although no special requirements must be met to form a partnership, it is customary and desirable to prepare a partnership agreement. Most state partnership laws are now based on the Revised Uniform Partnership Act. The limited partnership, which came into use in the early 19th century, arose as a result of difficulties encountered in obtaining corporate charters and because of concerns over the unlimited liability of partners in a general partnership. The limited partnership is generally viewed as a mixture of the partnership and corporate forms of business organization. Most of the states have adopted the Uniform Limited Partnership Act.

The corporation is the dominant form of business organization in the United States. The association of individuals in a single legal organization has existed since ancient times. Under Roman law, corporations were able to do many of the things that individuals could do, such as own, sell, or inherit property; acquire assets; and incur liabilities. These early forms of corporations influenced the development of English law, which is the basis for corporate law in the United States.

Corporations as we know them today date back to the late 1700s, when state legislatures began to authorize their formation and operation. The separate entity concept of the corporation is at the heart of its distinct legal status. Most state corporation laws are based on the Revised Model Business Corporation Act, which was drafted in 1984.

Future regulation of business organizations is likely to concentrate on the corporation. In the last several decades, several proposals have suggested the development of federal corporate law to displace state regulation of corporations. Proponents argue that the states are more interested in attracting corporations than in regulating them and that the country needs a uniform corporate law. Although there has been little movement toward the adoption of such proposals, federal securities and environmental laws increasingly affect corporate activities.

As the 20th century draws to a close, many corporations throughout the world seem to be engaged in significant restructuring. Corporations merge with each other; divisions are sold off or realigned; employees are laid off; contributions to pension and health care plans are reduced; new management groups purchase control of corporate segments and affiliates; and joint ventures and strategic alliances with foreign corporations and firms in related industries are actively pursued. As the structure and concerns of the corporate world change, major modifications in corporation law will inevitably follow.

The Forms of Business Organization

The basic forms of business organizations in the United States are the sole proprietorship, partnership, and corporation. More specialized entities, such as the joint venture, the limited partnership, the Subchapter S corporation, the professional corporation, and the limited liability company, havc evolved from these three basic forms. Franchise businesses also play a unique role in the organization of business activities, as some special laws govern certain aspects of franchise operations.

As you read this chapter, keep in mind the various characteristics and the formation processes for each of the different forms of business organization. Many small businesses face a choice among organizing as a proprietorship, partnership, or corporation. Today, Subchapter S, limited liability company, and limited partnership often also represent viable alternative organizational forms. When examining these alternatives, a number of factors should be compared. Figure 14–1 provides a basis for comparing and contrasting some of these factors for the most common forms of business organization.

The Proprietorship Form of Business Organization

sole proprietor An individual who is the sole owner of a business.

An individual who is the sole owner of a business is called a **sole proprietor.** Of course, as the business of a sole proprietor grows, he or she must hire employees to perform the work and hire agents to conduct transactions with other businesses.

FIGURE 14-1 Comparison of the Forms of Business Organization

	Sole Proprietorship	General Partnership	Limited Partnership	Limited Liability Company	Corporation
Ease and expense of formation	No formalities or expenses are required other than those specific to the business to be operated.	No formalities or expenses are required other than those specific to the business to be operated. A written agreement among the partners is advisable.	Must file a formal certificate. Written agreement is normal as roles of limited partner must be distinguished from general partner(s).	Must file articles of incorporation. Formation expense comparable to that of corporation.	Expense and time required to comply with statutory formality. Must receive charter from state. Usually required to register and pay fees to operate in states other than the state of incorporation.
Tax	Profits are taxed as ordinary income to the proprietor; losses are deducted by the proprietor.	A federal income return is filed by the partnership for informational purposes. Profits are taxed to each partner as ordinary income; losses are deducted by each partner. Profits and losses are shared equally unless the partnership agreement provides otherwise.	No tax on entity; tax liability flows through to partners. Partner cannot offset regular income with passive tax loss.	If it does not possess all the attributes of a corporation, it is taxed like a partnership.	Profits taxed first as income to the corporation and a second time as dividends are distributed to owners. Losses are deductible only by the corporation.
Liability	Sole proprietor has unlimited personal liability.	Each partner has unlimited personal liability for partnership debts.	General partner has unlimited liability; limited partners' liability is limited to capital contribution.	Liability of shareholders is limited to loss of capital contribution unless an extraordinary event requires piercing the corporate veil.	Liability of shareholders is limited to loss of capital contribution unless an extraordinary event requires piercing the corporate veil.
Control considerations	Sole proprietor has total control.	Each partner is entitled to equal control unless the partners provide otherwise in the partnership agreement.	General partner exercises all management powers. Written consent from all partners usually required for new general or limited partners.	All members can participate in management; can have numerous shareholders.	Separation of ownership and control. Owner generally has no control over daily management decisions.
Transferability of ownership	Transferable with sale of assets and business.	Nontransferable unless the partners unanimously agree.	Interest of partners are assignable, but new partners cannot	Members can limit transferability of shares.	Freely transferable unless shareholder agreements provide

FIGURE 14-1 (concluded)

	Sole Proprietorship	General Partnership	Limited Partnership	Limited Liability Company	Corporation
			be admitted without consent unless in partnership agreement.		otherwise.
Continuity	Limited to life of the proprietor.	Limited to life of the partners.	Limited partners can be added or dropped; change in general partner causes dissolution unless agreement provides otherwise.	If one member drops out, all others must agree to continue; similar to general partnership.	Unlimited.

Characteristics of a Proprietorship

A sole proprietorship is not considered to be an entity separate from its owner. If the business is sued, the suit is filed against the owner, though the name of the business is usually also indicated. For example, "Charles Smith, doing business as (D/B/A) Charley's Crabhouse" is a form often used. Charles Smith, not just the business organization, is the defendant, so all of his assets, whether derived from the business or from other sources, are exposed to liability for any legal judgment. A sole proprietorship has no legal status apart from that of its owner.

All the profits of a sole proprietorship belong to the owner. Thus, a sole proprietor generally does not need to file a separate income tax return for the business. Instead, income derived from the business is determined on a separate schedule (Schedule C for the federal income tax) of the owner's individual tax return. The income or loss from the business is combined with any other income of the owner to determine the owner's income tax liability. Approximately 80 percent of U.S. business organizations are sole proprietorships or partnerships.

Creation of a Proprietorship

A sole proprietorship is easier to form than any other kind of business organization. A special name may be used for the business, provided that a certificate for doing business under an assumed name is filed. Generally, the certificate is filed in the county in which the business operates. For example, Charles Smith's restaurant might do business under the name of "Charley's Crabhouse." If an owner wants to open several stores or branches of the same business, the certificate must generally indicate the location of each store. Registration of such trade names is discussed in Chapter 7.

Numerous local, state, and federal laws require the owner of any business, regardless of its form of organization, to comply with certain governmental regulations. For example, retail restaurants must usually obtain a permit from a local health department before it begins operating. Local zoning ordinances or land use regulations, referred to in Chapter 7, must also be met.

Usually, the restaurant will also need a sales tax permit from the state so that it is authorized to collect the sales tax from customers for food it sells. Manufacturing firms will also need special permits. A permit issued by state authorities may be required if the business emits pollutants or manufactures hazardous products. Businesses must meet state insurance requirements for unemployment compensation and worker's compensation requirements.

Both federal and state taxes must be withheld from the wages of employees. Firms conducting business across state lines may need the approval of federal regulatory agencies for some of their activities. Despite all of these requirements, which are also imposed on other business organizations, the sole proprietorship is the easiest to form and is usually subject to less government regulation than any other kind of business organization.

The Partnership Form of Business Organization

Although partnership law was developed through case-by-case decisions under common law, today almost all of the states have adopted the provisions of the Uniform Partnership Act (UPA). Thus, most of today's case law concerning partnerships reflects the UPA. While the UPA has been in effect since 1914, a revised partnership law, the Revised Uniform Partnership Act, was drafted several years ago and it is now under review by state legislatures.

Revised Uniform Partnership Act

The Revised Uniform Partnership Act (RUPA) is similar to the UPA in most respects. The objective of the RUPA is to amend the UPA by following case law and by simplifying partnership law so that the common provisions found in most well-planned partnership agreements become a part of the new law. For example, the RUPA adopts the entity theory for all partnerships except as is necessary for partnerships to retain the "flow-through" tax treatment (the partnership income or losses flow through to the partners; they, not the partnership itself, are taxed on any income and realize any losses) now provided by the Internal Revenue Code. Similarly, partnership dissolutions are treated as "breakups" under RUPA, abandoning the confusing "dissolution" process. After a partner withdraws, the other partners can more readily choose either to continue or discontinue business operations without concern for whether the business must be liquidated. Finally, the RUPA permits the partnership agreement to vary the partners' rights among themselves and achieve a mutually acceptable governance structure. The RUPA will probably be adopted by most states during this decade and will eventually replace the UPA.

Characteristics of a Partnership

The Uniform Partnership Act defines a **partnership** as an association of two or more persons who intend to carry on a business for profit as co-owners. The first requirement of a partnership is that there be an "association of two or more persons." The designation of business associates as partners has an important impact because each partner is both a principal, as a part of the partnership, and an agent, when acting on

partnership
An association of two or more persons who intend to carry on a business for profit as co-owners.

behalf of the partnership. Thus, the liability of a principal for the acts of an agent and the duties of an agent toward its principal become part and parcel of partnership law.

The UPA defines corporations and other partnerships as persons; thus, these entities can join with other persons or other entities to form a partnership. The law does not require a signed written partnership agreement, but the partners must consent to work together. Of course, sound business practice should lead the parties to set out their rights and responsibilities in writing. Through consultation with an attorney, a written agreement helps to ensure that the parties focus their attention on the problem areas that their partnership agreement should address.

Second, the partners must intend to carry on their business as co-owners. This requirement does not mean that the parties must contribute equal amounts of property and capital to the business. Rather, the parties have a community of interest in sharing the management responsibilities and the profits and losses of the business. If the owner of a business hires a manager to run the business and the manager does not share in the profits or losses of the business, these parties are not partners. Even if an employee receives a bonus based on business profits, there is no partnership because the employee does not also share in business losses. Although partners can make their own agreements regarding the sharing of profits, in the absence of special provisions, the law presumes partners will share profits and losses equally, even if their work or capital contributions are unequal.

Third, the objective of the parties must be to make a profit. People who act together in a nonprofit organization are not considered partners. Of course, the law does not require that a profit be made; it only requires that profit making be the intent or motive of the parties. If the partnership incurs losses, each partner must share those losses in some proportion. Should a married couple automatically be considered partners if they conduct business operations together? The following case illustrates the application of the criteria for a partnership to the business activities of a married couple.

Miller v. City Bank & Trust

266 N.W. 2d 687 (1978)
Michigan Court of Appeals

Mr. and Mrs. Miller married in 1959. Mr. Miller had operated a nursery business before his marriage, and Mrs. Miller joined him in the business soon after their marriage. When Mr. Miller died in 1974, the once marginal business was prosperous.

The land on which the Millers conducted their nursery business was owned by Mr. Miller. The Millers filed a business registration certificate in 1960 indicating the business was operated as a partnership, and a similar certificate was filed when some of the land was subdivided. That certificate, however, expired in 1971. The annual tax forms and schedules listed the business as a sole proprietorship and gave Mrs. Miller's occupation as housewife. Periodically, both the Millers received equal payments from the business. Household expenses were taken out of the business account.

Mrs. Miller testified that Mr. Miller referred to her as his partner. The Millers had no partnership agreement. Although Mrs. Miller made no capital contribution to the business, she kept all the books, hired and fired employees, and actively worked in the business operations. Upon Mr. Miller's death, Mrs. Miller claimed she was the sole owner of the business and the subdivided land as the sole surviving partner of the partnership. The bank as personal representative of Mr. Miller's estate claimed the land and nursery business were owned solely by Mr. Miller and thus passed to his heirs, but not solely to Mrs. Miller. The trial court held for the bank and Mrs. Miller appealed.

Danhof, Chief Judge

The determination of whether a partnership exists is a question of fact. The burden of proof is on the one alleging the partnership and the burden is stricter when relatives are alleged partners.

The elements of a partnership are generally considered to include a volunteer association of two or more people with legal capacity in order to carry on, via co-ownership, a business for profit. Co-ownership of the business requires more than merely joint ownership of the property and is usually evidenced by joint control and the sharing of profits and losses.

It is not disputed that the parties were involved in a business venture for profit and had the legal capacity to form a partnership. However, the evidence relating to co-ownership does not indicate that a legal partnership was contemplated. Prior to the marriage Mr. Miller operated the business and owned all the property. Mrs. Miller made no capital contribution except her services. Even though plaintiff worked long hours, this does not establish a partnership. . . .

Co-ownership is also indicated by profit sharing. In fact, profit sharing is prima facie evidence of a partnership. However, the court did not find an agreement to share the profits and we cannot say this was clearly erroneous. Mr. and Mrs. Miller's receipt of monthly payments from the nursery checking account does not establish profit sharing. The payments could also be reasonably viewed as salary or wages. . . .

Another indicia of co-ownership is mutual agency and control. That Mrs. Miller kept the books, wrote checks, and hired and fired, does not establish any control other than that which might be given to a trusted employee. No evidence of an agreement with respect to mutual control was presented.

The intention of the parties who enter into a partnership comprising the above mentioned elements is the controlling interest in this case. The filing of the business registration papers listing the business as a partnership gives support to plaintiff's claim. However, since the registration certificate filed for the subdivision operation expired in 1971, it does not raise a presumption of a partnership. Mrs. Miller claimed that the parties entered into an oral agreement and that Mr. Miller had told her "she was the best partner he ever had.". . . Mr. Miller could have meant that she was the best partner in marriage rather than in the business.

The evidence against these claims indicated that the deceased did not intend to form a legal partnership with his wife. First, there is no written agreement. . . . The income tax returns and schedules listed the business as a sole proprietorship, listed Mr. Miller's income as wages and Mrs. Miller's occupation as housewife. Other forms listed the business as a sole proprietorship. All the capital contributions came from Mr. Miller and the property remained in his name and none was transferred to the partnership. Although none of these factors are conclusive, they are all factors to be weighed in the decision.

Affirmed.

Case Questions

1. Mrs. Miller suggests the business and the subdivided lots were owned as a partnership. What hypothesis is made to counter that suggestion?
2. What assumption does this court make as to whether married people own their property or business interests as partners?
3. What specific actions could Mrs. Miller have undertaken while her husband was alive to help ensure that she was regarded as a partner of the nursery business?

Formation of a Partnership

Because a partnership involves at least two people, there is a sharing of rights and responsibilities. A partnership is usually created by the parties through a partnership agreement that defines their respective rights and duties. Such businesses as accounting firms and law firms frequently choose the partnership form of business organization. Some partnerships involve numerous parties with complex business transactions, whereas others involve only a few parties sharing in the operations of a single small business. As a result, the formalities of creating a partnership vary greatly, ranging from complex written articles of partnership to a simple verbal agreement between two partners.

Partnerships Compared to Joint Ventures

joint venture
An agreement among two or more parties to cooperate together for a specified time period and in specific, limited activities.

While the joint venture shares some characteristics with the partnership form of organization, there are also several features that distinguish it from the partnership. The partnership and joint venture are similar in that both involve two or more persons who join together in some business activity. However, they differ in their scope and duration. A partnership is created to carry on business activity for an indefinite period, whereas a **joint venture** is limited to a specified time period. Further, the joint venture, unlike the partnership, does not envision cooperation of the parties as associates in a number of different, but perhaps related, projects. Joint adventurers seek to cooperate in one specific venture and are not considered associates or partners in other ventures.

For example, IBM, Motorola, and Apple Computers have agreed to work together on a joint venture to design a computer chip using some substantially different materials than is currently used. Once their commitment with regard to this venture has expired, they may elect to cease working together on any business activity. Meanwhile, they will continue to compete on other projects involving the manufacture and sale of computer software equipment. Because the joint venture is limited in scope and duration, it is not used for long-term business activities.

Corporations from different countries often form joint ventures. Two large European advertising agencies, New Saatchi Agency headquartered in London and Publicis Communications, a unit of a French-based firm with offices in 56 countries, recently formed a joint venture. The French firm will provide logistical and technical services, planning, and media strategy, while the British firm will provide creative input and account management services. Such corporations do not intend to be partners in all of their business transactions. Instead, they act together in a limited setting for a specified time. Although an international joint venture can be formed by contract, typically it is formed by means of a separate corporate organization. A more detailed discussion of the role of joint ventures in international business transactions is provided in Chapter 3.

Partnerships Compared to Limited Partnerships

limited partnership
A partnership in which some of the partners are allowed to limit their liability to the amount of their original investment; each limited partnership must have at least one general partner with unlimited liability and at least one partner with limited liability.

In a **limited partnership,** unlike a general partnership, some of the partners are allowed to limit their liability to the amount of their original investment. Each limited partnership must have at least one general partner with unlimited liability and at least one partner with limited liability. The limited partner, like the corporate shareholder, has limited liability; but unlike the corporate shareholder, the limited partner has no voice in the control or management of the business. In fact, if the limited partner does participate in the management of the business, the legal protection of limited liability may be lost.

Limited partnership ownership interests can be made transferable, so the death or withdrawal of one limited partner does not affect the continuity of the partnership. Although a limited partnership interest may be transferred, often the partnership agreement limits that transferability so as to help maintain the flow-through tax nature of this form of organization. The resale market for a limited partnership interest is usually small, informal, and dispersed.

The general partner or partners in a limited partnership have essentially the same status as the partners in a general partnership. Each general partner may act on behalf of the limited partnership, and each can be held personally liable for partnership activities. However, the general partner or partners in a limited partnership do not have the authority to admit new general partners without the consent of the limited partners unless the limited partnership certificate gives them this authority.

Limited partnerships are frequently used to raise capital for the development of special projects. This enables, for example, a wealthy limited partner to invest significant funds in such a project without risking his or her other assets to creditors of the project. Oil wells, drilling ventures, Broadway shows, shopping centers, movies, and other rather risky ventures are often organized as limited partnerships.

The general partnership and the limited partnership also differ in the requirements for their creation. General partnerships can be created by the parties without a written agreement, whereas both the Uniform Limited Partnership Act (ULPA) and the Revised Uniform Limited Partnership Act (RULPA) require the filing of a certificate. The certificate must contain information regarding the partnership business, the names of the partners, and the amount of their capital contributions. Either the ULPA or the RULPA has been adopted in all of the states except Louisiana.

The ULPA also states that a limited partner's name may not be used in the partnership name. Moreover, the partnership name must include the words *limited partnership* or the abbreviation *LP* so that third parties will realize that it comprises one or more limited partners who are not liable for partnership activities beyond their capital contributions.

A Partner's Duties toward Other Partners

Each partner in a partnership has both rights and duties toward the other partners. Essentially, each partner acts both as an agent for other partners and as a principal when other partners are agents for partnership purposes. A partner's relations with third parties is based on agency law. In dealing with a third party, the responsibilities of a partner are based on the authority, actual or apparent, given the partner by the partnership.

The duties of a partner to other partners and to the partnership are defined in the partnership agreement and are This inferred from the agency relationship between the partnership as principal and the partners as agents. Each partner is both an agent and a principal for the other partners. The partnership is regarded as the principal, and each partner, as a part of the partnership, has the obligations of a principal with regard to the activities of other partners. For instance, the partnership must reimburse a partner who spends personal money in buying supplies for the partnership. The partners as a group owe the expenses incurred by an individual partner.

As an agent, each partner owes the partnership the fiduciary duties that an agent owes to his or her principal.

Fiduciary Duties Owed by the Partner as an Agent of the Partnership

1. The duty of loyalty.
2. The duty to communicate information.
3. The duty to obey instructions.

4. The duty to use reasonable care.
5. The duty to render an account.

If a partner violates any of the fiduciary duties owed to the partnership, the other partners can require that partner to account for any damages or for any profits. What duty do partners owe the partnership for a profit that only some of the partners received in the conduct of business activities? The following case illustrates the trust that is expected of all partners as fiduciaries of the partnership and of one another.

Van Hooser v. Keenon

271 S.W. 2d 270 (1954)
Kentucky Court of Appeals

Van Hooser, the defendant, and Keenon, the plaintiff, were partners with several other parties in the operation of a bus line. Several years after the partnership began business, Van Hooser began discussions with a representative from Greyhound, Inc., about the possible acquisition of the partnership business by Greyhound. As a result of these discussions, Greyhound gave Van Hooser $37,500 to be used as a partial payment for a controlling interest in the partnership business if that business could be converted into a corporation.

An agreement with Greyhound specified that if Greyhound later decided not to purchase the business, the money could be retained by Van Hooser and several of his partners. Van Hooser induced his partners to convert their partnership into a corporation, but Greyhound later decided not to purchase the bus line. When Keenon found out that Van Hooser and others had personally retained the Greyhound payment, he sued Van Hooser, claiming that the money given to Van Hooser belonged to the partnership. The trial court found for Keenon, and Van Hooser appealed.

Stewart, Justice

The case was referred to the master commissioner of the Fayette Circuit Court, who found that when Greyhound, Inc., paid $37,500 for an option to purchase a 60 percent interest in the partnership this included 60 percent of every partner's interest therein and that the money paid for the option inured to the benefit of all the members of the partnership in proportion to their ownership. . . . This finding was approved by the circuit judge and he rendered judgment solely against defendants Van Hooser and Utter, for the 25 percent due plaintiffs.

We should state, at the outset, that there is no relation of trust or confidence known to the law that requires of the parties a higher degree of good faith than that of a partnership. Each partner is the confidential agent of all the others and each has a right to know all that the others know. Nor will one partner be permitted to benefit at the expense of the firm. No undue advantage of one over another by misrepresentation or concealment will receive the approval of the law.

A court of equity will always grant relief to the partner who has suffered from a breach of the obligation. One partner will not be permitted to obtain secretly any right that should belong to the partnership and put it to his own individual profit. Of such character is the securing of a contract. The criterion is not an actual evil motive, for the courts look to the results of any such action regardless of evil intent. If such action results in profit or advantage, the courts will require an accounting.

Applying the foregoing basic rules of the common law to the admitted facts of this case, we conclude as did the lower court, and the evidence abundantly supports our conclusion, that the five defendants were and are under a legal obligation as partners to share proportionately with plaintiffs the option money which was obtained by the optioners by virtue of the partnership relationship. The important factor is that these defendants received money which should have gone into the partnership treasury and then should have been divided proportionately among all of the partners. The excuse advanced by them that they were compelled to keep the Keenons in the dark, in order for their plan to work, certainly furnishes no legal basis under the circumstances for their retention of all the money.

Furthermore, we believe it was proper to render judgment against the two appealing defendants alone for the full amount due plaintiffs. They initiated and consummated the option deal with Greyhound, Inc., and they collected and divided up among the five optioners the cash benefits from the transaction. . . . The mere fact that the five optioners have already apportioned the $37,500 among themselves does not relieve the appealing defendants of their obligation to settle with plaintiffs for their proportionate part.

We therefore conclude the lower court correctly disposed of the issues raised.

Therefore, the judgment is affirmed.

Case Questions

1. What reasons led the court to decide that the money received from Greyhound belonged to the partnership?
2. What assumption exists regarding payments made by a third party to a partner? What counter assumption does Van Hooser suggest applies to the payment he received?

Partners' Rights in a Partnership

The rights and responsibilities of the partners in the operation of a partnership are generally established in their partnership agreement. If not, the UPA and the RUPA grant certain property rights to each partner.

A Partner's Property Rights

- Rights in specific partnership property.
- An interest in the partnership.
- The right to participate in the management.

Partnership activities generally involve the use of property, either furnished by the partners or purchased by partnership resources. For example, a partnership of lawyers needs desks, books, telephones, file cabinets, computers, and other items of property. It is important to distinguish the property of the partnership from the personal and individual property that is owned by each partner but is used in the activities of the partnership.

Rights in Specific Partnership Property If property is owned by the partnership, its use by an individual partner may be restricted. Further, if partnership property is sold, the proceeds may be retained by the partnership or distributed according to the partnership agreement. For example, if a partnership sells its desks, the proceeds belong to the partnership and are distributed according to the partnership agreement. The proceeds from a desk used by a partner will not necessarily be distributed to that partner. On the other hand, if a partner owns a desk that the partnership uses, the proceeds from the sale of that desk belong to the individual partner, not to the partnership.

partner's right in partnership property A partner's right, shared equally with other partners, to possess and use partnership property for partnership purposes.

A **partner's right in partnership property** gives each partner an equal right with other partners to possess and use partnership property for partnership purposes. On the death of a partner, that partner's right to partnership property passes to the surviving partners, not to the partner's heirs.

partner's interest in the partnership A partner's share of the profits and surplus; this interest is considered personal property.

An Interest in the Partnership The second aspect of a partner's property rights concerns the partner's interest in the partnership itself. The UPA states that a **partner's interest in the partnership** is "his share of the profits and surplus, and the same is personal property." This interest is an asset that can be transferred, that can be seized by creditors of the individual partner, and that becomes a part of the individual partner's estate at death.

Partnership agreements often prohibit the transfer of an individual partner's interest to someone outside the partnership until the partnership or other partners have been given the opportunity to purchase it. Even when that interest is transferred, the transferee receives only a right to participate in the firm's profits; he or she does not have a right to participate in the firm's management or to become a partner.

For example, if one of the three partners in a pizza business transfers her interest to you, you receive only the right to share in the profits or losses of the business. You do not have a right to make decisions about the operation of the business or to act on behalf of the other partners. Furthermore, the transferor remains obligated to perform services for the business unless the remaining partners consent to the delegation of that duty to you, and you agree to assume it.

Partnership creditors, not the creditors of an individual partner, have first claim on partnership property needed to satisfy debts. Creditors of an individual partner may seize that partner's share of the profits but not any specific partnership property. Through a court approved *charging order,* the creditor may take the individual partner's share of the business but may not interfere in the operations of the business.

partner's right to participate in the management The right of each partner, in the absence of any contrary agreement made by the partners, to have an equal right to manage and conduct the business of the partnership.

Right to Participate in the Management The third aspect of a partner's property rights is the **partner's right to participate in the management** of the partnership business. If no contrary agreement is made by the partners, each partner has an equal right to manage and conduct the partnership business. By majority rule, the partners may make decisions regarding the operational aspects of running the business. The majority cannot, however, exclude the other partners, and it must act in good faith. Extraordinary changes, such as admitting a new partner, entering a different business, or relocating the business, cannot be made without the unanimous consent of all the partners. Generally, partnerships of more than several people alter these rules in the partnership agreement. For example, the partnership agreement of a large accounting or law firm typically specifies that new partners may be admitted by majority vote of the senior partners, that one partner may make most of the day-to-day management decisions for the firm, or that a small committee has the authority to change the firm's location.

A Partner's Relations with Third Parties

Partnership law can be viewed as an extension of agency law. A partner has the implied authority to engage in transactions for carrying on the normal partnership business. A partner can contract to hire employees, borrow money, and purchase items needed to operate the business. Thus, a third party that negotiates with a partner in selling goods, lending money, or transacting other normal business of a partnership can look to the partnership for payment. The contract made by a partner is the contract of the partnership, not the contract of the individual partner.

The partnership must inform third parties of any restrictions imposed on a partner's ability to make such contracts. Otherwise, the RUPA provides that third parties are not affected by such limitations. For example, if only specific partners are authorized to purchase furniture for a partnership, the partnership must inform the furniture stores with which it deals. If it does not, and if an unauthorized partner makes a purchase from a furniture store, the furniture store can still look to the firm for payment.

A partnership and all of its partners are liable to injured third parties for the torts of any partner who acts in the ordinary course of business or with the authority of the other partners. If a partner commits a tort outside the carrying on of his or her normal business activities, the partnership is not liable. Thus, the general rules of *respondeat superior* affecting the principal-agent relationship, as discussed in Chapter 13, determine a partnership's liability for the torts of individual partners.

Because partners are individually liable to third parties for all of the firm's financial obligations, a partnership must be careful about its commitments. The Lloyds of London insurance firm is one of the best known partnership organizations. The Lloyds firm specializes in providing reinsurance to other insurance firms that underwrite risks that are sometimes too big for one firm to manage. When both a hurricane in southern Florida and an earthquake in Oakland, California, caused deaths and millions of dollars in damaged property, the assets of the firm were not sufficient to meet its contracted obligations. As a result, the partners of the Lloyds firm (referred to as *the names*) were obligated to use their own assets to provide compensation to those with valid Lloyds commitments.

Termination of a Partnership

Termination of a partnership is a two-stage process involving dissolution and winding up. The Uniform Partnership Act defines dissolution as "a change in the relation of the partners caused by any partner ceasing to be associated in the carrying on . . . of the business." Thus, the death, withdrawal, or retirement of a partner technically dissolves the original partnership. In most cases, however, the dissolution does not affect the continuation of the business because the remaining partners wish to carry on. Instead, the books and records of the partnership are revised to reflect the dissolving of the old partnership and the beginning of a new one; meanwhile, the normal business of the partnership continues. Under the Revised Uniform Partnership Act, partnership dissolutions are treated as "breakups." After a partner withdraws, the other partners can more readily choose to continue business operations without concern for whether the business must be liquidated.

If the business is not going to be continued, a winding up of the business takes place. In these cases, the existing partnership must wind up, or terminate, the business by paying its debts, liquidating or selling its assets, and distributing the remaining proceeds among the partners. All third parties must be notified of the firm's dissolution, and creditors with whom the business has dealt are entitled to specific notice. The partners involved in winding up a business have no authority to continue the business; they are only authorized to complete the transactions that have been started, to collect assets, and to pay off debts. When the partnership's business is wound up, assets are distributed to (1) creditors who are not partners; (2) creditors who are partners; (3) partners to repay capital contributions; (4) partners entitled to profits.

Partnerships in Civil Law Countries

In most civil law countries, every form of business organization, including a partnership, is a company. In some countries, such as France, a partnership is regarded as a separate entity and can own property and be a litigant in its own name. By contrast, in Germany, a partnership is not a separate entity, and so, as in the United States, the partners essentially own the property of the partnership. The limited partnership is also recognized in civil law countries. In fact, limited partnerships flourished in Europe before becoming popular in the United States.

Franchises and Business Organizations

franchise
A privilege granted or sold, such as the privilege of using a name or process to sell products or services agreed upon between two parties: the franchisor and the franchisee.

A franchise may be considered a type of business organization because it defines how a firm's assets are financed, controlled, and distributed. However, a **franchise** is a privilege granted or sold, such as the privilege of using a name or process to sell products or services agreed upon between two parties: the franchisor and the franchisee. The *franchisor* develops a product or service, often protected by a trademark or a trade name, and then licenses this product or service to *franchisees* as a uniform method of doing business. Each of the parties to a franchise generally has its own form of business organization. Frequently, the franchisor consists of several commonly owned corporations. Franchisees invest in their own business operations and usually organize their own corporations.

Distinctive Characteristics of a Franchise

The most distinctive characteristic of a franchise is the franchisor's exercise of substantial control over a business owned by the franchisee. In exchange for allowing the franchisee to use the franchisor's unique trade name, trademarks, and special products and techniques, the franchisee permits the franchisor to establish the products that may be sold, the hours of operation, and the types of equipment that are to be used. Although fast-food franchises such as Wendy's, Little Caesar's Pizza, and Burger King are highly visible, franchises are common in many service businesses, such as the motel industry (Holiday Inn and Hilton), the tax preparation business (H & R Block), the muffler business (Midas and Tuffy), and even the legal business (Hyatt Legal Services). A franchise agreement usually provides that the franchisee will pay an established percentage of its gross sales to the franchisor as compensation for the use of the franchisor's trademark and business methods. Chapter 17 discusses the antitrust aspects of other forms of franchise compensation and the level of control that franchisors may exercise. That discussion includes the *Principe v. McDonald's* case, which illustrates why such control is permitted by the franchisor.

Typically, the franchise contract requires that the franchisee conform to the standard operating procedure specified by the franchisor. For example, the hamburgers must be cooked in a specified manner, and only certain kinds of potatoes can be used for the french fries. Failure to follow those requirements is usually grounds for termination of the franchise. Recall too that the discussion in Chapter 8 of the tort of negligence included an excerpt from *Martin v. McDonald's,* in which McDonald's was held liable because it prepared a security manual for its franchisees and also followed up with inspections to see if the procedures it suggested were being implemented. The control McDonald's exercised in that case led to it being liable for the negligent performance of the duty it had assumed.

In the franchise agreement, the franchisor (generally a large corporation such as Pillsbury, the owner of the Burger King trademark) frequently agrees to provide managerial assistance to the franchise, to select the site for operating the franchise, and to regulate the purchasing, advertising, and record keeping of the franchise. The franchisee, generally a local firm, agrees to provide the monetary investment in the business, to establish the desired business organization, and to operate the franchise in accordance with the terms of the franchise agreement.

Franchise Legislation

Many of the states have enacted legislation aimed at protecting the franchisee. One set of state laws require the franchisor to disclose specific information to a prospective franchisee prior to any sale. Most states use the *Uniform Franchise Offering Circular,* which requires balance sheet and income statements from the franchisor along with material terms of the franchise agreement. It also mandates that the franchisor provide a description of any territorial restrictions imposed on franchisees and the circumstances under which the franchisor can unilaterally terminate the franchise.

Other state statutes typically require the franchisor to notify the franchisee of problems with the franchisee's operations prior to termination. Many of these statutes limit the franchisor's right to cancel the franchise agreement. In addition to general laws enacted for the benefit of prospective or existing franchisees, some states also have laws aimed at particular industries. The Automobile Dealer Day in Court Act and the Petroleum Parties Act exemplify such statutes. State securities laws also are applicable to franchises because the franchises are viewed as involving the marketing of securities.

At the federal level, the Federal Trade Commission's Franchise Rules has established new guidelines for all Uniform Franchise Offering Circulars (UFOC) filed after the beginning of 1995. The new guidelines will force all franchisors to revise the information provided to prospective franchisees. The guidelines are intended to protect prospective franchisees from misrepresentations in the initial sale of franchises. For example, certain franchisors must disclose specific information on average franchise revenue, required supply purchases, number of new franchisees, and certain historical data to potential franchisees at least 10 days prior to entering into any agreement with them. Further, a franchisor's estimates of potential earnings must be supported by documents showing the basis for its estimates of gross sales and income.

Whether the franchisor is using hypothetical examples or actual sales income from existing franchisees, cautionary warning notes in large, bold-faced print must be included for the potential franchisee's benefit. The warning must note that there is no assurance that a prospective franchisee will do as well as the figures used by the franchisor indicate and that it must assume the risk that any given franchise will not perform as well as an "average" franchisee if it relies on the franchisor's figures.

Federal antitrust laws may also impact the franchise relationship. A brief discussion of the application of antitrust laws to vertical restraints imposed by a franchisor on its franchisees is found in Chapter 17.

The Corporation Form of Business Organization

corporation A separate entity that is legally distinct from its shareholder owners who generally enjoy limited liability for the corporation's debts.

Although the corporation is now the dominant form of business organization in the United States, it did not arrive on the U.S. scene until the late 18th century. The **corporation,** a separate entity distinct from its shareholder owners, is sometimes traced to ancient Greece or Rome. The early use of corporations influenced English law, which eventually became the basis for corporate law in the United States. Although the American colonists originally did not favor incorporations, the right of individuals to form a common business organization eventually became recognized in this country.

The Role of the Corporation Today

Although corporations account for less than 20 percent of the number of business organizations in the United States, they are responsible for almost 90 percent of total sales and annual revenue. The size and dominance of the corporation as a business organization could not have been envisioned 100 years ago. In recent years, mergers between such firms as Warner Communications and Time, Inc., and between Mitsubishi Bank and Bank of Tokyo have created even larger corporate entities. In banking, communications, transportation, and pharmaceuticals, larger corporations have acquired smaller ones. In countries such as Japan, Canada, Australia, and the countries of the European Union, corporations have become dominant through mergers within and across national boundaries.

INTERNATIONAL PERSPECTIVE AND COMMENTARY

ESTABLISHING FOREIGN CORPORATIONS

Although each state in the United States has its own laws for establishing business organizations, the various state laws do not differ dramatically from each other. However, a U.S. firm considering international investment will meet significantly different corporation laws. If the investment occurs in a country without a firmly established market economy, restrictions may be imposed on entry into particular industries, controls may be imposed on operations, and limitations may be imposed on the withdrawal of capital or profits.

In many European countries, there are two forms of business organization, one for closely held corporations and one for public corporations. Thus once a firm has decided to use the corporate form of business organization, it then must decide which form of organization will best fit its purposes. (These are briefly discussed in Chapter 3.) The laws and regulations governing each are quite different. For example, a U.S. firm contemplating establishing a German subsidiary corporation will find that Germany has two forms of corporations: the GmbH and the AG. The GmbH is used for small corporations, whereas the AG is for public corporations. Several basic differences between the two forms are noted below.

	GmbH	AG
Minimum capital	50,000 marks	100,000 marks
Minimum number of incorporators	1	5
Transfer of shares	Cannot be traded on stock exchange	Can be traded on stock exchange
Board of directors	No special requirements if fewer than 500 employees	Required to have both a supervisory board (representing employees and employers) and a management board
Accounting procedures	No special requirements	Public disclosure

Characteristics of the Corporation

At least four essential characteristics make the corporate form desirable for firms that have large capital needs and want to create a separate entity that can endure for many years. State laws determine how corporations must be formed; the documents generally required to form a corporation are noted below. Later sections discuss several types of corporations and examine the various roles of shareholders, directors, and corporate officers.

separate entity theory The characteristic of the corporation that gives it a legal life of its own, making it responsible for paying its own taxes and holding it accountable for its own torts and in some cases for crimes.

Separate Entity The first characteristic of the corporation is its status as a **separate entity** or person. The law gives the corporation a legal life of its own. It is responsible for paying its own taxes, and it can be held accountable for its own torts and in some cases for the commission of crimes. Several of the U.S. Constitution's provisions protecting persons also apply to corporations, including the due process clause, the prohibition of unreasonable searches and seizures of property, the access to courts, and the ability to buy, sell, and hold property rights.

limited liability A corporate characteristic provides that although corporate shareholders may lose their investment if the shares of stock they hold in the corporation become worthless, they generally cannot be held personally liable for corporate debts.

Limited Liability A second corporate characteristic, the **limited liability** of each individual shareholder who owns a portion of the corporation, is frequently the primary reason for incorporation as distinguished from organizing as sole proprietorships and general partnerships. The corporation's status as a separate entity shields its owners from personal liability for corporate debts. Although shareholders may lose their investment if the shares of stock they hold in the corporation become worthless, generally they cannot be held personally liable for corporate debts.

pierce the corporate veil The concept of breaking through the limited liability usually granted to corporate shareholders and making them liable if there is fraud or other reason to hold an individual owner liable for corporate obligations.

In some unusual cases, the concept of limited liability is disregarded. These cases usually involve closely held corporations in which the dominant shareholder is also active as a director or officer of the corporation. In such cases, the courts may **pierce the corporate veil of liability** and hold some individual, often a shareholder, liable for acts of the corporation. For example, a court held that a cab driver who was the sole owner, officer, and employee of a corporation that owned two cabs could not escape individual liability for his negligent operation of a cab owned by the corporation.[1]

What conditions might permit a court to disregard the limited liability of an individual shareholder? The next case discusses such conditions and reviews the theories used to pierce the corporate veil.

Mills Co. v. Crawfish Capitol Seafood

569 So. 2d 1108 (1990)
Court of Appeals of Louisiana

Henry Mills Company, Inc., filed suit against Crawfish Capitol Seafood, Inc., and its incorporators, Champagne, Melancon, and Peltier for money due for work done in renovating a building that the corporation planned to use in processing seafood. The individual defendants, who were also the corporation's only members of the board of directors and officers, claimed that the contract was made by the corporation and that as

[1] *Walkovszky v. Carlton*, 18 N.Y.2d 414 (1966).

individuals they could not be held liable for the corporation's debts. The trial court found for Mills against the corporation, but held that the individuals were not liable for the corporation's debts. Mills appealed.

Domengeaux, Chief Judge

The general rule that corporations are distinct legal entities, separate and distinct from the individuals who compose them, is statutory in origin and well recognized in Louisiana jurisprudence. Thus, shareholders are not individually responsible for the debts due by the corporation.

In *American Bank of Welch,* this court discussed the limited exceptions to the rule of nonliability of shareholders for the debts of corporations. One exception involves the corporation's failure to conduct its business on a corporate footing, thereby disregarding the corporate entity to such an extent that the corporation ceases to be distinguishable from its shareholders. In such situations, the corporation is referred to as the *alter ego* of its shareholders, and the court may *pierce the corporate veil* and impose personal liability on the shareholders.

In deciding whether to pierce the corporate veil, the totality of the circumstances must be examined. This determination is primarily a factual finding for the court to make. In deciding whether to pierce the corporate veil, the factors to be considered by the court include, but are not limited to: commingling of corporate and shareholder funds, failure to follow statutory formalities for incorporation and the transaction of corporate affairs, undercapitalization, failure to provide separate bank accounts and bookkeeping records, and failure to hold regular shareholder or directors' meetings. . . .

In the case before us, Mills must prove that Champagne and Peltier disregarded the corporate entity to such an extent that it ceased to be distinguishable from themselves. This is a heavy burden of proof. When fraud or deceit is absent, other circumstances must be so strong as to clearly indicate that the corporation and shareholders operated as one.

. . . In reaching a determination of whether the corporate veil should be pierced in the instant case, the trial court discussed the five factors listed in *Daley.* Concerning the commingling of corporation and shareholder funds, the record reflects corporate funds were used to renovate a restaurant where the crawfish would be cooked prior to processing and packaging for resale. The restaurant was leased to Melancon individually. Before the crawfish operations began, Melancon used the facility as a restaurant business in which Crawfish Capitol Seafood had no interest. The operation lasted two to three weeks.

We, like the trial judge, find this insignificant. . . . While it is true that the restaurant was renovated with corporate funds, we do not believe Melancon's personal use of the facility for two to three weeks constitutes commingled assets to the extent required to pierce the corporate veil.

Considering other relevant circumstances, the trial judge found, and the record supports her finding, that the statutory formalities required for incorporation and the transaction of corporate affairs were met. The Certificate of Incorporation and the Articles of Incorporation were included in the record.

Although bylaws were not written, bylaws are not required by law. The failure to issue stock certificates is likewise insignificant; each shareholder owned a one-third interest in the corporation in exchange for services to be rendered to the corporation, which can include management, labor, and technical expertise, as well as supplies or equipment.

The testimony reveals that the shareholders met regularly; although minutes of these meetings were not kept, minutes are not required by law. Crawfish Capitol Seafood had its own bank account from which numerous checks were drawn. Bookkeeping records were not available, but because the corporation never actually started doing business, its bookkeeping records would be sparse, if existent at all.

The remaining factor discussed by the trial court is Mills' contention that Crawfish Capitol Seafood was undercapitalized. The record does not support that contention. Crawfish Capitol Seafood obtained interim financing of $160,000 from Breaux Bridge Bank and Trust. The State of Louisiana approved a loan application for permanent financing. For reasons which were not made a part of the record, the permanent financing fell through. . . . Furthermore, when its permanent financing fell through, Crawfish Capitol Seafood ceased operations and incurred no additional financial obligations.

The circumstances presented in this case are insufficient to clearly indicate that the shareholders and the corporation were acting as one and therefore do not justify piercing the corporate veil.

In light of the totality of the circumstances of this case, and after reviewing the testimony of Champagne, Melancon, and Peltier, we cannot conclude that the corporation and the shareholders were indistinguishable. Therefore, the trial court did not err in failing to disregard the corporate entity of Crawfish Capitol Seafood.

Affirmed.

Case Questions

1. What assumption does the court make as to whether an individual owner of a corporation generally may be held liable for debts of the corporation?
2. What finding does the court make for each of the five factors it reviews to determine if an individual can be held liable for the corporation's debts?
3. Explain what is meant by the terms *alter ego* and *pierce the corporate veil.*

Freely Transferable Ownership A third corporation characteristic is the *freely transferable* nature of its ownership. An interest in a corporation, represented by shares of stock, can usually be transferred without disrupting business activities. The sale of an interest in a partnership or the sale of a proprietorship often does interrupt normal business activities.

Perpetual Life Finally, the *perpetual life* of a corporation is another characteristic that distinguishes it from the sole proprietorship or partnership. Unlike the sole proprietorship or partnership, the corporation's existence is not dependent on the lives of its owners. Changes in ownership generally do not affect the operations of the firm's business.

CHARACTERISTICS OF A CORPORATION

1. Separate entity.
2. Limited liability of owners.
3. Freely transferable ownership.
4. Perpetual life distinct from owners.

Corporate Formation

A corporation is formed when the state of incorporation grants a corporate charter. The first decision affecting the formation of a corporation is the selection of the state in which to incorporate. Although the Revised Model Business Corporation Act provides some degree of similarity in the corporation laws of the states, there are distinct differences among them.

Many corporations choose to incorporate in the state where their business originates. However, they may choose to incorporate in a state whose corporate laws they view more favorably, such as Delaware. Delaware's legislative provisions and court decisions enable corporations to conduct their internal affairs with few restrictions. The law of the state of incorporation is usually applied in litigation concerning a corporation's internal activities and its relations with its shareholders, so choosing the state in which to incorporate is an important aspect of forming a corporation.

incorporators
Persons who apply to the state for incorporation.

articles of incorporation
Document filed by the incorporators with the secretary of state or department of commerce to organize a corporation.

bylaws
Rules governing the internal aspects of the corporation's activities that are adopted by either the shareholders or the board of directors.

The persons who apply to the state for incorporation are called **incorporators.** They are required to pay certain filing fees and to file a document, called the **articles of incorporation,** that is reviewed by the secretary of state or the state commerce department. Incorporators generally have to comply with several requirements before the articles of incorporation or corporate charter is approved. To avoid confusing parties that deal with the new corporation, its name cannot be too similar to that of another corporation. The corporate name must include a special term such as *incorporated, limited,* or *company,* or an abbreviation of one of those terms, to indicate that the firm is a corporation. This requirement is imposed so that people dealing with the firm will know that it has limited liability.

Other requirements include the naming of a registered agent for the corporation and the designation of the corporation's principal place of business. These requirements permit all persons dealing with the corporation to contact it by mail and to deliver legal papers to its agent. Many states require that the officers and directors of the corporation be listed in the articles of incorporation. The corporation must begin with a minimum capitalization, typically $1,000. Its capital structure must indicate the rights of each class of shareholders.

After the articles of incorporation have been approved, the shareholders attend an organizational meeting. At this meeting, they elect the board of directors, which establishes corporate policies. Either the shareholders or the board of directors adopts **bylaws,** rules governing the internal aspects of the corporation's activities. The officers who will conduct the business of the corporation are then selected by the board of directors, and stock certificates are issued to the shareholders.

TYPES OF CORPORATIONS

Although this chapter focuses on the business corporation, which is created to make a profit, most of the state corporation laws provide for a number of types of entities that can be organized in the corporate form. A corporation may be public or private, organized for profit or nonprofit, publicly or closely held, professional or nonprofessional, and foreign or domestic. Each of these categories focuses on some special characteristic of the corporate form of organization.

Public and Private Corporations

This classification refers to the purpose for which the corporation has been created. Business corporations such as IBM, Xerox, and General Motors are private corporations that were created by private individuals for private purposes. The Federal Home Loan Bank, many of the state universities, and numerous municipal water or school districts are public corporations that governments created and funded to serve public purposes.

Profit and Nonprofit Corporations

This classification focuses on the operational objectives of the corporation. A for-profit corporation seeks to make money for its shareholders. The corporation distributes profits to the shareholders as dividends or retains them for its further growth. If the corporation's assets are sold, the net assets are divided among the shareholders.

A nonprofit corporation does not have shareholders and does not seek to pay dividends or operate at a profit. The League of Women Voters, the Boy Scouts, and the Sisters of Saint Joseph are examples of nonprofit corporations. Such corporations carry over any surplus of receipts over disbursements to the following year.

Publicly or Closely Held Corporations

This classification concerns the degree to which the stock ownership of a for-profit corporation is spread among owners. The ownership of a publicly held corporation, such as ATT or IBM, is widely diffused rather than concentrated among a few individuals. Publicly owned stock can be traded from one owner to another through stock exchange transactions. In order to issue stock to the public, a corporation must comply with federal and state laws and regulations imposed on the issuing and trading of corporate securities. These problems are discussed further in Chapter 15.

A closely held corporation, such as one formed by the owners of a local department store, has stock that is not sold to or traded by the public at large. The stock of a closely held corporation is owned by only a few people who are generally active in the management or who are relatives of the founder. In closely held corporations, unlike publicly held corporations, management and ownership are not separated.

While most state laws affecting private corporations apply equally to public and closely held corporations, some special laws affect only the closely held companies. Closely held firms may use several forms of business organization. Instead of forming a regular corporation, a firm may select to form either a limited liability company (LLC) or a Subchapter S corporation. Both offer owners limited liability and taxation of the owners' earnings, not that of the corporate entity. Some of the similarities and differences in these two forms of business organization are noted below.

Subchapter S corporation
A creature of the federal income tax laws; viewed as a hybrid between the corporation and the general partnership.

The Subchapter S Corporation The **Subchapter S corporation,** or **S corporation,** is a creature of the federal income tax laws. For tax purposes, it is viewed as a hybrid between the corporation and the general partnership. Several restrictions are imposed on Subchapter S corporations, but not on limited liability companies. For example, an S corporation can have no more than 35 shareholders, each of whom must agree to use the S corporation form of business organization. Another restriction is that an S corporation may not own more than 80 percent of another corporation. Neither of these restrictions is imposed on the limited liability company. An S corporation has two important attributes: (1) It is viewed as a corporation for purposes of liability, and (2) it is taxed like a partnership. With few exceptions, the shareholders of an S corporation cannot be held liable for its debts.

For income tax purposes, the S corporation is treated like a partnership. Its income is considered to belong to the shareholders not the corporate entity. Its losses can be used to offset income earned by its individual shareholders. For example, each of five equal shareholders of an S corporation with a $50,000 loss in a given year may use $10,000 of that loss to offset individual income they derived from other sources. Thus, if one of them had $50,000 in taxable income from other sources that year, that shareholder's net taxable income would be $40,000.

The income of an ordinary for-profit corporation is treated differently; it is not considered income of its shareholders until they receive it as dividends. Assume that you are one of five equal shareholders of a corporation that earns $50,000 in a given year. The corporation may retain much of that money as working capital and distribute only a small portion, say $5,000, as dividends. Your share of those dividends, $1,000, would be the amount of your taxable income from the corporation. Income not distributed by the corporation may be retained for growth or future distribution. This cannot occur with the income of either an S corporation or limited liability company because these entities must distribute all of their income to their shareholders and members.

limited liability company
A business organization used by owners of a closely held business that is organized like a corporation but taxed as a partnership if it lacks some of the essential characteristics of a corporation.

The Limited Liability Company A **limited liability company** is a business organization used by owners of a closely held business that is organized like a corporation but taxed as a partnership if it lacks some of the essential characteristics of a corporation. There are several differences between the limited liability company (LLC) and the S corporation. We have noted that while the S corporation can have only 35 shareholders and may not own more than 80 percent of another corporation, no such restrictions exist for the LLC. The limited liability company may also be used if there are foreign investors; they are normally barred from S corporations.

LLCs don't limit the number or type of owners, as S corporations do, except for a two-owner minimum. Another difference between these two forms of business organization is that a corporation may be a shareholder of a limited liability company but not of a Subchapter S corporation.

Another difference is that unlike the S corporation shareholder, the 20 percent owner of an LLC or partnership that losses money will not necessarily have a 20 percent loss. The LLC owners are allowed to annually reallocate income and deductions among themselves to fit their individual needs, a practice that the Subchapter S provisions do not permit. Thus, an LLC member's percent of the firm's profits or losses may differ from his or her share of ownership.

For tax purposes, a limited liability company, like an S corporation, may be treated as a partnership. According to treasury regulations, to be taxed as a partnership, the limited liability firm must possess no more than four of the following six corporate attributes:[2]

1. Associates.
2. An objective to carry on business and divide gains.
3. Limited liability.
4. Centralized management.
5. Continuity of life.
6. Free transferability of interests.

By establishing a limited life for the firm and imposing some restrictions on the transfer of interests, a firm is likely to meet the tests expressed in the treasury regulation.

Professional and Nonprofessional Corporations

The professional corporation—the use of the corporate form of business organization by people practicing the same profession—is a rather recent development. Physicians, attorneys, or accountants may organize their business activities as a professional corporation. A law firm known as Smith, James, and Jones, P.C., is a professional corporation. Usually, people who are not licensed to practice the particular profession are not allowed to be shareholders of such a corporation, and the corporation is

[2] Treasury Regulation, section 301. 7701–2 (a)(1).

permitted to engage only in the activity for which its shareholders are licensed. Special state laws usually govern professional corporations.

A nonprofessional corporation is a corporation whose services do not require licensed professionals. Since dry cleaners, for example, are not licensed professionals, if the owners of a dry cleaning business form a corporation, it is considered a nonprofessional corporation.

Foreign and Domestic Corporations

Clearly, a corporation organized in France would be regarded in the United States as a foreign corporation. However, in the United States the terms *foreign* refers both to corporations incorporated outside the United States and to corporations incorporated outside a given state. Thus, Pennsylvania laws regard a corporation incorporated in Michigan as a foreign corporation.

Even if a corporation does business within a state, it may be regarded as a foreign corporation if it was incorporated in another state. Because General Motors was incorporated in Delaware, even Michigan, where its corporate offices are located, could regard it as a foreign corporation. However, although the classification of a corporation as foreign or domestic is generally based on its place of incorporation, many state laws and most laws of countries other than the United States use a different criterion in classifying corporations as domestic or foreign. Often, that criterion is the location of the corporation's center of management. On this basis, most laws probably regard General Motors as a Michigan corporation.

The Role of Corporate Participants

The **shareholders** of a corporation are its owners. They have the power to sell or dissolve the corporation and to determine who will be responsible for managing it. The **directors** of a corporation are the managers of its business. They determine the corporation's overall strategy, and they select the **officers** who are in charge of conducting the corporation's day-to-day business.

shareholder
The owners of a corporation; they make major corporate decisions and determine who will be its managers.

director
The managers of a corporation's business; they determine the corporation's overall strategy and select the people who are in charge of daily activities.

officers
The people who are in charge of conducting the corporation's day-to-day business.

The relationship among these corporate representatives is illustrated by Figure 14–2. In large corporations, different people occupy the roles of shareholders, directors, and officers. In smaller businesses, the same people may perform more than one of these functions. If this occurs, corporate records should clearly indicate the actions taken by the shareholders, directors, and officers, as they each have separate and distinct legal responsibilities in the corporation. Failure to keep accurate corporate records may result in the imposition of tax, contract, or tort liability on those who appear to be responsible for a corporation's business activities, regardless of their actual role in the corporation.

Shareholder Rights

Although *shareholders* own the corporation, in most large corporations they do not play an active role in corporate management. The shareholders in a large corporation perform several tasks. First, they elect the board of directors, whose members are entrusted with the management of the corporation. Second, they vote to approve or disapprove extraordinary transactions of the corporation. For example, shareholder approval is required if the corporation is to sell most of its assets, change its principal

FIGURE 14-2 Relationships among Corporate Officers, Directors, and Shareholders

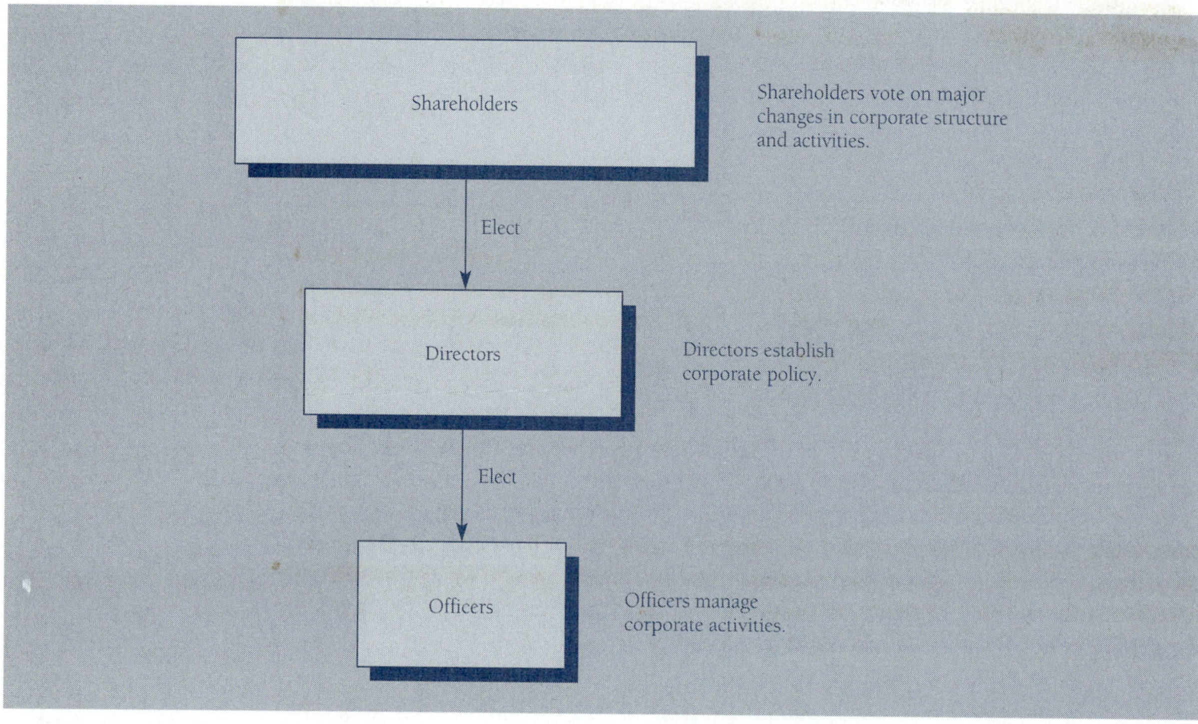

place of business, or merge with another corporation. Some shareholders are also seeking to require that the compensation of executive officers of corporations be established or approved by shareholders rather than by the board of directors.

Shareholders also have the right to inspect the books and records of the corporation and the right to sue the corporation in the event of improper action. For example, they may sue the corporation for agreeing to sell part of its assets if that action was not in their best interests. Finally, if the corporation is dissolved, the profits of the corporation are distributed to the shareholders.

proxy
A substitute vote on behalf of a shareholder at a corporate meeting when the shareholder of record is unable to attend.

A shareholder who is unable to attend a shareholders' meeting can exercise his or her rights by means of a **proxy,** which gives someone else the right to vote for the shareholder at the meeting. Shareholder proxies are generally solicited by the corporate officers. In corporations with publicly held shares, most of the shareholders' votes are usually cast by proxies granted to these officers. Proxy fights occur when individuals or groups outside the corporation solicit the proxies of shareholders. During such fights, shareholders are asked to elect new members to the board of directors or to sell their shares to individuals or groups that are seeking to take over the management of the corporation.

A shareholder of one share of stock in a corporation is generally entitled to one vote. Thus, the holder of 100 shares of stock can cast 100 votes. If the corporation's bylaws permit cumulative voting, when a shareholder with 100 shares of stock is voting for three directors, the shareholder has 300 votes. This system permits a shareholder to cast 300 votes for one director or to give 100 votes to each of three directors. Cumulative voting is favored by those who seek to protect minority shareholders.

These shareholders can cast all of their votes for one director, whereas the votes of the majority are being split among a group of directors. Most of the states require a corporation to conduct at least one shareholders' meeting each year; however, a few states, notably Delaware, have no such requirement.

Role of the Board of Directors

The board of directors is legally responsible for the management of corporate activities. If a corporation acts in an illegal or improper manner, the members of its board of directors can be held liable. The Revised Model Business Corporation Act requires that the business activities of a corporation be managed under the direction of its board of directors. The board usually delegates to corporate officers the responsibility for managing day-to-day corporate activities. It formulates and supervises management policies and strategies. Frequently, it authorizes some of its members to act for the entire board in certain matters. For example, an executive committee of the board of directors may make critical financial decisions and an audit committee may select and review the activities of auditors.

The board of directors interacts with the shareholders in several ways. It is responsible for calling shareholders' meetings, and it determines how large the dividends should be and when they should be paid to the shareholders. It is elected by the shareholders, and it must receive shareholder approval for mergers or other extraordinary corporate activities.

The board elects corporate officers and thereafter interacts with them to ensure the implementation of its policies. As members of the board, directors owe the duties of an agent to the corporation, including the duty of loyalty and the duty of reasonable care. Corporate officers or directors who neglect their duties can be held liable. However, many states shield directors from liability by applying the **business judgment rule.** Under this rule, directors are not held liable for errors in business decisions if they exercise reasonable business judgment. They are liable only for fraud, oppression, or arbitrary actions. The following commentary discusses the cost of settling lawsuits brought against corporate officers and directors.

business judgment rule The rule that corporate directors are not held liable for errors in business decisions if they exercise reasonable business judgment.

COMMENTARY

Costs of Settlements Reach Record in Suits Against Directors, Officers

Wade Lambert

A study says the cost of fending off lawsuits against corporate directors and officers hit a record last year, giving more ammunition to proponents of legislation that would curb frivolous shareholder litigation.

The cost of settlements in suits against directors and officers rose 39% to an average of $4.6 million for the nine-year period that ended in 1994, from an average of $3.3 million for the nine-year period ending in 1993, according to Wyatt Co., a Washington consulting firm. And settlement of shareholder suits—the most common and expensive claims—climbed 43% to $7.7 on average, from $5.4 million a year earlier.

"The numbers are pretty staggering," said Phillip Norton, a Wyatt risk-management consultant who conducted the survey of 1,231 companies. . . .

In addition to the actual settlement payments, companies are also forking over record amounts to outside law firms to fight the claims, the study found. For each claim—including those that companies won without paying a settlement—the average spending on outside counsel was $967,000, up 28% from $750,000 in the 1993 survey. Work on cases ranged from a few months to several years before the claims were resolved. The figures don't include the cost of in-house attorneys also assigned to a case.

The Wyatt survey found that small companies, especially technology companies, have seen a sharper increase in lawsuits against directors and officers than large corporations. Mr. Norton said that less stable stock prices make smaller companies more vulnerable to suits alleging that the failure to disclose information affected the stock price. . . .

The cost of lawsuits against directors "is a hot issue in Silicon Valley," said Eric Keller, chief financial officer of Ventritex Inc., a Sunnyvale, Calif., company that makes implantable medical devices. Avoiding such suits is difficult, Mr. Keller said, "unless you can ensure that your stock [price] is always increasing." . . .

The study indicates some possible trends in new litigation. . . . For instance, the number of employment lawsuits against directors and officers jumped by more than a third to 212 for the nine years that ended last year, from 157 for the nine years that ended in 1993. The average settlement cost of employment claims—including job-discrimination and harassment suits—was $247,000.

Source: Wade Lambert, "Costs of Settlement Reach Record in Suits Against Directors, Officers," Reprinted by permission of *The Wall Street Journal,* March 10, 1995, p. B10.

Role of the Officers

Corporate officers are the managers of the corporation's day-to-day business activities. They are responsible for carrying out the policies established by the board of directors. The board is responsible for determining the compensation paid to corporate officers and for detailing their duties. Corporate officers are agents of the corporation and owe the corporation a fiduciary duty of loyalty. As the *Cooke* case that follows illustrates, the fiduciary duty of a corporate officer is especially exacting where the corporation is closely held.

It is wrong for a corporate officer to appropriate a corporate opportunity for personal gain. For example, if an opportunity arises for a corporation to purchase the stock of another corporation, a corporate officer who learns of the opportunity is prohibited from purchasing that corporation's stock as a personal investment unless his or her corporation consents.

Corporate officers should also be diligent in carrying out corporate affairs. A corporate officer cannot be negligent or careless in performing the tasks of his or her office, but must use reasonable business judgment. For example, a corporate treasurer must take reasonable steps to safeguard and invest the corporate monies. It would be negligent for that officer to lend corporate funds to a friend involved in a risky business.

If, as an agent, a corporate officer uses reasonable care in acting on the corporation's behalf, that officers' activities are considered the activities of the corporation. The corporation is obligated to reimburse any loss suffered by an officer who is sued by a third party for an act done on the corporation's behalf. Thus, if a shareholder sues the treasurer because a reasonable investment in the stock market did not produce the expected gain, the corporation would be obligated to pay the treasurer's legal expenses in defending that suit.

The rights and duties of corporate officers are often spelled out in an employment agreement. However, the law of agency also imposes duties on and grants rights to any corporate agents, including corporate officers. For example, agency law imposes on corporate officers the duty to disclose information that they receive in their capacity as corporate agents, and it grants them the right to be indemnified or reimbursed for costs they incur while acting on the corporation's behalf. What if a corporate officer in a closely held company did not disclose the terms of his employment agreement to the company's board of directors? Is that agreement still valid?

Cooke v. Lynn Sand & Stone Co.

640 N.E. 2d 786 (1994)
Massachusetts Court of Appeals

Lynn Sand & Stone Company (Lynn Sand) was a family owned company in the business described as crushed stone and ready mixed concrete manufacturing. It was founded in 1918 by the plaintiff's grandfather. After the founder's death, the plaintiff's father, Theodore Cooke, took over. Although Theodore retired in 1978, he served thereafter as chairman of the board of directors.

Plaintiff James Cooke joined the company in 1955, working under his father and then under Raymond Pybus who was president from 1968–1975. Cooke became president and assumed active management of the company in 1975. He worked closely with Robert Prosperi (not a member of the Cooke family), who as vice president, assisted Cooke in the day-to-day activities. The other officers of the firm included a bother and sister of the plaintiff; each was a vice president. The board of directors of the firm consisted of Theodore as chairman of the board, the plaintiff, the brother and sister of the plaintiff, and Mr. Prosperi. Theodore Cooke owned about 33 percent of the company and controlled additional shares, the plaintiff owned a little over 20 percent, and the remainder was primarily in the hands of other family members.

In 1979, Prosperi asked for a contract to stabilize his position in the firm. The company counsel prepared a five-year contract for him. It was approved by Theodore, and the members of the board of directors knew about it even though it was not submitted to the board for approval. A new five-year contract was prepared for Prosperi in 1981, it was then signed by the plaintiff as president and by Prosperi as employee. The plaintiff asked Prosperi to prepare a similar contract for the plaintiff. The plaintiff asked Theodore about the contract, and he suggested the plaintiff show it to the other board members. Several weeks after the plaintiff passed the draft to the board for review, Theodore told the plaintiff that he was a member of the family and didn't need a contract. (No family member had ever had a written contract.)

When Prosperi's contract was again revised in 1982, the plaintiff asked Prosperi to write a similar contract (with different salary terms) for him. That contract was signed by Prosperi as the employer and plaintiff James Cooke as employee. This contract was not shown to the board of directors, and no mention of it was made in the company's report to its shareholders. In 1983, several firms made offers to purchase Lynn Sand. As one of the offers included a takeover of the company's contracts, the plaintiff sent a memo to the prospective buyer and to the board outlining the terms of his and Prosperi's employment contracts. Theodore and

Phillips, the plaintiff's brother, told the prospective buyer they thought the plaintiff's contract was not valid. Theodore told the buyer it would have to find a place for plaintiff in the firm but said that was for goodwill purposes, not as a legal obligation. Once the sale went through, the buyer agreed to hire the plaintiff at a reduced salary for a year, but the plaintiff sued to enforce his 1982 five-year employment contract. The trial court found for the plaintiff, and the company appealed.

Kaplan, Justice

Entering upon a contract nominally with the corporation, the plaintiff was bound to make full contemporaneous disclosure of it to the other director-shareholders so that they might judge the transaction and pass on it; the rule is that of the proverbial goldfish bowl. Instead, the plaintiff deliberately withheld the information, saw to its exclusion from financial statements rendered to the director-shareholders and let the cat out of the bag . . . only when it would have been very hazardous for him to do otherwise. The plaintiff's secretiveness is especially deplored when one considers that he was on notice through his failed effort in 1981 that the idea of a contract was not popular and would probably have met opposition in 1982 as it did earlier.

An insider contract starts out suspect because of a question or doubt whether the interests of the corporation have had any true representative, whether the contract resulted from anything on the order of an arm's-length negotiation. Here, it was Prosperi who signed for the corporation, but his situation was equivocal, to say the least. He was the plaintiff's subordinate and had been asked to copy the terms of the contract he had written for himself, when he had been seeking his own advantage, not the corporation's. . . . The swapping of roles, with the plaintiff endorsing Prosperi's contract, and Prosperi doing the same for plaintiff, adds an element of unintended comedy rather inapposite to the discharge of the plaintiff's fiduciary duty.

The foregoing is enough to invalidate this contract, but we have to add that its essential soundness and fairness given the business setting is much in doubt. Although there was no movement on foot in the company actually to displace the plaintiff as president, there was no disposition to ensure him a place for a period of five years. The plaintiff knew this from the episode in 1981, and the secret contract was an attempt to foist on the company a regime the plaintiff's associates had rejected as a proposed business arrangement and, as far as appears, would continue to reject if given a chance.

There is nothing in the Addendum that represents a ratification by Lynn Sand of the contract and no such action was ever taken by the board of directors or the shareholders—the votes, of course, would not have been there.

The judge's findings can be briefly characterized. They were bland, general rather than specific in style, and treated the transactions to the extent described as routine and correct. . . . In our view the findings of fact were clearly erroneous and the conclusions of law were unwarranted and incorrect.

Judgment reversed.

Case Questions

1. What assumption exists as to contracts between a corporate officer and a closely held corporation?
2. Who in the corporation would have authority to approve this contract—the chairman of the board, the entire board, the shareholders?

COMMENTARY

ETHICS AND THE BOARDROOM

Corporate scandals that have occurred in the United States, Japan, and the United Kingdom indicate that unethical behavior and violation of fiduciary duties knows no geographical boundaries.

In the United States, Salomon Brothers securities firm acknowledged that it had violated the agreement established for direct purchase of Treasury notes. The government allows five or six firms to participate as direct purchasers of Treasury notes; these firms then resell the notes to their clients and to other brokerage firms. Each participating firm agreed that it would purchase no more than 25 percent of the notes at any one sale. Salomon Brothers broke this agreement on several occasions, apparently purchasing 80 percent of the notes at one particular sale. Salomon Brothers breached its duty to the government and to the other firms by not disclosing its violation of the rules.

In Japan, several brokerage firms went to the extreme to ensure that their favored clients would continue to do business with them. These firms refunded the money lost on stocks purchased by their top customers. The losses of their other customers, however, were not refunded. Brokers as agents owe a duty of loyalty and a duty to use their best efforts for their clients. There is a clear breach of duty and conflict of interest when a broker represents that he or she acts on behalf of all clients but in fact gives preferential treatment to some without disclosing that fact to others or to the government.

In the United Kingdom, Robert Maxwell, who was chairman of Maxwell Enterprises and owner of newspapers on three continents (Australia, Europe, and North America) was found dead in the water near his yacht off the Canary Islands. After his death, authorities discovered that Maxwell had taken money belonging to public corporation pension accounts and transferred it to privately owned firms to keep them from falling into bankruptcy. His shell game, moving assets from one firm to another, was more extensive than anyone realized. The pension fund monies were there for the employees of the public firms, not for Maxwell's use with other firms. Maxwell's unethical actions certainly breached duties he owed to the expectant pensioners and no doubt also violated several laws.

Ethical Dilemmas for Corporate Management

Ethical Dilemma

Corporate managers, officers, and directors have access to valuable and confidential corporate information regarding discoveries from corporate research and development, the design of products, plans about products, strategies about marketing, impending takeovers, and corporate financial performance. Managers who seek to use such information for personal gain breach their ethical obligations if they place their personal interests before the interests of shareholders.

In recent years, corporations have changed the composition of their boards of directors in order to increase the board's supervision of corporate managers. The boards of most publicly traded corporations have several members who are independent of management; these members work for other corporations, banks, customers, suppliers, universities, or labor unions. Such diversity of membership is intended to enhance the "open forum" character of board meetings. A strong executive is less likely to force subordinates to make unethical decisions if independent board members are present.

Many corporations now have special subcommittees, mostly composed of independent members, that make decisions in areas of management compensation, litigation, and mergers. Independent board members arguably prevent insiders from taking advantage of their position to abuse shareholders or misappropriate corporate assets. However, is it ethical for inside managers to select only close friends as board members? Is this designed to merely give the appearance of independence?

Many observers allege that the "independent" board members are too closely tied to the chief executive officer or other insiders to effectively monitor management. Furthermore, since such members often lack expertise in the corporation's line of business, they may not be able to effectively advise the corporation.

Comparison of Business Organization Forms

Many small and medium-sized businesses face a choice as to the best form of business organization for them. The alternatives often include organizing as a sole proprietorship, partnership, limited partnership, limited liability company, or general corporation. This concluding section examines the taxation, liability, control, and continuity treatment that the law gives each of these forms of business organization. Any of these four features may determine which form is most appropriate in a given situation. Figure 14–1 on page 483 provides a synopsis of the major attributes of these different forms of business organization.

Any small business, regardless of its form of organization, generally needs to obtain financing to begin its operations, to allow it to continue in difficult economic times, and to finance expansion. Figure 14–3 depicts some of the sources of financing used by many small businesses.

Taxation

When individual tax rates are at or near historically low levels, taxation may lead a business to select the proprietorship, partnership, limited partnership, or limited liability business form. None of these forms of business organization is taxed as an entity, as is a corporation. The profits of a proprietorship are taxed as ordinary income to the proprietor, and the losses of a proprietorship are deducted from the gains the proprietor derives from other income sources.

A partnership files a return on which it reports income or losses and distributions to the partners. The partners then report their individual shares of the partnership income on their separate returns; any tax liability due from a partner is based on his or her overall income. The parties in a limited partnership and in a limited liability company are usually taxed in a manner similar to the partners in a general partnership.

Several tax benefits arise from selecting the sole proprietorship or partnership form rather than the corporate form. First, many of the states levy a separate franchise tax on the authorized shares of corporations doing business in the state. This tax is not imposed on sole proprietorships or partnerships.

Second, because the income derived by a proprietor or partner from the operation of a business is taxed only when received, it is not subject to double taxation (taxation of both the organization and the individual owner), as is corporate income distributed to a shareholder. For example, if a corporation earns $100 and distributes $25 of that amount to its shareholders as dividends, the corporation will be taxed on the $100 it earned and the shareholders will be taxed on the $25 they receive. Thus, a total of $125 is taxed.

If a proprietorship or a partnership earns $100, that total is taxed to the proprietor or to all of the partners. In either case, the total amount subject to tax is only $100. As corporate and individual income tax rates vary over time, the prevailing tax rates must

FIGURE 14-3

Sources of Financing for Small Businesses

1. Private Sources

   These include personal funds from relatives and friends. In addition, there may be some private placement money available from venture capitalists—those willing to invest in a business in exchange for a guaranteed return or a partial ownership of the business. As venture capitalists want to have limited liability, they are more likely to invest in corporations, limited companies, or limited partnerships than in partnerships or proprietorships.

2. Trade Sources

   A business may obtain funds from its suppliers by having the supplier make short-term or long-term credit available. The supplier will be guaranteed some future income and a new customer, and the business will obtain some needed credit.

3. Institutional Sources

   Firms needing capital may approach finance or leasing companies. Rates from these sources are generally higher than at commercial banks, but a continued source of funds may be obtained if the business continues to operate profitably. Firms may also obtain loans from commercial banks. Some banks specialize in short-term loans, whereas others offer either short- or long-term loans. Because the partner or proprietor is personally liable for loans made to the business, whereas the corporation is not, the owner of a small corporation may find that he or she will have to personally guarantee the repayment of loans made to the corporation.

4. Governmental Sources

   The Small Business Administration (SBA) may be helpful in obtaining financing. The SBA may make a loan to a bank or a direct loan to the firm. These loans are usually long-term and at low interest rates.

5. Other Sources

   Insurance companies are a good source of financing for firms with substantial collateral, such as real estate, to secure the loan. Investment bankers may be a good source of financing for the well-known large corporations.

be examined to determine which form of business organization is most desirable from a tax viewpoint. Several proposals seek to remove or minimize this double taxation of corporate income distributed to shareholders as dividends. Readers may find this area of tax law changed in the near future.

Finally, because the income from a sole proprietorship or a partnership may be only a part of the proprietor's or partner's overall income, losses from other sources may reduce the business income subject to tax. However, because the corporation is a separate entity for tax purposes, the owner of a corporation cannot offset corporate profits with individual losses or use corporate losses to offset individual profits.

Because the corporation is a separate entity and the current individual income tax rates increase as the amount of income increases, forming a separate entity to pay a portion of the taxes due on certain activities can be beneficial. Splitting income between two entities—the corporation and the individual—may lower taxes. However, the current relatively low tax rate for individual income makes the formation of a separate corporate entity less desirable.

Liability

Liability considerations often result in the selection of the corporate, limited liability company, or the limited partnership form rather than the proprietorship or partnership form of business organization. The sole proprietor is liable for all of his or her business activities and obligations. All the members of a general partnership are liable for the debts, claims, or judgments of the partnership to the full extent of their total personal assets.

Thus, the proprietorship or partnership form is usually not desirable for a business that is subject to significant tort liability exposure for injuries to customers, employees, or other parties. The limited liability of limited partners is essential to attracting their investment in a limited partnership. Similarly, a firm manufacturing or selling chemicals, pesticides, or dangerous industrial machines likely would select the corporate form of organization because of its limited liability.

Control

The sole proprietor, of course, has total control of his or her business. Control in a partnership is relatively easy both to obtain and to maintain. The partnership agreement can establish the control that the initial partners are to exercise. Although majority rule usually controls the partnership's ordinary operations, a court will refer to the partnership agreement provisions if the partners indicate a contrary desire. When a partnership contains an even number of partners, it becomes essential to determine how deadlocks will be resolved. Because the admission of new partners generally requires the unanimous consent of all the existing partners, maintaining the control usually does not pose a problem for the partnership. In the limited partnership, the general partner(s) exercise control of the firm. In the limited liability company, the firm is usually closely held, and control is easy to maintain.

Control can be easy for the small corporation but difficult for the large one. This is because the shares of the small corporation are usually not freely traded. The existing shareholders can restrict the transferability of their shares by requiring that the corporation or existing shareholders be given the first option to purchase any shares from a person desiring to sell them. The large corporation issues so many shares that it usually cannot restrict their transferability. Thus, although the original owners of a corporation can take measures to ensure their ownership of enough shares to counteract any other shareholders, in recent years many corporate takeovers have been effected by outsiders who bought shares of selected publicly traded corporations.

Continuity

Continuity is a problem for both the proprietorship and the partnership. A sole proprietor's business must be liquidated on the owner's death unless it can be quickly sold to a new owner who will continue to operate it. Every time a partner dies, resigns, or leaves a partnership, the existing partnership is automatically dissolved, though a new one may be created to continue the business. Dissolution sometimes requires notification of all the creditors of the partnership. The withdrawing partner's capital must be paid off by the old partnership.

A partnership agreement can simplify some of the problems of partnership continuity. Transitions can be eased by the partnership's purchase of life insurance on the partners, with the partnership as the beneficiary, or by the maintenance of separate funds for payment to a withdrawing partner. Unlike dissolution of the proprietorship, dissolution of the partnership generally does not require it to liquidate or to cease doing business. However, the partnership must be able to pay off the withdrawing partner and prepare a new partnership agreement among the remaining partners.

Dissolution of a partnership can sometimes be handled internally by making adjustments in its financial and accounting records that do not adversely affect its business operations. Nevertheless, both the proprietorship and the partnership face continuity problems that must be dealt with. On the other hand, the corporation's existence is generally perpetual, and its continuity is unaffected by the withdrawal of any one shareholder, key officer, or employee. While a limited liability company often does not have perpetual existence, it is easier to change members than with a partnership. New limited partners may be easily added to a limited partnership, but the addition of a general partner generally requires the approval of existing partners.

SUMMARY

A variety of types of business organization are reviewed in this chapter: the proprietorship, the limited partnership, the general partnership, the limited liability company, the Subchapter S corporation, and the general corporation. The proprietorship, partnership, and corporation represent the basic types of organizations. The proprietorship, which is the easiest to form, has no special legal status distinct from that of its owner. The partnership involves two or more persons who jointly carry on a business for profit. It is generally formed by a partnership agreement specifying the duties of the partners toward other partners and third parties.

Several other types of businesses are similar to the partnership. The joint venture and the limited partnership are used in special situations by persons who seek to combine partnership characteristics with attributes of other business organizations. Because a partner in a partnership may act as both its principal and its agent, he or she has duties and rights that define the relationships among the partners. The partners generally have authority to bind the partnership in normal business activities, and the partnership is liable for contracts made or torts committed by the partners.

The corporation is a desirable form of organization for many business activities. Essential characteristics of the corporation are its separate entity status, its limited liability, its ease of ownership transfer, and its perpetual life. A corporation is formed by filing articles of incorporation in a state office. Large for-profit private firms are the most noticeable corporations, but nonprofit corporations, professional corporations, public corporations, and closely held corporations, including limited liability companies and S corporations, are also common.

The bylaws of a corporation determine how it is organized. Shareholders, directors, and officers each perform distinct roles in the activities of the corporation. The shareholder-owners select the board of directors and vote to ratify or reject extraordinary corporate decisions. The directors are responsible for formulating and overseeing the corporation's management policies. The officers are responsible for the corporation's day-to-day operations.

In determining whether a proprietorship, a partnership, or a corporation is most suitable in a given situation, four factors are often examined. The taxation, liability, control, and continuity aspects of these forms of business organization generally are critical to a determination of the form that best fits the needs of a particular business.

Critical Thinking Review Questions

1. Match each of the forms of business organizations listed in Column A with the appropriate statement in Column B.

A	B
1. Franchise	a. An artificial being created by the state
2. Proprietorship	b. Created when shareholders elect to be treated as partners for tax purposes
3. Partnership	c. An entity in which some partners are treated like shareholders for liability purposes
4. Limited partnership	d. Created by an agreement between two or more persons who agree to share its profits and losses
5. Corporation	e. Owned by one person who is personally liable for all of its losses
6. S corporation	f. A privilege granted or sold, such as the privilege of using a name or a process to sell products or services agreed upon between two parties
7. Joint venture	g. Two or more persons joined in a business activity that is limited to a specified period

2. A and B, two sisters, operate a decorating firm using the name Decorators Den. The business was begun by Sister A, but as it grew, Sister B also worked full-time at the firm. They advertise under the firm name in the local newspaper and on letterhead stationery. Sister A recruits most of the firm's clients and contracts for its major jobs. Sister B keeps the books and records of the firm. When the time comes to divide the firm's profits, Sister B sues Sister A, claiming that they had formed a partnership and that the profits should be divided equally. Sister A says she hired Sister B as an employee in her business. Explain the assumptions each is making and decide who is correct and why.
3. Joe and Tom are partners in the classic car business. While Joe is driving a customer in a Jaguar that is part of the inventory of the business, he is involved in an accident in which the customer is injured. The customer sues the partners individually and the partnership. Who can be held liable?
4. Jones, a limited partner in a fast-food franchise, invests $100,000 in the limited partnership. Explain (a) the requirements for the formation of the limited partnership, (b) whether Jones may transfer his partnership interest to his wife on his death, and (c) whether or to what extent the limited partner may be held liable for partnership debts.
5. John and Richard are wealthy businessmen in a high-income tax bracket. They wish to enter into a business venture with a high risk of potential product liability suits. They expect a loss for the first three years of the business, owing to significant capital expenses and the difficulty of entering the market. What form of business organization would be best for them? Explain.
6. A, B, and C are partners in a delivery business. The partnership owns three delivery trucks. Jones, a creditor of C, obtains a judgment against C and asks the court to attach one of the delivery trucks. Does Jones have the right to attach the partnership's delivery truck and to sell it to pay off C's debt?

Critical Thinking Exercises

1. A and B are partners in a small business. B borrows $50,000 at the bank to purchase a new Mercedes for his personal use. Subsequently, B defaults on the loan amount, and the bank repossesses and sells the Mercedes. However, the proceeds of the sale are insufficient to pay off the remaining loan amount. May the bank seek the remaining loan amount from the partnership?
2. Roberta Goza owned 100 percent of the shares of the Alan Mills, Inc., corporation. She was in charge of the day-to-day operations of the corporation and wrote checks on the corporation's

account both to a business owned by her son and to herself. She says the transactions between herself and the corporation were legitimate business transactions. There is no evidence of any fraud or wrongdoing regarding any of those transactions. As a part of its business activities, Alan Mills corporation had signed promissory notes to Wright. When the corporation was unable to pay Wright, he sued Ms. Goza. Can Wright hold Ms. Goza liable on the notes? Why? *Wright v. Alan Mills, Inc.*, 567 So. 2d 1318 (Ala., 1990).

3. Figuerdo located undeveloped land in Orange County, Florida, that he thought would be a good investment. Figuerdo then formed a corporation under the laws of the Netherlands Antilles (a tax haven) to purchase the land. He told the investors that the cost of purchasing the land would be over $66,000 per acre and offered stock to investors in the corporation that took title to the land. Meanwhile, Figuerdo made a tentative agreement to pay the owners approximately $43,000 an acre for the land. Figuerdo and the sellers agreed to have the documents show his cost of acquiring the land was $66,000 per acre instead of $43,000, and they split the difference between them. Once the investors found that Figuerdo had profited, they sued Figuerdo for the profits. Figuerdo then proved that the actual value of the land he acquired for $43,000 had risen to well over $66,000 an acre. He asserts that the investors have no claim because they did not lose money. Do you agree? Why? *Tinwood N.V. v. SunBanks, Inc.*, 570 So. 2d 955 (1990).

4. In 1984, Wright Furniture Mills (Wright) sold furniture to the Bedtime Sleep Shop. The Shop was incorporated in 1983 and purchased by Sherill in 1985. Although Sherill did not keep great records of the corporation's activities, there is no evidence that Wright believed it was doing business with Sherill rather than with the Shop corporation. Wright sold its account receivable (the right to receive payment from the Shop) to Commonwealth Financial Corporation. That corporation sued Sherill individually for the corporation's debt. Can it collect? *Commonwealth Financial Corp. v. Sherill*, 398 S.E. 2d 438 (Ga. App., 1990).

5. Assume you are an executive in a small office furniture firm. A former classmate you knew while studying at Alpha University asks you to become a member of the board of directors of the computer software firm he and another associate founded. After serving on the board for several years, you find that your former classmate and friend is making misstatements to banks and other potential investors in the firm regarding the firm's present work on several specialized projects. You also suspect that financial documents given to these parties by your friend, the chief operating officer of the firm, are incomplete.

   Do you discuss what you know and suspect with your friend, the corporate officer? Should you reveal this information to the banks and potential investors? If you were asked for your opinion regarding the status of the company and the integrity and ability of its officers by bank officials or potential investors, what would you say?

6. You and two friends want to form a partnership business that will import certain textiles from several companies in Southeast Asia. One of these friends already has an import business that deals with several of these companies in different but related products. That friend wants to continue his own separate importing business. You worry that the Asian firms might sometimes deal with your friend in his own business rather than with the partnership. What ethical problems could confront your friend if he operates both businesses? What possible solutions could be recommended?

CHAPTER

15

Securities Regulations

Critical Thinking Questions

- What is presumed in the public policy underlying the securities laws which holds that fairness in the securities markets is needed so firms can reliably raise capital?
- What factors are similar among traditional corporate stocks and bonds that define novel investment contracts as new forms of securities?
- What ambiguities are there in enforcing the insider trading prohibition? Why is insider trading considered a form of securities fraud under Rule 10b-5?
- What issues of corporate governance are addressed by the proxy rules? What information is required from proxy solicitors to permit responsible voting by shareholders?
- How do the disclosures required by the Williams Act regulate tender offers and provide shareholders with advantages in responding to a tender offer's terms?

Introduction... Past, Present, Future

Before the Great Depression, there was little regulation of the securities markets. Laissez-faire allowed the markets to police themselves supplemented only by state common law remedies for fraud and breach of contract. This unregulated market ideal was abandoned after the 1929 stock market crash when governments took responsibility for reducing the securities fraud that had been rampant during the "Roaring Twenties." Today, the U.S. securities markets are probably the most efficient and liquid in the world. This means there are usually enough buyers and sellers present to satisfy any trader's supply or demand at prices reflecting intrinsic value. Today, the growth in other nations' securities markets is rapidly producing a global capital market.

Despite this growing strength, the world's markets are in turmoil over the persisting difficulties in accessing capital or investment opportunities worldwide. Revelations of insider trading and financial fraud reduce the credibility of some capital markets. Skepticism about the excesses of the influence of high-rolling and free-wheeling speculators erodes investor confidence. Stock scandals in the United States, Japan, and Europe are constantly in the news. Beliefs that takeover activity and speculation is excessive has led to restrictions on takeover tactics, leveraged buyouts (LBOs), and numerous trading strategies. Regulators and the securities exchanges have installed computerized systems to track transactions that identify the parties, participating floor traders, actual trade timing, and prevailing prices. New enforcement mechanisms are emerging to deter insider trading, financial fraud, and conflicts of interest. Securities firms continue reducing their staffs worldwide because of industry consolidation and lower projected activity.

In the future, the investment markets will continue to become more globalized. Investors in one nation will quickly and easily make trades in other nations' markets. Most nations have "bourses" (stock markets), and there has been considerable new market creation in the emerging markets of the Pacific Rim and the former communist nations. Twenty-four-hour trading will occur in many stocks somewhere in the world, and considerable trading will occur electronically. Investment industry regulation over the activities of investment advisors, investment companies (mutual funds), financial planners, and investment bankers will increase. Regulators of the various nations' capital markets will adopt similar regulations. This will become a form of regulatory equilibrium as more stringent regulations ease and lax regulations increase. Nations with guarded markets will be unable to attract the cross-border flow of capital. The U.S. securities laws will continue as the model for the world, although changes in the United States are also inevitable. This chapter examines the United States and samples foreign securities laws for their effect on raising capital.

ETHICAL DILEMMA

Ethical Dilemmas in the Securities Markets

Should management use its control over corporate affairs to hide its performance from shareholders and the public? Corporate information is owned by the firm and is ultimately produced for the benefit of shareholders and to encourage efficient capital markets. Material inside information may not be misappropriated for personal use by anyone, such as for a manager's inside trading. The securities markets, exchanges, and securities professionals serve the public and the economy by providing places for firms to raise capital and for investors to trade reliably and with confidence that the markets are fair. Actions that compromise these fiduciary duties show an unethical advantage taken over the beneficiaries of the trust. Accurate periodic financial disclosure is needed to prevent subversion of the capital markets. The securities laws legislate corporate morality. Managers have a disclosure duty that limits secrecy, making them more responsive to shareholders and improving the integrity of the capital markets, creating a "fair game."

The Primary Federal Securities Statutes

There are two main securities laws and several related amendments and ancillary laws. Other nations generally have some form of primary securities law, although they may differ widely in form and substance. For example, U.S. forces occupying Japan after World War II insisted that Japan's national legislature, the Diet, enact securities laws nearly identical to U.S. law. However, because Japan relies more heavily on consensus building than on governmental enforcement, their securities laws are not as rigorously enforced. Nevertheless, as investors realize that unregulated markets become rigged and unfair, capital will tend to move into markets where comprehensive and just securities laws protect investors.

Securities Act of 1933

The Securities Act of 1933 (1933 Act) is the original federal securities law passed as part of President Franklin D. Roosevelt's New Deal. The 1933 Act requires firms that issue new securities in **initial public offerings (IPOs)** must disclose financial information. New securities issues are registered with the Securities and Exchange Commission (SEC). For example, when Apple Computer first went public, its stock was registered before sale to public investors.

initial public offering (IPO)
First public solicitation and sale of new securities.

Securities Exchange Act of 1934

The Securities Exchange Act of 1934 (1934 Act) created the SEC to administer the 1933 Act and added some new provisions. The 1934 Act regulates the secondary trading markets for securities traded on an exchange, such as the New York Stock Exchange or the American Stock Exchange. The 1934 Act outlaws fraud in securities transactions, prohibits insider trading, and regulates corporate democracy under the proxy and tender after provisions. Brokers, dealers, investment advisors, issuers, and securities exchanges must register with the SEC. Continuous disclosure is required of pertinent corporate financial information (e.g., annual reports).

Securities and Exchange Commission The SEC is responsible for licensing, securities professionals, collecting disclosure information, and enforcing the various securities law requirements and prohibitions. Most nations have some regulator like the SEC, although their powers vary greatly. For example, as a result of the "kick-back" scandals implicating several Japanese brokerage houses in 1991, Japan is seriously considering an agency independent of the Ministry of Finance to regulate its securities markets. Canadian securities markets are regulated largely by Canadian provincial regulators, not by the Canadian central government.

Other Regulators The investment markets are also regulated by the states and other federal agencies. All the states regulate securities offerings to their residents with their so-called *blue sky* laws. Insurance and banking investments are regulated by various regulators. The futures markets are regulated by the Commodities Futures Trading Commission (CFTC), which has jurisdiction over standardized, exchange traded commitments for the future delivery of commodities. Traditionally, futures involved crops, livestock, processed commodities, building materials, petroleum, and metals. However, the biggest growth has occurred in financial futures. Critics charge the CFTC's lax enforcement of financial futures contribute to excessive market volatility that increasingly impacts the securities markets. For example, *program trading*, simultaneous offsetting transactions in stocks while also trading financial futures, is allegedly harmful. Controversy also rages over increasing speculation in relatively unregulated *derivatives.* These are investment contracts that fluctuate as the value of some underlying financial asset changes. Huge derivative losses have been reported by large corporations (e.g., Procter & Gamble) and governments (e.g., California's Orange County). Such controversy may eventually lead to a merger of the CFTC into the SEC.

The SEC has considerable power to promulgate regulations, investigate alleged violations, and bring civil enforcement actions either within the SEC or in the federal courts. The SEC also oversees the *self-regulation* used by various participants in the securities industry. Most investor complaints against brokers are settled by mandatory binding arbitration conducted by private arbitrators. In recent years, there has been considerable controversy over licensing and disciplining "rogue" brokers and dealers. The SEC helps refine the securities arbitration process to avoid unfairness to investors in disputes with their brokers. Arbitration is currently overseen by the National Association of Securities Dealers (NASD). The NASD also licenses securities brokers and dealers and operates the huge electronic over-the-counter (OTC) securities market known as the NASDAQ. The New York Stock Exchange (NYSE) and the other physical securities exchanges regulate their members, who perform the actual trading. The accounting rules (GAAP) used for corporate financial disclosure are generally set by the Financial Accounting Standards Board (FASB), and auditing standards (GAAS) are set by the American Institute of Certified Public Accountants (AICPA). Both accounting self-regulators are overseen by the SEC.

INTERNATIONAL PERSPECTIVE AND COMMENTARY

SECURITIES REGULATORS

The SEC is aggressively expanding its influence over international securities transactions through its Office of International Affairs. The International Securities Enforcement Cooperation Act of 1990 encourages the SEC to cooperate with other nations' securities regulators. The SEC negotiates Memoranda of Understanding (MOU) with foreign securities regulators to facilitate investigation of cross-border securities violations and enforcement by either nation. The SEC actively works to harmonize the differences between U.S. and foreign securities laws. Big differences attract illegal activities to those nations with lax regulations. Most nations are beginning to recognize that this is a "race to the bottom" that inevitably harms investors with intermarket distortions leading to a loss of investor confidence.

REGISTRATION OF SECURITIES

issuer
Firm creating and selling investment claims known as securities.

underwriter
Purchasers of securities with a view to public distribution.

prospectus
Any notice, circular, advertisement, letter, or communication that offers or confirms a security sale.

The initial public offering of new securities raises funds from the investing public to finance business operations. *Underwriting* is the process used to initially distribute a new issue of securities. Often, a closely held corporation like Apple Computer (the **issuer**) negotiates an underwriting contract with a group of underwriters, known as the *investment banking syndicate.* Underwriters can make a firm commitment to sell the whole issue if the syndicate takes the risk that the securities may not sell well by promising the issuer a specified amount of proceeds. Firms that are not yet well established may not be able to use this "wholesaling" form of underwriting, so the underwriter may act only as a sales agent promising to make its "best efforts" to sell all the securities.

The 1933 Act broadly defines **underwriters** to include (1) any person who purchases from an issuer with a view to distribute the security or (2) any person who offers or sells any security for the issuer's benefit in the distribution. Underwriters must take great care because they may be liable for violating the 1933 Act. Unintentional liability is also possible if someone is inadvertently designated as an underwriter. Underwriting occurs whenever an individual or firm receives compensation for selling an issuer's securities for the issuer's benefit.

Registration Statement and Prospectus

Issuers must provide investors with sufficient financial information to make an informed investment decision. The 1933 Act requires issuers to provide a **prospectus** (Figure 15–1). The prospectus is the primary sales and promotional tool in securities sales.

FIGURE 15-1

Prospectus Sample

Information contained herein is subject to completion or amendment. A registration statement relating to these securities has been filed with the Securities and Exchange Commission. These securities may not be sold nor may offers to buy be accepted prior to the time the registration statement becomes effective. This prospectus shall not constitute an offer to sell or the solicitation of an offer to buy nor shall there be any sale of these securities in any State in which such offer, solicitation or sale would be unlawful prior to registration or qualification under the securities laws of any such State.

(b)

NUVEEN

PROSPECTUS

Subject to Completion
May 3, 1989

10,000,000 Shares

Nuveen Performance Plus Municipal Fund, Inc.

Common Stock

Nuveen Performance Plus Municipal Fund, Inc. (the "Fund") is a newly organized, closed-end, diversified management investment company. The Fund's primary investment objective is current income exempt from Federal income tax, and its secondary objective is the enhancement of portfolio value through the selection of tax-exempt bonds and municipal market sectors that, in the opinion of the Fund's investment adviser, are undervalued. *See* "Investment Objectives and Policies." The Fund will seek to achieve its investment objectives by investing in a diversified portfolio of investment grade quality tax-exempt Municipal Obligations (as defined herein). No assurances can be given that the Fund's investment objectives will be achieved. The Fund's principal office is located at 333 West Wacker Drive, Chicago, Illinois 60606, and its telephone number is (312) 917-7825. Investors are advised to read this Prospectus and retain it for future reference.

The Fund's Board of Directors may in the future authorize the issuance of shares of preferred stock in order to provide leverage to the Common Stock, if the Board should determine that such leverage would be advantageous to the Common Shareholders under then existing and projected market conditions. No decision has yet been made by the Board to issue preferred stock, and the Fund does not anticipate the issuance of preferred stock under current market conditions. *See* "Special Leverage Considerations" and "Description of Capital Stock."

Prior to this offering, there has been no public market for the Common Stock. Application will be made to list the Common Stock on the New York Stock Exchange.

THESE SECURITIES HAVE NOT BEEN APPROVED OR DISAPPROVED BY THE SECURITIES AND EXCHANGE COMMISSION NOR HAS THE COMMISSION PASSED UPON THE ACCURACY OR ADEQUACY OF THIS PROSPECTUS. ANY REPRESENTATION TO THE CONTRARY IS A CRIMINAL OFFENSE.

	Price to Public	Underwriting Discounts and Commissions	Proceeds to the Fund(1)
Per Share	$15.00	$	$
Total(2)	$150,000,000	$	$

(a)

(1) Before deduction of expenses payable by the Fund, estimated at $

(2) The Fund has granted to the Underwriters an option, exercisable for 30 days from the date of this Prospectus, to purchase up to 1,500,000 additional shares to cover over-allotments, if any. To the extent that such option is exercised in full, the total Price to Public will be $172,500,000, total Underwriting Discounts and Commissions will be $, and total Proceeds to the Fund will be $. *See* "Underwriting."

The Common Stock is offered by the several Underwriters, subject to prior sale, when, as and if delivered to and accepted by them, and subject to the right of the Underwriters to reject any order in whole or in part. It is expected that delivery of the shares will be made at the offices of Alex. Brown & Sons Incorporated, Baltimore, Maryland, on or about , 1989.

Alex. Brown & Sons
Incorporated

John Nuveen & Co.
Incorporated

A. G. Edwards & Sons, Inc.

Blunt Ellis & Loewi
Incorporated

Dain Bosworth
Incorporated

Legg Mason Wood Walker
Incorporated

The date of this Prospectus is , 1989.

Issuers must also file a *registration statement* with the SEC. Both documents must include or refer to the issuer's financial statements. The *statutory* or *formal prospectus* is a specific document that contains basic information for use in evaluating the securities. Well-established issuers may omit certain financial information by referring to it if contained in a current annual and quarterly report. The issuer must first negotiate with the underwriting syndicate while preparing the prospectus and registration statement. The *prefiling period* ends when the registration statement is filed with the SEC.

Information Required in a Prospectus

1. Audited financial statements.
2. Five years of comparative financial information.
3. Management's discussion and analysis of financial condition.
4. Information describing the issuer's management.
5. A description of the security offered.
6. An explanation of how the proceeds will be used.

The Registration Process

Sales of securities are not permitted in the United States until the securities are registered with the SEC. *Sales* include contracts of sale or transfers of any interest in a security for value. "Gun-jumping" (preconditioning the market) during the prefiling period is prohibited to the issuer, its underwriter, and syndicate members. *Preconditioning* occurs with public statements suggesting a new securities offering is imminent. For example, press releases or speeches that predict, project, forecast, or estimate the value of the new security are prohibited preconditioning because they can create demand before an adequate evaluation of the issuer's prospects. However, the issuer should continue to advertise its products and respond truthfully to inquiries by shareholders or securities analysts. The appearance of business as usual should be maintained during the prefiling period because publicity about the new securities must be avoided. Exceptions permit limited preconditioning like by small issuers.

The *waiting period* begins when the issuer files a registration statement with the SEC. No sales are permitted during this period. However, *statutory offers* are permitted as long as the offer only indicates the interest to sell or buy. Other permissible communications during the waiting period include (1) *tombstone ads*, which are simple announcements with lined borders resembling tombstones, usually appearing in the financial press; (2) the preliminary or *red herring prospectus,* which conspicuously disclaims any formal offer; (3) *formal oral offers* that have not yet been accepted; and (4) the *summary prospectus,* which contains condensed information. All other forms of sales effort are illegal during the waiting period.

The effective date of the registration statement starts the *post-effective period* when actual sales may begin. This usually begins 20 days after the registration statement is filed unless the SEC accelerates the effective date or threatens to halt sales. A fully amended final prospectus must be sent along with all confirmations of sale, all deliveries of securities, written offers, and distributions of supplementary sales literature. The issuer, underwriters, dealers, and brokers are responsible for delivering a prospectus to all potential buyers. The initial sales period lasts for about 40 days or until all of the new issue is sold. The SEC's review of the registration statement does not ensure the accuracy of the issuer's claims, nor does the SEC verify the securities as good investments. The three stages of SEC registration are illustrated in Figure 15–2.

shelf registration Securities preregistered for sale when conditions are optimal.

Traditionally, the issuer must attempt to sell all the securities immediately after the registration becomes effective. However, **shelf registration** is an alternative process, permitting the issuer to comply with the complex registration procedures well in advance of the need for the proceeds. These preregistered securities are held in inventory "on the shelf" until financing is needed and market conditions become optimal. Issuers often sell shelf securities directly to investors and can thereby save some underwriting costs.

FIGURE 15-2

SEC Registration Process

	Prefiling Period	Filed with SEC	**Waiting Period**	Registration effective	**Posteffective Period**
			20 days or until SEC accelerates effective date of registration statement		40 days or until all the securities have been sold to investors
Prohibited actions	No contracts to sell securities No announcements conditioning the market (gun jumping)		No contracts to sell securities		No preliminary or "red herring" prospectuses
Permitted/ required actions	Can contact investment bankers for advice Can negotiate with underwriters for possible participation in underwriting syndicate Must prepare registration statement, preliminary prospectus, and supporting documents for SEC filing Must maintain "business as usual" communications with security holders, customers, suppliers, the press, and securities analysts		Can publish or distribute statutory offers to buy or sell securities, including: Tombstone ads Preliminary prospectus Formal oral offers Summary prospectuses Distribution of preliminary "red herring" prospectus		Must forward formal prospectus before or with all confirmations of sales, deliveries of securities Must attempt to sell all of the newly registered securities unless registered as a shelf offering

Global Securities Trading

International Perspective and Commentary

Initial public offerings (IPOs) in some foreign nations do not follow the complex and costly process described above. For example, even though the securities laws of the EU require IPO registration similar to the United States, the Germans have received an exception for their practice of "universal banking." German commercial banks also function as investment bankers by operating an underwriting syndicate. Such dual purpose banking is illegal in the United States under the Glass-Stegall Act. New IPO securities are generally not registered in Germany. Therefore, issuers disclose far less financial information to potential shareholders than in the United States, particularly about management's activities. Efforts in the United States to permit universal banking are currently uncertain. However, the U.S. financial reforms made thus far open some competition among U.S. firms in the finance businesses: insurance, pension administration, mutual funds, investment banking, commercial banking, and brokerage.

How do citizens of one nation trade on foreign stock exchanges or invest in securities of other nations' firms? Traditionally, U.S. citizens have invested in *American Depository Receipts (ADRs),* certificates that represent foreign securities held by a foreign trustee. ADRs must be registered as securities under the 1933 Act.

Some foreign firms' securities are registered to trade directly on U.S. exchanges. The big brokerage firms from most industrialized nations have established foreign branch offices to execute trades ordered by customers in other nations. Trading links are developing between various foreign securities exchanges, permitting brokers to receive price quotes and last-sale information on a foreign nation's securities exchange. Outside the United States, the world's major stock exchanges include Canada (Toronto and Montreal), the United Kingdom (London), Japan (Tokyo), Hong Kong, Australia (Sydney), Germany (Frankfurt), France (Paris), Switzerland (Zurich), Italy (Milan), Netherlands (Amsterdam), Sweden (Stockholm), Belgium (Brussels), and Spain (Madrid). Emerging markets are developing in nations of the Pacific Rim and Eastern Europe. Dealing with foreign brokers is one of several risks inherent in trading foreign securities. Other risks include changes in exchange rates, delays in settlement and clearance procedures (payment and delivery of security certificates), high withholding taxes, and high transactions costs.

The SEC has liberalized access to U.S. capital markets for foreign issuers. Regulation S permits registration of new IPOs by foreign issuers, with significantly reduced disclosure requirements. Rule 144A permits nearly unlimited resales of certain privately placed securities among *qualified institutional buyers (QIB)*. A QIB is a sophisticated institutional investor that manages a large portfolio over $100 million. Under these schemes, foreign issuers need disclose only the same type of information as required in their home nation. The 2,000 or so U.S. QIBs constitute a smaller secondary market for private placements. QIBs are interconnected with the screen-based quotation system known as PORTAL. Other liberalizations for publicly traded foreign corporations listed on U.S. exchanges became effective in 1993 so that nearly 600 foreign firms from over 40 nations are now traded in the United States.

What Is a Security?

The securities laws regulate only those investments known as *securities*. In the abstract, a security may be considered an intangible transaction or contract right requiring one party to make payments or future performances to another party. While *security* can also mean collateral or reduced risk and danger, the securities laws use the narrower meaning because it triggers strict SEC regulation.

SECURITY

The term *security* means any note; stock; treasury stock; bond; debenture; evidence of indebtedness; transferable share; investment contract; voting trust certificate; certificate of deposit for a security; fractional undivided interest in oil, gas, or other mineral rights; any put, call, straddle, stock option, or warrant; or, in general, any interest or instrument commonly known as a *security*.

Any instrument on this statutory list is covered by the securities laws, with a few exceptions. For example, purely commercial, consumption, or consumer transactions are exempted. Also exempt are short-term commercial paper (corporate IOUs maturing in 9 months or less) and notes that facilitate trade credit, sales of minor or consumer assets, or correct the seller's cash flow difficulties. Additionally, these exceptions extend to any note that bears a "family resemblance" to those just listed. *Reves v. Ernst & Young*[1] held that notes are securities depending on the following four factors: (1) the parties' purposes, (2) the seller's distribution plan, (3) the public expectation for securities law protection, and (4) whether another factor reduces the instrument's risk so the protection of the securities laws becomes unnecessary. The securities issued by banks, government agencies, and charities are also exempt. Several other instruments have been designated securities, including limited partnership interests, equipment trust certificates, some franchises, variable annuity insurance policies, and pyramid selling schemes. How is the "catch all" of investment contracts to be analyzed to determine if it is really a regulated security? The following case illustrates the elements of nontraditional securities, which are defined as (1) an investment of money, (2) in a common enterprise, (3) from which the investor is led to expect profits, (4) derived solely from the promoter's efforts.

SEC v. Howey

328 U.S. 293 (1946)
United States Supreme Court

Several investors purchased parcels of a common orange grove in Florida as part of the capital-raising efforts of the W.J. Howey Company. Each of the prospective purchasers was offered both a land sale contract and a separate service contract for planting, harvesting, and marketing the crop offered by Howey-in-the-Hills, a subsidiary of W.J. Howey. Such services were provided for 85 percent of the land sales. The 10-year service contracts granted Howey-in-the-Hills full and complete possession of the acreage. The various parcels of land were contiguous, and no fences or markers divided the investors' land. The harvested crop was pooled; purchasers shared profits in proportion to the land they owned. Most investors were nonresident professionals with no expertise in citrus growing and were guests of an adjacent hotel that assisted in marketing these investments. The SEC challenged the sales as the sale of unregistered securities.

Justice Murphy delivered the opinion of the Court.

Section 2(1) of the Act defines the term "security" to include the commonly known documents traded for speculation or investment. This definition also includes "securities" of a more variable character, designated by such descriptive terms as "certificate of interest or participation in any profit-sharing agreement," "investment contract" and "in general, any interest or instrument commonly known as a 'security.' " The legal issue in this case turns upon a determination of whether, under the circumstances, the land sales contract, the warranty deed and the service contract together constitute an "investment contract" within the meaning of §2(1). An investment contract came to mean a contract or scheme for "the placing of capital or laying out of money in a way intended to secure income or profit from its employment." An investment contract for purposes of the Securities Act means a contract, transaction or scheme whereby a person invests his money in a common enterprise and is led to expect

[1] *Reves v. Ernst & Young,* 494 U.S. 56 (1990).

profits solely from the efforts of the promoter or a third party, it being immaterial whether the shares in the enterprise are evidenced by formal certificates or by nominal interests in the physical assets employed in the enterprise. It embodies a flexible rather than a static principle, one that is capable of adaptation to meet the countless and variable schemes devised by those who seek the use of the money of others on the promise of profits.

The transactions in this case clearly involve investment contracts as so defined. The respondent companies are offering something more than fee simple interests in land, something different from a farm or orchard coupled with management services. They are offering an opportunity to contribute money and to share in the profits of a large citrus fruit enterprise managed and partly owned by respondents. They are offering this opportunity to persons who reside in distant localities and who lack the equipment and experience requisite to the cultivation, harvesting and marketing of the citrus products. Such persons have no desire to occupy the land or to develop it themselves; they are attracted solely by the prospects of a return on their investment. Indeed, individual development of the plots of land that are offered and sold would seldom be economically feasible due to their small size. Such tracts gain utility as citrus groves only when cultivated and developed as component parts of a larger area. A common enterprise managed by respondents or third parties with adequate personnel and equipment is therefore essential if the investors are to achieve their paramount aim of a return on their investments. Their respective shares in this enterprise are evidenced by land sales contracts and warranty deeds, which serve as a convenient method of determining the investors' allocable shares of the profits. The resulting transfer of rights in land is purely incidental.

Thus all the elements of a profit-seeking business venture are present here. The investors provide the capital and share in the earnings and profits, the promoters manage, control and operate the enterprise. It follows that the arrangements whereby the investors' interests are made manifest involve investment contracts, regardless of the legal terminology in which such contracts are clothed. The investment contracts in this instance take the form of land sales contracts, warranty deeds and service contracts which respondents offer to prospective investors. And respondents' failure to abide by the statutory and administrative rules in making such offerings, even though the failure results from a bona fide mistake as to the law, cannot be sanctioned under the Act.

Case Questions

1. What four elements are presumed to be common to all "investment contracts"?
2. Why designate a land sale as within the definition of a security?
3. What role was played in the Court's decision that investors need protection from the securities laws? Would these reasons change for sophisticated local citrus growers?

Later cases have refined the *Howey* concept when applied to novel and innovative instruments. For example, a security was offered when a seller issued warehouse receipts to each purchaser of aging scotch whiskey.[2] The receipts were to be repurchased later and the scotch blended by the seller for resale. The sale of all the common stock of a business to a buyer who intended to personally run the business was not considered exempt, rejecting the so-called *sale of business* doctrine.[3] However, there has been no security in other instances. For example, an employee's interest in a noncontributory and compulsory pension plan is not a security. The so-called stock, which permitted a tenant to lease a publicly subsidized co-op apartment, was not a security. These "stock certificates" lacked the traditional aspects of a security such as the right to vote, a share in profits, or the potential for capital gains appreciation.

[2] *SEC v. Haffenden-Rimar Intl., Inc.*, 496 F.2d 1192 (4th Cir. 1974).

[3] *Landreth Timber Co. v. Landreth*, 471 U.S. 681 (1985).

Questions have been raised about regulation of the burgeoning market for *derivative* investments that derive their value from some underlying financial asset or security. To the extent the derivative is an investment contract with a security as the underlying financial asset, the derivative is also a security. For example, options on securities (e.g., puts, calls) are derivatives regulated as securities. However, many derivatives are privately negotiated through commercial or investment bankers exempting them from registration. *Swaps* are a common derivative in which two parties exchange cash flows, either receivables or payables. The CFTC and SEC are beginning to regulate some derivatives and require the banks who arrange them to disclose more about the risk.

Exemptions from 1933 Act Registration

The IPO registration process is extremely costly; fees for registration, accounting, legal services, and printing often cause months of delay. However, Congress and the SEC believe the securities markets should be available to both small and large businesses. The 1933 Act includes some transactional *exemptions* that reduce the cost for issues of small size and limited scope or distribution. Issuers must be careful to establish their exemption because the sale of nonexempt unregistered securities is prohibited. There are also transaction exemptions, such as for "any *security exchanged* by the issuer with its existing security holders exclusively when no commission . . . is paid." This exemption affects three types of corporate reorganizations: (1) voluntary recapitalizations; (2) reorganizations made by the federal courts, bankruptcy courts, or authorized state agencies; and (3) securities issued in a merger, consolidation, or other transfer of assets approved by shareholders.

Intrastate Exemption The intrastate offering exemption allows a complete relaxation of all registration requirements. Based on the federalism principle, it defers to state securities laws. The SEC's Rule 147 exempts intrastate sales that meet strict requirements. First, all purchasers must be residents of the state. Second, the issuer must be domiciled and doing business within the state. Third, the issuer must satisfy three 80 percent rules: (1) at least 80 percent of the issuer's gross revenues are derived in the state, (2) 80 percent of the issuer's assets are located in the state, and (3) 80 percent of the proceeds will be spent in the state. A restrictive legend must be placed directly on intrastate security certificates warning that resale is restricted in intrastate sales. For example, consider a Pennsylvania corporation, PennCorp, which manufactures asphalt used almost exclusively to resurface Pennsylvania highways. PennCorp may avoid expensive registration if it issues stock only to Pennsylvania residents and the three 80 percent limitations are satisfied.

Small Issue Exemption Because small businesses are generally limited to raising capital through bank loans, partnerships, government loan guarantees, or venture capital, the small issue exemption opens the capital markets to small firms. Regulation A, the short form, permits the issuance of $5 million of securities without a complete registration statement. Only an *offering statement* must be filed that includes unaudited financial statements and a description of the issuer and the securities offered. An *offering circular* containing similar information must be delivered to all potential buyers solicited. Issuers may test the waters by soliciting investor interest before registration. This is an illegal practice for regular IPOs because it is considered preconditioning the market.

Private Placement Exemption The market for the private placement of securities with large institutional investors is growing rapidly. Historically, this was a market mostly for small or risky firms that issued securities such as junk bonds. Today, this market is evolving to include healthy blue-chip corporations. Private placements permit more efficient capital raising and the avoidance of most SEC regulations. Many leveraged buyout loans and asset-backed securities are privately placed and can be kept confidential, which is attractive to issuers suffering from adverse publicity. The most popular form is Regulation D, which combines aspects of small issues with private placements. Generally, sales may be made to an unlimited number of *accredited investors*. These are parties with financial sophistication and sufficient net worth, who have experience with and knowledge of investments so they are able to withstand the risk. They include certain institutional investors, employee benefit plans, corporations, the issuer's upper management, and certain well-to-do individuals.

Rule 504 permits unregistered offerings by nonpublic issuers for amounts up to $1 million and defers to registration under state blue-sky law. Rule 505 limits offerings to $5 million, and Rule 506 has no upper dollar limit. Sales under both Rule 504 and 505 may be made to no more than 35 nonaccredited and any number of accredited investors. There is no specific disclosure requirement when sales are made to accredited investors; however, the issuer must provide them with the information they request. Publicly traded issuers must provide their current annual reports when sales are made to nonaccredited investors.

Integration of Exempt Offerings The securities sold in several separate exempt transactions could really be a single plan of financing. The SEC may *integrate* or combine several separate exempt offerings if they are made too close in time and the proceeds are used for the same general purpose. Consider the example of a Michigan corporation that issued $4 million of stock under Rule 505. Soon thereafter, it made a separate intrastate offering of $2 million in promissory notes to Michigan residents, claiming the two offerings were separate. If the proceeds of both sales had been used to renovate a factory, the SEC would have integrated the two offerings. Because the $6 million total exceeded the dollar limit of Rule 505, the two separate sales became unlawful after integration.

Resale Restrictions

There are resale restrictions on securities sold under any one of the exemptions just discussed. Resale restrictions discourage an issuer from circumventing the registration requirements. For example, the issuer might first sell new securities as exempt but intend for the initial purchasers to immediately resell them to the public. Unsuspecting investors would be deprived of adequate disclosure. An initial buyer who intends to purchase only for a short time and resell immediately at a profit is considered an *underwriter,* triggering potential liability. Under Rule 144, initial purchasers may resell exempt securities only if they have *investment intent,* the desire to hold the securities for longer-term investment purposes. Initial purchasers of exempted securities must hold them for a minimum period of time, periodically reselling only small quantities. The SEC requires a boldface warning of resale restrictions on exempt securities. Proposed revisions may relax these rules.

Securities Act Liabilities

The 1933 Act remedies encourage compliance with the registration procedures. Investors may return nonexempt unregistered securities to the issuer and demand return of their investment. Investors may also bring private damage suits against those responsible for material omissions or misstatements. Persons subject to this liability include the issuer, its underwriters, control persons, and any individual who signs the registration statement, such as an officer, director, or auditor. Securities litigation reform efforts underway at this writing may make such suits more difficult, however. The *due diligence* defense may be used by defendants accused of making misstatements if they prove they reasonably believed the registration statement disclosures were true. Must the various responsible parties conduct a reasonable investigation to be protected by the due diligence defense? The following classic case illustrates the nature of fraud in initial public offers and the responsibilities of the various participants.

Escott v. BarChris Construction Corp.

283 F. Supp. 643 (S.D.N.Y. 1968)
United States District Court

Purchasers of the convertible debentures of BarChris Construction Corporation sued several persons, claiming that the BarChris registration statement was false and misleading. BarChris financed and built bowling alleys during the 1960s expansion of the bowling alley industry. The public offering of debentures was necessary to deal with a cash flow problem BarChris suffered after the industry became overbuilt. Buyers of bowling alleys began to default on their payments to BarChris. There were significant errors and omissions in the financial statements concerning BarChris's cash flow, sales, income, earnings per share, assets, and liabilities. The opinion addresses each party's role in the IPO and their due diligence defense.

McLean, District Judge

Russo. Russo was, to all intents and purposes, the chief executive officer of BarChris. He was a member of the executive committee. He was familiar with all aspects of the business. He was personally in charge of dealings with the factors. He acted on BarChris's behalf in making the financing agreements. In short, Russo knew all the relevant facts. He could not have believed that there were no untrue statements or material omissions in the prospectus. Russo has no due diligence defenses.

Vitolo and Pugliese. They were the founders of the business who stuck with it to the end. Vitolo was president and Pugliese was vice president. Pugliese in particular appears to have limited his activities to supervising the actual construction work. Vitolo and Pugliese are each men of limited education. It is not hard to believe that for them the prospectus was difficult reading, if indeed they read it at all. But whether it was or not is irrelevant. The liability of a director who signs a registration statement does not depend upon whether or not he read it or, if he did, whether or not he understood what he was reading. Vitolo and Pugliese were not as naive as they claim to be. They were members of BarChris's executive committee. At meetings of that committee BarChris's affairs were discussed at length. They must have known what was going on. Certainly they knew of the inadequacy of cash in 1961. They knew of their own large advances to the company which remained unpaid. They knew that they had agreed not to deposit their checks until the financing proceeds were received. They knew and intended that part of the proceeds were to be used to pay their own loans.

Kircher. Kircher was treasurer of BarChris and its chief financial officer. He is a certified public accountant and an intelligent man. He was thoroughly familiar with BarChris's financial affairs. He knew of the customers' delinquency problem. He knew how the financing proceeds were to be applied and he saw to it that they were so applied. He arranged the officers' loans and he knew all the facts concerning them.

Kircher's contention is that he had never before dealt with a registration statement, that he did not know what it should contain, and that he relied wholly on Grant, Ballard and Peat, Marwick to guide him. He claims that it was their fault, not his, if there was anything wrong with it. He says that all the facts were recorded in BarChris's books where these "experts" could have seen them if they had looked. He says that he truthfully answered all their questions. In effect, he says that if they did not know enough to ask the right questions and to give him the proper instructions, that is not his responsibility. Kircher has not proved his due diligence defenses.

Birnbaum. Birnbaum was a young lawyer, admitted to the bar in 1957, who, after brief periods of employment by two different law firms and an equally brief period of practicing in his own firm, was employed by BarChris as house counsel and assistant secretary in October 1960. Unfortunately for him, he became secretary and a director of BarChris on April 17, 1961, after the first version of the registration statement had been filed with the Securities and Exchange Commission. He signed the later amendments, thereby becoming responsible for the accuracy of the prospectus in its final form. He did not participate in the management of the company. As a lawyer, he should have known his obligations under the statute. He should have known that he was required to make a reasonable investigation of the truth of all the statements in the unexpertised portion of the document which he signed. Having failed to make such an investigation, he did not have reasonable ground to believe that all these statements were true. Birnbaum has not established his due diligence defenses except as to the audited 1960 figures.

Auslander. Auslander was an "outside" director, i.e., one who was not an officer of BarChris. He was chairman of the board of Valley Stream National Bank in Valley Stream, Long Island. In February and early March 1961, before accepting Vitolo's invitation [to accept a place on the board], Auslander made some investigation of BarChris. He obtained Dun & Bradstreet reports which contained sales and earnings figures for periods earlier than December 31, 1960. He caused inquiry to be made of certain of BarChris's banks and was advised that they regarded BarChris favorably.

Auslander was elected a director on April 17, 1961. The registration statement in its original form had already been filed, of course without his signature. On May 10, 1961, he signed a signature page for the first amendment to the registration statement which was filed on May 11, 1961. This was a separate sheet without any document attached. Auslander did not know that it was a signature page for a registration statement. He vaguely understood that it was something "for the SEC."

In considering Auslander's due diligence defenses, a distinction is to be drawn between the expertised and nonexpertised portions of the prospectus. As to the former, Auslander knew that Peat, Marwick had audited the 1960 figures. He believed them to be correct because he had confidence in Peat, Marwick. He had no reasonable ground to believe otherwise.

As to the nonexpertised portions, however, Auslander is in a different position. He seems to have been under the impression that Peat, Marwick was responsible for all the figures. This impression was not correct, as he would have realized if he had read the prospectus carefully. Auslander made no investigation of the accuracy of the prospectus. He relied on the assurance of Vitolo and Russo, and upon the information he had received in answer to his inquiries back in February and early March.

Section 11 imposes liability in the first instance upon a director, no matter how new he is. He is presumed to know his responsibility when he becomes a director. He can escape liability only by using that reasonable care to investigate the facts which a prudent man would employ in the management of his own property. In my opinion, a prudent man would not act in an important matter without any knowledge of the relevant facts, in sole reliance upon representations of persons who are comparative strangers and upon general information which does not purport to cover the particular case. Auslander has not established his due diligence defense with respect to the misstatements and omissions in those portions of the prospectus other than the audited 1960 figures.

The Underwriters and Coleman. The underwriters other than Drexel made no investigation of the accuracy of the prospectus. One of them, Peter Morgan, had underwritten the 1959 stock issue and had been a director of BarChris. He thus had some general familiarity with its affairs, but he knew no more than the other underwriters about the debenture prospectus. They all relied upon Drexel as the "lead" underwriter.

The facts as to the extent of the investigation that Coleman made may be briefly summarized. He was first introduced to BarChris on September 15, 1960.

Thereafter, he familiarized himself with general conditions in the industry, primarily by reading reports and the prospectuses of the two leading bowling alley builders, American Machine & Foundry Company and Brunswick. These indicated that the industry was still growing. He also acquired general information on BarChris by reading the 1959 stock prospectus, annual reports for prior years, and an unaudited statement for the first half of 1960. He obtained a Dun & Bradstreet report on BarChris on March 16, 1961. He read BarChris's annual report for 1960 which was available in March. After Coleman was elected a director on April 17, 1961, he made no further independent investigation of the accuracy of the prospectus. In any event, it is clear that no effectual attempt at verification was made. The question is whether due diligence required that it be made. Stated another way, is it sufficient to ask questions, to obtain answers which, if true, would be thought satisfactory, and to let it go at that, without seeking to ascertain from the records whether the answers in fact are true and complete?

The purpose of Section 11 is to protect investors. To that end the underwriters are made responsible for the truth of the prospectus. If they may escape that responsibility by taking at face value representations made to them by the company's management, then the inclusion of underwriters among those liable under Section 11 affords the investors no additional protection. In order to make the underwriters' participation in this enterprise of any value to the investors, the underwriters must make some reasonable attempt to verify the data submitted to them. They may not rely solely on the company's officers or on the company's counsel. A prudent man in the management of his own property would not rely on them. It is impossible to lay down a rigid rule suitable for every case defining the extent to which such verification must go. It is a question of degree, a matter of judgment in each case. In the present case, the underwriters' counsel made almost no attempt to verify management's representations. I hold that was insufficient.

Case Questions

1. What is the issue in a securities fraud defendant's defense of "due diligence"? Compare due diligence for insiders (e.g., officers, directors) with due diligence for outsiders (e.g., underwriters, auditors)?
2. What reasons justify holding signatories and preparers of the registration statement liable for omissions or misstatements? How does this raise the cost of IPOs?

Persons found guilty of intentional fraud in a securities offering are liable for both civil damages and criminal penalties. Under Section 12 of the 1933 Act, it is illegal to offer or sell an unregistered security, to fail to deliver a prospectus, or to use an illegal prospectus in making illegal offers or sales during the prefiling or waiting periods. These provisions are quite successful because most issuers are careful to follow the registration and prospectus delivery requirements. The 1933 Act liabilities apply only to IPOs.

Insider Trading

The 1934 Act requires firms that are publicly traded on national securities exchanges or in the OTC market to disclose material information. Fraud is outlawed in connection with purchases or sales of securities. In the 1980s, the SEC and the Justice Department focused enforcement attention on insider trading as an illegal form of fraud. *Insider trading* is the practice whereby a person's access to confidential and nonpublic information gives them an unfair advantage over others in trading a firm's securities. Their silence while trading with unsuspecting investors based on confidential information is a form of fraud by omission.

COMMENTARY

THE CONTROVERSY OVER INSIDER TRADING

Insider trading enforcement is quite controversial. Proponents of restricting insider trading argue it is unfair because insiders have an informational advantage that outsiders cannot overcome no matter how much they research the firm. As insider trading proliferates, a perception becomes widespread that capital markets are unfair and that the public will lose confidence. They also point to the loss of confidence after the Great Depression as evidence of this detrimental effect.

On the other side of this controversy are those who oppose restricting insider trading. They claim it is a victimless crime because the firm's shareholders can simply prohibit the practice. Some even argue insider trading is part of a corporate manager's implied compensation. Proponents argue that insider trading is beneficial by contributing to a more efficient market because insider trading sends a "signal" to the market about the direction the firm's stock price should move. Insiders buy on good news and sell on bad news, so the market may infer that some traders have access to confidential nonpublic information by observing the insider's trading activity. This arguably makes the market a more accurate reflection of underlying value.

The opponents of restricting insider trading apparently ignore the reality of shareholder democracy. Shareholders are probably unable to detect insider trading and any corporate rule prohibiting it would be rather ineffective. The victim of insider trading would probably insist on trading at a price adjusted for the insider's nonpublic information after the information became known publicly. If insider trading were considered an implied compensation or perk, this would encourage employees to manipulate the release of corporate information to enhance their profit opportunities such as by increasing the firm's price volatility. Some insiders could profit from the firm's misfortunes. Such market manipulation is inconsistent with an employee's fiduciary duty. Opponents of insider trading argue that management will be forced to release information more quickly if they cannot trade on inside information. Despite this controversy, many market professionals, Congress, the courts, the SEC, and the presidential administration oppose insider trading, making it illegal.

Short Swing Profits: Section 16(b)

Congress first restricted some forms of insider trading with §16(b) of the 1934 Act. Short swing profits made by specified insiders are illegal and must be paid to the corporation. These occur when the insider both purchases and sells the issuer's equity securities (stock) within any six-month period. *Insiders* are defined as officers, directors, and 10 percent shareholders. Their unlawful trading profits must be paid to the issuer.

Insiders: Officers, Directors, and 10 Percent Shareholders Section 16(a) requires that insiders report trades in their company's equity securities to the SEC to facilitate enforcement and to make them available to the public. Some commentators have speculated that §16(a) reports are the most commonly violated provisions of the securities laws. The SEC addressed this problem by passing new reporting rules, which now require companies to disclose when their officers' or directors' reports are delinquent. Violations can be remedied by internal SEC administrative action.

Brokerages and banks often give "officer-like" titles to middle-level managers. However, if these employees do not perform significant corporate executive decision-making functions, they are not statutory insiders. The SEC now interprets the "officer" title to include the president, any vice president in charge of a principal business function, other officers of the issuer's parent or subsidiaries who perform policy-making functions for the issuer, the principal financial officer, and the principal accounting officer.

There are "interlocking directors" who hold seats on the boards of two or more corporations. This may cause either corporation to also be considered an insider of the other corporation, thereby restricting it from short-swing trading in the other corporation's equity securities. Interlocking directors are considered "deputies" of both corporations because they may be a convenient conduit to transfer inside information.

There are similar definitional problems with 10 percent shareholders. For example, a shareholder could buy stock in the name of a spouse, minor child, or other relative living in the shareholder's household. Although it would appear the shareholder owned less than 10 percent, they would actually *control* more stock. To avoid this, the SEC has developed the concept of *beneficial ownership*. All the shares in which a related group has a pecuniary interest are presumed to be owned by one person. This presumption is rebuttable if the shareholder can prove no actual control was exercised over the relative's shares.

Short-Swing Profit Liability A sliding six-month scale is applied to capture *any* purchase and sale transactions within *any* six-month period. A purchase or sale occurs when there is an actual transfer or even a contract to purchase or sell an equity security. Options and other derivative securities (e.g., warrants, convertible securities, stock appreciation rights) are considered purchased when they are acquired, so exercise or conversion is exempt; they are considered sold when the converted security is sold.

Short-Swing Damages The corporation or any shareholder acting in its behalf may sue to recover an insider's trading profit. Damages are computed as the difference between the purchase and sale prices. These damages belong to the corporation, not to any shareholder personally. In computing short-swing profits, the courts do not apply the FIFO (first in, first out) method of matching particular stock certificates. That is, the prices of shares purchased first are not always compared with the prices of shares sold first to determine damages. Instead, the lowest purchase price is matched to the highest sale price within any six-month period, maximizing the measure of illegal trading profit. Assume an insider sells 100 shares at $10 in January and purchases 100 shares in March at $5. Thereafter, the insider purchases another 100 shares in April at $4. The profit realized is $600 ($10 – $4 = $6 per share) even though the sale occurred first. The comparison between the $5 purchase and the $10 sale is ignored because the lower purchase price of $4 occurred within six months of the $10 sale, as illustrated in Figure 15–3.

The computation of profit liability is intentionally maximized to hold insiders to a high standard of conduct by imposing a potent deterrent effect. The law prohibits sales before purchase because insiders could profit from bad news by "selling short" the issuer's securities. Although §16 is Congress' original and objective prohibition of insider trading, much of the emphasis has shifted to the subjective approach under SEC Rule 10b-5.

FIGURE 15-3 Short-Swing Profit Liability

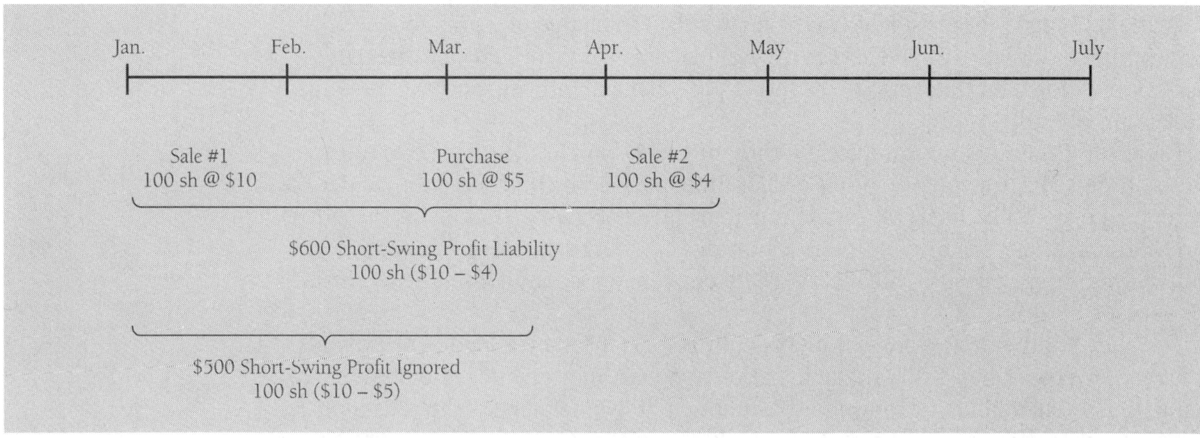

Insider Trading under the Common Law and Rule 10b-5

Even before Rule 10b-5 was used extensively, the common law developed a restriction against insider trading that combined the tort of deceit with the fiduciary duty concept. Insider trading was prohibited in certain "special circumstances" in the landmark 1909 case of *Strong v. Repide*.[4] A controlling stockholder failed to disclose pending merger negotiations when he purchased stock from minority shareholders.

Rule 10b-5
SEC rule prohibiting fraudulent omissions and disclosures, insider trading, and market manipulation.

The SEC originally passed **Rule 10b-5** in response to rumors that "the president of some company in Boston . . . is going around buying up the stock of his company from his own shareholders at $4 a share . . . telling them that the company has been doing very badly, whereas in fact the earnings are going to be quadrupled and will be $2 a share."[5] Rule 10b-5 has become the most pervasive antifraud provision in the securities laws.

SEC Rule 10b-5

It shall be unlawful for any person, directly or indirectly, by the use of any means or instrumentality of interstate commerce, or of the mails, or of any facility of a national securities exchange,

1. to employ any device, scheme, or artifice to defraud,
2. to make any untrue statement of a material fact or to omit to state a material fact necessary in order to make the statements made, in the light of the circumstances under which they were made, not misleading, or
3. to engage in act, practice or course of business which operates or would operate as a fraud or deceit upon any person, in connection with the purchase or sale of any security.

[4] *Strong v. Repide,* 213 U.S. 419 (1909).

[5] Statement of Milton Freeman in American Bar Association, Section of Corporation, Banking and Business Law. Conference on Codification of the Federal Securities Laws, 22 Bus. Law. 793, 921–23 (1967).

Rule 10b-5 requires corporate officers, directors, and any other insider to either *disclose* their inside information before trading or to *abstain* from trading altogether. This is the so-called *disclose or abstain* rule. This seemingly simple choice actually places the insider in a dilemma. The fiduciary duty of loyalty to the corporation usually prohibits a corporate insider from revealing secret information before trading if disclosure would divulge important confidential corporate information.

This problem arose in a leading insider trading case, *SEC v. Texas Gulf Sulphur Company*.[6] The Texas Gulf Sulphur Company (TGS) made a substantial mineral discovery in Canada. In order to acquire the mineral rights on land surrounding the discovery site at favorable prices, TGS publicly denied rumors of the discovery. At the same time, some TGS employees who knew about the discovery purchased TGS stock. If these employees had disclosed the mineral discovery before purchasing TGS stock, they would have violated their fiduciary duty of confidentiality. These employees were guilty of illegal insider trading and TGS was guilty of securities fraud in making materially misleading disclosures. While TGS employees had no duty to inform surrounding landowners of the discovery before acquiring their mineral rights, a stronger duty applies to corporate insiders when trading in the securities markets.

Ethical Dilemmas in Insider Trading

Ethical Dilemma

The disclose or abstain duty poses a false dilemma for managers in using the corporation's confidential inside information. If it is material financial information, management must disclose it to shareholders in periodic quarterly or annual reports. Before such reports are distributed, insiders must refrain from personal trading on it unless they first disclose the information. However, competitors can gain an advantage if such premature release reveals a corporate trade secret or strategic plan. Releasing sensitive confidential information is a breach of the manager's fiduciary duty. The profit incentive is strong, yet a manager cannot trade on the information without committing acts that are both illegal and an unethical breach of duty.

Under Rule 10b-5, insider trading is illegal in any security, debt or equity, whether the issuer is publicly traded or closely held. Defrauded sellers or purchasers may sue for civil damages, the SEC may bring enforcement actions and seek civil fines, and the Justice Department may prosecute insider traders by seeking fines and prison terms.

Elements of Rule 10b-5 Insider Trading Case

1. Identify the insider.
2. Hold liable persons making or receiving stock tips (tippers or tippees).
3. Determine the role of fiduciary duties in insider trading actions.
4. Determine the materiality of the misstatements or omissions.
5. Show reliance by the victims on the misrepresentations.
6. Show knowledge of the falsity of the statements by the misrepresentor.
7. Identify persons entitled to sue.
8. Measure the damages or penalty for insider trading.

---

[6] *S.E.C. v. Texas Gulf Sulphur Company*, 401 F.2d 833 (2d Cir. 1968).

insiders
Employees of an issuer or its consultants with access to confidential information.

Who is an "Insider"? Under Rule 10b-5, **insiders** include employees at lower levels in addition to officers and directors. Rule 10b-5 prohibits insider trading by *any* employee with access to confidential information. It also applies to certain tippees who receive inside information from insiders. The SEC established criteria for the identification of an insider in the leading case of *Cady, Roberts & Co.*[7] The trading restriction applies where (1) a relationship gives access to information, (2) information is intended only for corporate purposes, and (3) the information is used unfairly for the personal benefit of the insider.

Since the 1960s, a possession theory has circulated, first prohibiting *any* trading by persons with mere possession of nonpublic information. Then the Supreme Court appeared to reverse this *parity of information* theory in the famous *Chiarella*[8] case. A financial printer invested in takeover targets, which he identified by misappropriating the information from his employer. Without any evidence of wrongfulness, the mere possession of nonpublic information is not sufficient to prohibit trading. The *Chiarella* rule preserves the incentive for securities analysts to do research and investment analysis. Today, most employees possessing nonpublic information have a duty to maintain confidentiality. If they trade, the mere possession of inside information taints their trading, shifting to them the burden of proving they did not actually *use* the information in deciding to trade.[9]

Tippee Liability There is a trend toward expanding insider trading liability to noninsiders. Often outside tippees receive inside information from a tip originating with an insider. What circumstances taint inside information so that outsider tippees may not trade on the information? The following case establishes the criteria for tippee liability.

SEC v. Dirks

463 U.S. 646 (1983)
United States Supreme Court

Dirks was a securities analyst for a New York broker-dealer firm. He received information from Secrist, a former officer of Equity Funding of America, that the assets of Equity Funding were vastly overstated as the result of fraudulent corporate practices. Secrist urged Dirks to investigate further, so Dirks visited the corporate offices and interviewed several officers who denied any wrongdoing. However, some employees confirmed the fraud. Before Dirks notified the SEC, he openly discussed his findings with clients and fellow brokers at his firm, who in turn notified clients to liquidate nearly $16 million in Equity Funding holdings. During this period, the price of Equity Funding stock plummeted from $26 to $15. The New York Stock Exchange halted trading in Equity Funding, the SEC filed a complaint, and it eventually went into receivership. Dirks was censured for transmitting the inside information but was not disciplined more severely by the SEC because of his assistance in uncovering the fraud.

---

[7] *In re Cady, Roberts & Co.*, 40 SEC 907 (1961).
[8] *Chiarella v. United States,* 445 U.S. 222 (1980).
[9] *United States v. Teicher,* 987 F.2d 112 (2d Cir.1993).

Justice Powell delivered the opinion of the Court.

In the seminal case of *In re Cady, Roberts & Co.,* the SEC recognized that the common law in some jurisdictions imposes on "corporate 'insiders,' particularly officers, directors, or controlling stockholders" an "affirmative duty of disclosure . . . when dealing in securities." Unlike insiders who have independent fiduciary duties to both the corporation and its shareholders, the typical tippee has no such relationships.* In view of this absence, it has been unclear how a tippee acquires the *Cady, Roberts* duty to refrain from trading on inside information.

The SEC's position, as stated in its opinion in this case, is that a tippee "inherits" the *Cady, Roberts* obligation to shareholders whenever he receives inside information from an insider. This view differs little from the view that we rejected as inconsistent with congressional intent in *Chiarella.*

Imposing a duty to disclose or abstain solely because a person knowingly receives material nonpublic information from an insider and trades on it could have an inhibiting influence on the role of market analysts, which the SEC itself recognizes is necessary to the preservation of a healthy market. It is commonplace for analysts to "ferret out and analyze information," and this often is done by meeting with and questioning corporate officers and others who are insiders. And information that the analysts obtain normally may be the basis for judgments as to the market worth of a corporation's securities. The analyst's judgment in this respect is made available in market letters or otherwise to clients of the firm. It is the nature of this type of information, and indeed of the markets themselves, that such information cannot be made simultaneously available to all of the corporation's stockholders or the public generally.

The need for a ban on some tippee trading is clear. Not only are insiders forbidden by their fiduciary relationship from personally using undisclosed corporate information to their advantage, but they also may not give such information to an outsider for the same improper purpose of exploiting the information for their personal gain.

Thus, some tippees must assume an insider's duty to the shareholders not because they receive inside information, but rather because it has been made available to them *improperly.* And for Rule 10b-5 purposes, the insider's disclosure is improper only where it would violate his *Cady, Roberts* duty. Thus, a tippee assumes a fiduciary duty to the shareholders of a corporation not to trade on material nonpublic information only when the insider has breached his fiduciary duty to the shareholders by disclosing the information to the tippee and the tippee knows or should know that there has been a breach. As Commissioner Smith perceptively observed in *In re Investors Management Co.:* "[T]ippee responsibility must be related back to insider responsibility by a necessary finding that the tippee knew the information was given to him in breach of a duty by a person having a special relationship to the issuer not to disclose this information. . . ."

In determining whether a tippee is under an obligation to disclose or abstain, it thus is necessary to determine whether the insider's "tip" constituted a breach of the insider's fiduciary duty. . . . In some situations, the insider will act consistently with his fiduciary duty to shareholders, and yet release of the information may affect the market. For example, it may not be clear—either to the corporate insider or to the recipient analyst—whether the information will be viewed as material nonpublic information. Corporate officials may mistakenly think the information already has been disclosed or that it is not material enough to affect the market. Whether disclosure is a breach of duty therefore depends in large part on the purpose of the disclosure. Thus, the test is whether the insider personally will benefit, directly or indirectly, from his disclosure. Absent some personal gain, there has been no breach of duty to stockholders. And absent a breach by the insider, there is no derivative breach. As Commissioner Smith stated in *Investors Management Co.:* "It is important in this type of case to focus on policing insiders and what they do . . . rather than on policing information *per se* and its possession. . . ."

* [Footnote #14] Under certain circumstances, such as where corporate information is revealed legitimately to an underwriter, accountant, lawyer, or consultant working for the corporation, these outsiders may become fiduciaries of the shareholders. The basis for recognizing this fiduciary duty is not simply that such persons acquired nonpublic corporate information, but rather that they have entered into a special confidential relationship in the conduct of the business of the enterprise and are given access to information solely for corporate purposes. When such a person breaches his fiduciary relationship, he may be treated more properly as a tipper than a tippee.

For such a duty to be imposed, however, the corporation must expect the outsider to keep the disclosed nonpublic information confidential, and the relationship at least must imply such a duty.

As the facts of this case clearly indicate, the tippers were motivated by a desire to expose the fraud. In the absence of a breach of duty to shareholders by the insiders, there was no derivative breach by Dirks. Dirks therefore could not have been "a participant after the fact in [an] insider's breach of a fiduciary duty." We conclude that Dirks, in the circumstances of this case, had no duty to abstain from use of the inside information that he obtained.

The judgment of the Court of Appeals therefore is *Reversed.*

Case Questions

1. What are the factors that dictate when a "tippee" inherits an insider's duty to "disclose or abstain" from trading?
2. What would happen to analysts' incentive to investigate if *Dirks* had been decided differently?
3. What alternative scenarios might be sufficient to constitute an "improper" motive for transferring inside information to an outsider?

The now famous *Dirks* footnote #14 established a new category of *temporary insiders,* including underwriters, accountants, lawyers, and other outside consultants. They owe a fiduciary duty to their employer and ultimately to the issuer. A firm may expect its consultants to keep confidential any information discovered in the consulting engagement.

A tippee inherits the insider's duty to disclose or abstain if the tippee knows or has reason to know of the insider's fiduciary breach in tipping the information. Dirks was not guilty as a tippee because Secrist, the insider, breached no fiduciary duty in revealing the Equity Funding fraud. A tippee is restricted from trading only if the insider conveyed the inside information *improperly,* such as when the insider expects a personal benefit from the tippee. For example, it is improper if the tip is a gift or there is an unspoken expectation that the tippee will return the favor in the future with another tip.

misappropriation theory Theory condemning insider trading that uses information stolen by employees or fiduciaries.

The Misappropriation Theory Under the **misappropriation theory,** it is irrelevant whether nonpublic information originates from inside or from outside the issuer whose shares are traded. It is a common misconception that insider information can originate only from inside the issuer. However, secret information about tender offers is generally known only by outside takeover bidders, their consultants, and employees. Similar damage to the markets may occur with tender offer insider trading.

Any person, whether an insider or an outsider, who breaches their fiduciary duty by misappropriating nonpublic, confidential information may be liable for insider trading. Under the misappropriation theory, a financial printing firm employee who trades on information misappropriated from the employer is guilty of insider trading. Employees of law firms or investment banks that represent takeover participants are restricted from trading on nonpublic information learned from their employer. The misappropriation theory was established in *United States v. Newman.*[10] Employees at several investment banking firms traded on confidential takeover information they secretly exchanged before the information became public. The court in that case stated the following:

> In a tender offer situation, the effect of increased activity in purchases of the target company's shares is to drive up the price of the target company's shares; but this effect is damaging to the offering company because the tender offer will appear commensurately less attractive and the activity may cause it to abort. The deceitful misappropriation of confidential information by a

[10] *United States v. Newman,* 664 F.2d 12 (2d Cir. 1981).

fiduciary, whether described as theft, conversion, or breach of trust, has consistently been held to be unlawful.

The Supreme Court has unanimously approved insider trading prosecution based on the misappropriation theory if the case is predicated on the federal mail and wire fraud statutes. However, the Supreme Court was evenly split, four to four, in the famous *Wall Street Journal* "Heard on the Street" case, on whether misappropriation suits can be based on Rule 10b-5. Considerable attention in the late 1980s focused on the insider trading and securities fraud enforcement actions brought by the SEC and Justice Department against Dennis Levine, Ivan Boesky, Michael Milken, and the firm Drexel Burnham Lambert. In these cases, investment bankers and other Wall Street consultants established networks to regularly exchange inside information about companies involved in takeovers or restructuring. Although a few related convictions were reversed on technical grounds, these prosecutions may have slowed the pace of insider trading. Figure 15–4 compares the differences between the insider trading prohibitions under Rule 10b-5 and §16(b).

FIGURE 15-4 Insider Trading Comparison: Section 16(b) versus Rule 10b-5

	Section 16(b)	Rule 10b-5
Potential plaintiffs	Issuer or shareholder suing derivatively	SEC, Justice Department, and shareholders who trade contemporaneously with insider
Potential defendants	Statutory insiders: officers, directors, and 10 percent shareholders and deputies, nominees, or others performing officer-like or director-like duties	Any employee of the issuer, temporary insider, or misappropriator and certain tippees
Proof of access to and use of inside information	No proof required: access and use presumed for statutory insiders	Proof required: misappropriation or tippee status
Securities covered	Any registered equity security	Any security, registered or not
Disclosure required	Statutory insiders must report all changes in shareholdings within 15 days after any month in which a purchase or sale transaction occurs	Insider must publicly disclose inside information or abstain from trading
Tippee liability	No tippee liability	Tippee liable for insider trading if: Tippee knows or has reason to know that the tipper (insider) breached a fiduciary duty in tipping, and Tippee transferred tip for an improper purpose (i.e., personal benefit)
Damages recoverable	Match highest sale and purchase or purchase and sale within any six-month period	Disgorge illegal insider trading profit; SEC actions: ITSA treble penalty paid to U.S. Treasury; damages held in escrow for victims claimants
Criminal penalties	No criminal penalties; SEC may refer insider trading evidence to Justice Department	Justice Department may prosecute under rule 10b-5 or mail and wire fraud statutes; penalties of up to 10 years' imprisonment and $1million fine for individuals, $2,500,000 fine for firms

Additional Insider Trading Laws

Between 1984 and 1990, Congress enacted three laws affecting insider trading prosecutions. The Insider Trading Sanctions Act of 1984 (ITSA) imposes a civil penalty of up to three times the insider's trading profit. The SEC has discretion to sue for the full treble penalty or for a lesser amount, which is payable into the federal treasury. ITSA actions are tried only by a judge, not a jury. The ITSA does not affect existing remedies under §16(b), Rule 10b-5 or Rule 14e-3. ITSA damages are the "profit gained or loss avoided" through illegal insider trading, computed as the difference between the insider's purchase price and the trading price right after the inside information is disclosed publicly.

The ITSA penalties are cumulative with other insider trading liabilities. For example, Ivan Boesky paid a double penalty under the ITSA and paid damages to investors who sold stock to him at lower prices than prevailed after public disclosure of the tender offers. Investors who traded contemporaneously with the insider are entitled to such damages. However, the statute of limitations applicable to civil insider trading cases for private damages requires these cases be brought within one year after the wrongful act is discovered. The SEC usually sets aside a fund for payment of disgorged profits to private insider trading victims. Boesky was also found guilty of criminal insider trading.

Congress further toughened the insider trading penalties and enforcement powers in the Insider Trading and Securities Fraud Enforcement Act of 1988 (ITSFEA). This law (1) increases criminal penalties, (2) provides for payment of a bounty to informants, (3) requires brokers and dealers to supervise their employees to prevent tipping or insider trading, (4) establishes a statutory right for injured investors to sue for damages, and (5) gives the SEC authority to assist foreign investigations of international securities fraud.

The Enforcement Remedies and Penny Stock Reform Act of 1990 further expands the SEC's civil enforcement powers applicable to insider trading and other securities law violations. The SEC may seek money penalties and disgorgement in SEC administrative proceedings without prosecuting the defendants in federal court. Officers and directors may be debarred from practice before the SEC, effectively preventing their employment in that capacity for publicly traded companies. The SEC may issue cease and desist orders against repeat offenders. The Act significantly restructured the penny stock industry by nearly eliminating it. The Act gives the SEC powers over program trading and emergency enforcement powers over securities firms. Reform legislation is proposed to limit securities fraud suits because it is alleged that too many baseless suits impose social cost.

INTERNATIONAL PERSPECTIVE AND COMMENTARY

INSIDER TRADING ABROAD

The insider trading laws in the United States are the most stringent in the world. Most nations have traditionally permitted insider trading as an innocent executive perk, or they simply ignore it or consider it no more than unethical. Insider trading enforcement in other nations is lax, and few nations have cooperated fully with the SEC's enforcement of insider trading. For example, in a 1983 case involving Santa Fe International Corp., the Swiss Supreme Court refused to adopt the misappropriation theory. As in the U.S. Supreme Court's *Chiarella* opinion, the Swiss find no direct fiduciary relationship between two strangers trading anonymously through brokers on the impersonal stock exchange.[11]

[11]*The Santa Fe Case*, 22 Intl. Leg. Mat. 785 (1983).

Some commentators have argued that the U.S. insider trading laws are excessively stringent, and that U.S. markets will therefore lose some trading volume to other nations' securities markets. However, there were damaging insider trading and securities fraud scandals in the early 1990s in the United Kingdom, Ireland, France, Germany, and Japan. This has aroused criticism that investors are not treated fairly in these markets because insider trading is not well regulated. Therefore, most nations are reevaluating their insider trading rules, many are prohibiting it, and some are even enforcing their new laws. The SEC has negotiated bilateral accords with several nations to cooperate in enforcement.

Proxy Solicitations and Tender Offers

There is a market for corporate control in which individual financiers, takeover specialists, other corporations, and dissident shareholders struggle to control corporations. The SEC proxy and tender offer rules regulate how management and outsiders advocate shareholder action in proxy contests and how takeovers are effected through tender offers.

Proxy Solicitations

The proxy process is regulated by both state corporation statutes and the federal security laws. State law primarily regulates closely held corporations. The 1934 Act regulates proxy solicitations of shareholders in publicly traded corporations. The term *proxy* has several different meanings. Generally, it means the intangible agency or power of attorney a shareholder gives to another to vote. Corporate law refers to both the written ballot and the person who actually votes. The 1934 Act confines the term *proxy* to "any proxy, consent, or authorization to vote shares."

Proxy solicitations involve electioneering to convince shareholders to vote for particular proposals or director candidates, and that may affect corporate control. The federal regulatory scheme attempts to maintain fairness by promoting full disclosure, prohibiting fraud, and facilitating shareholder proposals. A proxy solicitation is usually made by either management or dissident shareholders or both. Proxy solicitations include a wide variety of communications, and they trigger special duties under the 1934 Act. For example, proxy solicitations include any request to give or revoke a proxy; the furnishing of the proxy form itself; advertising in newspapers, print, or other media; and direct mail solicitations. They all must comply with the SEC's proxy rules.

proxy solicitation Electioneering by management or insurgent shareholders to win proxy votes in a corporate election.

Proxy Statements Any person soliciting proxies must file a proxy statement containing certain information to inform shareholders of the issues and of the solicitor's motives.

Information Required in a Proxy Statement

1. Identity of the solicitor.
2. Legal terms of the proxy itself.
3. Information concerning the election of directors.
4. Specific details about extraordinary corporate transactions (merger, recapitalizations).
5. The issuer's financial statements.

Management annually solicits proxies in directors' elections, so the SEC requires the issuer to distribute its latest annual report. Upper management's compensation must be juxtaposed against shareholder return for recent years to highlight their pay/performance experience. Management has potential proxy fraud liability for inaccuracies or misstatements in the annual report. If management decides not to solicit proxies for director elections, it must nevertheless distribute an *information statement* containing the same information.

The proxy itself must be formatted much like a standard ballot, with a blank date line and boxes for each proposition permitting the shareholders' vote of approval, disapproval, or abstention (see Figure 15–5). A proxy solicited by the board of directors or one permitting the directors to vote incomplete proxies must conspicuously state these facts directly on the proxy.

Shares are often held in *street name,* that is, in the name of a broker-dealer or nominee. These shares actually belong to the investor but are held in street name to facilitate quick settlement of trades, or the shares are held as collateral for the margin loans the investor borrows to purchase the securities. The issuer and broker-dealer must forward all proxy solicitation materials to the beneficial or actual owner.

Proxy Contests Proxy contests are used increasingly in battles for control of corporations. Shareholders are best served by receiving accurate information from all proxy solicitors. Preliminary drafts of proxy solicitation materials must be filed with the SEC.

Corporate management has the most effective access to voting shareholders because management's proxy solicitation expenses are paid by the corporate treasury, and management alone possesses accurate lists of eligible shareholder voters. Dissident shareholders who oppose management have a more difficult time soliciting proxies. SEC regulations attempt to facilitate shareholder proxy solicitations in two ways. First, dissidents can pay for their own solicitation. Management can either provide a shareholder list to the dissident solicitor, or the corporation will mail the dissidents' solicitation to shareholders at the dissidents' expense. The direct-mailing alternative makes it difficult for dissidents to contact shareholders individually with follow-up electioneering.

Mandatory Shareholder Proxy Proposals The second shareholder solicitation method requires the corporation to pay expenses. Management must include certain shareholder proposals in management's own proxy mailing. This procedure is limited to use by small shareholders to give them at least a minimal voice in corporate elections.

Some shareholders abused this process in the 1960s by airing their personal political and social views arguably unconnected to the issuer's operations. For example, one shareholder opposed the Vietnam War and proposed a charter amendment prohibiting corporate production of napalm. The proxy process is not designed for such "political grandstanding," so the SEC tightened these requirements. Now, the dissident shareholder must have a serious financial interest in the corporation. This exists when the shareholder has held the shares for at least one year and owns at least 1 percent or $1,000 in market value of the voting securities. The dissident can make only one proposal per year. If management desires, it can limit the dissident's proposal to no more than 500 words. Sometimes management may omit a particular shareholder proposal if management determines the proposal violates the guidelines of SEC Rule 14a-8(c) listed below. While either the SEC or the shareholder may challenge an

FIGURE 15-5 Sample Proxy

Proxy

P
R
O
X
Y

This Proxy Is Solicited on Behalf of the Board of Directors

The undersigned hereby appoints and and each of them, with full power of substitution, the proxies of the undersigned to vote all shares of Common Stock of which the undersigned is entitled to vote at the Annual Meeting of Stockholders of the corporation to be held at the principal corporate office, , on April , 19 , at 10:00 A.M. and at any adjournments or postponements thereof, with the same force and effect as the undersigned might or could do if personally present thereat.

1. ELECTION OF DIRECTORS ☐ FOR all nominees listed below *(except as marked to the contrary below)* ☐ WITHHOLD AUTHORITY to vote for all nominees listed below

(The Board of Directors recommends a vote FOR)

This proxy will be voted in the Election of Directors in the manner described in the Proxy Statement for the Annual Meeting of Stockholders

(INSTRUCTION: To withhold authority to vote for one or more individual members, write such name or names in the space provided below.)

---

2. PROPOSAL TO AMEND THE CERTIFICATE OF INCORPORATION of the Company to increase the authorized number of shares of Preferred Stock, \$ 01 par value, from 1,000,000 to 10,000,000. (The Board of Directors recommends a vote FOR.)

   ☐ FOR ☐ AGAINST ☐ ABSTAIN

3. PROPOSAL TO RATIFY THE SELECTION OF , as independent public accountants for the corporation for the fiscal year ending December , 19 (The Board of Directors recommends a vote FOR)

   ☐ FOR ☐ AGAINST ☐ ABSTAIN

4. In their discretion, the Proxies are authorized to vote upon much other business as may properly come before the meeting.

(Continued on other side)

- -

(Continued from other side)

This proxy when properly executed will be voted in the manner directed herein by the undersigned stockholder. If no direction is made, this proxy will be voted FOR Proposals 1, 2, and 3.

Please sign exactly as name appears below. When shares are held by joint tenants, both should sign. When signing as attorney, executor, administrator, trustee or guardian please give full title as such. If a corporation, please sign in full corporate name by president or other authorized person. If a partnership, please sign in full partnership name by authorized person.

DATED____________________________19

____

Signature

____

Signature if held jointly

PLEASE MARK, SIGN, DATE AND RETURN THE PROXY CARD PROMPTLY USING THE ENCLOSED ENVELOPE exclusion, the SEC is abandoning its former active role. The SEC will now refrain from ruling on which proposals can be excluded as within the purview of management's ordinary business decisions.

Management Exclusion of Shareholder Proposals: Rule 14a-8(c)

1. Proposal is illegal.
2. Proposal violates SEC proxy rules.
3. Proposal furthers a personal grievance.
4. Proposal is unrelated to the seller's business.
5. Proposal concerns issuer's ordinary business operations.
6. Proposal duplicates another pending proposal.
7. Proposal is moot.
8. Proposal attempts to censure a particular director.
9. Proposal requires declaration of a dividend.

Liability for Proxy Violations Management, dissident solicitors, or others may be liable for violating the proxy rules. Proxy Rule 14a-9 is an antifraud provision prohibiting false or misleading proxy solicitation statements. Proxy fraud is judged by the "total mix" of communications made to shareholders from all sources. Proxy solicitors are also liable for negligent misstatements or omissions, a great potential liability.

The proxy rules exempt proxy solicitations by foreign issuers, issuers in bankruptcy or reorganization, and public utility holding companies. Most proxy rules do not apply to tombstone ads or to small solicitations of 10 or fewer persons. Misstatements or omissions must be material (e.g., significant) to be actionable as proxy fraud or in any other securities fraud context. What types of misstatements might constitute proxy fraud? The following case discusses the fundamental threshold of proxy fraud materiality. It also sets the standard for materiality used in other securities fraud contexts.

TSC Industries v. Northway

426 U.S. 438 (1976)
United States Supreme Court

After National Industries acquired 34 percent of TSC Industries' voting shares, five of National's nominees were placed on the TSC board of directors. The new board proposed to sell National all of TSC's assets and to buy out the remainder of TSC's shareholders with National preferred stock and warrants. A joint proxy statement was issued by both corporations, and all of the shareholders approved the transaction, so TSC was liquidated and dissolved. Northway, a former TSC shareholder, sued, claiming that the proxy statement was false and misleading. The proxy statement failed to state that National's president was on the TSC board when proxies were solicited and that National might be deemed the "parent" corporation of TSC under SEC rules. However, the proxy statement indicated that National had substantial influence over TSC. The proxy statement was allegedly deficient in failing to note some " bad news" in a letter from an investment banker concerning the size of the "premium" that the TSC shareholders would receive in the exchange transaction. A final omission was that a mutual fund, on whose board a National employee sat, made large purchases of National before the exchange transaction. Northway alleged that disclosure of these factors might have indicated a conspiracy to manipulate National's price upward to make the transaction appear favorable to TSC shareholders. The Court of Appeals found the omissions to be "material."

Justice Marshall delivered the opinion of the court.

The question of materiality, it is universally agreed, is an objective one, involving the significance of an omitted or misrepresented fact to a reasonable investor. Variations in the formulation of a general test of materiality occur in the articulation of just how significant a fact must be or, put another way, how certain it must be that the fact would affect a reasonable investor's judgment.

The disclosure policy embodied in the proxy regulations is not without limit. Some information is of such dubious significance that insistence on its disclosure may accomplish more harm than good. The potential liability for a Rule 14a-9 violation can be great indeed, and if the standard of materiality is unnecessarily low, not only may the corporation and its management be subjected to liability for insignificant omissions or misstatements, but also management's fear of exposing itself to substantial liability may cause it simply to bury the shareholders in an avalanche of trivial information—a result that is hardly conducive to informed decision-making.

The general standard of materiality that we think best comports with the policies of Rule 14a-9 is as follows: An omitted fact is material if there is a substantial likelihood that a reasonable shareholder would consider it important in deciding how to vote. This standard is fully consistent with *Mills'* general description of materiality as a requirement that "the defect have a significant *propensity* to affect the voting process." It does not require proof of a substantial likelihood that disclosure of the omitted fact would have caused the reasonable investor to change his vote. What the standard does contemplate is a showing of a substantial likelihood that, under all the circumstances, the omitted fact would have assumed actual significance in the deliberations of the reasonable shareholder. Put another way, there must be a substantial likelihood that the disclosure of the omitted fact would have been viewed by the reasonable investor as having significantly altered the "total mix" of information made available. Rule 14a-9 is concerned only with whether a proxy statement is misleading with respect to its presentation of material facts. If, as we must assume on a motion for summary judgment, there was no collusion or manipulation whatsoever in the National and Madison purchases—that is, if the purchases were made wholly independently for proper corporate and investment purposes, then by Northway's implicit acknowledgment they had no bearing on the soundness and reliability of the market prices listed in the proxy statement, and it cannot have been materially misleading to fail to disclose them.

Case Questions

1. What factors define "materiality" of facts for antifraud liability?
2. What reasons support defining fraud liability only for material misrepresentations?
3. Compare and contrast this materiality standard. Is it a qualitative or rather a quantitative economic standard like that used by auditors?

Tender Offers

After the wave of conglomerate mergers in the 1960s, American financiers adopted the British practice of using the *takeover bid* or *tender offer*. A tender offer typically involves a public offering of cash and/or securities in exchange for a controlling interest in a target corporation. Thereafter, the bidder can restructure the target firm or merge it into the bidding firm. For example, a takeover was effected when Standard Oil Co. of California (Chevron) made a tender offer for Gulf Oil Co. Traditionally, tender offers occurred very quickly, leaving shareholders little time to evaluate the transaction. Before 1968, shareholders had little notice of tender offers and often became panicked into selling their shares without making a careful evaluation. Many institutional investors and large block shareholders took advantage of limited tender offers made for less than all outstanding shares. These Wall Street participants allegedly crowded out small shareholders who did not learn of the tender offer until it was too late. This prompted Congress to amend the 1934 Act with the 1968 Williams Act to improve tender offer disclosure and slow the process so shareholders could better consider the tender offer.

Reasons for Takeovers Many economists argue that the threat of takeovers disciplines existing management into acting more efficiently. Takeover targets are often characterized as undervalued firms with inefficient management. Takeover prices are often higher than the firm's stock price beforehand because the market expects the takeover bidder will better manage the target after the takeover. Proponents of freewheeling takeover activity insist it is beneficial and creates "new wealth."

There are other explanations for tender offers and takeovers. *Synergism* may result from a merger between two firms with complimentary products and facilities. The combination may be more valuable than the sum of its parts. This may result from *economies of scale* obtained when the merging firms eliminate unused administrative personnel or productive capacity. A *portfolio effect* may explain how the cash flows of two firms complement each other after a merger by providing earnings stability. Despite these alleged benefits, many critics claim the real motive to merge comes from the psychological benefits of a larger firm and the profits made by leveraging the firm.

Opponents of increased tender offer activity argue that the resulting mergers make the industry anticompetitive. Considerable tender offer jargon has built up to graphically illustrate the emotional and financial pressures of a tender offer (see Figure 15–6).

FIGURE 15-6

Tender Offer Jargon	Meaning
Saturday night special	Quick, surprise tender offer
White knight	Merger partner who helps target avoid a hostile takeover by an unfriendly bidder
Leveraged buyout (LBO)	Takeover using target's borrowing power to buy target's shares; results in a few individuals or institutional investors owning target
Shark repellent	Defensive maneuver to avert hostile takeover
Poison pill	Large target debt liability that arises after takeover making target financially unattractive or the takeover becomes too expensive
Golden parachutes	Highly favorable management termination contracts; ousted management receives financial cushion if replaced after a takeover
Greenmail	Premium paid by target corporation to buy back a large block of stock from a hostile bidder
Standstill agreement	Agreement by hostile bidder not to attempt another takeover after payment of greenmail

Williams Act Notifications Requirements The Williams Act requires disclosures to balance the target management's power with shareholder emotion. A Schedule 13D gives an early warning to potential takeover targets and their shareholders. It identifies a possible takeover bidder who has accumulated a large block of the target's stock. Shareholders holding more than 5 percent of any equity security must make this disclosure when they acquire 2 percent or more of any registered equity security and the purchase results in their ownership of 5 percent or more. Schedule 13D must disclose the purchaser's background and identity, the source and amounts of funds used, any present or likely future plans to control the target, the number of shares owned, and any contracts they have concerning the issuer's securities (e.g., options). An inadvertent and unintentional failure to file a Schedule 13D is not improper if the SEC is notified and the 5 percent shareholder does not immediately make a tender offer.

When a tender offer begins, the offeror must file a Schedule 14D-1 *tender offer statement* with the SEC, telephone it to the exchanges, and hand deliver it to the issuer. Schedule 14D-1 includes the same disclosures required in a Schedule 13D but must also describe the tender offeror's negotiations with the issuer, state the bidder's purpose, indicate the bidder's plans for the target, include certain bidder's financial statements, state the actual tender offer terms, and include any letters sent to shareholders or press releases used during the tender offer. Management must immediately advise shareholders in a Schedule 14D-9 of management's opinion concerning the tender offer. These regulations apply even if management supports the tender offer because shareholders are usually still under pressure, or management may be coerced to support the offer.

What Is a Tender Offer? *Tender offer* has no statutory or regulatory definition, so its meaning developed in cases and SEC interpretations. Tender offers usually involve a widespread public announcement and solicitation of shareholders, not privately negotiated stock purchases. Tender offer bidders usually attempt to acquire a large block of shares by paying a premium price over the prevailing market price. Tender offers remain open only for a short time, and their terms are usually nonnegotiable. All this creates pressure to sell.

Although a corporation can be controlled with less than 100 percent ownership, the tender offer is usually made contingent on receiving all the shares the bidder seeks. The bidder can refuse to purchase any shares tendered unless the minimum amount sought is tendered. Some hostile bidders have terminated their undersubscribed tender offers and refused to purchase any shares tendered. Immediately thereafter, a bidder might purchase a substantial block of the target's shares in large privately negotiated transactions. The SEC believes these *street sweeps* have the same impact as a tender offer.

Mechanics of the Tender Offer Although a tender offer will probably be publicly disclosed by the press, it must be separately and personally communicated to all shareholders. This is based on the proxy solicitation model, so the target corporation's management usually distributes the tender offer documents. The target's management may either provide a shareholder list to the offeror or directly mail the tender offer at the bidder's expense.

Tender offers must remain open for at least 20 days. If more shares are tendered than the bidder requests, all shares must be accepted pro rata. Thus, if a limited tender offer is oversubscribed, all tendering shareholders may still own some of their original shares after acceptance. Tendering shareholders may withdraw their shares within 15 business days after tender. During the tender offer, it is illegal for the bidder to trade the target's shares on the stock market. Tender offer insider trading and manipulation of the target's stock are illegal. Shareholders may not *short tender* by tendering borrowed shares.

Tender Offer Liabilities Violators of the tender offer rules may be liable for fraud, for failure to file the required schedules, or for the commission of any manipulative acts. Although the Williams Act originally was passed to protect tendering shareholders, other parties such as the SEC, target corporations, or competing bidders may also enforce the rules.

State Tender Offer Regulations Most states, including Delaware, have passed some type of tender offer legislation. Some observers believe these statutes are really intended to retain the target corporation's employment and tax base within the state. Such laws may also attract businesses that seek protection from hostile tender offer bidders. Some of these state statutes interfere with the Williams Act and SEC rules. An Illinois antitakeover statute was invalidated in *Edgar v. MITE Corp.*[12] because it created delays inconsistent with the Williams Act. However, later cases have validated state antitakeover statutes that are specifically directed only at regulating corporate shareholder democracy. The Indiana Control Share Acquisition Act was validated in *CTS Corp. v. Dynamics Corp. of America.*[13] It has become a model followed by other states.

The control share acquisition provisions of the Indiana statute in *CTS* permit other shareholders to vote to withhold voting powers to the takeover bidder after a large or "control" block of stock is acquired. This is justified because the states have a traditional role in structuring corporations and shareholder rights. Some statutes include defensive provisions in addition to the control share provisions mentioned above. For example, some laws require the target management to consider the interests of corporate constituencies other than shareholders. Some permit takeovers only at "fair prices" that are reviewable by the courts. Some statutes prohibit the bidder from merging with the target until after a long time elapses. These laws impede hostile takeovers and force the bidder to negotiate with the target's management. These laws clearly shift power to the target's management and may also benefit the target management financially.

ETHICAL DILEMMA

ETHICAL DILEMMAS IN CORPORATE CONTROL CONTESTS

The corporate control processes are susceptible to ethical abuses by managers and minority shareholders. Managers may spend an excessive amount of corporate resources to win a proxy contest or defend against a hostile takeover bid. Managers have a personal incentive to hide the shareholder list from dissident shareholders. If management fears the loss of their position, pay, or jobs, this creates an incentive to oppose a proxy solicitor or tender offer bidder, irrespective of any benefits for shareholders.

It is arguably unethical for management to follow its self-preservation motive at the shareholders' expense. However, it is difficult to judge when management's

---

[12] *Edgar v. MITE Corp.*, 457 U.S. 624 (1982).

[13] *CTS Corp. v. Dynamics Corp. of America,* 481 U.S. 69 (1987).

opposition to an outsider is selfishly motivated. Similar ethical dilemmas exist for bidders who expect to be paid greenmail or for minority shareholders who use the proxy process to simply air their personal political beliefs unrelated to the firm's financial success. The proxy and tender offer processes are designed to balance the powers and legitimate interests of management and shareholders. Nevertheless, opportunities remain for unethical behavior even for those who comply with the law.

Miscellaneous Securities Laws

The SEC administers several specialized laws in addition to its primary responsibility for the 1933 and 1934 Acts. In 1935, Congress passed the Public Utility Holding Company Act to correct abuses in the financing and operations of gas and electric utilities with pyramid-type capital structures. In 1939, Congress passed the Trust Indenture Act to prevent conflicts of interest by bond indenture trustees and to assure fair treatment of corporate bondholders. After the "back office" paperwork crisis that brokerage firms experienced in the late 1960s, Congress passed the Securities Investor Protection Act of 1970 (SIPA). The SIPA established the Securities Investor Protection Corporation, an insurance fund to protect investors' securities and accounts from broker negligence or bankruptcy. Two other laws impact the securities industry and are discussed further in Chapter 22: the Racketeer Influenced Corrupt Organizations (RICO) provisions of the Organized Crime Control Act (OCCA) and the Foreign Corrupt Practice Act (FCPA).

The regulation of securities industry professionals has a long and enduring history. The Investment Advisors Act of 1940 requires licensing of persons and firms who advise others about securities transactions. The Investment Company Act of 1940 requires special registration and disclosures by mutual funds and money market funds. The SEC has recently stepped up enforcement efforts to discourage broker abuses of customers and to improve fairness in the near-mandatory securities arbitration of customer disputes with brokers.

Summary

The 1933 Act and 1934 Act are intended to reduce fraud in securities trading. Issuers of new nonexempt securities must register the securities before any public sale by filing a registration statement and distributing the prospectus. Before registration, new securities may not be sold, and the market may not be preconditioned. The SEC reviews the offering documents during the waiting period. Actual sales may commence during the posteffective period after clearance by the SEC. Shelf registration permits issuers to preregister securities long before sales are expected.

The securities laws apply only to "securities" such as stocks, bonds, notes, and options. The catch-all phrase "investment contract" defines new investments as securities as needed. An investment contract is a security if a person invests money in a common enterprise or scheme and is led to expect profits will be derived primarily from the efforts of the promoter. This costly registration process is exempted if securities are sold intrastate, in a private placement, or in small dollar volumes. Usually these securities may not be resold immediately to others. Issuers are liable in damages for securities fraud. Considerable criminal penalties exist for the illegal sale of unregistered securities.

Insider trading is prohibited if nonpublic, confidential information is misappropriated. Section 16(b) insiders, officers, directors, and 10 percent shareholders must report their trading activity and refrain from making short-swing profits. Rule 10b-5 prohibits securities fraud and restricts insider trading. Any person within or outside the issuer is prohibited from buying or selling securities based on inside information. Persons in possession of material, nonpublic, misappropriated information have the choice of disclosing the inside information or abstaining from trading. Tippees may not trade on misappropriated information or information improperly received from an insider.

Proxy solicitations are regulated, requiring all solicitors to file a proxy statement stating various information about the solicitation. SEC rules provide two alternate methods for shareholder proxy solicitations. Small shareholders solicitations are included with management's solicitation at the corporation's expense. Larger solicitors pay their own expenses. There is liability for proxy fraud.

The 1968 Williams Act regulates tender offers. Takeover bidders and the issuer's management are placed on an even footing so shareholders can make reasoned choices about tendering. Tender offer disclosures are required, including (1) Schedule 13D by 5 percent shareholders, (2) Schedule 14D-1 by the tender offeror when the tender offer commences, and (3) Schedule 14D-9 by the target management. There are penalties for tender offer fraud, failure to disclose as required, or the commission of manipulative acts. States may validly regulate the shareholder voting aspects of takeovers and tender offers.

Critical Thinking Review Questions

1. Under the Securities Act of 1933, there are three important periods that affect the offering of securities for sale. Name and describe these three periods and give reasons for their apparent importance in the public policy on regulating the securities markets.
2. What factors are presumed to be part of every "security?" Give three examples of transactions other than the sale of stock or bonds that have been interpreted as involving the sale of a security and explain why these are considered securities.
3. Compare and contrast the basic distinctions between common law fraud and the statutory fraud provisions against insider trading. What is the importance of this distinction?
4. Rule 10b-5 of the Securities Exchange Act of 1934 is of fundamental importance in the law of securities regulation. Restate this rule in your own words and describe its purposes.
5. Congress has attempted to clarify insider trading enforcement with two statutes passed in the 1980s. Describe those statutes and compare their coverage and implementation.

Critical Thinking Exercises

1. Claiming the intrastate exemption of the Securities Act of 1933, Jones Investment Company did not register its offering of shares with the SEC. Jones Investment is a Georgia corporation whose only offices are in that state. It sold shares only to Georgia residents. However, the funds were raised to finance the company's real estate developments in Florida. Is the intrastate exemption available for Jones Investment? Why or why not? *See Busch v. Carpenter,* 827 F.2d 653 (10th Cir.1987)
2. Liability under Section 16(b) arises only if there is a purchase *and* a sale of equity securities within a six-month period. Profits are calculated by matching the lowest purchase price for a class of securities against the higher sales price. This yields the highest possible profit. Insiders may not offset their losses. Consider the following example, and calculate the short-swing profits:

   On January 1, insider purchased 100 shares of Atlantic stock at $30 a share.

   On February 28, insider sold 100 shares of Atlantic stock at $20 a share.

   On April 15, insider purchased 100 shares of Atlantic stock at $40 a share.

   On May 20, insider sold 100 shares of Atlantic stock at $50 a share.

3. John Smith is a junior executive of the Widget Company. In the course of his employment, he has accumulated $25,000 of its common stock (at its current market value of $12.50 per share), having first received a stock bonus eight years ago and having last made a purchase of 200 shares at $10 per share four months ago. During the last four months, since a new president was brought in from the outside, he has felt that the company was drifting downhill. Some rather weak executives have been hired, apparently because they were friends or relatives of the new president. A disappointment is in the offing because a new device that was rumored to be a breakthrough (and was prominently mentioned in the trade journals) is having production difficulties that will probably prevent it from being offered in the market for a long time to come.

   Smith thinks that when the facts about the new device are announced, Widget stock will go down several points. It is unlikely, however, to descend to its level of a year ago for some time, perhaps not until its annual financial report is released in about seven months. Smith would like to sell his stock as soon as possible and would also like to advise some friends who have followed his lead and invested heavily in it to do so, too. He asks you whether this is possible. Outline the issues in the case. Which statutes apply? *See Shapiro v. Merrill Lynch, Pierce, Fenner & Smith,* 495 F.2d 228 (2d Cir.1974).
4. How would you apply the misappropriation theory to the fact pattern in the question above? For example, suppose that John Smith passed on the information to his friends and that the friends tipped off other outsiders. Would this violate Rule 10b-5? *See U.S. v. Chestman,* 947 F.2d 551 (2d Cir.1991).
5. James Jones has access to information on Atlantic Company that is not available to the general investor. He wants to buy stock in the company, and he is also preparing a proxy statement that is to be distributed to all of its shareholders. What standard should he apply to determine whether the information in his possession is "material" so that he cannot invest in his company prior to its public release? What standard should he apply to determine whether the information should be included in the proxy statement?
6. Contrast the analytical steps taken to evaluate the legal and ethical problems of the following securities markets activities:
   a. Stock parking, the practice of acquiring and holding large blocks of the stock of potential takeover targets through friends, family, and business associates in order to conceal the identity of the acquirer.
   b. Trading on inside information acquired from corporate employees of another firm by promising to return the favor with a tip of inside information on the trader's company.
   c. Disclosure of false information about your company's lower expected earnings for the next quarter in order to sell your holdings in the stock before the market price plunges.
   d. Falsifying the accounting records of your company to show a profit so that the company can float a new issue of bonds to secure financing that may help turn around the company's ill fortunes.
   e. Failing to disclose in management's proxy solicitation, which urges approval of a merger, that the officers of the company currently own large amounts of corporate stock and have lucrative "golden parachutes" (huge severance pay bonuses). Approval of the merger will trigger the officers' rights to these stock profits and severance bonuses. However, the officers have not secured any advice on a fair merger price from an independent investment banker and the merger price is far below the company's true value.

PART 6

Antitrust Law and Business

16 Monopolies and Mergers

17 Restraints of Trade, Price Discrimination and Unfair Trade Practices

CHAPTER

16

Monopolies and Mergers

Critical Thinking Questions

- What are the assumptions behind the policy of antitrust law suggesting it might help maintain a competitive economy with the prohibition of monopolistic practices or mergers that concentrate market power?
- What are the biases of the two major antitrust enforcement schools in their prescription of enforcement strategies?
- For what reasons do the antitrust laws exempt many actions of the following industries: regulated financial institutions, the insurance industry, labor unions, and professional baseball?
- What ambiguities are there is the analysis of monopolization through the exploration of market power in a particular geographic and product market?
- Compare and contrast the various forms of merger: horizontal, vertical, conglomerate. Discuss how the analytical processes for each are similar and different.

Introduction... Past, Present, Future

After the Civil War, a period of industrial expansion revolutionized the U.S. economy. The corporate form was increasingly accepted, and the capital markets were expanded. Early investment bankers helped concentrate wealth, power, and productive capacity in the hands of fewer persons. Fewer and larger companies produced most goods. For example, Andrew Carnegie created the largest steel company, U.S. Steel, during this period. Small business, the heart of American capitalism, became unable to compete with larger firms, which had economies of large-scale production and installed labor-saving machinery that displaced many skilled craftsmen.

The work ethic and the equal opportunity theories underlying the U.S. Constitution have always been a dominant force. Americans believe they have a "right" to pull themselves up by their own bootstraps according to their abilities and without undue governmental intervention. Thus, in the 19th century, business was regulated only by market competition. By the close of the 19th century, however, the new industrialism created a widening income disparity between classes, threatening the emerging middle class and raising fundamental questions of fairness. Mechanized factories allowed the production of better goods in less time by less-skilled workers. Skilled craftsmen and artisans lost economic power as large factories and concentrated businesses took over their markets. Many local businesses felt the shock of competition from more efficient production and began to mistrust big business.

Fewer and larger firms won larger market shares, resulting in a concentration of wealth and power. As these firms increased their control over resources and workers, these firms' owners could dictate prices. In response, a new political movement—*populism*—developed among the individualists, farmers, and small-business owners in the agrarian West. The populists claimed that large businesses were corrupt and oppressed those involved in the traditional economy.

Some large businesses brought on these criticisms by employing monopolistic practices. For example, the railroads came under federal regulatory power in 1888 because they paid secret rebates to a few favored customers, resulting in price discrimination between shippers. Some large businesses temporarily priced their products below cost to eliminate competition, then later raised prices to recoup losses. Other large businesses created monopolies by buying up competitors. Standard Oil and U.S. Steel obtained the largest market shares in their industries by pressuring their customers, competitors, and suppliers. Many people believe such domination is undesirable. Without vigorous competition, a large company can arbitrarily set prices and production policies for a whole industry. Big businesses prevented small competitors from advertising, purchasing supplies, or selling to their customers by threatening their suppliers and customers into boycotting the small competitors. Critics argued that the success of big business was too often due to these abusive practices and not to increased efficiency. Eventually public reaction led to passage of the antitrust laws.

Although the primary goal of the antitrust laws is to maintain a competitive economy, there are other goals: liberty, fairness, and opportunity. These goals are also influential. The populists hoped that the system of small, independent business units would preserve the American dream. They thought that further concentration of political and economic power would encourage the growth of power centers, reminiscent of feudalism, that might eventually rival the power of government. They considered the diffusion and decentralization of political and economic power necessary to preserve democracy. The antitrust laws were intended to encourage fairness and vigorous competition, thereby ensuring equitable allocation of resources and eliminating favoritism or prejudice.

The populists' discontent with industrial concentration highlighted how ineffective the common law was in dealing with monopolies. Since the common law was primarily state law, there was no uniformity among the states, and the outcome of litigation against large firms was unpredictable. Congress passed the Sherman Act in 1890, deriving its principles from the state common law.

Today, the economic efficiency argument dominates most descriptions of antitrust goals. The Supreme Court has stated this normative theory as the primary justification for the antitrust laws.

Economic Efficiency Theory Underlying the Sherman Act

The Sherman Act was designed to be a comprehensive charter of economic liberty aimed at preserving free and unfettered competition. . . . [I]t rests on the premise

> that unrestrained interaction of competitive forces will yield the best allocation of our economic resources, the lowest prices, the highest quality, and the greatest material progress.[1]

Under the economic efficiency theory, antitrust laws are justified as an incentive to innovate, maintain productive efficiency, and maximize the range and selection of goods. Monopolies are considered damaging because they impose limitations on production, heighten the danger of deterioration in quality, and give the monopolist power to fix prices and exclude competitors. These outcomes conflict with the basic premise that competition can provide incentives and disincentives consistent with maximum efficiency. Antitrust laws are justified as a way to move toward the perfect competition model and thereby maintain a competitive environment.

Antitrust laws are now enforced by state and federal regulators and by private plaintiffs. The Federal Trade Commission and the Justice Department are responsible for monitoring the economic environment and maintaining competition. However, the courts and these regulators have been responding to new theories of competition that justify many acts previously considered anticompetitive.

In the future, antitrust enforcement may increase. The use of complex economic analysis to gauge the anticompetitive effects of suppliers' control over their distribution chains is expected to grow. Such analysis involves a structured set of inquiries requiring expert testimony by economists and industry experts. However, the increased interdependence of the world's economies will reduce the need for the traditional intense antitrust enforcement efforts. Nevertheless, predatory acts will probably be prohibited for many years. A growing body of competition laws in other nations, particularly the EU, suggests that the policies of antitrust are spreading throughout the developed world.

Antitrust law is clearly important to decision making by both upper management and line managers. Such statutes as the Sherman Act, the Clayton Act, and the Federal Trade Commission Act largely define considerable conduct by business. This chapter explores the history, content, economic theory, and criticisms of antitrust laws by first focusing on monopolies and mergers. As with other legal areas, the statutes provide only a starting point. Court interpretations and administrative agencies provide other critical information about how management can avoid liability. Chapter 17 covers other antitrust offenses: price discrimination, restraints of trade, and unfair trade practices.

Thought Questions

1. What underlying conditions caused the political and popular presumptions underlying the antitrust laws concerning the quality of life and economic opportunity in the 19th century in the United States?
2. Why and how did the populist movement react to the evolution of 19th century capitalism and the Industrial Revolution?

---

[1] *Northern Pacific Railway Co. v. United States,* 365 U.S. 1 (1958).

U.S. Antitrust Laws

The U.S. antitrust laws broke new ground by directly regulating restraints of trade and monopolies. The early common law only indirectly prohibited those restraints that limited the ability to practice one's profession. The courts reasoned that their lack of earnings would burden society. The common law of contracts also provided an indirect model for antitrust law in declaring illegal covenants not to compete. As introduced in Chapter 9, a restraint is illegal if an employee is unreasonably prohibited from competing with a former employer. Similarly, the seller of a business or professional practice should not be unreasonably restrained from competing with the buyer. The antitrust rule of reason is a direct descendent from these principles. The contract law concepts of duress and economic duress underlie other antitrust laws such as the prohibition on tie-in sales and boycotts. However, these common law principles were unsuitable to encourage competition as the industrial revolution progressed. Contract law failed to protect the competitive structure of the economy because many of the customers, competitors, and suppliers of monopolists lacked privity and therefore had no remedy under contract law. These common law shortcoming and the pressures from populists eventually spawned the federal and state antitrust laws. The major U.S. antitrust laws and amendments are summarized in Figure 16–1.

The Sherman Act

Sherman Act
First antitrust law, passed in 1890, outlawing monopolization.

The **Sherman Act,** passed in 1890, prohibits anticompetitive devices that restrain trade and erect the barrier of monopoly to any trade or other aspect of interstate commerce. Sections 1 and 2 of the Sherman Act are the most pertinent.

Sherman Act, Section 1: Restraints of Trade

Section 1 of the Sherman Act makes it an unlawful criminal act to enter into a "contract, combination . . . or conspiracy in restraint of trade."

Sherman Act, Section 2: Monopolization

Section 2 of the Sherman Act states that "every person who shall monopolize, or attempt to monopolize, or combine or conspire with any other person or persons, to monopolize any part of the trade of commerce among the several states, or with foreign nations shall be deemed guilty of a felony."

The Clayton Act

Initially, the federal courts were quite lenient in their interpretations of the Sherman Act. One early case held that manufacturing was not commerce, so it could not be federally regulated.[2] Although that view was soon abandoned, it illustrates the courts' initial hostility to the Sherman Act. Congress responded to mounting criticism of this

[2] *United States v. E.C. Knight Co.,* 156 U.S. 1 (1896).

FIGURE 16-1 Summary of Federal Antitrust Laws

Law	Effect	Enforcement (discussed later)
Sherman Act (1890)	Illegal to enter contract, combination, or conspiracy in restraint or trade Outlaws monopolization, attempts to monopolize, or conspiracies to monopolize interstate commerce Criminal fines: for corporations, up to $1 million; up to $100,000 for noncorporations Prison sentences: up to three years for individuals	Justice Department: criminal and civil prosecutions FTC: no powers Private plaintiffs: civil damage suits State attorneys general: civil prosecutions
Clayton Act (1914)	Illegal to require another by contract to boycott a competitor if this substantially lessens competition or tends to create a monopoly (effectively prohibits tying and exclusive dealing) Prohibits mergers or purchase of assets if effect is to substantially lessen competition or create a monopoly Prohibits interlocking directorates	Justice Department: civil prosecutions FTC: civil prosecutions Private plaintiffs: civil damage suits
Federal Trade Commission Act (1914)	Creates FTC Empowers FTC to enforce FTC and Clayton acts Prohibits unfair methods of competition or deceptive trade practices	Justice Department: no powers FTC: civil prosecutions Private plaintiffs: no powers
Robinson-Patman Act (1936)	Price discrimination declared illegal if it tends to create a monopoly or lessen competition	
Celler-Kefauver Act (1950)	Acquisition of corporate assets included as a form of merger	Closed sale of assets loophole
Tunney Act (1973)		Federal District Court review of Justice Department settlements to assure they serve "the public interest"
Hart-Scott-Rodino Antitrust Improvements Act (1976)	Pre-merger notification to regulators	Permits regulator analysis of proposed mergers before consummation

leniency by passing the **Clayton Act** in 1914. It was written in more specific terms, outlawing particular anticompetitive activities. Whereas the Sherman Act requires proof of completed anticompetitive effects, the Clayton Act is violated earlier, when anticompetitive tendencies arise from conduct even before competition is damaged. Section 7 of the Clayton Act is discussed in this chapter. It prohibits interlocking directorates and mergers or stock acquisitions that result in a substantial lessening of competition. Sections 3 is covered in the next chapter. It prohibits tie-in sales, exclusive dealing arrangements, and requirements contracts that "substantially lessen competition or tend to create a monopoly."

Clayton Act Second antitrust law, passed in 1914, enumerating particular offenses.

Federal Trade Commission Act

The Federal Trade Commission Act, also passed in 1914, created the Federal Trade Commission (FTC). The FTC is given broad powers to prosecute "unfair methods of competition" and "unfair or deceptive acts or practices," and enforce the Sherman and Clayton Acts. The FTC Act protects businesses from the predatory and anticompetitive acts of their competitors and protects consumers from the deceptive acts of sellers.

Additional Antitrust Laws

In later years, Congress strengthened the antitrust laws several times. In 1936, price discrimination was specifically outlawed by the Robinson-Patman Act. In 1952, the Celler-Kefauver Act closed a loophole by extending the merger prohibition to corporate acquisitions in which the assets of another firm are purchased. In 1976, the Hart-Scott-Rodino Antitrust Improvement Act expanded the investigative powers of the Department of Justice (DOJ). Hart-Scott-Rodino requires public notice of mergers prior to their completion, and it permits the prosecution of antitrust violations by the attorneys general of the states for damages allegedly caused to state citizens. The Tunney Act (1973) was passed after Congress became suspicious of antitrust enforcement by President Nixon's Justice Department. There was concern the DOJ might settle antitrust suits by favorably approving mergers and monopolization activities conducted by corporations that were substantial campaign contributors. The Tunney Act requires federal district court review of antitrust settlements negotiated between the DOJ and antitrust defendants.

State Antitrust Laws

Most states have antitrust laws that parallel the federal antitrust laws. Typically, state antitrust laws outlaw particular anticompetitive acts such as restraints of trade, price-fixing, exclusive dealing, and tying. In recent years, state attorneys general have increased enforcement efforts under both state and federal antitrust laws. For example, various state attorneys general combined to challenge a price-fixing scheme by several national insurance companies, alleging that the companies fixed premiums and colluded in refusing to offer certain types of insurance. Critics charge that some of this activism is politically motivated. Nevertheless, business must not be lulled into complacency over antitrust enforcement even if federal regulators temporarily relax their vigilance. State attorneys general and private parties may use state laws as an alternate basis for antitrust litigation, making enforcement less susceptible to ideological shifts in Washington.

INTERNATIONAL PERSPECTIVE AND COMMENTARY

International Perspective on Competition Laws

During the 20th century, most nations have had weaker antitrust enforcement than the United States. Many nations promote domestic monopolies so they can compete more effectively in international commerce. For example, there is a South Korean government agency called the "Office of Monopoly," which promotes domestic industry. Many educated people in developing nations are torn between the two extremes of monopoly and competition. On one hand, popular nationalism motivates governments to grant monopolies to strengthen domestic industry. On the other hand, many of these supporters also denounce the inevitable decline in their personal standard of living caused by paying high monopoly prices for a variety of domestic products and services. This tension has led to anticompetitive and protectionist laws regulating foreign trade, discriminatory taxes, tariffs, quotas, and excessive inspections. There is often hostility toward foreign competition, particularly by large foreign firms. This suggests there are strong parallels between the efforts of GATT negotiations to reduce international trade barriers and antitrust enforcement targeting industry restraints of trader. They are remarkably the same problem at different levels. Many U.S. firms believe that the difficulties of opening foreign markets through trade negotiations leave antitrust enforcement as the only alternative. Nevertheless, many nations remain hostile to U.S.-style antitrust laws.

The EU and some other successful industrialized economies are increasingly adopting new antimonopoly laws that resemble existing U.S. laws. The Treaty of Rome, which created the EU, includes prohibitions against collusion among competitors to fix prices, control production, allocate markets, or limit the development of products or geographic markets. The EU business competition law prohibits tying, monopolization, and the use of discretionary supply contract terms. In recent years, the EU's Directorate General who is responsible for enforcing the competition laws has increased enforcement considerably by imposing large fines for price-fixing and for collusive exchanges of sensitive price information within trade associations. New interpretive regulations from the EU Merger Task Force require premerger competitive analysis and requires a much deeper understanding of the affected markets before regulators approve mergers and joint ventures. However, the EC imposes fewer restraints on the intracorporate activities of related multinational corporate groups.

There is a realization among some academics and policymakers that the U.S. economy no longer acts in isolation and is becoming an increasingly influential part of the global marketplace. The interdependence of the world's economies has implications for the stringent antitrust enforcement of the past. Excessive enforcement could weaken U.S. competitors, particularly where foreign competitors receive government sponsorship. Many foreign nations subsidize their sole producer of products for reasons of nationalistic pride or perceived self-sufficiency. This evolving reality suggests it may be necessary for some industries to consolidate and become larger to gain the needed economies of scale to effectively compete internationally. Perhaps the structures of particular industries, the efficiencies of scale within each industry, and the efficiency of foreign competition should be analyzed before there is antitrust enforcement.

Trusts and Monopolies

As corporations develop, economic power becomes more concentrated, bringing productive capacity under the control of fewer persons. Concentration can also involve the creation of *pools,* in which groups of businesses agree to split up the available business among their members. For example, where markets are separated geographically, sales in each market may be allocated to a local producer. This *division of markets* reduces competition among pool members. Pooling contracts are illegal but they are inherently weak because it is difficult to discipline members who breach the pool agreement. A disciplinary problem of this kind weakened OPEC's efforts to control oil output and set worldwide oil prices. In the late 19th century, trusts provided a more permanent and more enforceable bond than a pool.

Characteristics of a Trust

trust
Trustor conveys legal title on property to trustee who makes decisions about the property; used to bring former competitors under unified control of a single trustee.

A **trust** is an organizational form in which *trustors (settlors)* convey property (*res*) to a *trustee* who holds legal title (ownership) to the assets transferred. The trustor or other beneficiary retains beneficial ownership of the property, leaving the trustee responsible for decision making. The trust device is most justifiable when the beneficiaries have limited investment or business expertise. However, the restraint of trade was the primary purpose of these 19th century business trusts. These early business trusts stripped shareholder voting privileges to consolidate corporate control in the trustees. Shareholders were the trust beneficiaries who retained the right to receive dividends. Trusts were assembled into monopolies when the stockholders of several competing corporations transferred their stock to a board of trustees. The trustees exchanged *voting trust certificates* for the shares. Figure 16–2 illustrates both simple and monopolistic trusts.

Standard Oil Company was originally organized as a trust that drew together the major oil producers from Ohio (Sohio, now BP), New Jersey (Exxon), New York

FIGURE 16-2 Trust Origin of the Antimonopoly Laws

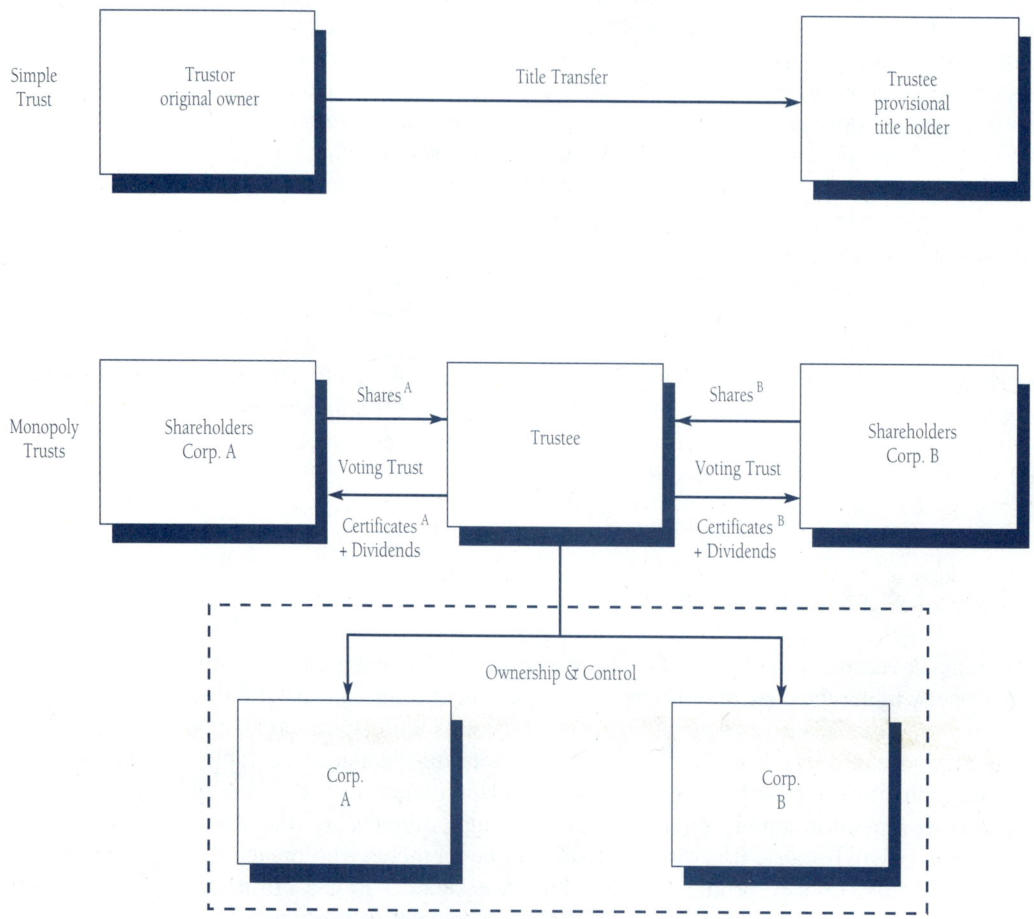

Monopoly business organization structure

(Mobil), Indiana (Amoco), California (Chevron), and several other smaller oil companies. The Standard Oil monopoly was eventually broken up into separate companies. Eventually, all large, monopolistic business organizations that tended to crush competitors became known as trusts even if organized as a corporation without using the trust form.

Market Structures

Traditional economic analysis defines five basic market structures (and several subforms): perfect competition, monopoly, oligopoly, monopolistic competition, and monopsony. This analytic model is used to predict the purchasing behaviors of consumers and the pricing, production, and collusive behaviors of sellers.

Under **perfect competition** there are a large number of buyers and sellers. No individual firm or consumer has sufficient market power to influence prices or the quantity of production. Perfect competition presumes low barriers to entry, uniform products, and perfect information concerning market conditions shared equally by all. These are unrealistic assumptions in the real world, but perfect competition is still useful as a model for economic analysis. As real-world markets are encountered, it becomes necessary to modify its implications. The securities markets and the markets for gasoline or groceries in larger cities often come close to the perfect competition model.

perfect competition
Market in which there are numerous buyers and sellers so there is no market power in any one; supply and demand allocate resources optimally.

Monopoly describes a market dominated by one large seller. Typically, there are no close substitutes for the seller's product. Usually there are high *barriers to entry:* the difficulties other firms face in trying to enter the market and produce similar products. Legal barriers to entry include patents, copyrights, franchises, international trade barriers, and licenses limiting the use of the monopolist's technology. Natural barriers to entry include the need to purchase a large amount of assets to produce the product or high transportation costs. Most utilities have natural monopolies in their service areas because of the expense to duplicate the generators and distribution wiring. The pricing and output decisions of utilities are regulated to reduce their monopolistic tendencies.

monopoly
Market dominated by one large seller with market power to dictate prices and supply.

Oligopoly conditions exist where there are a small number of sellers and high barriers exist to the entry of new producers. This gives strong sellers sufficient market power to influence prices and quantity. The U.S. domestic steel market was long regarded as an oligopoly. The steel obtainable from most producers was virtually interchangeable. There was little price competition although producers competed with a subtle variety of features, service, shipping costs, or advertising. Prices tend to be higher and output lower in oligopolistic markets than under perfect competition, although less restricted than under monopoly.

oligopoly
Market dominated by a few sellers that have the power to dictate prices and supply.

Monopolistic competition involves markets with few sellers offering somewhat substitutable but differentiated products. Examples include automobiles, soft drinks and beers. Each automaker tries to distinguish its models in consumers' minds even though most autos are somewhat interchangeable for the basic transportation purpose. Monopolistic competitors possess some market power, are slow to innovate, and spend more on marketing than those more perfectly competitive markets.

monopolistic competition
Market dominated by a few large sellers with some market power offering functionally similar but differentiated products.

Monopsony exists when a single buyer possesses monopoly buying power. **Oligopsony** exists when a few buyers have market power. For example, the employer in a company town is a monopsonist because, as the predominant buyer of labor, it can affect prices (wages), setting them lower than under perfect competition. These economic models are illustrated in Figure 16–3. They are the basis for most traditional antitrust analysis.

monopsony
Market dominated by one large buyer with market power over demand.

oligopsony
Market dominated by a few large buyers, each of which has some market power over demand.

FIGURE 16-3 Basic Market Structures

Market Structure	Primary Characteristics	Effects	Examples
Perfect competition	Numerous buyers and sellers; low barriers to entry; perfect information; numerous substitutes; elastic demand	Allocative efficiency	U.S. financial markets; retail gasoline and grocery businesses
Monopoly	Single seller; high barriers to entry; no adequate substitutes; inelastic demand	Seller's market power: seller may raise price and lower output; abnormal monopoly profits; no innovation	Public utilities; patent or trade secret
Oligopoly	Few sellers; high barriers to entry; inadequate substitutes	Seller's market power: abnormal monopoly profit; slow innovation	Breakfast cereals
Monopolistic competition	Few sellers; high barriers to entry; substitutes "appear" distinguishable in consumers' minds	Seller's market power: abnormal monopoly profits; slow innovation	Aerospace, automobiles
Monopsony	Single buyer; high barriers to entry	Buyer has market power to set low prices	Single employer in a company town

Enforcement of Antitrust Law

There are four basic antitrust law enforcers. First, the Department of Justice (DOJ) oversees antitrust enforcement. The DOJ Antitrust Division is the only enforcer with both criminal and civil enforcement powers. The Sherman Act gives DOJ these powers, and the Clayton Act gives DOJ additional civil enforcement powers. The DOJ is directed by the attorney general, a cabinet member, and is often a close confidant of the president.

The FTC may bring civil enforcement actions for violations of the Clayton Act. The FTC has sole enforcement authority of the FTC Act. The FTC is a quasi-independent regulatory agency headed by five commissioners appointed by the president and confirmed by the Senate. The FTC's composition and powers were introduced in Chapter 12.

Private parties injured by Sherman or Clayton Act violations may bring civil damage suits. A private party may wait to sue until a government agency successfully prosecutes the violator. This tactic often increases the private plaintiff's success because the government's successful enforcement action provides convincing evidence of guilt. In certain limited situations, if several individuals are harmed in a similar way by the defendant's conduct, a *class action* suit may be instituted.

State attorneys general may sue in their *parens patrie* role on behalf of their state's consumers or competitors. This enforcement activity has become well known in the 1980s and 1990s because of the concerted efforts of state attorneys general to prove anticompetitive acts in several industries such as insurance. Congress permitted this broad antitrust enforcement to promote vigorous enforcement of the antitrust laws.

Criminal Penalties

There are substantial penalties to deter anticompetitive conduct. The Sherman Act imposes criminal sanctions on individuals, including fines of up to $100,000 or prison sentences of up to three years or both. Corporations may be fined up to $1 million per occurrence. However, there are no criminal sanctions under the Clayton or FTC Acts. Criminal convictions require proof of criminal intent, which means that the defendant must have had "knowledge of the probable consequences" of the anticompetitive action. The intent and burden of proof requirements make it difficult to obtain criminal convictions so the predominant enforcement emphasis is in civil suits and the review and clearance of mergers by various government agencies.

Private Rights of Action

The Clayton Act grants standing to "any person . . . injured in his business or property by reason of anything forbidden in the anti-trust laws," under either the Sherman or Clayton Acts. Private plaintiffs may recover *treble damages* (three times the actual damage sustained) plus litigation costs, including reasonable attorneys' fees. Treble damages are similar to punitive damages because private parties have a greater incentive to sue. Injured competitors, consumers, suppliers, state attorneys general and even foreign governments may sue for treble damages. However, only direct purchasers may sue for treble damages. Indirect purchasers, those who purchase further down the distribution chain, are not directly injured by the anticompetitive action. In *Illinois Brick Co. v. Illinois,*[3] the Supreme Court rejected the state's treble damage claim made for downstream consumers. The suit alleged that concrete block manufacturers illegally fixed prices charged to building contractors. The added costs were allegedly "passed through" to the ultimate consumers through higher prices charged by the contractors. Despite the *Illinois Brick* rule, treble damages claims by such downstream indirect purchasers are permitted under some state antitrust laws.[4]

Civil Enforcement by Regulators

Both the FTC and the Justice Department use two enforcement devices to obtain innovative remedies. First, equitable relief may be obtained through an injunction to restrain and prevent future antitrust violations. This broad power permits the federal courts to restrain particular conduct, compel divestiture of subsidiaries, dismember monopolies to create more competitive industries, cancel a merger, order licensing of patents with reasonable royalty payments and cancel existing contracts.

Second, *consent decrees* permit the government and the defendant to avoid trial by agreeing to a settlement. Typically, the defendant voluntarily agrees to cease its anticompetitive actions, neither admitting nor denying any violation of the law, and the court enters a permanent injunction against future violations and approves the settlement. Consent decrees avoid costly litigation and appeals. Subsequent damage suits by private plaintiffs may not take advantage of the consent decree as proof of any violation. Later plaintiffs must prove their cases independently following a consent decree.

Settlements and consent decrees can be controversial. The Tunney Act requires federal court review of settlements to avoid politically inspired collusion and assure

[3] *Illinois Brick Co. v. Illinois,* 431 U.S. 720 (1977).

[4] *California v. ARC America Corp.,* 490 U.S. 93 (1989).

settlements are in the public interest. The federal judge overseeing the breakup of the Bell System still prohibits ATT and the "baby Bells" from some activities. For example, as of this writing, the settlement still prohibits the "baby Bells" from offering long distance services. The 1995 DOJ settlement with Microsoft was found not to be in the public interest. Microsoft's alleged "vaporware" and other exclusionary practices were not addressed in the settlement. This disappointed competing software companies who alleged Microsoft restrains trade and monopolizes the software and operating system markets.[5] However, antitrust regulators are limiting the duration of consent decrees to 20 years at the FTC. DOJ orders average only 10 years. There are nearly 100 such old decrees that restrain U.S. companies from more aggressive international competition. For example, General Electric had been barred for almost 90 years from selling private label light bulbs. GE was allegedly guilty of patent misuse in sales practices using its light bulb patents to prevent the entry of competitors. A similar decree restrains IBM's marketing decisions and its parts business. One court recently overturned a decree prohibiting Kodak from entering the private label film business. The courts and regulators realize that global competition requires a rethinking of traditionally aggressive antitrust enforcement.

COMMENTARY

APPROACHES TO ANTITRUST ENFORCEMENT

Although the laissez-faire economic theory has established the ethic that government should not intervene in markets, many observers believe there are market failures and shortcomings in business performance that justify some government regulation. They argue that market-based systems often yield poor results, such as the natural tendency to develop monopolies. However, it is difficult to design a regulatory system that stops short of destructive interference with the beneficial activities of markets.

industrial organization Study of optimal relations between sellers and buyers and optimal number of buyers and sellers within particular markets.

Economists and antitrust lawyers have developed theories of **industrial organization** that attempt to explain the performance and shape of markets by describing the relations among competing firms and with their suppliers and customers. Three basic approaches to government intervention have evolved: the structuralist approach, the conduct approach, and performance analysis. The *structuralist approach* looks primarily at the organization of each industry to identify particular structural characteristics that lead toward anticompetitive effects. This requires close examination of the number of buyers and sellers to determine the degree of industry concentration. The size and the geographic distribution of sellers determines a seller's market power. Structuralists analyze the degree of differentiation among competing products to identify substitute products. The barriers to entry for potential competitors are studied for signs that they could stifle new competition.

Taking the middle ground are adherents of the *conduct approach,* who would focus enforcement on the actual behavior of firms. Business practices are identified that reveal inefficiencies or breakdowns in competition. Pricing and production policies of firms are reviewed for anticompetitive practices. The intentional commission of illegal acts and conduct in advertising, research, and innovation are also relevant to enforcement.

[5] *United States v. Microsoft Corp.* (Civ. No. 94-1564), 1995 W.L. 59580 (D.D.C.).

The actual outcomes or end results of a firm's conduct are the focus of *performance analysis*. There is no emphasis on anticompetitive potential or conduct as there is under the other approaches. Instead, performance analysts are concerned with how well the market performance meets the antitrust goals of economic efficiency. Attention is directed toward the economic efficiency of industries, levels of technological innovation, reasonable profit performance, and reasonable barriers to entry. Complex economic analysis of costs, investments, investment return, innovation, and sales activities in particular industries is important.

The "optimal" approach to antitrust enforcement has been the subject of continuing debate among academics. Big business often supports performance analysis because it permits greater freedom of action. They argue that small firms cannot afford to invest enough in R&D to remain efficient. Technological developments eventually create new substitute products eliminating any short-term monopolies of large firms. However, structuralists counter this with evidence that large firms in many industries are less efficient than medium-sized firms. Additionally, large advertising and marketing expenses of many large firms divert scarce resources away from R&D.

Despite the antitrust enforcement debate, most commentators believe that monopolies are necessary in some industries to avoid inefficient duplication of facilities. For example, utilities operate most efficiently if only a single set of distribution facilities is built (e.g., power lines, telephone cables, and pipelines for water, natural gas, and sewers). State regulatory agencies usually control prices and services to prevent monopolistic behavior of these *natural monopolies*.

There are two schools of thought on antitrust enforcement policy: the Harvard (or traditional) school and the Chicago school. The Harvard school prefers vigorous antitrust enforcement to maintain atomized competition among numerous independent businesses. It argues that concentration of economic power will nearly always lead to monopolistic behaviors and to less than optimal distribution of goods and services. By contrast, the Chicago school insists on using a separate economic analysis in every antitrust case. It would tolerate some monopolistic behaviors if the anticompetitive effects were short-term, the monopolist competed internationally, or the monopoly profits were used for innovation. This approach encourages natural monopolies if they are more efficient than perfect competition where the monopolist becomes the least-cost producer.

During most of the 20th century, the traditionalists have guided antitrust enforcement. Since the mid-1970s, however, adherents of the Chicago school have become more influential, primarily in the federal agencies responsible for antitrust enforcement and to a somewhat lesser extent as their law and economics approach has been applied in the courts.

Enforcement of Antitrust Law

Ethical Dilemma

Antitrust law represents a national ethical principle to encourage competition and efficiency among participants in the economy. Some people believe this principle is similar to a basic work ethic. Arguably, monopolies and restraints of trade remove beneficial incentives for innovation or risk taking. Antitrust law may be viewed as a basis for economic ethics in a competitive society.

The criminal penalties for antitrust violations pose numerous ethical dilemmas for managerial decision making. It is difficult to detect many antitrust violations.

This reality may encourage violations by those who hope to go unnoticed. Most monopolies or mergers are too well publicized to be ignored. However, the participants in an agreement in restraint of trade could maintain silence, making the results less obvious. Therefore, practices like secret price-fixing, division of markets, group boycotts, illicit trade association activities, and intimidation of customers or suppliers becomes an ethical problem of illicit secrecy.

There is a national schizophrenia concerning antitrust enforcement. The Harvard and Chicago schools have had alternating successes in influencing antitrust enforcement by administrators, prosecutors, and courts. This poses ethical dilemmas for business managers, who find it difficult to know what is required of them. It encourages companies to test the limits of the current mood of antitrust enforcement by going beyond what is apparently permissible and by seeking to influence enforcement through campaign contributions. It is also argued that smaller firms misuse the antitrust laws to intimidate larger firms. Ethical questions are clearly presented whenever the legal process is subverted for private gain in such ways.

Antitrust Exemptions

Antitrust regulation of some industries, such as insurance companies and financial institutions, is the responsibility of government agencies other than the FTC. This prevents duplicative and unnecessary antitrust enforcement in these industries. To ensure their survival, some industries are permitted to more freely use restraints of trade than would be legal for other industries. For example, intellectual property owners receive government-granted monopolies. The holders of patents, copyrights, and trademarks are encouraged to innovate by granting them exclusive rights to exploit the product of their creativity by receiving monopoly profits. Congress and the courts have also granted antitrust exemptions to certain industries. These exemptions are narrowly construed under the strict constructionism policy. Courts have little flexibility to exempt new variations of an exempt activity unless the new variant is almost identical to the original exempt activity. A number of laws create exemptions for the encouragement of exports, R&D, and production joint ventures and are discussed in Chapter 17.

Agricultural Cooperatives The Clayton Act specifically exempts nonprofit agricultural cooperatives organized to provide mutual assistance to farmers. The *Capper-Volstead Act* extended this exemption to "persons engaged in the production of agricultural products such as farmers, planters, ranchmen, dairymen, or nut and fruit growers." Fishermen's cooperatives are also exempt. The exemption applies only to "persons engaged in agricultural production" and not to packing houses or associations involved in both production and distribution. The court's unwillingness to extend this exemption to packing houses illustrates strict constructionism.

Labor Organizations The *National Labor Relations Act,* discussed further in Chapter 19, is considered a sufficient regulatory program for labor unions. The antitrust laws do not apply to most labor union activities that pursue their members' welfare. However, court action may be appropriate if labor unions conspire to restrain trade. Labor union activities that provide aid to nonlabor groups or that tend to create monopolies or control marketing are not exempt. For example, labor agreements that require the employer to avoid dealing with a supplier or a customer may be anticompetitive. Such agreements will be enforceable only if they are designed to protect a legitimate labor union interest.

State Action Restraints of trade or monopolizations that result from valid governmental actions are exempt from the Sherman Act under the **state action** exemption.[6] For example, state licensing of liquor stores or firearm sales often creates oligopolies that restrict the number of sellers, an anticompetitive condition. These are not illegal restraints of trade because the state licenses are for the public's protection. It is believed that adequate supervision provided by the state's regulation justifies the exemption.

state action
Exemption under the antitrust laws for valid governmental actions.

For the state action exemption to apply, there must be a clearly defined state policy permitting or requiring the particular activity or restraint. The exemption does not apply to nongovernmental functions the state supplies by itself. For example, the state action exemption did not protect (1) alleged conspiracies by municipally owned utilities to exclude the services from utilities outside the municipality and (2) a conspiracy between a city's sports stadium and its airport authority to exclude a particular brand of beer sold at both facilities. The Sherman Act was violated when the city of Boulder, Colorado, prevented a cable television company from expanding its service territory.[7] Boulder's action in that case was not taken pursuant to a valid and clearly articulated state policy.

Regulated Industries Prior to 1944, the insurance industry was not considered a part of interstate commerce, so antitrust regulation of insurance was prohibited. The McCarran-Ferguson Act passed in 1945 to continue this special exemption if there is state regulation of premium rates, selling and advertising of policies, and insurance agent licensing. However, the insurance industry is not exempt for activities outside the sale of policies. For example, it may be illegal for an insurance company to boycott, coerce, or intimidate its competitors.

Stock exchanges have a limited form of antitrust exemption because they are considered necessary to support the regulatory framework of the securities laws. Bank and other financial institution mergers are exempt from antitrust laws because they are regulated by federal and state agencies, such as the Federal Reserve Board, the Comptroller of the Currency, the Federal Deposit Insurance Corporation, and the Office of Thrift Supervision. The exemption for formerly regulated transportation industries is largely removed now although there is uncertainty about which regulator has jurisdiction. A similar problem will probably accompany deregulation of telecommunications.

Professions and Sports For many years, some professionals such as lawyers and engineers were also exempt from antitrust enforcement. However, there was no overwhelming justification for this exemption. As a result, local bar associations' "minimum-fee schedules" for attorneys' services are now considered illegal as price-fixing.[8] The ethical code of engineers once prohibited competitive bidding for engagements to avoid unsafe cost cutting. However, the rule effectively created an illegal agreement among competing engineers to refrain from discussing price with customers.

Most professional sports involve at least some restrictive actions among club owners, players' representatives, and facility owners (e.g., arenas, stadiums). For

---

[6] *Parker v. Brown,* 317 U.S. 341 (1943).

[7] *Community Communications Co. v. City of Boulder, Colorado,* 455 U.S. 40 (1982).

[8] *Goldfarb v. Virginia State Bar,* 421 U.S. 773 (1975).

example, the limits on "free agency" prohibit players from moving between teams. Except for baseball, none of the professional sports are entitled to antitrust exemption. The Supreme Court exempted professional baseball in 1922, 1953, and again in 1972. However, the baseball exemption is probably an aberration inconsistent with other laws, and the 1994–1995 baseball strike has raised concern that the exemption should be repealed. Some argue that the owners colluded to impose the salary cap.

Political Action Groups of businesses may join together to take mutually advantageous political action without violating the Sherman Act. The Supreme Court has refused to apply the Sherman Act to bona fide political activities of competitors even if their objective is noncompetitive legislation, regulations, or administrative action. The *Noerr-Pennington* doctrine is based on two First Amendment rights: freedom of speech and the right to petition the government for redress of grievances.[9] However, a *sham* exception to the Noerr doctrine has developed that does not exempt intentional efforts to harass a competitor. For example, the purposeful interference with potential competitors' access to either the courts or regulatory agencies is not protected under *Noerr.* Conspiracy with a foreign government agency to restrain competition is also not protected.

INTERNATIONAL PERSPECTIVE AND COMMENTARY

EXTRATERRITORIAL ANTITRUST ENFORCEMENT

The Sherman and Clayton Acts have broad applicability to both domestic and foreign anticompetitive acts if there is an impact in the United States. From time to time, regulators, private parties, and commentators argue that U.S. antitrust laws should apply to foreign firms' anticompetitive practices. However, as discussed in Chapter 2, U.S. courts examine several factors before applying U.S. antitrust law to the activities of foreign firms. There are also several principles of international law that restrict antitrust litigation against foreign firms. The *act of state* doctrine and *sovereign immunity* prevent U.S. courts from extraterritorial application of U.S. laws if the foreign activity is sponsored by a foreign government. For example, these principles prevent challenges to collusion among Japanese firms because these activities are promoted by MITI, Japan's Ministry of Trade and Industry. Under the principle of *comity,* a foreign court will generally refuse to apply U.S. antitrust laws unless the nation has similar laws. However, a foreign firm's operations may have assets on U.S. soil. These may be held liable for antitrust violations if there is an anticompetitive impact in the United States. Strong U.S. antitrust enforcement also risks trade retaliation by foreign governments.

Foreign nations can frustrate U.S. antitrust suits against their home industries with *blocking laws* that prohibit compliance with U.S. pretrial discovery requests. These laws were passed in the 1970s by nations like Canada, France, and the United Kingdom after some aggressive U.S. antitrust enforcement efforts against the uranium cartel. For example, it is common for antitrust plaintiffs to request numerous documents from foreign firms crucial to proving their case. Blocking laws often require precompliance notification to the foreign government, enabling

[9] *Eastern Railroad Presidents Conference v. Noerr Motor Freight, Inc.,* 365 U.S. 127 (1961).

foreign regulators to bar compliance with a U.S. production of documents request. This effectively frustrates the antitrust suit.

Despite these obstacles, U.S. antitrust regulators are becoming tougher when the anticompetitive activities of foreign companies and their governments restrain U.S. exports. For example, when the DOJ can exercise jurisdiction within the bounds of international comity, it is bringing cases against foreign entities involved in group boycotts, collusive pricing, and exclusionary activities. This policy was changed during the Bush administration to protect U.S. producers. The previous policy barred enforcement unless U.S. consumers suffered harm. The DOJ is now pressuring the Japanese Fair Trade Commission (JFTC) into permitting private suits against Japanese companies by U.S. citizens. The DOJ is also pressuring the JFTC into permitting U.S. companies to join the Japanese trade associations that make and enforce restrictive trade rules.

MONOPOLIES

Monopolies are the basic ill the Sherman Act sought to cure. Monopoly power enables the monopolies to fix or control prices, reduce output, and exclude competitors. Under the Sherman Act, an illegal monopoly arises when monopoly power is intentionally exercised by acts of monopolization.

Monopoly Power

The most fundamental question in a monopoly case concerns the existence of monopoly power and its exercise by the defendant. Economists define monopoly power on the basis of the *elasticity of demand.* Perfectly competitive markets are highly elastic; thus, when the price of a product rises, consumers can quickly switch their purchases to similar or substitute products. Conversely, when the price of a product falls, consumers can quickly shift to purchase that product. The markets for investment securities and certain foodstuffs are fairly elastic. There is seldom significant monopolization in highly elastic markets.

In an *inelastic market,* consumer demand is relatively unresponsive to small price changes. The greater market power of firms in inelastic markets enables them to control prices to a greater extent. An *imperfect market,* characterized by inelastic demand, lends varying degrees of monopoly power to monopolists, oligopolists, and monopolistic competitors. Firms of these kinds may raise their prices without losing all of the customers because substitute products are not suitably equivalent as replacements. The market for patented or copyrighted component parts (microprocessor chips) is often inelastic because buyers cannot easily substitute the functionally different chips made by other manufacturers. Defining the relevant market is the first step in measuring monopoly power.

Relevant Market

The idea of a monopoly cannot make sense without some boundary on the alleged monopoly in a market being defined. The monopolist's illegal use of market power must exist over (1) an identifiable geographic area and (2) a particular product. The plaintiff must define this **relevant market** in cases involving monopolies, mergers,

relevant market
First determination in assessing monopoly power in a product line and geographic region.

and restraints of trade. The relevant market comprises all the producers of products or services that are functionally interchangeable and reasonably available to the same pool of consumers.

Geographic Market The monopolist's alleged illegal exercise of market power is relevant only to the specific geographic area within which that behavior affects competition. Usually, evidence is presented concerning the buying patterns of existing consumers. A region constitutes a geographic market if it is reasonable for consumers within the region to obtain the product or service produced from any seller including the alleged monopolist. A particular geographic market may be local (e.g., city, county, metropolitan area), regional (e.g., state, multiple states), or national. Generally, geographic markets are limited or bounded by the costs of transportation and by the ease with which consumers can gain access to other sellers. Within a particular geographic market, there may also be *submarkets* in which a group of local sellers compete more directly. For example, the shops in a neighborhood commercial area could comprise a submarket within a broader city geographic shopping market.

Product Market The product market is determined by consumers' preferences and by their willingness to substitute physically different products for the same basic purpose or use. The issue is usually whether two products are perceived as reasonably interchangeable or substitutable. Courts examine the price, use, and quality of all reasonable substitutes to make this determination.

cross-elasticity of demand
Substitutability between two substitute products, computed as percentage change in demand for one product divided by percentage change in the price of substitute.

The determination of **cross-elasticity of demand** is a method of analysis that measures the relationship between two possible substitutes. Cross-elasticity of demand is defined as the percentage of change in the quantity demanded of one product divided by the percentage of change in the substitute product's price. Where cross-elasticity is positive, the two goods compared are somewhat substitutable for each other and may be considered part of the same market (e.g., butter versus margarine). Negative cross-elasticity characterizes complementary products that are not substitutable for each other, but are often purchased together (e.g., automobiles and tires). Cross-elasticity analysis is not a perfect method of determining product markets because consumers' willingness to substitute dissimilar products may change significantly at different price levels. For example, someone may be willing to ride a bus to work only if doing so is significantly cheaper than commuting by automobile.

As more positive cross-elasticities are discovered between the monopolist's products and other products, the relevant market expands. On the other hand, if there are no reasonable substitutes (low cross-elasticities of demand), the relevant product market will be small. A particular firm's market share in a market with many direct competitors and/or many substitutes is usually small. By contrast, a particular firm's market share in a market with few competitors and substitutes may be large. There is a natural tendency for plaintiffs to allege there are few substitutes (low cross-elasticities), and defendants usually allege there are many substitutes (high cross-elasticities). How might cross-elasticities analysis be used in a case involving a common household product such as food wrap? The following classic case illustrates the dilemma faced by courts attempting to define a relevant product market.

United States v. E.I. du Pont de Nemours & Co.

351 U.S. 377 (1956)
United States Supreme Court

Du Pont produced almost 75 percent of the cellophane (plastic food wrap) sold in the United States. Cellophane sales constituted less than 20 percent of all "flexible packaging material." The DOJ challenged du Pont's market dominance on cellophane, arguing other flexible wraps (e.g., wax paper, aluminum foil) were neither substantially interchangeable in use nor priced similarly. Under §2 of the Sherman Act, du Pont was convicted of monopolization in the cellophane market rather than the flexible packaging material market.

Justice Reed delivered the opinion of the Court.

If cellophane is the "market" that du Pont is found to dominate, it may be assumed it does have monopoly power over that "market." Monopoly power is the power to control prices or exclude competition. It seems apparent that du Pont's power to set the price of cellophane has been limited only by the competition afforded by other flexible packaging materials. Moreover, it may be practically impossible for anyone to commence manufacturing cellophane without full access to du Pont's technique. However, du Pont has no power to prevent competition from other wrapping materials. The trial court consequently had to determine whether competition from the other wrappings prevent du Pont from possessing monopoly power in violation of §2. Price and competition are so intimately entwined that any discussion of theory must treat them as one.

If a large number of buyers and sellers deal freely in a standardized product, such as salt or wheat, we have complete or pure competition. Patents, on the other hand, furnish the most familiar type of classic monopoly. As the producers of a standardized product bring about significant differentiations of quality, design, or packaging in the product that permit differences of use, competition becomes to a greater or less degree incomplete and the producer's power over price and competition greater over his article and its use, according to the differentiation he is able to create and maintain. A retail seller may have in one sense a monopoly on certain trade because of location, as an isolated country store or filling station, or because no one else makes a product of just the quality or attractiveness of his product, as for example in cigarettes. Thus one can theorize that we have monopolistic competition in every nonstandardized commodity with each manufacturer having power over the price and production of his own product. However, this power that, let us say, automobile or soft-drink manufacturers have over their trademarked products is not the power that makes an illegal monopoly. Illegal power must be appraised in terms of the competitive market for the product.

Determination of the competitive market for commodities depends on how different from one another are the offered commodities in character or use, how far buyers will go to substitute one commodity for another. For example, one can think of building materials as in commodity competition but one could hardly say that brick competed with steel or wood or cement or stone in the meaning of Sherman Act litigation; the products are too different. This is the interindustry competition emphasized by some economists.

On the other hand, there are certain differences in the formulae for soft drinks but one can hardly say that each one is an illegal monopoly. Whatever the market may be, we hold that control of price or competition establishes the existence of monopoly power under §2.

The Relevant Market—When a product is controlled by one interest, without substitutes available in the market, there is monopoly power. Because most products have possible substitutes, we cannot give "that infinite range" to the definition of substitutes. Nor is it a proper interpretation of the Sherman Act to require that products be fungible to be considered in the relevant market.

But where there are market alternatives that buyers may readily use for their purposes, illegal monopoly does not exist merely because the product said to be monopolized differs from others. If it were not so, only physically identical products would be a part of the market. To accept the Government's argument, we would have to conclude that the manufacturers of plain as well as moistureproof cellophane were monopolists, and so with films such as Pliofilm, foil, glassine, polyethylene, and Saran, for each of these wrapping materials is distinguishable.

An element for consideration as to cross-elasticity of demand between products is the responsiveness of the sales of one product to price changes of the other. If a slight decrease in the price of cellophane causes a considerable number of customers of other flexible wrappings to switch to cellophane, it would be an indication that a high cross-elasticity of demand exists between them; that the products compete in the same market. The court below held that the "[g]reat sensitivity of customers in the flexible packaging markets to price or quality changes" prevented du Pont from possessing monopoly control over price. The record sustains these findings.

We conclude that cellophane's interchangeability with the other materials mentioned suffices to make it a part of this flexible packaging material market.

Case Questions

1. What is cross-elasticity of demand? How is this measure used to determine the relevant market?
2. What approach should be used to determine market share in cases in which the defendant is the only producer of the product? How would the answer be different if you presumed the defendant held a valid patent on the product?
3. How might the cross-elasticity analysis have been conducted differently if the Court had considered the different price ranges of the flexible wrapping products?

Refinement of the Product Market Analysis Although the Supreme Court's analysis in *du Pont* advanced the understanding of relevant product markets significantly, there seem to be obvious flaws in the analysis. When considering all forms of flexible package wrap, the Court should have considered specific consumer preferences between any two products for a particular use. Some substitute products are clearly not substitutable for some uses. For example, only aluminum foil can be used in barbecue grilling, whereas microwave ovens usually require nonmetallic food wrap. The Supreme Court's inclusion of all aluminum foil sales in the market makes the impossible assumption that all aluminum foil users could switch to cellophane or wax paper for all their uses of aluminum foil. A better analysis than that of the Supreme Court would provide for adjustments in the calculation of demand for substitute products that reflect reasonable estimates of the amount of nonsubstitutability. Nonsubstitutability helps explain why consumers are seldom indifferent in choosing between substitutes, a fact reflected in the calculation of cross-elasticity of demand. If this refinement in analysis had been used in the *du Pont* case, a smaller overall product market than *all* "flexible wrapping material" would have been used, and du Pont might have been found closer to monopolization.

The cross-elasticity analysis used may be flawed for another reason. If a monopolist is already charging monopoly prices, consumers may be willing to switch to less perfect substitutes only if the substitutes are much lower in price. This suggests that imperfect substitutes are not acceptable if the price of the more perfect monopolized product is still at historically "reasonable" levels. Consider the packaging of sandwiches. Resealable plastic bags are generally considered superior to wax paper. If the two products are priced the same, most people will use plastic bags. Only if wax paper is significantly cheaper will some people substitute it for plastic bags. In the *du Pont* case, the alleged substitutes were not perfectly substitutable. Thus, du Pont's control over the cellophane market was somewhat closer to monopolization of the flexible packaging material market than the Court held.

The *du Pont* case exemplifies how courts can expand the relevant market to protect alleged monopolists from prosecution. In some later cases, cross-elasticity analysis was restricted somewhat, resulting in a narrower product market definition. For example, professional championship boxing matches are considered a market distinct from other boxing matches. Championship matches are the "cream" of the boxing business, appealing to a broader audience than other boxing matches. A similar analysis could be used to separate the major league baseball market from the minor leagues. Gospel music is considered a market distinct from popular music. A sub-market for the leasing of large IBM mainframes was differentiated from the market for purchasing the same computers.

Market Share

Once the court has defined the relevant product and geographic markets, it must determine the alleged monopolist's market power within that market. Market power is typically measured as the percentage of the relevant market the alleged monopolist controls: the **market share.** This requires computing a fraction; the numerator is the defendant's unit sales, and the denominator is the total unit sales of all competitors. There is no litmus test for determining what market share constitutes a monopoly. Such percentages as 90 percent, 85 percent, and 75 percent are usually considered monopolies. Market shares of 20 percent or 50 percent usually are not. However, in the analysis of mergers, discussed later in this chapter, a lower market share resulting after the merger may be sufficient to prohibit the merger.

market share
Percentage of the relevant market held by the firm in question.

Monopolization

The mere existence of monopoly power does not violate the Sherman Act. Indeed, some industries (e.g., utilities) are more efficient when operated as a monopoly. A monopoly becomes illegal when market power is used illegally. This is a **monopolization,** which represents the intentional use of monopoly power to gain an illegal monopoly.

monopolization
Intentional acts to obtain and maintain an illegal monopoly.

The *abuse theory of monopoly* is derived from the conduct enforcement approach. Monopolies exist only where a firm with monopoly power abuses its market power by undertaking purposeful acts to harm competitors and consumers. Market power that is acquired by historical accident or obtained or maintained by selling better products, using business savvy, or applying superior skill, foresight, and industry is neither illegal nor abusive. What inferences may be drawn from a producer's purposeful acts to forestall the entry of competitors into the market? The following case illustrates how the proof of monopolistic intent may be inferred from circumstantial evidence.

United States v. Aluminum Co. of America

148 F.2d 416 (2d Cir. 1945)
United States Court of Appeals, Second Circuit

Up to the time of suit, Aluminum Company of America (Alcoa) was the only producer of "virgin" aluminum ingot (not from recycled scrap) in the United States. Alcoa argued that it was not a monopolist because markets existed for imported and recycled aluminum ingot. Alcoa also argued that it had not acquired its position of market dominance through illegal exclusionary acts. Alcoa's profit margins of about 10 percent were not considered as high as a monopolist's profit. Nevertheless, an illegal monopolization can exist even with lower than monopolist profit. The DOJ sought to have Alcoa dissolved but had to appeal from a trial court decision in favor of Alcoa.

Hand, Circuit Judge

Many people believe that possession of unchallenged economic power deadens initiative, discourages thrift and depresses energy; that immunity from competition is a narcotic, and rivalry is a stimulant, to industrial progress; that the spur of constant stress is necessary to counteract an inevitable disposition to let well enough alone. Such people believe that competitors, versed in the craft as no consumer can be, will be quick to detect opportunities for saving and new shifts in production, and be eager to profit by them. In any event the mere fact that a producer, having command of the domestic market, has not been able to make more than a "fair" profit, is no evidence that a "fair" profit could not have been made at lower prices. True, it might have been thought adequate to condemn only those monopolies which could not show that they had exercised the highest possible ingenuity, had anticipated every conceivable improvement, simulated every possible demand. No doubt, that would be one way of dealing with the matter, although it would imply constant scrutiny and constant supervision, such as courts are unable to provide. Be that as it may, that was not the way that Congress chose; it did not condone "good trusts" and condemn "bad" ones; it forbade all. Moreover, in so doing it was not necessarily actuated by economic motives alone. It is possible, because of its indirect social or moral effect, to prefer a system of small producers, each dependent for his success upon his own skill and character, to one in which the great mass of those engaged must accept the direction of a few.

It does not follow because "Alcoa" had such a monopoly, that it "monopolized" the ingot market; it may not have achieved monopoly; monopoly may have been thrust upon it. If it had been a combination of existing smelters which united the whole industry and controlled the production of all aluminum ingot, it would certainly have "monopolized" the market.

This notion has usually been expressed by saying that size does not determine guilt; that there must be some "exclusion" of competitors; that the growth must be something else than "natural" or "normal"; that there must be a "wrongful intent," or some other specific intent; or that some "unduly" coercive means must be used.

What engendered these compunctions is reasonably plain: persons may unwittingly find themselves in possession of a monopoly, automatically so to say; that is, without having intended either to put an end to existing competition, or to prevent competition from arising when none had existed, they may become monopolists by force of accident.

A market may, for example, be so limited that it is impossible to produce at all and meet the cost of production except by a plant large enough to supply the whole demand. Or there may be changes in taste or in cost which drive out all but one purveyor. A single producer may be the survivor out of a group of active competitors, merely by virtue of his superior skill, foresight and industry. In such cases a strong argument can be made that, although the result may expose the public to the evils of monopoly, the Act does not mean to condemn the resultant of those very forces which it is its prime object to foster. The successful competitor, having been urged to compete, must not be turned upon when he wins.

It would completely misconstrue "Alcoa's" position in 1940 to hold that it was the passive beneficiary of a monopoly, following upon an involuntary elimination of competitors by automatically operative economic forces.

There were at least one or two abortive attempts to enter the industry, but "Alcoa" effectively anticipated and forestalled all competition, and succeeded in holding the field alone. True, it stimulated demand and opened new uses for the metal, but not without making sure that it could supply what it had evoked. There is no dispute as to this; "Alcoa" avows it as evidence of the skill, energy and initiative with which it has always conducted its business; as a reason why, having won its way by fair means, it should be commended, and not dismembered.

The only question is whether it falls within the exception established in favor of those who do not seek, but cannot avoid, the control of a market. . . . It was not inevitable that it should always anticipate increases in the demand for ingot and be prepared to supply them. Nothing compelled it to keep doubling and redoubling its capacity before others entered the field. It insists that it never excluded competitors; but we can think of no more effective exclusion than progressively to embrace each new opportunity as it opened, and to face every newcomer with new capacity already geared into a great organization, having the advantage of experience, trade connections and the elite of personnel. Only in case we interpret "exclusion" as limited to maneuvers not honestly industrial, but actuated solely by a desire to prevent competition, can such a course, indefatigably pursued, be deemed not "exclusionary." So to limit it would in our judgment emasculate the Act; would permit just such consolidations as it was designed to prevent.

In order to fall within §2, the monopolist must have both the power to monopolize, and the intent to monopolize. To read the passage as demanding any "specific" intent makes nonsense of it, for no monopolist monopolizes unconscious of what he is doing. So here, "Alcoa" meant to keep, and did keep, that complete and exclusive hold upon the ingot market with which it started. That was to "monopolize" that market, however innocently it otherwise proceeded.

We may start therefore with the premise that to have combined 90 percent of the producers of ingot would have been to "monopolize" the ingot market; and, so far as concerns the public interest, it can make no difference whether an existing competition is put an end to, or whether prospective competition is prevented.

Case Questions

1. What evidence of Alcoa's interference with the development of competitors could be termed "monopolization"? Would these actions have been legal if Alcoa did not already have a monopoly position?
2. What evidence could be used to prove intent to monopolize? Which of Alcoa's actions were circumstantial evidence of this intent?
3. What is the alternative of how a producer might have market dominance "thrust upon" it? How does this justify holding a monopoly?

The types of monopolistic acts that constitute a monopoly vary considerably. Whenever a monopolist engages in predatory and coercive conduct in direct violation of the antitrust laws, monopolization intent can easily be inferred. However, acts considered legal in many circumstances may be illegal if the monopolist's market power is employed with monopolistic intent. For example, conduct that is intended to prevent the entry of competitors, such as systematically increasing production capacity in anticipation of new demand, is illegal. In another case, IBM's policy of leasing but never selling computers was considered exclusionary and unlawful. It is alleged that Microsoft monopolizes several of the PC software markets by preannouncing software products long before they are ready to sell to preempt consumer purchases from competitors, the so-called vaporware problem. Microsoft's intentional efforts at monopolization also allegedly include selectively giving other software firms advance copies of operating systems, tying favorable prices on operating systems to PC manufacturers that promise only to offer Microsoft's systems. These practices allegedly harm rival operating systems and give Microsoft an alleged advantage in developing its own word processors, spreadsheets, and other PC applications.

Predatory Pricing *Predatory pricing,* pricing below the producer's marginal cost, may also constitute deliberate and purposeful acts of monopolization. Although predatory pricing results in losses on sales, it often forces competitors out of business, thereby permitting later price increases to recoup earlier losses. If a monopolist lowers prices to undercut or restrict the entry of competitors, the intent to monopolize may be inferred. *Marginal cost* is the manufacturer's additional expense to produce one more unit beyond the number produced up to that point. *Average variable cost* is the average of all the variable expenses for all of the units produced. Some commentators have urged that pricing below average variable cost should be presumed predatory.

Predatory pricing is monopolistic if it tends to immediately eliminate rivals, thus creating a monopoly that enables the seller to recoup losses later. A similar tactic is to charge monopoly prices in one geographic market or in another product market and then lower prices in another market to drive out competitors. Discriminatory pricing allows the monopolist to undercut potential competition by taking temporary losses that are made up with profits taken at other times or profits made in other geographic or product markets.

Attempts to Monopolize

The Sherman Act prohibits "attempts to monopolize" even in cases in which the alleged monopolist does not possess clear monopoly power. The plaintiff must prove that the defendant employed methods, means, and practices that would, if successful, accomplish monopolization and that, though falling short of monopolization, nevertheless approached it so closely as to create a dangerous probability of monopolization.

The defendant in such cases must be proved to have had the specific intent of excluding competitors through the exercise of monopoly power. The "specific intent" standard requires a higher burden of proof than in monopolization cases. Intent may be inferred from unfair conduct. For example, inducing others to boycott a competitor's product, using discriminatory pricing, or refusing to deal with a particular customer are evidence of the specific intent to attempt monopolization. If two or more persons combine to do such acts, their agreement may also constitute a separate crime: the illegal *conspiracy* to monopolize.

MERGERS

Mergers receive considerable attention from several perspectives. Mergers typically involve struggles between insiders and outsiders for corporate control. Many of these corporate control battles occur in the securities markets so SEC regulation is involved. Most mergers must be approved by shareholders involving state corporate law. Mergers also fundamentally involve antitrust law if the merged firm thereby obtains monopoly power. Antitrust law poses a difficult question of industrial organization: Will the market structure resulting from a merger or an acquisition create an illegal monopoly?

Types of Mergers and Business Combinations

Mergers are only one of several methods of expansion. Firms may raise capital to finance growth by generating cash flow internally or externally in the public securities markets. However, it is often quicker and easier to acquire an existing firm through a merger, consolidation, purchase of assets, or acquisition of a subsidiary. A *merger* brings together two independent firms of which one survives and the other is dissolved. A *consolidation* combines two independent firms; both are terminated and replaced by a newly created combined entity. A *purchase of assets* involves the transfer of an acquired firm's assets to the acquiring firm without the necessity of dissolving either firm. In an *acquisition,* a firm acquired by another firm may operate as a separate division or subsidiary, though a merger may eventually result. Although these distinctions can be important under corporation and securities laws, for the purposes of antitrust analysis, all of these transactions are considered mergers.

Early interpretations of the Sherman Act held that mergers destroyed the competition that previously existed between the merged firms. Thus, most mergers were prohibited based simply on the concentration of power that would result. However, the courts eventually refused to use the Sherman Act to restrict mergers. Congress then passed the Clayton Act to specifically prohibit mergers tending to lessen competition.

Clayton Antitrust Act, §7

> . . . no person engaged in commerce, or in any activity affecting commerce shall acquire, directly or indirectly, the whole or any part of stock or other share capital . . . [or]
>
> . . . the whole or any part of the assets of another person engaged also in commerce or in any activity affecting commerce, where in any line of commerce or in any activity affecting commerce in any section of the country, the effect of such acquisition may be substantially to lessen competition, or tend to create a monopoly.

Section 7 was amended in 1950 by the Celler-Kefauver Act to (1) prohibit noncompetitive market structures (e.g., oligopolies, monopolistic competition), (2) encourage internal growth and expansion, and (3) preserve local industrial control and small business viability. Celler-Kefauver also closed a major loophole in the Clayton Act by including the sale of assets as covered activity. The amendments apply to all three of the basic merger variations: horizontal mergers between competitors, vertical mergers between suppliers and customers, and conglomerate mergers with firms in other industries.

Horizontal Merger Analysis

Although many mergers have aspects of a horizontal, vertical, or conglomerate nature, it is most useful to first examine **horizontal mergers.** These are combinations of firms that compete at the same level of production in the same industry, as shown in Figure 16–4. Regulation of horizontal mergers is the least controversial and employs the basic method used in all merger analysis. Merger analysis is very similar to monopoly analysis because the court must determine the relevant market and market share controlled by the merged firms. A merger may be prohibited if the change in market dominance results in a substantial lessening of competition in the relevant market.

horizontal merger Combination of two competing firms at the same level of production.

Relevant Geographic Market In a merger analysis, the court must first define the relevant "line of commerce." Each line of commerce has a geographic parameter and a product parameter. Mergers are prohibited when they tend to substantially lessen competition in a particular "section of the country." The product markets are defined on a local, regional, or national basis and geographic submarkets may also exist. Usually, an inquiry is undertaken into geographic substitutability for the particular region claimed as the relevant market. For example, evidence that buyers have shifted purchases between regions would tend to permit combination of the regions into a

FIGURE 16-4 Horizontal Merger

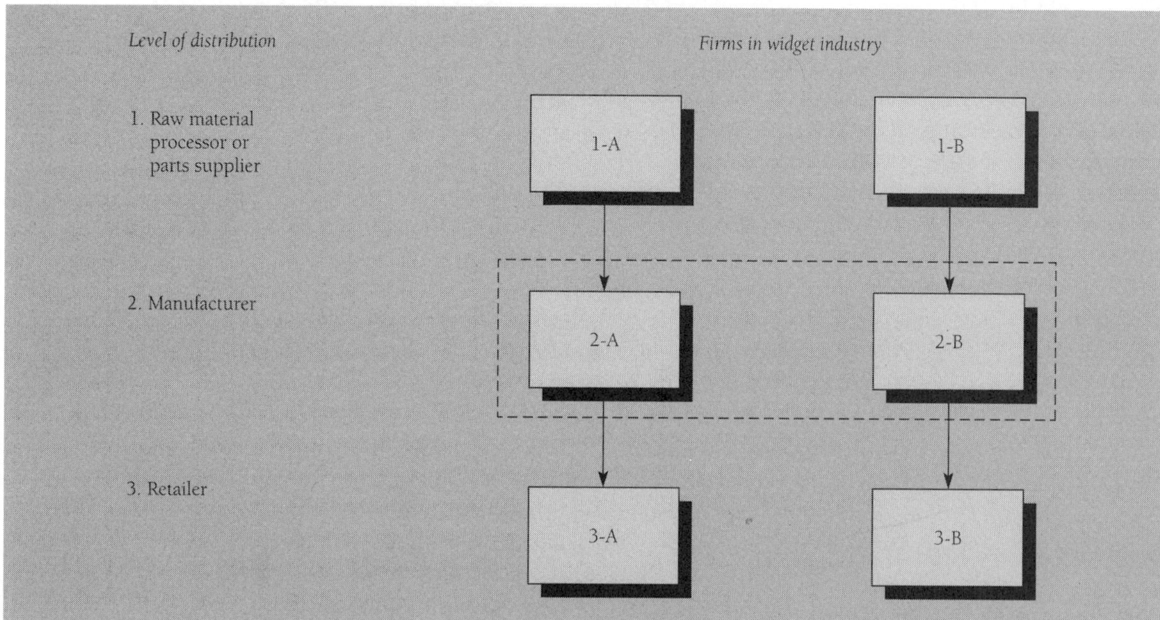

Horizontal mergers occur between competitors at the same level of distribution in the same industry—here the widget industry. Horizontal mergers may reduce competition among competitors, permitting producers to control price, production quantity, quality, and other features (e.g., services).

single market. However, as transportation costs increase, it becomes more difficult for customers to switch between producers in different regions. When highly correlated changes in product prices occur in two neighboring regions, this implies the regions are geographically substitutable.

Relevant Product Market The next step examines the relevant product market. Substitute products and their cross-elasticities of demand are identified, and consumers' perceptions of product substitutability are examined. There may also be inquiries into the correlation of price movements between similar products, suggesting substitutability.

In merger cases, it is necessary to identify all of the major firms that produce in a relevant market and to compute their individual market shares. Firms may also be included if they are capable of (1) switching to produce the relevant product, (2) reconditioning other products to make them good substitutes for that product, or (3) vertically integrating into the relevant product market. As in monopolization cases, defendants have an incentive to expand the market definition so that their merger will appear insignificant.

Justice Department Merger Guidelines Since the 1982 revision of its merger guidelines, DOJ approves or opposes mergers on the basis of *market concentration,* an indication of the potential for exercise of monopoly power. Greater concentration is found where there are fewer firms, each with larger market shares. There is less concentration where more firms compete. As the number of firms grows, the market approaches the antitrust objective of perfect competition.

The *Herfindahl Index* is used to calculate market concentration by summing the squares of each firm's individual market share. High Herfindahl numbers result if the market is dominated by monopolists or oligopolists with large market shares. For example, if just one firm in the relevant market had 75 percent of the market, the Herfindahl Index would be at least $75^2 = 5{,}625$. By contrast, if 10 firms in the relevant market each possessed a market share of 10 percent, the Herfindahl Index would be $10^2 + 10^2 + 10^2 + 10^2 + 10^2 + 10^2 + 10^2 + 10^2 + 10^2 + 10^2 = 10 * 100 = 1{,}000$. The Herfindahl Index can range from 10,000 in the case of a pure monopoly (100^2) to less than 1 in a perfectly competitive market.

It is unlikely that DOJ will attack any mergers for which the Herfindahl Index remains below 1,000. If the index lies between 1,000 and 1,800, DOJ will challenge a merger that results in an increase of 100 or more Herfindahl points. For index numbers above 1,800, DOJ will challenge a merger that results in an increase of more than 50 points. Markets with Herfindahl indexes greater than 1,800 are considered highly concentrated. The Herfindahl Index does not have the force of law, but it is used by DOJ to indicate when prosecution should be undertaken. DOJ can adjust its challenges to mergers by simply changing these thresholds. For example, it would be more lenient to raise the thresholds to 1,200 and 2,000 and more strict to lower them to 800 and 1,500.

Substantial Lessening of Competition Courts hearing merger cases must determine whether or not the resulting market share of the combined firms will probably lead to a substantial lessening of competition. Courts usually determine whether, as a preventive measure, a merger should be prohibited. Unlike court action under the Sherman Act, there is no necessity to prove attempts at predatory conduct or monopolistic acts. Probabilities, not "ephemeral possibilities," must be demonstrated by the party attacking the merger. DOJ considers the competitive impact of most mergers. Most parties will not pursue a merger if DOJ publicly opposes it.

The standard used by the federal courts to judge the anticompetitive effect of a merger is often different from the DOJ's standard to challenge a merger. Courts prohibit mergers if the newly created firm "controls an undue percentage share" of the relevant market and it results in "a significant increase in concentration." In one case, a prohibited merger would have resulted in a combined firm with a 30 percent market share. In another case, the absorption of a small, aggressive, and innovative firm by Alcoa was prohibited because the merger adversely affected competition.

In *United States v. Von's Grocery Co.*,[10] the Supreme Court upheld a DOJ challenge to a merger between two grocery store chains in the Los Angeles area: Von's and Shopping Bag. The combined sales of the two chains would have been only 7.5 percent of the metropolitan Los Angeles grocery market. However, the Court noted that these two firms had experienced tremendous growth and the mom and pop grocery stores were in steady decline. Merger analysis may consider industry trends toward consolidation to prevent a merger with short-term procompetitive effects but which would result in a concentration permitting collusion in the future. Even though mom and pop stores resemble the atomized perfect competition model, this form raises the question of whether they can produce the lowest consumer prices.

[10] *United States v. Von's Grocery Co.*, 384 U.S. 270 (1966).

FIGURE 16-5 Vertical Merger

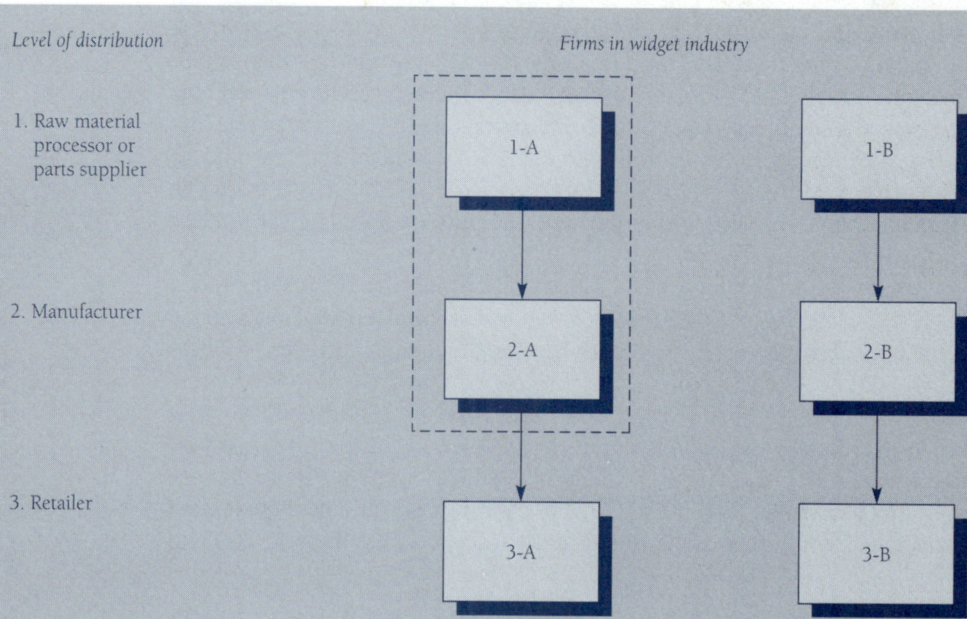

Vertical mergers occur between firms in the same chain of distribution, in the same industry—here the widget industry. Vertical mergers may erect harmful barriers to entry, futher industry concentration, and remove the beneficial discipline that comes from active competition at all levels of production.

Vertical Merger Analysis

vertical merger
Combination of two firms in supplier–customer relationship.

Vertical mergers combine firms that stand in a supplier-customer relationship along the same chain of distribution, as illustrated in Figure 16–5. The term *vertical integration* has come to describe the result of expansion of producers into the retail or supplier levels. There is a natural tendency for businesses to desire control over customers and suppliers. Vertical mergers enable the resulting firm to squeeze out unintegrated competitors, to limit future competition, and to erect barriers to entry. Vertically integrated firms tend to exclude competitors from sources of supply or from customers, causing a *supply squeeze.* They may also refuse to deal with nonintegrated firms and give preferential allocation of products to their subsidiaries. Allegedly, vertically integrated firms discriminate in price and favor captive customers over nonintegrated competitors.

Mergers between companies attempting vertical integration are subjected to analysis similar to that of horizontal mergers. First, the relevant geographic and product markets are determined. Second, the probable effect of the merger on the foreclosure of competition due to acquisition of excessive market share is analyzed. Third, the courts analyze historical trends toward concentration, the nature and purpose of the merger, and resulting barriers to entry.

Vertical mergers do not immediately result in more concentrated markets, so the analysis of a vertical merger's impact on competition is more difficult than in horizontal merger analysis. The potential foreclosure of competition and resulting barriers to entry by new firms is more important. Barriers to entry from vertical integration are objectionable if potential competitors must thereafter integrate vertically to compete effectively against the merged firm. This makes their entry more difficult. Challenge of vertical mergers is controversial if the vertical integration makes the industry more efficient.

DOJ will challenge a vertical merger if it facilitates collusion in a highly concentrated *upstream market* (concentration at the supplier level). For example, if suppliers own their retail outlets, the prices of competing suppliers are easily seen when the competing suppliers try to sell to another supplier's retail outlets. This can facilitate price-fixing among all suppliers. However, if there are independent and disruptive buyers, then suppliers may be forced to compete for the business of these buyers. Should a vertical merger be prohibited if it might reduce competition among suppliers? The next case illustrates how the potential loss of market discipline and the industry's trend toward concentration are used in the analysis of a vertical merger.

Brown Shoe Co. v. United States

370 U.S. 284 (1962)
United States Supreme Court

The Justice Department brought suit to block a merger between Brown Shoe Company, Inc. (Brown) and G.R. Kinney Company, Inc. (Kinney) as a violation of Section 7 of the Clayton Act. Both companies manufactured shoes and owned or controlled some retail outlets. The trial court found that the proposed merger would substantially lessen competition in the retail shoe market.

Chief Justice Warren delivered the opinion of the Court.

Economic arrangements between companies standing in a supplier–customer relationship are characterized as "vertical." The primary vice of a vertical merger or other arrangement tying a customer to a supplier is that, by foreclosing the competitors of either party from a segment of the market otherwise open to them, the arrangement may act as a "clog on competition," which "deprive[s] . . . rivals of a fair opportunity to compete." Every extended vertical arrangement by its very nature, for at least a time, denies to competitors of the supplier the opportunity to compete for part or all of the trade of the customer-party to the vertical arrangement. However, the Clayton Act does not render unlawful all such vertical arrangements, but forbids only those whose effect "may be substantially to lessen competition, or to tend to create a monopoly" "in any line of commerce in any section of the country."

We agree with the parties and the District Court that insofar as the vertical aspect of this merger is concerned, the relevant geographic market is the entire Nation. The relationships of product value, bulk, weight and consumer demand enable manufacturers to distribute their shoes on a nationwide basis, as Brown and Kinney, in fact, do. The anticompetitive effects of the merger are to be measured within this range of distribution.

The present merger involved neither small companies nor failing companies. In 1955, the date of this merger, Brown was the fourth largest manufacturer in the shoe industry with sales of approximately 25 million pairs of shoes and assets of over $72,000,000, while Kinney had sales of about 8 million pairs of shoes and assets of about $18,000,000. Not only was Brown one of the leading manufacturers of men's, women's, and children's shoes, but Kinney, with over 350 retail outlets, owned and operated the largest independent chain of family shoe stores in the Nation. Thus, in this industry, no merger between a manufacturer and an independent retailer could involve a larger potential market foreclosure. Moreover, it is apparent both from past behavior of Brown, and from the testimony of Brown's President that Brown would use its ownership of Kinney to force Brown shoes into Kinney stores. Thus, in operation this vertical arrangement would be quite analogous to one involving a tying clause. Another important factor to consider is the trend toward concentration in the industry.

Brown argues, however, that the shoe industry is at present composed of a large number of manufacturers and retailers, and that the industry is dynamically competitive. But remaining vigor cannot immunize a merger if the trend in that industry is toward oligopoly. It is the probable effect of the merger upon the future as well as the present which the Clayton Act commands the courts and the Commission to examine.

The District Court's findings convince us that the shoe industry is being subjected to just such a cumulative series of vertical mergers which, if left unchecked, will be likely "substantially to lessen competition."

We reach this conclusion because the trend toward vertical integration in the shoe industry, when combined with Brown's avowed policy of forcing its own shoes upon its retail subsidiaries, may foreclose competition from a substantial share of the markets for men's, women's, and children's shoes, without producing any countervailing competitive, economic, or social advantages.

Case Questions

1. What analytic steps should be taken in a vertical merger case?
2. What impact on vertical merger analysis should be given as evidence of the industry's trend toward vertical integration?

Conglomerate Merger Analysis

conglomerate merger Mergers not classified as horizontal or vertical; usually between firms in different industries or at different levels of production.

Conglomerate mergers include all types of mergers that cannot be classified as horizontal or vertical; they are illustrated in Figure 16–6. Typically, they involve the acquisition of firms in other industries or other product lines and at any level of production. *Product extension* conglomerate mergers allow a firm to acquire complementary product lines that can be used with existing products. For example, a computer manufacturer's acquisition of a software producer would be a product extension merger because software is used with computers. *Market extension* mergers enable the merging firm to operate in new geographic markets. Totally unrelated mergers are often referred to as *diversification mergers.* The diversified firm may smooth out its cash flows, permitting it to profit in other markets when its main market suffers a downturn.

Mergers that result in conglomerates appear to involve little or no anticompetitive effect. However, some structuralists argue that conglomerate mergers tend to reinforce oligopoly conditions in some industries. This further weakens independent firms, eventually leading to the elimination of competition. Large acquiring firms often bring financial resources and the goodwill of popular brand names to the merged firm. This makes it more difficult for independent firms to compete or enter the market. After a conglomerate merger, the larger merged firm may use discriminatory and exclusionary practices to discipline smaller competitors, thereby lessening competition.

potential entrant effect Firm apparently able to enter market so it exerts competitive discipline on existing competitors.

It is also argued that conglomerate mergers eliminate the **potential entrant effect,** or *potential competitor effect.* As long as competitors perceive that outsiders may come into the market, they are disciplined to remain efficient and price their products below monopoly levels to discourage new entrants. Potential entrants "waiting in the wings" create an *edge effect,* pressuring existing competitors to become more competitive. If the potential entrant simply merges with an existing firm, the edge effect is eliminated. Also, a merger with a potential entrant may eliminate future procompetitive deconcentration.

FIGURE 16-6 Conglomerate Merger

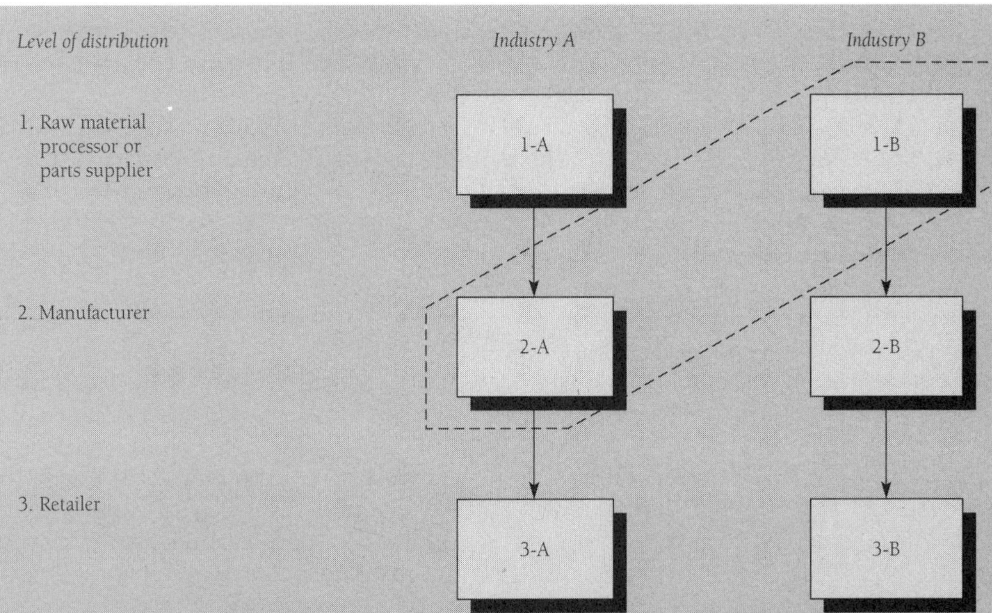

Conglomerate mergers occur between firms either at different levels of distribution and/or in different industries. Conglomerate mergers may eliminate the market discipline that a potential entrant imposes on existing firms (the "edge effect").

If, instead of merging, that firm had entered the market on its own *(de novo),* it would reinforce competitive discipline by increasing the number of competitors.

A plaintiff challenging conglomerate mergers must first prove that existing competitors perceived and were influenced by the potential entrant. Second, the acquiring firm must have had reasonable means to enter the given market without merging. Third, the number of potential entrants cannot be excessive; otherwise, the elimination of only one would have insignificant impact on competitive discipline. What effect does a large potential entrant have on the marketing practices of existing firms? The next case illustrates the effect of a large conglomerate's financial resources on one product market.

Federal Trade Commission v. Procter & Gamble Co.

386 U.S. 568 (1967)
United States Supreme Court

In 1957, Procter & Gamble (P&G), a large, diversified consumer products firm, acquired the assets of Clorox Chemical Company, the largest manufacturer of fabric bleach. Clorox had nearly half of the fabric bleach market in most markets and larger shares in some markets. The top three bleach firms had 80 percent of the market; the remainder was held by some 200 small firms. P&G was a dominant producer of cleansers, soaps, and detergents and has the largest advertising budget of any consumer products firm. The FTC challenged the conglomerate merger as anticompetitive because P&G was considered a potential entrant into the bleach market. The FTC alleged that the presence of P&G in the bleach market through the acquisition of Clorox would (1) intimidate new entrants from entering the bleach market, (2) discourage active competition among existing competitors for fear of retaliation by P&G, and (3) reduce competition by eliminating P&G as the most likely new competitor. Liquid bleach was considered the product market, and the nation was considered the relevant geographic market (with several submarkets). The FTC appealed an appeals court reversal of the trial court verdict. The trial court had held the acquisition was anticompetitive.

Justice Douglas delivered the opinion of the Court.

Since all liquid bleach is chemically identical, advertising and sales promotion are vital. In 1957 Clorox spent almost $3,700,000 on advertising, imprinting the value of its bleach in the mind of the consumer. In addition, it spent $1,700,000 for other promotional activities. The Commission found that these heavy expenditures went far to explain why Clorox maintained so high a market share despite the fact that its brand . . . retailed for a price equal to or, in many instances, higher than its competitors.

Prior to the acquisition, Procter was in the course of diversifying into product lines related to its basic detergent-soap-cleanser business. Liquid bleach was a distinct possibility since packaged detergents—Procter's primary product line—and liquid bleach are used complementarily in washing clothes and fabrics, and in general household cleaning.

The decision to acquire Clorox was the result of a study conducted by Procter's promotion department designed to determine the advisability of entering the liquid bleach industry. The initial report noted the ascendancy of liquid bleach in the large and expanding household bleach market, and recommended that Procter purchase Clorox rather than enter independently. Since a large investment would be needed to obtain a satisfactory market share, acquisition of the industry's leading firm was attractive. "Taking over the Clorox business . . . could be a way of achieving a dominant position in the liquid bleach market quickly, which would pay out reasonably well." The initial report predicted that Procter's "sales, distribution and manufacturing setup" could increase Clorox's share of the markets in areas where it was low.

The Commission found that the substitution of Procter with its huge assets and advertising advantages for the already dominant Clorox would dissuade new entrants and discourage active competition from the firms already in the industry due to fear of retaliation by Procter. The Commission thought it relevant that retailers might be induced to give Clorox preferred shelf space since it would be manufactured by Procter, which also produced a number of other products marketed by the retailers. There was also the danger that Procter might underprice Clorox in order to drive out competition, and subsidize the underpricing with revenue from other products. The Commission carefully reviewed the effect of the acquisition on the structure of the industry, noting that "[t]he practical tendency of the . . . merger . . . is to transform the liquid bleach industry into an arena of big business competition only, with the few small firms that have not disappeared through merger eventually falling by the wayside, unable to compete with their giant rivals." Further, the merger would seriously diminish potential competition by eliminating Procter as a potential entrant into the industry. Prior to the merger, the Commission found, Procter was the most likely prospective entrant, and absent the merger would have remained on the periphery, restraining Clorox from exercising its market power. If Procter had actually entered, Clorox's dominant position would have been eroded and the concentration of the industry reduced. . . . The liquid bleach industry was already oligopolistic before the acquisition, and price competition was certainly not as vigorous as it would have been if the industry were competitive.

The acquisition may also have the tendency of raising the barriers to new entry. The major competitive weapon in the successful marketing of bleach is advertising. Clorox was limited in this area by its relatively small budget and its inability to obtain substantial discounts. By contrast, Procter's budget was much larger, and, although it would not devote its entire budget to advertising Clorox, it could divert a large portion to meet the short-term threat of a new entrant. Procter would be able to use its volume discounts to advantage in advertising Clorox. Thus, a new entrant would be much more reluctant to face the giant Procter than it would have been to face the smaller Clorox.

Possible economies cannot be used as a defense to illegality. Congress was aware that some mergers which lessen competition may also result in economies but it struck the balance in favor of protecting competition.

It is clear that the existence of Procter at the edge of the industry exerted considerable influence on the market. First, the market behavior of the liquid bleach industry was influenced by each firm's predictions of the market behavior of its competitors, actual and potential. Second, the barriers to entry by a firm of Procter's size and with its advantages were not significant. There is no indication that the barriers were so high that the price Procter would have to charge would be above the price that would maximize the profits of the existing firms. Third, the number of potential entrants was not so large that the elimination of one would be insignificant. Few firms would have the temerity to challenge a firm as solidly entrenched as Clorox. Fourth, Procter was found by the Commission to be the most likely entrant. These findings of the Commission were amply supported by the evidence.

The judgment of the Court of Appeals is reversed and remanded with instructions to affirm and enforce the Commission's order.

Case Questions

1. What factors distinguish a pure conglomerate merger from a product extension merger?
2. What market discipline is presumed from a potential entrant to influence existing competitors? How did P&G's acquisition of Clorox change this discipline?
3. What legal alternative strategy could P&G have pursued to avoid this outcome? Why would this alternative be considered better than P&G's acquisition of Clorox?

In recent years, some plaintiffs have argued that a conglomerate merger between an outsider and the leading seller in a concentrated industry is also anticompetitive. They have argued that if the outsider must merge to gain entry, it should instead acquire a smaller firm whose market position could be improved over time. This is known as a *toehold acquisition.* Such an acquisition is preferable because it might preserve the opportunity for deconcentration in an oligopolistic market.

Merger Defenses

A legal challenge to merging firms may be turned away with a merger defense. For example, it is not uncommon for merging firms to claim that the merger will result in greater efficiency. Another merger justification is the **failing firm defense.** The defendant may argue that one of the merger partners will soon be insolvent, making the merger necessary for the failing firm's survival. For this defense to apply, the failing firm must be unable to reorganize successfully under Chapter 11 of the bankruptcy laws. In addition, the failing firm must have made unsuccessful good faith efforts to find other merger partners that might reduce market concentration. Another defense recognizes that purchases of another corporation's stock *solely for investment* does not substantially lessen competition.

failing firm defense Defense in conglomerate merger case that target firm must be acquired to avoid insolvency.

Merger Enforcement Priorities and Procedures

DOJ antitrust enforcement priorities change with the presidential administration. Since the attorney general is a cabinet-level officer appointed by the president, DOJ is likely to pursue the president's antitrust philosophy. By contrast, the FTC is a quasi-independent federal agency not directly under the president's control. Its prosecutorial efforts are more likely to reflect the philosophies of the various FTC commissioners, who may have been appointed prior to the existing president's term. The courts' attitudes may reflect another set of priorities.

Most recent merger have been approved after submission for approval to the FTC, DOJ, or another agency closely regulating the industry in question. For example, airline or railroad mergers have been overseen by the Department of Transportation. Bank mergers are overseen by federal banking regulators. Premerger negotiations are subject to scrutiny by federal agencies and the press, which affect merger activity by indicating approval or threatening a court challenge. Hart-Scott-Rodino premerger notification is required if the acquiring firm has sales or assets exceeding $100 million and the target has sales or assets exceeding $10 million. Notice must be made at least 30 days before the merger and contain basic information to aid in the evaluation of the acquisition. The EU is becoming more strict with European mergers that lessen competition.

SUMMARY

Antitrust laws are intended to foster a competitive business environment, but they can profoundly affect the structure and conduct of business. The term *antitrust* arose from reactions to the trust form, under which many separate producers gave authority to a central management's use of anticompetitive practices. The Sherman Act was passed in 1890 to break up trusts. Markets with many producers and buyers are less likely to be affected by the anticompetitive practices of any one seller, so prices in such markets are more likely to be set by the market forces of supply and demand, and the distortions of centralized economic decision making are more likely to be limited.

There are two basic approaches to antitrust enforcement. The Harvard school uses a structuralist approach to define harmful anticompetitive practices. The Chicago school analyzes the performance of competitors and would restrain enforcement activity unless long-term anticompetitive effects are apparent. The compliance responses of business to antitrust law are often dictated by which school of thought controls the antitrust enforcement agencies.

The Sherman Act outlaws contracts in restraint of trade and conspiracies to monopolize. Lackluster enforcement of the Sherman Act led to passage of the Clayton Antitrust Act and the FTC Act in 1914. The Clayton Act outlaws anticompetitive actions that tend to create a monopoly and prohibits other anticompetitive practices. The FTC Act created the FTC and gave it enforcement powers to define and prosecute unfair methods of competition and deceptive trade practices. Amendments now prohibit price discrimination, outlaw certain mergers accomplished through sales of corporate assets, and permit private parties and state attorneys general to sue. Persons convicted under the antitrust laws may be subject to civil and criminal penalties. Certain industries and activities are exempt from these laws; patents, copyrights, trademarks, agricultural cooperatives, labor unions, the insurance industry, political action, the stock markets, and baseball are all exempt to a certain degree.

The Sherman Act prohibits monopolies created when a defendant possessing monopoly power undertakes purposeful acts of monopolization. In order to be actionable, a monopolist's illegal market power must exist over a relevant market that has both geographic and product parameters. When two products have a high cross-elasticity of demand, they may be considered reasonably interchangeable as substitutes, expanding the product market. The alleged monopolist's percentage domination over a particular geographic and product market, called market share, is used to determine the existence of a monopoly. The intent to monopolize can be inferred from exclusionary conduct, predatory pricing, or attempts to monopolize.

Mergers are subject to antitrust law because they may result in the acquisition of monopoly power. The Clayton Act prohibits mergers, acquisitions, or sales of assets that tend to create a monopoly. This prohibition includes horizontal mergers between direct competitors, vertical mergers between suppliers and customers, and conglomerate mergers. Merger analysis is similar to the market share analysis used in monopolization cases. If a merger results in the acquisition of a market share large enough to create the probability of a substantial lessening of competition, the courts may prohibit the merger.

In vertical merger analysis, the courts consider historical trends toward concentration and the resulting barriers to entry. Vertical mergers may result in the imposition of discipline on suppliers or on customers' product pricing. Conglomerate mergers that eliminate the edge effect of a potential entrant may be illegal if competitors perceive the loss of the potential entrant's influence on market pricing and efficiency. If a single potential entrant has a reasonable means of entering the market on its own, its merger with an existing firm may be anticompetitive.

Merging firms may attempt to justify their merger with a merger defense. Proof that a merger will result in greater efficiency, that one of the merged firms is failing and needs the merger to survive, or that the acquisition is for investment purposes may permit the merger.

Critical Thinking Review Questions

1. Compare and contrast the three antitrust enforcement approaches.
2. For what reasons are foreign nations less likely to vigorously enforce U.S.-style antitrust laws against their own nationals and their own firms? How do foreign nations resist enforcement of U.S. antitrust laws?
3. For what reasons did Congress pass additional antitrust legislation and create a new trade regulation agency in 1914?
4. What is presumed about the potential anticompetitive impact of conglomerate mergers when a large marketing firm acquires a smaller producer of related products that the large firm might have produced itself? Explain how this presumption might impact enforcement.

Critical Thinking Exercises

1. The Justice Department challenged a merger between two waste disposal companies: Waste Management, Inc., and EMW Ventures, Inc. Both were large and dominant firms in this business. The merged firm would have a nearly 50 percent market share, with a Herfindahl Index of over 2,700. Barriers to entry were rather low, market entry by mom and pop waste disposal firms was easy—only a home office and a waste disposal truck were needed. On what basis could the merger be challenged? What defense might the firms offer to justify the merger? *United States v. Waste Management, Inc.*, 743 F.2d 976 (2nd Cir. 1984).
2. Big Oil Corp. was approached by a chemical engineer, William Carbs, with a new fuel injection device that promised to revolutionize gasoline automobile engines. The system adds air and water to the gasoline fuel mix and completely atomizes the mixture as it is injected into the cylinder. This permits nearly compete combustion, increasing miles per gallon on average automobiles by over 35 percent. The system also reduces pollutants well below federal EPA standards, eliminating the need for catalytic converters on the exhaust. Big Oil had recently purchased a substantial number of platinum futures contracts on the expectation that the price would rise now that European nations are requiring catalytic converters containing platinum. If developed into a commercially exploitable form, Carbs' invention would reduce the world's need for oil and platinum simultaneously. Big Oil acquired Carbs' small development corporation, including Carbs' patents. Thereafter Big Oil refrained from developing the fuel system altogether. Comment on the legal and ethical problems triggered by this merger.
3. A computer manufacturer designed a central processing unit that was demonstrably better than any other central processing unit on the market. It then designed peripherals (units that plug into the

central processing unit) and redesigned the central processing unit so that no other peripherals could be used with it. A peripherals manufacturer sued the computer manufacturer for monopolization under Section 2 of the Sherman Act. Did the computer manufacturer violate the Sherman Antitrust Act? Discuss. See *Telex Corp. v. IBM,* 367 F. Supp. 258 (N.D. Okla. 1973).

4. Cola Company produces a cola soft drink that is much like Coke and Pepsi. After considerable effort, it obtained 62 percent of the cola market, and it is now charged with monopolization. The company contends that its market should be defined as the market for all soft drinks (root beer, orange drink, lemon-lime soda, etc.), of which it has only 6 percent. What are the relevant considerations in determining the market for Cola Company's soft drink?
5. Eau Claire, Wisconsin, received funds to build a sewage treatment plant. Three neighboring towns were unable to build their own plants and sought to use Eau Claire's new facility. Eau Claire refused their participation unless voters in the three other towns agreed to become annexed as part of Eau Claire and also use Eau Claire's sewage removal and transportation services. Is the action of Eau Claire unlawful as monopolization? Explain whether an antitrust defense should apply? *Town of Hallie v. City of Eau Claire,* 471 U.S. 34 (1985).
6. RSR was the second largest lead recycling firm with 12.6 percent market share. Quemetco was fifth largest with 7 percent of the lead recycling market. If the merger of these two firms is challenged, what analytical steps are taken? If lead can also be produced from virgin ore, should the relevant market be defined as lead production or just lead recycling? *RSR Corp. v. FTC,* 9th Cir. 1979).

CHAPTER

17

Restraints of Trade, Price Discrimination and Unfair Trade Practices

Critical Thinking Questions

- What are the conceptual and practical differences between the assessment of restraints of trade under the per se rule as opposed to the rule of reason?
- What was presumed by Adam Smith in condemning communications between direct competitors who stand in a horizontal relationship?
- How do vertical restraints of trade between suppliers and customers protect the manufacturer's goodwill, involve restrictions on resale prices, maintain exclusive dealerships, territorial restrictions, or tying arrangements?
- What are the anticompetition issues presented by the three different forms of price discrimination for injuries at the primary line (seller's level), the secondary line (buyer's level), or the tertiary line (buyer's buyer level)?

Introduction... Past, Present, Future

The populists' desire for economic decentralization went unsatisfied because the courts refused to enforce the Sherman Act aggressively. At the turn of the century, the concentration of wealth and economic decision making continued to become concentrated, raising demands for more specific prohibitions of anticompetitive actions than the Sherman Act provided in its vague prohibition of "monopolization." Numerous anticompetitive horizontal and vertical restraints of trade were prohibited by the per se rule and new provisions of the Clayton and FTC Acts.

Today, the most controversial areas of antitrust enforcement pertain to horizontal and vertical restraints of trade and price discrimination. The "new learning" of law and economics suggests that overzealous antitrust enforcement may sometimes hinder competition. These advocates recommend shifting from the per se analysis to the rule of reason. Expansive interpretation of the price discrimination provisions may reduce competition if quick pricing responses to changing market conditions are prohibited. Changes in distribution channels, the rise of direct marketing, and volume discounters pit consumer choice against the traditional use of high-profit/high-service small, local retailers.

In the future, many of the innovations in economic analysis will become more readily accepted. The Supreme Court may nearly abandon per se analysis altogether and begin to analyze vertical restraints with the rule of reason on a case-by-case basis. Proof of violations will be increasingly subjected to structured economic analysis. There will be much less enforcement based on mere conjecture about anticompetitive effects. The size of relevant markets will be broadened to recognize internationalization so any one firm will have a narrower impact from their alleged domestic wrongdoing.

Both the Clayton and Sherman Antitrust Acts apply to a wider range of anticompetitive practices than the monopolies and mergers previously discussed. This chapter first examines restraints of trade resulting from horizontal relationships between competitors, such as price-fixing, division of markets, and group boycotts. Next, vertical relationships between suppliers and customers are examined, including resale price maintenance, refusals to deal, exclusive dealing, tying, and franchising. Although a few restraints are illegal per se—that is, illegal in all instances—most restraints have some economic justification and are prohibited only if unreasonable. The chapter concludes with a review of the FTC's powers to prosecute anticompetitive actions.

Thought Questions

1. What factors motivated the populists to seek more antitrust laws?
2. How do the Clayton and FTC Acts respond to criticism levied at the courts' enforcement of the Sherman Act?

Horizontal Combinations and Restraints of Trade

Horizontal restraints of trade arise when competitors in the same industry collaborate. They are considered the least justifiable restraints. Adam Smith, the famous laissez-faire economist, strongly urged that government should actively ensure competition in order to counteract competitors' natural tendency to collude.

Adam Smith's Observations about Collusion

> People in the same trade seldom meet together, even for merriment and diversion, but [that] the conversation ends in a conspiracy against the public, or in some contrivance to raise prices.

Early Supreme Court interpretations of the Sherman Act were so broad that "every contract, combination . . . or conspiracy in restraint of trade" was condemned. Later cases modified this approach by recognizing that some restraints are reasonable. There are two tests for restraints. The per se rule requires a strict interpretation of the Sherman Act's "plain meaning." Per se violations leave no room for any defense or justification. The rule of reason emerged from 19th-century contract law outlawing only unreasonable restraints. Horizontal restraints of trade are depicted in Figure 17–1.

Rule of Reason

The Sherman Act, in Section 1, literally prohibits "every contract, combination . . . or conspiracy in restraint of trade." If this provision is applied too strictly, every contract would be illegal because trade is restrained in some way. For example, goods or

FIGURE 17-1

Horizontal Restraint of Trade

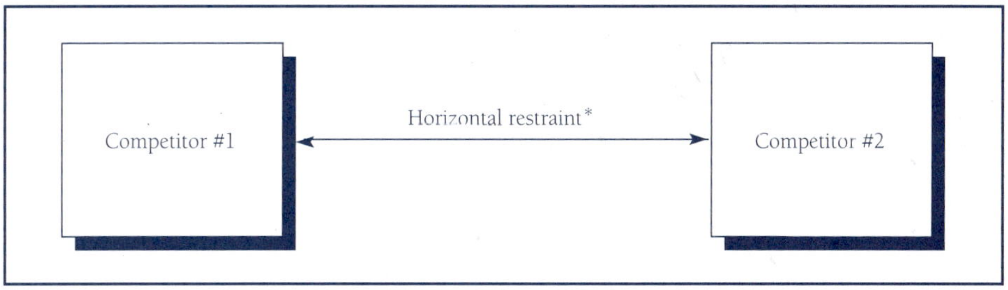

*Price-fixing; division of markets; limited production; trade association activities; limit on innovation or features.

services purchased by one person are unavailable to others, and the buyer does not purchase them from a competitor. The Sherman Act is intended to encourage free markets and should not prohibit such a small restraint. Trade is restrained even more by outputs or requirements contracts, exclusive dealing or supply contracts, and by covenants not to compete. Yet these are usually economically justifiable.

The rule of reason exception prohibits only contracts intended to unreasonably restrict competition. In 1918, Justice Brandeis announced the proper inquiry for rule of reason analysis in *Chicago Board of Trade v. United States.*[1]

Rule of Reason Analysis of Restraints of Trade

> The true test of legality is whether the restraint imposed is such as merely regulates and perhaps thereby promotes competition or whether it is such as may suppress or may even destroy competition. To determine that question, the court must ordinarily consider the facts peculiar to the business to which the restraint is applied; its condition before and after the restraint was imposed; the nature of the restraint and its effect, actual or probable. The history of the restraint, the evil believed to exist, the reason for adopting the particular remedy, the purpose or end sought to be obtained, are all relevant facts.

The **rule of reason** permits courts to be more flexible by using a less rigorous market share analysis than was used in monopolization or merger cases. This practice is justified because Section 1 of the Sherman Act requires no analysis of market power.

rule of reason Justification of restraint of trade judged by reasonability.

Per Se Violations

Courts have encountered many antitrust cases justifying a return to the plain meaning of the Sherman Act. Certain types of agreements are almost always unjustifiable as substantial restraints of trade. The rule of reason can be inefficient and time-consum-

[1] *Chicago Board of Trade v. United States,* 246 U.S. 231 (1918).

ing to apply anew in each case. Certain types of business agreements, such as price-fixing, are designated illegal per se and considered unreasonable in all instances. This means that the inquiry ends after the plaintiff or prosecutor proves the per se violation. Trials are shortened and simplified by avoiding unnecessary attempts to justify the restraint. The **per se rule** improves judicial efficiency and provides business managers with definite guidance. Per se offenses include price-fixing, division of markets, group boycotts, concerted refusals to deal, and tie-in relationships.

per se rule
Restraint of trade that is always illegal; no justification exists.

The courts first determine whether the conduct in question falls within a per se category; then no further analysis is necessary, and the anticompetitive effect is presumed. For example, if two competitors agree to restrict competition, the per se rule applies. However, if the conduct in question does not clearly fall within a per se category, the court must carefully apply the rule of reason and permit the defendant to prove some justification. For example, a particular restraint might make the market more competitive or increase market efficiency. To determine whether the restraint is legal, the court must balance its perceived anticompetitive effect against its benefits.

Price-Fixing among Competitors The most direct way for competitors to reduce competition is to agree to set prices artificially. Contracts to fix prices among competitors at the same level of production are illegal per se. **Price-fixing** tends to eliminate competition and passes on the inefficiencies of oligopoly to consumers. Price-fixing is never justified by good intentions to set "reasonable" prices or eliminate "ruinous" competition.

price-fixing
Agreement of competitors to set artificially prices high.

The courts broadly interpret the per se prohibition of price-fixing. Agreements among competitors to fix minimum prices are illegal. For example, at one time state and local bar associations enacted minimum fee schedules requiring lawyers to charge a minimum price for a particular service, such as writing a will or drafting a contract. Such schedules are illegal per se as price-fixing. It is also illegal to set maximum resale prices even though fixing "low" prices might not seem harmful. Low prices drive out competitors and reduce nonprice competition for optional features, improvements, or additional services. A price ceiling tends to stabilize prices. Illegal stabilization of prices also arises when automobile dealers agree to use negotiable list prices. Even where negotiable prices are not enforceable, they operate as a starting point for customer bargaining and tend to stabilize prices. Some critics charge the auto industry's practice of "no haggle" pricing may be price fixing. Agreements among sellers to limit production or among buyers to limit purchases also manipulates prices and are illegal per se.

Credit terms are an inseparable part of a product's price, so fixing these terms is illegal per se. In one case, an agreement among beer distributors to eliminate trade credit to retailers was illegal price-fixing equivalent to an agreement to eliminate discounts. Several plywood producers allegedly agreed to charge a uniform freight rate irrespective of the source of supply or the destination. This illegal scheme is known as *phantom freight* because it equalizes freight charges without reference to the actual costs for the distance transported. It eliminates competition based on the purchaser's closeness to the source of supply. Is an agreement among competitors to buy excess supplies of a commodity equivalent to a price-fixing arrangement? The next case is a classic illustration of the way price-fixing can be disguised and of how the Supreme Court analyzes its illegality.

United States v. Socony-Vacuum Oil Co., Inc.

310 U.S. 150 (1940)
United States Supreme Court

Numerous oil companies allegedly conspired to raise and maintain wholesale gasoline prices. These companies operated an organized program for discovering the amounts of surplus gasoline on the spot market, assigning portions of this surplus among the co-conspirators, and purchasing it at the going price. These intentional actions tended to stabilize and raise wholesale and retail prices of gasoline. Wholesalers and consumers paid higher prices than they would have under competitive conditions.

Justice Douglas delivered the opinion of the Court.

The elimination of so-called competitive evils is no legal justification for such buying programs. The elimination of such conditions was sought primarily for its effect on the price structures. Fairer competitive prices, it is claimed, resulted when distress (excess supply) gasoline was removed from the market. But such defense is typical of the protestations usually made in price-fixing cases. Ruinous competition, financial disaster, evils of price cutting and the like appear throughout our history as ostensible justifications for price-fixing. If the so-called competitive abuses were to be appraised here, the reasonableness of prices would necessarily become an issue in every price-fixing case. In that event the Sherman Act would soon be emasculated; its philosophy would be supplanted by one which is wholly alien to a system of free competition; it would not be the charter of freedom which its framers intended.

The reasonableness of prices has no constancy due to the dynamic quality of business facts underlying price structures. Those who fixed reasonable prices today would perpetuate unreasonable prices tomorrow, since those prices would not be subject to continuous administrative supervision and readjustment in light of changed conditions. Those who controlled the prices would control or effectively dominate the market. And those who were in that strategic position would have it in their power to destroy or drastically impair the competitive system. But the thrust of the rule is deeper and reaches more than monopoly power. Any combination which tampers with price structures is engaged in an unlawful activity. Even though the members of the price-fixing group were in no position to control the market, to the extent that they raised, lowered, or stabilized prices they would be directly interfering with the free play of market forces. The Act places all such schemes beyond the pale and protects that vital part of our economy against any degree of interference. Congress has not left with us the determination of whether or not particular price-fixing schemes are wise or unwise, healthy or destructive. It has not permitted the age-old cry of ruinous competition and competitive evils to be a defense to price-fixing conspiracies.

Under the Sherman Act a combination formed for the purpose and with the effect of raising, depressing, fixing, pegging, or stabilizing the price of a commodity in interstate or foreign commerce is illegal *per se*. Where the machinery for price-fixing is an agreement on the prices to be charged or paid for the commodity in the interstate or foreign channels of trade, the power to fix prices exists if the combination has control of a substantial part of the commerce in that commodity. Where the means for price-fixing are purchases or sales of the commodity in a market operation or, as here, purchases of a part of the supply of the commodity for the purpose of keeping it from having a depressive effect on the markets, such power may be found to exist though the combination does not control a substantial part of the commodity. In such a case that power may be established if as a result of the market conditions, the resources available to the combinations, the timing and the strategic placement of orders and the like, effective means are at hand to accomplish the desired objective. But there may be effective influence over the market though the group in question does not control it. Price-fixing agreements may have utility to members of the group though the power possessed or exerted falls far short of domination and control. Monopoly power is not the only power which the Act strikes down, as we have said. Proof that a combination was formed for the purpose of fixing prices and that it caused them to be fixed or contributed to that result is proof of the completion of a price-fixing conspiracy under §1 of the Act.

Case Questions

1. What assumption is made once the per se nature of the price-fixing is determined concerning the defendant's attempt to justify the practice? What arguments are used to justify price-fixing?
2. Is a monopoly a necessary condition to price-fixing? Explain.

In recent years, some restraints of trade involving incidental price-fixing have been judged under the rule of reason; in such cases, cooperation is deemed necessary to advance the market. For example, it is impractical for copyright owners of music to separately negotiate licensing fees for every performance of their works on television, radio, or in public. The Supreme Court applied the rule of reason to the blanket fee arrangement between the Broadcast Music, Inc. (BMI) and the American Society of Composers, Authors, and Publishers (ASCAP) because these organizations provide clearinghouse services essential to effective licensing. Their arrangement does not restrain trade but, rather, actually encourages the licensing and enforcement of music copyrights.[2]

In another case, the rule of reason was used to judge a price-fixing scheme illegal. The National Collegiate Athletics Association (NCAA) negotiated television contracts for all college football games between 1982 and 1985. However, television fees paid to schools were based neither on the size of the viewing audience nor on the popularity of the teams. The NCAA contracts with ABC and CBS limited the number of televised games and precluded price negotiation between the networks and schools. The NCAA scheme was invalid price-fixing under rule of reason analysis because both price and output were restrained, thereby effectively raising television fees above competitive prices with a system unresponsive to viewer demand. The per se rule was inapplicable because some horizontal restraint in athletics is essential to make the product available at all.[3]

Trade Association Activities The price-fixing prohibition is so strong that competitors must be careful about their collective activities. Competitors' exchange of price information generally makes price-fixing easier. An unreasonable restraint may arise if a trade association tempts its members to collude or it acts as a clearinghouse for competitors to exchange price information. Trade association activities may also violate the Sherman Act §1 as a concerted activity in restraint of trade or FTC Act §5 as an unfair and deceptive trade practice. However, there are critics of this approach who charge that to remain competitive in world markets, competitors should be permitted to "network" by joining legitimate trade associations and to promote their collective success and improve product quality. For example, trade associations can provide legitimate services for industry groups in the areas of political lobbying, public affairs, and access to information about suppliers and new production technologies. Nevertheless, the FTC and DOJ have stepped up enforcement of anticompetitive trade association activities in recent years.

[2] *Broadcast Music Inc. v. CBS,* 441 U.S. 1 (1979).

[3] *NCAA v. Board of Regents of the University of Oklahoma,* 468 U.S. 85 (1984).

Despite the good intentions of trade associations, some have acted as fronts to distribute price information. In the 1920s, for example, 365 hardwood manufacturers exchanged details of individual sales, production, inventories, and current price lists through their trade association. An expert analyst constantly warned members against overproduction. When hardwood prices increased sharply, the plan was found illegal. By contrast, the maple flooring trade association circulated average costs, freight rates, and past transaction information without identifying individual buyers or sellers. This exchange was not illegal because future prices were never discussed. In a more recent case, the paper box industry voluntarily exchanged price quotes that identified transactions with particular customers; the plan was held illegal because it tended to stabilize prices. Information exchanges should avoid revealing sensitive confidentes like price, costs, profits, or the identity of suppliers and customers.

Exchange of information through trade associations is not illegal so long as it is not intended to lessen competition. For example, a cement manufacturers' association distributed a list of construction contractors that abused the free delivery of cement. The exchange was considered justifiable because it helped prevent fraud on the cement manufacturers. However, information should not urge group boycotts of tough competitors. For example, the travel agents trade association agreed to stop urging the boycott of travel service providers not paying a standard commission rate. Baby product manufacturer associations agreed to stop threatening boycott of manufacturers selling through discount channels.

Bidding rings may arise among construction contractors. Sometimes contractors preselect a different winner for each of several successive construction projects. The designated "losers" agree to bid high, and the selected winner rigs its bid to be the "lowest." Although the selected winner's price seems lower than others, it is typically higher than would result with genuine competitive bidding. Bidding rings are considered illegal per se as a form of price-fixing. In Japan, it has been a common practice among construction contractors to consult each other before bidding on public works projects. This is allegedly a form of bid-rigging. The JFTC is supposed to function like the U.S. FTC but has only recently prohibited bid rigging and only under U.S. trade negotiation pressure to discontinue locking out foreign firms from bidding.

When trade associations influence their members to standardize products, the result may be improved quality and safety, interchangeability, and simplicity—to the benefit of customers. However, standardization can be anticompetitive if it is a hidden way to fix prices or thwart innovation. Standard setting should be based on technical and scientific standards, be couched in performance rather than design terms, be voluntary rather than mandatory standards, and emanate from an objective process. Otherwise trade association standards impose a barrier to entry and can throttle innovation.

Some trade associations limit their membership. This may be pro-competitive if membership is conditioned on integrity, quality, or reliability. Trade guilds and the apprenticeship system has been justified on this basis. However, the practice becomes anticompetitive if it is used to limit the number of competitors or if it limits access to some valuable association facility. For example, most local real estate associations operate multiple listing services that compile listings and enhance members' opportunities to sell listed properties. Denying membership or limiting nonmember access to multiple listing services reduces competition, particularly in commission rates. Real estate commissions show price rigidity, with little discounting from the 6–8 percent range prevailing nationwide.

ETHICAL DILEMMA

ETHICAL DILEMMAS IN TRADE ASSOCIATION CODES OF ETHICS

Self-regulation by industry trade groups is gaining favor as an alternative to government regulation and costly litigation. However, some "industry codes of conduct" are disguised methods to fix prices or otherwise reduce competition. For example, the National Society of Professional Engineers once prohibited its members from bidding competitively on design projects. The prohibition allegedly supported professional ethics and maintained the quality of engineering services by discouraging engineers from cutting corners in their design work. Minimum fee schedules formerly required by most local lawyers' bar associations were similarly justified as necessary to ensure a minimum standard of effort, competence, and quality in lawyers' services. These organizations argued that without these restraints, some members would be forced by ruinous price competition into the unethical cutting of corners, ultimately degrading the quality of services. Is it ethical for a profession to use codes of ethics to fix prices? Excessive discipline of a highly competitive member suggests that other members are really just suppressing competition. This is an ironic and unethical misuse of a professional association's powers, particularly when rationalized as an ethical rule. Trade association activities found illegal under the antitrust laws may subject both the association and its members to liability.

division of markets Competitors' allocation of customers or geographic markets; prohibited as anticompetitive.

Division of Markets Competitors may attempt to divide markets so that only certain producers serve particular regions or specified customers. This territorial allocation or **division of markets** is illegal per se because it gives the producer in each market segment an effective monopoly. Even if other competitors still sell in the affected region, the preferred firm generally exerts some market power. In one case, a group of independent local grocers formed a group buying chain. However, their joint exercise of buying power was considered illegal because they also caused many members to limit the location of their stores to designated territories. This division of markets was not justified by the grocers' intent to compete more effectively against larger chain stores.

group boycott Collusive agreements not to buy from or sell to certain individuals.

Group Boycotts Individuals are usually free to deal with whomever they please. But when groups of competitors agree to boycott a certain individual or group, the action may be illegal. Although most courts consider **group boycotts** to be illegal per se, sometimes illegality is tested by the rule of reason. For example, it may be illegal for competing sellers to agree not to sell to a particular customer, reseller, or class of persons. A group of buyers with market power (monopsony or oligopsony) may also be guilty of an illegal boycott if certain sellers are avoided. In one case, an apparel manufacturers' trade association urged its members to boycott any retailers selling pirated designs (e.g., fake designer jeans). In another case, a National Football League rule required a team to compensate the former team of a free agent if the player changed teams. Both actions were illegal, concerted refusals to deal. At one time, the American Medical Association had rules of ethics that prohibited doctors from participating in prepaid medical plans or from receiving a salary for practicing medicine. Those rules were illegal because they tended to destroy competition among professional groups. How would this affect current evolving health care systems?

Group boycotts generally are horizontal agreements used to force vertical restraints on suppliers or customers with whom a horizontal group is dissatisfied. Some boycotts are legal under the First Amendment as legitimate noneconomic political expression. For example, no anticompetitive boycott was found when the National Organization of Women caused a boycott of convention hotels in states that had not ratified the Equal Rights Amendment. However, the Supreme Court found illegal per se a boycott by members of a Washington, D.C., trial lawyers association who refused to continue accepting court appointments to represent indigent defendants.[4] Ninety percent of the group's attorneys agreed to cease taking court appointments until the city doubled their fees. This action was clearly motivated by desires for personal economic gain and hardly constituted protected political speech.

Joint Ventures A *joint venture* is a form of partnership in which two entities (e.g., persons, partnerships, corporations) enter into a limited business activity. Joint ventures are subject to rule of reason analysis because they are sometimes justifiable, such as when the purpose and effect is economic efficiency. The test is whether the restraint is really necessary to achieve the lawful purpose. The courts balance the joint venture's potential anticompetitive effects against its alleged efficiency. For example, the Associated Press is a cooperative wire service with thousands of members. Access to this service is often critical to effective competition. At one time, the bylaws of the Associated Press contained a veto clause permitting any member to blackball a competitor who sought membership. Because this clause excluded competitors from the joint venture and posed a substantial barrier to entry for new firms in the newspaper business, it was held to be illegal under rule of reason analysis. A joint ownership of theaters by moviemaking companies was also held illegal because new releases were not freely available to nonmember theaters, substantially lessening competition.

International Perspective on Joint Ventures

International Perspective and Commentary

Today, the development of increasingly complex technology may necessitate a pooling of resources and the efforts of several competitors. In international commerce, the primary vehicle for imports of goods and technology is an international joint venture. How can the antitrust law prohibitions against the competitive restraints of cooperative joint operations be reconciled with the need for international competitiveness? Does the threat of per se rule application discourage joint ventures? Firms unwilling or unable to make huge new investments to establish marketing channels or productive capacity in foreign nations often find that joint ventures with domestic firms are cost-effective. Such joint ventures are not illegal when reasonable and limited in scope and duration. For example, Toyota was initially unwilling to produce automobiles in the United States without some assurance of quality and efficient production. Toyota joined with General Motors to convert GM's idle plant in Fremont, California, for joint production of vehicles. The result was NUMMI, a production joint venture that builds Toyota Corollas and Geo Prisms for a limited time.

[4] *F.T.C. v. Superior Court Trial Lawyers Assn.*, 493 U.S. 411 (1990).

Congress passed the National Cooperative Research Act in 1984. The act reinforced the principle that research and development joint ventures are to be judged by the rule of reason, not the per se rule. Similar legislation passed for international shipping joint ventures and is proposed for production joint ventures.

Proof of an Illegal Agreement or Combination

Participants in an illegal horizontal restraint or price-fixing are probably careful not to leave any clear trail of evidence. Illegal contacts between co-conspirators would be hidden off the record. Clandestine tactics such as secret meetings or secret codes might be used. Because the Sherman Act's criminal provisions require proof beyond a reasonable doubt, it would be difficult to prove such hidden guilt with direct evidence. Instead, illegal concerted activity is usually inferred from circumstantial evidence of participation in suspect trade association activity, conscious paralleling of competitors' price movements, and interlocking directorates.

conscious parallelism Tacit agreement among competitors to mimic one another's pricing behaviors.

Conscious Parallelism In monopolistic competitive or oligopolistic industries firms may mimic pricing decisions of an industry leader. This is **conscious parallelism,** which may replace an overt agreement. In 1939, the Supreme Court stated: "[i]t is enough that, knowing that concerted action was contemplated and invited, the distributors [of feature films] gave their adherence to the scheme and participated in it." This is the *Interstate formula,* which permits proof of an illegal agreement if there is conscious parallelism.[5] Conscious parallelism may also constitute an unfair method of competition under §5 of the FTC Act. For example, a standard form contract emerging in a highly complex industry suggests that no proof of an actual illegal agreement may be necessary.

The more modern formulation of conscious parallelism is more forgiving, such as when legal conduct might incorrectly appear to be conscious parallelism. Businesses must often respond quickly to changes in market conditions or to new contract terms offered by their competitors. For example, changes in the price of crude oil often quickly lead to similar changes in the gasoline pump prices charged by independent gasoline retailers.

The American steel industry allegedly exhibited all the characteristics of conscious parallelism in the mid-1900s. Typically, the price leader, U.S. Steel, would raise or lower prices, and the other steelmakers would follow suit within a matter of days or weeks. This pricing behavior was never successfully prosecuted.

Test of Conscious Parallelism

> . . . the crucial question is whether the respondents' conduct . . . stems from an independent decision or from an agreement, tacit or expressed. But, this court has never held that proof of parallel business behavior conclusively establishes agreement.[6]

---

[5] *Interstate Circuit, Inc. v. United States,* 306 U.S. 208 (1939).

[6] *Theatre Enterprises v. Paramount Film Distributor Corp.,* 346 U.S. 537 (1954).

Interlocking Directorates Section 8 of the Clayton Act outlaws certain **interlocking directorates,** that is, the same person sitting on the board of two competitors.

interlocking directorates Illegal potential collusion if one director sits on the boards of two competitors.

CLAYTON ACT, SECTION 8: INTERLOCKING DIRECTORATES

> No person shall at the same time be a director in two or more corporations, any of which has capital . . . aggregating more than one million dollars . . . if such corporations are or shall have been theretofore, by virtue of their business and location of operation, competitors, so that the elimination of competition by an agreement between them would constitute a violation of any of the provisions of any of the antitrust laws.

The theory underlying the prohibition against interlocking directorates recognizes that a common director between competitors could provide a communication conduit for collusion. The FTC has been quite lax in enforcement permitting directors in the few reported cases to resign one of their board seats. By contrast, DOJ has been more aggressive, extending the interlocking directorate provision to firms engaged in "related businesses." For example, an illegal interlocking directorate could exist if a single individual sat on the boards of a computer mainframe manufacturer and a manufacturer of computer software. Figure 17–2 illustrates an interlocking director.

Exceptions Interlocking directorate law is best known for its exceptions. Interlocking directorates may exist between firms that are in a vertical relationship or in different industries. It is common for suppliers and customers to solidify their relationship with common directors. Indirect interlocks are permissible. For example, a bank employee may legally sit on the boards of two competing industrial firms. A nondirector employee of one firm may sit on the board of a competing firm. For example, a nondirector employee of Firm A may sit on the board of directors of its competitor, Firm B, without violating §8. All these interlocks are actively used in Japanese Keiretsu or "feudal families of firms."

Given the current trend toward holding directors liable for negligent decisions, it is an increasing challenge to attract competent and experienced directors. Vigorous enforcement of §8 could impair the overall quality of corporate management and directorships. Section 8 may also be inconsistent with the closer contacts firms may need to assure total quality and technological compatibility from their suppliers.

VERTICAL RESTRAINTS OF TRADE

Vertical restraints of trade are significantly different from horizontal restraints. Vertical relationships are intended to restrict certain activities along the chain of distribution between manufacturers, wholesalers, and retailers with an ultimate impact on consumers. Vertical restraints usually include resale price maintenance, restrictions on territorial or customer access, or restrictions on the freedom to sell competing brands. Vertical restraints may also require the purchase of less desirable goods in order to receive desirable ones. Figure 17–3 illustrates vertical restraints.

FIGURE 17-2 Interlocking Directorates

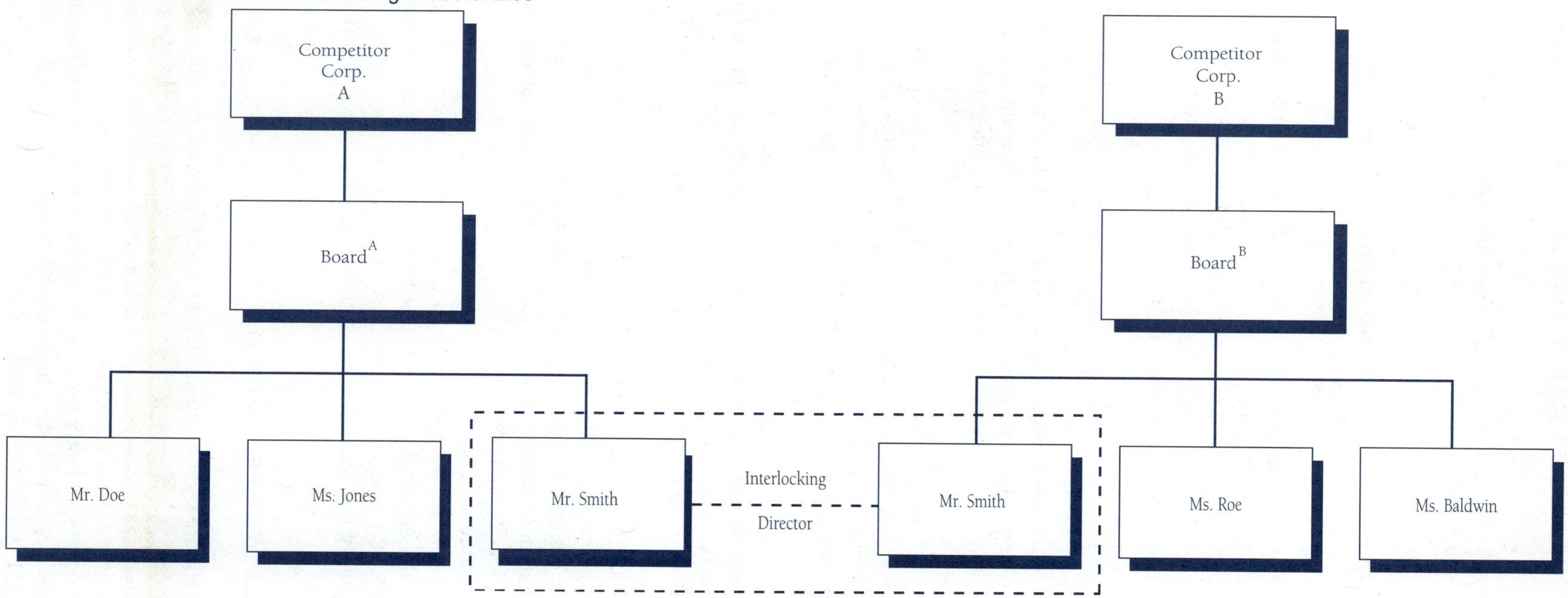

FIGURE 17-3 Vertical Restraint of Trade

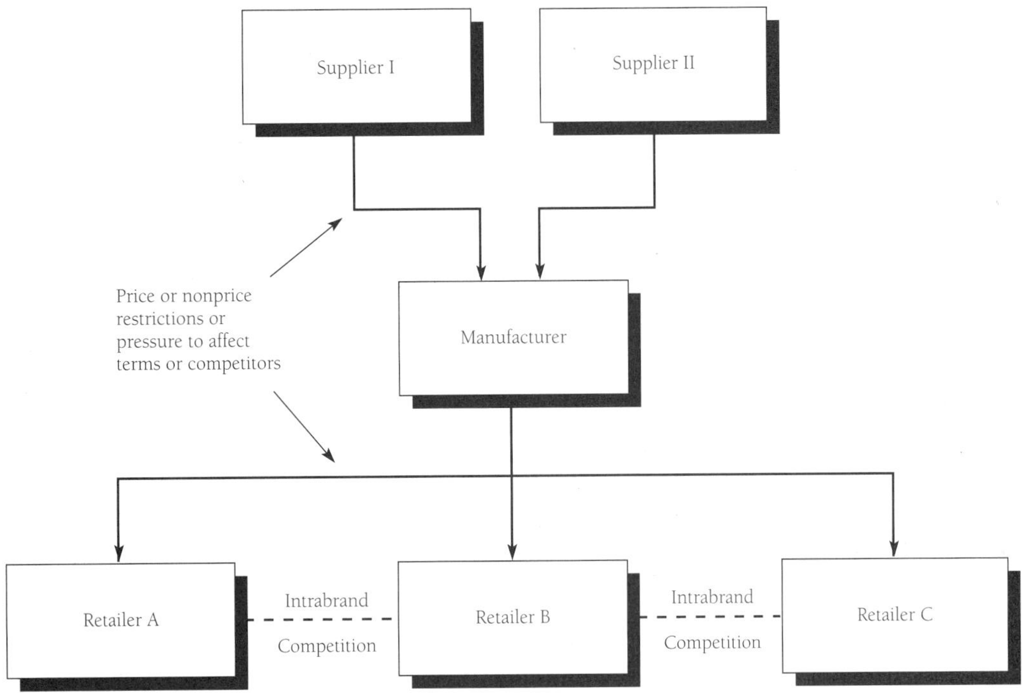

Vertical Restraint Controversy

COMMENTARY

Why should vertical restraints be illegal? Manufacturers and suppliers impose vertical restraints of trade to maximize their profits. Suppliers strive for long-term survival of their product line by limiting both the upper and lower bounds of retailers' profits. Abnormally high retail profits may deter consumer purchases because the product is overpriced. Retailers with abnormally low profits may exert less sales effort, advertise less, and provide poorer customer service. High prices create a quality image, whereas low prices suggest a cheap product image. Vertical restraints induce the retailer to make the distribution process more efficient and favorable for the manufacturer. High profit sales encourage retailers to hire trained sales and service technicians, provide customers better service and technical expertise, and provide better promotional support with more advertising, larger inventories, broader goods selection, and more display space devoted to the manufacturer's products.

A **free rider** problem arises when the same goods are sold by both high-profit retailers and discount stores. Customers may learn about technically complex products from the more proficient sales personnel at high-priced retailers but then purchase the products from low-overhead discounters. The discounters "ride free" on the promotional and technical expenditures of the higher-profit retailers. If free riding becomes widespread, higher-profit retailers are forced out of business, leaving little technical expertise available. Manufacturers of complex products

free rider
One who benefits from the expenditures of others, such as a competitor's service, advertising, and promotional activities.

dislike free riding and argue that it is detrimental to customer satisfaction. The free-rider problem has plagued the consumer electronics and personal computer markets in recent years. Manufacturers or suppliers often impose vertical restraints to prevent widespread free riding. Manufacturers may require minimum resale prices, grant exclusive dealerships, or impose territorial restrictions on dealers to reduce cutthroat competition and foster retail prices that permit adequate levels of customer service. However, widespread vertical restraints reduce price competition.

Because of the free-rider problem, some argue that it is better to enhance interbrand competition than intrabrand competition. *Intrabrand competition*—competition among sellers of the same brand—is reduced or eliminated by vertical restraints. Proponents insist that this enhances *interbrand competition*—competition among different brands of the same type of product—thereby making retailer service an important product feature. In this environment, consumers may select a different mix of service and price only by buying a competing brand from another dealer specializing in that brand.

Despite the arguments in their favor, vertical restraints that discipline retailers and reduce intrabrand competition are an exercise of market power of suppliers. If products do not need extensive customer service, vigorous intrabrand competition passes beneficial price reductions on to consumers. Vertical restraints may be considered illegal under both the Sherman and Clayton Acts. Although some vertical restraints are illegal per se, the clear trend is to apply the rule of reason.

Vertical Price Restraint: Resale Price Maintenance

resale price maintenance
Supplier requirement that goods be resold at a set price.

The most direct vertical restraint is the manufacturer's *vertical price-fixing*. The retailer is required to charge consumers a specified retail price. The specified price is usually a minimum price, but even a maximum price is considered **resale price maintenance.** This is no longer a per se violation because the courts increasingly apply the rule of reason. Some retailers secretly seek a minimum price requirement as a hidden method to achieve horizontal price-fixing. The retailers then falsely allege the pricing is forced on them by the supplier's market power. A specified maximum retail price often becomes an unspoken minimum price, so all retailers sell only at that price. What type of concerted activity constitutes illegal resale price maintenance? The following case illustrates a modern scheme the participants tried to justify as a state liquor regulation.

California Retail Liquor Dealers Assn. v. Midcal Aluminum, Inc.

445 U.S. 97 (1980)
United States Supreme Court

A California statute required all wine producers to file fair trade contracts (price schedules) with the state, showing the price at which wine must be sold. Although the state had no direct control over wine prices, wholesalers were subject to fine, license suspension, or revocation for selling below the posted prices. Midcal Aluminum, a wholesale distributor of wine, allegedly sold wines below the price posted by Gallo Winery. The California Court of Appeal ruled that the California wine-pricing system restrained trade in violation of the Sherman Act.

Justice Powell delivered the opinion of the Court.

California's system for wine pricing plainly constitutes resale price maintenance in violation of the Sherman Act. The wine producer holds the power to prevent price competition by dictating the prices charged by wholesalers. As Mr. Justice Hughes pointed out: such vertical control destroys horizontal competition as effectively as if wholesalers "formed a combination and endeavored to establish the same restrictions . . . by agreement with each other."

Thus, we must consider whether the State's involvement in the price-setting program is sufficient to establish antitrust immunity under *Parker v. Brown* . . . Several recent decisions have applied *Parker's* analysis. In *Goldfarb v. Virginia,* the Court concluded that fee schedules enforced by a state bar association were not mandated by ethical standards established by the State Supreme Court. The fee schedules therefore were not immune from antitrust attack. "It is not enough that . . . anticompetitive conduct is 'prompted' by state action; rather, anticompetitive activities must be compelled by direction of the State acting as a sovereign."

Petitioner contends that even if California's system of wine pricing is not protected state action, the Twenty-first Amendment bars application of the Sherman Act in this case. Section 1 of that Amendment repealed the Eighteenth Amendment's prohibition on the manufacture, sale, or transportation of liquor. The second section reserved to the States certain power to regulate traffic in liquor: "The transportation or importation into any State, Territory, or possession of the United States for delivery or use therein of intoxicating liquors, in violation of the laws thereof, is hereby prohibited."

These decisions demonstrate that there is no bright line between federal and state powers over liquor. The Twenty-first Amendment grants the States virtually complete control over whether to permit importation or sale of liquor and how to structure the liquor distribution system. Although States retain substantial discretion to establish other liquor regulations, those controls may be subject to the federal commerce power in appropriate situations. The competing state and federal interests can be reconciled only after careful scrutiny of those concerns in a "concrete case."

The federal interest in enforcing the national policy in favor of competition is both familiar and substantial.

> Antitrust laws in general, and the Sherman Act in particular, are the Magna Carta of free enterprise. They are as important to the preservation of economic freedom and our free-enterprise system as the Bill of Rights is to the protection of our fundamental personal freedoms.

We have no basis for disagreeing with the view of the California courts that the asserted state interests are less substantial than the national policy in favor of competition. That evaluation of the resale price maintenance system for wine is reasonable, and is supported by the evidence cited by the State Supreme Court in *Rice.* Nothing in the record in this case suggests that the wine pricing system helps sustain small retail establishments. Neither the petitioner nor the state Attorney General in his *amicus* brief has demonstrated that the program inhibits the consumption of alcohol by Californians. We need not consider whether the legitimate state interests in temperance and the protection of small retailers ever could prevail against the undoubted federal interest in a competitive economy. The unsubstantiated state concerns put forward in this case simply are not of the same stature as the goals of the Sherman Act.

We conclude that the California Court of Appeal correctly decided that the Twenty-first Amendment provides no shelter for the violation of the Sherman Act caused by the State's wine pricing program. The judgment of the California Court of Appeal, Third Appellate District, is *Affirmed.*

Case Questions

1. What are the two issues presented in the *Midcal* case?
2. What is the logical connection between the California statute controlling the liquor business and the national policy of antitrust enforcement?
3. Would the state statute be a defense to prevent antitrust enforcement if the regulatory system were designed to further a compelling state interest? Consider the alternate hypothesis that controlling liquor consumption through raising prices outweighs the national interest in promoting competition.

State Fair-Trade Laws Political pressure from small retailers coerced Congress to overrule the per se illegality of resale price maintenance. In 1937, the Miller-Tydings

Act permitted the states to legitimize resale price maintenance by statute when the restriction was included in the manufacturer's supply contract with retailers. After the Great Depression, there was a proliferation of chain stores that forced many small retailers and wholesalers out of business. Small businesses insisted that products should be sold at higher "fair prices" that would allow them a fair rate of return. By the early 1950s, 45 state statutes permitted resale price maintenance agreements. At its height, over 1,500 manufacturers enforced the fair-trade laws through agreements with retailers that required them to charge at least the "list price." Congress reinforced these agreements in 1952 with the McGuire Act which extended resale price maintenance even to those retailers that never signed the agreements under the so-called *nonsigner provisions.*

Resale price maintenance prevented discounting of many consumer goods, such as name-brand clothes, furniture, cameras, and consumer electronics. By the 1960s, however, mail-order houses began to proliferate in the few states without fair-trade laws eroding resale price maintenance. Discounting became very popular among consumers and eventually Congress repealed both the Miller-Tydings and McGuire Acts in 1975. This again permitted intrabrand competition. From time to time, legislation is introduced to reinstate or prohibit resale price maintenance; such efforts are currently underway.

Refusals to Deal After resale price maintenance was again prohibited, manufacturers developed other disciplines for retailers who refused to observe minimum prices. Manufacturers often initiated a *refusal to deal* with disruptive retailers. In *United States v. Colgate,*[7] the Supreme Court permitted certain refusals to deal so long as there was no contract agreement requiring sales at specific prices. The Colgate Company announced publicly that it would refuse to deal with distributors that failed to participate in its announced resale price maintenance policy.

Later cases have severely limited the *Colgate* doctrine, though they have not overruled it. Under the modern view, a refusal to deal is illegal and coercive if there is any active harassment or monitoring of the retailer's pricing behaviors or if the manufacturer uses a suspension or reinstatement system to discipline retailers. For example, Parke Davis distributed its pharmaceuticals through wholesalers and drug retailers.[8] Its wholesale catalog announced a refusal to deal to sellers that sold below the announced prices. Parke's retail prices often included a 50 percent markup. Parke Davis's wholesalers ceased filling orders for several retailers who advertised discounted prices on vitamins. The Supreme Court held that Parke Davis went beyond mere announcement of a refusal to deal by implementing an illegal resale price maintenance combination and conspiracy.

INTERNATIONAL PERSPECTIVE AND COMMENTARY

INTERNATIONAL PERSPECTIVE ON VERTICAL RESTRAINTS

The Japanese often divert criticism about the market entry barriers to foreign consumer goods by apologizing for problems caused by their "unique" distribution system. Most retail shops are small and often receive restocking deliveries several times each day; the Japanese claim that this is a useful "just-in-time" inventory method. High prices are necessary for profitability at the several wholesale levels

[7] *U.S. v. Colgate,* 250 U.S. 300 (1919).

[8] *U.S. v. Parke Davis & Co.,* 362 U.S. 29 (1960).

between manufacturers and traditional mom-and-pop retailers. Japan has a strong anti-chain-store law, making it difficult for large discounters to get started, expand, or continue operations. Widespread resale price maintenance is enforced through threats and intimidation by sellers and organized crime and even through discriminatory actions by regulators. Refusals to deal help to perpetuate this system. The number of small retail stores in Japan is beginning to decline, and discounters are on the rise. However, the Japanese resale price maintenance system effectively thwarts competition (both intrabrand and interbrand), discourages competitive imports, and passes huge overpricing on to consumers. Japanese consumer competition is tightly confined to perpetuate this system of inefficient small retailers, excessive levels of wholesale distributors, higher profits for all sellers, and a lower standard of living for Japanese consumers. Nevertheless, resale price maintenance is disappearing in Japan and Europe, so their consumers are beginning to discover U.S.–style discounting.

Consignments A *consignment sale* is a contingent transaction in which the manufacturer retains title to the goods (ownership) until the retailer resells them to the ultimate consumer. The consignee-retailer acts only as an agent for the consignor-manufacturer, so the retailer can be required to sell only on the manufacturer's prescribed sale terms and price. Manufacturers may try consignments as a legal form of resale price maintenance. In an early case, General Electric Company sold light bulbs through retailers on consignment, setting the retail price and paying the retailers a commission. Because GE owned the patent on light bulbs, it was held a legitimate agency relationship. GE retained title, risk of loss, and economic risk in the light bulb market. Today, the courts look more closely at consignments to avoid disguised resale price maintenance. After the GE patents expired, these consignment arrangements were held illegal per se under the Sherman Act. Today, some consignment arrangements can still have legitimate purposes. For example, it is legitimate for a supplier to retain title to goods as collateral. If the consignee-retailer goes bankrupt, the manufacturer can still recover the goods.

Vertical Nonprice Restraints

Manufacturers, unable to take advantage of resale price maintenance, often seek other nonprice restraints for similar control over retailers. One method prevents retailers from selling to discounters for resale. Another imposes territorial limitations prohibiting retailers from engaging in intrabrand competition. Both of these devices are vertical nonprice restraints. While nonprice restraints may have legitimate purposes, they can be used to enforce illegal resale price maintenance.

Exclusive Dealing The term *exclusive dealership* indicates some sort of restriction in the resale arrangement. Although the word *exclusive* often refers to fashionable or privileged status, in antitrust law it means two different things. First, the sole right to sell a manufacturer's products within a given region is known as an *exclusive distributorship*. This excludes all other dealers from selling the manufacturer's products in the same region. An exclusive distributor could also sell competitors' products. Manufacturers generally have wide freedom to pick their retailers or wholesalers. However, an exclusive distributorship is not always justified. If there are few substitutes for a manufacturer's products, exclusive distributorships may prevent all competition. Exclusive distributorships have been judged by the rule of reason, though some recent cases hold they are illegal per se. For example, it is illegal for one distributor to pressure the manufacturer to terminate sales to the only competing distributor.

The second use of the term *exclusive* relates to *exclusive dealing,* which requires the buyer to resell only the products of a single manufacturer. Exclusive dealing is illegal under §3 of the Clayton Act if it tends to create a monopoly or substantially lessens competition.

Clayton Act, §3: Exclusive Dealing

> It shall be unlawful for any person engaged in commerce to lease or make a sale . . . of . . . commodities . . . on the condition, agreement or understanding that the lessee or purchaser thereof shall not use or deal in . . . commodities of a competitor . . . of the lessor or seller, where the effect of such . . . [agreement] may substantially lessen competition or tend to create a monopoly in any line of commerce.

Quantitative Substantiality Manufacturers and suppliers cannot generally insist that a retailer refuse to carry competitor's products. Exclusive dealing contracts are judged by the *quantitative substantiality* test which presumes exclusive dealing adversely effects competition when it covers a substantial dollar volume. Thus, a violation may exist with a far lower percentage of market control than would be considered a monopoly or merger violation. In recent cases, a trend has emerged to focus this test on the actual market share foreclosed rather than the simple dollar volume.

Adequate Representation A more subtle way to enforce an exclusive dealing arrangement is to rely on the protection of the *Colgate* doctrine by simply refusing to sell to nonexclusive dealers. Manufacturers seeking this protection have replaced exclusive dealing language in their supply contracts with an *adequate representation clause.* This requires retailers to make substantial efforts to market the manufacturer's products. Manufacturers can terminate dealers if they do not expend the required efforts in advertising, inventory maintenance, service, or sales calls as specified in their contract.

Customer and Territorial Restrictions Manufacturers' efforts to restrict retailers from selling to particular customers or in specific territories are probably illegal. Arrangements that restrict retailers' sales to a geographic region or that require retailers to sell only to particular customers on a list deny retailers the right to sell to others, so they are illegal. At first, such arrangements were considered illegal per se under the *Schwinn* rule.[9] In 1977, however, this rule was replaced with the rule of reason. Now nearly all vertical nonprice restrictions are illegal only if unreasonable. The EU has banned territorial restraints in an effort to lower the barriers imposed by national borders within the EU. Some vertical nonprice restrictions are valid because they enhance interbrand competition. There are two important questions in the analysis of territorial or customer restrictions.

Vertical Nonprice Restriction Factors

1. Does the vertical restriction tend to limit competition?
2. Are there legitimate economic and business objectives for the vertical restriction?

[9] *United States v. Arnold Schwinn & Co.,* 288 U.S. 365 (1967).

Vertical nonprice restrictions may be illegal if there is little interbrand competition, if the manufacturer has considerable market power, or if high barriers to entry exist for new producers. In *Continental T.V., Inc. v. GTE Sylvania, Inc.*,[10] GTE Sylvania limited the number of retail franchises within specified geographic territories to strengthen its retail network. Franchised retailers could sell GTE Sylvania products only at particular locations. Continental was one of Sylvania's most successful retailers in San Francisco. It complained when Sylvania granted a franchise to another local retailer. Sylvania had refused to give Continental a franchise in Sacramento after Continental canceled a large Sylvania order. The U.S. Supreme Court overruled the *Schwinn* per se rule and justified Sylvania's actions after the Court recounted many of the competitive advantages discussed above that vertical restrictions give to interbrand competition.

Dealer Terminations Manufacturers have the freedom to choose or terminate their dealers when the dealer is unsuccessful, breaches key provisions in the distributorship agreement (e.g., adequate representation), or deviates from announced pricing or when the manufacturer changes its marketing strategy. However, the dealer termination power is not unlimited. Both federal and state laws protect against some types of arbitrary franchise termination. For example, the Automobile Dealer's Day in Court Act and the Petroleum Marketing Practices Act restrict arbitrary dealer terminations. State laws require manufacturers to exercise "good faith" or limit them to "just cause" terminations. Many foreign nations provide similar protection for local dealers of foreign-made goods.

1984 antitrust cases permit dealer terminations if no concerted action is taken to maintain resale prices. *Monsanto Co. v. Spray-Rite Service Corp.*[11] reaffirmed per se analysis of resale price maintenance but subjects vertical nonprice restrictions to the rule of reason. Can a manufacturer terminate a dealer who fails to comply with vertical nonprice restrictions? The following case permits manufacturers even wider latitude to terminate dealers.

Business Electronics Corp. v. Sharp Electronics Corp.

485 U.S. 717 (1988)
United States Supreme Court

Business Electronics was initially the exclusive dealer for Sharp calculators in the Houston market, but Hartwell was later added as a Sharp retailer. After continued discounting by Business Electronics, Hartwell threatened to quit selling Sharp products unless the Business Electronics dealership was terminated. Sharp terminated Business Electronics, which then sued Sharp for conspiracy in restraint of trade under §1 of the Sherman Act. The court of appeals reversed a jury verdict against Sharp for treble damages.

---

[10] *Continental T.V., Inc. v. GTE Sylvania, Inc.*, 433 U.S. 36 (1977).
[11] *Monsanto Co. v. Spray-Rite Service Corp.*, 465 U.S. 752 (1984).

Justice Scalia delivered the opinion of the Court.

Departure from the rule of reason standard must be justified by demonstrable economic effect, rather than formalistic line drawing. Departure from [the *GTE Sylvania* standard] must be justified by economic effect, such as the facilitation of cartelization, that interbrand competition is the primary concern of the antitrust laws, and that rules in this area should be formulated with a view towards protecting the doctrine of *GTE Sylvania.*

There has been no showing here that an agreement between a manufacturer and a dealer to terminate a "price cutter," without a further agreement on the price or price levels to be charged by the remaining dealer, almost always tends to restrict competition and reduce output. Without an agreement with the remaining dealer on price, the manufacturer retains both its incentive to cheat on any manufacturer-level cartel (since lower prices can still be passed on to consumers) and cannot as easily be used to organize and hold together a retailer-level cartel.

Any agreement between a manufacturer and a dealer to terminate another dealer who happens to have charged lower prices can be alleged to have been directed against the terminated dealer's "price cutting." In the vast majority of cases it will be extremely difficult for the manufacturer to convince a jury that its motivation was to ensure adequate services, since price cutting and some measure of service cutting usually go hand in hand. Accordingly, a manufacturer that agrees to give one dealer an exclusive territory and terminate another dealer pursuant to that agreement, or even a manufacturer that agrees to terminate another dealer for failure to provide contractually obligated services, exposes itself to the highly plausible claim that its real motivation was to terminate a price cutter. Manufacturers would be likely to forgo legitimate and competitively useful conduct rather than risk treble damages and perhaps even criminal penalties.

All vertical restraints have the potential to allow dealers to increase prices and can be characterized as intended to achieve just that. Vertical nonprice restraints only accomplish the benefits identified in *GTE Sylvania* because they reduce intrabrand competition to the point where the dealer's profit margin permits provision of the desired services. The term "restraint of trade" refers not to a particular list of agreements, but to a particular economic consequence, which may be produced by quite different sorts of agreements in varying times and circumstances. Economic analysis supports the view that a vertical restraint is not illegal per se unless it includes some agreement on price or price levels.

Affirmed.

Case Questions

1. What additional conduct between Sharp and Hartwell would be required before their activity would have constituted a per se violation?
2. What was the likely competitive effect of Sharp's termination of Business Electronics? How would Hartwell have likely behaved after the termination?
3. How does this decision change communications in supplier–customer relations and enhance their mutual fortunes?

---

tying
Supplier requires buyer to purchase undesired product to get the desired product; illegal under the rule of reason.

Tying Arrangements The Clayton Act has been interpreted to outlaw most tying arrangements. **Tying,** a tie-in agreement, requires customers to purchase certain commodities or goods. Typically, the seller refuses to sell a desirable, or *tying,* product, unless the customer agrees to purchase a less desirable, or *tied,* product. The tie-in relationship coerces buyers to purchase less desirable products if they want to obtain more desirable products. This effectively ties their main purchases to supplementary goods. A tie-in is effective only when the seller has some market power in the desirable or tying product, perhaps resulting from a patent or a secret process. The Clayton Act prohibits tying only of goods, not services or land sales. However, tying could also be illegal under the Sherman Act and apply more broadly to real estate, intangibles, and services.

Tying usually arises in one of three types of relationships. First, the tied and tying products are used together in fixed proportions (e.g., nuts and bolts, tires on automobiles). Second, the tied product may be necessary for use with the tying product (e.g., computer cards, disks or peripherals with a computer). Third, the products may be only loosely usable together and may even be used separately (e.g., seed and fertilizer).

Analysis of Tying For tying to be considered illegal, three elements must be established. First, there must be a tying product and a tied product. This requires evidence of the seller's sale of one product conditioned on the purchase of another. Second, the seller must have sufficient economic or market power to force the tie-in. This may be shown where buyers clearly prefer the seller's tying product. If several buyers agree to a coercive tie-in, the seller may be presumed to have market power. Third, the level of competition restricted in the tied (less desirable) product must be more than an insubstantial amount. This requires proof that there is a substantial amount of commerce in the tied product. For example, $500,000 of the salt market and $60,000 of the film market have been considered substantial irrespective of the market shares involved.

Effects and Motives for Tying Tie-in relationships force buyers to purchase tied products in larger quantities than they would purchase without the tie-in. Absent a tie-in, purchasers could probably obtain the tied product or some substitute more cheaply from other sellers. Tying reduces the buyer's freedom to use the lowest-cost vendor for each product. This probably permits the tying seller to charge near-monopoly prices for the tied product. Tying raises barriers to entry for potential producers of the tied product and reinforces the tying seller's market power in the tying product.

Sellers often use the tying relationship to extend their market power from the tying product to the tied products. Sometimes, manufacturers seek to protect their goodwill by restricting the use of tied products of allegedly inferior quality produced by outside vendors. Tying makes it possible to exercise a type of price discrimination by selling the tying product cheaply but receiving abnormally high profits from the tied product.

Justifications for Tying Although tying was once illegal per se, the courts increasingly permit sellers to justify it. DOJ has relaxed its stiff opposition to tying in recent years. In some instances, there is only one product, not two, so there can be no claim of tying. For example, both a picture tube and the accompanying television set or an automobile and its built-in radio can be viewed as either separate or single products. The real question here is whether there is a substantial market for the installation of the tied product into the tying product. There is only a replacement and repair market for television picture tubes, but a healthy and competitive installation aftermarket exists for car radios and stereos. Auto manufacturers may be guilty of an illegal tie-in of higher-priced and/or lower-quality car radios (tied product) to automobiles (tying product). Although some automakers permit buyers to delete standard equipment radios for a credit, at least one domestic automaker still makes it difficult to purchase stereos in the aftermarket by making its electrical system technically incompatible with aftermarket stereos.

In one case, U.S. Steel (now U.S.X.) attracted buyers of high-priced prefabricated homes by providing low-cost loans. Homes and loans are obviously not a single product. However, consumers might be willing to pay higher prices for the less desirable prefabricated homes (the tied product) if they receive desirable low-cost loans (the tying product). Today, many automobile and appliance manufacturers have captive finance companies (e.g., GMAC, FOMOCO Credit, GE Credit) that validly provide low-cost financing without violating antitrust policies against tying.

Tying relationships can be justified if they result in economic efficiency. During start-up, for example, new businesses may need to assure the proper functioning of their complex products. However, once a business has become established, the tying relationship is no longer justified. For example, a cable TV antenna manufacturer required the purchase of service contracts with the purchase of its equipment. This tie-in was justified only until the business had become well established.

Tying relationships are also justified if the quality of the tied product is higher than that of competitors' similar products. The seller may claim that without the tie-in the goodwill it derives from the tying product will suffer. This argument is seldom successful. At one time, IBM required that only the IBM brand of computer punch cards be used with its computers. Although other vendors sold similar punch cards at far lower prices, IBM argued that only the IBM punch cards could prevent fouling of the IBM card readers. The Bell System used a similar argument when it required that its customers use only Western Electric telephones and switching equipment. In both instances, the alleged low quality of competitors' products could be solved by other reasonable means, such as measurable design and performance specifications. For example, specifications concerning the thickness and resilience of computer punch cards are sufficient to prevent damage to IBM's leased computers. Likewise, specifications concerning the electronic characteristics of telephone instruments are sufficient to prevent damage to the Bell System's equipment. This quality control argument is weak if the company is well established and specifications can ensure the compatibility of the tied products with the tying products. How far may product tie-ins be legally used to maintain product quality and the firm's goodwill? The following case illustrates why franchises may use vertical restraints illegal for nonfranchise businesses. (Franchises were also discussed in Chapter 14.)

Principe v. McDonald's Corp.

631 F.2d 303 (4th Cir. 1980)
United States Court of Appeals

The Principes operated two McDonald's restaurant franchises in Virginia. McDonald's denied their request to acquire a third franchise on the ground that the additional franchise would impair the quality of the Principes' existing operations. Thereafter, the Principes sued McDonald's, alleging an illegal tying relationship. McDonald's required franchisees to pay royalties for use of the franchise and also required franchisees to rent the McDonald's store from an affiliate.

Phillips, Senior Circuit Judge

At the time this suit was filed, McDonald's consisted of at least four separate corporate entities. McDonald's Systems, Inc. controlled franchise rights and licensed franchisees to sell hamburgers under the McDonald's name. Franchise Realty Interstate Corporation (Franchise Realty) acquires real estate, either by purchase or long-term lease, builds McDonald's hamburger restaurants, and leases them either to franchisees or to a third corporation, McOpCo. McOpCo, which is not a party to this suit, operates about one-fourth of the McDonald's restaurants in the United States as company stores.

McDonald's is not primarily a fast-food retailer. While it does operate over a thousand stores itself, the vast majority of the stores in its system are operated by franchisees. Nor does McDonald's sell equipment or supplies to its licensees. Instead its primary business is developing and collecting royalties from limited menu fast-food restaurants operated by independent business people.

McDonald's develops new restaurants according to master plans that originate at the regional level and must be approved by upper management. Regional administrative staffs meet at least annually to consider new areas into which McDonald's can expand. Once the decision is made to expand into a particular geographic area, specialists begin to search for appropriate restaurant sites. McDonald's uses demographic data generated by the most recent census and its own research in evaluating potential sites. McDonald's attempts to analyze and predict demographic trends in the geographic area.

This process serves a twofold purpose: (1) McDonald's hopes to determine whether the residents are likely to buy fast food in sufficient quantities to justify locating a restaurant there; (2) by anticipating future growth, McDonald's seeks to plan its expansion to maximize the number of viable McDonald's restaurants within a given geographic area. Based on a comparison of data for various available sites, the regional staffs select what they believe is the best site in each geographic area. Occasionally no available site suits McDonald's requirements and expansion must be postponed.

As part of the planning process, McDonald's decides what type of store to build on each site and where to locate it on the land. Differences in lot size and shape necessitate adjustments in store and parking lot configurations. Projected market size dictates dining room size. Land elevation, sign restrictions, store visibility and local setback requirements control restaurant placement.

Meanwhile, Franchise Realty acquires the land, either by purchase or long-term lease, and constructs the store. Acquisition and development costs averaged over $450,000 per store in 1978. All McDonald's restaurants bear the same distinctive features with a few exceptions due to architectural restrictions: the golden arches motif, the brick and glass construction, and the distinctive roofline. According to the defendants, these features identify the stores as a McDonald's even where zoning restrictions preclude other advertising or signs.

As constructed, McDonald's restaurants are finished shells; they contain no kitchen or dining room equipment. Furnishing store equipment is the responsibility of the operator, whether a franchisee or McOpCo. McDonald's does provide specifications such equipment must meet, but does not sell the equipment itself.

Having acquired the land, begun construction of the store and selected an operator, McDonald's enters into two contracts with the franchisee. Under the first, the franchise agreement, McDonald's grants the franchisee the rights to use McDonald's food preparation system and to sell food products under the McDonald's name. The franchisee pays a $12,500 franchise fee and agrees to remit 3 percent of his gross sales as a royalty in return. Under the second contract, the lease, McDonald's grants the franchisee the right to use the particular store premises to which his franchise pertains. In return, the franchisee pays a $15,000 refundable security deposit (as evidence of which he receives a 20-year non-negotiable non-interest-bearing note) and agrees to pay 8.5 percent of his gross sales as rent. These payments under the franchise and lease agreements are McDonald's only sources of income from its franchised restaurants. The franchisee also assumes responsibility under the lease for building maintenance, improvements, property taxes and other costs associated with the premises. Both the franchise agreement and the lease generally have 20-year durations, both provide that termination of one terminates the other, and neither is available separately. The Principes argue McDonald's is selling not one but three distinct products, the franchise, the lease and the security deposit note. The alleged antitrust violation stems from the fact that a prospective franchisee must buy all three in order to obtain the franchise.

As evidence that this is an illegal tying arrangement, the Principes point to the unfavorable terms on which franchisees are required to lease their stores. Not only are franchisees denied the opportunity to build equity and depreciate their property, but they must maintain the building, pay for improvements and taxes, and remit 8.5 percent of their gross sales as rents. In 1978 the gross sales of the Hopewell store generated about $52,000 in rent. That figure nearly equaled Franchise Realty's original cost for the site and corresponds to more than a fourth of the original cost of the entire Hopewell restaurant complex. At that rate of return, the Principes argue, Franchise Realty will have recouped its entire investment in four years and the remainder of the lease payments will be pure profit. The Principes contend that the fact the store rents are so high proves that McDonald's cannot sell the leaseholds on their own merits.

Nor has McDonald's shown any need to forbid its licensees to own their own stores, the Principes say. Appellants contend that McDonald's is the only fast-food franchiser that requires its licensees not only to pay royalties but to lease their stores from the franchisor.

A separate tied product is the note that evidences the lessee's $15,000 security deposit, according to the appellants. The Principes argue the security deposit really is a mandatory contribution to McDonald's working capital, not security against damage to the store or breach of the lease contract. By tying the purchase of these $15,000 twenty-year non-negotiable non-interest-bearing notes to that of the franchise, McDonald's allegedly has generated a capital fund that totaled over $45 million in 1978. It is argued that no one would purchase such notes on their own merits. The Principes assert that only by requiring franchisees to purchase the notes as a condition of obtaining a franchise has McDonald's been able to sell them at all.

As support for their position, the Principes rely primarily on the decision of the Ninth Circuit in *Siegel v. Chicken Delight, Inc.,* one of the first cases to address the problem of franchise tie-ins. Chicken Delight was what McDonald's characterizes as a "rent a name" franchisor: it licensed franchisees to sell chicken under the Chicken Delight name but did not own store premises or fixtures. The company did not even charge franchise fees or royalties. Instead, it required its franchisees to purchase a specified number of cookers and fryers and to purchase certain packaging supplies and mixes exclusively from Chicken Delight. These supplies were priced higher than comparable goods of competing sellers. A class composed of franchisees challenged the tying arrangement as a violation of the Sherman Act. . . . In the court's view, Chicken Delight had attempted "to extend trademark protection to common articles (which the public does not and has no reason to connect with the trademark)," a classic kind of illegal tying arrangement.

Without disagreeing with the result in *Chicken Delight,* we conclude that the court's emphasis in that case upon the trademark as the essence of a franchise is too restrictive. Far from merely licensing franchisees to sell products under its trade name, a modern franchisor such as McDonald's offers its franchisees a complete method of doing business. It takes people from all walks of life, sends them to its management school, and teaches them a variety of skills ranging from hamburger grilling to financial planning. It installs them in stores whose market has been researched and whose location has been selected by experts to maximize sales potential. It inspects every facet of every store several times a year and consults with each franchisee about his operation's strengths and weaknesses. Its regime pervades all facets of the business, from the design of the menu board to the amount of catsup on the hamburgers; nothing is left to chance. This pervasive franchisor supervision and control benefits the franchisee in turn. His business is identified with a network of stores whose very uniformity and predictability attracts customers. In short, the modern franchisee pays not only for the right to use a trademark but for the right to become a part of a system whose business methods virtually guarantee his success. It is often unrealistic to view a franchise agreement as little more than a trademark license.

Applying this standard to the present case, we hold the lease is not separable from the McDonald's franchise to which it pertains. McDonald's practice of developing a system of company-owned restaurants operated by franchisees has substantial advantages, both for the company and for franchisees. It is part of what makes a McDonald's franchise uniquely attractive to franchisees.

First, because it approaches the problem of restaurant site selection systematically, McDonald's is able to obtain better sites than franchisees could select. Armed with its demographic information, guided by its staff of experts and unencumbered by preferences of individual franchises, McDonald's can wield its economic might to acquire sites where new restaurants will prosper without undercutting existing franchisees' business or limiting future expansion. Individual franchisees are unlikely to possess analytical expertise, undertake elaborate market research or approach the problem of site selection from an area-wide point of view.

Second, McDonald's policy of owning all of its own restaurants assures that the stores remain part of the McDonald's system. McDonald's franchise arrangements are not static: franchisees retire or die; occasionally they do not live up to their franchise obligations and must be replaced; even if no such contingency intervenes, the agreements normally expire by their own terms after 20 years. If franchisees owned their own stores, any of these events could disrupt McDonald's business and have a negative effect on the system's goodwill. Buildings whose architecture identified them as former McDonald's stores would sit idle or be used for other purposes. Replacement franchisees would have to acquire new and perhaps less desirable sites, a much more difficult and expensive process.

Third, because McDonald's acquires the sites and builds the stores itself, it can select franchisees based on their management potential rather than their real estate expertise or wealth. Ability to emphasize management skills is important to McDonald's because it has built its reputation largely on the consistent quality of its operations rather than on the merits of its hamburgers. A store's quality is largely a function of its management.

Finally, because both McDonald's and the franchisee have a substantial financial stake in the success of the restaurant, their relationship becomes a sort of partnership that might be impossible under other circumstances. McDonald's spends close to half a million dollars on each new store it establishes. Each franchisee invests over $100,000 to make the store operational. Neither can afford to ignore the other's problems, complaints or ideas.

Case Questions

1. What are the tie-in issues in the typical franchise relationship?
2. What justifies a franchisor requiring the franchisee to purchase a particular site, equipment, or supplies specified by the franchisor?
3. What were the alleged tying and tied products in the *McDonald's* case?

Reflections of Keiretsu[12]

COMMENTARY

Keiretsu is a Japanese industrial organization form that has been both praised and criticized in recent years. Firms within a Keiretsu share links among firms in different industries and between firms that stand in vertical relationships. Japanese firms within a Keiretsu tend to solidify their relationships through various links and affiliations, such as cross shareholdings, interlocking directorates, social structures among top management, financial commitments, joint affiliation within commercial and investment banks, joint R&D activities, technology transfers, primary or exclusive customer supplier relationships, and unspoken social norms, creating expectations for all employees to concentrate their personal purchases only from Keiretsu members. Keiretsu critics argue it is a cartel-like industrial organization structure that resembles a feudal family of firms.

Antitrust Barriers to Keiretsu

Western critics commonly allege that Japanese-style Keiretsu behave like cartels. This strongly suggests that illegal restraints of trade or monopolization activities accompany some aspects of Keiretsu relationships. On its face, the description of common Keiretsu relations suggest that threats and intimidation by lead industrial firms are anticompetitive practices that exert monopolization pressures on Keiretsu members. Contracts and practices that prohibit suppliers from selling outside their Keiretsu channel or boycott outside suppliers potentially violate U.S. and Japanese antitrust law.

As the Japanese economy has grown and there are numerous viable competitors in each industry, the Keiretsu have evolved from horizontal or intermarket Keiretsu into vertical structures. This means that Keiretsu are probably most vulnerable to

[12]John W. Bagby, *Reflections of Keiretsu,* Working Paper 92-1, Smeal College of Business Administration, Pennsylvania State University (1992).

allegations of vertical restraints of trade, up and down the chain of distribution. Under U.S. law, the classic analysis of prohibited vertical restraints of trade focus on a lead firm and its downstream pressures on distributors. While such pressures exist in Japanese-style Keiretsu relationships, it is alleged that the greater pressures are focused upstream toward suppliers. Therefore, the traditional U.S. vertical restraint of trade analysis is somewhat inappropriate to applications on Japanese Keiretsu.

Exclusive Distributorships Exclusive distributorships invert the coercion upstream from distributor or other reseller to a supplier. When the retailer has the sole right to sell goods produced by a particular manufacturer or sold through a particular distributor, this is known as an "exclusive distributorship." Effectively, this grants a geographic monopoly over that manufacturer's brand. Japanese-style Keiretsu can be enhanced by exclusive distributorships because this reinforces the community of interest within the Keiretsu chain of distribution and enhances competition only with other Keiretsu.

Customer or Territorial Restrictions A suppliers' restriction on which resellers may sell to particular customers or within particular regions are considered customer or territorial restrictions. They provide a minimum incentive to other resellers by permitting oligopoly profits and tend to favor some distribution channels over others. They are considered illegal when they tend to limit competition and have no legitimate economic or business objective. Therefore, the rule of reason applies to customer territorial restrictions. In Japanese-style Keiretsu, such restrictions probably proliferate. The continuation of relations with a particular supplier are threatened unless certain customers or territories are ignored by the reseller. This permits the distribution network for the lead industrial firm to be strengthened in pieces and prevents the growth of large, powerful, and potentially insurgent retailers or distributors downstream from the lead industrial firm.

Concerted Refusal to Deal U.S. antitrust laws prohibit a concerted refusal to deal as a method to enforce other vertical price and nonprice restrictions. This discipline assists in maintaining resale price maintenance. However, it is illegal to actively harass downstream resellers into following a resale price maintenance scheme. Any illegal monitoring, rather than a simple refusal to deal, is prohibited. The shunning activity of Keiretsu members against disruptive suppliers or distributors is similar to a concerted refusal to deal. Concerted refusals to deal in Keiretsu generally force compliance with exclusive dealing, exclusive distributorship, and price discrimination schemes. They are not usually intended to support a price floor as is typical in U.S. violations.

Price Discrimination

price discrimination Seller's illegal practice of charging different prices for commodities of like grade and quality.

Price discrimination is a seller's practice of charging different prices to different buyers for goods of like grade and quality. Where price discrimination substantially lessens competition or tends to create a monopoly, it is illegal under the Robinson-Patman Act. The FTC has enforcement powers under Robinson-Patman, and a private right of action exists for competitors or buyers damaged by a price discrimination.

Price discrimination would be impossible in a perfectly competitive market. Any buyer faced with a higher price than offered to others would simply buy from another seller. However, few markets are perfectly competitive, some buyers or sellers usually have some market power, and some buyers lack pricing information.

Ethical Dilemmas in Price Discrimination

ETHICAL DILEMMA

The Robinson-Patman Act prohibition against price discrimination was passed to protect small businesses competing with chain stores that had oligopsony or buyer's market power. Congress supported "atomized" markets despite evidence that such markets are inefficient in many markets. However, Congress sought to preserve small business and prevent secret rebates and kickbacks. The balance drawn by antitrust laws reflects a conscious legislative choice to discourage some forms of unethical behavior and to encourage and establish economic self-reliance as an ethical policy. Although some contemporary ethical systems make efficiency the sole criteria for ethical judgments in economic matters, the antitrust laws exemplify a richer heritage that also includes popular societal norms as a basis for ethical judgments. Nevertheless, critics claim that Robinson-Patman has outlived its ethical and economic usefulness.

Conditions Leading to Price Discrimination

Price discrimination is usually sustainable only while buyers or sellers have imperfect information. Buyers are often ignorant of the prices paid by other buyers. If buyers had better information, they could simply boycott the seller who charges higher prices. Price discrimination may occur when some buyers are given secret price concessions. Antitrust laws may impose conflicting and confusing standards. Whereas the Sherman Act prohibits active communication of price information among sellers to avoid the appearance of price-fixing, the Robinson-Patman Act suggests that the lack of price visibility may encourage price discrimination.

Proof of Price Discrimination

To establish a violation of the Robinson-Patman Act, a plaintiff or the FTC must prove six elements.

Establishing Price Discrimination

1. Discrimination in price,
2. Between two different purchases,
3. Affecting interstate commerce,
4. Concerning sales of commodities of like grade and quality,
5. Causing a substantial lessening of competition or a tendency to create a monopoly,
6. Causing injury to competitors of the seller or the buyer or to their customers.

The two discriminatory transactions must occur within a contemporaneous time period; transactions separated by an excessively long time probably reflect changing market conditions. The price discrimination is usually proved by reference to two different sales prices as stated in the contracts of sale, although different nonprice terms may also discriminate. For example, preferential credit terms given to one buyer but not offered to others are prohibited as price discrimination. Quantity discounts theoretically open to all purchasers but in practice denied to small buyers are also discriminatory.

Commodities of Like Grade and Quality The Robinson-Patman Act is inapplicable to intangibles, services, and mixed sales of goods and services. It is lawful to discriminate in the price charged for securities, mutual fund shares, patents, licenses, real estate leases, and consulting services. Air fares and hotel rates are commonly discriminatory. However, a price discrimination in intangibles or services could conceivably violate the Sherman Act as a restraint of trade or an attempt to monopolize. Such discriminations could also violate the FTC Act if they are found to be an unfair method of competition.

The goods sold must be of like grade and quality; that is, their physical and chemical composition must be similar. If buyers willingly substitute two seemingly different products as interchangeable, they may be of like grade and quality. Subtle differences in the brand names or labels of two similar products will usually not justify price discrimination if consumers perceive the two products as functionally similar in performance. Arguably, higher prices may be charged for name-brand goods, even if the seller manufactures a lower-quality, generic equivalent to account for cost differences in advertising or promoting a name brand.

Competitive Injuries from Price Discrimination

Price discrimination is prohibited if it substantially lessens competition or tends to create a monopoly or if it injures, destroys, or prevents competition. A critical element of proof is the actual injury to competition. Liability arises when any person either discriminates or knowingly benefits from a discrimination, thereby causing lost profits or missed business opportunities. The level of the business suffering the injury must be identified. Injuries may occur at the seller's level, buyer's level, or the level of the customers of the buyer. Injuries at these levels are respectively referred to as primary-line injuries, secondary-line injuries, and tertiary-line injuries.

Primary-Line Injury Price discriminations tending to injure those in competition with the discriminating seller are *primary-line injuries.* A discriminating seller operating in two distinct geographic regions damages its competitors in the lower-priced region. The seller may discriminate between regions in order to drive competitors out of business in one region by charging higher-than-normal prices in another region where it has greater market power. It recoups profits lost in the lower-priced market with profits in the high-priced market, temporarily cross-subsidizing losses in the underpriced market. Figure 17–4 illustrates Seller A's market power to charge higher prices in its primary market, Pennsylvania. The same goods are sold in Michigan at prices lower than Seller B can match, injuring Seller B at the primary line because B competes with A in Michigan. A similar effect occurs between nations. Dumping exported goods at lower prices than in the seller's home market can eliminate competitors by making high profits in the seller's home market.

Secondary-Line Injury Price discriminations between two buyers competing for the same customers may injure buyers, a *secondary-line injury.* If two buyers have

FIGURE 17-4 Primary-Line Injury

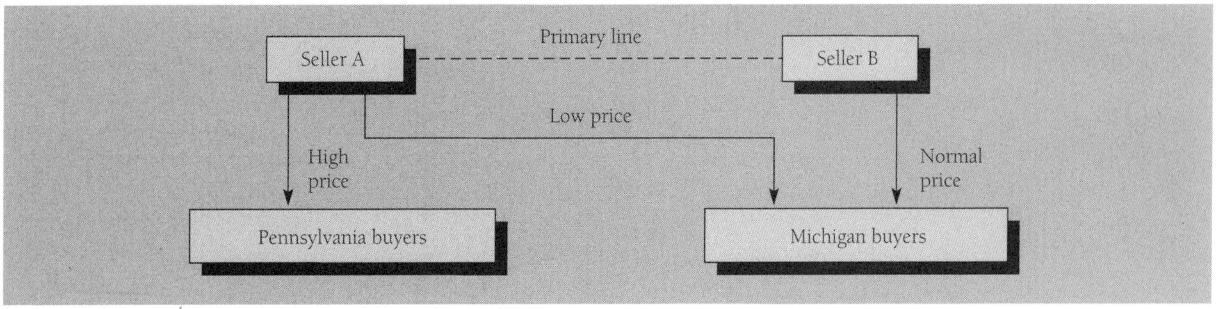

different costs for the same goods, the buyer paying higher prices suffers because the buyer paying lower prices can pass the savings on to its customers. In Figure 17–5, Buyer B pays the seller a lower price and can pass this cost savings on to its customers through lower retail prices. Buyer A cannot compete effectively if it cannot pass on its higher costs. Customers with a choice between A and B will prefer B's lower prices.

If Buyer A and Buyer B were in distinct geographic markets, no secondary-line injury would occur because their two sets of customers could not practically choose one over the other. This condition existed in *Utah Pie Co. v. Continental Baking Co.*[13] Several national bakers sold pies in the Salt Lake City market at lower prices than they charged in other markets, suffering losses on many sales. The Supreme Court upheld a jury's conclusion that Utah Pie, a local baker, suffered secondary-line injury even

FIGURE 17-5 Secondary-Line Injury

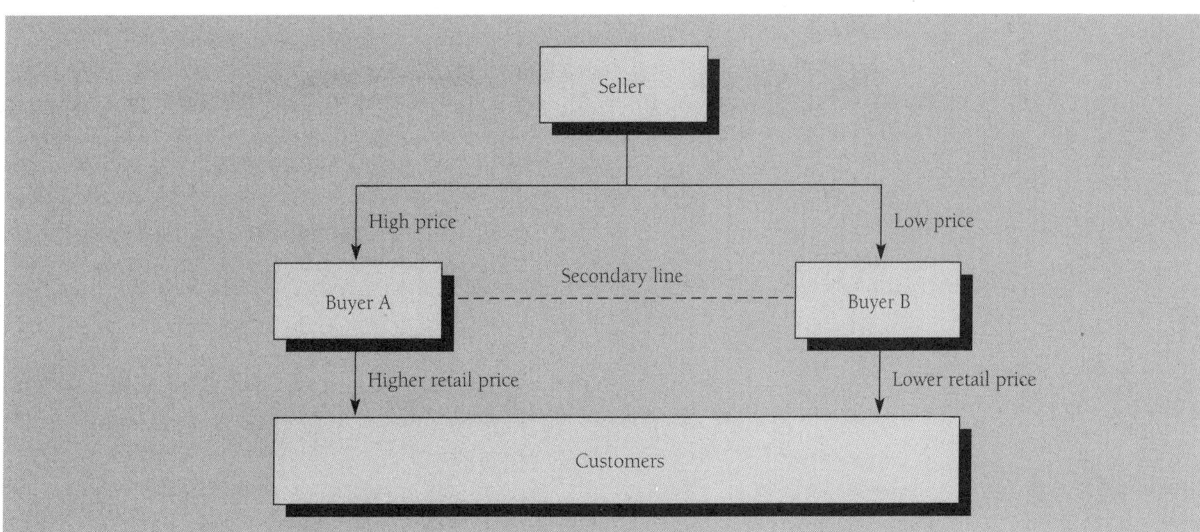

[13] *Utah Pie Co. v. Continental Baking Co.*, 386 U.S. 685 (1967).

FIGURE 17-6 Tertiary-Line Injury

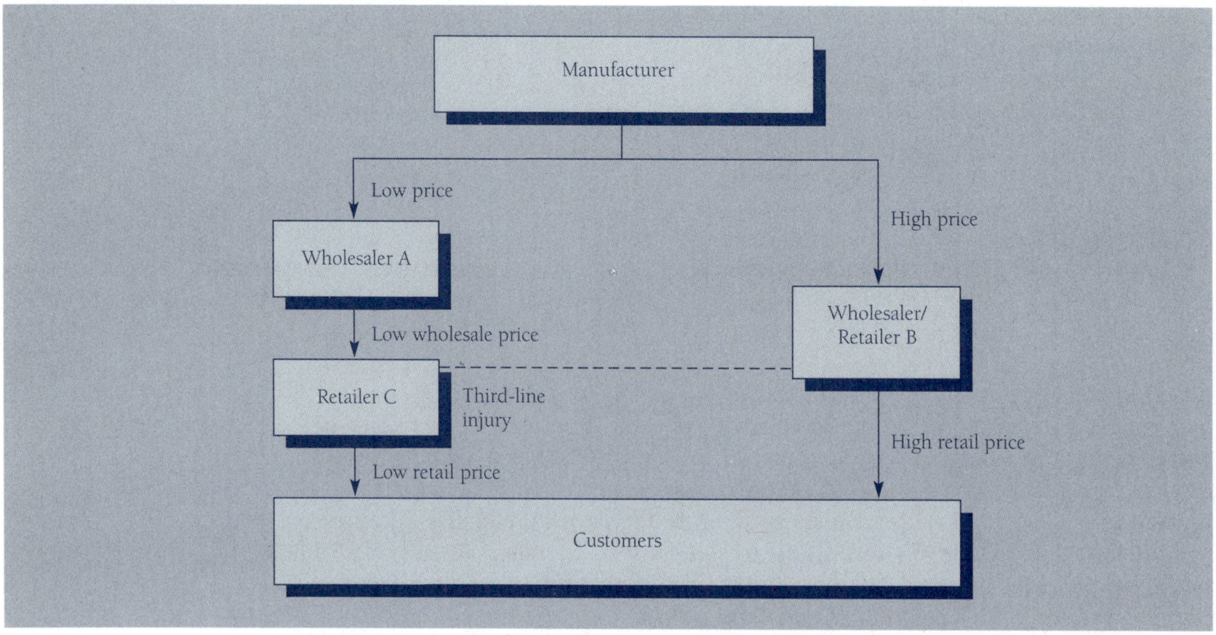

though it was profitable at the time of suit. Price discrimination that slowly erodes competition due to a drastically declining price structure is sufficient evidence of past conduct to project future competitive injury.

Tertiary-Line Injury A more controversial theory of price discrimination involves injury to the buyer's customers. Theoretically, injury may occur at any level of distribution, no matter where price discrimination occurs in a long chain of distribution. A *tertiary-line injury* may occur if customers of the buyers are injured by price discrimination because the cost savings are passed on through wholesalers to retailers. In Figure 17–6, a *third-line injury* occurs between the customers in two chains of distribution. The manufacturer has sold at a higher price to B, an integrated wholesaler/retailer, which passes the higher costs on to customers as higher retail prices. Because Wholesaler A receives a lower price, it charges a low wholesale price to Retailer C, which passes the lower costs on as lower retail prices to customers. B's ability to compete with A and C is undermined in sales made to the same customer base. Third-line injury occurs between B and C.

Price Discrimination Defenses

Price discrimination may be justified with an affirmative defense. The seller may attempt to show that the competitive effect of differential pricing was trivial, effectively rebutting evidence of competitive injury. For example, sales to a government or a nonprofit institution may be made at different prices unless the resale is intended in the retail market. Export sales are exempted because the Robinson-Patman Act applies only to "commodities . . . sold for use, consumption, or resale within the United

States." There are also three statutory defenses: changing conditions, cost differential, and meeting the competition in good faith.

Changing Conditions Section 2(a) of the Robinson-Patman Act provides a defense to allegations of illegal price discrimination when the market has changed so that prices previously charged are no longer realistic.

Robinson-Patman Act, §2(a): Changing Conditions Defense

> . . . nothing herein shall prevent price changes from time to time in response to *changing conditions* affecting the marketability of the goods concerned, such as (but not limited to) actual or imminent deterioration of perishable goods, obsolescence of seasonal goods, distress sales under court process, or sales in good faith in discontinuance of business.

The changing conditions defense is confined strictly to temporary situations in which the physical nature of the commodity requires a distress sale. A classic example is the lowering of retail automobile prices on the leftover inventory of the prior model year. After significant inventories of the new year's model arrive on dealer lots, conditions have changed sufficiently to permit lowering the price of the year-old "new" models.

Cost Differential Another defense provided in §2(a) recognizes that various sales contracts may have different costs.

Robinson-Patman Act, §2(a): Cost Differential Defense

> . . . nothing herein contained shall prevent differentials which make only *due allowance* for differences in the cost of manufacture, sale, or delivery resulting from the differing methods or quantities in which such commodities are sold or delivered.

Although this justification would appear significant, in practice it has been difficult for sellers to rely on. One problem is that there is no universal definition of costs. Robinson-Patman was designed to prevent predatory pricing in which one producer subsidizes low-priced sales from profits earned elsewhere and later raises prices above competitive levels after competitors are driven from the market. Predatory pricing may be demonstrated through the circumstantial evidence of average variable costs. Price-cutting below average variable costs is strong evidence of predatory pricing. Computation of average variable costs requires that an allocation be made of indirect costs (e.g., overhead), a complex and controversial process. The amount of overhead allotted to each unit in addition to average variable costs varies under different assumptions.

The cost differential defense is most often successful when discriminatory pricing is based on legitimate quantity discounts. The defense is more reliable when there are actual savings in packaging, handling, and transportation costs. Should "functional" discounts be permitted if some buyers provide these marketing functions? The next case illustrates how some sellers allege discounts for some buyers are illegitimate and destructive to buyers paying higher prices.

Texaco v. Hasbrouck

110 S. Ct. 2535 (1990)
United States Supreme Court

Texaco supplied gasoline to both independent filling stations and to distributors that owned their own stations in Spokane, Washington. Independent retailers paid Texaco a higher retail tank wagon price than was paid by groups of stations operated as a chain: Gull and Dompier. Gull sold Texaco gasoline through its own stations under the Gull trade name, and Dompier later entered the Spokane market, selling Texaco gasoline through its own stations under the Texaco name. Texaco charged them lower "functional" discount prices than it charged the independents. Dompier's Texaco stations were restocked by Dompier's tanker trucks. However, Texaco prohibited the independents from hiring their own trucks to transport gasoline from Texaco at the lower discount price. The independents' sales volume fell significantly, and Dompier's grew rapidly after it entered the market. The independents sued for treble damages, claiming that Texaco's pricing violated Robinson-Patman. Texaco claimed that its "functional" discounts were legitimate and as seller it was not responsible for the pricing behavior of its wholesale customers.

Justice Stevens delivered the opinion of the Court.

In order to establish a violation of the Act, respondents had the burden of proving four facts: (1) that Texaco sales to Gull and Dompier were made in interstate commerce; (2) that the gasoline sold to them was the same grade and quality as that sold to respondents; (3) that Texaco discriminated in price between Gull and Dompier on the one hand and respondents on the other; and (4) that the discrimination had a prohibited effect on competition.

In *F.T.C. v. Morton Salt Co.,* we held that an injury to competition may be inferred from evidence that some purchasers had to pay their supplier "substantially more for their goods than their competitors had to pay." Texaco, as supported by the United States and the FTC as *amici curiae,* argues that this presumption should not apply to differences between prices charged to wholesalers and those charged to retailers. Moreover, they argue that it would be inconsistent with fundamental antitrust policies to construe the Act as requiring the seller to control his customers' resale prices. The Report of the Attorney General's National Committee to Study the Antitrust Laws (1955) wrote:

> Suppliers granting functional discounts should not be held responsible for any consequences of their customers' pricing tactics. Price-cutting at the resale level is not "the effect of" a differential that merely accords due recognition and reimbursement for actual marketing functions.
>
> On the other hand the law should tolerate no subterfuge. Where a wholesaler–retailer buys only part of his goods as a wholesaler, he must not claim a functional discount on all. Only to the extent that a buyer actually performs certain functions, assuming all the risk, investment, and costs involved, should he legally qualify for a functional discount.

In this case, there was no substantial evidence indicating that the discounts to Gull and Dompier constituted a reasonable reimbursement for the value to Texaco of their actual marketing functions. Indeed, Dompier was separately compensated for its hauling function, and neither Gull nor Dompier maintained any significant storage facilities.

The evidence indicates that Texaco affirmatively encouraged Dompier to expand its retail business and that Texaco was fully informed about the persistent and marketwide consequences of its pricing policies. Indeed, its own executives recognize that the dramatic impact on the market was almost entirely attributable to the magnitude of the distributor discount and the hauling allowance. Yet at the same time that Texaco was encouraging Dompier to integrate downward, Texaco was inhibiting upward integration by the respondents. The special facts of this case thus make it peculiarly difficult for Texaco to claim that it is being held liable for the independent pricing decisions of Gull and Dompier.

One would expect that most functional discounts will be legitimate discounts that do not cause harm to competition. A functional discount that constitutes a reasonable reimbursement for the purchasers' actual marketing functions will not violate the Act. Not every functional discount is entitled to a judgment of legitimacy, and it will sometimes be possible to produce evidence showing that a particular functional discount caused a price discrimination. When such anticompetitive effects are proved—as we believe they were in this case—they are covered by the Act.

Affirmed.

Case Questions

1. What level of injury was established in this case?
2. What kind of evidence is needed to prove the legitimacy of a discount? Can a functional discount be distinguished from a volume discount?

Meeting the Competition in Good Faith Section 2(b) of the Robinson-Patman Act also permits a seller to discriminate in price if the lower price "was made in good faith to meet an equally low price of a competitor." The price discriminator must have a reasonable belief that granting the lower price is necessary to win the sale. The lower price must exactly meet, but not beat, the competitor's price.

The problem of conflicting antitrust goals is also involved in satisfying the competition defense. Communications with competitors concerning price strongly suggests price-fixing. Good faith is crucial to the competition defense because price discrimination and price-fixing enforcement must be harmonized. Sellers may show good faith if they investigate the truth of a buyer's claim that a competitor charges a lower price. For example, some retailers require buyers to bring in the competitor's ad or estimate or prove that a lower price is available to the buyer.

When the necessity of meeting the price has ceased and market conditions return to normal, the seller must cease discriminatory pricing. To fall within the competition defense, sellers may discriminate only in meeting their own competition and may not discriminate to assist a customer in meeting its competition. The competitor's price must be met within a short time frame.

Seller and Buyer Liability

The Robinson-Patman Act applies to both buyers and sellers. It is unlawful for "any person . . . knowingly to induce or receive a discrimination in price." Thus, if the buyer has knowledge that the price it obtained was discriminatory, either the buyer or the seller may be held liable. A buyer inducing a price discrimination may take advantage of any defense the seller has. For example, the A & P foodstore rejected as too high a bid made by Borden to supply A & P with "private label" milk products. Borden made a revised lower bid in a good faith effort to meet the competition, so its price discrimination was justified by the "meeting the competition in good faith" defense. Because Borden had this defense, A & P was not liable as a buyer for inducing a price discrimination.[14]

Indirect Concessions

The Robinson-Patman Act also prohibits price discriminations effected through indirect price concessions. It is unlawful for "any person to pay, grant, or receive any brokerage or allowance in lieu thereof except for services rendered in connection with the sale or purchase of goods." This provision prohibits a buyer from persuading a

---

[14] *Great Atlantic and Pacific Tea Co., Inc. v. FTC*, 440 U.S. 69 (1979).

seller to pay a brokerage fee to a person who splits the payment with the buyer, an illegal form of kickback. Fictitious brokerage fees represent a secret discount. However, a brokerage fee is permissible if the buyer or a third party actually performs legitimate brokerage-type services, such as preparing documents or arranging transportation.

Robinson-Patman also prohibits the seller from discriminating in providing payments, services, or facilities, such as giving only select customers some special assistance, allowance for advertising, or display materials. The disadvantaged buyer needs to prove (1) that the promotional service or allowance was provided only to other purchasers or (2) that a competitor was favored in its "business stature." Such services are permissible if triggered at specified dollar volumes or are equally available to all buyers.

Discrimination in Freight Charges Price discrimination may also occur when shippers charge discriminatory freight rates. If the quoted sale prices in two sales are identical, but either customer pays more or less than the actual cost of shipment, then there is an indirect price discrimination. There is no discrimination if the buyer must pay all freight and delivery charges. However, some informal "delivered price" quotes include freight charges. If all buyers pay the same freight charges, as part of a uniform delivered price, then buyers geographically closer to the seller's plant pay higher freight charges per mile than do buyers located farther away.

Equal freight rates charged for unequal delivery distances may constitute *phantom freight,* an illegal price discrimination. Phantom freight is classified as (1) a single-basing point system if the freight is actually shipped from another place, (2) zone pricing if the same freight rates are imposed on all customers within a zone, regardless of the distance, or (3) a multiple-basing point system if the nearest of several base points of origin governs the freight charge. In devising policies on pricing, additional service provisions, freight rates, brokerage commissions, or any other nonprice allowances, careful consideration must always be given to the possibility that a buyer might argue that the practices used are discriminatory.

The Future Regulation of Price Discrimination

The Robinson-Patman prohibition against price discrimination is generally regarded as one of the most violated provisions of antitrust law. Critics argue it perpetuates inefficient small retailers, reduces price competition, and raises consumer prices to uniform levels. However, it should be recognized that many of the international fair-trade laws, particularly the antidumping rules, are essentially price discrimination regulations. *Dumping,* as discussed in Chapter 2, is a foreign firm's practice of selling in another nation's market at prices lower than those prevailing in that firm's home market. The same arguments are made against both practices, dumping and price discrimination, because they encourage cross-subsidies that drive out competitors, leaving the discriminator with a monopoly.

Unfair Trade Practices

The Sherman and Clayton Acts do not cover other activities arguably resulting in unfair trade practices. Congress granted the FTC powers to remedy other practices in the FTC Act. Section 5 gives the FTC extensive powers to prohibit "unfair methods of competition and unfair or deceptive acts or practices in or affecting commerce."

Practices that are not clearly illegal under the antitrust laws may be ruled illegal by the FTC. The rulemaking power of the FTC permits it to fill in the gaps of the antitrust laws. In addition, most states have similar powers to prohibit some of these practices.

Federal Trade Commission Powers and Procedures

The FTC Act empowers the FTC to investigate and pursue complaints of unfair trade practices. The FTC often resolves such complaints with a *consent decree,* settling charges without an admission or denial. Defendants must usually promise to refrain from the practice in the future. The FTC may also issue *cease and desist orders,* which are somewhat stronger than injunctions. Cease and desist orders require the defendant to stop an unfair trade practice and bear the stigma of a repeat offender.

FTC proceedings usually involve an internal hearing held before an administrative law judge. Appeals may be taken to the FTC commissioners and ultimately to the U.S. Court of Appeals and the U.S. Supreme Court. FTC orders may be enforced with contempt citations, including fines and imprisonment.

Federal Trade Commission's Informal Guidance

The FTC attempts to provide guidance on the manner in which it will exercise its powers. This gives businesses notice of what the FTC considers unfair trade practices. In addition, parties may request the FTC to issue an *advisory opinion* regarding the legality of specific proposed conduct.

From time to time, the FTC issues comprehensive industry *guidelines.* These guidelines create *safe harbors* for specific conduct. The FTC promises not to prosecute a business that conforms its transactions to the guidelines. However, FTC advisory opinions and guidelines do not have the force of law and may be reinterpreted by the courts. The FTC may also issue specific trade regulation rules that do have the force of law. For example, the courts sustained the FTC's requirement that gasoline retailers post octane numbers on gas pumps. The deceptive advertising aspects of this rulemaking power were discussed in Chapter 12.

The FTC uses standards of fairness in giving advisory opinions, issuing guidelines, promulgating rules, and prosecuting violations. The FTC often considers (1) whether public policy is offended by the alleged unfair trade practice, (2) whether the practice is immoral, unethical, oppressive, or unscrupulous, and (3) whether the practice causes substantial injury to consumers, competitors, or others in business.

In *FTC v. Brown Shoe Co.,*[15] the FTC interpreted its mission as the extension of the philosophy of the Sherman and Clayton Acts. Brown Shoe had promised special benefits to retailers that agreed not to sell other brands of shoes. The Supreme Court upheld the FTC's exercise of power to stop trade restraints in their incipiency, without proof that those restraints violated the Clayton or Sherman Acts.

Summary

The rule of reason and the per se rule are used to judge the legality of restraints of trade. Under the rule of reason, the defendant can attempt to justify a restraint of trade. Only unreasonable restraints of trade are illegal under the Sherman Act. Horizontal combinations among direct competitors are illegal

[15] *F.T.C. v. Brown Shoe Co.,* 384 U.S. 316 (1966).

restraints of trade and the least justifiable. In certain repetitive and unjustifiable circumstances, restraints of trade are always considered illegal per se; these include price-fixing, division of markets, group boycotts, concerted refusals to deal, and tying. Recently, several per se violations have been judged under the rule of reason.

Agreements among direct competitors to set prices at artificial levels are illegal per se. There is no justification for price-fixing even if the competitors are well intentioned, attempt to set maximum prices, or argue the necessity for professional ethics. Fixing credit or freight terms is also illegal. Trade associations must be careful to avoid exchanges of price information that might facilitate price-fixing. Competitors that divide markets among one another commit a per se violation. Boycotts by groups of competitors are also illegal per se. Joint ventures are judged by the rule of reason.

Proof of conspiracies in restraint of trade is difficult because violators seldom leave an evidentiary trail. Circumstantial evidence often sustains the burden of proving criminal guilt beyond a reasonable doubt. Businesses that mimic the pricing behaviors of competitors under a tacit agreement may be committing illegal conscious parallelism.

Vertical restraints of trade impose tying arrangements and restrict resale prices, territorial access to markets, and the freedom to sell competing brands. Resale price maintenance agreements are illegal. A manufacturer's limited refusal to deal with retailers disregarding suggested list prices may be legal if there is no harassment, price monitoring, or conspiracy. Legitimate consignment sales may impose resale price maintenance.

Vertical nonprice restraints may be illegal. Exclusive dealing contracts are illegal if they substantially lessen competition or tend to create a monopoly. Adequate representation clauses may permit manufacturers to drop retailers that fail to adequately promote their products. Vertical nonprice restrictions, such as customer or territorial restrictions, are judged by the rule of reason. Franchising is a method that may legally use many vertical restrictions to protect the franchiser from trademark infringement.

The Clayton Act prohibits tying in which sellers require customers to buy less desirable, tied products in order to buy desirable, tying products. Tying may be justified where there is actually only one product, by a start-up company to ensure its product quality or where tied products of low quality would interfere with the tying product.

Price discrimination is illegal under Robinson-Patman if (1) two different purchasers, (2) in interstate commerce, (3) pay different prices, (4) for similar commodities, and if (5) the price discrimination substantially lessens competition or tends to create a monopoly and (6) causes damage. Primary-line injury resulting from price discrimination occurs to competitors of the seller. Secondary-line injury occurs to the buyer paying the higher prices. Tertiary-line injury occurs to the customers of the buyer when the price discrimination occurs at the level of the buyer's buyer. Sellers may justifiably discriminate in the prices they charge when market conditions change, legitimate quantity discounts are made, or lower prices of competitors are met in good faith. Both the seller granting the price discrimination and the buyer inducing it may be held liable.

The FTC Act fills in the regulatory gaps created by the Sherman and Clayton Acts and by the states' antitrust laws. Section 5 of the FTC Act prohibits unfair methods of competition and unfair and deceptive trade practices. The FTC may settle unfair trade practice claims with consent decrees or may prosecute in the courts.

Critical Thinking Review Questions

1. Describe the source and reasoning behind the rule of reason and the per se rule. Compare and contrast the reasoning for each of the per se categories.
2. Compare and contrast conscious parallelism with concerted action. How does the term *agreement* apply to conscious parallelism?
3. Discuss the differences between horizontal and vertical restraints of trade.

Critical Thinking Exercises

1. Licensed physicians belong to a nonprofit corporation, the Maricopa Foundation for Medical Care (Maricopa), which was intended to provide an alternative medical coverage plan to traditional health insurance systems. Maricopa set a maximum fee schedule, which its members agree to follow as a method to control health care costs. Insurers using Maricopa physicians agree to pay up to the limit. What type of restraint of trade do these activities constitute? What is the reasoning behind the court's decision? What constraint does this decision place on national health care design? *Arizona v. Maricopa County Medical Society,* 457 U.S. 332 (1982).
2. The Goldfarbs contracted to buy a home in Virginia, and the mortgage company that was to lend them the money for the purchase required a title examination before the deal was closed. Only a licensed attorney could conduct such an examination. The Goldfarbs contacted 36 attorneys, all of whom indicated that their fee for such services was the one recommended by the Bar Association of Virginia. Generally, charging lower than the Bar Association's recommended fees was a ground for disciplinary action against attorneys. The Goldfarbs sued, claiming that the fee arrangement violated §2 of the Sherman Act. With what result, and why? *Goldfarb v. Virginia State Bar,* 421 U.S. 773 (1975).
3. Mutt and Jeff are both sole proprietors of building cleanup services in Atlanta. They have been friends for several years. Recently, they discussed an idea of mutual interest: the possibility of coordinating their pricing so that downtown office building managers didn't pit them against each other in bidding for cleanup jobs. What are the antitrust implications? What would a competitor have to prove in order to show that it is illegal?
4. The publishers of over 12,000 newspapers are members of the Associated Press (AP), which collects and assembles news and distributes news stories to its members. The bylaws of the AP prohibited its members from selling news to nonmembers and set up a system by which AP members could block nonmember competitors from joining. The United States filed a complaint charging that these provisions violated §1 of the Sherman Antitrust Act. With what result, and why? *Associated Press v. U.S.,* 326 U.S. 1, 1945.
5. Your company, Run Company, manufactures running shoes and sells them to sporting goods stores. *Runing Magazine* recently rated your WINGS brand "excellent" and your other brand, PLOP, "worthless." The sporting goods stores are clamoring for shipments of WINGS. You notify these retailers that if they want WINGS, they must order an equal quantity of PLOP. Why does your lawyer complain when he hears what you have done?
6. Your company, Run Company, needs shoelaces to make WINGS and PLOP running shoes. You persuade a shoelace manufacturer to sell you shoelaces at a price lower than the price it charges Nike, your major competitor. Why does this trouble your lawyer?
7. Allen sells his product in both Georgia and Florida, while Ben sells his competing product only in Florida. Allen lowers his price in Florida but leaves it the same in Georgia. Is this an example of a primary-line, secondary-line, or tertiary-line injury? Why?
8. Seller A charges Buyers Y and Z a different price for its product. Buyers Y and Z, in turn, sell the product to other purchasers, but Buyer Z must charge a higher price than Buyer Y because of the higher price it paid Seller A. Is this an example of a primary-line, secondary-line, or tertiary-line injury? Why?
9. Stacy Corporation produces a unique "add-on" software program that enhances spreadsheet analysis of differing budget alternatives. Usually, budget categories must be painstakingly replicated in most spreadsheets, and the alternative assumptions of sales, expenses, interest rates, and overhead expense must be entered manually. Stacy's product, Budget-Ease, automatically projects different assumptions for the variables mentioned above, greatly reducing the time spent on projecting budget alternatives. However, Stacy insists that customers must purchase Stacy-Calc, the company's own spreadsheet program, in order to use Budget-Ease. Compare and contrast the legal and ethical analyses of this problem.

PART 7

Employment Law and Business

18 Terms and Conditions of Employment

19 Labor–Management Relations

20 Equal Employment Opportunities

CHAPTER

18

Terms and Conditions of Employment

Critical Thinking Questions

- How are the laissez-faire principles underlying the employment-at-will doctrine reconciled with the due process ethic in U.S. law?
- What reasons have been used to justify passage of the federal laws to regulate employment standards and compensation?
- Compare and contrast the various state unemployment compensation schemes with the desire for a federal scheme for retirement income and pension plan uniformity.
- What ambiguities plague the workers' compensation system? What are the arguments surrounding the calls for workers' compensation reform?
- What assumptions underlie the establishment of uniform safety standards under the Occupational Safety and Health Act (OSHA)?
- What biases might be introduced into worker safety standards if the National Institute for Occupational Safety and Health (NIOSH) or the Occupational Safety and Health Review Commission (OSHRC) were not reasonably independent of politics?

Introduction... Past, Present, Future

Statutes governing the wages and hours of employment and character of the workforce were among the first legal regulations of the employment relationship. These statutes were passed in response to the perception that employers early in the industrial revolution took advantage of child workers, immigrants, and the poor. Employees worked long workdays but were provided only subsistence wages. Early state laws passed in the mid-19th century were intended to achieve "a fair day's work." However, many were invalidated on the constitutional grounds that the laws deprived employers of their property without due process or unduly interfered with contracts. Few employment laws passed until the New Deal legislation of the 1930s, when Franklin D. Roosevelt pushed for legislation imposing minimum wages and maximum working hours.

Since the early 1900s, most states have enacted workers' compensation laws to provide workers with minimal injury compensation and supplement their immediate cash needs after injury. The perceived failure of these early workers' compensation laws and of the labor markets to improve workplace safety led Congress to a more comprehensive employment safety scheme with the Occupational Safety and Health Act (OSHA) of 1970. In an efficient employment market, employees are compensated for safety risks through income and work time adjustments. However, some labor economists argue that the labor markets are often inefficient. There cannot be efficiency unless all parties voluntarily assume the risks after acquiring perfect knowledge about all relevant job factors such as safety risks. Employees fully informed of those risks might be willing to accept them if sufficiently paid. The real-world labor markets have imperfections; both workers and employers have difficulty identifying workplace risks or analyzing the information available. Some observers argue that employers have an incentive to withhold information about job risks just as some employees may hide their incompetencies. Society suffers a burden if workers are injured and become unable to support their families and if productivity declines.

Labor market imperfections led to the passage of major employment standards and safety laws. The centerpiece of employment standards legislation is the Fair Labor Standards Act of 1938 (FLSA). It is intended to stabilize the economy by (1) placing a floor under wages with the minimum wage and (2) encouraging broader-based employment of more workers by imposing a "standard workweek," with maximum regular working hours and higher pay required for overtime. Employment safety regulation has experienced varied enforcement under different presidential administrations. However, by specifying particular hazards, OSHA supplements the financial incentives of state workers' compensation statutes to achieve safety.

In the future, many employment compensation and safety issues will be settled by means of uniform federal legislation rather than piecemeal state legislation or union contracts discussed in Chapter 19. Legislation may address issues such as mandatory medical benefits, rising minimum wages, a lower minimum wage for teenagers, and child care facilities or benefits. Such legislation would add significantly to employers' costs and/or government spending. Therefore, public policy should reconcile the cost burden of the legislation with the need to attract competent employees. Employers may be expected to continue the trend toward using more part-time or temporary employees and independent contractors. This permits the employer to reduce the employment costs of personnel administration functions (e.g., tax withholding) and it reduces costs of employee benefits and any long-term employment. Some observers have called this evolution a virtual corporation or temporary organization assembled only for short-term projects. After completion, all participants go their own way with no further employment responsibilities.

Will safety regulation receive greater emphasis in the future? Business can be expected to lobby for reductions in the cost burden of additional federal safety laws. Nevertheless, there may be more extensive notification of workplace health risks. The costs of employment standards and safety regulation will probably increase for both employers and the federal government, with some employees winning ever greater benefits. This chapter first discusses the employment-at-will concept and then covers state and federal laws on employment compensation, privacy, employee benefits, and unemployment compensation. It concludes with state and federal workplace safety laws.

The Employment-at-Will Doctrine

Before the 20th century, employment contracts were based on laissez-faire economic theory. Broad freedom of contract was given to both employers and employees. Either party could terminate the employment relationship at any time and without any cause or justification. Today, this freedom of contractual association, known as the **employment-at-will** doctrine, applies to nearly two-thirds of the workforce. It is justified as a symmetrical laissez-faire relationship. First, it would be slavery to force individuals to work involuntarily for an employer. Second, if employees have the right to quit, mutuality suggests the employer should have the right to fire them. Additionally, it would be unfair to require the employer to accept substandard services or retain an untrusted employee.

employment-at-will Either employer or employee may terminate an employment contract without the other's consent and without breach of contract.

Rationale for the Employment-at-Will Doctrine

> [Individuals] must be left, without interference, to buy and sell as they please, and to discharge or retain employees at will for good cause or for no cause, or even for bad cause, without thereby being guilty of an unlawful act per se. It is a right which an employee may exercise in the same way, to the same extent, for the same cause or want of cause as the employer.[1]

Erosion of Employment-at-Will

About 45 states have tort-like remedies or contract exceptions affecting employment-at-will. These protect employees from arbitrary dismissal. The first exception involves wrongful discharge under the *public policy exception.* In many states, an employee may not be fired for refusing to obey a supervisor's order to violate the law or other clearly articulated public policies. For example, an employee may not be fired for reporting that the employer is committing crimes. This type of abusive discharge is often referred to as the *whistle-blower exception.* Another public policy favors employees' participation in the justice system through service on juries. Employees are often protected from discharge if their absence from work was necessary to perform jury duty.

In some states, an employee's job is protected where the employer makes an express or *implied contract guarantee* of continued employment. For example, employers often issue written personnel policy guidelines or personnel manuals. Policies stated in such guidelines or manuals become implied terms of the employment contract. Many personnel manuals state that employees will be discharged only for "good cause" or "just cause." Some employers promise continued employment as long as employees "do the job." In such cases, the employer may be required to prove good or just cause, such as the discharged employee was insubordinate, incompetent, intoxicated, or drug impaired on the job; had excessive absences; or performed poorly. Some employers have responded to such restrictions by removing "just cause" language from personnel manuals. Others have required employees to sign a document agreeing they are employed-at-will or that the personnel manual is not part of the employment contract. An employee's rights are sometimes reinstated if the employer later makes an oral promise of good faith and fair dealing or promises terminations only for just cause.

A classic case illustrating employment security except for just cause as an implied contract term is *Toussaint v. Blue Cross & Blue Shield of Mich.*[2] Toussaint, a middle manager at Blue Cross for five years, was discharged unexpectedly despite his

---

[1] *Payne v. Western and Atlantic Railroad Co.*, 82 Tenn. 507, 518 (1884).

[2] *Toussaint v. Blue Cross & Blue Shield of Mich.*, 292 N.W. 2d 880 (Mich. 1980).

supervisor's assurance of continued employment as long as he was "doing the job." The Blue Cross Personnel Manual stated that company policy was to terminate employees "for just cause only." The Michigan Supreme Court found his termination was unjust, stating:

> Employers are most assuredly free to enter into employment contracts terminable at will without assigning cause [but] [w]hen a prospective employee inquires about job security and the employer agrees that the employee shall be employed as long as he does the job, a fair construction is that the employer may discharge only for cause. . . . While an employer need not establish personnel policies or practices, where an employer makes them known to its employees, the employment relationship is presumably enhanced. The employer secures an orderly, cooperative and loyal work force, and the employee the peace of mind associated with job security and the conviction that he will be treated fairly. . . . A promise to terminate employment for cause only would be illusory if the employer were permitted to be the sole judge and final arbiter of the propriety of the discharge. There must be some review of the employer's decision if the cause contract is to be distinguished from the satisfaction contract. . . . An employer who agrees to discharge only for cause need not lower its standard of performance. . . . The employer's standard of job performance can be made part of the contract. Breach of the employer's uniformly applied rules is a breach of the contract and cause for discharge. In such a case, the question for the jury is whether the employer actually had a rule or policy and whether the employee was discharged for violating it.

A few states give stronger protections with an implied *covenant of good faith and fair dealing* in the employment contract. In one case, a salesman was terminated just prior to becoming qualified for retirement benefits. Because the employer did not act in good faith, the court ordered the benefits paid. Some states protect workers from sexual harassment under this exception, although sexual harassment claims are more often brought under the federal equal employment laws, discussed in Chapter 19.

There are several state and federal statutes that prohibit unjust terminations. The National Conference of Commissioners on Uniform State Laws has issued the Uniform Employment Termination Act (UETA) for the state legislatures to consider. The UETA would impose the public policy and retaliatory termination exceptions, require good cause for terminations, and impose arbitration or other nonjudicial dispute resolution. Montana is one of only a few states to adopt any statutory exceptions to employment-at-will. A few states are limiting the employee's right to punitive damages by designating abusive discharge suits as based on breach of contract rather than tort law.

Federal law prohibits private employers from firing employees who exercise certain statutory rights. Employees are protected from discharge (1) for their first wage garnishment, (2) if they cooperate with government officials in legal proceedings brought against the employer for pollution or work safety violations, (3) if they exercise self-organization rights under the labor laws or their federal employment law rights governing minimum wages, overtime pay, or discrimination, (4) to avoid vesting of their pension rights, (5) for service on federal juries, (6) if they refuse a lie detector test, or (7) for taking a leave of absence for family health purposes. Many of these topics are detailed later in this and other chapters. Public employees generally have much greater protection against unjust terminations than do private sector employees. This is largely based on the various civil service systems initiated to prevent political *graft.* These systems provide job security to prevent newly elected politicians from rewarding political allies with government jobs vacated when the former employees were unjustly terminated.

These and the other employment, labor, and employment discrimination laws discussed in Chapters 18, 19, and 20 may be violated even if the employee is not overtly discharged. A *constructive discharge* occurs when working conditions become intolerable, forcing the employee to quit. Most courts use an objective test, the reasonable person standard, to determine if the working conditions were really intolerable. A few courts grant the employee relief only if the employer's grievance procedures are first exhausted. To avoid liability for back pay (past), front pay (future), or reinstatement, employers should forthrightly implement grievance procedures, train supervisors in employment law, document all complaints, and brief new employees on company policies when first hired.

Many other nations prohibit terminations without just cause and then only after notice of several weeks or months. Although the U.S. is not a signatory, many other nations are parties to the International Labor Organization's Convention on Termination at the Initiative of the Employer. The Convention imposes a just cause rule for employee terminations giving employees a form of vested right in the job.

Moral Dilemmas for Whistle-Blowers

In one unjust termination case, George Geary was fired by U.S. Steel after telling upper management that some tubular steel products were unsafe and unable to withstand normal operating stress. After several admonitions from his superiors, Geary continued to complain about these products. A Pennsylvania court upheld U.S. Steel's firing of Geary under the employment-at-will doctrine despite Geary's claim that an exception applied for so-called whistle-blowers.[3] While this doctrine is still applied in many states, federal law protects some types of whistle-blowing.

Plant Closing Law Effective since 1989, Congress constrained the freedom of many employers to decide exactly when plants might be closed down. The federal *plant closing law* requires employers to give notice of plant closings to give employees an opportunity to adjust. The Worker Adjustment and Retraining Notification Act of 1988 (WARN) requires employers of 100 or more employees to give at least 60 days' notice of a plant closing or layoff. Notice must be given for (1) *mass layoffs* of at least one-third of the full-time workforce or at least 500 employees at a single site and (2) permanent or temporary *plant closings* when 50 or more full-time employees will lose employment during any 30-day period. Notice must be given to unions representing the employees or to individual employees if they are nonunionized. Local governments must be notified to ease the adverse impact that mass layoffs and plant closings have on the surrounding community.

Exemptions Several exemptions to the plant closing law reduce the 60-day notification period. First, notice may be reduced if the employer is actively seeking capital or new business necessary to continue the plant's operations, and the employer believes in good faith that public notice would frustrate these efforts. Second, plant closings or mass layoffs caused by business circumstances that are not reasonably foreseeable permit reduction of the 60-day notification period. Third, no notice is required for closings due to natural disasters, such as floods, earthquakes, or drought. In these circumstances, the employer must give as much notice as is practical and explain why 60 days' notice was impossible. No notice is required when a temporary facility is closed or when a particular project has been completed and the employees knew that their employment was limited to that project. In addition, notice is not required for closings or layoffs during strikes or plant lockouts that are legal under the labor laws.

---

[3] *Geary v. United States Steel,* 319 A.2d 174 (Pa. 1975).

Employer Liability Employers in violation of the plant closing law are liable for back pay and benefits to each terminated employee. A penalty of $500 must be paid for each day that notice is not given to the local government if the employees are not paid within three weeks after the closing or layoff. Damages and penalties may be reduced if a federal court finds the employer acted in good faith. Attorneys' fees may be awarded to the prevailing party. The Department of Labor has rulemaking authority to enforce the law and interpret vague terms such as what constitutes a single *facility.*

Employee Privacy

employee privacy Controversial balancing of employee rights to secrecy with the employer's property rights and liberty.

Employers increasingly use tests and gather other information to predict the performance of new hires and existing employees. The equal employment laws discussed in Chapter 20 require that aptitude tests and other information used to project job performance must be directly related to the actual job tasks. Former employer references and information about an individual's lifestyle, habits, use of substances, and past behaviors may indicate a prospective employee's honesty and predictable future performance. A former employer may be liable for defamation if reference letters contain damaging false information. However, many people view some tests and background investigations as an excessive intrusion into their privacy. Some tests have questionable validity, resulting from scientifically fallacious techniques or slipshod testing procedures. The **employee privacy** controversy illustrates a growing tension between employers and employee rights advocates.

Many employers require interviewees to take batteries of tests, including psychological, medical, drug, intelligence, and skills tests. Psychological testing may reveal an applicant's work ethic, criminal tendencies, ability to work with others, performance under stress, and aptitude for leadership. Intelligence and skills tests may reveal an applicant's knowledge and capabilities to perform the tasks necessary for the job. Medical tests may reveal an applicant's predisposition to certain diseases that require expensive treatment. For example, mandatory HIV tests for the AIDS virus are a controversial procedure disapproved by some courts.[4] Some employers have even considered genetic testing to predict an applicant's honesty, criminal tendencies, or future health care burden. The use of intrusive tests, many without a scientific consensus on reliability, raises profound public policy, legal, and privacy issues.

Substance Abuse There is considerable empirical evidence that employees' abuse of certain substances can adversely impact their performance, productivity, and health as well as workplace safety. For example, tobacco use is strongly linked to lung cancer and emphysema. Whereas workplace smoking bans and hiring bans on smokers are probably legal, firing smokers may not be legitimate. Thousands of local ordinances and employer work rules regulate smoking. The Occupational Safety and Health Administration, discussed later, may further regulate workplace smoking. Alcohol and drug abuse is directly related to on the job accidents and diminished capacity, productivity, and public safety. Nearly all the Fortune 100 companies have drug testing programs, many for prospective new hires, usually performed through urinalysis or the assay of hair samples.

Drug testing poses numerous legal issues. Policies covering unionized employees must be negotiated with the union as a term or condition of employment. Random drug testing of existing employees is often impermissible. There are some exceptions for federal employees, where there is "reasonable suspicion" or "probable cause" that

---

[4] *Glover v. Easter Nebraska Community Office of Retardation,* 686 F.Supp. 243 (D.Neb.1988).

drug abuse has impaired the employee's job performance. The justification for random drug tests may be clearest when the employee's job impacts public safety, such as with operators of dangerous equipment or transportation workers: pilots, train engineers, air traffic controllers, bus drivers. A long history of low privacy expectations and the role model function of athletes have justified random testing of high school athletes. The Drug-Free Workplace Act of 1988 requires private contractors supplying the federal government to establish and enforce drug-free policies, although the Act neither requires drug testing nor rehabilitation services. Does the state policy of privacy protect employees from random drug testing? The following case illustrates how some states balance drug prevention with privacy.

Twigg v. Hercules Corp.

406 S.E.2d 52 (W. Va.1990)
West Virginia Supreme Court

Twigg performed his job satisfactorily as a material planner at Hercules's Allegany Ballistics Laboratory in Mineral County West Virginia. Twigg protested but submitted to two random drug urinalyses in 1986. Both tests were negative. However, Twigg was discharged by Hercules after refusing to submit to a third test in 1987. Twigg challenged his discharge in federal district court, which sought clarification of West Virginia privacy policy from the West Virginia Supreme Court of Appeals.

Workman, Justice

This court first dealt with the issue of employers being held liable where an employee's discharge contravenes a substantial public policy in *Harless v. First National Bank in Fairmont.* In *Harless,* a bank employee was allegedly discharged after he attempted to bring to the attention of the bank's vice-presidents, and a member of the bank's board of directors, the fact that the bank "had intentionally and illegally overcharged customers on prepayment of their installment loans and intentionally did not make proper rebates," all in violation of state and federal consumer credit and protection laws. We recognized in the Harless case a new cause of action for at-will employees who are discharged when the employer's motives for such discharge contravene a substantial public policy.

Subsequently, in *Cordle v. General Hugh Mercer Corp.,* we dealt with whether the discharge of an employee for refusal to take a polygraph test as a condition of employment violated substantial public policy. In applying the holding of the *Cordle* case to the present case, it is unquestionable that since we do recognize a "legally protected interest in privacy" and have previously found that requiring employees to submit to polygraph examinations violates public policy based upon this privacy right, we likewise recognize that it is contrary to public policy in West Virginia for an employer to require an employee to submit to drug testing, since such testing portends an invasion of an individual's right to privacy.

We do, however, temper our holding with two exceptions to this rule. Drug testing will not be found to be violative of public policy grounded in the potential intrusion of a person's right to privacy where it is conducted by an employer based upon reasonable good faith objective suspicion of an employee's drug usage or where an employee's job responsibility involves public safety or the safety of others.

The reasoning behind drug testing was best explained by the Supreme Court of Alaska in *Luedtke v. Nabors Alaska Drilling, Inc.* The court in Luedtke reasoned

> we think this right (to privacy) must yield when it interferes in a serious manner with the health, safety, rights and privileges of others or with the public welfare. No one has an absolute right to do things in the privacy of his own home which will affect himself or others adversely. Indeed, one aspect of a private matter is that it is private, that is, that it does not

adversely affect persons beyond the actor, and hence is none of their business. When a matter does affect the public, directly or indirectly, it loses its wholly private character, and can be made to yield when an appropriate public need is demonstrated.

Where a business is engaged in an activity which involves either public safety or safety concerns for others, we find that there exists a legitimate reason for the implementation of a drug testing program since a drug-impaired employee would potentially increase the risk of harm to others. However, there must be a showing by the employer that the employees required to undergo such testing have responsibilities or duties which are connected to the safety concerns of others. Thus, in the present case, it is obvious that a company involved in manufacturing highly explosive and dangerous fuels does employ individuals who, if drug-impaired, could increase the risk of harm to others, whether they are members of the general public or other employees.

Generally, courts have held that "(t)he proscription against unauthorized searches and seizures embodied in . . . the Fourth Amendment to the United States Constitution . . . applies exclusively to government or state action. Therefore, generally a private employer can conduct drug testing without having to concern themselves with requirements of the Fourth Amendment. Thus we recognize that the imposition of an obligation upon the employer to meet the high standards of probable cause before conducting a drug test on an employee would place an intolerable burden upon the employer. That is why we choose to impose the lesser standard of reasonable suspicion upon the employer.

In placing this minimum standard upon the employer which must be met prior to conducting drug testing we acknowledge not only the employer's right to ensure the efficient and proper operation of his or her particular workplace, but also the employer's right to be free from potential liability brought on by an employee's drug usage which may ultimately result in harm to the others or in mismanagement, misfeasance or incompetence in the workplace. We refuse to allow an employer to intrude upon this right of his employee absent some showing of reasonable good faith objective suspicion, unless the employer can articulate either a public safety concern or concern for the safety of other employees. To hold otherwise would effectively render an employee's right to privacy meaningless.

Case Questions

1. For what reasons is it legitimate to override an employee's right to privacy with a drug or lie detector test?
2. What alternate explanation is there to challenge an employer's presumption that when any employee refuses a drug test, the employee is a bad employment risk because the employee is a regular drug user?

Employers should take great care in establishing drug testing policies because the law is still unsettled. Employers should assure privacy and reliability of drug tests and maintain the confidentiality of test results. Additionally, employers are best advised to retest any employee with positive test results, provide rehabilitation services, and sanction only repeat offenders. Care must be taken to research the reputation and then choose only from among qualified outside vendors if assistance is needed to provide testing services.

Federal Lie Detector Prohibitions The Employee Polygraph Protection Act prohibits most employers' use of lie detectors unless there is reasonable suspicion of losses caused by employees. A lie detector test may be conducted if the employer provides a written statement showing a reasonable suspicion that the employee had access to damaged or missing material and was involved in the matter. The questions must relate only to the alleged misconduct and may not be the only basis for an employee's dismissal. Employers may not retaliate against employees who refuse to take a lie detector test. Violators are subject to liability for punitive damages, civil fines, and attorneys' fees. Some exemptions exist for governments, government defense contractors, drug producers, and security protection companies. While employer surveillance of employee electronic mail (E-mail) is subject to the wiretapping laws, there can be little real expectation of E-mail privacy.

The Fair Labor Standards Act

The Fair Labor Standards Act (FLSA) applies to all employers engaged in interstate commerce. Typically, it covers employees in the manufacturing, transportation, and communications industries as well as employees in any "enterprise" with gross annual sales in excess of $250,000. The FLSA does not apply to federal government employees or government contractors, for whom there are similar but separate statutes.

The determination of which workers are treated as *covered employees* under the FLSA involves an important qualification test. For example, the Act does not cover *independent contractors,* so their employers are not regulated by the FLSA. If an employer retains the right to control both the means used by the employee and the outcome obtained, then the FLSA applies. As discussed in Chapters 8 and 13, true independent contractors control their own work and most of their own scheduling; only the contract objective (outcome) is controlled in the employment contract.

Several exemptions have arisen from time to time under the FLSA. For example, a *white-collar provision* exempts "executive, administrative, and professional" employees. This exemption includes the traditional professions of law and medicine as well as artistic professions and positions that require the exercise of discretion and judgment. Certain workers in agriculture, commercial fishing, household domestic service, retail establishments, and white-collar jobs must be paid a salary to be exempt. If exempted by the secretary of labor, the wage rate paid to apprentices, handicapped workers, and students may be set below the minimum wage. For example, there was a "training wage" at 80 percent of the full minimum wage from 1990 to 1993.

Computation of the Minimum Wage

The FLSA sets standards and methods for the computation of minimum wages, overtime pay, and compensable time. The **minimum wage** has stayed at $4.25 since 1991. It may be reduced by an amount equal to "reasonable costs of food, lodging, and other facilities" furnished to the employee. The employer may treat up to half of tips over $20 per month received by employees to satisfy the minimum wage.

minimum wage Federally mandated lowest hourly wage.

The overtime pay provisions require the payment of time and a half of the regular rate of pay for each hour worked in excess of the standard 40-hour workweek. For example, an employee working 45 hours at the minimum wage would receive $170 for the 40 hours at the regular pay rate ($4.25 × 40) and an additional $31.88 for the 5 overtime hours paid at time and a half (1.5 × $4.25 × 5), totaling $201.88. No overtime has to be paid if a 40-hour week contains workdays with more than eight hours. Overtime pay computation becomes more complex if the employee receives nonstandard compensation in addition to the hourly wage. For example, regularly earned bonuses or incentive pay must be included in the base pay rate to which the time and a half premium is applied. Overtime premiums do not apply to bonuses or expense reimbursements.

COMMENTARY

Controversy over Raising the Minimum Wage

From its beginnings, the minimum wage was hotly debated. Proponents argue it is necessary to provide a minimum standard of subsistence living to unskilled workers. They believe that without the minimum wage, the earnings of unskilled workers would plunge below coverage of minimal living expenses and thereby increase the welfare rolls. Opponents argue that the minimum wage distorts the labor markets by lowering demand for unskilled labor, shifts jobs overseas to low-priced labor markets, deprives teenagers of summer and part-time employment, and hastens employers' move to automation. Recent empirical studies are in conflict on whether employment really behaves as predicted after changes in the minimum wage. Given the stakes, it seems likely that changes in the minimum wage will remain a hot political question.

Transportation to and from the employer's place of business is not considered "compensable time." However, the minimum wage and overtime standards are applied to preliminary and postliminary activities. *Preliminary* activities include preparatory activities such as a butcher's time spent sharpening knives or workers assembling for transportation by the employer to the work site. *Postliminary* activities are efforts to wind up the work, including cleanup or transportation back from the work site by the employer. Do the minimum wage provisions cover executive and administrative personnel? The next case illustrates that although overtime provisions are inapplicable to supervisors, it can be difficult to apply this exemption.

Donovan v. Burger King Corp.

675 F. 2d 516 (2d Cir. 1982)
United States Court of Appeals

Burger King's assistant managers usually performed managerial and supervisory functions. However, they also performed production activities during peak service hours at mealtime. They were not given any overtime pay for the hours they worked in excess of 40 hours per week. Burger King argued that these employees were exempt from the overtime record-keeping and pay provisions of the FLSA because they were genuine "executives." The Secretary of Labor sued to include them within the overtime provisions of the FLSA.

Ralph K. Winter, Jr., Circuit Judge

Judge Sifton found as a fact that the Burger King Assistant Managers "spent at least half of their time doing the same work as the hourly employees." This was a direct consequence of a deliberate corporate policy at the regional level which dictated "ideal" ratios of hourly labor to production and thereby required Assistant Managers to serve as an "extra hand" during high volume meal periods. Were the Assistant Managers to abstain from production work, more hourly employees would be needed, "thereby 'blowing payroll'—that is, spending more than the store's budgeted amount for hourly labor."

The regulations provide a different test for employees earning at least $250 per week. Such employees are exempt if their "primary duty consists of management of the enterprise . . . or of a . . . subdivision thereof . . . and includes the customary and regular direction of the work of two or more employees. . . ."

We agree with Judge Sifton that the "short test" Assistant Managers have, as their "primary duty," managerial responsibilities. Five factors must be weighed in determining an employee's primary duty: (1) time spent in the performance of managerial duties; (2) relative importance of managerial and nonmanagerial duties; (3) the frequency with which the employee exercises discretionary power; (4) the employee's relative freedom from supervision; and (5) the relationship between the employee's salary and the wages paid employees doing similar non-exempt work.

The record fully supports Judge Sifton's finding that the principal responsibilities of Assistant Managers, in the sense of being most important or critical to the success of the restaurant, are managerial. Many of the employees themselves so testified and it is clear that the restaurants could not operate successfully unless the managerial functions of Assistant Managers, such as determining amounts of food to be prepared, running cash checks, scheduling employees, keeping track of inventory, and assigning employees to particular jobs, were performed.

Such employees also exercise discretionary powers. They schedule work time for employees according to estimates of business based on factors such as weather and local events and assign them to particular work stations. They have the power, which they exercise, to move employees from task to task and to see that they are performing their jobs. They represent management in dealings with employees when they are in charge of the restaurant and, while they do not exercise the power to hire and fire frequently, there are some instances thereof in the record. Given that the ten to twenty-five employees under their direction are teenagers, many on their first job, this supervision is a not insubstantial responsibility. Assistant Managers order supplies in quantities based on their judgments as to future sales and are responsible for dealing with the public.

We do not understand the Secretary to dispute the existence of these powers and responsibilities so much as to disparage them as wholly dictated by the detailed instructions issued by Burger King. We fully recognize that the economic genius of the Burger King enterprise lies in providing uniform products and service economically in many different locations and that adherence by Assistant Managers to a remarkably detailed routine is critical to commercial success. The exercise of discretion, however, even where circumscribed by prior instruction, is as critical to that success as adherence to "the book." Burger King, of course, seeks to limit likely mistakes in judgment by issuing detailed guidelines, but judgments must still be made. In the competitive, low margin circumstances of this business, the wrong number of employees, too many or too few supplies on hand, delays in service, the preparation of food which must be thrown away, or an underdirected or undersupervised work force all can make the difference between commercial success and failure.

The record also shows that for the great bulk of their working time, Assistant Managers are solely in charge of their restaurants and are the "boss" in title and in fact. Finally, the evidence in the record is that the employees doing exclusively non-exempt work were paid the minimum wage. Assistant Managers earning $250 or more were paid substantially higher wages even taking their longer hours into account.

Case Questions

1. What reasons support application of FLSA provisions only to hourly employees but not to administrators, professionals, or supervisors?
2. What justification is there for Burger King to require assistant managers to perform both managerial tasks and hourly production worker tasks?
3. What factors most clearly make these assistant managers exempt as "supervisors"?

Child Labor Provisions

The FLSA includes provisions intended to prevent the abuse of children's labor. During the early industrial revolution, child laborers worked 12 or more hours a day for pennies an hour. They often endured the dangerous and unhealthful aspects of mining and heavy industry. In 1938, child labor provisions were added to the FLSA prohibiting the shipment of goods in interstate commerce if produced by an employer involved in "oppressive child labor." Child labor laws are also designed to encourage school attendance.

There are exceptions to the FLSA child labor provisions. Generally, children under 13 may not be employed. Children 14 or 15 years old are restricted to nonhazardous, nonmanufacturing jobs during nonschool hours such as in retail stores, food service establishments, and gasoline service stations. Children 16 or 17 years old may not be employed in hazardous industries (mining, explosives, roofing, logging, excavation).

Children may engage in agricultural employment if their parents give consent. Child actors may work with parental consent, but state laws often require an approved school-like tutorial training.

FLSA Administration

The Wage and Hour Division of the Employment Standards Administration was created under the FLSA as a part of the Department of Labor. The Division's administrator, who is responsible for passing and interpreting its regulations and restrictions, is appointed by the president with advice and consent of the Senate. The division investigates alleged violations and may file lawsuits to enjoin future violations, collect damages on behalf of individual claimants, or initiate criminal charges. Injured employees may also sue to collect unpaid minimum wages, overtime compensation, and penalty damages equal to twice the unpaid compensation. Both the federal and state courts may hear such suits against employers.

INTERNATIONAL PERSPECTIVE AND COMMENTARY

VARIATIONS IN WORK TIME AND PRODUCTIVITY

There was considerable controversy in the early 1990s about work time, vacation, leave, and productivity variations among the industrialized nations. On the one hand, some Japanese leaders have charged that American workers are lazy and illiterate. On the other hand, workers in most industrialized nations are legally entitled to longer annual paid vacations than are U.S. workers. Some measures put U.S. productivity at the top in the world, having increased steadily throughout the 20th century.

These seemingly contradictory assertions raise questions about employment standards for the workweek, overtime, vacation time, family and maternity leave policies, child care, and other related terms and conditions of employment. Should these matters be left to market forces, permitting the employer and employee to negotiate terms and conditions of employment? Free market adherents argue that further regulation of employment terms would harm productivity and ultimately hurt U.S. competitiveness. However, critics charge that the United States stands alone among industrial nations in not mandating vacation, child care, and family leave benefits by law. They maintain that increased leisure and worktime flexibility may actually increase productivity. German workers' high productivity is said to support this argument.

The Japanese, Koreans, and other Asian nationals are known for working hard and long hours. Some nations have adopted a survivalist and nationalistic work ethic to gain a competitive advantage over larger industrialized nations. Their work ethic provides the drive to enhance their collective competitive advantage and raises national productivity and strength. The Japanese reported workweek averages 45–46 hours but may actually be much longer due to chronic underreporting. The American workweek averages about 40 hours, while some European nations average less than 40 hours per week.

Critics of Japanese work practices ask whether such long work hours can be sustained for long, given mounting evidence that overwork eventually lowers productivity and job satisfaction while raising harmful stress. Some critics charge the United States and Japan with pursuing what the Japanese call *karoshi,* or death by overwork. These critics suggest that increased leisure time would give workers time to "recharge their batteries," which would increase productivity.[5]

Vacation time seems to be important to workers: 70 percent of working Americans surveyed would willingly give up one day's pay to get an added vacation day. Certainly the German workforce at the end of World War II was successful in rebuilding its postwar economy, yet during this period, most German workers enjoyed up to 7 weeks of vacation per year. In the United States, some employers believe that concepts such as job sharing, flextime, compressed workweek, sabbaticals, telecommuting, maternity/paternity leave, and expanding part-time work raise the costs of administering the workforce. Adding extra employees initially raises the administrative expenses of training, unemployment compensation, workers' compensation, and tax withholding.

Resolution of this debate will help determine whether competitive pressures will force worldwide working conditions to adopt the hard work model followed in the United States and Japan or to follow the lead of some European nations in meeting employee desires for free time while perhaps increasing (or decreasing) national per hour productivity.

Unemployment Compensation

During the Great Depression, nearly a third of the workforce became unemployed. Such tremendous hardship was suffered that Congress gave states an incentive to alleviate the suffering under the Federal Unemployment Tax Act (FUTA). It devised a tax offset incentive system that reduces the social security withholding tax (FICA) in states imposing an unemployment compensation tax on payrolls. All of the states have such taxes. Employers usually support such statutes because employers must pay a 3 percent federal excise tax if the state has no unemployment compensation law.

Employer Qualifications

The **unemployment compensation** system provides benefits to the employees of covered employers. It applies to all employers with at least one employee working one day a week for 20 weeks per year or having a quarterly payroll of at least $1,500, including employers that are charitable, educational, and scientific nonprofit organizations. It also applies to former military service personnel but not to the self-employed. Employers must pay at least 6.2 percent of the first $7,000 of each employee's annual wages into a state-operated fund. The rate varies among the states because employers get a credit of up to 5.4 percent for amounts paid to the state.

unemployment compensation
State insurance system intended to replace unemployed workers' income.

The states may adopt one of a variety of unemployment compensation programs. Most states have set a maximum period during which the unemployed may collect benefits, but the length of that period varies with changing economic conditions. The total benefits payable to each unemployed worker are based on a percentage of that worker's average base earnings while employed. Typically, this is set as the highest pay rate earned by the worker during the previous one or two quarters, but is usually limited to $200 or $300 per week for 26 weeks. The worker must also have had

[5]See Juliet B. Schor, *The Overworked American: The Unexpected Decline of Leisure* (New York: Basic Books, 1992).

earnings of a minimum amount in the preceding year to qualify. These limits are intended to prevent misuse of the unemployment compensation system by persons who have not had recent employment or whose employers have not paid into the system. Congress extended the benefit period twice during the 1991–1992 recession.

To qualify for benefits, the applicant must be actively seeking employment, be available and able to work, and follow the statutory procedure for claims processing. Applicants may be disqualified if they refuse to accept new employment, if they have quit without just cause, or if they have been fired either for serious misconduct or as the result of a labor dispute. Unemployment compensation is usually not available to fired strikers.

The circumstances surrounding the dismissal of employees affect the outcome of unemployment compensation hearings and the tax rate paid by employers. Employers that have low employee turnover rates generally pay lower premiums; this is known as *experience rating.*

Some state laws permit employers to disregard seniority systems as a method of limiting claims. In a reduction of force during times of economic downturn, for example, a participating employer might retain a larger percentage of the workforce than might be permitted if the employer adhered strictly to union seniority systems. If seniority systems are circumvented in this way, all employees must work fewer hours, and each employee collects unemployment compensation benefits for the lost time. Thereby, the employer avoids laying off trained workers and saves retraining costs for replacements when later hired. Higher regular unemployment compensation premiums are necessary to cover these additional benefits. This trade-off between higher training costs and the temporarily higher unemployment compensation premiums is favorable for many employers. However, some senior employees oppose even temporary loss of their seniority rights, hoping to force all job dislocation on less senior workers.

ETHICAL DILEMMA

ETHICAL DILEMMAS IN CIRCUMSTANCES SURROUNDING EMPLOYMENT SEVERANCE

A terminated employee's right to receive unemployment compensation depends on the circumstances of the severance. Employees who quit without good cause or are fired for misconduct are denied benefits. This rule can cause supervisors and employees to negotiate on how to characterize the termination: as a dismissal or resignation. Employers may seek to avoid litigation or feel sympathy to a dismissed employee. For example, employees may be given the choice of resigning rather than being dismissed to avoid disparaging their employment record. Is it ethical to collect unemployment compensation for an ineligible severance and thereby shift the costs of the employee's personal misconduct to the unemployment compensation system? Is it ethical for the supervisor to misrepresent the reason for a severance when an employee's misconduct is clearly pertinent to future employers? Both tactics pose an ethical dilemma for managers and employees.

RETIREMENT INCOME AND PENSIONS

Social Security

Prior to 1935, very few workers had any form of old-age or retirement benefits except for personal savings. Many workers continued to work until they died or became disabled. In 1935, Congress passed the Social Security Act as a centerpiece of the New

Deal. Social security is intended to prevent severe economic hardship by providing benefit payments intended to supplement retirement income.

Social security covers nearly all American workers. Unlike the European retirement systems, however, it generally does not apply to persons who have never worked. The social security system is compulsory, requiring employers to withhold social security payments from the paychecks of most employees. Each employer must match the amount withheld, which effectively doubles the social security tax. The actual name of the social security system is Old-Age, Survivors, and Disability Insurance (OASDI). In recent years, private pension systems have developed as the more important source of retirement benefits.

social security Federal retirement income supplement funded by current employee contributions.

Social security taxes are paid into the Social Security Trust Fund under provisions of the **Federal Insurance Contributions Act (FICA).** The Internal Revenue Service (IRS) collects FICA taxes. This responsibility is similar to its responsibility over the withholding of periodic federal income tax payments from employees' paychecks.

Federal Insurance Contributions Act (FICA) Federal social security contributions.

FICA withholding does not become part of a savings or investment fund that is eventually repaid directly to the retiree. Instead, the system is designed on a "pay-as-you-go" basis. Contributions from current employees immediately pay benefits to current retirees. Contrary to the common misconception that these contributions are held for employees until they retire, the system remains solvent only if current contributions exceed current benefit payments. The solvency of the system is periodically questioned as the number of retirees increases and the number of paying employees remains constant or decreases. This problem is magnified by cost-of-living adjustments (COLAs), which automatically increase benefits if inflation triggers an increase in the consumer price index. This index allegedly misstates the impact of inflation on a typical retiree's expenditures.

Social Security Taxes Nearly all employees must pay the compulsory FICA tax. To compute that tax, the wage base must be determined and then the appropriate tax rate applied to it up to certain limits. The FICA tax is levied on each employee's earnings, which are known as the *wage base.* This amount equals the employee's actual pretax earnings up to a statutory maximum that has steadily increased in recent years; the maximum was $61,600 for 1995. The FICA tax is paid only on amounts up to the statutory maximum, so excess amounts are exempt. The *tax rate* is a percentage that is applied to the wage base to determine the amount of tax withheld. The tax rate was 6.2 percent in 1995 but has increased in most years. Both the employee who earns $25,000 in 1995 and the employer will pay 6.2 percent of that wage base into FICA (0.062 × $25,000 = $1,550.00). The FICA withholdings of employees who earned more than $61,600 in 1995 were limited to $3,819.20 (0.062 × $61,600) because FICA is capped at $61,600 for 1995.

Self-employed persons must also pay FICA taxes. When self-employed persons make their quarterly estimated federal tax payment in lieu of withholding and file their annual federal income tax return, they must pay FICA to the IRS in addition to their federal income tax. The FICA tax paid by self-employed persons is more than double that paid by employed persons. Self-employed persons pay all the FICA taxes, Medicare taxes, and the employer's contribution. In 1995, the FICA tax of self-employed persons was 15.3 percent up to the statutory maximum but not on earnings of less than $400 per year.

Social Security Benefits The social security system provides retirement income primarily to those who have actively participated in the workforce. A worker's eligibility and amount of benefits are based on the worker's income level and on the work credits given while employed. *Fully insured* employees receive full old-age and survivors benefits. To qualify, the employee must have worked at least one-fourth of the time since 1950 or since reaching the age of 21, whichever is lowest. This is determined by giving the employee credit for each quarter of a year (three-month period) in which the employee was paid at least $50 by an employer or made at least $100 if self-employed. In addition, the employee must have worked a number of calendar quarters that equals or exceeds the number of years since attaining the age of 21 or since 1950, whichever is less.

Reduced benefits are available to employees who worked at least 6 calendar quarters in the previous 13 quarters if this time period ends in retirement, disability, or death. This results in *currently insured status.* Another type of reduced benefits may be paid to persons with *disability status.* Reduced benefits are paid if an employee worked for at least 20 quarters within the 40 quarters preceding disablement.

Benefits can be paid monthly to retired persons after age 62 according to their base pay during their work life. Spouses and children of deceased workers may receive half of the retired worker's benefit amount. The amounts paid tend to be a higher percentage of the base pay for lower-income workers and a lower percentage for upper-income workers. Social security recipients with annual incomes of over $25,000 pay federal income tax on half of their social security benefits.

Disability benefits may be paid to any former employee with a medically determined physical or mental impairment. The Social Security Administration, the agency responsible for benefit payments, automatically recognizes several severe impairments, such as loss of limbs or sight. An impairment not regularly recognized may qualify if the impairment is expected to be fatal or to last for more than a year. New impairments are determined on a case-by-case basis. Disability criteria under social security are different from those used under workers' compensation. Some disabled persons may receive both social security and workers' compensation payments.

Medicare

Since 1965, health insurance for the aged and disabled has been available for all qualified persons in the system known as Medicare. Health insurance pays for many hospital expenses. Persons over 65 years of age may qualify for such insurance even if they are not eligible for social security. Optional supplementary and medical insurance coverage is available to beneficiaries who pay additional premiums. Since Medicare does not pay enough to defray all medical costs, an active private insurance system has arisen to supplement Medicare coverage. For 1995, both employers and employees each contribute 1.45 percent of each employee's wage base (self-employed pay 2.9 percent) as a Medicare payroll tax.

COMMENTARY

MEDICARE AND HEALTH CARE REFORM

The costs of health care are skyrocketing, assuming up to a quarter of GDP. Health care expense is becoming the largest growing component of employment costs. As currently configured, most Americans receive health care benefits, including medical insurance, dental insurance, and catastrophic health care coverage, through group health plans purchased by their employer. However, not all employers provide their employees with full coverage. Particularly smaller firms claim they cannot afford the high health care premiums. Many part-time workers also have no coverage. In all, nearly 20 million Americans have no health insurance. This contrasts starkly with other industrialized nations that have some form of national health insurance. When the Clinton administration attempted to fundamentally change the health care system in 1994, special interest groups fostered suspicion that patients would be unable to select their own doctors or health care facilities. The U.S. health care system arguably provides superior service, at least for those patients who are covered, when compared with most other nations.

Early efforts were probably misguided because they moved reform toward an extensive regulatory program. Nevertheless, reform is progressing in some states and in the private sector. Most successful reform methods use some form of "managed care." For example, health care plans that service large employers provide the predominant coverage for large employee groups and their families. These groups enlist major physician groups, hospitals, and testing facilities to provide most of their group's health care.

Several forms of health networks are developing, led by health maintenance organizations (HMO). HMOs use three chief means to hold down escalating health care costs. First, the health insurer pays for all or a high percentage of medical services provided by doctors participating in the HMO and less for services provided by nonnetwork doctors. In return for this captive market, doctors must hold down charges. Second, doctors must implicitly limit expensive treatments and marginally useful tests to patients who indisputably need treatment. Most patients are first screened by a primary care physician, family doctor, or general practitioner before the insurer will pay for any care or services of a specialist. HMOs are less successful delivering on their third promise, to use preventative medicine to avoid the expense of preventable illness. Many doctors argue that HMOs may eventually suffer higher malpractice liability because most cost savings come from limiting care.

Managed care and ever higher payroll taxes may be needed to keep Medicare solvent after the turn of the century. Some predict that between 2010 and 2020, the bulk of baby boomers will reach retirement and their claims on Medicare may force its insolvency. Perhaps the federal government should use Medicare as a prototype for health care reform. However, the retiree lobby is so strong that significant changes to reign in escalating Medicare and social security costs are politically difficult.

Private Pension Plans

Although private pension plans have existed for over a century, their growth as a major source of retirement benefits has occurred mainly in the last half of the 20th century. Pension payments were first made largely at the employer's discretion, so they were often terminated or reduced at the employer's will. These payments were considered gratuitous rewards given only to faithful employees, not as part of a regular and mandatory compensation package. This arbitrary, discriminatory, and unpredictable character of private pensions led Congress to pass the Employee Retirement Income Security Act (ERISA) in 1974 to qualify and standardize retirement plans. ERISA regulates eligibility for pension benefits and the taxation of pension plan earnings and benefit payments. Private pension plans that meet ERISA requirements are entitled to tax-free treatment in the years that employers and employees make contributions to the plans.

The Plan Administrator's Fiduciary Duties Qualified pension plans must be administered by a person responsible for handling the pension funds. This person is a fiduciary who must carefully invest the funds and act only in the beneficiaries' best interest, using the skill and care of a reasonably prudent person. Pension administrators must diversify their investments to minimize the risk of large losses. They must disclose certain information to the Labor Department and to the plan's beneficiaries: the terms of the plan, annual financial reports, and annual summaries of each beneficiary's interest.

pension vesting ERISA requirement that a pension beneficiary's interest become irrevocable after a minimum employment period of 5–10 years.

Vesting and Participation Before ERISA was passed, pension plan beneficiaries often lost all their benefits. For example, a beneficiary whose employment was terminated prematurely or interrupted by a temporary layoff could have benefits denied or severely limited. As a result, ERISA established the **pension vesting** concept, requiring that the beneficiary's interest become irrevocable after employment for a minimum time period. Pension plans need not give the employee full irrevocable rights to the employer's contributions until the employee has worked for the employer for at least 10 years. However, many plans permit vesting in a shorter time. Of course, the employee has a right to eventually receive all of his or her own contributions. Gradual vesting in partial amounts for fewer than 10 years of service may also occur if the plan permits.

Many ERISA plans are *defined benefit plans.* Such plans provide specific payments based on the employee/beneficiary's age, earnings, and length of service. By contrast, a *defined contribution plan* requires each employee or employer to make particular contributions during employment. This allows for the payment of different retirement benefit amounts depending on the plan's investment successes.

ERISA established the Pension Benefit Guaranty Corporation (PBGC) to insure pension plans. PBGC funds underwrite the payment of vested benefits to beneficiaries of plans that are terminated prematurely. If a terminated pension plan has insufficient assets to satisfy the beneficiaries' future claims, the employer may be liable to PBGC for deficiencies. The PBGC provisions apply only to defined benefit plans, not to retirement annuities with variable payouts.

Other Retirement Plans

Individuals operating small businesses may establish less formal pension plans called *Keogh plans.* In addition, many employed individuals may also contribute limited amounts per year into individual retirement accounts (IRAs). IRA earnings are tax free until their withdrawal during retirement. Additional withholdings from wages that are also sheltered from taxation may be paid into deferred payment annuities (DPA or 401(k) plans). The tax advantages of these plans were reduced drastically by the 1986 Tax Reform Act. The benefits paid by all pension plans, Keogh plans, IRAs, and DPAs are taxable when funds are withdrawn and are subject to substantial penalties for early withdrawal. Periodically, there are proposals to stimulate the national savings rate by reinstating some IRA tax advantages.

Workers' Compensation

workers' compensation State insurance plans providing cash benefits for workers' job injuries.

Workers' compensation developed because the common law system of negligence torts imposed huge barriers on employee suits for injury compensation. Employees had the difficult burden of proving their employer's negligence. Three common defenses to negligence suits imposed further difficulties on injured workers. First, the *fellow servant* *doctrine* prevented an injured employee's suit where a fellow employee negligently contributed to the injury. Second, the *assumption of risk* defense prevented suits where the injured employee voluntarily accepted the job's risks. An injured employee who was aware of the job site risks was barred from recovery. Finally, the *contributory negligence* defense barred an injured employee's suit if the employee in any way contributed to the dangerous condition. Because this negligence "fault system" provided very limited remedies, the states created no-fault, employer-financed workers' compensation systems. Workers' compensation benefits are "exclusive remedies," preventing employees' suits against their employers for compensatory, pain and suffering, or punitive damages.

Workers' compensation laws create a form of compulsory insurance. Depending on the particular state's law, an employer may self-insure, purchase private insurance, or participate in a state-managed fund. Employers that take effective steps to minimize job risks may pay reduced premiums. The risk-adjusted employer premiums of this *merit rating system* provide incentive for employers to maintain a safe work environment.

Workers' Compensation Coverage

The first issue in a workers' compensation claim is whether the employee's injury is work related. Employees are covered by workers' compensation only while on the job; off-the-job injuries are covered by traditional tort law. Workers' compensation is applicable where the employer has the right to control the employee, so independent contractors are not covered. Independent contractors retain full access to the tort system. If the employer may control only the outcome but not the means used by a particular person, the person is an independent contractor. This determination of "scope of employment" is similar to the respondeat superior doctrine discussed in Chapters 8 and 13.

Most workers' compensation benefits are restricted to injuries occurring "in the course of and arising out of employment." Employees en route to or from the workplace are usually not covered, the *going and coming rule.* Workers' compensation coverage is generally limited to the employee's time at the employer's a work site located at a fixed and limited place. Employees are covered only after their arrival at the employer's premises. For example, employees are covered after parking in the employer's lot, while walking to a locker room to put on safety gear, and while being shuttled by the employer to the job site.

Problems may arise if employees must leave the employer's workplace as part of their job. Employees are usually covered by workers' compensation if they must leave the premises to eat lunch or must travel away from the employer's premises. If a worker is hurt by a co-worker's intentional act, some states distinguish between assaults, which are not covered by workers' compensation, and simple horseplay, which is covered. In *Murray v. Industrial Commission of Illinois,* the court overturned the Industrial Commission's decision that Murray's injuries were not work related.[6] Murray's co-worker hit him behind the knees, causing them to buckle, which caused Murray to slip on oil on the floor. Murray's horseplay injuries were compensable under workers' compensation. What acts of personal hygiene or neatness are job related? The next case discusses this.

---

[6] *Murray v. Industrial Commission of Illinois,* 516 NE.2d 1039 (Ill. App. 3d Dist. 1987).

United Parcel Service v. Fetterman

336 S.E.2d 892 (Va. 1985)
Supreme Court of Virginia

Randall Fetterman, a UPS driver, was required to load, unload, and deliver packages as part of his job duties. While unloading packages one day, Fetterman noticed his shoe was untied so he raised his foot to the back of the truck and bent over to tie the shoe. Fetterman immediately noticed an acute back pain; he had suffered an accidental lumbosacral strain. The deputy commissioner of the Virginia Industrial Commission denied Mr. Fetterman's unemployment claim, holding that his injury did not arise out of employment because it was not traceable to employment as a proximate cause and was not a natural incident of the work. Mr. Fetterman's claim was reinstated by the full commission, prompting an appeal by UPS and its insurer.

Per Curiam

An accident arises out of employment where there is a causal connection between the claimant's injury and the conditions under which the employer requires the work to be performed. Under this test, an injury arises "out of" the employment when it has followed as a natural incident of the work and has been a result of the exposure occasioned by the nature of the employment. Excluded is an injury that comes from a hazard to which the employee would have been equally exposed apart from the employment. The causative danger must be peculiar to the work, incidental to the character of the business, and not independent of the master-servant relationship. The event must appear to have had its origin in a risk connected with the employment and to have flowed from that source as a rational consequence.

The injury did not arise out of the claimant's employment. Under these circumstances, the act of bending over to tie the shoe was unrelated to any hazard common to the workplace. In other words, nothing in the work environment contributed to the injury. Every person who wears laced shoes must occasionally perform the act of retying the laces. The situation of a loose shoelace confronting the claimant was wholly independent of the master-servant relationship. Award reversed, application dismissed.

Case Questions

1. Compare and contrast this case with a situation where a loose shirttall becomes caught in a workplace conveyer, dragging an employee into an injury.
2. How should the decision be different if the employer supplied special protective gear or clothing and Mr. Fetterman's injury was caused by his reaching to fix it?

Workers' Compensation Benefits

Workers' compensation benefits are paid out of the workers' compensation insurance fund directly to the employee or the employee's family. Benefits can include medical payments and disability or death benefits. Medical payments are made for the services of physicians and nurses, hospitalization, drugs, and rehabilitation equipment. Disability benefits indemnify employees for wages lost during their convalescence, often ranging from one-half to two-thirds of the employee's normal wages.

Specific *scheduled benefits* are paid for the loss of certain bodily functions and reflect the disability's extent and duration. For example, *temporary total disability* prevents the employee from working at all for a while. *Temporary partial disability* prevents the employee from performing certain activities for a while. Partial disability might affect only eyesight, hearing, or the use of an arm or leg. *Permanent partial disability* prevents the employee from performing certain activities for the remainder of his or her work life. Finally, *permanent total disability* prevents the employee from ever working again. Permanent disabilities include total losses such as both eyes, hands, or legs or total paralysis. It also includes less drastic losses where the impairment prevents work.

Death benefits are usually limited; they are paid to the employee's next of kin to cover only burial expenses, typically a few thousand dollars. A few states pay substantial death benefits to surviving family members to replace the decedent's lost wages. Usually, life insurance is still needed for survivors to adequately replace the employee's lost income.

Compensable Injuries

Sudden and obvious injuries such as a loss of limb or bodily functions are clearly compensable injuries. However, many other conditions and diseases are more controversial. In many early cases, benefits were denied for occupational diseases.

Physical Injuries Today, workers' compensation benefits apply to *occupational diseases* but not to the ordinary diseases of life. Ordinary diseases are contracted away from the job site or communicated by co-workers. The difficult issue is determining the precise cause of an employee's disease. The employee must prove specific job hazards that were positively linked to the disease. For example, occupational exposures are difficult to link to cancer because it takes so long to develop and its causes are often conjectural. Cancer and allergic reactions are compensable only if the employee proves job-related exposure and causation.

Mental Injuries The cause of mental injuries is also quite difficult to prove. Courts have been increasingly providing benefits for diseases caused by the pressures of employment. Before ordering payment, most courts require that a physical impact accompany any alleged mental injury. For example, anxiety depression resulting in numbness of hands and feet, high blood pressure, and vertigo are compensable physical injuries. These injuries must arise out of and in the course of employment, causing total and permanent incapacity due to the traumatic and repetitious activities of the job. Mental injuries resulting from a physical blow or trauma are also covered. Should the ordinary strain of work without physical injury or eventual physical effect be covered under workers' compensation? The following case exemplifies how the courts place limits on work-related anxiety and depression claims.

Joseph Albanese's Case

389 N.E.2d 83 (Mass. 1979)
Supreme Court of Massachusetts

Joseph Albanese was a "working foreman" at Atlantic Steel Company for 20 years. After unionization in 1969, Atlantic Steel eliminated overtime pay. This often required Albanese to "go out into the shop and prod the men to expedite the work." He was also required to relay unpopular information to employees, causing considerable friction. Joseph's supervisor often reversed these decisions, undercutting Joseph's authority. After a heated discussion over one employee's claim to overtime pay, the plant manager again changed a decision to not pay overtime and told Albanese to pay the employee. Albanese immediately "became distressed, developed chest pains, nausea." He did not work thereafter and continually experienced pains, sweatiness, shortness of breath, headaches, and depression. His condition was later diagnosed as "a chronic anxiety state mixed with depression and somatized reaction and . . . neurocirculatory asthenia." Albanese's workers' compensation claim was granted by the hearing examiner, reversed by the review board, and then reinstated by the Massachusetts Superior Court.

Abrams, Justice

On appeal, the insurer does not dispute the fact that Albanese has become disabled as a result of a mental or emotional disorder, but argues that Albanese's condition is the result of gradual "wear and tear" and thus is not a compensable personal injury under the statute as interpreted by this court.

However, subsequent to the board's decision and to the proceedings in the Superior Court we held that "the term 'personal injury' also permits compensation in cases involving mental disorders or disabilities causally connected to mental trauma or shock arising 'out of the employment looked at in any of its aspects.' . . . There is no valid distinction which would preclude mental or emotional disorders caused by mental or emotional trauma from being compensable."

The insurer concedes that "the lack of a sudden episode does not of itself disqualify an employee's claim for personal injury." Instead, the insurer argues that in Albanese's case there is no evidence of shock or stress greater than ordinary and hence Albanese's disability is solely the result of general wear and tear.

Contrary to the insurer's claim of general wear and tear, the board did not find that Albanese's injury was the result of general stress or the wear and tear of working. The reviewing board found as fact both the existence of a series of specific stressful episodes and a causal nexus between Albanese's working conditions and his emotional disorder. Thus his injury is not "[a] disease of mind or body which arises in the course of employment, with nothing more, [and which] is not within the act'."

Based on the board's findings, we conclude that Albanese's injury was not the result of everyday stress or "[b]odily wear and tear resulting from a long period of hard work." Rather, it resulted from a series of identifiable stressful work-related incidents occurring over a relatively brief period of time, compared with his twenty-year employment. Therefore, Albanese is entitled to workmen's compensation for his disability.

Case Questions

1. What reasons support expanding compensation to mental injuries?
2. What reasons support creating an exception from workers' compensation claims for the ordinary stress or wear and tear of working?

Administration of Workers' Compensation

Most of the states have established a separate administrative agency to administer the workers' compensation statute. These agencies have such titles as the state *industrial commission* or the state *workers' compensation bureau* or *board.* The agencies perform legislative, executive, and judicial functions, adjudicating workers' compensation claims and managing the receipt and disbursement of funds.

Injured workers begin processing their claims by applying for benefits at the state administrative agency. Typically, a claims examiner investigates to verify the extent of the compensable injury. Most of the legitimate claims are quickly certified, with payment following almost immediately. However, if the agency disallows claims, contested cases are heard by a hearing officer in an informal proceeding. After review in the agency, novel questions and the coverage of new diseases are usually appealed through the state court system. Benefits must be paid after a claim is proved.

Controversy over Workers' Compensation Costs

COMMENTARY

Fundamental problems plague the workers' compensation system, bringing it close to collapse in several states. Thousands of claims go unpaid, and the systems' cost to employers continues to rise. Premiums averaged 2.3 percent of payroll in 1990 and up to 40 percent of payroll in dangerous industries. Some employers are relocating from high-cost to lower-cost states. Some insurers pay out more in claims than is received in premiums, bankrupting some insurers. Many state boards refuse to permit premium increases; other insurers are exiting the business. Injured employees do not collect compensation as promptly and completely, so they litigate their claims. The pressure to increase productivity forces employers to speed up the work and to introduce new and complex production systems with unknown dangers. Job-related accidents are still high in several industries: construction, mining, agriculture, fishing, forestry, transportation, and public utilities.

A proliferation of abuses by claimants also raises workers' compensation costs. For example, because claimants are generally free to use a physician of their choice, some claimants make false claims that are supported by sympathetic physicians who may falsely certify serious disabilities. Some workers make false claims for injury outside their jobs if not fully covered by other insurance. Some retirees make workers' compensation claims to supplement their retirement income.

Reformers argue that more rigid and responsive state administration would speed payments, reduce uncertainty and litigation, and thereby reduce system costs. Costs might be better controlled by adapting a technique from HMOs and preferred provider health care systems: restricting the employee's right to choose a physician. For example, some employers now require prescreening diagnoses by company physicians. Increasing employees' co-payment and deductible payments could also help minimize the "moral hazard" and thereby reduce fraud.

Occupational Safety and Health Act

In the 1950s and 1960s, there was a growing public sentiment that workers' compensation and other incentives to reduce workplace risks were ineffective to stop industrial accidents. This pressure accelerated as new manufacturing technologies were introduced with new and incalculable risks. For example, microwaves, atomic energy, lasers, new chemicals, and high-speed processing machinery significantly reduced the safety of workplaces. The problem was heightened by the inadequacy or absence of workplace safety regulations in most states.

In 1970 Congress passed the **Occupational Safety and Health Act (OSHA).** The act is intended to "insure so far as possible every working man and woman in the nation safety and healthful working conditions to preserve our human resources." The Act applies to any employer with at least one employee engaged in a business affecting interstate commerce. Exemptions exist for industries regulated under other safety laws

Occupational Safety and Health Act (OSHA) Federal statute regulating workplace safety and health hazards.

such as the Coal Mine Safety Act, Railway Safety Act, and Nuclear Regulatory Act. Domestic household employees and the religious activities of religious organizations are also exempt.

Administration of OSHA

OSHA created three new federal agencies: the Occupational Safety and Health Administration (OSHA Administration), the National Institute for Occupational Safety and Health (NIOSH), and the Occupational Safety and Health Review Commission (OSHRC). The OSHA Administration is authorized to implement the act by promulgating regulations and setting safety standards. The agency also inspects employers' premises for compliance with its safety standards. The OSHA Administration is responsible to the Department of Labor, a cabinet-level department controlled by the president.

NIOSH is responsible for conducting research into health and safety hazards and for recommending new regulations and safety or health standards to the OSHA Administration. It is also responsible for educating and training employers and employees to make the workplace safe. NIOSH is housed in the Department of Health and Human Services. OSHRC is an independent commission that conducts appeals from determinations made by the OSHA Administration. It is not directly controlled by any cabinet-level department, by another regulatory agency, or by the presidential administration. Its independence is designed to reduce bias that might be exerted by employers, employee groups, or the political system. OSHRC members are appointed by the president for staggered six-year terms and must be confirmed by the Senate.

Congress intended for the three agencies created by OSHA to increase workplace safety by involving both employers and employees in the process. In addition to other responsibilities, both employers and employees must keep records and report on the procedures used to investigate and remedy job-related injuries and illnesses.

The Employer's Duty of Safety

OSHA requires employers to provide a safe work environment and prevent unreasonably hazardous conditions that arise from the employment relationship. There must also be a general recognition in the industry in question that such hazards exist and could cause serious physical harm. Finally, it must be feasible, within the limits of modern technology, to prevent harm from the hazards. OSHA establishes an employer's *general duty* to make a safe workplace. The OSHA Administration may also promulgate specific health and safety standards. These standards impose a *specific duty* on employers to modify particular workplace safety and health conditions.

Health and Safety Standards

NIOSH research into workplace hazards eventually leads to recommendations for "legally enforceable regulations governing conditions, practices, or operations to assure safe and healthful workplaces." The OSHA Administration is not bound by NIOSH suggestions and may promulgate regulations on its own initiative. In OSHA's first year of existence, Congress required the OSHA Administration to adopt nearly 4,400 "consensus standards" drawn from existing federal regulations and from voluntary industry codes. However, many standards were already obsolete, raising criticism of OSHA.

Design versus Performance Standards During the 1970s, the OSHA Administration replaced the original consensus standards with more stringent *design standards,* which provide minimum specifications for safety equipment. For example, a design standard for a face mask might require construction from a particular material and a minimum thickness. However, experience shows that design standards stifle innovation and prevent the use of more effective or less costly means to achieve the same level of protection.

The recent trend in OSHA regulations has been to provide *performance standards,* which focus on a level of protection (end) rather than a particular device (means) to achieve the necessary protection. Performance standards would permit any type of face mask as long as the particular design sufficiently reduced the substance to be filtered.

Safety versus Health Regulations Another trend in OSHA regulations has been away from the primary focus on safety regulations and toward protecting employee health. Unsafe conditions are obvious dangers because they cause sudden and obvious disability. However, *delayed manifestation diseases* are becoming linked to low-level workplace exposure to hazardous or toxic substances. OSHA's performance standards now tend to provide increased protection from health hazards, overlapping the environmental regulations discussed in Chapter 21.

Health and Safety Rulemaking Process The OSHA Administration follows the same rulemaking procedure imposed on federal regulatory agencies discussed in Chapter 6. Typically, a NIOSH investigative study reveals a safety or health hazard. NIOSH then recommends action to the OSHA Administration. If the OSHA Administration agrees that a safety or health hazard exists, it drafts a proposed regulation and publishes it in the *Federal Register.* This begins a comment period that permits the affected industry, its workers, and other interested parties to express views about the proposed rule's adequacy or feasibility. This may result in revisions to the rule, as illustrated in Figure 18–1.

Cost-Benefit Analyses All new OSHA regulatory proposals must provide societal benefits greater than the expected costs. The president's Office of Management and Budget (OMB) interacts with the OSHA Administration to assure the accuracy and relevance of this analysis. OMB also assures that OSHA rule proposals are consistent with policies of the president's administration.

It may be impossible to completely eliminate certain harmful substances from the work environment. This becomes a particularly difficult problem when the OSHA Administration, NIOSH, or commenting parties insist there is no safe exposure level for a substance. Such a problem arose when OSHA attempted to reduce the level of occupational exposure to Benzene, a known cancer-causing carcinogen. The OSHA Administration had set safe levels of Benzene exposure at no more than 1 part per million (ppm). Benzene exposures above 10 ppm had been scientifically linked to blood disorders, leukemia, and other cancers. However, there was no reliable evidence that reductions in the standard from 10 ppm to 1 ppm would result in significant health improvements. The Supreme Court held, in *Industrial Union v. American Petroleum Institute,*[7] that the OSHA Administration must determine that a particular level of

[7] *Industrial Union v. American Petroleum Institute,* 448 U.S. 607 (1980).

FIGURE 18-1 OSHA Procedures

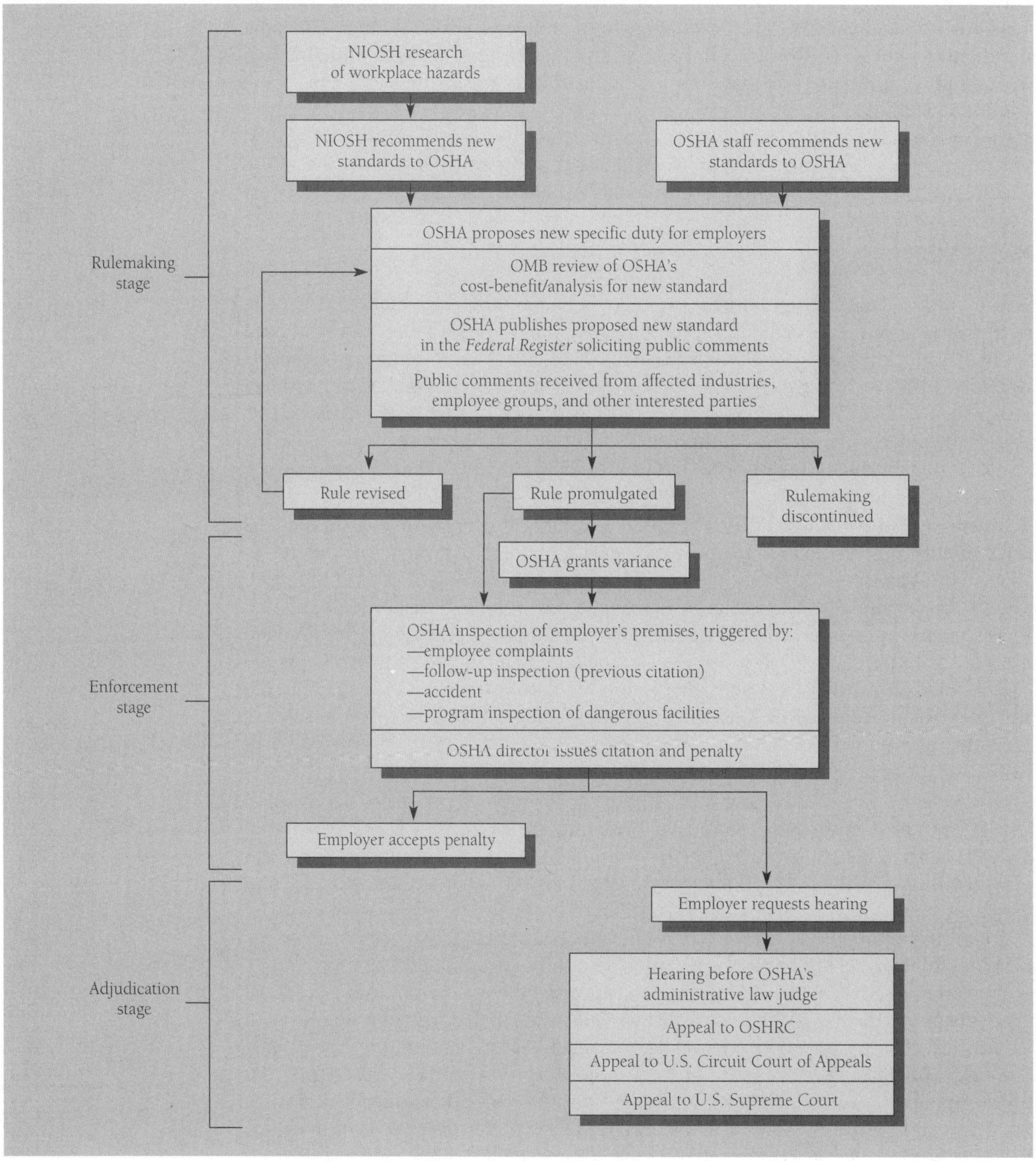

exposure to a hazardous substance posed a "significant risk" of material health impairment before imposing specific limits on exposure.

A similar controversy arose over workers' exposure to cotton dust, which can cause "brown lung" disease. In *American Textile Manufacturers Institute v. Donovan,* the Supreme Court required only a feasibility analysis rather than a more stringent cost-benefit analysis.[8] Today, Executive Order 12,291 requires a full cost-benefit analysis before most new OSHA regulations are imposed. Regulatory reform may add further costs and procedures to OSHA rulemaking.

Variances

Employers may avoid compliance with safety and health standards if a variance is granted. An employer unable to comply immediately with a new OSHA standard may seek a *temporary variance* if more time is needed to implement the standard. To qualify, the employer must assure that all available and feasible safety measures are in place until full compliance can be obtained. A *permanent variance* may be granted to an employer that proves use of alternative safety or health measures will provide at least equal levels of workplace safety. Employees may contest a variance. Although compliance costs are considered in setting standards initially, they are not considered in granting variances.

Strict compliance may also be excused if the safety or health equipment interferes with production. Isolated instances of employee misconduct or violation of safety rules may justify temporary noncompliance with OSHA's standards. For example, some employees may refuse to wear heavy masks or protective clothing if it is uncomfortable or causes excessive perspiration.

OSHA Enforcement Procedures

The OSHA Administration enforces OSHA and the agency's own regulations by collecting information submitted by employees and employers and from on-site inspections. The OSHA Administration may issue citations for violations and assess penalties for more serious violations.

Record-Keeping and Reporting Requirements OSHA requires employers to report unsafe incidents, accidents, fatalities, lost workdays, job transfers and terminations, medical treatments, and restrictions of work. These reports must be filed with the Secretary of Labor. Detailed logs of all recordable incidents must also be maintained. Employers with fewer than 11 employees are exempt from record keeping. OSHA must be notified within 48 hours following an accident if it results in a fatality or in the hospitalization of more than four employees. OSHA requires employers to post information regarding OSHA rights and obligations for all employees to review.

OSHA Inspections The OSHA Administration also conducts on-site inspections. The Supreme Court has said that only businesses with a long history of close regulation (e.g., the liquor industry, sellers of firearms, sellers of foods and drugs) are subject to warrantless searches. Therefore, surprise OSHA inspections violate the Fourth Amendment's protection against unreasonable searches and seizures. Employers may legally refuse OSHA Administration inspectors access to search their prem-

---

[8] *American Textile Manufacturers Institute v. Donovan,* 452 U.S. 490 (1981).

ises unless the inspectors have a search warrant issued by a federal magistrate. This principle, established in *Marshall v. Barlow's, Inc.,* was discussed in Chapter 6.[9]

The employer's work site may be inspected if the OSHA Administration inspector has a search warrant, the violation is in "plain view," or the employer consents. Typically, the employer or one of its representatives accompanies the OSHA inspector during the visit. The OSHA inspector may confer directly with employees unless an employee representative accompanies the inspector (e.g., a union shop steward); in that case, any conferring must be with the representative.

OSHA Administration inspectors may conduct four types of investigations: (1) *accident investigations* usually follow reports of fatalities and catastrophes; (2) *employee complaints* trigger one-third of all investigations; (3) *programmed inspections* are conducted in industries with a history of dangerous hazards. Inspections are typically routine in industries with higher-than-average injury reports; and (4) the OSHA Administration often conducts *follow-up inspections* where it has previously issued citations for violations of safety standards.

OSHA Citations The OSHA Administration may issue written citations and impose penalties for violations of safety standards. The penalties may involve monetary fines, and the employer is usually required to remove the violation. The area director of the OSHA Administration also issues citations and imposes penalties. These penalties may vary according to the size of the business, the employer's good faith and safety record, and the severity of the violation. Citations must be posted prominently near the location of the violation to give employees notice.

OSHA Violations and Penalties OSHA violations have several levels of seriousness, and this permits the OSHA Administration to impose different penalties. *De minimis violations* have no direct relationship to safety, so the employer is usually notified, and no penalty is imposed. For example, the lack of private toilet facilities or waste containers and the availability of only used paper cups have been considered *de minimis* violations.

Nonserious Violations A *nonserious violation* relates to job safety but is unlikely to cause death or serious physical harm. A monetary penalty for nonserious violations may be levied at the discretion of the director of the OSHA Administration. Examples include a hazard of tripping due to poor housekeeping and a failure to provide instructions for the safe use of machinery.

Serious Violations Violations that pose a substantial probability of death or serious physical harm are *serious violations.* Repeat violations and violations that might lead to imminent danger of likely death or serious physical harm carry penalties of up to $10,000 and/or up to six months in jail. Willful repeated violations carry a $20,000 fine and up to one year imprisonment.

Protection from Employer Retaliation Employers are forbidden to discharge or discriminate against employees who report safety violations. The secretary of labor is empowered to investigate and determine whether employer retaliation has occurred. Should an employer be required to reinstate a fired employee and give back pay or

[9] *Marshall v. Barlow's, Inc.,* 436 U.S. 307 (1978).

other relief to replace benefits of which a wrongfully discharged employee has been deprived? The following case illustrates how OSHA protects employees who report safety or health violations.

Whirlpool Corp. v. Marshall

445 U.S. 1 (1980)
United States Supreme Court

The secretary of labor adopted a regulation interpreting the employee retaliation law. The new regulation permitted employees to refuse an assigned task if a reasonable apprehension existed that death or serious injury would result from its performance. Two Whirlpool employees refused to perform assigned maintenance work, fearing that a wire mesh used to prevent objects from falling from an overhead conveyer was unsafe. The employees were sent home without pay for insubordination, and their refusal to work was noted on their records. The court of appeals reversed the district court's finding that the regulation was invalid.

Justice Stewart delivered the opinion of the Court.

The Act itself creates an express mechanism for protecting workers from employment conditions believed to pose an emergent threat of death or serious injury. Upon receipt of an employee inspection request stating reasonable grounds to believe that an imminent danger is present in a workplace, OSHA must conduct an inspection. In the event this inspection reveals workplace conditions or practices that "could reasonably be expected to cause death or serious physical harm immediately or before the imminence of such danger can be eliminated through the enforcement procedures otherwise provided by" the Act, the OSHA inspector must inform the affected employees and the employer of the danger and notify them that he is recommending to the Secretary that injunctive relief be sought. At this juncture, the Secretary can petition a federal court to restrain the conditions or practices giving rise to the imminent danger. By means of a temporary restraining order or preliminary injunction, the court may then require the employer to avoid, correct, or remove the danger or to prohibit employees from working in the area.

To ensure that this process functions effectively, the Act expressly accords to every employee several rights, the exercise of which may not subject him to discharge or discrimination. An employee is given the right to inform OSHA of an imminently dangerous workplace condition or practice and request that OSHA inspect that condition or practice. He is given a limited right to assist the OSHA inspector in inspecting the workplace and the right to aid a court in determining whether or not a risk of imminent danger in fact exists. Finally, an affected employee is given the right to bring an action to compel the Secretary to seek injunctive relief if he believes the Secretary has wrongfully declined to do so.

In the light of this detailed statutory scheme, the Secretary is obviously correct when he acknowledges in his regulation that, "as a general matter, there is no right afforded by the Act which would entitle employees to walk off the job because of potential unsafe conditions at the workplace." By providing for prompt notice to the employer of an inspector's intention to seek an injunction against an imminently dangerous condition, the legislation obviously contemplates that the employer will normally respond by voluntarily and speedily eliminating the danger. And in the few instances where this does not occur, the legislative provisions authorizing prompt judicial action are designed to give employees full protection in most situations from the risk of injury or death resulting from an imminently dangerous condition at the worksite.

As this case illustrates, however, circumstances may sometimes exist in which the employee justifiably believes that the express statutory arrangement does not sufficiently protect him from death or serious injury. Such circumstances will probably not often occur, but such a situation may arise when (1) the employee is ordered by his employer to work under conditions that the employee reasonably believes pose an imminent risk of death or serious bodily injury, and (2) the employee has reason to believe that there is not sufficient time or opportunity either to seek effective redress from his employer or to apprise OSHA of the danger.

The regulation clearly conforms to the fundamental objective of the Act—to prevent occupational deaths and serious injuries. The regulation thus on its face appears to further the overriding purpose of the Act, and rationally to complement its remedial scheme. In the absence of some contrary indication in the legislative history, the Secretary's regulation must, therefore, be upheld, particularly when it is remembered that safety legislation is to be liberally construed to effectuate the congressional purpose.

Case Questions

1. What alternative outcomes are likely if OSHA regulations are circumvented by employers threatening employees with discipline or dismissal for seeking protection?
2. What are better methods to discover workplace hazards than an employee's refusal to work under unsafe conditions?

In recent years, the business community has leveled considerable criticism against the OSHA Administration's enforcement of OSHA. One basic problem involves the lack of efforts by employees to minimize their own exposure to risks. Employees often defeat the effectiveness of safety equipment or refuse to wear safety clothing. Improvements in employee training and supervision probably would help. Some other nations require the installation of state-of-the-art technology, periodic inspections by environmental engineers, testing of exposure to toxic substances, and training of safety personnel. Other nations have suggested a tax on employers for unsafe conditions.

State Occupational Safety Laws

There are numerous additional state and federal laws with an impact on safety, environmental concerns, and health conditions in the workplace. Numerous "right-to-know" laws have been enacted, requiring employers to inform employees of the toxic, carcinogenic, or potentially harmful chemicals and other substances used in the workplace. The OSHA Administration has made these disclosures uniform by requiring employers to develop *material safety data sheets* for all of the chemicals they use. In addition, employers must post notices of the chemicals used in each facility and educate employees on safe methods of handling chemicals. OSHA funds state safety regulation programs.

There has been significant controversy over OSHA's preemption of state criminal laws. Local prosecutors in Illinois, Texas, New York, and other states have brought criminal charges against high-level company officials for work-related injuries and deaths. These charges can be based on murder, negligent homicide, assault, or reckless endangerment. Greater local prosecutorial activity is expected until either Congress strengthens the OSHA Administration's criminal penalties or the Supreme Court or Congress clarifies whether OSHA leaves any room for state law.

Summary

Laws regulating the employment relationship began to supplement private contracts as businesses grew in size and relationships became more impersonal. With some exceptions, employment is continued only at the will of both the employer and the employee. Federal law prohibits the use of lie detector tests by the employer. The plant closing law requires employers to give employees 60 days' notice of mass layoffs or plant closings.

The Fair Labor Standards Act (FLSA) requires the minimum wage and establishes a standard 40-hour workweek. It applies only to employees, not to independent contractors or professionals. Overtime is computed at time and a half of the regular wage rate for compensable time over 40 hours per week. In response to child labor abuses during the industrial revolution, child labor is significantly restricted.

State unemployment compensation statutes allow employees with an established record of employment to withdraw benefits for a fixed time period unless they are not seeking employment or were fired for serious misconduct or during a strike. Employers with low employee turnover rates may pay lower premiums into state insurance funds than are paid by employers with higher turnover rates.

Social security supplements retirees' income. Employers must withhold FICA taxes from employees' wages for payment to the IRS. These payments provide benefits to current retirees. Limited medical benefits are paid under Medicare to older persons. Private pension plans are a significant source of retirement income. ERISA regulates private plans by standardizing their vesting provisions, payments, contributions, and taxability. Additional retirement devices, such as Keogh plans, IRAs, and deferred payment annuities, receive special tax treatment to encourage retirement savings.

Workers' compensation and OSHA regulations give employers an incentive to reduce workplace dangers and compensate employees for workplace injuries. Workers' compensation is a compulsory, no-fault, employer-financed insurance system that covers the injuries of employees while they are "on the job" at the worksite. Money benefits are paid to the injured employee or to the deceased employee's family for medical expenses, lost wages, loss of bodily functions, or death. The uncertainty about the cause of physical or mental diseases causes litigation over workers' compensation benefits. State workers' compensation agencies process claims, investigating and verify compensable injuries.

The Occupational Safety and Health Act of 1970 applies to all employers in interstate commerce with at least one employee unless an exemption applies. The OSHA Administration establishes safety standards, NIOSH researches safety hazards, and the OSHRC provides an independent process for appeals from OSHA Administration determinations. OSHA regulations impose duties on both employers and employees to follow OSHA procedures and maintain a safe workplace.

The OSHA Administration sets health and safety standards. New OSHA regulations are increasingly based on performance standards to encourage innovation in achieving a given level of protection. Many physical safety hazards have been eliminated so emphasis has turned to preventing the delayed manifestation of occupational diseases. New regulations must be feasible, must be directed against verifiable and significant health risks, and must provide societal benefits greater than the costs of implementation.

The OSHA Administration may grant variances that permit employers to use alternative methods of compliance. Employers must compile detailed accident records and submit them to the OSHA Administration so that it can monitor compliance. An OSHA Administration inspector may visit the employer's worksite only if the employer consents or if the inspector has a search warrant. OSHA Administration investigations usually follow an accident or an employee complaint. Reinspections occur after citations for noncompliance are issued and may occur regularly in certain dangerous industries. Fines and abatement orders are issued by the area directors of the OSHA Administration. OSHA violations have several levels of seriousness. Employers may not retaliate against employees who report violations.

Critical Thinking Review Questions

1. Compare and contrast the relationship between workers' compensation and OSHA safety and health efforts.
2. Discuss the presumptions underlying the qualifications that an employee must meet in order to receive unemployment compensation.
3. Explain the reasons why the common law system of negligence torts imposed barriers on employee suits for injury compensation.

Critical Thinking Exercises

1. Galvcoat Metals Co. uses numerous toxic chemicals in its metal coatings business. Technicians recently discovered that applications of increased concentrations of sulfuric acid (SO^2) improved the preparation of the sheets of raw steel for the electroplating process applied by Galvcoat. However, management considered the new technique a "trade secret," so it refused to disclose the higher SO^2 concentrations to employees or to provide additional protective gear as required by OSHA regulations. This failure to disclose helped conceal the reason Galvcoat metals performed better than competitors' products. This enabled Galvcoat to charge higher prices for its "superior" products. However, Galvcoat paid for none of the additional safety expenses needed to protect workers from the higher concentrations of SO^2. Comment on the ethical and legal problems presented here.
2. Hauck sued his former employer, Sabine Pilot Service, for wrongful discharge, claiming he was discharged for refusing to pump the bilges of the boat on which he worked. He had been told by an official of the U.S. Coast Guard that pumping bilges into the water was illegal. Sabine Pilot Service claimed Hauck was discharged for insubordination and for refusing to swab the deck and not following through on other duties. Should Hauck be able to recover on a claim of the tort of wrongful discharge? Discuss the application of the employment-at-will doctrine. *Sabine Pilot Service, Inc. v. Hauck,* 687 S.W.2d 733 (Tex. 1985).
3. TWA, a major commercial air carrier, trained all TWA flight attendants at its training academy, located in Kansas. Flight attendant positions were highly desirable, and TWA received thousands of applications for these positions each year. It carefully selected trainees from a large group of applicants. During the four-week training period, most of the trainees resided in dormitory-like accommodations located on the grounds of the training academy. They did not receive any wages from TWA at that time, but TWA did provide them with meals, lodging, and good ground transportation.

   Trainees were not permitted to work on regular commercial flights or to supplement the work of regular flight attendants until they had completed the training course. Completion of the course qualified them as flight attendants, but TWA did not guarantee that all of the successful trainees would be hired upon graduation. Were the TWA flight attendant trainees "employees" within the meaning of the Fair Labor Standards Act? *Donovan v. Transworld Airlines, Inc.,* 726 F.2d 415 (8th Cir. 1984).
4. GMAC, which provided financing for buyers of General Motors automobiles, had employees at each of its offices whose job was to collect overdue accounts and repossess cars. These employees put in long and irregular hours, and they usually worked on their own and without direct supervision. The upper management of GMAC regularly encouraged the accurate reporting of hours worked. However, lower-level supervisors set strict limits on the number of hours that could be reported. These supervisors gave the collection employees substantially more work than could be done in a 40-hour week but generally permitted them to report only 40–42 hours. On the average, the collection employees actually worked about 53 hours per week. The U.S. Department of Labor filed a suit claiming that GMAC had violated the overtime provision of the Fair Labor Standards Act. With what result and why? *Brennan v. GMAC,* 482 F.2d 825 (1973).
5. Communication Workers of America (CWA) recommended a nationwide strike of Bell Telephone in 1971. In New York State, the strike continued for seven months. Since the state's unemployment insurance law provided no exemption for striking workers, the 38,000 striking CWA members in New York State filed for and received unemployment compensation. The amounts they received were charged back to the employer under the state's system of establishing employer contributions. Bell Telephone filed suit, claiming that the New York law had been preempted by the National Labor Relations Act. Did the National Labor Relations Act implicitly prohibit the state of New York from paying unemployment compensation to strikers? *New York Telephone Co. v. New York Department of Labor,* 440 U.S. 519 (1979).
6. A collective bargaining agreement between General Tire and the union included a supplemental unemployment benefits plan (SUB) administered

by General Tire and designed to supplement unemployment insurance benefits to laid-off employees. General Tire had the right to terminate the plan when the agreement expired, provided that the assets remaining in the plan were used to pay benefits until they were exhausted. Adams and the other plaintiffs were laid-off union members who had been receiving benefits under the plan. When the collective bargaining agreement expired and the union called a strike, General Tire suspended all SUB payments. Was this a breach of its fiduciary duty? *Adams v. Rubber Co.,* 794 F.2d 164 (4th Cir. 1986).

7. Jane was an employee of Oxford Industries. One day, she noticed that the safety guard on the cutting machine she operated was dislocated. If her hand slipped, she could suffer a serious injury. Jane reported the matter to her foreman, but nothing was done about it. Finally, out of anger and fear, she walked off the job, refusing to work until the safety guard on the cutting machine was repaired. The company immediately fired her. Does Jane have a remedy?

CHAPTER

19

Labor–Management Relations

Critical Thinking Questions

- What historical reasons have led to prohibiting employers and unions from interfering with union organization or committing other unfair labor practices?
- Why is a forum like the National Labor Relations Board (NLRB) provided to oversee labor's rights to self-organization? What is the purpose and effect of NLRB unfair labor practice charges against employers or unions?
- What is the impact on labor contracting from the requirement that the employer and the union meet at reasonable times to bargain in good faith over mandatory bargaining topics, wages, hours, and other terms and conditions of employment?
- What negotiating power is created if employees may legally engage in concerted activities, including peaceful picketing and striking for lawful mutual aid or protection?
- What are the presumptions in making the union the exclusive bargaining agent for all employees in the appropriate bargaining unit?
- What is presumed when employees are restricted from pressuring employers other than their own?

Introduction... Past, Present, Future

Prior to the 20th century, the employment relationship was governed largely by private contracts. Employers negotiated employment face-to-face with prospective employees. But as businesses grew larger, employment relationships became more impersonal and complex. This left many new problems unaddressed by the law of contracts and torts. Unions argued that employees needed unity in their bargaining power to correct market failure. That is, labor needed stronger negotiating powers to become better balanced when negotiating with employers that have monopsony power—a buyer's monopoly over employment contracting. The Clayton Act provided the first piece of federal labor law by exempting most union activities from antitrust liability. This was necessary because union collective action arguably acts like a cartel of employees who fix the prices of their wages.

Contemporary labor law seeks to balance two goals. First, it encourages industrial peace and stability through collective bargaining and reasonable dispute settlement. Second, it more nearly equalizes the balance of bargaining power between workers and management. This relationship was unbalanced in the past. After the Civil War, industrial empires were managed by a few powerful men who dominated the American economy. The laissez-faire policies of the 19th century did little to enhance employees' economic standing or job security. The Industrial Revolution served only to widen the distance between employers and employees. Craft societies, or guilds, the forerunners of unions, arose in the early 1800s to help skilled workers refine their crafts. By the turn of the century, the American Federation of Labor (AF of L) had increased the bargaining power of skilled workers. Under the AF of L umbrella, the member unions gained exclusive jurisdiction over a particular craft or a range of similar jobs. However, the AF of L never organized unskilled workers, leaving this to another group, the Congress of Industrial Organizations (CIO).

As early as 1806, the Pennsylvania state courts impeded unions by designating them illegal combinations. Union members were considered participants in a criminal conspiracy. This approach changed by the mid-1800s as many courts subdued unions by issuing injunctions against union activities considered "inimical to the public welfare." For example, court orders prohibited strikes, the use of force to compel union membership, and union attempts to prevent substitute workers (i.e., scabs) from replacing strikers. Interstate railroads became the first major battleground for unionization. Congress could not effectively regulate unionization because the courts considered manufacturing an intrastate activity. However, this changed after 1893 when the American Railway Union organized railroad workers despite strong management resistance. A violent strike erupted when the Pullman Palace Car Company refused to negotiate with this union. Congress quickly appointed a federal strike commission that reported favorably on unionization. At the turn of the century, many employers resisted the rise of unions by using spies, blacklisting union sympathizers, and threatening reprisals against union members.

Unions made some advances during World War I. President Wilson created the National War Labor Board to prevent labor disputes from disrupting war production. This temporarily gave employees the right to form unions and bargain collectively with employers. However, after the war AF of L membership declined, and the power of big business grew. Management began to apply "scientific management" techniques of industrial engineers, using time and motion analysis of job tasks to define "a fair day's work for a fair day's pay." Only railroad workers permanently won the right to bargain collectively. Congress passed the Railway Labor Act (RLA) in 1926, which was the first federal legislation regulating labor–management bargaining relations. Under it, railroad workers may organize into labor unions, and railroad employers must bargain collectively with them. Today, the RLA also covers airline employees.

The first comprehensive federal labor statute was the Norris-LaGuardia Act of 1932. It prohibits the federal courts from enjoining labor disputes unless unlawful acts are threatened or committed or a union strikes in violation of a valid no-strike agreement. Courts cannot enjoin most strikes, walkouts, labor union meetings, membership in labor unions, peaceful public assembly, publicity, payment of strike or unemployment benefits, or giving advice to others. Before 1932, federal injunctions against these activities demoralized strikers. Even if the strikers were later exonerated, injunctions usually undermined their impact. Norris-LaGuardia also outlaws yellow-dog contracts that prohibit employees from union membership. The Act requires proof that a union official participated in the violence before a union is held liable for damages.

Norris-LaGuardia does not require employers to collectively bargain with unions. Collective bargaining is required under the 1935 National Labor Relations Act (NLRA or Wagner Act). The NLRA has three important provisions. First, §7 gives employees the right to form, join, or assist labor organizations; the freedom to bargain collectively with the employer; and the right to engage in concerted activity.

Second, employers must bargain collectively with the employees' certified bargaining representative (union). Third, it creates the National Labor Relations Board (NLRB) as the principal regulatory body responsible for administering the act.

After World War II, the public believed unions had gained excessive political and economic influence and that this power permitted unions to intimidate adversaries. Public sympathy toward unions diminished as many people suspected that organized crime had some influence in union politics. While most unions were anti-Communist, some Communist party members became leaders of several CIO unions. After this fact became widely publicized in the 1940s, public pressure mounted to reign in unions' increasing power. The Taft-Hartley Act passed in 1947 and the Landrum-Griffin Act passed in 1959 address these concerns. These laws prohibit unions from engaging in certain unfair labor practices, prohibit undemocratic union self-governance, and prohibit unions from bullying their members. The antiunion climate finally caused the AF of L and the CIO to merge in 1955, during the Eisenhower years, to slow their loss of power and to confront rising antiunion hostility. The major federal labor laws are summarized in Figure 19–1.

Today, employers must bargain with unionized employees over such issues as working hours, retirement security, hiring and firing practices, and job health and safety conditions. Employers must be aware of many complex statutes, administrative regulations, and judicial interpretations that affect the terms and conditions of employment. Even nonunion employers must know these laws to avoid committing unfair labor practices if their employees should ever begin unionization. The

FIGURE 19–1 Principal Federal Labor Laws

Date	Name of Law	Purposes and Provisions
1926	Railway Labor Act	Comprehensive coverage of collective bargaining between railroad or airline employers and unions representing their employees
1932	Norris-LaGuardia Act	Prevents federal courts from enjoining collective union activities (e.g., meetings, picketing, strikes) during labor disputes unless unlawful acts occur
		Outlaws yellow-dog contracts
		Permits unionization activities
1935	National Labor Relations Act (NLRA or Wagner Act)	Comprehensive coverage of collective bargaining for all employers not covered by Railway Labor Act
		Give employees the right to form, join, or assist labor organizations
		Requires collective bargaining
		Created National Labor Relations Board (NLRB)
1947	Labor-Management Relations Act (Taft-Hartley Act)	Defines unfair labor practices of unions, such as discrimination and failure to bargain in good faith
1959	Labor-Management Reporting and Disclosure Act (Landrum-Griffin Act)	Requires fair and democratic procedures for elections of union officials
		Requires disclosure by union officials, unions, and employers to avoid embezzlement and conflicts of interest

potential for unionization continues to discipline the employment market, requiring both employers and unions to consider the impact that their bargaining decisions have on employees and on the success of the business.

Labor unions face numerous challenges in the future. Unionism is still strong in some basic industries (e.g., automobile manufacturing, rubber, steel, mining, oil, chemicals), and unionism is spreading rapidly to government and to white-collar workers. Nearly 40 percent of government workers are unionized. However, total union membership has declined to under 16 percent of the workforce from its high of over 35 percent during World War II when nearly 20 million workers were union members. Today, there are just 15 million union members. The traditional bargaining power of employees over their employer's business has diminished as assembly lines have been automated and many component parts are imported. Employers now often claim that because high wages diminish competitiveness, employees must scale back their wage demands to maintain their jobs. Employees may become disenchanted with unions and may increasingly prefer nonunion status, a trend now under way, particularly in the U.S. Sunbelt.

There is a growing trend toward both state and federal legislation on matters that unions traditionally bargained for. This will probably continue to create statutory rights for employees, replacing much of the unions' role in protecting employee rights and improving working conditions. Employment laws covering discrimination, health and safety regulations, privacy and compensation were discussed in Chapter 18. The perception that unions pursue unrealistic goals in an overly adversarial style may further hasten their decline and eliminate their role in negotiating many issues previously addressed in collective bargaining. Unions' influence on such matters may be confined to lobbying. For example, unions apply political pressure to limit the influx of immigrant labor and helped to delay ratification of NAFTA as they believed this might slow the loss of jobs to Mexico.

This chapter discusses the law governing labor's relations with management. Labor law is a federal regulatory scheme that largely displaces conflicting state law, so it eliminates most incentives for businesses to move to states with less restrictive labor law. Collective bargaining and union election relationships are governed solely by federal law, though there are gaps that the states may fill. For example, state or local police may intervene whenever labor disputes result in physical threats or actual violence. If labor disputes bring about malicious defamation, trespassing, or intentional infliction of emotional distress, state tort law may apply. State unemployment benefit laws may provide workers certain benefits during labor disputes. Several states have passed right-to-work laws, permitting employees to refrain from supporting unions, which has further weakened unions.

International Perspective and Commentary

Confrontation versus Cooperation between Unions and Management

Adversarial relations dominate the labor movement history in many nations, including countries in North America, Western Europe, and Southeast Asia. Using this confrontational approach, the parties bring economic pressure on their adversaries to influence the bargaining process. Proponents argue that confrontation produces an optimum compromise that becomes embodied in their collective bargaining agreement. However, some other nations use a cooperative approach. Unions become involved in some management decisions, either formally, as in Germany, or informally, as in Japan.

In Germany, union representatives become involved in setting corporate policy under the *codetermination* system discussed later in this chapter. Although this system does not prevent strikes, it does force management to consider workers' well-being. The Japanese culture encourages cooperation by prizing the appearance of harmony. Japanese labor relations confine unions to the role of refining workers' craft. Japan's lifetime employment system reduces adversarial relations between management and labor and encourages the two groups to share information. *Quality circles* are Japanese worker groups dedicated to increasing quality and eliminating production problems. Managers implement decisions after a consensus is developed in these worker groups.

However, in some other developing nations, union efforts to maintain harmony tend to work against workers' immediate interests. For example, Mexican unions are dominated by the ruling political party, so these unions allegedly hold down wages to check inflation. Much of Latin America will probably see unions taking on workers' immediate demands more aggressively. Unions in the emerging economies of eastern Europe were an important force in political reform but have generally not taken strong adversarial positions in labor negotiations. Aggressive and confrontational unionization may be coming to the developing economies of the Pacific Rim. In nations such as China, Indonesia, and Vietnam, strikes are increasing, demands are mounting for wage raises, and there is rebellion against the feudal-like labor conditions that still use slave or prison labor. Many developing nations have successfully held down wage demands by attracting new industries seeking low wages. While such nationalism concerns have been successful up to now, some of these nations take shortcuts in worker safety. The mounting disasters are triggering demands for better working conditions and benefits.

It may be ironic that U.S. labor history is now being mirrored in many developing nations, just as U.S. labor relations are finally turning towards cooperation. There is an increasing use of arbitration and collective bargaining to replace divisive and costly strikes and lockouts. Some of this evolution was encouraged by the Labor Management Cooperation Act of 1978, which funded research to improve labor relations and uses the Federal Mediation and Conciliation Service to explore alternative dispute resolution.

Role of the NLRB

Several organizational activities must precede collective bargaining between unions and employers, including the grouping of employees into a bargaining unit, the election of a bargaining representative (union), and the employer's recognition of the union as the valid employee representative. These activities are overseen by the **National Labor Relations Board (NLRB).** The NLRB certifies the selection of a particular union as the employees' bargaining representative. The NLRB is intended to provide a forum for worker protection away from undue pressures by the employer or the union.

National Labor Relations Board (NLRB)
Federal agency administering the labor laws.

Organization of the NLRB

The NLRB is organized into two major divisions: the board itself and the Division of General Counsel. The board consists of five members appointed by the president and confirmed by the Senate. Each member serves a five-year term; the members' terms are staggered to provide continuity. Board members may be removed by the president only for "malfeasance in office or neglect of duty." Although the board may sit as a full panel of five members, it often expedites cases by delegating power to a three-member subpanel. Trial-like hearings about labor matters are first heard by NLRB administrative law judges (ALJ) who sit in the various regional NLRB offices. The Division of General Counsel is headed by counsel independent of the NLRB. The general counsel is appointed for a four-year term by the president with Senate confirmation. This office has "final authority, on behalf of the Board, in respect to the investigation of the charges and issuance of complaints and with respect to the prosecution of complaints before the Board."

NLRB Procedures

NLRB procedures are usually begun after one person files a charge that another person committed an unfair labor practice. Typically, field examiners investigate the matter, taking affidavits (sworn statements) to discover facts supporting or denying the charge. Even if the person filing the charge withdraws the complaint, the NLRB may continue prosecution. A charge must be filed within six months after the event in question, or it is barred by the statute of limitations.

NLRB charges may be settled either in an informal settlement proceeding or at an ALJ hearing. The ALJ hearing is very similar to a court trial because the parties present their cases, and the rules of evidence apply. An appeal from the ALJ hearing may be made to the whole board. In unfair labor practice cases, appeal beyond the NLRB may be taken to the appropriate federal court of appeals. In representation and election cases, however, appeal to the courts is prohibited because the NLRB has primary jurisdiction, making it the final authority in designating bargaining representatives.

The NLRB has a history of quasi-independence and near neutrality. However, many labor scholars argue that the board became politicized during the Reagan administration years, favoring management and turning against even-handed treatment of labor disputes. Currently, the board is returning to the political center. Nevertheless, the lack of political balance for board appointees, as required for many other quasi-independent agencies, suggests it will continue to vacillate with the politics of the presidential administration. Most other nations have labor regulators performing some of the same functions as the NLRB. For example, the EU has separate labor administrative courts that regulate unionization matters as well as other employment regulation issues that the United States has delegates to other regulators, as discussed in Chapter 18.

Representation Elections

representation election Employees' election to certify a particular union as their bargaining representative.

Representation elections are the predominant procedure used to select a particular union as the employees' bargaining representative. The NLRB has power to oversee representation elections through its regional directors.

Responsibilities of NLRB Regional Directors

1. Ordering elections.
2. Determining the appropriate bargaining unit.
3. Certifying the election results.
4. Deciding close representation questions.

The first step in a representation election is the filing of a petition with the NLRB, which evaluates the petition to ensure the satisfaction of statutory requirements. A hearing is then held to schedule the election. After the election, the NLRB rules on its effect. For example, a fairly conducted election will probably be ruled valid. However, if there is evidence of coercion or threats, the NLRB may order a new election.

Many elections are initiated by employees who file petitions requesting a representation election. Many employees then assist some uncertified union in its organizational efforts. A union's petition must show support from at least 30 percent of the bargaining unit members. If an employer reasonably believes some union has employee support, the employer may initiate an election by filing a petition once the union has demanded recognition.

Types of Representation Elections

There are several types of representation elections. A *consent election* is held if the employer and the proposed union agree on which employees are in the bargaining unit and on the time and place of the election. However, if they disagree on these matters, a *contested election* is held. A *Globe election* is held when a group of employees chooses between merging into a larger bargaining unit or operating separately.

A *certification election* is held when an employer willingly recognizes and bargains with a union that claims support from employees. A certification election prevents rival unions from interfering with the certified union for one year following the election. A *decertification election* is held when employees become dissatisfied with an existing union and seek to remove it. Several unions were decertified during the 1980s. A *deauthorization election* permits employees to retain a certified union but remove a portion of its bargaining powers. For example, a certified union may be deauthorized from agreeing to a type of contract term that the membership does not want. A *runoff election* may be necessary when several competing unions are on one ballot and none receive a majority.

Appropriate Bargaining Unit

The **appropriate bargaining unit** includes all "employees" in a group who have similar interests in employment conditions and should be entitled to vote together as a unit. The unit should be represented by a single bargaining representative to ensure the fullest freedom of its members to exercise their rights. Eligible voters include any persons employed during the payroll period preceding the election, as well as most striking employees. Bargaining representatives are selected for each appropriate bargaining unit. Employers must bargain with only a single bargaining representative for any group of workers. Of course, a large employer with many separate employee groups may have to bargain with several unions representing different bargaining units. For example, one union may represent production workers, another may

appropriate bargaining unit
Employees sharing similar employment conditions, entitled to vote together as a unit.

represent truck drivers, and a third may represent maintenance workers. The NLRB selects the bargaining unit to ensure that the employees in it have similar economic interests, job classifications, and bargaining powers.

In determining the appropriate bargaining unit, the NLRB usually considers the similarity of interests among the employees within a potential bargaining unit; skills, wages, hours, and working conditions are considered the most important factors. Sometimes the NLRB also considers employees' desires, existing employee groupings, and collective bargaining history. The National Labor Relations Act also requires that the employees within an appropriate bargaining unit have similarities at the level of the employer, the craft unit, or the plant unit or within a recognized subdivision of these levels. For example, professional employees may not be included with nonprofessionals unless a majority of the professionals consent. Similarly, plant guards, who must protect the employer's property, may not be included with other employees because during intense labor disputes there might be a conflict of interest between plant guards and employees.

Alternative Union Selection Processes

Employer recognition occurs when an employer agrees to negotiate with a particular union after the union gives notice it has support from a majority of employees in a potential bargaining unit. An employer can avoid a costly and divisive election by simply recognizing the union. For example, a union can gain legitimate majority support by polling the employees. *Employee authorization* may be established if the union can show sufficient support with membership cards, authorization cards, petitions, or applications for membership.

Election Tactics Unions may need an employee list to conduct an effective campaign. At a nonunion plant, employers often frustrate unionization by denying the union access to the premises and by denying the union a list of employees' names. However, the *Excelsior* rule requires the union be given an employee list at least seven days prior to an election if the union cannot reach all of the other employees without great expense. Even when a union receives petitions signed by enough employees to hold an election, it may not have enough employee support to win the election. Seven days is often insufficient time for effective electioneering, so some unions immediately cease campaign efforts after receiving the list. This gives them more time to contact other employees, but the union must wait six months before beginning another election campaign.

ETHICAL DILEMMA

ETHICAL DILEMMAS IN LABOR–MANAGEMENT RELATIONS

Ethical, good faith, and reasonable conduct is at the heart of the national labor relations policy. However, the labor relations environment provides numerous opportunities for unethical behavior. During the initial organization of an employer's facility, there are often misrepresentations and intimidation, sometimes by the union and sometimes by the employer. The NLRA and the Taft-Hartley Act prohibit unfair labor practices that tend to deprive employees of reasonable "laboratory conditions" in making union selection decisions. It is unfair and unethical to use misrepresentations in electioneering. For example, some employers may insist, in bad faith, that their business will fail after unionization. This can coerce employees with implied threats of a plant closing or economic reprisals, an unethical means to avoid labor negotiations. Unions can be guilty of similar unfair electioneering tactics, particularly when some workers intimidate co-workers to gain support for the union.

Employer Interference with Union Organization

Employers are prohibited from interfering with, restraining, or coercing employees in the exercise of their self-organization rights. Employers who act on their incentive to disrupt union organization can be sanctioned with **unfair labor practice** charges. Employers guilty of any unfair labor practices listed in Figure 19–2 inhibit their employees' free choice to unionize.

unfair labor practice Prohibited actions of employer or union that impedes employees' self-organization rights.

Employer Unfair Labor Practices

Certain conduct by employers intimidates workers and thus upsets the ideal or "laboratory" conditions required for representation elections. Although employers may legitimately ask employees about the union's progress in organizing the workforce, an employer's intimidating interrogation is an unfair labor practice. This is coercive if the employee believes that the employer will retaliate for their union support.

The employer's polling of employees is an unfair labor practice unless the employer simply seeks to verify that a majority of employees supports the union. The employer must use secret ballots to protect employees from reprisal. The employer's use of spies or informers during any phase of self-organization is prohibited. A representation election may be set aside if the employer engages in interrogation or surveillance or any other unfair labor practice. Limits on an employer's use of lie detectors are discussed in Chapter 18.

Interference with Solicitation of Employees A union usually begins a campaign to organize a particular group of employees by having union representatives from the

FIGURE 19–2

Unfair Labor Practices of Employers

1. Interfering with employee efforts to form, join, or assist labor organizations.
2. Interfering with employees' concerted activities for mutual aid or protection.
3. Dominating a labor organization.
4. Supporting a labor organization.
5. Discriminating in hiring, firing, benefits, or other conditions of employment due to employee's union affiliation.
6. Discriminating due to employee's exercise of rights under the labor law.
7. Refusing to bargain collectively and in good faith with a duly certified labor organization.
8. Agreeing with a labor organization to conduct a secondary boycott.
9. Failing to reinstate unfair labor practice strikers.

national headquarters of a local union chapter visit employees. They may distribute literature to build support for unionization. Union representatives may ask employees about their dissatisfaction with the employer and then attempt to build on any negative sentiments. In all but the smallest towns, where most employees know one another, it is difficult for union officials to contact employees effectively. Unions are usually forced to electioneer on or near the employer's property. However, the presence of nonemployees on the employer's land is a trespass that violates the employer's property rights.

Employers must tolerate *some* inconvenience during union organization. However, reasonable nondiscriminatory restrictions may be imposed. For example, the congregation of too many nonemployees in work areas could interfere with work or risk safety hazards. Employers may restrict nonemployee union officials from trespassing in such work areas, effectively limiting work-site solicitations to those by co-workers. Co-workers may contact fellow workers during free time, before or after work, or during breaks and meals. Off-work-site solicitations may be made anytime and by anyone.

Employers may restrict the distribution of pro-union literature and union authorization cards to nonworking areas, such as exits, parking lots, cafeterias, and rest rooms. They may also prohibit nonemployees and off-duty employees from soliciting on company premises. Sometimes these restrictions discriminate against unions, so the employer's prohibition of solicitation must be a rule that applies to everyone. For example, the prohibition must apply equally to fund-raising by charities or membership drives by clubs and may not simply target unionization. If the employer prohibits solicitation, reasonable alternatives for the distribution of union materials must be available.

Union Activities at Shopping Centers Union activities on private shopping center property are particularly troublesome. The union's free speech rights seem to conflict with the owner's property rights. Consider a retail store employer located in the shopping center. Shopping centers are "dedicated to a public use," and the public access areas include the walkways, streets, and parking lots. Originally, under the *Logan Valley* rule, a union's free speech rights prevailed over the rights of a shopping center owner.[1] Therefore, such union activities as solicitation and picketing were permitted in shopping centers. More recently, however, the courts have limited these solicitation rights somewhat. In *Central Hardware Co. v. N.L.R.B.*, the mere fact that a large hardware store was open to the public did not mean that its private property was equivalent to a shopping center.[2] As long as alternative methods exist to communicate with retail store employees, unions have no constitutional right to trespass on private property.

Shopping centers are unique in that they are owned by commercial land developers that lease space to retailers. In many communities, shopping centers have nearly replaced the public downtown shopping districts, where union activities are generally permitted. Union organizational efforts directed at an employer/retailer may intimidate the customers that shopping centers are intended to attract. How should an employer's rights be reconciled with employees' self-organization rights? The next case distinguishes between employee and nonemployee presence on the employer's premises.

[1] *Amalgamated Food Employees Union, Local 590 v. Logan Valley Plaza, Inc.*, 391 U.S. 308 (1968).

[2] *Central Hardware Co. v. N.L.R.B.*, 407 U.S. 539 (1972).

Lechmere v. National Labor Relations Board

502 U.S. 527 (1992)
United States Supreme Court

Nonemployee members of the United Food and Commercial Workers Union attempted to organize employees of Lechmere, Inc., by handbilling car windshields in Lechmere's employee parking lot. Lechmere's manager ordered union organizers off the property, citing Lechmere's prohibition on solicitation or handbill distribution. The organizers relocated to a public grassy strip lying between the adjoining highway and Lechmere's parking lot to distribute pro-union handbills as employees drove by. Approximately 20 percent of Lechmere's employees received pro-union mailings after their addresses were identified by the Connecticut Department of Motor Vehicles from their license plate numbers. The union failed to organize Lechmere's employees and filed an unfair labor practice charge with the National Labor Relations Board (Board) charging that it had been illegally barred from Lechmere's private parking lot.

The court of appeals sustained an NLRB cease and desist order prohibiting Lechmere from enforcing the solicitation ban, and Lechmere appealed.

Justice Thomas delivered the opinion of the Court.

Section 8(a)(1) of the NLRA makes it an unfair labor practice for an employer "to interfere with, restrain, or coerce employees in the exercise of rights guaranteed by §7."

[In the *Babcock* case] we explained that the Board had erred by failing to make the critical distinction between the organizing activities of employees (to whom §7 guarantees the right of self-organization) and nonemployees (to whom §7 applies only derivatively). Thus, while "[n]o restriction may be placed on the employees' right to discuss self-organization among themselves, unless the employer can demonstrate that a restriction is necessary to maintain production or discipline, no such obligation is owed nonemployee organizers." As a rule, then, an employer cannot be compelled to allow distribution of union literature by nonemployee organizers on his property. As with many other rules, however, we recognized an exception. Where "the location of a plant and the living quarters of the employees place the employees beyond the reach of reasonable union efforts to communicate with them," employers' property rights may be "required to yield to the extent needed to permit communication of information on the right to organize."

To gain access, the union has the burden of showing that no other reasonable means of communicating its organizational message to the employees exists or that the employer's access rules discriminate against union solicitation. In practice, nonemployee organizational trespassing had generally been prohibited except where "unique obstacles" prevented nontrespassory methods of communication with the employees. So long as nonemployee union organizers have reasonable access to employees outside an employer's property, the requisite accommodation has taken place. It is only where such access is infeasible that it becomes necessary and proper to take the accommodation inquiry to a second level, balancing the employees' and employers' rights.

The exception to *Babcock's* rule is a narrow one. It does not apply wherever nontrespassory access to employees may be cumbersome or less-than-ideally effective, but only where "the location of a plant and the living quarters of the employee place the employees beyond the reach of reasonable union efforts to communicate with them." Classic examples include logging camps, mining camps, and mountain resort hotels. *Babcock's* exception was crafted precisely to protect the §7 rights of those employees who, by virtue of their employment, are isolated from the ordinary flow of information that characterizes our society. The union's burden of establishing such isolation is "a heavy one," and one not satisfied by mere conjecture or the expression of doubts concerning the effectiveness of nontrespassory means of communication.

Because the employees do not reside on Lechmere's property, they are preemptively not "beyond the reach," of the union's message. Although the employees live in a large metropolitan area (Greater Hartford), that fact does not in itself render them "inaccessible" in the sense contemplated by *Babcock.* Their accessibility is suggested by the union's success in contacting a substantial percentage of them directly, via mailings, phone calls, and home visits. Such direct contact, of course, is not a necessary element of "reasonably effective" communication; signs or advertising also may suffice. Access to employees, not success in winning them over, is the critical issue—although success, or lack thereof, may be relevant in determining whether reasonable access exists. The union in this case failed to establish the existence of any "unique obstacles," that frustrated access to Lechmere's employees. The Board erred in concluding that Lechmere committed an unfair labor practice by barring the nonemployee organizers from its property.

The judgment of the First Circuit is therefore reversed, and enforcement of the Board's order denied.

Case Questions

1. Compare how an employer must treat employees seeking unionization differently from nonemployee union officials in organizing the employer's workforce.
2. What is the presumption of unique inaccessibility that triggers the *Babcock* rule permitting nonemployee trespass?

Employer Electioneering

The First Amendment to the U.S. Constitution permits both employers and employees to exercise free speech by electioneering during union organization. However, there is a strong potential for misuse, given the employer's considerable economic power over employees. An employer's antiunion sentiment may influence voting far more than statements of union organizers. Coercive employer statements are unfair labor practices unprotected under the First Amendment. For example, an employer commits an unfair labor practice in threatening reprisal or in promising benefits to employees if they reject the union. The NLRB judges the employer's statements in their context by examining (1) the action threatened, (2) whether the threats could be taken seriously, and (3) how broadly the threats are communicated to workers.

Employees are a "captive audience." The employer may give antiunion speeches at the work site and on company time because the employer may use its property and its employees' paid time as a forum to express its views. There is no requirement that the union be given equal time. Within the 24 hours preceding a representation election, however, both the employer and the union are prohibited from making speeches unless employees attend voluntarily. Less coercive, nonpersonal communications (literature, noncoercive radio messages) are permitted throughout this period.

Threats Employers must carefully word speeches to ensure that they are not coercive. Such statements as "I intend to deal hard with the union" or "You may be replaced if you strike" are not automatically coercive. However, predictions of future consequences if the union is certified are considered coercive unless they are reasonable forecasts of objective facts over which the employer has no control. Predictions based on factors within the employer's control are coercive because the employer has the power to implement such predictions unilaterally. For example, an employer's promise to close a plant down if the union is approved is coercive. By contrast, it is not coercive if the employer simply recites facts about unionization events at other plants, such as bombings, shootings or violence, so long as the employer remains willing to bargain with the union. Both unions and employers must avoid making misrepresentations.

Benefits Positive statements by either the employer or the union can also be coercive. If an employer attempts to confer economic benefits on workers just prior to an election, it looks like a bribe to influence the outcome. Promises of such benefits as paid holidays, vacation time, and higher overtime pay have been called the "iron fist in the velvet glove" because they remind employees that the employer controls their economic fortunes. During the preelection campaign, the employer must maintain "business as usual" in its personnel policies. How can an employer effectively campaign against unionization if no representation election is held and the union gains support more secretly? The next case illustrates this dilemma yet sets certain limits for employer electioneering.

N.L.R.B. v. Gissel Packing Co., Inc.

395 U.S. 575 (1969)
United States Supreme Court

The union waged an organizational campaign and obtained authorization cards from a majority of the employees, then demanded recognition by the employer. The employer refused to bargain, claiming that authorization cards were inherently unreliable, and carried out a vigorous antiunion campaign. After a hearing, the NLRB held that the employer had engaged in unfair labor practices and that the authorization cards were valid and entitled the union to recognition to bargain with the employer.

Chief Justice Warren delivered the opinion of the Court.

Almost from the inception of the Act, then, it was recognized that a union did not have to be certified as the winner of a Board election to invoke a bargaining obligation. It could establish majority status by other means . . . by showing convincing support, for instance, by a union-called strike or strike vote, or, as here, by possession of cards signed by a majority of the employees authorizing the union to represent them for collective bargaining purposes. The acknowledged superiority of the election process does not mean that cards are thereby rendered totally invalid, for where an employer engages in conduct disruptive of the election process cards may be the most effective—perhaps the only—way of assuring employee choice.

The employers argue that their employees cannot make an informed choice because the card drive will be over before the employer has had a chance to present his side of the unionization issues. Normally, however, the union will inform the employer of its organization drive early in order to subject the employer to the unfair labor practice provisions of the Act; the union must be able to show the employer's awareness of the drive in order to prove that his contemporaneous conduct constituted unfair labor practices on which a bargaining order can be based if the drive is ultimately successful. Further, the employers argue that without a secret ballot an employee may, in a card drive, succumb to group pressures or sign simply to get the union "off his back" and then be unable to change his mind as he would be free to do once inside a voting booth. But the same pressures are likely to be equally present in an election, for election cases arise most often with small bargaining units where virtually every voter's sentiments can be carefully and individually canvassed. And no voter, of course, can change his mind after casting a ballot in an election even though he may think better of his choice shortly thereafter.

We do note that an employer's free speech right to communicate his views to his employees is firmly established and cannot be infringed by a union or the Board. Thus, an employer is free to communicate to his employees any of his general views about unionism or any of his specific views about a particular union, so long as the communications do not contain a "threat of reprisal or force or promise of benefit." He may even make a prediction as to the precise effects he believes unionization will have on his company. In such a case, however, the prediction must be carefully phrased on the basis of objective fact to convey an employer's belief as to demonstrably probable consequences beyond his control or to convey a management decision already arrived at to close the plant in case of unionization. If there is any implication that an employer may or may not take action solely on his own initiative for reasons unrelated to economic necessities and known only to him, the statement is no longer a reasonable prediction based on available facts but a threat of retaliation based on misrepresentation and coercion, and as such without the protection of the First Amendment. We therefore agree with the court below that "[c]onveyance of the employer's belief, even though sincere, that unionization will or may result in the closing of the plant is not a statement of fact unless, which is most improbable, the eventuality of closing is capable of proof." . . .

The Board found that petitioner's speeches, pamphlets, leaflets, and letters conveyed the following message: that the company was in a precarious financial condition; that the "strike-happy" union would in all likelihood have to obtain its potentially unreasonable demands by striking, the probable result of which would be a plant shutdown, as the past history of labor relations in the area indicated; and that the employees in such a case would have great difficulty finding employment elsewhere. In carrying out its duty to focus on the question: "[W]hat did the speaker intend and the listener understand?" the Board could reasonably conclude that the intended and understood import of that message was not to predict that unionization would inevitably cause the plant to close but to threaten to throw employees out of work regardless of the economic realities. In this connection, we need go no further than to point out (1) that petitioner had no support for its basic assumption that the union, which had not yet even presented any demands, would have to strike to be heard, and that it admitted at the hearing that it had no basis for attributing other plant closings in the area to unionism; and (2) that the Board has often found that employees, who are particularly sensitive to rumors of plant closings, take such hints as coercive threats rather than honest forecasts.

Case Questions

1. What alternative methods to certification elections can be used to show employee support for the union is sufficient to require the employer to bargain with it?
2. What problems underlie the use of authorization cards as a method of union certification?

Employers commit an unfair labor practice if they withhold customary periodic wage increases from employees who are attempting to unionize. However, the employer who announces that increased benefits will take effect after an election is not committing an unfair labor practice so long as the changes were planned prior to the election campaign. Just before the election at issue in *N.L.R.B. v. Exchange Parts*, the employer granted an additional "floating holiday."[3] At a dinner he held for employees, he lectured that the election would "determine whether [they] wished to hand over the right to speak and act for themselves." Later, he charged that the union had distorted the facts and reminded the employees of benefits they had obtained without a union. "The company puts things in your envelope. . . . It didn't take a union to get you any of those things." Thereafter, the union lost and a new election was ordered. Elections should be held in an atmosphere uncontaminated by promises of benefits that are clearly intended to influence the outcome.

[3] *N.L.R.B. v. Exchange Parts,* 375 U.S. 405 (1964).

Employer Domination or Support of a Union

In the 1920s, some employers created *company unions,* which were weak and favored the employer's goals. Employees were often unaware of the employer's secret support. Today, employers are prohibited from dominating or interfering with labor organizations. For example, it is an unfair labor practice for employers to provide financial or other support to unions. The test of unlawful employer domination is whether the union is truly independent in representing employees in disputes with the employer. Such support may arise from various activities. For example, solicitation by the employer or supervisors to join a particular union is an unfair labor practice. Undue assistance to a particular union may also be unlawful. For example, an unfair labor practice arises if the employer takes an active part in establishing a union by helping it draft its bylaws or by actively opposing a competing union. There have been unfair labor practices where employers gave one union access to legal counsel, office space, secretarial services, printing services, and other financial support while denying such assistance to a competing union. Union bylaws may not give the employer a voice or vote in the union's self-governance. Throughout the process of self-organization, the employer must maintain neutrality to avoid charges of domination, favoritism, or other interference with the employees' selection of a union.

INTERNATIONAL PERSPECTIVE AND COMMENTARY

CODETERMINATION AND LABOR HARMONY

German law requires *codetermination,* a system permitting labor union representation on each employer's corporate boards to implement the German ideal of labor harmony. In the United States, this practice could be construed as an unfair labor practice if it encouraged the employer's domination or support of the union. German corporate law requires two types of boards: the *supervisory board* and the *managing board.* Union representatives must constitute 5 of the 11 managing board members and one of the three supervisory board members. Shareholders elect 5 managing board members and an 11th is elected by the other 10 members to represent the public interest, mediate disputes, and cast tie-breaking votes. One management representative from sales and one from production also sit on the three-member supervisory board.

The inclusion of various constituencies in corporate policy making has arguably resulted in more peaceful industrial relations in Germany than in many other nations. Observers argue that Germany suffers less downtime from strikes and has better employee morale and working conditions than historically prevalent in the United States. Japanese unions also have harmonious relations with Japanese employers, a closeness that could also violate the NLRA prohibition against employer domination. The Japanese use *quality circles,* groupings of union employees and management supervisors to monitor quality control, provide a forum for discussing work refinement, and suggest implementation of improvements. There are difficulties for U.S. firms in implementing similar techniques if these worker committees function too much like unions in framing proposals for changes in wages, hours, or other terms and conditions of employment.[4] Considering the Japanese and German economic successes, however, policymakers might suggest adapting such innovations to U.S. labor relations.

---

[4] *In re Electromation, Inc.*, 309 N.L.R.B. 163 (1992).

Employer Discrimination

It is illegal for an employer to slow unionization by discriminating in hiring, firing, or job tenure. Employers may not grant promotions or pay raises to nonunion employees while withholding such benefits from union employees. This undermines the union.

Business Purpose In most discrimination situations, the employer claims a business purpose for a particular hiring, firing, or promotion decision. That claim must be supported by strong, independent evidence showing that there is no anitunion motive. For instance, well-documented records of employee insubordination, chronic tardiness, poor performance, or misbehavior prior to union involvement is strong evidence. However, an antiunion motive may be inferred if a large percentage of discharged employees had good work records but were engaged in union activities. Circumstantial evidence may also be derived from the timing of employee dismissals. If employees are fired during or immediately after unionization activities, the employer must show strong evidence that a reasonable basis existed for the dismissals.

Discrimination in hiring or firing on the basis of an employee's union affiliation is clearly unlawful. Decisions to lay off, demote, transfer, or change work assignments are illegal if they are based on antiunion considerations. In one case, an employer committed an unfair labor practice when it offered 20 years of seniority to strike-breaking employees.

Plant Closings It is legal for an employer to lock employees out of the plant if there are valid economic justifications and if negotiations have reached an impasse. These plant closings bring economic pressure on the employees to settle by depriving them of income.

A more drastic action occurs when the employer permanently closes the whole operation or moves to another locality. For example, an employer may want to slow unionization by starting new operations in an economically depressed region. Union contracts that add costs could make a union plant noncompetitive. A clear trend in the 1980s was to outsource parts from nonunion or foreign suppliers to lower costs. If the employer moves only part of the business to a new location and the employer's purpose is to discourage unionization, the action is unlawful. By contrast, employers have an absolute right to terminate their entire business for any reason whatsoever (including antiunion sentiments). If sound economic considerations support outsourcing or the movement of a plant, the employer need not bargain over the move, and there is no unfair labor practice. This has been called the *runaway shop* problem. However, if the employer has a clear antiunion motive, it is an unfair labor practice to move a plant far enough to require the hiring of a new workforce. As discussed in Chapter 18, notice of plant closings must be given to unions and employees under the WARN Act.

Interference, Restraint, and Coercion by Unions

The NLRA also prohibits unions from coercing employees in the exercise of their self-organization rights. Unions have somewhat broader latitude during organization. Unions must refrain from inflammatory racial or ethnic slurs during unionization and may express opinions so long as these are not coercive. However, such statements as "Those who do not join the union will eventually lose their job" and "We have ways of handling people that argue against the union" are unfair labor practices. Threats of

FIGURE 19-3

Unfair Labor Practices of Unions

1. Restraining or coercing employees who are exercising self-organization rights.
2. Coercing an employer to discriminate against nonunion employees.
3. Refusing to bargain in good faith with an employer if the union is certified as the employees' representative.
4. Engaging in illegal strikes, picketing, or secondary boycotts.
5. Charging excessive or discriminative dues in a union shop.
6. Featherbedding—requiring the employer to pay for work not actually performed.
7. Picketing to coerce the employer to recognize a noncertified union.
8. Agreeing with an employer to engage in a secondary boycott.
9. Failure to represent all members of the appropriate bargaining unit without regard to their union membership status.

violence made against employees who fail to cooperate with the union are also unlawful. When a union directs violence against the employer and destroys company property, it commits an unfair labor practice. In such a case, employees can reasonably infer that they are also threatened if they attempt to enter the plant.

Unions may be prohibited from other, more subtle forms of economic pressure. In one case, a union administered the employees' health fund, which was financed with employee contributions. The union acted unlawfully by threatening that only its members would receive benefit payments in an attempt to coerce nonmembers to join. In another case, the union's promise to waive or reduce union membership fees or dues was unlawful. Any union pressure on the employer to discriminate between union members and nonmembers is also illegal. Although picketing as such is not illegal coercion, it may be coercive if it is done on a massive scale that intimidates nonunion employees from approaching the work site. For example, forcefully blocking plant entrances and exits is clearly unlawful. Unfair labor practices must be remedied through settlement or administrative hearings before an election can be validated. Unfair labor practice hearings are first held before ALJs at the NLRB, who make recommendations to the whole board. The NLRB then makes fact-findings and may issue a cease and desist order or issue an affirmative order. In extreme cases, the NLRB may seek a restraining order or injunction in the U.S. District Court. Union unfair labor practices are listed in Figure 19–3.

The Labor Negotiation Process

After an appropriate bargaining unit selects a particular union as its bargaining representative, both the employer and the union must bargain in good faith. **Good faith bargaining** is an interactive process in which each side makes offers and counteroffers in an effort to reach an agreement over wages, hours, and other terms and conditions of employment. The labor negotiation process fulfills the five basic functions for society, listed below. It reflects the overall social and economic pressures from the financial, product, and labor markets. The labor contracts negotiated during this process allow labor markets to reach economic equilibrium.

good faith bargaining Interactive proposals for union contract between an employer and the bargaining unit.

Functions of the Labor Negotiation Process

1. Establishes work rules.
2. Selects the form and mix of employee compensation.
3. Provides uniformity among competitors.
4. Sets priorities for both labor and management.
5. Permits economic pressures to shape labor–management relations.

Collective Bargaining and Negotiation

collective bargaining Union contract negotiations between employer and employees' certified bargaining representative.

Collective bargaining is an interactive process between two parties that often have opposite goals. In many instances, gains made by one party represent losses for the other party, a zero-sum game. Except for incentive pay plans, there are few opportunities for both parties to "win" on compensation issues. Typically, one party will compile a set of proposals into a first offer. For example, the union may select a team of representatives (the bargaining committee) who seek to improve or maintain the pay scale and benefits that employees currently receive. The union's offer usually specifies an amount of compensation for each classification of employees, a designation of the work hours and overtime contingencies, a package of fringe benefits, and a classification of all the employees. Unions often seek to establish systems of seniority, grievance processes, protections against the loss of work to outside contractors or the cessation of business, and work and shift scheduling. Wage-related proposals include base salaries, cost-of-living and productivity increases, a wage scale rewarding seniority and skill levels, and fringe benefits such as medical insurance or pensions.

In most negotiations, the early offers from either party are more favorable to the offeror and less favorable to the opposing party. As a result, the opposing party may either decline the initial offer or make a counteroffer with terms more favorable to itself. Eventually, most negotiations result in a compromise in which the disagreements are reconciled by reaching some middle ground.

Bargaining Positions: Strengths and Weaknesses

It is customary for the negotiating teams representing management and the union to be well prepared for their first meeting. Elaborate financial statements and cost projections often accompany both the union's demand for higher wages and management's refusal to grant increases. The parties may study each other's negotiating history, particularly if the same negotiators are involved. Both parties need to be well versed in the nuances of the labor law to avoid committing unfair labor practices. Negotiations held on either party's "home turf" may provide a "home court advantage," so neutral premises are often selected. Negotiations are often held behind closed doors because public exposure or adverse publicity may cause a damaging and inflammatory atmosphere.

The parties often negotiate the noneconomic items first because their expectations are often closer on such items. For example, the existing grievance procedures, no-strike clauses, seniority provisions, and work assignments have often been acceptable to both sides. However, in recent years many employers have found the prevailing work rules and assignments are too costly. When absenteeism is high, production processes must be changed quickly. Restrictive work rules may permit overqualified workers to remain idle or can prevent underqualified workers from advancing into more complicated assignments. Many new contracts now remove these barriers to the employer's production flexibility.

Typically, each party's initial offer or counteroffer contains terms that are more favorable to itself than the terms it expects to achieve. For example, unions often demand higher salary raises than they realistically expect. By asking for "too much," each party is able to give up something during negotiations, thus appearing to compromise. Most negotiators would be satisfied if they could reach agreement on their fallback position, getting somewhat less than their initial demands. Astute third-party intermediaries, such as mediators, can facilitate cooperative negotiations and avoid adversarial relations. These persons act as conflict resolvers by reducing irrational feelings and pointing out the parties' unreasonable demands. They may generate alternative solutions or provide graceful retreats that permit the negotiators to save face. Such intermediaries also keep both parties focused on the important issues and remind them of the high costs of disagreement.

The teams representing both management and the union must have sufficient authority to bargain. The employer's representatives must have the authority to act as its agents in making offers or accepting union proposals. This requirement is less a problem for union negotiators because rank-and-file employees generally must approve the contract in a ratification vote. The employees may not immediately disavow their representatives after a certification election; this permits a newly elected union to establish itself.

A certified union has exclusive authority to represent all of the employees in the bargaining unit. Individual employees may not enter into separate bargains with the employer that are inconsistent with the collective bargaining agreement. For example, if the collective bargaining agreement covers all compensation issues, an individual union employee may not cut a separate deal to receive higher pay. Individual employees are considered third-party beneficiaries of the collective bargaining contract. In return for its exclusive bargaining right, the union must bargain fairly and equally on behalf of all bargaining unit employees, both union members and nonmembers. The laws in Switzerland and Germany are similar. But in Italy the union's negotiations apply only to union members, providing many workers with an incentive to join the union.

Duty to Bargain in Good Faith

The NLRA requires the union and employer to meet at reasonable times and confer in good faith with respect to wages, hours, and other terms and conditions of employment. It is an unfair labor practice for either party to refuse to bargain collectively. Neither party may engage in fictitious or surface bargaining if it has no real intent of reaching agreement. They must do more than just go through the motions.

Bad Faith Bargaining

Although bad faith is difficult to prove, it may be inferred. The parties should be willing to meet at reasonable times, put their agreement in writing, negotiate with each other, and bargain on mandatory subjects: wages, hours, and other terms and conditions of employment. The total course of conduct of each party's bargaining behavior is carefully examined. For example, it may be bad faith to offer totally unreasonable proposals or make an offer that is too quickly withdrawn before the other side can evaluate it.

The parties are often required to furnish information potentially relevant to bargaining. For example, the employer may be required to provide financial statements to substantiate its inability to pay higher wages. The disclosure duty is not unlimited so the employer can withhold information such as that might reveal confidential trade secrets. The union's need for such sensitive data may be balanced against the employer's need for confidentiality or privacy.

Bad faith may be inferred from other bargaining conduct, such as the failure to offer meaningful counterproposals, the refusal to discuss economic terms until noneconomic issues are resolved, attempts to delay meetings or to move the meeting place to a burdensome location, the withdrawal of earlier concessions, the refusal to bargain until the opposing party has withdrawn an unfair labor practice charge, or the launching of an adverse publicity campaign. It may be difficult to distinguish between permissible "hard bargaining" and impermissible "surface bargaining."

Boulwareism Can either party simply impose its judgment of what is reasonable and refuse to bargain further? This take-it-or-leave-it position is disfavored by the law and has been termed *Boulwareism* after Lemuel R. Boulware, a GE vice president who approached bargaining as though marketing a product.[5] He gathered comments on the levels and types of benefits expected by employees and researched the cost-effectiveness of these benefits to formulate a "product" of bargaining proposals acceptable to employees. GE then aggressively "sold" the proposals in an "avalanche" of publicity. GE stated that its proposals were firm, "fair offers," so that there was no need for union pressure or strikes. GE heavily publicized the unreasonableness of the union's proposals and refused to honor the union's request for cost estimates. During the negotiations, GE unilaterally instituted a 3 percent wage increase for nonunion employees and implemented its insurance and pension proposals for all employees. A strike ensued, and GE publicly criticized the personal conduct of the union negotiators, threatening to lay off strikers who did not return to work. Eventually, the union capitulated to all of GE's proposals. The U.S. Court of Appeals held that these activities amounted to an unfair labor practice by failing to respect the union's status as exclusive bargaining representative. GE's tactics were inherently divisive; they made negotiations difficult and uncertain and subverted the cooperation necessary to sustain a responsible and meaningful union leadership.

Remedies for Bad Faith Bargaining If either party refuses to bargain, the NLRB may order it to bargain or may issue a cease and desist order to refrain from bad faith bargaining. In unusual situations, the NLRB has ordered compensatory damages. In one case, for example, one party's refusal to bargain was so flagrant that the NLRB ordered the payment of litigation expenses to the innocent party. However, neither party may be forced to accept a particular agreement or provision. Nothing in the good faith bargaining obligation requires a party to make concessions.

Successor Employers When an employer experiences fundamental changes in its corporate structure, the question often arises whether existing labor contracts must be recognized. A firm in bankruptcy reorganization may have all of its contracts changed drastically, including its union contracts. Thus, the old labor contract may become unenforceable and employees may be required to accept a new, typically less favor-

---

[5] *N.L.R.B. v. General Electric Co.,* 418 F.2d 736 (2d Cir. 1969).

able, collective bargaining agreement. Congress amended the bankruptcy law in 1984, effectively limiting the effect of *N.L.R.B. v. Bildisco*.[6] The new law requires the bankruptcy judge's approval before an existing labor contract may be nullified. The bankruptcy judge must find that the labor contract modifications are "necessary" to the bankrupt's survival. Labor contracts may not be rejected unless (1) all creditors are treated fairly and equitably, (2) the union refused the bankrupt's proposed contract modification "without good cause," and (3) the equities favor rejecting the existing union contract.

When a corporation is merged with another corporation or its assets are purchased by another corporation, should the surviving corporation respect the terms of existing union contracts? The Supreme Court has held the surviving corporation must generally bargain with a duly certified union if there is substantial continuity of operations from the predecessor to the successor. But the successor is not bound by the terms unless it expressly or impliedly assumes the predecessor's collective bargaining agreement.[7] Clearly, this provides an incentive to merge or sell assets to invalidate unfavorable terms in a union contract.

Subjects of Bargaining

There are three basic categories of bargaining subjects. First, **mandatory collective bargaining subjects** include "wages, hours, and other terms and conditions of employment, or the negotiation of an agreement, or any questions arising thereunder." The parties are required to bargain over these subjects because the employment relationship is most directly affected by them. Bargaining on these subjects may continue to the point of impasse. Mandatory subjects include wages, merit increases, pension retirement benefits, vacations, rest periods, work assignments, seniority, no-strike provisions, and major grievances concerning working conditions. Safety rules and practices may also be considered mandatory subjects even if otherwise regulated. In one instance, Ford Motor Company was required to bargain over food prices charged in its employee lunchrooms. Food prices were a significant part of the employment relationship, and the whole automobile industry bargained over them. In France, such major bargaining subjects are not settled through collective bargaining but are set by government regulation. French unions bargain primarily to communicate employees' concerns to management.

mandatory collective bargaining subjects Unions and employers must bargain over subjects of wages, hours, and other terms and conditions of employment.

The second category includes *permissive subjects*. These subjects are "bargainable," but only if both parties voluntarily agree. Permissive subjects include company or union policies that only indirectly affect the employment relationship. For example, these could include modifications of an existing labor contract before it expires, public policies such as the employer's contributions to charities, the organization or size of the employer's corporation, the types of supervisors, general business practices, or the location of production facilities. Neither party may refuse to bargain on mandatory subjects in an attempt to force bargaining on permissive subjects.

Some employers seek to reduce their operations and eliminate union jobs. If company supervisors perform production work and this deprives union members of overtime pay, the employer must bargain. Many employers have started to contract out, or outsource, work formerly performed by union employees on the premises. This

[6] *N.L.R.B. v. Bildisco*, 466 U.S. 513 (1984).

[7] *Fall River Dyeing & Finishing Corp. v. N.L.R.B.*, 482 U.S. 27 (1987).

can lead to plant closure or to the sale or transfer of business operations. Employers have an incentive to reduce in-house work that an outsider paying lower wages can do more cheaply.

Managerial business judgments are considered mandatory subjects only to the extent that they directly affect the employment relationship. For example, managerial decisions to retrain or transfer employees or to give employees severance pay are usually considered mandatory subjects. In the *Fibreboard* case, an employer's unilateral decision to contract out maintenance work previously performed by employees was considered a mandatory subject.[8] The employer should have first given the union an opportunity to help reduce the maintenance labor costs before unilaterally contracting them out, particularly where there were no other alterations in the company's basic operations. By contrast, in *First National Maintenance*, the employer decided to discontinue certain operations.[9] First National had contracted to supply housekeeping and maintenance services to a nursing home. When it lost the contract, it decided to discontinue those operations altogether. Since the employer did not intend to replace the union employees it discharged, the cessation of operations was not considered a mandatory bargaining subject.

Either party may ask the other party to modify or terminate an existing agreement before its expiration date. However, neither party is required to bargain to modify an existing agreement. The party seeking a modification must notify the other party in writing at least 60 days before the agreement expires or 60 days before it wants the modifications to be effective and then must bargain in good faith.

The third category includes *illegal and prohibited subjects.* For example, the employer may not insist that the union bargain away its status as bargaining representative, and the employer must recognize a certified union. Some subjects may never become part of any collective bargaining agreement. For example, no collective bargaining agreement may prohibit employees from distributing union literature on company property or require that employees become union members before they are hired.

Impasse

The parties must continue to bargain in good faith and attempt reconciliation until an impasse is reached. An *impasse* is a deadlock in which neither party can make an offer on terms any more favorable to the opposing party. The duty to bargain continues during a strike, shutdown, lockout, or layoff, as these are not impasses. After an impasse has been reached, the employer may solicit striking employees to return to work based on the old contract terms or based on any terms previously rejected by the union negotiators.

The employer's communications to strikers during an impasse must not be coercive. If the employer offers strikers a wage increase above the level that the employer offered during negotiations, this may be an unfair labor practice because it tends to undermine the union's bargaining position. A temporary impasse does not necessarily signify a breakdown in negotiations, so the duty continues to bargain in good faith. Impasses are seldom permanent in negotiations between several employers and a national or parent union representing several local unions. This is called *pattern bargaining,* which is optional in the U.S. but mandatory in Germany and Belgium.

---

[8] *Fibreboard Paper Products Corp. v. N.L.R.B.*, 379 U.S. 203 (1964).

[9] *First National Maintenance Corp. v. N.L.R.B.*, 452 U.S. 666 (1981).

Labor Dispute Resolution: Concerted Activities

The NLRA grants employees the right to engage in "concerted activities for the purpose of collective bargaining or other mutual aid or protection." When a particular union becomes the certified bargaining representative for a bargaining unit, employees must use the union's grievance procedures. Even unorganized employees with no certified union representative are entitled to engage in concerted activity. To gain legal protection for concerted activities, employees must act as a group and not merely as individuals. Thus, one employer committed an unfair labor practice by firing nonunion employees who walked off the job to protest extremely cold working conditions.

Not all concerted activities are protected; they must be lawful, advanced in good faith, and directed toward a specific objective. The objective must be nonviolent, cannot constitute a breach of the union contract, and must concern a work-related matter. For example, employees may become involved in political responses to labor legislation or be politically active in elections. The objectives of these activities are sufficiently work-related to gain protection. However, the employee's political freedom is balanced against the loyalty that employees must show to their employers. In one case, some employees discouraged the public from patronizing their employer. Since the employees failed to connect the boycott to a specific grievance or to benefits that they sought, their concerted activity was disloyal and unprotected, permitting the employer's reasonable discipline.

Union Security Agreements

Concerted activities have greater economic impact when the union is strong and employees are not easily replaced. For many years, unions have sought to include provisions in collective bargaining agreements to strengthen the union. For example, all of the employees in the bargaining unit might be required to join the union or at least to pay union dues. Such union security devices must not be too restrictive. Before 1947, many unions successfully negotiated **closed shop agreements** requiring each new hire to join the union before work. Closed shop clauses gave unions extensive power over the pool of available workers and were effectively used to regulate and discipline union members. For fear of losing their jobs, unions members often blindly accepted the policy decisions of union officials without dissent. For these reasons, closed shop agreements are now illegal. It is also illegal for employers to hire only workers recommended by the union. This is a disguised form of the closed shop agreement. However, it is permissible to have a system of job referrals from unions that operate a *hiring hall* such as the practice of some unions to provide employers with lists of qualified union members.

closed shop agreement Illegal term in collective bargaining agreement requiring union membership before hiring.

Union Shops The **union shop** agreement is a legal device that makes union membership compulsory *after* an employee is hired. Union membership may be required after the employee has worked a probationary period of at least 30 days. The period may be as short as 7 days in the construction industry because work is often short-term and seasonal. In a union shop, full-fledged union membership is not necessary. Instead, employees may only be required to pay dues and initiation fees if the amounts are reasonable. A *checkoff* provision requires the employer to deduct the union dues from employees' paychecks and then forward them to the union. If an

union shop Union contract term requiring all employees to join the union.

employee has a bona fide religious objection to financial support for labor organizations, the employee may be required instead to pay an equivalent amount to a nonreligious, nonlabor, tax-exempt charity.

Agency Shop An *agency shop* does not require union membership, but only payment of a service fee or a *bargaining assessment.* This amount may be used to cover union representation activity expenses and is often less than regular union dues. Under a *maintenance of membership agreement,* union members may renounce their membership within a specified period after joining. For example, employees may decide to renounce union membership to avoid the union's discipline while still retaining benefits of union bargaining. Without these exceptions, the union could force the employer to discharge employees who are not union members or refuse to pay dues or other fees.

right-to-work laws State laws prohibiting union or agency shops that mandate union membership.

Right-to-Work Laws Section 14(b) of the Taft-Hartley Act permits state legislatures to prohibit certain union security agreements. State **right-to-work laws** may validly restrict or prohibit union or agency shops. Nearly half the states, predominantly in the West, South, and Sunbelt, have right-to-work laws. Most of the states in the Midwest and the industrial Northeast permit union security agreements. Some observers argue that the right-to-work states are better able to attract new industry because unionization in those states is slower, and unions are weaker. States may not override union security agreements that are valid under the Railway Labor Act.

Union's Duty of Fair Representation

The certified union has a special status as the "exclusive" bargaining representative of all the employees in the bargaining unit. The employer must bargain with the certified union. The certified union owes a duty of *fair representation* to all employees in the bargaining unit, including employees who voted against the union, are not union members, disagree with the union leaders, or are members of minority groups. The duty of fair representation began in the 1940s and 1950s as a response to racial discrimination by some unions. In one case, a union induced the employer to give job referrals to U.S. citizens rather than Mexican nationals, even though both were in the bargaining unit.[10] It is an unfair labor practice for unions to discriminate against any employee on the basis of "invidious or arbitrary classifications" such as citizenship, sex, race, or national origin.

Although ordinary negligence does not constitute a breach of the fair representation duty, a union's gross negligence or its arbitrary or reckless disregard of an individual employee's rights may constitute a breach. What is the union's responsibility in maintaining industrial peace, and how does it fulfill that responsibility? This is the key issue discussed below in defining the responsibilities of the postal worker's union to fairly advance a postal worker's grievance.[11]

> Fundamental to federal labor policy is the grievance procedure. It promotes the goal of industrial peace by providing a means for labor and management to settle disputes through negotiation rather than industrial strife. Adoption of a grievance procedure provides the parties with a means of giving content to the collective-bargaining agreement and determining their rights and obligations under it.

[10] *N.L.R.B. v. International Longshoremen's Assn.,* 489 F.2d 635 (5th Cir. 1974).

[11] *Bowen v. United States Postal Service,* 459 U.S. 212 (1983).

Although each party participates in the grievance procedure, the union plays a pivotal role in the process since it assumes the responsibility of determining whether to press an employee's claims. The employer, for its part, must rely on the union's decision not to pursue an employee's grievance. For the union acts as the employee's exclusive representative in the grievance procedure, as it does in virtually all matters involving the terms and conditions of employment.

There is no unfairness to the union in this approach. By seeking and acquiring the exclusive right and power to speak for a group of employees, the union assumes a corresponding duty to discharge that responsibility faithfully—a duty which it owes to the employees whom it represents and on which the employer with whom it bargains may rely. When the union, as the exclusive agent of the employee, waives arbitration or fails to seek review of an adverse decision, the employer should be in substantially the same position as if the employee had had the right to act on his own behalf and had done so. Indeed, if the employer could not rely on the union's decision, the grievance procedure would not provide the "uniform and exclusive method for [the] orderly settlement of employee grievances," which the Court has recognized is essential to the national labor policy.

Regulation of Strikes

Strikes are concerted activities of employees who stop work simultaneously to pressure their employer. Although there is no Supreme Court decision that squarely sanctions strikes, several constitutional provisions are often cited to infer the right to strike. For example, the First Amendment ensures freedom of speech, press, and assembly; the Fifth Amendment prohibits the deprivation of life, liberty, or property without due process; and the Thirteenth Amendment prohibits slavery and involuntary servitude. The Constitution has been interpreted to protect employees involved in a strike over wages, hours, or conditions of labor; the discipline or discharge of an employee; the employment of nonunion labor; and employees striking in aid of others engaged in such a controversy. The NLRA right to "engage in concerted activity" is also cited as guaranteeing the right to strike. Some state statutes give government workers the right to strike, and laws in many foreign nations sanction strikes.

strikes
Simultaneous work stoppage to pressure employer to settle a labor dispute.

Illegal Strikes Unions must notify the employer at least 60 days before engaging in an economic strike and must offer to negotiate a new or modified contract. The 60-day notice is designed to prevent hasty decisions based on emotion or hysteria. Violation of the notice provision is an illegal strike. Illegal strikes also involve violence, discrimination against certain employees, violation of a cooling-off period, seeking to compel the acceptance of featherbedding or hot cargo provisions, attempting to coerce recognition of a noncertified union when another union has already been certified, or violating a statute.

Featherbedding agreements require the employer to pay for services that are not actually performed. In the 1950s, for example, many railroads complained that retaining firemen on diesel locomotives was featherbedding. Unlike the firemen who shoveled coal on steam locomotives, firemen on diesel locomotives perform little real work. Today, the fireman's position has been eliminated altogether. Featherbedding is narrowly construed so that contracts requiring "make-work" jobs are enforceable if workers perform at least some minimal services.

Hot cargo clauses attempt to require the employer to terminate its business with another employer with which the union has a dispute. Collective bargaining agreements may not prohibit the employer from buying or reselling goods produced by nonunion employers.

Rival unions sometimes get into *jurisdictional disputes* in which each union seeks to have certain jobs assigned to it. Striking to force assignment of such disputed jobs is an unfair labor practice. Although the NLRB usually decides jurisdictional disputes, some union contracts opt to have joint arbitration boards settle them. If a strike is legal, nonstriking employees may recognize the picket lines of striking employees and refuse to cross them unless they are restricted by a valid no-strike clause.

In illegal *sit-down strikes,* employees at the job site suddenly refuse to work. In such strikes, the employees typically occupy the employer's premises by sitting down at their workstations. Strikers engaging in violence may be discharged by an employer. Sporadic or disruptive shutdowns or partial work stoppages are also illegal. *Wildcat strikes* are illegal because the striking employees fail to give the employer the required advance notice and lack the approval of other union members. Strikes are also illegal for many government employees, air traffic controllers, health care workers or if the strike violates a valid no-strike clause in the union contract.

Unfair Labor Practice Strikes It is an unfair labor practice for an employer to interfere with legitimate concerted activities, including strikes. Most strikers may not be fired just for participating in a legal strike. However, the employer may hire temporary replacements because it is legitimate to continue business operations during any strike. After a strike ends, a dispute often arises over the strikers' reinstatement. Strikers are entitled to reinstatement during or immediately after an unfair labor practice strike, a strike in protest against an employer's unfair labor practice, even if this means that temporary replacements are not needed or must be fired. Strikers are entitled to back pay beginning on the date that they were fired for striking.

Economic Strikes Economic strikes concern matters other than the employer's unfair labor practices. Economic strikers have no right to reinstatement if replacements are hired. They are entitled only to nondiscriminatory review of a reapplication for their old jobs. However, from the union's perspective, if permanent replacements are hired, the employer may not simply presume the replacements are antiunion.[12] This means the employer must continue recognizing the union unless it is decertified.

Economic strikes typically involve the efforts of employees to gain increased benefits or improved working conditions. Striking employees take the risk of permanent replacement if a strike is considered economic. Alternatively, the employer may abolish the positions or the whole work unit of strikers if economic or business conditions radically change. For example, if the employer loses key customers because of the strike, the struck plant may be shut down permanently. By contrast, the employer hiring permanent replacements may risk breach of contract liability if the strike is misjudged to be an economic rather than an unfair labor practice strike. Following most economic strikes, the union insists that the new contract include a term requiring nondiscriminatory reinstatement of all replaced strikers. In March 1995, President Clinton issued Executive Order No. 12,954 barring the federal government from doing business with private firms that have federal contracts for over $100,000 if they hire permanent replacements for economic strikers.

---

[12] *N.L.R.B. v. Curtin Matheson Scientific, Inc.,* 494 U.S. 775 (1990).

COMMENTARY

The Controversy over Firing Economic Strikers

Strikes impose powerful economic pressures on management if they shut down the employer's business, erase expected profits, or force the employer to breach contracts to its customers. The effectiveness of economic strikes varies by industry, by the skill levels of striking employees, and by the availability of qualified replacements. For example, compare the employers' ability to permanently replace professional athletes as opposed to flight attendants. After the failure of the 1994–1995 major league baseball strike, all striking players were reinstated. With a few exceptions, all the "scab" replacement players who played during the 1995 spring season were released. This illustrates the power of unique and highly skilled employees to gain reinstatement. By contrast, some TWA flight attendants abandoned their strike and crossed the picket line as crossover replacements during their 1986 strike. When the strike ended, the Supreme Court refused to replace either crossovers or newly hired replacements with more senior strikers who had sought reinstatement.[13] Labor experts believe that this case gives employers a powerful counterbalance against the strike threat. More senior employees might hesitate to support a strike if they could lose seniority, or even their jobs, to crossover and newly hired replacements. This comparison also illustrates the weakness of a strike threat by less skilled employees or when sufficient qualified replacements are available in the labor pool.

No-Strike Clauses Some labor contracts contain no-strike clauses, which obligate the union to refrain from striking or from causing work stoppages or slowdowns during the life of the contract. A local union may be liable for breach of contract damages to individual employees or to the national or international union if it conducts a wildcat strike in violation of such a clause. Unions often agree to no-strike clauses in return for the employer's agreement to arbitrate grievances. Although the Norris-LaGuardia Act prohibits federal court injunctions against strikes, if the grievance is arbitrable unions may be enjoined from striking in violation of a valid no-strike clause.

National Emergency Strikes The Taft-Hartley Act includes a cooling-off provision that is intended to prevent severe strikes that might impair the national health or safety. If a threatened strike or lockout is expected to affect an entire industry, then the U.S. president has special powers. First, the president may appoint a board of inquiry to investigate the causes and circumstances of the labor dispute. The board investigates the facts and reports its recommendations. Thereafter, the president may direct the attorney general to seek a federal court injunction prohibiting the threatened activity. The issue at the trial is whether that activity will impair the national health or safety.

If an injunction is issued, the 80-day cooling-off period begins. During that period, the parties may freely engage in negotiations and, it is hoped, reach an agreement. The Federal Mediation and Conciliation Service aids the parties in their negotiations by attempting to reconcile their differences. However, if no agreement is reached, the strike or lockout may resume after 80 days. Congress is then left with the responsibility for curing the national emergency or addressing its underlying causes.

[13]*Trans World Airlines v. Indep. Fed. of Flight Attendants*, 489 U.S. 426 (1989).

In 1963, Congress used this power when railroad unions threatened to strike following an attempt by railroad companies to unilaterally change work rules. Congress averted a national transportation disaster by passing a law requiring compulsory arbitration over railroad work rules that temporarily required the retention of firemen on diesel locomotives and specified the minimum number of train crew members.

Regulation of Picketing

picketing
Gathering and patrolling by persons to inform others of a labor dispute.

Picketing, if conducted in a peaceful manner and for a lawful objective, is another concerted activity protected by the Constitution. **Picketing** generally involves a gathering and patrolling of persons who intend to inform or disrupt others. It is typically done near the employer's place of business. Picketing may be enjoined as unlawful if it (1) violates federal law, (2) represents an unfair labor practice, or (3) violates state law, for example, it is not peaceful. Picketing may involve confrontations between the picketers and other employees of the picketed employer. Simply posting signs may not be sufficient to constitute confrontation, but confrontation may arise if the picketers remain close to the posted signs, because verbal or threatening exchanges are more likely.

Types of Picketing The picketing of an employer by its employees is considered *primary picketing* and receives the greatest degree of constitutional protection. *Stranger picketing*—that is, picketing by nonemployees—is protected only if it is done for a lawful purpose and in a peaceful manner. Whereas state law may regulate picketing by strangers, picketing as part of an uncertified union's campaign to organize the bargaining unit receives constitutional protection.

Secondary picketing takes place at a business site other than the site of the employer with which the picketing employees have a dispute. For example, a restaurant owner who wishes to build a second restaurant at a new site might hire a nonunion construction contractor. It is illegal secondary picketing for construction workers to picket at the site of the original restaurant to pressure the restaurant owner into pressuring the contractor to hire union construction laborers.

Limits on Picketing Mass picketing by large numbers of picketers may be illegal if it imposes implicit coercion on employees who are attempting to enter the work site. The obstruction of plant entrances is illegal if it is intended to limit nonstrikers' access to the employer's premises. In *Carnegie-Illinois Steel Corp. v. United Steelworkers of America,* for example, several hundred strikers stood three deep across an entrance gate to the steel plant.[14] Workers and supervisors were denied access through the gate. The trial court stated: "Picketing which results in the intimidation and coercion of officers and employees . . . is not legal picketing." The state courts may enjoin mass picketing by employees if it intimidates other employees. Both the NLRB and the courts carefully examine the degree of violence that arises during a strike or picketing program. Minor and isolated instances of misconduct are probably not illegal under the NLRA.

It is unlawful for an uncertified rival union to picket an employer if the employer currently recognizes a certified union and a valid union certification election was held less than 12 months prior to the picketing. However, recognition and organizational picketing by a rival union before or after the 12-month period is permissible. By contrast, *informational picketing* is designed to inform the employer's customers

[14] *Carnegie-Illinois Steel Corp. v. United Steelworkers of America,* 353 Pa. 420 (1946).

about a labor dispute. It may be legal even if it results in a consumer boycott of the employer. Informational picketing becomes illegal when it disturbs deliveries or physically disrupts customer access to the employer's premises.

Regulation of Secondary Pressure

secondary pressure Union activity directed at another employer with which the union has no dispute.

Secondary pressure is a union's concerted activity directed toward some other employer. An employer with which the union has no dispute is a *secondary employer.* For example, a union may seek to pressure the employer with which it has a dispute—the primary employer—by inconveniencing that employer's customers or suppliers, which are secondary employers. Secondary pressure exerted through picketing, strikes, or boycotts is generally prohibited.

A *secondary boycott* usually results from union pressure, threats, coercion, and other concerted activities aimed at a secondary employer. Such activities are illegal if the union strikes or refuses to handle goods or induces nonmembers to strike or refuse to handle goods. For example, although employees may legally strike or picket their own employer, picketing the employer's customers or suppliers is an illegal secondary boycott. Secondary boycotts intended to force a secondary employer to enter into a hot cargo agreement or to assign work to a rival union are also illegal. It is not an illegal secondary boycott to request employees of a neutral employer to refrain from crossing picket lines if the union in the primary dispute is certified and the strike is authorized.

The courts define secondary activities on a case-by-case basis. These activities are prohibited where an innocent secondary employer is forced into a labor dispute. In one case, longshoremen refused to handle grain shipments that were to be loaded onto ships headed for the Soviet Union. The refusal was part of a political protest against the Soviet Union's invasion of Afghanistan. The action was illegal because the longshoremen's refusal to work burdened secondary employers: shipowners, grain sales agents, and dock owners who had no direct labor dispute with the boycotting longshoremen.

Common Situs Problems A construction project located on a single work site serviced by several subcontractor employers is known as a *common situs.* Picketing and strike activity at a common situs raises some ambiguity as to secondary pressure. When employees of one subcontractor picket a common situs, it may be difficult to determine which employer is the object of the concerted activity. In the *Moore Drydock* case, the sailors' union struck against the owner of a ship that was being serviced at a dry dock facility owned by a secondary employer.[15] The NLRB created the *Moore Drydock* rules to draw a balance between union interests and the interests of secondary employers. Picketing or strike activity at a secondary employer's situs may be restricted if the striking union has a secondary motive, as tested by the *Moore Drydock* rules, regardless of which employer owns the situs.

MOORE DRYDOCK RULES

1. Picketing may occur only when the primary employer is engaged in its ordinary business activity.
2. The primary employer must be located at the secondary situs.

[15] *In re Sailors Union of the Pacific,* 92 NLRB 547 (1950).

3. Picketing is limited to an area physically close to the situs of the primary employer.
4. Picketing signs must clearly state that the dispute is only with the primary employer.

Employers often attempt to blunt the negative effects of common situs picketing by isolating the activities of primary employers. For example, the owner of a common situs may require each employer's workers to enter the premises through a separate gate. This permits them to confine the picketing of a primary employer to its assigned area, which reduces the impact on secondary employers. However, the primary employer must actually use only the designated gate. Construction sites involve these problems for the landowner, lessees, the prime contractor, and the numerous subcontractors.

Ally Doctrine In some instances, the secondary employer may not be neutral or innocent. A secondary employer economically linked to or aiding or abetting the primary employer is not protected from secondary pressure. For example, secondary pressure is legal if the secondary employer provides replacements for the primary employer's striking employees. A general contractor that hires temporary replacements from a subcontractor (the primary employer) to avoid work stoppage may validly be subjected to secondary pressure. A secondary employer may be considered an ally of the primary employer if its business operations are closely related to those of the primary employer. For example, a primary and secondary employer owned or controlled by the same parent corporation actually form two parts of the same business. Secondary picketing of such affiliated parties is permissible.

Consumer Boycotts Nothing prohibits a union from using nonpicketing means to advise the public about the products of the employer with which the union has a dispute. For example, a union's distribution of informational leaflets outside the primary employer's plant is permissible. Moreover, informational distributions conducted at a shopping mall are legal if the union is not picketing, patrolling, or engaged in other intimidating conduct. Such *handbilling* activity may advocate a consumer boycott of all the mall's stores even if the union's dispute is only with a contractor that is building a shop for a single mall tenant.[16]

A union's campaign to provide the public with information may be prohibited in certain more coercive situations. Under the Tree Fruits doctrine, such a campaign is illegal if it tends to cause a work stoppage or interfere with deliveries to a secondary employer.[17] For example, a union that has a dispute with a food processor may choose to picket a supermarket that resells the food processor's products. The Tree Fruits doctrine permits this secondary picketing only if it causes no interference with suppliers' deliveries or customers' shopping. The secondary picketing permitted under Tree Fruits must be noncoercive and peaceful, and it must be designed only to induce customers to refrain from buying the boycotted product.

Remedies for Illegal Concerted Activities

Illegal strikes, boycotts, and picketing are remedied through the filing of unfair labor practice charges against the union. Such charges receive priority over all other NLRB cases. The regional director of the NLRB may immediately seek an injunction against

[16] *DeBartolo Corp. v. Florida Gulf Coast Building and Construction Trades Council,* 485 U.S. 568 (1988).
[17] *N.L.R.B. v. Fruit and Vegetable Packers and Warehousemen, Local 760,* 377 U.S. 58 (1964).

the illegal activity. If violence is involved, the state or federal courts may issue injunctions. In some instances, the courts have ordered unions to pay damages to the secondary employer or to its customers or suppliers. For example, a union may be ordered to pay lost profits if its illegal secondary pressure had a direct and adverse impact on a secondary employer's sales.

Grievance Procedures and Arbitration

Employers often seek to include procedures in collective bargaining agreements for settling work floor disputes between workers and supervisors that could lead to strikes or picketing. Many collective bargaining agreements now include arbitration clauses delegating to independent and neutral third parties the authority to settle grievances in the final step of the proceedings.

The processing of a gricvancc usually begins with a hearing by lower-level managerial personnel. Eventually, the grievance may be reviewed or appealed to higher management levels and ultimately to an arbitrator. Typically, the union is responsible for processing employee grievances. Arbitrators are selected from neutral agencies, although in national emergencies mediators from the Federal Mediation and Conciliation Service are used. They attempt to facilitate negotiations and to persuade the disputing parties to reach an agreement on their own. Unlike arbitrators, federal mediators do not issue binding decisions but only attempt to create a negotiation atmosphere conducive to settlement.

The Arbitration Process and Its Effects Arbitrators need not be lawyers, but they should be familiar with labor policies and labor disputes. They are paid jointly by the employer and the union, who together select the time and place for arbitration. The American Arbitration Association suggests the use of certain procedures for informal arbitration hearings, although the arbitrator selects the particular procedures used. During arbitration, other forms of concerted activity or economic pressure are prohibited.

The arbitrator's authority is typically controlled by the collective bargaining agreement, which usually permits the arbitrator to settle disputes involving interpretation or application of contract provisions. This power is construed broadly, permitting the arbitrator to decide the facts but not to make rulings on questions of law. An arbitrator may dccide only "arbitrable" issues. This condition often raises the legal question of whether the arbitrator has exceeded the authority granted. Although arbitrators, unlike judges, are not bound by precedents, they generally follow patterns derived from their own experience or from earlier awards between the same parties. The NLRB may refuse to review an arbitrator's award on appeal.

Basis for NLRB Refusal to Hear Arbitration Appeal

1. All of the parties had agreed to the arbitration.
2. The arbitration was conducted in a fair and regular manner.
3. The arbitrator decided only factual issues.
4. The arbitrator's award is not clearly repugnant to the purposes and policies of labor law.

Any party to a labor arbitration may appeal the award based on the arbitrator's incompetence or bias or on the violation of any of the four requirements listed above. The courts respect the awards of arbitrators so long as the parties followed the prescribed arbitration procedures and the union provided fair and adequate representation of the employee's interests. However, if a union delays the arbitration process or shows hostility toward the employee, a court may intervene or overturn an arbitration award. Should the federal courts defer to an arbitrator's fact findings? The next case discusses this problem.

United Paperworkers Int'l Union v. Misco, Inc.

484 U.S. 29 (1987)
United States Supreme Court

The collective bargaining agreement between Misco, Inc., and the United Paperworkers International Union included arbitration procedures for settling grievances about contract interpretation. Isiah Cooper was caught in the backseat of another's car while it was filled with marijuana smoke. A marijuana cigarette was also found in the front seat ashtray. Based on this evidence, Misco exercised its right to apply its disciplinary rules by discharging Cooper for allegedly possessing or using controlled substances on company property. Later, Misco learned a police search of Cooper's car found marijuana gleanings or traces removed from interior surfaces while it was parked on Misco property. Cooper filed a grievance, and the claim was arbitrated as required under the union contract. The arbitrator found Misco had insufficient proof that Cooper used marijuana on Misco property based solely on the cigarette incident. The arbitrator ordered Cooper reinstated and refused to consider the gleanings evidence because Cooper was discharged before Misco learned of it. The court of appeals affirmed the trial court's overruling of the arbitrator's decision, and Cooper appealed.

Justice White delivered the opinion of the Court.

Collective-bargaining agreements commonly provide grievance procedures to settle disputes between union and employer with respect to the interpretation and application of the agreement and require binding arbitration for unsettled grievances. The Court made clear almost 30 years ago that the courts play only a limited role when asked to review the decision of an arbitrator. The courts are not authorized to reconsider the merits of an award even though the parties may allege that the award rests on errors of fact or on misinterpretation of the contract. "The federal policy of settling labor disputes by arbitration would be undermined if courts had the final say on the merits of the awards."

The reasons for insulating arbitral decisions from judicial review are grounded in the federal statutes regulating labor–management relations. These statutes reflect a decided preference for private settlement of labor disputes without the intervention of government.

The courts have jurisdiction to enforce collective-bargaining contracts; but where the contract provides grievance and arbitration procedures, those procedures must first be exhausted and courts must order resort to the private settlement mechanisms without dealing with the merits of the dispute. Because the parties have contracted to have disputes settled by an arbitrator chosen by them rather than by a judge, it is the arbitrator's view of the facts and of the meaning of the contract that they have agreed to accept. Courts thus do not sit to hear claims of factual or legal error by an arbitrator as an appellate court does in reviewing decisions of lower courts. To resolve disputes about the application of a collective-bargaining agreement, an arbitrator must find facts and a court may not reject those findings simply because it disagrees with them.

Under the Arbitration Act, the federal courts are empowered to set aside arbitration awards on such grounds only when "the arbitrators were guilty of misconduct . . . in refusing to hear evidence pertinent and material to the controversy." If we apply that same standard here and assume that the arbitrator erred in refusing to consider the disputed evidence, his error was not in bad faith or so gross as to amount to affirmative misconduct. Finally, it is worth noting that putting aside the evidence about the marijuana found in Cooper's car during this arbitration did not forever foreclose the Company from using that evidence as the basis for a discharge.

A refusal to enforce an award must rest on more than speculation or assumption. In any event, it was inappropriate for the Court of Appeals itself to draw the necessary inference. To conclude from the fact that marijuana had been found in Cooper's car that Cooper had ever been or would be under the influence of marijuana while he was on the job and operating dangerous machinery is an exercise in fact-finding about Cooper's use of drugs and his amenability to discipline, a task that exceeds the authority of a court asked to overturn an arbitration award. The parties did not bargain for the facts to be found by a court, but by an arbitrator chosen by them who had more opportunity to observe Cooper and to be familiar with the plant and its problems. Nor does the fact that it is injuring into a possible violation of public policy excuse a court for doing the arbitrator's task. The judgment of the Court of Appeals is reversed. So ordered.

Case Questions

1. Are there plausible alternative explanations for the gleanings from Cooper's car other than his use of controlled substances on company time or property?
2. For what reasons should the courts defer to fact-finding by arbitrators selected by the parties?

Internal Union Democracy

The post-World War II union scandals led to passage of two laws designed to balance the union's need for authority over its members against the members' rights to monitor the performance of union officials. A union may validly discipline its members for conduct interfering with the union's economic well-being, such as engaging in wildcat strikes, working for wages below union scale, or spying for the employer. However, the Taft-Hartley Act protects union employees from coercive discipline by union leaders. A union may not punish employees for pursuing their civic duties. For example, it may not punish an employee for testifying before judicial or congressional committees or for reporting violations of law by union members or officials.

Ethical Dilemmas for Union Officials

Ethical Dilemma

Union officials face numerous ethical dilemmas in and out of the bargaining context. When union officials condone a wildcat strike or a walkout in which the employer is not given notice, they abuse the union's position of power. Condoning violence in picketing or intimidation of nonunion employees is also unethical. Illegal picketing and secondary boycotts that bring innocent employers into disputes or that intimidate retail customers are unethical. In some instances, union officials have made personal use of union treasury pension funds or have used these funds for illegal political purposes. Such actions constitute an abuse of position and a clear breach of the officials' fiduciary duties.

Labor's Bill of Rights

The Landrum-Griffin Act created Labor's Bill of Rights to prevent abuses by union officials. Unions are prohibited from restricting a member's rights of free speech, assembly, or participation in union elections. Unions may increase dues, fees, and assessments only after reasonable notice and after all members are given an opportunity to vote by secret ballot. A union member must exhaust reasonable internal union procedures and remedies before suing a union official. Unions may not discipline a member for not paying dues until notified of specific charges and afforded time to prepare defenses in an impartial hearing.

Although the early common law prohibited court interference with union elections, the Landrum-Griffin Act now guarantees fair union elections by creating minimum standards of voting and candidacy. First, all union members in good standing must be permitted to vote. Second, elections for local officers must be held at least every three years. Third, secret balloting procedures must be followed in local elections, though delegates to a national or international union convention may cast open votes. Secret local ballots preserve anonymity and help prevent coercion by co-workers. Fourth, a reasonable opportunity to nominate candidates must be given to all eligible voting members. Fifth, the qualifications for candidate eligibility must be reasonable. The court in *United Steelworkers of America v. Usery* invalidated a union eligibility rule that required candidates for union office to attend at least half of all union meetings during the three years prior to an election.[18] This rule was considered unreasonable because it barred 97 percent of the union's members from candidacy.

Union elections must be designed to maximize the participation of union members. Candidates may not be denied access to membership lists or prohibited from distributing campaign literature. The Secretary of Labor and the federal district courts may overturn union elections in which these safeguards are absent. Legal problems in connection with union elections are often avoided by having independent and impartial nonunion election officials conduct the balloting and vote counting.

Landrum-Griffin addresses union corruption by requiring certain disclosures by unions, employers, and union officials. Unions must report to their members the names of officers, the union's financial condition, and certain election procedures. Financial transactions between a union officer or a union employee and the employer must be disclosed by the officer, employee, and employer. Violation of these reporting duties is punishable by fines of up to $10,000 and imprisonment of up to one year.

Union officers, agents, shop stewards, and other employee representatives are considered fiduciaries. They owe a duty of the highest and utmost faith to the union and its members. Any misappropriation of union funds by these parties is illegal. Litigation expenses of union officials may be paid by the union, but only if these officials are exonerated in the lawsuit. Unions are subject to damage suits or may be required to present an accounting of union transactions if there is good cause to suspect improprieties.

In extraordinary circumstances, a local union chapter may lose control over its own affairs. If local union officials misappropriate union assets, are corrupt, fail to provide democratic procedures, or fail to carry out the union's legitimate objectives, the national or international union may impose supervision through a *trusteeship*. Trusteeship is regulated today because in the past some national union leaders used the

[18] *United Steelworkers of America v. Usery,* 429 U.S. 305 (1977).

process to prevent dissent by local chapters or officials or to plunder local union treasuries. Landrum-Griffin requires trustees to file semiannual reports with the Secretary of Labor to ensure that the trusteeship process is not abused. Any financial assessments imposed by the national union on local chapters must be reasonable.

SUMMARY

Several statutes provide nearly exclusive federal regulation of labor relations. The Clayton Act exempts collective labor action from the antitrust laws. The Railway Labor Act governs the collective bargaining of railroad and airline employees with their employers. The Norris-LaGuardia Act prohibits the federal courts from enjoining labor activities. The National Labor Relations Act requires employers to bargain collectively with certified unions and refrain from coercing employees during union organization activities.

The NLRB administers unfair labor practice and representation cases. Representation elections are the primary method for union selection. Elections are ordered when employees file a petition covering an appropriate bargaining unit, the unit comprising employees with similar legal rights and economic interests. The employer may agree to bargain with a union that claims majority support or that presents authorization cards, petitions, or applications for union membership signed by a majority of employees.

Both employers and unions can commit unfair labor practices by interfering with employees' rights to self-organize. There is an unfair labor practice if either the employer or the union makes coercive speech, threats, or promises of benefits to employees. Employers may not financially support or dominate a particular union, discriminate against employees for antiunion motives, or provide benefits to employees opposing a union. Lockouts and plant closings are legal if they are not based on antiunion bias.

Collective bargaining negotiations must be conducted in good faith by both unions and management. Good faith bargaining is an interactive process in which the parties make offers and counteroffers until reaching a compromise on wages, hours, and other terms and conditions of employment. Both the employer and union negotiators must have authority to bargain. A union must bargain equally on behalf of all union and nonunion employees in the bargaining unit. It is bad faith bargaining if either party refuses to meet and confer over the mandatory subjects of bargaining: wages, hours, and other terms and conditions of employment. The parties may be required to provide information to each other. Neither party may adopt a "take-it-or-leave-it" approach, though neither party must accept any particular proposal or make concessions. The parties are not required to bargain over permissive subjects. The parties cannot bargain over prohibited subjects, such as a closed shop agreement, recognition of a certified union, or prohibitions of employee distribution of union literature. Existing agreements may be renegotiated if both parties consent. Bargaining must continue in good faith until impasse. The employer may then solicit striking workers to return to work on terms no better than those the union previously rejected.

Congress passed the Taft-Hartley Act in 1947 and the Landrum-Griffin Act in 1959 to control union corruption and curb unions' excessive power over workers. Employees may engage in concerted activities for mutual aid, but those activities must be lawful, made in good faith, nonviolent, and directed toward work-related matters and must avoid violating the union contract. Closed shop agreements are illegal. However, union hiring halls may provide employers with lists of qualified workers, and union shops may legally require union membership or payment of dues after a probationary period. Almost half of the states have passed right-to-work laws restricting union shops. Agency shops require only the payment of a bargaining assessment.

The union must represent all employees in a bargaining unit equally and impartially. It is an unfair labor practice for the union to discriminate or cause the employer to discriminate against any employee on the basis of race, citizenship, sex, or union membership. Strikes are concerted employee actions that temporarily halt work. Illegal strikes include strikes that are conducted during a national emergency; strikes that violate a no-strike clause, cooling-off period, or statute; sit-down or wildcat strikes; and strikes that seek to coerce the employer into agreeing to prohibited practices.

The labor law protects employees who gather for informational purposes and conduct peaceful and lawful picketing. Mass picketing and violent picketing are illegal. Picketing an employer other than the primary employer is usually illegal secondary picketing. It is illegal for employees to picket an employer's customers. Where several employers utilize a common situs, picketing at some entrance gates may be prohibited. Picketers at a common situs must clearly identify which employer their dispute is with.

Arbitration clauses are used to resolve grievances and reduce the probability of strikes or picketing. Arbitrators are independent hearing officers who determine disputed facts.

Extensive disclosures by unions, union officials, and employers are required; they include financial transactions between the employer and the union or its officials or employees. Officials of a union are fiduciaries owing the utmost and highest faith to the union and its members. The national union can replace local officials with trustees if the local officials become corrupt or fail to maintain democratic procedures.

Critical Thinking Review Questions

1. StrongSuit Airways operates the Western Air Shuttle, the high-volume passenger flight service between San Francisco, Los Angeles, and San Diego. To lower costs, Donald Strongsuit, the airline's owner and CEO, expected that when the new high-speed rail service commenced between these three cities, it would undercut fares on the Western Air Shuttle. He demanded that his flight attendants' union, the Amalgamated Flight Tenders (AFT) union, accept a 20 percent pay and benefit reduction two years before their contract was due to expire. Donald reasoned that the pay givebacks were necessary to remain competitive on the profitable western corridor passenger route. In response, AFT officials successfully enlisted the unions of the pilots and air traffic controllers that served all western U.S. airlines, as well as the unions of the locomotive engineers and switchmen for the passenger railroads in the region, to join in a sympathy strike. This effectively shut down all public passenger transportation between western corridor cities, except for automobile and bus service. Comment on the ethical and legal problems confronting the AFT officials in soliciting this form of secondary pressure. Is Donald ethically entitled to seek renegotiation of the AFT contract when the Shuttle confronts new competition from high-speed rail?
2. J. Steve Peevens, CEO of Peevens Textiles, hated all unions. Although he believed his employees were treated fairly well, many employees sought union representation. J. Steve instructed his supervisors to conduct a negative publicity campaign against the United Textile Employees (UTE) union, which was attempting to organize the Peevens facility. In an effort to discredit the UTE, one supervisor falsified documents to wrongly show that UTE officials at other mills gambled with the pension funds of their union members.

   Compare and contrast the overlapping and separate ethical and legal analyses of these problems. What ethical and legal problems would exist for UTE officials if the allegations of Peevens' supervisor were true?

Critical Thinking Exercises

1. Identify whether each of the following activities is legal or illegal. Which statute applies in each situation?
   a. An employer requires an employee to sign a contract stating that he will refrain from joining a union if he is hired by the employer. Signing the contract is a condition of working for the employer.
   b. An employer is unionized, and the collective bargaining agreement between the employer and the union prohibits the discharge or discipline of employees without just cause. As part of its investigation of a theft, the employer attempts to interview an employee. The employee refuses to be interviewed unless his shop steward (union representative) is present.

Is the refusal protected? *N.L.R.B. v. Weingarten, Inc.* 420 U.S. 251 (1975).

2. Action Automotive, Inc., a retail automobile parts and gasoline dealer with stores in several Michigan cities, is a closely held corporation owned equally by the three Sabo brothers. The brothers serve as the corporation's officers, make all policy decisions, and retain ultimate authority for the supervision of every department. The union files a petition with the NLRB requesting a representation election. Action and the union agree to elections in two bargaining units: one comprising the employees at the company's nine retail stores, and the other comprising the clerical employees at the company's headquarters. After the election, the union challenges the ballots of Diane and Mildred Sabo. Diane Sabo, the wife of Action's president, works as a general ledger clerk at the company's headquarters. Mildred Sabo, the mother of the three Sabo brothers, is employed as a full-time cashier at a company store. Mildred lives with one of her sons, James Sabo, secretary-treasurer of the corporation, and she regularly sees or telephones her other sons and their families. Should the NLRB exclude Diane and Mildred Sabo from the collective bargaining units? Is it necessary that the NLRB find that the relatives enjoyed job-related privileges? *N.L.R.B. v. Action Automobile, Inc.,* 469 U.S. 490 (1985).
3. As plant manager for Westex Company, you are concerned that some employees are huddling near the rest room, whispering over their tables at lunch break, and passing notices around when they should be working. With regard to employees' solicitation on company property, you can't decide whether to draft a rule stating "No solicitation during working hours" or "No solicitation during working time." Does the wording make a difference? Which of these two choices is legal? Discuss.
4. The union and the company were at a bargaining impasse. The major issue in dispute was whether to include an arbitration clause in their new contract. The company operated radio station WBT in Charlotte, North Carolina. Several union members picketed the radio station and distributed handbills attacking the company's method of operation and quality of programming. The handbills read: "Is Charlotte a second-class city? You might think so from the kinds of programs being presented over WBT. . . . There are no local programs being presented by WBT. . . . Why doesn't the company purchase the needed equipment to bring you the same type of programs enjoyed by other leading American cities?" The company fired the picketers. Was the firing an unfair labor practice? How did the use of handbills in this case differ from their use in a conventional strike? *NLRB v. Local 1229, International Brotherhood of Electrical Workers,* 346 U.S. 464 (1953).
5. Cabot Carbon Company established an in-plant employee committee system. The company prepared committee bylaws, which were then adopted by a majority vote of the employees. According to the bylaws, the committees were created to consider ideas and problems of mutual interest to the employees and management. The bylaws established a fixed term for committee membership, handled grievances at nonunion plants, and provided for regular elections of employees to the committees. The NLRB challenged the establishment of the in-plant committees, arguing that they were the equivalent of a company union. What was the result. Why? *N.L.R.B. v. Cabot Carbon Co.,* 360 U.S. 203 (1959).
6. Sure-Tan, Inc., sent a letter to the Immigration and Naturalization Service (INS), asking it to check the immigration status of five employees who had supported the union at the company. INS agents discovered that the five employees were Mexican nationals working illegally in the United States. They were arrested, and they later accepted the INS grant of voluntary departure as a substitute for deportation. The union argued that Sure-Tan had in effect discharged the employees in retaliation for their support of the union. Did the employer commit an unfair labor practice by reporting the undocumented alien employees to the INS in retaliation for their participation in union activities? *Sure-Tan, Inc. v. N.L.R.B.*, 467 U.S. 883 (1984).
7. A union shop agreement between the union and Western Airlines required all of Western's clerical workers to join the union within 60 days of employment. As the agreement was interpreted, these employees did not have to become formal union members, but they had to pay an "agency fee" equal to the dues of members. The union, in turn, "rebated" to employees with full membership privileges a pro rata share of the dues to

employees objecting. Certain employees objected to the plan, claiming that union expenditures left out of the rebate plan and paid for by the objecting employees went for the union's convention, litigation expenses, publications, social activities, and general organizing efforts. Were these activities "collective bargaining activities," and could the objecting employees be required to support them? *Ellis v. Brotherhood of Railway, Airline and Steamship Clerks, Freight Handlers, Express and Station Employees,* 466 U.S. 435 (1984).

8. A majority of the employees of Linden Lumber Company signed authorization cards, and the union requested recognition by the company. The company refused to bargain, so the union filed an unfair labor practices charge. There was no allegation that the company had engaged in any unfair labor practice other than the refusal to bargain. Was the company guilty of a refusal to bargain in good faith? *Linden Lumber Company v. N.L.R.B.,* 419 U.S. 301 (1974).

CHAPTER

20

Equal Employment Opportunities

Critical Thinking Questions

- What assumptions are made in the equal opportunity laws: statutes from the 1960s and 1970s, portions of the U.S. Constitution, state laws, presidential executive orders and post–Civil War statutes?
- How is statistical data from disparate treatment, disparate impact, or pattern or practice discrimination used to prove the illegality of employment discrimination on the basis of race, color, religion, national origin, disability or sex?
- Why is limited discrimination lawful when based on narrow exceptions: bona fide occupational qualification, performance on professionally developed aptitude tests, or pursuant to a valid and nondiscriminatory seniority system?
- What are the ambiguities in the Equal Employment Opportunity Commission's (EEOC) guidelines prohibiting sexual harassment in the workplace?
- Why is the EEOC the primary enforcement body for the antidiscrimination laws? Contrast the EEOC's procedures from rulemaking, investigation, and adjudication administration by state antidiscrimination authorities.
- What was the political pressure for the Civil Rights Act of 1991 expansion of private damage actions for unlawful discrimination and placing the burden on the employer to prove that unintentional discrimination is a business necessity?
- What issues led to the Americans with Disabilities Act (ADA), which prohibits employment discrimination against qualified but disabled workers and requires that employers provide reasonable accommodation and ready workplace accessibility?

Introduction... Past, Present, Future

Although several constitutional provisions are aimed at preventing discriminatory treatment of U.S. citizens, considerable discrimination has existed throughout U.S history. During the Reconstruction period that followed the Civil War, the Fourteenth Amendment was adopted, and Congress passed civil rights laws in 1866 and 1871. These measures were designed to correct the discriminatory abuses of the pre–Civil War period by giving all persons the same rights to make and enforce contracts, to sue, and to give evidence at trial. Full and equal benefit of all laws must be given to all people. However, these 19th century laws prohibit only racial discriminations; discrimination based on religion or sex is not specifically covered. As a result, pervasive discrimination continued through the 20th century. The only major antidiscrimination measure that was adopted between the Reconstruction period and the 1960s was the Nineteenth Amendment, which gave women the right to vote. Significant empirical evidence suggests there is still extensive discrimination in the housing and labor markets.

Unequal opportunities and discriminatory practices in employment, promotions, working conditions, and compensation systems work against minorities and women. Some economists argue that this failure to reward productive activity misallocates labor resources, causing imperfections in the labor markets. For example, imperfect labor markets send the wrong signals, incorrectly matching skills with jobs. In addition, it relegates potentially productive workers to less skilled jobs, leaving an important pool of talent unused. In response to the economic and moral arguments against discrimination, Congress has passed several more antidiscrimination laws since the 1960s. Today, these laws significantly affect all employment decisions made by managers. These and other major equal employment laws are discussed in this chapter and are summarized in Figure 20–1.

FIGURE 20-1 U.S. Employment Discrimination Laws

Act	Date	Major Provisions	Enforcement/Remedies
U.S. Const. Art. I §9	1788	Permitted Congress to (1) tax slave trade and (2) prohibit slave importation after 1807.	Ended slave importation
U.S. Const. 5th Amend.	1791	Due process clause prohibits deprivation of life, liberty or property without due process.	Private actions against federal government for discrimination.
U.S. Const. 13th Amend.	1865	Abolished slavery.	Empowered Congress to implement abolition.
Civil Rights Act of 1866 & 1870	1866	Prohibits private sector discrimination based on race, color, or national origin in employment, contracts, and housing.	Private actions for: reinstatement, compensatory damages, and punitive damages, injunction, attorney's fees
U.S. Const. 14th Amend.	1868	Due process of 5th Amend. applicable to the states; Equal protection clause prohibits state denial of equal protection of laws to all persons	Private actions against states for discrimination.
Equal Pay Act	1963	Prohibits gender-based pay discrimination between two jobs substantially similar in skill, effort, and responsibility under similar working conditions.	Fines up to $10,000, imprisonment up to six months or both; enforced by Equal Employment Opportunity Commission (EEOC); private actions for double damages up to three years wages, liquidated damages, reinstatement or promotion.
Civil Rights Act of 1964 Title VII	1964	Prohibits discrimination based on race, color, religion, sex, or national origin in employment decisions: hiring, pay, working conditions, promotion, discipline, or discharge.	Enforced by EEOC; private actions for back pay, front pay, reinstatement, restore seniority and pension benefits, injunction, attorneys' fees and costs.
Executive Order No. 11246 & No. 11375	1965	Requires equal opportunity clauses in federal contracts; prohibits employment discrimination by federal contractors based on race, color, religion, sex, or national origin.	Creates Office of Federal Contract Compliance to investigate violations; empowered to terminate violator's federal contracts.
Age Discrimination in Employment Act	1967	Prohibits employment discrimination based on age for persons over 40; restricts mandatory retirement.	EEOC enforcement, private actions for reinstatment, back pay, front pay, restore seniority and pension benefits; double unpaid wages for wilful violations; injunctions, attorneys fees and costs.
Equal Employment Opportunity Act	1972		Expands EEOC enforcement powers.
Vocational Rehabilitation Act	1973	Requires affirmative action by all federal contractors for persons who are handicapped; defines handicaps as physical or mental impairments that substantially limit major life activities.	Federal contractors may not discriminate in hiring the handicapped for jobs capable of performance after reasonable accommodation.
Pregnancy Discrimination Act	1975	Included pregnancy as discrimination based on sex in Title VII; prohibits mandatory pregnancy leaves.	Title VII private actions for employment discrimination based on pregnancy; both women and men covered.

FIGURE 20-1 (continued)

Act	Date	Major Provisions	Enforcement/Remedies
Immigration Reform & Control Act	1986	Requires employers to verify identity and employment eligibility of all hirees; prohibits compliance through discrimination based on citizenship or national origin.	Immigration & Naturalization Service (INS), Dept. of Labor, National Labor Relations Board (NLRB) & U.S. Attorney have separate duties.
Americans with Disabilities Act	1990	Extends affirmative action provisions of Vocational Rehabilitation Act to private employers; requires workplace modifications to facilitate disabled employees; prohibits discrimination against disabled.	EEOC enforcement; private actions for Title VII remedies.
Civil Rights Act of 1991	1991	Clarifies Title VII requirements: disparate impact suits, "business necessity," "job related," shifts burden of proof to employer, permits punitive damages and jury trials	Compensatory damages, punitive damages limited to sliding scale only in intentional discrimination based on sex, religion, and disability.
Family & Medical Leave Act	1991	Requires 12 weeks unpaid leave for medical or family needs: paternity, family member illness.	Private actions for lost wages and other expenses, reinstatement.

In the future, there may be additional workplace and political conflicts over how co-workers' and managers' attitudes cause discrimination. Major steps have already been taken to eliminate housing and job-entry discrimination; in the future, the more insidious stereotyping and discriminatory attitudes will be addressed. However, these sources of discrimination are difficult to prove, so the initial approaches to eliminating them may appear to unfairly favor certain minority groups and may therefore arouse resentment. Until the public willingly accepts more widespread nondiscriminatory attitudes, the effectiveness of legal controls and affirmative action plans may be limited and sometimes unpopular.

Thought Questions

1. How do the antidiscrimination laws address presumptions of the perfect competition model as applied to the labor markets?
2. Develop hypotheses for explaining what forces and rationales were used to support the succession of various antidiscrimination laws.

Equal Pay Act

The Equal Pay Act of 1963 amended the Fair Labor Standards Act by prohibiting unequal pay for equal work by either sex. The Equal Pay Act is enforced by the Equal Employment Opportunity Commission (EEOC). It does not apply to discrimination in hiring, promotions, or firing on the basis of sex, which is regulated by the Civil Rights Act of 1964. Instead, if one of two substantially similar jobs is held by a male and the other by a female, the employer is prohibited from paying the two employees at different rates. For this prohibition to apply, the two jobs must require "equal skill, effort, and responsibility . . . [if] performed under similar working conditions." A recurring issue under the Equal Pay Act is the content analysis of jobs. Employers must specify a *job description* for each job, so that if two jobs are substantially similar, the equality of the pay given for performing them can be determined.

Permitted Pay Differentials

The Equal Pay Act does not apply to legitimate pay differentials resulting from factors other than sex, such as bona fide seniority systems, bona fide merit systems, or the quantity or quality of output. For example, *shift differentials*—pay differentials based on the time of a work shift—are usually valid. However, such differentials may be illegal if there are no shift differences in working conditions and one shift is staffed predominantly by males and another by females. New workers involved in training programs may be rotated through several departments and perform work substantially similar to that done by workers permanently assigned to the departments. Pay differentials between these trainees and permanent workers are not illegal so long as the training programs are open equally to both sexes.

comparable worth Theory of pay equalization comparing two jobs not substantially equivalent in tasks but requiring similar skill, effort, and responsibility.

Comparable Worth From time to time, courts are urged to reexamine an old theory of equal pay known as **comparable worth**. Under this theory, male and female workers who are not performing substantially equal jobs under the same working conditions may nevertheless be required to receive equal pay. The comparable worth theory arose during World War II in an effort to equalize pay. It has resurfaced because of longtime discriminatory patterns that have forced females into clerical and service positions, reserving positions of higher pay for males. Arguably, the comparable worth theory could also apply to wage comparisons based on suspect classifications other than sex.

Analyses of job classifications often indicate that two very different jobs have roughly equal levels of responsibility and difficulty. Members of one sex may predominantly hold a lower-paying job, the worth of which is comparable to that of another job predominantly held by members of the opposite sex. Some people insist that the courts should order equalization in the pay for any two such jobs. For example, a salesperson and an administrative assistant performing different tasks may have equal responsibilities and skills. If they receive different pay for their work, a comparable worth program would adjust the pay structure to reflect the inherent equality of the two jobs.

Many economists have argued that a comparable worth system limits the way the free market operates to set prices (wages) according to the demand for particular jobs by the supply of qualified applicants. Comparable worth sends incorrect signals to individuals to enter professions of administratively determined "high value" even if they have an excessive supply of those workers. Entry is deterred into jobs the market finds more valuable. Therefore, enforcement of pay scales between different jobs could distort the allocation of resources while imposing extraordinary expenses to administer such programs.

In *County of Washington v. Gunther*,[1] the Supreme Court suggested that Title VII of the Civil Rights Act of 1964, not the Equal Pay Act, might form the basis for comparable worth systems if the gender-based discrimination is intentional. More recently, the lower federal courts have been less receptive to the comparable worth

[1] County of Washington v. Gunther, 452 U.S. 161 (1981).

theory. However, some states and local governments have comparable worth statutes for government workers. Canada applies the concept to both public and private workers. Any attempt to apply comparable worth to private employers in the United States will fundamentally affect the whole employment market unless a "market conditions" defense develops. Comparable worth should be carefully monitored.

The Civil Rights Act of 1964

Title VII of the Civil Rights Act of 1964 has the greatest impact on the employment relationship of all the discrimination laws. It prohibits discrimination by employers with 15 or more employees, by unions that bargain with such employers or operate hiring halls, and by employment agencies. Title VII makes it illegal to discriminate in hiring, firing, or compensation or in the terms, conditions, or privileges of employment if based on race, color, religion, national origin, or sex. Any classification of employees based on their membership in a *protected class* is prohibited if it deprives persons in that class of employment opportunities. Liability will attach to employers whose discrimination results in (1) disparate treatment or (2) disparate impact.

Generally, *discrimination* is the practice of choosing or differentiating among alternatives based on distinguishable characteristics. Discrimination becomes illegal when employment decisions are based on bias or prejudice about a person's membership in a protected class. Discrimination is also illegal if it perpetuates prior discrimination. Illegal discrimination arises when applicants or employees are separated by demographic class, constructively discharged by class (resignation prompted by harassment), paid differently by class, or subjected to different standards for personal characteristics by class (e.g., personal conduct, appearance, lifestyle).

Ethical Dilemmas in Employment Discrimination

Ethical Dilemma

Is it ethical for a manger to permit personal prejudices or preferences to influence promotion or hiring decisions? Discrimination in promotion or hiring poses ethical dilemmas because managers must use their personal discretion. Decisions may be unethical if based on conflicts between the manager's personal bias or peer pressures and the optimal use of human resources based on past and expected performance. Most employees expect employment decisions to be based on merit, not on the employee's race, color, national origin, sex, religion, handicap, or age. Equality of opportunity, not equality of result, is the essence of fairness as set out in the Declaration of Independence, the Constitution, and a number of constitutional amendments, including the Bill of Rights.

Title VII does not require an employer to hire or promote any particular person. Of course, employers may legitimately discriminate among job applicants on the basis of their ability to perform or their prospects for success. It is important to recognize that Title VII outlaws only "discrimination" predicated on a person's membership in a protected class: race, sex, religion, color, and national origin. Discriminations based on measurable differences in qualifications closely related to job performance are necessary, justifiable, and legal. The three theories of illegal discrimination—disparate treatment, disparate impact, and pattern or practice—are summarized in Figure 20–2.

FIGURE 20-2 Theories of Unlawful Discrimination under Title VII of the Civil Rights Act of 1964

Discrimination Theory	Disparate Treatment Theory	Disparate Impact Theory	Pattern or Practice Theory
Statement of theory	Employer, union, or employment agency announces and/or uses intentional discriminatory policies that are more favorable to one group than to a protected class.	Employer, union, or employment agency uses job selection standards that appear neutral, yet result in a disparate impact on a protected class.	Employer, union, or employment agency's track record reveals a pattern or practice of discrimination affecting a protected class of persons rather than a specific individual.
Proof required	Intent to discriminate. Inferences are allowed from circumstantial evidence. Employment of a qualified applicant from a protected class is rejected, and job remains unfilled afterward. Burden of proof shifts to employer to justify actions.	No proof of discriminatory intent required. Adverse effect on protected class; statistical proof may be used. Employer unable to justify the employment practice as job related. Evidence of disparate treatment unavailable.	No proof of discriminatory motive required. Inference from statistical analysis: Compare the percentage of suspect class members in the employer's workforce with its percentage in job applications and among the general public. Employer's work force contains a substantially lower percentage of suspect class members than of members of other groups.
Examples	Biased hiring, firing, and promotion practices. "Blacks need not apply." "This is a man's job."	General intelligence or achievement tests covering background rather than specified job skills. Unjustified height restrictions or high school diploma requirement.	Qualified persons in the protected class deterred from applying due to employer's reputation for discrimination. Low utilization of protected class applicants. Pay differences between members of protected class and members of other groups in comparable jobs. Similar pattern or practice of discrimination by other employers.

Disparate Treatment

disparate treatment Intentional use of discriminatory employment policies.

Title VII prohibits discriminatory policies of an employer, union, or employment agency that treat one group of employees or job applicants more favorably than members of a protected class. An illegal **disparate treatment** occurs when an employer intentionally conducts discriminatory hiring, promotion, or firing policies. Proof of such a discrimination would be easy if the employer overtly stated, for example, "Blacks need not apply" or "This is a man's job." Today, overt practices are rare. Disparate treatment typically results from more subtle conduct, so courts accept inferences based on circumstantial evidence.

Plaintiff's Required Proof of a Prima Facie Case of Disparate Treatment

1. Membership in a protected class.
2. Qualification for the job sought.
3. Rejection despite adequate qualifications.
4. Position remained open after the plaintiff was rejected.

In a disparate treatment trial, the plaintiff must first establish a prima facie case (the basic elements); then, the burden of proof shifts to the defendant, who must prove there was a legitimate reason for the disparate treatment. Often the plaintiff may rebut this justification by showing statistical evidence of a pattern of discrimination by the employer, which also constitutes disparate treatment. What if an employer has a mixture of legal and illegal discriminatory reasons for an employment decision? The next case illustrates the Supreme Court's analysis of such a situation.

Price Waterhouse v. Hopkins

490 U.S. 228 (1989)
United States Supreme Court

Ann Hopkins, a senior manager at the Washington, D.C., office of the Price Waterhouse accounting firm was proposed by the partners in her office for a promotion to partner in 1982. However, her candidacy was held over for reconsideration to the following year and thereafter dropped. At the time only 7 of a total of 662 Price Waterhouse partners nationwide were women, and Hopkins was the only woman of 88 candidates for partner that year. Both her supporters and opponents indicated that Hopkins was "overly aggressive, unduly harsh, difficult to work with, and impatient with staff." Hopkins was described as "macho" and "overcompensating for being a woman." She was advised to take a "course at charm school" and to walk, talk, and dress "more femininely, wear make-up, have her hair styled, and wear jewelry." Price Waterhouse claimed that the decision was based primarily on legitimate interpersonal factors. The trial court held that Price Waterhouse had unlawfully discriminated against her on the basis of sex by consciously giving credence to sexually stereotyped comments.

Justice Brennan delivered the opinion of the Court.

In passing Title VII, Congress made the simple but momentous announcement that sex, race, and national origin are not relevant to the selection, evaluation, or compensation of employees. The statute does not purport to limit the other qualities and characteristics that employers may take into account in making employment decisions. The critical inquiry in this case is whether gender was a factor in the employment decision at the moment it was made. Title VII was meant to condemn even those decisions based on a mixture of legitimate and illegitimate considerations.

To say that an employer may not take gender into account is not the end of the matter. Title VII preserved the employer's remaining freedom of choice. The employer shall not be liable if it can prove that, even if it had not taken gender into account, it would have come to the same decision. In saying that gender played a motivating part in an employment decision, we mean that, if we asked the employer at the moment of the decision what the reasons were and if we received a truthful response, one of those reasons would be that the applicant or employee was a woman. An employer who acts on the basis of the belief that a woman cannot be aggressive has acted on the basis of gender. We are beyond the day when an employer could evaluate employees by assuming or insisting that they match the stereotype associated with their group.

An employer who objects to aggressiveness in women but whose positions require this trait places women in an intolerable and impermissible Catch-22: out of a job if they behave aggressively and out of a job if they do not. Title VII lifts women out of this bind. Price Waterhouse invited partners to submit comments; some of the comments stemmed from sexual stereotypes; the Policy Board's decision on Hopkins was an assessment of the submitted comments; and Price Waterhouse in no way disclaimed reliance on the sex-linked evaluations. The defendant may avoid a finding of liability only by proving by a preponderance of the evidence that it would have made the same decision even if it had not taken the plaintiff's gender into account. [After remand on whether Price Waterhouse would have made the same decision without considering sex stereotyping, the trial court ordered that Ms. Hopkins be made a partner.]

Case Questions

1. How can an employer avoid liability in mixed-motive decisions? What standard is used to judge how the decision was made?
2. Should it be relevant to Price Waterhouse's decision if client comments indicated that Hopkins's aggressive behavior was inappropriate or if clients requested she be replaced on their assignment?

The Civil Rights Act of 1991 modified the *Hopkins* holding where the applicant's sex was a motivating factor but other factors were sufficient for an adverse employment decision. In such cases, the plaintiff is entitled to an injunction and attorney's fees but is not entitled to backpay or the promotion.

Disparate Impact

disparate impact Apparently neutral job selection standards that negatively impact a protected class.

Title VII allows the plaintiff to bring a legal action even if direct or circumstantial evidence of disparate treatment is unavailable. A violation may be found if it can be shown that a **disparate impact** resulted from the employer's hiring policies or evaluation process. Violations may result where hiring standards and employment practices fail to deal adequately with a suspect class, resulting in a disparate impact. Sometimes the use of apparently neutral employment policies causes a disparate impact. Certain achievement tests or job qualifications may initially appear neutral yet cause a disparate impact on a particular class. For example, height restrictions often result in the exclusion of women or Asians. General intelligence tests often discriminate in favor of those whose background is most closely tested. For example, it is argued the Scholastic Aptitude Test (SAT) discriminates against African Americans. Some courts have enjoined the use of allegedly biased tests used in employment or admission decisions. Unless physical requirements or general intelligence tests are directly related to necessary job qualifications, they may result in a disparate impact.

Statistical Evidence Both disparate impact cases and the pattern or practice cases discussed in the next section may be proved by statistical evidence. Usually a comparison is made between a segment of the employer's workforce and the pool of qualified applicants available for work in that segment. However, such comparisons are susceptible to error from numerous arbitrary classifications. For example, who should be placed in the pool of potential applicants for comparison with the employer's workforce?

Wards Cove Packing Co. Inc. v. Antonio[2] illustrates how a prospective employee could be treated unfairly by an employer's use of overinclusive or underinclusive classifications. In that case, applicants excluded from consideration for higher paid and skilled "noncannery jobs" claimed discrimination in hiring and promotions that caused a disparate impact on nonwhites. The discriminatory acts allegedly included: nepotism, rehire preferences, lack of objective hiring practices, not promoting from within, and separate hiring channels established for lower paid and unskilled "cannery jobs" held predominately by nonwhites and "noncannery" jobs held primarily by whites. The plaintiffs proved discrimination at the trial court using statistics showing a higher percentage of nonwhite workers in the cannery jobs and a lower percentage of nonwhites in the noncannery positions. However, the Supreme Court criticized this as an invalid comparison. The proper comparison is between the racial composition of the jobs at issue and the racial composition of the qualified population in the relevant labor market. The employer's employment practices should not be held responsible if there are insufficient qualified minorities in the available labor pool. The cannery workforce in no way reflected the pool of qualified job applicants or the qualified population in the labor force. The court labeled it "nonsensical" to measure the alleged discrimination in selecting skilled noncannery workers, such as accountants, managers, boat captains, electricians, doctors, and engineers, by comparing the number of nonwhites occupying these jobs to the number of nonwhites filling unskilled cannery jobs. The comparisons urged by the plaintiffs would force employers to defensively adopt racial quotas to avoid litigation. The *Wards Cove Packing* case also ruled that employees have the burden of proving a specific employment practice caused a disparate impact on a particular class. However, the Civil Rights Act of 1991 shifted the burden of proof to the employer to prove the employment practice was a business necessity.

Pattern or Practice of Discrimination Where the employer's discrimination affects a whole class of persons rather than a specific individual, suit may be based on the *pattern or practice theory.* Evidence of such systematic discrimination is usually circumstantial and derived from statistical inference like in other disparate impact cases. It may be inferred that significantly lower percentages of employees from the protected class result from a pattern or practice of discrimination. Congress refrained from setting a definitive percentage for comparison, leaving it to the courts to establish standards on a case-by-case basis. An employer may rebut the inference of pattern or practice discrimination with evidence of serious methodological flaws in the statistical comparison used similar to the *Wards Cove Packing* rationale above.

If a plaintiff successfully proves that an employer is involved in a pattern or practice of discrimination, a presumption arises in favor of all job applicants in the protected class. Some of the people in that class may have been deterred from applying for jobs with the discriminating employer. A pattern or practice suit is strengthened when the plaintiff proves disparate impact or disparate treatment. Some personnel policies are especially likely to lead to a pattern or practice suit. These include low utilization of available minorities, disparate pay treatment of minorities or women, and disparate pay for minorities in comparable jobs. Some employers are large and influential enough to encourage other employers to mimic

[2] *Wards Cove Packing Co. Inc. v. Antonio*, 490 U.S. 642 (1989).

their pattern or practice discrimination. Such parallelism tends to broaden the disparate impact of the discrimination. If an employer with high turnover rates fails to hire available members of minorities, EEOC guidelines suggest there is a pattern or practice of discrimination.

Protected Classes

protected class Demographic classification of persons historically subjected to discrimination, including: race, color, religion, national origin, sex, disability, and age.

Title VII of the Civil Rights Act of 1964 prohibits discrimination in employment practices on the basis of membership in a protected class. A **protected class** is a demographic variable or classification of persons who have historically been subjected to discrimination in hiring. The protected classes include race, color, religion, national origin, sex, disability, and age. An employment practice is prohibited if it discriminates against an applicant on the basis of his or her membership in a protected class and this results in disparate treatment, disparate impact, or a pattern or practice of discrimination.

Race Both the Civil Rights Act of 1866 and the Civil Rights Act of 1964 are intended to prohibit racial discrimination. Although the original focus of these acts was to prohibit discrimination against blacks, both of the acts also apply to all other races. All persons are members of a particular race, religion, or sex and have a particular national origin, so the antidiscrimination laws apply to both whites and blacks. Thus, *reverse discrimination* may be illegal; this occurs when *preference* is given to members of protected classes that historically suffered discrimination. This principle was established in 1978 in a famous Supreme Court case, *Regents of the University of California v. Bakke*.[3] In that case, the University of California admitted minority applicants whose admission test scores were lower than that of Bakke, a white applicant. Reverse discrimination is discussed further later in the chapter.

Religion A fundamental concern addressed in the Constitution is discrimination based on religious practices and beliefs. The separation of church and state and the First Amendment freedoms of religion form a protected zone for religious beliefs. In addition, the 1964 Act prohibits employment discrimination on the basis of religion. The term *religion* is easiest to define when it refers to standard denominations. From the standpoint of the law, however, the term also includes sets of ethically or morally based beliefs that are sincerely held. Thus, in addition to protecting the traditional religions—Christianity, Judaism, Islam, Buddhism, and Hinduism—Title VII protects such beliefs as atheism and agnosticism.

A recurring problem in religious discrimination cases is the extent of an employer's duty to accommodate employees' religious observances. Where an employee's religious practices tend to interfere with the employer's business, a delicate balance must be drawn between hardships on the business and hardships on the employee's beliefs. Where an employer convincingly demonstrates that accommodating an employee's religious beliefs would impose undue hardship on the business, discrimination on the basis of religion is permitted. How can an employee's observance of the Sabbath be reconciled with a union's seniority system and an employer's need for 24-hour shift schedules? The following case illustrates this problem.

---

[3] *Regents of the University of California v. Bakke*, 438 U.S. 265 (1978).

Trans World Airlines, Inc. v. Hardison

432 U.S. 63 (1977)
United States Supreme Court

Hardison worked for TWA maintenance, which operated 24 hours a day. The union collective bargaining agreement gave the most senior employees some choice of job and shift assignments. Hardison used his seniority to opt out of work on Saturday, his Sabbath. However, his seniority dropped after his transfer to another department, forcing him to work Saturdays. TWA discharged Hardison after he refused to do work Saturdays. Hardison sued for an injunction under Title VII, claiming that the discharge constituted unlawful religious discrimination. Both the trial court and the Court of Appeals agreed with Hardison; TWA appealed to the Supreme Court.

Justice White delivered the opinion of the Court.

The Court of Appeals held that TWA had not made reasonable efforts to accommodate Hardison's religious needs under the 1967 EEOC guidelines in effect at the time the relevant events occurred. In its view, TWA had rejected three reasonable alternatives, any one of which would have satisfied its obligation without undue hardship. First, within the framework of the seniority system, TWA could have permitted Hardison to work a four-day week, utilizing in his place a supervisor or another worker on duty elsewhere. That this would have caused other shop functions to suffer was insufficient to amount to undue hardship in the opinion of the Court of Appeals. Second—according to the Court of Appeals, also within the bounds of the collective-bargaining contract—the company could have filled Hardison's Saturday shift from other available personnel competent to do the job, of which the court said there were at least 200. That this would have involved premium overtime pay was not deemed an undue hardship. Third, TWA could have arranged a "swap between Hardison and another employee either for another shift or for the Sabbath days." In response to the assertion that this would have involved a breach of the seniority provisions of the contract, the court noted that it had not been settled in the courts whether the required statutory accommodation to religious needs stopped short of transgressing seniority rules, but found it unnecessary to decide the issue because, as the Court of Appeals saw the record, TWA had not sought, and the union had therefore not declined to entertain, a possible variance from the seniority provisions of the collective-bargaining agreement. The company had simply left the entire matter to the union steward who the Court of Appeals said "likewise did nothing."

We disagree with the Court of Appeals in all relevant respects. It is our view that TWA made reasonable efforts to accommodate and that each of the Court of Appeals' suggested alternatives would have been an undue hardship within the meaning of the statute as construed by the EEOC guidelines.

It appears to us that the [seniority] system itself represented a significant accommodation to the needs, both religious and secular, of all of TWA's employees. As will become apparent, the seniority system represents a neutral way of minimizing the number of occasions when an employee must work on a day that he would prefer to have off. Additionally, recognizing that weekend work schedules are the least popular, the company made further accommodation by reducing its work force to a bare minimum on those days.

Any employer who, like TWA, conducts an around-the-clock operation is presented with the choice of allocating work schedules either in accordance with the preferences of its employees or by involuntary assignment. Insofar as the varying shift preferences of its employees complement each other, TWA could meet its manpower needs through voluntary work scheduling.

It was essential to TWA's business to require Saturday and Sunday work for at least a few employees even though most employees preferred those days off. Allocating the burdens of weekend work was a matter for collective bargaining. In considering criteria to govern this allocation, TWA and the union had two alternatives: adopt a neutral system, such as seniority, a lottery, or rotating shifts; or allocate days off in accordance with the religious needs of its employees. TWA would have had to adopt the latter in order to assure Hardison and others like him of getting the days off necessary for strict observance of their religion, but it could have done so only at the expense of others who had strong, but perhaps nonreligious, reasons for not working on weekends. There were no volunteers to relieve Hardison on Saturdays, and to give Hardison Saturdays off, TWA would have had to deprive another employee of his shift preference at least in part because he did not adhere to a religion that observed the Saturday Sabbath.

Title VII does not contemplate such unequal treatment. The repeated, unequivocal emphasis of both the language and the legislative history of Title VII is on eliminating discrimination in employment, and such discrimination is proscribed when it is directed against majorities as well as minorities.

To require TWA to bear more than a *de minimis* cost in order to give Hardison Saturdays off is an undue hardship. Like abandonment of the seniority system, to require TWA to bear additional costs when no such costs are incurred to give other employees the days off that they want would involve unequal treatment of employees on the basis of their religion. By suggesting that TWA should incur certain costs in order to give Hardison Saturdays off, the Court of Appeals would in effect require TWA to finance an additional Saturday off and then to choose the employee who will enjoy it on the basis of his religious beliefs. While incurring extra costs to secure a replacement for Hardison might remove the necessity of compelling another employee to work involuntarily in Hardison's place, it would not change the fact that the privilege of having Saturdays off would be allocated according to religious beliefs.

Case Questions

1. What alternative accommodations could be made to permit employees' observance of religious holidays?
2. How much economic hardship must an employer undergo to provide religious accommodation?
3. How does the collective bargaining agreement balance employer economic hardship against employee religious accommodation?

National Origin Discrimination based on the country in which a person was born or from which the person's forebears came is *national origin* discrimination. Refusing to hire persons whose surnames are typical of a particular national origin is an example of such discrimination. It is sometimes legal for employers to indirectly discriminate against aliens or noncitizens. For example, some jobs may require fluency in English, particularly those involving communication with customers, suppliers, or fellow employees. However, if fluency in English is not required by business necessity, it may be prohibited to make fluency a qualification if this has an adverse impact on certain groups.

Immigration Laws and Anti-Discrimination Laws The 1986 amendments to the immigration laws thoroughly revised U.S. policy. Employers are prohibited from hiring, recruiting, or referring for a fee any known illegal alien. The work eligibility of all employees hired in after November 6, 1986, is required, usually by examining original documents that "reasonably appear genuine." Form I-9 (Employment Eligibility Verification Form) must be filed with the Immigration and Naturalization Service (INS) within three days after hiring every new employee. Verification is required for all full-time, part-time, temporary, and casual employees but not for independent contractors. I-9 forms must be retained for three years for Labor Department or INS inspection. Employers are subject to civil fines for failing to verify all newly hired employees, for failing to retain I-9 forms, or for hiring illegal aliens.

Discriminatory hiring practices prohibited under Title VII are explicitly restated in the antidiscrimination provisions of the immigration law. Congress included this

"Frank Amendment" out of concern that the law might encourage or excuse employment discrimination on the basis of national origin or citizenship. For example, an employer might refuse to hire individuals who "look foreign" or speak with a foreign accent. It is an unfair employment practice to discriminate on the basis of national origin or to hire only U.S. citizens. The antidiscrimination provisions of the immigration law apply to employers of 4 to 14 persons; they do not apply to employers of 3 or fewer persons. Title VII prohibits employers of 15 or more persons from national origin discrimination, and the immigration law requires them to refrain from discrimination on the basis of citizenship. The burden of illegal immigration on public services and the deflating pressure it allegedly has on wages should continue to present tough political issues over the next few years.

Sex It is illegal to discriminate on the basis of sex. This prohibition was originally designed to correct the stereotypical societal roles of the sexes, which tended to discriminate against women. However, the prohibition protects both women and men. The employment advances made by women probably result from several factors: (1) the Civil Rights Act of 1964, (2) the evolution of the economy from a manufacturing base to a service base, and (3) a blurring of the distinctions between sex roles. A clear trend of the 20th century has been the enlargement of the economic activities of women. Today, women comprise approximately 40 percent of the workforce.

Pregnancy Discrimination Congress passed the Pregnancy Discrimination Act in 1978 to assure women of protection against employment discrimination during pregnancy. Over 70 percent of all women who become pregnant were working during that time; half of these women return to work after the newborn reaches three months of age, and almost three-fourths return by the child's first birthday. The act prohibits employers from requiring that pregnant employees take leaves of absence if they are still qualified to do the job. Pregnancy leaves may not be treated differently from other temporary disability leaves. Employers may not specify different lengths of post-delivery leaves of absence from those applied to other disability or illness. Pregnant women may not be denied a promotion or job assignment on the basis of their pregnancy. The act applies to both married and unmarried employees and to both sexes. How could it apply to men? Well, if the employer provides family medical coverage, it cannot provide lesser pregnancy benefits to spouses of male employees than to female employees.

Fetal Protection Policies In more hazardous jobs, employers are becoming concerned that pregnant employee exposure to toxic substances or radiation could lead to liability for infertility, miscarriages, or birth defects. Some employers have reacted defensively by refusing employment or terminating the jobs of women of childbearing age. However, in *International Union v. Johnson Controls*[4] the Supreme Court found that such practices were discriminatory on the basis of sex. This case places a substantial and uncertain burden on employers to discover and monitor the workplace for numerous toxic agents, to inform employees, and to undertake costly protective measures. Employers' potential liability for such injuries can be incalculable yet substantial.

Sex-Plus Discrimination Sex-plus discrimination occurs when an employer requires additional qualifications of one sex. For example, one airline required that female

---

[4] *International Union v. Johnson Controls*, 499 U.S. 187 (1991).

flight attendants be unmarried, yet hired married male flight attendants, an illegal sex-plus discrimination. Similarly, permitting one sex to retire earlier, smoke on the job, or receive desirable overseas assignments while denying such rights to employees of the other sex is illegal discrimination.

Family Leave Congress passed the Family and Medical Leave Act in 1993 to supplement the growing number of states and employers setting policies to secure the employment for those compelled by family obligation to take temporary work release. Private employers with 50 or more employees and all governments must permit up to 12 weeks of unpaid leave for employees after childbirth, adoption, or the serious illness of a parent, child, or spouse of the employee. The employee must give advance notice where practical but cannot be terminated for taking such leaves. Additionally, employees' medical insurance coverage must remain in effect during the leave, and the same or a similar job must be made available on their return to work. Exemptions permit employers to deny leave to (1) employees of less than one year who have not yet worked at least 1,250 hours and (2) the top 10 key employees, presuming their leave would economically injure the employer. Many U.S. employers offer some period of paid leave for family emergencies or postnatal care. European nations have generally taken the lead with generous family leave policies.

sexual harassment Unwelcome sexual advances, requests for sexual favors, and other verbal or physical conduct of a sexual nature made explicitly or implicitly a term or condition of an individual's employment, used as the basis for employment decisions, unreasonably interfering with individual's work performance, or creating an intimidating, hostile, or offensive work environment.

Sexual Harassment Title VII does not specifically outlaw **sexual harassment.** However, making submission to sexual harassment a condition of employment may be prohibited as discriminatory. Due to the difficulties in distinguishing between non-offensive social gestures and unlawful sexual harassment, it can be difficult to fairly judge behavior in this area. Indeed, many observers allege that if an employee has been promoted or given pay raises as the result of sexual relations with a supervisor, an unlawful sexual harassment has caused discrimination on the basis of sex. Employees who quit a job as the result of sexual harassment may also maintain an action as a *constructive discharge* on the basis of sexual harassment.

The EEOC has issued guidelines on sexual harassment. These apply the general principles of Title VII to employers and supervisors irrespective of whether the sexually harassing acts are authorized. An employee experiences harassment when unwelcome sexual advances are encountered, requests for sexual favors are received, or verbal or physical conduct of a sexual nature is received. If the surrounding circumstances either explicitly or implicitly make submission to the sexual advances a term or condition of employment, the action is illegal. This is often called *quid pro quo* sexual harassment. A right of action arises if an employee is not granted a promotion or a pay raise because a less qualified person who granted sexual favors was promoted instead. Although few other nations rigorously prohibit sexual harassment, the European Union (EU) has adopted a nonbinding restriction, and Japan has started taking legal actions against sexual harassment. The following excerpt from *Bundy v. Jackson*[5] the EEOC Guidelines' definition of sexual harassment.

EEOC Sexual Harassment Guidelines

"The Final Guidelines of Sexual Harassment in the Workplace (*Guidelines*) issued by the Equal Employment Opportunity Commission on November 10, 1980 . . .

[5] *Bundy v. Jackson*, 641 F.2d 934 (D.C. Cir. 1981).

define sexual harassment broadly: Unwelcome sexual advances, requests for sexual favors, and other verbal or physical conduct of a sexual nature constitute sexual harassment when (1) submission to such conduct is made either explicitly or implicitly a term or condition of an individual's employment, (2) submission to or rejection of such conduct by an individual is used as the basis for employment decisions affecting such individual, or (3) such conduct has the purpose or effect of unreasonably interfering with an individual's work performance or creating an intimidating, hostile, or offensive work environment."

Even less blatant actions may constitute sexual harassment. Sexual innuendo that creates an intimidating, offensive, or *hostile working environment* is also prohibited. In *Meritor Savings Bank v. Vinson*,[6] a bank employee repeatedly submitted to her supervisor's sexual advances out of fear of losing her job. Although the employer had a policy against sexual harassment and there was a grievance procedure, the Supreme Court found that a sexually harassing atmosphere nevertheless existed. Employers that know or should know about the sexually harassing acts of employees may be held responsible and liable for damages if they fail to take appropriate corrective action. Employer liability can also be based on principles of agency law that require adequate supervision. The problem is magnified where superiors with supervisory authority to hire, fire, promote, and discipline facilitate a hostile work environment. A higher standard of responsibility is developing for permanent, high-level supervisors than for the actions of temporary or low-level supervisors and for co-workers. The employer's knowledge of a hostile working environment triggers a duty to take reasonable steps to eliminate it. Clearly, employers should establish prevention programs and complaint procedures, facilitate the discovery of hostile environment developments, respond to notice with genuine investigatory and disciplinary efforts, and then eliminate harassing conditions.

The EEOC also regards prevention as the best way to eliminate sexual harassment and encourages employers to take all necessary steps to sensitize employees to the problem. Many firms conduct seminars or discussion groups on sexual harassment or use video enactments of sexually harassing behavior. What constitutes a "hostile" or "abusive" working environment? The following case illustrates how sexual intimidation may be harassing and how an employer is responsible for remedying the situation.

Harris v. Forklift Systems, Inc.

114 S.Ct. 367 (1993)
United States Supreme Court

Theresa Harris worked as a manager at Forklift Systems. Charles Hardy was Forklift's president. Throughout Harris's time at Forklift, Hardy often insulted her because of her gender and often made her the target of unwanted sexual innuendos. Hardy told Harris on several occasions, in the presence of other employees, "You're a woman; what do you know?" and "We need a man as the rental manager"; at least once, he told her she was "a dumb ass woman." He suggested that the two of them "go to the Holiday Inn to negotiate (Harris's) raise." Hardy occasionally asked Harris and other female employees to get coins

[6] *Meritor Savings Bank v. Vinson*, 477 U.S. 57 (1986).

from his pants pocket. He threw objects on the ground in front of Harris and other women, and asked them to pick the objects up. Harris complained to Hardy. Hardy said he was surprised that Harris was offended, claimed he was only joking, and apologized. He also promised he would stop. Based on this assurance, Harris stayed on the job. But in early September, Hardy began anew: While Harris was arranging a deal with one of Forklift's customers, he asked her, again in front of other employees, "What did you do, promise the guy . . . some (sex) Saturday night?" On October 1, Harris collected her paycheck and quit. Harris then sued Forklift, claiming that Hardy's conduct had created an abusive work environment for her because of her gender.

Justice O'Connor

Title VII of the Civil Rights Act of 1964 makes it "an unlawful employment practice for an employer . . . to discriminate against any individual with respect to his compensation, terms, conditions, or privileges of employment, because of such individual's race, color, religion, sex, or national origin."

The phrase "terms, conditions, or privileges of employment" evinces a congressional intent "to strike at the entire spectrum of disparate treatment of men and women in employment," which includes requiring people to work in a discriminatorily hostile or abusive environment. When the workplace is permeated with "discriminatory intimidation, ridicule, and insult," that is "sufficiently severe or pervasive to alter the conditions of the victim's employment and create an abusive working environment. This standard, which we reaffirm today, takes a middle path between making actionable any conduct that is merely offensive and requiring the conduct to cause a tangible psychological injury. "Mere utterance of an . . . epithet which endangers offensive feelings in a employee," does not sufficiently affect the conditions of employment to implicate Title VII. Conduct that is not severe or pervasive enough to create an objectively hostile or abusive work environment—an environment that a reasonable person would find hostile or abusive—is beyond Title VII's purview. Likewise, if the victim does not subjectively perceive the environment to be abusive, the conduct has not actually altered the conditions of the victim's employment, and there is no Title VII violation.

But Title VII comes into play before the harassing conduct leads to a nervous breakdown. A discriminatorily abusive work environment, even one that does not seriously affect employees' psychological well-being, can and often will detract from employees' job performance, discourage employees from remaining on the job, or keep them from advancing in their careers. The very fact that the discriminatory conduct was so severe or pervasive that it created a work environment abusive to employees because of their race, gender, region, or national origin offends Title VII's broad rule of workplace equality. The appalling conduct alleged in *Meritor* merely present some especially egregious examples of harassment. They do not mark the boundary of what is actionable.

The District Court erred in relying on whether the conduct "seriously affect(ed) plaintiff's psychological well-being" or led her to "suffe(r) injury." Such an inquiry may needlessly focus the factfinder's attention on concrete psychological harm, an element Title VII does not require. So long as the environment would reasonably be perceived, and is perceived, as hostile or abusive, there is no need for it also to be psychologically injurious. This is not, and by its nature cannot be, a mathematically precise test. Whether an environment is "hostile" or "abusive" can be determined only by looking at all the circumstances. These may include the frequency of the discriminatory conduct; its severity; whether it is physically threatening or humiliating, or a mere offensive utterance; and whether it unreasonably interferes with an employee's work performance. The effect on the employee's psychological well-being is, of course, relevant to determining whether the plaintiff actually found the environment abusive. But while psychological harm, like any other relevant factor, may be taken into account, no single factor is required. We therefore reverse the judgement of the Court of Appeals, and remand the case for further proceedings consistent with this opinion. So ordered.

Justice Scalia, Concurring

"Abusive" (or "hostile," which in this context I take to mean the same thing) does not seem to me a very clear standard—and I do not think clarity is at all increased by adding the adverb "objectively" or by appealing to a "reasonable" person's notion of what the vague word means. Today's opinion does list a number of factors that contribute to abusiveness, but since it neither says how much of each is necessary (an impossible task) nor identifies any single factor as determinative, it thereby adds little certitude. As a practical matter, today's holding lets virtually unguided juries decide whether sex-related conduct engaged in (or permitted by) an employer is egregious enough to warrant an award of damages.

Be that as it may, I know of no alternative to the course the Court today has taken. I know of no test more faithful to the inherently vague statutory language than the one the Court today adopts. For these reasons, I join the opinion of the Court.

Justice Ginsburg, Concurring

Today the Court reaffirms the holding of *Meritor Savings Bank v. Vinson*. As the Equal Employment Opportunity Commission emphasized, the adjudicator's inquiry should center, dominantly, on whether the discriminatory conduct has unreasonably interfered with the plaintiff's work performance. To show such interference, "the plaintiff need not prove that his or her tangible productivity has declined as a result of the harassment." It suffices to prove that a reasonable person subjected to the discriminatory conduct would find, as the plaintiff did, that the harassment so altered working conditions as to "ma(k)e it more difficult to do the job." Title VII declares discriminatory practices based on race, gender, religion, or national origin equally unlawful.

Case Questions

1. How might the standard for harassing environment be ambiguous in application?
2. What is the standard for harassing activities that might constitute an "interference" with job performance?

The test for a hostile or abusive work environment is determined objectively by the "reasonable person" standard, not by a "reasonable woman" standard as many observers had previously suggested. However, the *Forklift* decision also requires courts to consider the victim's subjective perception of whether the environment is abusive. Factors relevant to this determination include (1) the frequency of the discriminatory conduct, (2) the severity of the conduct (3) whether the conduct is physically threatening or humiliating as opposed to being merely an offensive utterance, and (4) the unreasonableness of the interference with the employee's work performance.

Ethical Dilemmas Involving Sexual Harassment

Ethical Dilemma

Blatant forms of sexual harassment pose ethical dilemmas. Sexual harassment clearly arises if supervisors abuse their positions to gain sexual favors from subordinates. Requests for such favors are usually made under the implied or overt threat that the supervisor will make adverse promotion, hiring, or firing decisions unless the subordinate complies. Hearings on the confirmation of Supreme Court Justice Clarence Thomas exposed the disparity between male and female perceptions about what sexual harassment is and how it tips the balance of power to the harasser.

Despite the appearance of clear prohibitions, there is much ambiguity in less clear-cut cases. For example, norms have only begun to emerge concerning the extent to which joking behavior leads to the creation of a chilling and harassing work atmosphere. What kinds of behavior should expose firms and supervisors to damage liability? What "tasteless" behaviors are serious enough to be unethical? Are there workable standards for identifying a chilling atmosphere? Are such standards generally recognized or capable of precise measurement? Any form of discrimination that is not based on clear performance measures may be unethical. Wherever a supervisor abuses a position of authority to make decisions that are based on the supervisor's biases but are unconnected with performance and economic efficiency, an ethical dilemma arises.

Age Discrimination on the basis of an employee's age is not a prohibited activity under Title VII, but the Age Discrimination in Employment Act of 1967 now protects persons over 40 from some forms of age discrimination. The act is enforced by the EEOC. It applies to both public and private employers of 20 or more employees. Numerous age discrimination claims have been brought by middle-aged, professional, white males often dismissed in favor of lower-paid, younger workers.

Some employers prefer younger workers to older ones because seniority systems tend to raise wage costs with age. Other employers insist on the perceived strength and appearance of younger workers. However, researchers find that older workers usually have more experience, may be more loyal, and experience less absenteeism than younger workers. Where an employer imposes physical fitness standards that are directly related to job activities, a pattern or practice of discrimination against older workers may be justified. For example, where public safety is involved, performance tests may be used even if this results in the hiring of fewer persons over 40 (e.g., bus drivers, firefighters, police officers). Pilots may be forced to retire or may be moved to less physically demanding positions such as flight engineer after age 60 because empirical evidence shows health declines after that age. Although it once seemed justifiable to require all employees to retire between 65 and 70, the Age Discrimination in Employment Act has prohibited this since 1986 with a few exceptions, most of which expired after 1993.

Disability Title VII did not originally include handicapped workers as a protected class. However, two later federal laws are gradually including many disabilities as part of a separate protected class. In 1973, Congress passed the first law, the Vocational Rehabilitation Act, requiring employers that receive federal contracts simply to *consider* handicapped job applicants if they can adequately perform the job after a reasonable accommodation has been made. The 1973 law does not require the hiring of the disabled.

The first law defined *handicaps* as physical or mental impairments that substantially limit one or more of a person's major life activities or that create the perception of impairment. Handicaps, now *disabilities,* that result from diabetes, epilepsy, deafness, disfigurement, heart disease, cancer, retardation, blindness, paraplegia, quadriplegia, alcoholism, or drug abuse are protected. So long as the disability does not adversely affect successful job performance, the employer may not take it into consideration in offering employment. For example, persons with many communicable diseases are disabled. In *School Board of Nassau County Florida v. Arline,*[7] Gene Arline was discharged from her position as a school teacher after her inactive tuberculosis became active. The Supreme Court held that because the risk of transmitting the disease was slight, Arline was still qualified as a teacher. Employers must make reasonable

[7] *School Board of Nassau County Florida v. Arline,* 480 U.S. 273 (1987).

accommodation for diseased employees to continue employment. Courts have only started to deal with the many difficult questions raised by discrimination against HIV positive persons. HIV and genetic testing for predisposition to disease or dishonesty, and drug testing for substance abuse may eventually reveal additional disabilities. The privacy issues of such testing were discussed in Chapter 19. Finally, at least one court has suggested that obesity is also a disability.[8]

The second law is the **Americans with Disabilities Act of 1990 (ADA).** The ADA expands the coverage of the Rehabilitation Act to most private employers. The definition of handicap is transformed to the newer term disability. The ADA makes all Title VII remedies and procedures applicable to persons with disabilities. This means that discrimination in employment decisions based on the disability of an applicant or employee is prohibited. Only valid tests or measures of performance directly relevant to the particular job tasks may be considered. The ADA now applies to large companies and to many smaller companies including companies with 15 to 24 workers, which were formerly exempted until 1994. Operators of public facilities such as motels, hotels, restaurants, theaters, passenger trains and busses, and retail stores must ensure that their premises accommodate access by the disabled. Early critics of the ADA claimed it would be too costly for U.S. businesses, particluarly during the early transition years. However, many firms have made reasonable accommodations without much cost.

Americans with Disabilities Act (ADA) 1991 federal law making disability a protected class.

Reasonable Accommodation

Adjusting the job application and screening processes to consider the disabled, modifying the work environment or expected job performance to permit a disabled person's performance, making facilities readily accessible to the disabled, and restructuring work schedules, examinations, equipment, and training to accommodate the disabled.

Statutory Exceptions to Title VII

There are three major statutory exceptions to prohibited discrimination under Title VII. These exceptions permit employers to discriminate against employees on the basis of sex, age, national origin, and religion, but seldom on the basis of race. The exceptions are: (1) bona fide occupational qualification, (2) professionally developed aptitude tests, and (3) valid, nondiscriminatory seniority systems.

Bona Fide Occupational Qualification The first exception permits an employer to discriminate where religion, national origin, or sex is a **bona fide occupational qualification (BFOQ).** Discrimination is permitted if an applicant's membership in one of these protected classes is a **business necessity,** that is where employment of persons from other groups would undermine the business. The employer must prove that hiring persons outside the BFOQ class entails more than mere inconvenience. Race discrimination is never justified by a BFOQ.

Religious institutions may validly require that candidates for certain jobs have certain religious characteristics. For example, churches may hire only ordained minis-

bona fide occupational qualification (BFOQ) Permitted discrimination if employer has a business necessity.

business necessity Where employment of persons from some protected class would undermine the business.

[8] See *Cook v. State Department of Mental Health, Retardation and Hospitals,* 10 F.3d 17 (1st Cir.1993).

ters, and kosher slaughterhouses may require Jewish butchers. Female models may be required to display women's fashions. Fluency in a particular language may be necessary for tour guides or for persons working with the public or with co-workers.

BFOQs are not granted easily by the courts, and the employer must show absolute business necessity. For example, airlines may not insist on female flight attendants even though females may be superior to males in providing reassurance to anxious passengers, giving courteous personalized service, or making flights more pleasurable. Similarly, the preference of gourmet restaurant customers for male waiters does not justify a BFOQ for males only. Ethnic restaurants may not insist on waiters or waitresses of a particular national origin by arguing that this makes for a better ambience.

A valid BFOQ requires female locker-room attendants in a female exercise club. By contrast, it is discriminatory to exclude female sportswriters from the male locker rooms of professional sports teams. This is probably because sportswriters spend only short times in the locker room but locker-room attendants spend most of their time there.

Professionally Developed Ability Tests The second major exception permits employers to discriminate on the basis of an applicant's performance on professionally developed ability tests. The employer may require certain education qualifications or require demonstration of the skills needed on the job. These qualifications must be directly related to the job and constitute a business necessity. The qualifications or tests must be validated as accurate and reliable predictors of job performance. These requirements have made it difficult for employers to use tests that are not scientifically designed or have not been proven to offer direct evidence of successful job performance.

Disparate impact analysis and the necessity of validating qualification tests were originally established in *Griggs v. Duke Power Co.*[9] That case invalidated the requirement that janitorial workers possess a high school diploma or pass an intelligence test. The Wonderlick Aptitude test used by the employer in *Griggs* tended to reward the experiences of whites over blacks. The test had no bearing on success in the janitorial job in question but only to a generally "intelligent work force." As a result of *Griggs,* tests must be validated as significantly related to successful job performance. Tests that disqualify members of a protected class at a rate substantially higher than the rate at which they disqualify other persons may not be used unless the test's validity is established, a complex task for industrial psychologists.

The EEOC has issued guidelines to assist employers in designing valid tests. Tests that have an adverse impact on a protected class must be validated by any one or more of three test validation methods. The first requires that *criterion validity* be established. Tests with criterion validity demonstrate a strong statistical relationship between test results and observed job performance. *Content validity* exists when the test contains a representative sample of the job tasks that are part of the job description. *Construct validity* exists when the test measures the characteristics that are considered useful on the job. For example, a typing test would exhibit both criterion and content validity for a typist's position. The test would identify good typists when typing is the primary job activity. Construct validity might exist for a test to establish a police officer's emotional stability or leadership ability. A psychological test that demonstrates these traits might serve this purpose.

[9] *Griggs v. Duke Power Co.,* 401 U.S. 424 (1971).

The EEOC guidelines require employers to publish *job descriptions* that carefully catalog the tasks required for each job. The employer may use only tests that validly discriminate between applicants who can successfully accomplish the tasks listed in a job description. This restriction leads to a more careful analysis of job requirements and to greater precision in specifying job characteristics.

Seniority Systems The third major Title VII exception permits job discrimination pursuant to a bona fide seniority system if it is not designed to discriminate. In decisions to lay off (reductions in force), promote, or give merit raises, employers may legitimately discriminate in favor of more senior employees if the union contract includes a seniority provision. Such provisions are intended to eliminate favoritism and permit the employer to retain its more experienced employees.

Some seniority systems may tend to perpetuate the effects of discrimination because the newest workers were typically hired under conditions of less discrimination than existed when many of the older workers were hired. During times of economic downturn, more recently hired workers are laid off first even though they represent higher percentages of protected class members. As a result, seniority systems may tend to frustrate the goals of the antidiscrimination laws. How should the antidiscrimination laws and the goals of the National Labor Relations Act be reconciled? The following case illustrates that bona fide seniority systems prevail over discrimination laws.

International B'hd of Teamsters v. United States

431 U.S. 324 (1977)
United States Supreme Court

The United States brought suit against the Teamsters Union and a trucking company employer, alleging a pattern or practice of discrimination against blacks and persons with Spanish surnames. These persons were hired in lower-paying and less desirable driving jobs than those of the long-haul and over-the-road drivers. The collective bargaining agreement between the employer and the Teamsters provided for a seniority system that perpetuated and locked in the effects of past discrimination. The district court ordered a complex subsectioning of the labor force to reduce this discrimination. The Court of Appeals reversed the district court's decision, eliminating the new seniority system. Instead, it gave retroactive seniority to blacks and Hispanics to secure the better jobs. The union appealed to the Supreme Court.

Justice Stewart

The primary purpose of Title VII was "to assure equality of employment opportunities and to eliminate those discriminatory practices and devices which have fostered racially stratified job environments to the disadvantage of minority citizens." To achieve this purpose, Congress "proscribe[d] not only overt discrimination but also practices that are fair in form, but discriminatory in operation." Thus, the Court has repeatedly held that a prima facie Title VII violation may be established by policies or practices that are neutral on their face and in intent but that nonetheless discriminate in effect against a particular group.

Were it not for §703 (h), the seniority system in this case would seem to fall under the *Griggs* rationale. The heart of the system is its allocation of the choicest jobs, the greatest protection against layoffs, and other advantages to those employees who have been line drivers for the longest time. Where, because of the employer's prior intentional discrimination, the line drivers with the longest tenure are without exception white, the advantages of the seniority system flow disproportionately to them and away from Negro and Spanish-surnamed employees who might by now have enjoyed those advantages had not the employer discriminated before the passage of the Act. This disproportionate distribution of advantages does in a very real sense "operate to 'freeze' the status quo of prior discriminatory employment practices."

Although a seniority system inevitably tends to perpetuate the effects of pre-Act discrimination in such cases, the congressional judgment was that Title VII should not outlaw the use of existing seniority lists and thereby destroy or water down the vested seniority rights of employees simply because their employer had engaged in discrimination prior to the passage of the Act.

The seniority system in this litigation is entirely bona fide. It applies equally to all races and ethnic groups. To the extent that it "locks" employees into non-line-driver jobs, it does so for all. The city drivers and servicemen who are discouraged from transferring to line-driver jobs are not all Negroes or Spanish-surnamed Americans; to the contrary, the overwhelming majority are white. The placing of line drivers in a separate bargaining unit from other employees is rational, in accord with the industry practice, and consistent with National Labor Relations Board precedent. It is conceded that the seniority system did not have its genesis in racial discrimination, and that it was negotiated and has been maintained free from any illegal purpose. In these circumstances, the single fact that the system extends no retroactive seniority to pre-Act discriminates does not make it unlawful.

Because the seniority system was protected by §703 (h), the union's conduct in agreeing to and maintaining the system did not violate Title VII. On remand, the District Court's injunction against the union must be vacated.

Case Questions

1. Compare and contrast the requirements of a seniority system and the impact of the antidiscrimination laws.
2. Does the Civil Rights Act permit seniority systems that might arguably have a discriminatory effect?
3. Identify factors in seniority system design that can help to avoid discrimination claims.

Enforcement of the Antidiscrimination Laws

Equal Employment Opportunity Commission (EEOC) Federal agency responsible for enforcement of anti-discrimination laws.

The **Equal Employment Opportunity Commission (EEOC)** was created by the Civil Rights Act of 1964 and was granted additional powers by the Equal Opportunity Act of 1972 and the ADA in 1990. The EEOC may investigate, conciliate, and litigate grievances filed by existing and prospective employees who claim violation of the various employment discrimination laws. It is also authorized to issue rules implementing the antidiscrimination laws. Approximately 45 states have similar fair employment practice laws with widely varying provisions. They typically establish a state fair employment practices commission with powers paralleling those of the EEOC. State commission procedures dovetail directly with EEOC procedures.

Record-Keeping Requirements

The EEOC requires record keeping and disclosure to provide evidence for pattern or practice and disparate impact suits. Employers, union, and employment agencies covered by the record-keeping regulations must keep biographical and demographic records concerning all applicants for new positions and concerning promotions, demotions, transfers, layoffs, and pay rate changes. These records must be made available whenever an employment discrimination suit arises. Each year, employers must audit their minority populations. A notice must be posted describing the various rights available under Title VII so that employees know how to pursue these rights.

EEOC Investigations

An EEOC right of action is first triggered when an aggrieved employee perceives that an unlawful discrimination has occurred. If the state in which the alleged discrimination occurred has an antidiscrimination statute, the aggrieved employee must initially file charges with the so-called "706" agency, a state regulator that agrees with EEOC to process such claims. If the state agency takes no action within the following 60 days, the employee may file charges with the federal EEOC. EEOC filings must be made within 180 days after the discriminatory act or within 300 days if the state antidiscrimination law requires a local filing first. This is a shorter statute of limitations than for most other legal rights.

The EEOC must notify the employer of the discrimination charges and then investigate the incident by visiting the employer's premises and questioning the employer and employees. It may subpoena any documents relevant to the investigation. If reasonable cause exists for believing that a Title VII violation has occurred, the EEOC then notifies the employer of its intent to seek a form of mediated settlement known as conciliation. Otherwise, the EEOC dismisses the charges and advises the aggrieved employee that it will not pursue them, but that the employee may proceed. This "right to sue letter" permits the employee to file suit within the next 90 days in federal district court or state court.

Conciliation

Most EEOC complaints are settled by the alternative dispute resolution process known as *conciliation.* Typically, a confidential proceeding is conducted between the EEOC and the employer outside the aggrieved person's presence. During this proceeding, the EEOC represents the aggrieved person. If the EEOC presents convincing evidence of a discriminatory pattern or practice or a resulting disparate impact, both the employer and the EEOC may voluntarily agree to a remedy.

A conciliation agreement is binding on both parties; neither party may turn to the courts except to enforce the agreement. If no agreement is reached, the EEOC regional office may have its litigation counsel bring suit in a federal district court. Remedies awarded by the court may include the victim's reinstatement into the old job, back pay, litigation costs, attorney's fees, or some affirmative action. Figure 20–3 illustrates these EEOC procedures. In private damage actions, compensatory and punitive damages may be granted for intentional discrimination.

Affirmative Action

The Civil Rights Act of 1964 specifies certain remedies, but in some cases the courts have implied additional rights, permitted proactive antidiscrimination remedies, or encouraged voluntary or privately negotiated solutions. These remedies may require employers to use more positive approaches to reduce the underlying conditions leading to discrimination by actively encouraging the employment of minorities and women. In its conciliation process, the EEOC has often taken such more proactive, "affirmative

FIGURE 20-3 EEOC Procedures

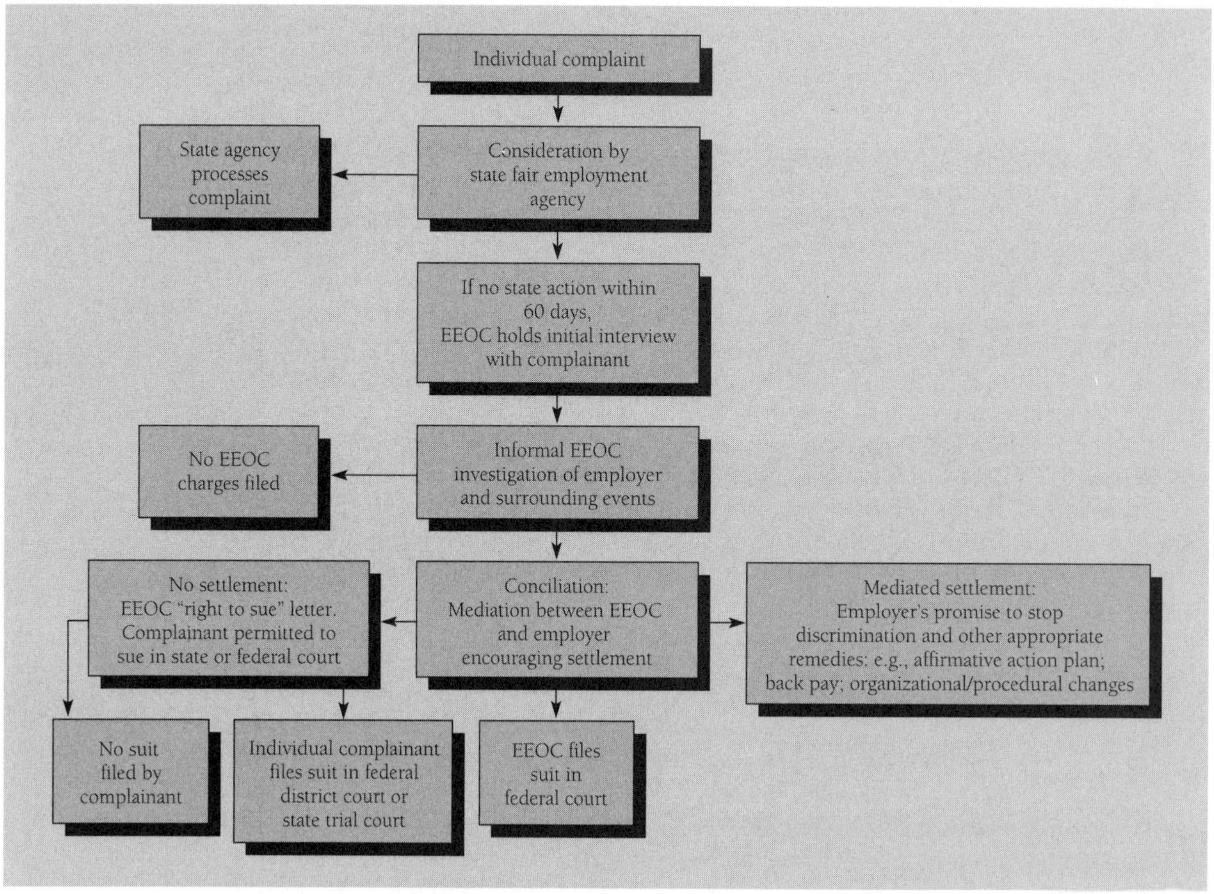

affirmative action programs Actively recruiting of minorities, goals and timetables for greater minority employment.

action" to achieve equal employment opportunities. **Affirmative action programs** actively recruit minorities and may establish goals and timetables for greater employment participation among certain employers by members of suspect classes that have historically suffered patterns of discrimination. Affirmative action plans are also adopted voluntarily or can result from a negotiated collective bargaining agreement with unions. Affirmative action plans are required for most federal contractors.

Affirmative action programs can lead to charges of *reverse discrimination.* Qualified white male applicants are sometimes displaced by less qualified women or members of minorities who are given preference in hiring by these programs. Some affirmative action programs have been invalidated because they unnecessarily "trammeled" nonminority employees in hiring, firing, or promotion decisions. For example, provisions in labor union contracts giving minorities preference to avoid layoffs violate the equal protection clause of the Fourteenth Amendment. Hiring quotas foreclose only one of many employment opportunities to the better qualified applicant. However, layoff preferences impose the entire burden of achieving racial equality on the particular individuals laid off. The disruption of these individuals' lives is unacceptable, and other means of achieving equality, such as affirmative action hiring plans, should be used.

Should the courts approve privately negotiated affirmative action plans between employers and unions to achieve racial balance? The type of program that may receive court approval is illustrated in the next case.

United Steelworkers of America v. Weber

443 U.S. 193 (1979)
United States Supreme Court

The 1974 master collective bargaining agreement between Kaiser Aluminum & Chemical Corporation and the United Steelworkers of American (USWA) included an affirmative action plan to eliminate conspicuous racial imbalances. The enrollees in Kaiser's in-plant craft-training programs were almost exclusively white. The affirmative action plan was to reserve 50 percent of the openings in these programs for blacks until the percentage of black craftworkers in the Kaiser workforce came up to the percentage of blacks in the local labor force. In the first year, seven blacks and six whites were selected for the training program at one plant on the basis of seniority. However, the most senior black selected had less seniority than several white workers who had been rejected for the program, including Weber. Weber claimed reverse discrimination on the basis of race because he was rejected for the training program. The Court of Appeals affirmed the district court's finding of reverse discrimination in the affirmative action plan, and the Steelworkers union appealed to the Supreme Court.

Justice Brennan delivered the opinion of the Court.

Respondent [Weber] argues that Congress intended in Title VII to prohibit all race-conscious affirmative action plans. Respondent's argument rests upon a literal interpretation of §§703 (a) and (d) of the Act. Those sections make it unlawful to "discriminate . . . because of . . . race" in hiring and in the selection of apprentices for training programs.

Respondent's argument is not without force. But it overlooks the significance of the fact that the Kaiser-USWA plan is an affirmative action plan voluntarily adopted by private parties to eliminate traditional patterns of racial segregation.

Congress' primary concern in enacting the prohibition against racial discrimination in Title VII of the Civil Rights Act of 1964 was with "the plight of the Negro in our economy." Before 1964, blacks were largely relegated to "unskilled and semi-skilled jobs." Because of automation the number of such jobs was rapidly decreasing.

As a consequence, "the relative position of the Negro worker [was] steadily worsening. In 1947 the nonwhite unemployment rate was only 64 percent higher than the white rate; in 1962 it was 124 percent higher."

Congress feared that the goals of the Civil Rights Act—the integration of blacks into the mainstream of American society—could not be achieved unless this trend were reversed.

Given this legislative history, we cannot agree with respondent that Congress intended to prohibit the private sector from taking effective steps to accomplish the goal that Congress designed Title VII to achieve. The very statutory words intended as a spur or catalyst to cause "employers and unions to self-examine and to self-evaluate their employment practices and to endeavor to eliminate, so far as possible, the last vestiges of an unfortunate and ignominious page in this country's history," cannot be interpreted as an absolute prohibition against all private, voluntary, race-conscious affirmative action efforts to hasten the elimination of such vestiges. Nothing contained in Title VII "shall be interpreted to *require* any employer . . . to grant preferential treatment . . . to any group because of the race . . . of such . . . group on account of" a *de facto* racial imbalance in the employer's work force. The section does *not* state that "nothing in Title VII shall be interpreted to permit" voluntary affirmative efforts to correct racial imbalances. The natural inference is that Congress chose not to forbid all voluntary race-conscious affirmative action.

We need not today define in detail the line of demarcation between permissible and impermissible affirmative action plans. It suffices to hold that the challenged Kaiser-USWA affirmative action plan falls on the permissible side of the line. The purposes of the plan mirror those of the statute. Both were designed to break down old patterns of racial segregation and hierarchy. Both were structured to "open employment opportunities for Negroes in occupations which have been traditionally closed to them."

At the same time, the plan does not unnecessarily trammel the interests of the white employees. The plan does not require the discharge of white workers and their replacement with new black hirees. Nor does the plan create an absolute bar to the advancement of white employees; half of those trained in the program will be white. Moreover, the plan is a temporary measure; it is not intended to maintain racial balance, but simply to eliminate a manifest racial imbalance. Preferential selection of craft trainees at the Gramercy plant will end as soon as the percentage of black skilled craftworkers in the Gramercy plant approximates the percentage of blacks in the local labor force.

Case Questions

1. What is the purpose of an affirmative action plan?
2. Compare and contrast the protections of the Civil Rights Act with the freedom of contract in light of the Supreme Court balancing.
3. How long must affirmative action plans persist?

Periodic review of an affirmative action plan that permits revisions to account for its success may be a redeeming feature. In *Johnson v. Transportation Agency, Santa Clara, California,*[10] the court held that plans should be limited to "attaining" racial balance but not intended to maintain permanent numerical quotas. Government- or court-sponsored plans may constitutionally employ racial classifications essential to remedy unlawful treatment of minorities. Plans should consider neutral alternative remedies and maintain the plan's flexibility by waiving quotas when no qualified minority candidates are available.

Minority set-asides are another device challenged as reverse discrimination. Such programs involve government quotas requiring that a certain minimum percentage of federal contracts or other valuable government privileges be reserved for minority groups. For example, a federal program that reserved at least 10 percent of subcontracts on certain federal construction projects for minority business enterprises was held constitutional.[11]

However, the future for set-aside programs is deteriorating. Some state government programs have been invalidated where race-neutral alternatives existed. The Federal Communication Commission (FCC) has a "multicultural" broadcast license program that gives preference to minority or women applicants for TV and radio broadcast licenses. The FCC's program is designed to promote diversity in programming, station ownership, and management to enhance viewers' rights. Although a 1990 decision supported the concept,[12] a 1992 decision invalidated a license granted in that program because preference was given to the applicants due to their gender.[13] In *Adarand Constructors, Inc. v. Pena*[14] a minority subcontractor set aside was judged by the strict

[10] *Johnson v. Transportation Agency,* Santa Clara, Calif., 480 U.S. 616 (1987).
[11] *Fullilove v. Klutznick,* 448 U.S. 448 (1980).
[12] *Metro Broadcasting, Inc. v. F.C.C.,* 110 S.Ct. 2997 (1990).
[13] *Lamprecht v. F.C.C.* 958 F.2d 382 (D.C. Cir. 1992).
[14] *Adarand Constructors, Inc. v. Pena,* 115 S.Ct. 2097 (1995).

scrutiny standard of equal protection, discussed in chapter 5. Some commentators argue this case may hasten the demise of affirmative action quotas because they can withstand strict scrutiny only when justified by expensive studies proving past discrimination by an industry or employer. The ruling creates a dilemma for federal contractors still required by Executive Order No. 11,246 to institute affirmative action. However, voluntary goals (not quotas) are probably still valid.[15] Nevertheless, some members of congress are seeking to repeal the Executive Order.

Ethical Dilemmas in Affirmative Action

ETHICAL DILEMMA

Another ethical issue has emerged from affirmative action programs. Some statutes and labor union contracts require hiring and promotion decisions to bring minority participation into balance with the overall population. Many opponents claim that these are quotas essentially requiring reverse discrimination. They are highly unpopular among some segments of the population. Is it ethical to correct the discriminatory abuses of many years in a short time span? Does affirmative action redress past wrongs, or does it unfairly treat the qualified applicants who are not selected?

Executive Order Program

Since the passage of the Civil Rights Act of 1964, several presidents have issued executive orders dealing with discrimination by the federal government or by private employers that contract with the federal government. Executive Order 11,246 requires that all contracts between the federal government and federal contractors include a provision prohibiting discrimination on the basis of race, color, creed, or national origin. More recently, executive orders have also prohibited age and sex discrimination. Federal contracts must also include a provision requiring nondiscriminatory hiring practices. If discriminatory practices are proved, federal contracts may be canceled or suspended and contractors declared ineligible for future contracts.

Executive Order 11,246 and 11,375 created the Office of Federal Contract Compliance Programs. This agency oversees the affirmative action programs required of most federal contractors. The larger federal contractors must develop affirmative action programs to remedy imbalances among protected classes in their workforce. Typically, a federal contractor must analyze its minority employee profile as compared to that of the workforce in general or of the population at large. To implement the affirmative action programs, federal contractors often establish goals and timetables for hiring from protected classes.

Local, state, and federal agencies issue bonds through Wall Street investment bankers. Many governments are demanding to see detailed profiles of minority and female participation in these firms' executive ranks before granting underwriting business to a firm. This may force Wall Street firms to dismantle the "glass ceiling," (artificial barrier to women's advancement) given the enormity of the government and municipal bond markets. Such practices complement the executive order programs by placing a similar market-based pressure on firms to avoid discrimination or else forgo lucrative government business.

---

[15] *Wygant v. Jackson Board of Education*, 476 U.S. 267 (1986).

FIGURE 20-4

Damage Caps under Civil Rights Act of 1991

Number of Employees	Upper Limit on Damages (Compensatory and Punitive)
0–14	No damages allowed
15–100	$ 50,000
101–200	100,000
201–500	200,000
over 500	300,000

Other Remedies

State statutes, court decisions, and other federal laws establish enforcement mechanisms to supplement EEOC enforcement, state agency enforcement, affirmative action programs, and the executive order program techniques just discussed. For example, the EEOC has negotiated court-approved *consent decrees* with employers charged with widespread discriminatory practices. The employer typically agrees to adopt new employment practices, often involving affirmative action plans. EEOC and state agency remedies include *reinstatement* for an individual dismissed or constructively discharged by the discrimination. *Back pay* (with interest) is often ordered to compensate for earnings lost by the individual while he or she was denied the job or promotion. Awards of *retroactive seniority* are also made from the time of the discrimination.

The *Civil Rights Act of 1991* authorized recovery of punitive damages for intentional, malicious, or reckless indifference to the discrimination laws. Claimants may also receive compensatory damages other than back pay, which can include future income losses, pain and suffering, mental anguish, and other noneconomic damages. However, punitive and compensatory damages are capped, or limited in dollar amount, in all but race discrimination suits. These caps are scaled according to the size of the discriminating employer's workforce, as indicated in Figure 20–4. Critics charge the damage caps were a political compromise that violate equal protection by discriminating in favor of race and against other protected classes.

The Civil Rights Act of 1991 changed other aspects of employment discrimination litigation. In disparate impact cases, the employer has the burden of proving that its employment practices are job related and have a business necessity when they have an unintended disparate impact. This reverses the Supreme Court's shift of the burden of proof in unintentional discrimination cases to the employee, as discussed earlier in the *Ward's Cove Packing* case. An employer's claim that a particular employment practice is a business necessity is not a defense to an intentional discrimination. The new law permits either party to demand a jury trial. The law also prohibits "test norming"—the adjustment of test scores or providing different test score cutoffs to favor a protected class.

International Enforcement Employment discrimination laws present particularly difficult international enforcement problems. Discrimination is closely tied with each nation's self-image, its culture, its view of "ethnic purity," any historical hostility towards its enemies, competition between its citizens and foreigners for jobs, and each sovereign's assertion of control over economic activity within its own borders. This raises several questions about whether a nation's discrimination laws should apply outside its borders. Generally, comity under international law prevents the extraterritorial reach of any nation's laws, including antidiscrimination laws, to the foreign operations of foreign firms. Of course, U.S. employment law applies to the domestic operations of domestic and foreign firms. This may pose problems as foreign firms establish U.S. facilities and insist on applying their tradition of confining the role of women or reserving upper-management positions for their own nationals. The Civil Rights Act of 1991 reversed a Supreme Court decision that had permited U.S. firms to discriminate against U.S. citizens in their foreign operations.[16] However, U.S. firms must comply with any foreign discrimination law even if it conflicts with U.S. law. International treaties are applying antidiscrimination laws in the European Union and in other nations.

International Perspectives on Employment Discrimination

International Perspective and Commentary

Few other nations show as much concern for equal employment opportunities as does the United States. Many observers cite cultural diversity and the varied immigrant ancestry as the driving force behind the economic and social successes of the United States. By contrast, many nations seek to remain "ethnically pure" by consciously resisting integration with other races or people of other national origins. For example, critics charge that the low-paying and undesirable jobs in Japan are relegated to immigrants from other Asian nations. Some sociologists have argued that the Japanese presume their economic success is due to their racial homogeneity.

Many other nations have similar discriminatory policies or practices. For example, Northern Ireland, a predominantly Protestant nation, still has no comprehensive prohibition against religious discrimination. Israel permits only Jews to vote in national elections. The Israeli Jewish clergy determines who is a Jew and, therefore, who can participate in their democracy. The role of women in Japan, in the Muslim world, and in most other nations is far more restricted than in the United States.

Although, many nations are now adopting antidiscrimination laws; these laws are generally rather ineffective and are poorly enforced. However, the European Union has adopted an equal pay policy that should soon permit freer movement of workers, licensed professionals, and the self-employed throughout the European Union. While it is difficult to attain and maintain diversity and equal opportunity without discrimination or bigotry, the United States arguably demonstrates the potential for ultimate success from such egalitarian policies. Worldwide, discrimination is changing, albeit rather slowly.

Summary

Equal opportunity laws are intended to prevent discrimination against protected individuals. The Equal Pay Act prohibits paying the sexes unequally for the performance of equal work. Employers establish accurate job descriptions that permit the comparison of work performed. Comparable worth theories would equalize the pay of different jobs with different tasks but with roughly equal responsibility and difficulty.

Title VII of the Civil Rights Act of 1964 prohibits employment discrimination in hiring, firing, promotion, and the terms of employment based on race, color, religion, national origin, sex, age, or disability. It prohibits disparate treatment—discriminatory policies that treat one group of employees or job applicants more favorably than a protected class. Disparate impact arises when apparently neutral

[16] See *EEOC v. Arabian American Oil Company*, 499 U.S. 244 (1991).

selection criteria have adverse effects on a protected class. Pattern or practice discrimination affects a whole protected class. These may be proved by statistical inferences from comparisons between the proportion of protected class members in the general population and those in the employer's workforce.

There are three exceptions that permit employers to legally discriminate against members of a protected class. First, discrimination is permitted if there is a bona fide occupational qualification, though race is never a BFOQ. Second, employers may discriminate on the basis of professionally developed aptitude tests if these are validated as accurate predictors of job performance. Third, employers may discriminate when a valid union contract imposes a seniority system for employees in a bargaining unit.

Sexual harassment is the unlawful requirement of requiring submission to sexual advances or the creation of a hostile sexual environment. Although sexual harassment is not specifically outlawed by Title VII, it is illegal to make submission to sexual advances a condition of employment. EEOC guidelines have separately outlawed sexual harassment. Employers may be held liable for not monitoring the activities of supervisors guilty of sexual harassment.

The EEOC is responsible for enforcement of the antidiscrimination laws through investigation, rulemaking, and adjudication. It requires extensive record keeping to facilitate such enforcement. Although most EEOC complaints are settled through conciliation, the EEOC or the victim may also sue in a federal court. In some cases, affirmative action programs are valid to achieve greater employment participation for protected classes that have historically suffered patterns of discrimination. Federal contractors may not discriminate and must implement affirmative action programs.

Critical Thinking Review Questions

1. What defenses are available to an employer under the Equal Pay Act? For what reasons are certain pay differentials permitted?
2. What is the proper comparison of racial composition in disparate impact cases?
3. When employees make out a prima facie case of disparate impact, what further inquiries become necessary?

Critical Thinking Exercises

1. Ace Airlines required an applicant for flight officer to have a college degree for employment. Joan Jones, a woman who did not have a college degree but was otherwise qualified for this position, applied for the position and was denied employment. She filed a complaint with the EEOC. At the hearing, Ace Airlines testified: "All flight officers undergo a rigorous training program on being hired and then are required to attend intensive refresher programs at six-month intervals in order to remain at peak performance ability. Possession of a college degree indicates that the applicant is able to understand and retain the concepts and information imparted in a classroom atmosphere and is more apt to cope with these programs than a person without a college degree." Will Joan win? Identify and discuss the issues that the court would probably consider.
2. Weeks, a woman, worked for the telephone company in Georgia for 19 years before requesting that she be given the job of switchman. She was told that women were not eligible for this job because it was strenuous and because it required employees be on 24-hour call. A Georgia statute prohibited women from employment that required the lifting of over 30 pounds. Weeks claimed that her employer had illegally discriminated on the basis of sex. The telephone company contended that sex was a BFOQ for the job. Analyze any violation of Title VII. *Weeks v. Southern Bell & Telegraph Co.,* 408 F.2d. 228 (1969).
3. The Los Angeles Department of Water and Power provided an employee retirement program in which benefits were funded by employer and employee contributions and computed on the basis of monthly salary and years of service. Because standard mortality tables showed that the average woman would live longer and thus receive more benefits than the average man, female employees were required to make monthly contributions that were almost 15 percent higher than the contributions of male employees. Manhart, a female em-

ployee, filed a class action suit alleging that this differential contribution requirement constituted sex discrimination in violation of Title VII of the 1964 Civil Rights Act. Analyze the problem, discuss the presumptions, and give reasons for the outcome. *Los Angeles Department of Water and Power v. Manhart,* 435 U.S. 702 (1978).

4. Discuss how the following fact situations present a legal problem.
   a. X company is laying off employees, starting with the employees who have least seniority. The first group to be laid off consists of 25 white women and 15 black men and women.
   b. A company refuses to hire male receptionists, maintaining that business callers, mostly male, want to see a "pretty face" in the reception area.
   c. X company has traditionally hired males to do its assembly-line work. The assembly-line positions include some jobs that require lifting and some that do not. Males are rotated between these jobs, all male assembly-line workers being on the same pay scale. The company has recently started to hire women for the assembly line, but they work only in nonlifting positions. For this reason, they are paid a lower wage scale than the men. The female assembly line workers sue.
5. Coburn was 43 years old and had worked for Pan Am for 17 years when he was discharged due to a reduction in the workforce caused by Pan Am's financial difficulties. The airline argued that, on the basis of a fair and nondiscriminatory evaluation process to assess productivity, it had concluded Coburn was the least productive employee in his peer group. Pan Am's policies with regard to the layoffs were formal and rigorous, and they were applied uniformly. Did Pan Am discriminate against Coburn on the basis of age? Identify the elements of an age discrimination case, and discuss their application here. Coburn v. Pan American World Airways, 711 F.2d 339 (1983).
6. Philbrook, a teacher, had religious beliefs that required him to miss six workdays each year. The Ansonia Board of Education allowed him to use three personal leave days, requiring him to take the other three days as unauthorized leave for which he received no pay but was not otherwise disciplined. The school board refused Philbrook's request to allow him to pay for a substitute teacher and not have his pay docked. Discuss the school's likely arguments that it fulfilled its duty to accommodate Philbrook's religious beliefs and Philbrook's likely response. *Ansonia Board of Education v. Philbrook,* 479 U.S. 60 (1986).
7. Ms. Rawlinson applied for a position as a correctional counselor in a male maximum security prison in Alabama. The Alabama Board of Corrections adopted a rule forbidding women to be employed in "contact" positions requiring close physical proximity to inmates. Rawlinson sued under Title VII. What will be the likely result and why? *Dothard v. Rawlinson,* 433 U.S. 321 (1977).
8. In 1983, the Richmond city council adopted an ordinance requiring that minority subcontractors (MBEs) receive 30 percent of the dollar amount of each city construction contract. MBEs were defined as businesses 51 percent owned or controlled by "blacks, Spanish-speaking [persons], Orientals, Indians, Eskimos or Aleuts." At public hearings on the proposed set-aside program, it was noted that although Richmond's population was 50 percent black, only .67 percent of the city's prime construction contracts had been won by minority firms during the previous five years. J. A. Croson Company, a mechanical plumbing and heating firm, attempted to bid on a project for urinals and water closets in the city jail. Despite efforts to find a minority subcontractor, Croson ultimately submitted a bid without minority participation, seeking a waiver of the set-aside requirement on the ground that no qualified minority subcontractor was available. A minority firm, however, tardily submitted a somewhat higher bid than Croson's. The city denied Croson's waiver request and resolved to rebid the project. Croson sued in federal court, claiming that the Richmond ordinance was unconstitutional on its face. What will be the likely result and why? *City of Richmond v. J. A. Croson,* 488 U.S. 469 (1989).
9. Supervisors may place their co-workers and subordinates in uncomfortable ethical dilemmas by attempting to cover up discriminatory bias in job decisions. This practice may be an unspoken expectation for those involved in evaluating candidates for new jobs or for promotion to conform their judgments to the supervisor's discriminatory bias. Is it ethical for such co-workers and subordinates to submit to these pressures or to alter their honest hiring/promotion evaluations and documents to substantiate the supervisor's false claim that hiring was nondiscriminatory? Discuss the ethical analysis and presumptions.

PART 8

Societal Powers Affecting Business

21 Environmental Law

22 The Social Responsibility of Business

CHAPTER

21

Environmental Law

Critical Thinking Questions

- What roles should local, state, federal, and international regulations play in protecting the environment?
- What assumption underlies the need for an environmental impact statement?
- Some federal and state lawmakers want to return to the states many powers now exercised by the federal government. What arguments would support granting to the federal Environmental Protection Agency dominant powers? What arguments would support placing most of the powers in the hands of state lawmakers and administrators?
- The Clean Air Act requires motor vehicle producers selling in California to have a certain percentage of their fleet cars meet very minimal air pollution standards. What are the reasons why the legal system should demand that producers meet tough standards in the future so as to promote technological changes? What arguments suggest the law should wait until the marketplace brings about those changes?
- What reasons support using a permit system for water pollution? What alternative methods for control exist?
- Which of the federal regulations seeking to protect the environment—air, water, land—are most effective? Why?

Introduction...Past, Present, Future

In the past, only nuisance, trespass, zoning, and land use laws sought to regulate actions affecting the environment. The dumping of solid, liquid, and gaseous products into streams and harbors, on land, and into the air was largely unregulated. Medical science was unaware of the effects on health of waste, pollution, and decaying products. Centuries ago, the London smog was in evidence when soft coal became a common fuel. Venice has encountered serious water and air pollution problems for centuries. For decades, the water from lakes and rivers near many cities throughout the world has been virtually undrinkable due to the wastes dumped into them by residents and business firms.

The first federal legislation aimed at water pollution was the River and Harbors Act of 1886. This act established a permit system for the discharge of such refuse as sewage, rubbish, or litter into navigable waters. Although it focused on items that could obstruct navigation in the nation's primary waterways, it also became a means for attacking some sources of water pollution.

Modern water pollution law originated in the 1948 Water Pollution Control Act, which sought to eliminate all discharges of pollutants into the nation's waterways. After the Act had been amended on several occasions, the Clean Water Act, a comprehensive plan for maintaining and restoring the quality of the nation's waterways, was adopted in 1972.

Environmental law now comprises pervasive federal regulation. The Clean Water Act, Clean Air Act, Superfund legislation, Solid Waste Disposal Act, and Toxic

Substances Control Act are recent statutory laws intended to address environmental problems. Yet environmental law seems ineffective. Billions of dollars can clean up only a few of the hundreds of sites that present critical environmental problems. The states charged with providing regional sites for hazardous waste disposal respond, Not in my backyard (NIMBY). Oil spills, illegal dumping, and acid rain all threaten the fragile ecosystem.

Recent global environmental tragedies include the oil spill from the *Exxon Valdez* tanker in Alaska, Iraq's deliberate spilling of oil in the Persian Gulf and setting ablaze oil wells in Kuwait during the Persian Gulf War, and the massive cutting of trees and clearing of land in the Brazilian rainforests. U.S. and Canadian lakes and streams have been polluted by acid rain resulting from power plant emissions. The potentially devastating consequences of the **greenhouse effect**, the warming of the lower atmosphere caused by emissions of carbon dioxide, are being studied. The depletion of the ozone layer, caused at least in part by the use of fluorocarbons, has led to state and federal regulation and international agreements mandating the gradual decrease of their use. However, some environmentalists claim that the existing efforts are too little, too late.

greenhouse effect
The warming of the earth's lower atmosphere caused by emissions of carbon dioxide; its specific causes and consequences are being studied.

Environmental law is increasingly important for business managers. Paper, glass, aluminum, and other recycled products often provide less expensive material costs. Monitoring pollution abatement activities and providing environmentally sensitive products helps enhance corporate goodwill. On the other hand, substantial penalties may be assessed, and a growing number of criminal actions are being brought against firm managers when intentional violations of environmental laws are discovered. Most of the major environmental laws contain criminal enforcement provisions, and a governmental crackdown on environmental crimes has begun. In the last decade, over 500 indictments have been brought by the environmental section of the Department of Justice.

The Environment and Legal Regulation

The environment consists of all of the surrounding physical conditions and influences that affect the development of living things. Environmental law regulates our interaction with the surrounding air, water, and land through limitations imposed by law. Despite the deregulation movement of the 1980s, public concern over the deteriorating environment is increasing, not decreasing. Serious environmental threats to human health have become too common and too dangerous to ignore. The laissez-faire attitude toward the use of the environment that prevailed throughout the first half of the 20th century led to the dumping of wastes in waterways, the burning of low-grade coal, and lead emissions from millions of cars. The role of law in protecting the environment is much more likely to increase than to decrease.

Mexico City's rapid urbanization has created some of the most acute pollution problems in the world. In Estonia, a republic of the former Soviet Union, the emissions from a cement factory descend from the air and cake village rooftops. The waste from the four million inhabitants of Athens, Greece, is dumped untreated into the Mediterranean Sea. Air pollution in some cities in the former East Germany has been measured at 50 times higher than national German standards. As China's cities continue to attract millions of farmers from the countryside, building projects increase, existing green space disappears, and air pollution from motor vehicles, residential coal fires, and small factories becomes almost unbearable.

The greenhouse effect and the depletion of the ozone layer are environmental concerns that affect the entire planet. Although pollution differs from region to region, its effects do not stop at state or national borders. Pollution problems and environmental regulations aimed at addressing them are neither merely national in scope nor totally recent in origin. Environmental laws clearly need to be coordinated and enforced internationally if they are to be effective. Nevertheless, in this chapter our emphasis is on environmental regulation in the United States. Dramatic changes have occurred in the last several decades and in many, but not all, respects, the scope of environmental protection in the United States is extensive compared to the protection elsewhere on the globe. The cornerstone of environmental regulation in the United States is the Environmental Policy Act.

The National Environmental Policy Act

The 1970 National Environmental Policy Act (NEPA) makes it federal policy to consider the environmental impact of various activities. It also establishes the Council of Environmental Quality, which gathers information on the environment, reviews and recommends changes in federal policies, and makes annual reports on environmental conditions. The purposes of NEPA include the following: to declare a national policy that will encourage productive and enjoyable harmony between humans and their environment, to promote efforts that will prevent or eliminate damage to the environment and the biosphere and stimulate the health and welfare of human beings, and to enrich our understanding of the ecological systems and national resources important to the nation.

The Environmental Protection Agency (EPA) was created in 1970 to coordinate the federal government's environmental policies. Congress recognized that the problems of air pollution, water pollution, and solid waste disposal were interrelated. Subsequent laws addressed control of pesticides, ocean dumping, and hazardous waste problems. The EPA is headquartered in Washington, D.C., but it also has 10 regional offices throughout the country. Although the EPA is the nation's primary federal environmental agency, the Nuclear Regulatory Commission (one of the litigants in the *Metro Edison* case, below) and the Department of Interior also have specific environmental responsibilities.

Environmental Impact Statements

The NEPA **environmental impact statements** are studies of the effects that certain proposed federally financed or approved projects will have on the environment. Such statements have to be prepared for major projects that are likely to have a significant effect on the quality of the human environment. When the federal government plans to build a dam or power plant, the appropriate federal agency must prepare an environmental impact statement. State roads or prisons built with federal funds also require the preparation of such a statement. Private companies that receive federal contracts or that are granted permits to cut timber or drill for oil on federal property may be required to assist in preparing environmental impact statements.

environmental impact statement
Studies of the effects that certain proposed federally financed or approved projects will have on the environment; the NEPA requires such statements be prepared for major projects that are likely to have a significant effect on the quality of the human environment.

The Content of an Environmental Impact Statement

A significant provision of NEPA requires the preparation of an environmental impact statement before any major federal action is taken that can significantly affect the quality of the human environment. Such a statement must contain the following information:

1. The environmental impact of the proposed action.
2. Any adverse environmental effect that can be avoided should the proposed action be implemented.
3. Alternatives to the proposed action.
4. The relationship between local short-term use of the environment and the maintenance and enhancement of long-term productivity.
5. Any irreversible and irretrievable commitments of resources that would be involved should the proposed action be implemented.

Environmental impact statements are submitted to the president and the Council on Environmental Quality and disclosed to the public. What concerns must be addressed in such statements? After an accident damaged a nuclear reactor at one of Metropolitan Edison's two nuclear power plants, both of the plants were shut down. The following case deals with an environmental impact statement that would be needed prior to starting up the other plant at the facility near Three Mile Island, Pennsylvania.

Metro Edison v. People Against Nuclear Energy

406 U.S. 766 (1983)
United States Supreme Court

Metropolitan Edison (Metro) owned two nuclear power plants at Three Mile Island, near Harrisburg, Pennsylvania. In March 1979, one of these plants, TMI-2, suffered a serious accident that damaged its nuclear reactor. After the accident, the Nuclear Regulatory Commission (NRC) ordered Metro to also keep TMI-1, the other plant, shut down until a determination was made as to whether it could be operated properly. The NRC then published a notice of a hearing regarding several safety-related issues. The notice stated that the NRC had not determined whether to consider psychological harm and other indirect effects of the accident in deciding whether to permit the renewed operation of TMI-1. People against Nuclear Energy (PANE) contended that restarting TMI-1 would cause severe psychological damage to persons in the area, but the NRC decided not to consider such evidence at its hearing. PANE argued that the National Environmental Protection Act required agencies to consider various effects on health in making a decision. Metro intervened on the side of the NRC. The court of appeals found for PANE, and Metro appealed to the Supreme Court.

Justice Rehnquist delivered the opinion of the Court.

The issue in these cases is whether petitioner Nuclear Regulatory Commission (NRC) complied with the National Environmental Policy Act of 1969 (NEPA), when it considered whether to permit petitioner Metropolitan Edison Co. to resume operation of the Three Mile Island nuclear power plant near Harrisburg, Pa. Both plants were licensed by the NRC after extensive proceedings, which included preparation of Environmental Impact Statements.

All the parties agree that effects on human health can be cognizable under NEPA, and that human health may include psychological health. The Court of Appeals concluded that these propositions were enough to complete a syllogism that disposes of the case: NEPA requires agencies to consider effects on health. An effect on psychological health is an effect on health. Therefore, NEPA requires agencies to consider the effects on psychological health asserted by PANE.

PANE, using similar reasoning, contends that because the psychological health damage to its members would be caused by a change in the environment (the renewed operation of TMI-1), NEPA requires the NRC to consider that damage. Although these arguments are appealing at first glance, we believe they skip over an essential step in the analysis. They do not consider the closeness of the relationship between the change in the environment and the "effect" at issue.

Section 102(C) of NEPA directs all federal agencies to "include in every recommendation or report on proposals for legislation and other major Federal actions significantly affecting the quality of the human environment, a detailed statement by the responsible official on—

"(i) the environmental impact of the proposed action, [and]

"(ii) any adverse environmental effects which cannot be avoided should the proposal be implemented. . . ."

To paraphrase the statutory language in light of the facts of this case, where an agency action significantly affects the quality of the human environment, the agency must evaluate the "environmental impact" and any unavoidable adverse environmental effects of the proposal. The theme of section 102 is sounded by the adjective "environmental": NEPA does not require the agency to assess every impact or effect of its proposed action, but only the impact or effect on the environment. We think the content of the statute shows that Congress was talking about the physical environment—the world around us, so to speak.

The statements of two principal sponsors of NEPA illustrate this point:

> "What is involved [in NEPA] is a congressional declaration that we do not intend, as a government or as a people, to initiate actions which endanger the continued existence or the health of mankind: That we will not intentionally initiate actions which do irreparable damage to the air, land and water which support life on earth." (remarks of Sen. Jackson). "We can now move forward to preserve and enhance our air, aquatic, and terrestrial environments . . . to carry out the policies and goals set forth in the bill to provide each citizen of this great country a healthful environment." (remarks of Rep. Dingell).

To determine whether section 102 requires consideration of a particular effect, we must look at the relationship between that effect and the change in the physical environment caused by the major federal action at issue. This requirement is like the familiar doctrine of proximate cause from tort law. The issue before us, then, is how to give content to this requirement. This is a question of first impression in this Court. The federal action that affects the environment in this case is permitting renewed operation of TMI-1. The direct effects on the environment of this action include release of low-level radiation, increased fog in the Harrisburg area (caused by operation of the plant's cooling towers), and the release of warm water into the Susquehanna River. The NRC has considered each of these effects. Another effect of renewed operation is a risk of a nuclear accident. The NRC has also considered this effect.

PANE argues that the psychological health damage it alleges "will flow directly from the risk of [a nuclear] accident." But a risk of an accident is not an effect on the physical environment. A risk is, by definition, unrealized in the physical world. In a causal chain from renewed operation of TMI-1 to psychological health damage, the element of risk and its perception by PANE's members are necessary middle links. We believe that the element of risk lengthens the causal chain beyond the reach of NEPA.

For these reasons, we hold that the NRC need not consider PANE's contentions.

Case Questions

1. What assumption did PANE make in its argument that the NRC was required to consider PANE's evidence? Why did the court reach a contrary finding?

2. Did the NRC have to assess the possible damages caused by the risk of nuclear accident when considering the restarting of TMI-1?

Environmental Compliance Audits

environmental auditing A systematic, documented, periodic, and objective review by regulated entities of facility operations and practices related to meeting environmental regulations.

As business firms may face significant penalties and possible criminal punishment for not complying with environmental regulations, many firms today are using environmental risk audits to better understand the risks presented by environmental laws for their facilities. The Environmental Protection Agency defines **environmental auditing** as a systematic, documented, periodic, and objective review by regulated entities of facility operations and practices related to meeting environmental regulations.

Audits can be designed to evaluate a facility for compliance with national, state, and local laws and regulations as well as company policies and appropriate environmental operating procedures. Usually, such audits are performed by attorneys, consultants, and company personnel. Attorneys are involved so that, where possible, attorney–client privileges may be used to protect environmental auditing documents created in the audit. Currently, five states have passed environmental audit privilege legislation: Colorado, Illinois, Indiana, Kentucky, and Oregon. Similar legislation is pending in a number of states. Consultants and company personnel bring engineering and company-specific information and expertise to the audit team.

Environmental risk audits are performed for a variety of reasons including the following:

- Audits can provide data to managers charged with prioritizing investments among environmental projects.
- Early discovery of violations or risky practices can minimize the cost of responding or the likelihood of incurring liability.
- Voluntary discovery and correction can minimize or eliminate enforcement actions and possible criminal sanctions.
- Compliance audits may meet disclosure requirements of the Securities and Exchange Commission and of insurance company mandates.

The requirements for an effective environmental vary with the activities of the facilities being audited. Nevertheless, an effective audit usually contains the elements depicted in Figure 21–1.

Air Pollution

The first federal statute dealing with air pollution was passed in 1955. The Clean Air Act was passed in 1963 and amended in 1970, 1977, and most recently in 1990. That act requires the EPA to set **national ambient air** (atmospheric air as opposed to air

FIGURE 21-1

Elements of an Effective Environmental Compliance Audit

Element	Comment
1. Top management support	A written policy articulating support for the audit and compliance with all regulations is vital. Follow-up comments should also be distributed in the firm.
2. Independence of audit	There should be no conflict of interest, and auditors should be free from interference or possible retribution.
3. Adequately trained auditors	Audits should have appropriate knowledge and skill and should demonstrate currency in technical and analytical components.
4. Clear objectives and adequate resources	Compliance with all regulations and evaluation of company policies, practices, and training should be clear objectives.
5. Process for collection, analysis, and interpretation of data	Information should be sufficient, reliable, relevant, and useful to provide a basis for audit findings and recommendations.
6. Process to report on findings and to correct problems	Reports should be sent within firm to persons responsible for follow-up activities and externally to appropriate regulators.

Source: This chart is based on an article by Robert Zayro, "Compliance Audits Can Limit a Facility's Environmental Risk," *Michigan Lawyer's Weekly*, March 27, 1995, p. 44.

inside buildings) **quality standards (NAAQS)** for such pollutants as carbon monoxide, hydrocarbons, lead, nitrogen oxide, ozone, and sulfur dioxide. Each state was required to develop a **state implementation plan (SIP)** to demonstrate how it would achieve a level of air pollution below the maximum level specified by EPA standards. States also were required to inform the EPA about the methods they would use to achieve the standards for each industrial plant and meet the attainment dates. If a state's plan was found to be inadequate, the EPA had authority to withhold federal funds, halt construction of new sources of air pollution, or take steps to implement alternative plans.

The EPA controls both mobile and stationary sources of pollution. Mobile sources of pollution account for over 50 percent of the air pollution in the United States. Motor vehicles are subject to emission and fuel standards established by the EPA. The use of unleaded gasoline has diminished the amount of lead in the air. Manufacturers' installation of pollution control devices has lessened the emission of carbon monoxide and hydrocarbons (a source of smog) from cars, trucks, and buses. Stationary sources of pollution, such as industrial plants, are more difficult to control. Heavily industrialized areas have been unable to attain air quality standards set by the EPA.

national ambient air quality standards (NAAQS) EPA standards required by the Clean Air Act establishing maximum levels in the air of such pollutants as carbon monoxide, hydrocarbons, lead, nitrogen oxide, ozone, and sulfur dioxide.

state implementation plan (SIP) A state's plan as to how it will achieve a level of air pollution below the maximum level specified by EPA standards.

The Pre-1990 Clean Air Act

At first, the Clean Air Act prohibited new plants or modifications to existing ones in **nonattainment areas**—areas not meeting the EPA standards. Strict enforcement could have halted new construction in practically all industrial areas. The 1977 amendments allowed new construction or modification if state permits were first

nonattainment areas Geographic areas not meeting the EPA NAAQS standards.

best available technology Standard for pollution-controlling devices used in industrial plants constructed in areas with air that met the national ambient air quality standards.

emissions offset policy The policy that allows the construction of a plant with pollution emissions in an area that does not meet the NAAQS when there is a more than equal reduction in the emission from other plants in that area.

bubble concept The concept that allows states to treat all pollution-producing devices within a plant as a single unit—as if they were all under one bubble. A new plant that fails to meet standards could be permitted if the total pollutants under the bubble do meet the standard.

obtained. The permit requirements varied depending on the air quality in the area of the proposed addition or change.

New construction in areas with clean air—air of better quality than that specified by the national standards—could be undertaken as long as the resulting increase in pollutants did not cause these areas to exceed the allowable maximum. New industrial plants in these areas were required to install the **best available technology.** In areas with more air pollution than the national standards allowed, firms wishing to construct new facilities were required to meet stricter standards.

Pollution Control Standards in Polluted Areas

1. The facility must use technology designed to obtain the lowest achievable emissions rate.
2. The firm must prove that all of the other major sources of pollution within the state that are under the firm's control meet the state implementation plan (SIP).
3. The increased emissions from the new facility may not exceed the allowance for growth identified in the SIP, or, alternatively, there must be a more than equal reduction in the emission of similar pollutants from other plants in that area. The second option is known as the **emissions offset policy.**

In 1981, the EPA regulations permitted the states to adopt a plantwide definition of the term *stationary source of pollutants*. Thus, even if individual machines or emission points within a plant failed to meet the established standards, a firm could meet permit requirements if the total pollutants emitted from the plant did not increase. This **bubble concept** treats all of the pollution-producing devices within a plant as a single unit—as if they were all under one bubble. Industry favors expansion of the bubble concept to permit the combining of numerous facilities and communities. Is the bubble concept consistent with the National Environmental Protection Act? The next case established the bubble concept as a precedent in determining a "stationary source."

Chevron, USA, Inc. v. Natural Resources Defense Council, Inc.

467 U.S. 837 (1984)
United States Supreme Court

In 1977, Congress passed amendments to the Clean Air Act that required the states to address stationary sources of air pollution. Under the act, the Environmental Protection Agency (EPA) was to establish modified standards with regard to air pollution from stationary sources that the states had to meet. The EPA's standards allowed the states to treat all air pollution-emitting devices within the same industrial grouping as a single "source." The EPA published a regulation containing the plantwide definition, referred to as the *bubble concept*. The Natural Resources Defense Council filed a petition in the court of appeals for a review of that rule, and the court of appeals set aside the EPA rule. Chevron had an industrial plant that would be adversely affected if the proposed rule was not adopted, so it appealed to the Supreme Court.

Justice Stevens delivered the opinion of the Court.

The question presented by this case is whether EPA's decision to allow States to treat all of the pollution-emitting devices within the same industrial grouping as though they were encased within a single "bubble" is based on a reasonable construction of the statutory term "stationary source."

Section 109 of the 1970 Amendments directed the EPA to promulgate National Ambient Air Quality Standards (NAAQS's), and section 110 directed the States to develop plants (SIP's) to implement the standards within specified deadlines. In addition, section 111 provided that major new sources of pollution would be required to conform to technology-based performance standards. Section 111(e) prohibited the operation of any new source in violation of performance standards.

Section 111(a) defined the terms to be used in setting and enforcing standards of performance for new stationary sources. It provided: "For purposes of this section: (3) The term 'stationary source' means any building, structure, facility, or installation which emits or may emit any air pollutant."

Nonattainment

The 1970 legislation provided for the attainment of primary NAAQS's by 1975. In many areas of the country, particularly the most industrialized states, the statutory goals were not attained. The Clean Air Act Amendments of 1977 were a lengthy, detailed, technical, complex, and comprehensive response to a major social issue. A small portion of the statute expressly deals with nonattainment areas. Most significantly for our purposes, the statute provided that each plan shall: "(6) require permits for the construction and operation of new or modified major stationary sources."

The 1977 Amendments contain no specific reference to the "bubble concept." Nor do they contain a specific definition of the term "stationary source," though they did not disturb the definition of "stationary source" contained in section 111(a)(3) of the Act. Significantly, the EPA expressly noted that the word "source" might be given a plantwide definition for some purposes and a narrower definition for other purposes. In 1981 a new administration took office and initiated a "Government-wide reexamination of regulatory burdens and complexities." The EPA concluded that the term should be given the same definition in both nonattainment and PSD (Preventing Significant Deterioration) areas.

Statutory Language

The definition of the term *stationary source* in section 111(a)(3) refers to "any building, structure, facility, or installation" which emits air pollution. The definition in section 302(j) sheds virtually no light on the meaning of term "stationary source."

The meaning of a word must be ascertained in the context of achieving particular objectives, and the words associated with it may indicate that the true meaning of the series is to convey a common idea. The language may reasonably be interpreted to impose the requirement on any discrete, but integrated, operation which pollutes. This gives meaning to all of the terms—a single building, not part of a larger operation, would be covered if it emits more than 100 tons of pollution, as would any facility, structure, or installation. Indeed, the language itself implies a bubble concept of sorts: each enumerated item would seem to be treated as if it were encased in a bubble.

In this case, the Administrator's interpretation represents a reasonable accommodation of manifestly competing interests and is entitled to deference: the regulatory scheme is technical and complex, the agency considered the matter in a detailed and reasoned fashion, and the decision involves reconciling conflicting policies. We hold that the EPA's definition of the term "source" is a permissible construction of the statute which seeks to accommodate progress in reducing air pollution with economic growth. The Judgment of the Court of Appeals is reversed.

Case Questions

1. What did the 1977 amendments to the Clean Air Act require the states to do regarding stationary sources of pollution?
2. What did these amendments say regarding the term *stationary source of pollution?*
3. What reasons does the Court give for supporting the administrative agency's interpretation of the legislative language?

The 1990 Amendments to the Clean Air Act

Reduction of Ozone and Carbon Dioxide (SMOG) The 1990 Amendments to the Clean Air Act impose additional requirements for the nation's urban areas that were not in compliance with the standards for ozone and carbon monoxide. Ninety-six cities were given deadlines for meeting the federal standards. Those classified as having marginal or moderate problems have until 1996 to meet the federal standards. Areas that are worse than moderate must reduce their smog by 15 percent by 1996. The goal is that all but nine areas meet the standards before the year 2000. Figure 21–2 depicts the target cities.

FIGURE 21-2 Target Cities of the Clean Air Act

A total of 96 cities and communities with the worst ozone smog problems have been targeted to meet stricter federal standards.

- Cities with marginal problems that were to meet the standards by November 1993:

Albany, NY
Allentown, PA, nearby NJ
Altoona, PA
Birmingham, AL
Buffalo, NY
Canton, OH
Columbus, OH
Erie, PA
Essex County, NY
Evansville, IN, nearby KY
Fayetteville, NC
Greenbrier County, WV
Greenville-Spartanburg, SC
Hancock County, ME
Harrisburg, PA
Indianapolis, IN
Johnson City-Kingsport-Bristol, TN
Johnstown, PA
Kansas City, KS
Kansas City, MO
Knoxville, TN
Lake Charles, LA
Lancaster, PA
Lewiston, ME
Lexington, KY
Lincoln County, ME
Manchester, NH
Montgomery, AL
Norfolk, VA
Owensboro, KY
Paducah, KY
Poughkeepsie, NY
Scranton, PA
South Bend, IN
Stockton, CA
Sussex County, DE
Tampa, FL
Waldo County, ME
York, PA
Youngstown, OH-Sharon, PA

- Cities with moderate problems that must meet the standards by November 1996:

Atlantic City, NJ
Bowling Green, KY
Charleston, WV
Charlotte, NC, nearby SC
Cincinnati, nearby KY and IN
Cleveland
Dallas
Dayton-Springfield, OH
Detroit, MI
Grand Rapids, MI
Greensboro, NC
Jefferson County, NY
Kewaunee County, WI
Knox County, ME
Louisville, KY, nearby IN
Memphis, TN, nearby AR and MS
Miami, FL
Modesto, CA
Nashville, TN
Pittsburgh, PA
Portland, ME
Raleigh-Durham, NC
Reading, PA
Richmond, VA
Salt Lake City
San Francisco-Oakland-San Jose
Santa Barbara, CA
Smyth County, VA
St. Louis, nearby IL
Toledo, OH
Visalia, CA
Worcester, MA

- Cities with serious problems that must meet the standards by November 1999:

Atlanta, GA
Bakersfield, CA
Baton Rouge, LA
Beaumont, TX
Boston, nearby NH
El Paso, TX
Fresno, CA
Hartford, CT
Huntington, WV, nearby KY and OH
Parkersburg, WV, nearby OH
Portsmouth, NH, nearby ME
Providence, RI
Sacramento, CA
Sheboygan, WI
Springfield, MA
Washington, nearby MD and VA

- Cities with severe problems that must meet the standards by November 2005:

*Baltimore, MD
Chicago, nearby IN and WI
Houston
Milwaukee
Muskegon, MI
*New York, nearby NJ and CT
San Diego
Philadelphia, nearby NJ, DE, and MD

*These cities have until 2007 to meet the standards.

- The city with extreme problems that must meet the standards by November 2010:

Los Angeles

Acid Rain The 1990 Amendments also addressed the acid rain problem for the first time. The emission of sulfur dioxide from over 100 power plants in 21 states must be reduced by 5 million tons by 1995. (A two-year extension is possible in some cases.) Further reductions must be accomplished by the year 2000. The use of the bubble concept led to the introduction of a market-based trading system to reduce pollution without unduly burdening businesses. Under the **smog swapping system,** companies whose emissions are cleaner than the levels allowed by law are able to sell their credits to emit sulfur dioxide to other companies who are having difficulty meeting the standards. For every 1.2 pounds of pollution eliminated by the selling company, the program allows the creation of one pound of pollution by the purchasing company. Any trading of credits must be approved by the Environmental Protection Agency.

smog swapping system The system permitting companies whose emissions are cleaner than the levels allowed by law to sell their credits to emit sulfur dioxide to other companies who are having difficulty meeting the standards.

Businesses argue that the market-based trading of pollution credits will work to reduce pollution. Critics contend a system that allows companies to purchase the right to pollute the environment is unethical. Despite some criticism, the market-based trading of pollution credits is becoming institutionalized. The Chicago Board of Trade is planning to offer future contracts on pollution credits. Companies buying credits could ensure that they will continue to have the right to emit pollution in the future.

Toxic Emissions Toxic air pollution is also significantly affected. While the pre-1990 law identified and regulated only seven chemicals, the current law provides that firms that emit 189 chemicals must use their best technology to reduce emissions by 90 percent before the end of the decade.

Alternative Fuels Finally, the most striking legacy of the 1990 Clean Air Amendments will probably be the use of alternative fuels. The law requires that by 1998 fleets of 10 or more cars must run 80 percent cleaner than 1990 autos; trucks must be 50 percent cleaner. By the end of 1995, all gasoline in the nation's nine smoggiest cities will have to be cleaner burning, with 15 percent less hydrocarbons and toxic pollutants. Car manufacturers must produce at least 150,000 super-clean cars and light trucks a year, cars and trucks that run on methanol, electricity, or other alternative fuels. Although there are several current proposals to delay or alter these requirements, no modifying legislation has yet been enacted.

Another provision inserted into the 1990 Clean Air Amendments made it unlawful to tamper with existing devices on automobile exhaust systems that were installed to reduce the emission of carbon monoxide and hydrocarbons. In the case that follows, several arguments are presented by the muffler center that was sued by the EPA. Note that the law provides for a fine of up to $2,500 per violation. Do you think such a fine is too stiff?

United States of America v. Economy Muffler & Tire Center, Inc.

762 F. Supp. 1242
United States District Court (Va. 1991)

Economy Muffler operates an automobile repair shop in Richmond, Virginia, that routinely services motor vehicle exhaust systems. On 32 occasions during the past five years, Economy Muffler service personnel replaced three-way catalytic converters with two-way catalytic converters on a total of 51 motor vehicles. Motor vehicles with two-way converters got better gas mileage than did those equipped with three-way converters.

Two-way catalytic converters contain platinum and palladium, chemical substances that reduce the emissions of carbon monoxide and hydrocarbons. Three-way catalytic converters also contain rhodium, a chemical substance that reduces the emissions of nitrogen oxides. Since the early 1980s, most passenger cars sold in the United States have been equipped with three-way converters, in accordance with Environmental Protection Agency (EPA) emission control standards.

Economy Muffler representatives regularly received and signed certificates, also known as "statement forms," labeled "Notice[s] to Professional Installers." The statement forms contained the following excerpt from the Section 203(a)(3)(B) enforcement policy published by the EPA on August 5, 1986:

> In order not to be considered a violation of Section 203(a)(3) of the Clean Air Act, the converter must be the same type of converter as the original (i.e. oxidation, three-way, or three-way plus oxidation) and be the proper converter for the vehicle application as determined and specified by the Catalog.

The United States sued Economy Muffler, charging violations of Section 203(a)(3)(B) of the Clean Air Act of 1990, and seeking penalties of up to $2,500 for each violation. The trial court's decision follows.

Williams, District Judge

Section 203(a)(3)(B) of the Clean Air Act of 1990, known as "the tampering provision," prohibits "any person engaged in the business of repairing [or] servicing . . . motor vehicles" from "knowingly . . . removing or render[ing] inoperative any device or element of design installed on or in a motor vehicle . . . in compliance with regulations under this title." In *United States v. Haney Chevrolet, Inc.*, (1974), a Florida District Court held that a service manager violated Section 203(a)(3)(B) by removing an automobile's original carburetor and accompanying idle speed solenoid and installing a new carburetor without the idle speed solenoid. The Court reasoned that the transmission control spark system and the idle speed solenoid are emission control devices or elements of design within the meaning of the statute. The replacing of the original carburetor with a different carburetor that lacked the idle speed solenoid rendered the solenoid inoperative.

The same reasoning is applicable here. Three-way catalytic converters contain rhodium, a "device" or "element of design" without which a motor vehicle's exhaust system cannot reduce emissions of nitrogen oxide. Replacing a three-way converter with a two-way converter effectively removes rhodium or renders it inoperative and is therefore subject to civil penalties under the Clean Air Act.

The legislative history of the Act suggests that Congress intended the statute to be interpreted in this manner. The Senate Report explains that the provision does not prohibit the use of aftermarket parts "except where the use of such parts or the service performed would adversely affect the emission control system of the vehicle." Installing a two-way converter in place of a three-way converter adversely affects a vehicle's emission control system by destroying its capacity to prevent the harmful emission of nitrogen oxides.

The EPA has consistently interpreted the statute to bar the replacement of three-way catalytic converters with two-way catalytic converters. The tampering enforcement policy published by the EPA on August 6, 1986, and reproduced on statement forms distributed to repair shops specifically requires that a replacement converter "be the same type of converter as the original." As the agency responsible for Clean Air Act enforcement, the EPA's interpretation of the statute is entitled to "considerable deference."

Defendant argues that the tampering policy imposes a new set of legal obligations not contained in the statute and, for this reason, should have been enacted or promulgated as regulations in accordance with the

Administrative Procedure Act's notice and comment rulemaking requirements. The defendant's characterization of the EPA enforcement policy is inaccurate. The tampering enforcement policy falls under Administrative Procedure Act Section 553(b)(3)(A), which exempts interpretive rules, general statements of policy, and rules of agency organization, *procedure*, and practice from the APA's rulemaking requirements.

Economy Muffler also claims that its employees did not knowingly violate the Clean Air Act because they were not aware of the Act's requirements with respect to converters. In adopting the 1977 amendments to the Clean Air Act, the House Committee on Interstate and Foreign Commerce endorsed the construction of the term "knowingly," given by the Federal District Court in *United States v. Haney Chevrolet, Inc.* The Court in Haney accepted the well-settled view that "an act is done knowingly when it is done voluntarily or intentionally, and not by mistake." The term "knowingly" modifies the verbs "remove" and "render" and applies not to the law but to the offensive act. Both the United States Supreme Court and the Fourth Circuit Court of Appeals have established that the inclusion of the term "knowingly" in an environmental statute does not "carve out an exception to the general rule that ignorance of the law is no excuse."

Finally, Economy Muffler challenges the statute as void for vagueness. In reviewing a business regulation for vagueness, "the principal inquiry is whether the law affords fair warning of what is proscribed." Fair warning is interpreted more loosely in the context of economic regulation because businesses, which face economic demands to plan behavior carefully, can be expected to consult relevant legislation in advance of action. The company president's claim that he and other employees were unaware of the legal requirements even though they had received and signed dozens of statement forms bearing the text of the enforcement policy strains credibility.

For these reasons, the defendant's motion for summary judgment is *denied* and the government's motion for partial summary judgment is *granted*.

Case Questions

1. Why does replacing a three-way converter with a two-way converter violate the Clean Air Act?
2. How did the EPA notify firms like Economy Muffler that replacing converters would violate the Clean Air Act?
3. What are the assumptions each party makes regarding the interpretation of the word "knowingly" in the statute? Do you agree with the court that the employees did knowingly violate the Act?

International Perspective and Commentary

Air Pollution Problems

Canadian government leaders have long sought to have more control over the acid rain that falls on Canada from the northeastern and midwestern United States. The 1990 Clean Air Amendments indicate that the United States has decided to take some action to address this regional problem.

Scientists claim that fires in the Amazon Basin caused by burning of the rainforest are destroying not just the region but perhaps the planet. The loss of trees and foliage also reduces the photosynthesis capacity to take in carbon dioxide. Approximately 7 percent of the carbon dioxides that are said to be responsible for global warming are spewed from the Amazon region.

At a 1990 London conference, almost 60 nations agreed to eliminate by the year 2000 the production of chlorofluorcarbons (CFCs) and other chemicals that damage the ozone layer. Data examined by some scientists in early 1992 suggest even that response may not be strong enough. There is evidence that the ozone layer is breaking up over the Arctic far faster than had been anticipated. Accordingly, many nations have pledged to eliminate CFCs by the end of 1995 instead of waiting until the year 2000.

International agreements are the only way to address some of these worldwide environmental problems. The environmental and international legal environment noted in Chapter 3 are likely to be increasingly intertwined in the coming years.

WATER POLLUTION

The Clean Water Act (CWA)

The Clean Water Act requires a permit before pollutants can be discharged into navigable waters from any point source, regardless of whether the discharge existed prior to the legislation. Criminal sanctions may be imposed if pollutants are discharged without a permit. Permits are required for any private or public source of discharge into navigable waters. A firm with a discharge permit must monitor its own performance regarding the discharge of pollutants and report the results to the state and the EPA. The states have the option of administering the permit program themselves or allowing the EPA to do so.

best practicable technology (BPT) The Clean Water Act standard that required plants initially to meet in installing water pollution control devices; factors such as the cost of the equipment, the amount of time required to install it, and the severity of the pollution were considered in determining whether a firm complied with this requirement.

best available technology economically achievable (BAT) The Clean Water Act's more stringent standard, which now requires firms to install the most effective water pollution control equipment available.

For both private and public organizations discharging pollutants into the nation's waters, the Clean Water Act establishes two standards: the **best practicable technology (BPT)** and the best available technology economically achievable (BAT). All plants were required to install water pollution control devices representing the best practicable pollution control technology by 1977. Such factors as the cost of the equipment, the amount of time required to install it, and the severity of the pollution were considered in determining whether a firm had complied with this requirement.

The Clean Water Act provided that a more stringent standard of **best available technology economically achievable** had to be met by 1987. Firms must now install the most effective water pollution control equipment available. Less effective alternatives are not acceptable even if they are significantly less expensive.

The Federal Water Pollution Control Act (FWPCA)

The FWPCA establishes minimum water quality standards, but it also allows the states to adopt more stringent standards. Once the EPA has approved such state standards, those standards must be met by all persons in the state that seek permits. Are the states free to consider any factors they choose in establishing more stringent state water quality standards? Consider the excerpt from the *Homestake Mining* case, which examined water quality standards established in South Dakota:

> The FWPCA states that "standards shall be established taking into consideration" the various factors listed. The applicable federal regulation states that "the State should take into consideration" the various factors. It must, therefore, be determined what the phrase "taking into consideration" requires. Nothing in the statute seems to indicate that the states must give equal weight to all the factors listed. The *Weyerhaeuser* case indicates that the amount of weight to give each individual factor is within the State's discretion.
>
> In *United States Steel Corporation v. Train*, the Court dealt with the issue of more stringent state standards. The Court held that the FWPCA was not designed to inhibit the states from adopting more stringent standards and in forcing industry to create more effective pollution control technology. Furthermore, the Court held that EPA has no authority to set aside or modify state standards which are more stringent than those mandated by the Act.
>
> The FWPCA clearly indicates that the states are to play a significant role in the reduction of water pollution. The statute itself and the case law make it clear that the states can adopt more stringent standards and can force technology. South Dakota was not required to consider economic and social factors, and thus its failure to do so does not invalidate its water quality standards. EPA's approval of those standards was not arbitrary and capricious or violative of the Act.[1]

[1] *Homestake Mining Co. v. U.S. Environmental Protection Agency*, 477 F. Supp. 1279 (S.D. 1979).

Ocean Dumping

The Marine Protection Research and Sanctuaries Act of 1972 is a U.S. law that establishes a permit system to regulate dumping of materials into the ocean. Internationally, over 60 countries have signed the 1990 London Dumping Convention. The signatory nations agreed to abide by a 1995 global ban on ocean dumping of industrial waste.

The March 1989 oil spill by the *Exxon Valdez* in the waters of Prince William Sound, Alaska, showed that neither Exxon nor the oil industry was prepared to respond to the emergency. The first cleanup barge did not reach the site until 14 hours after the oil spill and the oil eventually contaminated over 1,000 miles of shoreline. The Oil Pollution Act of 1990 was Congress's reaction. Administered by the Coast Guard, the act requires new oil tankers to have double hulls and compels tanker owner-operators to establish an oil pollution cleanup contingency plan. The Coast Guard must issue a certificate to a tanker owner-operator before oil is brought to the United States. The certificate will not be issued unless the tanker owner-operator proves it is fully insured to cover any liability.

Land Pollution

Pollution of the earth is caused by the disposal of toxic and nontoxic solid wastes. Millions of tons of solid wastes are generated each year and are disposed of in open dumps or landfills. Trash from residences and small businesses is usually taken by disposal companies to county or municipal landfills. However, some solid wastes are burned by the individuals or firms generating them. The largest portion of solid wastes comes from agricultural operations. The waste consists of chemical fertilizer residues, manure from farm animals and the leavings from crops, bushes and plants. Solid wastes generated by mining operations are another significant factor in land pollution. Solid waste disposal is not only a land pollution problem. Burning solid wastes contributes to air pollution, and dumping solid wastes in or near sources of water may contaminate waterways, lakes, and streams. Many sources of pollution fit into more than one pollution category.

Until very recently, the federal government gave less attention to solid waste disposal than to air and water pollution. Today, however, three federal statutes are concerned with land pollution: the Resource Conservation and Recovery Act (RCRA), the Toxic Substance Control Act (TSCA), and the Comprehensive Environmental Response, Compensation, and Liability Act (CERCLA) which was amended by the Superfund Amendments and Reauthorization Act (SARA).

Resource Conservation and Recovery Act (RCRA)

The Solid Waste Disposal Act This Act, enacted in 1965 and amended in 1970, sought to assist states and municipalities in addressing waste disposal problems. Grants from the federal government were made for waste disposal studies and for the construction of facilities that turn solid waste into energy. Several events occurring in the 1970s focused the attention of Congress on the need for more specific regulation of the use and disposal of certain types of wastes. For example, the land and water contamination caused by the improper disposal of chemical wastes in New York

State's Love Canal and by the improper disposal of an insecticide in Virginia received significant attention.

The Resource Conservation and Recovery Act In 1976, the Resource Conservation and Recovery Act (RCRA) amended the Solid Waste Disposal Act, creating a federal permit system. All businesses that use, transport, or store hazardous wastes are required to comply with its standards. **Hazardous wastes** are wastes that contribute significantly to a serious, irreversible illness or pose a hazard to human health when improperly managed. Firms that generate such wastes must keep records of their disposal. Hazardous wastes must be packaged and labeled. If they are transported off-site for disposal, a manifest must identify the nature and quantity of the wastes and the names of both the transporter and the firm receiving them. The transporter must make entries on the manifest and is responsible for intentional or accidental waste discharges occurring during transportation. Firms generating hazardous wastes must submit annual reports.

hazardous wastes Wastes that contribute significantly to a serious, irreversible illness or pose a hazard to human health when improperly managed.

Facilities for the disposal of hazardous wastes must have a permit. Such permits are issued only if certain performance standards are met. A disposal facility of this kind must sign the manifest it receives from the transporter of hazardous wastes and return the manifest to the generator of the wastes. Each disposal facility has an EPA identification number. Representative samples of the hazardous wastes must be analyzed before the wastes are stored or treated. EPA inspectors are authorized to enter the disposal facilities at reasonable times to conduct inspections or review records. Currently, less than half of the states have commercial dumps for hazardous waste. Although several of these states have attempted to limit out-of-state waste from being dumped at their facility, federal courts have consistently found such laws to interfere with the freedom of interstate commerce. Restrictions in Alabama, Ohio, and South Carolina have been struck down by courts in the last several years. For example, in a 1991 South Carolina case, the federal court of appeals judges wrote in their unanimous ruling, "The effect of every state designating particular limits and bars for out-of-state waste would be catastrophic. . . . Such barriers threaten national economic union."[2]

Hazardous and Solid Waste Amendments In 1984, the Hazardous and Solid Waste Amendments amended RCRA to increase the EPA's regulatory powers. Many small waste generators that were exempt from RCRA are now required to use the manifest system for tracking the use, transport, and disposal of hazardous wastes. The 1984 amendments also established a timetable for the gradual elimination of landfills as sites for the disposal of many hazardous substances. Beginning in 1987, existing landfills were required to use specific equipment to limit the harmful effects of leakage. A regulatory program for underground storage tanks was established, and the protection of groundwater is now being addressed by a national commission.

The scope of the 1984 amendments indicates the increasing concern with land pollution from hazardous waste disposal. How does an environmental concern covered by one statute affect environmental concerns covered by other statutes? Although the following case deals primarily with land pollution, it also deals with water pollution and public nuisances.

---

[2] See Milo Geyelin and Jeff Bailey, "Court Says South Carolina Can't Stop Waste Disposal There from Out of State," *The Wall Street Journal*, September 25, 1991, p. A16.

O'Leary v. Moyer's Landfill, Inc.

523 F. Supp. 642 (Pa. 1981)
United States District Court

The plaintiffs were citizens who claimed that the defendants' disposal practices included the addition of pollutants to U.S. waters in violation of the Clean Water Act and open dumping in violation of RCRA. They also sued under several state pollution control laws.

Pollack, District Judge

The complaint alleges the landfill's responsibility for: (1) the discharge of leachate (i.e., contaminated liquid) into nearby Skippack Creek; (2) the contamination of water used by the landfill's neighbors for drinking and other purposes; (3) the release of mal odors and loose trash; and (4) the illegal inclusion of toxic wastes among the waste materials accepted for disposal.

Plaintiffs' claims under the Clean Water Act and RCRA are brought under the "citizen suit" provisions contained in each statute. Plaintiffs' claims under RCRA are brought under both the "hazardous waste" and the "solid waste" provisions. The complaint seeks declaratory judgment and enforcement of RCRA's requirement that notification be given to EPA of the storage or disposal of hazardous waste and enforcement of the proscription of "open dumping" of solid waste.

This [Clean Water] Act prohibits the unlicensed discharge of any pollutant. The definitions define an "open dump" as a facility that does not comply with the requirements there set forth. My determination of point source pollution also leads to a finding that RCRA has been violated.

The hazardous waste provisions of RCRA require any operator of a site for the storage or disposal of hazardous waste to give notice of the activity to EPA or the state before undertaking the activity. Hazardous wastes include the carcinogens found to be escaping in the landfill's leachate (the solution that results when soluble waste is dissolved). Indeed, leachate from hazardous waste is an important target of RCRA. And the regulatory definition of a "discarded" waste, which in turn includes materials "disposed of," points directly to contaminated leachate.

A material is "disposed of" if it is discharged, deposited, injected, dumped, spilled, leaked, or placed into or on any land or water so that such material or any constituent thereof may enter the environment or be emitted into the air or discharged into ground or surface waters. The evidence of toxic chemicals in leachate from Moyer's Landfill is compelling evidence that those chemicals were "discarded" at the landfill.

However, defendants accurately note that such chemicals, even if discarded, are not "hazardous" unless the chemicals were "commercial chemical product" or "off specification" commercial product. These categories encompass the commercially pure grade of the chemical, any technical grades of the chemical that are produced or marketed, and all formulations in which the chemical is the sole active ingredient.

It is fairly clear from EPA's comments to the regulations that the limitation to commercial product was meant to exclude materials that simply contained such a chemical but which were not themselves the product. Plaintiffs adduced no evidence that the discarded toxic chemicals were materials disposed of in their commercial form rather than, for example, materials which were the residue of other waste. Accordingly, I cannot conclude that the landfill is a noncomplying hazardous waste site.

[Discussion of the violation of the Clean Water Act is omitted.]

The findings underlying my conclusion that pollutants have been discharged into the waters of the United States under the Clean Water Act also lead me to conclude the pollutants have been discharged into Commonwealth waters, which include "any and all rivers, streams, creeks . . . " within this state. Accordingly, I find the defendants have violated the Pennsylvania Clean Streams Act.

Plaintiffs have advanced other claims under the state statutes, which declare a violation of their provisions to be a "public nuisance." Public nuisances may be civilly prosecuted by private plaintiffs only if these plaintiffs allege and prove specific injury "over and above the injury suffered by the public generally." A private nuisance may be abated when the plaintiff's use and enjoyment of his land are substantially diminished by defendant. While plaintiffs have urged findings of both public and private nuisance, there is insufficient evidence showing significant contamination of plaintiffs' drinking water, and there is virtually no evidence showing that the existing contamination of drinking water is a result of the landfill operations.

I have concluded that defendants are in violation of the Clean Water Act and the open dumping provisions of the Resource Conservation and Recovery Act. The accompanying Order (1) declares the defendants to be in violation of the Clean Water Act and the Resource Conservation and Recovery Act; (2) directs defendants forthwith to repair all damaged elements of the existing leachate collection system; and (3) directs the parties, after consultation with EPA and DER, promptly to submit a proposed further Order outlining the long-range steps defendants will be required to take to halt all leachate leakage from the landfill at the earliest possible date.

Case Questions

1. What was the basis for the court's finding that the defendants had violated the federal Clean Water Act?
2. What was the basis for the court's finding that the defendants had not violated the hazardous waste provisions of the RCRA?

The Toxic Substances Control Act

Congress enacted the Toxic Substances Control Act in 1976 to identify, test, and control chemicals that were believed to pose an unreasonable risk of injury to health or the environment. Many chemicals that are manufactured for useful purposes, such as dioxins, PCBs, and Agent Orange, pose grave dangers to human health and to the environment for years after they have been discarded. Initially, the EPA was charged with developing a comprehensive list of all manufactured chemicals, including thousands of chemicals used in industry and agriculture.

The Toxic Substances Control Act requires manufacturers to test toxic chemicals. The EPA can halt the manufacture of high-risk substances and can issue regulations concerning the manufacture, distribution, commercial use, or disposal of toxic chemical substances.

Pesticides The Toxic Substances Control Act does not cover pesticides because these are regulated under the Federal Insecticide, Fungicide, and Rodenticide Act (FIFRA). This federal law regulates the sale and use of chemicals intended to be used as pesticides and herbicides.

International Toxic Waste Over 100 nations have signed an international agreement on toxic waste exports. The international accord requires the government of any country exporting toxic waste to obtain written permission from the government of any country to which the waste is to be shipped. Both industrial and developing countries are concerned about toxic waste exports. The waste from industrial countries has often found its way to developing countries that have been willing to accept it in exchange for much-needed hard currency. Although developing countries may not have the technical know-how to safely dispose of the waste they accept, they realize it is dangerous. The treaty provides them with greater assurance that there will not be secret dumping of foreign waste in their territory.

The Comprehensive Environmental Response, Compensation, and Liability Act (CERCLA) and the Superfund Amendments and Reauthorization Act (SARA)

The Comprehensive Environmental Response, Compensation, and Liability Act (CERCLA) Until 1980, most of the environmental laws enacted by Congress were aimed at preventing future environmental problems. However, the CERCLA legislation was intended to regulate and identify hazardous sites. It also specified that responsible parties could be held liable. CERCLA also created a fund for the cleanup of hazardous waste disposal sites. The money for the fund is raised through taxes levied on manufacturers of certain dangerous chemicals.

Approximately $1.6 billion was used over a five-year period from 1980 to 1985, mostly for cleaning up hundreds of emergency oil and tank car spills. By the end of that period, less than 2 percent of the 679 sites on the national priority list had been cleaned up.

The Superfund Amendments and Reauthorization Act (SARA) In 1986, Congress provided an additional $8.5 billion for cleanup during the 1986–1990 period. In 1990, another $5.1 billion was authorized for 1990–1994. It is estimated that over the next 50 years more than $100 billion will be required to clean up waste sites.

An important aspect of the Superfund legislation is its compensation and liability provisions. Owners and operators of polluting facilities or vessels, as well as those who generate, treat, and dispose of hazardous waste, are held strictly liable for all cleanup costs. These costs include the government's response costs and the damage to natural resources. Owners who cooperate in cleanup and whose acts are not willfully negligent have limited liability. A due diligence defense exists if commercial developers run tests and examine EPA records and title documents to discover previous toxic dumping.

The imposition of liability on the "owner and operator" of polluted sites caused banks to severely limit their commercial real estate lending. After complaints from businesses that were affected by the "credit crunch" brought about by the Superfund liability provisions, the EPA made some modifications in the liability portions of the law.

The Superfund legislation does not make polluters liable for injuries to private persons, though such persons may bring private suits in state courts under common law rules. In addition, persons injured by hazardous waste may make a limited claim for compensation from the Superfund if the owner of the hazardous waste site is unknown.

The Right-to-Know Act Congress also amended the Superfund law in 1986 when it passed the Emergency Planning and Community Right-to-Know Act. The Act was passed in response to the chemical plant disaster in Bhopal, India, that resulted in over 3,000 deaths. The Act requires companies to notify the government if they release any extremely hazardous chemicals into the environment. Inventories of hazardous substances must be submitted to the government, and state and local planning to deal with emergencies is required.

Other Federal Environmental Concerns

Figure 21–3 depicts the major federal environmental laws, while several other federal environmental laws are noted in this section. Some states have laws providing compensation for hazardous waste victims. Other state and local environmental concerns are discussed in the final section of the chapter.

Two other environmental concerns that have been addressed by significant federal legislation are nuclear energy and wildlife preservation. In the early days of nuclear energy, the federal government had a monopoly on its use and would not allow its use for civilian purposes. More recently, the federal government's concerns with nuclear energy have focused on nuclear accidents and nuclear waste. Since wildlife is regarded as subject to federal regulation under the commerce clause, the state laws affecting wildlife are subject to preemption by federal laws. Some of the federal laws that seek to protect wildlife from both governmental and private interference are noted in this section.

FIGURE 21-3

Major Federal Environmental Laws

Act	Coverage
Clean Air Act (CAA)	Protects ambient (outdoor) air quality through national ambient air quality standards, state implementation plans, and controls on both stationary (point source) and moveable (automotive) sources.
Clean Water Act (CWA) and Federal Water Pollution Control Act (FWPCA)	Protects quality of surface water by setting water quality standards and limiting industrial and municipal discharges into those waters by a permit system.
Comprehensive Environmental Response Compensation and Liability Act (CERCLA)	Identifies and provides funding for cleanup of hazardous waste sites; imposes liability for cleanup on those who generate, treat, and dispose of hazardous waste.
Superfund Amendments and Reauthorization Act (SARA)	Establishes a superfund to clean up hazardous waste sites.
Marine Protection, Research, and Sanctuaries Act (MPRSA)	Regulates dumping of all materials into ocean waters.
Nuclear Waste Policy Act (NWPA)	Establishes a national plan for nuclear waste disposal.
Resource Conservation and Recovery Act (RCRA)	Establishes a regulatory system for the generation, transportation, and disposal of hazardous waste; also deals with solid waste problems.
Toxic Substance Control Act (TSCA)	Requires testing of toxic chemicals and provides for regulation of those chemicals that pose an unreasonable risk to health or the environment.

Nuclear Power and Nuclear Waste

Nuclear power is a controversial source of energy in the United States and, to a lesser extent, throughout the rest of the world. Although it has the potential for supplementing fossil sources of energy such as coal and oil, significant dangers are posed by the possibility of nuclear radiation, nuclear accidents, and terrorist acts against nuclear power plants. Nuclear power currently provides approximately 10 percent of the energy used in the United States, over 30 percent of the energy used in Japan and Great Britain, and close to 65 percent of the energy used in France.

The Regulation of Nuclear Power Plants Nuclear power has been heavily regulated by the federal government since the beginning of the atomic age during World War II (1941–1945). The Atomic Energy Act was amended in 1954 to authorize the Atomic Energy Commission (now the Nuclear Regulatory Commission) to license a variety of private, commercial uses for nuclear energy. In 1959, Congress permitted the states to establish restrictions regarding the location of nuclear power plants and the disposal of nuclear wastes. Under the Clean Air Act, the states may also establish limits for the emission of radioactive particles by nuclear power plants. Some states have such restrictive standards with regard to the use of nuclear power that nuclear power plants cannot be constructed in them.

Since the 1986 disaster at the Chernobyl, Russia, nuclear power facility, it has been clear that a nuclear accident can cause substantial damage and injury to thousands of people. Although the most disastrous consequences are felt by those close to the accident site, radiation in the atmosphere and in the food supply adversely affects the lives of millions of people in distant locations.

Regulation of Nuclear Waste The accumulation of nuclear wastes is a second concern associated with nuclear energy. Radioactive wastes are created as the fissions of uranium release energy in nuclear reactors. Since those wastes may take centuries to become harmless, the need for safe storage or disposal sites is critical. In 1982, Congress passed the Nuclear Waste Policy Act to establish a national plan for the disposal of highly radioactive nuclear wastes. The construction of several appropriate storage facilities was to begin in the 1990s. As communities targeted for the facilities have objected to their construction, no new facilities for nuclear waste have yet been constructed. It is intended that the cost of constructing and operating the facilities will be paid for by fees levied on nuclear energy generators.

Wildlife Protection

Numerous federal laws seek to protect wildlife. The most comprehensive of these laws is the Endangered Species Act. The Act, enforced by the Environmental Protection Agency and the Department of Commerce, protects endangered and threatened animal species. It prohibits the taking of any animal on the endangered species list. Harassing, harming, pursuing, hunting, shooting, trapping, collecting, and capturing are considered the taking of an animal. Federal projects must not adversely affect endangered species or their habitats. It is a federal offense to buy, sell, or possess any species listed as endangered or threatened or any product made from such a species. For example, the Endangered Species Act prohibits the sale or purchase of garments made from some furs or of products made from reptile skins.

The Migratory Bird Treaty Act, the Fishery Conservation and Management Act, and the Marine Mammal Protection Act are among the federal laws designed to protect wildlife. The states also enact laws to protect wildlife within their borders. The granting of state hunting and fishing permits is often dependent on the need to protect state fishing and gaming resources.

ETHICAL DILEMMA

Yew Trees—Environment versus Medicine

Sometimes protecting the environment isn't easy. Thirty thousand women in the United States struggle with ovarian cancer; 12,000 are likely to die of the disease this year. An experimental drug, taxol, has achieved a very good response rate in advanced ovarian cancer cases. But, taxol is derived from a rare Pacific yew tree. Because only a small amount of taxol is available from each tree, tens of thousands of the trees, which grow in old forests and provide refuge to some endangered wildlife, would have to be cut down to meet the demand for the drug. Conservationists oppose large-scale sacrificing of the trees, while medical researchers say the yew trees' taxol is the most promising chemotherapy to appear in a decade. How should we decide what action to take?

State and Local Concerns

State Environmental Protection Laws

Most states have detailed legislation that requires environmental impact statements regarding actions by state or local governments that will affect environmental quality. This legislation generally also requires private industrial and commercial firms to prepare such statements regarding actions of this kind on their part. Some states are addressing environmental concerns that are more appropriately handled on a state level. Solid waste bans for yard waste, mandatory use of recyclable materials, and higher limits for automobile emissions are among the proposals being addressed by the states. One example of an action brought under a state environmental law is provided in the case that follows.

West Michigan Environmental Action Council, Inc. v. Natural Resources Commission of the State of Michigan

275 N.W.2d 538 (1979)
Supreme Court of Michigan

The Michigan Department of Natural Resources (DNR)* sold oil and gas leases covering 500,000 acres of state land, including part of a state forest. After filing an environmental impact statement, the DNR permitted Shell Oil Company and several other oil companies

*While the Michigan Department of Natural Resources is governed by the Natural Resources Commission, this case treats the Commission and the DNR as one.

to drill exploratory wells in a portion of the state forest. The plaintiffs filed a complaint under the Michigan Environmental Protection Act, claiming DNR's agreement with the oil companies did not properly consider the environmental impact of the drilling on wildlife, particularly the elk. The trial court upheld the agreement, and the plaintiffs appealed to the Supreme Court of Michigan.

Moody, Justice

Perhaps the single most revealing piece of evidence is the Environmental Impact Statement for Potential Hydrocarbon Development in the Pigeon River County State Forest, prepared by the DNR. Many of the EIS's conclusions directly apply to the effects of exploratory drilling.

Testimony before the trial court indicated that six of the ten proposed sites were not adjacent to any road, requiring that roads be built to such sites. The EIS cites studies in Montana which concluded that "[e]lk avoid roads even when there is no traffic." The EIS also observed that "[w]hether the elk will return to their former range following completion of the last seismic survey work is unknown."

Some quantification of the adverse impact of exploratory drilling on the elk can be gained from comparing the EIS's Matrix for Proposed Hydrocarbon Development in the Southern Portion of the Forest with Dr. Inman's testimony. Dr. Inman, who participated in the development of the EIS, testified that a slow recovery time is considered to be 40 to 50 years or more, a short recovery time less than 20 years, and a great recovery time is 100 years or more.

The Environmental Impact Matrix defines a significant adverse impact as "a change in the element that is impacted from its present status to a status that may take a long time for recovery, at least during the duration of the project." Applying Dr. Inman's definitions of what constitutes a slow recovery time to the matrix predictions, it would appear that elk would avoid the impacted areas for 40 to 50 years.

We recognize that virtually all human activities can be found to adversely impact natural resources in some way or other. The real question before us is, when does such impact rise to the level of impairment or destruction? The DNR's environmental impact statement recognizes that "[e]lk are unique to this area of Michigan" and that the herd is "the only sizable wild herd east of the Mississippi River. Several attempts to introduce elk elsewhere in Michigan have been unsuccessful."

It is estimated that the herd's population, which numbered in excess of 1,500 in 1963, now probably lies between 170 and 180. Expert testimony has established that the Pigeon River County State Forest, particularly unit 1 in which the exploratory drilling is to take place, provides excellent habitat for elk and that the elk frequent this area. Furthermore, it is clear from the record that available habitat is shrinking.

In light of the limited number of the elk, the unique nature and location of this herd, and the apparently serious and lasting, though unquantifiable, damage that will result to the herd from the drilling of the ten exploratory wells, we conclude that defendants' conduct constitutes an impairment or destruction of a natural resource. Accordingly, we reverse the remand to the trial court for entry of a permanent injunction prohibiting the drilling of the wells.

Case Questions

1. Why would the exploratory drilling damage the elk?
2. If it is impossible to drill without adversely affecting some animals, would drilling ever be permitted?

Antilitter Laws

A few states have enacted laws aimed at reducing the litter along state highways. Litter is frequently in the form of disposable beverage bottles or cans. Some states have passed **bottle laws** requiring purchasers to pay a cash deposit on all beverage containers. The purchaser receives a return of the deposit for empty containers returned to any authorized center. Usually, stores selling beverages must also handle returns and refund the deposit. The states with bottle laws have significantly decreased roadway litter.

bottle laws
State laws requiring purchasers to pay a cash deposit on all beverage containers; states with bottle laws have significantly decreased roadway litter.

nuisance laws
Common laws used by state and local governments to deal with environmental problems; any substantial and unreasonable interference with the use and enjoyment of a person's interest in property is a tort and both damage to private and public facilities are actionable wrongs.

trespass
An unlawful interference with the property of another; trespass invades the property owner's exclusive right of possession, whereas a nuisance interferes with the property owner's use and enjoyment of the property.

Nuisance, Trespass, and Land Use Laws

Nuisance Laws Common law **nuisance laws** have long been used by state and local governments to deal with environmental problems. A *nuisance* is a substantial and unreasonable interference with the use and enjoyment of a person's interest in property. A public nuisance causes damage to the property of many people or to public facilities, whereas a private nuisance is a use of property that deprives other property owners of their right to use and enjoy their property. Both public and private nuisances are discussed in Chapter 7.

Trespass A **trespass** is an unlawful interference with the property of another. The person who sets foot on the property of another is a trespasser, but so is the firm that causes soot, dust, or other particles to intrude onto the land of another. Trespass invades the property owner's exclusive right of possession, whereas a nuisance interferes with the property owner's use and enjoyment of the property. If the cement dust from a nearby factory is deposited on another's land, a trespass has occurred because something else is now on that land. Since trespass and nuisance often overlap, it is generally less important to determine which exists than to determine whether either has occurred.

Land Use Laws Zoning ordinances and land use regulations have recently begun to play a larger role in the addressing of environmental problems. As Chapter 7 indicates, municipalities enact zoning ordinances to control the use of land. State laws may require municipalities to prepare land use plans or allow them to determine how differing uses of land will be accommodated.

Summary

Environmental laws regulate human interaction with the surrounding air, water, and land. These laws impose limitations on the use of products and manufacturing processes that can adversely affect the natural environment. Most of the environmental laws in the United States are fairly recent federal laws. The 1970 National Environmental Policy Act declared a national policy of protecting the environment. Its most significant provision requires that an environmental impact statement be prepared before any major federal action that will significantly affect environmental quality. The Environmental Protection Agency is responsible for enforcing federal laws regulating air, water, and land pollution.

The Clean Air Act is the primary federal statute directed at air pollution. It establishes standards for air quality, and it requires each state to develop a plan for achieving an air pollution level lower than those standards. The 1990 Amendments to the Clean Air Act concern smog, acid rain, toxic emissions, and alternative fuels.

The Water Pollution Control Act seeks to eliminate water pollution, and the Clean Water Act requires permits for discharges of pollutants into navigable waters from any source. Like the Clean Air Act, the Clean Water Act establishes standards that are to be met and allows the states to administer a permit program.

Three federal statutes address land pollution: the Resource Conservation and Recovery Act (RCRA), the Toxic Substance Control Act (TSCA), and the Comprehensive Environmental Response, Compensation, and Liability Act (CERCLA), which was amended by the Superfund Amendments and Reauthorization Act (SARA). The Resource Conservation and Recovery Act establishes a permit system regulating the use, transport, or storage of hazardous wastes. The Toxic Substances Control Act regulates the manufacture, distribution, commercial use, and disposal of chemical substances that pose an unreasonable risk of injury to health or the environment. The CERCLA and SARA legislation provides money for the identification and cleanup of hazardous waste disposal sites. It places liability for cleanup costs associated with the treatment or disposal of hazardous wastes on the waste generator or landowner. Nuclear power and wildlife protection are important environmental issues addressed by other federal laws.

Although the most significant environmental legislation is found at the federal level, state and local laws also seek to protect the environment. State environmental protection laws are modeled on, and permitted by, the National Environmental Policy Act. Special state resources are also protected by state laws. A few states have enacted bottle laws that require deposits for cans or bottles of beverages sold in the state; such laws seek to reduce litter from these containers by encouraging their return and recycling. The common law doctrines of nuisance and trespass are also used to deal with environmental problems. Zoning ordinances at the local level also regulate land use.

Critical Thinking Review Questions

1. What are the reasons why government regulation of the environment is important to the business community?
2. Your firm has been hired to build a new federal post office near a large neighborhood. A group of residents oppose the building of the new government facility. What factors must you consider in an environmental impact statement (EIS)?
3. What is the difference between an individual machine emission point source and a "bubble concept" source?
4. What does it mean to say that the Clean Air Act is "technology forcing"? What purpose does technology forcing serve?
5. What are three requirements that are a part of the 1990 Clean Air Act? Which one(s) do you think will have the greatest effect on business practices? Why?
6. Why has the federal government enacted extensive legislation in the environmental area? Do you favor international regulation instead of national regulation? Federal regulation instead of state regulation? Why?

Critical Thinking Exercises

1. As part of its mushroom farming business, Frezzo Brothers, Inc., produces compost to provide a growing base for mushrooms. The Frezzos were discharging pollutants through the runoff overflow from their mushroom farm. The government brought criminal actions against their firm. May criminal sanctions be used as a means of enforcement under the Clean Water Act? What must one prove for there to be criminal liability? *United States v. Frezzo Brothers, Inc.*, 602 F.2d. 1123 (1979).
2. The city of Chicago enacted an ordinance banning the use of detergents containing phosphates. Procter & Gamble lost $4.8 million in sales in the Chicago area during the first five months following enactment of this ordinance because a number of Chicago-area wholesalers that sold in midwestern states other than Illinois refused to carry phosphate-based detergents. Procter & Gamble sued, alleging that the ordinance resulted in an impermissible interference with interstate commerce. Do you think that state and local governments should have the power to regulate such products as phosphates? *Procter & Gamble v. City of Chicago*, 501 F.2d. 69 (1975).
3. The U.S. Forest Service manages the country's national forests, and it has the authority to issue special use permits to allow private companies to operate on federal lands. Methow Recreation, Inc. (MRI) wants to develop and operate a ski resort on Sandy Butte, a 6,000 foot mountain located in a national forest, and on adjacent land MRI owns. Sandy Butte is presently a pristine undeveloped area with a large animal population. Does the

proposed project require an environmental impact statement even if some of the development occurs on MRI lands? Why? *Robertson v. Methow Valley Citizens Council*, 490 U.S. 332 (1989).

4. One of the methods for mining for gold in Alaska is known as placer mining. Miners remove soil, mud, and clay from streambeds and separate that material from other matter by forcing water through the dirt. The water that is discharged into the stream affects the water quality level in the area and at downstream sites. Toxic metals such as arsenic, lead, and zinc are found in higher concentrations where mining in streams occurs. The EPA issued rules requiring those using placer mining techniques to use the best available control technology (BACT) to control the discharge of toxic pollutants. The BACT standard requires the construction of settling ponds (ponds for the water to settle in while much of its mineral content is being removed) for recycling water prior to the water returning to the streambeds. The Alaska Miner's Association challenges the EPA's rule. Who should win?
5. Water pollution caused by oil spills in the waters of Alaska, Texas, and Delaware occurred in 1989. In the summer of 1988, numerous beaches on the eastern coast of the United States were inundated with medical debris that apparently had been discarded from hospitals or medical clinics. In some cases, the polluter responsible for an oil spill is a corporation that has little insurance or assets and is thus unable to pay for the cleanup costs. In other cases, it is impossible to trace the debris dumped into an open sea to one or more polluters.

   What should the government policy be in these cases? Should the government absorb the cost of cleanup? Should the cost be spread among all manufacturers of certain products or to all waste disposal firms, even if many are not polluters? What if the cost of cleanup to private industry or to a particular polluting firm will cause that firm to go bankrupt or to reduce employment? Is the benefit derived from having the firm pay for its pollution worth the cost to society of having the firm go out of business? Will enforcing pollution laws make U.S. firms less competitive with foreign firms that may not have to bear such costs? If so, should the laws still be strictly enforced?

CHAPTER

22

The Social Responsibility of Business

Critical Thinking Questions

- Compare and contrast how normative ethical standards, religious precepts, and community mores provide managers with guidance in making ethical decisions. How do proscriptive criminal laws contribute to prohibiting unethical conduct?
- Identify the corporations' duties to various stakeholders including which groups deserve the consideration of managers.
- By what means does business exert political influence on candidates, legislation, and ballot issues? How does the Federal Elections Campaign Act campaign-finance law impact these activities?
- Codes of professional responsibility have been adopted by nearly all professions and many business groups. For what reasons are there few general codes of corporate honor? What challenges are there for managers to recognize ethical dilemmas and choose the right course of conduct absent definitive codes?

Introduction ... Past, Present, Future

Public concern with the social responsibilities of business has increased greatly in recent decades. During the 1950s, the public began to consider the view that the role of corporations should go beyond maximization of shareholders' welfare. During the 1960s and 1970s, concern over the scandals of Watergate and the weapons used in the Vietnam War heightened public demand that business become more socially responsible. Seventy percent of Americans polled in one survey believe that "business has an obligation to help society, even if it means less profit."[1] Another survey indicated that "most respondents have overcome the traditional ideological barriers to the concept of social responsibility and have embraced its practice as a legitimate and achievable goal of business."[2] The recent banking, savings and loan, insider trading, stock manipulation, Iran-Contra, government securities, and defense contractor scandals have reinforced public demands on both business and government.

In the future, business must recognize that significant new scandals or evidence of widespread unethical behavior will be met with strong political pressure. Unless business managers act in good faith, laws to reregulate may be enacted hastily

---

[1] "Mounting Public Pressure for Corporate Social Responsibility," in *ORC Public Opinion Index* (Princeton, N.J.: Opinion Research Corporation, January 1974), reprinted in Lyman E. Ostlund, "Attitudes of Managers toward Corporate Social Responsibility," *California Management Review* (Summer 1977), p. 25.

[2] Steven N. Brenner and Earl A. Molander, "Is the Ethics of Business Changing?" *Harvard Business Review* (January-February 1977), pp. 57, 59.

amid an atmosphere of overreaction. Business can avoid ill-conceived regulatory reactions to unethical behavior by instilling ethical standards in all employees. The adoption of ethical codes, the close supervision of employees, and strict enforcement of ethical standards can go far to alleviate the threat of new regulation. Much of the criticism of the unethical behavior of business concerns fraud, collusive conduct, corporate crimes, and bribery. Legal and ethical principles reflect an evolution in society's expectations through the setting of public policy. Society's reactions cause public issues that require constant attention by managers.

In order to facilitate learning business administration, decision making is presented as a separate subject from the laws affecting business. However, few business decisions can be so neatly and simply compartmentalized. Business transactions and the relations among firms are becoming increasingly complex. Therefore, the study of business social responsibility should be viewed as a complex and multifaceted set of constraints and opportunities that influence nearly every aspect of business. Any important decision may have contractual, regulatory, employment, financing, production, or competitive considerations. Each of these may be affected by various aspects of social responsibility: resolution of ethical dilemmas, avoidance of criminal liability, the need for stakeholder analysis, political interaction, and self-regulation. As you review the following materials on the social responsibility of business, consider how these matters may impact business decision making. It is important to integrate this form of analysis into the wide range of legal and business issues developed in this course and in other business courses.

White-Collar Crime

Society increasingly believes it is wrong for business to generate undesirable side effects. Unique temptations and opportunities encourage some business crimes. Criminal acts are often blended with legitimate transactions to avoid detection. Enforcement is frustrated because existing laws do not address all aspects of corporate crime. Many laws target individual conduct or organized crime groups while ignoring the unique attributes of criminality within the business firm. Increasingly, however, new laws specifically address **white-collar crime**—illegal, nonviolent behavior by business employees—and **corporate crime**—illegal behavior intended to benefit business firms.

white-collar crime Illegal, nonviolent behavior by businesses and their employees.

corporate crime Illegal behavior intended to benefit business firms.

As white-collar crime becomes more prevalent, prosecutors more actively apply these laws to business activities. Consequently, managers should work to understand criminal law and its procedures and should diligently direct their firms' attorneys to review proposed transactions to avoid unintended criminal exposure. This section discusses the criminal law process, some common types of crime applicable to business, and special crimes of increasing concern to business. As you study white-collar crime, you should also review the material concerning the legal process and the defendant's constitutional rights under the Bill of Rights, previously discussed in Chapters 1 through 5.

Ethics and the Criminal Law

For many centuries, both religious principles and laws have been a primary source of ethical guidance. Religious precepts and ethical standards outline the ideal behavior of persons. These standards are often called *normative* principles because they suggest ideal goals for conduct. Laws, by contrast, are *prescriptive* because they do more than suggest normative or "ought to" standards; they require, or prescribe, minimal levels of conduct.

Criminal law is usually *proscriptive* because it forbids certain actions that society views as unacceptable. Society constantly makes choices between flexible ethical standards and the less flexible criminal laws. This dilemma poses both threats to free choice and opportunities for responsive businesses. Nearly every business decision can be analyzed for ethical impact (see Chapter 1).

Corporate Crime

Law has not proven to be a sufficiently effective control over aberrant corporate behavior.[3] Some structural and procedural aspects of law reduce its effectiveness as a motivator of corporate responsibility. For example, business crimes tend to affect much larger financial interests than do personal crimes. In addition, judges tend to be more lenient with corporate wrongdoers than with "common" criminals. There have been several explanations for this leniency. Corporate officers are usually upstanding community members with reputations for responsibility and can usually afford to hire the best lawyers. Defendants charged with corporate crime often claim that their actions were motivated not by personal greed or hatred but by the goal of business survival.

Many corporate crimes involve fraud or labor, environmental, or manufacturing violations that are not immediately obvious. Unlike the more common "street crimes" of murder or larceny, corporate crimes often go undetected because their effects do not surface immediately. The traditional law enforcement emphasis on immediate and personal crimes tends to shield corporate crime from attention.

Criminal Procedure

The criminal procedure followed by state and federal law enforcement officials varies somewhat according to which governmental units have jurisdiction and on the seriousness of the alleged crime. Criminal prosecutions differ from civil cases because the plaintiff is a local prosecutor, state attorney, or United States attorney bound to protect the public, rather than a private party vindicating a personal right. Private citizens, however, often do report business crimes to prosecutors and nor seek to initiate prosecution. Detection of a criminal act initially prompts an investigation and arrest by law enforcement officials. Thereafter, the investigation may continue with interviews of the accused and potential witnesses and seizure of documents or other hard evidence. Finally, criminal charges may be initiated with an affidavit, complaint, accusation, or information against the person or persons implicated in the crime.

Pretrial Procedures After charges are filed, the accused defendant makes the first appearance before a judge or other magistrate at an *arraignment.* The defendant may then file a *plea:* not guilty, guilty, or *nolo contendere* (no contest, no admission of guilt but submitting to court resolution). A defendant who does not plead not guilty may be immediately sentenced. Indigent defendants may be assigned a free public defender

[3] *See* Christopher D. Stone, *Where the Law Ends: The Social Control of Corporate Behavior* (New York: Harper Colophon Books, 1975).

under the constitutional right to counsel. Bail may be set to ensure that the defendant will appear at the trial. Bail is often provided by a bail bondsman or in some cases may be waived if the judge believes the defendant will not flee, thereby releasing the defendant on his or her own recognizance. The defendant may waive the right to a preliminary hearing or review by the grand jury. The U.S. Constitution requires that the defendant be given an appearance before a judge without unreasonable delay, and the defendant must receive a speedy trial.

Before any criminal trial is held, there are prescreening processes to prevent law enforcement officials from abusing the criminal process or bringing false charges against innocent accused defendants. At a *preliminary hearing,* the prosecutor must demonstrate the existence of probable cause that the evidence connecting the defendant to a crime is sufficient to "hold the defendant over" for prosecution. A *grand jury,* consisting of numerous local citizens, performs a similar function by issuing an *indictment* when there is sufficient evidence against the defendant. Some states use only one of these prescreening processes, although both are used in some serious cases. Many defendants agree to settle the charges in a *plea bargain agreement,* pleading guilty to a lesser offense or to only some of several charges. This process conserves public resources when the defendant understands that the prosecution could win a conviction on the charge or charges.

The Criminal Trial Criminal trials follow a sequence similar to civil trials: (1) a jury is impaneled, (2) both sides make opening remarks, (3) the prosecution presents its case-in-chief by examining and cross-examining witnesses and presenting tangible evidence, (4) the defense similarly presents its case-in-chief, (5) both sides make closing remarks, (6) the judge instructs the jury with the applicable law, (7) the jury deliberates, and (8) the jury renders its verdict. If the verdict is not unanimous, then a "hung jury" results, necessitating either another trial or the defendant's release.

The defendant may be sentenced immediately if the law requires mandatory sentences. However, sentencing may be postponed in capital crimes or where sentencing guidelines give the judge discretion. In such cases, a later hearing is held to consider further evidence regarding the crimes seriousness and the defendant's background and likelihood of recidivism (return to crime). Generally, the defendant may appeal a conviction. Appeal may be automatic in capital punishment cases. The appeals court may permanently dismiss the charges or order a new trial. Absent a trial court error, the double jeopardy constitutional protection prohibits another prosecution on the same charges.

Proof of Criminal Guilt

Criminal prosecutors must usually prove two elements of an alleged crime to gain a conviction. First, a *criminal act* defined by the criminal code must have been committed by the defendant. Second, the defendant must have had the *intent* to commit the criminal act. These elements must be proved *beyond a reasonable doubt,* a much higher burden of proof than the *preponderance of the evidence* standard used to evaluate civil offenses.

Corporate criminal prosecutions are further limited by the difficulty of assessing individual responsibility. Because businesses are large organizations that perform complex acts in which many persons have a part, the legal determination of criminal intent is problematic. It is difficult to assign direct responsibility for the overall effect of such complex behavior. This point was exemplified in Chapter 12 in the *U.S. v Park* case. Parent corporations are increasingly held liable for crimes committed by subsidiaries under the civil theory of piercing the corporate veil, introduced in Chapter 14. When the parent so controls the subsidiary's decision making, courts reason that it would be inequitable to shield the parent from responsibility for the deeds of a related corporation within the larger unified enterprise.[4]

Business Crimes

Although a business crime might be defined as any crime committed by or against a business, the term is used here to include only those business activities that have a criminal impact. This section discusses some common, nonviolent business crimes: embezzlement, computer crime, mail and wire fraud, racketeering, and bribery. These crimes are separate from any criminal sanctions for violating the civil or regulatory laws discussed previously as well as some intentional torts; patent, copyright, or trademark infringement; unfair or deceptive trade practices; antitrust violations; securities fraud; environmental pollution; or tax evasion.

Embezzlement

Embezzlement is the wrongful appropriation of property entrusted to an individual. Embezzlement differs from larceny in that the embezzler is given rightful possession of the misappropriated property. A thief has no rightful possession of stolen property. Therefore, embezzlement is committed by persons who are entrusted with another's property: agents, brokers, consultants, accountants, attorneys, or corporate officials. Consider, for example, cashiers, who receive currency from customers as payment for goods or services. A cashier can rightfully possess the cash during working hours, even though it really belongs to the employer. However, it becomes embezzlement when the cashier takes money from the cash register while on the job. By contrast, it is larceny for a cashier to steal cash out of the employer's unguarded safe because the cashier has no right to possess that money.

Computer Crime

Because computers are an integral part of nearly every business, numerous computer crimes are now possible. These include embezzlement by computerized funds transfer; industrial espionage or misappropriation of confidential computer files; theft of valuable computer-use time; sabotage through tampering with computer files or destroying data, programs, or hardware; fraud in making misrepresentations in computer-collected data; or criminal infringement. Computer crimes are difficult to detect because the more artful "hackers" carefully cover their tracks to conceal any "audit trail." Firms must be vigilant in using effective computer security controls (e.g., access to computer hardware, passwords, ID codes). Until recently, the enforcement of computer crime has simply required the extension of existing law. Several states have, however, customized computer laws to accommodate these unique problems. The following case illustrates the problems of adapting existing law to either white-collar crime in general or computer crime in particular.

---

[4] See *U.S. v. NYNEX*, 788 F.Supp. 16 (D.D.C.1992).

State v. McGraw

480 N.E.2d 552 (Ind. 1985)
Indiana Supreme Court

The City of Indianapolis leased computer services at a flat-rate fee, which was irrespective of the actual on-line processing time used. McGraw, a city employee, was authorized to access the system from his desktop terminal. City employees were forbidden to make unauthorized use of city property. McGraw began moonlighting by selling the direct marketed product NaturSlim to his co-workers. He used the city's computer system to keep the associated business records: correspondence, client lists, inventory records. McGraw was reprimanded for making sales during office hours and was eventually terminated for poor job performance. After his discharge, McGraw requested a former co-worker make a printout of his personal business records and delete all associated computer files from the city's system. The former co-worker provided the printout to McGraw's supervisor, who then investigated McGraw's criminal theft of computer time. The state appealed the trial court's dismissal of his conviction for the theft.

Judge Prentice

It is fundamental that penal statutes must be construed strictly against the State. They may not be enlarged by implication or intendment beyond the fair meaning of the language used and may not be held to include offenses other than those which are clearly described, notwithstanding that the court may think the legislature should have made them more comprehensive. The Act provides: "A person who knowingly or intentionally exerts unauthorized control over property of another person with intent to deprive the other of any part of its value or use commits theft, a class D felony."

It is immediately apparent that the harm sought to be prevented is a deprivation to one of his property or its use—not a benefit to one which, although a windfall to him, harmed nobody. The Court of Appeals focused upon Defendant's unauthorized use of the computer for monetary gain and upon the definition of "property" as used in the statute. We think that it would be more accurate to say that the information derived by use of a computer is property. Having determined that Defendant's use was property, was unauthorized and was for his monetary benefit, it concluded that he committed a theft. Our question is, "Who was deprived of what?"

There is no evidence that the City was ever deprived of any part of the value or the use of the computer by reason of Defendant's conduct. Defendant's unauthorized use cost the City nothing and did not interfere with its use by others. He extracted from the system only such information as he had previously put into it. He did not, for his own benefit, withdraw City data intended for its exclusive use or for sale. Thus, Defendant did not deprive the City of the "use of computers and computer services" as alleged. We find no distinction between Defendant's use of the City's computer and the use, by a mechanic, of the employer's hammer or a stenographer's use of the employer's typewriter, for other than the employer's purposes. Under traditional concepts, the transgression is in the nature of a trespass, a civil matter—and a de minimis one, at that. Defendant has likened his conduct to the use of an employer's vacant bookshelf, for the temporary storage of one's personal items, and to the use of an employer's telephone facilities for toll-free calls. The analogies appear to us to be appropriate.

Intent is a mental function and, absent an admission, it must be determined by courts and juries from a consideration of the conduct and natural and usual consequences of such conduct. There was no evidence presented from which the intent to deprive, an essential element of the crime, could be inferred. A companion statute to the theft statute, proscribing conversion, [states] as follows: "A person who knowingly or intentionally exerts unauthorized control over property of another person commits criminal conversion, a class A misdemeanor."

The only difference between the statutory definitions of theft and criminal conversion is that the definition for conversion omits the words "with intent to deprive the other of any part of its value or use." At most, the evidence in this case warranted a conviction for criminal conversion. The decision and opinion of the Court of Appeals are ordered vacated, and the judgment of the trial court is affirmed.

Judge Pivarnik (dissenting)

I must dissent from the majority opinion. In the first place, intent is clearly shown in that Defendant used the City computer system for his personal business, well knowing that he was doing so and well knowing that it was unauthorized. I think the Court of Appeals properly focused upon Defendant's unauthorized use of the computer for monetary gain and upon the definition of property as used in the statute. Time and use are at the very core of the value of a computer system. To say that only the information stored in the computer, plus the tapes and discs and perhaps the machinery involved, are the only elements that can be measured as the value or property feature of that system is incorrect.

It is irrelevant that the computer service was leased to the City at a fixed charge and that the tapes or discs upon which the imparted data was stored were erasable and reusable. The fact is the City owned the computer system of all the stations including the defendant's. The time and use of that equipment at that station belonged to the City. Thus, when the defendant used the computer system, putting on data from his private business and taking it out on printouts, he was taking that which was property of the City and converting it to his own use, thereby depriving the City of its use and value. I therefore would allow the Court of Appeals opinion to stand.

Case Questions

1. What is the wording and perspective taken in the Indiana statute which is not readily adaptable to the type of computer crime in this case?
2. How could a new statute be written to specifically eliminate the ambiguities inherent in applying traditional criminal law to computer crime?

Mail and Wire Fraud

Federal statutes make it a criminal offense to perpetrate fraud by communicating misrepresentations in the mail or over the telephone, telegraph, radio, television, or other electronic telecommunication means. These laws prohibit the use of the mail or wire to conduct an intentional scheme or artifice to defraud in order to obtain money or property. Most businesses communicate to potential clients or customers by mail, over the phone, and increasingly by some electronic means (e.g., electronic data interchange, computer modem, satellite, E-Mail, Internet). If any such communication is used in the fraud, or even as a mere incidental part of perpetrating the fraud, the businessperson may be liable for mail and wire fraud. These crimes carry stiff penalties of fines up to $1,000 and imprisonment for up to five years per count. Elaborate fraudulent schemes may constitute numerous separately punishable crimes also illegal under the racketeering laws discussed in the next section.

Mail and wire fraud is often combined with the prosecution of other regulatory crimes. For example, the mail and wire fraud statutes were used in the infamous insider trading case involving *The Wall Street Journal*'s "Heard on the Street" columnist. The Supreme Court decisively outlawed the participants' insider trading under the misappropriation theory when prosecuted under the mail and wire fraud statutes.[5] Insider trading is illegal as mail or wire fraud if confidential information is misappropriated and trades are made by mail or co-conspirators are tipped by phone or wire. These activities are separately illegal under Rule 10b-5 of the Securities Exchange Act of 1934.

---

[5] Carpenter v. United States, 484 U.S. 19 (1987).

COMMENTARY

ETHICAL AND CRIMINAL PROBLEMS OF THE INTERNET

Communications technology is fast changing the conduct of business, advertising, knowledge dissemination, and information retrieval. The internet is fast becoming the centerpiece for a national information superhighway. The "net" is a decentralized patchwork collecting hundreds of separate connections and networks linking servers and client users. The internet permits the near cost-free transfer of documents, E-Mail, video and audio programs, and nearly every other type of copyright-protected expression.

The power of the "net" poses some interesting ethical and criminal problems. Critics charge that many "postings" violate legal rights and legal or ethical duties: defamation (libel and slander), privacy, infringement of copyright and trademarks, fraud, obscenity, incitement, treason, terrorism, solicitation and stalking. Proponents of an unimpeded net claim that regulation of the net is invalid under the First Amendment, arguing that all net expressions are protected speech. Nevertheless, many state and local governments are using existing law to prosecute net offenders. As conflicting local standards proliferate, choice of law problems will increase, such as the case of an "adult" bulletin board operated from California; the operator was convicted of obscenity and sentenced to a three-year prison term in Tennessee. Although some regulators are monitoring the net for fraud, critics charge that the most strident lawmakers are naive about the net's technology. One federal proposal is vague and will lead to extensive litigation. Many net supporters argue that private ethical codes and parental oversight is better than the heavy hand of ill-conceived regulation. The ethical and regulatory issues of the internet should continue to be important for years to come.

Racketeer Influenced and Corrupt Organizations (RICO)

RICO
Racketeer influenced corrupt organizations, crime of repeated and related underlying federal crimes.

A portion of the Organized Crime Control Act of 1970 is known as **RICO,** an acronym for that law's Racketeer Influenced and Corrupt Organizations provisions. RICO permits private plaintiffs to sue for civil treble (triple) damages against persons found guilty of racketeering activities. RICO outlaws a pattern of illegal activities involving the so called *predicate offenses* of securities fraud, murder, arson, extortion, drug dealing, fraud, bribery, loan sharking, and other enumerated state and federal crimes.

A RICO action requires the private plaintiff to prove the following essential elements to win triple damages: (1) the defendant committed at least two prohibited predicate acts (2) that constituted a pattern (3) of racketeering activity (4) by which the defendant (5) invested in, maintained an interest in, or participated in (6) an enterprise (7) that affected interstate or foreign commerce. Critics claim RICO has been expanded to cover many activities that were not traditionally considered part of organized crime.

It is unlawful to invest proceeds derived from racketeering activities. In one case, the proceeds from the sale of a firm tainted by securities fraud were invested in another firm, triggering a RICO claim. In another case, a fraud by general partners who sold their brokerage business constituted RICO activity. The pattern of racketeering activity outlawed by RICO may be proved, for example, by the artificial inflation of a company's market price. Nearly half the states have passed RICO-type statutes. The state laws combined with the expansive federal RICO provision make significant liabilities possible in business litigation. In addition, the RICO criminal procedures provide for stiff penalties and permit prosecutors to freeze the defendant's assets during a criminal RICO trial. This tactic has allegedly been used to bully investment banking firms accused of stock manipulation and securities fraud into settling RICO charges.

Ethical Dilemmas in Accusing Racketeers

Ethical Dilemma

RICO and state racketeering laws are susceptible to unethical abuse. Courts have permitted private plaintiffs and prosecutors to broaden RICO's reach into crimes or activities of legitimate businesses that were never part of the traditional mobster-type organized crime. Recent cases have charged racketeering in contract disputes, securities investments, religious protests, retirement village mismanagement, abortion clinic protests, and commodities speculation. RICO coverage of these more common political and business disputes are often based on broad predicate offenses, such as mail and wire fraud.

Congress intended RICO to provide civil plaintiffs the treble damage incentive to aid law enforcement efforts against racketeers and thereby prevent the use of illegal racketeering profits to finance legitimate businesses. When racketeering operations exist, other legitimate businesses are placed at a considerable competitive disadvantage and may suffer injuries. However, RICO's powerful penalties and vagaries give this "supercrime" an increasingly abusive profile. For example, plaintiffs and prosecutors may threaten RICO suits to bludgeon settlements from defendants even if they are chargeable with only two of the prohibited predicate offenses. The Supreme Court may have slowed the RICO misuse somewhat in *H.J. Inc. v. Northwestern Bell Telephone Co.* by requiring better proof of a relationship between the predicate offenses, such as the same or similar purpose, results, participants, victims, or methods of commissions.[6] There is no "pattern" from two isolated events that do not pose a threat of continuity. In *Reeves v. Ernst & Young,* the Supreme Court relieved most auditors, investment bankers, and legal counsel from RICO liability for such crimes as securities fraud committed by their clients. RICO requires that the defendant must "participate" in committing the predicate offense to be held liable, so the RICO threat on auditors of fraudulent financial statements is eliminated unless they knowingly participate in management or operations of the client.[7] *Reeves* goes far to eliminate the RICO paranoia of many professional consultants.

RICO's special powers and penalties promise treble damages and attorney's fees to civil plaintiffs. Criminal conviction can carry fines of up to $25,000 and/or imprisonment for up to 20 years per violation. RICO and other criminal statutes authorize judges to order the defendant to forfeit any property acquired with the illegal racketeering profits. This permits prosecutors to request a pretrial freeze or seizure of the defendant's assets. This powerful settlement inducement was allegedly used to bring down the "junk bond king" Michael Milken and his investment banking employer Drexel, Burnham, Lambert. Financial firms such as Drexel would have difficulty operating if their capital were frozen during a lengthy RICO trial. Drexel settled the RICO claims to avoid such a financial squeeze. The subsequent fall of the junk bond market imperiled the solvency of numerous banks, thrifts, insurance companies and retirement annuity companies that were too heavily invested in junk bonds.

Critics charge that RICO's pretrial forfeitures are unreasonable. However, defendants charged with street crimes commonly submit to pretrial forfeitures of their liberty such as arrest, jail, or high bail. Similarly, drug defendants' vehicles are confiscated in prosecutions under the Comprehensive Crime Control Act of 1984. Forfeitures deter defendants from fleeing or disposing of assets and become permanent only if the defendant is ultimately convicted.

Business managers must be aware of their potential personal and corporate liability under RICO. These threatening powers create a strong "settlement value" and incentive to win treble damages or for a prosecutor's desire for political visibility. The use of RICO's considerable powers constitutes an ethical dilemma for prosecutors and plaintiffs. They must weigh RICO's adverse consequences for individuals and firms against the benefits to society from punishing and deterring genuine racketeering.

Bribery and the Foreign Corrupt Practices Act

Following the Watergate scandal, which led to President Nixon's resignation, the public focused inquiry on the misuse of corporate funds for unethical and illegal purposes. In the mid-1970s, the SEC investigated several questionable payments by domestic firms, including bribery of domestic and foreign officials, campaign contributions, and kickbacks. Subsequently, in 1977, Congress passed the **Foreign Corrupt Practices Act (FCPA),** which it later clarified with the Foreign Corrupt Practices Act Amendments of 1988. The FCPA outlaws foreign bribery and establishes accounting standards to prevent bribery. Among other things, the FCPA was intended to prevent bribery because it is unethical. In addition, the FCPA tends to restore investors' confidence in corporations whose securities are traded in the financial markets. The FCPA outlaws foreign bribery by all *domestic concerns.* Domestic bribery is also a criminal offense under various state and federal laws.

Foreign Corrupt Practices Act (FCPA) U.S. foreign bribery law prohibiting bribing foreign officials to win business.

Domestic Concern

> . . . any individual who is a citizen, national, or resident of the United States; and any corporation, partnership, association, joint-stock company, business trust, unincorporated association, or sole proprietorship which has its principal place of business in the United States, or which is organized under the laws of a state of the United States or a territory, possession, or commonwealth of the United States.

Prohibited Bribery The FCPA antibribery provisions outlaw any corrupt payments, offers to pay, and offers to give anything of value to foreign officials to influence decisions to grant business. *Foreign officials* include persons with discretionary powers (rather than ministerial or clerical responsibilities), foreign political parties, and candidates for foreign public office.

---

[6] *H.J. Inc. v. Northwestern Bell Telephone Co.*, 492 U.S. 229 (1989).

[7] *Reeves v. Ernst & Young*, 113 S.Ct. 1163 (1993).

Grease or facilitating payments are not considered bribes under the FCPA. *Grease* is usually a payment made to a lower-echelon foreign agent without discretionary power. In some foreign countries, for example, customs officials routinely expect a "gratuity" to expedite the clearance of incoming goods. If a domestic concern made such a payment so that perishable goods were quickly cleared through foreign customs, the payment would probably not be an illegal bribe if it were legal in the foreign country. Bona fide promotional expenditures and contract performance expenses, including lodging for foreign officials, are not illegal.

Accounting Standards The FCPA accounting standards provisions are intended to prevent the accumulation of funds for use as bribes. These provisions apply only to publicly traded firms, requiring them (1) to maintain accurate records and (2) to maintain a system of internal accounting controls. *Internal accounting controls* are procedures for reconciling and overseeing corporate books and assets. These procedures provide reasonable assurance that transactions are executed as authorized and that assets are adequately safeguarded. Records must be reconciled so that accurate financial statements can be prepared. When independent auditors find weaknesses in a firm's accounting system and internal controls, the firm should remedy them. Accounting controls reinforce corporate ethics through supervision of employees to avert the misuse of corporate funds.

Two SEC rules support these accounting provisions. First, it is unlawful to falsify accounting records. Second, misrepresentations to an accountant are prohibited. The FCPA accounting standards and the SEC rules reinforce the FCPA as an ethical code.

FCPA Enforcement The FCPA gives enforcement powers to both the SEC and the Department of Justice (DOJ). The DOJ conducts criminal investigations, prosecutes criminal bribery, and may seek injunctions. The SEC has civil enforcement powers over publicly traded firms and enforces the accounting standards provisions of the FCPA. Publicly traded corporations that violate the FCPA bribery provisions are subject to fines of up to $2 million; individual violators are subject to fines of up to $100,000 and/or imprisonment for up to five years. The SEC may assess civil penalties of up to $10,000 for individuals. The employer may not pay an individual violator's fine. Most of the cases brought by the SEC have been settled by *consent decree.* This usually means the publicly traded corporation and the individual defendants consent to certain undertakings without admitting or denying guilt. The 1988 amendments give the attorney general power to issue guidelines to assist firms in complying and the power to issue opinions on the legality of specific proposed conduct by domestic concerns. The Enforcement Remedies Act of 1990 also gives the SEC considerably greater enforcement powers.

Ethics and Foreign Bribery

International Perspective and Commentary

The FCPA represents a confluence of important international management and policy issues. These include ethical dilemmas, the clash of cultures, the conduct of foreign contract negotiations, growing uniformity in accounting and auditing standards, and whether U.S. practices should be exported abroad. Bribery contradicts the basic assumptions underlying the perfect competition model by diverting transactions from freely negotiated market outcomes into suboptimal transactions based on factors other than price, service, and quality. Bribery receives varying degrees of acceptance in other nations. Firms may be induced to bribe foreign officials to gain business in nations where bribery is tolerated by the culture or by self-interested government officials. These foreign officials act unethically when other nations' firms must bribe them to gain business. The officials' personal profiteering occurs at the expense of their citizens and their own nations.

Nearly all nations outlaw bribery. Therefore, bribery becomes possible only where there are primitive control systems and lax accountability and enforcement, or concealment. The FCPA has established a higher standard in law and accounting by requiring internal corporate accountability. Critics charge the FCPA is simply an effort to export U.S. ethics. Further, they argue it is an ill-conceived plan because firms from nations without tough antibribery laws will simply fill the foreign orders that U.S. firms cannot win through bribery. Although there is conflicting evidence, U.S. exports have grown steadily since the FCPA passage.

The FCPA appears to be exporting accountability as U.S. accounting and auditing standards are implemented worldwide. Some major U.S. accounting firms have merged with foreign accounting firms, so these accounting practices are multinational. U.S.-trained auditors supervise audits of foreign firms and expect FCPA-style accounting controls. This eventually raises the ethical standards intrinsic in the foreign firms' accounting systems. Generally accepted auditing practices will eventually become standardized as the world's capital markets merge. Capital will be attracted mainly to markets with accountable firms, which investors will perceive as carrying a lower risk.

Perquisites: Ethical and Legal Analysis The FCPA accounting standards provisions have been used in ethical contexts other than foreign bribery. They have been applied to upper management in situations involving excessive perquisites, or perks. *Perks* are profits or benefits that an employee receives in addition to regular compensation. Perks arguably help to more closely identify the personal interests of employees with the interests of the firm. Some observers say that they can help "perk up" employees' performance. However, some upper managers are tempted to abuse their position by taking excessive perks. Accountability for the use of corporate assets by executives is often more relaxed than for other employees. An executive's misuse of corporate assets is a classic case of unethical behavior. When does an executive's personal use of perks conflict with the firm's interests? The following case illustrates that accountability for excessive use of perks may be maintained under the FCPA even if state law fails to address such ethical abuses.

In re Playboy Enterprises, Inc.

S.E.C. Admin. Proc. File No. 3–5951 (1980)

The SEC held an administrative hearing concerning Playboy Enterprises, Inc., to determine whether certain perks given to its president, Hugh Hefner, were excessive. In addition to Hefner's use of the Playboy mansion, described below, Hefner, his family, and his friends had extensive use of limousine service, personal tax and legal consulting services, insurance policies, flights on the Playboy DC-9 jet plane *Big Bunny,* automobile use, hotel and Playboy club charges, and loan guarantees. Although Hefner personally paid for some of these expenses, many were paid from the Playboy corporate treasury.

The Securities and Exchange Commission

Hefner, the company's founder, is Chairman of the Board of Directors and Chief Executive Officer. Since Playboy became a publicly held company, Hefner has owned approximately 72 percent of the company's common shares issued and outstanding. The company has approximately 25,000 other stockholders of record.

The federal securities laws require registrants to fully disclose, among other things, all forms of remuneration provided to their officers and directors, as well as company transactions in which officers, directors or 10 percent shareholders have a direct or indirect material interest. Possible conflicts of interest and the use of corporate assets for the personal benefit of officers or directors are required to be disclosed in a wide variety of filings with the Commission, including prospectuses, proxy statements and annual reports to the Commission. Since becoming a public company in 1971, Playboy has in significant respects failed to make [these] disclosures.

Playboy's Audit Committee determined that the total amount of all such benefits received over a period of approximately eight years was in excess of $2 million. Playboy's Audit Committee determined that Hefner should have been charged $212,749 for his basic accommodations for the period 1971–1978, $65,199 more than the amounts he paid for rent during this period.

The Chicago Mansion consists of two separate buildings. The principal building is a four-story, 54-room stone structure containing 13 apartments and bedrooms; a number of common areas, including a large ballroom and restaurant-type kitchen; and a six-car garage. After purchasing the building, Playboy added a swimming pool (with adjacent "underwater bar"), sauna, and recessed grotto. Playboy also converted first-floor space into a game-room and exercise room, and installed a wide assortment of electronic gadgetry, consisting of a variety of audio/visual equipment and extensive security apparatus.

The second, 20-room building comprises three additional bedrooms, a board room, an office for Hefner, and additional office and storage space. A dormitory with room for thirty Playboy Club Bunnies occupies the top floor of the two buildings. Improvements consisted of general refurbishing and the installation of a single-lane bowling alley on the building's lower level. Playboy's improvements to the Chicago Mansion, completed over the period from 1959 to 1977, cost approximately $3.2 million. Playboy absorbed the total cost of operating the Chicago Mansion, less Hefner's rent and rent by the Playboy "Bunnies" residing in the dormitory. The total amount spent by Playboy on operating costs for the Chicago Mansion during the period 1971 to 1978 was approximately $9.15 million.

Hefner's accommodations comprised a master bedroom suite, consisting of a bedroom, bathroom, living room and sitting room. Located on the first floor and accessible through Hefner's bathroom is the "Roman Bath," an elaborate bathing/sleeping area. Adjoining the suite are a study, library/work area and conference room, which were available to Hefner for use as office space.

Playboy Mansion West [PMW] consists of a 30-room Tudor-style stone structure set on 5 wooded acres. The main floor consists of a two-story hall, living room (with built-in movie screen and antique pipe organ), library, dining room, breakfast room, and kitchen/servants' dining area. The second floor comprises a master bedroom suite, five furnished guest rooms, and four offices. Above the master bedroom is an attic, converted to an office for Hefner. The master bedroom suite consists of a bedroom, bathroom, and dressing area. The bedroom contains an extensive array of audio/visual equipment, which is monitored through a small electronics control room. Two one-story outbuildings within the Mansion complex serve as a separate guest house and a game house. On the landscaped Mansion grounds are a lighted tennis court, a barbecue area, a swimming pool with a bathhouse/cabana/sauna and grotto, an animal shelter, and a greenhouse/aviary. The grotto, a cavern with underwater access and multiple sitting areas, contains individualized Jacuzzi systems and a stereophonic sound system.

Playboy undertook substantial renovation of PMW. [T]he first stage [of] improvements totaled approximately $5 million, [and] the [second stage] is $2.6 million, of which $1,035,000 is attributable to Hefner's quarters. PMW operating costs during the period 1971 through 1978 were approximately $11.5 million.

Personal guests of Hefner have stayed at the Mansions for extended periods of time. They included Hefner's family members, Hefner's girlfriends, and other friends and associates. The expenditure of corporate funds on these personal guests served no business purpose to the company. All Mansion guests enjoyed a wide variety of services and amenities. In addition to meals and beverages, they received the use of extensive recreational facilities, including swimming pools, a bowling alley, game rooms, and a tennis court. Playboy's Audit Committee found that, out of at least 21,949 overnight guest "stays" at the Mansions, some 6,020 such stays were personal to Hefner and thus should be reimbursed to the company.

Playboy has spent substantial amounts on sophisticated video equipment, commercial films, blank films, and tape cassettes for on-premises taping. This equipment is used by Hefner primarily for business purposes and much of it is located in his bedroom suite at PMW. The equipment purchased by Playboy has included four wide-screen projection systems, five video-replay/recorder units, three color TV monitors, and three low-light cameras. On occasion, Hefner has used some of this equipment for purely personal purposes. Playboy has also purchased an extensive collection of erotic films and cassettes, which the Audit Committee found to serve the company's editorial needs.

Hefner hosted frequent parties at the Chicago Mansion and PMW [including] an open bar and buffet dinner followed by the screening of a movie or prize fight. A 1974 management study showed that the direct cost of such parties ranged from $1,000 to $7,000 per party.

Playboy has taken and continues to take the position that such expenditures are "promotional" in nature and thus benefit the company's business activities. . . . The Commission has taken into consideration the argument that expenditures on parties and social gatherings given by Hefner at the Mansions and the substantial expenditures on lavish improvements to the Mansions are business-related because they are designed to promote the Playboy "image" and thus produce a benefit to Playboy, albeit one of indeterminate value. This argument has been accepted in large part by Playboy's Audit Committee, which concluded that, while Playboy's promotional success "is not solely or even primarily attributable to activities at the Mansions," management had a reasonable basis for believing that promotion of the Mansions was part of a "highly successful corporate strategy."

Finally, the argument that expenditures on Hefner are "promotional" in nature and thus are business-related has no application to the undisclosed benefits to company executives who are not in the "public eye" and thus whose receipt of benefits at corporate expense could not be deemed part of some sort of promotional program. Playboy lacked an adequate system of internal accounting controls for distinguishing between business and nonbusiness expenditures at the Mansions and between reimbursable and nonreimbursable expenses of officers. . . . Playboy's Annual Reports since 1972 have omitted disclosure of management remuneration and affiliated transactions. Playboy's proxy statements have inadequately disclosed the matters discussed. No disclosure of the benefits received by persons other than Hefner was made.

[Playboy settled the SEC charges by making forthright disclosure of these perks, reinforcing its internal control over these assets, electing an additional outside director, and having these matters audited independently.]

Case Questions

1. What legal and ethical safeguards are presumed to prevent corporate asset misuse?

2. What might justify a president receiving perks such as those described in this case?

3. Criticize the misuse of the FCPA in the perk area if perks have little or no connection with foreign bribery. What factors might better connect perks to foreign bribery?

Corporate Social Responsibility

There have been various stages in the development of the social responsibility of American business. Before the 20th century, the corporate form was seldom used. Without the limited liability of the corporate form, business owners were personally liable for business debts. The discipline on business was felt directly by owners who had no shield from personal liability. As the limited liability concept became more widespread during the latter 1800s, the next stage of business responsibility developed. Passive investors were encouraged to provide the capital needed for industrial expansion. As the use of the corporate form widened, the ownership and control of business were separated. This created new ethical dilemmas for managers in their shareholder relations because they were insulated from many of the consequences of their decisions. It also suggests that managers should remain aware of the interest and power over corporate affairs that various groups can wield.

Corporate Stakeholders

In performing strategic planning, business should be aware of the diverse expectations of numerous groups. Business can actively identify its stakeholders and attempt to understand their reaction to and influence on corporate actions. **Corporate stakeholders** are groups or entities affected by the firm's activities. Society actively monitors the impact that business has on its stakeholders. For many of these stakeholders, there are significant measures of business performance other than the firm's profitability.

corporate stakeholders Persons or entities affected by corporate activities.

Identifying Stakeholders Numerous parties that have direct or indirect contact with business may consider themselves corporate stakeholders. Consumers, customers, wholesalers, employees, and retailers are the predominant stakeholders because they contract with the corporation. Participants in the distribution chain expect the corporation to act responsibly in satisfying their concerns. They evaluate the corporation's responsibility by the quality of its products or services, by its work environment, and by its honesty in describing products and services. Employees and suppliers expect fair dealing and prompt payments. These audiences usually receive considerable attention from firms.

The financial community is another audience that demands the attention of corporations. It consists of shareholders, creditors, investment advisers, investment bankers, and potential investors. Firms must provide sufficient and accurate information concerning their financial status and prospects. Contributors of capital may use the legal system to remedy irresponsible behaviors of firms. If a firm's management becomes unresponsive, shareholders can take over the firm or use its proxy process to oust its management or change its policies.

Another audience is the local community near the firm's facilities. For example, nearby homeowners and businesses can bring pressure on the firm through the legal system, deny needed zoning or operating permits, and influence the public with adverse publicity. Firms should monitor the attitudes of their major audiences and modify their policies to avoid detrimental reactions by these stakeholders. Figure 22–1 suggests how these stakeholders interact with business.

Stakeholders' Expectations and Influence Business is expected to refrain from having a negative impact on various stakeholders. Some stakeholders expect business to generate favorable benefits, sometimes called *positive externalities.* For example, corporate philanthropy, economic growth, freedom from pollution or industrial accidents, and beneficial research are considered by many to be the responsibility of business. If some audiences of a firm have sufficient political or economic power to pressure it to act in a "responsible" manner, the firm should consider their influence in its decision making. To avert costly regulation, business managers must understand the

FIGURE 22-1 Corporate Stakeholder Influences

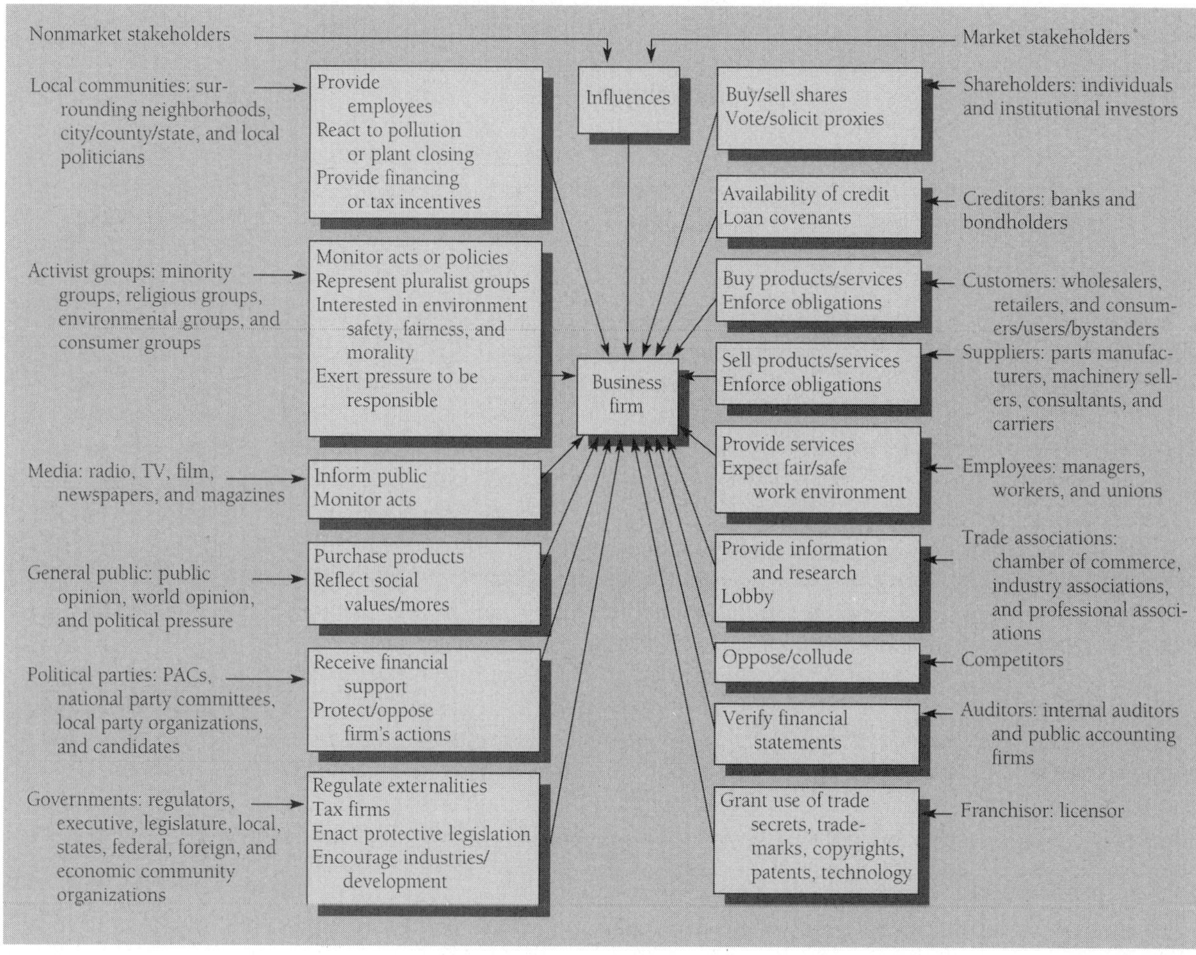

complex power structure of government and the relationships among the participants in government who affect the legal environment of business.

Campaign Finance Laws and Political Action Committees

Advocacy during political campaigns or referenda is a primary method by which business can exert political influence. Today, federal elections are often won by the candidates who spend the most. Political consultants and pollsters, television advertisements, and electioneering visits to voters are costly. Many businesses are able to make large political contributions. Numerous observers argue that such contributions pervert the political process by making politicians beholden to special interests.

In the late 19th century, some businesses made large direct money contributions in elections. Society believed that the political influence of these businesses was excessive, so in 1907 Congress passed the Tillman Act, which prohibited corporations from directly contributing to candidates in federal elections. Some of the states passed similar laws. To bypass the Tillman Act, some business executives were paid large bonuses that they were expected to use as political contributions. Corporate staff, facilities, and consultants have sometimes been provided to candidates. In recent elections, some candidates have had their debts canceled or have been given free rental cars or secret contributions.

Federal Election Campaign Act In 1971, Congress reinforced the Tillman Act with the Federal Election Campaign Act (FECA). The FECA established the Federal Election Commission (FEC) to administer the campaign finance laws. The FEC requires disclosure of political contributions, receipts, and expenditures by both contributors and candidates. The FECA permits the formation of political action committees to solicit campaign contributions from particular groups.

The FECA prohibits individuals from contributing more than $1,000 to the election of any federal candidate. Individuals may contribute no more than $5,000 per year to a single political action committee or $20,000 per year to the national committee of a political party. An aggregate limit of $25,000 per year is imposed on contributions by an individual to all recipients of political contributions. There are no limits on an individual's personal campaign expenditures. The expenditures made by the national committees of political parties are also limited: $17,500 per year to Senate candidates, $1,000 per election for House candidates, and $5,000 per year to other committees (e.g., PACs).

political action committees (PACs) Groups of like-minded political contributors concentrating electioneering resources for candidates and causes.

Political action committees (PACs) are groups formed by individuals, labor unions, corporations, trade associations and other special interest groups. A PAC officially exists when it receives political contributions from more than 50 people and either spends or receives over $1,000 per year. PACs must file regular financial reports with the FEC, identifying their contributors and recipients. The organization establishing a PAC may pay the PAC's expenses for rent, salaries, or postage without violating the FECA. PACs advocate policies favorable to their members. They channel contributions received from management, employees, stockholders, or other members for or against the causes or candidates they target.

PACs may not contribute more than $5,000 to any one federal candidate during primary elections. They may contribute another $5,000 to the same candidate during the general election. PACs may give up to $15,000 per year to national party committees and up to $5,000 per year to other PACs. Although corporations with several facilities may establish separate PACs for each facility, the contributions of these PACs are combined in determining whether they have remained within the contribution limits.

After a presidential candidate has received federal matching funds for an election campaign, PAC contributions are prohibited. However, PACs may make an unlimited amount of "independent" expenditures, called *soft money,* in favor of particular candidates or causes. These expenditures must not be made with the candidate's cooperation or knowledge. Therefore, PACs may independently buy TV ads to promote a candidate. This technique has been used in several recent negative campaigns to oust several key members of Congress. The PAC chairperson or treasurer may be subject to criminal prosecution for violations. The PAC system is coming under criticism for controlling legislation favorable to their industries' interests. Although, some critics seek to prohibit PACs altogether or at least limit soft money expenditures, campaign finance reform seems unlikely to pass through Congress anytime soon.

THE DIVERGENT GOALS OF BUSINESS AND SOCIETY

Before the New Deal era, Supreme Court interpretations of the U.S. Constitution reinforced the United States's historical preference for free market decision making. This philosophy was founded on the colonists' contempt for the British crown's authoritarian rule and the economic restraint imposed by British merchantilism. The constitutional framers included provisions in the Constitution and in the Bill of Rights pronouncing broad social, political, and economic freedoms to encourage **laissez-faire** free markets and other libertarian ideals. These principles limited the role of federal, state, and local governments in the economy and thereby minimized government's intrusion on business. Today, U.S. economic freedom starkly contrasts with the intrusive government decision making throughout most developed and developing economies.

laissez-faire
Non-interventionalist freedom of contract theory underlying free-market capitalism.

Laissez-faire capitalism is founded on freedom of contract. Contemporary implementation of this theory by economists like Milton Friedman argue that a corporation's sole social responsibility is strict adherence to the profit motive, which leads to an optimal allocation of goods and services. Competition leads to the success of efficient firms and the failure of inefficient ones. The ideal of free choice is enhanced because it determines the types and quantities of goods produced. In this system, managers are motivated to succeed by heeding market signals and influences.

The best known statement of the traditional laissez-faire model is attributed to Adam Smith's 1776 publication *The Wealth of Nations.* He predicted that the "invisible hand" of capitalism implemented through self-interested economic actors would "naturally" drive the market to optimize social welfare. Private property would provide incentives to take risks and innovate as long as the actors are entitled to the profits of their effort. Competition would discipline participants to become efficient, attracting new competitors as abnormally high profits become available. The four primary economic questions would be answered with *allocative efficiency:* what is produced, how is it produced, who receives that production, and how production is changed.

Adam Smith's model makes further assumptions, such as those underlying the **perfect competition model:** markets must have numerous rational buyers and sellers, all market participants have perfect information, there are no barriers restricting new firms' entry into markets, only standardized products are sold, and no participant possesses market (monopoly) power. The market "clears" (exhausts available supply) for quantities and at prices that form an *equilibrium.* Adam Smith believed there is only limited justification for government intervention in free markets because government intrusion is "unnatural." In his view, government has only three legitimate duties: (1) provide for *national defense,* (2) *administer the justice system* to preserve property rights and facilitate enforcement of transactions and (3) establish public works or other *public goods* that are valuable throughout society but which private enterprise might neglect (e.g., roads, dams, parks).

perfect competition model
Market system allocating resources through acts of numerous buyers and sellers, each with perfect information, none possessing market power, selling only standardized products, with no significant barriers to entry.

Market Failures

Considerable experience with the operation of markets illustrates that Adam Smith's assumptions are difficult to achieve in the real world. The market seldom operates just as predicted; sometimes it produces market inefficiencies or **market failure.** Many observers argue market failure suboptimizes society's welfare, emphasizing the injuri-

market failure
Failure in the assumptions or operation of markets, producing suboptimal results.

ous side of self-interest. For example, a polluter can often hide the **externalities** or *side effects* of their industrial processes, eventually harming society. While democratic market economies such as that of the United States prefer market systems, critics often justify government intervention to correct market failures through regulation. Additionally, some observers argue that a competitive market system is incapable of addressing many social and public policy preferences generated by a pluralistic democracy. Public consensus often pressures government to reduce externalities, eliminate asymmetrical information, more equitably distribute income, conserve natural resources, eliminate minority discrimination, pursue nationalistic goals, stabilize economic volatility, or instigate various other social policies. The natural conflict among self-interested ideologies and reality has led to business involvement in philanthropy and efforts at self-regulation.

externalities
Costs or benefits from a firm's activities absorbed by outsiders.

Corporate Philanthropy

Many firms seek to act responsibly by giving educational or research grants or engaging in other philanthropic efforts. In some early court decisions, judges prohibited corporate philanthropy holding that it was an improper corporate goal. Is a corporation permitted to intentionally provide societal benefits? Some Ford shareholders questioned Henry Ford's goals of corporate social responsibility. Henry Ford had a controlling interest in Ford Motor Company. As Ford expanded and the Model T automobile became immensely popular, Ford was able to pay large quarterly dividends and a total of $41 million in special dividends. In October 1915, however, Henry Ford declared that special dividends would be discontinued. He publicly declared his altruistic vision to "employ still more men, to spread the benefits of this industrial system to the greatest possible number, to help them build up their lives and their homes."[8] Thereafter, Ford profits were primarily plowed back into the business. The Dodge brothers, who together owned one-tenth of all Ford Motor Company stock, sued the company, complaining that a dividend should be paid. The Michigan Supreme Court established the "goal of the firm" as maximizing shareholder wealth.

Traditional Goal of the Firm

> A business corporation is organized and carried on primarily for the profit of the stockholders. The powers of the directors are to be exercised in the choice of means to attain that end, and does not extend to change in the end itself, to the reduction of profits, or to the nondistribution of profits among stockholders in order to devote them to other purposes. . . It is not within the lawful powers of a board of directors to shape and conduct affairs of a corporation for the merely incidental benefit of shareholders and for the primary purpose of benefiting others.

The judicial attitude toward corporate philanthropy has evolved since the early 20th century; today, many firms make charitable contributions. A firm's ultimate successes may be enhanced by its reputation for responsible acts. Philanthropy may actually be in a firm's best interests if it leads to favorable public impressions of the firm. In an

[8] *Dodge v. Ford Motor Co.*, 170 N.W. 668 (Mich.1919).

early 1950s case, a group of stockholders alleged that a corporation's donation of $1,500 to Princeton University was beyond the corporation's powers.[9] However, such gifts are upheld today because they legitimately advance the corporation's interests.

Justification for Corporate Philanthropy

"[i]ndividual stockholders'. . . interests rest entirely upon the well-being of the . . . corporation, [and these stockholders] ought not be permitted to close their eyes to [the corporation's] high obligation as a constituent of our modern social structure."

Universities provide educated employees and research discoveries that are used directly by business. However, philanthropic contributions are permissible even if business receives less direct benefits. Over half the states, including Delaware, have adopted "corporate constituency" takeover legislation permitting corporate boards to consider the effect of its operations and corporate control transactions on surrounding communities, customers, suppliers, and others. In *Schlensky v. Wrigley,* a minority shareholder in the Chicago Cubs sued Philip K. Wrigley and the Cubs's corporate directors, claiming management was not maximizing shareholder wealth.[10] Wrigley Field, the Cubs's home park, had no field lights, prohibiting lucrative night games that all other major league teams enjoyed. Without night games, the Cubs allegedly could not maximize attendance, limiting their profitability. The Illinois court sustained the board's decision not to install lights, stating:

> It appears to us that the effect on the surrounding neighborhood might well be considered by a director who was considering the patrons who would or would not attend the games if the park were in a poor neighborhood. Furthermore, the long-run interest of the corporation in its property value at Wrigley Field might demand all efforts to keep the neighborhood from deteriorating.

Of course, there are lights now at Wrigley Field that further hasten the demise of baseball as a "day sport," a fear voiced by Philip K. Wrigley. Today, modern constituency statutes would not even require that a board connect the firm's financial interests so directly to the condition of the surrounding community. The modern goal of the firm includes serving the interests of a variety of stakeholders in addition to shareholders.

Codes of Responsibility and Ethics

ethical code
Compilation of prohibited activities for members of a firm or industry.

Regulatory responses are often initiated when self-discipline is perceived as insufficient or nonexistent. Government initiates many of these responses, but there has also been a trend toward the imposition of **ethical codes** by firms. Although professional codes are not always laws, they may nevertheless become an issue in trials. The determination of professional malpractice liability often depends on professional standards. For example, an auditor's failure to follow generally accepted auditing standards, a real estate agent's violation of the realtor's code of ethics, or a lawyer's violation of the attorney's code of conduct is often evidence of malpractice.

---

[9] *A.P. Smith Mfg. Co. v. Barlow*, 98 A.2d 581 (N.J.1953).
[10] *Schlensky v. Wrigley*, 237 N.E.2d 776 (Ill. 1968).

Some industry groups have also adopted codes of responsibility. For example, many advertisers, broadcasters, many trade associations, and purchasing managers voluntarily abide by codes of conduct. Typically, these codes require professionals to be loyal to their clients' interests and to avoid conflicts of interest. Professionals must exercise their best efforts for every client. Confidential relationships with clients must be maintained and due care exercised in all efforts made on behalf of clients.

Unfortunately, "business" has never been considered a separate profession and has not yet developed a comprehensive and universal code of conduct for general application. Many firms have developed specific in-house codes with varying degrees of success. A "model" code of business responsibility, developed by Charles E. Harris of the Florida Bar, is reproduced below.[11] Much of this model code can be derived from or related to an "abuse of position" or fiduciary duty discussed in chapters 13–15. The *canons* are general statements of broad applicability. The *ethical principles* focus attention on more specific behaviors.

Code of Business Responsibility

Canon 1. A Professional Manager Should Assist in Maintaining the Integrity and Competence of the Business Community.

Ethical Principles

EP 1.1. The public and shareholders of this Company have a right to expect that the business of this Company will be efficiently and competently performed by our officers and employees. A professional manager should strive for excellence in performing his or her duties.

EP 1.2. A professional manager should maintain a high level of integrity in business conduct and should encourage other managers to do likewise. A manager should refrain from all illegal conduct in personal and business affairs. In doing so, the manager should support and obey both the language and the spirit of the law, avoiding efforts to circumvent the law by devious means or questionable interpretations. A professional manager should be able to rely upon the opinions of lawyers, accountants, and other outside experts, but should not shirk the final responsibility of making the business decisions associated with those opinions.

EP 1.3. A professional manager should disclose, as may be necessary and appropriate, any illegal or unethical business activities by any director, officer, or employee that are likely to have an adverse effect upon the business reputation or affairs of the Company. Although the manager should respect the Company's organizational structure if possible, the integrity and interests of the Company, its shareholders, and our business community may dictate that the manager report such illegal or unethical activity directly to the Company's audit committee, board of directors, or legal counsel, or, as a last resort, to appropriate governmental authorities.

Canon 2. A Professional Manager Should Preserve the Confidential Nature of Business and Customer Information.

Ethical Principles

EP 2.1. A professional manager should ensure that all confidential and proprietary information relating to the Company, its shareholders, and its existing and

[11] Charles E. Harris, "Restructuring a Workable Business Code of Ethics," *University of Florida Law Review*, 30 (1978), p. 310. Reprinted with the permission of the University of Florida Law Review. Copyright 1978.

prospective customers and suppliers, acquired in the course of duty, is used solely for Company purposes and is not provided to unauthorized persons or used for the purpose of furthering a private interest or making a personal profit.

EP 2.2. A professional manager should ensure that all material nonpublic information concerning the securities, financial condition, earnings, and other performance of the Company remains confidential, unless and until it is fully and properly disseminated to the public.

EP 2.3. The obligation of a professional manager to preserve the confidential nature of business and customer information continues after termination of the manager's employment with the Company.

Canon 3. A Professional Manager Should Place the Interests of the Company ahead of Any Private Interests and Should Disclose the Facts in Any Situation where a Conflict of Interest May Appear.

Ethical Principles

EP 3.1. A professional manager should ensure that none of his or her outside personal, business, or investment activities unreasonably conflict with the interests of the Company. In all situations where an actual or potential conflict of interest exists or may appear to others to exist, the manager should disclose all details of the activity and conflict.

EP 3.2. A professional manager should not use his or her position with the Company for personal gain. Likewise, a professional manager should separate personal interests and considerations from activities and decisions relating to the Company and its affairs.

EP 3.3. Except where expressly authorized by the terms of the manager's employment agreement or compensation arrangements with the Company, a professional manager should not directly or indirectly solicit or accept any fee, commission, entertainment, gift, gratuity, property, discount, or loan for himself or herself or his or her affiliates or immediate family as compensation for performing duties with the Company or for making, or causing the Company to make, any business decision.

EP 3.4. Except where expressly authorized by the Rules of Conduct, a professional manager should not directly or indirectly solicit or accept any fee, commission, entertainment, gift, gratuity, property, discount, or loan for himself or herself or his or her affiliates or immediate family from any existing or potential customer, competitor, or supplier of the Company.

EP 3.5. Except where expressly authorized by the Rules of Conduct, neither a professional manager nor his or her affiliates or immediate family should directly or indirectly solicit or receive any bequest or legacy from any customer, competitor, or supplier of the Company, or serve as executor, personal representative, trustee, or guardian of an estate, trust, or guardianship established by a customer, competitor, or supplier of the Company.

Canon 4. A Professional Manager Should Avoid Even the Appearance of Impropriety in Business Matters.

Ethical Principles

EP 4.1. Continuation of the American free-enterprise system requires that the public have confidence in this system and, particularly, in the ethical conduct of its business leaders. Consequently, a professional manager should strive to promote public confidence in our business system by avoiding not only ethical impropriety but also the appearance of ethical impropriety in business matters.

EP 4.2. A professional manager should exercise prudence and restraint in personal financial affairs, including speculative investments and margin accounts, in order to avoid debts or other financial obligations that are, or might appear to be, significantly out of proportion to the manager's financial statement and personal or family financial condition.

EP 4.3. Although a professional manager should be encouraged to participate freely and actively in the political process, the manager should ensure that such activities are separated from those of the Company. Except where expressly permitted by the Rules of Conduct, no Company assets, funds, or loans should be used for political purposes. All contributions for political purposes should be made pursuant to law and accurately reflected in the Company's books.

EP 4.4. Except for campaign contributions and lobbying expenditures designated as such and authorized or permitted by applicable law in the jurisdiction for which the election is held, no fee, commission, property, bribe, or any other compensation should be offered or paid directly or indirectly by a professional manager to, for, or on behalf of any elected, appointed, or ruling government official or head of state, in the United States or abroad, for the purpose of influencing in any way any decision by or within the influence of such official or head of state.

EP 4.5. If a professional manager has previously performed government or public service, or is presently performing such service, the manager should not perform activities for the Company in connection with any specific matter for which the manager had or has substantive responsibility as a government or public servant.

Canon 5. A Professional Manager Should Be Honest in Dealing with the Public and with the Company's Officers, Directors, Employees, Experts, and Customers.

Ethical Principles

EP 5.1. A professional manager should be open and honest in his business relationships with other officers and employees of the Company, the board of directors of the Company, and the lawyers, accountants, and other professionals retained by the Company. In this regard, honesty requires the furnishing of all information that the manager has that would be material to a given decision. The failure to furnish information that is known or thought to be necessary, or the provision of information that is known or thought to be inaccurate, misleading, or incomplete, is unacceptable.

EP 5.2. In order to preserve confidence in the information and advertising disseminated by our nation's businesses, a professional manager should strive to ensure that all information, advertising, and other statements released to the public by the Company are not misleading and do not omit to state any material fact necessary to make the information, advertising, or statements not misleading under the particular circumstances involved.

In recent years, numerous corporations have instituted codes of ethics for their employees. These codes are usually enforced with disciplinary sanctions and termination for serious violations. Typically, corporate codes of conduct prohibit employees from taking or making bribes or kickbacks. They usually prohibit conflicts of interest, illegal political contributions, and other general violations of the law. Other prohibitions that appear less frequently in such codes include misappropriation of inside information and insider trading, bribery, falsification of records, antitrust or FCPA violations, and work for other firms. The Organization of Economic Cooperation and Development (OECD) developed an international code of conduct for multinational corporations in 1976.

Two important factors help raise compliance with corporate codes of conduct. First, it must be clear that upper management endorses the code and appears to comply. This means that the tone from the top must signal a policy of commitment to ethical conduct in general and specifically to the firms own code. Second, the system for investigating and punishing violations must be perceived as providing fair due process. It must also routinely punish violations. If exceptions are made for guilty personnel, other employees may lose respect for the code and this could affect compliance.

Legal Effect of Corporate Codes of Conduct

The accelerating trend toward corporate codes of conduct may be due to several factors. First, codes are sometimes adopted to appease regulators. For example, some defense contractors found guilty of overcharging the U.S. government have agreed to develop, implement, and strongly enforce codes of conduct in order to retain their defense contracting business. Alternatively, codes have been instituted under consent decrees made with various regulators. Second, codes probably improve the firm's public image.

The proliferation of codes poses questions about their legal effect on the criminal, tort, and regulatory liability of both employers and employees. If strictly enforced, codes may sometimes reduce legal obligations. The *respondeat superior* doctrine of tort law holds the master vicariously (indirectly) liable for a servant's torts committed within the scope of employment. Respondeat superior is often applied in criminal prosecutions to punish a firm for its employees' crimes. However, several factors may influence leniency among prosecutors, judges, and juries, particularly if the firm cooperates in the investigation and strictly enforces its code of conduct. Comment C to the Restatement of Agency (Second) §230 suggests there should be a corporate code exception from employer liability when employees violate the code:

> [The corporate code prohibition] accentuates the limits of the servant's permissible action and hence makes it more easy to find that the prohibited act is entirely beyond the scope of employment.

Although codes generally parallel the law, they may actually trigger additional legal obligations. In the insider trading context, a corporate code or other work rules that prohibit insider trading actually trigger the misappropriation theory discussed in Chapter 15. This means that employees who violate corporate codes prohibiting misappropriation of information may be liable for insider trading or for revealing confidential nonpublic information. Investment banking firms that enforce such codes may avoid some vicarious liability for their employees' insider trading. For example, the firm's liability is reduced if *Chinese wall* procedures are implemented to prevent the leak of inside information from the firm's underwriting division to its brokerage division. Other provisions of the securities laws eliminate vicarious liability if firms have effective compliance programs and the firms act in *good faith* with no knowledge of the illegal activities of the person(s) they control (e.g., employees). Should a jury consider leniency for a firm that strictly enforces its code of conduct? The following case illustrates this problem.

United States v. Beusch

596 F.2d 871 (9th Cir. 1979)
United States Courts of Appeals

The California subsidiary of Deak & Co., the world's largest foreign currency exchange dealer, and its president, Beusch, were convicted of 377 misdemeanor violations of the

Bank Secrecy Act. Deak failed to report these money shipments to the Treasury Department, as required by the Act for transactions over $5,000 received in cash from outside the United States. Beusch had initiated contact with two Filipinos who sent numerous, large, cash shipments to Deak for further dispersal throughout the world. Deak appealed the conviction, contending the trial jury was improperly instructed to hold the firm vicariously liable for the violations of its employee, Beusch.

James M. Carter, Circuit Judge

Deak's final contention is that one of the instructions given to the jury prior to its deliberation was erroneous because, in effect, it imposed strict liability on Deak for Beusch's acts in spite of the requirement of specific intent. The challenged instruction reads as follows:

> "A corporation may be responsible for the acts of its agents done or made within the scope of its authority, even though the agent's conduct may be contrary to the corporation's actual instruction or contrary to the corporation's stated policies."

We have examined all of the instructions related to vicarious responsibility and find that, read in context, the challenged instruction does not mean what Deak says it means. It does not impose strict liability on Deak without proof of intent. Rather, it suggests that a corporation *may* be liable for acts of its employees done contrary to express instructions and policies, but that the existence of such instructions and policies may be considered in determining whether the employee in fact acted to benefit the corporation. Merely stating or publishing such instructions and policies without diligently enforcing them is not enough to place the acts of an employee who violates them outside the scope of his employment. It is a question of fact whether measures taken to enforce corporate policy in this area will adequately insulate the corporation against such acts, and we see no reason to disturb the jury's finding in this regard.

Case Questions

1. Why does the law require the court to consider the firm's efforts to enforce its corporate code? What weight should be given the firm's enforcement efforts?
2. What can a firm do to prove its enforcement efforts should be a mitigating factor in determining vicarious criminal liability?

U.S. Sentencing Guidelines A variation of the approach suggested in the *Beusch* case was adopted in the U.S. Sentencing Commission Guidelines, effective November 1991. Firms with a strictly enforced compliance program or corporate code of conduct may receive credits that reduce the firm's criminal sentence to as low as 15 percent of the potential penalty for their employees' violations. To qualify, such programs must be reasonably designed, implemented, and enforced in such a way as to be generally effective in preventing and detecting criminal conduct. This "mitigation" of the corporate penalty depends on whether the firm (1) reported the violation voluntarily, (2) instituted an effective compliance program (code of conduct and enforcement) before and after the violation, (3) had no high-level policy-setting official with knowledge of the violation, (4) cooperated fully with the government's investigation, and (5) accepted responsibility and took prompt, reasonable steps to remedy the harm. The sentencing guidelines add force to the trend to adopt and enforce corporate codes of conduct.

Legal Standards as Ethical Norms

In addition to the ethical norms discussed in Chapter 1 to aid in ethical analysis, there are several well-established legal standards that form a major basis for ethical analysis. First, the *fiduciary duty* standard, generally introduced for agents in Chapter 13 and then applied to acts of partners and corporate managers in Chapter 14, is the most fundamental legal/ethical principle. Agents owe their principals a duty of loyalty, which prohibits conflicts of interest and requires confidentiality. Second, there are several laws, most notably the UCC, that require commercial parties dealing at arms length to act in *good faith*. This means they must act honestly in fact in the transaction in question. Dishonesty and bad faith are often specifically penalized in commercial litigation.

A third legal/ethical principal prohibits persons from *misappropriation* of others' assets. While this legal/ethical standard seems to be stated clearly enough in the criminal law of theft, larceny, or embezzlement, it also applies to intangibles. For example, information is property that should not be misappropriated by another. The laws of insider trading, unfair competition, trade secrets, and intellectual property infringement make it illegal to misappropriate information for personal use or for communication to an outsider. A fourth legal/ethical standard is the requirement that everyone and every entity act with *due care*. The tort of negligence requires that all activities be undertaken with reasonable consideration of the possible external impact on others. Physically dangerous or financially damaging activities must be performed with due diligence. Finally, *respect for others' rights* must be observed. This legal/ethical norm also requires evaluation of how one's acts impact others and requires steps be taken to avoid infringing on the rights of others. Most ethical dilemmas can be resolved by reference to one of these five legal/ethical norms.

SUMMARY

Society increasingly expects business firms to act in a socially responsible manner. Managers seeking to avoid society's negative reactions should use ethical analysis in making decisions. Ethical principles create normative standards for ideal behavior. They contrast with the proscriptive standards of criminal law, which impose a required minimum base for behavior. Procedural and personal biases involved in the prosecution of corporate crimes make the law less effective as a deterrent to corporate crimes. Therefore, a greater role exists for proactive social responsibility analysis by decision makers to avert additional government regulation. Ultimately, a firm's chief officers are responsible for enforcing codes of conduct and compliance with the law and may be held criminally liable.

Business must identify its audiences and consider the effect that its decisions will have on various stakeholders. The influence of business on the political process is often criticized, so campaign finance laws were passed to diffuse their financial influence. Limits on political contributions and the development of PACs tend to spread rather than concentrate this influence. There is growing criticism over campaign financing and the influence of PACs.

Some people see a natural difference between the profit motive of business and society's perception of its best interests. Where business can externalize its costs, society often reacts through regulation to force internalization. Some people believe that the only legitimate goal for corporations is to maximize their profits and enhance their shareholders' welfare. Increasingly, business is held responsible to society. Philanthropic acts are legitimate corporate actions because they indirectly enhance corporate interests.

An important trend toward borrowing ethical codes from the learned professions has been developing in business. Firms and trade associations avert new regulation by imposing self-regulation promoting better public perception. Well-enforced codes may help shield firms from criminal liability. Business decision making requires adherence to ethical/legal analysis from ethical principles, codes of ethics, criminal laws, and civil laws.

Critical Thinking Review Questions

1. Discuss why the law has not proven to be the most effective control over aberrant behavior.
2. What does the term *corporate social responsibility* mean to business managers?
3. Discuss how the corporate stakeholders in your industry affect the doctrine of corporate social responsibility.
4. There are thousands of political action committees (PACs) in existence. Candidates for Congress increasingly look to these special interest groups for campaign financing. What is the role of PACs, and how does this role relate to the Federal Election Campaign Act?

Critical Thinking Exercises

1. Discuss the two main sections of the Foreign Corrupt Practices Act of 1977.
2. McClean and Uriarte were employees of International Harvester Company. International Harvester supplied equipment and acted as a subcontractor to Crawford Enterprises, which had contracted to build a plant for the National Petroleum Company of Mexico. McClean and Uriarte were indicted for violating provisions of the Foreign Corrupt Practices Act and for bribing officials of the National Petroleum Company. They filed motions to dismiss the charges against them on the grounds that the failure to convict their employer was a bar to their prosecution. Does the Foreign Corrupt Practices Act permit the prosecution of an employee if his employer has not been, and cannot be, convicted of similarly violating the act?
3. Discuss the structural changes that have been suggested to control irresponsible corporate behavior.
4. Many companies have codes of responsibility and ethics to govern the behavior of their key executives and employees. Discuss how such codes are enforced.
5. Nestlé Corporation allegedly used questionable marketing practices to sell baby formula in Third World countries. Some mothers in these countries watered the formula to make it go further. As a result, babies were unable to receive adequate nutrition. Certain groups urged a consumer boycott of Nestlé's products, claiming that Nestlé contributed to causing malnutrition and even death of babies in lesser developed countries. As Nestlé's vice president for marketing, how would you respond to this accusation?
6. Discuss the major elements you would use in a code of ethics for your company.

A

The Constitution of the United States of America

Preamble

We the People of the United States, in Order to form a more perfect Union, establish Justice, insure domestic Tranquility, provide for the common defense, promote the general Welfare, and secure the Blessings of Liberty to ourselves and our Posterity, do ordain and establish this Constitution for the United States of America.

Article I

Section 1 All legislative Powers herein granted shall be vested in a Congress of the United States, which shall consist of a Senate and House of Representatives.

Section 2 The House of Representatives shall be composed of Members chosen every second Year by the People of the several States, and the Electors in each State shall have the Qualifications requisite for Electors of the most numerous Branch of the State Legislature.

No Person shall be a Representative who shall not have attained to the age of twenty five Years, and been seven Years a Citizen of the United States, and who shall not, when elected, be an Inhabitant of that State in which he shall be chosen.

Representatives and direct Taxes shall be apportioned among the several States which may be included within this Union, according to their respective Numbers, which shall be determined by adding to the whole Number of free Persons, including those bound to Service for a Term of Years, and excluding Indians not taxed, three fifths of all other Persons.[1] The actual Enumeration shall be made within three Years after the first Meeting of the Congress of the United States, and within every subsequent Term of ten Years, in such Manner as they shall by Law direct. The Number of Representatives shall not exceed one for every thirty Thousand, but each State shall have at Least one Representative, and until such enumeration shall be made, the State of New Hampshire shall be entitled to choose three, Massachusetts eight, Rhode-Island and Providence Plantations one, Connecticut five, New York six, New Jersey four, Pennsylvania eight, Delaware one, Maryland six, Virginia ten, North Carolina five, South Carolina five, and Georgia three.

When vacancies happen in the Representation from any State, the Executive Authority thereof shall issue Writs of Election to fill such Vacancies.

The House of Representatives shall chuse their Speaker and other Officers; and shall have the sole Power of Impeachment.

Section 3 The Senate of the United States shall be composed of two Senators from each State, chosen by the Legislature thereof,[2] for six Years; and each Senator shall have one Vote.

Immediately after they shall be assembled in Consequence of the first Election, they shall be divided as equally as may be into three Classes. The Seats of the Senators of the first Class shall be vacated at the Expiration of the second Year, of the second Class at the Expiration of the fourth Year, and of the third Class at the Expiration of the sixth Year, so that one third may be chosen every second Year; and if Vacancies happen by Resignation, or otherwise, during the Recess of the Legislature of any State, the Executive thereof may make temporary Appointments until the next Meeting of the Legislature, which shall then fill such Vacancies.[3]

No Person shall be a Senator who shall not have attained to the Age of thirty Years, and been nine Years a Citizen of the

[1] Changed by the Fourteenth Amendment.

[2] Changed by the Seventeenth Amendment.

[3] Changed by the Seventeenth Amendment.

United States, and who shall not, when elected, be an Inhabitant of that State for which he shall be chosen.

The Vice President of the United States shall be President of the Senate, but shall have no Vote, unless they be equally divided.

The Senate shall chuse their other Officers, and also a President pro tempore, in the Absence of the Vice President, or when he shall exercise the Office of President of the United States.

The Senate shall have the sole Power to try all Impeachments. When sitting for that Purpose, they shall be on Oath or Affirmation. When the President of the United States is tried, the Chief Justice shall preside: And no Person shall be convicted without the Concurrence of two thirds of the Members present.

Judgment in Cases of Impeachment shall not extend further than to removal from Office, and disqualification to hold and enjoy any Office of honor, Trust or Profit under the United States: but the Party convicted shall nevertheless be liable and subject to Indictment, Trial, Judgment and Punishment, according to Law.

Section 4 The Times, Places and Manner of holding Elections for Senators and Representatives, shall be prescribed in each State by the Legislature thereof; but the Congress may at any time by Law make or alter such Regulations, except as to the Places of chusing Senators.

The Congress shall assemble at least once in every Year, and such Meeting shall be on the first Monday in December, unless they shall by Law appoint a different Day.[4]

Section 5 Each House shall be the Judge of the Elections, Returns and Qualifications of its own Members, and a Majority of each shall constitute a Quorum to do Business; but a smaller Number may adjourn from day to day, and may be authorized to compel the Attendance of absent Members, in such Manner, and under such Penalties as each House may provide.

Each House may determine the Rules of its Proceedings, punish its Members for disorderly Behaviour, and with the Concurrence of two thirds, expel a Member.

Each House shall keep a Journal of its Proceedings, and from time to time publish the same, excepting such Parts as may in their Judgment require Secrecy; and the Yeas and Nays of the Members of either House on any question shall, at the Desire of one fifth of those Present, be entered on the Journal.

Neither House, during the Session of Congress, shall, without the Consent of the other, adjourn for more than three days, nor to any other Place than that in which the two Houses shall be sitting.

Section 6 The Senators and Representatives shall receive a Compensation for their Services, to be ascertained by Law, and paid out of the Treasury of the United States. They shall in all Cases, except Treason, Felony and Breach of the Peace, be privileged from Arrest during their Attendance at the Session of their respective Houses, and in going to and returning from the same; and for any Speech or Debate in either House, they shall not be questioned in any other Place.

No Senator or Representative shall, during the Time for which he was elected, be appointed to any civil Office under the Authority of the United States, which shall have been created, or the Emoluments whereof shall have been encreased during such time; and no Person holding any Office under the United States, shall be a Member of either House during his Continuance in Office.

Section 7 All Bills for raising Revenue shall originate in the House of Representatives; but the Senate may propose or concur with Amendments as on other Bills.

Every Bill which shall have passed the House of Representatives and the Senate, shall, before it becomes a Law, be presented to the President of the United States; If he approves he shall sign it, but if not he shall return it, with his Objections to that House in which it shall have originated, who shall enter the Objections at large on their Journal, and proceed to reconsider it. If after such Reconsideration two thirds of that House shall agree to pass the Bill, it shall be sent, together with the Objections, to the other House, by which it shall likewise be reconsidered, and if approved by two thirds of that House, it shall become a Law. But in all such Cases the Votes of both Houses shall be determined by Yeas and Nays, and the Names of the Persons voting for and against the Bill shall be entered on the Journal of each House respectively. If any Bill shall not be returned by the President within ten Days (Sundays excepted) after it shall have been presented to him, the Same shall be a Law, in like Manner as if he had signed it, unless the Congress by their Adjournment prevent its Return, in which Case it shall not be a Law.

Every Order, Resolution, or Vote to which the Concurrence of the Senate and House of Representatives may be necessary (except on a question of Adjournment) shall be presented to the President of the United States; and before the Same shall take Effect, shall be approved by him, or being disapproved by him, shall be repassed by two thirds of the Senate and House of Representatives, according to the Rules and Limitations prescribed in the Case of a Bill.

Section 8 The Congress shall have Power To lay and collect Taxes, Duties, Imposts and Excises, to pay the Debts and provide for the common Defence and general Welfare of the United States; but all Duties, Imposts and Excises shall be uniform throughout the United States.

To borrow Money on the credit of the United States;

To regulate Commerce with foreign Nations, and among the several States, and with the Indian Tribes;

To establish an uniform Rule of Naturalization, and uniform Laws on the subject of Bankruptcies throughout the United States;

To coin Money, regulate the Value thereof, and of foreign Coin, and fix the Standard of Weights and Measures;

[4] Changed by the Twentieth Amendment.

To provide for the Punishment of counterfeiting the Securities and current Coin of the United States;

To establish Post Offices and post Roads;

To promote the Progress of Science and useful Arts, by securing for limited Times to Authors and Inventors the exclusive Right to their respective Writings and Discoveries;

To constitute Tribunals inferior to the supreme Court;

To define and punish Piracies and Felonies committed on the high Seas, and Offences against the Law of Nations;

To declare War, grant Letters of Marque and Reprisal, and make Rules concerning Captures on Land and Water;

To raise and support Armies, but no Appropriation of Money to that Use shall be for a longer Term than two Years;

To provide and maintain a Navy;

To make Rules for the Government and Regulation of the land and naval Forces;

To provide for calling forth the Militia to execute the Laws of the Union, suppress Insurrections and repel Invasions;

To provide for organizing, arming, and disciplining, the Militia, and for governing such Part of them as may be employed in the Service of the United States, reserving to the States respectively, the Appointment of the Officers, and the Authority of training the Militia according to the discipline prescribed by Congress;

To exercise exclusive Legislation in all Cases whatsoever, over such District (not exceeding ten Miles square) as may, by Cession of particular States, and the Acceptance of Congress, become the Seat of the Government of the United States, and to exercise like Authority over all Places purchased by the Consent of the Legislature of the State in which the Same shall be, for the Erection of Forts, Magazines, Arsenals, dock-Yards, and other needful Buildings;—And

To make all Laws which shall be necessary and proper for carrying into Execution the foregoing Powers, and all other Powers vested by this Constitution in the Government of the United States, or in any Department or Officer thereof.

Section 9 The Migration or Importation of such Persons as any of the States now existing shall think proper to admit, shall not be prohibited by the Congress prior to the Year one thousand eight hundred and eight, but a Tax or duty may be imposed on such Importation, not exceeding ten dollars for each Person.

The Privilege of the Writ of Habeas Corpus shall not be suspended, unless when in Cases of Rebellion or Invasion the public Safety may require it.

No Bill of Attainder or ex post facto Law shall be passed.

No Capitation, or other direct, Tax shall be laid, unless in Proportion to the Census of Enumeration herein before directed to be taken.[5]

No Tax or Duty shall be laid on Articles exported from any State.

No Preference shall be given by any Regulation of Commerce or Revenue to the Ports of one State over those of another: nor shall Vessels bound to, or from, one State, be obliged to enter, clear, or pay Duties in another.

No Money shall be drawn from the Treasury, but in Consequence of Appropriations made by Law; and a regular Statement and Account of the Receipts and Expenditures of all public Money shall be published from time to time.

No Title of Nobility shall be granted by the United States: And no Person holding any Office of Profit or Trust under them, shall, without the Consent of the Congress, accept of any present, Emolument, Office, or Title, of any kind whatever, from any King, Prince, or foreign State.

Section 10 No State shall enter into any Treaty, Alliance, or Confederation; grant Letters of Marque and Reprisal; coin Money; emit Bills of Credit; make any Thing but gold and silver coin a Tender in Payment of Debts; pass any Bill of Attainder, ex post facto Law, or Law impairing the Obligation of Contracts, or grant any Title of Nobility.

No State shall, without the Consent of the Congress, lay any Imposts or Duties on Imports or Exports, except what may be absolutely necessary for executing its inspection Laws: and the net Produce of all Duties and Imposts, laid by any State on Imports or Exports, shall be for the Use of the Treasury of the United States; and all such Laws shall be subject to the Revision and Controul of the Congress.

No State shall, without the consent of Congress, lay any Duty of Tonnage, keep Troops, or Ships of War in time of Peace, enter into any Agreement or Compact with another State, or with a foreign Power, or engage in War, unless actually invaded, or in such imminent Danger as will not admit of delay.

Article II

Section 1 The executive Power shall be vested in a President of the United States of America. He shall hold his Office during the Term of four Years, and, together with the Vice President, chosen for the same Term, be elected, as follows

Each state shall appoint, in such Manner as the Legislature thereof may direct, a Number of Electors, equal to the whole Number of Senators and Representatives to which the State may be entitled in Congress: but no Senator or Representative, or Person holding an Office of Trust or Profit under the United States, shall be appointed an Elector.

The Electors shall meet in their respective States, and vote by Ballot for two Persons, of whom one at least shall not be an inhabitant of the same State with themselves. And they shall make a List of all the Persons voted for, and of the Number of Votes for each; which List they shall sign and certify, and transmit sealed to the Seat of the Government of the United States, directed to the President of the Senate. The President of the Senate shall, in the Presence of the Senate and House of Representatives, open all the Certificates, and the Votes shall

[5] Changed by the Sixteenth Amendment.

then be counted. The Person having the greatest Number of Votes shall be the President, if such Number be a Majority of the whole Number of Electors appointed; and if there be more than one who have such Majority, and have an equal Number of Votes, then the House of Representatives shall immediately chuse by Ballot one of them for President; and if no Person have a Majority, then from the five highest on the List the said House shall in like Manner chuse the President. But in chusing the President, the Votes shall be taken by States, the Representation from each State having one Vote; A quorum for this purpose shall consist of a Member or Members from two thirds of the States, and a Majority of all the States shall be necessary to a Choice. In every Case, after the Choice of the President, the Person having the greatest Number of Votes of the Electors shall be the Vice President. But if there should remain two or more who have equal Votes, the Senate shall chuse from them by Ballot the Vice President.[6]

The Congress may determine the Time of chusing the Electors, and the Day on which they shall give their Votes; which Day shall be the same throughout the United States.

No Person except a natural born Citizen, or a Citizen of the United States, at the time of the Adoption of this Constitution, shall be eligible to the Office of President; neither shall any Person be eligible to that Office who shall not have attained to the Age of thirty five Years, and been fourteen Years a Resident within the United States.

In Case of the Removal of the President from Office, or of his Death, Resignation, or Inability to discharge the Powers and Duties of the said Office, the Same shall devolve on the Vice President, and the Congress may by Law provide for the Case of Removal, Death, Resignation or Inability, both of the President and Vice President, declaring what Officer shall then act as President, and such Officer shall act accordingly, until the Disability be removed, or a President shall be elected.[7]

The President shall, at stated Times, receive for his Services, a Compensation, which shall neither be encreased nor diminished during the Period for which he shall have been elected, and he shall not receive within that Period any other Emolument from the United States, or any of them.

Before he enter on the Execution of his Office, he shall take the following Oath or Affirmation:—"I do solemnly swear (or affirm) that I will faithfully execute the Office of President of the United States, and will to the best of my Ability, preserve, protect, and defend the Constitution of the United States."

Section 2 The President shall be Commander in Chief of the Army and Navy of the United States, and of the Militia of the several States, when called into the actual Service of the United States; he may require the Opinion, in writing, of the principal Officer in each of the executive Departments, upon any Subject relating to the Duties of their respective Offices, and he shall have Power to grant Reprieves and Pardons for Offences against the United States, except in Cases of Impeachment.

He shall have Power, by and with the Advice and Consent of the Senate, to make Treaties, provided two thirds of the Senators present concur; and he shall nominate, and by and with the Advice and Consent of the Senate, shall appoint Ambassadors, other public Ministers and Consuls, Judges of the supreme Court, and all other Officers of the United States, whose Appointments are not herein otherwise provided for, and which shall be established by Law; but the Congress may by Law vest the Appointment of such inferior Officers, as they think proper, in the President alone, in the Courts of Law, or in the Heads of Departments.

The President shall have Power to fill up all Vacancies that may happen during the Recess of the Senate, by granting Commissions which shall expire at the End of their next Session.

Section 3 He shall from time to time give to the Congress Information of the State of the Union, and recommend to their Consideration such Measures as he shall judge necessary and expedient; he may, on extraordinary Occasions, convene both Houses, or either of them, and in Case of Disagreement between them, with Respect to the Time of Adjournment, he may adjourn them to such Time as he shall think proper; he shall receive Ambassadors and other public Ministers; he shall take Care that the Laws be faithfully executed, and shall Commission all the Officers of the United States.

Section 4 The President, Vice President and all civil Officers of the United States, shall be removed from Office on Impeachment for, and Conviction of, Treason, Bribery, or other high Crimes and Misdemeanors.

Article III

Section 1 The judicial Power of the United States, shall be vested in one supreme Court, and in such inferior Courts as the Congress may from time to time ordain and establish. The Judges, both of the supreme and inferior Courts, shall hold their Offices during good Behaviour, and shall, at stated Times, receive for their Services, a Compensation, which shall not be diminished during their Continuance in Office.

Section 2 The judicial Power shall extend to all Cases, in Law and Equity, arising under this Constitution, the Laws of the United States, and Treaties made, or which shall be made, under their Authority;—to all Cases affecting Ambassadors, other public Ministers and Consuls;—to all Cases of admiralty and maritime Jurisdiction;—to Controversies to which the United States shall be a party;—to Controversies between two or more States;—between a State and Citizens of another State;[8]—between Citizens of different States;—between

[6] Changed by the Twelfth Amendment.

[7] Changed by the Twenty-fifth Amendment.

[8] Changed by the Eleventh Amendment.

Citizens of the same State claiming Lands under Grants of different States, and between a State, or the Citizens thereof, and foreign States, Citizens or Subjects.

In all Cases affecting Ambassadors, other public Ministers and Consuls, and those in which a State shall be Party, the supreme Court shall have original Jurisdiction. In all the other Cases before mentioned, the supreme Court shall have appellate Jurisdiction, both as to Law and Fact, with such Exceptions, and under such Regulations as the Congress shall make.

The Trial of all Crimes, except in Cases of Impeachment, shall be by Jury: and such Trial shall be held in the State where the said Crimes shall have been committed; but when not committed within any State, the Trial shall be at such Place or Places as the Congress may by Law have directed.

Section 3 Treason against the United States, shall consist only in levying War against them, or in adhering to their Enemies, giving them Aid and Comfort. No Person shall be convicted of Treason unless on the Testimony of two Witnesses to the same overt Act, or on Confession in open Court.

The Congress shall have Power to declare the Punishment of Treason, but no Attainder of Treason shall work Corruption of Blood, or Forfeiture except during the Life of the Person attainted.

Article IV

Section 1 Full Faith and Credit shall be given in each State to the public Acts, Records, and judicial Proceedings of every other State. And the Congress may by general Laws prescribe the Manner in which such Acts, Records and Proceedings shall be proved, and the Effect thereof.

Section 2 The Citizens of each State shall be entitled to all Privileges and Immunities of Citizens in the several States.

A Person charged in any State with Treason, Felony, or other Crime, who shall flee from Justice, and be found in another State, shall on Demand of the executive Authority of the State from which he fled, be delivered up, to be removed to the State having Jurisdiction of the Crime.

No Person held to Service or Labour in one State, under the Laws thereof, escaping into another, shall, in Consequence of any Law or Regulation therein, be discharged from such Service or Labour, but shall be delivered up on Claim of the Party to whom such Service or Labour may be due.[9]

Section 3 New States may be admitted by the Congress into this Union; but no new State shall be formed or erected within the Jurisdiction of any other State; nor any State be formed by the Junction of two or more States, or Parts of States, without the Consent of the Legislatures of the States concerned as well as of the Congress.

[9] Changed by the Thirteenth Amendment.

The Congress shall have Power to dispose of and make all needful Rules and Regulations respecting the Territory or other Property belonging to the United States; and nothing in this Constitution shall be so construed as to Prejudice any Claims of the United States, or of any particular State.

Section 4 The United States shall guarantee to every State in this Union a Republican Form of Government, and shall protect each of them against Invasion; and on Application of the Legislature, or of the Executive (when the Legislature cannot be convened) against domestic Violence.

Article V

The Congress, whenever two thirds of both Houses shall deem it necessary, shall propose Amendments to this Constitution, or, on the Application of the Legislatures of two thirds of the several States, shall call a Convention for proposing Amendments, which, in either Case, shall be valid to all Intents and Purposes, as Part of this Constitution, when ratified by the legislatures of three fourths of the several States, or by Conventions in three fourths thereof, as the one or the other Mode of Ratification may be proposed by the Congress; Provided that no Amendment which may be made prior to the Year One thousand eight hundred and eight shall in any Manner affect the first and fourth Clauses in the Ninth Section of the first Article; and that no State, without its Consent, shall be deprived of its equal Suffrage in the Senate.

Article VI

All Debts contracted and Engagements entered into, before the Adoption of this Constitution, shall be as valid against the United States under this Constitution, as under the Confederation.

The Constitution, and the Laws of the United States which shall be made in Pursuance thereof; and all Treaties made, or which shall be made, under the Authority of the United States, shall be the supreme Law of the Land; and the Judges in every State shall be bound thereby, any Thing in the Constitution or Laws of any State to the Contrary notwithstanding.

The Senators and Representatives before mentioned, and the Members of the several State Legislatures, and all executive and judicial Officers, both of the United States and of the several States, shall be bound by Oath or Affirmation, to support this Constitution; but no religious Test shall ever be required as a Qualification to any Office or public Trust under the United States.

Article VII

The Ratification of the Conventions of nine States, shall be sufficient for the Establishment of this Constitution between the States so ratifying the Same.

Done in Convention by the Unanimous Consent of the States present the Seventeenth Day of September in the Year of our Lord one thousand seven hundred and eighty seven and of the Independance of the United States of America the Twelfth. In witness whereof We have hereunto subscribed our Names.

Amendments

[The first 10 amendments are known as the "Bill of Rights."]

Amendment I (Ratified 1791)

Congress shall make no law respecting an establishment of religion, or prohibiting the free exercise thereof; or abridging the freedom of speech, or of the press; or the right of the people peaceably to assemble, and to petition the Government for a redress of grievances.

Amendment 2 (Ratified 1791)

A well regulated Militia, being necessary to the security of a free State, the right of the people to keep and bear Arms, shall not be infringed.

Amendment 3 (Ratified 1791)

No Soldier shall, in time of peace be quartered in any house, without the consent of the Owner, nor in time of war, but in a manner to be prescribed by law.

Amendment 4 (Ratified 1791)

The right of the people to be secure in their persons, houses, papers, and effects, against unreasonable searches and seizures, shall not be violated, and no Warrants shall issue, but upon probable cause, supported by Oath or affirmation, and particularly describing the place to be searched, and the persons or things to be seized.

Amendment 5 (Ratified 1791)

No person shall be held to answer for a capital, or otherwise infamous crime, unless on a presentment or indictment of a Grand Jury, except in cases arising in the land or naval forces, or in the Militia, when in actual service in time of War or public danger; nor shall any person be subject for the same offence to be twice put in jeopardy of life or limb; nor shall be compelled in any criminal case to be a witness against himself, nor be deprived of life, liberty, or property, without due process of law; nor shall private property be taken for public use, without just compensation.

Amendment 6 (Ratified 1791)

In all criminal prosecutions, the accused shall enjoy the right to a speedy and public trial, by an impartial jury of the State and district wherein the crime shall have been committed, which district shall have been previously ascertained by law, and to be informed of the nature and cause of the accusation; to be confronted with the witnesses against him; to have compulsory process for obtaining Witnesses in his favor, and to have assistance of counsel for his defence.

Amendment 7 (Ratified 1791)

In Suits at common law, where the value in controversy shall exceed twenty dollars, the right of trial by jury shall be preserved, and no fact tried by a jury, shall be otherwise re-examined in any Court of the United States, than according to the rules of the common law.

Amendment 8 (Ratified 1791)

Excessive bail shall not be required, nor excessive fines imposed, nor cruel and unusual punishments inflicted.

Amendment 9 (Ratified 1791)

The enumeration in the Constitution, of certain rights, shall not be construed to deny or disparage others retained by the people.

Amendment 10 (Ratified 1791)

The powers not delegated to the United States by the Constitution, nor prohibited by it to the States, are reserved to the States respectively, or to the people.

Amendment 11 (Ratified 1795)

The Judicial power of the United States shall not be construed to extend to any suit in law or equity, commenced or prosecuted against one of the United States by Citizens of another State, or by Citizens or Subjects of any Foreign State.

Amendment 12 (Ratified 1804)

The Electors shall meet in their respective states, and vote by ballot for President and Vice-President, one of whom, at least, shall not be an inhabitant of the same state with themselves; they shall name in their ballots the person voted for as President, and in distinct ballots the person voted for as Vice-President, and they shall make distinct lists of all persons voted for as President, and of all persons voted for as Vice-President, and of the number of votes for each, which lists they shall sign and certify, and transmit sealed to the seat of the government of the United States, directed to the President of the Senate;—The President of the Senate shall, in the presence of the Senate and House of Representatives, open all the certificates and the votes shall then be counted;—The person having the greatest number of votes for President, shall be the President, if such number be a majority of the whole number of Electors appointed; and if no person have such majority, then from the persons having the highest numbers not exceeding three on the list of those voted for as President, the House of Representatives shall choose immediately, by ballot, the President. But in choosing the President, the votes shall be taken by states, the representation from each state having one vote; a quorum for this purpose shall consist of a member or members from two-thirds of the states, and a majority of all the states shall be necessary to a choice. And if the House of Representatives shall not choose a President whenever the right of choice shall devolve upon them, before the fourth day of March next following, then the Vice-President shall act as president, as in the case of the death or other constitutional disability of the President.[10]—The person having the greatest number of votes as Vice-President, shall be the Vice-President, if such number be a majority of the whole number of Electors appointed, and if no person have a majority, then from the two highest numbers on the list, the Senate shall choose the Vice-President; a quorum for the purpose shall consist of two-thirds of the whole number of Senators, and a majority of the whole number shall be necessary to a choice. But no person constitutionally ineligible to the office of President shall be eligible to that of Vice-President of the United States.

Amendment 13 (Ratified 1865)

Section 1 Neither slavery nor involuntary servitude, except as a punishment for crime whereof the party shall have been duly convicted, shall exist within the United States, or any place subject to their jurisdiction.

Section 2 Congress shall have power to enforce this article by appropriate legislation.

Amendment 14 (Ratified 1868)

Section 1 All persons born or naturalized in the United States, and subject to the jurisdiction thereof, are citizens of the United States and of the State wherein they reside. No State shall make or enforce any law which shall abridge the privileges or immunities of citizens of the United States; nor shall any State deprive any person of life, liberty, or property, without due process of law; nor deny to any person within its jurisdiction the equal protection of the laws.

Section 2 Representatives shall be apportioned among the several States according to their respective numbers, counting the whole number of persons in each State, excluding Indians not taxed. But when the right to vote at any election for the choice of electors for President and Vice President of the United States, Representatives in Congress, the Executive and Judicial officers of a State, or the members of the Legislature thereof, is denied to any of the male inhabitants of such State, being twenty-one[11] years of age, and citizens of the United States, or in any way abridged except for participation in rebellion, or other crime, the basis of representation therein shall be reduced in the proportion which the number of such male citizens shall bear to the whole number of male citizens twenty-one years of age in such State.

Section 3 No person shall be a Senator or Representative in Congress, or elector of President and Vice President, or hold any office, civil or military, under the United States, or under any State, who, having previously taken an oath, as a member of Congress, or as an officer of the United States, or as a member of any State legislature, or as an executive or judicial officer of any State, to support the Constitution of the United States, shall have engaged in insurrection or rebellion against the same, or given aid or comfort to the enemies thereof. But Congress may by a vote of two-thirds of each House, remove such disability.

Section 4 The validity of the public debt of the United States, authorized by law, including debts incurred for payment of pensions and bounties for services in suppressing insurrection or rebellion, shall not be questioned. But neither the United States nor any State shall assume or pay any debt or obligation incurred in aid of insurrection or rebellion against the United States, or any claim for the loss or emancipation of any slave; but all such debts, obligations and claims shall be held illegal and void.

Section 5 The Congress shall have power to enforce, by appropriate legislation, the provisions of this article.

Amendment 15 (Ratified 1870)

Section 1 The right of citizens of the United States to vote shall not be denied or abridged by the United States or by any State on account of race, color, or previous condition of servitude.

Section 2 The Congress shall have power to enforce this article by appropriate legislation.

Amendment 16 (Ratified 1913)

The Congress shall have power to lay and collect taxes on incomes, from whatever source derived, without apportion-

[10] Changed by the Twentieth Amendment.

[11] Changed by the Twenty-sixth Amendment.

ment among the several States, and without regard to any census or enumeration.

Amendment 17 (Ratified 1913)

The Senate of the United States shall be composed of two Senators from each State, elected by the people thereof, for six years; and each Senator shall have one vote. The electors in each State shall have the qualifications requisite for electors of the most numerous branch of the State legislatures.

When vacancies happen in the representation of any State in the Senate, the executive authority of such State shall issue writs of election to fill such vacancies: *Provided,* That the legislature of any State may empower the executive thereof to make temporary appointments until the people fill the vacancies by election as the legislature may direct.

This amendment shall not be so construed as to affect the election or term of any Senator chosen before it becomes valid as part of the Constitution.

Amendment 18 (Ratified 1919; Repealed 1933)

Section 1 After one year from the ratification of this article the manufacture, sale, or transportation of intoxicating liquors within, the importation thereof into, or the exportation thereof from the United States and all territory subject to the jurisdiction thereof for beverage purposes is hereby prohibited.

Section 2 The Congress and the several States shall have concurrent power to enforce this article by appropriate legislation.

Section 3 This article shall be inoperative unless it shall have been ratified as an amendment to the Constitution by the legislatures of the several States, as provided in the Constitution, within seven years from the date of the submission hereof to the States by the Congress.[12]

Amendment 19 (Ratified 1920)

The right of citizens of the United States to vote shall not be denied or abridged by the United States or by any State on account of sex.

Congress shall have power to enforce this article by appropriate legislation.

Amendment 20 (Ratified 1933)

Section 1 The terms of the President and Vice President shall end at noon on the 20th day of January, and the terms of Senators and Representatives at noon on the 3d day of January, of the years in which such terms would have ended if this article had not been ratified; and the terms of their successors shall then begin.

Section 2 The Congress shall assemble at least once in every year, and such meeting shall begin at noon on the 3d day of January, unless they shall by law appoint a different day.

Section 3 If, at the time fixed for the beginning of the term of the President, the President elect shall have died, the Vice President elect shall become President. If a President shall not have been chosen before the time fixed for the beginning of his term, or if the President elect shall have failed to qualify, then the Vice President elect shall act as President until a President shall have qualified; and the Congress may by law provide for the case wherein neither a President elect nor a Vice President elect shall have qualified, declaring who shall then act as President, or the manner in which one who is to act shall be selected, and such person shall act accordingly until a President or Vice President shall have qualified.

Section 4 The Congress may by law provide for the case of the death of any of the persons from whom the House of Representatives may choose a President whenever the right of choice shall have devolved upon them, and for the case of the death of any of the persons from whom the Senate may choose a Vice President whenever the right of choice shall have devolved upon them.

Section 5 Sections 1 and 2 shall take effect on the 15th day of October following the ratification of this article.

Section 6 This article shall be inoperative unless it shall have been ratified as an amendment to the Constitution by the legislatures of three-fourths of the several States within seven years from the date of its submission.

Amendment 21 (Ratified 1933)

Section 1 The eighteenth article of amendment to the Constitution of the United States is hereby repealed.

Section 2 The transportation or importation into any State, Territory, or possession of the United States for delivery or use therein of intoxicating liquors, in violation of the laws thereof, is hereby prohibited.

Section 3 This article shall be inoperative unless it shall have been ratified as an amendment to the Constitution by conventions in the several States, as provided in the Constitution, within seven years from the date of the submission hereof to the States by the Congress.

Amendment 22 (Ratified 1951)

Section 1 No person shall be elected to the office of the President more than twice, and no person who has held the office of President, or acted as President, for more than two years of a term to which some other person was elected President shall be elected to the office of the President more than once. But this Article shall not apply to any person

[12] Repealed by the Twenty-first Amendment.

holding the office of President when this Article was proposed by the Congress, and shall not prevent any person who may be holding the office of President, or acting as President, during the term within which this Article becomes operative from holding the office of President or acting as President during the remainder of such term.

Section 2 This Article shall be inoperative unless it shall have been ratified as an amendment to the Constitution by the legislatures of three-fourths of the several States within seven years from the date of its submission to the States by the Congress.

Amendment 23 (Ratified 1961)

Section 1 The District constituting the seat of Government of the United States shall appoint in such manner as the Congress may direct:

A number of electors of President and Vice President equal to the whole number of Senators and Representatives in Congress to which the District would be entitled if it were a State, but in no event more than the least populous State; they shall be in addition to those appointed by the States, but they shall be considered, for the purposes of the election of President and Vice President, to be electors appointed by a State; and they shall meet in the District and perform such duties as provided by the twelfth article of amendment.

Section 2 The Congress shall have power to enforce this article by appropriate legislation.

Amendment 24 (Ratified 1964)

Section 1 The right of citizens of the United States to vote in any primary or other election for President or Vice President, for electors for President or Vice President, or for Senator or Representative in Congress, shall not be denied or abridged by the United States or any State by reason of failure to pay any poll tax or other tax.

Section 2 The Congress shall have power to enforce this article by appropriate legislation.

Amendment 25 (Ratified 1967)

Section 1 In case of the removal of the President from office or of his death or resignation, the Vice President shall become President.

Section 2 Whenever there is a vacancy in the office of the Vice President, the President shall nominate a Vice President who shall take office upon confirmation by a majority vote of both Houses of Congress.

Section 3 Whenever the President transmits to the President pro tempore of the Senate and the Speaker of the House of Representatives his written declaration that he is unable to discharge the powers and duties of his office, and until he transmits to them a written declaration to the contrary, such powers and duties shall be discharged by the Vice President as Acting President.

Section 4 Whenever the Vice President and a majority of either the principal officers of the executive departments or of such other body as Congress may by law provide, transmit to the President pro tempore of the Senate and the Speaker of the House of Representatives their written declaration that the President is unable to discharge the powers and duties of his office, the Vice President shall immediately assume the powers and duties of the office as Acting President.

Thereafter, when the President transmits to the President pro tempore of the Senate and the Speaker of the House of Representatives his written declaration that no inability exists, he shall resume the powers and duties of his office unless the Vice President and a majority of either the principal officers of the executive department or of such other body as Congress may by law provide, transmit within four days to the President pro tempore of the Senate and the Speaker of the House of Representatives their written declaration that the President is unable to discharge the powers and duties of his office. Thereupon Congress shall decide the issue, assembling within forty-eight hours for that purpose if not in session. If the Congress, within twenty-one days after receipt of the latter written declaration, or, if Congress is not in session, within twenty-one days after Congress is required to assemble, determines by two-thirds vote of both Houses that the President is unable to discharge the powers and duties of his office, the Vice President shall continue to discharge the same as Acting President; otherwise, the President shall resume the powers and duties of his office.

Amendment 26 (Ratified 1971)

Section 1 The right of citizens of the United States, who are eighteen years of age or older, to vote shall not be denied or abridged by the United States or by any State on account of age.

Section 2 The Congress shall have power to enforce this article by appropriate legislation.

Amendment 27 (Ratified 1992)

No law, varying the compensation for the services of the Senators and Representatives, shall take effect, until an election of Representatives shall have intervened.

APPENDIX

B

Uniform Commercial Code (Excerpts from the Official Text—1990)*

Title

An Act

To be known as the Uniform Commercial Code, Relating to Certain Commercial Transactions in or regarding Personal Property and Contracts and other Documents concerning them, including Sales, Commercial Paper, Bank Deposits and Collections, Letters of Credit, Bulk Transfers, Warehouse Receipts, Bills of Lading, other Documents of Title, Investment Securities, and Secured Transactions, including certain Sales of Accounts, Chattel Paper, and Contract Rights; Providing for Public Notice to Third Parties in Certain Circumstances; Regulating Procedure, Evidence and Damages in Certain Court Actions Involving such Transactions, Contracts or Documents; to Make Uniform the Law with Respect Thereto; and Repealing Inconsistent Legislation.

ARTICLE 1 GENERAL PROVISIONS

§1—203. Obligation of Good Faith

Every contract or duty within this Act imposes an obligation of good faith in its performance or enforcement.

§1—205. Course of Dealing and Usage of Trade

(1) A course of dealing is a sequence of previous conduct between the parties to a particular transaction which is fairly to be regarded as establishing a common basis of understanding for interpreting their expressions and other conduct.

(2) A usage of trade is any practice or method of dealing having such regularity of observance in a place, vocation or trade as to justify an expectation that it will be observed with respect to the transaction in question. The existence and scope of such a usage are to be proved as facts. If it is established that such a usage is embodied in a written trade code or similar writing the interpretation of the writing is for the court.

(3) A course of dealing between parties and any usage of trade in the vocation or trade in which they are engaged or of which they are or should be aware give particular meaning to and supplement or qualify terms of an agreement.

(4) The express terms of an agreement and an applicable course of dealing or usage of trade shall be construed wherever reasonable as consistent with each other; but when such construction is unreasonable express terms control both course of dealing and usage of trade and course of dealing controls usage of trade.

(5) An applicable usage of trade in the place where any part of performance is to occur shall be used in interpreting the agreement as to that part of the performance.

(6) Evidence of a relevant usage of trade offered by one party is not admissible unless and until he has given the other party such notice as the court finds sufficient to prevent unfair surprise to the latter.

ARTICLE 2 SALES

Part 1 Short Title, General Construction and Subject Matter

§2—104. Definitions: "Merchant"; "Between Merchants"; "Financing Agency"

(1) "Merchant" means a person who deals in goods of the kind or otherwise by his occupation holds himself out as having knowledge or skill peculiar to the practices or goods involved in the transaction or to whom such knowledge or skill may be attributed by his employment of an agent or broker or other intermediary who by his occupation holds himself out as having such knowledge or skill.

(2) "Financing agency" means a bank, finance company or other person who in the ordinary course of business makes advances

against goods or documents of title or who by arrangement with either the seller or the buyer intervenes in ordinary course to make or collect payment due or claimed under the contract for sale, as by purchasing or paying the seller's draft or making advances against it or by merely taking it for collection whether or not documents of title accompany the draft. "Financing agency" includes also a bank or other person who similarly intervenes between persons who are in the position of seller and buyer in respect to the goods (Section 2—707).
(3) "Between merchants" means in any transaction with respect to which both parties are chargeable with the knowledge or skill of merchants.

Part 2 Form, Formation and Readjustment of Contract

§2—201. *Formal Requirements; Statute of Frauds*

(1) Except as otherwise provided in this section a contract for the sale of goods for the price of $500 or more is not enforceable by way of action or defense unless there is some writing sufficient to indicate that a contract for sale has been made between the parties and signed by the party against whom enforcement is sought or by his authorized agent or broker. A writing is not insufficient because it omits or incorrectly states a term agreed upon but the contract is not enforceable under this paragraph beyond the quantity of goods shown in such writing.
(2) Between merchants if within a reasonable time a writing in confirmation of the contract and sufficient against the sender is received and the party receiving it has reason to know its contents, it satisfies the requirements of subsection (1) against such party unless written notice of objection to its contents is given within 10 days after it is received.
(3) A contract which does not satisfy the requirements of subsection (1) but which is valid in other respects is enforceable

(a) if the goods are to be specially manufactured for the buyer and are not suitable for sale to others in the ordinary course of the seller's business and the seller, before notice of repudiation is received and under circumstances which reasonably indicate that the goods are for the buyer, has made either a substantial beginning of their manufacture or commitments for their procurement; or

(b) if the party against whom enforcement is sought admits in his pleading, testimony or otherwise in court that a contract for sale was made, but the contract is not enforceable under this provision beyond the quantity of goods admitted; or

(c) with respect to goods for which payment has been made and accepted or which have been received and accepted (Section 2—606).

§2—202. *Final Written Expression: Parol or Extrinsic Evidence*

Terms with respect to which the confirmatory memoranda of the parties agree or which are otherwise set forth in a writing intended by the parties as a final expression of their agreement with respect to such terms as are included therein may not be contradicted by evidence of any prior agreement or of a contemporaneous oral agreement but may be explained or supplemented

(a) by course of dealing or usage of trade (Section 1—205) or by course of performance (Section 2—208); and

(b) by evidence of consistent additional terms unless the court finds the writing to have been intended also as a complete and exclusive statement of the terms of the agreement.

§2—204. *Formation in General*

(1) A contract for sale of goods may be made in any manner sufficient to show agreement, including conduct by both parties which recognizes the existence of such a contract.
(2) An agreement sufficient to constitute a contract for sale may be found even though the moment of its making is undetermined.
(3) Even though one or more terms are left open a contract for sale does not fail for indefiniteness if the parties have intended to make a contract and there is a reasonably certain basis for giving an appropriate remedy.

§2—205. *Firm Offers*

An offer by a merchant to buy or sell goods in a signed writing which by its terms gives assurance that it will be held open is not revocable, for lack of consideration, during the time stated or if no time is stated for a reasonable time, but in no event may such period of irrevocability exceed three months; but any such term of assurance on a form supplied by the offeree must be separately signed by the offeror.

§2—206. *Offer and Acceptance in Formation of Contract*

(1) Unless otherwise unambiguously indicated by the language or circumstances

(a) an offer to make a contract shall be construed as inviting acceptance in any manner and by any medium reasonable in the circumstances;

(b) an order or other offer to buy goods for prompt or current shipment shall be construed as inviting acceptance either by a prompt promise to ship or by the prompt or current shipment of conforming or nonconforming goods, but such a shipment of nonconforming goods does not constitute an acceptance if the seller seasonably notifies the buyer that the shipment is offered only as an accommodation to the buyer.
(2) Where the beginning of a requested performance is a reasonable mode of acceptance an offeror who is not notified of acceptance within a reasonable time may treat the offer as having lapsed before acceptance.

§2—207. *Additional Terms in Acceptance or Confirmation*

(1) A definite and seasonable expression of acceptance or a written confirmation which is sent within a reasonable time operates as an acceptance even though it states terms additional to or different from those offered or agreed upon, unless acceptance is expressly made conditional on assent to the additional or different terms.

(2) The additional terms are to be construed as proposals for addition to the contract. Between merchants such terms become part of the contract unless:

(a) the offer expressly limits acceptance to the terms of the offer;

(b) they materially alter it; or

(c) notification of objection to them has already been given or is given within a reasonable time after notice of them is received.

(3) Conduct by both parties which recognizes the existence of a contract is sufficient to establish a contract for sale although the writings of the parties do not otherwise establish a contract. In such case the terms of the particular contract consist of those terms on which the writings of the parties agree, together with any supplementary terms incorporated under any other provisions of this Act.

Part 3 General Obligation and Construction of Contract

§2—302. *Unconscionable Contract or Clause*

(1) If the court as a matter of law finds the contract or any clause of the contract to have been unconscionable at the time it was made the court may refuse to enforce the contract, or it may enforce the remainder of the contract without the unconscionable clause, or it may so limit the application of any unconscionable clause as to avoid any unconscionable result.

(2) When it is claimed or appears to the court that the contract or any clause thereof may be unconscionable the parties shall be afforded a reasonable opportunity to present evidence as to its commercial setting, purpose and effect to aid the court in making the determination.

§2—305. *Open Price Term*

(1) The parties if they so intend can conclude a contract for sale even though the price is not settled. In such case the price is a reasonable price at the time for delivery if

(a) nothing is said as to price; or

(b) the price is left to be agreed by the parties and they fail to agree; or

(c) the price is to be fixed in terms of some agreed market or other standard as set or recorded by a third person or agency and it is not so set or recorded.

(2) A price to be fixed by the seller or by the buyer means a price for him to fix in good faith.

(3) When a price left to be fixed otherwise than by agreement of the parties fails to be fixed through fault of one party the other may at his option treat the contract as cancelled or himself fix a reasonable price.

(4) Where, however, the parties intend not to be bound unless the price be fixed or agreed and it is not fixed or agreed there is no contract. In such a case the buyer must return any goods already received or if unable so to do must pay their reasonable value at the time of delivery and the seller must return any portion of the price paid on account.

§2—306. *Output, Requirements and Exclusive Dealings*

(1) A term which measures the quantity by the output of the seller or the requirements of the buyer means such actual output or requirements as may occur in good faith, except that no quantity unreasonably disproportionate to any stated estimate or in the absence of a stated estimate to any normal or otherwise comparable prior output or requirements may be tendered or demanded.

(2) A lawful agreement by either the seller or the buyer for exclusive dealing in the kind of goods concerned imposes unless otherwise agreed an obligation by the seller to use best efforts to supply the goods and by the buyer to use best efforts to promote their sale.

§2—310. *Open Time for Payment or Running of Credit: Authority to Ship Under Reservation*

Unless otherwise agreed

(a) payment is due at the time and place at which the buyer is to receive the goods even though the place of shipment is the place of delivery; and

(b) if the seller is authorized to send the goods he may ship them under reservation, and may tender the documents of title, but the buyer may inspect the goods after their arrival before payment is due unless such inspection is inconsistent with the terms of the contract (Section 2—513); and

(c) if delivery is authorized and made by way of documents of title otherwise than by subsection (b) then payment is due at the time and place at which the buyer is to receive the documents regardless of where the goods are to be received; and

(d) where the seller is required or authorized to ship the goods on credit the credit period runs from the time of shipment but post-dating the invoice or delaying its dispatch will correspondingly delay the starting of the credit period.

§2—312. *Warranty of Title and Against Infringement; Buyer's Obligation Against Infringement*

(1) Subject to subsection (2) there is in a contract for sale a warranty by the seller that

(a) the title conveyed shall be good, and its transfer rightful; and

(b) the goods shall be delivered free from any security interest or other lien or encumbrance of which the buyer at the time of contracting has no knowledge.

(2) A warranty under subsection (1) will be excluded or modified only by specific language or by circumstances which give the buyer reason to know that the person selling does not claim title in himself or that he is purporting to sell only such right or title as he or a third person may have.

(3) Unless otherwise agreed a seller who is a merchant regularly dealing in goods of the kind warrants that the goods shall be delivered free of the rightful claim of any third person by way of infringement or the like but a buyer who furnishes specifications

to the seller must hold the seller harmless against any such claim which arises out of compliance with the specifications.

§2—313. Express Warranties by Affirmation, Promise, Description, Sample

(1) Express warranties by the seller are created as follows:

(a) Any affirmation of fact or promise made by the seller to the buyer which relates to the goods and becomes part of the basis of the bargain creates an express warranty that the goods shall conform to the affirmation or promise.

(b) Any description of the goods which is made part of the basis of the bargain creates an express warranty that the goods shall conform to the description.

(c) Any sample or model which is made part of the basis of the bargain creates an express warranty that the whole of the goods shall conform to the sample or model.

(2) It is not necessary to the creation of an express warranty that the seller use formal words such as "warrant" or "guarantee" or that he have a specific intention to make a warranty, but an affirmation merely of the value of the goods or a statement purporting to be merely the seller's opinion or commendation of the goods does not create a warranty.

§2—314. Implied Warranty: Merchantability; Usage of Trade

(1) Unless excluded or modified (Section 2—316), a warranty that the goods shall be merchantable is implied in a contract for their sale if the seller is a merchant with respect to goods of that kind. Under this section the serving for value of food or drink to be consumed either on the premises or elsewhere is a sale.

(2) Goods to be merchantable must be at least such as

(a) pass without objection in the trade under the contract description; and

(b) in the case of fungible goods, are of fair average quality within the description; and

(c) are fit for the ordinary purposes for which such goods are used; and

(d) run, within the variations permitted by the agreement, of even kind, quality and quantity within each unit and among all units involved; and

(e) are adequately contained, packaged, and labeled as the agreement may require; and

(f) conform to the promises or affirmations of fact made on the container or label if any.

(3) Unless excluded or modified (Section 2—316) other implied warranties may arise from course of dealing or usage of trade.

§2—315. Implied Warranty: Fitness for Particular Purpose

Where the seller at the time of contracting has reason to know any particular purpose for which the goods are required and that the buyer is relying on the seller's skill or judgment to select or furnish suitable goods, there is unless excluded or modified under the next section an implied warranty that the goods shall be fit for such purpose.

§2—316. Exclusion or Modification of Warranties

(1) Words or conduct relevant to the creation of an express warranty and words or conduct tending to negate or limit warranty shall be construed wherever reasonable as consistent with each other; but subject to the provisions of this Article on parol or extrinsic evidence (Section 2—202) negation or limitation is inoperative to the extent that such construction is unreasonable.

(2) Subject to subsection (3), to exclude or modify the implied warranty of merchantability or any part of it the language must mention merchantability and in case of a writing must be conspicuous, and to exclude or modify any implied warranty of fitness the exclusion must be by a writing and conspicuous. Language to exclude all implied warranties of fitness is sufficient if it states, for example, that "There are no warranties which extend beyond the description on the face hereof."

(3) Notwithstanding subsection (2)

(a) unless the circumstances indicate otherwise, all implied warranties are excluded by expressions like "as is," "with all faults" or other languages which in common understanding calls the buyer's attention to the exclusion of warranties and makes plain that there is no implied warranty; and

(b) when the buyer before entering into the contract has examined the goods or the sample or model as fully as he desired or has refused to examine the goods there is no implied warranty with regard to defects which an examination ought in the circumstances to have revealed to him; and

(c) an implied warranty can also be excluded or modified by course of dealing or course of performance or usage of trade.

(4) Remedies for breach of warranty can be limited in accordance with the provisions of this Article on liquidation or limitation of damages and on contractual modification of remedy (Section 2—718 and 2—719).

§2—317. Cumulation and Conflict of Warranties Express or Implied

Warranties whether express or implied shall be construed as consistent with each other and as cumulative, but if such construction is unreasonable the intention of the parties shall determine which warranty is dominant. In ascertaining that intention the following rules apply:

(a) Exact or technical specifications displace an inconsistent sample or model or general language of description.

(b) A sample from an existing bulk displaces inconsistent general language of description.

(c) Express warranties displace inconsistent implied warranties other than an implied warranty of fitness for a particular purpose.

§2—318. Third Party Beneficiaries of Warranties Express or Implied

Note: If this Act is introduced in the Congress of the United States this Section should be omitted. (States to select one alternative.)

Alternative A

A seller's warranty whether express or implied extends to any natural person who is in the family or household of his buyer or who is a guest in his home if it is reasonable to expect that such person may use, consume or be affected by the goods and who is injured in person by breach of the warranty. A seller may not exclude or limit the operation of this section.

Alternative B

A seller's warranty whether express or implied extends to any natural person who may reasonably be expected to use, consume or be affected by the goods and who is injured in person by breach of the warranty. A seller may not exclude or limit the operation of this section.

Alternative C

A seller's warranty whether express or implied extends to any person who may reasonably be expected to use, consume or be affected by the goods and who is injured by breach of the warranty. A seller may not exclude or limit the operation of this section with respect to injury to the person of an individual to whom the warranty extends.

§2—319. F.O.B. and F.A.S. Terms

(1) Unless otherwise agreed the term F.O.B. (which means "free on board") at a named place, even though used only in connection with the stated price, is a delivery term under which

(a) when the term is F.O.B. the place of shipment, the seller must at that place ship the goods in the manner provided in this Article (Section 2—504) and bear the expense and risk of putting them into the possession of the carrier; or

(b) when the term is F.O.B. the place of destination, the seller must at his own expense and risk transport the goods to that place and there tender delivery of them in the manner provided in this Article (Section 2—503);

(c) when under either (a) or (b) the term is also F.O.B. vessel, car or other vehicle, the seller must in addition at his own expense and risk load the goods on board. If the term is F.O.B. vessel the buyer must name the vessel and in an appropriate case the seller must comply with the provisions of this Article on the form of bill of lading (Section 2—323).

(2) Unless otherwise agreed the term F.A.S. vessel (which means "free alongside") at a named port, even though used only in connection with the stated price, is a delivery term under which the seller must

(a) at his own expense and risk deliver the goods alongside the vessel in the manner usual in that port or on a dock designated and provided by the buyer; and

(b) obtain and tender a receipt for the goods in exchange for which the carrier is under a duty to issue a bill of lading.

(3) Unless otherwise agreed in any case falling within subsection (1)(a) or (c) or subsection (2) the buyer must seasonably give any needed instructions for making delivery, including when the term is F.A.S. or F.O.B. the loading berth of the vessel and in an appropriate case its name and sailing date. The seller may treat the failure of needed instructions as a failure of cooperation under this Article (Section 2—311). He may also at his option move the goods in any reasonable manner preparatory to delivery or shipment.

(4) Under the term F.O.B. vessel or F.A.S. unless otherwise agreed the buyer must make payment against tender of the required documents and the seller may not tender nor the buyer demand delivery of the goods in substitution for the documents.

§2—320. C.I.F. and C. & F. Terms

(1) The term C.I.F. means that the price includes in a lump sum the cost of the goods and the insurance and freight to the named destination. The term C. & F. or C.F. means that the price so includes cost and freight to the named destination.

(2) Unless otherwise agreed and even though used only in connection with the stated price and destination, the term C.I.F. destination or its equivalent requires the seller at his own expense and risk to

(a) put the goods into the possession of a carrier at the port for shipment and obtain a negotiable bill or bills of lading covering the entire transportation to the named destination; and

(b) load the goods and obtain a receipt from the carrier (which may be contained in the bill of lading) showing that the freight has been paid or provided for; and

(c) obtain a policy or certificate of insurance, including any war risk insurance, of a kind and on terms then current at the port of shipment in the usual amount, in the currency of the contract, shown to cover the same goods covered by the bill of lading and providing for payment of loss to the order of the buyer or for the account of whom it may concern; but the seller may add to the price the amount of the premium for any such war risk insurance; and

(d) prepare an invoice of the goods and procure any other documents required to effect shipment or to comply with the contract; and

(e) forward and tender with commercial promptness all the documents in due form and with any indorsement necessary to perfect the buyer's rights.

(3) Unless otherwise agreed the term C. & F. or its equivalent has the same effect and imposes upon the seller the same obligations and risks as a C.I.F. term except the obligation as to insurance.

(4) Under the term C.I.F. & C. & F. unless otherwise agreed the buyer must make payment against tender of the required documents and the seller may not tender nor the buyer demand delivery of the goods in substitution for the documents.

§2—326. Sale on Approval and Sale or Return; Consignment Sales and Rights of Creditors

(1) Unless otherwise agreed, if delivered goods may be returned by the buyer even though they conform to the contract, the transaction is

(a) a "sale on approval" if the goods are delivered primarily for use, and

(b) a "sale or return" if the goods are delivered primarily for resale.

(2) Except as provided in subsection (3), goods held on approval are not subject to the claims of the buyer's creditors until acceptance; goods held on sale or return are subject to such claims while in the buyer's possession.

(3) Where goods are delivered to a person for sale and such person maintains a place of business at which he deals in goods of the kind involved, under a name other than the name of the person making delivery, then with respect to claims of creditors of the person conducting the business the goods are deemed to be on sale or return. The provisions of this subsection are applicable even though an agreement purports to reserve title to the person making delivery until payment or resale or uses such words as "on consignment" or "on memorandum." However, this subsection is not applicable if the person making delivery

(a) complies with an applicable law providing for a consignor's interest or the like to be evidenced by a sign, or

(b) establishes that the person conducting the business is generally known by his creditors to be substantially engaged in selling the goods of others, or

(c) complies with the filing provisions of the Article on Secured Transactions (Article 9).

(4) Any "or return" term of a contract for sale is to be treated as a separate contract for sale within the statute of frauds section of this Article (Section 2—201) and as contradicting the sale aspect of the contract within the provisions of this Article on parol or extrinsic evidence (Section 2—202).

§2—328. Sale by Auction

(1) In a sale by auction if goods are put up in lots each lot is the subject of a separate sale.

(2) A sale by auction is complete when the auctioneer so announces by the fall of the hammer or in other customary manner. Where a bid is made while the hammer is falling in acceptance of a prior bid the auctioneer may in his discretion reopen the bidding or declare the goods sold under the bid on which the hammer was falling.

(3) Such a sale is with reserve unless the goods are in explicit terms put up without reserve. In an auction with reserve the auctioneer may withdraw the goods at any time until he announces completion of the sale. In an auction without reserve, after the auctioneer calls for bids on an article or lot, that article or lot cannot be withdrawn unless no bid is made within a reasonable time. In either case a bidder may retract his bid until the auctioneer's announcement of completion of sale, but a bidder's retraction does not revive any previous bid.

(4) If the auctioneer knowingly receives a bid on the seller's behalf or the seller makes or procures such a bid, and notice has not been given that liberty for such bidding is reserved, the buyer may at his option avoid the sale or take the goods at the price of the last good faith bid prior to the completion of the sale. This subsection shall not apply to any bid at a forced sale.

Part 4 Title, Creditors and Good Faith Purchasers

§2—401. Passing of Title; Reservation for Security; Limited Application of This Section

Each provision of this Article with regard to the rights, obligations and remedies of the seller, the buyer, purchasers or other third parties applies irrespective of title to the goods except where the provision refers to such title. Insofar as situations are not covered by the other provisions of this Article and matters concerning title become material the following rules apply:

(1) Title to goods cannot pass under a contract for sale prior to their identification to the contract (Section 2—501), and unless otherwise explicitly agreed the buyer acquires by their identification a special property as limited by this Act. Any retention or reservation by the seller of the title (property) in goods shipped or delivered to the buyer is limited in effect to a reservation of a security interest. Subject to these provisions and to the provisions of the Article on Secured Transactions (Article 9), title to goods passes from the seller to the buyer in any manner and on any conditions explicitly agreed on by the parties.

(2) Unless otherwise explicitly agreed title passes to the buyer at the time and place at which the seller completes his performance with reference to the physical delivery of the goods, despite any reservation of a security interest and even though a document of title is to be delivered at a different time or place; and in particular and despite any reservation of a security interest by the bill of lading

(a) if the contract requires or authorizes the seller to send the goods to the buyer but does not require him to deliver them at destination, title passes to the buyer at the time and place of shipment; but

(b) if the contract requires delivery at destination, title passes on tender there.

(3) Unless otherwise explicitly agreed where delivery is to be made without moving the goods,

(a) if the seller is to deliver a document of title, title passes at the time when and the place where he delivers such documents; or

(b) if the goods are at the time of contracting already identified and no documents are to be delivered, title passes at the time and place of contracting.

(4) A rejection or other refusal by the buyer to receive or retain the goods, whether or not justified, or a justified revocation of acceptance revests title to the goods in the seller. Such revesting occurs by operation of law and is not a "sale."

§2—402. Rights of Seller's Creditors Against Sold Goods

(1) Except as provided in subsections (2) and (3), rights of unsecured creditors of the seller with respect to goods which have been identified to a contract for sale are subject to the buyer's rights to recover the goods under this Article (Section 2—502 and 2—716).

(2) A creditor of the seller may treat a sale or an identification of goods to a contract for sale as void if as against him a retention of possession by the seller is fraudulent under any rule of law of the state where the goods are situated, except that retention of possession in good faith and current course of trade by a merchant-seller for a commercially reasonable time after a sale or identification is not fraudulent.

(3) Nothing in this Article shall be deemed to impair the rights of creditors of the seller

(a) under the provisions of the Article on Secured Transactions (Article 9); or

(b) where identification to the contract or delivery is made not in current course of trade but in satisfaction of or as security for a pre-existing claim for money, security or the like and is made under circumstances which under any rule of law of the state where the goods are situated would apart from this Article constitute the transaction a fraudulent transfer or voidable preference.

§2—403. Power to Transfer; Good Faith Purchase of Goods; "Entrusting"

(1) A purchaser of goods acquires all title which his transferor had or had power to transfer except that a purchaser of a limited interest acquires rights only to the extent of the interest purchased. A person with voidable title has power to transfer a good title to a good faith purchaser for value. When goods have been delivered under a transaction of purchase the purchaser has such power even though

(a) the transferor was deceived as to the identity of the purchaser, or

(b) the delivery was in exchange for a check which is later dishonored, or

(c) it was agreed that the transaction was to be a "cash sale," or

(d) the delivery was procured through fraud punishable as larcenous under the criminal law.

(2) Any entrusting of possession of goods to a merchant who deals in goods of that kind gives him power to transfer all rights of the entruster to a buyer in ordinary course of business.

(3) "Entrusting" includes any delivery and any acquiescence in retention of possession regardless of any condition expressed between the parties to the delivery or acquiescence and regardless of whether the procurement of the entrusting or the possessor's disposition of the goods have been such as to be larcenous under the criminal law.

(4) The rights of other purchasers of goods and of lien creditors are governed by the Articles on Secured Transactions (Article 9), Bulk Transfers (Article 6) and Documents of Title (Article 7).

Part 5 Performance

§2—501. Insurable Interest in Goods; Manner of Identification of Goods

(1) The buyer obtains a special property and an insurable interest in goods by identification of existing goods as goods to which the contract refers even though the goods so identified are nonconforming and he has an option to return or reject them. Such identification can be made at any time and in any manner explicitly agreed to by the parties. In the absence of explicit agreement identification occurs

(a) when the contract is made if it is for the sale of goods already existing and identified;

(b) if the contract is for the sale of future goods other than those described in paragraph (c), when goods are shipped, marked or otherwise designated by the seller as goods to which the contract refers;

(c) when the crops are planted or otherwise become growing crops or the young are conceived if the contract is for the sale of unborn young to be born within twelve months after contracting or for the sale of crops to be harvested within twelve months or the next normal harvest season after contracting whichever is longer.

(2) The seller retains an insurable interest in goods so long as title to or any security interest in the goods remains in him and where the identification is by the seller alone he may until default or insolvency or notification to the buyer that the identification is final substitute other goods for those identified.

(3) Nothing in this section impairs any insurable interest recognized under any other statute or rule or law.

§2—502. Buyer's Right to Goods on Seller's Insolvency

(1) Subject to subsection (2) and even though the goods have not been shipped a buyer who has paid a part or all of the price of goods in which he has a special property under the provisions of the immediately preceding section may on making and keeping good a tender of any unpaid portion of their price recover them from the seller if the seller becomes insolvent within ten days after receipt of the first installment on their price.

(2) If the identification creating his special property has been made by the buyer he acquires the right to recover the goods only if they conform to the contract for sale.

§2—504. Shipment by Seller

Where the seller is required or authorized to send the goods to the buyer and the contract does not require him to deliver them at a particular destination, then unless otherwise agreed he must

(a) put the goods in the possession of such a carrier and make such a contract for their transportation as may be reasonable having regard to the nature of the goods and other circumstances of the case; and

(b) obtain and promptly deliver or tender in due form any document necessary to enable the buyer to obtain possession of the goods or otherwise required by the agreement or by usage of trade; and

(c) promptly notify the buyer of the shipment. Failure to notify the buyer under paragraph (c) or to make a proper contract under paragraph (a) is a ground for rejection only if material delay or loss ensues.

§2—507. Effect of Seller's Tender; Delivery on Condition

(1) Tender of delivery is a condition to the buyer's duty to accept the goods and, unless otherwise agreed, to his duty to pay for them. Tender entitles the seller to acceptance of the goods and to payment according to the contract.

(2) Where payment is due and demanded on the delivery to the buyer of goods or documents of title, his right as against the seller

to retain or dispose of them is conditional upon his making the payment due.

§2—508. Cure by Seller of Improper Tender or Delivery; Replacement

(1) Where any tender or delivery by the seller is rejected because non-conforming and the time for performance has not yet expired, the seller may seasonably notify the buyer of his intention to cure and may then within the contract time make a conforming delivery.
(2) Where the buyer rejects a non-conforming tender which the seller had reasonable grounds to believe would be acceptable with or without money allowance the seller may if he seasonably notifies the buyer have a further reasonable time to substitute a conforming tender.

§2—509. Risk of Loss in the Absence of Breach

(1) Where the contract requires or authorizes the seller to ship the good by carrier

(a) if it does not require him to deliver them at a particular destination, the risk of loss passes to the buyer when the goods are duly delivered to the carrier even though the shipment is under reservation (Section 2—505); but

(b) if it does require him to deliver them at a particular destination and the goods are there duly tendered while in the possession of the carrier, the risk of loss passes to the buyer when the goods are there duly so tendered as to enable the buyer to take delivery.

(2) Where the goods are held by a bailee to be delivered without being moved, the risk of loss passes to the buyer.

(a) on his receipt of a negotiable document of title covering the goods; or

(b) on acknowledgment by the bailee of the buyer's right to possession of the goods; or

(c) after his receipt of a non-negotiable document of title or other written direction to deliver, as provided in subsection (4)(b) of Section 2—503.

(3) In any case not within subsection (1) or (2), the risk of loss passes to the buyer on his receipt of the goods if the seller is a merchant; otherwise the risk passes to the buyer on tender of delivery.
(4) The provisions of this section are subject to contrary agreement of the parties and to the provisions of this Article on sale on approval (Section 2—327) and on effect of breach on risk of loss (Section 2—510).

§2—510. Effect of Breach on Risk of Loss

(1) Where a tender or delivery of goods so fails to conform to the contract as to give a right of rejection the risk of their loss remains on the seller until cure or acceptance.
(2) Where the buyer rightfully revokes acceptance he may to the extent of any deficiency in his effective insurance coverage treat the risk of loss as having rested on the seller from the beginning.
(3) Where the buyer as to conforming goods already identified to the contract for sale repudiates or is otherwise in breach before risk of their loss has passed to him, the seller may to the extent of any deficiency in his effective insurance coverage treat the risk of loss as resting on the buyer for a commercially reasonable time.

§2—512. Payment by Buyer Before Inspection

(1) Where the contract requires payment before inspection non-conformity of the goods does not excuse the buyer from so making payment unless

(a) the non-conformity appears without inspection; or

(b) despite tender of the required documents the circumstances would justify injunction against honor under the provisions of this Act (Section 5—114).

(2) Payment pursuant to subsection (1) does not constitute an acceptance of goods or impair the buyer's right to inspect or any of his remedies.

§2—513. Buyer's Right to Inspection of Goods

(1) Unless otherwise agreed and subject to subsection (3), where goods are tendered or delivered or identified to the contract for sale, the buyer has a right before payment or acceptance to inspect them at any reasonable place and time and in any reasonable manner. When the seller is required and authorized to send the goods to the buyer, the inspection may be after their arrival.
(2) Expenses of inspection must be borne by the buyer but may be recovered from the seller if the goods do not conform and are rejected.
(3) Unless otherwise agreed and subject to the provisions of this Article on C.I.F. contracts (subsection (3) of Section 2—321), the buyer is not entitled to inspect the goods before payment of the price when the contract provides

(a) for delivery "C.O.D." or on other like terms; or

(b) for payment against documents of title, except where such payment is due only after the goods are to become available for inspection.

(4) A place or method of inspection fixed by the parties is presumed to be exclusive but unless otherwise expressly agreed it does not postpone identification or shift the place for delivery or for passing the risk of loss. If compliance becomes impossible, inspection shall be as provided in this section unless the place or method fixed was clearly intended as an indispensable condition failure of which avoids the contract.

Part 6 Breach, Repudiation and Excuse

§2—601. Buyer's Rights on Improper Delivery

Subject to the provisions of this Article on breach in installment contracts (Section 2—612) and unless otherwise agreed under the sections on contractual limitations of remedy (Sections 2—718 and 2—719), if the goods or the tender of delivery fail in any respect to conform to the contract, the buyer may

(a) reject the whole; or

(b) accept the whole; or

(c) accept any commercial unit or units and reject the rest.

§2—602. Manner and Effect of Rightful Rejection

(1) Rejection of goods must be within a reasonable time after their delivery or tender. It is ineffective unless the buyer seasonably notifies the seller.

(2) Subject to the provisions of the two following sections on rejected goods (Sections 2—603 and 2—604),

(a) after rejection any exercise of ownership by the buyer with respect to any commercial unit is wrongful as against the seller; and

(b) if the buyer has before rejection taken physical possession of goods in which he does not have a security interest under the provisions of this Article (subsection (3) of Section 2—711), he is under a duty after rejection to hold them with reasonable care at the seller's disposition for a time sufficient to permit the seller to remove them; but

(c) the buyer has no further obligations with regard to goods rightfully rejected.

(3) The seller's rights with respect to goods wrongfully rejected are governed by the provisions of this Article on Seller's remedies in general (Section 2—703).

§2—603. Merchant Buyer's Duties as to Rightfully Rejected Goods

(1) Subject to any security interest in the buyer (subsection (3) of Section 2—711), when the seller has no agent or place of business at the market of rejection a merchant buyer is under a duty after rejection of goods in his possession or control to follow any reasonable instructions received from the seller with respect to the goods and in the absence of such instructions to make reasonable efforts to sell them for the seller's account if they are perishable or threaten to decline in value speedily. Instructions are not reasonable if on demand indemnity for expense is not forthcoming.

(2) When the buyer sells goods under subsection (1), he is entitled to reimbursement from the seller or out of the proceeds for reasonable expenses of caring for and selling them, and if the expenses include no selling commission then to such commission as is usual in the trade or if there is none to a reasonable sum not exceeding ten per cent on the gross proceeds.

(3) In complying with this section the buyer is held only to good faith and good faith conduct hereunder is neither acceptance nor conversion nor the basis of an action for damages.

§2—606. What Constitutes Acceptance of Goods

(1) Acceptance of goods occurs when the buyer

(a) after a reasonable opportunity to inspect the goods signifies to the seller that the goods are conforming or that he will take or retain them in spite of their non-conformity; or

(b) fails to make an effective rejection (subsection (1) of Section 2—602), but such acceptance does not occur until the buyer has had a reasonable opportunity to inspect them; or

(c) does any act inconsistent with the seller's ownership; but if such act is wrongful as against the seller it is an acceptance only if ratified by him.

(2) Acceptance of a part of any commercial unit is acceptance of that entire unit.

§2—608. Revocation of Acceptance in Whole or in Part

(1) The buyer may revoke his acceptance of a lot or commercial unit whose non-conformity substantially impairs its value to him if he has accepted it

(a) on the reasonable assumption that its non-conformity would be cured and it has not been seasonably cured; or

(b) without discovery of such non-conformity if his acceptance was reasonably induced either by the difficulty of discovery before acceptance or by the seller's assurances.

(2) Revocation of acceptance must occur within a reasonable time after the buyer discovers or should have discovered the ground for it and before any substantial change in condition of the goods which is not caused by their own defects. It is not effective until the buyer notifies the seller of it.

(3) A buyer who so revokes has the same rights and duties with regard to the goods involved as if he had rejected them.

§2—609. Right to Adequate Assurance of Performance

(1) A contract for sale imposes an obligation on each party that the other's expectation of receiving due performance will not be impaired. When reasonable grounds for insecurity arise with respect to the performance of either party the other may in writing demand adequate assurance of due performance and until he receives such assurance may if commercially reasonable suspend any performance for which he has not already received the agreed return.

(2) Between merchants the reasonableness of grounds for insecurity and the adequacy of any assurance offered shall be determined according to commercial standards.

(3) Acceptance of any improper delivery or payment does not prejudice the aggrieved party's right to demand adequate assurance of future performance.

(4) After receipt of a justified demand failure to provide within a reasonable time not exceeding thirty days such assurance of due performance as is adequate under the circumstances of the particular case is a repudiation of the contract.

§2—610. Anticipatory Repudiation

When either party repudiates the contract with respect to a performance not yet due the loss of which will substantially impair the value of the contract to the other, the aggrieved party may

(a) for a commercially reasonable time await performance by the repudiating party; or

(b) resort to any remedy for breach (Section 2—703 or Section 2—711), even though he has notified the repudiating party that he would await the latter's performance and has urged retraction; and

(c) in either case suspend his own performance or proceed in accordance with the provisions of this Article on the seller's right to identify goods to the contract notwithstanding breach or to salvage unfinished goods (Section 2—704).

§2—611. Retraction of Anticipatory Repudiation

(1) Until the repudiating party's next performance is due he can retract his repudiation unless the aggrieved party has since the repudiation cancelled or materially changed his position or otherwise indicated that he considers the repudiation final.

(2) Retraction may be by any method which clearly indicates to the aggrieved party that the repudiating party intends to perform, but must include any assurance justifiably demanded under the provisions of this Article (Section 2—609).

(3) Retraction reinstates the repudiating party's right under the contract with due excuse and allowance to the aggrieved party for any delay occasioned by the repudiation.

§2—613. Casualty to Identified Goods

Where the contract requires for its performance goods identified when the contract is made, and the goods suffer casualty without fault of either party before the risk of loss passes to the buyer, or in a proper case under a "no arrival, no sale" term (Section 2—324) then

(a) if the loss is total the contract is avoided; and

(b) if the loss is partial or the goods have so deteriorated as no longer to conform to the contract the buyer may nevertheless demand inspection and at his option either treat the contract as avoided or accept the goods with due allowance from the contract price for the deterioration or the deficiency in quantity but without further right against the seller.

Part 7 Remedies

§2—701. Remedies for Breach of Collateral Contracts Not Impaired

Remedies for breach of any obligation or promise collateral or ancillary to a contract for sale are not impaired by the provisions of this Article.

§2—702. Seller's Remedies on Discovery of Buyer's Insolvency

(1) Where the seller discovers the buyer to be insolvent he may refuse delivery except for cash including payment for all goods theretofore delivered under the contract, and stop delivery under this Article (Section 2—705).

(2) Where the seller discovers that the buyer has received goods on credit while insolvent he may reclaim the goods upon demand made within ten days after the receipt, but if misrepresentation of solvency has been made to the particular seller in writing within three months before delivery the ten day limitation does not apply. Except as provided in this subsection the seller may not base a right to reclaim goods on the buyer's fraudulent or innocent misrepresentation of solvency or of intent to pay.

(3) The seller's right to reclaim under subsection (2) is subject to the rights of a buyer in ordinary course or other good faith purchaser under this Article (Section 2—403). Successful reclamation of goods excludes all other remedies with respect to them.

§2—703. Seller's Remedies in General

Where the buyer wrongfully rejects or revokes acceptance of goods or fails to make a payment due on or before delivery or repudiates with respect to a part or the whole, then with respect to any goods directly affected and, if the breach is of the whole contract (Section 2—612), then also with respect to the whole undelivered balance, the aggrieved seller may

(a) withhold delivery of such goods;

(b) stop delivery by any bailee as hereafter provided (Section 2—705);

(c) proceed under the next section respecting goods still unidentified to the contract;

(d) resell and recover damages as hereafter provided (Section 2—706);

(e) recover damages for non-acceptance (Section 2—708) or in a proper case the price (Section 2—709);

(f) cancel.

§2—704. Seller's Right to Identify Goods to the Contract Notwithstanding Breach or to Salvage Unfinished Goods

(1) An aggrievated seller under the preceding section may

(a) identify to the contract conforming goods not already identified if at the time he learned of the breach they are in his possession or control;

(b) treat as the subject of resale goods which have demonstrably been intended for the particular contract even though those goods are unfinished.

(2) Where the goods are unfinished an aggrieved seller may in the exercise of reasonable commercial judgment for the purposes of avoiding loss and of effective realization either complete the manufacture and wholly identify the goods to the contract or cease manufacture and resell for scrap or salvage value or proceed in any other reasonable manner.

§2—706. Seller's Resale Including Contract for Resale

(1) Under the conditions stated in Section 2—703 on seller's remedies, the seller may resell the goods concerned or the undelivered balance thereof. Where the resale is made in good faith and in a commercially reasonable manner the seller may recover the difference between the resale price and the contract price together with any incidental damages allowed under the provisions of this Article (Section 2—710), but less expenses saved in consequence of the buyer's breach.

(2) Except as otherwise provided in subsection (3) or unless otherwise agreed resale may be at public or private sale including sale by way of one or more contracts to sell or of identification to an existing contract of the seller. Sale may be as a unit or in parcels and at any time and place and on any terms but every aspect of the sale including the method, manner, time, place and terms must be commercially reasonable. The resale must be reasonably identified as referring to the broken contract, but it is

not necessary that the goods be in existence or that any or all of them have been identified to the contract before the breach.
(3) Where the resale is at private sale the seller must give the buyer reasonable notification of his intention to resell.
(4) Where the resale is at public sale

(a) only identified goods can be sold except where there is a recognized market for a public sale of futures in goods of the kind; and

(b) it must be made at a usual place or market for public sale if one is reasonably available and except in the case of goods which are perishable or threaten to decline in value speedily the seller must give the buyer reasonable notice of the time and place of the resale; and

(c) if the goods are not to be within the view of those attending the sale the notification of sale must state the place where the goods are located and provide for their reasonable inspection by prospective bidders; and

(d) the seller may buy.

(5) A purchaser who buys in good faith at a resale takes the goods free of any rights of the original buyer even though the seller fails to comply with one or more of the requirements of this section.
(6) The seller is not accountable to the buyer for any profit made on any resale. A person in the position of a seller (Section 2—707) or a buyer who has rightfully rejected or justifiably revoked acceptance must account for any excess over the amount of his security interest, as hereinafter defined (subsection (3) of Section 2—711).

§2—708. Seller's Damages for Non-Acceptance or Repudiation

(1) Subject to subsection (2) and to the provisions of this Article with respect to proof of market price (Section 2—723), the measure of damages for non-acceptance or repudiation by the buyer is the difference between the market price at the time and place for tender and the unpaid contract price together with any incidental damages provided in this Article (Section 2—710), but less expenses saved in consequence of the buyer's breach.
(2) If the measure of damages provided in subsection (1) is inadequate to put the seller in as good a position as performance would have done then the measure of damages is the profit (including reasonable overhead) which the seller would have made from full performance by the buyer, together with any incidental damages provided in this Article (Section 2—710), due allowance for costs reasonably incurred and due credit for payments or proceeds of resale.

§2—709. Action for the Price

(1) When the buyer fails to pay the price as it becomes due the seller may recover, together with any incidental damages under the next section, the price

(a) of goods accepted or of conforming goods lost or damaged within a commercially reasonable time after risk of their loss has passed to the buyer; and

(b) of goods identified to the contract if the seller is unable after reasonable effort to resell them at a reasonable price or the circumstances reasonably indicate that such effort will be unavailing.

(2) Where the seller sues for the price he must hold for the buyer any goods which have been identified to the contract and are still in his control except that if resale becomes possible he may resell them at any time prior to the collection of the judgment. The net proceeds of any such resale must be credited to the buyer and payment of the judgment entitles him to any goods not resold.
(3) After the buyer has wrongfully rejected or revoked acceptance of the goods or has failed to make a payment due or has repudiated (Section 2—610), a seller who is held not entitled to the price under this section shall nevertheless be awarded damages for non-acceptance under the preceding section.

§2—711. Buyer's Remedies in General; Buyer's Security Interest in Rejected Goods

(1) Where the seller fails to make delivery or repudiates or the buyer rightfully rejects or justifiably revokes acceptance then with respect to any goods involved, and with respect to the whole if the breach goes to the whole contract (Section 2—612), the buyer may cancel and whether or not he has done so may in addition to recovering so much of the price as has been paid

(a) "cover" and have damages under the next section as to all the goods affected whether or not they have been identified to the contract; or

(b) recover damages for non-delivery as provided in this Article (Section 2—713).

(2) Where the seller fails to deliver or repudiates the buyer may also

(a) if the goods have been identified recover them as provided in this Article (Section 2—502); or

(b) in a proper case obtain specific performance or replevy the goods as provided in this Article (Section 2—716).

(3) On rightful rejection or justifiable revocation of acceptance a buyer has a security interest in goods in his possession or control for any payments made on their price and any expenses reasonably incurred in their inspection, receipt, transportation, care and custody and may hold such goods and resell them in like manner as an aggrieved seller (Section 2—706).

§2—712. "Cover"; Buyer's Procurement of Substitute Goods

(1) After a breach within the preceding section the buyer may "cover" by making in good faith and without unreasonable delay any reasonable purchase of or contract to purchase goods in substitution for those due from the seller.
(2) The buyer may recover from the seller as damages the difference between the cost of cover and the contract price together with any incidental or consequential damages as hereinafter defined (Section 2—715), but less expenses saved in consequence of the seller's breach.

(3) Failure of the buyer to effect cover within this section does not bar him from any other remedy.

§2—713. Buyer's Damages for Non-Delivery or Repudiation

(1) Subject to the provisions of this Article with respect to proof of market price (Section 2—723), the measure of damages for non-delivery or repudiation by the seller is the difference between the market price at the time when the buyer learned of the breach and the contract price together with any incidental and consequential damages provided in this Article (Section 2—715), but less expenses saved in consequence of the seller's breach.
(2) Market price is to be determined as of the place for tender or, in cases of rejection after arrival or revocation of acceptance, as of the place of arrival.

§2—714. Buyer's Damages for Breach in Regard to Accepted Goods

(1) Where the buyer has accepted goods and given notification (subsection (3) of Section 2—607) he may recover as damages for any non-conformity of tender the loss resulting in the ordinary course of events from the seller's breach as determined in any manner which is reasonable.
(2) The measure of damages for breach of warranty is the difference at the time and place of acceptance between the value of the goods accepted and the value they would have had if they had been as warranted, unless special circumstances show proximate damages of a different amount.
(3) In a proper case any incidental and consequential damages under the next section may also be recovered.

§2—715. Buyer's Incidental and Consequential Damages

(1) Incidental damages resulting from the seller's breach include expenses reasonably incurred in inspection, receipt, transportation and care and custody of goods rightfully rejected, any commercially reasonable charges, expenses or commissions in connection with effecting cover and any other reasonable expense incident to the delay or other breach.
(2) Consequential damages resulting from the seller's breach include

(a) any loss resulting from general or particular requirements and needs of which the seller at the time of contracting had reason to know and which could not reasonably be prevented by cover or otherwise; and

(b) injury to person or property proximately resulting from any breach of warranty.

§2—723. Proof of Market Price: Time and Place

(1) If an action based on anticipatory repudiation comes to trial before the time for performance with respect to some or all of the goods, any damages based on market price (Section 2—708 or Section 2—713) shall be determined according to the price of such goods prevailing at the time when the aggrieved party learned of the repudiation.
(2) If evidence of a price prevailing at the times or places described in this Article is not readily available the price prevailing within any reasonable time before or after the time described or at any other place which in commercial judgment or under usage of trade would serve as a reasonable substitute for the one described may be used, making any proper allowance for the cost of transporting the goods to or from such other place.
(3) Evidence of a relevant price prevailing at a time or place other than the one described in this Article offered by one party is not admissible unless and until he has given the other party such notice as the court finds sufficient to prevent unfair surprise.

§2—725. Statute of Limitations in Contracts for Sale

(1) An action for breach of any contract for sale must be commenced within four years after the cause of action has accrued. By the original agreement the parties may reduce the period of limitation to not less than one year but may not extend it.
(2) A cause of action accrues when the breach occurs, regardless of the aggrieved party's lack of knowledge of the breach. A breach of warranty occurs when tender of delivery is made, except that where a warranty explicitly extends to future performance of the goods and discovery of the breach must await the time of such performance the cause of action accrues when the breach is or should have been discovered.
(3) Where an action commenced within the time limited by subsection (1) is so terminated as to leave available a remedy by another action for the same breach such other action may be commenced after the expiration of the time limited and within six months after the termination of the first action unless the termination resulted from voluntary discontinuance or from dismissal for failure or neglect to prosecute.
(4) This section does not alter the law on tolling of the statute of limitations nor does it apply to causes of action which have accrued before this Act becomes effective.

APPENDIX

C

Spanish-English Equivalents for Important Legal Terms

abatement of nuisance eliminación de an estorbo
abstract of title resumen de título
acceptance aceptación
accession accesion
accommodation paper documento de favor
accord and satisfaction acuerdo y satisfacción
act of state Acto de Gobierno
adjudicate juzgar, adjudicar
administrator administrador
adverse possession posesión adversa
affirm affirmar
affirmative action acción affimativo
agent agente
allege alegar
allegation alegato
answer contestación
anticipatory breach infraccion anticipador
appelle apelado
arbitrate arbitrar
assignee cesionario
assignment cesion
assignor cedente
bailee depositario
bailment deposito, entrega
bailor depositante
bankruptcy bancarrota
bearer portador
beneficiary beneficiario
bid oferta
bill of lading conocimiento de embarque
blue sky laws el nombre popular de leyes estatales hechos a proteger a inversionistas en la venta de valores
brief breve, escrito
bulk transfer transferencia a granel
burden of proof carga de la prueba
case law leye de causas, precedentes
cashier's check cheque de caja, cheque bancario
cause of action derecho de acción
caveat emptor tenga cuidado el comprador
caveat venditor tenga cuidado el vendedor
certification certificación
certified check cheque certificado
check cheque
C.I.F. costo, seguro y flete
civil action acción civil
class action litigio entablado en representación de un grupo
C.O.D. "Cash on Delivery" entrega contra pago
code codigo
codicil codicilo, cambio a un testamento
common carrier transportador público
compensatory (see damages) compensatario
complaint queja, demanda
composition with creditors concordato con acreedores
condition condición
condition precedent condición precedente
condition subsequent condición subsigiente
conditional gift regalo condicional
consignee consignatario
consignment consignación

Prepared by Roberto Cisneros, Jr., Chaviano & Associates, Ltd., Chicago, Illinois.

consignor consignador
contract contracto
conversion conversión
corporation corporacion, sociedad automoma
counterclaim contrademanda
counteroffer contraoferta
custody custodia
D/B/A Haciendo negocio como
damages danos y perjucios
debtor deudor
deceit engaño
decision decisión
deed escritura, titulo
defendant accusado, demandado
defraud estafar
deliver entregar
de novo, trail jucio de nuevo
deposition deposición
derivative action accion derivado de an accionista a beneficio de la corporación
dictum opinión expresado por un tribunal
directed verdict veredicto dirigido por el juez
discharge in bankruptcy extinción de una obligacion en bancarrota
dismiss despedir, rechazar
donee donatario
donor donante
dower los bienes del esposo fallecido que le corresponden a las viuda
draft letra de cambio
drawee girado
duress por cumpulsion
easement servidumbre
en banc en el tribunal
equity equidad, valor liquido
equity of redemption derecho de rescate de una propiedad hipotecada
estoppel impedimento por actas propios
ex ship enviar al gasto y riesgo del venededor
exculpatory clause clausa exculpatoria
executor albacea
executory por complirse
executrix albacea
F.A.S. Franco Muelle
felony felonia, crimen
fiduciary fiduciario
financing statement declaracion de seguridad
fixture instalación fijo
F.O.B. libre a bordo
fungible goods bienes fungibles
garnishment embargo
gift un regalo
good faith buena fe
guarantor garante
guaranty garantia
heirs herederos
holder in due course tenedor de buena fe
illusory illusorio
implied warranty garantia implicita
incapacity incapacidad
Independent Contractor contratista independiente
indorsement endorso
injunction interdicto judicial
inpersonam contra la persona
insolvency insolvencia
in status quo en stata quo
instrument instrumento
jointly conjuntamente
jointly and severally conjuntamente y independientemente, solidariamente
joint tenancy tenencia conjunta
judgment jucio
judgment N.O.V. sentencia contraria al veredicto
jurisdiction jurisdicción
law merchant derecho commercial
lease contrato de arrendamiento
legal legal
lien gravamen, carga
litigant litigante
magistrate juez, magistrado
mechanic's lien gravamen de constructor
mens rea intención criminal
minitrail mini jucio
minor menor
misdemeanor delito, ofensa menor
mistrial jucio nulo
mitigation of damages mitigación de danos
mortgage hipoteca
necessaries necesarios
negligence negligencia
negotiable negociable
negotiable instrument instrumento negociable
negotiation negociación
no arrival, no sale sino llegan los bienes, no hay pago por ellos
nolo contendere no contestare
non compos mentis incapacitado mentalmente
novation novación
oath juramento
obligee obligante

obligor obligado
objection objeción
offer oferta
offeree quien recibe una oferta
offeror oferente
opinion opinión
option opción
ordinance ordenanza
parol evidence prueba extrínseca
partners socios
payee tenedor, beneficiaro de pago
per curiam por el tribunal
perjury perjurio
petition (bankruptcy) petición de bancarrota
plaintiff demandante
plea alegato
polygraph aparato para detectar mentiras
positive law ley positiva
post dated check cheque posfechado
Power of Attorney poder actual
precedent precedente
privity relacion juridica o contractual
probate validacion de testamento
promisee a quien se promete
promisor prometedor
promissory estoppel impedimento promisorio
promoters promotores
prospectus prospecto
proximate cause causa immediata
quasi contract cuasicontracto
ratification ratificacion
rebuttal refutación
recorder registrador, grabador
redemption redención
remand devolver
remedy remedio
res asunto
respondent respondiente
satisfaction satisfación
scienter a sabiendas
security agreement accuerdo de seguridad
shareholder accionista
sovereign immunity inmunidad soberana
specific performance ejecucion de lo estipulado en un contrato
Stated Capital dicha capital
stare decisis acaturse a los precedentas judiciales
status quo el estado de las cosas en un momento dado
stockholder accionista
subpoena citacion
summary judgment sentencia sumaria
summons emplazamiento
testimony testimonio
tort daño legal
tortious dañoso
trail jucio
transcript transcripción
treble damages danos triplcados
trustee in bankruptcy sindico concursal
unliquidated debt deuda no liquidado
ultra vires act acta fuera de la facultad de una corporacion
usury usura
venue lugar de jurisdicción
verdict verdicto
versus contra
void nulo
voidable anulable
waive renunciar
waiver renuncia
warranty garantia
whistleblowing un empleado que informa sobre actividades ilicitas en su empresa
writ orden judicial
writ or certiorari auto de avocación
writ of executional (or garnishment) ejecutoria, mandamiento de ejecución

GLOSSARY

acceptance Conduct reasonably indicating approval and commitment to a proposed contract.

accord and satisfaction An agreement and its performance that discharges a previous obligation.

actual authority The authority granted to an agent from a principal, based either on express statements or implied from those statements or actions of the principal.

adjudicatory function The performance of a judicial-type function of an administrative agency that holds hearings to determine facts and the application of laws and regulations to those facts.

administrative agency In the United States, a governmental body that is not defined by the Constitution as being part of the executive, legislative, or judicial branch.

administrative law The law that governs the grant of powers to administrative agencies, specifies the procedures they are to use in carrying out their operations, and determines the extent to which courts review their actions.

Administrative Procedure Act (APA) The legislative statute that establishes the methods or procedures by which administrative agencies are to perform their adjudicatory or rulemaking function as well as determining the extent of judicial review of those actions.

administrative process The methods used by administrative agencies to perform a wide variety of activities.

adversarial process A process in which the parties have the responsibility for developing evidence that will prove their claims; parties also determine which witnesses to call and when to object to opposing evidence.

affirmative action programs Actively recruiting of minorities, goals and timetables for greater minority employment.

agency coupled with an interest The interest of an agent whose reimbursement depends on the continuation of his or her authority to act as an agent.

agency relationship The relationship that arises whenever two people agree that one of them, the agent, may act on behalf of the other, the principal.

agent A person who acts on behalf of another person or firm and who has duties to further that person or firm's interests; unlike a distributor, an agent sells the principal's products, not products owned by the agent.

alternative dispute resolution Various methods for resolving disputes that are alternatives to litigation; the term usually refers to arbitration, mediation, minitrials, and private trials.

Americans with Disabilities Act (ADA) 1991 federal law making disability a protected class.

annual percentage rate of interest (APR) Standardized computation of the interest cost of credit required by TILA.

answer A document filed by the defendant that responds point by point to the allegations in the plaintiff's complaint.

antidumping duties Antidumping duties are levied when imported goods are sold in a foreign market at a price lower than in their principle market.

Anti-Federalists Early states' rights advocates in the United States.

apparent authority The authority of an agent that exists when the principal creates a reasonable appearance of authority in an agent, even though it does not grant the agent actual authority.

appropriate bargaining unit Employees sharing similar employment conditions, entitled to vote together as a unit.

arbitration A process for resolving disputes that uses an individual or panel, often selected for their expertise, authorized by the parties to make a binding decision after hearing evidence presented through established procedures similar to those used in litigation.

Articles of Confederation First form of U.S. constitution used between 1781 and 1789.

articles of incorporation Document filed by the incorporators with the secretary of state or department of commerce to organize a corporation.

assignment The transfer by a tenant of all his or her rights in a leasehold estate to another person.

assumption of risk The defense to negligence or strict liability that prevents plaintiff's recovery if he or she knew or should have known of the risk inherent in a particular situation and voluntarily assumed that risk.

attachment Creation of a security interest through written agreement or the secured party's possession of the collateral.

attorney-at-law A person who acts for someone else in legal matters; attorneys are licensed by state law.

attorney–client privilege Provides that an attorney cannot be forced to divulge confidential information regarding his or her client.

bailment The transfer of possession and custody of property without a transfer of ownership.

bait and switch Deceptive trade practice by seller of placing ads for inexpensive "bait" while intending to "switch" consumers to higher-profit merchandise.

battle of the forms Nonconformity of contract terms between buyer and seller's forms, often resolved in goods sales by UCC §2-207.

best available technology Standard for pollution-controlling devices used in industrial plants constructed in areas with air that met the national ambient air quality standards.

best available technology economically achievable (BAT) The Clean Water Act's more stringent standard, which now requires firms to install the most effective water pollution control equipment available.

best practicable technology (BPT) The Clean Water Act standard that required plants initially to meet in installing water pollution control devices; factors such as the cost of the equipment, the amount of time required to install it, and the severity of the pollution were considered in determining whether a firm complied with this requirement.

bilateral treaty An agreement between two nations that is generally given national and international effect.

bill of lading Document of title entitling holder to delivery of goods in transit.

bill of lading The document that represents both a receipt for goods being transported and a title to the goods; if it is negotiable, the goods can be delivered to whomever has the document.

bona fide occupational qualification (BFOQ) Permitted discrimination if employer has a business necessity.

bottle laws State laws requiring purchasers to pay a cash deposit on all beverage containers; states with bottle laws have significantly decreased roadway litter.

branch (foreign branch) A branch is not a separate firm, but a part of another firm; a foreign branch is not in the same country as the main office of the firm, but it is a part of that firm.

brief A short summary of a case.

bubble concept The concept that allows states to treat all pollution-producing devices within a plant as a single unit —as if they were all under one bubble. A new plant that fails to meet standards could be permitted if the total pollutants under the bubble do meet the standard.

burden of proof The standard as to the amount of proof needed to find the defendant guilty or liable; in a civil case, the standard is by the preponderance of the evidence; while in a criminal case, the standard is beyond a reasonable doubt.

business ethics Application of traditional ethical analysis to business decisions.

business judgment rule The rule that corporate directors are not held liable for errors in business decisions if they exercise reasonable business judgment.

business necessity Where employment of persons from some protected class would undermine the business.

bylaws Rules governing the internal aspects of the corporation's activities that are adopted by either the shareholders or the board of directors.

C & F The term stands for costs and freight and is a transportation term expressing the seller's obligation to pay these expenses, while the buyer pays any insurance needed to protect the goods.

case or controversy Constitutional requirement for genuine adversariness in litigation.

caveat emptor "Let the buyer beware."

caveat venditor "Let the seller beware."

CIF The term standing for costs, insurance, and freight, which are totaled together in determining the price of goods for foreign buyers; the CIF term is the most common transportation term used in international sales.

civil law Laws that concern the rights and duties of people in a society; civil laws seek to have a wrongdoer compensate the injured party for his or her loss.

civil law legal system The legal system that has a code of law as the primary source of law in the society; the customs that became recognized as legal rules in the society were organized and codified into one source or code of law.

Clayton Act Second antitrust law, passed in 1914, enumerating particular offenses.

closed shop agreement Illegal term in collective bargaining agreement requiring union membership before hiring.

collective bargaining Union contract negotiations between employer and employees' certified bargaining representative.

collective bargaining agreement employment contract negotiated between employer and union, covering employees in the bargaining unit.

common law The law based on court decisions in a common law legal system.

common law legal system The legal system that originated in England and that recognizes courts as creators of law.

comparable worth Theory of pay equalization comparing two jobs not substantially equivalent in tasks but requiring similar skill, effort, and responsibility.

comparative negligence The negligence defense that weighs the relative negligence of the plaintiff and the defendant and holds defendant liable only for a portion of plaintiff's damages.

complaint The document a plaintiff files to begin a civil lawsuit. It gives the plaintiff's version of the facts, shows the court's jurisdiction, and requests a remedy by its prayer for relief.

computer crime Any illegal act that requires knowledge of computer technology or the use of a computer.

computer law Laws related to the protection of computer hardware or software or to the illegal use of computers or computer technology.

conditions Express or implied contract terms that trigger a party's performance duty.

confederation Loose aggregation of autonomous states for limited mutual benefits.

conflict of law rules Rules that establish criteria to determine what law governs transactions involving different states or countries.

conglomerate merger Mergers not classified as horizontal or vertical; usually between firms in different industries or at different levels of production.

conscious parallelism Tacit agreement among competitors to mimic one another's pricing behaviors.

consideration Test for contract enforceability that judges the seriousness of the promises made.

contract An enforceable set of mutual obligations for which the law provides a remedy, recognizes a duty, or provides for court enforcement.

contributory negligence The negligence defense that even though the defendant may have been negligent, as plaintiff was also somewhat negligent, plaintiff cannot recover.

copyright The protection granted to protect the original work of authors, musicians, and painters that makes it illegal to copy their work without permission.

corporate crime Illegal behavior intended to benefit business firms.

corporate opportunity doctrine Prohibits the diversion of business opportunities by corporate directors, officers, or key employees if the corporation has an expectancy in the opportunities.

corporate stakeholders Persons or entities affected by corporate activities.

corporation A separate entity that is legally distinct from its shareholder owners who generally enjoy limited liability for the corporation's debts

corrective advertising FTC remedy requiring ads to undo misimpression from former ads.

countervailing duties A countervailing duty is imposed by an importing country to counteract a subsidy for certain goods from the exporting country.

course of dealing Precedents in performing prior contracts between parties giving special meanings to terms.

course of performance Precedents in performing prior installments in a contract between parties giving special meanings to terms.

courts of law Courts originally organized to give a remedy to a specific problem, one mentioned in a writ.

criminal law Laws that seek to protect society as a whole; their aim is to protect society and to punish the wrongdoer.

cross-elasticity of demand Substitutability between two substitute products, computed as percentage change in demand for one product divided by percentage change in the price of substitute.

deceptive advertising Illegal advertising under the Wheeler-Lea Act if capable of deceiving the typical ordinary consumer.

deductive reasoning The process of examining general principles derived from induction or legislation and applying them to specific situations.

delegation The transfer of powers by one governmental branch to another or to an administrative agency.

deposition Testimony that a witness gives under oath and outside the courtroom; depositions are used to find out prior to trial the testimony of opposing witnesses and to preserve that testimony for use at trial if the witness is unavailable.

direct investment An international direct investment is one in which the investing firm purchases or owns all (or almost all) of the stock of a foreign firm.

director The managers of a corporation's business; they determine the corporation's overall strategy and select the people who are in charge of daily activities.

disclosed principal One whose existence and identity is known by the third party when it contracts with the agent.

discovery procedures The methods used by litigants to uncover facts or documents in the exclusive knowledge of the opposing party or that party's witnesses.

disparate impact Apparently neutral job selection standards that negatively impact a protected class.

disparate treatment Intentional use of discriminatory employment policies.

distributor An individual or firm who purchases products from the seller and who assumes the economic and legal risk of selling them.

division of markets Competitors' allocation of customers or geographic markets; prohibited as anticompetitive.

dower interest The interest in land owned by a decedent granted to his or her surviving spouse.

draft Three-party instrument in which the drawer issues a draft ordering drawee (bank) to pay money to a payee.

drawee Party directed to make payment on a draft.

drawer Party directing drawee to make payment on a draft.

duty of care The duty imposed on all individuals and businesses to act carefully toward others when it is foreseeable that a lack of reasonable care could cause injury.

easement A nonpossessory interest in land allowing its owner to make limited use of some portion of another's property.

electronic data interchange (EDI) Computerized commercial contracting through telecommunications.

electronic fund transfers (EFT) Paperless electronic money transfer often through ATM machines and telephone transfer.

eminent domain The power of the government to take private land for public purposes if adequate compensation is paid.

emissions offset policy The policy that allows the construction of a plant with pollution emissions in an area that does not meet the NAAQS when there is a more than equal reduction in the emission from other plants in that area.

employee privacy Controversial balancing of employee rights to secrecy with the employer's property rights and liberty.

employer-independent contractor relationship A relationship between a person or firm that hires another to perform specific tasks but whose activities are not subject to control by the hiring party.

employment-at-will Either employer or employee may terminate an employment contract without the other's consent and without breach of contract.

enabling act Legislative provisions that grant powers to agencies, enabling them to perform a wide variety of functions.

environmental auditing A systematic, documented, periodic, and objective review by regulated entities of facility operations and practices related to meeting environmental regulations.

environmental impact statement Studies of the effects that certain proposed federally financed or approved projects will have on the environment; the NEPA requires such statements be prepared for major projects that are likely to have a significant effect on the quality of the human environment.

Equal Employment Opportunity Commission (EEOC) Federal agency responsible for enforcement of anti-discrimination laws.

equity courts Courts established to hear cases that could not be adequately addressed by the law courts; the chancellor decided by referring both to law and equity.

estate The nature, quantity, and quality of a person's interest in real property.

ethical analysis Studying ehtical concepts and theories and applying them to particular situations.

ethics A field of philosophy that examines motives and actions from the perspective of moral principles.

executive agency An agency of the government that is subject to control by the executive branch.

executive branch The chief executive (president or governor), cabinet, and administrative agencies that derive their authority from the executive.

exhaustion of administrative remedy The requirement that before seeking review by a court, a person challenging an administrative action first must use any and all available administrative methods to review that action.

export The selling of a domestically produced good or service to a foreign purchaser.

expropriation Expropriation occurs when private property is taken by a government and no, or clearly inadequate compensation is paid to its former owner.

externalities Costs or benefits from a firm's activities absorbed by outsiders.

extraterritorial law The law of one nation that seeks to regulate activities or conduct outside its geographic border because of the consequences occurring within its territory.

failing firm defense Defense in conglomerate merger case that target firm must be acquired to avoid insolvency.

failure to warn Liability theory against seller who fails to warn consumers of known product hazards.

FAS The term stands for free alongside and expresses the buyer's obligation to deliver the goods to or alongside a ship, but not to pay to have them loaded onto the ship.

Federal Insurance Contributions Act (FICA) Federal social security contributions.

Federal Register The source where proposed rules, final rules, and certain policies of federal administrative agencies are published; the *Federal Registers* when bound together become the *Code of Federal Regulations (CFR).*

federalism Debate over best place for government power: centrally or locally.

federalism The concept of shared lawmaking powers between the federal and state or local governments.

Federalists Early advocates of strong central or national government in the United States.

fiduciary relationship A relationship based on trust and confidence that gives rise to duties being imposed on the person who acts on behalf of another.

firm offer UCC (§2-205) option that makes an offer irrevocable, enforceable without consideration, if made by a merchant in a signed writing.

fixtures Personal property that has become real property through attachment to land or buildings.

FOB The term stands for free on board, which describes an international seller's obligation to deliver the goods for a stated cost on board a common carrier (ship, truck, etc.) at a named destination; thereafter, any further transportation or insurance is to be paid by the buyer. The destination may be at the buyer's end (destination) or at the seller's end (shipper).

foreign affiliate A foreign affiliate is a firm that is located in a country other than the firm that owns it; usually it is organized in the country where it transacts business.

Foreign Corrupt Practices Act (FCPA) U.S. foreign bribery law prohibiting bribing foreign officials to win business.

foreign direct investment The purchase by a person or firm from one country of at least 10 percent of the ownership of a firm in another country.

foreign portfolio investment The purchase by a person or firm from one country of less than 10 percent of the ownership of a firm in another country.

foreign sales corporation A foreign sales corporation is a corporation that is organized under U.S. laws and that derives almost all of its income from foreign sales; often, it is practically a paper corporation established primarily for tax reasons.

franchise A privilege granted or sold, such as the privilege of using a name or process to sell products or services agreed upon between two parties: the franchisor and the franchisee

free rider One who benefits from the expenditures of others, such as a competitor's service, advertising, and promotional activities.

Freedom of Information Act (FOIA) The law that provides access to information held by administrative agencies for private citizens and firms.

full warranty Magnuson-Moss Act requires that a full warranty provide reasonable repair, refund, or replacement rights and not limit implied warranties.

garnishment Statutory debt collection procedure from debtor's wages.

global legal environment Laws, institutions, and legal processes that affect private business firms.

good faith bargaining Interactive proposals for union contract between an employer and the bargaining unit.

gratuitious agency A relationship in which one person acts on behalf of another without any expectation of being compensated.

gray-market goods Gray-market goods are goods that are imported into a country without the consent of the trademark holder.

greenhouse effect The warming of the earth's lower atmosphere caused by emissions of carbon dioxide; its specific causes and consequences are being studied.

group boycott Collusive agreements not to buy from or sell to certain individuals.

hazardous wastes Wastes that contribute significantly to a serious, irreversible illness or pose a hazard to human health when improperly managed.

horizontal merger Combination of two competing firms at the same level of production.

incorporators Persons who apply to the state for incorporation.

independent contractor A person employed by a business solely to do a particular job without the business having any control over how the job is to be done.

inductive reasoning The process of examining specific situations to determine if they have some common attributes.

industrial organization Study of optimal relations between sellers and buyers and optimal number of buyers and sellers within particular markets.

informal actions The performance by administrative agencies of activities, such as determining eligibility for government benefits or grants, that are neither adjudicatory nor rulemaking functions.

initial public offering (IPO) First public solicitation and sale of new securities.

inquisitorial process A process in which the judge, with the assistance of the parties, investigates the facts and determines the evidence to be presented in a trial.

insiders Employees of an issuer or its consultants with access to confidential information.

intangible property Personal property that does not have a physical existence.

intellectual property Intangible property that is created by mental rather than physical effort.

intentional tort An intentional, wrongful act causing injury to another person.

inter vivos gift A gift of personal property made by a living person.

interlocking directorates Illegal potential collusion if one director sits on the boards of two competitors.

international law Laws governing conduct among nations.

interrogatories Written questions submitted to the opposing party that must be answered under oath.

intestacy laws The state laws that provide for the distribution of property of a decedent who died without a valid will.

intrastate commerce Commercial activities conducted wholly within one state and having negligible impact on other states.

issuer Firm creating and selling investment claims known as securities.

joint tenancy with right of survivorship The ownership of property by at least two people that automatically transfers the interest of one party to the other upon that party's death.

joint venture An agreement among two or more parties to cooperate together for a specified time period and in specific, limited activities.

joint venture An international joint venture is formed when two or more participating firms agree to share in a common project with limited scope and duration; usually, a separate firm is created and is jointly owned by the two parties.

judgment The judge's determination or decision at the end of a trial; it may be different from the jury's verdict. If the judgment is not appealed within a certain time, it becomes final.

judicial branch The courts, which have the power both to interpret laws made by other branches and to make laws when deciding cases.

judicial review Power of courts to review legislation or the acts of administrative agencies.

jurisdiction A court's power to hear and decide cases.

laissez-faire Non-interventionalist freedom of contract theory underlying free-market capitalism.

law Established standards or guidelines for action or behavior in a society, whether they originate from a higher authority or from the common practices and customs of people.

law merchant The law governing the sale of goods for international traders that was first used in the 17th century and that today forms the foundation for today's international convention on the sale of goods.

law merchant Evolution of merchants' customs and practices from the middle ages into modern commercial law.

leasehold estate A possessory interest in property that allows a person to possess real property for a designated term.

legal analysis The study of court cases that solve specific disputes by applying general legal principles.

legal environment of business The study of the legal, regulatory, and political institutions and processes affecting business activities.

legal environment of international business The international, regional, and national laws that affect global business transactions.

legal institutions The institutions in a society that create or apply a society's law; these institutions are one of the components of a society's legal system.

legislative oversight committee A committee that reviews and scrutinizes agency activities, particularly when the agency is requesting legislative funding.

legislative veto The exercise by Congress of its disapproval of administrative rules; by law, the veto belongs to the legislature as a whole, not to only one segment of the legislature.

legislature An officially selected body of persons responsible for making laws for a political unit such as a state or nation.

letter of credit A bank document indicating the bank will pay for goods if the seller submits the prescribed documents to the bank; if the bank issues an advising rather than a confirming letter of credit, the bank will review the documents but will not guarantee payment.

letter of credit (L/C) Document promising a bank will make a payment to a third party for the bank's customer.

license A nonpossessory interest in land, personal in nature and revocable by its grantor, which allows the owner of the license the right to use the land of another (the grantor) for a limited purpose.

license Can be either the permit to sell, assemble, manufacture, or use property belonging to someone else or the permit to enter upon or make use of another person's real property.

license A license is a certificate or document that permits a licensee to make use of the licensor's property.

lien An interest in property, real or personal, that gives one person a collateral-like interest in another person's property.

life estate An interest in real property that gives a person the right to use it for as long as some designated person is alive.

limited liability A corporate characteristic provides that although corporate shareholders may lose their investment if the shares of stock they hold in the corporation become worthless, they generally cannot be held personally liable for corporate debts

limited liability company A business organization used by owners of a closely held business that is organized like a corporation but taxed as a partnership if it lacks some of the essential characteristics of a corporation.

limited partnership A partnership in which some of the partners are allowed to limit their liability to the amount of their original investment; each limited partnership must have at least one general partner with unlimited liability and at least one partner with limited liability.

litigation A process for solving disputes involving presentation of evidence by parties through attorneys before a jury and judge.

maker Party promising to pay amount stated in note.

mandatory collective bargaining subjects Unions and employers must bargain over subjects of wages, hours, and other terms and conditions of employment.

market failure Failure in the assumptions or operation of markets, producing suboptimal results.

market share Percentage of the relevant market held by the firm in question.

market share liability Relieves product liability plaintiff of strict proof of causation against manufacturer(s) of defective product when precise manufacturer cannot be determined.

master-servant or employer-employee relationship The relationship between an employer and an employee whose physical conduct is subject to the employer's control and direct supervision.

material breach Failure of contract obligee to perform as promised, triggers the obligee's remedies.

mediation A dispute resolution process whereby a third party seeks to persuade the disputing parties to settle their differences; unlike arbitration, the recommendation or decision of the mediator is not binding on the parties.

memorandum Written contract minimally sufficient to satisfy the statute of frauds.

merchant Seller or buyer who deals in goods like those involved in the contract; also someone who professes expertise in the trade.

merchants Persons who deal in goods of kind, profess to be experts, or hire expert agents to conduct their business; the UCC implies special duties on merchants.

minimum wage Federally mandated lowest hourly wage.

minitrial A dispute resolution process involving informal presentation of the evidence regarding a dispute to the senior executives of the firms that are parties to a dispute; occasionally, an independent adviser observing the minitrial may make settlement recommendations to the executives of the disputing parties.

misappropriation theory Theory condemning insider trading that uses information stolen by employees or fiduciaries.

misuse Product liability defense for an unreasonable and unintended product use.

monopolistic competition Market dominated by a few large sellers with some market power offering functionally similar but differentiated products.

monopolization Intentional acts to obtain and maintain an illegal monopoly.

monopoly Market dominated by one large seller with market power to dictate prices and supply.

monopsony Market dominated by one large buyer with market power over demand.

moral reasoning The process of moving from premises to conclusions in determining the right course of action.

morality Human behavior that is found to be good and just.

mortgage The lien interest in property retained by an individual or firm providing financing to the purchaser of the property.

national ambient air quality standards (NAAQS) EPA standards required by the Clean Air Act establishing maximum levels in the air of such pollutants as carbon monoxide, hydrocarbons, lead, nitrogen oxide, ozone, and sulfur dioxide.

National Labor Relations Board (NLRB) Federal agency administering the labor laws.

nationalization Nationalization is the taking of private property and making it public or governmental property; when property is nationalized, the former owner of the property receives compensation.

necessaries Necessities of life for which quasi-contractual liability exists even if an incompetent disaffirms that contract.

negligence per se Applies when the plaintiff uses the defendant's violation of a criminal statute as a presumption of defendant's negligence.

negligence tort Occurs when a person breaches a duty to use reasonable care toward others, and the breach of duty causes injury.

nonattainment areas Geographic areas not meeting the EPA NAAQS standards.

nontariff barrier Any governmental restriction that discriminates against imports or favors exports is a nontariff barrier.

note Two-party instrument in which one party promises to pay a specified amount in the future.

nuisance laws Laws that provide that an owner of real property cannot use it in a way that injures others.

nuisance laws Common laws used by state and local governments to deal with environmental problems; any substantial and unreasonable interference with the use and enjoyment of a person's interest in property is a tort and both damage to private and public facilities are actionable wrongs.

Occupational Safety and Health Act (OSHA) Federal statute regulating workplace safety and health hazards.

offer Proposal to contract, containing all the necessary contract terms communicated to the offeree.

officers The people who are in charge of conducting the corporation's day-to-day business.

oligopoly Market dominated by a few sellers that have the power to dictate prices and supply.

oligopsony Market dominated by a few large buyers, each of which has some market power over demand.

option A contract making an offer irrevocable, gives the offeree a specified time to further consider the offer.

parol evidence rule Evidence rule prohibiting admission of contradictions to an integrated written contract intended to be the whole and complete agreement.

partially disclosed principal One whose existence is known by the third party, but whose identity is unknown; the third party knows the agent is acting for someone else but does not know the identity of the principal.

partner's interest in the partnership A partner's share of the profits and surplus; this interest is considered personal property

partner's right in partnership property A partner's right, shared equally with other partners, to possess and use partnership property for partnership purposes

partner's right to participate in the management The right of each partner, in the absence of any contrary agreement made by the partners, to have an equal right to manage and conduct the business of the partnership

partnership An association of two or more persons who intend to carry on a business for profit as co-owners.

patent A new and nonobvious process, machine, manufactured item, or composition of matter that is protected by national law.

payee Party named to receive payment in note or draft.

pension vesting ERISA requirement that a pension beneficiary's interest become irrevocable after a minimum employment period of 5–10 years.

per se rule Restraint of trade that is always illegal; no justification exists.

perfect competition Market in which there are numerous buyers and sellers so there is no market power in any one; supply and demand allocate resources optimally.

perfect competition model Market system allocating resources through acts of numerous buyers and sellers, each with perfect information, none possessing market power, selling only standardized products, with no significant barriers to entry.

perfection Public notification of a security interest establishing priority for the secured party.

personal property Moveable property that has a physical existence and property without a physical existence.

picketing Gathering and patrolling by persons to inform others of a labor dispute.

pierce the corporate veil The concept of breaking through the limited liability usually granted to corporate shareholders and making them liable if there is fraud or other reason to hold an individual owner liable for corporate obligations

police power Laws that allow state or local governments to impose reasonable regulations that promote the public health, safety, morals, and general welfare of a community.

police power State reserved legislative power to protect the health, safety, welfare, and morals of the people.

political action committees (PACs) Groups of like-minded political contributors concentrating electioneering resources for candidates and causes.

potential entrant effect Firm apparently able to enter market so it exerts competitive discipline on existing competitors.

preexisting legal duty Repromising an old duty is insufficient consideration for a new contract.

pretrial conference A meeting of attorneys and the judge prior to trial held to narrow the issues in dispute and to move the controversy toward trial or settlement.

price discrimination Seller's illegal practice of charging different prices for commodities of like grade and quality.

price-fixing Agreement of competitors to set artificially prices high.

primary jurisdiction When both a court and an administrative agency are authorized to review some administrative action, the concept that the court will defer to the agency because it should have the first chance to review such matters.

principal A person or firm that has other people, agents, acting on its behalf and representing its interest.

principal-agent relationship The relationship between a person or firm (principal) who authorizes another (agent) to carry out a broad range of activities subject to the general control of the first person.

private law Law that concerns relations between individuals or firms in a society such as contract, property, and tort law.

private trial A dispute resolution process using a retired judge or senior attorney selected by the parties to resolve a dispute. While the parties generally agree that the decision will be binding, private trial judgments usually are not enforced by public officials unless state law recognizes such judgments.

privity of contract Direct relationship between parties, usually by contract, suggesting mutual responsibilities.

probate laws The laws defining the process for determining if a decedent had a valid will and what property is transferred and who inherits it at the decedent's death.

procedural law The law that enforces a society's substantive law and details the methods by which those duties and rights are enforced; it constitutes a third component of a society's legal system.

prohibition A prohibition totally restricts imports into a country.

property The bundle of rights that people have in things.

property law The law that describes the legally enforceable relationship between people or businesses and things in which they have a property interest.

prospectus Any notice, circular, advertisement, letter, or communication that offers or confirms a security sale.

protected class Demographic classification of persons historically subjected to discrimination, including: race, color, religion, national origin, sex, disability, and age.

proximate cause The standard used in negligence cases to establish the required causal relationship between the defendant's nonperformance or breach of duty and the plaintiff's injury.

proxy A substitute vote on behalf of a shareholder at a corporate meeting when the shareholder of record is unable to attend.

proxy solicitation Electioneering by management or insurgent shareholders to win proxy votes in a corporate election.

public law Law that concerns the relationship between people and their government, such as constitutional or administrative law.

quasi-contract Contract-like duty imposed to prevent unjust enrichment after a benefit is conferred.

quota A quota limits the number of specified goods that may enter a country.

ratification The act by a principal of approving an unauthorized action of an agent; ratification may occur by express action or be implied from the principal's retention of benefits.

rational basis Equal protection test of legislation validity requiring a rational connection between a permissible governmental purpose and the statute in question.

real property Land and everything attached to it, including the air above and the minerals below.

rejection Offeree's refusal to contract on the offered terms.

relevant market First determination in assessing monopoly power in a product line and geographic region.

reorganization Continuation of business in bankruptcy without liquidation.

representation election Employees' election to certify a particular union as their bargaining representative.

res ipsa loquitur Means "the thing speaks for itself"; in some situations, circumstantial evidence is used to establish a first-impression case of negligence.

resale price maintenance Supplier requirement that goods be resold at a set price.

respondeat superior The term, meaning let the superior respond, is used to describe the liability of the principal for the torts of its agent when the agent is acting in the scope of its authority to further the principal's interests.

restrictive convenant Private agreement restricting the use of real property.

revocation Offeror's withdrawal of an offer terminating the offeree's power of acceptance.

RICO Racketeer influenced corrupt organizations, crime of repeated and related underlying federal crimes.

right-to-work laws State laws prohibiting union or agency shops that mandate union membership.

ripeness The requirement that an issue that relates to a challenge to an action taken by an administrative agency is sufficiently final and ready for court determination.

rule of reason Justification of restraint of trade judged by reasonability.

Rule 10b-5 SEC rule prohibiting fraudulent omissions and disclosures, insider trading, and market manipulation.

rulemaking The process by which an administrative agency exercises a legislative-type function in making rules of general applicability.

secondary pressure Union activity directed at another employer with which the union has no dispute.

secured transaction Contract granting lien on collateral as security for a loan.

separate entity theory The characteristic of the corporation that gives it a legal life of its own, making it responsible for paying its own taxes and holding it accountable for its own torts and in some cases for crimes

separation of powers The splitting of lawmaking authority at one level of government among the executive, legislative, and judicial branches.

sexual harassment Unwelcome sexual advances, requests for sexual favors, and other verbal or physical conduct of a sexual nature made explicitly or implicitly a term or condition of an individual's employment, used as the basis for employment decisions, unreasonably interfering with individual's work performance, or creating an intimidating, hostile, or offensive work environment.

shareholder The owners of a corporation; they make major corporate decisions and determine who will be its managers.

shelf registration Securities preregistered for sale when conditions are optimal.

Sherman Act First antitrust law, passed in 1890, outlawing monopolization.

smog swapping system The system permitting companies whose emissions are cleaner than the levels allowed by law to sell their credits to emit sulfur dioxide to other companies who are having difficulty meeting the standards.

social security Federal retirement income supplement funded by current employee contributions.

sole proprietor An individual who is the sole owner of a business.

sovereign immunity doctrine International law principle. Courts of one state do not have jurisdiction to determine cases against another sovereign state; there is a recognized exception for commercial activities of a sovereign state.

SQ3R A study method whose name stands for survey, question, read, recite, and review.

standards A legislative provision that establishes the specific concerns an agency is to address in performing its functions.

standing The requirement that a person or organization have a sufficient stake in the outcome of an agency activity before challenging it in an administrative proceeding or in court.

stare decisis The concept that a judge's decision in a common law legal system sets a precedent for future cases because it is recognized as a primary source of law.

stare decisis "Let the decision stand."

state action Exemption under the antitrust laws for valid governmental actions.

state implementation plan (SIP) A state's plan as to how it will achieve a level of air pollution below the maximum level specified by EPA standards.

state-of-the-art defense Product liability defense that manufacturer used all known safety improvements at the time the product was designed.

statute of frauds Requirement for written contracts in the sale of interests in land, guarantee contracts, contracts not to be performed within one year, and sales of goods of $500 or more.

statute of repose Limitation period for the technological useful life of products.

statute of repose Time limitation on the period during which products should be defect free.

statutory law The law based on legislative enactments.

strict constructionism Ideology limiting judicial interpretation.

strict liability tort Occurs if one person does something dangerous that injures another person who is within the scope of risk; some product liability cases now are based on this standard.

strict scrutiny Equal protection test of legislation validity requiring the legislation be necessary to and the only means to achieve a compelling governmental interest.

strikes Simultaneous work stoppage to pressure employer to settle a labor dispute.

Subchapter S corporation A creature of the federal income tax laws; viewed as a hybrid between the corporation and the general partnership.

sublease The transfer by a tenant of some but not all of his or her rights in a leasehold estate to another person.

subpoena Government order requiring a witness to testify.

substantial performance Slightly defective but still acceptable contract performance which entitles obligor to an adjusted payment.

substantive law The law that regulates the activities of people in a society by defining their rights and duties; it constitutes a second component of a society's legal system.

summons A court order giving the defendant notice of a lawsuit and a certain time period in which to respond or face a judgment by default.

sunset laws Laws that provide for an automatic periodic review of agency activities.

taking Government appropriation of private property for which just compensation is usually due.

tangible property Personal property that has a physical existence.

tariff A tax on imported goods; the tax may be based on the value of the goods (ad valorem) or simply be levied on goods of a certain type (flat rate).

tenancy in common An interest in property owned by two or more people that gives each an undivided right to possess the property and gives the property to a party's heirs upon death.

the act of state doctrine Established by the U.S. Supreme Court. U.S. courts will not judge legality of a politically sensitive act of a foreign court; will defer to other branches of the U.S. government.

tort law Imposes duties on people to act in a reasonable manner toward others and to refrain from intentionally causing others to be injured.

trade secret A valuable formula, process, or compilation of information that is known only to its developers.

trademark A distinctive mark on goods that designates their origin and distinguishes them from those of competitors.

trespass An unlawful interference with the property of another; trespass invades the property owner's exclusive right of possession, whereas a nuisance interferes with the property owner's use and enjoyment of the property.

trust Trustor conveys legal title on property to trustee who makes decisions about the property; used to bring former competitors under unified control of a single trustee.

tying Supplier requires buyer to purchase undesired product to get the desired product; illegal under the rule of reason.

unconscionability Unfair adhesion contract with inadequate consideration; can be canceled by a court under the UCC.

underwriter Purchasers of securities with a view to public distribution.

undisclosed principal One whose existence and identity is unknown to the third party when it contracts with the principal's agent.

unemployment compensation State insurance system intended to replace unemployed workers' income.

unfair labor practice Prohibited actions of employer or union that impedes employees' self-organization rights.

union shop Union contract term requiring all employees to join the union.

universal theory Defines actions as morally good if those actions can be undertaken by everyone in good conscience.

usage of trade Customary business practices unique to an industry giving special meanings to terms.

utilitarian theory Defines an action as morally right and ethical if it produces the greatest amount of good for the greatest number of people.

verdict The jury's decision at the end of a case based on instructions regarding the law from the judge and the jury's determination of the facts.

vertical merger Combination of two firms in supplier–customer relationship.

vicarious liability The liability of the business for the actions of its agents.

warehouse receipt Document of title entitling holder to possession of goods held in a warehouse.

warranty Affirmation of fact or a promise of performance made in any product sale under the UCC.

warranty deed The deed a seller of property usually transfers to a purchaser; it warrants that the title is good and free of claims by others.

white-collar crime Illegal, nonviolent behavior by businesses and their employees.

workers' compensation State insurance plans providing cash benefits for workers' job injuries.

zoning ordinances A local law that restricts the use of real property in furtherance of benefiting the general public.

Case Index

Cases appearing in italic type are excerpted in the text; others are discussed or cited.

A

Action Automobile, Inc., N.L.R.B. v., 703
Adams v. Rubber Co., 665
Albanese's Case, Joseph, 653–654
Allied Structural Steel Co. v. Spannaus, 170–171
Allison v. Fiscus, 26
Aluminum Co. of America, United States v., 575–577
Amalgamated Food Employees Union, Local 590 v. Logan Valley Plaza, Inc., 676
Amax, Inc. v. Water Quality Control Commission, 209–211
American Academy of Pediatrics v. Heckler, 200–202
American Bell International v. Islamic Republic of Iran, 368n
American Textile Manufacturers Institute v. Donovan, 659
Anheuser-Busch, Inc. v. Stroh Brewery Co., 237–239
Ansonia Board of Education v. Philbrook, 737
A.P. Smith Mfg. Co. v. Barlow, 787n
Apablasa, J. v. Merritt & Co., 303–304
Arizona v. Maricopa County Medical Society, 628
Arnold Schwinn & Co., United States v., 610
Associated Press v. United States, 629
Atari Games Corp. v. Nintendo of America Inc., 240–243

B

Batson v. Kentucky, 123
Beusch, United States v., 792
Bibb v. Navajo Freight Lines, Inc., 168
Bildisco, N.L.R.B. v., 687
Blanton v. North Las Vegas, 34–35
Board of Curators of the University of Missouri v. Horowitz, 182
Board of Regents of State College v. Roth, 229–230
Bowen v. United States Postal Service, 690n
Bowsher v. Synar, 51–52
Brennan v. GMAC, 664
Broadcast Music Inc. v. CBS, 598n
Brooks v. Brooks, 35–37, 59
Browing-Ferris Indus. v. Kelco Disposal, 184
Brown Shoe Co., FTC v., 627
Brown Shoe Co. v. United States, 583–584
Brown v. Board of Education, 35
Buck v. Kuykenclall, 168
Bundy v. Jackson, 720
Business Electronics Corp. v. Sharp Electronics Corp., 611–612

C

Cabot Carbon Co., N.L.R.B. v., 703
Cady, Roberts & Co., In re, 536
California Retail Liquor Dealers Assn. v. Midcal Aluminum, Inc., 606–607
California v. ARC America Corp., 565n
Capua v. City of Plainfield, 293
Carnegie-Illinois Steel Corp. v. United Steelworkers of America, 694
Carpenter v. United States, 775n
Carter v. Jury Commission of Greene County, 124
CBS v. Stokely-Van Camp, Inc., 478
Central Hardware Co. v. N.L.R.B., 676
Central Hudson Gas & Electric Corp. v. Public Service Commission, 175–176
Chada, INS v., 196–197
Chevron, USA, Inc. v. Natural Resources Defense Council, Inc., 748–749
Chiarella v. United States, 536
Chicago Board of Trade v. United States, 595
Cipollone v. Liggett Group, Inc., 391–393
Citizens to Preserve Overton Park v. Volpe, 214–215
City of Richmond v. J. A. Croson, 737

Coates v. City of Cincinnati, 183
Coburn v. Pan American World Airways, 737
Colgate, United States v., 608
Colgate-Palmolive Co., FTC v., 420n
Commonwealth Financial Corp. v. Sherill, 515
Community Communications Co. v. City of Boulder, Colorado, 569n
Conklin Development v. Acme Markets, Inc., 250
Conoco, Inc. v. Norwest Bank Mason City, 371
Continental TY, Inc. v. GTE Sylvania, Inc., 610
Cooke v. Lynn Sand & Stone Co., 507–508
Cook v. State Department of Mental Health, Retardation and Hospitals, 725n
County of Washington v. Gunther, 710
Crouch v. Crouch, 36
CTS Corp. v. Dynamics Corp. of America, 548
Curtin Matheson Scientific, Inc., N.L.R.B. v., 692n

D

Darby, United States v., 166
Daves v. Reed, 287
Dean Milk Co. v. Madison, 169n
DeBartolo Corp. v. Florida Gulf Coast Building and Construction Trades Council, 696n
Dirks v. SEC, 536–538
Dodge v. Ford Motor Co., 786n
Dolan v. City of Tigard, 159–161, 258–260
Donovan v. Burger King Corp., 642–643
Donovan v. Trans World Airlines, Inc., 664
Dorton v. Collins, Aikman Corp., 370
Dothard v. Rawlinson, 737

E

Eastern Advertising Co. v. McGaw & Co., 324
Eastern Dist. Co., Inc. v. Flynn, 316–317
Eastern Railroads Presidents Conference v. Noerr Motor Freight, Inc., 570n
Eastman Kodak Company v. Polaroid Corporation, 234n
E.C. Knight Co., United States v., 558n
Economy Muffler & Tire Center, Inc., United States v., 751–753
Edgar v. MITE Corp., 548n
Edmonson v. Leesville Concrete Company, Inc., 123–126
EEOC v. Arabian American Oil Company, 735
E.I. du Pont de Nemours & Co., United States v., 573–574
E.I. du Pont de Nemours & Co. v. Christopher, 234n, 235
Ellis v. Brotherhood of Railway, Airline and Steamship Clerks, Freight Handlers, Express and Station Employees, 704
Erickson v. FTC, 421n
Erie R. Co v. Tompkins, 41
Escola v. Coca-Cola Bottling of Fresno, 401–402
Escott v. BarChris Construction Corp., 529–531
Exchange Parts, N.L.R.B. v., 680

F

Fall River Dyeing & Finishing Corp. v. N.L.R.B., 687n
Federal Deposit Insurance Corporation v. Texas Bank of Garland, 452–454
Feldman v. Lederle Laboratories, 410
Fiberboard Paper Products Corp. v. N.L.R.B., 688
First English Evangelical Lutheran Church of Glendale v. Los Angeles County, 161n
First National Bank of Boston v. Bellotti, 176
First National Maintenance Corp. v. N.L.R.B., 688
Fort Gratiot Sanitary Landfill, Inc. v. Michigan Dept. of Natural Resources, 168n
Frezzo Brothers, Inc., United States v., 765
Fruit and Vegetable Packers and Warehousemen, Local 760, N.L.R.B. v., 696n
FTC v. Brown Shoe Co., 627
FTC v. Colgate-Palmolive Co., 420n
FTC v. Morton Salt Co., 624
FTC v. Procter & Gamble Co., 585–587
FTC v. Superior Court Trial Lawyers Assn., 600n
Fullilove v. Klutznick, 732n

G

Gallagher & Ascher v. Simon, 203–204
Geary v. United States Steel, 637n
General Electric Co., N.L.R.B. v., 686
Gibbons v. Ogden, 165, 166
Gissel Packing Co., Inc., N.L.R.B. v., 679–680

Glover v. Easter Nebraska Community Office of Retardation, 638n
Goldfarb v. Virginia State Bar, 569n, 607, 629
Great Atlantic and Pacific Tea Co., Inc. v. FTC, 625n
Griggs v. Duke Power Co., 726
Grimshaw v. Ford Motor Co., 399n
Griswold v. Connecticut, 273
Guth v. Loft, 462n
Guzman, United States v., 150

H

Haagen-Dazs Co., Inc., In re, 419n
Haffenden-Rimar Intl., Inc., SEC v., 526n
Haldeman, United States v., 122
Haney Chevrolet, Inc., United States v., 752
Harless v. First National Bank in Fairmont, 639
Harris v. Forklift Systems, Inc., 721–723
Haven v. Randolph, 478
Heart of Atlanta Motel, Inc. v. United States, 166
Hennis v. O'Connor, 293
Hensley v. Sherman Car Wash Equipment Co., 403–404
H.J. Inc. v. Northwestern Bell Telephone Co., 776–777
Hoffman v. Red Owl Stores, Inc., 309–310
Hornestake Mining Co. v. U.S. Environmental Protection Agency, 754n
Howey, SEC v., 525–526
Humphrey's Executor v. United States, 52

I

Illinois Brick Co. v. Illinois, 565n
Industrial Union v. American Petroleum Institute, 657
In re Cady, Roberts & Co., 536
In re Haagen-Dazs Co., Inc., 419n
In re Investors Management Co., 537
In re Playboy Enterprises, Inc., 780–782
In re Sailors Union of the Pacific, 695n
In re Union Carbide Corp. Gas Plant Disaster, 269
In re U.S. Financial Securities Litigation, 150
INS v. Chada, 196–197
International Assn of Machinists v. OPEC, 79–81
International B'hd of Teamsters v. United States, 727–728
International Longshoremen's Assn., N.L.R.B. v., 690n
International Union v. Johnson Controls, 719
Interstate Circuit, Inc. v. United States, 602n
Investors Management Co., In re, 537

J

Johnson v. Transportation Agency, Santa Clara, Calif., 732
Joseph Albanese's Case, 653–654
Joseph v. Norman's Health Clubs, Inc., 428–429

K

Kassel v. Consolidated Freightways Corp. of Delaware, 168n
Katko v. Briney, 25–26, 28–29
Katzenbach v. McClung, 167
Kewance Oil Co. v. Bicron Co., 235n

L

Lamprecht v. FCC, 732n
Landreth Timber Co. v. Landreth, 526n
Lechmere v. National Labor Relations Board, 677–678
Linden Lumber Company v. N.L.R.B., 704
Local 1229, International Brotherhood of Electrical Workers, N.L.R.B. v., 703
Los Angeles Department of Water and Power v. Manhart, 737
Lucas v. South Carolina Coastal Council, 161n
Luedtke v. Nabors Alaska Drilling, Inc., 639–640
Lykins Oil Co. v. Fekkos, 370

M

Macke Co. v. Pizza of Gaithersburg, Inc., 324–325
MacPherson v. Buick Motor Co., 376–377, 409
Marbury v. Madison, 163
Marshall v. Barlow's, Inc., 205–206, 660
Martin v. McDonald's Corp., 281–282, 494
Massey v. Tube Art Display, Inc., 475–476
Masterson v. Sine, 320–321
McCabe v. L. K. Liggett Drug Co., 381–382
McGowan v. St. Regis Paper Co., Inc., 287–288
McGraw, State v., 774–775
McQuade v. Tucson Tiller Apartments, Ltd., 256–257
Meinhard v. Salmon, 458
Meritor Savings Bank v. Vinson, 721

Merrill Lynch, Pierce, Fenner & Smith, Inc. v. Boech, 458–461
Metro Broadcasting, Inc. v. FCC, 732n
Metro Edison v. People Against Nuclear Energy, 744–745
Micro-Managers, Inc. v. Gregory, 370
Microsoft Corp., United States v., 566n
Miles v. Perpetual Savings & Loan, 464
Miller Brewing Co. v. G. Heileman Brewing Co., 236n
Miller Brewing Co. v. Jos. Schlitz Brewing Co., 237
Miller v. City Bank & Trust, 486–487
Mills Co. v. Crawfish Capitol Seafood, 497–499
Minnesota v. Clover Leaf Creamery Co., 180
Mitsubishi Motors Corp. v. Soler ChryslerPlymouth, Inc., 91–92, 136–137
Moncur v. City of Los Angeles Dept. of Air, 280
Monsanto Co. v. Spray-Rite Service Corp., 611
Moren v. Samuel M. Langston Co., 398
Morton Salt Co., FTC v., 624
Murray v. industrial Commission of Illinois, 651
Myers v. United States, 52

N

Nachtigal, United States v., 34–35
National Collegiate Athletic Ass'n v. Tarkanian, 182n
NCAA v. Board of Regents of the University of Oklahoma, 598n
Nelson v. Hydraulic Press Mfg. Co., 400
Newman, United States v., 538
New York Telephone Co. v. New York Department of Labor, 664
Nixon v. Administrator of General Services, 273
N.L.R.B. v. Action Automobile, Inc., 703
N.L.R.B. v. Bildisco, 687
N.L.R.B. v. Cabot Carbon Co., 703
N.L.R.B. v. Curtin Matheson Scientific, Inc., 692n
N.L.R.B. v. Exchange Parts, 680
N.L.R.B. v. Fruit and Vegetable Packers and Warehousemen, Local 760, 696n
N.L.R.B. v. General Electric Co., 686
N.L.R.B. v. Gissel Packing Co., Inc., 679–680
N.L.R.B. v. International Longshoremen's Assn., 690n
N.L.R.B. v. Local 1229, Brotherhood of Electrical Workers, 703
N.L.R.B. v. Weingarten, Inc., 703
Nollan v. California Coastal Commission, 161n
Northern Pacific Railway Co. v. United States, 557
Northern Plumbing Supply, Inc. v. Gates, 383

O

O'Leary v. Moyer's Landfill, Inc., 757–758
Orkin Exterminating Co. v. FTC, 426–427

P

P. Lorillard v. FTC, 421n
Pacific Mutual Life Ins. Co. v. Halsip, 184–186
Palmer v. A.H. Robins Co., Inc., 410
Palmer v. United States, 116–117
Palsgraf v. Long Island Railroad Co., 293
Park, United States v., 440–441
Parke Davis & Co., United States v., 608n
Parker v. Brown, 569n, 607
Payne v. Western and Atlantic Railroad Co., 635
Perez v. United States, 166–167
Playboy Enterprises, Inc., In re, 780–782
Plessey v. Ferguson, 35
Powell, United States v., 179
Powers v. Ohio, 124
Price Waterhouse v. Hopkins, 713–714
Princeton Graphics v. NEC Home Electronics, 422n
Principe v. McDonald's Corp., 494, 614–616
Procter & Gamble Co., FTC v., 585–587
Procter & Gamble co. v. City of Chicago, 765

Q

Quill Corp. v. North Dakota, 169n
Quinnipiac Council, Boy Scouts of America, Inc. v. Commission on Human Rights and Opportunities, et al., 60–63

R

Rappaport v. Playtex Corp., 478
Rasmussen v. South Florida Blood Service, 272–274
Reeves v. Ernst & Young, 525n, 777
Regents of the University of California v. Bakke, 716
Regina v. Dudley, 24
Rickey v. Chicago Transit Authority, 283

Robertson v. Methow Valley Citizens Council, 755
Robinson v. Merrill Lynch, Pierce, Fenner & Smith, Inc., 459
RSR Corp. v. FTC, 590

S

Sabine Pilot Service, Inc. v. Hauck, 664
Sailors Union of the Pacific, In re, 695n
Santa Fe Case, The, 540n
Schechter Poultry Corp. v. United States, 194
Schlensky v. Wrigley, 787
Schoenberger v. Chicago Transit Authority, 454–455
School Board of Nassau County Florida v. Arline, 724
Schweiger v. Loewi & Co., Inc., 459
Science Accessories v. Summagraphics, 462–464
Sears, Roebuck & Co. v. FTC, 419n
SEC v. Haffenden-Rimar Intl., Inc., 526n
SEC v. Howey, 525–526
SEC v. Texas Gulf Sulphur Company, 535
Shearson/American Express, Inc. v. McMahon, 133
Siegel v. Chicken Delight, Inc., 615
Sindell v. Abbott Laboratories, 378
Smith v. American Express Travel Services, 472–474
Socony-Vacuum Oil Co., Inc., United States v., 597–598
Sony Corp. v. Universal City Studios, 239n
South Carolina State Highway Dept. v. Barnwell Bros., 168
South-Eastern Underwriters Ass'n, United States v., 162n
Southern Pac. Co. v. Arizona, 168
State v. McGraw, 774–775
Stouffer Foods Corp., 419n
Strong v. Repide, 534
Superior Court Trial Lawyers Assn., FTC v., 600n
Sure-Tan, Inc. v. N.L.R.B., 703
Sztejn v. J. Henry Schroder Banking Co., 365–367

T

Telex Corp. v. IBM, 590
Texaco, Inc. v. Hasbrouck, 623–624
Texaco, Inc. v. Pennzoil Co., 275–277
Texas Gulf Sulphur Company, SEC v., 535
Theatre Enterprises v. Paramount Film Distributor Corp., 602n
Thiel v. Southern Pacific Co., 149
Thomas v. Winchester, 377
Thompson Printing Machinery Co. v. B.F. Goodrich Co., 338–339
Timberlane Lumber Co. v. Bank of America, 76–78
Tinwood N. V. v. SunBanks, Inc., 515
Totem Marine Tug & Barge, Inc. v. Alyeska Pipeline Service Co., 313
Toussaint v. Blue Cross & Blue Shield of Michigan, 635–636
Town of Hallie v. City of Eau Claire, 590
Trans World Airlines, Inc. v. Hardison, 717–718
Trans World Airlines, Inc. v. Indep. Fed. of Flight Attendants, 693n
T.S.C. Industries v. Northway, 544–545
Twigg v. Hercules Corp., 639–640

U

Underhill v. Hernandez, 80
Union Carbide Corp. Gas Plant Disaster, In re, 269
United Paperworkers Int'l Union v. Misco, Inc., 138n, 698–699
United Parcel Service v. Fetterman, 652
United States Steel Corp. v. Train, 754
United States v. Aluminum Co. of America, 575–577
United States v. Arnold Schwinn & Co., 610
United States v. Beusch, 792
United States v. Colgate, 608
United States v. Cranton, 34–35
United States v. Darby, 166
United States v. E. C. Knight Co., 558n
United States v. Economy Muffler & Tire Center, Inc., 751–753
United States v. E.I. du Pont de Nemours & Co., 573–574
United States v. Frezzo Brothers, Inc., 765
United States v. Guzman, 150
United States v. Haldeman, 122
United States v. Haney Chevrolet, Inc., 752
United States v. Microsoft Corp., 566n
United States v. Nachtigal, 34–35
United States v. Newman, 538
United States v. Park, 440–441
United States v. Parke Davis & Co., 608n
United States v. Powell, 179
United States v. Socony-Vacuum Oil Co., Inc., 597–598
United States v. South-Eastern Underwriters Ass'n, 162n
United States v. Von's Grocery Co., 581

United States v. Waste Management, Inc., 589
United Steelworkers of America v. Usery, 700
United Steelworkers of America v. Weber, 731–732
Upjohn v. United States, 129–130
U.S. Financial Securities Litigation, In re, 150
Utah Pie Co. v. Continental Baking Co., 621

V

Van Hooser v. Keenon, 490–491
Virginia State Board of Pharmacy v. Virginia Citizen's Consumer Council, 174n, 189
Von's Grocery Co., United States v., 581

W

Walkovsky v. Carlton, 497n
Wards Cove Packing Co., Inc. v. Antonio, 715
Warner-Lambert Co. v. FTC, 421n
Waste Management Inc., United States v., 589
Waterson v. General Motors Corp., 405
Weeks v. Southern Bell & Telegraph Co., 736
Weingarten, Inc., N.L.R.B. v., 703
Westinghouse Electric Corp. v. Nutt, 397–398
West Michigan Environmental Action Council, Inc. v. Natural Resources Commission of the State of Michigan, 762–763
Whalen v. Roe, 273
Whirlpool Corp. v. Marshall, 661–662
Wickard v. Filburn, 166, 189
Williams on Behalf of Williams v. Bowen, 212–213
Williams v. Jackson Co., 278–279
Wisconsin Public Intervenor v. Mortier, 47–49, 60
Wright v. Alan Mills, Inc., 515

INDEX

Ability testing, 726–727
Acceptance
  contract law, 300–305
  sales of goods, 336
Accord and satisfaction, 308
Account, duty to, 465
Acid rain, 751
Act of state doctrine, 79
Actual authority, 449–450
Adjudicatory functions, 197, 198
Administrative agencies
  adjudication, 197, 198, 202
  business interaction, 215–217
  control, 195–198
  creation, 192–193
  criticism of regulation by, 217–218
  delegation of authority, 194
  deregulation, 218–219
  executive controls, 197
  general functions of, 198–199
  informal actions, 199
  informal activities, 204–205
  judicial review, 206–211
  public controls, 197–198
  role, 193–194
  rulemaking, 198, 199–201
Administrative law, 192. *See also* Administrative agencies
Administrative Procedures Act (APA), 195, 200
Adversarial process, 109–110
Advertising regulation, 418–424. *See also* Commercial speech
  comparative advertising, 422
  corrective advertisements, 421–422
  deceptive advertising, 418–422
Affectation doctrine, 165
Affiliate, 96
Affirmative action, 729–733
Age Discrimination in Employment Act, 708, 724
Agency coupled with interest, 456
Agency law. *See also* Employment law
  agent defined, 448
  agent's duties to principal, 457–465
  authority, 449–451
  contract liability, 467–470
  creation of agency, 449–456
  principal's duties to agent, 465–467
  ratification, 454
  termination, 456–457
  tort liability, 470–475
Agency relationship, 449
Agency shop, 690
AIDS, testing, 638
Ally doctrine, 696
Alternative dispute resolution (ADR), 132–147
  arbitration, 134–138
  in corporate arena, 133
  defined, 132
  ethics, and, 146–147
  litigation compared with, 142–145
  mediation, 133–134, 138–140
  minitrial, 133, 140
  private trial, 141
  pros and cons of, 146
Alternative fuels, 751
Ambiguity, in critical thinking, 12
American Federation of Labor (AFL), 667, 668
Americans with Disabilities Act of 1990, 709, 725
Andean Pact (ANPAC), 67
Anglo-American legal system, 32–38
Annual percentage rate of interest (APR), 428
Answer, 112
Antidumping duties, 85
Antitrust law. *See also* Clayton Act; Federal Trade Commission Act; Mergers; Monopolization; Restraints of trade; Sherman Antitrust Act
  acts compared, 559
  enforcement, 564–572
  enforcement theories, 556, 566–567
  exemptions, 568–570
  international, 99
  market structures, 563–564
Apparent authority, 451
Appeal to authority, 14
Appellant, 27
Appellee, 27
Appropriate bargaining unit, 673–674
Arbitration, 134–138
  court-mandated, 137–138
  defined, 134
  enforcement, 138
  international, 90, 135–136
  labor law, 697–698
  voluntary agreements to arbitrate, 135–136
Arbitration agreements, 138
Arbitration offer, 134
Articles of Confederation, 157
Articles of incorporation, 500
Assault, 270
Association of Southeast Asian Nations (ASEAN), 67, 74
Assumption of risk, 286, 403, 651
Atomic Energy Act, 761
Atomic Energy Commission, 761
Attachment, 119, 355–356
Attorneys, 126–129
  privilege, 128–129
Auction sales, 336–337

B

Bailey, Jeff, 756n
Bailments, 246

Bait and switch, 425
Banking. *See also* Commercial paper
  relations with customers, 354
Bankruptcy, 356–361
  corporate reorganization, 360–361
Bankruptcy Reform Act of 1994, 361
Barter, 368
Battery, 271
Battle of forms, 335
Best available technology (BAT), 748
Best available technology economically achievable (BAT), 754
Best practicable technology (BPT), 754
Bilateral treaty, 72
Bill of lading, 82–83, 339–340
Black's Law Dictionary, 8
Board of directors of corporation, 505
Boesky, Ivan, 539
Bona fide occupational qualification (BFOQ), 725–726
Bottle laws, 763
Boulwareism, 686
Boycotts
  consumer, 696
  group, 600
  secondary, 695
Branch of corporation, 97
Brenner, Steven N., 769n
Bribery, 777–779
Brief, 15
  sample, 28–29
Briefing cases, 15, 27–28
Bubble concept, 748
Burden of proof, 41
Business ethics, 22. *See also* Ethics
Business judgment rule, 505
Business necessity, 725
Bylaws, 500

C

Capper-Volstead Act, 568
Cardozo, Benjamin, 458
Case opinions, 15
Case or controversy, 162
Caveat emptor, 375
Caveat venditor, 376
Cellar-Kefauver Act, 560, 579
C&F, 82
Chicago school, antitrust theory, 568
Child labor, 641–642, 643–644
CIF, 82
Circular reasoning, 14
Citation, 27
Civil law, 39–41
  legal system, 5, 38, 75
Civil litigation
  appellate process, 119–120
  pleadings, 111–113
  prelitigation, 111
  pretrial, 113–115
  remedies, 119
  trial, 115–119
Civil Rights Act of 1866 & 1870, 708
Civil Rights Act of 1964, 708
  discriminatory pattern or practice, 715–716
  disparate impact, 714–716
  disparate treatment, 712–713
  enforcement, 728–733
  equal employment opportunity. *See* Equal employment opportunity
  protected classes, 716–725
  statutory exceptions, 725–728
Civil Rights Act of 1991, 709, 734
Clayton Act, 579. *See also* Mergers; Restraints of Trade
  enactment, 559
  enforcement, 564–566
  exclusive dealing, 609–610
  interlocking directorates, 602–604
Clean Air Act, 741, 746–754, 761
  amendments (1990), 750–751
Clean Water Act, 741, 754–755
Closed shop agreement, 689
Closing statements, 118
Collateral estoppel, 172
Collective bargaining, 683–688. *See also* Labor-management relations
  defined, 684
Commercial paper, 346–355
  definitions, 347
  liabilities of parties, 353–355
  negotiability, 347–349
  transfer of, 349–353
Commercial speech, 174–175
Commodities Futures Trading Commission (CFTC), 519
Common law, 41–42
  contracts, 333
Common law legal system, 5, 10, 33–38, 75
  defined, 33
Commonwealth of Independent States (CIS), 71
Communicate information, duty to, 464
Community, use of ADR in, 133–134
Community property, 251–252
Comparable worth, 710–711
Compensate, duty to, 465–466
Competition, perfect competition model, 786
Complaint, 111
Comprehensive Environmental Response, Compensation, and Liability Act (Superfund), 741, 759–760
Computer law, 244–246, 773
Conditions, to contract, 325
Condominium ownership, 252
Conflict of law, 59, 172
Congress of Industrial Organizations (CIO), 668
Conscious parallelism, 601
Consideration, 337
Consignment sale, 608–609
Constitutional law, 155–187
  commerce clause, 164–167
  contract clause, 169–170
  due process, 179–186
  Fifth Amendment, 179–187
  First Amendment, 173, 174–178
  Fourteenth Amendment, 179–187
  Fourth Amendment, 178–179
  full faith and credit clause, 171–172
  judicial review, 162–163
  necessary and proper clause, 167–169
  privileges and immunities clause, 172–173
  procedural due process, 182–183
  substantive due process, 183
  supremacy clause, 47
  Tenth Amendment, 159

Consumer Credit Protection Act, 414, 427
Consumer financing, 427–438
Consumer Leasing Act, 437–438
Consumer Product Safety Act, 439
Consumer Product Safety Commission (CPSC), 439
Contract
  classification, 297–298
  defined, 297
  implied, 298
  mutual assent, 298–305
  offers, 298–305
Contract law. *See also* Uniform Commercial Code (UCC)
  acceptance, 300–305
  capacity, 310–311
  consideration, 305–310
  duress, 312–313
  illegality, 313–317
  interpretation, 319–320
  mailbox rule, 304–305
  misrepresentation, 311–312
  mistake, 312
  parol evidence rule, 319
  performance, 325–327
  promissory estoppel, 308–310
  remedies, 325–327
  statute of frauds, 317–319
  third-party rights, 321–324
  and tort law, 267
Contributory negligence, 651
Conversion, 274
Cooperative ownership, 252
Copyrights, 99–100, 239–240
Corporate opportunity doctrine, 462
Corporate reorganization, 360–361
Corporation(s), 495–510
  characteristics, 497–499
  closely held, 501–502
  compared, 510–513
  corporate crime, 770, 771–773
  defined, 495
  domestic, 503
  foreign, 503
  formation, 499–500
  nonprofessional, 503
  participants, 503–507
  philanthropy, 786–788
Corporation(s)—*Cont.*
  professional, 502–503
  S corporations, 501–502
  social responsibility, 782–793
  stakeholders, 782–784
  use of ADR by, 133
Cost-benefit analysis, OSHA, 657–659
Costs, insurance, and freight (CIF), 82
Costs and freight (C&F), 82
Counterpurchase, 368
Countertrade, 368
Countervailing duties, 85
Course of dealing, 343
Course of performance, 343
Court-annexed mediation, 139
Court-mandated arbitration, 137–138
Creditors' rights, 355–362
  bankruptcy, 356–361
  secured financing, 355–356
Criminal law, 39–41, 268
  business crimes, 773–782
  and ethics, 770–771
  procedure, 771–772
  proof of guilt, 772–773
Critical legal study, 18
Critical thinking skills, 11–15
Cross-elasticity of demand, 572

D

Damages, 327
  caps, 291
  compensatory, 270, 327
  liquidated, 327
  punitive, 183–186, 270, 327
  treble, 565
Deductive reasoning, 10–11
Deed, 253
Defamation, 271–272
Default, secured transactions, 356
Defendant, 27
Deontological theories, 20
Deposition, 113
Deregulation, 218–219
Direct investment, 92, 94–95
Director of corporation, 503
Discharge of debts, 359
Disclosed principal, 468
Discovery procedures, 113
  international, 114–115
Discrimination. *See* Civil Rights Act of 1964; Equal employment opportunity
Disparagement, 275
Dispute resolution, 43
  ADR compared with litigation, 142–145
  alternative methods. *See* Alternative dispute resolution (ADR)
  civil litigation process. *See* Civil litigation
Dissent, 28
Distributor, 457
Diversity of citizenship, 58
Division of markets, 561, 600
Documentary sales, international, 363–369
Documents of title, 339–342
Domestic corporations, 503
Double jeopardy, 172, 268
Dower, 248
Draft, 347
Drawee, 347
Drawer, 347
Drexel Burnham Lambert, 539
Drug-Free Workplace Act of 1988, 639
Duties, 85
Duty of care, 279

E

Easement, 251
Economic legal theory, 17–18
Elasticity of demand, 571–572
Electronic data interchange (EDI), 369
Electronic funds transfer, 354–355, 435
Electronic Funds Transfer Act, 354–355, 435
Eminent domain, 159, 255, 258
Emissions offset policy, 748
Emotional language, 14
Employee Polygraph Protection Act, 640
Employee Retirement Income Security Act (ERISA), 649–650
Employer-employee relationship, 448
Employer-independent contractor relationship, 449

Employment law. *See also* Agency law; Fair Labor Standards Act; Labor-management relations
employee privacy, 638–640
employer-employee relationship, 448
employment-at-will, 634–637
Enabling acts, 194
Endangered Species Act, 761
Endorsement, commercial paper, 350–352
Environmental auditing, 746
Environmental law
air pollution, 745–756
background, 741–742
bubble concept, 748
environmental impact statements, 743–744
land pollution, 755–760
National Environmental Policy Act, 743–744
nuclear waste, 761
state laws, 762–764
water pollution, 754–755
wildlife protection, 761–762
Environmental Protection Agency (EPA), 743
Equal Credit Opportunity Act, 428, 434–435
Equal employment opportunity
background, 708
Civil Rights Act of 1964. *See* Civil Rights Act of 1964
enforcement, 728–733
federal laws, 708
immigration reform, 718–719
Equal Employment Opportunity Act, 708
Equal Employment Opportunity Commission (EEOQ), 709, 728–733
Equal Pay Act, 708, 709–711
Equal protection policies, 719
Equity courts, 42
Erie doctrine, 42
Estate, 248
Ethical analysis, 20
Ethics
codes, 788–792

Ethics—*Cont.*
defined, 19
ethical theories, 5–6, 19–22
legal standards for, 793
European Union (EU), 67, 71, 74
Evaluation of evidence, in critical thinking, 12
Evidence, 117–118
Exclusive dealing, 609–610
Executive Order No. 11246 & No. 11375, 708
Executive orders, 55, 708, 733
Exhaustion of administrative remedy, 208
Export laws. *See* International business
Expropriation, 99
Externalities, 786
Extraterritorial law, 76

F

Facts, of case, 27
Failure to warn, 387
Fair Credit and Charge Card Disclosure Act, 428
Fair Credit Billing Act, 427, 432
Fair Credit Reporting Act, 427, 432–433
Fair Debt Collection Practices Act, 428, 436–437
Fair Labor Standards Act (FLSA), 634, 641–645
Fair-trade laws, 607
Falling firm defense, 587
False dilemma, 14
False imprisonment, 271
Family leave, 720
Family & Medical Leave Act, 709
FAS, 82
Featherbedding, 691
Federal Arbitration Act, 133, 134
Federal Aviation Administration (FAA), 439
Federal Election Campaign Act, 784
Federal Election Commission, 784
Federal Food, Drug, and Cosmetic Act, 438–439
Federal Insurance Contributions Act (FICA), 647

Federalism, 45–48, 156
Federal judicial system, 57–59
Federal question, 57
Federal Register, 200
Federal supremacy, 47
Federal Trade Commission Act, 414. *See also* Advertising regulation; Consumer financing; Mergers; Restraints of trade
antitrust enforcement, 564–566, 618, 626
enactment, 560
functions, 414–417
informal guidance, 627
unfair trade practices, 626–627
Federal Trade Commission (FTC), 414–417
Federal Unemployment Tax Act (FUTA), 645
Fellow servant doctrine, 650
Fiduciary duties, 457–461, 489–490
Fiduciary relationship, 457
Firm offer, 335
Fishery Conservation and Management Act, 762
Fixtures, 227–228
FOB, 82
Food and Drug Administration (FDA), 438–439
Force majeure clauses, 326
Foreign branch, 97
Foreign commerce, regulation of, 164–165
Foreign corporations, 503
Foreign Corrupt Practices Act, 550, 777–780
Foreign direct investment, 69
Foreign portfolio investment, 69
Foreign sales corporation (FSC), 84, 96–97
Foreign subsidiary, 96
Forgery, 354
Franchises, 494–495
Franchisor, liability of, 395
Free alongside (FAS), 82
Freedom of Information Act (FOIA), 197–198
Freely transferable ownership, 499
Free on board (FOB), 82

G

Garnishment of wages, 119
Geary, George, 637
General Agreement on Tariffs and Trade (GATT), 69, 81
Geyelin, Milo, 756n
Gifts, 247
Global legal environment, 68
Global marketplace, 563
Good faith bargaining, 683
Goods
  defined, 333
  leases of, 346
  sales of, 331–346
Gratuitous agency, 466
Gray-market goods, 88
Greenhouse effect, 742
Gulf Cooperation Council (GCC), 67

H

Harris, Charles E., 788n
Hart-Scott-Rodino Antitrust Improvement Act, 560
Harvard school, antitrust theory, 568
Hazardous and Solid Waste Amendments, 756–757
Hazardous wastes, 756
Hearsay testimony, 118
Herfindahl index, 581
Holder in due course, 352–353
Holder-in-due-course rule, 353, 424–425
Holding, of case, 27–28
Holmes, Oliver Wendell, 17
Home Equity Loan Consumer Protection Act, 428, 429–431

I

Immigration and Naturalization Service (INS), 718
Immigration Reform & Control Act, 709
Implied warranties
  fitness for particular purpose, 382–383
  merchantability, 380–381
Import laws. *See* International business
Imports, 84–86
Incorporators, 500
Indemnification, duty of, 466
Independent contractor(s), 266. *See also* Agency law; Employment law
Individual retirement accounts (IRAs), 649
Inductive reasoning, 10
Infliction of mental distress, 272
Initial public offering, 519
Inquisitorial process, 110
  international, 110
Insider trading. *See* Securities Exchange Act of 1934
Insider Trading and Securities Fraud Enforcement Act (ITSFEA), 540
Insider Trading Sanctions Act (ITSA), 540
Intangible property, 228
Intellectual property, 6, 230–243. *See also* Computer law; Copyrights; Patents; Trademarks
  defined, 230
Interlocking directorates, 602–604
International business. *See also* International law
  documents, 82–83
  exports, 81–84
  forms of organization, 95–97
  franchising and licensing, 83, 86–89
  imports, 84–86
  investment, 69, 92–100
  joint ventures, 93–94
  legal environment of, 68
  sales of goods, 362–369
  sales transactions, 82–83
  trade, 69, 81–88
International Convention for the Protection of Industrial Property (Paris Union), 100
International law. *See also* International business
  act of state doctrine, 79
  defined, 68
  dispute resolution, 89–90
  extraterritoriality, 76
  sources, 70–72
  sovereign immunity, 78–79
International Monetary Fund (IMF), 81
Interrogatories, 114
Interstate Commerce Commission (ICC), 192
Inter vivos gift, 247
Intestacy laws, 247
Intrastate commerce, 164
Intrastate exemption, 527
Invasion of privacy, 272
Investment Advisors Act of 1940, 550
Investment Company Act of 1940, 550
Involuntary petition, 357
Islamic legal system, 5, 38, 75
Issue(s)
  of case, 27
  in critical thinking, 12

J

Joint and several liability, 290–291
Joint tenancy, 251
Joint ventures, 488, 600–601
Judgment, 119
Judicial restraint, 162
Judicial review, 162–163, 206–214
Juries, 115–117, 121–123
  role of, 53
Jurisdiction, 56–59

K

Kant, Immanuel, 21
Keiretsu, antitrust barriers to, 617–618
Keogh plans, 650

L

Labor laws, international business, 98–99
Labor-management relations. *See also* Employment law; Unions
  acts compared, 669
  collective bargaining, 683–688
  excelsior lists, 674
  federal labor policies development, 668–670
  grievance procedures and arbitration, 697–698
  Labor-Management Relations Act (Taft-Hartley Act), 668–669

Labor-management relations—*Cont.*
  Labor-Management Reporting and Disclosure Act (Landrum-Griffin Act), 669, 700–701
  National Labor Relations Act (Wagner Act), 668
  NLRB role, 671–672
  Norris-LaGuardia Act, 668–669
  picketing regulation, 694–695
  Railway Labor Act, 668
  representational elections, 672–675, 678–679
  secondary pressure regulation, 695–696
  strike regulation, 691–694
  unfair labor practices
    employers, 675–684
    unions, 682–683, 696
Labor-Management Relations Act (Taft-Hartley Act). *See* Labor-management relations
Labor-Management Reporting and Disclosure Act (Landrum-Griffin Act). *See* Labor-management relations
Laissez-faire, 785
Landrum-Griffin Act. *See* Labor-management relations
Land use laws, 764
Lanham Act, 236, 422
Law. *See also* Legal systems
  classification, 38–42
  defined, 8
  and equity, 42, 115
  and ethics, 5–6, 18–22, 770–771
  legal environment of business, 6–7, 9–10
  legal theories, 5, 15–18
Lawmaking
  administrative agencies, 55
  executive branch, 54–55
  judicial branch, 55–63
  legislative branch, 54
Law merchant, 81, 295, 331
Leasehold estate, 248
Leases, 248–250
  of goods, 346
Legal analysis, 5, 10–15
  defined, 10
Legal environment of international business, 68
Legal institutions, 33
Legal positivism, 16
Legal standards for ethics, 793
Legal systems, 32–38
  civil law, 38, 75
  common law, 33–38, 75
  functions, 43–45
  Islamic, 5, 38, 75
Legislative history, 60
Legislative oversight committee, 196
Legislative veto, 196
Legislature, 54
Letter of credit, 83, 363–368
Levine, Dennis, 539
Liabilities of parties, commercial paper, 353–355
Liability, 497
  of retailer, 395
Licenses
  intellectual property, 230–231
  products, 83, 86–89
  real property, 251
Lien, 119, 251
Life estate, 248
Limited liability, 497
Limited liability companies, 502
Limited partnerships, 488–489
Liquidation, bankruptcy, 358–359
Litigation. *See also* Dispute resolution
  ADR compared with, 142–145
  adversarial process, 109–110
  avoidance of, 130–131
  extent, 106–109
  inquisitorial process, 110
  participants, 120–132
  parties, 130–132
Logical fallacies, in critical thinking, 14–15
London Dumping Convention, 755
Long arm statute, 56
Loss, risk of, 342
Loyalty, duty of, 461–462

M

McGuire Act, 607
Magnuson-Moss Warranty Act, 384–386
Mail and wire fraud, 775
Mailbox rule, 337
Maker, 347
Mandatory collective bargaining subjects, 687
Manufacturer, liability of, 394
Marine Mammal Protection Act, 762
Marine Protection Research and Sanctuaries Act, 755
Market failure, 786
Market share, 575
Market share liability, 378
Master-servant relationship, 448, 467
Material breach of contract, 326
Mediation, 133–134, 138–140
Mediators, 133
Medicare, 648–649
Merchant, defined, 333, 380
Mergers. *See also* Antitrust law
  classification, 578–579
  competitive effect, 581
  conglomerate, 584–587
  defenses, 587
  enforcement, 587–588
  guidelines, 580–581
  horizontal, 578–581
  relevant market, 579–580
  vertical, 582–583
Migratory Bird Treaty Act, 762
Milken, Michael, 539
Miller-Tydings Act, 607
Minimum wage, 641–642
Minitrial, 133, 140
Minority set-asides, 732
Mirror-image rule, 303
Misappropriation theory, 538
Misrepresentation
  contracts, 311–312
  product liability, 389
Misuse (product liability defense), 404
Molander, Earl A., 769n
Monopolistic competition, 563
Monopolization, 575. *See also* Antitrust law
  combination or conspiracy, 578
  intent, 575–578
  monopoly power, 563, 571
  relevant market, 571–575
Monopsony, 563
Moore Drydock Rules, 695–696
Morality, 19–20

Moral reasoning, 19–20
Mortgages, 251, 253

N

National ambient air quality standards (NAAQS), 746–747
National Institute for Occupation Safety and Health, 656
Nationalization, 99
National Labor Relations Act (NLRA) (Wagner Act), 568; *See also* Labor-management relations
National Labor Relations Board (NLRB), 671–672
National Traffic and Motor Vehicle Safety Act, 442
Natural law, 15–16
Necessaries, 311
Negligence, 387. *See* also Torts
  comparative, 285–286, 403
  contributory, 285, 403
  per se, 284
Negotiability, of commercial paper, 347–349
Nonattainment areas, 747
Nonprofessional corporations, 503
Nontariff barrier, 85–86
Norris-LaGuardia Act. *See* Labor-management relations
North American Free Trade Agreement (NAFTA), 74
Note, 347
Nuclear Regulatory Commission (NRC), 761
Nuclear Waste Policy Act, 761
Nuisance, 255–256, 964

O

Obedience, duty of, 465
Occupational Safety and Health Act, 633, 655–662
Occupational Safety and Health Administration (OSHA), 655–662
Occupational Safety and Health Review Commission, 656
Ocean Dumping Ban Act, 755
Offer, firm offer, 335
Office of Federal Contract Compliance Programs, 708, 733
Office of Management and Budget (OMB), 657
Officers of corporation
  defined, 503
  role of, 506–507
Old-Age, Survivors, and Disability Insurance (OASDI), 647
Oligopoly, 563
Oligopsony, 563
Open terms, 335
Option contract, 301–302
Organization of Petroleum Exporting Countries (OPEC), 67
Organized Crime Control Act, 776
Ostlund, Lyman E., 769n
Ownership, freely transferable, 499

P

Partially disclosed principal, 468–469
Parties to litigation, 130–132
Partnership property, partner's right in, 492
Partnerships. *See also* Agency law
  compared, 510–513
  defined, 485
  fiduciary duties, 489–490
  and joint ventures, 488
  and limited partnerships, 488–489
  participation in management, 492
  partner's interest in, 492
  rights, 491–492
  rights in partnership property, 492
  termination, 493
Patents, 99–100, 233–234
Payee, 347
Pension Benefit Guaranty Corporation (PBGC), 650
Pension plans, 649–650
Peremptory challenge, 123
Perfect competition, 563
Perfect competition model, 786
Perfection, 356
Performance
  of contract, 325–327
  course of, 343
  Uniform Commercial Code, 325–327, 342–345
Perpetual life of corporation, 499
Per se negligence, 284
Per se violations, 595–601
Piercing the corporate veil, 497
Plain meaning of statute, 60
Plaintiff, 27
Plant closings, 637–638, 682
Pocket veto, 54
Police power, 159, 257
Political action committees (PACs), 784–785
Political speech, 176–177
Pollution. *See* Environmental law
Pools, 561
Posner, Richard, 17
Potential entrant effect, 584
Potential entrant theory, 584–587
Predatory pricing, 577–578
Preexisting legal duty, 307
Preferential transfers, 358
Pregnancy Discrimination Act, 708, 719
Pretrial conference, 115
Price discrimination. *See also* Restraints of trade
  competitive injury, 620–621
  defenses, 621–625
  defined, 618
  elements of offense, 619–620
Price-fixing, 596–599
Primary jurisdiction, 208
Primary liability, 353
Principal
  defined, 448
  disclosed, 468
  partially disclosed, 468–469
  undisclosed, 469
Principal-agent relationship, 448–449. *See also* Agency law
Priorities, bankruptcy, 359
Private law, 42
Private placement exemption, 527–528
Private trial, 141
Privity
  of contract, 376
  warranties and, 386
Probate laws, 247
Procedural due process, 182–183
Procedural law, 33, 39
Product liability
  affirmative defenses, 402–404

Product liability—*Cont.*
criminal liability, 393
defects, 396–402
duty to warn, 400
limitations on suits, 377–378
misrepresentation, 389
negligence, 387
parties, 393–396
product safety regulation, 438–442
reform, 405–407, 410–411
risk management, 408–409
strict liability, 387–388
warranty liability, 379–386
Professional corporations, 502–503
Prohibition on imports, 84
Property, defined, 226
Property law
creation in former socialist countries, 45
defined, 227
intellectual property, 6, 230–243
personal property, 228–229, 246–247
real property, 227–228, 247–258
Proximate cause, 280
Proxy, 504
Proxy solicitations, 541–544
Proxy statements, 541–542
Public law, 42
Public Utility Holding Company Act, 550
Puffing, 379, 420
Punitive damages, 291
Purchase money security interest, 355

Q

Quasi-contract, 298
Quotas
EEO, 733
imports, 85

R

Racketeer Influenced and Corrupt Organizations Act (RICO), 550, 776–777
Railway Labor Act, 668
Rationale, of case, 28
Realism theory, 17
Reasonable care, duty to use, 465
Reasoning errors, in critical thinking, 14–15
Reasons, in support of conclusion, 12
Refusal to deal, 608, 618
Reimburse expenses, duty to, 466
Rejection of offer, 302
Remedies
of buyer, 344–345
of seller, 345
Representation election, 672–673
Resale of securities, 528
Resale price maintenance, 605–606
Res ipsa loquitur, 284
Res judicata, 172
Resource Conservation and Recovery Act, 756
Respondeat superior, 471, 493, 791
Restatement (Second) of Contracts, 295
Restatement (Second) of Torts
state-of-the-art defense, 404
strict liability, 388
Restraints of trade. *See also* Antitrust law; Federal Trade Commission Act
concerted action, 601
division of markets, 600
exclusive dealing, 609–610
group boycotts, 600
horizontal, 600
per se violations, 595–601
price discrimination, 618–626
price-fixing, 596–599
resale price maintenance, 605–606
rule of reason, 594–595
tying arrangements, 612–616
vertical, 604–618
Restrictive covenant, 257–258
Restrictive endorsement, 351
Retailer, liability of, 395
Reverse discrimination, 730
Revised Model Business Corporation Act, 482
Revised Uniform Partnership Act, 481, 485
Revocation of offer, 301
Right-to-work laws, 690
Ripeness, 207
Risk of loss, 342
Rival hypotheses, in critical thinking, 14
Rivers and Harbors Act, 741
Robinson-Patman Act, 560, 618–620, 622–626
Roman law, 38
Rule 10b-5, 534
Rule of law, 28
Rule of reason, 594–595
Rules of evidence, 118
Rustad, Michael, 186n

S

Safe working conditions, duty to provide, 466
Sales. *See* Contract law; Property law; Uniform Commercial Code (UCC)
Sales contract, 334–338
Sales of goods, 331–346
international transactions, 362–369
S corporations, 501–502
Secondary liability, 353
Secured transaction, 355
Securities Act of 1933, 519. *See also* Securities regulation
exemptions, 527–528
liability, 528–531
registration requirements, 520–523
Securities and Exchange Commission (SEC), 519. *See also* Securities regulation
Securities Exchange Act of 1934, 519–520. *See also* Securities regulation
insider trading, 531–540
proxy solicitations, 541–544
short-swing profits, 532–533
tender offers, 541, 545–548
Securities Investor Protection Act (SIPA), 550
Securities regulation. *See also* Securities Act of 1933; Securities Exchange Act of 1934
federal statutes, 518–520, 540, 547, 550
security defined, 524–527
Security agreement, unions, 689–690
Self-incrimination, 186–187
Seniority systems, 727
Separate entity theory, 497

Separation of powers, 45, 49–51
Sex-plus discrimination, 720
Sexual harassment, 720–724
Shareholders of corporation, 503
  rights of, 503–505
Shelf registration, 522
Sherman Antitrust Act, 558. *See also* Mergers; Monopolization; Restraints of trade
  enactment, 558
  enforcement, 564–572
  per se violations, 595–601
  rule of reason, 594–595
Short-swing profits, 532–533
Small-issue exemption, 527
Smith, Adam, 594
Smog, 750–751
Smog swapping system, 751
Socialist legal system, disintegration of, 44–45
Social responsibility of business, 782–793
Social Security Act, 646–648
Social Security Administration, 648
Sociological theory, 16–17
Sole proprietor, 582
Sole proprietorships, 482–485
  compared, 510–513
Solid Waste Disposal Act, 741, 755–756
Southern Common Market (MERCOSUR), 67
Sovereign immunity doctrine, 78–79
Special endorsement, 351
Specific performance, 327, 344
SQ3R (survey, question, read, recite, and review), 5, 11
Stakeholders of corporation, 782–784
Standards, in legislation, 194–195
Standards for review, 208
Standing, 207
Stare decisis, 10, 33–35, 59, 172
State action, 569
State implementation plan (SIP), 747
State judicial systems, 56–57
State-of-the-art defense, 404
Statute of frauds, 317–319
  Uniform Commercial Code, 337–338
Statute of repose, 378, 404
Statutory interpretation, 60
Statutory law, 41–42
Stone, Christopher D., 771n
Straight bankruptcy, 357
Strict constructionism, 162
Strict liability
  product liability, 387–388
  torts, 288–290
Strict scrutiny, 180
Strikes. *See also* Labor-management relations
  constitutional issues, 691
  illegal, 691–692
  regulation, 691–694
Sublease, 249–250
Subpoena, 178–179
Subpoena duces tecum, 178
Substantial performance of contract, 326
Substantive due process, 183
Substantive law, 33, 39
Summons, 111
Sunset laws, 196
Superfund (Comprehensive Environmental Response, Compensation, and Liability Act), 741, 759–760
Supremacy clause, 47
Swap, 368

T

Taft-Hartley Act. *See* Labor-management relations
Takeover bids. *See* Tender offers
Tangible property, 228
Tariff, 85
Taxation
  business organizations, 510–511
  foreign investments, 97–98
  social security, 647
Teleological theories, 20
Tenancy in common, 251
Tender offers, 541, 545–548
Testimonial, 14
Tillman Act, 784
Title
  documents of, 339–342
  of property, 339
  warranty of, 342
Torts
  and contracts, 267
  deceit or fraud, 416
  defined, 265
  intentional, 270–275
  negligent, 277–290
  strict liability, 288–290
  tort law reform, 290–291
  vicarious liability, 266–267, 791
Toxic Substances Control Act, 741–742, 758
Trade, international, 69
Trade associations, price-fixing and, 598–599
Trademarks, 99–100, 236
Trade secrets, 234–235
Transfer, of commercial paper, 349–353
Trespass, 274, 764
Trials. *See* Dispute resolution; Litigation
Trustee, bankruptcy, 357–358
Trust Indenture Act, 550
Trusts, 562–563
Truth-in-Lending Act, 427, 428–429
Tying arrangements, 612–616

U

Unconscionability, 337
Undisclosed principal, 469
Unemployment compensation, 645–646
Unfair labor practices, 675–684, 696
Uniform Commercial Code (UCC), 295–296, 331. *See also* Contract law
  commercial paper, 346–355
  consideration, 310
  creditors' rights, 355–362
  duress, 312–313
  interpretation, 319–320
  misrepresentation, 311
  offers, 300–305
  performance, 325–327, 342–345
  realism theory and, 17
  remedies, 325–327
  sales contract, 334–338
  sales of goods, 331–346
  statute of frauds, 317–319, 337–338

Uniform Commercial Code (UCC)—*Cont.*
  summary of articles, 332
  title of property, 339
  warranties, 379–386
Uniform Consumer Credit Code (UCCC), 437
Uniform Copyright Convention, 100
Uniform Employment Termination Act (UETA), 636
Uniform Limited Partnership Act, 481
Uniform Partnership Act, 485
Unions. *See also* Labor-management relations
  collective bargaining, 683–688
  duty of fair representation, 690–691
  elections, 672–675, 678–679
  grievance procedures, 697–698
  interference and coercion, 675–684
  internal democracy, 699–701
  officer duties, 700
  security agreements, 689–690
  strikes, 691–694
Union shop, 689
United Nations Commission on International Trade Law (UNCITRAL), 90, 333
United Nations Convention on Contracts for the International Sale of Goods, (CISG), 81
United Nations Convention on the Recognition and Enforcement of Foreign Arbitral Awards, 90
United States Constitution
  Article I, 708
United States Constitution—*Cont.*
  Fifth Amendment, 708
  Fourteenth Amendment, 708
  Thirteenth Amendment, 708
Universal ethical theory, 6, 21
Usage of trade, 342–343
Usury laws, 437
Utilitarian ethical theory, 6, 20–21

V

Value-added tax (VAT), 84
Values, in critical reasoning, 15
Verdict, 118–119
Vertical integration. *See* Mergers
Vicarious liability, 266–267. *See also* Respondeat superior
Vienna Convention for the International Sales of Goods (CISG), 331, 333
Vocational Rehabilitation Act, 708, 724
Voire dire, 122
Voluntary petition, 357

W

Wagner Act. *See* Labor-management relations
Warehouse receipt, 340
Warranties, 379
  exclusions, 383–384
  express warranty, 379–380
  full warranty, 386
  implied warranties
    fitness for particular purpose, 382–383
    merchantability, 380–381
Warranties—*Cont.*
  in international commerce, 386–387
  Magnuson-Moss Warranty Act, 384–386
  privity and, 386
  of title, 342
Warranty deed, 253
Water Pollution Control Act, 741
Webster's Third New International Dictionary, 8
Wheeler-Lea Act, 414
Whistleblowing, 635, 637–638
White collar crime, 770
Wholesaler, liability of, 395
Williams Act, 547
Worker Adjustment and Retraining Notification Act, 637
Workers' compensation
  administration, 654–655
  benefits, 652–653
  compensable injuries, 653
  coverage, 651
World Bank (WB), 81
World Trade Organization (WTO), 81
Writ of mandamus, 163

Y

Yellow-dog contracts, 668

Z

Zoning, 257, 764